BRITAIN'S INDUSTRIAL REVOLUTION

FRONTISPIECE

The counterpoint between continuity and rapid change – one of the themes
of this book – is clearly exemplified in this watercolour of Ely Cathedral,
attributed to Edward Duncan and painted about 1850. The Benedictine house
in Ely, one of the richest in England in the Middle Ages, occupied the site of
a monastery built for Queen Ethelfleda in 673. The great Norman nave of the
church was constructed in the early twelfth century at about the time it became a
cathedral. Its fourteenth-century octagon above the crossing is as daring a feat of
engineering as any described in the chapters that follow. The cathedral acted as
a landmark for lightermen carrying inland coal brought to King's Lynn from the
Tyne and the Wear, for Derbyshire men tending Butterley Co. engines pumping
water to drain the Fens, and for Owenite colonists seeking Utopia at Manea
in the 1830s. Duncan portrays some of the agencies of change: the navigable
river Great Ouse, the tollhouse on the turnpike road authorised in 1763, and the
Eastern Counties Railway, opened to Ely in 1845.

BRITAIN'S
INDUSTRIAL
REVOLUTION

The making of a
manufacturing people,
1700–1870

**BARRIE
TRINDER**

For Barbara

Britain's Industrial Revolution: The making of a manufacturing people, 1700–1870

Copyright © Barrie Trinder, 2013

First edition

First published in 2013 by
Carnegie Publishing Ltd
Chatsworth Road
Lancaster LA1 4SL
www.carnegiepublishing.com

British Library Cataloguing-in-Publication data
A catalogue record for this book is available from the British Library

ISBN 978-1-85936-175-7   *hardback*
ISBN 978-1-85936-219-8   *softback*

Designed, typeset and originated by Carnegie Publishing
Printed and bound in China by Latitude Press

Contents

Part II   Creating the 'workshop of the world'

Part III   Towns, cities, and communities

Acknowledgements

I am indebted for many insights and ideas to colleagues, students and friends with whom I have explored Britain's industrial past from the 1960s, and to friends from TICCIH who have introduced me to the history of other countries. I have been fortunate over the years to have enjoyed the advice and assistance of many archivists and librarians, and am particularly grateful to John Powell, librarian at the Ironbridge Gorge Museum for his help with this and many other projects. I am indebted to Alan Godfrey for providing me with opportunities to explore places with which I was previously unacquainted while writing introductions to his historical maps.

This is a work of synthesis and I must acknowledge my debt to the many scholars of the industrial revolution whose works are listed in the bibliography. Finally I should record my gratitude to Alistair Hodge and his colleagues at Carnegie, and particularly to Dr Alan Crosby, for their initial support of this project, and for all they have added to it.

Picture acknowledgements

The publishers have incurred many debts of gratitude in assembling such a large number of illustrations. Most of the photographs of industrial remains are taken from the author's own extensive library of slides and prints. Apart from these images, the owner of each specific illustration is credited at the end of the caption. In particular, however, we would like to thank the staff at the Ironbridge Gorge Museum Trust, for allowing us to photograph and to reproduce items from their collections. The Science & Society Picture Library holds extensive historic collections relating to industrial history, including some rare gems such as early photographs, patent drawings and artefacts: and more than 150 items from their collections are reproduced here. The Museum of London, as always, was able to supply a number of pertinent and attractive images from their collections, while some repositories, notably the Lancashire Record Office and the National Library of Scotland, provided historic maps, and several industrial museums supplied images, paintings, engravings and photographs.

Thank you to all who have helped make this book so attractively illustrated.

Preface

'Clearer than Scafell Pike, my heart has stamped on The view from Birmingham to Wolverhampton. ... Long, long ago, when I was only four, Going towards my grandmother, the line Passed through a coal-field. From the corridor I watched it pass with envy, thought "How fine! Oh how I wish that situation mine." Tramlines and slagheaps, pieces of machinery, That was, and still is, my ideal scenery.'

W.H.AUDEN, 'LETTER TO LORD BYRON'

In the past half-century there has been a dramatic change in attitudes to Britain's industrial past. In 1960 it would have seemed scarcely credible that places such as Cromford, Blaenavon, the mines of Cornwall, New Lanark, Pontcysyllte Aqueduct and Ironbridge might attract visitors, or that they would be inscribed on UNESCO's World Heritage List. This development is one of which my generation can perhaps feel modestly satisfied. Britain's industrial World Heritage Sites represent a coming to terms with an inherited industrial past that in some respects is uncomfortable and challenging. For with industrialisation came a factory system and mines whose worst aspects included dangerous and unhealthy working practices; many industries were also polluting to humans and to the environment; the economic and financial system that underpinned the industry helped produce inequality and hardship as well as a gradual lifting, over time, of living standards. The objective of this book is to focus attention on those places, both celebrated and obscure, which directly experienced the economic and social changes between 1700 and 1870 that are customarily encapsulated in the term 'industrial revolution'.

This study incorporates decades of exploration of industrial landscapes. I grew up in Banbury, not the most industrial of towns but one where effects of the industrial revolution could readily be observed. I know that former colleagues who grew up in Nottingham, Jarrow, the Potteries, Rochdale, St Helens or Swansea have different perspectives. Banbury's principal employer in the 1940s was an aluminium plant, an archetypal twentieth-century industry but one which, in its shift system — a constant topic of conversation in shops and across garden fences — retained the kind of work discipline that had its origins with Richard Arkwright. My school friends included members of families from Kirkby-in-Ashfield, Barnsley, Oldham and Merthyr, in a sense refugees from the consequences of the industrial revolution, who in the 1930s were drawn to work at the aluminium plant. Family walks often passed the borough waterworks, from which issued the asthmatic panting of a James Watt & Co. steam engine of 1893. Another sound of my childhood was the putt-putt-putting of the engines of narrowboats bearing the name Fellows, Morton & Clayton that carried coal along the Oxford Canal. At most hours of the day men could be observed in the streets where we lived, heading for the former Great Western Railway engine shed, to study traffic notices, lubricate valve motions and drive locomotives, many of them hauling coal southwards. A cycle ride eastwards revealed southbound coal trains at Culworth

Junction, Bletchley, Wellingborough and Sandy, and on Wednesdays it was possible to go to see steam locomotives under construction at Swindon. In my last years at university I travelled with like-minded friends on some railways that were about to be closed, and saw industrial landscapes around Swadlincote, in the South Wales valleys and in central Scotland that seem extraordinary now from the perspective of the twenty-first century. A term spent in Yorkshire brought an acquaintance with mill towns on both sides of the Pennines, with York's cathedral-scale station and with the main lines through Derbyshire and south Yorkshire of the Midland and Great Central railways, bordered with collieries, ironworks and by-product plants, and choked with queuing coal trains. I spent three years in the Black Country, when I explored canals, looked out of my teaching room towards the Grand Junction Railway and the lofty cone of a colliery waste tip, and taught children whose families had escaped from the condemned mining villages of west Durham. Subsequently I spent forty years in Shropshire, and came to know the landscape of the Severn Gorge and the documents that reveal its history, as well as exploring Shrewsbury, Bridgnorth, Ludlow and the Clee Hills. From 1980 until 1995 I taught at the Ironbridge Institute at a time when many local authorities sought regeneration through the conservation of industrial monuments, hoping to become 'another Ironbridge'.

From my base in Shropshire I was privileged to explore Cromford, New Lanark, Manchester, Glasgow, Newcastle-upon-Tyne, Sunderland, the Sankey Valley and Blaenavon, to see steel being rolled at Priorslee and on an epic scale at Scunthorpe, the rolling of brass in central Birmingham, copper wire being produced at speed at Prescot, and iron being poured in the New Foundry at Stourbridge, as well as watching fabrics being woven at Saltaire, mules spinning in Stanley Mill in Gloucestershire, doubling machines at Masson Mill, and rope being spun at Chatham. With colleagues I was able to explore the Pennine lead mines, and copper mines in Cornwall, Anglesey and Co. Cork, and to experience industrial heritage projects at Helmshore, Abbeydale, Wortley Top, St Helens, Caphouse, Stoke-on-Trent and Kew Bridge. Involvement in the TICCIH (The International Conference for the Conservation of the Industrial Heritage), whose first meeting was at Ironbridge in 1973, brought opportunities to explore Eisenheim and Duisburg in the Ruhrgebiet, Falun and Engelsberg in Dalarna (Sweden), the Erzberg in Styria, the *fereira* at Pescia Fiorentina in Tuscany, La Arboleda in the Basque Country, Lawrence and Lowell in New England, the Cité Ouvrière at Mulhouse and les Forges de St Maurice in Quebec, all of which have influenced my thinking.

Industrialisation in England, Ireland, Scotland and Wales took place in 'old countries'. This study is written with an awareness that in 1700 the places which were involved in mining and manufacturing already had histories, which shaped those developments as much as geological resources or the availability of energy. While the analysis of an industrial community need not necessarily go as far back as Anglo-Saxon charters or runic inscriptions, previous generations created not just landscapes but attitudes which did affect those developments – deference or defiance towards landlords, partiality towards Cavaliers or Parliamentarians in a distant civil war, hostility towards neighbouring parishes, different occupational groups or the English. Edward Gibbon understood the creative power that came from observing historical paradox:

It was at Rome, on the 15th of October, 1764, as I sat musing amidst the ruins of the Capitol, while the barefooted friars were singing vespers in the Temple of Jupiter, that the idea of writing the decline and fall of the city first started to my mind.

Lord Torrington in 1787 was similarly aware of the paradox that colliers were making their homes in the odd corners of what had once been Neath Abbey and its mansion house. This sense of paradox and these tensions recur in every section of this book.

Barrie Trinder, 2012

1

Introduction:
a manufacturing people

'It will be seen that a manufacturing people is not so happy as a rural population, and this is the foretaste of becoming the "Workshop of the World".'

SIR JAMES GRAHAM TO EDWARD HERBERT, 2ND EARL OF POWIS,
31 AUGUST 1842

'From this foul drain the greatest stream of human industry flows out to fertilise the whole world. From this filthy sewer pure gold flows. Here humanity attains its most complete development and its most brutish; here civilisation works its miracles, and civilised man is turned back almost into a savage.'

ALEXIS DE TOCQUEVILLE ON MANCHESTER, 1835

BRITAIN'S national census of 1851 reveals that just over one half of the economically active population were employed in manufacturing (including mining and construction), while fewer than a quarter now worked the land. The making of textiles alone employed well over a million men and women. The number of factories, mines, metal-working complexes, mills and workshops had all multiplied, while technological innovations had vastly increased the number of, and improved the capabilities of, the various machines that were housed in them. Production and exports were growing, and the economic and social consequences of industrial development could be felt throughout the British Isles. The British had become 'a manufacturing people'. These developments had not happened overnight, although many of the most momentous had taken place within living memory.

By the 1850s commentators were already describing this momentous shift as an 'industrial revolution'. The phrase obviously struck a chord, and is now deeply ingrained. Yet the term is, in fact, somewhat perplexing. It has no precise or universally accepted meaning, and can only ever be used in the loosest sense. Under 'revolution' in the *Shorter Oxford English Dictionary*, indeed, there is no definition whatever relating to this type of phenomenon. Is it, therefore, really a help or a hindrance to rely on it to describe the many new developments in manufacturing that occurred in Britain during the late eighteenth and nineteenth centuries? The idea of a 'revolution' conveys the impression that economic, social and industrial change was everywhere profound and sudden – apocalyptic even – and that old or traditional methods of production were discarded overnight, rendered obsolete by a host of new inventions or the sudden arrival of huge new mills and innovations in factory working. Rarely was this actually what happened. The 'industrial revolution' never was a deterministic force, like a volcanic eruption. Nor was it some plot, whether well intentioned or malevolent, hatched by a coterie of eighteenth-century inventors and entrepreneurs. Industrialisation might have appeared inexorable, but it was hardly planned in any sense. It did not follow a single, linear path and was often patchy or chaotic in its stuttering progress. It was neither sudden nor total.

In this book, therefore, the phrase 'industrial revolution' is used sparingly, sometimes as a convenient way of distinguishing the period under review from the twentieth century or the Middle Ages, sometimes deliberately to emphasise that while many developments took place gradually, at some times and in some places changes *were* revolutionary, such as when water-powered cotton-spinning mills transformed the Derwent Valley in the 1770s and 1780s, or when the building of blast furnaces created dramatic new landscapes around Coatbridge in the 1830s.

The term 'industrial revolution' was popularised by Arnold Toynbee who, in lectures published the year after his early death in 1881, saw the causes of change as developments in economic thought. 'The essence of industrial revolution,' he wrote, 'is the substitution of competition for the medieval regulations which had previously controlled the production and distribution of wealth.' But the phrase has a more venerable lineage than this. One of the earliest published uses – albeit in German rather than English – appeared in the mid-1840s in the first edition of Friedrich Engels' *Condition*

'Richard Arkwright's Cotton Mill' at Cromford, by William Day, *c.*1789. Arkwright's legacy was, perhaps, summarised best by the engineer James Watt: 'He is, to say no worse, one of the most self-sufficient, ignorant men I have ever met with, yet, by all I can learn, he is certainly a man of merit in his way … for whoever invented the spinning machine, Arkwright certainly had the merit of performing the most difficult part, which was the making it useful.'

Pontcysyllte Aqueduct is one of the enduring symbols of the early industrial age. Contemporaries were quick to recognise its importance in terms of innovative design, its use of new materials and techniques, and the very boldness of its conception: Sir Walter Scott spoke of it as 'the most impressive work of art he had ever seen'. Industrialisation comprised a broad range of complementary developments in areas as diverse as engineering, materials science, machine making, design, and finance, and a few large civil engineering structures such as Pontcysyllte captured the essence of the process and the spirit of the age. The aqueduct is now the centrepiece of a World Heritage Site.

PHOTOGRAPH BY COURTESY OF ADRIAN PINGSTONE, 2008

of the Working Class in England (a work that was not published in English until the 1890s). European radicals of this era were well versed in the terminology of political 'revolution', and the use of the word to describe the economic and social changes that Engels had observed at first hand while in Manchester must have come naturally:

> The history of the proletariat in England begins with the second half of the last [i.e. eighteenth] century, with the invention of the steam-engine and of machinery for working cotton. These

inventions gave rise to an industrial revolution ['*zu einer industriellen Revolution*'], a revolution which altered the whole civil society …

Sixty years later, in 1909, another continental commentator, Paul Mantoux, introduced his survey of *The Industrial Revolution in the Eighteenth Century* with a similarly straight-forward explanation:

> The modern factory system originated in England in the last third of the eighteenth century. From the beginning its effects were

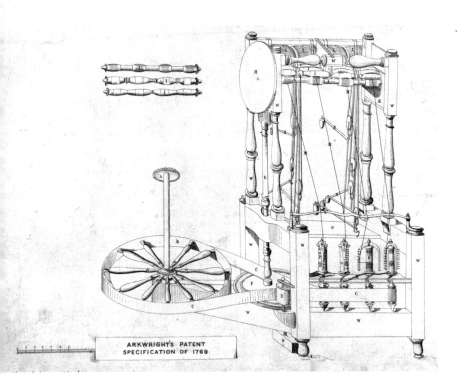

ARKWRIGHT'S PATENT
SPECIFICATION OF 1769

so quickly felt and gave rise to such important results that it has been aptly compared to a revolution, though it may be confidently asserted that few political revolutions have ever had such far-reaching consequences.

Until relatively recently this kind of narrative was widely accepted. In broad terms it ran thus. In the late eighteenth century British industry, particularly the manufacturing of cotton textiles, grew at a prodigious rate, largely as the result of technological innovations in the spinning of yarn, the harnessing of water and subsequently of steam power to drive machinery, and the adoption of new systems of management in which workers' time and effort were closely directed, measured and valued. In textiles and beyond, manufacturing production came to be accommodated in ever larger workplaces, in factories or mills of a whole new type. Receptive domestic and overseas markets enthusiastically welcomed the products of these new enterprises, which were often less expensive and of higher quality than what had been available before. Strong demand and improving supply spurred on higher rates of economic growth. Part of the improvement involved new systems of production, in which various processes were mechanised and powered by a single power source – epitomised by the Arkwright-style cotton-spinning mill. Such buildings involved the gathering together of much larger workforces. Spinning mills were built in many parts of Britain, and elements of the factory system they embodied came to be adopted in other sectors of industry. Alongside this industrialisation came urbanisation, as a fair proportion of manufacturing came to be concentrated in towns and cities, to which migrants were attracted by the apparent prospects of high wages, regular employment and the availability of housing; and some were driven away from rural society because of poverty, insecurity of tenure, uncertain and inadequate remuneration or, in some cases, obligatory deference towards social superiors. Some forms of domestic manufacturing were threatened as production was mechanised, but others continued to prosper for considerable periods because their raw materials, whether textile yarns or wrought-iron rods, became more abundant or less expensive as a result of new technology.

A handloom weaver is depicted (*left*) in the *Book of English Trades* (1804–05), while (*right*) we see a depiction of powerloom weaving in 1835, one of the plates used to illustrate Baines' *History of the Cotton Manufacture*. The transition from hand to power weaving came later than the mechanisation of spinning, and it took longer to accomplish, but the contrast between these images is striking. Ranks of powerlooms, seen here attended by young women operatives, were able to weave much more quickly and cost-effectively. Progressive mechanisation such as this was one of the principal features and drivers of industrial development.

The broad thrust of change which so excited the attention of contemporaries was that increasing numbers of workers had come to be tied to factory machines and to their employers' systems of time-keeping. Discipline and long hours of unremitting toil were the prices to be paid for regularity of work and high wages. There had been a remarkable, if not quite thorough, transition from domestic to factory production, and the change could be startling. Polite visitors from afar flocked to marvel at and write about 'palaces of industry'. Many came from overseas, from Sweden, Germany, France and America, from countries with their own entrenched or emergent industrial sectors. They recorded their observations because many were in Britain, formally or informally, to spy on new technologies and systems of production with a view to replicating them at home. Their detailed reports are also a reminder that throughout the period we call the industrial revolution British manufacturers faced potential competition from abroad. Such visitors naturally concentrated on the novel and the remarkable, and to many the cotton mills of Lancashire epitomised the whole phenomenon. According to Léon Faucher, a French Liberal politician, amateur historian and free-trade economist who spent time in Manchester in 1844, 'The birth of the manufacturing system, like that of Minerva, was sudden and complete; and in less than a century, its colossal, if not harmonious, proportions were fully developed ... Lancashire was its cradle.'

A manufacturing society had been born, and to many the change had taken place so quickly, and its nature was so novel, that it constituted much more than a simple increase in the rate of production. Alongside the statistics of growth, the industrial

Detail of 'East View of Derby', 1728, showing the silk mill on the river Derwent near the centre of the town. Lombe's mill possessed many of the characteristics of later textile mills: it was multi-storey; machinery was powered by a single power source; several different processes took place under one roof; and a large number of employees was gathered together in one workplace. Yet the Derby silk mill opened half a century before Arkwright's cotton-spinning mill at Cromford, demonstrating that industrialisation was not a straightforward, linear process.

revolution was a qualitative shift, affecting the whole of society and stimulating other developments within the British Isles and beyond, many of which increased the demand for manufactured goods. Technological developments, such as the steam engine, which at first were concerned with mining or manufacturing, were applied to the improvement of transport facilities, allowing the development of more distant markets. Similarly, cast iron, first used for constructional purposes in bridges, was employed in the frames of fireproof textile factories, which increased the output of fabrics and thread and the demands placed upon iron foundries. And industrial change was helped everywhere by a surprisingly broad range of enabling factors, such as improvements in machine making, better transport infrastructure, and from new forms of credit and financial transactions.

Recent generations have refined and re-evaluated the traditional narrative. The emphasis on inventions and revolutionary change had perhaps been excessive.

The industrial history of Britain was not all about big new factories and machinery. For instance, we now know that handloom weaving continued on a significant scale for more than half a century after the powerloom had been invented, and that a fair proportion of weaving still took place in domestic settings far into the middle of the nineteenth century: a salutary reminder that the date of invention was never the same as the date of widespread adoption or displacement of older practices. Similarly, although steam power did eventually become hugely influential, water power was still of greater significance and ubiquity in manufacturing until well into the nineteenth century.

Further, an objective analysis of most industrial sectors shows that large factories were not always the norm, and that the average size of firms and factories remained surprisingly small, especially in places such as Birmingham or Sheffield and in the trades producing consumer goods. Even in the 1870s, there were armies of domestic craft workers, some of them in large towns, who never saw the inside of a 'factory'. The typical production facility, right to the end of the nineteenth century, was more likely to be a small or medium-sized workshop rather than one of the mighty mills or factories whose novelty and size drew such attention at the time.

Further, we should remind ourselves that in one or two celebrated instances large-scale manufacturing facilities had existed *before* the classic period of industrial 'revolution': as early as the 1720s in Derby, for example, there was a large, water-powered textile mill that was in many crucial aspects a direct precursor of Arkwright's mills half a century later. And this Derby silk mill continued to operate profitably throughout our period. We should always be mindful of strands of continuity from earlier periods.

Coincident with this period of historical re-evaluation, Britain has continued to see its manufacturing sector decline as a proportion of the national economy. From the viewpoint of the early twenty-first century British industrialisation no longer appears, as it did to many of our forefathers, as a continual and inexorable process of expansion and growth that could be projected into the distant future. Rather, it now looks more like one fleeting phase of the country's long and complex history, rather like the protectorate of Oliver Cromwell or the rather longer period of the Roman occupation.

This may provide a good perspective from which to evaluate British industrialisation in a balanced manner. The aim of this book is to analyse the profound changes that certainly occurred as well as the strands of continuity that ran alongside them. Where, when and how industry came to be organised, located and managed are the principal concerns of this work. As we shall see, the rise of industry could provoke almost unbounded optimism, reflecting a characteristically Victorian sense of history as the march of progress. Industrialisation could also result in what Karl Marx called the 'immiseration' of the workers. It could bring dislocation and hardship, particularly during recessions in trade. Alongside the growth of manufacturing

⋎ For centuries the Greenfield Valley, near Holywell, where water gushed from a spring for about a mile down into the Dee Channel, was one of the most abundant sources of water power in the British Isles: in the 1720s the stream powered three corn mills, two snuff mills, a fulling mill and perhaps also an iron forge. The first cotton factory in the valley, known as the Yellow Mill, was constructed by John Smalley in 1777 from stones from the ruins of the medieval Basingwerk Abbey. Other cotton mills followed. From 1740 Thomas Patten, and from 1780 Thomas Williams and others built mills in the valley to fabricate copper into sheets and bars. This view of 1792 shows, in the centre, the six-storey Lower Cotton Mill of 1785, and to the left the buildings of a works where brass and copper wire were drawn for nail and pin making.
DRAWING BY I. INGLEBY ENGRAVED BY W. WATTS. AUTHOR COLLECTION

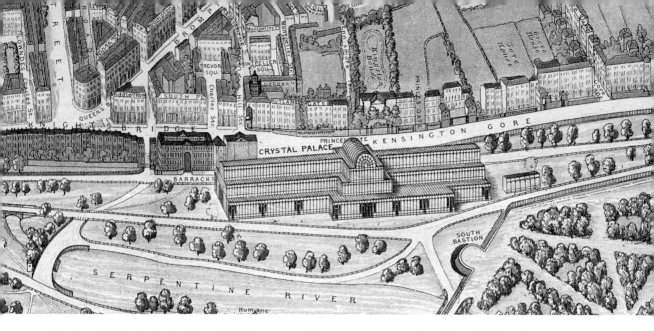

The Crystal Palace housing the Great Exhibition was opened on 1 May 1851, an occasion celebrated by the publication by Banks & Co. of an engraved 'Balloon View of London', of which this is one small detail. Joseph Paxton's design demonstrated that new materials – cast iron and glass – could be used to create a structure ideal for its function, with a subtlety and novelty of style that gave an identity to the whole exhibition project. The Exhibition was also an international event, and some exhibits from overseas, particularly from the United States, were a foretaste of the time when Great Britain would cease to be the only 'workshop of the world'.

came urbanisation, and in the worst parts of industrial towns the dearth, poverty and pain suffered by the poorest classes were unspeakable. Revolution or not, the period from 1700 to 1870 is perhaps the most remarkable and interesting in the history of the British Isles, and always merits re-examination.

There are many ways to approach this broad sweep of history. Economic historians can provide the perspective of numbers: increases in gross national product, fluctuations in interest rates, and, at least from the 1850s, tolerably accurate statistics of the amount of coal mined, the quantity of cotton imported, or the output of the nation's blast furnaces. Financial historians can explain the sources of the capital used to develop mines, factories and railways. Demographers point to sometimes radical movements in population, from countryside to town, or within coalfields, as well as to rapid increases, particularly in towns and cities, caused in part by the lowering of the age of marriage. Similarly, labour historians can compare wage rates in manufacturing cities with those in the rural counties, and historians of technology can explain the intricate details of the development of machinery, how the

Watt pumping engine or the Stephensons' *Rocket* were constructed, for example. Archaeologists and landscape historians in recent decades have located many previously unrecognised sites of industrial activity, including textile mills in remote Pennine dales, cottages in suburban Coventry with high-ceilinged lofts built to accommodate ribbon weavers' Jacquard looms, or the routes of eighteenth-century wooden railways in the coal districts of County Durham. This study acknowledges its debts to all such approaches and attempts to draw them together, examining industrialisation by identifying those areas where developments in mining and manufacturing took place, analysing some of them in detail, and identifying individuals and groups who were responsible for and were affected by such changes.

This book focuses on the ways in which the economy and society of the British Isles were transformed between 1700 and 1870. The subject is so large and the historical themes so numerous that it has not been possible to cover every aspect of industrialisation, about the building and construction trades, for example, or the activities of 'improving' agriculturalists.

It seems appropriate to begin with looking at some of the enabling technologies and innovations, those things that were possible by the 1860s that had been impossible in 1700: thus, Chapter 2 looks at the importance of energy and the harnessing of power to machinery; Chapter 3 looks at machine making, machine tools and what was sometimes referred to as 'mechanicking'; Chapters 4 and 5 deal with the crucial areas of civil engineering and transport, both of which were vital components of industrial development.

Part II of the book then moves on with a group of chapters dealing with the 'core sectors' of industrialisation: thus, Chapter 6 looks at coal mining and the range of industries that grew up on coalfields; Chapter 7 describes a broad range of iron-making communities and their associated industries, while Chapter 8 does a similar job in dealing with the important non-ferrous metals sector, including tin, brass, copper and lead; then, at the heart of the book, Chapter 9 details the various branches of the textile industries, from cotton to wool, linen and silk; and Chapter 10 discusses the often neglected industry of paper making.

Part III is a broad survey of towns, cities and industrial communities. First, Chapter 11 examines the particular features of the manufacturing and economic lives of some of the great industrial towns and cities. The unique characteristics of London, where there was a surprising amount of industry, are described in Chapter 12. The subsequent chapter is devoted to the emergence of the 'industry' that provided recreational facilities, not just for the wealthy but by the 1860s for increasing numbers of working people. Finally, Chapter 14 discusses community, and the understanding that can come from comparison between industrial and rural settlements, and from an analysis of utopian and marginal communities.

Throughout the book there is, very deliberately, a strong sense of place. In each chapter regional variations are discussed at some length, for the experiences of no two places were ever the same, and no understanding of industrialisation can be gained without acknowledging local circumstances and changes over time. This book is not aimed at economists, and so does not include the kind of theoretical analysis that may be found in such books as Robert C. Allen's recent

The British Industrial Revolution in Global Perspective. Allen explicitly seeks to explain *why* the industrial revolution happened in this country, contending that high wage levels and inexpensive energy produced an inevitable economic imperative towards power-driven, labour-saving innovations, and therefore industrialisation. The present book looks more at the what, the where, the how and the when rather than the why, and hopefully presents a nuanced and convincing description of what really happened on the ground. A by-product of this approach is the authenticity that comes from discussing actual people and real places.

Sir James Graham's letter, quoted at the head of this chapter, laments somewhat sadly that industrialisation had made Britain the 'Workshop of the World'. Graham was old-school: a landowner, educated at Westminster and Christ Church. He did recognise the importance of industry, but some of his social class were indignant that they were no longer accorded the respect that was their due, and yearned for an imagined medieval past. It was symbolic that the Eglinton Tournament in Ayrshire, a revival in 1839 of medieval jousting patronised by Tory aristocrats including the 13th Earl of Eglinton, was ruined by rain and traffic congestion, and that six years later, the brothers Baird, sons of a small farmer from Monkland, should have built blast furnaces within sight of Eglinton Castle. Signs of the times. Graham's remarks do not prove the Marxist concept of the immiseration of the proletariat. They do indicate an informed awareness of the scale of recent social and economic change whose significance was realised in the debate on the 'condition of England'. These changes, in communities across the British Isles, are the subject of this study.

Nine years after Graham wrote to Powis recent economic changes could appear in an optimistic light. Thomas Babington Macaulay, historian, MP for Leeds from 1832, and author of the criminal code for India, entered the Crystal Palace on Thursday 1 May 1851, the opening day of the Great Exhibition:

there must have been near three hundred
thousand people in Hyde Park at once. The
sight among the green boughs was delightful.
The boats and little frigates darting across

the lake; the flags; the music; the guns; — everything was exhilarating, and the temper of the multitude the best possible. … I made my way into the building; a most gorgeous sight; vast; graceful; beyond the dream of the Arabian romances; I cannot think that the Caesars ever exhibited a more splendid spectacle. I was quite dazzled, and I felt as I did on entering St Peter's.

The Great Exhibition, held in the Crystal Palace in Hyde Park between May and October 1851, attracted up to 6 million visitors. This great event seemed to be a high-water mark for those who were optimistic about the forces of economic 'progress' that had in many respects transformed the British economy and society. Significantly, many thousands gained their first experience of railway travel on the excursion trains that took them to London for the Exhibition. The creation of what was fast becoming a national rail network was itself one of the wonders of the age. 'Lord' George Sanger, the circus proprietor, thought that the Exhibition symbolised the improvement that had taken place in the condition of the English (although obviously not the Irish) nation in the fourteen years

since the accession of Queen Victoria, and that it demonstrated to people 'that they were living in times infinitely better than they could have imagined possible but a few short years before'. The construction of the Britannia Bridge over the Menai Straits, opened on 5 March 1850, attracted thousands of celebrating spectators, as did the opening in 1853 of Sir Titus Salt's Saltaire Mill near Bradford, which was built to incorporate 'every improvement that modern art and science have brought to light'. Even Sir James Graham recognised the impact of manufacturing industry, which, he told Parliament, 'is the tree to which our little isle owes its prosperity, which has diffused so much happiness over this great empire, and which has rendered this nation the most wealthy and the most civilised'.

In the vanguard of industrialisation were the textile industries described in Chapter 9. Famously, Richard Arkwright developed a 'water-frame' that could spin cotton yarn and which was powered by a waterwheel. More than this, he devised a whole new system of production which he went on to exploit commercially with spinning mills, at first in the Derwent Valley in Derbyshire, and subsequently in Manchester and elsewhere. He and his descendents became immensely rich. While they had a precursor in the Derby silk

Robert Stephenson's final design for the bridge opened in 1850 by which the Chester & Holyhead Railway was carried over the Menai Straits was ground-breaking: trains ran through gigantic wrought-iron tubes carried on three stone towers (the provision of anchorages in the towers for suspension chains that were never installed shows just how much this form of construction was a venture into the unknown). Great crowds gathered to see the tubes being lifted into place by a hydraulic press that was subsequently displayed in the Great Exhibition (see page 76). Queen Victoria travelled to North Wales especially to view the bridge in 1852, and thousands of her subjects were taken to see it by excursion trains. Like Saltaire Mill, it symbolised the optimism of the early 1850s.

Joseph Wright of Derby is often regarded as the artist who best portrayed the industrial revolution through individual and group portraits and landscapes. His acquaintances included Richard Arkwright, Erasmus Darwin, Jedediah Strutt, Josiah Wedgwood and John Whitehurst. In this view of Arkwright's mill at Cromford he expresses amazement that such a large building remained working and illuminated throughout the night (one of the very first uses of gas lighting was in textile mills such as this). Other visitors to Derbyshire including Lord Torrington were similarly impressed. Wright's portrayal of light seems to reflect the lasting impression made upon him by an eruption of Vesuvius that he had witnessed.

mill of the 1720s, Arkwright's mills dramatically demonstrated the potential of the new manufacturing systems, and they were widely imitated. They were imposing buildings with single power sources in which large numbers of closely managed operatives worked for fixed hours; the various phases of production took place in different parts of the building, and materials flowed efficiently and logically from one stage of manufacture to the next. In *The Wealth of Nation*, published in 1776, Adam Smith had theorised about the division of skills and labour and dissected the art of making pins into around eighteen distinct processes. At Cromford Arkwright had already put these theories into practice for the spinning of cotton yarn. As well as developing the machines themselves, Arkwright had brought into being a new, highly profitable 'factory system'.

One evening in 1790 John Byng recorded his impressions of Arkwright's mill at Cromford:

I saw the workers issue forth at 7'oClock ... a new set then goes in for the night, for the mills never leave off working. ... These cotton mills ... fill'd with inhabitants, remind me of a first rate man of war; and when they are lighted up, on a dark night, look most luminously beautiful.

This exact scene – an illuminated cotton mill in a pastoral landscape – was depicted by the artist Joseph Wright of Derby. But attractive, stone-built cotton mills nestling in a picturesque Derbyshire valley were one thing. Huge steam-powered mills in Manchester a few decades later were something else. There the mills were on constricted sites next to the canal and hard by some of the least salubrious housing in the country. Manchester, the cotton capital, was the 'shock city' of the industrial age. As Douglas Farnie noted, no objective or comprehensive history of the cotton

Manchester's first large cotton-spinning mill was probably Shudehill Mill, built in the north of the town around 1782 by partners of Richard Arkwright. That mill used a steam engine to raise water for the waterwheel. Ironically, however, the relatively high cost of Arkwright's water-frames meant that most late eighteenth-century Manchester mills were designed instead to accommodate spinning mules. This engraving of 1835 shows the impressive range of cotton mills on the banks of the Rochdale Canal in Ancoats. In 1814 these factories alone housed over 160,000 spindles. A gazetteer of cotton mills still standing in Greater Manchester in the mid-1980s numbered 1,112 in all. Lancashire and north-east Cheshire had become the heartlands of cotton. (See also page 415.)
CARNEGIE COLLECTION

industry in Manchester has yet been written, but there is no denying the strength of its impact, or the strong divisions of opinion that this industrial city provoked. Manchester's great spinning mills were untypically large (Murrays' Sedgwick Mill, for example, was eight storeys high) and, congregated together, they made a profound impression. Indeed, of urban–industrial sites Manchester was the archetype. There the ambition and optimism of the manufacturer could be found in abundance. Léon Faucher wrote in 1844:

> The men of Manchester conduct operations upon the most gigantic scale, such as the imagination can scarcely embrace. I know of a spinning-mill in Manchester, which employs 1500 hands. … And a Lancashire manufacturer has exclaimed, inspired by the contemplation of this industrial omnipotence, 'Let us have access to another planet, and we will undertake to clothe its inhabitants.'

'At the present day [1844], Lancashire possesses three-fifths of the establishments devoted to the spinning and weaving of cotton; and there are more than a hundred factories in the town of Manchester alone,' wrote Faucher. 'Nothing is more curious than the industrial topography of Lancashire. Manchester, like a diligent spider, is placed at the centre of the web …'

For those who prospered during these years they could be heady times. But such optimism was not universal, and it was not sustained. At precisely the time of Faucher's visit the German radical Engels was being guided around the slums and factories of Manchester by his young companion, the Irish millgirl Mary Burns. Engels was systematic in cataloguing the horrific living conditions he had encountered in cellars, courts and houses. In particular he condemned dwellings that had been thrown up by developers on land they held only on short leases: having to return the land (and everything they had constructed upon it) to the freeholder removed all incentive to build anything permanent or in any way decent. 'I shall present the English,' he wrote to Karl Marx in November 1844, 'with a fine bill of indictment. At the bar of world opinion I charge the English middle classes with mass murder, wholesale robbery, and all the other crimes in the calendar.' Visiting Manchester in the summer of 1835 Alexis de Tocqueville made some of the same points, albeit without the political venom: the seeming pursuit of money at all costs; the lack of regulation; the primacy of individualism and the concomitant weakness of society and social institutions in the face of mercantile or manufacturing interests; and, above all, the enormous contrast between rich and poor, between the great cotton factories – 'palaces of industry' as he describes them – and the 'hovels' of the workers near the mills and down by the river. It was the haphazard, dirty, half-built and half-decayed physical character of this new industrial town that impressed him so vividly: 'The fetid, muddy waters, stained with a thousand colours by the factories they pass … wander slowly round this refuge of poverty [Little Ireland]. They are nowhere kept in place by quays; houses are built haphazard on their banks … [the river] here is the Styx of this new Hades.'

Most of these early industrial towns lacked public authorities that could impose logical planning of developments or insist upon adequate sanitation, acceptable building standards, or even supplies of clean water. Cholera outbreaks in the 1830s and 1840s created alarm among all social classes. Subsequent agitation by the Health of Towns Association led to the Public Health Act of 1848 enabling the establishment of local boards of health which began the process, described in Chapters 4 and 11, of making towns healthy places in which to live, part of which involved the application of technologies developed in manufacturing and the construction of canals and railways. Nevertheless, it was many years before there were substantial improvements in the living conditions of many of the urban

working class, whose ways of life in 1870 still remained a mystery to most educated people. The Manchester journalist Robert Blatchford, writing in the 1880s, railed against the merchant princes of the city which was, in their words, 'the modern Athens', pointing out how they closed the curtains of their carriages as they passed through the teeming, squalid inner city, opening them again only when they had made good the leafy suburbs. He asked, rhetorically, 'How shall I attempt to paint the shame of modern Athens – the dwellings of her people … where a devilish ingenuity seems to have striven with triumphant success to shut out light and air.' Despite this, some Mancunians thought their town had had an unduly harsh press. In his *Manchester Handbook* of 1857, Joseph Perrin felt that, 'To the stranger Manchester is an enigma: it has been little understood and much misrepresented. Authors like Mrs [Frances] Trollope have maligned it; and even Charles Dickens, has … shown us but scant justice.' Somewhat plaintively, he announced that the town 'is not as bad as it is painted. … Even as regards the material picturesque, Manchester can boast of it. It needs artistic training, perhaps, to discern it, but it is, nevertheless, there.' In the eye of the beholder.

Poverty was not, of course, simply the consequence of industrialisation. In many parts of rural Britain in the early nineteenth century most of the population endured squalid living conditions and received meagre remuneration for their labours. The poor had suffered from over-crowding and economic insecurity

Apparently archaic modes of production for specialist fabrics persisted in the textile industry long after the advent of steam-powered factories and iron machines. This view of about 1920 of a factory in Darvel, East Ayrshire, portrays effectively the atmosphere of a weaving workshop where wooden-framed looms were operated by hand. The product in this instance was chenille (the French word for caterpillar), a fairly complex fabric characterised by a protruding pile, which could be made from silk, cotton or synthetic fibres.

▲ The Madeley Wood (or Bedlam) Ironworks was built in the late 1750s on the north bank of the river Severn a short distance from where the Iron Bridge was constructed some 20 years later. It was one of five groups of coke-fired blast furnaces built in the Shropshire Coalfield within less than five years, which marked a real revolution in the pattern of iron making in England. This view depicts the furnaces from downstream and shows in the foreground a sled, apparently being used to transport coal. Probate inventories confirm that the use of sleds was not uncommon in this part of Shropshire in the early eighteenth century.

IRONWORKS, COALBROOKDALE, 1805. AQUATINT, WILLIAM PICKETT AFTER P.J. DE LOUTHERBOURG. © SCIENCE MUSEUM/SCIENCE & SOCIETY PICTURE LIBRARY

in every great city from the times of classical antiquity. Indeed, some of the worst urban living conditions in the period under review were experienced in Dublin, the least industrialised of Britain's great cities. Nevertheless, the particular features of the great manufacturing towns, the imposing size of factories and of such structures as the railway viaduct that crosses Stockport, the flames that illuminated up every place where there were furnaces, the pervasive palls of smoke that respected no barriers of social class, caused many to react with horror as they reflected upon the lives of those who lived among such spectacles. As late as 1881 Henry George considered that the life of primitive peoples was preferable to that of the English poor, while in the decade that followed Andrew Mearns in *The Bitter Cry of Outcast London*, William Booth in *In Darkest England and the Way Out* and Charles Booth in *The Life and Labour of the People in London*, revealed the 'darkness' in which the 'submerged tenth' in London were condemned to live. As early as 1808 the poet William Blake coined the phrase '… among

these dark Satanic mills' as a counterpoint to the 'Jerusalem' that he predicted might be built in England. This memorable phrase has come to be interpreted as a condemnation of factory work in general, but it was probably written with regard to the Albion Flour Mill on London's south bank rather than the textile mills of the industrial North. In *News from Nowhere* (1890) William Morris concluded that from an idyllic medieval past England had become 'a country of huge and foul workshops and fouler gambling dens, surrounded by an ill-kept, poverty-stricken farm, pillaged by the masters of the workshops'. The economic changes of the industrial revolution could be interpreted between poles of optimism and pessimism. To understand the period it is necessary to acknowledge the intensity and validity of both kinds of judgement.

Over the last forty years or so it has become fashionable to look closely at the eighteenth-century economy in search of precursors of factory-based manufacturing. Ugly new words – 'protoindustry', 'protoindustrialisation' – are deployed, with mixed success, to describe the supposed progression from a system of domestic production to one based on mills and factories. In the eighteenth century, it is suggested, merchants developed and honed the practice of 'putting out' tasks to home-based workers – usually smallholders and yeomen families with small farms – and that this provided a springboard for later industrial developments. Rightly the role of merchants is given prominence, for they were indeed pivotal in facilitating or stimulating economic activity throughout the period. Quite rightly, too, historians have drawn attention to the importance of home-based work in the eighteenth century. In many sectors and regions, such as lace making in the East Midlands, boot-and-shoe making in Northamptonshire, hardware production in the Black Country, or, classically, handloom weaving in Lancashire and the West Riding, domestically organised production formed a significant part of the economy, allowing families to supplement agricultural incomes that were meagre or seasonal. Yet in most such places these practices had long histories, and in some areas domestic production continued – albeit often in straitened circumstances – into the late nineteenth century or even beyond. The problem with the theory of proto-industrialisation is that it is difficult to demonstrate any neat progression from one older, domestic system to a novel one based on new-style factories. Rather, it appears that mechanisation and the concentration of labour and capital in larger units developed alongside rather than in substitution for more venerable types of small-scale domestic manufacturing. Some forms of domestic work – for example the spinning of textile yarns – did virtually disappear, but domestic handloom weaving, although much diminished, continued on a significant scale in some places, as did the manufacture of hardware. Cottages at Dudley Wood in the Black Country, designed specifically for domestic chain making, were still being built between 1884 and 1906. Professor Carl Chinn has shown that many tasks in Edwardian Birmingham, including the pasting of matchbox labels and the stitching of sacks, were undertaken by poor women and their families on 'putting-out systems', and the same was true in other great cities. In the manufacture of many lowly consumer goods the classic 'industrial revolution' had little obvious effect.

The start of the eighteenth century is a logical point at which to begin a study of British industrialisation. By that date England's economy was already well developed. There were established patterns of trading in coal, from Northumberland and County Durham to London and along the east and south coasts, as well as down the Severn from Coalbrookdale, on the Aire & Calder Navigation and, within a few years, also on the Mersey and Weaver. Commercial links from London spread across the known globe, and ships from quite small ports were trading in distant waters. Overseas produce – tea, tobacco, spices and sugar – was sold at mercers' shops in every town. England was not self-sufficient in iron, but had a long-standing import trade with Sweden.

Even earlier, the potential of the British economy had been recognised by Andrew Yarranton, an officer in the parliamentarian army during the civil wars of the mid-seventeenth century, an ironmaster, and an improver of river navigations. He proposed the extension of inland navigation by the construction of canals, particularly a link from the Warwickshire Avon near Stratford to the Cherwell between Banbury and Oxford, and the creation of manufacturing settlements at waterway junctions and other locations, including Christchurch in Hampshire, Lechlade at the head of the Thames Navigation, Wellingborough on the river Nene, Slane on the river Boyne, and the Isle of Dogs. Yarranton also urged the encouragement of ship-building, fishing, linen manufacture and iron making, particularly tinplate manufacture. He commended methods of thread making at Dordrecht, bleaching technology at Haarlem, and schools in Saxony where girls were taught to spin. He asserted that England was well endowed with wool, tin, leather, iron, lead, flesh, corn and fish, with safe harbours and timber to build ships. His considered that England, 'should be the Empory and Store House of the World but it is not so'. His proposed 'improvements by sea and land' were intended 'to set at work all the poor of England' and 'to outdo the Dutch without fighting'. Yarranton died in 1684, but many of his visions were realised in the century and a half after his death. Clearly and not unreasonably he envisaged a planned and ordered economy, logically arranged with a tidy

↗ There were malthouses in every significant town in the eighteenth century, where local barley was used to produce malt for brewing. This example stands in Oundle, Northamptonshire. Ceiling heights on malting floors tended to be low, since the only activity that took place there was the spreading, turning and collecting of grain, while fenestration tended to be sparse, as in this building. The lucam to the right housed a hoist used to raise sacks of barley to the storage area, probably on the attic storey.

geography and rational social principles. The reality of what did emerge was very different. In contrast to other industrialising nations, Britain's burgeoning economy was subject to scarcely any central regulation. Nothing was planned, nothing was co-ordinated, nothing was rational except in the theoretical sense of the supposedly rational behaviour of the free market. The legacies of this almost anarchic freedom remain to this day, including in the incoherent settlement patterns of the former coalfields in the Black Country, Co. Durham or the central valley of Scotland, or in the relics of competing railway lines, the ruins of viaducts along the Derbyshire/Nottinghamshire border, of Duddeston viaduct that has never led anywhere (see page 187), or Manchester's Central Station being adapted as a conference centre.

The vitality of the eighteenth-century economy is illustrated by the characteristic 'manufactures' of many towns. The term was applied to goods which were made in particular places but traded nationally or exported. It is used by Daniel Defoe and other writers, including Stephen Whatley, who described as 'manufactures' the hats made in Dunstable, the locks produced at Wolverhampton, and the shoes sent beyond the seas from Northampton. The meaning he attached to the term is revealed when he placed malt among the 'manufactures' of Reading and Devizes. Malt was made in every town, but only in certain places in grain-growing areas was it made, for use by brewers elsewhere, on a sufficient scale for it to be described as a 'manufacture'.

This study ends around 1870, the beginning of a time of change during which the staples of the industrial revolution continued. Coal output, the production of iron (but increasingly of steel), cotton, woollen cloth and iron steamships increased, and nearly 7,000 route miles of new railway were laid in Great Britain between 1871 and 1914. Nevertheless, industrial output in Germany and the United States was increasing faster, while capacity in Belgium, France, the Austrian empire and Italy, though not matching Britain's, was developing significantly. In the years around 1870 pig iron output in Shropshire, South Wales and the Black Country peaked, and the final decline of metalliferous mining in upland regions began. During the 1870s the Solvay process for making alkali was introduced into Britain, and chemical manufacturing began to evolve into a science-based activity. The same period saw the beginnings of factory-based production of consumer goods, footwear, clothing, furniture and food, employing many women and using American technology. Many of the patterns set between 1700 and 1870 – the use of coal, its movement by canals and railways, the use of steam engines, the generation of coal gas, shift working, mule spinning and the puddling of iron, among others – continued into the twentieth century. Since 1950 all have effectively disappeared. In these respects the 'industrial revolution' might not be said to have ended until the 1980s. There are nevertheless good reasons for bringing this study to a close about 1870, summarised by the observation that, by then, Britain was no longer the world's only workshop.

During this period of industrialisation, between the 1700s and 1870, the British Isles experienced many changes other than those related directly to the economy and industry. One particular feature of

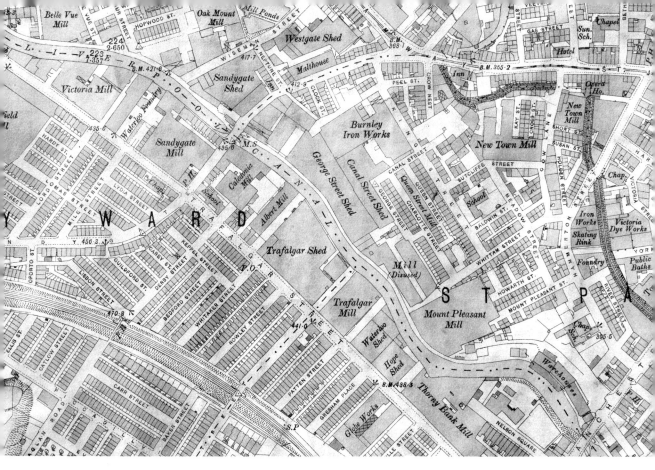

↙ This section of the large-scale Ordnance Survey map published in 1893 shows one of the astonishing concentrations of industrial buildings and living quarters that could be found in northern industrial towns, in this case in Burnley, Lancashire. Many of the factories cluster along the Leeds & Liverpool Canal which reached the town from Yorkshire in 1796 and was extended westwards in 1801, although it was not until 1816 that through navigation to Liverpool became possible. To the east of this section the canal crosses the valley on the Burnley Embankment, 1,256 yards long and 60 feet high, an outstanding feat of civil engineering. The 'sheds' seen here are single-storey weaving factories, most of which had characteristic 'north-lit' or 'saw-tooth' roofs, which admitted the maximum amount of light without creating glare from direct sunlight. Some back-to-back houses are shown north of the canal, but the majority of terraced dwellings south of the canal follow the simple rectangular plan characteristic of many towns in the second quarter of the nineteenth century. Burnley's principal occupation was cotton weaving and by the early twentieth century it was boasted that there were nearly 100,000 looms in the town. South of the map where Manchester Road crosses the canal is the celebrated Weavers' Triangle, where there is now a visitor centre.

PHOTOGRAPH BY CARNEGIE, REPRODUCED BY COURTESY OF THE COUNTY ARCHIVIST, LANCASHIRE ARCHIVES

Britain was that the proportion of the people of the British Isles engaged in agriculture, already low by European standards, continued to diminish, and the proportion making things increased substantially, as did the percentage living in towns and cities. It was perceived that manufacturing moved from people's homes to factories; this was generally true, although substantial numbers continued to ply their skills in domestic workshops into the third quarter of the nineteenth century. Their numbers also grew. The understanding of geology and chemistry, and of civil

and mechanical engineering, increased substantially, although industrial growth before 1870 owed less to pure science – except, perhaps, to geology – than to pragmatic technical advances. In manufacturing and in people's homes energy was consumed on an increasing scale, and much of it was derived from coal. Consequently, most towns were dirtier, sootier and more polluted than in the past. In Elizabeth Gaskell's novel *North and South*, published in 1854, Manchester is thinly disguised as 'Milton-Northern in Darkshire', and its pollution is powerfully conveyed: 'For several miles before they reached Milton, they saw a deep lead-coloured cloud hanging over the horizon in the direction in which it lay. … Nearer to the town, the air had a faint taste and smell of smoke.' And an anonymous visitor noted: 'The town of Sheffield is very large and populous, but exceedingly dirty and ill paved. What makes it more disagreeable is the excessive smoke from the great multitude of forges which this town is crowded with.'

The proliferation of machines – railway trains, hammers and rolling mills in forges, seemingly endless ranks of chattering powerlooms – made cities excessively noisy. De Tocqueville wrote that, 'a sort of black smoke covers [Manchester]. The sun seen through it is a disc without rays. Under this half daylight 300,000 human beings are ceaselessly at work. A thousand noises disturb this damp, dark labyrinth … the footsteps of a *busy* crowd, the crunching wheels of machinery, the shriek of steam from boilers, the regular beat of the looms, the heavy rumble of carts. … Never the gay shouts of people amusing themselves, or music heralding a holiday.' It was said that

This watercolour by Sean Bolan depicts the station at Chippenham about 1850 with *Iron Duke*, one of the celebrated 'Gooch Singles', the 4-2-2 locomotives designed by Sir Daniel Gooch that powered the express trains of the Great Western Railway from the time of their introduction in 1847 until the end of Brunel's broad gauge in 1892. Other locomotives in the class included *Lord of the Isles*, displayed in the Great Exhibition, and *Alma*, driven by Peter Mottershead (see page 198). Brunel introduced a broader gauge in order to increase stability and speed, but the inconvenience of having to transfer passengers and freight where the gauges met, as at Gloucester, Wolverhampton and Basingstoke, was too great, and from the 1860s the GWR was gradually converted to standard gauge.

Roofing materials changed dramatically as Lord Penrhyn and others began to exploit the slate resources of Gwynedd. This picture shows platforms suspended from the top of the quarry face from which workers could drill holes for gunpowder which, when fired, caused blocks of slate to fall to the quarry floor. These were worked by other quarrymen, and taken away by rail. The artist also depicts a group of spectators, and Lord Penrhyn's quarries certainly attracted a great deal of attention from travellers in North Wales. A watercolour by John Nixon, 1807.

Gayle Mill, on the southern outskirts of Hawes, was built in 1784–85 as a cotton-spinning mill, powered by a 24-foot waterwheel. It was just the sort of intrusion into the peace of the countryside that so offended the sensibilities of men such as Lord Torrington.

when approaching Manchester one could hear the town before one could see it.

Britain's population increased substantially, although growth in the eighteenth century was not uniform, and the Great Irish Famine was a demographic catastrophe, in which a million people are thought to have perished and another million emigrated. By the time of the 1851 census, 109,000 people of Irish birth were living in London, with another 84,000 in Liverpool, 53,000 in Manchester and at least 100,000 in the Scottish cities of Glasgow, Edinburgh and Dundee (in Dundee the extraordinary scale of displacement is highlighted by the fact that the Irish made up 19 per cent of the population).

It was a common perception that social relationships changed in the decades before 1840, that a perceived model of a deferential society was disintegrating, and that there was a growing awareness of differences of social class. Yet some of those communities where manufacturing and mining flourished had never conformed to this kind of deferential model, while some manufacturing settlements accepted paternalistic principles as much as any village nestling in the shade of its parish church and manor house. Many commentators pointed to the emergence of – or perhaps sometimes just the increased visibility of – a new factory working class, a proletariat of wage-earners newly migrated from the countryside or elsewhere in Britain or Ireland.

The wider contexts in which mining and manufacturing developed must also be borne in mind. The economic, technological and social changes discussed below were contemporary with the governments of the Duke of Newcastle, Pitt the younger, Lord Liverpool and Sir Robert Peel; with the preaching of John Wesley, Howell Harris, George Whitefield and John Henry Newman, with visits of Wolfgang Amadeus Mozart and Franz Joseph Haydn to London; with the writings of Samuel Johnson, George Eliot and

Charles Dickens; and with the architecture of Nicholas Hawksmoor, Robert Adam and George Gilbert Scott. Industry is but one thread in this broad pattern.

Several salient features of industrialisation are worthy of general comment. One is that manufacturing people were found not only in the great northern cities. Industrial change is often perceived as, or even confused with, urbanisation, although they are, of course, quite different phenomena. In some urban centres industry was pervasive, characterised by Pyne's engraving of the cotton factories alongside the Rochdale Canal at Ancoats, or the descriptions of nearby Little Ireland, a small concentration of poorly built back-to-back terraces in a loop of the Medlock. Manufacturing did help to create great cities, but in the eighteenth and early nineteenth centuries it also impacted on the geographical margins, transforming and bringing into the economic mainstream the slate quarries of Gwynedd and the copper mines of Cornwall, Anglesey and West Cork. And it was not just the extractive industries that affected rural areas. Lord Torrington, observing Askrigg in Wensleydale

Textile manufacturing developed during the industrial revolution through the contemporaneous establishment of large, steam-powered factories, and of workshops, some quite extensive in size, where machines were worked by hand or by animal power. The last decades of the eighteenth century were characterised in most textile regions by the proliferation of 'jenny shops', workshops accommodating small numbers of spinning jennies. Some continued in use, usually producing specialised yarns, into the twentieth century, such as this example at the works of Palmer Mackay at Trowbridge, Wiltshire, photographed about 1930.

© SCIENCE MUSEUM/SCIENCE & SOCIETY PICTURE LIBRARY

bell-ringing and the clamour of the mill all the vale is disturb'd; treason and levelling systems are the discourse, and rebellion may be near at hand.

Manufacturing also transformed less isolated areas which had also been marginal to the mainstream of the economy in 1700 – for example, the valleys around Manchester and the heathlands of the Black Country. Wetlands, the Fens of East Anglia and Lincolnshire and the Bog of Allen, were also affected by new technology, and found a new economic role as sources of food or fuel for cities.

Another feature that strikes the modern eye is the wide dispersal of industrial enterprises. Workshops, small factories and mines sprang up in many places that now seem wholly unpropitious. It is unsurprising that miners followed seams of metalliferous ores to such remote places as Dufton Hush, almost 3,000 feet above sea level in the northern Pennines, but there were also dozens of little water-powered bobbin mills on the streams that thread through the hills of upland Lancashire, as well as some spinning mills high up in the fells. There were mines, most of them small ones, in many parts of Ireland, and the streams of Ulster powered numerous spade-mills. There was a certain ubiquity of 'busy-ness' in eighteenth-century Britain. In the course of time some sectors became more concentrated geographically, as the size of individual manufacturing plants increased, as transport systems developed, and as proximity to coal supplies became more crucial. But, as subsequent chapters show, there is much more to British industrialisation than the towering factories of Manchester, Leeds or Glasgow.

Importantly, too, people's horizons were becoming broader. Mining and manufacturing developed in a country that increasingly recognised a British identity, particularly after the Act of Union between England and Scotland in 1707 and the Jacobite Risings of 1715 and 1745. Ireland was also an important part of the story: the common ownership by aristocrats of land in Great Britain and Ireland, the trade across the Irish Sea, and the tide of migration from Ireland in the mid-nineteenth century make it logical to examine Ireland in this study, not least because the Act of Union

in 1792, was aware that remote communities could be transformed by water-powered cotton mills:

> Sir Richard Arkwright may have introduced much wealth into his family and into the country; but, as a Tourist, I execrate his schemes, which, having crept in every pastoral vale, have destroy'd the course and beauty of Nature. Why, here now is a great flaring mill, whose back stream has drawn off half the water of the falls above the bridge. With the

(1800) brought Ireland under the administration of the Westminster Parliament.

Looking farther afield, by 1700 British merchants had become a significant force in world markets. Throughout the period under review, Britain was at the centre of an expanding empire, focused in the eighteenth century on the Atlantic Ocean and the eastern seaboard of America, but subsequently on India and more distant colonies and possessions. Historians casually use phrases such as 'global markets', 'international trade networks' and 'overseas trade', but the profound significance of Empire to Britain's industrial revolution can easily be understated. The development of the Empire re-orientated the patterns whereby raw materials came to these islands and the markets for the goods that were manufactured here. Merchants and manufacturers were helped in some respects by the Navigation Acts – repealed as late as 1849 – which prevented foreign merchant vessels for participating fully in trade with ports in Britain or its colonies. The Empire came with high costs: it constituted an enormous financial burden to the nation, and the true balance sheet, economic, moral, social and political, is impossible to calculate. Many goods produced in Britain were traded with African rulers in return for slaves, while slaves in the Americas provided the cotton, sugar and tobacco that were processed in British towns and cities, while British merchants and manufacturers profitably sold textiles, spirits, hardware and salted cod to plantation owners. The transportation by Europeans of between 11 and 12 million Africans to work in slave conditions in the Americas must be acknowledged as part of the background against which manufacturing developed in Britain, but the bold claim that the industrial revolution was financed by the Atlantic slave trade is an exaggeration.

Beyond the colonies British merchants found ready markets for manufactured goods of all kinds. The established export trade in textiles, originally in woollens but increasingly in cotton fabrics and yarn, continued to be important in the eighteenth century as it had been since the Middle Ages. Metals and metalwares too were widely traded. In antebellum America the West was won using Bowie knives and tools from Sheffield

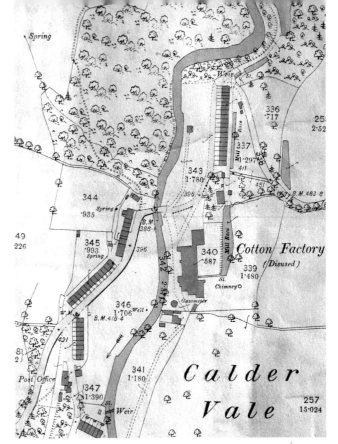

The potential of water power drew manufacturing entrepreneurs to sites in marginal locations even as late as 1835 when the Quaker brothers Richard and Jonathan Jackson established a cotton mill at Calder Vale, ten miles south of Lancaster. 'Calder' is Old English for a fast-flowing stream; this particular Calder rises on Bleasdale Moor on the western edge of the Forest of Bowland and flows into the river Wyre at St Michael's on Wyre. The map shows how weirs and leets were constructed to provide power for the mill, which, it appears, was lit by a small gasworks to the south of the complex. The Jacksons also built good-quality terraced housing for their workpeople, and in 1863 erected a church dedicated to St John, which lies south of the map. Part of the factory is shown as disused, but one of the mill buildings remains in production in 2012.

and the Black Country. In 1848 Wostenholms', cutlery manufacturers of Sheffield, opened their Washington Works, named in recognition of the importance to the company of their American markets. British merchants also participated in many profitable re-export trades, controlling for example the distribution of goods such as sugar, tobacco and pepper to other European markets. Comparing statistics from diverse sources over long periods is problematic, but after making

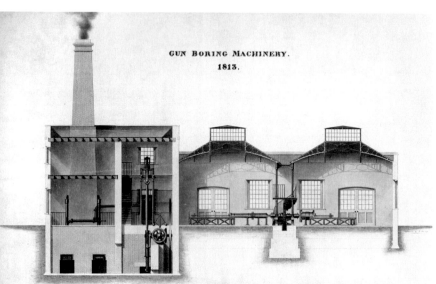

GUN BORING MACHINERY.
1813.

adjustments for inflation, and using official figures collected at port, one can estimate that British exports over the period 1700–1870 increased by a factor of 37.5, from £6.4 million to £240 million. British goods could be bought almost anywhere.

The crucial period of industrial development in Britain – between the beginning of the Seven Years War in 1756 and the end of the Napoleonic Wars in 1815 – was also the period of Britain's ascent to dominance as a maritime nation. The strength of the Royal Navy, which from 1805 was unchallenged by any other naval power, enabled British merchant ships to collect raw materials and deliver manufactured goods throughout the world in relative safety. Naval power was one part of a British hegemony that extended around the known world, a hegemony based on political, mercantile, military and financial muscle. Economic power grew throughout our period, helped by increasingly market-driven policies designed to promote free trade. Britain's power probably reached its zenith in the mid-nineteenth century when the nation's supremacy could be charted in several sectors. 'To Arkwright and Watt,

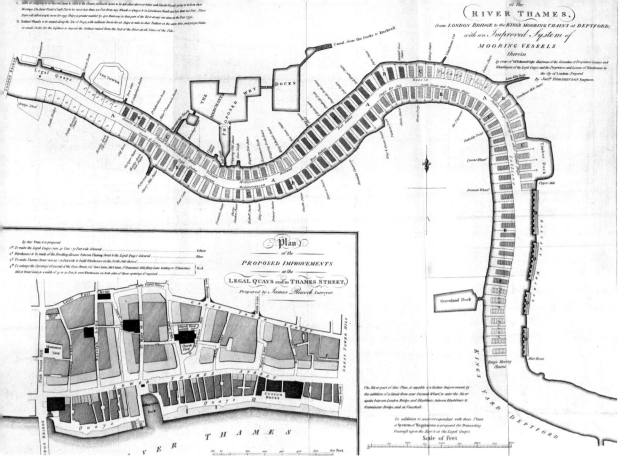

Throughout this period London was Britain's busiest port, handling a particularly broad range of goods. By 1796, when Edward Ogle drew this plan as part of his proposal to re-organise the handling of ships in the river, the limitations of the river wharfs and small existing docks were obvious. Ogle's management plan for the river was never implemented and instead there followed a major dock building programme by private investors and the East India Co. Despite this, most of the privately owned river wharfs remained busy and commercially viable right through to the middle of the twentieth century.

England is far more indebted for her triumphs than to Nelson and Wellington,' opined Edward Baines in 1835 as he contemplated the £570,000,000 worth of cotton goods that he calculated had been exported by British manufacturers in the previous half-century. But manufacturers and politicians were acutely aware that foreign competition was growing, and that industrial development was taking place in many other countries. Baines himself commented upon those who 'apprehend a competition [overseas] too formidable to be withstood, on the part of several foreign nations'. These included the USA, 'where the spinning machinery is equal to that of England', 'Belgium, Switzerland, and other countries of Europe, where the [cotton] manufacture exists, and is rapidly expanding', and the

'East Indies, where … the natives are supposed to have a great advantage, from their having so long been habituated to the employment, and from the excessively low rate of wages they require.' And during parliamentary debates on factory legislation MPs were quite aware that restrictive laws might erode the international competitiveness of British manufacturers. The industrial revolution was never an insular British phenomenon, for technology was transferable, and other nations were very keen to play catch-up.

Overseas trade and industrial growth were facilitated, or, indeed, made possible by the 'financial revolution' that followed the Glorious Revolution of 1688. The establishment of the Bank of England in 1694, and the founding of insurance companies, provided a measure of security for overseas traders and protection against the hazards of fire for merchants and manufacturers, as well as creating funds for investment. Recent writings by such historians as Jeremy Black have emphasised the importance of the security of financial transactions to the development of foreign trade. Also significant was the extra liquidity provided to British overseas traders by the ability of the Bank of England to construct sophisticated financial instruments that were no longer dependent upon actual bullion. British merchants could perform relatively complex transactions overseas with increasing peace of mind. Meanwhile during the eighteenth century 'country' banks were established in most market towns, continuing the practice by which local solicitors, often from the same families as the first generation of bankers, channelled their clients' money into potentially profitable investments, including manufacturing enterprises.

Indeed, no major industrial development would have been possible without money. Historians and other observers, seduced by the glamour of steam and the power of machinery, tend to overlook the fact that the less romantic conventions, practices and rules of accountancy and mechanisms for financial transfers underlay every activity described in this book. Manufactured goods had to be traded and sold for money which was the mechanism by which rents, suppliers' bills and workers' wages were settled. Historians have debated at length the processes involved in raising investment capital during the industrial revolution, but almost all are agreed that there was usually no shortage of money. Much of this capital was held in the provinces, and it is clear that many concerns were financed locally, or from contacts made within particular trades or from links established through religious bodies such as the Society of Friends or the Unitarians. Thousands of private individuals or small entrepreneurs sought to take advantage of the new investment opportunities being touted and promoted, and many did make handsome returns by way of capital growth or dividend. Many entrepreneurs spread risk by forming partnerships or by investing in several different enterprises, for limited liability for company shareholders was not introduced until the 1850s. Failure of a concern, often because of lack of cash, could be ruinous. Until

1860 only railway companies had the authority to seek funds from a large number of investors, and the consequent flow of capital into railway projects significantly aided the rapid construction of the national network. As will be revealed in several chapters below, some aristocrats also invested capital in order to develop their estates: there were fortunes to be made from the coal or ironstone that could be mined below them. Manufacturers might support canals or railways that could benefit their own enterprises as well as producing profits. Some provincial entrepreneurs found sources of finance in London, the availability of which might be determined by prevailing rates of interest. The detail of how capital was obtained is less significant than the big picture, which shows that the British Isles between 1700 and 1870 was overall a fertile nursery for enterprise, where new and varied sources of money for investment were available for those with ambitions to provide goods or services.

Change took place in a demographic as well as a financial context. In England there was a general, four-fold increase in population over the period from 1700 to 1870, from just over 5 million to rather more than 6 million in 1771, 8.6 million in 1801, 16.8 million in 1851, and 21.3 million in 1871. English demography was exhaustively analysed by Wrigley and Schofield, whose results were published in 1981. While the general upward trend is obvious, there are many refinements of detail. They showed that there were several crises in the first half of the eighteenth century, when mortality rates for particular months rose to at least 25 per cent above the trend, most notably in 1728, 1729 and 1742, and that there were lesser crises in the rest of the century, all of them impacting more severely at a national level than the much better publicised outbreaks of Asiatic cholera after 1832. There were no mortality crises in 1795 and 1800, years of agricultural shortage, which suggests that although food became expensive and even difficult to obtain, England by this date was effectively free of the threat of famine. The population of Scotland increased from 1.6 million in 1801 to 3.4 million in 1871, while that of Wales rose from 587,000 to 2.2 million in the same period. The population of Ireland rose in the eighteenth century from around 2.5 million in 1700 to about 5 million in

1801, and then increased exceptionally rapidly to 8.2 million by 1841. The Great Famine of 1845–48 caused catastrophic mortality and large-scale loss of population by emigration. By 1851 Ireland's population had fallen to 6.5 million, and it fell by another 1.1 million over the next two decades.

It is clear from the research of many scholars that population in England rose fastest where mining and manufacturing flourished and less rapidly in areas not directly influenced by industry. The availability of housing, whether by extension or multiplication of cottages in areas of open settlement or though provision by employers, appears to have been an incentive to early marriage. Wrigley and Schofield showed that the 'national average' female age at marriage fell from 26.2 to 23.4 between 1700 and 1820, which meant effectively one or two more children per marriage. Infant mortality diminished overall, although it remained high, and was part of most people's experience, even in the wealthiest classes.

The statistics of urban population growth in the early nineteenth century can be obtained from census returns and are frequently quoted, but overall figures do not convey the true level of over-crowding in some areas. In the early 1840s, for instance, Manchester and Liverpool had population densities, respectively, of 100,000 and 138,000 per square mile. Since antiquity the poorest quarters of every large city have been unhealthily over-crowded, but rarely in human history have so many people been crowded together more tightly or in worse sanitary conditions than in the poor areas of the booming cities that were created during Britain's industrial revolution.

Nevertheless, images of squalor in Glasgow or the east end of Leeds give only a partial impression of industrial communities. Many who migrated to industrial cities were drawn by the hope of better housing, increased income or greater regularity of employment. And there were keenly perceived gradations – even in Manchester – between neighbouring working-class residential areas, while more isolated industrial settlements built by entrepreneurs, such as Arkwright's Cromford, the Strutt family's Belper, Owen's New Lanark and Sir Titus Salt's Saltaire, were also significant components of the British experience.

What becomes clear throughout this book is that industrialisation was not a single phenomenon: and it certainly did not occur in the same form everywhere or at the same time. There were profound variations between different localities, even within individual sectors and trades, but some general points can safely be made. One is that the majority of those employed in new systems of manufacturing were young people. Obviously scandalous was the practice of employing very young children in mines or textile factories, before the Factory Acts sought to impose minimum age limits and maximum hours of work. Richard Oastler, the campaigner against child labour, referred in 1830 to 'those magazines of British infantile slavery – the worsted mills of the town and neighbourhood of Bradford'. Such children received a measure of attention and sympathy because early textile factories were the focus of such public interest, when they were a novelty in the 1770s and 1780s, or when some regarded them as a source of shame in the 1830s and 1840s. But children as young as eight could be found working in almost every sector of industry, loading brick kilns, breaking copper ore, hauling baskets of coal underground and assisting in the hand forging of nails or chains. In 1838 a summer thunderstorm flooded the Huskar Pit on Silkstone Common near Barnsley, sweeping 26 underground workers to their deaths. The inscription on the monument to the victims blames 'an awful Visitation of the Almighty'. It was truly awful, for the youngest victim was seven years of age, the oldest seventeen.

Some owners of textile factories, as detailed in Chapter 9, recruited 'factory apprentices', orphans, chiefly from city workhouses, who were housed in institution-like accommodation within mill boundaries. A British Parliament Report of 1819 revealed that 54.5 per cent of workers in cotton factories were aged 19 or less. In mining, similarly, around a third of underground workers in 1842 were found to be children or youths under the age of 20. The corollary or this was that in many occupations – not only the physically hardest of jobs such as mining – workers aged over 40 were considered old. Quite remarkable was Thomas Batty of Willington Colliery, who gave evidence in April 1841 to the Commission on Mines:

Aged 93 according to his own account and that of the agents. Went down a pit when he was about 6 or 7 years of age and was employed in and about pits up to about his 85th year and has always had good health and good fortune. About 40 years ago he was made an overman and has never worked himself since.

More typical of the commission's interviewees were children such as Janet Snedden, aged 9: 'Is a trapper in the Gartsherrie Pit [in Scotland], No. 1; comes down with Janet Ritchie, a single woman who hooks on and off the corves on the chain for drawing coal up the pit. Comes down a quarter before 6 and goes up again about 4 p.m.' Or Sally Fletcher, aged 8, who worked at Mr Stock's Windy Bank Pit: 'I have worked here short of three years. I cannot read or write. I never went to any school day or Sunday. I go to work between six and seven o'clock in the morning. I thrust corves with Josh Atkinson who is 10 years of age. I sometimes go home at three o'clock. Sometimes six. I don't go home to dinner. I get it at the pit mouth. I always have trousers and jacket on and also my clogs. I am not very tired when I go home at night. We sometimes hurry 20 corves and have 400 yards to hurry them.'

According to one source Engels talked to in the 1840s, 'of 22,094 operatives in diverse factories in Stockport and Manchester, but 143 were over 45 years old'. 'Mr Ashworth, a large manufacturer,' he goes on, 'admits in a letter to Lord Ashley, that, towards the fortieth year, the spinners can no longer prepare the required quantity of yarn, and are therefore "sometimes" discharged …' In many industries it was the nature of the job, the working environment or the long hours that produced ill-health, physical deformity or premature ageing. In a marginal note of 2 July 1835 de Tocqueville wrote that Manchester's working population were 'absorbed in material pleasures and brutalised'.

Titus Rowbotham, a mechanic who had first come to work in Manchester in 1801, would have agreed:

I have seen three generations of operatives. I know men who are of my age … who have passed their lives in tenting the *mule jenny*. Their intellect is enfeebled and withered like a tree. They are more like grown up children than the race of men I knew formerly. … The long hours of labour, and the high temperature of the factories, produce lassitude and excessive exhaustion. The operatives cannot eat, and seek to sustain life by the excitement of drink.

Official government documents rarely have such capacity to shock as the lengthy pages of the Children's Employment Commission (Mines) of 1842. This illustration was reproduced in the Leeds and Bradford report: 'The sketch given is intended to represent Ann Ambler and William Dyson, witnesses No. 7, hurriers at Messrs Ditchforth and Clay's Colliery at Elland in the act of being drawn up crosslapped upon the clatch iron by a woman … The turn wheel, as represented … is the least expensive, and certainly the most dangerous, as you are, upon all occasions, dependent on the man or it may be a woman, who works it … you are at the mercy of the winder.' At the time of the report William Dyson was 14 years of age, and had been working underground for eight years. Of his fellow-worker Ann, whose exact age is not given, Dyson testified: 'I have seen her thrashed many times when she does not please the [men]. They rap her in the face and knock her down. I repeat I have seen this many times. She does not like her work, she does not like that, I have seen her cry many times. The men swear at her often and she says she will be killed before she leaves the pit.'

A Large numbers of women worked in factories and workshops across Britain, but some also worked in more manual occupations such as sorting coal at the pithead. In the South Lancashire coalfield in particular, the 'pit brow lasses' of Wigan and elsewhere were frequently photographed in the later nineteenth century. This photograph was taken in 1865.

Like most migrant workers, Rowbotham had travelled to the town as a young man. As in all periods and places, those who chose to up-sticks and migrate in search of a better life were the youthful and the more dynamic of their communities. In sectors such as textiles, where production had formerly taken place in the family home, villages could be left with an ageing population of handloom weavers whose incomes were under threat from mechanisation but who would not have been able to make the change to factory work even had they been willing.

Factories did provide many opportunities for young women, although in mining and metal working the majority of workers were men. Collecting information for a parliamentary report in 1833 from 82 cotton factories, 65 wool factories, 73 flax factories, 29 silk factories, 7 potteries, 11 lace factories, 1 dyehouse, 1 glass works, and 2 paper mills throughout Great Britain, Dr James Mitchell calculated that, overall, considerably more than half of the workers (57 per cent) were female. More than half of the female workforce in these factories were less than 20 years old, and

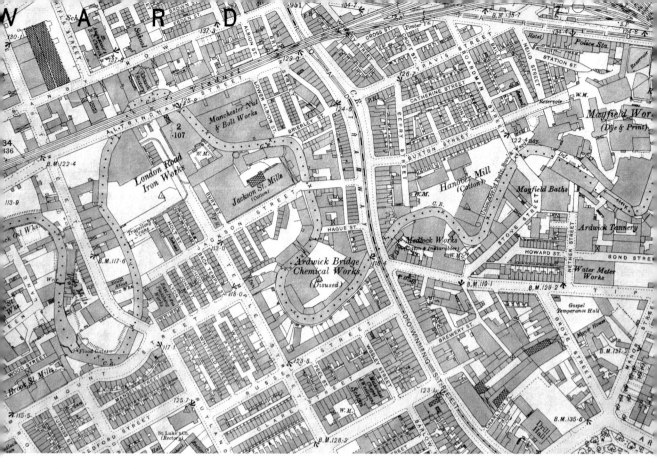

This map of 1893 of part of the centre of Manchester portrays vividly some of the characteristic features of a large nineteenth-century city. Many textile works had been built along the meandering banks of the river Medlock, but they tended to be those involved in finishing fabrics, particularly in dyeing, and used the river for process water, although there were some spinning factories which probably originally operated their machines by water power. There were also establishments linked with engineering, such as the London Road Iron Works and a manufacturer of nuts and bolts, as well as a tannery, the (by then disused) Ardwick Bridge Chemical Works, and a soap factory. There is some back-to-back housing in the north of the area, but to the south are many houses of simple rectangular plan, characteristic of the second quarter of the nineteenth century, as well as some tunnel-back houses of the kind built in large numbers in many towns after 1850.

PHOTOGRAPH BY CARNEGIE, REPRODUCED BY COURTESY OF THE COUNTY ARCHIVIST, LANCASHIRE ARCHIVES

of the teenagers he found working in the silk factories, he found that more than 84 per cent were women. In the parliamentary debate on hours of factory work on 22 March 1844, Sir James Graham suggested that women were keen to work hard: 'female adults, as well as male adults, tempted by a love of high wages, and honest gain, were disposed to flock to factories where labour might be obtained for a longer period than twelve hours.' The 1851 census shows 650,000 female workers in Britain's textile industries, compared to 661,000 men. Some women could also be entrepreneurs: an analysis of trade directories from several industrial towns found that the proportion of business owners who were female rose from around 9 per cent in the 1780s to around 12 per cent in the 1850s. Of the 'drapers, mercers and dealers of cloth' listed in a Manchester trade directory of 1788, no fewer than 15 (or 24 per cent), were women, as were 9 per cent of publicans and 13 per cent of shopkeepers. Some enterprising women even built and operated textile mills. Michael Baumber, the historian of Keighley and Haworth, cites the examples of Ann Illingworth, Rachel Leach and Betty Hudson, who did so in that part of the West Riding, while parliamentary papers in 1833 name a Mrs Doig who owned a powerloom factory in Yorkshire that employed 60 people.

Throughout the period of industrialisation neither national nor local government imposed any effective controls upon the development of manufacturing premises or of housing. Regulations did not exist about where industry could be sited, or how close to industry houses could be built; town planning, building regulations and development control were all much later innovations. Having said that, the nature of particular areas could be determined by landownership. It was possible for landowners such as the Russell family, dukes of Bedford, in the Bloomsbury area of London, or the owners of the Colmore and Calthorpe estates in Birmingham, to control development by releasing land gradually to house builders or industrial entrepreneurs or by the strict enforcement of the terms of leases. Nevertheless many well-intentioned plans for select middle-class terraces and villas, as in the west end of Leeds, were frustrated by the pressures of a land market in which there was an almost insatiable demand to build premises for manufacturing and for the accommodation of the families employed therein. There was no formal zoning, and in many parts of Manchester, Birmingham, Leeds and even London, industrial buildings stood cheek-by-jowl with workers' housing. The early Ordnance Survey maps of most towns show bewildering muddles of workshops, cottages, factories, canals, pigsties and slaughter-houses. There were elements of planning in a few areas, such as the grid of streets alongside the Rochdale Canal in Ancoats in Manchester where some of the city's largest spinning mills were built, but these were exceptional. The requirements of specific processes did lead to clusters of activity, for example along waterways: streams were used for water power, and activities that needed process water – such as dyeing, bleaching or tanning – congregated near to natural or man-made watercourses, while ease of access to transport led to other mills and factories also being built along the banks of canals or river navigations. But even here, where industrial premises were mostly highly concentrated, there were still plenty of workers' houses to be found, right next to the noxious waters of river, canal or drainage systems.

In the absence of any health and safety legislation until the mid-nineteenth century (and its minimal effectiveness for decades thereafter), industries of all sorts were potentially dangerous, and for many workers life was 'nasty, brutish and short'. We are familiar, and rightly so, with images of mining disasters and of industrial injury in mills and factories. An 1889 description of Wigan casually enumerated 11 local pit disasters in fifteen years, in which 525 men and boys had died. Such catastrophes were commonplace, and little regarded by the outside world except when something really spectacular happened – such as the 204 miners who suffocated in the Hartley pit disaster in Northumberland in 1862, or the 366 killed when the Oaks Pit near Barnsley exploded in December 1866. But early death through disease was insidious and ubiquitous. Among the lead-miners of Swaledale in the 1860s the average age at death was 42 years: for non-miners in the same communities it was 63. Lung diseases, from breathing the fine lead-laden dust, were largely responsible: at Allendale in Northumberland in 1862, 80 per cent of lead miners had chronic asthma or respiratory conditions. Some traditional industries were notoriously dangerous. In tanneries there were deep pits of noxious, slimy waters in which to drown. Foundry-workers were burned and scarred with splashes of white-hot metal, or had their lungs scorched by inhaling hot gases. Railwaymen were crushed between shunted waggons and lost limbs as they fell beneath locomotives. In mills the plethora of fast-moving unprotected machinery could be lethal to sleepy children and careless adults: in 1826 a Lancashire millworker, remembering the 1790s, wrote how, 'My Brother Joseph got his hand Catched in the factory, lost one finger & was much Cut & mangled – after that he sickend & died aged 11 years.' Such accidents were numerous beyond counting, and counted little except to the victims and their families … anyway, in most places there were plenty more where they came from.

Industrialisation was, in the main, the consequence of private enterprise. The role of the State in mining and manufacturing in Britain was modest in comparison to that of some governments in continental Europe. There was no British equivalent of Dijonval, the monumental state-sponsored broadcloth factory at Sedan, nor of the Fonderie Royale and the Cristallerie de la Reine, laid out as if components

△ This engraving which appeared in the *History of the Cotton Manufacture*, by Edward Baines, Jnr, published in 1835, is one of the best-known images of the industrial revolution. It shows the operation of spinning mules in the Fishwick mill of Swainson Birley, near Preston, Lancashire. The spinning mule had been invented by Samuel Crompton in 1779, combining the moving carriage of the spinning jenny with the rollers of Arkwright's water-frame; it was the most successful and widely used of the powered spinning machines and was developed into a fully mechanised, self-acting standardised machine by Richard Roberts between 1825 and 1830. The engraving shows that even the most up-to-date machinery posed dangers to the children who worked it, in this case being employed to crawl beneath the extended yarn to sweep up the cotton waste; children were also used to piece together broken ends of yarn.

of an ornamental park at Le Creusot in the 1780s. Some specific infrastructure projects were funded by town corporations, the most notable example probably being all of the enclosed docks at Liverpool (those at London, by contrast, were built with private capital, and no overall public body for the Thames existed until the Port of London Authority was created in 1908). Nonetheless, government was directly involved in the production of armaments. In 1700 there were naval dockyards at Deptford, Woolwich, Chatham and Portsmouth, and a recently founded establishment at Devonport which stimulated the growth of Plymouth. These were significant employers. In 1711 the dockyards together employed some 6,500 people. The yards grew and multiplied during the eighteenth century, and

their scale can be appreciated at Chatham, in covered building slips, a mould loft completed in 1755 which measures 119 feet × 55 feet (36.6 × 17 m) with mast and spar shops below, and a three-storey rope works of 1786–91 which is 1,140 feet long (351 m), and which could produce 24-inch (0.62 m) cables. An American Quaker in 1776 remarked at Portsmouth, 'The King's Dock is sufficient to strike terror in the enemies of England. Nothing can give one a higher idea of its strength and power. Rope makers, smiths, shipwrights, mast makers, all seem to move by clockwork.' Nevertheless, most of Britain's wooden merchant ships were built in small establishments along the coast and on river banks in many parts of the country, while significant numbers were actually constructed in North America and India. By 1814 the dockyards employed 17,500 people, including about 2,000 who worked in India, the Mediterranean and the Caribbean. The separately constituted Victualling Board supplied food and drink to the Royal Navy, and in the early nineteenth century built monumental depots – the Royal Victoria Yard at Deptford, the Royal Clarence at Gosport and the Royal William at Plymouth.

The army's principal manufacturing and logistics base was the arsenal at Woolwich, which originated with a military storage depot established in 1671 on a 31-acre site. This had grown to 104 acres by the late 1770s, when construction began of a 2½-mile boundary wall, originally 8 feet (2.5 m) high. Sir John Vanbrugh and Nicholas Hawksmoor designed buildings within the complex, and a gun foundry was established there in 1717. Close to the Arsenal were the Royal Military Academy and the headquarters of the Royal Artillery. Government was also involved in the manufacture of gunpowder, at mills at Faversham (sold in 1825) and a late eighteenth-century works at Ballincollig, Co. Cork. This was sold in 1833, after which the manufacture of explosives was concentrated at Waltham Abbey, purchased by the Crown in 1787 at the prompting of Lt General Sir William Congreve. The manufactory of small arms at Enfield Lock, opened in 1816, employed about a thousand people by 1860.

Military demands influenced the production of cannon, and consequently of other iron castings, the fabrication of copper, and the introduction of steam-propelled iron ships. Indeed, the order placed with Henry Maudslay for block-making machines designed by Sir Marc Brunel for Portsmouth Dockyard was a key event in the development of mechanical engineering. Brunel and Maudslay had both worked at the Royal Arsenal. By the 1820s, in another example of innovation in the military, the mass-production of ships' biscuits at the Royal Victoria Yard at Deptford

▸ The Royal Dockyards were among the most imposing industrial establishments in the British Isles. The yard at Deptford on the south bank of the river Thames downstream from London was founded in 1513 by Henry VIII, and Peter the Great of Russia studied there in 1698. The yard reached its zenith in the eighteenth century, and by the 1790s there were five slipways for warships in the yard. After the Napoleonic Wars the Deptford yard went into decline, since it was situated too far upstream to cope with the largest ships of the time; new ships were no longer built there from the 1830s, and it was closed in 1869. This painting of about 1750 is one of several of that period showing ships of the line being launched at Deptford. Such launchings were relatively rare events, and, as the picture shows, they attracted many spectators. The substantial brick building to the right of the ship being launched was the Grand Storehouse, and the dwelling house on the left, which still stands, was the home of the Master Shipwright. The ship was launched without its mast and rigging which might have been added at Deptford or at the nearby Royal Dockyard at Woolwich.

The British government played a relatively small role in manufacturing in the eighteenth and nineteenth centuries, but some installations that supplied the army or the Royal Navy had a grandeur that was rarely seen in private industry. Under the direction of Sir John Rennie the Royal William Victualling Yard at Plymouth was built between 1827 and 1835 to supply the Royal Navy.

The war in which Britain, France and Prussia confronted Russia and the Ottoman Empire broke out in October 1853, and on 15 March 1854 the Royal Navy despatched from Portsmouth a substantial fleet under the command of Sir Charles Napier which was to join a French squadron in attacking Russian installations in the Baltic. The campaign proved inconclusive since the commanders were apprehensive about attacking strong fortifications and the Russian use of mines had a considerable deterrent effect. At the centre of the picture is a wooden-walled ship of the line, possibly *Neptune*, flagship of the second-in-command, but Napier's flagship was the screw-propelled steamer *Duke of Wellington* which had a crew of more than 1,000 men. By this date the Royal Navy was turning more and more towards using steam-powered vessels. An oil painting by Wilhelm Melbye.

was establishing a technology that was later used by civilian manufacturers.

While the arsenal and the dockyards were evidence of military power, that power was for the most part exercised overseas, and for much of our period the military presence in much of Britain was scarcely noticeable, although not in the Scottish Highlands after Culloden in 1745, nor in Ireland in 1798. Nevertheless, press gangs influenced coastal and estuarial shipping, while the passage of columns of troops could momentarily disrupt towns of thoroughfare. To overseas visitors the lack of military visibility was as surprising as the absence of internal customs. The German Pastor

Moritz observed in 1782 that, 'Passing through an English town is very strange to a foreigner. ... There are no fortifications – town walls, gate or the like; no exciseman on the lookout, no menacing sentry to beware of; you pass through town and village as freely and unhindered as through wide-open nature.' The contrast with his homeland, where the gradual dismantling of inter-state customs under the *Zollverein* began only in 1818, was particularly marked.

Britain's industrial development was shaped in part by successive wars: that against Louis XIV which concluded with the Treaty of Utrecht in 1713; the War of the Austrian Succession between 1740 and 1748; the

Seven Years War of 1756–63; the War of American Independence; the wars against Revolutionary and Napoleonic France; and the Crimean War (1853–56). Manufacturing was affected by blockades that shut off supplies of raw materials or closed export markets, but modest commitments to land warfare meant that the drain on manpower was less than in Prussia or France, although the threat of militia service could shape the lives of individuals, as it did that of the engineer Richard Roberts, who about 1813 walked from London to Manchester to avoid conscription into the militia. The rapidity with which educated Englishmen flocked abroad after the signing of the short-lived Treaty of Amiens in 1802 indicates the extent to which they saw themselves as Europeans.

The war with France between 1793 and 1815, and its immediate aftermath, form a distinct phase in British history, a time of democratic aspiration and of repression by government, and in Ireland a period of awakened nationalism, repressed with less measured severity. Evangelical religion gained many adherents. Industrial labour was, relatively speaking, lavishly rewarded, but according to middle-class critics those rewards were squandered, rather than being saved for adverse circumstances. Child labour was callously exploited. The practices revealed in parliamentary enquiries of the 1830s and 1840s are disturbing, but textual analysis of evidence presented to those enquiries suggests that conditions had been worse between 1790 and 1815. London magistrates believed that there was less juvenile delinquency in the capital during the wars with France because with so many men serving as sailors more employment was available for children. Colquhoun in 1815 marvelled at the progress of manufactures after 1793, brought about by the improvement of steam engines and the deployment of ingenious machinery in the textile trades.

Some important technological developments were imported from the continent. In the early eighteenth century managers of copper plants at Bristol, Redbrook (on the river Wye near Monmouth), and Cheadle drew on the expertise of continental workers. Tinplate manufacture drew upon the research of the Frenchman René Réaumur, while the production of 'corrugated iron' in the Black Country from the 1830s followed the galvanising process patented in France in 1829 by Stanislas Sorel. The boring machines that shaped the cylinders of late eighteenth-century steam engines were derived from one built at Woolwich by the Dutchman Jan Verbruggen. The casting of plate glass was introduced from France to Ravenhead (St Helens) in 1773, and Robert Lucas Chance brought the hand cylinder method of making sheet glass from Lorraine to Smethwick. The Leblanc and Solvay processes for making alkali, the Jacquard loom and the Guibal ventilation fan were other technologies brought from the continent. Famously, the closely guarded secret of mechanised silk throwing was stolen from Italy by John Lombe, who cheekily went on to secure a British patent for his ill-gotten gain and established a large new mill in Derby to exploit it. On the other hand, British technology was itself of interest to foreign governments. John Harris has shown how spies recorded processes used in Britain and tempted skilled workers overseas. Several leading innovators and entrepreneurs were natives of continental Europe, or were descended from immigrants, including Sir Mark Brunel from Normandy, Andrew Kurtz from Würtemburg, Sir William Siemens from Hanover, Henry Bolckow from Mecklenburg, Sir Bernhard Samuelson from Hamburg, Sir John Brunner (son of a Swiss Unitarian), Ludwig Mond from Kassel, and Karl Friedrich Beyer from Saxony. A succession of British engineers founded concerns in Belgium, Russia, France and Austria. It was a two-way exchange. Furthermore the nineteenth century was a time of great migrations from Europe to the New World, and with those human tides went manufacturing knowledge and skills. Most notable of those who took their know-how abroad were the Cornish miners, who could be found throughout the Empire and in every continent, wherever there were metalliferous ores that merited extraction.

After 1789 the British were aware of continental Europe, not only because of war but also through the presence of French prisoners-of-war and royalist exiles, commemorated by memorials in Dorchester Abbey (Oxfordshire) and the parish church at New Alresford (Hants). Dartmoor Prison was built in 1809 to house Napoleonic prisoners, and a governor's house, a monument and earthworks provide evidence of the prisoner-of-war camp at Norman Cross near Peterborough. Cultural influences from the continent gradually extended throughout society. In cities, small towns and even in the remote countryside during the nineteenth century German and Italian musicians were familiar. There were 880 German musicians in England and Wales in 1881, mostly in bands of six to eight players. Many came from the barren lands of the western Palatinate around Kusel, but some from Hanover, Berlin and Frankfurt-am-Main. In 1861 they were recorded as staying at Bourne, Cambridge, Horncastle and Ironbridge among other places. Jewish sellers of 'Mizpah brooches', mostly born in present-day Poland, could be encountered throughout Britain. A group in the poorest part of Oxford in 1851 included a Hebrew writer, as well as jewellers from Nordhausen and Poznań (Posen), and in 1851 a Prussian-born jeweller was staying in a remote hamlet near Coalbrookdale. Some British forgemen and glassworkers found employment abroad, including residents in the Combe des Anglais at Le Creusot. Navvies building the Severn Valley Railway in 1861 had worked in Normandy and the Rhone Valley. International exhibitions attracted self-educated working men. A group in Banbury organised language classes to enable them to converse with their French *confrères* at the International Exhibition of 1862, while Joseph Gutteridge, a Coventry loom mechanic, visited the Paris exhibition of 1867 and studied textile manufactures in St Etienne, Lyons, Basle and Rouen.

The universities of Glasgow and Edinburgh are regularly mentioned in this study, but Oxford and Cambridge hardly at all. The latter, the only universities in England until the 1830s, excluded Dissenters, which may have driven some to Scotland or continental Europe. Dr Joseph Black, Professor of Medicine at Glasgow in 1756–66 and of Medicine and Chemistry at Edinburgh from 1766, was the academic who most influenced industrial development. His best-known research concerned latent heat. He encouraged the young James Watt, and William Reynolds attended his classes in Edinburgh. Some entrepreneurs and innovators gained experience abroad. Sir Isaac Lothian Bell studied at Edinburgh and the Sorbonne. William Losh

received part of his education in Hamburg; A. G. Kurtz and John Hutchinson were fellow students in Paris; and Angus Smith attended classes given by Justus von Liebig at Giessen. In fact few elements of economic development and even fewer technological innovations were products of the education system or of theoretical science. As Peter Mathias pointed out: 'Great determination, intense curiosity, quick wits, clever fingers, luck, capital, or employment and a backer to survive the period of experimenting, testing, improving were more important in almost all fields than a scientific training.' And Edward Baines lists many textile innovations that were made by practical men of modest formal training, including 'Mr Robert' (i.e. Richard Roberts, see Chapter 3, pages 77, 81–2), the 'extremely ingenious machine-maker of Manchester' who devised a successful form of self-acting mule; 'a person named Green, a tinsmith, of Mansfield, who was the first who conceived of the idea of attaching the movements of the spindle and bobbin together' in roving frames; and 'the patent [for the dressing-machine was taken out] … in the name of Thomas Johnson, of Bredbury, a weaver in [the company's] employment, to whose inventive talent the machine was chiefly owing.'

More influential in facilitating industrial growth than most academic institutions were the literary and philosophical societies of the industrial cities, the informal associations such as the Lunar Society, and industrial concerns that served as nurseries of talent, such as Henry Maudslay's workshop. James Keir, the chemist, was for a time an employee at the Soho Manufactory and a member of the Lunar Society. He wrote in 1789 that 'the diffusion of a general knowledge of, and of a taste for science over all classes of men in every nation of Europe or of European origin seems to be the characteristic feature of the present age'.

The unseen presence of America underlay developments throughout the period. Imports from America became increasingly significant – tobacco, sugar, timber, and above all cotton, until the mid-1860s slave-grown – while iron tools, hardware, textiles and printed books crossed the Atlantic in the other direction. Elihu Burritt, who grew up in Bristol, Connecticut, wrote in 1864:

All Americans who were boys forty years ago will remember three English centres of particular interest to them. These were Sheffield, Colebrook Dale and Paternoster Row. There was hardly a house or log cabin between the Penobscot and the Mississippi which could not show the imprint of these three places, on the iron tea-kettle, the youngest boy's Barlow knife and his younger sister's picture-book. To the juvenile imagination of these times, Sheffield was a huge jack-knife, Colebrook Dale a porridge pot, and Paternoster Row a psalm book.

From the time of the Pilgrim Fathers America was a refuge for the discontented and oppressed. After the War of Independence it was also a source of hope for those who had lost their means of livelihood, or whose political or religious views did not fit comfortably into British society. Some fled across the Atlantic because they had broken the law, others in groups organised by landowners anxious to reduce rural pauperism. People learned about America through literature and popular lectures. Frances Trollope (mother of Anthony) and Charles Dickens published best-selling books about their travels, while with the aid of lantern slides entertainers such as Henry Russell and Washington Friend provided audiences with impressions of 'the wondrous scenes of the distant west … the crowded city and the solitary forest … represented with a truthfulness which carried the imaginations of the lookers on to the shores of the Mississippi or the mighty plunge of Niagara.'

American evangelists such as Lorenzo Dow, Alexander Campbell (founder of the Disciples of Christ), Phoebe Palmer, Ira D. Sankey and Dwight L. Moody attracted crowds in Britain. Images of the United States were purveyed by nigger minstrels and by the circuses of Seth B. Howes & Joseph Cushing and Phineas T. Barnum. The significance of America emerges, for example, from the reminiscences of Adam Rushton, who learned to read at the Sunday school in Macclesfield and, on discovering the Pilgrim Fathers, 'fell into a sort of enchanted dream of a freer life in the American backwoods'.

The tomb of 'Poor Samboo, a faithfull Negro', a black cabin boy who served the captain of a ship which arrived at the tiny harbour at Sunderland Point, then an outport of Lancaster, in 1736. Sambo died shortly after the ship docked, and, since it was believed he had never been baptised, was buried in unconsecrated ground. This plaque and poem were added in 1796.

Another aspect of the imperial dimension was the presence in Britain of men and women who had grown up or worked in India, North America or the Mediterranean. Some, including many born in Spain and Portugal between 1808 and 1814, were the offspring of soldiers. Others were black people, of whom there were about 15,000 in Britain in 1800. Lord Torrington observed at Stockport in 1790 that, 'This inn is striped and barr'd with as much black timber as would build a man of war. The waiter likewise is black, a very Othello, a quick intelligent fellow who comes to swarth our breed.' In 1842 J. G. Kohl noted 'Hindoo' beggars on the streets of Manchester, while in the graveyard of the parish church of Bishop's Castle in remotest Shropshire is a stone inscribed, 'Here lieth the body of

I.D., a native of Africa, who died in this town on Sept 9th 1801. "God hath created of one blood all nations of men," Acts Ch. 17 verse 26.'

Many developments between 1700 and 1870 were dependent on technological innovation. It is not the intention of this study to break new boundaries in the history of technology, but rather to place technological developments in their appropriate contexts. Relationships with distant countries also involved technology. While cotton manufacturers in the eighteenth century learned much from India, and the Royal Navy built ships there, the capabilities of craftsmen in countries regarded as inferior were rarely recognised. Few heeded Samuel's Johnson's sage observation to Warren Hastings in 1774 that 'There are arts of manufacture practised in the countries in which you preside which are yet very imperfectly known here, either to artificers or philosophers'.

Early commentators were often quick to emphasise new technologies, techniques and mechanical devices. Some of these, such as the water-frame, the flying shuttle or Watt's separate condenser for the steam engine, were of momentous importance, but the speed of adoption of innovations could be variable, and it could take many years for new methods to displace the old. Inventions, not infrequently protected by patent, could take a long time to spread. For this reason among many, one needs to take a surprisingly long view of some of the processes involved, reinforcing the scepticism noted above of the usefulness of the term 'industrial revolution'.

Over the long term, however, the changes described did propel the national economy into an acknowledged position of international competitive superiority in the 1850s and 1860s. This is more a cause for reflection than an excuse for chauvinistic rejoicing, and in this book the use of such terms as 'world first', 'world centre of' and 'cradle of' will mostly be avoided. This study attempts to show awareness of the topography and past histories of communities within the British Isles. It does not focus unduly on celebrated places, and it attempts to heed William Cobbett's observation in 1825 that, 'Those that travel on turnpike roads know nothing of England – From Hascomb to Thursley almost the whole way is across fields, or commons, or along narrow lands. Here we see the people without any disguise or affectation. Against a great road things are made for show. Here we see them without any show.'

Despite half a century and more of retreat from manufacturing, Britain's industrial legacy is still with us. Some former mining and manufacturing sites have left little trace. Their buildings have been demolished and the 'brownfield' land re-used for housing or service industries. Other buildings have been adapted for new uses, for business or housing, or as museums. Indeed, places linked to the industrial revolution comprise about a third of Britain's UNESCO World Heritage Sites: the mining and iron-working landscape of Blaenavon; the tin and copper mines of Cornwall and west Devon; Derbyshire's Derwent Valley mills; the complex landscape of the Ironbridge Gorge; Robert Owen's New Lanark; Sir Titus Salt's mill and model village at Saltaire; and, inscribed as recently as 2009, the Pontcysyllte Aqueduct and the adjoining sections of the canal that passes over it. Yet the legacy goes deeper. Many towns that were once busily pre-occupied with mining or manufacturing have struggled to come to terms with the loss of industry: typical of such places are the iron-mining village of Cleator Moor in west Cumberland, Merthyr Tydfil in South Wales, some of the pit villages in Derbyshire, Nottinghamshire and south Yorkshire, and the cotton towns of east Lancashire. These and many other communities flourished because of the developments described in this book, and now have been left stranded, economically and socially, by the decline of mining and manufacturing in the twentieth century.

In some places, the legacy is also one of despoiled landscape or lingering pollution. Among the most ravaged was the lower Swansea Valley: its hillsides were stripped naked of vegetation by decades of toxic fumes that had poured from the copper works, smelters and tinplate works which had developed from the end of the eighteenth century; all around man-made mountains of slag and industrial waste hid the valley floor. The slopes of beautiful Swaledale were scarred by the deep ravines created by 'hushing', as torrents of water were released to flood down the hillsides to scour away the overburden and reveal – all being well – the lead-veins beneath. In the central valley of Scotland bright-pink conical 'bings', immense hills of burnt shale that was the waste product of the oil-shale industry, towered above coal-mining villages such as Addiewell and Tarbrax. Some of the lovely estuaries of Cornwall were choked with silts washed down from tin-streaming works upstream. At Widnes in the 1870s hydrochloric acid gas poured from alkali plants into the lungs of all who lived there, and when it rained corrosive acid dropped on to both people and buildings. In the towns and villages of mid-Cheshire houses and public buildings sank slowly and crazily into subsidence pits that had been created by underground salt workings. Ironically, we often now treasure the remaining evidence of such processes – hushes, pit heaps and lakes created by subsidence – and not simply for archaeological reasons. The oil-shale bings at Addiewell are now a National Nature Reserve. The 170-acre lake of Pennington Flash near Leigh, formed barely a century ago as the result of mining at Birkenshaw Colliery, now attracts more than 230 species of birds; the lake and surrounding country park are regarded as one of the premier bird-watching reserves in the North. In the Ironbridge Gorge, mean-while, the regeneration of woodlands and the return of wildlife after several centuries of despoliation by smoke and the dumping of waste are now appreciated as one of the most significant features of the landscape.

In 1791 Arthur Young, an informed witness who is often quoted below, took an optimistic view of changes in his lifetime, exhorting his readers to

> get rid of that dronish, sleepy and stupid indifference, that lazy negligence, which enchains men in the exact paths of their forefathers, without enquiry, without thought and without ambition, and you are sure of doing good. What trains of thought, what a spirit of exertion, what a mass and power of effort have sprung in every path of life from the works of such men as Brindley, Watt, Priestley, Harrison, Arkwright, and let me add my fellow-traveller Bakewell! Who will tell me that the buttons at Birmingham are not better made because the tups around are better

bred – because locks and sluices are better constructed, and that woollen cloth will not be better woven because cotton is spun in the beautiful invention of the mills? In what path of life can a man be found that will not animate his pursuit from seeing the steam engine of Watt?

He concluded, as he watched the Oxford Canal Company's engineer trying to remedy a shortage of water caused by increasing traffic, that: 'Undoubtedly the spirit of enterprise, the ardent, energetic and daring attempts that are every day made in this kingdom, are glorious exertions and do infinite honour to it.'

In the 1840s one member of the Manchester Athenaeum accepted the task of translating Léon Faucher's book about contemporary Manchester. In a short Preface, the translator, writing from the perspective of the free-trade capital of the world, gave us this:

> There is something mysterious in the rise and progress of the manufacturing system. A few mechanical discoveries, apparently insignificant in themselves, and almost unnoticed at the time of their appearance, form the nucleus of a system which grows steadily, and marches on silently, and yet, with such irresistible influence as to absorb in a few years, the olden features of society, developing new features, requiring new institutions in accordance with its new developments, and pointing to some new Destiny, ill-understood, yet instinctively believed in by all.

Marvellous and mysterious, this new 'manufacturing system' had changed the world.

Industrial change and expansion affected the British Isles profoundly between 1700 and 1870. In its wake it brought massive urbanisation, fundamental demo-graphic and social change, the transformation of landscapes and the reshaping of the economy. It was

Few scenes in industrial Britain in the nineteenth century were as awe-inspiring as a distant prospect of the blast furnaces at Merthyr Tydfil. The spectacle impressed the King of Saxony and his entourage in 1844 (see pages 311–12). This painting shows the Cyfarthfa Ironworks, constructed under the direction of Charles Wood in the late 1760s, and the property of the Crawshay family from the 1790s. In 1806 it was the most productive ironworks in Britain, and Richard Crawshay, 'Moloch, the Iron King', was conscious in 1790 that he belonged to a generation who had transformed the iron industry. The flame-topped blast furnaces, which still stand, are evident in the centre of the picture, and the numerous chimneys carried flues from the boilers of steam engines which powered blowing machines and rolling mills. Similar scenes could be observed in the mid-nineteenth century in the vicinity of Coalbrookdale, in the Black Country, in parts of Yorkshire and around Coatbridge.

'CYFARTHFA STEELWORKS AT NIGHT' BY THOMAS PRYTHERCH, BY COURTESY OF MERTHYR TYDFIL COUNCIL

one of the most important processes in world history, a period and a phenomenon of global significance. No part of the world has been unaffected by what happened in these islands a quarter of a millennium ago, and we live every day with the consequences. The object of this study is to survey as broadly as possible the experiences of those who witnessed and lived through these changes.

Industrial history is not primarily about machines, raw materials, processes and products. It is about the people who created, innovated, laboured, suffered, acquired, bought and enjoyed, became rich or died young, lived comfortably on the profits or were crushed by the harshness of it all. None of this would have happened without people, and that is why, throughout this book, they take centre stage.

PART I

'Illustrious followers of science'

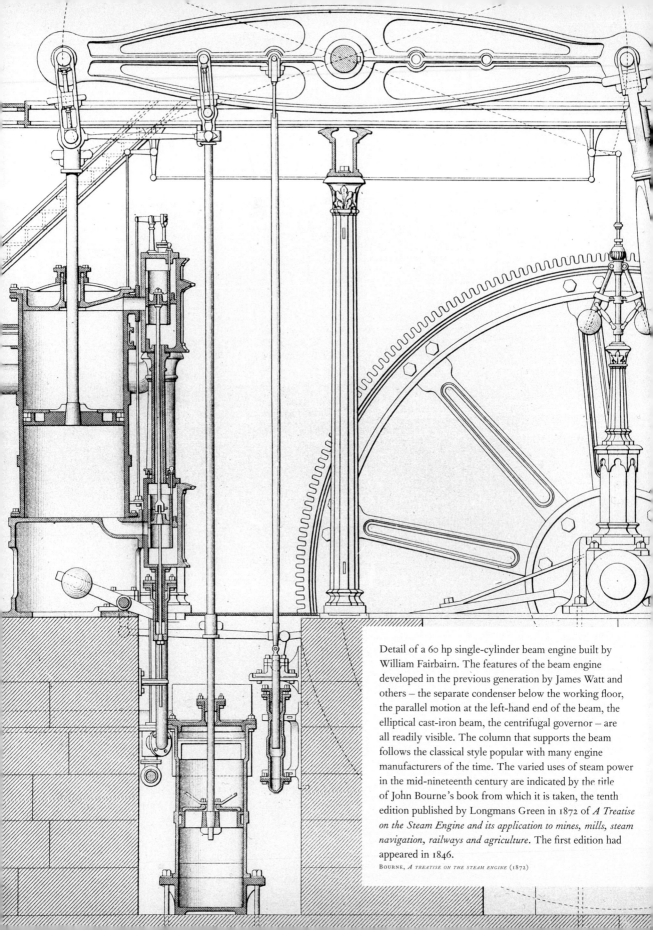

Detail of a 60 hp single-cylinder beam engine built by William Fairbairn. The features of the beam engine developed in the previous generation by James Watt and others – the separate condenser below the working floor, the parallel motion at the left-hand end of the beam, the elliptical cast-iron beam, the centrifugal governor – are all readily visible. The column that supports the beam follows the classical style popular with many engine manufacturers of the time. The varied uses of steam power in the mid-nineteenth century are indicated by the title of John Bourne's book from which it is taken, the tenth edition published by Longmans Green in 1872 of *A Treatise on the Steam Engine and its application to mines, mills, steam navigation, railways and agriculture*. The first edition had appeared in 1846.

BOURNE, *A TREATISE ON THE STEAM ENGINE* (1872)

2

Fuelling growth: energy and power for industry

'He enlarged the resources of his country, increased the power of man and rose to an eminent place among the most illustrious followers of science and the real benefactors of the world.'

MEMORIAL TO JAMES WATT, WESTMINSTER ABBEY

T HE AVAILABILITY OF ENERGY determines the prosperity of economies and the comfort of societies, as anyone who queued for coal at a snow-encrusted railway yard in January 1947, or saw lights go out during the three-day week of 1974, or observed the bitterness of the miners' strike of 1984–85, will be well aware. Affordable fuel contributes to domestic well-being and stimulates enterprise, while expensive fuel raises living expenses. In 1700 many urban activities depended on the availability of fuel, to provide heat for blacksmiths' hearths, maltsters' kilns, brewers' coppers, tallow chandlers' vats and brickmakers' clamps. There were profound changes between 1700 and 1870 in the sources of energy and the ways in which it was applied, which shaped the broader social and economic changes of the period.

Wood, peat and coal before the industrial revolution

In 1700 and to a lesser extent in 1870 woodlands and forests were sources of energy and raw materials. From them came naval timbers, beechwood for chairs, twigs for baskets and besoms, coopers' staves, hop poles, pit props and split wood for crates, as well as faggots for bakers, billets for fuel in distant places, and underwood for local fires. Forests were sources of charcoal, essential in smelting and forging iron until the mid-eighteenth century and still used in iron working in the 1860s. Lime kilns on the Sussex Downs were still fired with wood in the 1780s. Firewood cut in the Chiltern Hills was taken to wharfs on the river Thames, and carried downstream to London. As

early as 1689 Sir John Borlase had billets to the value of £350 stacked on one wharf at Medmenham, and wood worth £975 at Little Marlow. In 1690 William Willmott of Fingest had beech billets worth more than £230 stacked in his woods and on a Thamesside wharf. These are very large sums of money indeed. The woodlands of Buckinghamshire met much of the county's need for fuel, yet even Sir John Borlase had some coal.

Heathlands were also a source of energy. William Cobbett, visiting Thanet in September 1823, observed the paradox between the plentiful crops being gathered in and the poverty of the harvesters. He argued that

A peat cart in Langstrothdale, source of the uppermost reaches of the river Wharfe. The thin wheels enabled the cart to pass easily through turf. The author of *The Costume of Yorkshire* observed that in 1814 peat was the general fuel used in the mountainous and moorland districts of northern England, and that it was customarily dug or cut into pieces about the size of a common brick, before being dried by the sun and stacked before use. Hand-coloured aquatint by Robert Havell after George Walker.

'the more purely a corn country, the more miserable the labourers' and thought that labouring men fared better in 'the rabbit countries' where there were woods and heaths. Probate inventories reveal that before the 1750s faggots and logs were the usual fuels in central Essex. Pehr Kalm in 1748 watched furze being cut and bundled on Ivinghoe Common (Buckinghamshire), and beech twigs and bracken being collected as fuel for brick kilns on the Ashridge estate of the 3rd Duke of Bridgewater. A generation later, in the 1770s, Thomas Pennant observed that in the Severn Valley in Wales the rich burned wood while the poor used a wretched turf. The poor of Wigginton in Oxfordshire were supplied with fuel which, before enclosure in 1795, was usually bundles of furze from the parish heath, but thereafter coal. Many heathlands were enclosed during the eighteenth century, and the process continued in wetlands and uplands until the 1860s. The brothers la Rochfoucauld were surprised in 1774 to observe near London stretches of common overgrown with bracken where

'improvements', which they considered desirable, were delayed because the poor had immemorial rights to cut bracken and brushwood for firewood.

Some energy came from wetlands. Peat was the principal domestic fuel in parts of the Scottish Highlands, around the mosses of Cheshire and Lancashire, and in the Fens and the Isle of Axholme. It was being cut in marshes near Uxbridge in 1798. It was even tried as a fuel for blast furnaces in the eighteenth century, and used experimentally in finery forges in the 1820s. It was used to smelt lead ore in the Pennines, where the ruined peat store at Old Gang in Swaledale is monumental. By the mid-nineteenth century peat was supplanted by coal in the Lincolnshire Fens, but not in Cambridgeshire where 36 men were digging and carting peat at Burwell in 1861 and 50 at Isleham. Turf was particularly significant in Ireland where more than three million acres, or 16 per cent, of the land surface consisted of peat bog. Before 1946 almost all peat was cut with a spade called a slane or *sleaghan*.

Along with the properties they owned or occupied many Irishmen had rights to cut turf in particular places for their own use. Commercial exploitation grew from the late eighteenth century as the Grand Canal enabled peat to be carried from the Bog of Allen to Dublin. In Germany, Russia and Denmark peat was more than a marginal source of energy, and in the Netherlands the museum at Barger-Compascuum provides evidence of its significance.

At the start of the eighteenth century large areas of the country that were remote from coalfields or navigable water lacked energy to a significant extent. In 1698, for instance, Celia Fiennes travelled from Peterborough to Wansford and saw cakes of cow dung hung up to dry on cottage walls and observed 'it is a very offensive fewell but the country people use little else in these parts'. In his gazetteer, published in 1750–51, Stephen Whatley was impressed by the dearness of fuel around Northampton, where there was scarcely any woodland, and coals could not be supplied before the river Nene was made navigable, a process that was completed in 1761. Probate inventories illuminate the shortage of fuel around Banbury which lies 22 miles south of the Warwickshire coalfield and about the same distance north of Oxford, where Thames barges were able to deliver coal that had been imported via London from north-east England. Banbury's hinterland comprised rich arable and pasture land, but not much woodland, no peat-yielding wetlands and only small areas of open common. More than a hundred probate inventories survive for citizens who died between 1690 and 1724, of which 39 (36 per cent) record fuel, a higher proportion than in most towns. Twenty-seven refer unambiguously to 'coals', two of which value it at a shilling per hundredweight, or £1 per ton. Twenty-four inventories record firewood; seven refer to furze, five to faggots, one to broom and one to turfs, a hundredweight and a half of which were valued at 2s. 6d. In fact, coal was reaching the Banbury area, and its use was not confined to the wealthy. But it was expensive, and people also burned fuels from local woodlands and commons. The Shropshire market town of Bishop's Castle was situated a dozen miles from the nearest coal mines, but beyond hills that could be crossed only with difficulty

Locally dug peat was commonly used as fuel in the lead smelters of the Pennines. For example, there were four ore furnaces at the Old Gang complex in Swaledale, for which peat was kept in a storehouse 390 feet long and 21 feet wide (119 × 6.5 m), which could hold sufficient fuel to fire the smelter for three years. Just the pillars, foundations and end walls remain of this extraordinary building, set in a landscape where there are now few traces of any other human activity. (See also page 375.)

Charcoal was produced in large quantities in 1700 in woodlands throughout the British Isles. It was used in smelting iron ore in blast furnaces and in refining iron in forges, and also in working other metals, as well as in processes such as malting that required a smokeless fuel. For many purposes charcoal was superseded by coke or anthracite during the eighteenth century. In 1870 it was still used to refine wrought iron with particular qualities, to line moulds in foundries, and as a filter and a source of carbon in the chemical industry. The traditional way of making charcoal, by heating 'cords' of wood about 4 feet long under a blanket of earth or turf that excluded air, is demonstrated here at the Weald & Downland Museum in Sussex. Cords were trimmed before they were used. The resultant twigs were usually bundled into faggots for use in bakers' ovens, or used by local people as domestic fuel.

'Irish Peasantry: the Turf Footers'. Many Irishmen had, and many still have, rights to extract turf or peat from bogs in the parishes where they live. Cutting peat was a family activity, as indicated in this engraving of 1790.

© SCIENCE MUSEUM/SCIENCE & SOCIETY PICTURE LIBRARY

by wheeled vehicles. Of 100 inventories taken between 1690 and 1754, 27 refer to fuel, suggesting that means of heating were highly valued. Coal is listed on seven inventories, but wood for burning is mentioned on nine, while there are eight references to broom, gorse or faggots.

Coal was naturally plentiful in those areas where it was mined, but received wisdom in the mid-eighteenth century held that it could not profitably be carried more than about 15 miles from its source or from navigable water. The Portuguese traveller Don Manuel Gonzales remarked in 1730 that in Monmouth there were fires 'in the meanest cottage' because coal was so cheap. In the Shropshire coalfield it was so slightly valued that it was rarely recorded in probate inventories. The most significant effect of coal mining in 1700 was that it enabled London to enjoy cheap energy. Most overseas visitors the capital were unaccustomed to coal and smoke, and left London with vivid impressions of their effects. Gonzalez listed characteristic English smells: tar at Wapping, herring curing at Yarmouth, and smoke in London. Pehr Kalm found that smoke-induced London fog made him ill. The fashionable physician and philanthropist Dr John Radcliffe lived in Bloomsbury Square, and spent £88 8s. 4d. on coal out of household expenses of £1,503 in the year ending Lady Day 1710.

There are statistical records of the import of coal to London from 1700 onwards. The total received in that year was almost 430,000 tons, which increased threefold to almost 1,290,000 tons in 1800, and to more than 3,550,000 tons in the next fifty years. Almost all of London's coal came by sea from the North East, a trade which had began, on a large scale, in the sixteenth century. By contrast, the quantities carried to London by canal were never large – the peak was 72,000 tons in 1844 – but from 1845 deliveries by rail were recorded, which exceeded a million tons in 1855, two million tons in 1864 and three million tons in 1867, the first year in which carriage by rail exceeded that by sea, and totalled almost 4,450,000 tons in 1871. Coal from the North East was also carried to ports on the east coast and along the south coast as far west as Devon, as well as to the limits of navigation on rivers.

Diminishing supplies from heathlands and woodlands, and the incremental improvement of transport systems, led people to believe that by the 1790s coal had become the principal fuel in most parts of the country. That decade saw a substantial increase in coal output, made possible by the installation of steam winding engines at collieries and the opening of canals. Arthur Young observed that in the 1770s Essex farmers burned little else but wood, but that by 1813 coal was 'everywhere gaining ground upon wood'. French industrial spies in 1785 concluded that the combination of coal and the growing canal network, together with the absence of internal customs, gave Britain great commercial advantages, while William Blakey in 1791 thought that Birmingham had become 'the greatest magazine of hardware on earth', because fuel had 'given life to numbers of Manufactories, while many die upon the continent for want of firing'. In 1793 Lord Torrington, travelling towards Coalbrookdale, fantasised about what a man of the seventeenth century would make of contemporary England, and concluded that he would regret the disappearance of tapestry hangings and woodlands, that he would admire canals and new roads, and that coals would offend both his smell and his sight.

Between the mid-seventeenth century and 1800 the production of coal in Britain – still mainly in the north-east of England – had risen sixty-fold. Whereas the real cost of other fuels such as firewood had increased substantially over this period, the price of coal in London was more or less static, and fell in the coalfields. As we shall see in Chapter 6, by the end of the eighteenth century Britain was producing more coal than anywhere else in the world, and its low price – particularly in the coalfields and along the new transport arteries – became an increasingly important factor in stimulating the development of industry. Coal was set to become the principal fuel of industrialisation.

The enduring importance of muscle power, water and wind

A fundamental innovation of the industrial revolution was to be the use of heat energy to create mechanical power that could be applied to do useful work. In 1700 this had been impossible. Instead, it was human energy that wound minerals from many pits, and raised heavy loads at ports. The treadwheel crane preserved at Harwich was constructed in the naval dockyard in 1667, and the 'great crane' erected in 1735 in the Mud

⌃ Horses working machinery associated with the extraction and processing of clay for brick making could be observed on the edges of most English towns in the mid-nineteenth century. This 'wash-mill' is a large installation, operated by two horses turning a 'gin'. The man with the barrow appears to be taking prepared clay to brickmakers.

▽ A much smaller and more common machine used in brick making was the portable clay mill, produced by many market-town foundries, that could be operated by a single horse. This view dates from 1888.
© NMPFT/ROYAL PHOTOGRAPHIC SOCIETY/SCIENCE & SOCIETY PICTURE LIBRARY

➢ 'Interior of the Well House, Carisbrooke Castle, Isle of Wight', 1850s. This working donkey wheel, whose operations are watched by thousands of visitors every year, is a well-known example of animal power. It was installed in the late sixteenth century above a well 161 feet (49 m) deep. The wooden wheel has a diameter of 15 ft 6 ins (4.7 m) with the four main spokes of each set arranged tangentially about the shaft, with subsidiary framing at right angles to these main spokes.
© SCIENCE MUSEUM/SCIENCE & SOCIETY PICTURE LIBRARY

The tower mill at Kempsey, three miles south of Worcester was recorded in the early 1850s by the pioneer photographer Benjamin Brecknell Turner. It had a masonry tower, rebuilt after a fire in 1802 caused when a high wind caused the sails to rotate so rapidly that they generated too much friction and heat. The wooden cap could be turned by the wheel above the door and the pulley rope that dangles from it. The canvas sails were set for use. The mill was demolished in the 1870s, but the brick cottages to the right still stand.

Wilton Mill, near Marlborough in Wiltshire, dates from 1821, and is one of the best examples of the tower mills that were built during the Napoleonic Wars and the years that followed. The top and the shuttered sails are turned into the wind by a fan-tail, the invention of Edmund Lee in 1745. The mill has been restored and retains much of its original machinery.

The differences between tower mills (such as at Wilton) and post mills can be seen in this post mill built at Danzey Green, Warwickshire, about 1820, and rebuilt in 1969 at the Avoncroft Museum of Historic Buildings. The whole of this mill is rotated into the wind (or 'luffed') by the luffing pole, just visible to the rear. Flour is regularly ground on the single set of stones.

Dock by John Padmore, builder of the railway from Combe Down to Bath, was one of the sights of Bristol. The prison treadmill, invented by Sir William Cubitt, was first used at Bury St Edmunds in 1819. By 1850 such mills were installed in about 30 gaols, including Beaumaris in North Wales, where a wheel of 1829 is preserved. Treadwheels were also used to raise water from deep wells in the chalk country, as at Carisbrooke Castle, and Catherington, original site of the wheel now in the Weald & Downland Museum.

Throughout the period covered here animal power was used for a wide range of manufacturing purposes. Edge-runners, large wheels shaped from stone, running in circular tracks and powered by horses or donkeys, crushed cider apples and metallic ores and broke flax, and in Ireland pounded coal into dust to be formed into balls for domestic heating. Gins raised coal and ores from mines. Some were large: the apparatus installed at Walker Colliery on Tyneside in 1763 to raise coal from a 600-foot shaft was powered by eight horses. Horse-powered winding installations were still being constructed in the 1840s, such as that built for Langton Colliery, Nottinghamshire, now at Wollaton Hall. Horse mills were cheap to build and were widely used in the Scottish Highlands. Indeed, animal power made possible the initial development of mechanised textile-manufacturing processes. In the late eighteenth century a horse could work carding machinery supplying four spinners, while many workshops filled with spinning jennies were horse-powered. Horses also powered clay preparation machinery in suburban brickfields and threshing machinery on farms. Most market-town foundries made horse gins, and there were probably more in use in the 1860s than at any time previously.

Windmills of many shapes and sizes worked all over the British Isles in 1700 and in 1870. They were employed principally to grind grain, but they also drained wetlands and were used in smaller numbers for other purposes. In 1796, for instance, Charles Hatchet watched windmills pumping brine into evaporating pans at Northwich. Unsurprisingly, windmills were most numerous where winds were persistent and where fertile land yielded abundant crops, such as in the Fylde of Lancashire, Lincolnshire, and the coastal areas of Kent. County maps of the early nineteenth century mark 212 windmills in Essex, 79 in Kent and 66 in Sussex, while 250 have been counted on the first edition Ordnance Survey maps for Ireland, which were completed in the 1840s. Tower mills were fixed and are readily identified, but post mills could easily be moved, as evidenced by the two at Greasley in the Erewash Valley in the 1850s, one transported from Hucknall in the 1830s and the other from Nottingham in 1843.

The most eminent engineers of the late eighteenth century were involved in improving the efficiency of windmills. John Smeaton built a five-sail smock mill at Newcastle-upon-Tyne and received the Royal Society's Copley Medal in 1759 for research that included 'curious experiments concerning … windmill sails'; his treatise on milling was published posthumously and ran to several editions. Andrew Meikle, a Scottish engineer who was 'descended from a line of ingenious mechanics', invented the shuttered sail in 1772, while Sir William Cubitt in 1807 replaced canvas sails with self-regulating sails with lever-operated shutters.

The most significant application of wind power was the construction during the Napoleonic Wars and the years that followed of tower mills, which increased capacity for grinding grain during a period of rapid population growth. Of 28 dated tower mills identified by Falconer in 1980, 19 were constructed between 1780 and 1830, including those at Fulwell, Co. Durham; Lytham, Lancashire; Polegate, Sussex; and Wilton near Marlborough. Tower mills powering up to four sets of stones were built in considerable numbers in Ireland between 1770 and 1815. The best-known surviving example, 118 feet 6 inches (24.29 m) high and built between 1790 and 1810, is at the Guinness Brewery in Dublin. Some mighty tower mills were destroyed by the winds they were intended to harness. Others were commercial failures, including the 55-foot (17.76 m) tower built in 1796 by the millwright Joseph Jackson at Newport, Shropshire, which was sold in 1802 for less than half the cost of erection and soon demolished. By contrast there is the Union Mill at Cranbrook, Kent, a four-storey smock mill 72 feet (21.95 m) high on a three-storey octagonal brick base. Constructed by the

A waterwheel that appears to be driving by means of a crank a series of rods that probably powered pumps at a mine at some distance.

This waterwheel powered the bellows of three chafery hearths in one of the forges worked by the Hanbury family at Pontypool. In 1754 the Swedish industrial spy R. R. Angerstein, whose drawing this is, was impressed by the water supply system, remarking that 'the water driving the wheels flows out of the bottom of the pond through a pipe which then bends upwards by the wheel and takes the water to the same level as that in the mill pond. The water then flows out on to the undershot wheel paddles.' By this arrangement the wheels could be kept going as long as there was water in the pond.

The unconventional wheel that provides power for milling grain at Daniels Mill, Eardington, near Bridgnorth. There was a mill on this site from the fifteenth century, powered by a short stream that flows into the Severn. This wheel, 38 ft in diameter with a cast-iron hub and wrought-iron buckets probably dates from a rebuilding of the mill in 1854–55. Between the wheel and the mill wall is the wallower which transmits power to a horizontal shaft that drives three sets of stones.

The waterwheel at Midleton, Co. Cork, where the multi-storey building in the background was constructed as a woollen mill in 1796. It was never used for that purpose but was adapted as a distillery from 1825. The wheel is 16 ft wide and 19 ft in diameter.

millwright James Humphrey in 1814 at a cost of more than £3,500, and equipped with Cubitt's patent sails, it was reputedly the most powerful windmill in England and still works.

The power that could be gained from water was, ultimately, of much greater significance than wind. Water power had been in use for centuries throughout the British Isles, and in many areas a map of mills working in 1870 might not be very different from one of 1700 or even 1450. Water power made possible the take-off of coke-fired iron smelting in the 1750s, of silk throwing from 1721, of cotton spinning from 1771. It remained the principal source of power for manufacturing in 1800. That was no longer so by 1870, but many significant factories utilised water power systems inherited from previous generations.

The ways in which water power was generated varied between regions. Horizontal or 'Norse' wheels were commonly used in the West Highlands, Shetland, the Isle of Man and parts of Ireland. On the slow-moving rivers of lowland England, on the other hand, most mills used broad undershot waterwheels, while in the upland zone millwrights exploited the power of small, fast-flowing streams by erecting overshot wheels, some of substantial diameter. The amount of power that a mill could generate over time could be increased by the construction of additional dams, pools and leats in order to supply either a greater or a more consistent supply of water. Richard Arkwright used soughs that drained mines and pools created by damming the Bonsall Brook to provide water to power his cotton mills at Cromford, and the completion of the woollen mill at King's Stanley, Gloucestershire, in 1812–14, for example, was preceded by the excavation of a five-acre mill pool, the diversion of the river Frome, and the rationalisation of the ownership of adjacent plots. Similar investment went into other sites used for textile manufacturing or iron working. As well as streams and rivers, there were mills on most estuaries, powered by the tide. One of the most notable of these was Three Mills at Bromley-by-Bow, where there were four 20-foot (6.16 m) undershot wheels at the House Mill, rebuilt after a fire in 1802, and three at the Clock Mill of 1817, while the site of the third was adapted for distilling gin from 1872.

Steam power was successfully applied to grinding grain from the 1780s, but in the late eighteenth and early nineteenth centuries there is plenty of evidence of investment throughout the British Isles in water corn mills, including new buildings, new pools and leats, iron wheels and gearing. In 1780 Arthur Young was impressed by the corn mill at Slane on the river Boyne in Co. Meath, which had been constructed in 1763–66: 'a very large and handsome edifice such as no mill I have seen in England can be compared with'. The five-storey stone building survives today, 138 feet long and 54 feet wide (41.3 × 16.6 m), fed with water by a stone-lined leat. The mill drew in grain from a radius of ten miles, and produced up to 17,000 barrels *per annum* of flour, which was despatched by barge and by cart to Dublin and Newry. Slane Mill was eclipsed in size by Lee Mill in Cork, where six- and seven-storey buildings were constructed in 1825–31, with waterwheels made by the local Vulcan Ironworks and mill work by Peele, Williams & Peele of Manchester. Some 50 miles south of Dublin, the mill at Milford near Carlow, built in 1790, was much admired in 1860, after the installation of new machinery by William Fairbairn.

In regions where there was potential for manufacturing most of the sites suitable for generating power had been occupied by mills for many centuries, so eighteenth-century entrepreneurs seeking to use water power could only use those sites which happened to be on the market. At some places water power was abundant. At Ludlow, for example, a mill on the river Corve and six on the river Teme were used for grinding grain, dressing leather, making paper, blowing the cupola of a foundry, fulling woollen cloth, and throwing silk. The water that cascaded through the Greenfield Valley near Holywell in North Wales was employed by cotton-spinning mills, copper works, fulling mills and snuff mills. When Arthur Young visited Blarney, Co. Cork, in 1780 he found a textile printing works, a woollen manufactory, a leather-dressing works and a paper mill, as well as associated activities, such as handloom weaving, that did not require power. More than five miles of leats were dug between 1794 and 1809 at Ballincollig on the river Lee near Cork, providing power for twelve

The Upper Mill in the Cromford Mill complex built by Richard Arkwright from 1771 was originally a five-storey structure of local gritstone, extending over 11 bays, and was extended by four bays in the late 1780s. The two top storeys were removed after a fire in 1929. This view shows the tail race, from which water, having entered the mill across an aqueduct, originally of wood but from 1821 of cast iron, and passed over the mill's wheels, flows into the mill yard. (See also the site plan on page 395.)
PHOTOGRAPH: CARNEGIE

Once the water had passed out of the Upper Mill into the mill yard it was directed towards the Lower Mill, a 16-bay, six-storey building constructed from 1776, most of which was destroyed by fire. From about 1820 part of the flow was diverted by this weir into a channel that fed the nearby Cromford Canal.

The so-called 'Bear Pit' in Cromford village was part of the system by which Richard Arkwright controlled the flow of water to his mills. From this stone-lined pit some water flowed to power Cromford Mills, but some was diverted to Greyhound Pool, a reservoir in the centre of Cromford village. Water was diverted there at weekends so that there was a sufficient supply for the mills on Monday mornings.
PHOTOGRAPHS: CARNEGIE

New Lanark was notable not only as the scene of the social experiments of Robert Owen, but also as one of the most abundant sources of water power in the British Isles. The mills stood just downstream from the Falls of Clyde (the subject of one of the most memorable paintings of J. M. W. Turner), and water was fed to the waterwheels by a complex system of lades. This view shows the main lade; mill numbers 1–3 are on the left. (See also the map and photographs on pages 598–9.)
PHOTOGRAPH: CARNEGIE

The large corn mills built in Ireland in the late eighteenth century were regarded as examples for the rest of the world. The most celebrated was Slane Mill, built between 1763 and 1766 under the direction of David Jebb, who had supervised construction work on the River Boyne Navigation. It was a five-storey stone structure, reputedly the largest corn mill in Ireland, that could grind 15 tons of grain per day. It operated until the 1870s but could not withstand competition from roller mills. About 1918 it was adapted to scutch flax, and from 1935 it was used for weaving cloth for flour bags. In recent years it has been adapted as an hotel.

The *Lady Isabella* at Laxey on the Isle of Man is perhaps the most celebrated waterwheel in the British Isles and was always intended to be so. The 72 ft 6 in. (22 m) diameter pitchback wheel was installed in 1854 and operated pump rods that were carried over a viaduct of 34 stone arches to nearby lead mines. The wheel was designed as an eye-catching feature of the landscape that would attract visitors, who, many decades after the lead mines have ceased to work, still flock to see it and make use of the surrounding tea shops.

Part of the Three Mills complex on the river Lea at Bromley-by-Bow in east London. There were indeed three mills on the site in the Middle Ages, but only two by 1600. The ten-bay House Mill in its present form dates from 1776, and is a tide mill where sea and river water was trapped at high tide, and then used to turn the mill's four wheels, which operated 12 sets of mill stones. It ceased working in 1941. The adjacent Clock Mill, shown in this picture, dates from 1817, although the oast houses are probably earlier. It was associated with the trade in gin from the seventeenth century. Distilling ceased after bomb damage during the Second World War, but the buildings were used for bottling and storage until the 1980s. The Clock Mill has been adapted as film and television studios, while the House Mill is being restored by the River Lea Tidal Mill Trust.

The Melincourt Brook, a tributary of the river Neath, cascades down a fall of some 80 ft (24 m) near Resolven, and was recorded by many artists, including J. M. W. Turner. Below the falls are some buildings of one of the pre-industrial revolution ironworks in South Wales, a blast furnace that operated for about 100 years from 1708, and was out of use by 1819 when Thomas Hornor visited the site. Its bellows were powered by the overshot waterwheel shown in the picture, of unknown but considerable diameter. It was fed with water taken from a point higher up the stream by an aqueduct supported on high stone piers.

THOMAS HORNOR, 'TOUR THROUGH THE VALES OF GLAMORGAN', 1819

pairs of gunpowder mills. There were similar concentrations of water-powered manufacturing along the river Derwent in Derby, along the river Don and its tributaries which powered numerous grinding shops in the Sheffield area, in Carlisle and Galway, and around Edinburgh where the Water of Leith in the 1790s powered 71 mills.

Leading engineers concerned themselves with water power and its improvement. John Smeaton designed millwork for a fulling mill at Colchester in 1761, the blast furnaces at Carron near Falkirk from 1764, a forge and slitting mill at Kilnhurst in 1765, powder mills at Waltham Abbey, a paper mill at Thornton (Fife), and machinery at the Wanlockhead lead mine. He used wrought-iron waterwheel buckets and cast-iron gearing from the 1770s, and his posthumous treatise on millwork covered water as well as wind power. Thomas Telford wrote a paper on mills and collaborated with the ironfounder William Hazledine, who sprang from a mill-wrighting family and provided machinery for many watermills. William Fairbairn, an engineer of the following generation, introduced ventilated waterwheel buckets in 1828–29 and demonstrated the efficiency of the breastshot wheel. His treatise on mills ran to four editions between 1861 and 1878. Benôit Fourneyron from Le Creusot demonstrated an effective water turbine in 1827, and turbines were subsequently manufactured by British engineering companies. Williamson Bros (later Gilbert Gilkes & Gordon) of Canal Head, Kendal, established in 1853, made their first turbine in 1856 and employed 80 people by 1861. Turbines had replaced waterwheels at many mills by 1870.

Some celebrated wheels are evidence of the significance of water power in the early and mid-nineteenth century. One of the sights of South Wales was *Aeolus*, the 50-foot (15.4 m) waterwheel, designed by Watkin George, which powered the blowing cylinders of the blast furnaces at Cyfarthfa. In 1827 William Fairbairn designed two wheels 50 feet in diameter and 10 feet (3.1 m) wide, for the Catrine textile mills in Ayrshire which were equally famous and worked until the 1940s. The cotton mill at Egerton near Bolton, taken over in 1829 by the brothers Ashworth, was well known for its 62-foot (19 m) waterwheel, whose admiring spectators were invited to sign a visitors' book. The basement in which five waterwheels provided power for the machines at Stanley Mill, Gloucestershire, was intended, like the forehearth areas of some eighteenth-century French blast furnaces, to provide a sublime vision for spectators. The most spectacular British waterwheel was the 72 foot 6 inch (27.5 m) diameter *Lady Isabella*, built in 1854 to drain the metalliferous mines at Laxey in the Isle of Man. It was designed as an eye-catching monument, and attracted tearooms and guesthouses.

A revolution in power: the development of steam

In 1712 a steam engine was erected by Thomas Newcomen to pump water from coal mines at Coneygre near Dudley, the first economically significant application of steam power. Although Newcomen is one of the most famous of engineers, many aspects of his career are obscure. It is known that he was an ironmonger working in Dartmouth, and understood the need to drain mines in the west of England. He regularly purchased iron from forges in the Stour Valley, and had other links with the West Midlands through his Baptist faith. The 'atmospheric' engine that was to bear the name of Newcomen had a beam with a brass cylinder at one end and chains attaching it to a pump at the other. Steam at atmospheric pressure was admitted to the cylinder and then condensed by a water jet, allowing the piston in the cylinder to be forced down by atmospheric pressure, before being raised again by the force of the pump rod. The engine was the first self-acting machine apart from the clock, and employed no parts that were not comfortably within the manufacturing capacity of contemporary craftsmen. Little is known of the engine's evolution before 1712, but it is likely that experimental engines were constructed. *The Compleat Collier*, written in the North East and published four years before the Coneygre engine was built, makes the tantalising comment that 'there is one invention of drawing water by fire which we hear of'. The Newcomen engine was deemed to be covered

This engraving of 'The engine to raise water by Fire' was published in the *Universal Magazine* in September 1747, more than three decades after a Newcomen engine successfully began to pump water from a mine near Dudley in 1712. The Newcomen engine was thermally inefficient, but its impact can easily be underestimated. About 100 were working in England by 1733, and doubtless many more by 1747, and this was only one of several images that celebrated one of the most influential inventions of the early eighteenth century. In this example the cylinder is mounted above the boiler, from which a flue extends through the wall of the engine house. The beam is balanced on the opposite wall, and attached to it, outside the engine house, are rods operating pumps in a mine.

The replica Newcomen engine house at the Black Country Museum, showing the beam, balanced on a bob wall and attached to pump rods extending into the shafts of a mine.

by the patent granted in 1698 to Thomas Savery and controlled after his death until its expiration in 1733 by a consortium called 'the Proprietors of the Invention for Raising Water by Fire'.

The Newcomen engine was adopted quickly. There were more than a hundred in Britain by 1733, with examples in every major coalfield and the principal ore-mining regions. The first in Ireland was installed in the Kilkenny coalfield in 1740. Its inefficiency was of little consequence at collieries, where the engine's boilers could be fired with coal that was otherwise unsaleable, although there was more incentive to reduce its fuel consumption at ore mines, to which coal might well have to be transported over long distances. Nevertheless a Cornish miner reflected that 'Mr Newcomen's invention of the fire engine enabled us to sink our mines to twice the depth we could formerly do by any other machinery', and as many

as 70 engines might have been working in Cornwall by the 1770s. Some incremental improvements were doubtless made to the engine in the mid-eighteenth century, such as those carried out by John Smeaton at Chacewater in 1775, but it is difficult to assess either changes in technology or the number of engines built between 1733 and 1776. Their significance was recognised in 1747 by a Frenchman who wrote,

England has more than any other country of those machines so useful to the state which readily multiply men by lessening their work; and by means of which one man can execute what would take up to thirty without such assistance.

Newcomen engines were used for pumping water rather than powering machinery. Thus, from

▲ The construction of Newcomen engines continued after the introduction of the much more efficient Watt engines in the 1770s and well into the nineteenth century. With the use of cranks Newcomen engines could be adapted to provide rotative motion, and many of the hundreds of engines built in the 1790s to wind coal from pits were of the Newcomen type. They included this example built by the Coalbrookdale Company. On the right and in the centre are boilers supplying steam to a small engine whose workings are protected from the elements by a wooden shed rather than an engine house. The beam operates a drum which wound coal and probably men from the pit in buckets attached to a three-link wrought-iron chain. Ancient steam engines of several types were still working in the Coalbrookdale area in the late nineteenth century and attracted considerable interest from visiting engineers, and, in this instance, from a pioneer photographer.

September 1743 a Newcomen engine was employed at Coalbrookdale to pump water that had passed over the waterwheels of the ironworks in which Abraham Darby II was the principal partner, back up to the topmost pool in the system, an innovation which for forty years enhanced the effectiveness of water-power installations and enabled the builders of blast furnaces, forges and textile mills to use steam indirectly to produce mechanical power. Applying steam power directly to machinery was to come considerably later.

The history of steam power in the last quarter of the eighteenth century is necessarily dominated by the enigmatic figure of James Watt, not simply because he was an engineer of remarkable talents, but because the archive of the Boulton & Watt partnership is voluminous and, in the absence of other documentation,

is the principal source of evidence concerning their competitors. Understanding of developments is made difficult by the heroic status conferred on Watt by Victorian writers, and by the apparent impertinence of questioning aspects of the career of one who is commemorated by statues in Edinburgh, Glasgow and Birmingham and a colossal memorial in Westminster Abbey.

While working in Scotland in 1763–66 Watt developed a separate condenser for the steam engine, and secured a patent for it in 1769. In 1774, when Matthew Boulton accepted John Roebuck's share in the patent in settlement of a debt, he persuaded Watt to move to Birmingham. The following year their steam engine partnership was formalised, and Boulton used parliamentary contacts to obtain 'James Watt's Fire

The enigmatic figure of James Watt, a polymath and certainly a genius, but one whose concern to defend his patents and the interests of his partners may have inhibited the development of the steam engine in the 1790s. His historical reputation has been shaped in part by the survival of his company's copious archives. Engraving by C. Picart after a drawing by W. Evans. from the painting by Sir William Peechey.

'Mr Watt's Patent Rotative Steam Engine, as constructed by Messrs Boulton & Watt, Soho from 1787 to 1800, 10 Horse Power'. This drawing shows the essential features of the Watt rotative engine: the separate condenser, the parallel motion, the centrifugal governor and the sun-and-planet drive. This engine had the wooden beam that was usual until the development of the elliptical cast-iron beam by the Yorkshire engineer John Banks. The concept of horsepower as a means of expressing the power output of an engine was developed by James Watt.

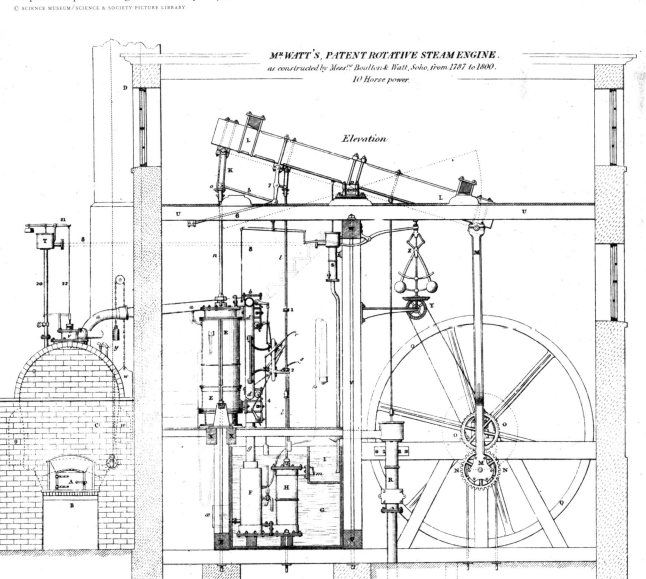

MR WATT'S, PATENT ROTATIVE STEAM ENGINE.
as constructed by Messrs Boulton & Watt, Soho, from 1787 to 1800.
10 Horse power.

Elevation

Scale of Feet for 10 horse power.

↗ The first Boulton & Watt engines, like contemporary Newcomen engines, provided only reciprocating motion, which could be used to operate pumps but not to drive machinery. In the early 1780s Watt used the 'sun-and-planet' motion to create a rotative engine which did not infringe the crank that had been patented by James Pickard. Watt also developed in this period the double-acting engine in which steam enters the cylinder at each end, forcing the piston up or down before it was exhausted out to the condenser, and he also began to utilise the centrifugal governor which ensured that an engine operated at a constant speed. This engine, which incorporates all these features, was used from 1788 to power metal-polishing machinery at Boulton & Watt's Soho Manufactory. It survives complete and essentially unaltered and is now displayed in the Energy Hall of the Science Museum, London.

Engines Patent Act' which extended the patent for the separate condenser until 1800. The first working engines were built in 1776, draining a colliery at Tipton and operating the bellows of John Wilkinson's blast furnace at Willey. In 1778 the first of many canal pumping engines was constructed at Spon Lane on the Birmingham Canal. Interestingly, the principal payments made by most customers for Boulton & Watt engines were annual premiums, calculated on the estimated saving over the use of a Newcomen engine. A strong demand for engines with greater efficiency came from mine owners in Cornwall – where the high price of coal was a major cost factor – and much of the partners' energy was expended there.

In the early 1780s Watt developed the double-acting engine, in which steam was applied on both sides of the piston stroke, and in 1784 patented parallel motion, his means of ensuring that the piston rod of a double-acting engine remained vertical. He wrote in 1808 that, 'I am more proud of the parallel motion than of any other mechanical invention I have ever made'. Parallel motion is a mechanism of remarkable mathematical beauty, and it made possible the elliptical cast-iron beam for steam engines which was developed by the Yorkshire engineer and scientific lecturer John Banks.

There was growing demand from entrepreneurs for a rotative engine that could wind coal up shafts, work hammers or drive rolling mills and textile machinery. The crank, the obvious means of creating rotative motion from a beam engine, had been patented in 1780 by a Birmingham engineer, James Pickard of Snow Hill, who built an engine driving a mill for grinding metals. It worked until 1879. In 1781 Watt

A monument that provides evidence for the continued construction of 'atmospheric' engines after James Watt took out his patent. This Newcomen engine was installed at the colliery at Elsecar in the West Riding of Yorkshire, probably in 1787, the date on the engine house. Its original wooden beam was replaced by a cast-iron beam in 1795. It worked regularly until 1923 and could still be steamed in the early 1950s.

devised the 'sun and planet' motion which achieved the same effect without infringing Pickard's rights. The partners produced some 'sun and planet' engines until 1802, although Pickard's patent expired in 1794, after which most engines were built with cranks.

The first Watt rotative engine operated a hammer at John Wilkinson's Bradley Ironworks near Wolverhampton, where it was working by May 1783. Others had contemplated applying cranks to Newcomen engines, and many did so in the 1790s. William Reynolds wrote in 1782 that he and his father considered using a 'common fire engine' (i.e. a Newcomen engine) to work a corn mill. Richard Arkwright was the first cotton spinner to employ steam power, installing Newcomen engines which recycled the water that powered machinery at Haarlem Mill, Wirksworth, in 1780 and Shudehill Mill, Manchester, in 1783, but the first rotative Boulton & Watt engine to work a cotton mill was completed at Papplewick, Nottinghamshire, in 1785. Matthew Boulton argued in 1790 that the Watt engine was 'the most powerful machine in the world'. It was, he claimed, the most tractable and the most regular, more uniform in its action than a waterwheel, that its power could be scientifically measured, that it could be applied 'to every purpose that requires either Rotative or Reciprocating motion', citing its use in weaving ladies' garters and fine muslins, spinning silk and cotton, drawing coals, copper, salt and men from deep mines, pressing oil and sugar, grinding corn, mustard, drugs and dyewoods, making paper, draining land and pumping water to make canals navigable.

In the British Isles between 1776 and 1800 the Boulton & Watt partnership was responsible for the erection of 183 reciprocating and 268 rotative engines, a total of 451, in addition to 24 built overseas. By 1825 the company had made 1,095 engines. It was once believed that the introduction of the Boulton & Watt engine halted the construction of Newcomen engines, and that Boulton & Watt's output represented the total number of steam engines working in 1800. But in 1967 John Harris showed that this assumption was untenable, and in 1980 Robey and Kanefsky, using cautious and conservative methodology, positively identified 2,191 engines constructed within that period, the majority of which were of the Newcomen type. Contemporary estimates of the numbers of engines in particular regions – about 200 in the Shropshire coalfield alone, for example – suggest that the total should be somewhat larger, perhaps about 3,500. Only 10 of the 43 English counties lacked at least one steam engine in 1800, and in Wales and Scotland there were significant concentrations on the coalfields. There were about a dozen in Ireland, and some Irish ironfounders circumvented patent restrictions by constructing 'pirate' engines before 1800. Many engines built in the

The Coalbrookdale Company's forge at Horsehay was one of the first such ironworks where the machinery was operated by steam power. Some of the first Boulton & Watt rotative engines were installed to work hammers in the forge in 1784–85, while the rolling mill was powered by an atmospheric engine adapted for rotative motion, which was replaced in 1809. This view of the forge dates from about 1840. I does not include the engine house, but steam power operated the hammer on the right, to which a worker appears to be taking a ball of iron from a puddling furnace, as well as the rolling mills, which are producing both round iron, in the centre, and iron plates to the left.

1790s were 'common' engines, erected at coal mines where fuel was available at minimal cost. One such was that constructed in 1795 at Elsecar, now the only Newcomen engine remaining on its original site.

In the 1790s James Watt and his partners were concerned about the way their patents were being infringed by the construction of 'pirate' engines with separate condensers, for which they were paid no royalties. Neo-conservative historians have suggested that the Boulton & Watt patent retarded the high-pressure steam engine – and hence economic development – for about sixteen years, but it may be doubted whether the patent inhibited either the technological development or the proliferation of engines. Innovations were stimulated as the capacity to build machines expanded in London, Manchester, Leeds, Cornwall and elsewhere. The sketchbook of the ironmaster William Reynolds, for instance, shows that engineers in the 1790s were experimenting with configurations other than the traditional beam engine. Nevertheless Boulton & Watt did significantly obstruct the activities of some of their competitors. Informers alerted them to infringements of their patents and provided details of the activities of other companies. Boulton & Watt purchased land next to Matthew Murray's Round Foundry in Leeds in the hope of constraining its extension, made threats to his craftsmen, and contested his patents. Edward Bull devised an inverted vertical engine in which the steam cylinder was placed directly above the pump. Boulton & Watt brought legal proceedings against this in 1793, and these continued until they obtained a favourable verdict in 1799, but only after Bull had died a broken man. Nevertheless, Bull engines worked successfully at waterworks and were still being installed in the 1850s – there were at least twelve in the London area, one of which is preserved at Kew Bridge.

Jonathan Hornblower also began experiments with steam power in 1776, and in 1781 was awarded a patent

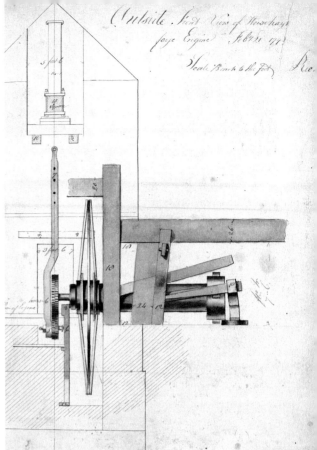

△ In the early 1780s Jonathan Hornblower developed a compound engine, in which steam having been used at high pressure in one cylinder was exhausted to be used at a lower pressure in another, before passing to the condenser. Hornblower was one of the engineers accused by Boulton & Watt of infringing Watt's patent for the separate condenser, which did not expire until 1800. The rightness of Hornblower's cause was affirmed by the ironmaster William Reynolds, but litigation impeded the adoption of his engines.

© SCIENCE MUSEUM/SCIENCE & SOCIETY PICTURE LIBRARY

▽ One of the engines that provided power for the machinery at the Horsehay forge; a drawing which shows the engine house in outline, the connecting rod linking the piston to the flywheel, and the shaft that conveyed power to the machinery. This sketch, dated 21 February 1793, appears in the Sketch Book collected by the ironmaster William Reynolds which records many of the outstanding innovations of the time.

SCIENCE MUSEUM. WILLIAM REYNOLDS SKETCH BOOK

for a form of compound engine of which about a dozen were built. Hornblower, with John Winwood, a Shropshire-born Bristol ironmaster who purchased a share in his patent, argued in a memorial in 1788 that the compound principle was not an infringement of the patent protecting the separate condenser. Threats of litigation from Boulton & Watt inhibited the building of further Hornblower engines in Cornwall. A decision by the Court of the King's Bench in January 1799 found that an engine built by Jonathan Hornblower's brother, Jabez Carter Hornblower, did indeed infringe the patent, and Boulton & Watt used the ruling to

enforce premium payments from users of Jonathan Hornblower's engines, although he was not concerned personally in this case. William Reynolds, who as a precocious 19-year-old in 1777 considered Watt 'one of the greatest philosophers in Europe', supported Hornblower, telling him in 1792 that his engine was much superior to that of Boulton and Watt. James Watt did not favour the use of high-pressure steam, and even after the expiry of the separate condenser patent his company, in which he was no longer an active partner, sought a bill in Parliament to deter Richard Trevithick from his experiments in this area.

The rate of engine building increased rapidly in the 1790s, and experimentation continued. In 1780 Watt wrote that 'every man who is obliged to live by his profession ought to keep the secrets of it to himself so far as is consistent with the use of them, it is only people of independent means who have a right to give away their inventions without attempting to turn them to their own advantage'. Concerned that posterity should give him his due, he asserted in a memorial in 1786 that, 'the General theory & Principles on which the perfection of Steam Engines depends, were first discovered by J. Watt at Glasgow in Scotland in the year 1763 & were the consequence of a laborious course of experiments that he made for that purpose'. He displayed elements of paranoia, but was clearly concerned that he would not spend his old age in penury, as many did including Andrew Meikle, Richard Trevithick and the brothers Fourdrinier.

James Watt senior retired in 1800 to Handsworth, where his fertile mind and dexterous hands were occupied in devising a means of replicating sculptures, but his company continued under the direction of the sons of the founders, M. R. Boulton, James Watt junior and Gregory Watt, who entered the partnership in 1794. After James Watt junior died in 1848 the firm was known as James Watt & Co.

The expiry of the separate condenser patent in 1800 stimulated innovation. The significance of the event was widely recognised. The Coalbrookdale partners promptly stopped their blast furnaces at Horsehay, between 21 September and 6 October 1800, 'to alter the engine to Watts'. The same year the Newcastle engineer Phineas Crowther patented a vertical winding engine that was used at many collieries in the North East. The grasshopper beam engine was patented by William Freemantle in 1803; then, in 1805, Matthew Murray introduced a side-lever engine that was developed to power ships; and two years later Henry

A drawing, believed to have been made by John Llewellyn of Pen-y-darren, showing Trevithick's tram engine, December 1803. Richard Trevithick was responsible for many innovations in steam technology, particularly for showing that steam could power locomotives to run on roads or railways. In 1802 he built a locomotive at Coalbrookdale designed for use on a plateway, but there is no evidence that it was used, perhaps because of the death of William Reynolds, the ironmaster, in 1803. He subsequently built a locomotive for another plateway, the 9½-mile Merthyr Tramway which served the Dowlais, Pen-y-darren and Plymouth ironworks. It had a single horizontal cylinder and an 8 ft flywheel, and displayed two innovations characteristic of subsequent steam railway locomotives: coupled wheels, and the exhausting of steam with smoke from the boiler up the chimney. The locomotive was demonstrated successfully in February 1804, but it broke the cast-iron plate rails upon which it ran. Merthyr's ironmasters continued to operate their tramways with horses, but in other parts of Britain engineers followed Trevithick's example in building locomotives, which, on stronger wrought-iron rails, achieved greater success. A model of the Pen-y-darren locomotive, built for the Welsh Industrial & Maritime Museum, is displayed at Cyfarthfa Castle.

TRAM ENGINE
4¾ Inches DIAᵗ of Cylinder
3 Feet Stroke
Decᵗ 1803

This locomotive *Puffing Billy* and its sister *Wylam Dilly* were built by William Hedley and Timothy Hackworth in 1813–14 for use on a 5 ft gauge railway at Wylam Colliery near Newcastle (see map on page 346), and provided the first practical demonstration that steam locomotives could effectively move substantial loads on rails. Investigations in 2008 by forensic mechanical engineers showed that *Puffing Billy* was the older of the two. The locomotive originally had eight wheels, but still tended to cause cast-iron rails to break. It was rebuilt with four wheels when wrought-iron rails were laid on the Wylam Railway about 1830. The two locomotives worked until 1862 when the railway was converted to standard gauge. They were photographed in that year, and *Puffing Billy* was first demonstrated at, and then sold for £200 to, the forerunner of the Science Museum, London, while *Wylam Dilly* went to Edinburgh and is now displayed in the Royal Museum. A working replica of *Puffing Billy* dating from 2006 is demonstrated at Beamish.

Maudslay patented the table engine, a configuration in which the cylinder was mounted upon a base of that shape. Arthur Woolf patented a boiler for producing high-pressure steam in 1803, and a compound engine in 1805.

Richard Trevithick was already developing a high-pressure engine by 1796 and used versions of it to power a steam carriage in 1801 and locomotives from 1802. He also designed the Cornish Engine, the first of which began work at Wheal Prosper in 1812. It proved to be an economical means of draining mines or pumping water or sewage. Many engineers made incremental improvements to it after Trevithick went to Peru in 1816 (to help introduce steam power to drain silver mines), and examples were still being built into the twentieth century.

Similarly, the steam locomotive underwent many changes between 1802 and 1829–30, at which point it became the motive power of the main-line railways. Trevithick experimented with a horizontal engine in 1802. Fears of uneven cylinder wear constrained development, but by the 1860s horizontal engines were being produced in large numbers. The basic form of the portable engine, a locomotive-style boiler mounted on wheels with an engine on top, was standardised by Ransomes of Ipswich from the 1840s, and thousands were built by engineers in towns all over Britain. Self-propelled versions, or traction engines, appeared in the 1850s and were developed in the 1860s by Fowlers of Leeds and Aveling & Porter of Rochester.

By 1840 it was easy to assume that steam engines supplied most of Britain's energy. Several

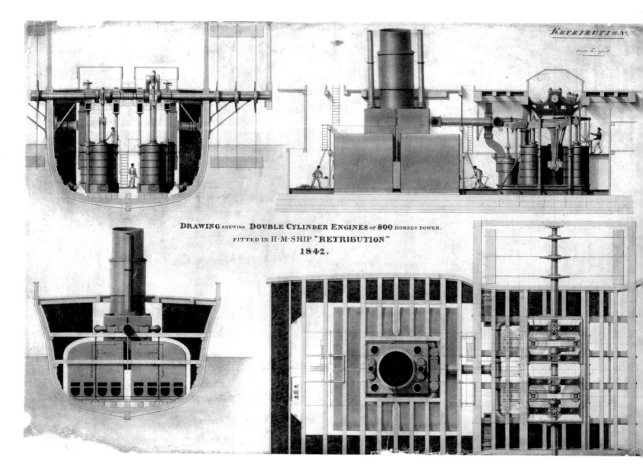

DRAWING SHEWING DOUBLE CYLINDER ENGINES OF 800 HORSES POWER.
FITTED IN H·M·SHIP "RETRIBUTION"
1842.

⌖ This engine, designed by Joseph Maudslay and supplied by Henry Maudslay & Co. to the Royal Navy to power the 1,641-ton wooden paddle frigate HMS *Retribution*, is of the twin-cylinder or 'Siamese' type, in which two vertical cylinders are arranged side by side, with their piston rods attached to a common T-shaped crosshead. The Siamese engine was intended to replace earlier side-lever engines, but proved only marginally smaller and lighter. Siamese engines were installed in several warships, but they were never built in large numbers. As ships became larger from the mid-nineteenth century some of the constraints on engine size were removed, and the vertical inverted direct-action engine in many forms, compound, triple- or quadruple expansion, came to be used in most steamships, and such engines continued to be installed until after the Second World War. *Retribution* was laid down as the *James Watt*, but was re-named on launching on 4 July 1844. She was deployed in the Black Sea and the Baltic during the Crimean War, and in the Far East during the Second Opium War in 1858–59. She was sold for scrap in 1864.

estimates were made of numbers in use. One source in 1825 counted 290 in London, 90 in Glasgow, 212 in Manchester, 83 in Bolton, 67 in Stockport, and 130 in Leeds. In 1838 there were 29 in Dublin, 50 in Belfast and 240 in Birmingham. Steam power after 1800 made possible the growth of mining and manufacturing, for in well-populated England most potential sites for water-powered mills were already occupied. Yet water power remained significant. It was calculated in 1838 that the textile industry drew its power from 3,053 steam engines and 2,230 waterwheels. Water power appeared to be eclipsed because on a national scale it could not fulfil the growing demand for energy of nineteenth-century manufacturers. William Fairbairn declared in 1864 that 'the time has not yet arrived when it can be dispensed with … in our own country'. In Scotland and Ireland, less densely populated than England, the use of water power went on increasing

⌐ The Great Western Railway's 4-2-2 locomotive *Tartar*, built at Swindon in 1848, was of the same class, designed by Sir Daniel Gooch, as *Iron Duke* (illustrated on page 18). It could haul trains of 100 tons and more at 80 mph and elegantly exemplified the progress made in locomotive design in little more than 30 years after the building of *Puffing Billy*. Watercoloured drawing by E. Rees.

⌐ Undated photograph of Springwell Colliery Engine No. 2, County Durham, a locomotive that was built by Robert Stephenson in 1826. Steam locomotives proliferated in the North East Coalfield in the decade after the construction of *Puffing Billy*, and in 1823 George Stephenson began to build a works specifically for the construction of locomotives in Forth Street (now South Street), Newcastle-upon-Tyne, which was managed by his son, Robert Stephenson, from whom it took its name. Some of the first locomotives constructed there, in 1826, were for the Springwell Colliery, about three miles south of Gateshead. They had long lives, and No. 2 survived to be photographed here, probably in the 1850s or 1860s. The metal leaf springs which are visible were probably not original features.

until the 1860s. The abandonment of many sources of water power after 1870 was in fact a consequence of increasing imports of grain. Flour production was concentrated in mills using roller-milling technology, most of them on the coast. At this time many ancient watermills ceased to grind flour, but manufacturers using water power employed it as long as their businesses flourished, replacing waterwheels with turbines, and from the 1880s using turbines to generate electric power. Amid mounting concern regarding climate change and energy production, the period between 1870 and, say, 2020 might come to be seen as a curious interval in the history of the British Isles, a time when the country's abundant water power was not utilised.

The choice of power sources available to factory masters in the early decades of the industrial revolution can be illustrated by the case of the cotton-spinning mill at Sutton-in-Ashfield, which was worked by the hosier Samuel Unwin. In the 1750s Unwin built a water-powered mill that was used for silk throwing, fulling woollen cloth, and twisting yarn for framework knitters. Then, in the 1770s he replaced it with what came to be known as 'the old Mill', a cotton-spinning factory where by 1784 120 people were employed. This mill's machinery was first operated by a horse capstan or possibly by oxen; subsequently it was worked by a 24 foot (7.4 m) diameter waterwheel fed from an enormous 8½-acre pond. A windmill on top of the mill worked pumps which returned water to the pool after it had passed over the wheel, and before 1790 this windmill was supplemented by a Newcomen pumping engine, probably by Ebenezer Smith & Co. of Chesterfield. Unwin explained in 1791 that its fuel costs were lower than those of a rotative engine since it was worked only when water supplies were low. Nevertheless shortly before he died in 1799 Unwin installed a rotative steam engine.

As well as providing heat and power for homes and industry, coal could produce flammable gas. The properties of coal gas were demonstrated in the closing years of the eighteenth century by William Murdock and others, and from the first decade of the nineteenth century gas lighting companies proliferated in British towns. The first commercially successful engines which used 'town gas' to produce mechanical power were built from 1860 by the Frenchman Etienne Lenoir. Gas engines were subsequently built by numerous British engineering companies and were economical sources of power for urban workshops and small factories which produced, for example, footwear and clothing.

With the proliferation of steam engines and manufacturing processes that required heat, the demand for coal increased hugely between the 1770s and the

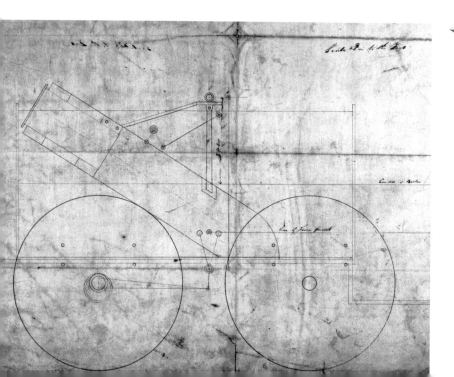

◁ Drawing showing the wheels of a steam locomotive designed by Robert Stephenson, possibly for the Canterbury and Whitstable Railway. The Canterbury and Whitstable Railway opened on 4 May 1830. Most of its 6-mile route consisted of inclined planes worked by stationary engines, but there was a 1¼ mile stretch of level track at Whitstable on which Stephenson's locomotive *Invicta* operated passenger trains. *Invicta* is now preserved in the Canterbury Heritage Museum.

The year 1810 saw the first recorded use of coal gas in Belfast. Work on this building on the Ormeau Road began in 1822. It was privately owned until 1874 when it was bought by the City Corporation. The gas undertaking prospered under municipal ownership and produced profits which subsidised the rates, other Corporation activities, electricity generation, parks, libraries and public baths, and they contributed substantially to the cost of building the City Hall. Several municipal gas concerns had prestigious office blocks like this one, and the gas payments office in central Birmingham is now part of the city's art gallery.
PHOTOGRAPH: CARNEGIE

From the first decade of the nineteenth century gasworks, initially intended primarily for providing gas for street or factory lighting, were established in most substantial towns and cities in the British Isles, and by 1870 there were gas suppliers in almost every community that had claims to urban status. By this time gas engines, more compact and more efficient than steam engines, were beginning to power the increasing numbers of factories of modest size that were manufacturing consumer goods. This illustration is a diagrammatic representation, published in 1819, of one of London's many gasworks. The retort house is on the right. This is one of the many images of gas production and distribution that form part of the extensive collection of industrial art, now held at Ironbridge, that was built up by Sir Arthur Elton.
© SCIENCE MUSEUM/SCIENCE & SOCIETY PICTURE LIBRARY

1860s, and the domestic needs of a growing population. The canal system transformed the pattern of distribution: by the 1840s there were few significant towns in England that were not within easy reach of navigable waterways, and in the 1860s almost every town in the British Isles could receive coal by rail. The demand generated by steam engines prompted a steady increase in coal production. The best estimates suggest that national output by 1871 had reached 115 million tons, by which date energy was available on a scale many times greater than it had been in 1700.

Such an increase in coal consumption inevitably brought significant problems. From a modern perspective the long-term implications for global warming are immediately obvious. Contemporaries, too, were well aware of the ill-health and misery that could be caused by the blankets of smoke around mines and factories and which hung in palls over towns and cities. Yet many regarded the steam engine as a source of prosperity and comfort. Sir John Sinclair wrote in 1825 that the steam engine

has increased indefinitely the mass of human comforts and enjoyments: and rendered the material of wealth and prosperity everywhere cheap and accessible. It has armed the feeble hand of man with a power to which no limits can be assigned; completed the dominion of mind over the most refractory qualities of matter; and laid a sure foundation for all those future miracles of mechanical power which are to aid and reward the labours of after generations.

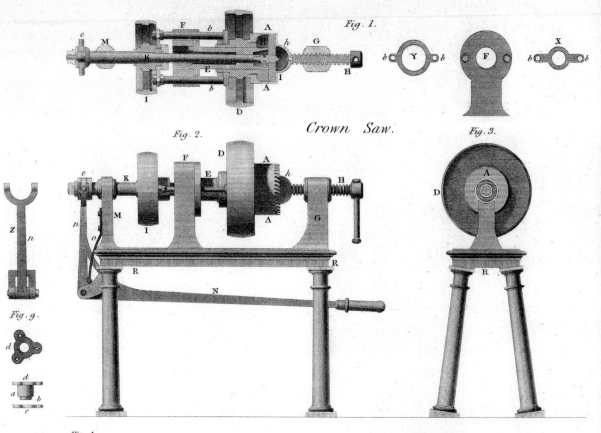

Fig. 1.

Crown Saw.

Fig. 2.

Fig. 3.

Fig. 9.

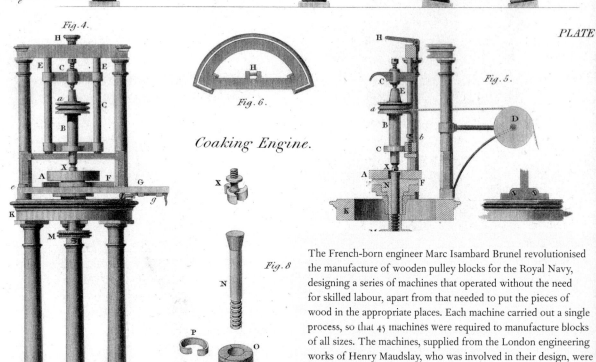

Fig. 4.

PLATE

Fig. 6.

Fig. 5.

Coaking Engine.

Fig. 8.

The French-born engineer Marc Isambard Brunel revolutionised the manufacture of wooden pulley blocks for the Royal Navy, designing a series of machines that operated without the need for skilled labour, apart from that needed to put the pieces of wood in the appropriate places. Each machine carried out a single process, so that 45 machines were required to manufacture blocks of all sizes. The machines, supplied from the London engineering works of Henry Maudslay, who was involved in their design, were installed in the Royal Dockyard at Portsmouth where they may still be seen. Engraving by Lowry after J. Farey, plate 2 from vol. 2 of *The Cyclopaedia, or Universal Dictionary of Arts*, by Abraham Rees (London, 1820).

3

Making machines

'Were we required to characterise this age of ours by any single epithet, we should be tempted
to call it, not an Heroical, Devotional, Philosophical, or Moral Age, but, above all others, the
Mechanical Age. It is the Age of Machinery. ... Nothing is now done directly, or by hand; all is
by rule and calculated contrivance.'

THOMAS CARLYLE, *SIGNS OF THE TIMES*, 1829

'The locomotive has not been the invention of any one man but of a race of mechanical engineers.'

GEORGE STEPHENSON

MACHINES made of iron and powered by wind, water or steam were fundamental components of the industrial revolution. During this period British engineers learned and honed the art of designing, making and using such machines. Writing in 1800, the Salford textile manufacturer George Augustus Lee was in no doubt that, 'If the incombustible plan of Building Mills becomes tolerably general and the Machinery is made of Iron which we are likewise adopting, the Consumption of that Metal here must become enormous'. Some, such as the historian and social commentator Thomas Carlyle, deplored the social and moral effects of mechanisation. Carlyle later developed his ideas more generally in his analysis of the 'condition of England', in which he attacked industrialisation and the economic divisions he saw as its consequences, but as early as 1829 he argued that the factory system and machines were turning people into automatons devoid of individuality and spirituality, workers whose very thought processes were mechanistic and lacking the ability to act freely.

But such reservations were not shared by everyone. Around the same time, in 1837, Sir George Head was commending machine shops:

> There can be no spectacle more grateful to the heart of an Englishman than viewing the interior of a manufactory of machinery, to observe the features of each hard working mechanic, blackened by smoke yet radiant with the light of intelligence, to contrast with his humble station the lines of fervid thought that mark his countenance and direct his sinewy arm, and to reflect that to such a combination of the powers of mind and body England owes her present state of commercial greatness.

These contemporary commentators were far from alone in perceiving the significance of the enormous

advances that were being made in the field of mechanical engineering. The usefulness and ingenuity of machines were widely praised, as was the primary role played in their development by British engineers and inventors. This chapter will look at these processes and their role in Britain's industrialisation. What follows focuses on mechanical engineering, but it should be pointed out that in the eighteenth century no distinction had yet been made between civil and mechanical engineering, and James Brindley, John Rennie and Robert Stephenson were all as distinguished for their constructional as for their mechanical skills.

In 1700 there were few machines in the modern sense of the word, and the larger ones were made principally of wood. The traditional water-cornmill – with its pit wheel, crown wheel, wallower and stone nuts – was itself a machine, with the mill building as its frame. Watermills and windmills were built and maintained by millwrights, and it is no coincidence that some of the first mechanical engineers sprang from millwrighting. Probate records in Lancashire show increasing numbers of millwrights, particularly after 1770. William Fairbairn recalled in 1864:

> The ordinary millwright was usually a fair arithmetician, knew something of geometry, levelling and mensuration, and in some cases

possessed a very competent knowledge of practical mathematics. He could calculate the velocities, strength and power of machines; he could draw a plan and section.

Clock making was another important source of expertise. There were clockmakers in almost every English town by 1750, with particular concentrations in London, Coventry and Prescot (Lancashire). Craftsmen in some small towns supplied national markets with clock parts. Small brass castings were made at Ashbourne, and springs at Pershore. In the mid-eighteenth century the influential Swedish metallurgist Reinhold Angerstein visited Daniel Mather in Prescot, who 'makes all kinds of steel hardware required for a watchmaker's shop'. He was able to observe Mather's ability to draw steel wire for making pinions in watches; his workshop also employed smiths whose tongs, pliers and watchmakers' hammers were reckoned to be the best in England. John Aikin, meanwhile, described the spinning frame as 'an aggregation of clockmakers' work most wonderful to behold'.

Mechanical engineers also sprang from those smiths who, venturing beyond the accustomed tasks of local farriers, shaped metal tools. There was a tradition of spade making in Ireland, where a spade mill from Coalisland is preserved at Cultra Manor. In 1744 James Fussell leased land at Mells, Somerset, with authority to erect 'a good, firme and substantiall Mill or Mills for Grinding Edge Tools and forging Iron Plates'. By 1800 his family operated six water-powered works near Mells, making scythes, sickles and spades for national and export markets. There were similar concerns elsewhere in southern England. At Deddington, Oxfordshire, Benjamin Mason and his brothers began to make wrought-iron axles in 1820 and employed 40 people in the 1860s. Such enterprises were of small significance compared with companies in the coalfields that made springs, couplings, wheels or boilers, but they show that the origins of mechanical engineering were not solely in areas conventionally regarded as 'industrial'. In December 1771 Arkwright advertised in the *Derby Mercury*:

Cotton Mill, Cromford
10th Dec. 1771
Wanted immediately, two Journeymen Clock-Makers, or others that understands Tooth and Pinion well: Also a Smith that can forge and file.—Likewise two Wood Turners that have been accustomed to Wheel-making, Spool-turning, &c. ... Weavers may ... have good Work. There is [also] Employment at the above Place, for Women, Children, &c. and good Wages.

An anonymous Lancashire mechanic recalled how, in the 1790s, an engineer who was superintending the erection of a spinning mill looked for millwrights, carpenters, smiths and clockmakers.

The agricultural implement manufactory of Messrs. Richard Hornsby & Son, from George Measom, *The Official Illustrated Guide to the Great Northern Railway* (London: Measom, 1861). Richard Hornsby entered business as a blacksmith in 1815 and soon began to make iron castings. By 1861 he had developed his Spittlegate Ironworks in Grantham into one of the largest market-town foundries. He showed seed drills, a winnowing machine and an oilcake crushing machine at the Great Exhibition in 1851, but the firm was most celebrated for its patent portable engines, of which a 6 h.p. example went to the Crystal Palace. Several such engines are depicted here in the works timber yard. Many agricultural machines of the period, especially threshing machines, incorporated wooden parts. The tall chimney probably led from the boilers of the steam engines that provided power for the works, while the building with long parallel rows of smaller flues would have accommodated lines of smiths working at hearths to manufacture wrought-iron components.

Casting, boring, forging and founding: the techniques of machine making

In 1700 most iron castings were made at blast furnaces or at adjacent air furnaces, but a foundry in Blackfriars (Southwark) was already making 'various things for millwrights' alongside pots and firebacks. Iron parts for Newcomen engines were cast before 1720, and iron cylinders by 1722. Cylinders were cast hollow but required boring to not especially accurate tolerances. By 1801 the Coalbrookdale Company was producing a range of components for mechanical engineers – air pumps, flywheels and cylinders for steam engines; axle trees for waterwheels; presses for making cheese, paper or cider; frames for lathes; and levers for weighing machines. Within a decade specialist companies in the Black Country were making springs, couplings and other components. From the 1750s millwrights had turned to cast-iron gearing, making their own castings, and some began to make agricultural machinery.

Some technical advances arrived in Britain from elsewhere. Jan Verbruggen had developed Swiss techniques for boring cannon from solid castings. In the early 1750s he was Master Founder of the state foundry at The Hague, but in 1770 he migrated to the Woolwich Arsenal where, surrounded in secrecy, he built a boring machine. The pioneering ironmaster John Wilkinson gained knowledge of it, and was granted a patent for a horizontal boring machine in 1774. He made a modified machine to bore steam engine cylinders, but since by the late 1770s cylinders could be as much as 58 inches (1.5 m) in diameter, they obviously could not be bored from the solid. The casting was fixed upon a supporting frame, and the revolving cutter bar, supported by bearings at each end, passed right through it. This innovation probably merited patent protection, but Wilkinson considered it to be covered by his patent of 1774. That was revoked in 1779, allowing others to use it.

The Soho Manufactory, on the northern side of Birmingham, designed for Matthew Boulton by William Wyatt and completed in 1761, was used for the manufacture of a variety of small metal objects, including buttons, buckles and plated items, collectively known as 'toys'. This factory, in which Boulton was in partnership with John Fothergill, was pioneering, pre-dating Richard Arkwright's cotton-spinning mills. Some water power was employed, provided by the Hockley Brook, although many tasks were done by hand. From 1788 metal polishing machinery was operated by a steam engine (illustrated on page 56). The Manufactory was also the base of the steam engine partnership that Boulton formed with James Watt after the latter's move from Scotland to Birmingham in 1774, although the partners themselves made only small parts for engines until they opened the Soho Foundry in Smethwick in 1796.

In 1790 most steam engines were assembled from cast iron, wrought iron, brass, copper and timber parts that had been fabricated by sub-contractors and which were assembled by erectors. However in the 1790s, as the pace of engine building increased, companies undertook to supply and install engines. These included Matthew Murray in Leeds and Bateman & Sherratt in Manchester. Boulton and Watt invested in the famous Soho Foundry at Smethwick near Birmingham in 1796, becoming suppliers of engines rather than designers and supervisors of construction. As the potential of the steam locomotive began to be appreciated in the 1820s several other companies offered to make them. A partnership including Robert Stephenson and George Stephenson, Edward Pease and Michael Longridge of Bedlington established a factory off Forth Street, Newcastle-upon-Tyne, in 1823 specifically to supply locomotives; they subsequently built *Locomotion No. 1*. Robert Stephenson with Charles Tayleur opened the Vulcan Foundry at Newton-le-Willows in Lancashire in 1828, with the intention of supplying the Liverpool & Manchester Railway, and completed two locomotives, *Tayleur* and *Stephenson*, in the following year. From the 1840s, however, most railway companies built their own rolling stock, and Robert Stephenson & Co., the Vulcan Foundry and others had to seek customers overseas.

The proliferation of engineering works was made possible by improved transport facilities. By 1820 most towns of consequence were within reach of navigable water, making materials such as coke and pig iron readily available. A parliamentary report in 1849 reveals that in most parts of England foundrymen had a choice of iron from the works in South Wales, Scotland, Shropshire, Staffordshire or Yorkshire. Everywhere, each industrial sector depended upon the work or innovations of others. Foundries depended upon the cupola furnace that had been developed by John or William Wilkinson in the 1790s, which

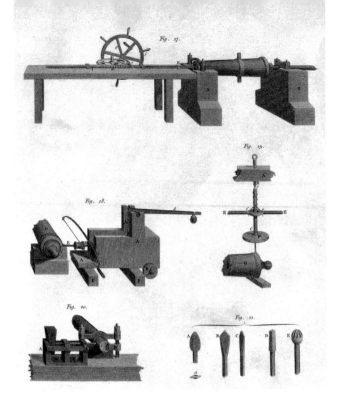

A machine for boring cannon from the solid was developed by Jan Verbruggen, Master Founder of the state foundry at The Hague, who built a similar machine after he moved to Woolwich Arsenal in 1770. The gun barrel rather than the boring bit was rotated, and the bit was pressed forward by a ratchet from the wheel visible in the picture. John Wilkinson knew of the machine and took out a patent in 1774 for a boring machine incorporating its essential features. In the mid-1770s he applied some of the principles to bore steam engine cylinders, believing that it was protected by the 1774 patent. When that patent was revoked in 1779 other ironfounders were able to use machines like his for boring both cannon and cylinders.

provided a straightforward means of melting pig iron or scrap. They used machine tools, which were chiefly obtained from engineers in London or Manchester. The growth of mechanical engineering also depended on the diffusion of knowledge among men with the ability to design machines and manage their construction, as well as the skills among those who fabricated components and fitted them together.

Machine tools

The significance of the machine-tool sector can hardly be over-estimated. By allowing and facilitating the mass production of components to precise tolerances it helped the development of a wide range of other processes and industries. Within the two generations between 1770 and 1830 British engineers gained the

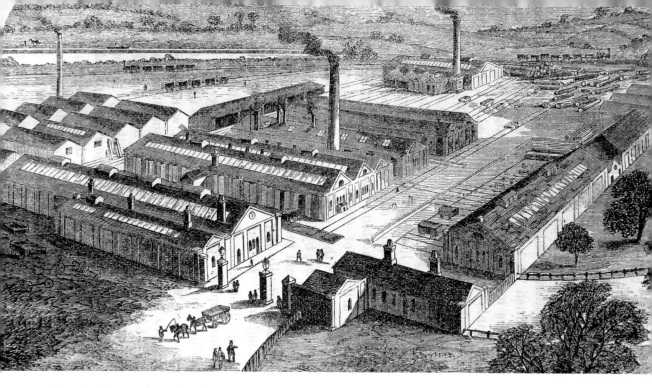

↗ The works of Mr Joseph Wright, Saltley, near Birmingham, from Measom, *The Official Illustrated Guide to the Great Western Railway* (London: Measom, 1865). Joseph Wright was a coach operator who from 1837 began to build carriages for the London & Southampton Railway. This side of his business prospered and in 1845 he leased six acres of meadow at Saltley to the east of Birmingham, alongside the railway to Derby, where he built a works for the construction of railway carriages. By 1853 he had 800 employees. The enterprise was continued after his death in 1859 by his sons Henry and Joseph, and in 1862–63 the firm became the Metropolitan Railway Carriage & Wagon Co. The works was expanded to cover 50 acres, and carriages were built for most of the principal British railway companies, and for many overseas. The factory closed in 2005 after completing an order for the 'Pendolino' trains used on the main line out of Euston.

capacity to produce such precision-made components for prime movers and many kinds of machine used throughout manufacturing and agriculture. Many of these machine tools were developed in Britain, but from 1800 the contribution of the machine shops of New England to this aspect of technology was influential, and that influence increased further after the Great Exhibition of 1851.

Machine tools took several forms and performed a variety of functions. As we have seen, boring machines that could work cylinders to adequate tolerances had been erected from the 1770s. Hammers that could shape wrought iron were traditionally operated by water power but from the 1780s began to be powered by rotative steam engines. A superior means of shaping forgings was the work of James Nasmyth, the Scottish engineer and inventor, who in 1839 designed a steam hammer that operated vertically and was powered by a cylinder in the apex of an A-frame. The first was used at Le Creusot, but from the 1840s many were built at the foundry that Nasmyth established at Patricroft west of Manchester.

Shaping materials while they are being rotated on a spindle is one of the oldest manufacturing techniques, and lathes – on which pieces of wood or metal could be shaped by tools – were known long before 1700. During the eighteenth century the basic industrial or 'engine' lathe was developed. This had a rigid frame, usually of cast iron, supporting a spindle, and could produce cylindrical, flat or conical surfaces. Henry Maudslay did much to develop the screw-cutting lathe, an example of which, made in 1800, is held in the Science Museum. Richard Roberts contributed substantially to the development of the lathe, and from the 1850s lathes were produced that could undertake repetitive tasks such as the mass production

↗ James Nasmyth, who worked at Henry Maudslay's workshop between 1829 and 1834, like many contemporary mechanical engineers, was concerned to develop the lathe and other machine tools. He popularised the slide principle which moved the piece of metal to be worked towards a rigidly held tool on the lathe, which made it possible to produce large metal components with greater precision. Lathes, with steam hammers, were some of the principal products of his Bridgewater Foundry at Patricroft, west of Manchester.

▽ Much of Henry Maudslay's life was devoted to the development of machine tools that could fashion pieces of metal into forms in which they could be incorporated into machines. He was best known for his work from 1810 in developing an all-metal lathe, which came to be used in engineering works in Britain and overseas. When his career began most lathes had been hand-worked, and tools used on them were hand-held. By the time he died in 1831 ranks of powered lathes in machine shops could produce parts for looms or steam engines in huge numbers.

of screws. The life stories of several eminent Victorian engineers, including Sir Daniel Gooch and Joseph Clement, record that they gained access as boys to lathes, upon which they were able to exercise their imaginations.

The principle of the planing machine, which could produce a flat surface on metal components, was patented by Joseph Bramah, Yorkshire locksmith and inventor (see page 76), in 1802. It was developed by Richard Roberts, whose works in Manchester supplied such machines to many other engineering companies. The milling machine, which shapes work by feeding it to a revolving toothed cutter, was developed in New England in the early nineteenth century, but was in fairly common use in Britain by the 1850s.

The slotting machine has a vertically reciprocating tool for cutting slots in pieces of metal, large or small. Early examples were built by Richard Roberts and James Nasmyth. Steam hammers of various sizes, lathes, and planing, milling and slotting machines were to be found in the machine shops of all the substantial mechanical engineering concerns that were prospering in Britain in the 1860s. The development of all these

machines was facilitated by the availability from the 1740s of crucible steel, used in cutting tools.

The development of a capacity to build machines also depended on the appreciation that came through the work of Maudslay of the necessity of high standards of precision, which could be achieved through the use of micrometers, gauges, sectors and callipers. The replacement of hand work by reliable machine tools enabled the production of hundreds of identical spinning mules, railway locomotives and threshing machines, with what were, in effect, interchangeable parts. Joseph Whitworth was among those concerned to standardise engineering practice, and his uniform system of screw threads, proposed in 1841, was in general use by 1860.

Machine shops have always been dependent upon hand tools to some extent, today as in earlier periods. New power systems often involved innovative means of transmitting power to machinery, but there were many manufacturers who continued to prosper through producing hand tools. The copious records of Peter Stubs of Warrington illuminate this well, documenting the manufacture of files in a region with a tradition of tool making. Stubs was a file maker by 1777, when he employed outworkers, but from 1802 he concentrated his activities in a substantial workshop. As well as files he made callipers, draw plates for wire making, and hand vices. He was landlord of the *White Bear* inn, where he brewed beer, and exploited connections gained through the inn to sell files. He used crucible steel principally from Sheffield, but also from Tyneside and the Calder Works in Scotland. Stage waggons and canal carriers distributed his files to all parts of Great Britain. His tools were also exported and many are held at the Davistown Museum in Maine. The accelerating pace of engineering manufactures is revealed by the occasional despatch by stagecoach of urgent orders to customers in London and Manchester. The principal centre of file manufacture was in the Sheffield area, from where filemakers migrated to settle around engineering works all over Britain.

New forms of power transmission

Means of transmitting energy from prime movers to machines changed after 1790. In the first mechanised textile mills and in contemporary machine shops power was conveyed by leather belts that were driven by rotating wooden drums. Cast-iron shafting was used by the 1790s and in 1817 William Fairbairn, when renewing the transmission system at Murrays' Mill, Manchester, substituted shafts of turned wrought iron. In the 1820s Fairbairn and James Lillie developed a system of power transmission that was used in innumerable manufactories, whereby power was conveyed through horizontal shafts and toothed gearing to vertical shafts which, through further gearing, drove horizontal shafts on each floor of a building, and thence individual machines by leather belts and pulleys. Horizontal line shafts were usually between 6 feet 6 inches (2 m) and 16 feet 6 inches (5 m) in length and coupled together, so that they could extend along a mill floor that might be as long as 200 feet (60 m). Shafts were carried on bearings mounted on hangers or brackets, which might be attached to the outer walls or to bolting faces – the flattened top sections of the cylindrical columns which supported the internal structure of the mill – such as those used in the 1820s at Beehive Mill, Manchester, and John Marshall's mill in Leeds. They were not commonplace until the 1850s. The system by which ropes conveyed power from grooved pulleys on the flywheel of a steam engine to shafting on each floor of a building was introduced in Belfast in the 1850s, but was not in common use until after 1875.

Joseph Bramah experimented with hydraulic principles in the late eighteenth century, but hydraulic

This picture is one of five pencil, pen and wash images by Thomas Allom of the monumental cotton mill of Swainson, Birley & Co. at Fishwick just outside Preston, Lancashire, published in 1834, which appeared in Edward Baines, jnr, *The History of the Cotton Manufacture in Great Britain* (London: Fisher, Fisher & Jackson, 1835). It shows women engaged in carding, drawing and roving cotton, and illustrates clearly the manner in which power was transmitted to individual machines by leather belts driven by pulleys on horizontal shafts that range the length of the floors in the mill. Safety guards were unknown at this period.
CARNEGIE COLLECTION

transmission did not become significant until the mid-nineteenth century through the work of Sir William Armstrong, the son of a Newcastle corn merchant. He had trained as a lawyer, but began experiments after being intrigued by a waterwheel while on holiday in 1835, and in 1845 demonstrated a hydraulic crane. He patented this the following year and in 1847 formed a partnership to produce hydraulic machines at Elswick, west of Newcastle, making hoists for the docks at Liverpool, underground haulage engines for coal mines, and machinery for dressing lead ore. In 1850–51 Armstrong invented the hydraulic accumulator, a storage vessel in which hydraulic fluid is held under pressure by a spring, a raised weight or compressed gas. The accumulator was a means of providing constant pressure in a power system and storing its energy, and examples of accumulator houses, with characteristically crenellated towers, remain in Bristol, London, Liverpool and other ports. During the Crimean War Armstrong established a munitions plant alongside the hydraulic works. In 1882 his company merged with that of Charles Palmer, the Jarrow shipbuilder, and in 1897 with the Manchester firm established by Joseph Whitworth, and as Armstrong Whitworth was one of the most powerful forces in British engineering in the first half of the twentieth century. Hydraulic machines operated cranes, lock gates and lifting bridges in ports, and elevators, traversers and capstans in railway depots. In some cities, including Manchester, hydraulic power systems were established as public utilities.

Strutt's Cotton Mill at Belper, Derbyshire, from *The cyclopaedia, or universal dictionary of arts, by Abraham Rees* (London, 1820). This celebrated image of the iron-framed North Mill at Belper (built in 1804) shows clearly how power was transmitted from a wide waterwheel by means of pit wheels to vertical shafts which, in turn, powered horizontal shafts running along each floor of the mill, from which machines were operated by means of pulleys and leather belts. Most textile mills were powered in this manner before 1870, although by that date the prime movers in most of them were steam engines rather than waterwheels. (See also the plan of the watercourses at Belper on page 424.)

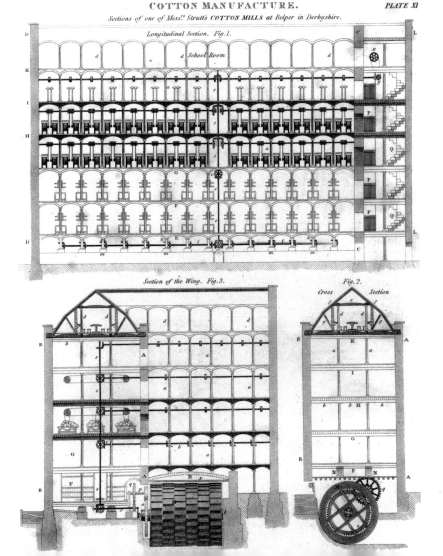

COTTON MANUFACTURE.   PLATE XI

Sections of one of Mess.rs Strutt's COTTON MILLS at Belper in Derbyshire.

Longitudinal Section. Fig.1.

School Room

Section of the Wing. Fig.3.

Fig.2.

Cross Section

Networks of engineers around the British Isles

During Britain's industrial revolution successful engineers and machine makers rarely worked in isolation. Between the 1770s and the 1830s there were several overlapping networks – perhaps the most influential of which centred upon London – which helped to advance the understanding of engineering principles and to diffuse new methods of working. Connections could be made and sustained over long time-frames and distances. Together these networks represented a remarkable web of connections, contacts, experience and skills.

To trace one such network, one can begin with Joseph Bramah. His memorial in All Saints' church, Silkstone (near Barnsley) records that, 'By rare genius and unusual perseverance [Bramah] advanced himself to considerable eminence as an Engineer and Machinist and matured several inventions of the greatest public utility'. Bramah had been apprenticed as a cabinet-maker in Yorkshire, but he spent his working life in the capital where he diversified from cabinet making to manufacture an improved type of water closet, for which he obtained a patent in 1778 (see page 139). In 1784 Bramah set up a company to make a patent lock, and from lock making he turned to machine tools, and designed a beer engine, a hydraulic press and a paper-making machine. In 1789 this talented engineer employed the young Henry Maudslay, a native of Woolwich who had worked at the Royal Arsenal. Nine years later Maudslay opened his own workshop off Oxford Street, and between 1801 and 1808 made 44 block-making machines designed by Sir Marc Brunel for Portsmouth Dockyard, which annually shaped 130,000 blocks for the rigging of sailing ships. While fulfilling the contract Maudsley met Joshua Field, a draughtsman who from 1810 was his partner at a workshop in Lambeth. Maudslay and Field improved the lathe, constructed marine engines, and supplied machine tools to others. Their workshop became, in effect, a staff college for engineers. Richard Roberts,

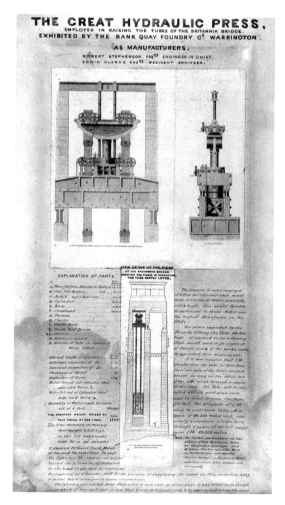

> Hydraulic power was developed from 1840s by William (later Sir William) Armstrong, who patented the hydraulic crane in 1846. Just two years later Jesse Hartley incorporated the new technology in the warehouses of Liverpool's Albert Dock. One of the most spectacular applications of hydraulic engineering was in the construction between 1846 and 1850 of Robert Stephenson's Britannia Bridge which carried the Chester & Holyhead Railway across the Menai Straits. Four hydraulic cylinders were cast by the Bank Quay Foundry at Warrington to lift into place the huge wrought-iron tubes that comprised the bridge (see page 10). It was reckoned they might lift 2,000 tons, but in the event the heaviest lift achieved during the construction of the bridge was 1,144 tons. The Bank Quay Foundry was established in the late 1830s, and taken over in 1847 by Charles and Edward Tayleur, locomotive builders, of the Vulcan Foundry at Newton-le-Willows, with the intention of using it for producing heavy castings such as these, for shipbuilding and for the production of armaments. It had a short life, ceasing production about 1854.

The disparate group of buildings that from 1810 formed the Lambeth workshops of Henry Maudslay & Co., which by 1851 had some 800 employees, many of whom, although relatively well paid, lived in squalid housing in the vicinity. The workshops stood on the site now occupied by Lambeth North Underground station, upon which a plaque commemorates Maudslay's achievements.

son of a shoemaker from Llanymynech, Shropshire, who had learned mathematics from the cartographer Robert Baugh and had served as a patternmaker at Bradley in the Black Country, worked at Lambeth for several years before 1816. From 1814 to 1817 Maudslay's chief draughtsman was Joseph Clement, son of a Westmorland weaver, who made precision instruments and advocated the standardisation of screw threads.

Maudslay also employed Samuel Seaward, who worked for his brother John Seaward from 1826 at the Canal Ironworks, Millwall, famous for marine engines and swing bridges. Joseph Whitworth from Stockport, previously a mechanic in cotton mills, assisted Maudslay between 1825 and 1833 in developing the means of making truly plane surfaces, and in the manufacture of the calculating machines designed by Charles Babbage. James Nasmyth, from Edinburgh, built a steam engine at the age of 18, worked for Maudslay between 1829 and 1834, and in 1830 undertook a tour during which he sketched *Rocket* near Liverpool and saw castings made at Coalbrookdale. Then, towards the end of Maudslay's life, between 1831 and 1836, he employed William Muir, son of an Ayrshire carrier, who built a steam carriage for Admiral Thomas Cochrane, 10th Earl of Dundonald, and established a works in Manchester. Maudslay's influence was not confined to those who worked for

him. In 1806 he took out a joint patent with Bryan Donkin for a differential motion that could be used for raising weights or driving a lathe. Donkin, whose status as a London engineer was second only to that of Maudslay, was the son of a Northumberland surveyor. In 1782 he was apprenticed to John Hall at Dartford, and was involved from 1801 in the production of Fourdrinier paper-making machines. In 1812 he set up a factory in Bermondsey for canning food, and made dredging machines for the Calder & Hebble Navigation, engines for the Caledonian Canal, and developed screw-cutting machines and later made gas distribution plant. There were other successful London engineers, of course, but the network of connections from Bramah and Maudslay shows how important the role of the capital could be in diffusing expertise.

The Soho Manufactory and the Soho Foundry of Matthew Boulton and James Watt formed the hub of another network. Watt had been born in Greenock, the son of a merchant. He trained as a maker of mathematical instruments in Glasgow, making a visit to London to gain professional experience in 1755–56. Dr Joseph Black described him as 'a young man possessing most uncommon talents for mechanical knowledge and practice'. Watt learned German and Italian, took an interest in the manufacture of porcelain, surveyed several Scottish waterways, and became interested in steam engines. After erecting several

△ Richard Trevithick was the pioneer of high-pressure steam. Son of a mine 'captain', he worked from his teens in Cornish mines. He demonstrated a steam road engine at Camborne in 1801, and built high-pressure engines at Coalbrookdale where in 1802 he constructed a steam railway locomotive. He demonstrated other railway locomotives at Merthyr in 1804, and in London (the *Catch-me-who-can*) in 1808. Several engineering companies, notably that of John Hazledine and John Urpeth Rastrick at Bridgnorth, supplied stationary engines to his design for varied applications. In 1812, with other Cornish engineers, he perfected the 'Cornish' pumping engine, which continued to be built for another century. From 1816 he travelled in South and Central America, returning penniless in October 1827. He did some work for John Hall at Dartford, where he died in 1833, his coffin being borne to a pauper's grave by his fellow engineers from Hall's works.

▽ Bryan Donkin was, after Henry Maudslay, the most eminent of London's mechanical engineers in the early nineteenth century. A Northumbrian, he was apprenticed to John Hall at Dartford and played an important role in developing paper-making machines. He was a pioneer in canning food, and his engineering works in Bermondsey produced a variety of machines, pumps used in the construction of the Thames Tunnel, steam engines, lathes, dredging apparatus and subsequently plant for gasworks. A global valve-making company based at Chesterfield continues to bear his name.

Newcomen engines in 1765–66 he took out his first patent – for the separate condenser – in 1769 at the age of 33. He might have developed his research at Carron, but the precarious financial situation of the company led him to move in 1774 to Birmingham, where he worked in partnership with Matthew Boulton, who in 1761 had built the Soho Manufactory, a three-storey, 19-bay building designed by the architect William Wyatt for the manufacture of small metal items (see illustration on page 70). The first steam engines incorporating Watt's improvements were erected in 1776. Initially Boulton & Watt supplied drawings, some key components such as valves, and the services of erectors, but in 1796 they opened the Soho Foundry where they produced engines themselves. Their erectors disseminated the principles of mechanical engineering.

In 1777 William Murdock, son of a millwright from Cumnock, Ayrshire, walked to Birmingham seeking work with Watt, who judged him 'a very sober, ingenious young man, who has a good deal of experience under us in putting engines together and knows all the little niceties, the omission of which might cause a bad performance'. From 1779 Murdock spent nearly twenty years representing the company in Cornwall. He returned to the Soho Foundry where in 1799 John Southern was astonished by 'the torrent of ingenuity which Murdock's genius pours forth'. Murdock discovered the illuminating powers of coal gas in 1792, and developed the company's business in lighting equipment. He designed machine tools for the Soho Foundry, and was admired by the craftsmen who worked there. John Southern, a draughtsman for Watt

▲ Matthew Boulton was one of the outstanding entrepreneurs of the industrial revolution, and one of the most influential figures in the development of Birmingham into one of the world's principal manufacturing cities. His Soho Manufactory, completed in 1761, set a pattern for the concentration of labour in large establishments, although many processes were hand-worked. According to Josiah Wedgwood Boulton was 'the Most Compleat Manufacturer in Metals in England'. His engine partnership with James Watt enabled the latter's enigmatic genius to flourish in the English Midlands, partly through the Lunar Society of which Boulton was a leading member. He was among those who set up the Birmingham Assay Office in 1773, which stimulated the working of precious metals in the city, and in 1788 began to make high-quality coins and metals at the Soho Mint.

▼ Henry Maudslay was a gifted engineer who contributed substantially to the development of machine tools, of machines used in manufacturing processes and of marine engines, but his principal contribution to the development of mechanical engineering was the welcome he accorded to young engineers at his works in south London. The founders of many of the principal engineering concerns of the mid-nineteenth century spent time working with Maudslay at Lambeth.

from 1782, became head of the drawing office at the Soho Manufactory and a partner in the company from 1810. He represented the company in conversations with Richard Arkwright and Joseph Wilkes. Until 1782 Henry Williams erected engines for Boulton & Watt at several Shropshire ironworks, but he then began to work for the ironmaster Richard Reynolds. Williams was subsequently surveyor to the Shropshire Canal, whose inclined planes he designed with John Lowdon; he also built part of the Holyhead Road near Oakengates, and in 1818 became a partner in the Ketley Ironworks. John Rennie, while working on his own account, was constantly in touch with Boulton and Watt, and represented them in London. Peter Ewart built engines in the 1790s for the partnership in the Manchester area and, when a textile entrepreneur,

maintained a correspondence about steamboats. William Creighton erected Boulton & Watt engines in Lancashire from 1795, and from 1815 succeeded John Southern as head of the drawing office at Soho. Thomas Barnes, viewer at the Walker Colliery, advocated the Watt engine, and provided the partnership with intelligence from the North East.

Another network was centred on the metalliferous mines of west Cornwall. James Watt and Matthew Boulton considered the market in Cornwall to be promising, since the high cost of coal – which had to be imported by sea from South Wales – gave the fuel-efficient Watt engine a major advantage over the atmospheric engines of Newcomen. Arthur Woolf, one of the best-known Cornish engine builders, was born in Camborne but worked in London for Joseph

Bramah. After patenting a compound engine in 1805 he returned to Cornwall in 1811. He became chief engineer for the foundry which had been established at Hayle in 1779 by the blacksmith John Harvey, and was subsequently managed by his son Henry Harvey.

Richard Trevithick, who developed the use of high-pressure steam, was Cornish by birth, but after 1800 worked at Coalbrookdale and Penydarren and for the foundry at Bridgnorth established by John Hazledine, where the Trevithick engine now in the Science Museum was constructed. As a young man Trevithick worked with another Cornish engineer, Edward Bull, on a pumping engine in which the steam cylinder was inverted over the pump, dispensing with the need for a beam. On returning to Cornwall Trevithick perfected the Cornish engine, the final development of the condensing single-cylinder beam engine which utilised some of the principles developed by Bull. The first of these was installed at Wheal Prosper in 1811–12. Trevithick married Harvey's daughter in 1797 and worked for a time at Hayle, but in 1816 settled in Peru, following steam machinery worth £16,152 that had been produced for him at Bridgnorth. He returned penniless in 1827. Meanwhile, Arthur Woolf developed the Cornish engine into a pumping machine that was both elegant and economical and for which a worldwide demand continued throughout the century. One of Woolf's successors was another Cornishman, William Husband, who was sent at the age of 21 to supervise the erection of an engine near Haarlem. He remained in the Netherlands, learned Dutch, and for four years from 1845 served as chief engineer of the Haarlemmermeer drainage works. He managed Harveys' London office from 1852 until 1854, when he returned to Hayle to take charge of engineering and to give support to the Royal Cornish Polytechnic Society.

The Perran Foundry at Perranarworthal on the banks of the Kenrial river near Falmouth was established in 1791 by the brothers Robert Were Fox and Charles Fox, members of the Quaker family who operated the Neath Abbey Ironworks. The Foxes were principally responsible for the founding in 1832 of the Royal Cornish Polytechnic Society, which from 1835 had its headquarters in a building at Falmouth designed by George Wightwick. Like the literary and philosophical societies of cities in the Midlands and the North, it served as a forum for the exchange of ideas about geology, mining technology and mechanical engineering. The society offered prizes for innovations, one of which was awarded to Michael Loam, a pupil of Arthur Woolf, who devised a man engine by which miners could descend and ascend shafts; the first was installed near Redruth in 1842.

The third outstanding engineering company in west Cornwall was the Copperhouse Foundry of Sandys, Carne & Vivian, which from about 1820 until 1867 occupied the site just east of Hayle where from 1758 the Cornwall Copper Co. had smelted copper. Harveys', Perran and Copperhouse were exceptional concerns, situated at a distance from supplies of iron, but deriving stimulation from a sustained local demand for engines and pumps. Their status was recognised in 1843 by the Children's Employment Commission, which reported that between them the three firms employed 644 adults, that they provided training for young men who went off to work at a distance but later returned, and that workers were accustomed to 12-hour shifts with hour-long dinner breaks during which they ate pasties. The three foundries did routine work for local mines, but from time to time they produced engines of international significance. For example, the Copperhouse Foundry was responsible for the 90 inch (2.3 m) Cornish engine of 1848 at Kew Bridge Steam Museum, where there are also two Harvey engines, a Bull engine of 1856–59 and a 100 inch Cornish engine of 1869–71. The Cruquius engine house built in 1849–52 near Haarlem contains an engine by Harveys' with a 144 inch (3.7 m) cylinder that operated 11 cast-iron beams balanced on its walls, working pumps supplied by Perran which drained the 45,000 acre Haarlemmermeer. Cornishmen exercised their mechanical skills throughout Britain. They included two 'practical engineers' from Redruth and Phillack, who in 1861 operated the pumping engines on the Kennet & Avon Canal at Crofton, one of 1812 by Boulton & Watt, the other, of 1846, by Harveys'.

Manchester was the centre of another network. In 1795 the antiquarian John Aikin detailed the impact on metal-working trades of the growth of textile manufacturing:

The prodigious extension of the several branches of the Manchester [cotton] manufactures had likewise increased the business of several trades and manufactures connected with or dependent upon them. ... To the ironmonger's shops, which are greatly increased of late, are generally annexed smithies, where many articles are made, even to nails. ... The tin-plate workers have found additional employment in furnishing many articles for spinning machines, as have also the braziers in casting wheels for the motion-work of the rollers used in them; and the clockmakers in cutting them.

Several manufacturers of steam engines flourished in Manchester in the 1790s, including the St George's Foundry at Knott Mill, in which the Shropshire iron-master Alexander Brodie was a partner, and that of James Bateman and William Sherratt in Salford. The millwright Thomas Hewes settled in Manchester in 1792. In 1811 he introduced the high breast-shot suspension waterwheel, combining cast-iron and wrought-iron components. From 1813 Hewes employed William Fairbairn, from Kelso, who had been apprenticed as a millwright in Northumberland where he had known George Stephenson. In 1817, with James Lillie, Fairburn set up Fairbairn & Lillie, engine makers, who improved line-shafting, and in the early 1840s devised the 'Lancashire' boiler, through which heat from the fire passed through two large tubes, which became the standard means of raising steam in almost every textile mill and in factories of many other kinds. Fairbairn was involved in the construction of more than 100 bridges, including the tubular structure designed by Robert Stephenson which carries the railway over the river at Conwy, and the similar Britannia Bridge which until 1970 took the

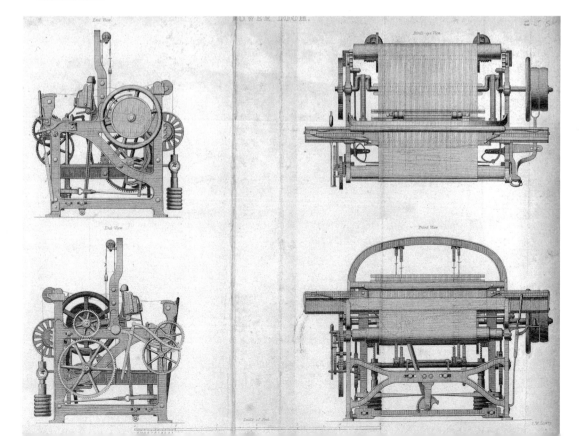

Early nineteenth-century power looms of the kind patented by Richard Roberts. Assembled almost entirely from cast- and wrought-iron parts, these were mass-produced by several Lancashire engineering works. From Baines, *The History of the Cotton Manufacture in Great Britain* (1835).

81

line to Holyhead across the Menai Straits. He was also responsible for the mechanical engineering at Saltaire mill. Between 1834 and 1848 he had a works at Millwall, London, where he built more than 80 iron ships and 400 railway locomotives. Richard Roberts returned to Manchester from London in 1816, and devised planing and slotting machines. However, his greatest impact on Lancashire was through his powerloom, an iron machine patented in 1822 (of which 4,000 were being manufactured annually within three years) and his

self-acting spinning mule that was patented in 1825. In 1826 he became a partner in Sharp, Roberts & Co., engineers, but his business abilities were limited, and the firm closed in 1852.

James Nasmyth also settled in Manchester after a spell with Henry Maudslay in Lambeth. From 1834 he built steam engines and machine tools on the first storey of a tenemented former cotton mill, the floor of which was insufficiently strong: it could not support the load of an engine beam being machined, and this

⟍ This Ordnance Survey map of 1893 portrays the great concentration of engineering capacity that grew up on the eastern side of Manchester in the mid-nineteenth century. Towards the north of the map runs the 1806 turnpike from Manchester to Ashton-under-Lyne; the Stockport Branch of the Ashton-under-Lyne Canal runs along the eastern edge. The first large manufacturing concern to be established in the area was the Openshaw works opened by Joseph Whitworth in 1833, producing machine tools and, later, armaments. The main line of the Sheffield, Ashton-under-Lyne & Manchester Railway was opened in 1845; two years later the company became part of the Manchester, Sheffield & Lincolnshire Railway which in 1848 built its locomotive and carriage works north of the main line and west of the canal. The installation marked as 'Gorton Yard' is the MSLR running shed that provided motive power for the company's trains around Manchester. The running shed south of the main line in the fork with the Sheffield & Midland Joint Railway (Asburys Junction–New Mills) was the Belle Vue depot of the Midland Railway which gained access by this route to London Road Station in Manchester. Gorton Foundry, to the south of the main line, was founded in 1854 by Richard Peacock, who left the employ of the MSLR the previous year, with Charles Beyer. This map marks many smaller iron-working concerns, but only two modest cotton works: Manchester was as much an engineering as a textile city.

The foundry of Kennan & Sons in Fishamble Street, Dublin, was established in the 1790s and by the 1860s was one of the principal engineering concerns in Ireland. It continued in production until the 1980s; the buildings on the street frontage are now occupied by the Contemporary Music Centre. The interior view, top, shows a line of smiths' hearths where wrought-iron components for machines were fabricated. George Measom, *The Official Illustrated Guide to the Great Southern & Western and Midland Great Western Railways of Ireland* (London: Measom, 1866).

crashed through into the stock of a glass worker. In 1836–38 Nasmyth built the Bridgewater Foundry, Patricroft, which specialised in the manufacture of machine tools, particularly the steam hammer which he had designed, although he also built locomotives and hydraulic presses. He retired in 1856 to pursue astronomical studies (a crater on the moon bears his name). A third engineer who settled in Manchester after experience with Maudslay was Joseph Whitworth, who set up as a toolmaker in 1833 and displayed machine tools at the Great Exhibition in 1851. Having developed his system of standardised screw threads, in 1854 he began to manufacture armaments. William Muir, with experience of Maudslay's workshop and the Copperhouse Foundry, worked for Whitworth from 1842, but left two years later to manufacture machines to make railway tickets, for Thomas Edmondson, their inventor. He subsequently opened a works at Strangeways, Manchester, which made machine tools. Carl Friedrich (Charles Frederick) Beyer, the son of a weaver from Plauen, Saxony, studied at the polytechnic in Dresden, settled in Manchester after 1834, and worked in the drawing office of Sharp, Roberts & Co. He became chief engineer in 1843, and was engaged in designing locomotives. In 1854 he set up a company in partnership with Richard Peacock and the ironmaster Henry Robertson. From 1841 Peacock was locomotive superintendent of the Sheffield, Ashton-under-Lyne and Manchester Railway, and laid out the company's workshops at Gorton in east Manchester, alongside which the partners built a factory designed by Beyer. In the 1850s and 1860s Beyer Peacock constructed locomotives for railways in Sweden,

Spain, Portugal and the Netherlands, and supplied machine tools for their maintenance, while Gorton became a noted centre of engineering talent.

Mechanical engineering also flourished in Ireland. Foundries in Dublin and Cork produced what Boulton & Watt regarded as pirate steam engines in the 1790s. Some Irish engineers competed successfully for contracts in England. Robert Mallett's works in Dublin, established in the 1820s, fabricated the building known as the 'Irish shed' at the Lancashire & Yorkshire Railway's locomotive depot at Newton Heath, Manchester. The company's method of riveting together pieces of iron to form rigid composite plates was used in the construction of St Pancras Station. From the 1860s Falls Foundry in Belfast was the principal manufacturer of flax-spinning machinery in the United Kingdom. About a third of the 2,300 steam locomotives used on Irish railways in the course of more than a century were built in Ireland. As early as 1836 the Dublin & Kingstown Railway had decided

⋏ The wrought-iron T-section rails that were designed by John Birkinshaw at Bedlington were influential in the spread of railways across Great Britain. Here redundant rails of this kind have been re-used in a fence alongside the Kennet & Avon Canal at Semington in Wiltshire.

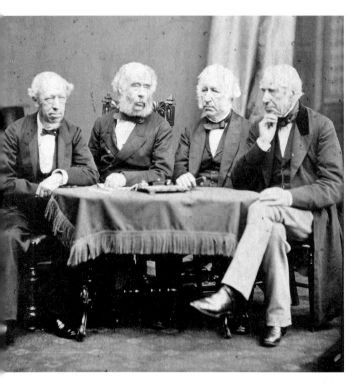

⋏ This photograph taken at the Manchester meeting of the Institution of Mechanical Engineers in 1866 encapsulates the role of the professional institutions in the diffusion of knowledge and expertise. Collectively, the four men pictured here had an enormous fund of understanding of engineering, particularly of marine engineering. They are, from left to right, John Penn, the marine engineer whose works in south London was one of the capital's largest engineering establishments, Joseph Whitworth, pioneer of standardised measurements, Robert Napier, shipbuilder, and William Fairbairn.

to build its own locomotives, and completed the first, *Princess*, in 1839. The works at Inchicore of the Great Southern & Western Railway was begun in 1851, when it had 96 workers. By 1900 it covered 52 acres and employed 2,000 men. It built 406 locomotives, while 132 were constructed at the works of the Midland Great Western Railway at Broadstone. In Belfast the Belfast & Northern Counties Railway built a works near its York Road terminus where it produced its first locomotive in 1870. The first Irish steamship was built at Passage West, Cork, in 1815, and by the 1840s iron vessels were being constructed at Waterford, Londonderry and Cork, while the Lagan Foundry in Belfast became Ireland's principal supplier of marine steam engines.

Other networks stimulated the growth of mechanical engineering, including those centred on Leeds (see pages 88–91) and those in Newcastle-upon-Tyne and Glasgow discussed in Chapters 5 and 6, and one in Shropshire that revolved around William Reynolds. The nature of such networks is illustrated by the career of Sir Daniel Gooch, who was born in 1816 at Bedlington, Northumberland, where his father worked at the ironworks that belonged to his cousins. Daniel spent his spare time at the ironworks or the neighbouring coal pit, where he enjoyed going underground to ride on the trams. The Gooches knew George Stephenson and John Birkinshaw, who worked at the Bedlington Ironworks and invented the T-section wrought-iron rail that was used on most of the first generation of main-line railways. The middle-aged Daniel Gooch noticed Birkinshaw rails on the Stratford & Moreton Railway when the GWR took it over in 1859. Gooch read books on mechanics from the age of 12, when his father bought him a lathe. The family moved to Tredegar in 1831, when the young Daniel began work at the ironworks, making cores in the foundry, repairing the valves of the blowing engines, and often venturing underground. He reflected in old age: 'Large works of this kind are by far the best school for a young engineer to get a general knowledge of what he needs in after life. It is, in fact, the foundation for all else. Every Englishmen ought to know and understand the manufacture of iron and working of mines.' He worked

Sir Daniel Gooch is best known as first chief mechanical engineer of the Great Western Railway from 1837 until 1864. He also did much as chairman of the company to retrieve its fortunes in the 1860s. He was also chief engineer of the Telegraph Construction Company, which, using the SS *Great Eastern*, laid the first successful transatlantic telegraph cable in 1865–66. His autobiography provides many illuminating insights into the training of engineers.

The ability of British mechanical engineers to manufacture machines to meet all kinds of new challenges is exemplified in this image of the cable-laying machinery on the deck of the SS *Great Eastern*, when the ship was being operated by Sir Daniel Gooch's Telegraph Construction Company in the mid-1860s.

at the Vulcan Foundry in 1834, and had experience making marine engines and flax-spinning machinery at Dundee, before a spell at Robert Stephenson's locomotive works at Newcastle. In 1836 he took up an appointment at the Gateshead locomotive works of Robert Hawkes, for whom he ordered machine tools from Joseph Whitworth. When he was only 21, I. K. Brunel gave him responsibility for the locomotives of the Great Western Railway. He subsequently designed the company's works at Swindon. Much of the development of mechanical engineering between 1700 and the dawn of main-line railways depended on talented but self-taught men. The 1840s saw the beginnings of new means of ensuring the maintenance of standards and promoting engineering training.

A formal network, the Institution of Mechanical Engineers, was established in Birmingham on 27 January 1847 after a 'conversation' among leading members of the profession, probably during the locomotive trials that took place on the Lickey Incline in 1846. The Institution's headquarters moved from Birmingham to London in 1877. Charles Beyer and Richard Peacock and the Birmingham tube makers George Selby and Archibald Slate were among the founders, and the Institution's presidents in its first decades included many prominent British engineers such as George and Robert Stephenson, William Fairbairn, Joseph Whitworth, Sir William Armstrong, Sir William Siemens and Sir Isaac Lothian Bell. Their achievements were matched by those of British engineers who worked overseas: William Cockerill, who established an iron-making and engineering concern near Liège; William Handyside, who worked in the imperial arsenal in Russia; Aaron Manby, who set up engineering works in France; and John Haswell, who built locomotives in Vienna.

George Stephenson epitomises the Victorian concept of self-help. He was born at Wylam, Northumberland, to illiterate parents, and began his working life at a nearby colliery, ending it living the life of a landed gentleman in north Derbyshire. He developed a safety lamp for miners and gained skills in the workings of steam engines, which he demonstrated by building the locomotive *Blücher* for the Killingworth colliery railway in 1814. He surveyed and supervised the construction of the Stockton & Darlington Railway which opened in 1825, its engine *Locomotion* being the first product of the locomotive works in Forth Street, Newcastle, of Robert Stephenson & Co., in which George was a partner. He was responsible for the construction of the Liverpool & Manchester Railway, opened in 1830. The company's Rainhill Trials held in October 1829 were won by the locomotive *Rocket*, largely the work of Robert Stephenson. George built more lines including the North Midland Railway between Derby and Leeds whose construction revealed seams of coal near Chesterfield. He invested much of his fortune in mining in the area and from 1832 until his death in 1848 leased the nearby mansion Tapton House. He was elected first President of the Institution of Mechanical Engineers in 1847.

© NMPFT/DAILY HERALD ARCHIVE/SCIENCE & SOCIETY PICTURE LIBRARY

A wide variety of engineering and mechanical skills

Networks are important, but engineering is more than the history of great men, whatever their practical skills or entrepreneurial genius. It is about teaching skills to sufficient people to give practical expression to ideas. The success of this between 1780 and 1850 is shown by the ease with which, in the 1830s and 1840s, the great railway companies established works for building and maintaining their locomotives in places without engineering traditions. One example, Wolverton, serves to illustrate what also occurred at Ashford, Crewe, Doncaster and Swindon. This village in Buckinghamshire was selected by the London & Birmingham Railway as the site for a locomotive repair depot because it lay approximately midway between its two termini. The works opened in 1838, and by 1845 the company had constructed an estate with more than 200 houses, a church and schools. The adjacent land in Stony Stratford, until 1838 a busy town of thoroughfare, was held by the Radcliffe Trustees, who were reluctant to sell, and houses in a settlement called New Bradwell were built during the

1850s. In 1864 the London & North Western Railway concentrated locomotive building and maintenance at Crewe and work on carriages at Wolverton, which led to large-scale movements of men and their families in each direction. The expansion of the works after 1864, and the realignment of the main line in 1880, led to the destruction of the earliest housing. In 1849 F. B. Head described Wolverton as

a little red-brick town composed of 242 little red-brick houses – all running either this way or that at right angles – three or four tall red-brick engine chimneys, a number of very large red-brick workshops, six red houses for officers, one red beer shop, two red public houses, and, we are glad to add, a substantial red schoolroom and a neat stone church, the whole being lately built by order of a railway board, at a railway station, by a railway contractor, for railwaymen, railway women and railway children; in short, the round, cast-iron

This engraving illustrates very well the relatively small scale of the first generation of locomotive-building works. The Grand Junction Railway, which ran from Newton-le-Willows to Birmingham built its works at Monks Coppenhall, later known as Crewe, where it made a junction with the Manchester & Birmingham Railway. Both companies subsequently became part of the London & North Western Railway. By 1848 the works employed more than 1,000 men and was able to produce one locomotive a week. Locomotives on the right seem to be nearing completion, while on the left it appears that frames have been laid for the construction of others. The cranes, unlike the overhead cranes of later works which could lift whole locomotives, were clearly capable only of lifting components.

plate over the door of every houses, bearing the letters LNWR is the generic symbol of the town.

To Samuel Sidney in 1851 it appeared to be an example of rational planning, where regularly employed and well-paid mechanics of above-average intelligence were able to make use of a reading room and mechanics' institute, but where other diverting recreations were lacking. In 1861 3,047 people lived in Wolverton and New Bradwell, but some railway engineers resided at Stony Stratford. The specialisation of labour at the locomotive works illustrates how effectively skills had been taught in earlier decades.

The workforce comprised a wide range of specialists, including angle-iron smiths, blacksmiths, boilermakers, brass finishers, brass founders, brass moulders, brass tube workers, copper smiths, engine smiths, strikers, engine turners, iron rolling mill workers, iron turners, locomotive engine erectors, machine smiths, mill sawyers, pattern makers, rivet carriers and steam hammermen. The majority were incomers. Engine fitters, the largest occupational group, included men from Aveling (Gloucestershire), Attercliffe (Sheffield, Yorkshire), Banbury, Barnsley, Barnstaple, Berwick-upon-Tweed, Birmingham, Bristol, Blyth (Northumberland), Bromsgrove, Calverton (Nottinghamshire), Camborne, Castleford, Chichester, Clitheroe, Darley Abbey (Derbyshire), Darlington, Devizes, Doncaster, Eccleshall (Staffordshire), Evesham, Exeter, Leeds, Leicester, Liverpool, Loughborough, Macclesfield, Mansfield, Newcastle-upon-Tyne, Newton-le-Willows, Nottingham, Radford (Nottinghamshire), Salisbury, Selby, Sunderland, Tanfield (Co. Durham), Taunton, Tavistock, Tiverton, Warwick, Wednesbury and York, as well as from Camden Town, Deptford, Lambeth, Lewisham, Nine Elms, Pimlico and Poplar in London, and from Scotland and Ireland. Nevertheless

by 1861 locally born young men had taken up skilled work in the factory.

The multiplier effects of a large engineering works are illustrated by the career of Edward Hayes, a Mancunian who began to work at Wolverton about 1840. Within ten years he had established the Watling Works at Stony Stratford, where he made agricultural machinery and portable engines and, from the 1860s, the steamboats for which he became famous.

Hayes was a conscientious educator whose household in 1861 included 13 apprentice mechanical engineers aged between 14 and 18, born in ten English counties, Calcutta, and the Isles of Scilly. In 1868 a previous apprentice, Belfast-born Osborne Reynolds, became the first professor of mechanical engineering at Owens College, Manchester.

Hunslet and Holbeck, southern suburbs of Leeds where iron had been shaped since the Middle Ages, became a notable concentration of mechanical engineering enterprise and expertise. The Middleton Railway and barges on the river Aire supplied the area with coal, and engineers could rely on an infrastructure of cotton waste and grease dealers, oil millers and makers of firebricks; Yorkshire textile entrepreneurs and mine owners were potential customers for machines. Matthew Murray, a millwright, worked with John Marshall from 1788 to improve flax-spinning machinery. In 1791 Marshall began construction of his flax-spinning complex in Water Lane, Leeds. Murray worked for him until 1795 when with David Wood (and from 1797 James Fenton) he formed an engineering company operating from workshops at Mill Green, and after 1802 from the purpose-built Round Foundry, south of the river Aire near Leeds Bridge.

James Watt junior observed on 14 June 1802 that 'Fame has not outdone the magnitude of Murray's new Edifice. It is a rotundo of about 100 feet in diameter with a magnificent Entrance. It is an excellent building.' Murray continued to supply machinery to Marshall, and contributed to the development of iron frames for textile mills. In 1812, working with John Blenkinsop, he completed *Salamanca*, the first of four steam locomotives for the Middleton Railway, which hauled coal trains until 1835. Murray took out further patents, including one for a finely adjustable hydraulic press for use in finishing woollen cloth, and supplied machine tools to other engineers. He died in 1826 and is commemorated by an obelisk at St Matthew, Holbeck. About 80 steam locomotives were built at the Round Foundry between 1831 and 1842.

ᵧ The two-mile long railway carrying coal into Leeds from the colliery at Middleton was opened in 1758. Steam-powered haulage was introduced in 1812 by the colliery manager, John Blenkinsop, who had patented the principle of the rack railway the previous year. *Salamanca*, the first locomotive employed on the line was built at the Round Foundry, and the cogs on its central wheels are clearly visible in this aquatint, entitled 'The Collier', by Robert Hovell. *Salamanca*'s boiler exploded in 1818, killing the driver, and again in 1831, after which the Middleton Railway relied on horse haulage until 1866 when tank locomotives were purchased from Manning Wardle. This image is perhaps best known from its use on the cover of one of the most influential books on the Industrial Revolution period, the Penguin edition of E. P. Thompson's *The Making of the English Working Class*, published in 1968.

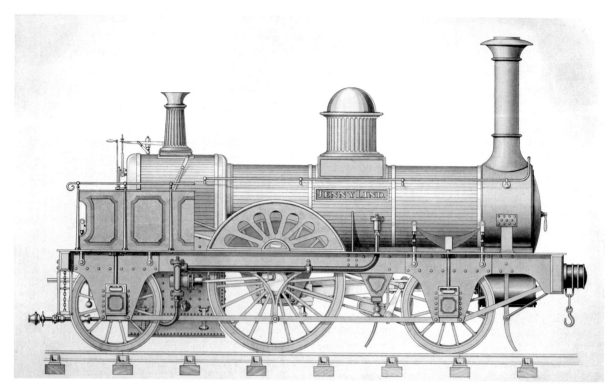

⚹ The Railway Foundry, in Pearson Street, Leeds, was founded in 1839 by Charles Todd, who until 1837 had worked at the Round Foundry, and John Shepherd. Todd was succeeded as partner in 1846 by Edward Brown Wilson who constructed a new assembly shop the following year. One of the first products of the assembly shop was this, the 2-2-2 locomotive *Jenny Lind*, designed by David Joy, and built for the London, Brighton & South Coast Railway. The Railway Foundry closed in 1858, but several of its engineers subsequently set up other enterprises in this part of Leeds.

In 1837 Charles Todd left the Round Foundry to establish an engineering concern with James Kitson and others alongside the Middleton Railway on Pearson Street. Their products included *Lion*, one of six locomotives for the Liverpool & Manchester Railway. The partnership had a short life. In 1839 Todd, with John Shepherd, opened the Railway Foundry on the south side of Pearson Street. Kitson, a publican's son who had been impressed by Nicholas Wood's *A Practical Treatise on Rail-roads*, joined a partnership which set up the Airedale Foundry on the opposite side of the road. Todd remained at the Railway Foundry until 1846 when he went to the Sun Foundry on Dewsbury Road. He was succeeded by Edward Brown Wilson, who opened a new assembly shop the following year. The company prospered during the

Railway Mania of the late 1840s, but closed in 1858, when its site attracted other locomotive builders. Two former managers of the Railway Foundry, Alexander Campbell and C. W. Wardle, purchased the intellectual property rights and goodwill of the company in 1858 and on part of the site established a new concern, Manning Wardle & Co., using capital provided by a clergyman, John Manning. The firm built small locomotives for industrial concerns and construction contractors, completing about 1,500 before 1900. Engines were supplied to Portugal and New South Wales in the early 1860s. The first Manning Wardle tram locomotive went to Brazil in 1866. From 1864 the adjacent plot was occupied by the Hunslet Engine Co., whose partners were John Leather, a civil engineer, and James Campbell, son of Alexander Campbell of

Manning Wardle. The company specialised in locomotives for narrow-gauge railways, such as those in the slate quarries of Gwynedd. Their tenth locomotive went to Java, and a lucrative trade with Australia began in the 1870s.

On the opposite side of Jack Lane the name 'Railway Foundry' was revived in 1860 by W. S. Hudswell and John Clarke, who had eleven employees in the following year. Some of their first locomotives went to the Cockermouth & Workington and North Eastern railways but, like its neighbours, the company specialised in industrial locomotives, completing about 1,600 by 1927. The adjacent property, no. 100 Jack Lane, was occupied from 1876 by the Midland Engine Works, which built traction and ploughing engines and road rollers.

The Airedale Foundry prospered. In 1854 James Kitson ensured a reliable supply of iron by establishing the Monk Bridge Ironworks on a nearby site. It was managed by his sons Frederick William and James Kitson II and in 1872 included 26 puddling furnaces and 8 rolling mills. The foundry made about 4,500 locomotives before its closure in 1938. James Kitson I was one of Leeds's most prominent citizens: Elmete Hall at Roundhay was built for him in 1865–68 by the architects Dobson & Chorley.

The manufacture of road engines and steam ploughing equipment in Hunslet began with John Fowler, a Quaker from Melksham, Wiltshire, who had married a daughter of Joseph Pease, son of the projector of the Stockton & Darlington Railway. Fowler won a prize for a steam ploughing engine at the Royal Agricultural Society's show in 1858, and subsequently ordered engines from James Kitson. In 1862 he established a works alongside Kitson's Airedale Foundry. After Fowler's death his successors made the company a celebrated supplier of steam engines and associated agricultural equipment.

Thus, each of the five major locomotive-building companies in Hunslet in the 1860s could trace their descent from the Round Foundry. In the early 1840s this had been taken over by Smith, Beacock & Tannett, who continued the tradition established by Matthew Murray of manufacturing machine tools. Robert Beacock employed nearly 600 men and boys in 1861.

The company won prizes at the Great Exhibition and manufactured a gigantic screwing machine for the shipyard at Barrow-in-Furness, which received a congratulatory mention in the *New York Times* in 1881.

There were other substantial engineering companies in Hunslet and Holbeck. In 1861 the machine maker John Pollard had 382 workers; John Longbottom and John Shepherd, makers of machine tools 150 each; William Wood, master millwright and engineer 100; and William Nichols, engineer and tool maker 85. These were the middle ranks of a hierarchy of companies in which the Airedale Foundry and Smith, Beacock & Tannett occupied the premier positions, but mechanical engineering in Leeds also derived strength from smaller concerns such as Luke Pool, screw manufacturer, who in 1861 had 36 employees. This census also shows that John Atkinson, wheelwright, smith, axle maker and ironfounder employed 49 people; William Bywater, machine-tool manufacturer had 45; and William Humphrey, boilermaker, 41. Benjamin Greaves, with 37 employees, was one of several filemakers who had migrated to Hunslet from Sheffield. Jonathon Merton, toolmaker, worked with nine others in a former pottery building, while Henry Craven and four other people made machines in the yard of Marshall's Mill.

Most small concerns of this kind occupied unremarkable premises, many of them having been adapted from other purposes. The products and services they offered were crucial to the prosperity of the large locomotive and machine building companies in this part of Leeds, and taken together they employed a significant number of the city's engineering workers. The engineering workforce in Holbeck and Hunslet, many of whom lived in insanitary back-to-back terraces, practised skills that had been unknown two generations earlier, tending slide lathes, planing-machines, slotting-machines, horizontal borers and steam hammers; making bolts, moulds, cores, axles, and compositions to case-harden iron; nicking screw heads, shearing boiler plates, casting brass, shaping copper, erecting locomotives, and fitting their wheels. In less than a century engineers had learned to make a wide range of machines that helped to transform the British economy and society. (See map of Leeds on page 249.)

Market-town foundries

Mechanical engineering expertise spread to almost every town of consequence in the British Isles between 1780 and 1850. As Richard Jefferies explained,

> Country towns of any size usually possess at least one manufactory of agricultural implements and some of these factories have acquired a reputation which reaches over the sea. The visitor to such a foundry is shown medals that have been granted for excellence of work exhibited in Vienna, and may see machines in process of construction which will be used upon the Continent.

Jefferies was aware of the migratory nature of engineering workers: 'Busy workmen pass to and fro, lithe men, quick of step and motion, who come from Leeds or some similar manufacturing town, and whose very step distinguishes them in a moment from the agricultural labourer.' At Cirencester, which Jefferies knew well, the 1871 census reveals four concerns employing, respectively, 6, 19, 33 and 36 men. Even in a town as small as Fairford, Gloucestershire, there was a maker of agricultural implements employing four men and a boy in 1861. In Kington, Herefordshire, one of the

most isolated of towns, can be seen the impressive quadrangular buildings of the foundry which John Meredith built about 1820 alongside the tramroad from Hay. At Horncastle, Lincolnshire, the buildings of the foundry buildings established by the Yorkshireman William Wheton, and the surrounding terraced housing, comprise a whole landscape of market town engineering.

Many engineering works specialised in machines which had markets in their particular regions. Thus, Martin Samuelson & Co. of Hull made hydraulic presses for making oilcake; Barrett, Exall & Andrewes of Reading manufactured biscuit-making machines; George Elliott of Farnham made equipment for bagging hops; Gimson & Co. of Leicester made machines that produced rubber and elastic threads; J. B. Whitehall of Nottingham manufactured Jacquard looms; George Tidcombe of Watford built Fourdrinier paper-making machines; and Joshua Horn of Castleford produced glass-making machinery. At Cork the Hive Iron Works, established in 1800 by Thomas Addison Barnes, made sieves for paper making and frames for the manufacture of gunpowder at Ballincollig.

Yet other towns developed specialisms unrelated to local demand. Leamington became the centre for the

Between 1780 and 1850 small foundries making agricultural implements were established in most market towns of significance, including such relatively small places as Horncastle in Lincolnshire, where this foundry, established by the Yorkshire-born William Whetton, employed six men in 1861.

Some market foundries made machines which were exported in large quantities to distant parts of the world, but most, whatever their other products, fulfilled the unspectacular needs of their neighbours, as did Barton's foundry at Sudbury (Suffolk) whose name is recorded on this unremarkable piece of fencing in the town.

One market-town foundry that grew to spectacular size was the Britannia Works of John Howard, located alongside the river Great Ouse at Bedford. This bill heading used in 1838 illustrates the ironmonger's shop, of the kind from which many such enterprises originated. The courtyard layout of the engineering works is characteristic of many of the early nineteenth century. The four flues along the south range indicate the position of the smiths' shops; the wide central flue is probably from the cupola furnace; the tall chimney is probably from the boilers which supplied the steam engine working the machine tools and the cupola fan. Several large wooden patterns are strewn across the yard. By 1861 John Howard was employing 450 men at the works, and it grew substantially in subsequent decades.

JOHN JOHNSON COLLECTION, BODLEIAN LIBRARY, BILL HEADINGS, BOX 15

manufacture of 'kitcheners', or kitchen ranges. When the canal through the growing spa town was opened in 1800 foundries were set up to supply cast-iron railings and verandas for its Regency houses. The iron-founders William and Sidney Flavel began to specialise in kitcheners, and by 1861 employed 100 workmen and were making 50 ranges a week. Their example was followed by Thomas Radcliffe and Joshua Harrison, and 'Leamington kitcheners' became a powerful brand nationally. Some market town engineering works grew to great size. James Howard's Britannia Ironworks at Bedford was described in 1861 as 'among the marvels of our wonder-producing age … so vast an industrial colony in the midst of a retired agricultural district'. At Leiston, Suffolk, the works of Richard Garrett & Sons is the best preserved of its kind; in the early 1870s its traction engines and agricultural machinery went to depots at Budapest, Barcelona, Cairo, Constantinople, Cologne, Calcutta, Hanover, Königsberg, Kiev, Madrid, Melbourne, Naples, Odessa and Sydney.

Conclusions: a diffusion of technical skills

The process of learning in mechanical engineering originated with individuals of genius, such as James Watt, whose discovery of parallel motion was a creative experience; the process was also taken forward by managers who, like Richard Arkwright, maximised the discoveries of others. The dissemination of knowledge, expertise and know-how was developed by figures such as Henry Maudslay, whose workshops were nurseries of talent, and by those who set up machine shops in areas such as Hunslet or in market towns. James Watt junior observed of Matthew Murray in 1802 that 'He employs altogether about 160 men. … Many are apprentices.' Some engineers, such as James Kitson II or James Howard, employed hundreds and received public acclaim, while others continued on a much more modest scale, shaping metal for the needs of their localities. All were part of a diffusion of skills that between 1800 and 1860 helped to create the 'workshop of the world'.

Working shaft, Kilsby Tunnel, Northamptonshire, 8 July 1837, a wash drawing by John Cooke Bourne, from a collection of views of the construction of the London & Birmingham Railway (LBR). In 1833 Robert Stephenson was appointed chief engineer of the LBR, the first railway into London. Running from Curzon Street Station, Birmingham, to Euston Station, London, the 112-mile long line took 20,000 men nearly five years to build, at a cost of £5.5 million. Extensive quicksands made the digging of the Kilsby Tunnel in Northamptonshire one of the most difficult engineering challenges on the route. Eighteen working shafts were sunk to construct the tunnel, which took two years to complete, cost three times the estimate, and claimed the lives of 26 workers. The LBR opened on 17 September 1838.

4

Comprehending structures:
the evolution of civil engineering

'Telford's is a happy life: everywhere making roads, building bridges, forming canals and creating harbours – works of sure, solid, permanent utility: everywhere employing a great number of persons.'

ROBERT SOUTHEY, 1819

ROWLAND HUNT was a canal shareholder and a Shropshire landowner. At the opening of the Pontcysyllte Aqueduct on 26 November 1805 he declared that 'Antiquity has produced no such structure as an Aqueduct which can compare with Pontcysyllte'. He was right to be impressed, for the aqueduct, which was built to carry the Ellesmere Canal over the river Dee near Wrexham, remains one of the great feats of nineteenth-century civil engineering. Inscribed in 2009 as a World Heritage Site, the aqueduct is still the longest and highest canal aqueduct in Britain, remarkable for its cast-iron arches and trough which are carried on hollow masonry piers almost 130 feet above the river. We know that Hunt was acquainted with the ancient Roman Pont du Gard, the Lisbon Aqueduct, the fountains at Versailles and the Canal du Midi, but he went on to make a broader point, discerning a moral purpose in contemporary civil engineering, and arguing that while the structures of antiquity had been designed for amusement or for domestic uses, 'Pontcysyllte is destined to convey the Riches of the mineral Kingdom into the World of Industry and thence to every part of the Universe'. Such early optimism was common – and came to be tempered in subsequent decades – but the importance of structures such as the Pontcysyllte Aqueduct can scarcely be overestimated: the economic changes of the 170 years after 1700 would have been inconceivable without the remarkable achievements of civil engineers.

These achievements were made possible by several factors. First, there was the growth of theoretical understanding in areas such as the geometry of arch construction, the load-bearing capacity of iron components, and the stability of embankments. Second, there was an increase in the number of suppliers, of quarries, brickworks, iron foundries and forges. Third, from the ranks of architects, surveyors, millwrights and sappers emerged professional civil engineers, who were able to design and direct large-scale projects and whose standards came to be upheld by professional organisations. Finally, building contractors established themselves, capable of engaging and directing large bodies of men, supplying them with materials and managing finances.

Sappers and architects

At the beginning of the eighteenth century the word 'engineer' related to sappers, that is those who built the fortifications of cities or destroyed them by mining. These were not activities at which the British then excelled. The fortifications of the civil wars of the 1640s, or those hastily put together during the Jacobite risings of 1715 and 1745, are feeble structures compared with Hadrian's Wall, Offa's Dyke or the castles of Edward I. By contrast, too, the defences at Strasbourg, Namur, Metz and Sedan, which were designed by the great seventeenth-century French military engineer Sebastien, Marquis de Vauban, show a comprehensive understanding of constructional problems and an ability to deploy large numbers of men to complete tasks to precise timescales. There were no comparable works in Britain. Nevertheless, in 1717 the Board of Ordnance established the Corps of Engineers, composed of commissioned officers whose task was to direct manual work undertaken by companies of civilians, an arrangement which foreshadowed the emergence of contracting companies.

The outstanding feat of military engineering in Britain was the creation of a system of roads through the Scottish Highlands by General George Wade, the Irish-born Commander in Chief in North Britain between 1725 and 1740. He directed gangs of up to 500 men who built several hundred miles of gravel-surfaced roads to a standard width of 16 feet (4.9 m). The most important of more than 30 bridges built under his direction crossed the river Tay at Aberfeldy, providing access to the eastern and central Highlands. Wade laid its foundation stone on 23 April 1733, and it was constructed during the summer by masons from all over northern England who had spent the previous winter preparing the stone. In spite of delays at the quarry and shortages of transport, the bridge was in use from October 1733, although it was not formally opened until 8 August 1735. With a principal arch of 60-foot span, it was designed and embellished with Baroque detailing by William Adam, an architect who worked on more than 40 Scottish country houses.

Many eighteenth-century bridges were designed by men of varied talents who, like Adam, are best known as architects. For example, Sir John Vanbrugh, soldier, playwright and architect, designed the Grand Bridge at Blenheim, construction of which began in 1711. The plan for Inveraray, a new town built near the head of Loch Fyne in Argyll from 1745 for the 3rd Duke of Argyll, was by Robert Mylne, architect of country houses and engineer of several canals; he also built Blackfriars Bridge in London between 1760 and 1769. William Adam's son Robert Adam designed bridges at Kedleston Park and Inveraray, as well as the famous Pulteney Bridge at Bath. Thomas Farnolls Pritchard, designer of the Iron Bridge over the river Severn near Coalbrookdale, was a carpenter in Shrewsbury before re-ordering several country houses in the West Midlands. John Gwynn, another Shrewsbury carpenter, designed the covered market, the workhouse and Magdalen Bridge in Oxford, as well as bridges over the Severn at Shrewsbury, Atcham and Worcester.

◁ The imposing bridge across the river Tay at Aberfeldy, designed by William Adam and built for General George Wade during the summer of 1733.

Designing new roads: turnpikes and the road to Holyhead

Britain's road system was transformed between 1700 and 1840. John Loveday, *en route* for Ireland in 1732, noted that, 'A causey wide enough for one horse runs from Shrewsbury with some Interruption for about 8 miles on the way to Welshpool'. It was difficult for wheeled vehicles to journey far into Wales. Nevertheless even in 1700 the road system sustained an effective network of carriers. Turnpike trusts were created in increasing numbers after 1700, a process which transferred the cost of maintenance from those who lived alongside roads, to those – horseriders and the drivers of vehicles or beasts – who used them. Roads were improved by countless minor schemes, and some entirely new routes were constructed. These included the road from Bath along the Limpley Stoke Valley with a viaduct at the bottom of Brassknocker Hill, completed in October 1834; the 'road through the fields' from Gateshead through Low Fell to Durham City, first traversed by a mail coach on 16 June 1826; and that from Belper to Matlock with its rock cutting through Arkwright's Cromford, which was finished in 1820. In Lancashire 189 of the 754 miles of turnpike road in 1842 had been built on completely new alignments; sometimes these were straighter than the old roads, but more often their designers were concerned to reduce the gradients and avoid the steep hills that could cause such problems for horse-drawn waggons.

Experienced travellers certainly thought that the system had been transformed. Arthur Young wrote in 1813:

> I remember the roads of Oxfordshire forty years ago, when they were in a condition formidable to the bones of all who travelled on wheels. The two great turnpikes which cross the county ... were repaired in some places with stones as large as they could be brought from the quarry; and when broken, left so rough as to be calculated for dislocation rather than exercise. At that period the cross roads were impassable but with real danger. A noble change has taken place. ... The turnpikes are very good, and where gravel is to be had, excellent.

Charles Dibdin recalled sudden changes brought about by two turnpike Acts of 1758 in Hampshire:

> I know that before 1755 there was no symptom of anything like a Turnpike between Winchester and Southampton; and that when it came to be set about, the improvement was as efficacious as it was incredible. A few months completely altered the face of the country. It was the old grown young. Everything wore a new aspect, and those chalky bottoms about Winchester which had been at times impassable, and those slippery declivities through which travellers climbed with so much difficulty ... soon wore the appearance of a sober and gradual ascent, scarcely perceptible to the traveller.

Turnpike trusts raised revenue by collecting tolls at gates, alongside most of which were cottages accommodating tollgate keepers, such as this weather-boarded example at Ticehurst, Sussex, which controlled a gate set up by the Mayfield and Wadhurst Trust.

The fourteen turnpike Acts relating to roads in north and mid-Wales that were passed between 1752 and 1782 brought great changes. Richard Warner observed in Merionethshire in 1798 that, before the turnpike road was formed, 'the use of wheels was scarcely known here, the sled being the only vehicle made use of'. By 1800 stage coaches could reach the coastal resorts.

The first turnpike roads in Scotland were within the county of Edinburgh (or Midlothian), for which an Act was obtained in 1712. The Great Post Road from Edinburgh to the south was turnpiked in 1750, and the principal Scottish manufacturing areas were served by turnpikes by 1790. Thomas Telford was commissioned in 1801 to prepare a report on communications in the Highlands, and spent the summer of that year in energetic investigation. In 1803 he was appointed engineer to the Commission for Highland Roads and Bridges, and in the next 18 years directed the building of 920 miles of new road, the realignment of 280 miles of Wade's roads, and the construction of numerous bridges and harbours. Telford also built 184 miles of road in the Lowlands. In 1814–15 he reported on the road between Glasgow and Carlisle, whose

improvement he subsequently directed, justifying the cost of £76,758 in terms of reducing the number of accidents and helping to avoid delays to the mail.

The turnpike system was introduced to Ireland in 1729, and by 1758 twenty-nine trusts controlled 1,216 miles of road. In 1800, immediately after the Act of Union, and two years after the rising of 1798, the Board of Works began to construct roads in the Wicklow Mountains, and from 1824 William Dargan rebuilt the road between Howth and Dublin following the specifications that Telford had used on the Holyhead Road. In the west between 1822 and 1836 Richard Griffith superintended the construction of over 200 miles of road in Kerry, Cork, Limerick and Tipperary.

But the most notable example of government intervention in road transport was the road from London to Holyhead, which, while the least typical of British roads, illuminates many aspects of the history of civil engineering. After the union of the parliaments of England and Ireland in 1800 MPs had to travel the tortuous and slow route from Dublin to London by the packet from Howth to Holyhead, the road across Anglesey, the ferry over the Menai Strait and the road through Snowdonia to Shrewsbury, from where several

⊻ The route of the London to Holyhead turnpike in North Wales.

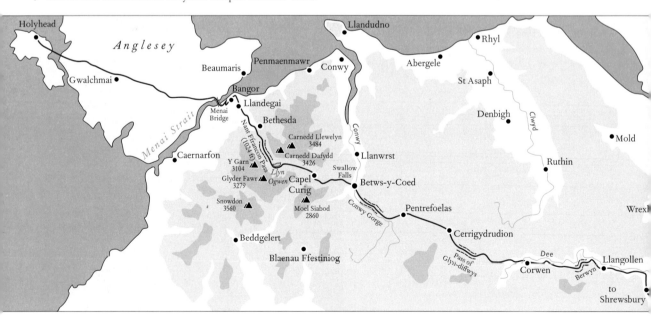

A civil engineer inspecting his works. Thomas Telford on tour in the Highlands, *circa* 1820. Telford is sitting in the trap with John Rickman, his biographer and the organiser of the first five censuses. Rickman's son William is driving, while the party is watched by a group of labourers with barrows.

routes could be taken to London. Stage-coach services from Shrewsbury to Holyhead were promoted from 1779 by Robert Lawrence of the town's *Lion Hotel*, who was among the promoters of a new turnpike from Pentrefoelas to Llandegai through Betws-y-Coed and Capel Curig, first used by coaches in the summer of 1805. Telford reported on the road in 1810, and found that on the 85 days between 1 January and 27 March of that year the mail was between one and five hours late on 71 occasions. He recommended that the road from London through Towcester, Coventry, Birmingham and Wolverhampton to Shrewsbury and across North Wales to Holyhead should be improved as the principal route to Dublin. The Holyhead Road Commission, whose inspiration was the Irish MP Sir Henry Parnell, was established in 1815. Telford became its engineer, and his reports provide copious documentation of the project. Legislation in 1819 established a new management structure. Between London and Shrewsbury the Commission worked with turnpike trusts, but from Shrewsbury to Holyhead the trusts relinquished their responsibility for the road to Ireland, which was managed directly by the Commission.

The Holyhead Road was improved with government capital that could never have been generated from toll revenue in such a sparsely populated region. As Telford observed, 'This road so essential for maintaining the communication between six or seven million of His Majesty's subjects on one side of the Irish Channel and twelve million on the other could never be put into a proper state of repair and safety if it is left to local interests to support and maintain it'. Sir Henry Parnell observed that few turnpike trusts could aspire to the standards achieved on the Holyhead Road. Telford defined his objective in 1824, 'that horses may easily and rapidly trot over the whole road, ascending or descending with a loaded coach', maintaining an average speed of 8 m.p.h. and ideally with no gradients steeper than 1 in 30. The projected average width of the road was 40 feet (12.3 m), and it was never to be less than 30 feet (9.2 m), with a minimum of 18 feet (5.5 m) of gravelled surface in the centre, and an elaborate system of side and cross

Sir Henry Parnell, the chairman of the Holyhead Road Commission, in an anonymous portrait.

In order to prevent damage to surfaces, turnpike trusts had to be able to impose weight limits on vehicles using their roads. In the eighteenth century weighing machines were like gigantic steelyards on which carriages and waggons were lifted up by chains slung beneath them. This example is in Soham, Cambridgeshire, and another survives at Woodbridge, Suffolk. By 1800 most had been replaced by weighbridges, with platforms flush with the road and supported in a pit by levers, in such a way that the weight could be read from an adjacent scale or dial.

Most turnpike acts stipulated that trusts should erect mileposts. For the Holyhead Road Thomas Telford took pains to design an elegant post that could be read from the window of a passing carriage. His specification provided for a pillar of limestone from Red Wharf Bay, Anglesey, 6 ft 11 ins high, of which 2 feet were to be buried foundations. The inscription took the form of a cast-iron plate set into a recess at the top of the pillar. The 106 milestones between Holyhead and Shrewsbury were installed in 1826–28 at a cost of five guineas each.

drains of the kind recommended by John Metcalf. Telford advocated solid stone foundations, in contrast to the view of his fellow Scot John Loudon Macadam that the base of a road should consist of layers of stone chips. Telford believed that roads should have footpaths, that overhanging trees should be felled, and hedges replaced by stone walls. Through the mountains the road was sustained by breast walls topped with parapets protecting travellers from ravines, matched by massive retaining walls designed to prevent landslips. Large embankments were built at Ty Nant through the pass of Glyn Diffwys, on the ascent from the crossing of the river Dee at Chirk, at the head of the Nant Ffrancon Pass below the Ogwen Falls, and from Anglesey to Holy Island, the Stanley Embankment. An iron arch crossed the Afon Conwy

at Betws-y-Coed; a suspension bridge carried the road over the Menai Strait; and numerous streams were spanned by masonry arches.

An unusual feature of the Holyhead Road was the provision of 'depots', recesses for the storage and measurement of road metals, at quarter-mile intervals, from which stones could be taken in hand barrows to where they were needed. Telford and Parnell recommended the use of ring gauges to ensure that stones used for dressing surfaces were appropriately small. The Commission installed weighing machines, whose booths remain by the tollhouses at Ty-isaf near Llangollen and Lon Isa near Bangor. Earlier weighing machines were gigantic steelyards of the kind that remain at Woodbridge (Suffolk) and Soham (Cambridgeshire); by 1800 most were weigh*bridges*, platforms flush with the road and supported in pits by levers in such a way that weights could be calculated from an adjacent scale or, in the machine patented in 1796 by Robert Salmon, on a dial.

For travellers the results of this massive engineering project were dramatic. In 1787 a four-horse post chaise could travel the 260 miles to Holyhead from London in four days. By 1808 a stage coach took 38 hours, a time that had been reduced to less than 27 hours by 1837.

Bigger and better structures: the development of arches and beams

Nicholas Hawksmoor, Vanbrugh's collaborator at Blenheim, discovered enlightening theories of bridge design in books by Antonio Palladio and Hubert Gautier. The most advanced contemporary thinking was expressed in the 11-arched bridge over the Loire at Blois, completed in 1724 to the design of Jacques Jules Gabriel, 'Premier Ingenieur' of the Corps des Ponts et Chaussées, an organisation of which there was no equivalent in Britain. The first structure in England derived from a similarly theoretical approach was Westminster Bridge over the river Thames, designed by Charles Labelye, begun in 1738 and opened on 18 November 1750. A native of Vevey, Switzerland, Labelye lived in England from about 1720. He was invited to advise on the bridge's foundations, and afterwards was appointed engineer for the project, introducing new practices in the use of centring, coffer dams and tie-bars, and insisting on weather-resistant finishes on the masonry. Westminster Bridge was described in 1752 as 'the most magnificent monument of our times', but it was subjected to ill-informed criticism, and, after justifying the design in 1751, Labelye settled in Paris where he became a friend of the bridge designer Jean-Rodolphe Perronet. He did, however, advise the Dublin architect George Semple on the construction of the Essex Bridge across the Liffey, which was opened in 1775.

William Edwards, from 1745 the pastor of a chapel near his birthplace in Glamorgan, contributed substantially to structural theory. His understanding of masonry and his influence in the community were utilised by Charles Wood during the construction of the Cyfarthfa Ironworks in 1766–67 (see page 314). Edwards made three attempts to bridge the river

The iron bridge across the river Wear at Sunderland, opened in 1796, was constructed on the same principles as a stone arch, but with voussoirs that were iron castings rather than wedge-shaped pieces of stone. This view of the bridge from the east shows the structure prior to the removing of the centring, the wooden scaffold on which the voussoirs were erected before the 'keystone' was put in place. The aquatint is by J. Raffield after an original by Robert Clarke.

To Rowland Burdon Esq. M.P. by whom this Excellent piece of Mechanism was invented, under whose Patronage it has been carried into Execution
This East View of the CAST IRON BRIDGE over the RIVER WEAR at Sunderland in the County of DURHAM previous to the Centre being taken down

An unspectacular and characteristic masonry aqueduct at James Bridge, Darlaston, carrying the Walsall Canal across a stream and Bentley Mill Lane. The structure bears the date 1797.

Two arches are visible in this photograph of Ewood Aqueduct in Blackburn. The splendid masonry arch at the top of the photograph supports the weight of the Leeds & Liverpool Canal as it crosses the river valley of the Darwen (whose channelled waters can just be glimpsed bottom right). When the aqueduct was completed in 1813–16 there was only a narrow path alongside the river, and the arch's shape was a virtually complete circle. In the 1920s, however, a new road (seen here) was built under the aqueduct, resulting in a more conventional shape to the main arch, and the river was culverted beneath.

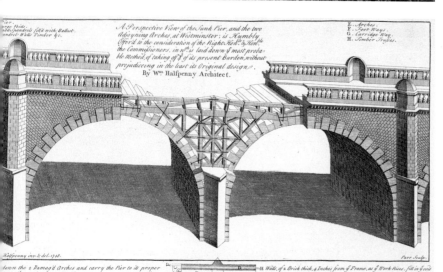

An engraving illustrating the principles of arch construction and the underwater piers used in the construction of Westminster Bridge, designed by the Swiss Charles Labelye and opened in 1750, which was a significant development in the application of theory to bridge building.

↲ The monumental stone aqueduct by which John Rennie carried the Lancaster Canal across the river Lune near Lancaster. The aqueduct, which was completed in 1797, is 664 feet long, and rises 53 feet above the normal river level. While this is one of the most imposing engineering features of the English waterways system, it is nevertheless of traditional masonry construction. An inscription reads: 'To Public Prosperity'.

Taff at Pontypridd before the construction in 1755 of the 140-foot (43.1 m) span structure that remains, in which he lightened the load on the arch by leaving three voids in the spandrels. He built other bridges in South Wales, and the Pontypridd bridge was visited by leading engineers, including John Smeaton in 1764.

Inevitably, the pace of bridge building quickened as the turnpike road system expanded, although most bridges remained the responsibility of the courts of quarter session, and toll bridges were constructed by boards of trustees established by Acts of Parliament. By 1800 some quarter sessions employed county surveyors, experienced freelance men who took responsibility for bridge building. Architects, too, continued to design some bridges. The elegant stone arch of the 1790s that crosses the river Great Ouse at Tyringham (Buckinghamshire), and the adjacent mansion, were designed by Sir John Soane for William Praed, chairman of the Grand Junction Canal Company. The great John Carr of York designed the bridge of 1797 that carries the Great North Road across the river Aire at Ferrybridge, while the bridges over the Thames at Swinford and Maidenhead (built respectively in 1769 and 1772–77) were designed by Sir Robert Taylor, who endowed the Taylorian Institution in Oxford.

Jean-Rodolphe Perronet, the son of a Swiss guardsman, directed the École des Ponts et Chaussées, managed the construction of no less than 1,550 miles of road in France, and in 1768–74 built the five-arch bridge over the Seine at Neuilly. He influenced the design of masonry arch bridges in Britain in several respects. Spans became longer, culminating in 1833 in the Grosvenor Bridge at Chester, a 200-foot (62 m) segmental arch designed by Thomas Harrison. The

There was no clear divide in the eighteenth century between architects and civil engineers, and many of the most celebrated bridges of the period were designed by men who were best known for their buildings. One example is the segmental arch across the river Great Ouse, designed in the 1790s by Sir John Soane on the approach to Tyringham House, Buckinghamshire.

One of the 128-foot elliptical arches of Isambard Kingdom Brunel's bridge that carries the main line of the Great Western Railway across the river Thames at Maidenhead which was completed in 1838. It was widely predicted that the bridge would collapse, but Brunel's confidence was justified, and when the number of tracks on the line was increased from two to four in 1890–93 the same methods of construction were used. The bridge still carries an intensive service of trains between London and the west of England. Through the arch can be seen part of the 13-arch bridge of Portland stone, erected in 1772–77 by which Sir Robert Taylor carried the Great West Road over the Thames.

Skerton Bridge over the river Lune, completed in 1788 and remarkable for its flat deck, was also designed by Harrison, and remains open to traffic. Foundations were improved with the aid of steam power, used to drain the areas behind coffer dams and later to drive in piles. Arches were designed with pointed cutwaters rounded at the shoulders, and sloping or chamfered edges, while the lines of roadways and parapets were generally horizontal or nearly so. Thomas Telford's Over Bridge, which crosses the river Severn at

Gloucester, has a single span of 150 feet (46.2 m) but bears many similarities to the Neuilly bridge. The Revd F. E. Watts wrote on 28 April 1829 that, 'It is very beautiful, light, graceful and imposing by its span ... I am persuaded it will remain for centuries a testimony of the profound science of Mr Telford.' It carried traffic until 1975 and remains open to pedestrians. The bridge by which I. K. Brunel carried the Great Western Railway across the Thames at Maidenhead similarly challenged conventional thinking. The two main elliptical arches were of 128 foot (39.4 m) span with a rise of only 24 feet 6 inches (7.5 m). The eastern arch showed signs of distortion after its completion early in 1838, which for a time was a cause for concern. The centring was left in place but was destroyed in a storm in the autumn of 1839, when the bridge remained standing, and still carries traffic. As a result of controversy over this structure papers on the theory of arches were published in 1846 by W. H. Barlow and George Snell.

Bridges, aqueducts and viaducts on canals and railways

For centuries county and local authorities had been responsible for most of the country's bridges, the majority of which were required to carry roads over streams and rivers. New forms of transport – canals, tramroads and railways – brought new challenges and opportunities to both designers and builders. One of the first was James Brindley's aqueduct which carried the Bridgewater Canal on three masonry arches over the river Irwell at Barton. Opened in 1761, the Barton Aqueduct was one of the wonders of the age. Its arch was built of masonry, as were those of most subsequent canal aqueducts. Many, such as the one on Brindley's Staffordshire and Worcestershire Canal at Great Haywood and the one over the Ashby-de-la-Zouch Canal at Shackerstone, near Nuneaton, were low structures crossing streams. Above the crowns of their arches, such aqueducts carried a layer of puddled clay, four feet thick, in order to waterproof the bed of the canal. Telford, by contrast, sealed the bottom of the 10-arch masonry aqueduct of 1796–1801 at Chirk with cast-iron plates, which gave a more elegant appearance.

Some canal aqueducts were magnificent structures. In 1794–97 John Rennie built the monumental, 61 feet high Lune Aqueduct to carry the Lancaster Canal over the river Lune on five large masonry arches. Rennie also built the Dundas Aqueduct of 1805 on the Kennet & Avon Canal, with three arches of Bath stone over the river Avon. The Kelvin Aqueduct on the Forth & Clyde Canal, designed by Robert Whitworth, was similarly imposing. When it opened in 1790 the *Scots Magazine* wrote that it exhibited to the spectators in the valley below 'the singular and new object of a vessel navigating 70 feet over their heads, a feature of this work which gives it a pre-eminence over everything of a similar nature in Europe'.

One of the most celebrated eighteenth-century bridges, the 105-foot (32.3 m) single-span Causey Arch of 1727, carried the Tanfield Waggonway, an important coalfield railway in County Durham (see

The elegantly proportioned Dundas Aqueduct, designed by John Rennie and opened in 1805, which carries the Kennet & Avon Canal over the river Avon three miles south of Bath, drawn by J. F. Burrell and engraved by J. Ashley. Some years later a plaque was placed on south face of the aqueduct to thank its Quaker superintendent of works: 'to the memory of John Thomas, by whose skill, perseverance and integrity, the Kennet and Avon Canal was brought to a prosperous completion.'

page 221), and from the 1820s builders of mainline railways used masonry arches as well as other forms of bridge. Many were accommodation bridges carrying rails over roads or vice versa, but others, such as Brunel's Great Western Railway bridge over the Thames at Maidenhead, were remarkable both for structural ingenuity and aesthetic appeal, in this case constructed in brick in the 1830s. Viaducts, sequences of masonry arches, were known to the ancient world, but with the arrival of the railways many more came to be built throughout Britain. One of the most dramatic is the Victoria Bridge, carrying the Durham Junction Railway across the river Wear and which was opened in June 1838. It consists of seven stone spans, the largest of 160 feet (49.3 m), and passes 130 feet (40 m) above the river. James Walker and Alfred Burges consciously based its design on the bridge built about AD 105 for the Emperor Trajan over the river Tagus at Alcántara. A comparable inspiration guided Sir John Macneill when, near Newry, he designed the 'Egyptian Arch' to resemble a pharaoh's headpiece. The Ballochmyle Viaduct that carries the Glasgow & South Western Railway across the river Ayr near Cumnock was designed by John Miller and completed in March 1848 after many people had marvelled at the massive timber centring used in its construction. The longest of its seven stone spans extends 181 feet (55.7 m) and rises 164 feet (50.5 m) above the water. Ballochmyle remains the highest railway viaduct in Britain.

The significance of early railways in the coalfield of County Durham is shown not just by the imposing structure of the Causey (or Tanfield) arch, the 105-foot span stone bridge built in 1727, but by its celebrity. This 'View of the Tanfield Arch in County Durham', by I. C. Stadler after an original by Joseph Atkinson was published in 1804, some 77 years after the bridge was completed.

This detail of a panoramic view of London published in the 1850s is dominated by the four-mile-long viaduct of 878 arches that carried the London & Greenwich Railway into London Bridge Station, which opened in 1836. Supposedly the many millions of bricks used in the structure were made at Sittingbourne, Kent, and transported to London by barge. Also visible are one of the first railway hotels, alongside the station, the London group of docks on the north side of the river Thames and the adjacent church of St George-in-the-East, the West India Docks across the isthmus of the Isle of Dogs, the viaduct of the London & Blackwall Railway and the Grand Surrey Canal.

Viaducts could extend to remarkable lengths. A lofty and lengthy viaduct, with dwellings in its arches and a roof above to keep them dry, carried a tramroad at Blaenavon by 1798, but was afterwards covered in spoil. Even more remarkable was the four-mile-long viaduct that takes the London & Greenwich Railway into London Bridge Station. This was opened in 1836 and consists of 878 arches, some of which were intended from the beginning to be leased as workshops. By comparison, the 41 arches of the 1,980 feet (600 m) Wicker Arches that carried the Manchester, Sheffield & Lincolnshire Railway over the Don river and valley into Sheffield was relatively modest. Similar viaducts carry the tracks of the Great Western Railway into Snow Hill Station, Birmingham, and those of the Manchester South Junction & Altrincham Railway.

Urban viaducts usually had detrimental effects on the districts through which they passed. One observer commented in 1866, 'I know no railway passing through a town on arches ... without it being to my mind a very serious detriment to the town property through which it passes'.

More lofty viaducts took railways across river valleys. The first and one of the most impressive was the Liverpool & Manchester Railway that passed over the Sankey Brook on nine 50-foot (15.4 m) arches, designed by William Allcard. The nearby Dutton Viaduct, designed by Joseph Locke and opened in 1837, carried the Grand Junction Railway across the river Weaver on twenty 60-foot (18.5 m) stone arches. In 1848 the young Henry Robertson took the Shrewsbury & Chester Railway 148 feet above the

▹ George Stephenson carried the Liverpool & Manchester Railway across the canalised Sankey Brook near Newton-le-Willows on the nine-arch Sankey Viaduct, built with local sandstone in 1828–30. The engraving shows a Mersey flat about to pass beneath the viaduct.
FROM A CONTEMPORARY PRINT

▹ The Wicker Arches is the name commonly given to a 41-arch, 660-yard long viaduct that carried the Manchester, Sheffield and Lincolnshire (from 1899 the Great Central) Railway across the valley of the river Don in Sheffield. The company's Victoria Station, seen here just right of centre, stood on the viaduct. The specifications for the structure were drawn up by the engineer Sir John Fowler, but the detailed design was by the local architects Miller, Blackie & Shortedge. Also visible are a working colliery within the city (right), and several steelworks with numerous cementation furnaces (see page 292) which produced the blister steel used in the manufacture of cutlery.
BY COURTESY OF SHEFFIELD GALLERIES AND MUSEUMS TRUST

▹ The Dutton Viaduct was built by Joseph Locke to designs by George Stephenson to carry the Grand Junction Railway (from Newton-le-Willows to Birmingham) over the valley of the river Weaver in Cheshire. It was completed on 9 December 1836 and opened to traffic the following July. It consists of 20 stone arches, has a total length of 1,284 feet and still carries main-line traffic.
© SCIENCE MUSEUM/SCIENCE & SOCIETY PICTURE LIBRARY

➤ The imposing viaduct on which
I. K. Brunel carried the broad-gauge Great
Western Railway through the Wiltshire
market town of Chippenham, portrayed
in John Cook Bourne's *History and
Description of the Great Western Railway*.

➤ A class Al 'Pacific' locomotive, No. 60127,
built in May 1949 and later named *William
Worsdell*, photographed crossing the Royal
Border Bridge in September 1950, with the
Queen of Scots Pullman train from London
via Leeds and Harrogate to Edinburgh.
Photograph by E. R. Wethersett. The
bridge was opened formally by Queen
Victoria on 29 August 1850. Rising 126
ft 6 ins above the river Tweed, it was
built by the York, Newcastle & Berwick
Railway Company to replace a temporary
trestle bridge that had carried the line for
two years. The main contractors for the
bridge was the Cumberland firm of McKay
& Blackstock, and they made use of
Nasmyth's newly invented steam-powered
pile driver. The bridge cost £184,143 and
still forms a key link in the main east-coast
line from London to Scotland.

© NATIONAL RAILWAY MUSEUM / SCIENCE & SOCIETY PICTURE
LIBRARY

➤ The 1,569 ft long, 100 ft high brick viaduct
at Welwyn, Hertfordshire, designed by
William Cubitt, that carries the main line
of the Great Northern Railway across
the valley of the river Mimram. The line
was formally opened on 8 August 1850,
and this watercolour by W. Humber was
completed the following September.

BY COURTESY OF THE IRONBRIDGE GORGE MUSEUM TRUST

river Dee on 19 arches of 60-foot span, a total length of 1,530 feet (4710 m) and on a scale that matches the nearby Pontcysyllte Aqueduct. Robert Stephenson's dramatic Royal Border Bridge, opened in 1850, carries the Newcastle & Berwick Railway across the river Tweed and has a total length of 2,160 feet (665 m), with 28 spans each of 61 feet 6 inches (18.9 m). The railway from Dublin to Belfast crosses the river Camlugh near Newry on a viaduct of 18 granite arches, each spanning 60 feet (18.5 m); designed by Sir John Macneill, it was opened in 1851. At Stockport the Manchester & Birmingham Railway crosses the valley of the Mersey in the centre of the town on a viaduct completed in December 1840 to the design of George W. Buck. It extends over 1,786 feet (550 m), and consists of 22 arches, with a maximum height of 111 feet (34.2 m). The 22-arch Saddleworth Viaduct on the Huddersfield & Manchester Railway, completed in 1848, includes three skew arches, in which every piece had to be worked to a compound curvature different from that of every other piece; one arch crosses the Huddersfield Narrow Canal. Railway engineers built masonry viaducts throughout the second half of the nineteenth century, including more than 20 on the Midland's 72-mile route through the Pennines between Settle and Carlisle; work on the project began in 1869, and the railway opened on May Day 1876. The route was hilly: a total of 3½ miles of line had to be tunnelled, and long sections of the line were built at gradients of 1 in 100. The most notable of the viaducts, at Ribblehead, was designed by John Sydney Crossley and consists of 24 arches. The viaduct not only curves but climbs 13 feet (4 m) from its southern to its northern end.

After completing its route to London, where St Pancras Station was opened in 1868, the Midland Railway decided to build its own route to Scotland, with a 72-mile line from Settle to Carlisle, where it exchanged traffic with two Scottish railways, the North British and the Glasgow & South Western. The construction of the line through the Pennine fells posed many difficulties. It passed through Dent, where the station, at 1,150 feet above sea level, is the highest on the British main-line system. It included more than twenty viaducts, of which the best known is this, the 24-arch structure at Ribblehead.

PHOTOGRAPH, CARNEGIE, 2005

Wooden bridges

Eighteenth- and nineteenth-century bridge builders also used timber, although there was no tradition in Britain, as there was in Switzerland and Quebec, of building wooden covered bridges. In the North East coalfield, where timber staithes were commonplace, wooden railway viaducts were built between 1750 and 1780 at Crawcrook, Killingworth and Wylam. The potentially dangerous state of the wooden bridges across the Thames, at Walton, Kew and Battersea, was a source of scandal in the late eighteenth century. At Coalport in Shropshire a two-arched wooden bridge across the river Severn was designed by William Hayward and opened in the spring of 1780, nine

months before the Iron Bridge, but as a wooden structure it lasted only 15 years. Then, in 1799–1800 Thomas Telford constructed a wooden trestle bridge across the Severn at Cressage, six miles above Iron Bridge, which lasted for more than a century. Such structures were uncommon.

The pioneer of timber bridges on main-line railways was John Green, who built two laminated timber viaducts on the Newcastle & North Shields Railway, opened in 1839. They were publicised in a paper delivered by his son Benjamin to the British Association in 1838. Impressed by Green's work, the directors of the Sheffield, Ashton-under-Lyne & Manchester Railway

⋏ The viaduct at Landore by which Isambard Kingdom Brunel carried the South Wales Railway, opened in 1850, across the valley of the river Tawe and into Swansea. It was originally about a third of a mile long and was constructed of Canadian pitch pine. The wrought-iron central span was inserted in 1889, and the viaduct has undergone successive rebuildings so that only four stone piers remain of the original structure.
© NRM/PICTORIAL COLLECTION/SCIENCE & SOCIETY PICTURE LIBRARY

➤ The constructional principles used by Isambard Kingdom Brunel in his timber viaducts on the Cornwall and West Cornwall railways are evident in this view of the Carvedras Viaduct, Truro. From each of the 15 stone piers radiated three fans of timber struts which supported beams which carried the tracks. This particular viaduct was 969 feet long and 86 feet high, and was replaced in 1902.
FROM A CONTEMPORARY POSTCARD

Another of Brunel's lofty timber viaducts on the Cornwall Railway.
AUTHOR COLLECTION

The timber viaduct at Liskeard was 720 feet long, 150 feet high and had eleven piers. It was opened, with the rest of the broad-gauge Cornwall Railway, in 1859. The timber spans were replaced in 1894.
© NATIONAL RAILWAY MUSEUM/SCIENCE & SOCIETY PICTURE LIBRARY

in 1842–44 commissioned Joseph Locke to construct two viaducts near Glossop, consisting of stone piers between which were laminated ribs of Memel fir. The timber spans were replaced with wrought iron in 1859. I. K. Brunel built a wooden trestle bridge over Sonning Cutting and laminated timber bridges over the Tawe at Landore and the Avon at Bath, but his outstanding wooden structures were in the west of England where he constructed 66 viaducts in Memel pine, mostly in the 1850s. The viaduct at Truro was 1,329 feet (409 m) long, and that at St Pinnock 151 feet high (46.5 m), more than 20 feet higher than the Pontcysyllte Aqueduct. Most were not replaced until after 1880, and one lasted until 1934.

The age of iron: new forms in civil engineering

A Yorkshire blacksmith constructed an ornamental bridge, probably in wrought iron, at Kirklees Hall in 1769, but the Iron Bridge at Coalbrookdale, designed by Thomas Farnolls Pritchard, built by Abraham Darby III, and opened on New Year's Day 1781, was perceived to be an innovation. Its peculiar form, an arch of five ribs with its parts held together by dovetails and shouldered joints, was never used again except in small replicas in France and Germany, but it did much to inspire subsequent engineers. In his oration at the Pontcysyllte Aqueduct in 1805 Rowland Hunt praised 'Mr Darby who erected the first Iron Bridge'.

The decorative properties of cast iron were exploited in bridges in ornamental parks, erected by the Coalbrookdale Company at Trentham Park (1794); Sydney Gardens, Bath (1800); and Oakpark, Co. Carlow (1816). By 1830 many foundries could cast bridges of modest size. The Horseley Company of Tipton made at least 16 towpath bridges for the Birmingham Canal Navigation and the Oxford Canal, as well as the larger Pelsall Works Bridge of 1824 on the Wyrley & Essington Canal and the Gallows Bridge of 1820 near Brentford on the Grand Junction.

Other iron bridges were of more consequence in the history of structures. Tom Paine, the political philosopher, returned to England from America in 1787 with plans to build bridges in iron. Walkers of Rotherham erected an experimental arch in their foundry, and in 1790 the *Yorkshire Stingo* public house in London displayed a bridge of 110 foot (33.9 m) span with six ribs, each made up of cast-iron voussoirs. In 1791 Paine published *The Rights of Man*. He was charged with sedition in 1792 and fled to Paris, but the link between the Walkers' foundry and iron bridges was established. The company provided castings for the 236-foot (72.7 m) bridge of 1793–96 over the river Wear at Sunderland, whose construction was due principally to Rowland Burdon of Castle Eden (see page 224). Its six ribs consisted of cast-iron voussoirs, and the erection was overseen by Thomas Wilson, a Sunderland architect who took out a patent in 1802 for arches constructed from connecting metallic blocks.

Walkers built bridges to his design in Jamaica and at Stratfield Saye, Berkshire, and in 1800–03 provided castings for his bridge across the river Thames at Staines – although it subsided when the centring was removed, and was replaced by a temporary wooden structure. Wilson's bridge over the river Tees at Yarm, built in 1805, collapsed with a concussive thud on 12 January 1806. The disasters at Staines and Yarm constrained the optimism about iron structures, which in 1801 had been expressed in a claim that the Coalbrookdale works could produce 'iron bridges of any span or height'.

The embodiment of such optimism was the remarkable Pontcysyllte Aqueduct, carrying the Ellesmere

⌐ The Iron Bridge across the river Severn near Coalbrookdale in Shropshire is rightly regarded as the inspiration for the innovative use of iron in the building of bridges and other structures which so characterised subsequent decades, although there was at least one earlier iron bridge of modest dimensions. The main half ribs of the bridge each weighed about seven tons, and the main components were held together by cast-iron radials to which they were attached by shouldered dovetailed joints. While the Iron Bridge was replicated on a small scale in parkland bridges in France and Germany, different constructional principles were employed when iron was used in subsequent bridges.

Canal 127 feet (39.1 m) above the river Dee in a cast-iron trough supported by 19 cast-iron arches erected between slender and hollow stone piers. There were earlier examples. Watkin George erected Pont-y-Cafnau at Cyfarthfa in 1793, but the aqueduct was not intended for navigation, while Telford, with William Reynolds, built an aqueduct at Longdon-on-Tern on the Shrewsbury Canal, opened in 1796, in which an iron trough was supported by iron columns and struts. But Pontcysyllte was of a different order. The Ellesmere Canal, authorised in 1793, was intended to link the river Dee at Chester with the river Severn at Shrewsbury through the North Wales coalfield. The company engineer was William Jessop, and Telford became its 'general agent'. Jessop, like Telford, had experience of iron structures. Benjamin Outram, his partner in the Butterley Company, completed an iron aqueduct on the Derby Canal at The Holmes in 1796, and in 1801, on the Huddersfield Canal at Stalybridge, replaced a damaged masonry structure with an iron trough. The Ellesmere's proprietors decided on 14 July 1795 to follow Jessop's recommendation to carry the canal on high aqueducts over the Dee at Pontcysyllte and the Ceiriog at Chirk. The foundation stone at Pontcysyllte was laid on 25 July 1795, but most of the construction took place after the

The king post truss structure known as Pont-y-Cafnau (the 'bridge of troughs') constructed in 1793 by Watkin George near the Cyfarthfa Ironworks outside Merthyr in South Wales. Its deck carried an edge railway conveying limestone to the furnaces. A trough beneath the deck took water to provide power to the furnaces and at its central point the bridge supported one of the trestles that carried the high and lengthy wooden aqueduct feeding the celebrated waterwheel *Aolus* that powered the furnace bellows.

The spectacular iron aqueduct on the Birmingham Canal Navigation by which Thomas Telford carried the feeder channel from the Rotton Park Reservoir across his new main line running north-west from Birmingham. The castings were made by the Horseley Co., and the aqueduct opened for traffic in 1830.

The Ellesmere Canal and other waterways in the Welsh Marches.

The great aqueduct at Pontcysyllte viewed from the air. At the top of the picture is the vast embankment on which the canal was carried from the village of Froncysyllte on to the iron aqueduct, which crosses the river Dee. At the end of the iron trough is the junction with the line to Llangollen which supplied the Ellesmere Canal with water at the Horseshoe Falls, and served several quarries where carboniferous limestone was extracted for ironworks in the Midlands. At the bottom of the picture is Trevor Basin where goods were transferred to the canal from early railways. The canal was intended to continue to Chester, but in the event was extended only a short distance beyond the basin to serve local industries. (See also the photograph on page 3.)

Chirk Aqueduct had been completed in 1801. The Pontcysyllte Aqueduct was opened on 26 November 1805 with an elaborate ceremony, devised by Telford as 'a beautiful picture of the harmony with which all ranks may unite in promoting the prosperity of the British empire and in diffusing general happiness', a significant objective in the light of what he called 'the singular and not infrequently alarming situation of Public Affairs since the commencement of the undertaking', and Rowland Hunt's observation that since 1791 'governments sanctioned for ages had been overthrown'. Telford carried responsibility for the final five years of construction but spent large parts of those years in Scotland, and was not the resident engineer. Jessop's formal link with the canal ceased in 1802 but the two shared responsibility for Pontcysyllte, and Hunt acknowledged 'our General Agent, Mr Telford, who with the advice and judgement of our eminent and much respected Engineer, Mr Jessop, invented and with unabating diligence carried the whole in execution'. The aqueduct was more than a utilitarian component of a coal-carrying canal. It was an expression of an optimism about iron structures that was already deflated by the time it opened. It was also an expression of what could be achieved by science and art. The company declared that it would 'gratify those who enjoy the effects of works of art when executed on a large scale', while for Sir Walter Scott it was 'the most impressive work of art I have ever seen'.

No subsequent iron aqueduct approached the scale of Pontcysyllte. In 1809–11 an iron trough was installed to carry the Grand Junction Canal over the river Ouse at Wolverton after the collapse of a masonry aqueduct. Three iron aqueducts were built on the Stratford-on-Avon Canal between 1812 and 1816, three on the Union Canal in Scotland in 1818–22 and two on the Montgomeryshire Canal. Telford built several carrying the Birmingham & Liverpool Junction and Macclesfield canals over roads, but in similar locations he achieved the same purpose with masonry arches.

Several iron bridges carried tramroads in South Wales. Three others were built in East Anglia by J. & R. Ransome of Ipswich, and several in Yorkshire by Aydon & Elwell. The Butterley Co. built several in the Fens, and provided castings for John Rennie's Southwark Bridge of 1811–19 and for James Walker's Vauxhall Bridge of 1813–18. Between 1810 and 1830 the most consistent style of iron bridge building was employed by Thomas Telford and the ironfounder William Hazledine, who from 1811 used two designs. The first, for structures spanning no more than about 100 feet, consisted of pairs of half-ribs, castings that incorporated ribs, spandrel-frames and deck-bearers in a grid pattern that rested in stone abutments. The first was built at Meole Brace, Shrewsbury, in 1811. The largest takes the Holyhead Road over the Afon Conwy at Betws-y-Coed. It is ornamented with roses, shamrocks, leeks and thistles, and an inscription recording its construction in the year the Battle of Waterloo was fought (1815), although it was not actually built until 1816. The ostentatious Engine Arm Aqueduct on the Birmingham Canal follows the same basic design. Larger bridges by Telford and Hazledine had

Thomas Telford's suspension bridge which carried the Holyhead Road across the Menai Straits, opened in 1826. One reason for the height of the bridge was the insistence of the Admiralty that fully rigged ships of the line should be able to pass through the Straits.

An example of an unexceptional bridge carrying a railway over a road, in this case the Reading–Reigate line of what became the South Eastern Railway over the London–Bath road near Reading. The line was commenced in 1847 and completed in 1849, and it is possible that James Gardner's patent form of construction was devised in reaction to the accident on the bridge over the river Dee at Chester in 1847.

AUTHOR COLLECTION

ribs made up from segments with the deck-bearers supported by vertical or inclined struts in the spandrels. The first, the 150-foot span of the bridge at Bonar (1811–12) united the counties of Ross and Sutherland across the Dornoch Firth (see also page 592). Telford and Hazledine built the 150-foot (46.2 m) span bridge that joins Banffshire to Moray across the river Spey at Craigellachie (1814), and the three-span bridge over the river Esk north of Carlisle in 1820. Two 150-foot bridges over the river Severn, built between 1823 and 1827 at Mythe near Tewkesbury and Holt Fleet near Worcester, were similar to the Scottish bridges.

The early nineteenth century saw the development of the suspension bridge, in which the deck was hung from cables anchored in the ground on each side of the structure, and slung across towers or piers at either end. The principle was scarcely applied in the West until James Finley built a bridge hung from wrought-iron chains at Jacob's Creek, Pennsylvania, in 1801. Captain Samuel Brown propounded the concept in Britain and in 1816 established the Newbridge Chain & Anchor Works alongside the Glamorganshire Canal near Pontypridd – it produced anchor chains until 1916. Brown designed the 449-foot (138.2 m) Union Bridge, across the river Tweed between Horncliffe in England and Fishwick in Scotland, and similar structures near Jedburgh and Melrose, at Welney in Norfolk, and at Shoreham-by-Sea. The same principles could be applied in the construction of piers, and Samuel Brown himself built the Trinity Chain Pier at Edinburgh, opened in 1821, and the Chain Pier at Brighton (see pages 556–7), completed in 1823 and memorably

painted about five years later by J. M. W. Turner. Telford's bridge carrying the Holyhead Road over the Menai Straits was the longest suspension bridge of its time, with a span of 579 feet (178.3 m). The chains, made by William Hazledine, were lifted into place between April and June 1825, and the bridge was opened to traffic on 30 January 1826. Telford, Hazledine, Sir Henry Parnell and William Provis met the first vehicle, the London mail coach which arrived at 01.30, crossed repeatedly on passing vehicles up to 9 o'clock, and for the rest of the day were delighted spectators, witnessing 'an uninterrupted succession of passing carriages, horsemen and pedestrians who had assembled to witness and enjoy the novelty'. The similar but smaller bridge at Conwy opened on 1 July 1826.

Railway engineers in the 1830s and 1840s built many iron arched or girder structures crossing lanes or streams. The outer members of some can still be seen, bearing such foundry names as 'Brymbo', 'Butterley' or 'Lilleshall'. Some were trussed girder structures in which wrought-iron bars joined and reinforced castings. One example was the bridge over the river Dee at Chester, designed by Robert Stephenson; it collapsed on 14 May 1847 as a train was passing over, resulting in five deaths. A parliamentary commission revealed severe deficiencies in engineers' understanding of the structural properties of iron, and many similar bridges were replaced in the 1850s. Cast-iron arches were not subject to such problems, and John Fowler and Benjamin Baker designed two particularly fine structures across the river Severn: the Royal Victoria

Bridge carrying the Severn Valley Railway at Arley, opened in 1862; and the Albert Edward Bridge near Coalbrookdale, which was completed the following year.

The development of a theoretical understanding of the structural properties of iron evolved in the context of buildings as well as of bridges and aqueducts. The size of public rooms in spas or town halls was constrained by the spanning capacity of timber beams, since floors extending more than about 20 feet tended to deflect, or 'bounce'. Among the buildings that Andrew Yarranton proposed in the late seventeenth century for his new industrial settlements at waterways junctions were seven-storey granaries in the Dutch style, more than 18 feet wide. The silk mill of 1721 at Derby was 39 feet (12 m) wide, but the 240 foot (73.9 m) long mill of 1753 at Congleton only 24 feet (7.4 m), while most early cotton-spinning mills extended no more than 30 feet. The cotton master William Strutt constructed a mill at Derby in 1792–93 in which brick arches sprang from timber beams which were supported by cast-iron columns, the unbalanced horizontal thrusts being restrained by wrought-iron tie rods. During the next two years he built two similar buildings: a warehouse at Milford and the West Mill

at nearby Belper. Strutt corresponded with Charles Bage of Shrewsbury, surveyor and wine merchant, who in 1796 designed the Ditherington Flax Mill as a partner with John Marshall and Thomas and Benjamin Benyon. This five-storey mill is 177 feet long and 39 feet 6 inches wide (54.5 × 12.2 m). Three lines of cruciform columns carry iron cross-beams from which spring brick jack arches sustaining the floors above.

The same principles were applied, with variations, in other mills. William Reynolds had been interested in the structural properties of iron from at least 1781 when, as a result of a conversation at Coalbrookdale with Erasmus Darwin and Richard Lovell Edgeworth, he made an experiment to determine whether a cast-iron bar could be broken with a hammer. Upright members designed for the Longdon Aqueduct were tested to destruction, and the findings were used by Charles Bage in designing the Ditherington mill, while Bage and Reynolds were consulted by Thomas Telford in 1800 when he proposed a single 600-foot (185 m) iron arch to replace London Bridge. He also sought opinions from William Jessop, John Rennie, James Watt, John Wilkinson, and Charles Hutton of the Royal Military Academy, who wrote the first book on iron bridges. Telford's bridge was never built, but

The fourth floor of the iron framed main building in the Ditherington Flax Mill complex, Shrewsbury, photographed in the 1970s when, as the barley spread on the floor indicates, it was used for malting.

⚞ Thomas Telford's overly ambitious plan of 1800 for a cast-iron arch of 600 foot span to replace the medieval London Bridge, which would have allowed ocean-going ships to progress farther up the river Thames. The proposal was a response to a perceived problem of congestion in the Port of London which was solved by a totally different means – by the construction of wet docks downstream from the Tower. The proposal symbolised the confidence in the use of iron for structural purposes that was prevalent around 1800; such enthusiasm was soon tempered by the collapse of the bridges at Staines and Yarm, in 1803 and 1806 respectively.

the project illustrates the evolution of the scientific appraisal of iron structures. In an essay published in 1803 John Banks, the itinerant lecturer on scientific subjects and designer of the elliptical beam for steam engines and employee of the Yorkshire ironfounders Aydon & Elwell, described experiments made to test the strength of cast iron, while the structural properties of iron were examined in publications by Charles Hutton in 1812 and Thomas Tredgold in 1824. The work of Eaton Hodgkinson was the basis of subsequent structural use of iron. He devised a form of I-section beam with equal flanges at top and bottom, first used in 1830 in the bridge which carried the Liverpool & Manchester Railway over Water Street in Manchester. Hodgkinson beams were subsequently employed by William Fairbairn in Travis Brook Mill, Stockport in 1834–35; Shaddon Mill, Carlisle (1836); and in the 1850s at Saltaire Mill. Nevertheless, between 1800 and 1850 most textile mills were of traditional construction and only a minority were iron-framed.

Some railway bridge builders used iron in innovative ways. Robert Stephenson carried the Newcastle & Darlington Junction Railway across the river Tyne on the High Level Bridge, consisting of six main cast-iron spans of 125 feet (38.5 m) between stone columns. The railway is carried on a deck supported on the arches, while a road deck is slung beneath them. The bridge stands on timbers driven 40 feet (12.3 m) through the bed of the river to solid rock, achieved by the use of a steam pile-driver supplied from James Nasmyth's works at Patricroft. Stephenson, William Fairbairn, Eaton Hodgkinson and others debated at length how to carry rails over the Menai Straits and, following experiments and theoretical calculations, decided to construct a tubular bridge. The wrought-iron tubes through which the trains ran were fabricated on shore

∧ This early photograph, of 1858, shows Brunel's Royal Albert Bridge, carrying the Cornwall Railway across the river Tamar from Plymouth to Saltash, with one of the main spans in place and the other waiting to be lifted into place. The bridge was opened to traffic in 1859. Major engineering works, such as this and the Deepdale Viaduct (pictured opposite), were favourite subjects for pioneering photographers.

and raised into position by hydraulic lifting tackle. With two spans of 460 feet (141.7 m) and two approach spans of 230 feet (70.8 m), the Britannia Bridge was opened in March 1850. The lions at its portals were designed by Francis Thompson. A smaller tubular bridge at Conwy was opened in 1849, and a wrought-iron box-girder bridge on the same principles, designed by William Le Fanu and fabricated by Fairbairn, carries trains over the river Suir near Cahir in County Tipperary. I. K. Brunel, meanwhile, took the South Wales Railway across the river Wye at Chepstow with a bridge on which the rail deck was supported by suspension chains from a pair of gigantic trusses fabricated from wrought-iron plates. The design of the Royal Albert Bridge carrying the Cornwall Railway across the river Tamar at Saltash was derived from the Chepstow Bridge, but there the two main spans are sustained by a cast-iron pier in the middle of the river.

The tubes in the trusses are oval rather than circular, and serve as arches sharing the load of the deck with the suspension chains. This was Brunel's last great work. Although ill, he superintended the floating out of the western truss on 1 September 1857, but he was unable to attend the formal opening by the Prince Consort on 2 May 1859. He was afterwards propelled slowly over the bridge on a flat truck, and died on 15 September 1859.

Innovative bridges of a different kind were built by Charles Nixon, T. W. Kennard and Thomas Bouch. Nixon designed the Chetwynd Viaduct on the Cork & Bandon Railway (1851), which crosses the Glasheen river on lattice bowstring girders with a central span of 117 feet (36 m). The Crumlin Viaduct, built between 1853 and 1857 to the design of Thomas William Kennard, carried the Taff Vale extension of the Newport, Abergavenny & Hereford Railway over

Ebbw Vale. The lattice beams followed the form of the triangular girder patented in 1848 by James Warren, in which diagonal members carry both tensile and compressive forces. The Crumlin Viaduct consisted of two viaducts, separated by the shoulder of a hill, and had a total length of 1,658 feet (510 m) and a maximum height of 200 feet (61.6 m). The piers were made up of circular cast-iron columns braced together with wrought-iron ties. Iron came from works in which Kennard's father, Robert William Kennard, had interests, a foundry at Falkirk, and the Blaenavon Ironworks, which supplied wrought iron which was forged and fabricated in workshops at Crumlin. The bridge was opened in June 1858, but the following year T. W. Kennard left Wales to prospect for gold in America. The workshops, managed until 1872 by his brother Henry Martin Kennard, fulfilled contracts for many subsequent bridges. Thomas Bouch designed two similar viaducts in the remote Pennines, at Belah and Deepdale on the South Durham & Lancashire Union Railway which opened in 1859, using standardised cast-iron and wrought-iron components assembled on the spot into piers and lattice girders. Crumlin, Belah and Deepdale were demolished in the 1960s, but similar structures of 1874 at Meldon (Devon) and 1879 at Bennerley (Derbyshire) still stand.

Lattice beam girders were used in railway bridges that reached less giddy heights. The first of note was the three-span structure with 15 masonry arches carrying the railway from Dublin to Belfast over the river Boyne at Drogheda, designed by J. B. MacNeill and completed in 1853. The bridges taking the South Eastern Railway across the Thames into Charing Cross and Cannon Street stations were designed by Sir John Hawkshaw and opened in 1864 and 1866. The Aethelfleda Bridge of 1868 (designed by William Baker) carries the London & North Western Railway over the Mersey between Runcorn and Widnes.

Iron, in the form of trusses fabricated from wrought- and cast-iron components, was also used in the construction of roofs. The pioneer of this style was the garden designer John Claudius Loudon who used it in glass houses, but its most sophisticated exponent was the Dublin engineer Richard Turner, who revised

⋏ The main railway line between Dublin and Belfast is carried across the river Boyne at Drogheda by a viaduct designed by Sir John MacNeill that was opened in 1855. It consisted of 12 stone arches to the south and three to the north, with a three-span wrought-iron structure crossing the river itself. The original iron structure was replaced by the present truss in the 1930s.
PHOTOGRAPH BY COURTESY OF JOHN POWELL

⋎ Deepdale Viaduct under construction, County Durham, c.1858. This lattice girder viaduct, supported by cast-iron piers, was designed by Thomas Bouch for the South Durham & Lancashire Union Railway's line between Barnard Castle and Tebay (usually known as the Stainmore Route). The masonry contractor was D. P. Appleby and the ironwork was by Kennard & Co. The viaduct, which crossed Deepdale Beck, was 740 feet long and 161 feet high. Bouch's Belah Viaduct was also on this railway; both were demolished shortly after the line closed in 1962.
© NATIONAL RAILWAY MUSEUM/SCIENCE & SOCIETY PICTURE LIBRARY

designs by Decimus Burton for the Palm House at Kew Gardens, and provided spectacular roofs for train sheds at several substantial stations including Lime Street in Liverpool, completed in 1850. Similarly ambitious overall roofs were designed for railway stations by other architects – that at Newcastle Central, completed by John Dobson in 1850, for instance, is outstanding – and for commercial buildings such as the Corn Exchange in Leeds, built under the direction of Cuthbert Brodrick in 1861–63.

Waterway engineering: the building of canals, locks, bridges and tunnels

Civil engineering expertise also developed through the building of waterways. Already by 1750 commercial vessels could use about 620 miles of naturally navigable river as well as about 680 miles that had been improved by engineers. During the next century canals were constructed in Britain with a total length of about 5,000 miles. Bridges and aqueducts were for the most part similar structures to those that were built by road and railway engineers, but canal builders contributed substantially to the understanding of elements such as cuttings, embankments and tunnels.

Canal engineering began to evolve from the late seventeenth century. In 1675–77 Andrew Yarranton extended the navigable portion of the Warwickshire Avon from Bidford to Stratford-on-Avon, when he was writing visionary proposals to connect the Avon with the river Cherwell near Oxford, and to establish settlements with granaries and linen manufactories at the junctions. Not long after, the improvement of the Aire & Calder Navigation between 1699 and 1703 was directed by John Hadley. Thomas Steers made the rivers Mersey and Irwell navigable to Manchester in 1722–25. Steers was a pivotal figure, involved in military and civil engineering as well as in river improvement and canal construction. He served in the army of William III and fought in 1690 at the Battle of the Boyne, and subsequently in the Netherlands where he acquired an understanding of military engineering. He built Liverpool's first enclosed dock – later known as the 'Old Dock' – in 1715, and from 1736 until 1741 worked on the Newry Canal in Ireland, the first in the British Isles to cross a summit, rising from the south by means of nine brick-built locks, each 44 feet (13 m) long. Henry Berry, who succeeded Steers as engineer at Liverpool and built further docks, was commissioned in 1754 to survey the Sankey Brook from the Mersey to St Helens. An Act was obtained in 1755 to make the brook navigable, but the plans were changed and the main line of the separate Sankey Canal opened to traffic two years later.

Earlier, Francis Egerton, 3rd Duke of Bridgewater, had been inspired by a visit to the Canal du Midi during his Grand Tour. In 1757, working with his agent John Gilbert and James Brindley, a millwright with experience of surveying, he planned a canal running from a basin adjoining coal workings at Worsley, across the river Irwell on an aqueduct at Barton, to a terminus at Castlefield in Manchester. The opening of the Bridgewater Canal immediately brought down the cost of coal in Manchester by about 50 per cent. The project, completed in 1761, was the nucleus of the narrow canals network of central England. By 1790 the Thames, Severn, Mersey and Trent navigations were linked by canals, and from 1816 boats could cross the Pennines by three routes (the Rochdale, the Huddersfield Narrow, and the Leeds & Liverpool). Other proposals for long-distance canals were made before 1760. Alexander Gordon, the Aberdeen-born antiquary and singer, surveyed a line between the firths of Clyde and Forth

↱ The aqueduct by which James Brindley took the Duke of Bridgewater's Canal across the river Irwell at Barton on its way from Worsley into Manchester was opened in 1759, and soon became a visitor attraction, and was reproduced on many engravings. It continued in use until the early 1890s when the Manchester Ship Canal, opened in 1894, was constructed along the line of the Irwell, and Bridley's structure was replaced by the spectacular swinging aqueduct which remains in use.

The Grand Canal in Ireland crosses the river Liffey on the five-arch Leinster Aqueduct, on the Bog of Allen, 3½ miles south of the cotton-spinning village of Prosperous. The canal was authorised in 1755 but only completed in 1804 after the proprietors had sought the advice of William Jessop. The structure is a characteristic aqueduct of the early period of canal building, accommodating a thick layer of puddled clay above the crowns of the arches to retain the water.

One of the most spectacular lock flights on the canal system, the Bingley Five-rise, on a section of the Leeds & Liverpool Canal opened in 1774. The five locks enable canal boats to rise 60 feet from the bottom of the flight.

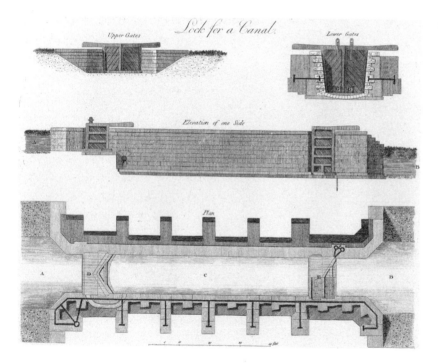

A diagram explaining the workings of a pound lock, of the kind used on most British and Irish canals of the late eighteenth century. The inclusion of this image in John Aikin's *A Description of the country from 30 to 40 miles round Manchester*, published in 1795, is evidence of the importance of the canal system to contemporary economic developments.

in 1726. The Grand Canal linking the river Liffey in Dublin with the river Shannon was proposed in 1755. Construction began after a grant of £20,000 from the Irish Parliament in 1757, but was not completed until 1804 after the company took advice from John Smeaton in 1773, and subsequently, over many years, from William Jessop.

Engineers who improved river navigations could construct pound locks, usually located where short side-cuts could carry a waterway past mills, or where cuts with locks could bypass shallows or meanders. The earliest pound lock in Britain had been built in the 1560s on the four-mile-long Exeter Canal, a lateral cut alongside the river Exe.

The 'dry hurries' on an extension of the Coalisland Canal in County Tyrone, completed in 1777 to the design of Davis Ducart with advice from John Smeaton, were the first inclined planes to operate on a waterway in the British Isles. They had a working life of only ten years, but their remains can still be recognised in the landscape outside the village of Drumnea Etra. Other canal inclined planes had longer lives, but those built before the late nineteenth century were capable of handling only the smallest vessels.

Wherever canals encountered rising terrain, or crossed watersheds, locks had to be built. To climb the slope east from Wigan to Aspull barges on the Leeds & Liverpool Canal had to negotiate a long series of 23 locks. In places the locks might be grouped in staircases, as in the flight of five, rising 60 feet (18.5 m), which was opened at Bingley, also on the Leeds & Liverpool Canal, on 21 March 1774; the 29-lock Caen Hill flight on the Kennet & Avon Canal of 1810, where John Rennie overcame the shortage of water by building side ponds; or the 36 locks at Tardebigge on the Worcester & Birmingham Canal opened in 1815. Flights of locks used large quantities of water, and slowed the progress of boats, and canal companies were tempted by speedier methods of raising and lowering vessels. The first on a canal in the British Isles were the inclined planes known locally as 'dry hurries' on an extension of the Coalisland Canal in County Tyrone, completed in 1777 by the Franco-Italian architect Davis Ducart (Daviso de Arcort), with the advice of John Smeaton. They were used for less than ten years. The six inclined planes on the canals of the Shropshire coalfield, which carried boats with a maximum capacity of only eight tons, were built from 1787, five of them to a design by John Lowdon and Henry Williams. The Hay incline lifted tub boats 207 feet (63.8 m) up and down the side of the Severn Gorge for about 100 years, and the Trench incline worked from 1794 into the twentieth century. The Blackhill inclined plane on the Monkland Canal worked from 1850 until 1887. Empty boats were taken in caissons down the 1,040 foot (320 m) length of the incline, while loaded boats ascended the 96-foot (29.6 m) rise by a flight of locks. Inclined planes

were also built on the Bude, Grand Western and Kidwelly canals. Experimental lifts installed on the Somersetshire Coal, Ellesmere, Worcester & Birmingham, and Dorset & Somerset canals were unsuccessful, but seven on the Grand Western worked for about 30 years from 1838. Inclines and lifts were not a significant part of the canal network before 1870, and were successful only with small boats. Their potential, once new materials became available, was demonstrated by the vertical lift between the river Weaver and the Trent & Mersey Canal at Anderton, completed in 1875; although several were built in continental Europe, the vertical lift concept was not repeated elsewhere in Britain.

Inclined planes, with some similarities to those on canals, were widely used on the 'hybrid' railways built between 1790 and 1840. These were designed like canals, with flat sections in the manner of canal pounds, worked by horses or later by locomotives, interspersed with inclines, sometimes steam-powered and sometimes self-acting. Such inclines were an essential feature of the 'Old Tram Road' at Preston, which linked the Lancaster Canal with a spur of the Leeds & Liverpool, as well as hybrid railways at Hetton Colliery, Severn & Wye, Pensnett, Stockton & Darlington, Stanhope & Tyne, Leicester & Swannington, Cromford & High Peak. During the early years of main-line railways inclines raised passenger trains out of Euston as well as from Crown Street Station, Liverpool.

Canal builders pioneered the construction of tunnels, the first being the 1,239 yard (1,115 m) tunnel at Preston Brook on the Trent & Mersey Canal, opened in 1775. By 1860 there were 36 miles of canal tunnel in Great Britain. Some took many years to complete, and

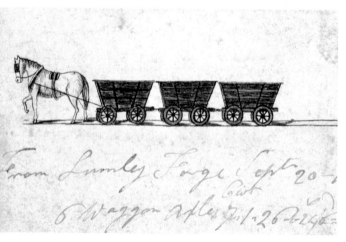

The bottom locks of the flight of five at Adderley, Shropshire, on the Birmingham & Liverpool Junction Canal (now the Shropshire Union), engineered by Thomas Telford, and opened in 1835. The flight carried the canal towards its summit on the watershed between streams draining into the river Severn and those running northwards toward the river Weaver.

A sketch from the notebook of the engineer Timothy Hackworth of 1827–28 showing a typical 'train' on a railway in the coalfield of north-east England, with a horse drawing three chaldron waggons of the kind that carried about 52 cwt of coal which could be discharged through bottom-opening doors at staithes in sea ports or along the rivers Tyne and Wear.
© SCIENCE MUSEUM/SCIENCE & SOCIETY PICTURE LIBRARY

The Cromford & High Peak Railway across the Derbyshire Pennines was a characteristic 'hybrid' railway, using locomotive haulage on flat sections and powered inclined planes to raise waggons between different levels. The incline at Middleton Top, opened in 1829, was operated using a steam engine built by the Butterley Co., which raised trains at a gradient of 1 in 8½ over a distance of 708 yards. The line continued in use until 1963. The engine house and steam engine have been conserved.
PHOTOGRAPH: CARNEGIE

in building them engineers learned to deal with quick-sands and with flooding from saturated strata. The longest was the 5,500 yard (5,030 m) Standedge Tunnel under the Pennines on the Huddersfield Canal. Other lengthy tunnels were at Harecastle on the Trent & Mersey Canal, 2,880 yards (2,633 m) long and opened in 1777 after eight years of excavation; Sapperton on the Thames & Severn Canal (3,817 yards, 3,490 m), opened in 1789; and Blisworth on the Grand Junction Canal (3,056 yards, 2,794 m), opened in 1805. The last

to be built was the 3,037 yard (2,786 m) Netherton Tunnel beneath the ridge of the Black Country; it had towpaths on each side and gas lighting, and was opened in 1858. Most tunnels did not have towpaths, and boats were propelled by professional 'leggers', who lived in the communities around the portals. It could take up to 1½ hours to 'leg' a barge — accomplished by lying on the boat and 'walking' on the tunnel side — through the mile-long Foulridge Tunnel on the Leeds & Liverpool. Tunnels were excavated by

VIEW of the RAILWAY from HETTON COLLIERY

To the DEPÔT on the BANKS of the RIVER WEAR near SUNDERLAND in the COUNTY of DURHAM, with the
LOCO-MOTIVE and other ENGINES used on the same.

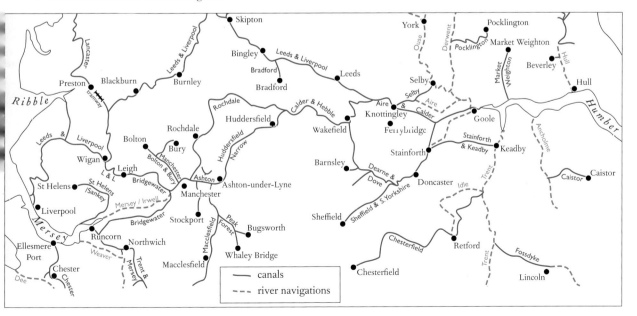

One of the most important railways built in the Co. Durham coalfield in the early nineteenth century ran eight miles from Hetton Colliery to the Hetton Staithes (see also pages 220, 227) on the south bank of the river Wear at Sunderland. The line was designed by George Stephenson and was one of the first upon which none of the sections was worked by horses. As the upper diagram shows, there were two steam-powered inclined planes which drew loaded coal waggons to the summit and five gravity inclines running down to the riverside, on which downward rakes of loaded waggons drew up the returning empties. Other sections were worked by five steam locomotives designed by Stephenson which were developments of those he used at Killingworth Colliery. The line opened in 1822, and by 1827 was carrying 120,000 loaded chaldron waggons per year to the staithes. In modified form the Hetton Railway remained in use until 1959.

© SCIENCE MUSEUM/SCIENCE & SOCIETY PICTURE LIBRARY

The canal network of northern England.

The Grand Junction Canal Company established workshops for the manufacture of such items as lock gates at Bulbourne in Hertfordshire in the early nineteenth century. They stood close to the junction of the main line of the canal with the 6.7-mile branch to Wendover, and near the wharf from which goods conveyed by canal were taken by road to and from Dunstable. The Grand Junction was one of several companies that amalgamated to form the Grand Union Canal Company in 1929, and this stretch of water is today called the Grand Union Canal.

The Claverton pumping station on the Kennet & Avon Canal near Bath, in which a 25 ft broad waterwheel, of 17 ft 6 in. diameter can raise 100,000 gallons of water per hour some 53 feet from the river Avon into the canal. The installation was designed by John Rennie and built between 1809 and 1813.

sinking vertical shafts about 18 feet (5.5. m) in diameter (there were 10 at Blisworth and 25 at Sapperton), from which digging extended in each direction. Spoil was sometimes used to build embankments, but at Crick on the Grand Union Canal the spoil tips lie over the well-preserved ridge-and-furrow of medieval fields.

On 25 July 1787 Lord Torrington passed through the stone façade of the tunnel by which the Thames & Severn burrows under the Cotswolds at Sapperton, and was dragged on a horse-drawn sledge to a working face where, enveloped in thick gunpowder smoke, he met miners from Derbyshire and Cornwall. Contractors continued to recruit miners for the construction of railway tunnels. Those digging at Bletchingley on the South Eastern Railway in 1841 were from Derbyshire, Staffordshire and Yorkshire, and the group excavating the tunnel that took the Severn Valley Railway beneath Bridgnorth in 1861 came from Shaw in Lancashire. In the Thames Tunnel, built with great difficulty between 1825 and 1843, Sir Marc and I. K. Brunel employed a shield, but most railway tunnels were constructed by the tried-and-tested methods used by canal builders.

Over a period of half a century canal engineers learned to excavate cuttings and to build stable embankments. A comparison between the sinuous contouring line of the Oxford Canal from Hawkesbury Junction to Banbury, designed by James Brindley but completed in 1778 after his death, and Thomas Telford's Birmingham & Liverpool Junction Canal, opened in 1835, which runs on embankments or in cuttings along most of its 39-mile course from Autherley Junction to Nantwich, shows the extent of the change. The remarkable 'straight mile' embankment that carries the Leeds & Liverpool Canal high above Burnley was designed by Robert Whitworth and opened in 1801. The cuttings near Chirk and the 2,000 foot (610 m) long, 75 foot (23 m) high embankment at the south end of the Pontcysyllte Aqueduct were excavated by William Evans, whose 'well-computed labours' were applauded at its opening. Evans was one of the first contractors to employ iron railways to move the spoil from cuttings to help form embankments farther along the route.

Engineers also learned to supply water to the summit levels of canals to cope with increasing traffic. To fill a narrow canal required four or five million gallons of water per mile, a high proportion of which would be lost whenever locks were used, as well as through leakage and evaporation. Initially, water was usually obtained by diverting streams, or from mine pumps. From the outset, though, canal engineers also used reservoirs to amass water, which was conveyed to canals along feeder channels. Motorists on the M6 in Cumbria might rest awhile next to the tranquil Killington Lake, little realising that this was built in 1819 as the head reservoir for the Lancaster Canal, while farther south on the motorway the extensive reservoirs of the Staffordshire & Worcestershire Canal

can be seen at Junction 12 near Gailey. A pumping engine was first used on a canal in 1778, at Spon Lane on the Birmingham Canal Navigation, when a 20 inch (0.5 m) Boulton & Watt engine was installed, to be followed in 1779 by a 32 inch (0.8 m) engine at Smethwick. Jim Andrew showed that about 80 canal pumping engines, most of them lifting water less than 50 feet, were installed between 1778 and 1860, as well as about a dozen water- or wind-powered pumping installations. They included the two at Crofton on the Kennet & Avon Canal, and the Leawood pumping engine on the Cromford Canal, made by Graham & Co. of Elsecar in 1849. Increasing traffic necessitated the installation of ten engines between Fenny Stratford and Tring on the Grand Junction Canal between 1837 and 1841.

There were several proposals in the early nineteenth century for canals that could be used by ocean-going ships. The Gloucester & Berkeley Canal, opened in 1827, enabled Gloucester to develop into a seaport. The Caledonian Canal provides a route for sea-going vessels, avoiding the hazards around the north of Scotland. It was constructed between 1803 and 1822 after a survey by William Jessop and Thomas Telford, and extends 62 miles through the Great Glen between Corpach near Fort William and Inverness, making use of Loch Dochfour, Loch Ness, Loch Oich and Loch Lochy. The canal disappointed the hopes of its promoters. The contractors, who appear to have believed that the project would never be finished, produced faulty work, and it attracted few ocean-going ships, but its 29 locks, including Neptune's Staircase at Banavie and the sea-locks at Clachnaharry are imposing.

Building ports, docks and harbours

Economic expansion depended on overseas trade and coastal shipping. All foreign and a high proportion of internal trade was carried by ship. As late as 1870 in some places cargoes were still being delivered by running a wooden ship of less than 200 tons on to a beach and, while the tide was out, shovelling coal, salt or grain into carts alongside. Nevertheless, most ports were radically changed in the 170 years after 1700.

Eighteen Acts of Parliament for improving harbours were passed between 1700 and 1750. Whitehaven is an eighteenth-century harbour created by building piers. Docks in which vessels could float had long been used for repairing ships, including the Duke of Bedford's notable Howland Great – or 'Greenland' – Dock at Rotherhithe which was built in the 1690s, but Thomas Steers built the pioneering Old Dock at Liverpool in

The Old Dock at Liverpool, built by Thomas Steers in 1715, one of the first such docks which allowed ships to be loaded and unloaded at any state of the tide. From *A South-west Prospect of Liverpool*, published by Samuel and Nathaniel Buck in 1728.

The Howland Great Wet Dock at Rotherhithe was another early example of a 'wet' dock. It was built on land owned by the Russell family, dukes of Bedford, in 1695–99, and was originally intended for the repair and re-fitting of ships. From the 1720s it was used by ships trading to Greenland, and from 1806 it became part of a series of docks and timber ponds developed by the Commercial Dock Company, intended for trade with northern Europe and the eastern seaboard of North America. The company merged with the Surrey Dock Co. in 1865 to form the Surrey Commercial Docks.

The Albert Dock, Liverpool, completed to the design of Jesse Hartley in 1845. The warehouses surrounding the dock are carried on massive cast-iron pillars. The limited clearances at the entrances prevented the larger ships of the late nineteenth century from entering the Albert Dock, but after a long period of dereliction the complex was adapted to new uses in the 1980s when it became one of Liverpool's principal attractions.

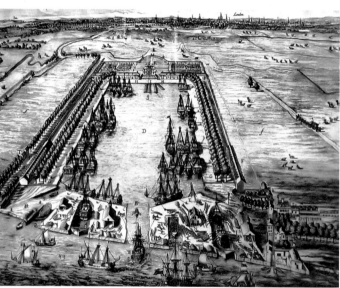

1715 which, in contrast to the riverside quays, allowed ships to be loaded and unloaded at any state of the tide. His successor, Henry Berry, built the Salthouse, George's and King's Docks, as well as the Queen's Dock at Hull. John Rennie demonstrated the essential principles of subsequent dock construction at Grimsby in 1796. The dock there was built on a timber raft and anchored with sheet piles at each end. Its floor was an inverted brick arch constructed to resist the upthrust of the mud beneath. John Smeaton used hydraulic cement made from argillaceous limestone – which will set under water – in the third Eddystone lighthouse in the 1750s. This was then employed by Rennie in the 1790s and by most subsequent dock engineers. In 1824, when Jesse Hartley became engineer to the port of Liverpool, there were 50 acres of enclosed docks,

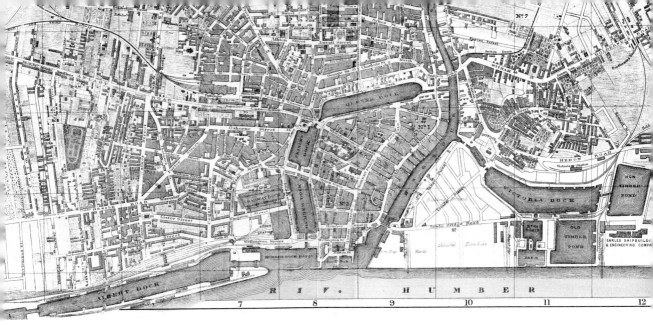

Hull lies 25 miles from the sea on the north bank of the river Humber around its confluence with the river Hull. During the eighteenth century it grew to be the third port in England. This map of the 1860s shows the network of wet docks that developed after what came to be called the Old Dock was opened in 1778.

ALL ILLUSTRATIONS CARNEGIE COLLECTION

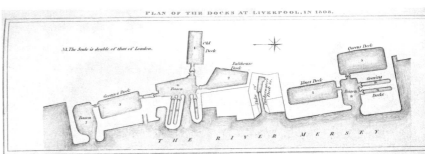

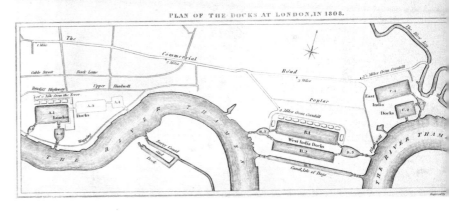

Plans published in *Rees's Cyclopaedia* of 1808 showing, uppermost, the first wet docks in the port of Liverpool, and, beneath, the West India Docks built across the isthmus of the Isle of Dogs in London. The physical characteristics of Britain's two largest ports were very different: by 1808 Liverpool's trade was conducted entirely from enclosed docks whose construction had been funded by the Corporation, while in London the docks were privately funded and the river wharfs in London remained of great importance.

© SCIENCE MUSEUM/SCIENCE & SOCIETY PICTURE LIBRARY

but over 200 acres when he retired in 1860. The Albert Dock, completed in 1845, was surrounded by warehouses in which four storeys of storage space were carried above ground floors supported on massive cast-iron pillars. The roofs are made of wrought-iron trusses covered with iron plates. Construction of wet docks continued at London and Liverpool after 1870 and they became characteristic of the ports of Hull, Leith, Bristol, Goole, Gloucester, Grangemouth, Greenock, Glasgow, Dundee, King's Lynn and Dublin.

Trade in the Port of London doubled between 1700 and 1770 and doubled again in the next 30 years. The wharfs became over-crowded and goods piled on the riverside quays could readily be taken by the least-practised of thieves, providing a satisfying source of income for hardened criminals. Telford's proposal

A panoramic view, looking westwards or upstream on the river Thames, of the West India Docks, built across the isthmus of the Isle of Dogs to the design of William Jessop under the supervision of Ralph Walker, and completed in 1800. Ships could remain afloat in such docks at all stages of the tide; goods could be loaded and unloaded directly from or to the surrounding multi-storey warehouses, and the whole site was protected by a high boundary wall. The image shows the installation as originally built, with two docks and a canal that was intended to allow ships an easy passage upstream, but the latter was subsequently adapted as another dock.

Copper ore was exported, principally to South Wales, from the harbour at Hayle in west Cornwall, and there was a return traffic in Welsh coal for Cornish mines and furnaces. A copper smelthouse was established in the harbour, and Hayle was also the location of some of Cornwall's principal mechanical engineering companies (see pages 79–80). The harbour wall at Hayle, photographed in 1980, is constructed from blocks of copper slag, the waste product from the smelthouse.

for a single iron arch to replace London Bridge was intended to make it possible for sea-going vessels to unload as far upstream as Blackfriars. It was decided instead to expand facilities downstream by improving the wharfs of the Pool of London and by creating a number of enclosed docks. Whereas the width of the Mersey at Liverpool allowed civil engineers to build all but one of the docks out into the river itself, on the Thames the docks had to be excavated from dry land. The first of these were the West India Docks across the isthmus of the Isle of Dogs. They were designed by William Jessop, constructed under the supervision of Ralph Walker, and opened in 1802. Two parallel rectangular docks of 30 acres and 24 acres were built — one used for imports and one for exports — with a 'canal' to the south which was ultimately adapted as a third dock. Warehouses lined the water's edge, and a forbidding boundary wall, pierced only by a controlled gateway, surrounded the premises. In the 1780s the East India Company constructed warehouses in Cutler Street on the edge of the City, which were subsequently linked by the East India Dock Road to quays near the mouth of the river Lea, where the company's dock complex opened on 4 August 1804. It was designed by Ralph Walker, with John Rennie as consultant, to take East Indiamen of about 1,000 tons. The Regent's Canal Dock at Limehouse opened in 1812 and was enlarged in 1820. The London Docks at Wapping were completed in 1805 to the design of John Rennie. Development of the Surrey Commercial Docks on the south bank of the river Thames followed the authorisation of the Grand Surrey Canal in 1801 and the opening of the Grand Surrey Basin in 1807. The principal engineer, the Falkirk-born Ralph Walker, is commemorated at Greenland Dock.

St Katharine's Dock, adjacent to the Tower of London, was designed by Thomas Telford, and involved the demolition of 1,250 houses occupied by more than 11,000 people. Work began in 1827, and the opening took place on 25 October 1828. After this no substantial docks were built until 1855, when the Royal Victoria Dock was constructed on Plaistow Marshes by Samuel Morton Peto. It was the first in London to have hydraulic power systems, railway sidings and finger piers. The Millwall Dock, in the centre of the Isle of Dogs, was designed by Sir John Fowler and opened in 1868.

The temporary passenger station of the Great Northern Railway at Maiden Lane, London, used between 1850 and the opening of the present King's Cross terminus on the Euston Road at the top of the picture. The station became part of the extensive King's Cross freight depot, which handled coal, grain, potatoes and many other commodities, and served as an place where goods were exchanged between rail and road transport and also between the railway and vessels on the Regent's Canal which passes through the site.

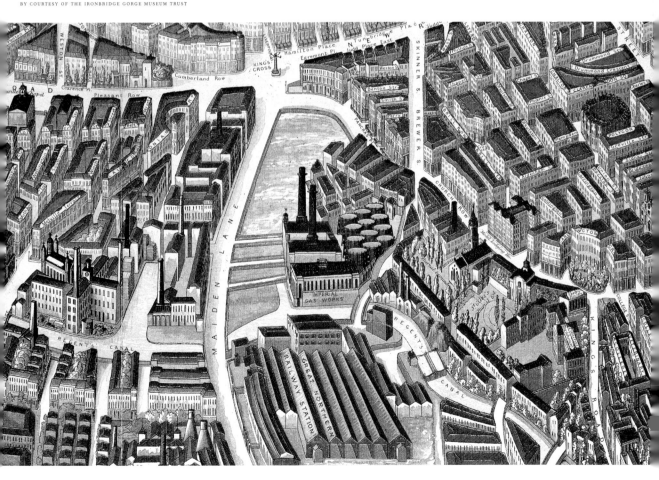

Draining land, controlling water

Controlling water while creating docks and digging new channels was one of the major challenges faced by civil engineers. Draining low-lying land in the name of agricultural improvement was another. In south-west Lancashire Thomas Fleetwood had attempted in the 1690s to drain the enormous Martin Mere by erecting sluice-gates that closed automatically when the incoming tide pushed against them and reopened on the ebb. The project failed because of rapid silting, however, and it was not until the introduction of steam pumping in the nineteenth century that Martin Mere was successfully drained. On a much broader scale, however, were the changes effected over a long period in the Fens of Lincolnshire and East Anglia, where civil engineers literally transformed the landscape. In the 1630s the Bedford Level Corporation employed the Dutchman Cornelius Vermuyden to carry out drainage works, under which 12,000 acres were made available to the king and 43,000 acres to investors in the company, while 40,000 acres provided revenue to maintain the infrastructure. Vermuyden built the 21-mile Old Bedford River, which provided a new course for the river Great Ouse between Earith and Salter's Lode Sluice. By 1748 in the middle section of the Fens alone more than 250 windmills raised water into rivers running through man-made channels sufficiently high to run off into the sea. In 1789 a correspondent of Boulton & Watt pointed out that current pumps could only work when there was wind, but that coals from Newcastle were available from Lynn, which should 'remind all Fen Men of the necessity of Steam Engines'. Steam power was applied for drainage purposes from about 1803, after which engines proliferated: 16 were installed between 1817 and 1835 and at least 24 more before 1852. A Butterley Co. steam engine of 1831 is preserved at Stretham on the Waterbeach Level, one of 1833 at Prickwillow, and one of 1856 at the Dogdyke pumping station near Tattershall. John Rennie drained Deeping Fen from 1800, worked on the river Witham from 1802, and directed the construction of the Eau Brink Cut on the river Ouse above King's Lynn which opened in 1821. Thomas Telford was also involved with the Eau Brink Cut, and was responsible for a new course of the river Nene between Wisbech and the Wash, opened in 1830, and the drainage of the North Level between Crowland and Guyhirn, completed in 1834.

A parallel activity which involved some of the same engineering skills and techniques was the supply of clean water to urban areas. This need had, indeed, stimulated some of the great engineering achievements of antiquity, including the Roman Pont du Gard in southern France and the aqueduct at Segovia, north of Madrid. By 1700 several notable schemes in Britain served that purpose. The 24-mile New River of 1613 conveyed water to London from springs near Hertford, and several monuments to the system remain in the square in Islington named after its builder, Sir Hugh Myddleton. In Shrewsbury a pipeline supplying a cistern in the town centre dated from the 1570s. In 1674–76 a 3-inch lead pipe was installed from Comiston Springs, three miles south of Edinburgh Castle, to

↗ Drainage works over several centuries linked many communities in the Fens with the waterways network. Burwell, in Cambridgeshire, was a medieval inland port, while the channel or 'lode' that links it with the river Cam may be Roman in origin. Transport facilities enabled this malthouse to flourish, together with boat-building and brick-making enterprises. From the mid-nineteenth century fertilisers were manufactured at Burwell from processed coprolite, ancient fossilised animal dung which was mined locally.

On the eastern edge of Padnall Fen is the Middle Fen Pumping House at Prickwillow, which housed a Butterley steam engine driving a scoop wheel when it was opened in 1833. A larger pump house was built alongside in 1880, but the Butterley engine continued to work until 1897. The engine house is open to the public and bears the inscription added in 1842:

In fitness for the urgent hours / Unlimited untiring power / Precision, promptitude command / The infant's will, the giant's hand / Steam, mighty Steam ascends the throne / And reigns lord paramount alone.

A pumping station of 1830 that drained Padnall Fen, north-east of Ely, in the angle between the river Great Ouse and the river Lark immediately upstream from their confluence.

Most of the great engineers of the late eighteenth and early nineteenth centuries were involved in drainage projects in the Fens. This is Thomas Telford's plan of the drainage system around The Wash, showing the outfalls of the three principal rivers, the Great Ouse to the east, the Nene in the centre and the Welland to the west.

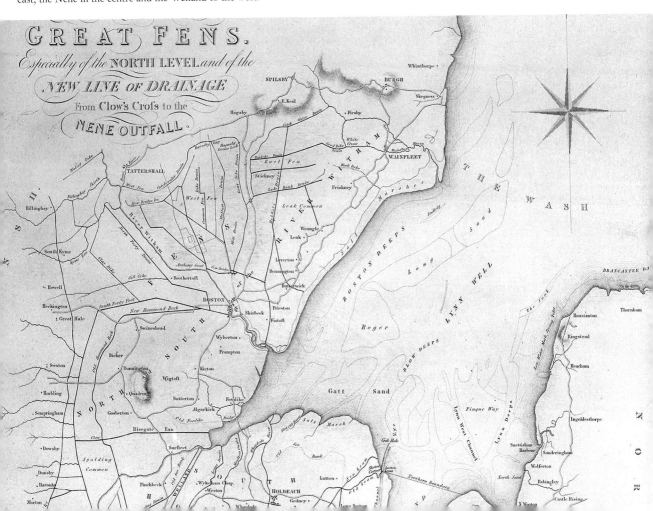

➤ The Netherbow Wellhead, Edinburgh, one of the cisterns
that supplied the city with drinking water from Comiston
Springs by way of a network of lead pipes laid out in 1674.

➤ The celebrated Newcomen engines that pumped water at
Chelsea for the City of Westminster. The first such engine
was installed nearby in 1726, but the bankruptcy of its
owners necessitated its removal six years later. The two
engines depicted in this 'A View of Chelsea Waterworks', by
Henry Cook after James Parsons, were installed in 1741–42
and were much visited, illustrating the role of the capital
city as a showcase for new technology. (See also pages
523–4.)

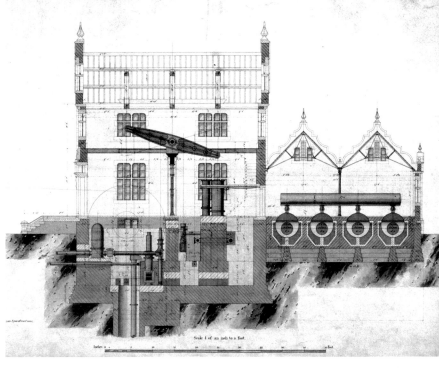

Nottingham Waterworks, 1856, a drawing (scale ¼ inch to 1 foot) showing a longitudinal section of the engine house and transverse section of the boiler house of the Nottingham Waterworks. Nottingham Waterworks Company built two new pumping stations in the 1850s, using 60 hp Cornish beam engines to pump water from wells sunk into aquifers in the sandstone upon which the city is situated. A third station was added in 1871.

a large cistern on Castle Hill; from there water was distributed via hollowed-out elm pipes to a series of elaborate stone wellheads down the High Street. As early as 1580 a Dutch engineer, Peter Morice, had installed an under-shot waterwheel beneath one of the northern arches of London Bridge, which was used to pump river water to a conduit at Leadenhall. From 1696 the London Bridge Company supplied water in London, using pumps operated by a waterwheel that could be raised and lowered to suit water levels. This technology was patented in 1693 by John Hadley and George Sorocold. Similar systems were soon installed at Bridgnorth, Bristol, Chester, Derby, King's Lynn, Leeds, Newcastle-upon-Tyne and Sheffield. The Chelsea Waterworks Company was established in 1723, 'for better supplying the City and Liberties of Westminster and parts adjacent with water' from the Thames. Between 1760 and 1830 water companies were established in most large cities. In London the Borough Company was established in 1770, the Lambeth in 1785, the West Middlesex and East London both in 1806, and the Grand Junction Company in 1811. The Cork Piped Water Company began pumping in 1768. The Glasgow Water Company was established by an Act of Parliament of 1806, and the rival Cranstonhill (Water) Co. in 1808, the Edinburgh Joint Water Co.

in 1819, the Birmingham Water Company in 1826, the Sheffield Waterworks Co. in 1830, and the Nottingham New Waterworks Co. in 1824.

Another major stimulus towards improving the supply of clean water to urban areas came as a response to the cholera epidemics that hit most towns across Britain in the two decades from 1832. In London the cholera epidemic of 1848–49 caused 14,137 deaths, while 10,738 died in the outbreak of 1853. In the 1849 *On the Mode and Communication of Cholera* Dr John Snow was able finally to pinpoint the cause of the disease and demonstrated, by removing the handle of a water pump in Broad Street, Soho, that those who drank water from it were prone to catch cholera. Snow also discovered that the Southwark & Vauxhall Waterworks Company had been taking water from polluted sections of the Thames, thereby distributing the cholera bacteria. The link between polluted water and disease, and the need for adequate supplies of clean water, had been established.

Making improvements to water supplies depended on technology. Robey and Kanefsky calculated that by 1800 36 steam engines had been installed at waterworks in Britain. George Sorocold invented a machine for boring the wooden pipes for water mains, but water suppliers began to install cast-iron pipes – the

Edinburgh company from 1790 and the Lambeth company from 1802. At Perth in 1832 Dr Adam Anderson designed a steam-powered waterworks, a building in the Ionic style with a domed cast-iron roof tank. The filtering of water was increasingly recognised as a crucial method of purification: for example, the waterworks at Paisley adopted filtration from 1829 under the direction of James Simpson. In the same year the Chelsea company began to purify the water it extracted from the river Thames by the slow sand filtration system, which was subsequently adopted, albeit slowly, by other suppliers. When the Grand Junction Company moved its waterworks from Chelsea to Kew Bridge in 1838 it installed filtering reservoirs and a 200 foot high tower to provide a head of water for its pipe system. The industry was increasingly subject to government control. The Metropolitan Water Act of 1852 forbade the extraction of water from the tidal stretch of the Thames, that is below Teddington Lock, causing the Chelsea and Lambeth companies to move to Surbiton. Filtration became compulsory in London in 1855. The Nottingham Water Act of 1845 amalgamated three companies, and the city's supply was thereafter directed by the celebrated engineer Thomas Hawksley. Some water-pumping stations of the 1860s, such as that at Ryhope near Sunderland, were 'temples of public health', buildings of impressive appearance internally and externally, set among flower beds, lawns and woodland in the manner of country houses.

In manufacturing cities there were few unpolluted sources of water, and engineers were obliged to bring pure water from the upper catchment areas of rivers. John Frederick Bateman (from 1883 John Frederic La Trobe Bateman), grandson of Benjamin La Trobe, founder of the Moravian community at Fairfield and nephew of Benjamin Latrobe who built the Capitol in Washington DC, practised as a civil engineer from 1833. His reservoirs on the river Bann in Ireland impressed William Fairbairn, whose daughter he married. He was consulted in 1844 on water supplies in Manchester and Salford, and in 1846 proposed reservoirs east of the city in Longdendale, from which water might flow into the Tame Valley through a 3,100 yard (2,835 m) tunnel at Mottram. The project was realised between 1848 and 1877, by which time

Manchester was also seeking supplies by pipe and aqueduct from Thirlmere, their new reservoir around 90 miles north of the city in the Lake District. Bateman gave advice on water supply to other cities including Belfast, Dublin, Perth, Wolverhampton, Buenos Aires, Naples, Constantinople and Colombo. In Glasgow rivalry between three companies in the 1840s stimulated a scheme to extract water from Loch Katrine, which was linked to the city by a 34-mile pipeline. Work began in 1856, and the system was opened by Queen Victoria in 1859 when it was said to 'bear comparison with the most extensive aqueducts in the ancient world, not excluding those of Rome'.

Establishing reservoirs in the uplands involved building dams, theoretical understanding of which was initially very limited. The engineer George Leather had an ill-defined relationship to those who built the Bilberry Dam above Holmfirth, between 1839 and 1843, but considered that he had terminated his connection with the project in 1845. The dam collapsed on 5 February 1852, causing 81 deaths and much destruction, and effectively ended Leather's career. In 1859 the Sheffield Waterworks Co. began to build four reservoirs around Bradfield, eight miles north-west of the city. The census of 1861 recorded the presence in the area of two contractors who between them employed 100 men. The Dale Dyke Dam, which impounded the first reservoir, collapsed on 11 May 1864, releasing 650 million gallons of water in a tremendous flood, which killed 250 people downstream. A committee of distinguished engineers subsequently found faults in the dam's construction and, as in other instances, a disaster accelerated the process of learning.

With growing knowledge and awareness about the links between polluted water and public health, civil engineers concerned themselves increasingly with the disposal of sewage. In some cities sewers, which might be centuries old, carried surface water and in some cases excrement, untreated, into rivers. In 1840, for example, more than 80 miles of sewers of this kind ran beneath London. In most towns, though, accumulations in earth closets were removed in the hours of darkness by 'scavengers' or 'night soil men' and used as fertiliser. By the late nineteenth century, for example, around 100,000 tons of animal and human

GENERAL VIEW OF THE ABBEY MILLS PUMPING STATION.

⋏ A water closet of the kind designed by Joseph Bramah, manufactured in 1880, the plunger mechanism by Tylor & Son of Newgate Road, London, and the ceramic bowl by John Bolding & Sons, also of London. The installation of such closets in middle-class and increasingly in working-class homes in the mid-nineteenth century increased the demand for piped water in cities, and did much to bring about improvements in public health. The quality of the workmanship reflects the traditional skills of London craftsmen.

© SCIENCE MUSEUM/SCIENCE & SOCIETY PICTURE LIBRARY

▽ The pumping station on Sir Joseph Bazalgette's Northern Outfall Sewer at Abbey Mills in east London, completed in 1868. The building, in the Italianate Gothic style, is cruciform in plan, housed two beam engines in each of its four bays (see also page 333), and is topped by a central lantern. Abbey Mills was one of the 'cathedrals of public health' of mid-Victorian England. The building remains, although the steam engines were removed and replaced by electric pumps in 1931–33.

manure were being transported on the Leeds & Liverpool Canal, much of it carried by barge from Liverpool to fertilise the market gardens of southwest Lancashire. At the beginning of the 1840s Edwin Chadwick advocated water carriage for sewage, via the water-closet reinvented by Joseph Bramah and networks of pipes glazed on the inside. Chadwick was largely responsible for the Public Health Act of 1848, and new authorities established under its provisions hesitantly set up effective systems, having to learn, for example, that sewage needed treatment, which might be provided on 'sewage farms', before it could be safely discharged into rivers. Engineers used glazed earthenware pipes for smaller sewers, but main sewers might be made of bricks or fabricated from cast- or wrought-iron segments. London's problems were demonstrated in 1858 by the 'Great Stink', caused by the accumulation of sewage in the Thames.

Sir Joseph Bazalgette directed the construction in 1858–65 of the Northern and Southern Outfall Sewers which ran west–east, cutting across existing sewers on north–south or south–north alignments, into the river Thames. The pumping stations at the eastern ends of the two systems, at Abbey Mills of 1868 and Crossness of 1865, are flamboyant 'temples of public health'. Bazalgette's Thames Embankment, built by Thomas Brassey between 1865 and 1870, incorporated a main sewer as well as the tunnels of the District Railway and a new road across 22 acres of reclaimed riverside land.

From drainage schemes to canal and railway building, and from dock construction to bridge and road design, civil engineers were responsible for many of the essential, and enduring, structures of the new industrial landscape. But who was it who undertook the tasks of organising and actually executing these designs and projects?

Contractors and navvies

Little is known about the contractors who built the first British canals or contemporary bridges and roads, or of the workers they employed. Nevertheless, we do know that by the 1770s there were men who could undertake the construction of bridges or sections of roads or canals, who were able to hire labour, provide tools and to ensure that the directions of engineers were followed. John Beswick, for example, employed up to 60 men building parts of the Staffordshire & Worcestershire Canal, and also worked on the Bridgewater Canal, the Calder & Hebble Navigation, and six other waterways. Denis Edson, meanwhile, worked on the Chester Canal, the Iron Bridge (probably building its approach roads), the turnpike road from Cainscross through Nailsworth to Bath, and later on the Stourbridge, Gloucester & Berkeley and Grand Surrey canals. The career of John Pinkerton, who worked on several canals including the Basingstoke, was markedly less successful: he displayed a consistent level of incompetence and was sued by several of the companies who employed him.

In order to undertake the strenuous manual work involved in major works such as these, building contractors would employ large numbers of 'navigators', known popularly by the sobriquet 'navvy'. Large groups of such workers would be assembled at a site, where they often invited, and in some cases deserved, a bad press for rowdiness, immorality and heavy drinking on days off. Sarah Lawrence, companion of the Evangelical Mary Fletcher of Madeley, was moved in the mid-1790s to prevent performances of offensive plays in the churchyard and discovered that the ringleaders were 'Navigators who were lately come into the Parish to work at the new Cut'. This was the Shropshire Canal, whose construction was directed by the ironmaster William Reynolds. The incident shows that even at this date there was already an itinerant labour force of specialist canal builders. When construction of the Birmingham & Liverpool Canal was about to begin in February 1827 between 300 and 400 men assembled to seek work at Market Drayton, and by the following August some 1,600 were employed in the area.

Several contractors worked on the Holyhead Road during most of its rebuilding. Thomas Evans, for example, built the double-arch bridge over the Afon Llugwy, the road through Llangollen, a long section on Rhysgog Hill, and the new line between Chirk Bridge and Gobowen. George Deas built the tollhouses at Ty-issa and Betws-y-Coed, Rhydllanfair Bridge and sections of road near Cerrig-y-drudion. Both appear to have been local men, and their tenders were consistently cheaper than those of their rivals. In 1817 Gill, Hodges & Co., whose work was praised by Telford in his *Autobiography*, undertook to build the road near Owen Glyndwr's Hill, and subsequently constructed the approaches to the Menai Bridge, much of the new road across Anglesey, and the Stanley Embankment, on which they employed 150 men.

The specialist masonry contractors employed by Telford are better documented. John Simpson was born in Midlothian and in 1790 became clerk of works at St Chad's church, Shrewsbury. He took over a building business in 1793 and before 1800 was involved in the construction of the Ditherington Flax Mill. He contracted with William Hazledine to build the Chirk Aqueduct, and was 'the accurate mason who erected the pillars' of the Pontcysyllte Aqueduct. Telford called him a 'treasure of talents and integrity' and acted as his executor. John Wilson, from Dalton, Cumberland, the stone mason who actually laid the stones of the piers of Pontcysyllte, worked on

The most elegant of Thomas Telford's masonry bridges in the Highlands crosses the river Tay at Dunkeld. It consists of seven spans, has a total length of 685 ft (211 m), and was opened in 1808.

To minimise gradients railway lines incorporated cuttings as well as embankments, and, as seen here, the spoil from the former would be transported to the end of the tracks to make up embankments there. This is Roch Viaduct on the Shawforth branch of the East Lancashire Railway, photographed on 7 November 1867. The viaduct has been completed and an embankment is being built up. The East Lancashire Railway ran from Bury to Rawtenstall, connecting with the line from Manchester to Bolton.

© NATIONAL RAILWAY MUSEUM/SCIENCE & SOCIETY PICTURE LIBRARY

the Gotha and Caledonian canals and, with his sons, constructed the stonework of the Menai Bridge. John Straphen, born at Inverkeithing, was clerk of works for Telford's bridge at Dunkeld, succeeded Simpson in his building business in Shrewsbury, built the columns on the Holyhead Road commemorating Lord Hill and the Marquis of Anglesey, and constructed the roads around Lake Ogwen and through the pass of Glyn Diffwys. Telford wrote to Jessop in 1804 proposing to employ John Simpson and John Wilson on the Caledonian Canal,

> the works being upon a scale of uncommon
> magnitude, and in a district of country
> unaccustomed to operations of this nature,
> I propose that such persons only shall be
> instructed with the chief superintendence and
> the execution of the principal works, as have to
> my own and your knowledge for ten years past,
> being employed upon works of a similar nature
> whose abilities may be relied on and who are
> likely to enter with zeal into the spirit of the
> undertaking …

Some navvies became contractors. Hugh McIntosh worked for Robert Whitworth on the Forth & Clyde Canal. Upon its completion in 1790 he, with other Scots, followed Whitworth to work on the Leeds & Liverpool Canal. In 1797 he undertook his first contract, for the Grand Trunk Canal, and in 1798 married the daughter of the company's agent at Cheddleton. He worked for the Grand Trunk until 1816, building the Leek Canal and the railway to Caldon Low. He subsequently undertook contracts on the Kennet & Avon, Gloucester & Berkeley and Stainforth & Keadby canals as well as on the Union Canal in Scotland. From 1803 he supervised the excavation of the East India Docks, and later built the Royal William Victualling Yard at Plymouth. He constructed the Highgate Archway and Vauxhall Bridge roads in London. Telford entrusted him with the erection of the Mythe Bridge over the Severn, and in 1825–27 he built Folly Bridge at Oxford to the design of Ebenezer Parry. He constructed the London & Greenwich Railway and carried out contracts on the Great Western, Manchester & Leeds and North Midland railways. He was appropriately described by Telford as 'a person of uncommon activities'.

Sir Alec Skempton calculated that the nine main railway lines built between 1834 and 1841, totalling some 660 route miles, involved the excavation of 70 million cubic yards (54 million m³) of material, most of which went into embankments elsewhere on the lines. During the early years of railway construction most material was moved by hand. This could only be achieved by the employment of large numbers of men. In July 1837 some 6,250 men and 450 horses were building the Great Western; 5,150 men and 510 horses worked on the Midland Counties Railway in 1839; and 6,210 men and 960 horses on the London, Brighton & South Coast Railway in 1840. John Cooke Bourne's engraving of Tring Cutting on the

London & Birmingham Railway, 2½ miles long, 57 feet (17.5 m) deep and excavated between September 1834 and December 1837, portrays the labour force of the contractor Thomas Townshend, who had also dug the Smethwick Cutting on the Birmingham Canal in 1827–30.

By 1851, despite periods of slowdown and instability, railway building was a colossal industry employing 38,675 men; it dwarfed past civil engineering ventures. By this date there were 6,266 route miles of main-line railway; another 3,180 miles were built in the next decade, and 3,942 in the 1860s. Before 1914 the total exceeded 20,000 miles. The construction of railways did depend on the trade cycle, but every year, somewhere in the British Isles, gangs of navvies were excavating cuttings, dumping spoil on embankments, driving tunnels and building stations, freight depots and locomotive sheds. Some of the navvies stayed in cheap inns and lodging-houses, or with fellow-navvies who rented houses, or with local residents glad of extra income. Others lived in shanties of stone, brick, mud and timber, roofed with tarpaulins. For example, 93 of the men who built the extension of the Erewash Valley line in 1861, and also 32 women, lived in wood or mud huts on South Normanton Common. Remains of navvy encampments have been identified on the moors above Woodhead Tunnel, and others have been partly excavated near Ribblehead.

Disputes between English and Irish navvies were endemic. Hugh McIntosh took the precaution of accommodating them separately when he was building the London & Greenwich Railway in the 1830s, and there was antagonism during the construction of the Shrewsbury & Birmingham in the 1840s. On the Great Western around Bath there was friction between Devonian and Cornish navvies. In 1838 around five hundred local mill workers and Irish navvies battled each other on the North Union line south of Preston, and one man was shot dead. In 1861 on the Severn Valley line, under construction between Bewdley and Shrewsbury, 23 per cent of the workers were Irish-born. One contractor observed that, 'Navvies were the pick of the agricultural districts through which the new railways were being made, both as regard physique and intelligence'. It was an occupation for young men. On the Severn Valley line,

Railway construction on an epic scale: the excavation of Tring Cutting in Hertfordshire on the London & Birmingham Railway, which was opened to traffic in 1838. The engraving by John Cooke Bourne shows the barrow runs up which navvies, with the aid of horse gins, would wheel excavated spoil to the top of the cutting, and which would probably be used for embankments elsewhere on the line. From J. C. Bourne, *Drawings on the London & Birmingham Railway*, London, Ackerman, 1839.

Navvies moving spoil and rubble from a construction site on the Metropolitan Railway, photographed by Henry Flather, about 1861. The Metropolitan Railway was celebrated as the world's first underground railway, but it was constructed using well-established 'cut-and-cover' techniques that had been used for tunnels of considerable size for many years. The busy streets of London in the 1860s provided very different challenges to those faced by the navvies in the much tougher circumstances in the Pennines during the building of the 3-mile long Woodhead Tunnel in the 1840s.

© NATIONAL RAILWAY MUSEUM/SCIENCE & SOCIETY PICTURE LIBRARY

57 per cent were under 30, and 27 per cent between 20 and 24. Typically a young man gained employment with a contractor building a line in his native area, but might then follow the contractor to other parts of the country. When his strength ebbed or he was inclined to marry and settle (60 per cent of those working on the Severn Valley line were bachelors), he would find regular employment, perhaps as a plate-layer or porter. The *Bath Chronicle* observed in 1839 that, 'The navigator appears to belong to no country, he wanders from one public work to another. … Go where he will, he finds some of his comrades whom he has met in some part of England before, and makes enquiries as to their mode of living the wages they were paid since they last met &c.'

In contrast with the dozens employed under the contractor's direct supervision in the eighteenth century, railway contractors employed thousands, often in widely separated parts of the country. The most celebrated, Thomas Brassey, operated on a global scale. A farmer's son born near Chester in 1805, Brassey worked in the 1820s under Telford's direction on the Holyhead Road. Later, while seeking stone for the Sankey Viaduct, he encountered George Stephenson, who encouraged him to tender for the Penkridge section of the Grand Junction Railway. He built other railways in England, and from the 1840s contracted for lines in France, Germany and the Netherlands, as well as the Grand Trunk Railway

of Canada, the Victoria Dock in London, and one of the principal London sewers. His son became an earl.

William Mackenzie, the Lancashire-born son of a Scots contractor, worked on the Leeds & Liverpool Canal, the bridge at Craigellachie and the Union Canal before overseeing the completion of the Gloucester & Berkeley Canal in 1822, and serving as resident engineer for the Mythe Bridge. He worked for Telford on the Birmingham Canal, and then, as contractor, undertook the construction of tunnels on the Liverpool & Manchester Railway, and work on the Midland Counties and Glasgow, Paisley & Greenock railways, and the Shannon Navigation. He also built railways in continental Europe in the 1840s.

Samuel Morton Peto was born to a family of London builders. With a cousin he built Nelson's Column and the two railway stations at Curzon Street, Birmingham, before constructing the section of the Great Western Railway that included the Wharncliffe Viaduct. He built lines in Kent and Sussex, and undertook contracts overseas. He went bankrupt during the financial crisis of 1866, and sold his estate at Somerleyton in Suffolk to the Halifax carpet manufacturer Sir Francis Crossley. Sir John Aird, the principal contractor of the next generation, was the son of a London mason and contractor whose company demolished the Crystal Palace and re-erected it at Sydenham. Aird later built gasworks and waterworks and several railway lines, and carried out many overseas contracts.

The 2,984-yard long Dove Holes Tunnel was built by the Midland Railway in 1860–65 on the line between Peak Forest and Chapel-en-le-Frith by which it gained access to Manchester. It proved to be one of the most difficult of railway construction projects, and six steam engines were needed to pump water from the workings.

© NRM/PICTORIAL COLLECTION/SCIENCE & SOCIETY PICTURE LIBRARY

Understanding the earth beneath

The proliferation of civil engineering projects from the mid-eighteenth century onwards stimulated understanding of the origins of the earth. Those who dug below the surface provided data for the practitioners of the infant science of geology, and their professional expertise was enlarged by what they learned from the scientists. William Hutton of the University of Edinburgh, who was known to Adam Smith and Joseph Black, published *The Theory of the Earth* in 1795. His principles were publicised by the mathematician John Playfair, brother of the engineer William Playfair, a draughtsman with James Watt. Another of Black's scholars, Robert Jameson, was given charge of the university's natural history collection and undertook fieldwork in the Scottish islands and in Ireland. He studied for a year at Freiberg with Abraham Gottlieb Werner before becoming Regius Professor at Edinburgh in 1804, and subsequently tutor to Charles Darwin. He also taught Richard Griffith, a founder member in 1808 of the Geological Society and Professor of Geology in Dublin from 1812, who published geological maps of Ireland, superintended road construction in the southern counties of Ireland from 1822 to 1830, and from 1850 was chairman of the Board of Works. William Reynolds, the Shropshire ironmaster, was said in 1802 to be 'very busy in

exploring the Bowels of Madeley'. He exchanged fossils with Richard Crawshay, and Erasmus Darwin visited his 'Tar Tunnel'.

The connection between excavating canals and geological knowledge is most clearly encapsulated in the career of William Smith, from Churchill, Oxfordshire, who trained as a surveyor, worked on Sapperton Tunnel, and after settling in Somerset in 1791 became engineer to the Somersetshire Coal Canal. He recalled:

> For six years I put my notions of stratification to the test of excavation; and I generally pointed out to contractors and others who came to undertake the work what the various parts of the canal would be dug through. ... This discovery of the mode of identifying the strata by the organized fossils respectively imbedded therein led to the most important distinctions.

Smith was dismissed in 1799, but in 1815 he published his *Geological Map of Britain*, regarded as the foundation of modern geology, which delineates strata and shows the canals, tunnels, tramways, roads and mines which provided his evidence. He was imprisoned for debt and on his release in 1819 made a modest

An example of how construction works led to geological discoveries. The remaining buildings of the Adamantine Clinker and Tile Works near Little Bytham, Lincolnshire, opened in 1854, which specialised in exceptionally hard bricks for use in paving. The bed of clay used at the works was discovered during the construction of the nearby Great Northern Railway which opened in 1851.

living as an itinerant surveyor, but in 1831 he was awarded the first Wollaston Medal of the Geological Society, when Adam Sedgwick, Professor of Geology at Cambridge, acknowledged him as the 'Father of English Geology'. Sedgewick's work was enlightened by research in quarries and mines, as were the studies of less exalted geologists. Thus, the Coventry weaver Joseph Gutteridge spent his leisure time in 1856–57 collecting fossils from the excavations for the Midland Railway's line from Leicester to Bedford.

Civil engineering: an evolving profession

John Smeaton was the first to call himself a civil engineer, intending by so doing to distinguish the work he did from that of the graduates of the Royal Military Academy, Woolwich. It was he who convened the Society of Civil Engineers in 1771, a social group that was renamed the Smeatonians after his death. In 1818 Henry Robinson Palmer, resident engineer at the London Docks, who had been apprenticed to Bryan Donkin, suggested the formation of a learned society for civil engineers. His proposal was supported by Joshua Field, who worked with Henry Maudslay, and William Provis, Telford's assistant on the Birmingham & Liverpool Junction Canal and the Holyhead Road. Provis proposed that Telford should be the inaugural president. The Institution of Civil Engineers was established in Whitehall in 1818 and in Great George Street from 1837. By 1851 there were 2,589 civil engineers in England and Wales. Anthony Trollope regarded civil engineers as 'tradesmen of an upper class, tradesmen with intellects', and the profession suffered from the condescension of those who held themselves aloof from manual labour, unlike Brunel who advised his pupils to avoid French theoretical works since 'a few hours spent in a blacksmith's and wheelwright's shop will teach you more practical mathematics'.

Those who by 1870 were called civil engineers transformed the landscape by building roads, canals and railways, by draining wetlands and by supplying water to and removing sewage from great cities. Their supreme achievement was perhaps the creation of a network of 6,000 miles of main-line railways in scarcely more than 20 years after 1830. Subsequently British engineers, contractors and navvies carried out similar tasks in continental Europe, the United States and throughout the Empire. They applied the results of a learning process involving constructional theory, management techniques and the application of technologies developed in other disciplines.

According to Henry Robinson Palmer the civil engineer was 'a mediator between the philosopher and the working mechanic'. Whether as designer or contractor the engineer had to communicate with the navvy, whose skills gave practical form to his proposals. He was sustained by 'philosophers' of whatever discipline, whose imaginative thinking enabled men to believe that roads might be improved, canals and railways constructed, and cities made healthy.

Driving wheel and nameplate of the locomotive *Rocket*, built by George and Robert Stephenson in 1829.

© NATIONAL RAILWAY MUSEUM/SCIENCE & SOCIETY PICTURE LIBRARY

5

———

Changing horizons:
transport in an industrial age

'Locomotive engines are destined to be the greatest civilisers on the face of our globe.'

HENRY ROBERTSON, 1884

T HE ABILITY to move people and goods more quickly and in greater numbers was one of the most profound changes in British society between 1700 and 1870, made possible by the growing understanding of mechanical and civil engineering described in the preceding chapter. Some changes happened quickly – such as the completion of the Holyhead Road in fifteen years, or the construction of a railway network of 6,000 route miles in little more than two decades, or the introduction from the 1850s of steam-powered iron ships. Others, such as the replacement in the lowlands of packhorses by wheeled vehicles, the multiplication of ships trading with distant countries, and the emergence of networks of country carriers, were more gradual, but they nevertheless contributed greatly in transforming people's possibilities and expectations. The object of this chapter is to examine the social and economic implications of all these changes.

To distant shores in little ships

Britain's fortunes in this period were sustained by overseas trade and coastal shipping. From the eighteenth century many new quays and piers were constructed. There were small wet docks in Liverpool and London in the early eighteenth century, but from the first years of the nineteenth century, when William Jessop was completing the West India Docks in London, they characterised most of the principal British ports. Growth and expansion could be seen everywhere. The opening of the Gloucester & Berkeley Canal in 1827 stimulated the growth of a new port at Gloucester. Three years later Francis Witts observed that the basin was crowded with vessels, that the completed warehouses were busy, and that others were under construction; salt was being exported, and timber brought in from North America, slates from Wales, and wine, wool and barilla from Spain and Portugal. Similarly, the opening in 1826 of a canal parallel to the river Aire, downstream from Knottingley, led to the development of the port of Goole.

Although they became ever more numerous, as late as 1870 the ships that carried most of Britain's trade were remarkably small. The most famous of all contemporary vessels, Nelson's flagship HMS *Victory*, can help make the point. *Victory* was launched at Chatham in 1765 and commissioned in 1778. She was in

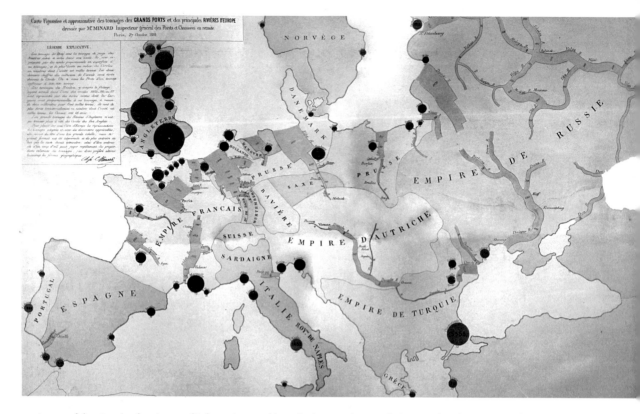

Carte Figurative et approximative des tonnages des GRANDS PORTS et des principales RIVIÈRES D'EUROPE dressée par M. MINARD Inspecteur général des Ponts et Chaussées en retraite.
Paris, 27 Octobre 1859.

LÉGENDE EXPLICATIVE.

⏶ A map of the 1850s by the pioneer of information graphics, Charles Joseph Minard, showing the relative status of sea and river ports in Europe. The preponderance of trade in the ports of the British Isles is immediately evident.

⏴ HMS *Victory* in Portsmouth harbour with a coal ship alongside, 1828, an etching after his own drawing by Edward William Cooke, of possibly the most famous warship in the history of the Royal Navy. *Victory* was the flagship of Admiral Lord Nelson at the Battle of Trafalgar in 1805. She was built at Chatham in 1759–65 to the design of Sir Thomas Slade, and then rebuilt between 1800 and 1803. At Trafalgar she carried a total of 102 guns. *Victory*'s active career ended in 1812, and in 1922 she was moved to Portsmouth dockyard, where she has been restored and attracts some 350,000 visitors a year as a tourist attraction. Illustration from Cooke's *Fifty plates of shipping and craft* published in London in 1829. The relatively small size of the collier alongside is immediately evident.

service until 1812 and then lay moored at Portsmouth until 1922, when she was placed in dry dock. *Victory*, one of three ships with more than 100 guns to fight at Trafalgar, is 227 feet (70 m) long overall, displaces 3,500 tons, and was one of the largest ships of her time. Later, when they were used as convict hulks in the river Thames, ships of her era and type towered above merchant sailing ships using the Port of London. Until late in the nineteenth century merchant ships were all much smaller than the *Victory*. Most long-distance trade was carried in three-masted sailing ships of a type not dissimilar to that developed in Europe in the fifteenth century.

Throughout the period from 1700 to 1860, at small shipyards on river banks and on the shores of sheltered harbours in many parts of Britain, were constructed wooden vessels for river navigations, coastal trade and ocean voyages. Constructional techniques changed slowly, and the most significant innovations did not involve new constructional techniques. Copper sheathing and bolts were applied to deter maritime pests, enabling warships and merchantmen to make longer voyages in distant waters (see also the section on copper, pages 363–4). Sir Marc Brunel's block-making machines installed at Portsmouth between 1801 and 1844 (see page 76) accelerated the production of essential components. Increasing quantities of wrought iron became available for anchors and for small fastenings

The first wet dock in the port of Bristol was built at Sea Mills in 1712, but was succeeded from 1768 by Champion's Wet Dock, later called Merchants' Dock, on the river Avon about a mile downstream from the city centre.

CARNEGIE COLLECTION

One of the main shipbuilding yards at Lancaster was begun by George Brockbank in the early eighteenth century and built ships on the riverbank here until 1822. The average tonnage of ships built was just 200 tons. After Skerton Bridge was built across the river Lune in 1788 Brockbanks purchased the old medieval bridge and in 1802 removed one arch, as can be seen here, so that their new vessels could be floated downstream. In the background can be seen the river quay and associated warehouses of this prosperous Georgian port.

BY COURTESY OF LANCASTER MARITIME MUSEUM

The 'East Indiamen', ships operated for the Honourable East India Company, were among the largest merchant vessels to sail in British waters. The *Herefordshire*, shown off Margate in 1813, was built in Bombay, had a crew of 130 men and was armed with 36 guns. As was common with pictures of vessels painted for their owners, she is shown in three positions on the same painting – broadside, from the bow and from the stern. She was built to the specifications of the company, but was privately owned.

Double-hulled pleasure steamboat, 1788, a lithograph by C. F. Cheffins after a drawing by John C. Bourne, after an oil painting by Alexander Nasmyth, of the boat which featured the first marine steam engine. Patrick Miller, an Edinburgh banker, commissioned mining engineer William Symington to build a steam engine to power this experimental craft. The engine had two single-action cylinders, with separate condensers, which drove two paddle shafts by chains and ratchets, and propelled the steamboat on Dalswinton Loch, near Dumfries, Scotland, at five knots. Symington's engine is now in the Science Museum. Illustration from 'A sketch of the origin and progress of steam navigation from authentic documents' by steam navigation pioneer Bennet Woodcroft, published in London in 1848.

and fittings. The ironmaster Alexander Brodie who had works near the Iron Bridge and in London began to manufacture cast-iron stoves that could heat cabins safely in rough weather. Shipyards were dependent on supplies of oak mostly supplied by river, brought down the Severn from mid-Wales to builders in the Ironbridge Gorge, Bridgnorth and Chepstow and carried from the High Weald to the yards along the Lower Medway. Shipbuilding also required 'naval stores', the collective name given to the softwoods, principally white pine, used as masts, spars and yard arms, the various derivatives of pine resin such as tar, pitch and turpentine, and hemp and flax necessary for cordage and sail making. Naval stores were imported from the Baltic, but during the eighteenth century the Atlantic coast of North America became the principal source of supply. Some sea-going vessels were constructed at considerable distances from the coast, a notable example being the *William*, built at Benthall in the Ironbridge Gorge in 1809, which was too large to work on the upper Severn, but made her living in the coastal trade in the Bristol Channel until she sank in 1939 while being towed from Cardiff to Bristol. The

naval yards at Chatham, Portsmouth and Plymouth were among the largest industrial concerns in Britain, but most shipbuilding concerns were of modest size employing only a dozen or so men.

Some of the ships that carried Britain's trade and maintained her naval superiority in distant waters were manufactured overseas. Shipbuilders in India could use teak, a timber more resistant than oak to pests and decay, and vessels built there could be expected to have a working life of more than 50 years. The East India Company established a shipyard in 1675 at Mumbai (Bombay) where a dry dock was constructed about 1750, and between 1735 and 1863 built there about 170 vessels for its own use. The Royal Navy ordered significant numbers of ships from Indian builders in the first half of the nineteenth century. Two were particularly notable for their longevity. HMS *Cornwallis*, a 75-gun vessel built at Bombay in 1813, was converted to screw propulsion in 1855, used as a jetty at Sheerness from 1865, and was not broken up until 1957. HMS *Ganges* was constructed at Bombay in 1821, passed into training use in 1905, and was broken up at Plymouth in 1930.

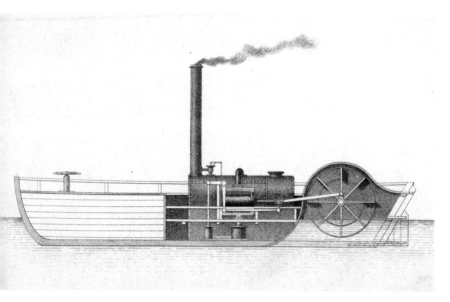

A diagram of the machinery of the *Charlotte Dundas*, 1803, a lithograph by C. F. Cheffins after a drawing by H. B. Barlow, of the 10 nominal horsepower engine designed and built by William Symington, British pioneer of marine steam propulsion. The *Charlotte Dundas* was used on the Forth & Clyde Canal by Lord Dundas of Kerse for experiments on the use of steam tugs instead of horses for towing vessels and barges.

Built of wood at Bristol to the plans of Isambard Kindom Brunel for the Great Western Steamship Company, the SS *Great Western* sailed between Bristol and New York 64 times in all between 1838 and 1846. She could accommodate up to 300 passengers and crew and was sold to the Royal Mail Steam Packet Co. Ltd to run between Southampton and the West Indies in 1847. She was broken up in 1857.

The launch of the SS *Great Britain* on 19 July 1843 from the same dock at Bristol in which she has been displayed to visitors since the 1970s. The *Great Britain* was laid down just three years after Brunel's *Great Western*, but during this period two important decisions were made: the first, inspired by a test voyage on the Channel packet *Rainbow*, was to build the hull of iron rather than of oak; the second, based on the success of London-built SS *Archimedes*, was to employ a screw propeller rather than paddle wheels.

At almost 19,000 tons the SS *Great Eastern* was the largest ship launched in the period covered by this book, vastly bigger than most merchant ships of the time; not surprisingly, during the 1850s the 'leviathan' under construction was one of the must-see sights of London. This view of the ship on the stocks on the banks of the Isle of Dogs is taken from *A Pictorial History of the Great Eastern Steam Ship*, published soon after she was launched on 12 January 1858. (See also page 542.)

The Maritime Provinces of Canada also built ships in considerable numbers. About 85 per cent of New Brunswick is forested and in the first half of the nineteenth century ships were built seasonally as speculations on beaches all along the shores of the province. Most were taken to St John for fitting by the smiths, ropemakers and sailmakers of the provincial capital. In December 1854 a sale of merchant vessels in Liverpool followed the death of the ship broker Edward Oliver a few months earlier. Of the 76 ships in the sale, 53 had been built in British North America, 19 in New Brunswick, 18 in Quebec, 14 in Nova Scotia and 2 on Prince Edward Island. The sale also illustrates the relatively small size of most merchant vessels; 35 were of less than 500 tons, 36 between 500 and 999 tons, and only seven of more than 1,000 tons.

Most traded goods in the 1860s travelled in wooden sailing ships, but steamships of iron construction were increasingly used in some trades, such as the carriage of coal from north-eastern England to London (see pages 221, 223–4). While the building of wooden ships was widely dispersed, the construction of iron steamships depended on the availability of wrought-iron (later steel) plates rolled to appropriate sizes and on engineering concerns that could supply engines. Iron ships could not be constructed on beaches, but required slipways or docks, and, as their size increased, they required investment in cranes and of ranges of workshops where rivets could be manufactured and plates prepared for fitting. The increasing size of vessels demanded access to deep water, which in part explains the decline of shipyards in London where the construction of iron ships had developed in the early nineteenth century (see pages 540–2). The industry came to be concentrated along the Clyde, the Tyne and the Wear, where it was interdependent with local ironmakers, but also on the Mersey and in Belfast where Sir Edward Harland and Gustav Wilhelm Wolff formed a partnership in 1861 and opened their yard on New Queen's Island in the following year. Building iron steamships was highly competitive which led to constant downward pressure on wages, and consequently to uneasy industrial relations.

The first successful experiments in steam propulsion of vessels were carried out in 1788 by William Symington, and the first practical steamship was the wooden-hulled *Charlotte Dundas*, which pulled two 70-ton barges on the Forth & Clyde Canal in 1802. *Comet*, designed by Henry Bell, began working as a tug between Glasgow and Greenock in 1812. Two years later *Margery* was the first steamship on the river Thames, and in 1816 became the first to cross the English Channel. *Rob Roy* began a regular service between Dover and Calais in 1821. The paddle steamer *Witham*, launched on 26 May 1816, began a packet service between Lincoln and Boston, and *Lady of the Shannon* commenced work on Ireland's eponymous principal river in the same year. *Savannah* crossed the Atlantic in 1819 using paddles to supplement her sails, but *Sirius*, which just beat I. K. Brunel's *Great Western* across the ocean in 1838, was the first vessel to do so using sustained steam power. Brunel's 3,675-ton SS *Great Britain*, launched at Bristol on 19 July 1843, was the first iron-hulled screw-driven vessel. She, and the 18,910 ton *Great Eastern*, launched at Millwall on 12 January 1858 and powered by sails, paddles and a screw propeller, presaged a future of large iron-hulled vessels driven by steam. Iron ships multiplied in the 1860s, but no larger vessel than the *Great Eastern* was launched until 1899, and sailing ships of advanced design, such as the 963-ton *Cutty Sark*, built of American elm planking bolted to an internal iron frame and launched at Dumbarton in 1868, continued to be built. The transition from sail to steam was inexorable, but it was not always speedy. As Professor Slaven points out in a new survey of the British shipbuilding industry: 'Even by 1850 sail tonnage represented 89 per cent of all output [of British shipbuilding yards], and wood provided 90 per cent of all hull tonnage. The wood and sail industry was then approaching its maximum scale, reaching that position in 1855.' Until as late as 1890 Liverpool, Britain's second largest port, was frequented by a greater number, and larger tonnage, of sailing vessels than of steam-powered ships. But iron ships powered by steam were much more productive than wooden sailing vessels of comparable size, and the superior modern technology was ultimately bound to prevail.

Coastal shipping

Dirty British coaster with a salt-caked smoke
   stack
Butting through the Channel in the mad
   March days,
With a cargo of Tyne coal,
Road-rail, pig lead,
Firewood, iron-ware and cheap tin trays.

These lines come from John Masefield's *Cargoes*, a poem first published in 1902. Significantly, perhaps, the poet saves his description of the humble British coaster for the final stanza, for these small, unremarkable vessels were often overshadowed by the great ocean-going liners and cargo vessels that took pride of place in the docks of London, Liverpool or New York. Yet, in the early nineteenth century Britain had dozens of little ports – many in seemingly remote or unlikely locations – which were visited by a wide range of small coastal traders as well as larger overseas vessels. The 1861 census, despite being inconsistent in its recording of vessels, shows the interdependence of coastal and overseas shipping. For example, the eight ships trading overseas which were moored at Gloucester at this time ranged from a 74-ton schooner to a barque of 320 tons. They included three registered at Sunderland, and others from South Shields, Plymouth, New Quay (Cardiganshire), Bridgwater and Wick. Twenty coasting vessels, ranging from 19 to 91 tons, originated from ports including Greenock, Barmouth, Aberystwyth, Padstow, Hayle and Weymouth. There were also 28 vessels involved in inland navigation, from such places as Ironbridge, Hereford, Lechlade, Stourport and Droitwich. In the same year, of 40 vessels on the river Medway near Maidstone 35 were

This picture, although of much later date than 1870, shows something of the nature of coastal shipping that was an important part of the transport system in the British Isles throughout the period covered by this book. The *Roman*, built by J. & J. Hay of Kirkintilloch in 1904, has been beached at Kilchattan Bay on the southern tip of the Isle of Bute, and is taking on a cargo of potatoes.

This picture of *circa* 1893 shows the SS *Robin* moored at the herring fishing station at Lerwick in the Shetland Islands, probably collecting a cargo of barrels of salted herring for export to continental Europe.

Sailing ships carried slate from the ports of Gwynedd all around the British coast and to many overseas destinations. Y Felinheli (previously Port Dinorwic), a small port on the Menai Strait between Bangor and Caernarfon was established in the late eighteenth century by the owners of the Dinorwig slate quarries five miles inland. The quarries were taken over in 1809 by a consortium of investors headed by Thomas Assheton-Smith. The new owners invested in 1812 in railways within the quarry, and in 1825 constructed a railway to the coast, which was replaced in 1842–43 by the 4 ft gauge Padarn Railway. This picture shows the vast numbers of slates that were in transit from the quarries of North Wales at any particular time.

Coastal and overseas trade at ports in the British Isles was controlled from custom houses, one of the most distinguished of which was the building in the Palladian style at Limerick, designed by Davis Ducart and completed in 1769. It now accommodates the city's Hunt Museum.

registered locally, 2 were from London, and the others from Boston, Goole and Hull. They were loading stone, chalk, cement, lime and bricks, while the *John & George* of Goole had delivered coal taken aboard at Sunderland, while the *Kent & Sussex* of Maidstone had brought general cargo from West India Dock. Only one vessel at Maidstone and one at Gloucester were powered by steam.

The interface between coasting and inland navigation is also apparent from the 1861 census in East Anglia. At King's Lynn there were 20 sea-going trading vessels, including one from Holland and two from Hanover, and about 20 lighters from the Fenland river ports of Cambridge, Earith, St Ives and Littleport. There were 21 sea-going ships at Wisbech, including one from Denmark, and the 90-ton *Idris* of Aberdyfi.

A Swedish ship with a crew of eight was moored at Wells-next-the-Sea alongside two local sloops recently arrived from Goole. Four vessels at Blakeney included the 98-ton coaster *Kingston* of Plymouth and the 71-ton *Omnibus* of Aberystwyth. There were five vessels at Snape in Suffolk, all locally registered, and eight at Woodbridge. The 53-ton *Germ* from Goole had entered the port from London and was loading at the Lime Kiln Quay, while the 54-ton *Maria* of London was taking on grain. The 13 vessels at Mistley, above Harwich, included three from Prussia and three from Denmark, others from Goole, Cromer, Rochester and Castletown, Isle of Man, and a Colchester-based river barge. There were 25 vessels at Maldon, including one from Norway and one from Fowey, recently arrived from Runcorn. Three had brought in coal – the 170-ton

The river Stour in Suffolk was made navigable as far upstream as the town of Sudbury in 1713. This warehouse at the head of navigation is of rather later date.

Maldon-based *Joanna* from Blyth, the 125-ton *Holker* from Seahouses, and the diminutive 5-ton *Caesar* of Colchester, from Sunderland. Several sprit-sail barges were loading hay and straw for London. The five trading vessels at Burnham-on-Crouch included a Norwegian vessel, the 34-ton *Azur* from Jersey, and *John Tinnell* of Rochester, which had arrived from Deptford and was engaged in the lime trade.

The bustle of a small port is depicted in Beatrix Potter's 'Stymouth', modelled on Lyme Regis which she visited in 1883. She saw coal being unloaded from the *Margery Dawe* of Sunderland and the *Jenny Jones* of Cardiff, while the *Pound of Candles* took aboard mixed cargo; fish boxes were stowed on a small steamer, the *Goldielocks* was discharging oranges, and the brig *Little Bo Peep* of Bristol was loading wool. There were five coasting vessels at Lyme Regis on 7 April 1861, ranging from a 25-ton sloop arrived from Paignton to a 128-ton schooner. The 76-ton *Henrietta* of Swansea had recently arrived from Berehaven, Co. Cork.

Other small ports were similarly busy. Eight trading vessels in Rye harbour included the 160-ton schooner *Emily* of St Ives and the 71-ton schooner *Leander* of Aberystwyth, as well as barges on the river. In Wainfleet Haven (Lincolnshire) were *William*, a 42-ton sloop registered at Boston, and *Effort*, a 37-ton coasting barge from Grimsby. The 42-ton sloop *William* of Liverpool and the 33-ton lugger *John* of Fleetwood were at Holker in Furness, which hardly merited the label 'port', while at Glasson Dock, as well as four barges from the Lancaster Canal, were a steamer and a schooner from Lancaster, a 67-ton coasting schooner from Wexford, and a 391-ton Liverpool-registered barque trading with North America.

River navigations extended upstream from the estuaries of the principal rivers, including the Mersey, the Severn, the Thames, the Humber, and the rivers draining into the Wash. Improvement schemes before 1800 made it possible for barges to reach Stamford on the Welland, Sudbury on the Suffolk Stour, Northampton on the Nene, Tonbridge on the Medway, and Manchester on the Irwell. Hallamshire cutlers and steel makers used the tiny, somewhat unlikely river port at Bawtry on the Idle, a tributary of the Trent, before the construction of the Don Navigation in the later eighteenth century. The vessels employed on each system – the 'boats', barges and trows on the Severn, the flats on the Mersey, the keels on the Humber – were all fairly similar sailing boats, but each had features which, whatever their size, distinguished them from those on other rivers. Some coastal flats were built with lowering masts so that they could negotiate bridges on inland waterways such as the Douglas Navigation in Lancashire, while the carvel construction and overall design of these vessels inspired early types of wooden canal barge. On the tidal Thames, meanwhile, large numbers of unpowered lighters were 'swept' up and down the river on the flow and tide, servicing the merchantmen that were moored in the river or tied up at the wharfs and even in the enclosed docks. Roads provided 'land bridges' between river navigations. Thus, it was established practice in the 1740s for goods bound from the upper Severn to London to be taken to John Jones's wharf at Gloucester, then by road to the Lechlade warehouses of Richard Ainge, successor in the trade to his father and grandfather, who took them down the Thames.

The Severn, a tempestuous river draining an enormous catchment in Wales, was an open and almost unobstructed navigation, since the difference between summer and winter levels was too great to make the construction of weirs and mills feasible. It could scarcely be navigated at times of flood, and loads had to be reduced when waters were low. General merchandise was taken downstream by two or three trows from Bewdley twice a month to meet the spring and neap tides at Gloucester, sailing onwards to Bristol or Bridgwater, although some boats also reached the estuary from ports farther upstream in Shropshire. Packhorses and waggons carried manufactured goods to the river ports at Bewdley and Bridgnorth, principally 'Manchester packs' with varied textile products, 'Staffordshire crates' filled with pottery from around Stoke-on-Trent, and hardware from Birmingham and the Black Country. Such traffic was transferred to the canals after the Staffordshire & Worcestershire Canal reached Stourport in 1772, and was carried in canal boats until the 1840s when it passed to the railways.

The port books of Gloucester give a valuable insight by showing the kinds of cargo that were carried in each direction by the boats of one family, the Beales, principal owners in Bewdley in the first half of the eighteenth century:

---

16 January (NS) 1724: *Hopewell*, of Bewdley, merchant John Beale;
master Thomas Steward, downstream from Bewdley to Bristol

35 tons iron & iron ware	10 packs/trusses Kidderminster stuff
30 cases/crates glass and glasses	20 reams paper
41 packs Manchester goods and thread	1 puppet show and materials
1 hogshead white leather	5 bags wick yarn
1 pack white leather	5 tons timber and timber stuff
1 ton tanned leather	3 dozen lanthorns
3 casks fish	10 boxes/chests millinery/hardware

30 June 1724: *Hopewell*, of Bewdley, merchant John Beale, master Thomas Steward,
upstream from Bristol

26 tons English iron	9 hogsheads train oil
5 tons grocery and saltery, 4 hogsheads	1 case white lead
2 tons brass and battery	2 bags corks
4 tons foreign iron and steel	4 trusses cloth and serge
2 tons coco wood	1 cwt soap, 2 boxes
1 ton lignum vitae	36 gallons Spanish wine
100 of ox and cow horns	1 ton earthenware
4 barrels tar	100 gallons British spirits, 1 hogshead
3 bags old wool cards	300 lb tobacco, 3 casks
6 packs girth web	200 dozen glass bottles
60 deal boards	3 cane chairs

We know from the researches of Mary Prior that there were two communities of boatmen on the Thames at Oxford, one at Grandpont near Folly Bridge who worked to London, the other at Fisher Row who sailed boats upstream to Lechlade. Defoe observed West of England barges at Reading lightening their loads before proceeding upstream, having brought coal, salt, groceries and tobacco from the capital. They returned with malt, meal and timber from the Chilterns, and *en route* loaded malt, meal and beechwood at Marlow. The river Great Ouse was navigable to Bedford, and communities of merchants grew up in St Ives and other riverside towns. The extension of drainage schemes allowed barges to reach almost every hamlet in the Fens. In 1811 William Gooch described how connected waterways served Peterborough, Ely, Stamford, Bedford, St Ives, Huntingdon, St Neots, Northampton, Cambridge, Bury St Edmunds and

Ely owed much of its prosperity in the eighteenth and nineteenth centuries to the river Great Ouse which gave it access to the sea through the port of King's Lynn, and to numerous inland towns. These warehouses, now adapted as apartments, would have been busy with trade in 1870.

The river Great Ouse at St Ives, in the ancient county of Huntingdon, immediately upstream from the town's medieval bridge. Several of the principal barge owners on the Great Ouse lived in St Ives, some of them in this row of houses fronting the river.

Thetford, bringing coal and salt from Newcastle, softwoods, iron and forest products from Scandinavia, and wine from Portugal, while despatching wheat, rye, oats and barley. On the Trent Defoe saw salt, hemp, flax and iron from northern Europe unloaded at Nottingham, and downstream traffic in lead, wood, cheese and corn. Cheese from Cheshire bound for London was either taken by coastal shipping round Land's End, or by road to Wilden Ferry on the Trent and thence by river and by sea from Hull. The coastal carriage of cheese persisted as late as 1804, when shares were being offered at Chester in four 125-ton cheese ships.

Transporting goods by canal and inland waterway

The range of inland navigation was greatly increased by the building of canals, of which some 4,000 miles were built in England and Wales between 1760 and 1850. However, it could be difficult for vessels to navigate both coastal and inland waterways, with the size of locks being one limiting factor. Canal building in Britain began 50 years after the Mediterranean and Atlantic coasts of France had been linked by the Canal du Midi. The first British canal, serving the collieries near Coalisland, Co. Tyrone, was built between 1730 and 1744. In England, as noted in the previous chapter (page 123), the Sankey Canal, completed in 1759, connecting the St Helens area to the Mersey and thus to Liverpool, enabled Lancashire coal to be carried to Cheshire saltmakers. The canal on the estate of the 3rd Duke of Bridgewater was completed in 1761, linking his collieries at Worsley with Castlefield on the edge of Manchester, and triumphantly bridging the river Irwell at Barton. The Bridgewater Canal became an object of curiosity, particularly from 1766 when packet boats began to carry passengers, including Jean-Jacques Rousseau, to view the mines at Worsley. Other coal-carrying canals that opened in the next 40 years were important over short distances. The Birmingham Canal was opened to Wednesbury in 1769, amid enthusiastic celebrations, its Old Wharf fronting Suffolk Street being a flamboyant symbol of canal prosperity. In front of the twin basins was a central three-storey octagonal building (with a broken pediment framing a medallion in the central bay) linked by a pair of arches – each with a room above lit by a Diocletian window – to two-storey blocks on either side, with Venetian windows on the first floor. The Coventry Canal began to deliver Bedworth coal to the city in 1771; the Monkland Canal carried coal into Glasgow from 1791; and the Derby and Nottingham canals opened in 1796. The supply of coal to Leeds was improved not by canal but by the Middleton Railway, originally a horse-drawn waggonway that was authorised by Parliament and which opened in 1758 (see pages 248–9).

From the 1760s a wider network that could distribute goods over greater distances began to be envisaged. A direct waterway link between Manchester and Liverpool was the intention of the Act of Parliament of 1762 which permitted the extension of the Bridgewater Canal from Longford Bridge at Stretford to the river Mersey at Runcorn; Runcorn thus became the first of the towns which developed where narrow canals met river navigations. In 1766 an Act was obtained for the Trent & Mersey – or Grand Trunk – Canal, which crossed the Midlands from Preston Brook on the Bridgewater Canal, passing

through the Harecastle Tunnel and the Potteries to join the Trent at Derwentmouth near Shardlow. A meeting of proprietors at Lichfield on 15 December 1769 settled the dimensions of the narrow boats for which locks on the Midlands canals were to be built: 70 feet long (21.34 m), 7 feet in beam (2.13 m), with a cabin 10 feet long (3.08 m) in the stern. The capacity could be 35 tons, but in practice most boats carried between 20 and 25 tons. Traders in towns were desperate to secure connections to the waterway networks, and a spate of parliamentary bills proposing new canals were approved in the early 1790s, the period of the 'canal mania'. A paper promoting the Lancaster Canal – one of the broad canals that were built in the North – in 1791 declared that 'a Canal is now become as necessary an Appendage to a Manufacturing or Commercial Town as a Turnpike Road'. Some Acts were never implemented, while other canals, such as the Ellesmere and the Lancaster, remained incomplete. The latter was begun in 1792 and reached Kendal in 1819, but the planned magnificent aqueduct across the Ribble at Preston was never built, partly, it was claimed, because of the huge cost of Rennie's Lune Aqueduct farther north. Instead, a horse-drawn tramroad, with a steam-driven incline up from the banks of the Ribble, filled the gap between the Lancaster and the Leeds & Liverpool throughout the canal's working life.

Vessels on the river Thomas depicted by J.C. Bourne near the bridge carrying the Great Western Railway at Basildon, Berkshire. Compared with the feverish activity of the lighters on the Thames in London, traffic on the river through the Home Counties was relatively sparse, but nonetheless important. In the eighteenth century 'West of England' barges, such as the one on the left of this group of vessels, took upstream shop goods and coal from the North East, returning with agricultural produce and wood from the Chilterns. After the opening of the Oxford Canal in 1790 narrow boats from the Midlands canals, such as the two shown by Bourne, were able to carry coal to communities along the Thames and its tributaries.
AUTHOR COLLECTION

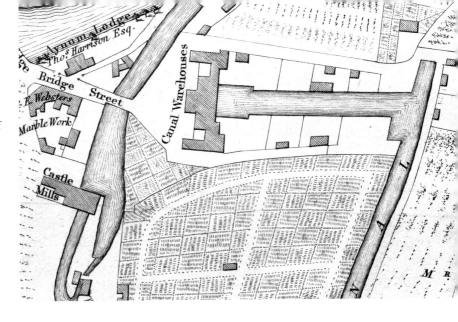

The Kendal terminus of the Lancaster & Kendal Canal, with adjacent mills and manufactories, depicted on a map of Kendal published in 1833 by John Wood of Edinburgh.

PHOTOGRAPH CARNEGIE, BY COURTESY OF WESTMORLAND RECORD OFFICE, KENDAL

By 1790 all the principal estuary navigations of southern Britain were connected by canal. In 1772 the 46½-mile Staffordshire & Worcestershire Canal was opened, linking the Grand Trunk at Great Haywood with the river Severn at Lower Mitton, where the town of Stourport grew up. At Aldersley Junction near Wolverhampton it was joined by the Birmingham Canal Navigation. In 1790 the completion of the Coventry and Oxford canals created a route from Fradley Junction near Lichfield on the Grand Trunk, past Hawkesbury Junction, and south through Banbury to the Thames at Oxford. It was joined to the Birmingham system at Fazeley. A more direct route from the Midlands to London opened in 1805 with the completion, after many tribulations, of the Blisworth Tunnel. The Grand Junction Canal extended 93½ miles from Braunston on the Oxford Canal to Brentford on the Thames. Braunston was linked to Birmingham by the Warwick & Napton and Warwick & Birmingham canals which opened in 1800. The Thames & Severn Canal opened in 1789 and with the Stroudwater Navigation created a route from Framilode on the Severn to Lechlade on the Thames, but it failed to generate significant traffic to and from London. The completion of the Kennet & Avon Canal in 1810 created a route from London to Bristol, while since the late 1770s the Dudley and Stourbridge canals had provided an outlet to the Severn from the Black Country coalfield. A five-mile branch of the Grand Junction from Blisworth to the river Nene at Northampton, opened in 1815, linked the Midlands with the waterways in eastern England.

Waterways in the North were mostly broad, built to allow vessels up to 14 feet in beam to use their locks. The first of these was the Aire & Calder Navigation, authorised in 1699. In time no fewer than three routes crossed the Pennines. First, the Huddersfield (narrow) Canal was authorised in 1794 and opened in 1811 from Ashton-under-Lyne to Cooper's Bridge near Huddersfield. The Rochdale Canal, also sanctioned in 1794, ran from Sowerby Bridge on the Calder & Hebble Navigation to join the Bridgewater Canal at Castlefield, and was opened in 1804. The Leeds & Liverpool Canal was authorised in 1770 and construction work began at both ends. By 1776 the canal had been completed from Liverpool to Wigan and from Leeds to Gargrave, but then the money ran out, and not until 1816 was the 116-mile route completed, at a cost of £878,000 – or almost four times the original estimate. In Ireland the 79-mile Grand Canal from Dublin to Shannon Harbour in Co. Offaly, authorised in 1755, was completed in 1804. Dublin was also linked with the Shannon at Cloondara by the Royal Canal, opened to Mullingar in 1806 and Cloondara in 1817, and extended to Longford in 1830.

Just as river traffic elided into coastal shipping, there were overlaps between the operations on canals and rivers such as the lower Severn, the waterways of Yorkshire and Lincolnshire and the Mersey estuary. On the Bristol Avon at Bath seven narrow boats kept company on census night in 1861 with a trow from Gloucester and a 50-ton barge from Bristol. There were 38 boats at Isleworth and Brentford where the Grand Junction Canal joined the river Thames. They included locally registered barges of up to 70 tons, carrying bricks, sand and lime, one of which had come upstream from West India Dock, a 37-ton barge involved in the 'country trade' on the Thames, two 70-ton barges recently arrived from Deptford and Gravesend, and 30 narrow boats, mostly from the Black Country.

New stretches of canal were still being built in the 1830s, the last major project on the network being the Netherton Tunnel in the Black Country, completed in 1858. The Grand Junction company built the steam-powered narrow boat *Pioneer* in 1859, and before long steam-tugs were in use towing trains of narrow boats through the longer tunnels which lacked towpaths, such as those at Braunston and Blisworth where tugging began in 1871. Yet most boats in 1870 were still drawn by horses, as indeed they were until the adoption of oil engines in the twentieth century.

It was the short-distance carriage of bulk materials, particularly coal, that sustained the first generation of canals. Industry in the Black Country grew up in locations that made it dependent on day-boats on the Birmingham Canal Navigation and, although it took 46 years to complete the Leeds & Liverpool Canal, the sections that were opened in Yorkshire and Lancashire in the 1770s quickly became busy with industrial traffic. In South Wales the Brecknock & Abergavenny, Monmouth, Glamorganshire and Neath canals made possible the remarkable growth of the iron industry, but had no direct links with the national network. In Scotland short-distance traffic in minerals on the Forth & Clyde Canal was more important than through-carriage from Grangemouth to Bowling's Bay.

Heavy industrial traffic did not constitute the full picture, however, and canal carriers, specialising in general commercial business, soon appeared. Thus, the completion of the Grand Trunk Canal in 1777 opened up the prospect of boats carrying shop goods and export consignments. The first canal-carrying concern appears to have been established by Hugh Henshall, a surveyor, and brother-in-law of James Brindley. He was involved with carrying by 1772, and Hugh

Henshall & Co., based at Stone, Staffordshire, became the carrying company of the Trent & Mersey proprietors. It built the Grocers' Warehouse at Castlefield, Manchester, in about 1780. The dominant carrying company in the North West was that managed by the Duke of Bridgewater's trustees, which worked several hundred canal and river boats from Worsley. The headquarters of the Manchester road-carrying concern established by James Pickford was relocated to London by his son in 1756. By 1777 the company was responsible for six weekly fly waggon departures in each direction, but canal carrying began in 1778 and already in the following year Pickfords had 28 boats, as well as 50 waggons and 400 horses. They began carrying by canal between Manchester and London in 1796, using the railway between Blisworth and Stoke Bruerne while the Blisworth Tunnel was being completed. In 1801 the company opened a warehouse at the Paddington basin of the Grand Junction Canal, and in 1820 moved its London operation to the City Road Basin on the Regent's Canal; in 1836 Pickfords were working 116 canal boats.

In the 1820s Thomas Monk of Tipton operated a fleet of 130 cabin boats carrying general cargoes from London to the Midlands, returning with bedsteads and other Black Country products, and also ran a service on three days a week from 1820 until 1853 'for the accommodation of Passengers & conveyance of Parcels' aboard the *Euphrates Packet*, which reached Birmingham in two hours from Tipton. In 1841 James Fellows, who began canal carrying at West Bromwich in 1837, transferred his base to Toll End, Tipton, and specialised in taking iron products to London. He had 50 boats by the 1860s, and in 1876 and 1889 his descendants combined the company with others to form Fellows, Morton & Clayton, the best-known canal carrying company.

By the early nineteenth century these, and other firms such as Crowley, Hicklin & Batty, Worthington Gilbert and many local concerns, were available to carry small consignments of merchandise almost anywhere on the national waterway network. Shropshire provides a good example. In the eighteenth century its towns were supplied with goods by barges on the Severn and by road transport, but

Roving bridges, by which horses towing boats could cross a canal where the towpath changed sides, were a common feature of British waterways. This example is near Hyde on the Peak Forest Canal.

Canal junctions usually attracted clusters of buildings where goods were handled and boats were serviced, and where those working on the waterway could find accommodation. At the junction of the Ashton-under-Lyne Canal, opened in 1796, and the Peak Forest Canal opened the following year grew up the complex known as Portland Basin. The brick warehouse in the background was built in 1834, has been restored since a damaging fire in 1973, and now houses a museum of social and industrial history. The arched stone bridge carrying the towpath over the Peak Forest Canal dates from 1835.

The picturesque flight of locks at Tring was part of the Grand Junction Canal from Braunston to Brentford that linked London with the Midlands from 1805.

from the 1790s onwards most consignments appear to have been delivered by road from canal wharfs at Wolverhampton. Then, in 1835, the county gained a direct link to the national network with the opening of the Newport Arm of the Birmingham & Liverpool Junction Canal. Accounts from Wappenshall Wharf on the estate of the 2nd Duke of Sutherland make it possible to examine traffic in detail. Iron-working companies despatched coal and iron, and brought in limestone from North Wales, but the inward traffic was diverse. Cargoes unloaded during March and April 1835, for example, included a very wide range of general goods: sugar, salt, slates, tobacco, bags of corks, coffee, rice, molasses, corn, glass, soap, flax, sulphur, malt, raisins, oranges, lemons, tallow, rum, currants, beans, wine, herrings, gunpowder, vinegar, treacle, shovels, hops, carpets, spades, seeds and sacking. An article in *Household Words* in 1858 described London's City Road basin as full of 'goods, bales, boxes, casks and cases', and of 'wagons, horses, cranes, bales and men', who included bargemen 'dressed in their short fustian trousers, heavy boots, red plush jackets, waistcoats with pearl buttons and fustian sleeves and gay silk handkerchiefs slug loosely round their necks'. Thirteen vessels with crews on board were moored in the basin on 7 April 1861, when ten boatmen employed by the Grand Junction slept at a nearby beerhouse.

From the late 1830s, as a national network evolved, railways began to capture much of the traffic in sundries, and virtually all the passenger trade. In 1847 Pickfords stopped using canal boats for traffic between London and Manchester and three years later withdrew from canal carrying altogether. The Grand Junction then began carrying on its own account and did so until 1881. Nevertheless, many of the patterns of canal trade established between 1790 and 1830 persisted for decades and in some cases – as with the carriage of Midlands coal to the paper mills around Oxford and in the Gade Valley (Hertfordshire) – into the mid-twentieth century. Coal, iron, limestone, clay and bricks were carried by canal boat over short distances in the major coalfields, in Yorkshire, Lancashire, the Black Country and South Wales, until changes in those industries removed the need for such journeys. As late as 1962 a horse-drawn boat, its day's work completed, could still be seen,

silhouetted against an autumn sunset, as it made its way home along the high embankment of the Tame Valley Canal near West Bromwich.

River navigation was constrained by custom, but most canals were open to all carriers, subject to the rules and tolls imposed by the companies. Coal merchants in market towns bought boats which they sent to colliery wharfs for supplies. When a saltworks near Middlewich was offered for sale in 1805 four boats navigating on the canal and four boat horses were included. The Coalbrookdale Company in 1805 began to operate its own fleet of barges carrying goods on the river Severn, but reverted in 1808 to sending them with an owner whose family had worked the river for generations. However, when the Birmingham & Liverpool Junction Canal opened to Wappenshall in 1835 the partners successfully operated their own narrow boats, as did other iron-working companies.

Living accommodation in 10-foot-long cabins was cramped, but from the early years of canal navigation families lived on some boats. Their number increased in the mid-nineteenth century when, with the onset of railway competition, some carrying companies ceased using canals and their vessels passed to owner-boatmen. On some canals, particularly those around Birmingham, and on all the Scottish canals, carrying was done by boats whose crews returned home nightly, but for any longer-distance journeys that was of course impractical. Communities of boatmen, boat builders and coal merchants grew up at isolated junctions such as Fradley or Welsh Frankton. Some village wharfs served the needs of neighbouring towns. The Grantham family established a coal business at Lower Heyford on the Oxford Canal which supplied the market town of Bicester six miles distant, and for a time paupers from the Bicester workhouse went to Heyford with wheelbarrows to fetch coal. Two of the Granthams' boats, *Prince* and *Miller*, were moored near Claydon summit on census night in 1871, when the wharf at Lower Heyford sheltered a flotilla of five vessels from the Abingdon area.

Canal communities developed as the waterways network expanded, with homes of watermen and boat builders, and as places of interchange for goods, and centres of administration for canal companies. Village canal wharfs, with paved or setted yards, piles of coal, warehouses for outgoing and incoming sundries, lime kilns, weighbridges and pillar cranes, became features of the landscape. Soon after the Trent & Mersey Canal opened a visitor commented that 'the market town of Stone from a poor insignificant place is now grown neat and handsome in its buildings and from its wharfs and busy traffic wears a lively aspect of a little seaport'. Mary Prior has shown how people from Fisher Row, the community in Oxford which worked the upper Thames, found work after 1790 on the Oxford Canal. Another boating community on the Thames was at Eynsham, where the Oxford Canal Company employed a wharfinger from 1792 and in 1800 leased an ancient wharf and built a flash lock to improve access for boats. From it the Parker family dealt in coal, corn, salt and bricks, and worked barges down the Thames to London. In 1861 boat people from Eynsham could be found along the length of the Oxford Canal, at Napton, Hillmorton, Wormleighton, Little Bourton and Adderbury, and farther afield at Moira, Stourport and Braunston. In Derbyshire Shardlow was the place of transshipment between the broad vessels used on the Trent and the narrow boats employed on the Grand Trunk. There were boat-building yards, warehouses

where the carrying companies redirected items of cargo, and specialist warehouses for salt, malt and iron. When sundries traffic declined after 1860 most of the warehouses were adapted as mills.

Tipton in Staffordshire was at the heart of the Birmingham Canal Navigation, and indeed of the great Midlands canal network. In 1861 there were 62 men and 27 women on board vessels in the parish on census night, while 248 boat people slept ashore. Fourteen men maintained canals and collected tolls, and 42 loaded and unloaded boats. Of 46 boat builders, 18 originated in the Black Country, the incomers including men from London, Stourport, Gloucester and Manchester. Demonstrating the two-way nature of traffic, Tipton-born boat people slept on vessels moored at Ellesmere, Market Drayton and Maesbury on the Shropshire Union; at Gayton, Heyford, Blisworth, Abbot's Langley, Marsworth, Hemel Hempstead and Brentford on the Grand Junction; at Fradley and Shardlow on the Trent & Mersey; and at Bull Bridge on the Cromford Canal.

Runcorn, with Ellesmere Port, Stourport and Goole, was one of the 'canal ports' defined by Porteous, developing at a place where cargoes were transferred between broad and narrow vessels. There

The main line of the Birmingham Canal Navigation at the foot of Factory Locks, Tipton. The name 'Factory' comes from James Kier's alkali works which stood on nearby Factory Road.

was previously no major settlement at Runcorn, but it grew into a town with manufacturing industries and a full range of urban facilities. It became the focus of a series of rival or separate canal projects, making it a central place on the regional waterways network. At Runcorn the Bridgewater Canal from Manchester and Worsley, opened in 1776, descended to the Mersey estuary by a flight of ten locks, described by Josiah Wedgwood as 'the work of titans'. The locks, which in 1826 were duplicated to accommodate increasing traffic, were overlooked by Bridgewater House, from which the 3rd Duke viewed their construction; it eventually became the headquarters of the canal company. The Mersey & Irwell Navigation had been completed to Manchester in 1736, and between 1799 and 1804 the river authorities built a new cut on the south side of the Mersey from Latchford, above Warrington, to a point about a mile east of the Runcorn locks, creating a rival interchange between inland and coasting craft. On the north shore the Sankey Brook Navigation opened in 1762 to Fiddler's Ferry, and was extended to Widnes, opposite Runcorn, in 1833. The Trent & Mersey Canal joined the Bridgewater at Preston Brook, four miles east of the lock flight, but initially no connection was made with the Weaver Navigation, completed in 1732 from the Mersey at Frodsham to Winsford in the Cheshire saltfield. In 1810 the Weaver Trustees completed a new outlet to the Mersey, a canal extending from Frodsham along the south bank of the estuary to deep water at Weston Point, Runcorn, where by the 1840s a sea-lock

Most of the canal lifts described in this book lifted tub boats of very modest size or were wholly unsuccessful. By the 1870s new materials, notably mild steel and steel rope, as well as hydraulic power, were available. The Anderton Lift at Northwich in Cheshire was completed in 1875 to the design of Edwin Clark, and was the prototype for a succession of other boat lifts in North America and continental Europe.
PHOTOGRAPH: MIKE PEEL, 2007 (WWW.MIKEPEEL.NET)

One of the many warehouses at Shardlow, close to the junction between the Grand Trunk Canal and the navigable River Trent, which became one of the hubs of merchandise traffic on the Midlands inland waterways network.

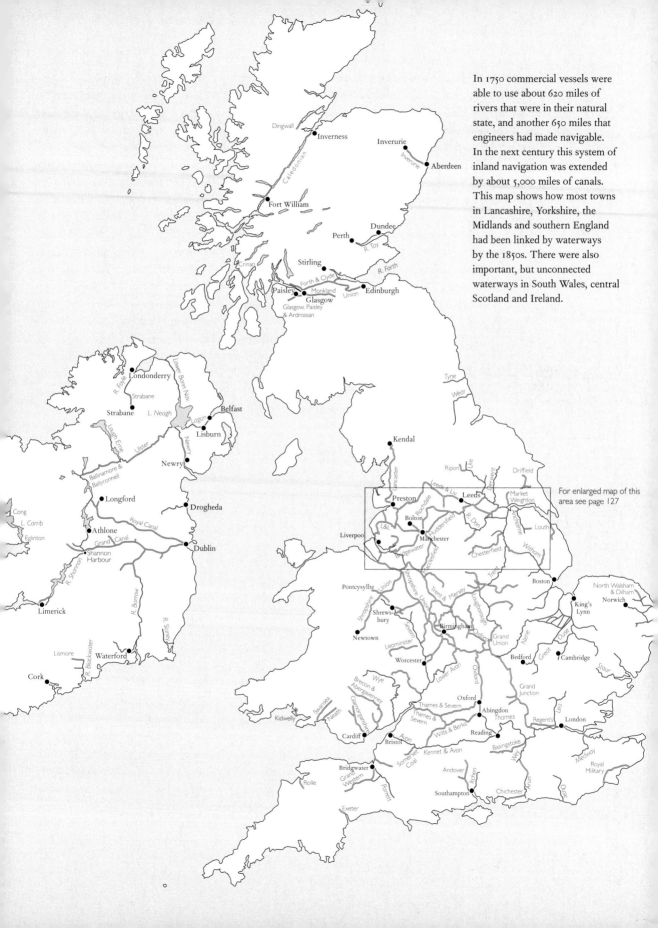

In 1750 commercial vessels were able to use about 620 miles of rivers that were in their natural state, and another 650 miles that engineers had made navigable. In the next century this system of inland navigation was extended by about 5,000 miles of canals. This map shows how most towns in Lancashire, Yorkshire, the Midlands and southern England had been linked by waterways by the 1850s. There were also important, but unconnected waterways in South Wales, central Scotland and Ireland.

For enlarged map of this area see page 127

and small basin had gradually expanded to become a significant dock complex. The Bridgewater Trustees took over the Mersey & Irwell Navigation in 1844, by which time some 160,000 tons of goods annually were being transferred from coasters to inland vessels. The docks were extended during the 1860s, although the focus of inland navigation and industrial development was changed utterly by the opening of the Manchester Ship Canal in 1894.

In the early nineteenth century Runcorn had aspirations to be a fashionable bathing resort. Riverside baths were built in 1822, and the handsome Belvedere Terrace, intended for visitors, was erected in 1831. But the presence of the canals inevitably brought industries which put paid to that ambition. Characteristic urban trades such as tanning, malting and brewing developed, but by the 1820s there were soapworks which, through a process of vertical integration, turned to making alkalis and then sulphuric acid. Chemical manufactures proliferated and came to be the area's principal industry. In 1861 the largest manufacturer, John Johnson of Bank House, was employing 1,281 men and boys. The oldest local industry was sandstone quarrying; the quarrymaster John Tomkinson employed 170 men. Other enterprises included Samuel Shaw Brown's works where 40 people were employed making elastic hosiery, belts and bandages; the iron foundry of Ebenezer Timmins with 58 men; a tar distillery; and a workshop where slates were trimmed and framed for use in schools. The population of Runcorn grew from 1,379 in 1801 to 8,688 in 1851 and 10,366 in 1861. Urban amenities included a weekly market (1811), town hall (1831), schools and a variety of churches and chapels, to be followed in the 1850s by a market hall, public library and courthouse. By 1860, while still a hub of inland navigation, the town had a self-sustaining economy.

Many residents of Runcorn and Weston in 1861 were employed on the waterways. About 350 were working boats, 270 in the docks; 160 were boat builders or makers of sails and blocks, more than 70 were clerks, porters or lock keepers on the waterside, and about 40 tended horses pulling boats. Seven 'boat drivers' lodged with a joiner on Old Quay, while nine horse-drivers on the Bridgwater Canal

stayed with a widow on Waterloo Road. The dominant figure in shipbuilding was Philip Whiteway of Grove House, who also owned vessels and employed 365 men. There were 14 boats at the Bridgewater Trustees' warehouses at Norton, three of them Mersey flats and the remainder narrow boats, mostly from the Black Country. At Preston Brook, the junction of the Bridgewater and Trent & Mersey, more than 60 men worked on the canals, 40 of them porters employed by carriers, others keeping books, tending the steam engine in the warehouse, and maintaining the 1,239-yard Preston Brook Tunnel. Twenty-one boats were moored there on the night of 7 April: three 50-ton flats and eighteen narrow boats.

The Weaver Navigation and the Trent & Mersey Canal both passed through the salt-working area around Northwich, where from 1875 they were linked by the Anderton Lift. Three vessels, two locally owned and one from the Lancashire coalfield, were moored at Pickering's Wharf, Dutton, on the Weaver Navigation, two with families on board. In 1861 there were about 140 salt miners in the townships that made up Northwich, and about 220 men boiling and making salt. The dependence of the industry on the waterways is shown by the presence of about 300 boatmen and 120 boat builders. Much carrying was done by day-boats, for only 17 vessels were recorded on the waterways at Northwich. Eight were Mersey flats on the Weaver, the largest the 105-ton *Four Brothers* which traded to Liverpool. Five were coal barges of between 38 and 48 tons, including one from St Helens, one from Leigh and one from Astley, while there were four narrow boats, one laden with earthenware. Around Winsford at the head of the Weaver Navigation, more than 600 people were employed making salt, about 140 in working boats, two dozen in hauling them and 63 in boat building. On the Trent & Mersey south of Northwich there were three narrow boats at Rudheath, and 16 were moored at Middlewich, six belonging to the North Staffordshire Railway Company which had taken over the canal in 1846, and two to the Anderton Company. Two were moored at Wheelock, and four at Malkin's Bank, two carrying coal and salt, one with earthenware and clay and the other with grain. There were five boats at Odd Rode and Thurlwood near

Alsager, four of them loaded with iron, and eleven around Church Lawton, three of which belonged to the Bunker's Hill Colliery at Talke, opened by William Rigby & Sons seven years earlier and linked to the canal by a rope-hauled tramway.

At Kidsgrove, just north of Harecastle Tunnel, the Trent & Mersey was joined by the Macclesfield Canal. South of the tunnel lay the most northerly wharf in the Potteries, at Tunstall. The 1861 census records 25 boats at the wharf or moored along the canal to the tunnel portal. Six were laden with potters' materials, one with earthenware, four with coal, four with iron, one with timber and one with sundries, and they came from all parts of the Midlands – Coventry, Runcorn, Ellesmere, Ruabon, Nottingham, Oxford and the Black Country.

From ancient, indeed prehistoric, times the most efficient method of transporting bulky goods had been by water. Right through the early decades of industrialisation in Britain the developing inland waterway and canal networks allowed the relatively economical transportation of an astonishing range of raw materials, fuels and finished products. Some canals had been promoted with a particular commodity in mind, such as coal or limestone, but after completion came to be used for many different purposes. The carrying of general merchandise, as we have seen, could be significant, and could add much to canal company profits. It is sometimes forgotten that for many years passenger traffic was also an important feature of Britain's canals.

Passenger traffic on the canal network

For more than a century inland waterways contributed to an evolving network of public passenger services. As early as 1747 the proprietors of a Worcester–London stage coach drew attention to connecting passenger wherries on the river Severn: two return journeys each week operated to and from Shrewsbury and five between Worcester and Gloucester. In 1755, 1760 and 1761 one traveller was Abiah, wife of Abraham Darby II, who completed journeys by wherry between Coalbrookdale and Worcester. By 1773 the service from Shrewsbury was extended to Gloucester, with overnight stays at Worcester going downstream and at Worcester and Bridgnorth in the opposite direction. Wherry services on the upper Severn ceased in the early nineteenth century, and by the 1830s market boats were the only vessels carrying passengers on that section of the river.

Packet boats also carried passengers in Yorkshire, between Chester and Liverpool, and between the principal towns of the Fenlands – in the 1830s there were twice-weekly services between Peterborough and Wisbech, daily departures from Mildenhall to Bury St Edmunds and Lynn, and a steam packet between Lincoln and Boston. By the 1820s passenger boats worked on the Trent from Gainsborough to Nottingham, and there were twice-weekly sailings from Gainsborough to Hull. Packet boats plied between the basin at Paddington, opened by the Grand Junction Canal Company in 1801, and Uxbridge. From Preston, Lancashire, passenger boats worked to Lancaster from 1798 and to Kendal after 1820, when the through journey took 14 hours. The introduction in 1833 of new vessels known as 'Water Witches', with finer lines and shallower draughts, reduced the journey time to 7¼ hours. In Scotland, meanwhile, the passenger boat *Flora McIvor* began to sail from Edinburgh to Ratho in 1822, immediately after the opening of the Union Canal, and by 1823 there was a daily service on the canal from Port Dundas to Port Hopetoun.

In 1776 the Bridgewater company began to build passenger boats at Bangor-on-Dee and later did so at Worsley and Runcorn. Its services grew steadily and in 1800 boats left Castle Quay at Manchester on alternate days for Runcorn, arriving at 17.00, connecting at Warrington for coaches to Liverpool and at Preston Brook for Chester. Another boat took customers from the Warrington area each Saturday to and from markets in Manchester, and a fourth worked daily into Manchester from Worsley. Boats also carried passengers between Manchester and Ashton-under-Lyne, Altrincham, Stockport and Bolton. After 1804, when its extension to Runcorn opened, the Mersey & Irwell Navigation began a packet service rivalling that on the Bridgewater Canal. In the 1830s, therefore,

A poster of 1834 advertising passenger and parcel services on the packet boat *Water Witch* on the Lancaster Canal between Preston and Kendal, with road coach connections to Manchester and Liverpool. The Lancaster Canal had very few locks and so was well suited to this type of passenger service.

The former hotel at Portobello, Dublin, one of five that served passengers on the packet boats of the Grand Canal of Ireland. The building is now adapted as offices.

Runcorn was the hub of passenger services which included twice-daily steam packets to Liverpool, daily services to Manchester by the Bridgewater and the Mersey & Irwell, with extra sailings in summer, and a daily service to Northwich. The short canal journey between Glasgow and Paisley on the Glasgow, Paisley & Johnstone Canal was an ideal candidate for a passenger service, and in one month alone – August 1836 – no fewer than 48,000 passenger trips were made.

Passenger boats even survived the initial challenge of railway competition. Sir George Head, when visiting Lancashire in 1835 – several years after the opening of the Liverpool & Manchester Railway – chose to travel between the towns not by train but by three different waterway routes, all of which he found well patronised. He began on the Bridgewater Canal, crossing the river Mersey from Liverpool by the steamer *Duke of Bridgewater* and joining the canal packet boat for Manchester at the summit of the locks at Runcorn, to which passengers' luggage was humped by porters. The next day he returned to Liverpool by the Leeds & Liverpool, departing initially on the Bridgewater Canal and crossing the Barton Aqueduct, lunching on salted sirloin of beef with fried onions, a salad and a 'good mild cheese', and passing through a 'compound of villainous smells' at Wigan. On the third day he left Liverpool by the *Eclipse* steamer, worked by the Mersey & Irwell Navigation, whose facilities at Runcorn did not equal those of the Bridgewater, and was perturbed by the failure of the crew to prevent 'rough' passengers from entering the first-class cabin.

Irish canals were also distinguished for their passenger services. Six 'passage boats' operated on the unfinished Grand Canal to Robertstown in 1784 and to Athy in 1791, and lighters with state and common cabins were introduced in 1834. They called at five hotels built between 1784 and 1806, of which those at Portobello (Dublin), Robertstown, Co. Kildare, and Shannon Harbour remain. Passenger boats worked from Dublin to Kilcock on the Royal Canal from 1796, and in 1801 the canal company built hotels at Broadstone, Dublin, and Moyvalley, Co. Kildare. In 1806 the canal was opened to Mullingar, whence in the following year there were two daily departures to

Dublin. In 1833 the company invested in vessels which permitted the journey between Mullingar and Dublin to be completed in eight hours, and road cars from Sligo, Carrick-on-Shannon and Athlone connected at Longford with the afternoon boat to Dublin. In 1837 the Royal Canal was carrying nearly 900 passengers a week, but passenger services on both canals had ceased by 1852.

Coaches and carriers: a golden age of road transport

In the 1720s Daniel Defoe remarked that his objective in describing his travels in England was to show that 'in almost every place of note through the whole island … it will be seen how this whole kingdom, as well the people as the land, and even the sea, in every part of it, are employ'd to furnishing something … to supply the city of London with provisions'. Dorian Gerhold has shown how this was made possible by the packhorse and waggon services which by 1700 were carrying goods to the capital from every county, while stage coaches, travelling about 50 miles a day in summertime, offered similar facilities to passengers.

The most significant indicator of the improvement of English roads in the early eighteenth century is that by the 1750s, following the growth of carrying by waggon in the 1740s, goods were no longer being taken to London by packhorse. Packhorses were still used on many difficult or inaccessible routes, for example among the lead workings on Alston Moor, where, until roads were improved in the 1820s, they formed trains of up to 30 animals, each headed by a leader with bells on his harness. In the southern Peak District hollow ways, paved causeys and narrow bridges enabled traders with packhorses, and some with carts, to carry iron, salt, grain and cheese between Yorkshire and Lancashire, to take millstones and lead from the mountains to navigable water, and to supply hill-dwellers with coal. Trains of packhorses continued to carry goods in areas such as the Lake District where there were few metalled roads, and they were still carrying coal, slate and lime in the hills of east Lancashire around Burnley and Clitheroe into the 1860s.

Trains of packhorses ceased to convey goods from distant parts of England to London between 1700 and 1750, an indication of the improvement of the road system, but packhorses remained in use for transport over shorter distances in mountainous regions. These little Galloway horses (named after the Galloway region of south-west Scotland) are shown carrying wood, probably for use in lead mines, either on Alston Moor or in Allendale. This is one of a series of 66 watercolours and pen-and-ink drawings by various artists, assembled into two volumes, illustrating all aspects of lead mining, both above and below ground, in the northern Pennines.

Porthmadog, Caernarfonshire, the port that was part of the programme of improvement carried out by W. A. Madocks after he obtained an Act of Parliament for the purpose in 1803 (see pages 587–8). The picture shows the Cob, the embankment that closed off the sands that he enclosed from the sea, which was completed in 1811. The first quays at Porthmadog were completed in 1825, and subsequently slate was delivered to the harbour by the Festiniog Railway which crossed the Cob.

In the early days, passengers on the Stockton & Darlington Railway were carried in horse-drawn coaches. The Union started operating in October 1826. This notice for passengers gives details of the new railway coach, including the stops the coach will make, the timetable for travel, tariffs and the amount of luggage that could be taken.

Stage coaches ran regularly between London and many provincial towns in 1700. Coaching developed slowly in the following decades, but more rapidly from the 1740s as roads were improved and vehicles were fitted with springs made of crucible steel. When Samuel Johnson and James Boswell left London for Harwich by stage coach early in the morning on 5 August 1763, they lunched *en route*, spent the night at Colchester and arrived at Harwich in daylight, so that Boswell could see Johnson on the beach as his sailing packet left for the Netherlands. Journey times were subsequently reduced as overnight stops were eliminated. The 150-mile journey to London from Shrewsbury took four days in 1753; only eleven years later this had been halved to two days, and in 1774 the fastest service was able to reach the capital in 24 hours. By the 1830s coaches were travelling from Shrewsbury to London in about 15 hours, an overall average of 10 miles per hour.

From the 1740s the system of 'posting' was regularised. A traveller could hire a post horse or a post chaise with horses, and change it, or them, at

Oxford is celebrated as the seat of one of England's two ancient university, as a centre of county and diocesan administration, and as a market town. It was also a port, where from 1790 the narrow boats of the Midlands canals met the broad-beamed barges that worked on the river Thames, and a busy town of thoroughfare where coaches plying the routes from Wales and the West Midlands shown here changed horses at inns on the High Street, and where pedestrian travellers crowded into the lodging-houses and low taverns of High Street St Thomas. This diagrammatic map highlights the role of Oxford as a town of thoroughfare in the eighteenth and early nineteenth centuries. Stage-coach services from London reached the city either through High Wycombe or through Henley, and on leaving Oxford served many towns in the West Midlands, the Borderland and Wales. Services in the rest of the county were relatively sparse.

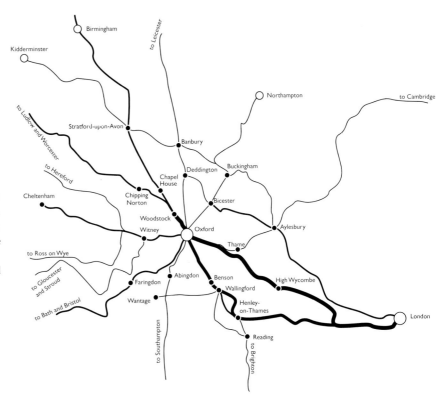

the next associated posting inn on his route. It was exceptionally expensive, though: the rates for posting in Chester in 1802 were 2s. per mile for a four-horse chaise, 1s. per mile for one with two horses, and 6d. a mile for saddle horses. Thoroughfare towns on the main roads were usually between 25 and 35 miles apart, such places as Dunstable, Northampton, Market Harborough, Leicester, Derby and Ashbourne on the road from London to Manchester. Some coaches also stopped at smaller towns such as Lutterworth, and some changed horses in thoroughfare villages, such as Hockliffe (Bedfordshire) where the Manchester road left Watling Street, Stilton on the Great North Road, and Benson on the Oxford road. Among the places identified as thoroughfare towns by Whatley in 1751 were Basingstoke, Bawtry, Chippenham, Dartford, Daventry, Lichfield and Maidenhead. He wrote of Chelmsford that, 'the chief support of this place … is the multitude of carriers and passengers constantly passing this way to London with droves of Cattle, provisions and manufactures'.

The Frenchman Baron d'Haussez considered inns among the wonders of English civilisation, finding them magnificent in large towns and good and well supplied in the smallest. Ludlow, nearly 150 miles from London, provides a viewpoint from which to begin a survey of this aspect of eighteenth-century road transport. The *Feathers*, a richly ornamented timber-framed house, was constructed about 1620 by a Pembrokeshire-born lawyer, and adapted as an inn by his son Thomas Jones. In 1713 it provided ten guest rooms, the best of which, bearing the name of the inn, was furnished to the value of £16. The cellars were well stocked with beer, ale and cider, but not with wine. The use of such an exceptional building as an inn testifies to the significance of road traffic. By 1749 the *Feathers* could reputedly find stabling for more than a hundred horses, because its landlords specialised in posting: the inn only became a calling point for stage coaches in 1849.

At Banbury in 1681 John Jordan worked a carrying concern from his *Hollybush* inn. When he died in

⌐ The *Bell* at Stilton in the ancient county of Huntingdon was one of the most celebrated inns on the Great North Road. The oldest parts of the present building date from 1642, and it was substantially re-built in 1736 and on several subsequent occasions. The *Bell* became famous in the eighteenth century for selling the blue-veined Stilton cheese.

⌐ The *Feathers* at Ludlow, built about 1620, adapted as an inn before 1700. In the late eighteenth century it was celebrated as a posting house and did not host stage coaches until the 1840s.

⌐ The courtyard of the *George* at Huntingdon, one of the principal coaching inns on the Great North Road. It includes buildings of many periods from the sixteenth century to the 1860s.

⌐ Long-distance stage coaches terminated their journeys to London at large inns, of the kind described in several Dickens novels. Most had courtyards surrounded by galleries that gave access to bedrooms. The only one to survive is the *George* just off Borough High Street, Southwark, which is now owned by the National Trust and leased to tenants, but the buildings which remain comprised only part of the original inn. In the mid-nineteenth century the property was acquired by the Great Northern Railway which used it as its warehouse in south London, and who demolished two of the principal ranges of buildings.

May 1689 there were three guest rooms, the fittings in the best of which were valued at £11. His waggon, horses, and 'such things as belong to a carrier', were worth £40, and he was owed good debts totalling more than £80, suggesting a flourishing business. In 1709 a summertime coach from the *Black Bull* in Holborn called at the spa at Astrop Wells, five miles before Banbury, before terminating at the *Three Tuns* in the town. A vivid impression of the inn is provided by the probate inventory of Henry Upton made in 1722. There were a dozen rooms for travellers, including some well-furnished garrets. The best room, the King's Chamber, was fitted with a curtained bedstead with feather-filled mattress and pillows, six matted chairs, a close stool, a looking glass and window curtains, valued at more than £20. There were 19 cane chairs and four oval tables in the dining room, a shuffleboard table and nine Turkey-work chairs in the hall, a stock of beer, cider, brandy and rum, as well as equipment for ninepins and bowls.

The inventory of Edward Marshall, an innkeeper at High Wycombe on the London to Oxford road, was taken in February 1698–99. This, too, gives good detail of such a building and its contents. There were 16 guest chambers and further accommodation in garrets. The *Great Antelope* chamber had a bed lined with silk and furnished with calico curtains, a cane-work couch and 12 Turkey-work chairs. Marshall had regular dealings with Oxford academics, and his appraisers despaired of retrieving 15 shillings owed to him by the Warden of All Souls. The 1742 inventory of William McConnell of Towcester concerns an inn on Watling Street (the modern A5), turnpiked between Old Stratford and Dunchurch in 1707. The inn had eleven guest rooms and further accommodation in a lodging room and six garrets. The two best chambers had feather mattresses weighing 100 lbs; the beds had quilts and curtains of varied colours and fabrics; and a portrait of Queen Elizabeth and a map of America hung in the public area. There were utensils for serving guests with tea, coffee and alcoholic drinks, including punch, for which there were seven glasses, the eighth of the set having been broken by the cat. In fact, Towcester's main street was lined with inns, the *Sun*, the *Old Bell*, the *Swan*, the *Talbot*, the *White Horse* and the *Pomfret Arms*. More than 60 stage and mail coaches were passing daily through the town by the early 1830s. A writer in 1874 observed that 'lofty gateways which now lead to tumbledown workshops or to small tenements led in olden time to spacious yards for the reception of merchandise and were surrounded with stabling, warehouses and dormitories'.

Defoe considered that the *George* in Northampton looked more like a palace than an inn, while in 1776 the American Quaker J. Maude Fisher praised the *Castle* at Marlborough for its 'high storeys, grand staircases, ceilings stuccoed, wainscots carved, and the furniture particularly elegant, with fine gardens, walks, images and fountains'. In Derbyshire the *Devonshire Arms*, a five-bay inn with stables able to accommodate a hundred horses, was built in 1795–1800, at the direction of the 5th Duke of Devonshire, at Newhaven, 14 miles north of Ashbourne at an isolated junction on the London–Manchester road. Andrew Blaikie in 1802 found the *Devonshire* an excellent inn where 50 gentlemen and their horses could be accommodated without being thronged. In nearby Bakewell the *Rutland Arms*, opened in 1805, formed part of a programme of town improvement carried out for the 5th Duke of Rutland.

Chapel House, built in the 1770s on the road from Oxford to Stratford-upon-Avon near Chipping Norton, was one of the grandest wayside inns. There, on 21 March 1776, Samuel Johnson expressed his preference for a good inn where there was a freedom from the anxiety which always attended a stay in a private house, concluding 'there is nothing which has yet been contrived by man, by which so much happiness is produced as by a good tavern or inn'. The brothers La Rochefoucauld found the parlours and bedrooms at *Chapel House* 'of a luxury and comfort that cannot be compared with anything in France', and learned that the innkeeper kept 52 post horses. Just three months later Lord Torrington found *Chapel House* 'quite a principality', that eclipsed all the inns of Chipping Norton, and with his travelling companion played bowls in the garden. In 1802 Andrew Blaikie was impressed by 'as civil a house as any in Britain', which supposedly could accommodate a troop of dragoons.

Some of the practicalities of working such an inn are shown by a plan of the *Talbot* fronting Market Street in Shrewsbury, an elegant building designed in 1775 by the architect Samuel Scoltock and financed by the Oteley family of Pitchford Hall. It was principally a posting establishment and in 1853 the property included the extensive inn yard and two other blocks, one incorporating the *Talbot Tap*, six dwellings, a brewhouse, carpenters' shops, two coach houses, stabling and a large yard, and another about 50 yards distant with further stables surrounding a yard.

Coaching derives some of its perceived glamour from nostalgic books published in the late nineteenth century. There was an air of drama around immaculately turned-out horses, coach names evocative of speed and current events, and idiosyncratic coachmen, of which Sam Weller's father, depicted in Charles Dickens's *Pickwick Papers*, is the archetype. George Eliot described a time when the glory had not yet departed from the old coach roads; the great roadside inns were still brilliant with well-polished tankards, the smiling glances of pretty barmaids, and the repartee of jocose ostlers. The mail still announced itself by the merry notes of the horn; the hedge-cutter or the

rick-thatcher might still know the exact hour by the unfailing yet otherwise meteoric apparition of the pea-green *Tally-ho* or the yellow *Independent*. Not all coach travel was comfortable, though. Carl Philip Moritz described a horrific journey from Leicester to London in 1782, in which he travelled on top of the coach with a young farmer and a young black man. The coach rolled on the stony road, frequently tossed the passengers into the air, and made him fear for his life. From Market Harborough to Northampton he was drenched with rain. After sleeping at Northampton he travelled inside the coach to London, hemmed in by farmers whose faces were bloated with beer and brandy.

In Ireland the turnpike trusts took control of some of the main roads between 1730 and the 1760s – by 1758 the 29 trusts controlled 1,216 miles of road – but after 1766 most new roads were financed through the 'presentment system', by which a county grand jury could authorise an individual to improve a road and, upon completion of the scheme, reimburse him from public funds. From 1831 the Irish Board of Public Works undertook the improvement of such trunk routes as the Great Coast Road from Larne to Ballycastle. Stage-coach services between the principal Irish cities were not unlike those in England, but provincial towns were linked by 'bians', vehicles on which passengers sat back-to-back in two rows, looking towards the roadsides, on either side of a central luggage well. The network was established by Charles Bianconi, a Lombard who had settled in Clonmel, Co. Tipperary. In aggregate his cars achieved 3,000 route miles per day by 1840, and were not completely superseded until branch railways reached the farthermost extremities of the island.

At the beginning of the eighteenth century long-distance stage waggons made their way slowly from most parts of the provinces to London. Some continued to do so until the late nineteenth century, although by then most of their trade had been lost to the railways. In the eighteenth century they carried cloth consigned to Blackwell Hall (see below, page 461), as well as agricultural produce. Thomas Ward Boss, who grew up in Banbury in the 1820s, described the waggons that worked to London. They measured 18 feet long by 7 feet 6 inches wide (5.5 m × 2.3 m), and the top was 12

A country carrier's cart from north Shropshire making its way up the hill into the centre of Shrewsbury, portrayed on an engraving published in 1838.

A hand-coloured aquatint from the *Costume of Great Britain*, published in 1808, showing one of the heavy waggons that were used to take agricultural and other produce from many parts of England to London. There were regional variations in the design of such waggons, but most had broad wheels, were drawn by eight horses, and had a punt for certain kinds of goods slung between the axles. Most waggon services of this kind ceased with the coming of railways, but a few, from areas such as the Chilterns, continued into the 1870s.

© SCIENCE MUSEUM/SCIENCE & SOCIETY PICTURE LIBRARY

feet (3.7 m) from the road. They had broad wheels and were drawn by eight horses, and a punt was suspended between the axles to accommodate live sheep, pigs and poultry, which were fed *en route*. Stout mohair curtains secured the back; bags with food for the horses hung at the front; a light ladder to reach to top of the load hung at the side; and two horn lanterns were carried, one in front and one behind the team. John Buckmaster, who travelled in a country waggon from Uxbridge towards Leighton Buzzard about 1840, was impressed by its 'Norman roof of tarpaulin'. After 1800 perishable goods were increasingly carried by speedier vans, but traditional waggons continued to make their way to London and other large cities from communities not served directly by railways. In south Oxfordshire Thomas Eustace remained the London carrier from Chinnor in 1861, and ten years later Henry Palmer, then in his eighties, continued to drive his waggon from Benson to the capital.

One consequence of the improvement of roads was the development of networks of country carriers, travelling with carts from villages into market towns and back again, delivering eggs, cheese, butter and poultry for sale in markets, collecting orders placed by country people with shops, and carrying passengers. In *The Woodlanders* Thomas Hardy described a cart, half-full of passengers, drawn by a single horse with hair of the roughness and colour of heather and driven by one

Mrs Dollery, with leggings under her gown and a felt hat tied down by a handkerchief. Perhaps 4 per cent of carriers were women.

It is difficult to measure the growth of carrying, since trade directories probably give an incomplete picture of services in the early nineteenth century, but it is likely that networks developed from the 1750s as roads were turnpiked. The size of networks indicates the intensity of trade in market towns. The largest market centres, county towns such as Reading, Derby and Leicester, were served by up to 500 carrier journeys per week in the 1850s, but some smaller towns, such as Banbury, Cirencester, Evesham and Newbury, had numbers out of proportion to their mere population, highlighting their wider importance as markets. The smallest centres, places such as Chipping Norton, Leominster and Leek, attracted between 10 and 20 journeys per week. The opening of railways usually reduced the number of services from villages which had stations, although routes were often reorientated to serve railheads. Despite the arrival of the railways, carrying remained buoyant in 1870 and in most areas did not decline significantly before 1900. Carriers' networks defined people's perceptions of the hinterlands of towns. When Mr Tulliver in *Mill on the Floss* was contemplating sending his son to boarding school, he concluded 'we won't send him out o'reach o'the carrier's cart'.

Railways: creating a national network for goods and passengers

One of the most important contributions to improving transport during the industrial age was the development in Britain of what eventually became an integrated, national network of railways. Their significance stemmed from several factors. First, they enabled goods and (crucially) passengers to be carried more quickly than any previous form of transport. Second, they added considerable extra capacity to the overall transport system. Despite what is sometimes asserted, the canals and roads were by no means rendered obsolete by the railways; rather, the new rail network gave traders and travellers an increasingly wide choice of routes and services. Third, the railways could be a powerful force in driving down the cost of transport,

particularly over longer distances and for certain bulk items. Finally, if perhaps least tangibly, the railways offered a much broader conception of what was possible: great new vistas of communication, travel, trade and commerce opened up, with cost-effective long-distance travel and trade now more feasible and affordable than ever. Passengers, raw materials, finished goods, the Royal Mail and many others made increasing use of the new system. Eventually, indeed, the railways themselves prompted the establishment of new communities: some, like Middlesbrough, dependent on handling rail-borne traffic; some, such as Rugby, on the employment generated at junctions; some, like Swindon and Ashford, on engineering

An oil painting by W. Wheldon showing a colliery with the waggonway that served it in the North Eastern coalfield, *circa* 1845. The empty chaldron waggons are being drawn back to the mine through the countryside on a cable-operated incline of the kind that could still be seen crossing the Team Valley in Co. Durham in the 1970s. In the foreground two miners are walking home after a shift at the coalface. The pithead installations include ovens for making coke for which the mines of Co. Durham were famous. It was the preferred fuel of foundry masters in many parts of southern England, and from the 1860s was carried by rail in great quantities to the blast furnaces of Furness and Cumberland.

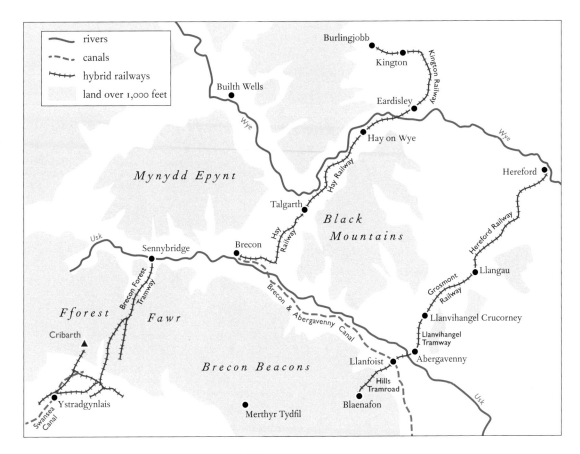

⋏ 'Hybrid' railways in the area north of the South Wales coalfield.

works established by railway companies; and others, such as Surbiton, on the burgeoning phenomenon of commuting that railways facilitated.

This transport revolution, which began in Britain in the 1830s before spreading to other countries, could trace its origins to earlier horse-drawn plateways and railways which had been constructed to move heavy raw materials. By the 1790s, for example, there were railways in every significant British coalfield, carrying coal for short distances, usually to navigable water. Short railways were built by many canal companies, too, and the versatility of rail transport was demonstrated by the operation in 1800–05 of a two-mile line connecting the completed parts of the Grand Junction Canal while Blisworth Tunnel was being excavated. When the tunnel was opened the track was relaid to form a link between the canal at Gayton and

Northampton. Furthermore, most lines working in 1800 were part of networks rather than single routes, mazes of lines around such industrial installations as the ironworks at Horsehay or Blaenavon or the Lambton drops on Wearside.

By the 1790s railways in South Wales, of varied gauges and with several kinds of rails, were delivering raw materials to blast furnaces. One of the first steam locomotives ran on a plateway at Penydarren near Merthyr in 1804, but the region's principal contribution to the development of railways was to demonstrate that they could be viable over considerable distances, even when running through countryside to towns that were not primarily industrial. The 24-mile Hay Railway, authorised in 1811 and completed in 1816, was a 3 foot 6 inch (1.08 m) gauge plateway from the Brecon wharf of the Brecknock & Abergavenny

Evidence that the use of early railways was not confined to the coalfields in the early nineteenth century: this engraving published in 1807 shows 'Mr Whitbread's Chalk Quarry at Purfleet [Essex]', and depicts a horse-drawn railway transporting chalk from quarries to lime kilns.

'Christ Church and Coal Staithe, Leeds', an engraving by T. Owen after an original by Nathaniel Whittock, published in 1829, which depicts the terminus of the Middleton Railway on the south bank of the river Aire near Leeds Bridge. (See also map of Leeds on page 249.) The church in the background is the recently completed Christ Church, which stood in Meadow Lane, Hunslet, and which was demolished in 1972.

Many early railways were built to link wharfs on newly opened canals with industrial installations, among them the Ticknall Tramway a 4 ft 2 in. gauge plateway that ran 12¼ miles from Willesley Basin on the Ashby Canal through Ashby-de-la-Zouch to the lime workings around Calke Abbey. It opened in 1802. The section serving Willesley Basin was closed in 1850; parts of the remainder were converted to a standard-gauge branch of the Midland Railway, but sections around the lime yard at Calke Abbey, shown here, were still in use in the late nineteenth century.

A crudely excavated cutting and tunnel on the Cromford & High Peak Railway near Longcliffe in upland Derbyshire. Although it was opened in 1831, the year after the Liverpool & Manchester Railway began operations, the C&HPR was a characteristic hybrid railway, originally with nine inclined planes and horse haulage on other sections.

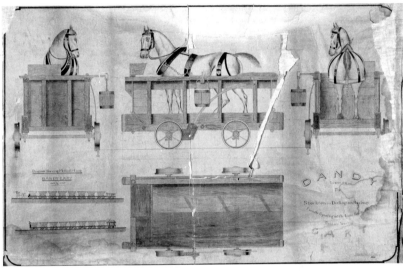

A dandy cart is a vehicle which enabled horses that had pulled trains on uphill or level sections of a railway to rest on downhill stretches. The horse could stand in the vehicle and was usually provided with fodder in a manger or nosebag. George Stephenson used such vehicles on the Stockton & Darlington Railway at a time when the line's steam locomotives were proving unreliable, and they were employed on the Festiniog Railway and on other lines with gravity-worked sections.

Canal to Eardisley. The following year the Kington Railway, a similar plateway, was authorised. Built by the Shrewsbury ironfounder William Hazledine and a local surveyor Morris Sayce, it extended the Hay Railway as far as Kington in 1820 and to lime kilns across the Radnorshire border in 1825. This railway carried goods 36 miles through sparsely populated countryside. Another project began with the construction of a 7¾-mile plateway from the Brecknock & Abergavenny Canal at Llanfoist to Llanvihangel. This opened in 1814 and was linked with the 5½-mile Grosmont Railway in 1821. An 11¾-mile extension to the Wye Bridge at Hereford was opened in 1829, completing a route 25 miles long. The most ambitious line was the Brecon Forest Tramroad, built from

1819, a route of about 36 miles across the high and remote uplands of Fforest Fawr (Great Forest) from the Swansea Canal at Ystradgynlais to Sennybridge on the upper Usk. From 1867 it was superseded by the Neath & Brecon Railway but, like the lines extending from the Brecknock & Abergavenny Canal, it demonstrated the thirst of colliery owners for new markets as well as the potential of the railway for stimulating economic growth.

Historians have described many of the lines that were built between 1800 and 1830 as 'hybrid' railways. Each displayed some, but not all, of the five attributes of main-line railways as defined by Michael Robbins: specialised track; the accommodation of public traffic; the conveyance of passengers; mechanical traction;

and some measure of public control. Some hybrid lines had specialised track but others ran alongside public roads. The Hetton Railway, which used the latest technology, was a private concern, but other lines accommodated public traffic, and a few, such as the Swansea & Mumbles Railway of 1807 and the Stockton & Darlington Railway of 1825, carried passengers. Most 'hybrid' railways used horse transport on some sections of their routes, but they also employed self-acting and steam-powered inclined planes and steam locomotives.

The Liverpool & Manchester Railway, a focus of popular attention during the Rainhill locomotive trials of 1829 and after its ceremonial opening in 1830, was the first railway with all five attributes. Its lines were segregated from public roads; it accommodated public traffic and conveyed passengers; its trains were hauled throughout by mechanical traction, by a powered inclined plane (at the Liverpool end) and steam locomotives; and its activities were controlled by Acts of Parliament. Although it incorporated practices from

North Eastern railways introduced by George and Robert Stephenson, in its civil engineering with its crossing of Chat Moss, in mechanical engineering with *Rocket* and other steam locomotives, and in the confidence expressed in its descent beneath a Moorish arch into Liverpool and in its terminus at Liverpool Road, Manchester, the Liverpool & Manchester Railway was a new phenomenon. Its impact was immediate and far-reaching – coaches such as the *Hawk* from Shrewsbury began to take passengers for Liverpool and Manchester to intermediate stations so that they could complete their journeys by rail – and it impressed all who saw it. The young James Nasmyth went to Liverpool in 1830 and sketched *Rocket*, while Alexander Somerville travelled on the line in 1832 and recorded his experience:

> ... at Manchester I saw a railway, locomotive engines and railway trains for the first time.
> ... The opening of that railway is an epoch in the history of the world. In memory ...
> it seems like an epoch of my life. All sights

A map showing the course of the Liverpool & Manchester Railway, one of a series of seven in a slip case which belonged to George Stephenson, and whose signature it bears.

An original share certificate, no. 2476, of the Liverpool and Manchester Railway Company, 28 December 1826. The image shows three goods trains and the Exchanges of Liverpool, on the left, and Manchester, on the right. The construction of Britain's main railway network was financed almost exclusively by private investment. Many of the early main-line schemes between centres of population were profitable, but the later branch-line routes were more marginal and proved to be a much shakier financial proposition for investors.

which I had seen in London or elsewhere – the beautiful, the grand, the wonderful – shrunk into comparative nothingness, when, after reaching Liverpool, I went into the country a week in the neighbourhood of Prescott, and saw (each day I sought to see it, each hour of the day I could have stood to see it again) the white steam shooting through the landscape of trees, meadows and villages, and the long train, loaded with merchandise, men and women and human enterprise, rolling along under the steam. I had seen no sight like that; I have seen nothing to excel it since. In beauty and grandeur, the world has nothing beyond it …

The Liverpool & Manchester Railway set the pattern for what became a network of main-line railways linking urban centres. During the fifteen years of its independent existence, the Liverpool & Manchester company paid an average dividend of 9½ per cent, just less than the maximum authorised by its Act. Not surprisingly, many of the private investors went on to invest enthusiastically in other railways in Lancashire and elsewhere; in 1860 as many as 40 per cent of the shareholders of the South Eastern Railway came from Lancashire and Cheshire, with around 25 per cent from London and the City. Between 1825 and 1835 Parliament passed 54 Acts sanctioning the building of railways. The construction of 'hybrid' railways continued in the 1830s and some, such as the Stanhope & Tyne, were of strategic economic importance, but by the end of that decade the beginnings of a main-line network were appearing even though the contemporary economic crisis reduced the pace of investment.

The Grand Junction Railway, opened in 1837, linked Birmingham with Newton-le-Willows, whence trains

The use of gunpowder in the construction of railways is illustrated in this picture of the construction of the London & Birmingham Railway at Linslade, Buckinghamshire. High explosives such as dynamite were not employed for this purpose in Britain until the 1880s. From J. C. Bourne, *Drawings on the London & Birmingham Railway*, London, Ackerman, 1839.

Bourne's print, based on drawings that must have been made around 1836, illustrates the scale of the engineering activity involved in the construction of main-line railways. The London & Birmingham Railway opened in April 1838 from Euston Station to Denbigh Hall in Buckinghamshire. Initially trains were hauled by a stationary steam engine out of the terminus, up the slope and over the Regent's Canal, to this spot at the top of Camden Bank. From J. C. Bourne, *Drawings on the London & Birmingham Railway*, London, Ackerman, 1839.

could head west to Liverpool or east to Manchester along the L&MR. From 1838 the Grand Junction was connected at Curzon Street in Birmingham with the London & Birmingham Railway, which terminated in the capital at Philip Hardwick's Euston Station. By this date travellers from the capital could journey by train from London to Birmingham, Liverpool, Manchester and Leeds. The success of these lines, and the improving economic situation after 1842, sparked the 'railway mania' of the mid-1840s. Capital investment in railways peaked in 1847 at £30 million, while the prospect of dazzling financial returns tempted thousands of small private investors into the market. In Britain the construction of most nineteenth-century railways was authorised by Act of Parliament and funded by subscription, private and City investment, and by some borrowing. The railway companies that built and operated principal routes could become extremely successful, paying out to shareholders regular and sometimes substantial dividends. According to Charles Dickens, the London & North Western Railway was

'wealthier than any other corporation in the world'. As a whole the railways were big business. By 1881 the total capitalisation of British railways had reached £881 million, a sum equal to the entire national debt. During the first half of Queen Victoria's reign railways came of age both financially and technologically, and they helped to transform the economic, industrial and social landscape of Britain.

Yet the network was not centrally planned. There was fierce competition between the promoters of railway companies in the 1840s, and in subsequent decades some lines were wastefully duplicated. One consequence of the rivalry between projects was the amalgamation of many of the first generation of companies. The London & North Western Railway of 1846 incorporated the Liverpool & Manchester, the Grand Junction and the London & Birmingham among others. The Birmingham & Derby Junction, the Midland Counties and the North Midland merged in 1844 to form the Midland Railway, and within a year took over the Birmingham & Gloucester. By

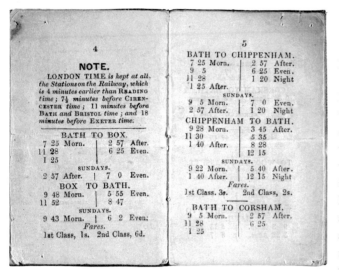

A Great Western Railway timetable of the early 1840s, which explains time differences between the towns that the company served, but affirms that the railway used only 'London time'. It was due to the establishment of the railway system that standard time was adopted throughout the country.

© NATIONAL RAILWAY MUSEUM/SCIENCE & SOCIETY PICTURE LIBRARY

1850 further amalgamations had created the London, Brighton & South Coast, the Lancashire & Yorkshire, and the North Eastern. Another consequence was increased parliamentary control of the railways, expressed in W. E. Gladstone's Railway Regulation Act of 1844. The Act is celebrated for imposing on companies the duty to run on each line a daily 'parliamentary train', calling at all stations and with a maximum fare of a penny a mile, but that was only one provision in a very lengthy piece of legislation.

The principal point of controversy during the Mania was the gauge question. Most lines were built to a gauge of 4 ft 8½ ins (1.435 m), which had been common on the Tyneside colliery railways and which was eventually regarded as standard. The exception was the Great Western Railway, authorised in 1835 and initially a line from Bristol to London. The directors had appointed the young Isambard Kingdom Brunel as the company's engineer in 1833, and he proposed a much broader gauge of 7 ft 0¼in. (2.15 m) with the rails laid on horizontal baulks of timber (rather than on transverse sleepers). The line opened from Paddington Station in London as far as Maidenhead in 1838 but only in 1841, with the completion of Box Tunnel near Bath, did it open throughout. The Great Western subsequently expanded, northwards to Oxford, Birmingham and Wolverhampton and towards Wales through Gloucester. It was possible for trains to run faster on the broad than on the standard gauge, and it was much more comfortable for passengers, but the prospect of a national network was not fully comprehended in 1833, and the problem of differing gauges emerged only with time and the success of the railways. Transshipment of goods and passengers created confusion wherever the two gauges met, at Basingstoke and Wolverhampton but notoriously at Gloucester. The extent to which the broad gauge should be allowed

A panoramic view that shows the route of Brunel's Great Western Railway through the city of Bath, incorporating two major bridges and a succession of viaducts. The railway did not, as had been anticipated, bring a new burst of prosperity to the resort (see page 553), but the low-lying area near the river, around Avon Street and near the Kennet & Avon locks, became a small but significant industrial area.

PHOTOGRAPH CARNEGIE, BY COURTESY OF BATH LIBRARY

to penetrate northwards was the subject of an inquiry in 1845, whose recommendations proved less influential than economic realities. At Gloucester the chaos around the interchange between the standard-gauge Birmingham & Gloucester and the broad-gauge Bristol & Gloucester Railway ceased from 1846, when the latter passed into the ownership of the Midland Railway which converted it to standard gauge.

The Great Western opened a branch from Didcot to Oxford in 1844, extended it to Banbury in 1850 and to Birmingham two years later, but it failed, in spite of permissions granted by Act of Parliament, to establish connections with lines to the north. Earthworks south of the village of Bishop's Itchington, adjoining the railway from Banbury, are the remnants of a junction by which the Great Western hoped to take the broad gauge to Rugby. The shallow cuttings and low embankments near Holmes House Farm are monuments to the Railway Mania just as the ridge-and-furrow in adjacent fields signifies the passing of open-field agriculture. Farther north, the rooftops of the Birmingham suburb of Duddeston are crossed by the arches of a viaduct intended to take Great Western trains on to the Grand Junction and Birmingham & Derby Junction lines, but the viaduct was never used. In 1854, when the Great Western was extended from Birmingham to Wolverhampton, it took over two standard-gauge companies, the Shrewsbury & Birmingham and the Shrewsbury & Chester, which provided it with a through route – albeit with a break of gauge – from London to Merseyside.

Meanwhile, the Oxford, Worcester & Wolverhampton Railway, the initial subject of the inquiry of 1845, though initially a Great Western protégé and surveyed by Brunel, operated as a standard-gauge line from its opening in 1853. For a time through standard-gauge trains to London travelled on the L&NWR line from Oxford via Bletchley but from 1863, after a series of takeovers, the OW&WR became part of the Great Western. To allow direct through trains to London, standard-gauge tracks (laid within the broad-gauge lines) were completed between Didcot and Paddington in 1861, and from 1 May 1869 broad-gauge trains to the north ceased completely. Meanwhile in 1856 standard-gauge

The line running north to south and marked 'G.W.R. (Disused) Viaduct' on this late nineteenth-century map of the south side of Birmingham crosses the Duddeston Viaduct, by which the company hoped to make contact with the lines to northern England, whose tangled junctions can be seen at the top of the map. The incompatibility between Brunel's broad gauge and the standard gauge used by the Grand Junction and Birmingham & Derby railways and their successors meant that the connection was never made. The viaduct was never brought into service but still stands today. The arches were let as workshops and some still serve that purpose. This map also shows the course of the Warwick & Birmingham Canal which crosses the river Rea on an aqueduct, as well as some metal-working shops for which Birmingham was famous, and numerous small groups of back-to-back houses.

△ Broad-gauge locomotives assembled at the GWR works at Swindon awaiting scrapping after the last broad-gauge operations on the company's line from London to Penzance ceased in 1892.

© NATIONAL RAILWAY MUSEUM/SCIENCE & SOCIETY PICTURE LIBRARY

tracks were installed on the GWR route from Reading to Basingstoke, opened in 1845, to enable freight from the north to be carried without transshipment to Southampton and other destinations on the London & South Western Railway. The branch to Hereford, which left the route from Gloucester to South Wales at Grange Court, was opened in 1855 but fourteen years later was converted to standard gauge – in just one week by a team of 300 navvies – the beginning of a process of contraction which culminated in 1892 with the demise of broad gauge when the main line from London through Bristol to Penzance was also converted to standard gauge.

Brunel's lines in Devon were yet more distinctive. The Bristol & Exeter Railway, which collaborated with the Great Western until the two amalgamated in 1876, opened in 1844. On the South Devon Railway,

which continued the route westward, Brunel determined to use the innovative atmospheric principle, which had been demonstrated on the new Dalkey Atmospheric Railway near Dublin, operated from 1843. In this system – once described by Robert Stephenson as 'a rope of air' – a cast-iron pipe was laid between the tracks, from which air was evacuated by means of a stationary steam pumping engine. The train was pulled along by a piston attached to the carriage by an arm which penetrated through a continuous hinged flap valve of leather, which was shut by rollers following the passage of the piston. Eight engine houses were constructed west of Exeter and the operation of atmospheric trains began in September 1847 to Teignmouth and to Newton Abbot in January 1848. By June 1848 it was evident that the system was unworkable, partly because the leather flap was already rotting, but also because of operating difficulties inherent in the system – particularly the complexity of shunting operations. Atmospheric traction was abandoned, though an Italianate pumping station at Starcross remains, together with two others at Torre and Totnes that were never commissioned. William Cubitt made experiments with atmospheric propulsion on the London & Croydon Railway in 1844–47 but they were quickly abandoned. In fact, the early failures of the atmospheric system precluded its application in what would have been a more appropriate application, on London's underground railways.

More than 6,000 route miles of railway were built in Great Britain between 1830 and 1851, one of the great achievements of British civil engineering. By 1851 London was linked directly with all the major provincial cities in Great Britain, albeit rather circuitously in the case of Aberdeen, while a well-developed cross-country network was emerging. By this time, too, shorter branches linking smaller towns with main lines were being promoted, often by local entrepreneurial interests, while companies anxious to see off competitive threats from rivals were developing secondary routes which linked and fed into their main lines. In 1861 the network covered almost 10,000 miles, it was approaching 12,000 miles in 1866, and exceeded 15,000 by the late 1870s, reaching a peak of more than 20,000 immediately before the First World War.

The first main-line railways in Ireland linked Dublin with the port of Dun Laoghaire (Kingstown) in 1834 and with Drogheda in 1844, and Belfast with Lisburn in 1839. These three lines were built to different gauges, and after an inquiry by the Board of Trade a compromise gauge of 5 ft 3 ins (1.6 m) was imposed by the Railway Regulation (Gauge) Act of 1846. By 1860 Dublin was linked by railway with the principal cities in Ireland, but most of the highly distinctive narrow-gauge lines, serving remote communities in counties such as Donegal, Kerry, Clare and Cork, were not constructed until after 1870.

The railway passenger station became part of the urban and rural landscape. The small scale of the original Manchester terminus of the Liverpool & Manchester Railway is evidence that early railway companies had only moderate expectations of passenger traffic,

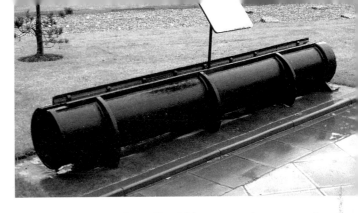

An iron pipe, cast by the Coalbrookdale Company, that was part of the atmospheric system tried on the London & Croydon Railway in 1844–47. It is displayed in the National Railway Museum, York.

The pumping house alongside the station at Totnes on the South Devon Railway, built when the company was intending to operate trains on the atmospheric system, which proved unworkable in 1847–48 on the section of line to the east. The pumping station was never used for its intended purpose but the buildings later served as a dairy.

Broadstone Station, Dublin, terminus of the Midland Great Western Railway, designed by J. S. Mulvaney, and completed in 1850. It was subsequently adapted as a bus station.

The railway system in the British Isles *circa* 1852, demonstrating the extraordinary achievement of engineers, contractors and entrepreneurs in creating within little more than two decades a 6,000-mile network that linked most of the nation's principal towns and cities.

A wayside station in a picturesque Gothic style, at Thurgarton, Nottinghamshire, on the line from Nottingham to Lincoln, which opened in 1846 and which formed part of the Midland Railway. The engraving is by W. L. Walton.

A wayside station on I. K. Brunel's broad-gauge Great Western Railway, at Pangbourne west of Reading, depicted in John Cook Bourne's *History and Description of the Great Western Railway*.

and the subsequent enthusiastic demand surprised railway managers. In some cases wayside accommodation was improvised – the Leicester & Swannington used rooms in three public houses near the lineside as booking offices, while at Moreton-on-Lugg the Shrewsbury & Hereford adapted a hollow tree for the purpose. Some early wayside stations, such as that at Hampton-in-Arden where the Birmingham & Derby Junction Railway joined the London & Birmingham, had the appearance of turnpike tollhouses. Companies often adopted distinctive architectural styles for their wayside stations. Benjamin Green chose Tudor Gothic for the Newcastle & Berwick Railway at Beal, Belford

and Christon Bank, while the North Staffordshire used red brick in a Jacobean style in village stations and at the hub of its system at Stoke-on-Trent.

How railways should negotiate towns and rapidly growing urban centres was problematic. In some cases, such as at Bath, Berwick-upon-Tweed or Conwy railways companies were authorised to build adjacent to, or indeed through or under, historic districts. Elsewhere, as at Edinburgh Waverley, the city's topography allowed relatively uninterrupted access to the centre, in this case over the site of the recently drained Nor' Loch. Elsewhere, vested property interests or high land prices resulted in the siting of termini some

A mid-nineteenth-century view of the Doric Arch at the entrance to the Euston terminus of the London & Birmingham Railway, opened in 1838. The arch, designed by Philip Hardwick, gave access to a courtyard and was intended to be 'a grand but simple portico'. It was constructed with stone from Bramley Fall Quarry in Yorkshire. The arch was demolished from December 1961 as part of the reconstruction of Euston Station. Many people had urged its preservation, but its destruction was the result of deliberate decisions at the highest levels of government.

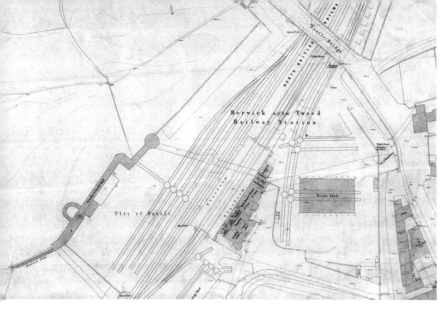

A mid-nineteenth-century map of the railway station at Berwick-upon-Tweed, showing the extensive use of waggon turntables to gain access to the goods shed and sidings. The map shows several historic locations, including the castle walls and the site of one of the city gates, are marked.

Since the early years of main-line railways York has been one of the country's principal junctions. George Hudson's York & North Midland Railway, which reached the city in 1839, originally had a temporary station, but in 1841 the station within the city walls shown on this map was opened. As the railway system developed it became one of the principal stations on the main line from London to Newcastle and Edinburgh but the need for long-distance trains to reverse was an operational inconvenience. In 1877 the present through-station was built outside the walls. The old station was subsequently used as carriage sidings, and from 1928 it housed the railway museum established by the London & North Eastern Railway after the centenary celebrations of the Stockton & Darlington Railway in 1925. The collection now forms part of the National Railway Museum in another part of the city, and the old station is about to be adapted for new uses.

CARNEGIE COLLECTION

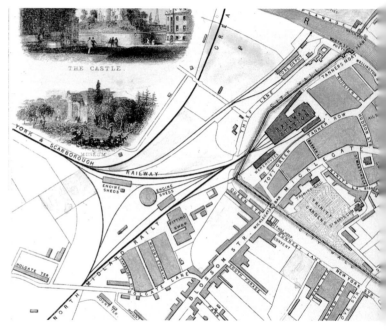

Lithograph by Newman & Co. after a drawing by John Lister junior. The Conwy Tubular Bridge (formerly known as Conway), which was built in 1849, was designed by Robert Stephenson (1803–59) as part of the Chester to Holyhead Railway. The main span of the bridge is 125 metres. As at Berwick and York, the railway line at Conwy was allowed to pierce the ancient fabric, in this case by tunnelling under part of the town, which caused damage to one of the towers of the medieval city walls.

Timothy Hackworth was born at Wylam in 1786, and trained as a blacksmith, but came to play a significant role in the development of the steam locomotive. He helped William Hedley in the construction of *Puffing Billy*, worked with George Stephenson on *Locomotion*, and in 1827 built a six-wheel locomotive *Royal George*. His *Sans Pareil* had a cracked cylinder and was unable to compete in the Rainhill Trials on the Liverpool & Manchester Railway. For a time Hackworth was manager of the Stockton & Darlington Railway but from 1833 established his own Soho Works making locomotives at Shildon. His house now accommodates displays that are part of Locomotion, the Shildon annexe of the National Railway Museum.

Thomas Brassey was the best known of the contractors who built the first generation of main-line railways in the British Isles. He also built several important lines in continental Europe and inspired great loyalty among some of the navvies whom he employed, who followed him from one contract to another.

BOTH IMAGES: © SCIENCE MUSEUM/SCIENCE & SOCIETY PICTURE LIBRARY

Isambard Kingdom Brunel's original terminus for the Great Western Railway at Temple Meads, Bristol, which opened for services to Bath in 1840 and for trains to London in 1841. Trains from the Bristol & Exeter Railway, which also opened in that year, had to reverse into the platforms, but from 1845 a through-platform was constructed for trains running through from London to Devon. Temple Meads was subsequently expanded as a through-station, and only local trains used Brunel's terminus until it ceased to be used in the early 1960s. Subsequently it has been used as a car park and as part of a museum but now awaits new uses.

CARNEGIE COLLECTION

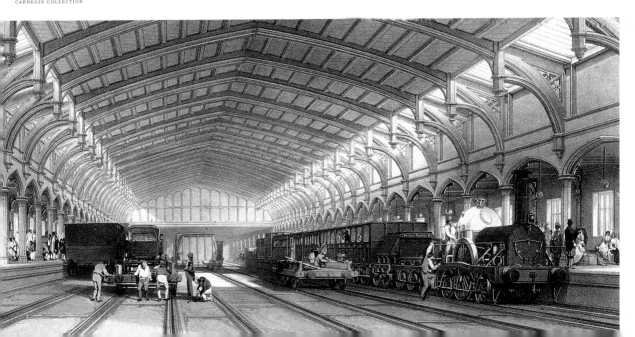

'The Last of the Coaches', a print by 'H' of about 1850 showing a Louth to London Royal Mail coach loaded on to a flat waggon at the rear of a train. The opening of main-line railways in the fifteen years before 1851 led to the demise of most mail coach services.
© NRM/PICTORIAL COLLECTION/SCIENCE & SOCIETY PICTURE LIBRARY

distance from the urban centre. In the case of London a ring of termini surrounded the City on all sides, with only Fenchurch Street Station being located within the ancient city limits. Euston, King's Cross and St Pancras all lie to the north of the turnpike road, New Road, along the north of the capital. To the east and south-east the lines into Fenchurch Street and London Bridge, like railways in Birmingham, Manchester and elsewhere, approached city-centre stations along viaducts which often had a blighting effect on the areas through which they passed (see above page 107).

Stations in cities were advertisements for particular companies and for railway travel in general. The London & Birmingham Railway terminus at Euston was the first to offer to passengers from London the prospect of long-distance travel. Designed by Philip Hardwick, it was seen as 'the greatest railway port in England', and his Doric Arch and the adjacent great hall conveyed impressions of the safety of the new form of transport and of the respectability and reliability of the company providing it. The terminus was less welcoming beyond the façade. Its waiting room was described in 1851 as 'mean' and its dining room as 'dungeon-like'. Equally impressive gateways to railway passenger travel were built outside London. Brunel's Great Western Railway terminus at Bristol Temple Meads has a timber roof that has the appearance of hammer-beam construction. Francis Thompson, an architect who worked in Britain and Canada, built the Italianate brick front of the station at Chester, and the elegant station buildings at Derby, as well as Regency-style wayside stations on the North Midland Railway. At Newcastle John Dobson completed in 1850 the spectacular Central Station, with a 600 foot (185 m) long façade in the Baroque style, and curving train sheds in wrought iron and glass. The termini in Dublin were likewise worthy of a capital city. Amiens Street (now Connolly) – the station for Belfast – was completed in 1844 to a restrained Italianate design by W. D. Butler. Kingsbridge (Heuston) – terminus of the line to Cork – is a Renaissance palace designed by Sancton Wood, who also designed stations at Cambridge and Stamford. Broadstone, terminus of the Midland Great Western Railway, completed in 1850 to the design of J. S. Mulvany, is an elegant five-bay building with Egyptian detailing. In London the first trains ran into Lewis Cubitt's station at King's Cross in 1852; a new terminus for the Great Western Railway at Paddington, designed by Brunel and Matthew Digby Wyatt, was opened in 1854; and in 1868 the Midland Railway opened its cathedral-like St Pancras, a symbol in the capital of the wealth and status of a provincial company, and harbinger of more comfortable rail travel.

The *Lord Warden Hotel* at Dover, which provided overnight accommodation for many wealthy people travelling to and from continental Europe. It was designed for the London, Chatham & Dover Railway by the London architect, Samuel Beazley, and opened in 1853. As new railways were built at Dover the hotel came to be entirely surrounded by tracks.

Substantial improvements in passenger comfort and safety began in the 1860s in the United States, and were emulated in Great Britain. Contact between passengers and drivers by means of a communication cord became mandatory in 1869. The continuous vacuum brake was invented by James Gardner in 1878, although it was not until 1893 that legislation enforced its use in passenger carriages. Steam heating was introduced in 1881, and the first carriages with electric lighting ran on the London, Brighton & South Coast Railway in the following year. Sleeping cars worked between London and Glasgow from 1873, and in 1874 the Midland Railway introduced luxury carriages operated by the American company established by George Pullman. Dining cars began to run on the Great Northern Railway in 1879.

For a generation the railways carried the wealthy in their own private carriages, secured on top of flat railway trucks. Francis Witts went from Gloucestershire to London by coach on 4 May 1839 and transferred at Maidenhead to a generously wide railway carriage while his luggage remained on the coach which was lashed to a flat waggon. On 22 June 1844 the king of Saxony travelled from one ducal household at Woburn to another at Chatsworth. His surgeon described how the carriages drove to Wolverton on the London & Birmingham Railway, where the party's vehicles were placed on trucks attached to a train from London. The king remained sitting in an open carriage. At Rugby the train passed on to the Midland Counties Railway and travelled to Derby. The trucks were then attached to a North Midland train which conveyed them to Chesterfield, where the carriages were unloaded for the drive over the moors to Chatsworth. The surgeon

enjoyed the journey under 'thundering bridges', over viaducts and through tunnels filled with smoke and steam, observing loaded boats on canals and trains passing in the other direction, one with oxen penned in carriages, and the 'wonderful pushing, going and coming, getting-out and getting-in' at stations. He was impressed with Derby's station, with the view of the Roundhouse (the shed in which 16 locomotives could be accommodated on tracks radiating from a turntable), and of the 'hospital' for engines that needed repair. It was 'a true railway day'.

Facilities for passengers improved gradually. Refreshment rooms and lavatories were provided at large stations: Queen Victoria had a chamber pot on board her GWR coach as early as 1848, but on-board lavatories did not become common until the advent of corridor coaches in the 1880s. Hotels, too, were soon constructed beside most principal stations. The Bridge House Hotel, built in 1835 on the approach to London Bridge, accommodated a lavish banquet when the London & Greenwich Railway's adjacent terminus opened on 14 December 1836. It was owned by John Humphrey, a city alderman and MP, and though it was in effect the hotel for London Bridge Station it remained independent of the railway companies. Two hotels, the Euston and the Victoria, were designed by Philip Hardwick on either side of the Euston arch, both with the appearance of plain Regency-style terraces. More imposing hotels were built by Lewis Cubitt at King's Cross in 1854 and by Francis Thompson at Derby. At Fleetwood in Lancashire – for a few years the place where railway passengers from the south disembarked to take the steamer to Glasgow – Decimus Burton built the revealingly named *North Euston Hotel*. More followed in the 1860s at Paddington, Charing Cross, Cannon Street, Victoria, Harwich, Southampton and at Millbay Docks in Plymouth.

Some hotels had the appearance of palaces, and Queen Victoria stayed in 1854 at the Paragon at Hull, completed four years earlier to the design of G. T. Andrews. The Lord Warden Hotel at Dover was designed for the London, Chatham & Dover Railway by Samuel Beazley and completed in 1853. Its 48 guests on census night in 1861 included two baronets, Sir Horace St Paul and Sir Charles Goring, two army officers, a banker, two lawyers and Archibald Tait, then bishop of London and from 1869 archbishop of Canterbury. The ultimate expression of a railway company's wish to impress was George Gilbert Scott's Midland Grand Hotel, which formed the Euston Road front of St Pancras Station and opened on 5 May 1873. All these hotels were places of transit, where the wealthy could pause on lengthy journeys which, before the introduction of sleeping carriages and restaurant cars, might take several days, but railway companies also built hotels such as those at Ilfracombe, Saltburn and Aberystwyth, intended to be the nuclei of resorts that might provide profitable traffic.

By 1870 railway companies were also carrying a high proportion of the freight traffic within the British Isles. The efficiency of the movement by sea of coal from the North East was transformed by iron steamships, but the railways nevertheless carried increasing quantities to London. While the principal canals remained viable, they did not pay the high dividends of previous years, and carrying on the more remote waterways dwindled. Significantly, new industries was

no longer being sited near to canals, and new mines, factories and quarries now had railway sidings rather than branch canals. Freight depots were built in most towns, and even small wayside passenger stations had goods yards with warehouses, cattle docks and sidings for unloading coal. Goods sheds were standardised on some lines, including the Oxford, Worcester & Wolverhampton, which constructed tarred wooden buildings at its stations along the Evenlode Valley.

Depots in cities were among the largest industrial sites. The one at King's Cross, which has been most thoroughly researched, was developed by Lewis Cubitt for the Great Northern Railway from 1851, and extended over 59 acres, including the site of the 'Top Shed' locomotive depot. Goods were exchanged with boats on the Regent's Canal as well as with road transport, for which extensive stable accommodation was provided. Cubitt built a six-storey granary in 1851, and roads ran through the site on viaducts whose arches accommodated stables. There were also transit sheds where small consignments of goods were interchanged between railway waggons and road vehicles. The nature of this kind of operation is conveyed vividly in *Freight 1935*, a film made by the London, Midland & Scottish Railway about its Camden depot, where the methods of operating had changed little from those of 1870. At King's Cross the temporary passenger station used until the main terminus opened in 1852 was adapted as a potato market, rivalling that in Tooley Street, Southwark, to which supplies were delivered by coastal shipping. By 1862 it was handling 85,000 tons annually, and in 1864–65 was enlarged by the addition of 39 small merchants' warehouses,

⊲ This multi-storey building in the Great Northern Railway's freight depot was known as the Granary, although cargoes other than grain were handled there at certain times. The depiction of barges on the Regent's Canal indicates the importance of the depot as an interchange between rail and water transport (see also page 133).

The original station of the London & Birmingham Railway was at Curzon Street, then on the edge of the city, and that of the Birmingham & Derby Junction Railway at nearby Lawley Street. By 1854 the former was part of the London & North Western Railway and the latter part of the Midland Railway. A joint through-station at New Street was opened in 1854. This picture shows the L&NWR platforms about 1870.

each with sidings approached by waggon turntables. A hydraulic system powering capstans and traversers, a new and untried technology, was installed when the depot was built. Much of the yard was occupied by coal drops, the earliest of which were installed in 1851, when the Great Northern was carrying coal to London in 7½-ton capacity hopper waggons which could discharge their loads through bottom doors. A legal decision in 1860 determined that the Great Northern had no authority to operate as a coal-trader itself, and merchants moved in to the drops and offices previously occupied by the company. One was Samuel Plimsoll, who prospered by bringing in coal and transferring it to canal boats that delivered it to London gasworks. In 1859 he patented a form of drop in which coal fell for a shorter distance, so that less of it broke into dust, and in 1865–66 the Great Northern built him a viaduct, incorporating 13 of the new style drops, facing Canley Street where in 1862 the Midland Railway had also built drops. After 1870 an increasing proportion of London's household coal was being delivered in box-type waggons to be unloaded by hand in railway yards in the suburbs.

Some passenger stations built on the edges of towns when railways opened were later replaced by central stations, and after closure were adapted as freight depots, including those at Liverpool Road, Manchester, Bricklayers' Arms in south London, and Lawley Street and Curzon Street in Birmingham.

Sidings for sorting waggons were operating by 1870, but most large marshalling yards were not laid out until after 1900. In 1870 locomotives were serviced at several hundred running sheds. Some were small installations at branch line termini, with buildings where two or three locomotives could receive the overnight attention of fitters, sidings with pits into which ashes could be raked from fireboxes, and space for waggons from which tenders and bunkers could be loaded with coal. At the other extreme, vast installations in cities, such as Stewart's Lane at Battersea, Holbeck in Leeds, or St Margaret's in Edinburgh, housed several hundred locomotives, and emitted sulphurous hazes that engulfed their neighbourhoods.

Stage-coach services between large towns closed as soon as railways opened, but the long-term effect of railways was substantially to *increase* horse-drawn road traffic. Railway passenger stations proved to be magnets for horse-drawn vehicles, hackney cabs, omnibuses conveying travellers to and from hotels, connecting coaches to places that the railway had yet to reach, and private carriages. Freight depots employed multitudes of horses. When the King's Cross yard opened in 1851 the Great Northern estimated that its operations would require 500 horses, but 600 were in use by 1860 and 1,500 forty years later. Many industrial concerns used waggons and carts for short distance traffic: when Mr Pickwick reached the Black Country he observed ponderous waggons which toiled along

'First class – the meeting', a painting by Abraham Solomon, an artist who made extensive use of railway subjects. The first version of this painting, shown in 1854, caused controversy as it showed a young man flirting with a young woman while her father was asleep. In this revised version the young man is shown talking to the father while exchanging glances with the young woman. The painting portrays effectively the upholstery of first-class accommodation in the 1850s, which was much more comfortable than that to be found in stage or mail coaches.

the road, laden with clashing rods of iron. It has been calculated that by the 1890s there were 3.5 million horses in England. Although many were employed in agriculture, a substantial proportion carried goods or people to and from railway stations.

Railways also became one of the country's largest employers. By 1850 nearly 60,000 men were working on the main lines, and the total more than doubled in the following decade, approaching 275,000 by 1873. Initially railways, like any new industry, drew in large numbers of young people, but employment structures became hierarchical and in some respects, such as the wearing of uniforms, drew upon military precedents. In 1860 George Measom told intending travellers on the Great Western that 'Every person employed on the line has a distinguishing number on the collar of his coat; if you have any complaint to make, write to the Secretary, designating the offender by his number.' In 1861 we know that 23 Great Western engine drivers were living in two blocks of streets near Paddington Station. Their mean age was 33, and nine originated from Northumberland and Durham.

The opportunities available to young men are illustrated by the career of Peter Mottershead, born at Burnage, Manchester, on 6 January 1835. Bored with school at the age of 11, he worked for three years in a brickyard before moving on to a grocer's shop in Manchester. In September 1853, at the age of 18 and with 'an inclination for railroading', he first applied for a post with the LNWR at Longsight and then was offered a job by the Shrewsbury & Chester Railway, cleaning locomotives at Shrewsbury. He was promoted to fireman in November 1854, after the Shrewsbury & Chester and its sister company the Shrewsbury & Birmingham became part of the Great Western. He fired for drivers from Fife and Lancashire, and for a man who had learned his trade on the Stockton & Darlington. Aged 22, he was transferred to Wolverhampton and became a driver in April 1857, and in 1860 was taking the daily freight train from Wolverhampton to Basingstoke. He moved to Birmingham where, as one of the last to work broad-gauge passenger trains, he received wages of 7s. 6d. per day. With his own locomotive, *Alma*, he could cover the 43 miles from Oxford to Leamington in 35 minutes. In 1869 he returned to Wolverhampton, when broad-gauge trains ceased to run to the north and in 1873, after 20 years, he resigned, took ship at Liverpool, and after a spell in Canada moved to the United States where in 1908 he was still driving locomotives, in Iowa, at the age of 73.

By the 1860s, little more than a generation after the first public line had begun services, the railways were the prime means of inland transport in the British Isles. Farmers at Knighton were told in 1862 that

Railways have increased the wealth of the merchant, and have equally benefited the poor man; distance has been annihilated, local markets have been brought into connection with the outports of the country, each district has derived the advantages of competition between the merchants of London, Liverpool, Bristol and other ports, for the supply of the commodities necessary for its wants. The manufactured goods of Lancashire and Yorkshire, by a reduction in the carriage of the raw material, have been produced at less cost, and carried by the same means to the most distant corners of the kingdom; and these products have been brought within the means

of the most needy, giving them comfort, health and happiness …

To this commentator the economic benefits of the railways – in reducing costs and increasing communications and trade over longer and longer distances – were obvious and profound. In the context of the industrial revolution the railways were vital: just as vital, indeed, as the creation of a viable system of inland waterways and canals had been in the eighteenth century, or the introduction of the shipping container was to be in the twentieth.

A transport revolution?

The transport history of the industrial revolution is more varied and complex than any simple chronology of innovation. There was no straight-forward, linear transition from one phase to another, from the use of packhorse to horse-drawn waggon, or from canal barge to railway carriage. Successive generations did see the introduction of new and improved forms of transport, but more often than not these supplemented existing systems, rather than replace them, at least for a time. For the crucial trade between Manchester and Liverpool, for example, the road network remained busy even as canal links were dramatically improved; neither road nor canal was rendered obsolete by the first railway link between the two cities in 1830, nor by the second, southern route via Warrington which was completed in the 1870s; and all routes between Liverpool and Manchester remained busy even after the Manchester Ship Canal was constructed in the 1890s.

As we have seen, one of the most profound of the early improvements was the substitution of wheeled vehicles for packhorses in the lowlands. Indeed, right through our period and beyond, the incremental improvement of turnpikes and other roads was one of the most ubiquitous and widespread of transport improvements. From the mid-eighteenth century inland waterways and canals sustained industrialisation for more than a generation, often reducing costs of carrying by 25 per cent. Many canals, indeed, remained in use for decades after the railways were

built. At sea, both for foreign and for coastal trade, the merits of iron ships and steam propulsion had been demonstrated, although the general adoption of such technologies did not really begin to transform the merchant shipping fleet until the 1860s. Whatever their type, ships were able to make use of the new systems of wet docks that had been constructed in the major ports, while there were new piers and quays in small harbours all around the coast. And then there arrived the railways. Revolutionary in many ways, even the railways were in fact the product of more than 170 years of development. And they could not operate or exist in isolation: their effective operation was dependent upon ships, barges, coaches, carts and waggons.

By the end of the period, the transport infrastructure of Great Britain was very different, and much more efficient and cost-effective than it had been at the beginning. The ability to move raw materials, finished goods and passengers quickly and relatively inexpensively was crucial to the pace and process of industrialisation.

Industry also required power, and as we have seen the surging demand for fuel was a major stimulus for some transport innovations, including the Duke of Bridgewater's pioneering canal and the horse-drawn waggonways of the North East. In the next chapter we will turn to consider the fuel that was so important to the industrialisation of the British Isles: coal.

PART II

Creating the 'workshop of the world'

Gosforth Colliery, on the west bank of the Ouse Burn, three miles
north of Newcastle, was sunk between 1825 and 1829 and worked
until 1884, when it was abandoned due to geological problems.
The image shows the twin shafts, each of which was wound by a
50 hp steam engine, while a 150 hp engine pumped water from the
workings. The chaldron waggons carried coal to staithes on the river
Tyne along a 3½ mile waggonway which was worked by stationary
steam engines.

6

Coal mining and
coalfield industries

'All the activity and industry of this kingdom is fast concentrating where there are coal pits.'

ARTHUR YOUNG, AT MEASHAM, 7 AUGUST 1791

ETWEEN 1700 AND 1870 the resources of Britain's coalfields were unlocked. When travelling from Durham to Newcastle in the 1720s Daniel Defoe observed that the area was an 'inexhausted store of coal and coal pits', but at this early date few other areas of the country were dominated by mining. Defoe was struck by the scene because it was extraordinary. Nowhere else in Europe produced anywhere near as much coal as Britain. There was a modest mining sector in southern Belgium, but nowhere else was coal the principal fuel source, and nowhere else was it mined in large quantities. At the end of the eighteenth century the vast majority of worldwide coal production was British, and most of that was in north-east England, where coalfield operations and development were stimulated principally by long-established seaborne coal shipments to London. British pits in 1700 were producing about three million tons *per annum*, but by 1830 output exceeded 30 million tons, an increase in annual consumption per head from 9 cwt to more than 37 cwt. In 1855 output was more than 75 million tons; it exceeded 100 million tons for the first time in 1865, and had reached 115 million tons by 1871, an annual *per capita* consumption of about 75 cwt. Britain's rapid growth in coal mining meant that both industrial and domestic consumers had ample and readily available supplies of what was, by international standards, comparatively inexpensive energy: a significant economic advantage which underpinned the growth or viability of many other industries. By the 1860s, too, there were distinct coalfield economies. Developing transport systems enlarged markets for domestic coal, while coal-using industries, such as salt extraction and associated chemical manufactures, the smelting and shaping of metals, glass making and ceramic production, developed on the coalfields. Coal was the principal fuel of industrialisation.

Working the seams

Most coal deposits can be found in horizontal, or sloping seams (unlike lead, which can generally be found in vertical seams). In some places the coal seams outcrop to the surface, but most have to be excavated. In 1700 some seams in most British coalfields were accessed by bell pits, shafts up to 30 feet deep from

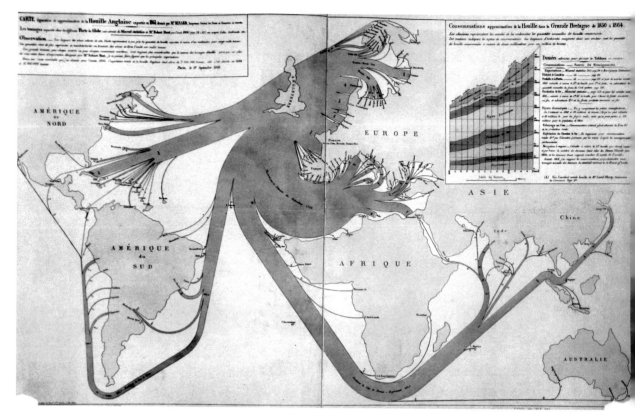

A diagrammatic map by the French cartographer Charles Joseph Minard showing exports of coal from Great Britain in 1864. It is evident that British mines supplied huge quantities of coal to many parts of continental Europe for industrial and domestic purposes, and that substantial quantities were carried to 'coaling stations' all over the world for fuelling the increasing numbers of British steamships which carried most international trade.

St Hilda's Colliery was sunk in 1825, and by 1844 had two 30 hp winding engines, a 90 hp pumping engine and a 20 hp engine situated in the underground working, probably used for haulage. Like most mines in the North East this colliery was served by a waggonway worked with chaldron waggons. It was closed in 1940 when the entry of Italy into the Second World War closed off its principal export market.

A German image, published in the mid-nineteenth century, of the bottom of the shaft at a coal mine near Newcastle-upon-Tyne. Coal in corves (baskets) is brought to the shaft along an underground railway before being raised up the shaft. In the North East coal was almost universally extracted by the pillar-and-stall system whereby each miner would be paid piece work for the coal he dug, and each basket would contain the output of a particular man. The boys employed as 'hangers-on', who attached corves to ropes, can be seen resting on the right.

© SCIENCE MUSEUM/SCIENCE & SOCIETY PICTURE LIBRARY

An illustration published in 1842 showing how coal was hauled underground by children using the girdle and chain method.

which coal was worked in a circular fashion, eventually forming bell-shaped voids. A shaft would be abandoned when the roof began to fall, and another would be dug nearby. Bell pits appear in the landscape on the Clee Hills in Shropshire, at Bentley Grange near Doncaster, and at Strelley, Nottinghamshire, as saucer-shaped depressions, while 77 were recorded in 2008 during tree felling at Wilsontown, Lanarkshire. Some were worked in the nineteenth century, but remains are difficult to date. Adit mines or drifts, in which miners advance horizontally from the surface outcrop of a seam, are still worked in the Forest of Dean and were employed throughout the period from 1700 to 1870. Adits form the 'second ways out' for the underground sections of the preserved Caphouse Colliery near Wakefield and Big Pit at Blaenavon.

Britain's earliest significant coalfield, the North East, was particularly important in nurturing mining skills. Men who had trained as colliery viewers (or managers) on Tyneside and Wearside were by the 1860s managing pits all over the British Isles. Despite this, the pillar-and-stall system of extraction which was characteristic of the North East, whereby headings were driven into the coal and columns were left to support the roof, was not used in most other areas. They, instead, favoured the longwall system,

Bearing Pits, West Linton, Peeblesshire. The evidence of Jane Peacock Watson, aged 40, coal bearer: 'I have wrought in the bowels of the earth 33 years and have been married 23 years, and had nine children. Six are alive, three died of typhus a few years since and I have had two dead born. They were so from the oppressive work. A vast number of women have dead children and false births which are worse, as they are no able to work after the latter. I have always been obliged to work below till forced to go home to bear the bairn, and so other women. We return as soon as we are able, never longer than 10 or 12 days, many less if they are needed. It is only horse work, and ruins the women. It crushes their haunches, bends their ankles, and makes them old women at 40. Women so soon get weak that they are forced to take the little ones down to relieve them; even children of six years of age do much to relieve the burthen. Knows it is bad to keep bairns from school but every little helps …'

EVIDENCE FROM THE EAST OF SCOTLAND REPORT OF THE 1842 COMMISSION

employed in Shropshire from the mid-seventeenth century, in which miners removed the whole of a seam as they advanced from or retreated towards a shaft, and propped the resulting void (sometimes called the *goof* or *gob*) with wooden pit props, and filling the space with slack or waste rock.

Flooding of coal workings was a persistent problem. During the eighteenth century the Newcomen engine became the principal means of pumping water from coal mines. Since unsaleable coal was readily available as boiler fuel, there were few incentives to install more

Bearing Pits, Harlaw Muir, Coaly Burn, parish of West Linton, Peeblesshire. (Rev. J. J. Beresford, Leaseholder and Heritor)

The evidence of Margaret Leveston, 6 years old, coal-bearer:

'Been down at coal-carrying six weeks; makes 10 to 14 rakes a-day; carries full 56lb. of coal in a wooden backit. The work is na guid; it is so very sair. I work with sister Jesse and mother; dinna ken the time we gang; it is gai [i.e. quite] dark. Get plenty of broth and porridge and run home and get bannock, as we live just by the pit. Never been to school; it is so far away.' [A most interesting child and perfectly beautiful. I ascertained her age to be six 24th May, 1840; she was registered at Inveresk.]

efficient steam engines. Until the 1780s coal was hoisted from the larger pits by horse gins or man-powered windlasses, but then a proliferation of steam winding engines from the 1780s allowed an acceleration in coal production. A Scottish ironmaster, reflecting in 1864 on the waste tips of small collieries worked by windlass and gin that remained among the new mines around Coatbridge, implied that it was the steam winding engine as much as the Monkland Canal that had stimulated growth in the area. Sometimes explicit evidence is available: the installation of a winding engine in 1804 at Middle Pit at Radstock, Somerset, for instance, raised daily output from 20 to 50 tons.

In the eighteenth century coal was raised up shafts in corves (baskets), which were drawn by hemp ropes. Wrought-iron chains, which were cheaper and more durable, were developed in the early nineteenth century. At Coalport, in about 1804, Gilbert Gilpin forged a three-link rattle chain, and several years later his neighbour Benjamin Edge used wooden keys to hold together three parallel chains. Wire ropes, first used at Clausthal in the Harz Mountains of Germany, were tried at the St Lawrence Colliery, Newcastle, from the late 1830s, emerged successfully from a trial in July 1844 at the Wingate Colliery, Co. Durham, and by the 1860s were widely used. Wooden headstocks

A list of deaths from accidents and explosions in the Bradford and Halifax district, compiled for the 1842 Commission on Mines. This is an unrepresentative sample, but it would appear that most accidents should have been preventable: well over half involved workers falling down the shafts or suffering objects fall upon them, while a good number involved accidents involving coal waggons and corves. The fate of William Drake (12) is particularly poignant: 'Deceased trying to ascend the shaft by taking hold [of] the axles of the corve, and letting go within a few yards of the top.'

No.	Date	Where	Name	Age	Verdicts
1	1837 Dec. 26	Saddleworth	Mills, Richard	..	Fell from a corve in ascending the shaft of a coal-pit. Deceased and another boy in the corve with a collier, and was properly cautioned.
2	1838 Jan. 2	Bierley	Thorp, Joseph	52	A banksman, fell down the shaft, in landing the corve neglected to slip the catch.
3	Feb. 1	Lindley	Walker, George	26	Fall of a stone from the shaft side. No neglect.
4	March 7	Bowling	Root, Edward	13	Fell from the corve in descending. Supposed to have caught at something on the pit's side.
5	March 22	Holmfirth	Hurst, Enoch	10	Killed by a piece of coal falling from the corve. No blame; he might have got out of the way.
6	April 28	North Bierley	Sugden, Abraham	9	Fall of ironstone from a corve. No blame or negligence.
7	May 2	Bradford Moor	Walker, William	16	Thrown from a corve to the bottom of the shaft by the rope breaking—the engineer neglecting to stop his rope in proper time; the boy coming up without notice, and contrary to the rules.
8	June 22	Wilsden	Binns, Abraham	15	Fall of scale from a corve hitting against the ledges of the shaft.
9	July 5	Northowram	Crossley, John	16	Ditto ditto, in consequence of wet weather.
10	July 10	Ditto	Crossley, Abraham	30	The like.
11	Aug. 3	North Bierley	Anson, Christopher	7	Accidental fall down a shaft; a "gin" driver. No blame.
12	Aug. 31	Halifax	Taylor, Francis	11	Explosion of fire-damp. Neglect of John Crossley, his master, in not going first in pit.
13	1839 April 17	Ditto	Lumley, James	9	The like. With caution there is no need of safety-lamps in this district.
14	April 22	Baildon	Craven, Joseph	7	Accidental fall in going down a shaft.
15	Oct. 9	Northowram	Oldfield, Thomas	48	The like, in consequence of machinery being out of gear. No blame.
16	March 1	Southowram	Gray, Joseph	11	Accidental fall of a stone from the roof of a pit.
17	March 25	Idle	Hardaker, John	8	Accidental fall down a shaft. Deceased a cart-driver.
18	April 19	Allerton	Stansfield, Joshua	30	The like.
19	April 26	Tong	Oates, Henry	..	Accidental fall down an old shaft. Afterwards filled up at request of jury.
20	May 11	Bowling	Tewdale, James	9	Fall from a corve in ascending a shaft.
21	Aug. 13	Kirkheaton	Drake, William	12	Deceased trying to ascend the shaft by taking hold the axles of the corve, and letting go within a few yards of the top.
22	Sept. 3	Holmfirth	Barraclough, Joseph	14	Unexpected explosion of fire-damp.
23	Oct. 4	North Bierley	West, Joshua	9	Fall from a corve in ascending a shaft contrary to rules.
24	Oct. 14	Northowram	Jennings, James	11	Accidental fall down a shaft by attempting to ascend by tackling without corve.
25	Nov. 19	Wilsden	Fetley, Benjamin	14	Ditto ditto of earth from the roof of a pit by deceased driving corve against a post.
26	Dec. 6	Bradford	Brook, Joseph	13	Ditto ditto of stone from the roof of pit.
27	1840 March 2	Bowling	Naylor, James	..	Fall of dirt from a corve. The corve not properly fastened by deceased.
28	April 6	Wyke	Marsden, William	42	Explosion of fire-damp, caused by deceased taking the top from his lamp.
29	April 11	Bowling	Beaumont, Benj.	..	Killed by coal-waggons. Cautioned to keep out of the way.
30	April 28	Lindley	Wilkinson, William	21	Accidental fall of earth from roof of pit.
31	May 18	Southowram	Cheatham, Charles	10	Explosion of fire-damp, Isaac Green, his employer, neglecting to fill up an old hole.
32	June 1	Thornton	Fearnsides, Thomas	20	Accidental fall from corve in descending the shaft.
33	June 11	Halifax	Sheard, William	30	Explosion of fire-damp. Deceased persisting in going into the pit, although against the fire-damp as he went on.
34	June 15	Ditto	Sheard, Joseph	..	Explosion of fire-damp. Deceased compelled to go in by Wm. Sheard, his employer.
35	Aug. 15	Bradley	Haigh, Reuben	12	Accidentally caught in a chain of a corve, and falling whilst drawing up.
36	April 6	North Bierley	Sharp, Joseph	33	Unexpected fall of coal from the roof of a pit.
37	Aug. 22	Lockwood	Haigh, David	..	Accidental explosion of fire-damp. Deceased aware of it, and fetching his tools contrary to order.
38	Ditto	Ditto	Jephson, Joshua	..	The like.
39	Sept. 15	Horton	Fieldhouse, Thomas	5	Accidental fall down a shaft by deceased playing near the pit in the absence of the workpeople.
40	Sept. 23	North Bierley	Worship, Noah	11	Killed in pit by a corve running over him, deceased going before instead of behind the corve.
41	Nov. 2	Northowram	Woodhead, John	29	Accidental fall from a corve in ascending the shaft.
42	Nov. 17	North Bierley	Smith, James	13	Killed in pit by a corve falling on him.
43	Dec. 18	Ditto	Brook, Jonas	38	Unexpected fall of earth from the roof of the pit.
44		Wike	Heaton, John	..	The like.
45	1841 Jan. 21	Tong	Thomas, Benjamin	12	Explosion of gunpowder, deceased intending to secrete a portion.
46		Bowling	Hill, John	..	Accidental fall down a shaft in landing a corve.
47	Jan. 22	Ditto	Sharp, Joseph	12	Ditto ditto ditto.
48	Feb. 26	Halifax	Sutcliffe, Jonathan	..	Accidental and unexpected explosion of fire-damp.
49	April 10	Northowram	Smith, Mathew	..	Fall down a shaft, deceased holding the clutch-irons without giving notice to draw up.
50	June 12	North Bierley	Kellett, David	14	Fall down a shaft. Deceased drawn over the pulley by his uncle and grand-father.

were combined as 'tandem headgears', such as the one now restored at Brinsley, Nottinghamshire. By the 1860s wrought-iron, and subsequently steel lattice, frames were installed over newly sunk shafts, but wooden headstocks, including that of 1876 at Caphouse Colliery, continued to be installed until they were prohibited by legislation in 1911. A 12-year-old from Ilkeston explained in 1842 that he helped his father, a 'hanger-on', attaching corves to chains at the shaft bottom so that they could be raised to the surface. Thomas Young Hall, viewer at South Hetton Colliery, replaced corves with iron tubs from 1833, and from 1834 applied shoes, guide rods and 'keps' upon which to rest cages while carriages were changed. His system was demonstrated in London in 1835.

Coal mining was a hazardous occupation. Even getting to the seam being worked was fraught with danger. In pits where chains were used for haulage it was customary for men, six or seven at a time, to descend and ascend the shafts on pieces of wood simply passed through the links of the chain. Nine miners, four of them under 15 years of age, were killed when a chain snapped as they were ascending the Brick Kiln Leasow pit in Madeley on 27 September 1864. Cages, in use from the 1840s, could make the miner's journeys from and to his workplace safer, but they were not universally adopted. Unlined shafts also represented a major hazard, as equipment and men passing up or down could snag on obstructions, while falls of rock or earth could endanger those below. John Buddle used cast-iron tubbing to line a shaft at Wallsend Colliery as early as 1792, and installed cast-iron bolted segments at Percy Main Colliery in 1796–97. In the 1840s viewers and government inspectors recommended filling the

spaces between the lining and the shaft walls with lime. Many deaths were caused by miners falling in to shafts or, even after lining was introduced, by loose bricks dropping on to 'hangers-on' or men waiting to ascend. Conscientious viewers ensured that curbing around shaft tops stopped the dislodgement of bricks and that fencing prevented falls into shafts. Such precautions were not costly, but their absence caused many deaths in every coalfield. Other ever-present dangers included the threat of roof falls, and scorching with fire damp. In old age – or what passed for old age in mining communities – many were stiffened by rheumatism or subject to asthma and lung diseases caused by the inhalation of coal dust.

The direct precursors of Britain's main-line railways may be found in its coalfields. The earliest recorded examples of the use of railways in English collieries date from the years around 1600, and they were commonplace in adit mines long before 1700. In the same period, two distinctive systems of surface railway were nurtured in the North East and Shropshire coalfields, and by the 1790s railways were transporting the produce of every significant coalfield. In 1765 Gabriel Jars observed that underground in the North East wooden rails were used on the horse roads along which coal was conveyed from faces to shafts. Subsequently these were replaced with iron rails. Vehicles were drawn by ponies or asses tended by boys, many of whom, in the 1860s, were aged between ten and twelve. Haulage or 'putting' between coal faces and horse roads might be undertaken by children pulling corves along rough surfaces by a rope or chain to which they were attached by a leather girdle. In 1787 John Curr, the Tyneside-born coal viewer who managed the Duke of Norfolk's collieries in Sheffield, introduced for the purpose iron 'plate rails', which were L-shaped in section. This innovation greatly ameliorated the suffering of children who worked in mines, and he was even commemorated in song:

> God bless the man in peace and plenty
> That first invented metal plates:
> Draw out his years to five times twenty,
> Then slide him through the heavenly gates.

The dangers of explosions caused by methane, or 'fire damp', were appreciated in the North East well before 1700, but the gas was still causing catastrophic accidents in the twentieth century. It was encountered increasingly as shafts became deeper. Sir Humphrey Davy's safety lamp, which employed a fine wire gauze through which flames could not penetrate, made mining feasible in places where previously it had been too hazardous. Davy's research was prompted by an explosion at Felling near Gateshead in 1812 that killed 91 men. The lamp was publicly displayed in 1815 and used at Hebburn Colliery the following year. George Stephenson designed a similar lamp that produced greater luminosity, and by 1870 the safety lamp was the usual means of lighting where methane was present. Carbon dioxide, or 'black damp', could cause the deaths of miners when it accumulated in the lowest parts of workings. Its presence in pits where there was no methane could be indicated when candles were extinguished by the gas, and in gassy mines by canaries, which keeled over if taken into concentrations of gas.

An illustration published in 1842 showing how coal was hauled underground by children using the girdle and chain method. '1. The candle holder. A socket of iron, having a spike at right angles for the convenience of sticking the light in the sides of the pit when stationary. The spike forms a handle when the light is carried before them. 2. The skull-cap, having a leather band into which the candle holder is thrust when the hands are employed in locomotion. 3. The girdle and hook for attaching to the chain. 4. Represents the position of the girdle.'

FROM THE REPORT ON THE EMPLOYMENT OF CHILDREN AND YOUNG PERSONS IN THE COLLIERIES OF SOUTH GLOUCESTERSHIRE, 1842

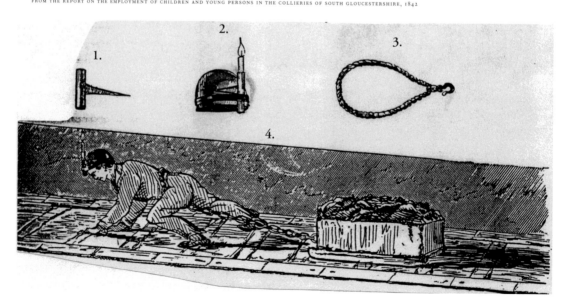

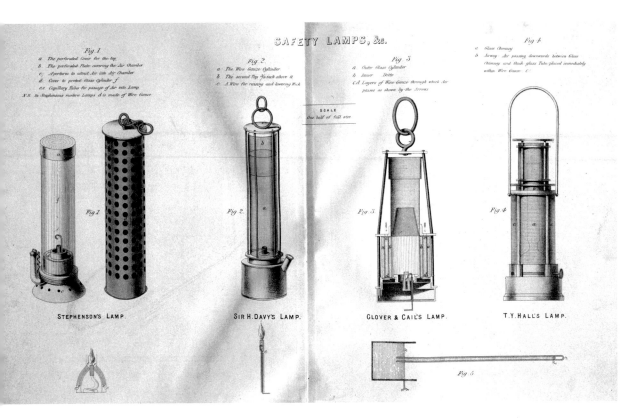

Diagrams of safety lamps designed by George Stephenson, Sir Humphrey Davy, Clover & Cail and T. Y. Hall. Until the development of safety lamps miners worked by the light of candles or other naked flames, which in some mines could ignite methane or 'fire damp'. From *A Practical Treatise on Mine Engineering*, by George Clementson Greenwell, published in 1869.

In order to prevent the accumulation of methane or CO_2 collieries had to be ventilated by the circulation of fresh air. Doors were installed to seal off particular areas and were opened only when vehicles or men passed through. The task of opening and shutting these ventilation doors usually fell to young boys, some as young as six years old. In 1843 the Children's Employment Commission reported that young boys were being employed in a range of duties below ground. As well as controlling ventilation doors, they were drawing corves to horse roads, or tending the ponies that hauled waggons to the shafts. The employment of children was justified on practical grounds, since they were small enough to perform tasks that adults could not do. The evidence given to the Commission suggests that the employment of very young children might already have been diminishing before the Mines Act of 1842 prohibited the employment of children under the age of ten to work underground, although the census returns of 1861 show that many ten-year-olds were still then being employed.

In many collieries fresh air was drawn down one shaft and foul air expelled up another, while in a single-shaft mine the good air could be drawn down one side of a shaft that was divided by a 'brattice', or wooden barrier, and expelled up the other side. At many collieries in 1860 air was being circulated by furnaces, in or adjacent to shafts, which by creating updrafts of hot air could lift stale air from the workings, but this method was slowly superseded by the use of powered fans, of which about 200 were working in Britain by the 1870s. William Brunton had installed a fan at one of the Navigation pits in South Wales in 1849, and James Nasmyth designed one that was in use at Elsecar from 1852. A fan of the type patented in 1862 by Theophile Guibal of Mons, Belgium, was installed at Elswick Colliery from 1864. The fan designed by John Roberts Waddle of Llanelli, was first used at Bouville's Court Colliery, Saundersfoot, also in 1864, and examples remain at Big Pit and Beamish, while a fan designed by the Glasgow engineer James Howden is conserved at Prestongrange.

Where a pit had only one access, miners' lives were endangered if it became blocked, as happened at Hartley Colliery, Northumberland, in 1862, when the beam of the pumping engine fractured and fell into the shaft: 204 men and boys were trapped and died of suffocation. Subsequent legislation enforced the provision of more than a single access in all pits of significant size.

In the North East by 1820 coal was being separated into different grades by screening. Eight collieries in Lancashire in 1849 were using Walker's patent cylindrical coal riddle, a steam-powered revolving screen for separating slack, and this technology was adopted by Yorkshire colliery owners as they looked to markets in London which demanded a better-graded and higher quality product. Nevertheless at many collieries in the 1860s gangs of women were still sorting coal by eye and hand, a practice that continued in the Wigan (where Pit Brow Lasses formed the subject of picture postcards) and St Helens area even in the 1950s.

As we have seen, the amount of coal being mined in British pits increased from 3 million tons to 115 million tons between 1700 and 1871, and there was a corresponding increase in employment. In 1700 there had been about 15,000 coal miners in Britain, about half of them working in Northumberland and Co. Durham. By 1841 there were almost 120,000, nearly 220,000 in 1851, 307,500 in 1864, and more than half a million by 1873. There was much internal migration within coalfields, particularly to newly opened collieries. Those who moved from agricultural areas might seek employment on the surface, since it was difficult to learn in mature years the sensitivity to surroundings that was necessary for safe working below ground. It was received wisdom, indeed, that mining coal was a way of life, not a set of skills that could be taught. In 1754, for instance, a Little

Wenlock man was esteemed highly because he had 'been brought up as a collier from a boy', while in 1821 'bred a collier' appeared on the settlement certificates of four men from Ketley. In 1842 an 80-year-old Derbyshire miner said that he had been a labourer before entering the pit at the age of 30. He never did 'boys' work', but his four sons were brought up to it, one entering the pit at the age of seven and two at eight. He believed that a man who had not mined coal as a boy could never become a collier equal to those who had been raised from childhood in the pits.

The terms and systems of employment varied both between and within coalfields. In some areas miners were employed directly by the colliery management, but elsewhere sub-contractors, commonly called 'butties', undertook to produce certain quantities of coal and then hired men to carry out the necessary tasks. The inquiry into the Chartist-inspired strikes of 1842 revealed dissatisfaction with that system, particularly over the allocation of workplaces, the definition of a day's work, truck shops, and being forced to wait for wages in pubs. In Derbyshire in the 1840s, sub-contracting was widespread but not universal: the coal-owners John and Charles Mold of Morley Park, for instance, were proud not to have used butties for 20 years. Abuses of the system may have been mitigated from the 1840s, but sub-contracting still remained widespread in the 1860s.

Throughout the eighteenth century Scottish miners fared even worse from a legal point of view, being 'bonded' to their employers under legislation that had been passed by the Scottish Parliament in 1606. Under this Act the owners of Scottish saltpans and collieries had been allowed to exercise wide-ranging control over their employees, a system that in 1775 was described as 'a state of Slavery or Bondage'. In the opinion of one historian, miners and saltworkers were subjected to 'a degradation without parallel in the history of labour in Scotland'. Evidence from the 1740s shows that some free men sold themselves into bondage, under which they, their families, and even their children yet to be born, were bound to particular collieries. Bonded miners could be loaned to other coalmasters, or set to do other work, and were pursued vigorously if they fled. Nevertheless, their wages were higher than those for most manual craftsmen and they were provided with housing that was at least no worse than that occupied by others. Legislation in 1775, stimulated by the case of a slave threatened with being returned to servitude in Grenada – who claimed that baptism in the Kirk made him a free man – enabled a gradual emancipation of the bonded miners. The 1775 Act stipulated that anyone beginning work as a collier after 1 July 1775 could not be bound. The change removed a major constraint on growth – since the prospect of bondage made men reluctant to enter the industry – but many Scottish miners remained bonded until the Colliers (Scotland) Act of 1799 made them wholly free.

The employment of females underground was prohibited by the Mines Act of 1842, by which time women worked below the surface only in Scotland, Lancashire and South Wales. It is possible that females accounted for a quarter of the underground labour force in eastern Scotland before 1843, but in the country at large fewer than 3 per cent of miners were women.

In the second half of the nineteenth century between 4,000 and 6,000 women worked above ground at coal mines, a small and declining proportion of an expanding labour force. In the East Midlands, Lancashire and Yorkshire coal mining co-existed with textile manufacturing, which readily provided employment for young women, although such complementary opportunities were lacking in most of the pit villages of the North East. There were also some employment opportunities in other extractive industries: thus in Shropshire iron ore occurs in nodules in bands of clay, which was mined by longwall methods and dumped on tips. After months of weathering, the nodules would be collected by gangs of women, who carried them to tramroads which took them to blast furnaces. Young women so employed traditionally migrated to the western fringes of London every May, where they found employment in hay making, and then in picking fruit, which they carried in baskets on their heads to Covent Garden. Women from South Wales and Staffordshire were similarly employed.

The industrial uses and consumers of coal

The mining of coal could be highly dangerous, expensive, and often presented considerable technical difficulties. These costs could only be justified if there were a ready and profitable market for the coal produced. Fortunately for mine owners, those markets were both diverse and increasing rapidly. Some were well established, such as the seaborne trade from the North East to London. In other areas a growth in production followed the opening up of new markets, such as those made accessible by the building of new transport systems. In others the increasing output was consumed by an expanding local manufacturing industry. For example, coal was used on a large scale in ironworks from the mid-eighteenth century, and the pattern of integrated coal- and iron-working companies, set in Shropshire in the 1750s, was followed elsewhere. Such companies used coal in brick making and lime burning and also sold some of the produce of their mines for domestic use. Over time coal production became the primary concern of some iron-making companies. Copper working also consumed coal, and

lead smelting provided a market for the meagre coal seams in the Pennine uplands.

Coke, the substance that remains after the volatile constituents have been removed from coal, is an almost smokeless fuel. Dr Robert Plot wrote in 1685 of, 'the coal … prepared by charring, they call coakes'. Houghton, writing in 1692, believed that Derbyshire maltsters had been using it from about 1650, and it was traded sufficiently often in the 1690s for a duty to be levied on, 'all cinders made of Pit-coal … [whether] shipped or water-born[e]'. Abraham Darby was using coke made in open heaps to smelt iron ore in 1709, but several ironmasters subsequently made coke in ovens. In the 1780s and 1790s Lord Dundonald retrieved tar and other volatile products by heating coal in ovens in which coke was left as a residue, but his process did not gain universal acceptance. The proliferation of foundries in provincial towns increased the demand for coke, and from the early nineteenth century the gasworks – which made use of the volatile components of coal that had previously been regarded as waste – provided coke, which to them was a residue, for local consumption. Until the early 1860s most railway locomotives were fired with coke, but then Charles Markham and others demonstrated that fireboxes could be designed to burn raw coal.

Salt and soda ash

The production of salt by boiling brine was long-established by 1700, and was important in Lancashire, on Tyneside and Wearside, in west Cumberland and in Scotland. Alkali – which in an industrial context means sodium carbonate (Na_2CO_3) or soda ash – is essential for the manufacture of soap and glass. In the eighteenth century it was obtained from barilla or kelp, but Archibald Cochrane, 9th Earl of Dundonald, and James Keir devised methods of making it from coal, salt and limestone which, though sound in chemical

157. BRICKFIELD, MOULDER'S BENCH, KILN, &c.

A substantial proportion of the coal extracted in Britain was used to fire kilns to make bricks, and the opening of canals and railways bringing in supplies of coal almost always stimulated brick making. This engraving shows a characteristic town-edge brickyard, with a pug mill (see also page 216), probably worked by a horse, a hovel where bricks were shaped, and a coal-fired kiln in the background.
BY COURTESY OF THE IRONBRIDGE GORGE MUSEUM TRUST

A colliery in the North East *circa* 1845 with a characteristic headstock, steam winding-engine house, coke ovens and chaldron waggons. The six-wheeled locomotive shows remarkable similarities to Timothy Hackworth's *Royal George* of 1827.
© SCIENCE MUSEUM/SCIENCE & SOCIETY PICTURE LIBRARY

terms, were never successfully applied. Before the War of 1812 some pearl ash (potassium carbonate) was imported from America, made by a process devised by Samuel Hopkins, of Pittsford, Vermont. An alternative process, developed by the Frenchman Nicholas Leblanc, was introduced at Newcastle-upon-Tyne in 1796 and in Lancashire from the 1820s. This required sulphuric acid, which was made from iron pyrites that occurred naturally in coal measures. Leblanc works consumed large quantities of coal, released hydrochloric acid gas into the atmosphere, and produced calcium sulphide, which was dumped to create the white 'alps' around St Helens and Widnes. The industry prospered, supplying soda ash to soap and glass manufacturers and overseas customers. Exports rose twenty-fold between 1840 and 1860, when there were 170 Leblanc works in Britain. The effects of

releasing acid gas into the atmosphere were to some extent mitigated by the introduction from 1836 of the tower devised by William Gossage (see below, pages 279–80). Gross and harmful pollution remained, however, and in the late 1850s a St Helens land-owner urged Edward Stanley, 14th Earl of Derby, to promote controlling legislation. The Alkali Works Regulation Act 1863 appointed an inspectorate to regulate discharge into the air of gaseous hydrochloric acid from Leblanc works. Robert Angus Smith, a Scot who had studied at Glasgow University, became the first inspector, and the Act set the pattern for legislative control of pollution. From the late 1870s the Leblanc process was superseded by that developed in 1865 by the Belgian, Ernest Solvay, which was introduced at Northwich in 1874 by John Brunner and Ludwig Mond.

Glass making

Glass is made by heating silica (usually sand), soda ash and lime (calcium oxide) at a high temperature. Red lead is incorporated to produce crystal glass for tableware. Glass can be shaped by blowing, pressing, rolling, moulding, drawing out or spinning, and can be decorated by cutting and engraving. Glass making, hitherto small in scale and centred on the Weald of Surrey and Sussex, had become a coalfield industry by 1700, and the imposition of a tax in 1696 is evidence of its widespread adoption for windows. Sheet glass could be made by blowing cylinders which were opened out into sheets while still hot and cut into shape, but by 1700 glassworkers in London were

making crown glass, by cutting a blown cylinder, spinning it into a disk, annealing it, then cutting it into panes. Concentric rings visible in window panes are evidence that they consist of crown glass.

A characteristic feature of most glassworks after 1700 was the English glass cone, a brick-built truncated cone up to 80 feet (24.6 m) high enclosing one or more furnaces and serving as a funnel by increasing the draught. Examples remain at Catcliffe near Rotherham, Newcastle-upon-Tyne, Stourbridge and Alloa. The manufacture of plate glass by casting, developed in France from 1688, was introduced at St Helens in 1773. The hand cylinder process of making

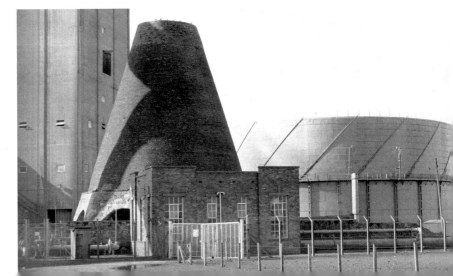

The remnants of the 65 ft (20 m) high English glass cone at Alloa, which formed part of a works founded in 1750 by Lady Frances Erskine. (For interior views of English glass cones see below, pages 214, 535.)

⌄ A rum glass of the 1850s, probably made in Sunderland, showing a merchant ship passing beneath the iron bridge of 1796 that linked Sunderland with Bishop's and Monks' Wearmouth, and a train crossing Robert Stephenson's High Level Bridge at Newcastle-upon-Tyne. It exemplifies not only the achievements of civil engineers in north-east England but also the significance of the region's glass industry.
BY COURTESY OF THE IRONBRIDGE GORGE MUSEUM TRUST

⌄ Interior and exterior views of the glass works of Jones, Smart & Company, Aston Hill, Birmingham, published by James Bissett of Birmingham in 1800. The exterior view shows a formal street frontage that could have been the façade of almost any kind of urban manufacturing establishment, but it is dominated from the rear by a lofty English glass cone. The interior view shows glass blowers taking molten glass from crucibles within the furnace at the base of the cone, whose structure acted as a funnel creating a strong draught to raise the temperature in the furnace.
© SCIENCE MUSEUM/SCIENCE & SOCIETY PICTURE LIBRARY

sheet glass was brought to England from Lorraine in 1832 by Lucas Chance, and in 1839 Sir James Chance developed a method of grinding and polishing sheet glass which enabled it to compete vigorously with crown glass in the market for window panes.

New methods were developed of rolling and drawing glass using tank furnaces, and by the 1860s glassmakers were using the regenerative furnaces developed by Sir William Siemens which ensured a continuous flow of glass from a tank. Bottles were being manufactured in large numbers by 1700, although before the 1890s all were blown by hand. In 1731 common black bottles were relatively expensive, costing 20s. a gross.

A view of *circa* 1860 of the glassworks that was established in 1822 at Smethwick by Robert Lucas Chance, which became one of the largest in Britain (see page 264). It lay alongside Telford's new line of the Birmingham Canal, built during the 1820s, and the Stour Valley Line of the London & North Western Railway. In 1832 the Chances adopted a French technology for the production of sheet glass, and the works provided glass for the Crystal Palace.

The principal glass-making area during the eighteenth century and into the 1830s was the North East coalfield, which paid 44 per cent of the excise duties raised on glass, compared with 18 per cent from Liverpool and Warrington, and 22 per cent from the Midlands, but by the 1860s works in Northumberland and Co. Durham were closing, while those in south Lancashire expanded dramatically.

Pottery

The ever-increasing output of pottery during the eighteenth and nineteenth centuries further increased demand for the coal that was used to fire kilns. Probate inventories suggest that at the beginning of the eighteenth century pottery was not highly valued in Britain, and that pewter and wooden vessels were still preferred, or were more readily available and affordable. Nevertheless, potters flourished in many parts of Britain, and their numbers increased as transport systems facilitated the distribution of coal. The most

Pug mills, introduced in the seventeenth century, comprised sets of mixing blades that rotated within a cylindrical container, an apparatus which was often put together by a cooper. They were most commonly rotated by horse power, and by 1850 were ubiquitous in all but the most primitive of brickyards in the coalfields and elsewhere. They were also employed in the preliminary stages of preparing clay for more sophisticated ceramic products.

A hand-coloured aquatint from *The Costume of Great Britain*, published in 1808, showing a potter making a large dish while his assistant turns the potter's wheel.

fashionable pottery in the early eighteenth century was delftware: hard, translucent and white-bodied, with bluish decoration and a tin glaze. Most delftware was produced in London, Bristol, Liverpool, Glasgow and Dublin. The rapid increase in tea- and coffee drinking generated growing demand for delicate wares, and the variety of pieces with other specialised functions, such as posset pots, punch bowls, spice jars, colander bowls and barbers' basins, suggests the development of a sophisticated clientele. By the 1770s creamware was more fashionable than delftware and was manufactured on a large scale into the nineteenth century. The *Universal British Directory* of the 1790s lists china and glass dealers in almost every town, revealing the existence of an effective distribution network.

Some probate inventories made around 1700 list china or 'cheny' wares, porcelain from China, originally brought to Britain as ballast and rarely valued highly. Porcelain was first manufactured in Europe at Meissen in 1710 and Sèvres from 1738. The works at Chelsea was established about 1743 by Nicholas Sprimont, a Huguenot from Liège who had worked in London as a silversmith. The Bow Works followed about four years later, managed by Thomas Frye, a potter who by 1758 supposedly employed 300 people. Bow closed in the 1760s and Chelsea in 1784, after both were acquired by William Duesbury, who transferred their stock to Derby. Bow and Chelsea used imported clay, but in 1746 William Cookworthy, a Quaker pharmacist, identified china clay, previously called moorstone, at Tregonning Hill in Cornwall, and in 1768 took out a patent for its use in making porcelain. Cookworthy was the first in England to make true porcelain, with materials which, when fired, produced white-bodied wares, in contrast to soft porcelains that are earthenwares made translucent by the addition of flux. Cookworthy set up a porcelain factory at Plymouth in 1768, removing it to Bristol in 1770 where he worked with his kinsman Richard Champion. The patent rights were sold to the Newhall Company in Staffordshire in 1778.

At the end of the seventeenth century potters prepared clay with the aid of pug mills, developed from the late seventeenth century, which were cylinders in which clay was mixed by rotating blades. Their use spread until by the 1850s they were found even in primitive brickyards. Pottery itself was made by throwing clay on a potter's wheel, by pressing it into prepared moulds, or, increasingly from the 1740s, by pouring slip (or liquid clay), prepared in a 'blunger', into plaster moulds. By the 1720s lathes were also being used in manufacturing pottery. Thomas Asbury, a potter of Shelton in Stoke, developed the use of ground flint to whiten fine earthenware. It was prepared in water-powered mills such as that which survives on the river Churnet at Cheddleton near Leek, and the same process prepared calcined bones for use in bone china at the steam-powered Etruscan Bone & Flint Mills of 1857, alongside the Trent &

Mersey Canal in Stoke-on-Trent. The decorating of pottery was revolutionised by transfer printing, supposedly first applied at Battersea in 1753 by John Brooks, an Irish engraver who lived in Birmingham.

The technology of firing was of course crucial in the development of the pottery industry. In 1700 the traditional conical oven, with an internal diameter of up to 7 feet, was usually built by the potter who used it, but ovens subsequently grew in size and were modified for particular purposes. By the 1740s it was usual to fire fine earthenware twice – first a biscuit firing, followed by a glost firing to fix the glaze. Developments in management separated production into a succession of stages which could readily be taught, and work became concentrated in factories. Josiah Wedgwood is the best known of the master potters who did this, although he followed earlier precedents.

Even in the mid-nineteenth century small country potteries were numerous, in the main working to produce wares for local, every-day use. For example, in Oxfordshire in 1861 red ware was made at Barford St Michael, Ipsden, and Nettlebed. However, most potters worked in the coalfields, because the ready availability of fuel in very large quantities was a key determinant of location. There were important potteries in Yorkshire, Lancashire, County Durham and Lanarkshire, but above all in north Staffordshire, which became synonymous with the trade in the popular imagination. There were 24,992 potters in the United Kingdom in 1841, of whom 17,825 (or 71 per cent) lived in and around Stoke-on-Trent. Master potters gained prestige from supplying aristocrats and royalty, but their prosperity owed much more to their ability to supply mass markets with the utilitarian wares necessary for the ever more popular practice of tea drinking, and with the toby jugs, ornamental dogs and figures of preachers and prize fighters which were purchased to adorn the mantel-shelves of working-class homes.

Limestone burning, brick making and other uses of coal

Carboniferous limestone occurs on the fringes of most coalfields, and was burned on a large scale until the use of lime was supplanted by Portland cement in the building industry from the mid-nineteenth century

onwards. Coal was also carried to fire lime kilns in areas such as Exmoor and the Dorset coast which were remote from the carboniferous measures, and since it was hazardous to transport quicklime by water, both coal and limestone from the coalfields were used in many river- and canal-side kilns. Bricks were made from coal measure clay in every coalfield, but those for common use were only rarely transported over long distances before the 1860s. The carriage of coal to the brickworks on the fringes of most towns was of more consequence.

It was appreciated by 1700 that different seams of coal had different qualities – for example, that smokeless coals, anthracite and culm, could be used for malting, while other coals could not. Celia Fiennes in 1698, and later travellers, were intrigued by the cannel coal mined in Wigan, which 'burns light as a candle' and which was carved into curiosities sold in London

as jet or black marble. From 1709 Abraham Darby I learned that of all the coals mined in Shropshire only the Clod seam could be used to make coke suitable for smelting iron ore. By the 1790s stratifications had been completed in most coalfields, sometimes with details of the uses to which various seams might be put. Robert Townson listed 70 strata that had been identified in a 550-foot depth in Shropshire, including 16 seams of coal, among them the Clod, the Flint and Little Flint, good burning coals, the Fungus, Stone, Top and Doubles for household use, the Randles, the best smiths' coal, and the Stinking Coal, consumed in burning bricks and limestone. Coals with particular qualities were carried over long distances, often

Limestone burning on a grand scale. The lime kilns at Llandybie, Carmarthenshire. The range of six kilns in the Gothic style was built in 1856 to the design of the architect Richard Kyrke Penson, in anticipation of the opening of the Llanelly Railway the following year.

Lime was exported from Sunderland in considerable quantities. Much of it was burned in this bank of lime kilns at Southwick, on the north bank of the river Wear just upstream from Wearmouth Colliery.

against the general flow of the trade. Thus in the 1720s Welsh smokeless coals were carried up the Severn to malthouses in West Midlands towns, passing *en route* Shropshire coal with different attributes that was heading downstream. There must have been a particular characteristic of coal from Dawley to have justified taking it down the Severn in 1756 and hauling it up the river Wye through the Forest of Dean to Monmouth. Coal was classified by its size at the point of sale. Domestic users demanded large coal, but small coal could be consumed in the boilers of pumping and winding engines, in ventilation furnaces, in the hearths of smiths who maintained miners' tools, and in brick- and lime kilns. A Northumbrian coal viewer in 1830 estimated that more than 13 per cent of the coal raised was consumed at the mines where it was raised. Coal production figures are imprecise, but every colliery certainly raised much more coal than it sold.

There were many contrasts between coalfield communities. The archetype might be regarded as an isolated mining village in which almost all the male inhabitants were employed in the pit, but many miners lived, too, in the developing industrial conurbations, alongside workers who followed other occupations, and some in equally varied company in communities which had originated as squatter settlements, on the tattered urban fringe or the edges of rural commons and heaths.

First and foremost: coal mining and industry in north-east England

The Great Northern coalfield, extending along the coast for 48 miles from the river Coquet to Hartlepool (see map on page 222), was the most productive in Britain. Already in 1700 it was supplying coal by sea to London and much of southern England, and produced more than 40 per cent of the coal mined in Britain, a proportion that had fallen to less than a quarter by 1830, although output had risen dramatically over this period, from about 1.3 million to 6.9 million tons *per annum*. There were more than 21,000 miners in Northumberland and Durham in 1831, nearly 39,000 in 1851, over 50,000 in 1861, and almost 75,000 ten years later. By 1914 the total reached 224,500.

The Compleat Collier, published in 1708, discussed the qualities of the coal in different seams in the North East and the problems encountered in sinking shafts, draining workings and dealing with methane. The diaries of the seventeenth-century coal viewers William Brown and Edward Smith reflect a similar scientific approach to mining and to sharing knowledge. The development of coal mining, railways, mechanical engineering, and metalliferous mining and processing was shaped by two generations of engineers and chemists from the North East, men such as Sir William Armstrong, Sir Isaac Lowthian Bell, Thomas Bell, John Buddle senior and junior, William Chapman, Thomas Young Hall, John and William Losh, Charles Mitchell, Charles Mark Palmer, Hugh Lee Pattinson, George and Robert Stephenson, John Vaughan, Thomas Wilson and Nicholas Wood. Newcastle-upon-Tyne was their forum. Its Literary and Philosophical Society was established in 1793, and in 1852 the appalling loss of life in colliery explosions stimulated the founding of the North of England Institute of Mining Engineers, whose objectives were 'to devise measures to avert or alleviate those dreadful calamities, which have so frequently produced such destruction to life and property … and to establish a Literary Institution … applicable to the theory, art and practice of mining'. The first president was Nicholas Wood, and in 1872 the Institute settled in Neville Hall, designed by Archibald Dunn.

In 1700 the deepest pits were sunk to around 360 feet (111 m), but as improved drainage systems made it possible to sink deeper shafts, methane gas became an increasing threat. One explosion at Stony Flat, Gateshead, in October 1705 cost more than 40 lives. The first steam engine known to have been erected in the North East drained a colliery at Tanfield Lea from 1715. In the 1730s plans for mines in the Ouseburn Valley (Jesmond Dene) north of Newcastle envisaged drainage by steam power, and three Newcomen engines were working there in 1744. Raistrick calculated that 137 engines were installed in the coalfield before 1778. Thomas Barnes, viewer at Walker Colliery, advocated the merits of Boulton & Watt

Production at the Hetton Colliery in Co. Durham began in 1822. By 1826 the colliery was reckoned the largest in England, producing more than 310,000 tons annually, much of which was carried to the Hetton Staithes (see page 227) along the 8-mile Hetton Railway which was built by George Stephenson. Three steam locomotives were built for the line, one of which appears in this view, but on some stretches waggons travelled on inclined planes.

A coal waggon on an early railway near Newcastle depicted in 'Description des Arts et Metiers, II, art d'exploiter les Mines de Charbon de Terre', published in 1773 by the Académie Royale des Sciences in Paris. The waggon is apparently going downhill with a boy sitting on it, operating the brake, with the horse that was used on uphill sections of the line following behind. In the background are staithes where coal was loaded on to keels – the small vessels also seen here – which carried coal to ocean-going ships at the mouths of the Tyne and the Wear.

engines, which enabled the sinking of shafts up to 850 feet (262 m) deep between 1790 and 1810 at Hebburn, Percy Main, Jarrow and South Shields.

'Waggonways', as railways were called along the Tyne and Wear, were central to the growth of the coalfield. A railway at Wollaton, Nottinghamshire, built between October 1603 and October 1604 to carry coal, was worked by Huntington Beaumont whose family owned the colliery at Coleorton in Leicestershire. He also had mines near the river Blyth in Northumberland, where he built railways between 1605 and 1608. After 1660 the technology he introduced was increasingly applied to carry coal from pithead to navigable water. The Tanfield Waggonway was built in the 1720s by the Grand Alliance, a partnership signed on 27 June 1726 to develop collieries in Co. Durham which would be deeper than 360 feet and whose produce could be carried to the Tyne by rail. This route included the Tanfield (or Causey) Arch, the 105-foot (32.3 m) span bridge that was an object of marvel from the time of its construction (see page 106). North East engineers also constructed wooden viaducts, and were particularly known for the riverside staithes, up to 390 yards (357 m) long. The 'chaldron' waggons used on local railways carried between 42 and 52 cwt. They ran out onto wooden staithes and discharged their coal through bottom-opening doors onto chutes that led directly to the holds of vessels. For most of the eighteenth century the chaldrons ran on wooden rails and worked singly, each pulled by a horse. Their flanged wheels were also of wood until, from the 1750s, foundries began to cast them in iron. Gauges varied from about 5 feet to about 3 feet 10 inches (1.54 m, 1.17 m). The route mileage of railways in the North East increased from about 40 in 1700 to some 146 in 1800. After 1790, as railways proliferated, steam-powered and self-acting inclined planes, iron rails, and the practice of linking waggons in trains were all adopted in the region. The last two enabled the use of the steam locomotive, whose nursery was Tyneside.

Coal was purchased from the mining companies by middlemen called 'fitters'. They sold it to the ship-owners or masters, who then marketed it. In the eighteenth century much of the coal mined in Northumberland and Co. Durham was taken by rail to the staithes on the Tyne and Wear and then carried by rowing boats, called keels, each with a capacity of about 21 tons, to be loaded onto sea-going ships at Sunderland or Shields. On the river Tyne the usual limit of navigation for keels was Lemington, upstream from its confluence with the Derwent; on the Wear it was Fatfield, near Chester-le-Street. In 1731 about 570,000 tons of coal were despatched from Newcastle to London, more than 35,000 tons to King's Lynn, 33,000 tons to Great Yarmouth, and more than 6,000 tons each to Hull, Southampton, Ipswich, Portsmouth, Rochester and Sandwich. Smaller quantities went to southern ports such as Cowes, Falmouth and Fowey, and as far north as Aberdeen and Fort William.

In 1700 about 100,000 tons of Tyneside coal was used annually in salt making. In 1732, when John Loveday went on an excursion from Newcastle in the lord mayor's boat, he could scarcely see the shore at North Shields, such was the thickness of smoke from the saltworks. There were reputedly 200 saltpans at Shields in 1767, but salt making apparently ceased there in 1787, perhaps because of competing demands for coal. In the 1720s local glassworks consumed half the 32,000 tons produced annually at one Tyneside colliery. There were 12 makers of bottles, sheet and crown glass in Newcastle in the 1820s, and the industry flourished on a similar scale on Wearside. In 1841 there were 1,346 glassmakers in the two counties, and Isaac Cookson & Co. at Newcastle and South Shields paid £61,000 in excise duty on glass, more than any other firm in Britain. More than 500 potters in Co. Durham made earthenware, and coal was also consumed in ironworks and lime kilns.

Walker township, east of Newcastle, covered 1,108 acres and was owned by the town's corporation. Its population reached almost 6,000 by 1861, when some areas were still farmland. Walker Colliery was sunk on land leased in the 1750s by William Brown, who installed two steam pumping engines. The first shaft, the Ann Pit, reached the High Main seam at 594 feet (183 m) in January 1762, an event marked by the issue of commemorative medals to the sinkers. A third pumping engine, with a 74 inch (1.88 m) cylinder, was supplied by the Coalbrookdale Company in 1763. In the 1790s, when two further shafts were sunk, the

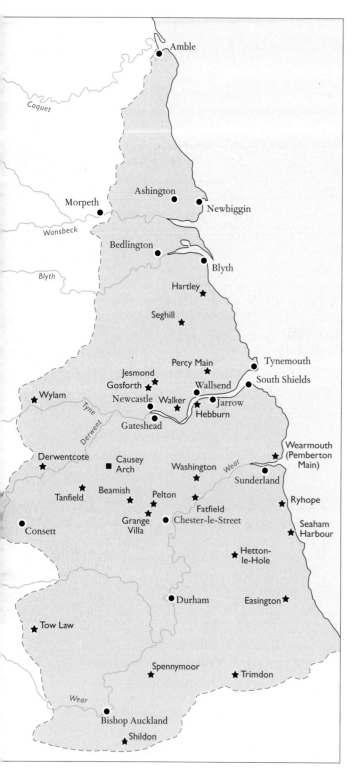

↗ The Great Northern coalfield.

colliery's viewer was Thomas Barnes, who laid a railway with 3 feet long T-section cast-iron rails. The colliery was always subject to danger from methane. Eight men were killed by an explosion in 1765, and ten in 1766, and in 1811 workings were temporarily abandoned. Mining resumed in 1818 after the Davy Lamp became available, and production continued until 1920. The quality of Walker Colliery's domestic coal was famous, and the extent of its markets is indicated by the presence of ships from Yarmouth, London, Rye, Teignmouth, Arbroath, Peterhead and Skye among the 28 moored there on 7 April 1861.

A salt spring at Walker Colliery was utilised from 1798 by John Losh and the 9th Earl Dundonald for the manufacture of alkali, a process observed in 1802 by Erik von Svedenstierna. From 1807 alkali was produced using the Leblanc process by a partnership consisting of John's brother William, who had studied in Hamburg and gained experience of industry in Sweden and France; Thomas Wilson, the poet who composed *The Pitman's Pay*; and Thomas Bell, alderman of Newcastle. By the late 1820s Losh, Wilson and Bell were trading in iron and coal, and from about 1830 made bleaching powder. About 1840 the partnership was joined by Bell's son Isaac (later Sir Isaac) Lowthian Bell, who had studied in Edinburgh and Paris. He remained for a decade and subsequently became an ironmaster both on Tyneside and in Cleveland. The company built a blast furnace at Walker in 1842–43 to smelt ore from Whitby, and subsequently invested in another four and also in a forge which produced wrought-iron plate for building ships. The labour force in 1861 included more than 50 Welsh puddlers, for whom a Merioneth-born minister officiated at a Welsh-speaking chapel. Ninety Irishmen, mostly from Co. Londonderry, lived in 20 houses in Hicks' Buildings.

Shipyards flourished at Walker. The first iron vessel built on the Tyne was the *Star*, a steamship launched at South Shields in 1839, and designed to carry passengers between Newcastle and North Shields. Interest in iron ships was stimulated in 1840 by the arrival of the Aberdeen-built collier *John Garrow*, and that year an Aberdonian, John Coutts, opened a shipyard at Walker where the *Prince Albert*, a passenger ship for use on the

The river Wear at Sunderland. On the high ground on the far (north) bank stands Wearmouth (or Pemberton Main) Colliery, sunk over many year from 1826, but 'the marvel of the district' after it was completed. On the far banks are the staithes where the produce of the colliery was dropped on to sea-going ships, with a small shipyard to the right. In the foreground are some of the Lambton Drops where coal that had been brought to the port by an early railway was placed on ships.

The same stretch of the river Wear in 1995.

river Thames, was launched on 23 September 1842 and an iron collier in 1844. His business did not prosper, but Charles Mitchell, another Aberdonian, opened a yard at Low Walker in 1852, and by 1857 was building warships for the tsar's navy. His business merged with that of Sir William Armstrong of Elswick in 1882.

Charles Mark Palmer, whose business education included four years in Marseilles, worked from 1838 in his father's timber business, and by 1845 was managing a colliery at Gateshead. He opened a shipyard at Jarrow whose first vessel was the steam tug *Northumberland*, completed in 1851. The 465-ton iron screw collier *John Bowes*, launched on 30 June 1852, could carry 650 tons of coal to London in two days and return in another two, completing in a week the work that would occupy a sailing collier for two months. The *John Bowes* was a response to the threat to the London market posed by rail-borne coal from the East Midlands, and was the pattern for subsequent generations of coasting colliers. Palmer took over a shipyard on the north bank of the Tyne in 1860 and the ironworks at Wallsend in 1856, and built blast furnaces at Jarrow from 1857. On a single day, 15 August 1863, he launched four iron ships on the afternoon tide.

The communities along the south bank of the Tyne between South Shields and Hebburn included many miners but also men involved in shipping coal, iron making and shipbuilding. In 1861 the census recorded seamen from Cuxhaven, Hamburg, Sweden, Denmark, New Orleans and Portland, Maine, as well as from Lerwick, Kirkwall, Wells-next-the-Sea, St Mawes, Plymouth, Montrose and Dumfries. There were shipbuilders, iron-ship hole-drillers, iron-ship riveters, iron-ship caulkers, holders-up, and ship painters. Keelmen and keel boys still lived at South Shields, while the port provided employment for coal

trimmers, pilots, ballast trimmers and the stokers who fired the engine of the ballast crane. Many blast-furnacemen lived in the 36 houses in Long Lane Row, including a furnace keeper from Round Oak in the Black Country and about 40 labourers from Ireland. Nearly 100 people manufactured plate glass and bottles, and a handful made brown earthenware.

The largest chemical plants in the region were associated with Hugh Lee Pattinson, who in 1833 perfected a process for separating silver from lead. His alkali works at Felling, established in 1834, employed about 1,000 men in the 1850s, and in 1852, with his son-in-law Isaac Lowthian Bell, he opened a works at Washington which produced white lead directly from galena, and also manufactured magnesium oxide, used in medicine and in refractories. Most of the workers lived in a new settlement called Pattinsontown.

By the 1860s some of the most productive North East collieries were along the coast, with shafts penetrating the magnesian limestone and workings extending

Coal from the collieries in Co. Durham of the Lambton family, earls of Durham, was conveyed to Sunderland by a railway that tunnelled underneath the Hetton Railway as it approached the south bank of the river Wear. The line terminated at a range of coal drops, a form of staithes on which coal waggons were lowered by counterbalanced platforms to the ship where the coal was discharged, thereby avoiding breakage of the coal. The drop was invented by William Chapman in 1800 and first used at Wallsend in 1812. The Lambton Drops were demolished in the early 1970s. In the background is Rowland Burdon's iron bridge, opened in 1796, while on the opposite bank of the river are some of the structures that formed part of Wearmouth Colliery. From T. H. Hair, *A Series of Views of the Collieries of Northumberland and Durham* (London: J. Madden, 1844).

The Wearmouth (originally Pemberton Main) Colliery became one of the most productive in Britain. This early view shows the engine house and shaft on top of the cliffs lining the river Wear, with a rake of four chaldron waggons descending the colliery waggonway to staithes on the river bank. At the foot of the cliffs is a yard where a wooden ship is under construction, while several keels – the small boats that conveyed coal from up-river staithes – are heading for the Sunderland harbour at the mouth of the Wear, where their cargoes will be transferred to sea-going ships. From T. H. Hair, *A Series of Views of the Collieries of Northumberland and Durham* (London: J. Madden, 1844).

beneath the North Sea. The existence of coal beneath the limestone was proved at Haswell in 1811, and it was first mined at Hetton Colliery, sunk to 900 feet in 1823. Svedenstierna in 1803 observed that all over England he had seen engravings of the celebrated iron bridge between Wearmouth and Sunderland, completed in 1796 at the instigation of Rowland Burdon. Keels glided down the river Wear, taking coal to sea-going vessels, and the banks adjacent to the iron bridge became intensely busy in the first half of the nineteenth century. In 1812 and 1822 two installations for the despatch of coal were constructed on the south bank – the Lambton Drops, where 11 coal-drops of the kind invented by William Chapman were supplied with coal by a railway which approached through a tunnel, and the Hetton Staithes, six coal drops and two spouts, to which coal was delivered by the Hetton Railway.

The Wearmouth (originally Pemberton Main) Colliery was sunk from May 1826 by Richard Pemberton, his two sons and two partners. After eight years, having penetrated the magnesian limestone, the sinkers found coal, which was worked from 1835, although not until 1846 did they reach the rich Hutton seam at 1,772 feet (540 m). This was then the deepest mine in Britain, 'the marvel of the district' according to a local writer in 1860. It was the first in Co. Durham to extend under the sea, and was regarded as the birthplace of the Durham Miners' Association, founded in 1869 when it employed 1,200 men. By 1844 an inclined plane took coal from the headstocks to staithes on the riverbank. The natural contours between the mine and the river were obscured in the 1850s and 1860s by the dumping of sand brought in as ballast by collier ships, and by waste from the mine. The colliery, having richly repaid the capital and the confidence of Pemberton and his partners, was regarded in 1993 as 'a pit for the future', but was closed the following year. Sunderland FC's Stadium of Light now occupies the site.

In 1861 nearly 13,000 people lived in the townships of Monkwearmouth and Southwick, of whom about

850 were coal miners and more than 500 were working in shipyards. Other industries included timber yards, iron foundries, an engine builder, an anchor smithy, a file works, as well as makers of sails, canvas, ropes, masts, blocks and galvanised nails. There were two banks of lime kilns, two glassworks with about 250 workpeople, earthenware potteries employing almost as many, a paper mill, a steam cornmill and stables where the North Eastern Railway kept the horses for the freight depot adjacent to the elegant Monkwearmouth Station of 1848. By 1870 the industrial installations were intermingled with single-storey terraced cottages and catslide houses. The largest glassworks in Sunderland, in Trimdon Street, was established by James Hartley whose Scottish father John worked at Nailsea and Smethwick. James and his brother moved to Sunderland in the 1830s and in November 1838 patented a method of rolling plate glass. He employed 700 people in the 1860s, when he produced about a third of British plate glass. He retired in 1868–69, but his successors adopted new technologies too slowly and the works closed in 1894.

Many substantial collieries in the North East lay in rural settings, despatching their produce by rail towards navigable water, past coppices and farms and through rolling fields. J. G. Kohl wrote in 1844 that

> Along the Tyne the whole country is covered with … collieries, lying like old smoky castles, among the green meadows and the teaming cornfields. … Two classes of men are seen mingled together – the miners and the husbandmen, whose pursuits, manners, customs and ways of thinking vary as much as it is possible to imagine. Close to the handsome farmhouses and the neat labourers' cottages lie the black, dismal openings to the pits. Here you see the seat of some wealthy landlord or capitalist, there a rural village peopled by agriculturalists, and a little further on, in a straight line, a regular uniform row of collieries cottages … to one who could take a bird's eye view of the country, it would seem to swarm like an anthill with locomotives, hurrying trains and long lines of coal wagons … despite this busy movement, the country looks everywhere so beautiful, so verdant, so hilly, so undulating, so charmingly wooded.

Kohl depicts the quintessential Durham pit village. Cottages were arranged in ranked terraces. Most were of brick burned from coal-measure clays, but the earliest in many settlements was a 'Stone Row', built of sandstone that had been recovered during sinking. In some villages deputies or overmen enjoyed more spacious accommodation, in a terrace called 'Quality Row'. Behind the cottages were ranks of detached pantries and 'netties' (earth closets), while allotments in a 'garden field' were dotted with pigeon crees, pigsties and hen coops. The largest buildings were Methodist chapels and public houses. A characteristic example is Grange Villa in Pelton parish west of Chester-le-Street, where the gabled house at the end of Stone Row bears the date 1873, and the adjacent Primitive Methodist chapel was completed in 1875. Commentators in the mid-nineteenth century were impressed by the cleanliness and tidiness of miners' cottages, which was perhaps the consequence of the scarcity of regular outside employment for women in isolated pit villages. A. B. Reach particularly admired 'the handsome beds, ample and polished chests of drawers and burnished teapots and candlesticks of the Northumberland and Durham pitmen'.

A study of Pelton illuminates patterns of migration. The parish was created in 1843, after landowners and colliery owners built Holy Trinity church, following the discovery of seams of coal that could be exploited, utilising the access to staithes at South Shields provided by the Stanhope & Tyne Railway. A group of about 100 cottages was named Perkins Villas, after the owners of one of the collieries, and about 130 cottages were ranked in nine rows in Pelton village. The population, which in 1851 was 1,207, rose to 2,797 by 1861, when 685 (25 per cent) were miners. As in most North East mining communities, the majority (in this instance, 88 per cent) had been born in Northumberland or Co. Durham. Most of the remainder were from Cumberland or Yorkshire, and there were some Irishmen and Scots – although more than 50 people living at Pelton in 1861, mostly

At the traditional staithes in the North East coal was discharged through the bottom doors of chaldron railway waggons onto chutes which conducted it to the holds of waiting keels or sea-going ships. By the early nineteenth century the more sophisticated installations such as the staithes on the south bank of the river Wear at Sunderland at the end of the Hetton Railway were covered. Only a small timber yard stood between the Hetton Staithes and the Lambton Drops, and the Wearmouth Colliery stood on the opposite bank of the river. From T. H. Hair, *A Series of Views of the Collieries of Northumberland and Durham* (London: J. Madden, 1844).

young adults, had migrated from a very different world, the rural villages of Tuddenham, Cavenham and Snailworth near Newmarket.

Hetton-le-Hole has particular significance in the history of the coalfield. Hetton Hall was the residence of Nicholas Wood, chronicler of early railways and viewer for the Hetton Colliery Company. On 19 December 1820 the company began sinking the shafts which in 1823 reached the Hutton Seam, and by 1826 the colliery, reckoned the largest in England, was producing annually more than 310,000 tons of coal, most of which was carried to the Hetton Staithes along the 8-mile Hetton Railway, built by George Stephenson and opened in the presence of large crowds on 18 November 1822. The railway was equipped with three locomotives, *Dart*, *Tallyho* and *Star*, but waggons were also hauled on self-acting and steam-powered inclines. Coal was raised by four high-pressure winding engines, while screens at the surface, manned largely by Irishmen, separated small coal from large. Hetton-le-Hole had a population of

fewer than 300 in 1801, but grew to 6,400 by 1861. More than 1,300 (21 per cent) of its inhabitants were coal miners, 83 per cent of whom were born in the North East. The largest identifiable groups among the immigrants were the 87 Irish, most of whom were from Co. Down, and 44 Yorkshiremen, some from the lead-mining villages of Grassington, Swaledale and Arkengarthdale. Nevertheless, even such a large mining community retained links with agriculture, for in 1843 miners' wives still helped to gather the harvest.

At Seaham, south of Sunderland, John Dobson, architect of Newcastle's Central Station and Grainger Market, planned a spectacular seaside town of crescents and terraces for the 3rd Marquis of Londonderry, who fought in the Peninsular Wars and served as a diplomat at the Congress of Vienna. Construction of a harbour, designed by William Chapman, began in 28 November 1828, and by the 1850s the port could accommodate 300 coasting vessels. The first cottages were made with rubble stone, from the excavation of the docks. The harbour was served by three railways,

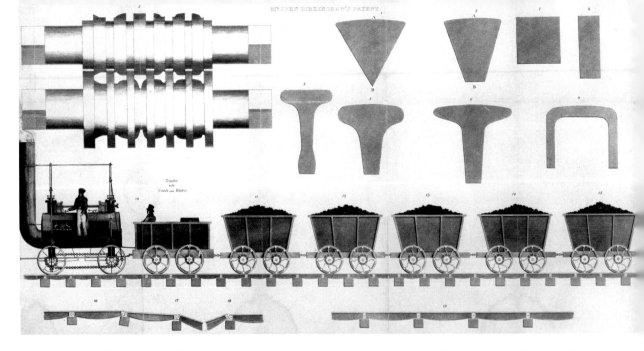

⚞ Plate from 'Specification of John Birkenshaw's patent for an improvement in the construction of malleable iron rails', 1824. The locomotive shown is of the type patented by George Stephenson and William Losh on 26 November 1816. The principal feature of the patent, no. 4067, was the steam springs. In 1820 John Birkenshaw rolled the first malleable iron rails made under his patent at the Bedlington Iron Works, Northumberland, of which Michael Longridge was proprietor.

the Rainton & Seaham, completed in 1831; the South Hetton & Seaham, which carried its first trains in 1833; and the Londonderry, Seaham & Sunderland, opened for passengers as well as coal trains in 1855. More than 2,000 people lived at Seaham by 1841 and more than 4,600 in 1851 after the sinking of Seaham Colliery. The Londonderry Bottle Co. employed about 200, and other enterprises included lime kilns, a foundry, an anchor forge, and shipyards. But Dobson's ambitious plans were never realised, for it was to be a grimy industrial community, not a fashionable coastal resort, that emerged on the low cliffs of the Durham coast.

Many collieries flourished between Newcastle and the river Coquet to the north. The population of the parish of Earsdon, which extended from the mouth of the Seaton Burn to the estuary of the river Blyth, increased from 3,651 in 1801 to 10,982 in 1851. A glass-works established at Hartley in 1763 had over 200 employees a century later, and Hartley Colliery was the scene of the notorious accident in 1862, when 204 men and boys suffocated. Several pits were sunk south of the river Blyth in the 1820s and 1830s – Barrington in 1821, Bedlington in 1838 and Choppington in 1857

– and were linked by waggonway to Blyth harbour, where more than 250,000 tons of coal were shipped in 1850. The 36 vessels moored there on 7 April 1861 included four from France, and others from Whitby, Lynn, Wells, Cley, Colchester, Whitstable and Aberdeen. The ironworks at nearby Bedlington began in 1736 as a slitting mill with nail-making shops. A blast furnace was constructed in the 1750s but was abandoned in the 1780s, when new owners developed a forge which in the nineteenth century was run by the Longridge family who also operated the nearby Glebe Colliery. In 1814 the works made wrought-iron boiler plates, axles and wheels for George Stephenson's locomotive *Blücher*, and in 1820 one of its employees, John Birkinshaw, patented the 15-foot T-section wrought-iron rail that was used on the first generation of main lines. Steam locomotives built between 1836 and 1855 included *De Arend* and *Bayard*, the first to be used, respectively, in the Netherlands and Italy. The works appears to have been inactive in 1861 and closed in 1867. The most northerly mines in the coalfield were near Amble at the mouth of the river Coquet, where 16 vessels were loading coal on 7 April 1861.

Industrial innovation on the Shropshire coalfields

The Coalbrookdale coalfield in Shropshire covers less than one tenth of the area of the Great Northern coalfield, yet it was the scene of important technological and managerial innovations and a critical component of the economy of western Britain. The coalfield extends a dozen miles from north to south, and from east to west is rarely more than three miles wide. Twenty-one of its coal seams have been profitably worked, together with eight seams of iron ore and clays suitable for making building bricks, refractory bricks, pottery and tobacco pipes; there are outcrops of Carboniferous limestone at Lilleshall, and of Silurian limestone farther south. The river Severn flows through the coal measures in a gorge 300 feet deep, created during the melting of the Devonian ice sheet about 15,000 years ago. The river provided transport opportunities that stimulated the development of mining, as did Watling Street, the Roman road that passed through Ketley and gave access to Shrewsbury.

Coal mining on a commercial scale began in the reign of Elizabeth I, and by the 1660s about 100,000 tons of coal were supposedly being extracted each year. The earliest evidence of the longwall system of mining is found in Shropshire, and by 1800 the deepest shafts extended to 600 feet (185 m). The first documented steam pumping engine in the area, draining mines in Madeley, began work in 1719, and three more were built by 1733. An engine at Ketley, valued at £200, was among the possessions of Jane, widow of the coalmaster Richard Hartshorne, in 1737. Minerals were traditionally raised from pits by horse gins, 15 of which were listed on Jane Hartshorne's inventory, the most valuable worth £14. The first steam engine successfully to raise coal in Shropshire was built by William Reynolds at Wombridge in 1787, and within 15 years about 100 winding engines were working in the coalfield. In 1801 a writer looking north from a rock above Coalbrookdale observed 'steam engines erected for the purposes of raising Coals, Ironstone &c from the Pits they being now in almost general use instead of horses', and in 1842 a miner in his sixties recalled his youth as the time when winding engines proliferated.

A wooden railway carried coal to the river Severn in 1605, and several more lines had been built by 1700. Dr Michael Lewis has shown that they differed in important respects from the railroads of the North East. They were usually of no more than 3 foot

A classic view of an eighteenth-century mine in the Shropshire coalfield, George Robertson's *The Mouth of a Coal Pit near Broseley*, published in 1788, which shows a horse gin used for winding coal up the shaft, a wooden railway and a pair of packhorses tended by a woman.

Much of the produce of coal mines in Shropshire was taken to customs in towns and villages along the river Severn as far downstream as Gloucester. This picture shows vessels moored at Bridgnorth, home of many of the bargemen who worked on the river. The waterwheel, seen here on the left, raised drinking water to High Town, laid out in the mid-twelfth century by Henry II, on top of the sandstone cliffs.

© SCIENCE MUSEUM/SCIENCE & SOCIETY PICTURE LIBRARY

From the 1760s the collieries and ironworks of the Coalbrookdale Coalfield were served by a network of canals which included, by 1797, six inclined planes. The vessels employed were mostly 'tub boats', about 20 feet long and 6 feet 4 inches wide, which could readily be carried on the inclined planes. From 1835 the tub-boat system was linked to the national waterways network by a branch of the Birmingham & Liverpool Junction (now called the Shropshire Union) Canal. The width and good condition of the waterway shown in this photograph of about 1900 suggests that it was the BLJC, along which some deliveries of coal to local customers were made by tub boat. By 1900 most of the tub-boat network was closed or in a ruinous condition.

© NATIONAL RAILWAY MUSEUM/SCIENCE & SOCIETY PICTURE LIBRARY

(0.91 m) gauge, and some extended into adits. The waggons had low sides, and minerals were held in place by wrought-iron bands. Iron wheels for railways were cast from 1729, the first probably being for a two-mile line from Little Wenlock to the Severn. Self-acting inclines were used by the 1740s, and from the 1750s ironmasters built railways. Some two-level wooden rails were employed, and in 1767–68 the Coalbrookdale partners replaced the top levels with crude bars of cast iron. In the late 1780s the operators of most railways in the coalfield began to use plate rails, the angled track devised by John Curr, which could be made in cast iron or wrought iron, and could be laid on wooden, stone, cast-iron or wrought-iron sleepers. Plateways remained the principal means of short-distance transport for minerals even in the 1860s.

Railways were supplemented from the 1760s by tub-boat canals. The first, on the estate of the 2nd Earl Gower, extended from mines at Donnington Wood to limestone workings at Lilleshall and a landsale wharf at Pave Lane. John Gilbert, agent at the Worsley estate of the earl's brother-in-law the 3rd Duke of Bridgewater, belonged to the partnership that built the canal. The ironmaster William Reynolds built two short private canals in 1787–88 at Wombridge and Ketley, and in 1788 an Act of Parliament authorised the building of the Shropshire Canal, extending eight miles from Donnington Wood to a junction north of Madeley, from which one line, never completed, was intended to pass through Coalbrookdale to the Severn, while the other terminated by the river Severn at a the place subsequently called Coalport. The network was extended to Shrewsbury by a canal completed in 1797, by which time the tub-boat system incorporated six inclined planes. The Shropshire Canal was heavily used for more than 50 years but was distorted by subsidence, and in 1860–61 a railway was laid over much of its course.

The Coalbrookdale coalfield supplied a market that in 1700 extended down the river Severn to Gloucester, and along the valley of the Warwickshire Avon from Tewkesbury to Stratford. Richard Cornes remarked of the Severn at Bridgnorth in 1739 that 'the most common freight upon it is pit coal from Broseley', while Samuel Simpson wrote in 1746 that coal mines employed thousands of men in and around the Severn Gorge, where he had seen 200 vessels waiting for cargoes. Demand for coal along the Severn increased during the eighteenth century, with the growth of salt production at Droitwich and the use of coal in iron forges, but sales were constrained by competition from Black Country coal after the opening of the Staffordshire & Worcestershire Canal in 1772 and the Worcester & Birmingham Canal in 1815. Nevertheless the 'Severn Sale' remained substantial. An approximate figure of 50,000 tons *per annum* despatched from Coalport was commonly quoted from about 1800, and is given credibility by statistics from individual companies. The Coalbrookdale Company despatched 18,000 tons in 1807, the Madeley Wood Company's 'Severn Sale' realised £1,600 in 1832, and the Old Park Company despatched an average of 19,000 tons *per annum* during the 1840s. The trade was subsequently destroyed by railway competition and had almost ceased by 1870.

Increased production in the coalfield after 1700 was stimulated by the use of coal for manufacturing. After 1709 Abraham Darby I used coke to smelt iron ore at Coalbrookdale, and from the 1750s at the Horsehay Ironworks his son, Abraham Darby II, produced coke blast iron that could be forged into wrought iron. He and his partners established a pattern of management that was followed elsewhere. Land for mining was leased from proprietors, and sub-contractors extracted coal and iron ore which, with limestone from quarries similarly leased and worked, was conveyed by railway to blast furnaces. Mines also produced coal for other purposes and for sale. Limestone was burned to produce lime for construction and agriculture, while bricks were made for general sale as well as for the company's own use. The new furnaces were a response to the state of the iron trade, but their construction can also be interpreted as a means of creating enduring markets for coal.

Most of the characteristic coalfield manufactures flourished in Shropshire. Thus, coal was the fuel used in salt production at Kingsley Wyche, where horse-operated pumps raised brine that was boiled, using blood from local butchers to accelerate the process, in wrought-iron pans made at the Lower Forge at Coalbrookdale. At Broseley in the 1690s Martin Eele produced tar, pitch and oil by distilling coal in ovens, and a similar process was used by Abraham Darby II in the 1740s. In the 1780s at the Benthall and Calcutts Ironworks Lord Dundonald introduced ovens for making coke and utilising the by-products, and around 1800 there were coke ovens at several ironworks. Nevertheless, most of the coke used in Shropshire in the 1860s was still made in open heaps. The chemist William Lewis observed in 1768 that 'British Oil' was manufactured from bituminous rocks alongside the road from Coalbrookdale to Horsehay. In 1786 miners employed by William Reynolds drove a tunnel north from the banks of the river Severn, intended for a canal to convey coal from newly sunk mines. They struck a spring of natural bitumen, producing up to 55 gallons per week, and this was collected, refined and sold in barrels until 1843. The 'Tar Tunnel' eventually extended more than 1,000 yards. It drained and ventilated mines, and a railway was laid through it in 1796.

In the Carboniferous limestone around Lilleshall, served by canal from the 1760s, there were underground workings up to 250 feet (77 m) deep in beds more than 60 feet (18.5 m) thick. Many kilns were built, some of which produced hydraulic cement, reputedly used in the building of Liverpool docks. The underground workings were flooded in 1860. There were also limestone mines at Steeraway, where a steam winding engine was employed in the nineteenth century in workings 100 feet (31 m) deep, while in the Severn Gorge there were quarries on Benthall Edge, and underground workings distorted Lincoln Hill on the eastern side of Coalbrookdale. There, the 32 kilns working in the 1840s produced lime far in excess of local needs; the surplus was carried away by river until 1854.

There were other small industries. A glasshouse at Snedshill, dating from the 1670s, was probably making window panes and bottles in 1700, but closed soon afterwards, while one with two English glass cones began production at Wrockwardine Wood in 1791 and continued until the 1840s. A plant at Wombridge, built to make sulphuric acid from iron pyrites, was adapted in 1799 to produce alkali. Lord Dundonald planned in 1800 to work with William Reynolds to build an integrated chemical plant on the slopes of the Severn Gorge, whose products would have included alkali, soap, dyes and fertiliser, but when Reynolds died in 1803 the project came to an end.

Abraham Darby I and his partners smelted copper and made brass in Coalbrookdale, but brass making ceased in 1714, and the copper smelter probably did not work after 1717. A lead smelter, built in 1731 at Benthall to use ore from mines at Llangynog (Montgomeryshire), was employed from 1739 for ores from the Bog mine on the Stiperstones in the Shropshire hills, and appears on early prints of the Iron Bridge. A visitor in 1746 observed, 'The Lead Works are vastly poisonous and destructive to everything near it'. Three other lead-smelters worked in the Severn Gorge, the last of which ceased soon after 1800.

After 1700 bricks superseded sandstone as the customary material for workers' cottages in the area, and from the 1750s the iron-working companies made building bricks and refractories on a large scale. From about 1800 works were established in the Severn Gorge, with sheds for clay preparation and moulding, round kilns and rectangular drying stoves. They produced bricks of a pinkish-grey hue, bearing 'kiss marks' from contact with other items during firing, and roofing tiles of the type branded from the 1880s as 'Iron Broseley'. They can be seen in buildings in Bridgnorth and Bewdley, and around the docks at Gloucester. Brick and tile production was buoyant in the 1860s, providing a staple traffic on the river Severn that persisted until the 1890s. In the ruins

of the Benthall Ironworks George and Arthur Maw began to make encaustic tiles for churches in 1852, and the manufacture of decorative tiles came to employ large numbers of people in the Severn Gorge. Henry Powell Dunnill took over a roofing tile works in 1867 and manufactured decorative tiles there from 1870; at the 1871 census he employed 89 people. Subsequently he and the Maws built factories on the banks of the river, whose products adorn, *inter alia*, state parliament houses in Australia and railway stations in India.

Significant production of earthenware pottery began in the Shropshire coalfield about 1710, and by the 1730s storage jars, chamber pots, and tea and coffee pots were being made at potteries with semi-courtyard layouts. In 1772 Thomas Turner began to produce porcelain at Caughley, where a prominent clock governed the days of the 100 workers. China clay and ball clay were brought from the west of England, and Turner enjoyed royal patronage. Further porcelain works, and a pottery producing quality earthenware, were established under the tutelage of William Reynolds at Coalport in the 1790s. By 1814 the Coalport and Caughley works were owned by the potter John Rose, and production was concentrated at Coalport, where 500 people were employed by 1851. Earthenware production continued on a modest scale. The making of clay tobacco pipes, for which Broseley was renowned before 1700, still employed 91 people in 1861.

The east Shropshire landscape was laid waste by the growth of industry between 1700 and 1870. By the 1840s spoil tips had covered 286 of the 518

◅ Holywell Lane in the parish of Little Dawley, less than two miles from Coalbrookdale, one of the archetypal squatter communities that housed many of the miners and ironworkers of the Shropshire coalfield.

The Iron Bridge, constructed in the summer of 1779 and opened to traffic on 1 January 1781, became the symbol of the booming industries of the Coalbrookdale coalfield in the late eighteenth century. This photograph of the late nineteenth century was taken long after the coalfield had passed its peak of prosperity. The barge photographed here was collecting bricks from the White Brickworks alongside the river, the last significant commercial traffic on the Severn, which came to an end in 1895.

acres of Wrockwardine Wood and over 400 acres in Donnington. Settlements grew up haphazardly on common land, or where proprietors were content for others to build cottages. Probate documents show that in the Severn Gorge many individual dwellings were extended into terraces of irregular appearance in order to accommodate the successive generations of families. Thus, the house of a collier who died in 1762 was divided between a son who inherited the kitchen, cellar and parlour, and his brother who had a little room, the room above it and the brewhouse. Because they had smallholdings and little plots of land those who lived in such dwellings were able to raise crops of potatoes, grain, and flax and hemp that could be spun into linen yarn, and to keep pigs or even a cow.

In 1772 Holywell Lane in Little Dawley consisted of six cottages in 'slangs', long narrow plots parallel to the thoroughfare. Two generations before, one of these had been the home of Edward Darrell, who was among those colliers that in 1709–10 supplied

coal for Abraham Darby at Coalbrookdale. Darrell died in 1726, when he had possessions worth less than £5, including an old cow, a spinning wheel and brewing and dairying equipment. By 1830 there were 30 cottages in the Lane, most of them intermingled in a grotesquely irregular terrace. There were also company terraces in the coalfield, the earliest of which were built in the 1730s. The rows built in the 1750s and 1830s by the Coalbrookdale partners alongside the pool at Horsehay, or Forge Row, erected by the Old Park Company in the 1790s, were of exemplary quality, but the terraces at Hinkshay and Dark Lane, provided by the Old Park partners in the 1820s and 1830s, were less spacious than those of 80 years previously. Some families remained in their homes in Holywell Lane for generations, changing jobs as circumstances altered, while those who lived in company housing were more inclined to take their skills elsewhere.

On New Year's Day 1781 the Iron Bridge across the river Severn was opened to traffic. It was much

The late eighteenth-century engine house from which water was pumped from one of the coal mines at Pontesford, south of Shrewsbury. The building was no longer used by 1828 and by 1842 had been adapted as a dwelling.

and admire the inclined planes that brought stone down the precipitous face of Benthall Edge. Near the Iron Bridge was a cornmill with a 60-foot wheel, depicted by Paul Sandby Munn, and near Coalport Bridge a larger wheel, 76 feet in diameter, powered machines for crushing linseed and grinding materials for potteries. Visitors watched eleven cannon being bored in the foundry of the Calcutts Ironworks. They could admire or ride the inclined plane on the canal at the Hay, and examine the porcelain made at Coalport. Some discussed geology and chemistry with William Reynolds. The Shropshire coalfield expanded in the nineteenth century, except at times of economic depression, and reached peaks of coal and iron production around 1870, but it was no longer perceived as nationally significant. Nevertheless, for a generation after 1779 the Ironbridge Gorge epitomised the heady excitement generated by mining and manufacturing.

Shropshire's other coalfields provide evidence of the role of coal in economic change. The Shrewsbury coalfield extends 15 miles from the river Severn at Preston Boats to the slopes of the Breidden Hills at Bragginton. Steam engines were used for pumping, the earliest at Westbury Colliery in 1781, and the surviving engine house at Pontesford was constructed before 1800. About 300 miners were employed when output reached a peak in the 1850s and 1860s. Most of the coal was sold from landsale wharfs on main roads, or consumed in lime kilns or brickworks, but that from the Pontesford pits was used to smelt ores from the lead mines at Snailbeach, an indication that coal mines – even if, as here, they were remote and had thin seams and complex faulting – could foster the growth of significant industries.

Titterstone Clee, the great hill between Bridgnorth, Bewdley and Ludlow, rises to 1,749 feet (533 m). Its landscape provides eloquent evidence of the role of squatter communities in industrial development. Coal and iron ore were being extracted in 1700, and as the scale of working grew the number of cottages in Snitton township increased between 1745 and 1778 from 49 to 68. Evidence of many bell pits can still be seen in the landscape, and the slopes of the hill are dotted with cottages, crudely built in local stone and extended into terraces, occupying plots delineated by low ramparts

more than a utilitarian link between the communities on the north and south banks of the river Severn. The bridge proprietors commissioned paintings of the structure by well-known artists, engravings of which were widely circulated, and urged travellers to arrange their itineraries in order to see the bridge. For two decades thereafter, from the bridge, visitors could see the flames of four blast-furnace complexes and a lead smelter. At Coalbrookdale many were shown two more blast furnaces and the foundries that surrounded them. They might see the labyrinthine workings in the limestone beneath Lincoln Hill, topped with hedges of holly, damson, crab apple and hazel. Coal was distributed by road, to Ludlow and westwards into Radnorshire. It was used in 1700 to burn lime, to fire kilns for pottery, bricks and tobacco pipes, and probably to make glass. Initially iron ore was transported by packhorse to blast furnaces around the hill at Bouldon, Bringewood and Charlcott, but two blast furnaces were later built on Titterstone Clee itself. One, on the Corndon Brook, worked between 1783 and 1810; the other, at Knowbury, was built about 1803, and worked, albeit spasmodically, until the 1840s. Its last owner, James George Lewis, migrated to New Zealand, where he arrived on 22 February 1854, and contributed to the development of the coalfield around Otago. A peak of production was reached about 1851 when 273 miners were living around Titterstone Clee, a number that had fallen to 186 ten years later, by which time mining was being eclipsed by the opening of rail-served quarries in the dolerite that overlies the coal measures.

Coal mining in Ireland

The Irish coalfields similarly show how modest fuel reserves could generate economic growth. In the 1860s there were 73 collieries in Ireland, most of them around Ballycastle and Coalisland in Ulster, and Castlecomer and Slieveardagh (or New Birmingham) in Kilkenny and Tipperary. Their combined output in 1854 was nearly 150,000 tons, less than 1 per cent of United Kingdom production, and most was used near the pitheads for domestic fuel, lime burning, malting and brick making. The first steam engine in Ireland pumped water from pits at Doonane, Co. Laois, in 1740, while a wooden railway was in use at collieries at Ballycastle by 1752.

In 1723 Francis Seymour leased land from the Archbishop of Armagh around Brackaville (later re-named Coalisland) in Co. Tyrone, and introduced sophisticated methods of mining. After the cutting of a canal to the river Blackwater, construction began in 1731 of the 18-mile Newry Navigation, which enabled vessels to reach the coast and deliver coal to Dublin. Newry was subsequently linked to the sea by a ship canal built between 1759 and 1767, which enabled the use of larger vessels. In the 1770s the Drumglass collieries were connected to the waterway by a canal that included three 'dry hurries', self-acting inclined planes completed in 1777 and designed by the Franco-Italian architect Davis Ducart with the advice of John Smeaton. Mining stimulated the growth of brickworks and spade mills. The Tyrone coalfield reached its peak in the 1830s and 1840s, when it was worked by the Hibernian Mining Co., and its principal pit employed 150 miners who raised about 500 tons of coal per week.

The expansion of coal working at Ballycastle, Co. Antrim, was one of a series of developments undertaken by Hugh Boyd, who inherited an estate in 1711 and took responsibility for mining from 1735. Salt boiling began at Ballycastle in the 1620s, but Boyd encouraged the building of new pans, parts of one of which remain at Pans Rocks. He built wooden and then stone piers, and constructed docks to which coal was delivered by a railroad, allowing ships to take it to Belfast and Dublin. He sponsored the Ballycastle Glass Co., which was formed in 1754, and in the following year built a 90 foot high English glass cone, where local sand, limestone and kelp were fired with coal, and bottles were produced. Boyd also built a soapworks and a brewery. The mines continued after his death, but the other enterprises were less successful and the glassworks had closed by 1784.

The mines in the Slieveardagh Hills between Kilkenny and Cashel produced anthracite, worked on a small scale in the eighteenth century. In 1802 Sir Vere Hunt, a distinguished soldier, published plans for the construction at Glengoole of an industrial community to be called New Birmingham, but he lacked capital and his plans were not realised. The Mining Company of Ireland, formed in 1824, opened a colliery at Mardyke where it built a Cornish engine and 25 terraced houses for its workers. By 1841 the company worked three mines employing 400 people, and new developments continued after the Famine of the late 1840s. Still to be seen are four distinctive brick 'steeples', 90 feet high, the chimneys of ventilation furnaces.

Industry on the fringe: the Cumberland coalfield

Much of the demand for coal in Ireland was met not from indigenous resources but from west Cumberland, where the coalfield operations were nurtured by seigniorial enterprise. The port of Whitehaven lay in the vast ancient parish of St Bees, which included much of the western fells of the Lake District. In 1851 the entire parish had a population of nearly 24,000, but of these two-thirds lived in Whitehaven town. In 1634 the main landowner, Sir Christopher Lowther, built the Old Quay, the nucleus of the harbour, and established coal-fired saltpans at Bransty. His son, Sir John Lowther, augmented his family's estate with a royal grant of the lands of the former Benedictine priory of St Bees, and in 1665 and again in 1687 extended the quay. Sir John was responsible for laying out the grid of streets around which Whitehaven developed, England's first planned town since the medieval period. By 1700 the population was about 2,000, and the coal export trade was thriving. In 1709 Sir James Lowther entrusted to trustees the government of 'the port harbour and town of Whitehaven', and his successors, the earls of Lonsdale, undertook further

developments. A new pier, built in 1733–35, was named the Sugar Quay, reflecting growing transatlantic trade – a sugar refinery was directed in 1754 by a migrant from Hamburg. In the 1740s Whitehaven was second only to London in its volume of tobacco imports, and the port handled most of the rum distilled in Antigua.

Carlisle Spedding, coal viewer on the Lowther estates, was a pioneer in the use of gunpowder in mining, and invented the steel mill, in which metal wheels striking flints provided illumination by producing showers of sparks, a means of illumination which, if not exactly safe, was much less hazardous than candles. His principal achievement was the sinking in 1729–31 of the Saltom Pit from a natural platform below the cliffs south of Whitehaven. It reached a depth of 456 feet (140 m), from which it extended under the sea, the first substantial British colliery to do so. Spedding's weather-battered Newcomen engine house remains on the shore. A wooden railway carried coal from Saltom to Whitehaven by 1735. To the north is the cap of the King Pit, sunk by Spedding in 1750, which by 1793 had reached a depth of 960 feet (296 m) and at the time was the deepest coal mine in Britain. The harbour is lined by monuments reflecting the power exercised by the dominant land-owning family. The tall Candlestick on the southern side was a chimney, designed by Sydney Smirke in 1850 as part of the ventilation system for the notoriously gassy and dangerous Wellington Pit, sunk in 1838. The adjacent crenellated building stands above a shaft of the Duke Colliery, which ceased production in 1844. It was taken over by the King Colliery and from 1870 housed a Guibal fan.

Coal-using industries flourished in Whitehaven, although a glasshouse that opened in 1732 had closed by 1738. The Whitehaven Pottery was producing quality earthenwares and soft paste porcelain by 1812, and achieved renown after 1820 under the ownership of John Wilkinson. Known as the 'White Pottery', it stood adjacent to the 'Brown Pottery', founded in 1740, which also produced earthenware. Peter Woodnorth from north Staffordshire built the Ladypit Pottery in 1813. The saltpans at Bransty ceased working in 1782,

The 'Candlestick' south of the harbour at Whitehaven, a ventilation chimney for the Wellington Pit, built in 1850 to the design of Sydney Smirke.

Carlisle Spedding installed a Newcomen engine at the Saltom mine, south of Whitehaven, in 1729–31. The remains of its engine house, battered by waves and onshore winds for nearly three centuries, still stand on the sea shore.

when their site was used by Daniel Brocklebank for a shipyard. Iron pyrites from coal workings was used to make sulphuric acid in the 1750s, while the 'Lime Quay' was built in 1754, and in the 1820s there was a 'lime office' at the Lowther estate headquarters. Lime was despatched to the ports of Galloway, distantly visible across the Solway Firth.

By the nineteenth century public health in Whitehaven had deteriorated from that experienced by earlier generations, because densely packed cottages were crowded on to land originally envisaged as open space. It was nevertheless prosperous, at least for its owners and managers. Coal was despatched in great quantities from its quays, while the export of iron ore justified the presence in the town of iron-ore merchants, agents and accountants. The Ironstone Quay formed part of the harbour, and proprietors of ironstone mines occupied substantial houses. The sugar trade had disappeared by 1861, but two tobacco manufacturers employed between them 82 workers. At the same date the shipyard of Lumley Kennedy had a workforce of 124, and could draw on the skills of local

makers of sails, ropes, anchors and blocks. The town's principal pottery remained in business, as did its cotton and flax mills.

All the characteristic coal-using manufactures flourished elsewhere along the Cumbrian coast. Humphrey Senhouse, another prominent landowner from an ancient family, developed Ellenfoot, a cluster of cottages around the estuary of the river Ellen, and in 1756 renamed it Maryport after his wife. Like Whitehaven, Maryport despatched coal to Ireland and attracted coal-hungry manufactures. There are remains of eighteenth-century saltpans on the shore at Crosscanonby, and in 1755 Angerstein observed a coke blast iron furnace and a glassworks. By the 1820s the town had a population of 3,500. Coal was being delivered to the harbour by tramroads; timber, flax and iron were imported from the Baltic and North America; shipbuilding, and textile production and pottery manufacturing prospered. In 1861 the coalmaster William Mulcaster employed more than 250 people. There were 'brown ware' potteries at Outgang, and shipyards were supported by the foundry of Thomas Tickle, who

⋏ The crenellated engine house of the Jane Pit, Workington, erected in 1844.

employed more than 20 people. A bonded warehouse was opened in 1842; the railway to Carlisle was opened in 1845; and the Elizabeth Dock was commissioned in 1857. Fifteen ships were moored in the harbour on 7 April 1861. Two, the *John C. Ives* of Maryport, a 244-ton schooner, and the *Currency* of Whitehaven, a 335-ton barque, were engaged in trade with North America. The *Thetis* from Norway and the *Alli* from Finland had arrived, probably laden with timber. Irish trade was represented by ships from Belfast and Dublin, and others came from Peel, Dumfries and Pwllheli.

In the early eighteenth century Workington, at the mouth of the river Derwent, was already an established town, with a market charter dating back to 1573. The Curwen family of Workington Hall were lords of the manor, and in the years around 1800 John Christian Curwen achieved national renown as an agricultural improver and maverick MP. Staithes at the mouth of the Derwent and the harbour at Harrington,

three miles to the south, were built from the 1750s, and in 1776 Sir James Lowther constructed a stone pier on the south side of the estuary. In 1800 six steam engines were working at collieries in Workington which employed 400 miners and by the mid-1820s annual shipments of coal totalled about 200,000 tons. Workington's growth was reflected in the building in 1823 of the church of St John the Baptist, designed by Thomas Hardwick in the style of Inigo Jones's St Paul, Covent Garden. Its first curate was a Curwen. The family's mining interests were developed from 1828 by Henry Curwen who, following a disaster at Chapel Bank Colliery in April 1837, in which 27 men and boys perished, erected the crenellated engine house of the Jane Pit and a ventilation chimney in a similar style bearing the date 1844. Jane Pit closed after another explosion in 1875. Methane made the coal workings in Cumbria notoriously hazardous. Coal exports declined by the 1890s to no more than 130,000 tons per year, but the loss of distant markets was matched by expanding demand from the ironworks that grew up from 1856–57. The shipbuilder Jonathan Fell had a workforce of more than 300 in 1861, and Charles Lambert employed more than 100 in his yards. Workington's population increased from 6,424 in 1861 to 8,386 in 1871, 14,350 in 1881 and 23,522 in 1891. The prosperity of those years is reflected in the French Renaissance-style villas overlooking the town from Park End Road.

The owners of the eighteenth-century blast furnaces at Little Clifton and Maryport used coke to smelt iron ore, and local haematite was exported, but it was not until the building of the blast furnaces at Cleator Moor in 1841, and the advent of the Bessemer process for making steel from 1856 onwards, that iron became the dominant feature in this coalfield economy. In 1860 there were fewer than 80 coal miners at Cleator Moor, compared with nearly 500 iron-ore miners, but the iron-works consumed 70,000 tons *per annum* of coal, much of it from other collieries. Between 1856 and 1878 some 50 blast furnaces were built along the coast between Maryport and Millom, and the coal trade with Ireland diminished. Textile mills provided a little employment for women, although some worked underground in the eighteenth century, and 'screen lasses' worked on the surface into the twentieth century.

Coal mining and industry in Scotland

For most of the period between 1700 and 1870 the Scottish coalfields produced between 10 and 15 per cent of the British output. Coal was mined in three principal areas: in Ayrshire, along the coast from Ayr to Saltcoats and extending inland to Kilmarnock, Cumnock and Muirkirk; in Lanarkshire, Renfrewshire, Dunbartonshire, Stirlingshire, Clackmannan, West Lothian and into Fife; and in the Lothians south and east of Edinburgh. The industry was relatively prosperous in 1700 and seven Newcomen engines – 9 per cent of the British total – were installed at Scottish mines before 1733. On both coasts coal was used in salt boiling, at Prestonpans, Bo'ness, Alloa, Methil and Culross around the Firth of Forth, and at Saltcoats in Ayrshire. Scottish coal-owners found markets for their coal in Glasgow, Edinburgh and other cities, but some east-coast towns, such as Peterhead and Arbroath, received supplies in the 1860s from north-east England.

Coal mining was stimulated by the cessation of

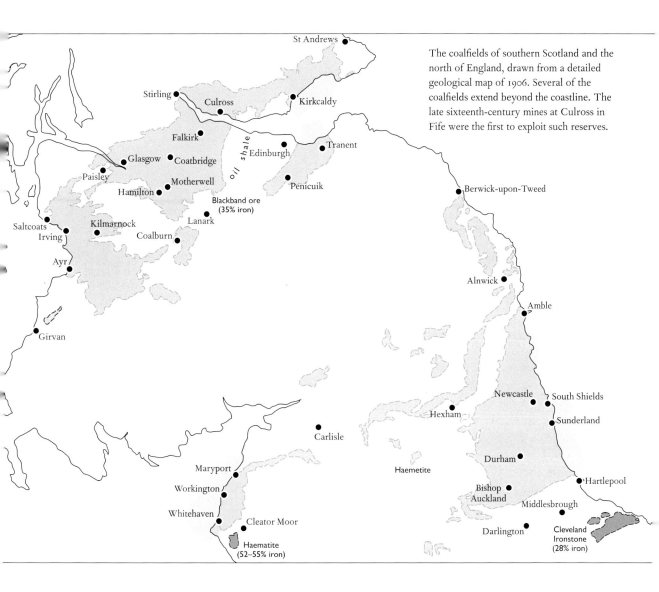

The coalfields of southern Scotland and the north of England, drawn from a detailed geological map of 1906. Several of the coalfields extend beyond the coastline. The late sixteenth-century mines at Culross in Fife were the first to exploit such reserves.

Coal had been mined at Tranent, 11 miles east of Edinburgh, for many centuries; a wooden waggonway carrying coal to Cockenzie on the coast was opened as early as 1722. This picture by Robert Sanderson dates from the late nineteenth century and shows how, as in other coalfields, some mines worked in rural settings. Here, labourers can be seen gathering in the corn harvest.

The Act authorising the building of the Glasgow & Garnkirk Railway received the royal assent in 1826, and the line was opened in 1831 (just a year after the Liverpool & Manchester), extended to Coatbridge in 1843, and taken over by the Caledonian Railway in 1844. It was originally of 4 ft 6 in. gauge. Passengers were carried from the opening, but the line was chiefly important for the carriage of coal into Glasgow in competition with the Monkland Canal, and was partially financed by the chemical manufacturers, Charles Tennant & Co., who were one of the railway's principal customers. The significance of the line's coal traffic is evident in this view of its Glasgow depot.

bondage from the 1790s (see pages 210–11), and by the building of canals. The 35-mile Forth & Clyde Canal was completed in 1790 from Bowling's Bay on the Clyde, round the northern edge of Glasgow and past Falkirk to the river Carron at Grangemouth on the Firth of Forth. It was joined at Port Dundas in 1791 by the Monkland Canal, which carried coal into Glasgow, and near Falkirk by the Union Canal, completed in 1822, which gave access to Edinburgh. Coal masters used railways, of which the first was probably the 2½-mile line from pits at Tranent to the harbour at Cockenzie. Built in 1722, it provided a defensive line during the battle in 1745 in which the Jacobite army led by Charles Edward Stuart defeated government forces under the command of Sir John Cope. It was still in use in 1815, when the track was relaid with cast-iron rails. The waggonway to the harbour at Alloa was built in the 1760s and worked until the 1930s; the Elgin Railway, serving the port of Charlestown on the north shore of the Firth of Forth, was built in 1768; and the Halbeath Railway, to Inverkeithing, was completed in 1783. There were banks of lime kilns at both harbours. On the west coast a plateway between Kilmarnock and Troon was completed in 1812. Many lines carried coal to wharfs on the Monkland Canal.

The variety of coal-using manufactures in eighteenth-century Scotland is illustrated at Prestonpans, eight miles east of Edinburgh, where monks had mined coal as early as 1184. There were fourteen salt makers at Prestonpans in the 1790s, eight in 1820s and four in 1860, and one continued working into the twentieth century. In 1749 John Roebuck established a sulphuric acid works to supply linen bleachers, but it closed in 1825–26 after the development of chlorine bleaching. Thomas Paterson began to make soap at Prestonpans in the mid-eighteenth century, using kelp as his source of alkali, and had three iron vats. His company continued for two centuries. William Morison opened a glassworks in 1698, which for three decades made bottles, and a pottery subsequently occupied the site. Eleven kiln foundations are displayed at Prestonpans, where there were three potteries in the 1790s. One of them, established in 1750 by William Cadell, worked until 1838, employed 125 people in 1792, and made creamware for export to the Baltic, the Mediterranean and North America. The West Pans Pottery, active between 1754 and 1817, made some porcelain, but its principal product was also creamware. There were brick and tile works in the area by the 1780s, and in 1803 Svedenstierna noted several coal-using industries around Edinburgh, including distilleries, potteries, glassworks, soapworks, steam-driven paper mills and lime kilns.

In 1841 662 people were employed making glass in Scotland, about 8.5 per cent of the total in the United Kingdom. The glassworks at Dumbarton, opened in 1777 and closed in 1850, was one of the largest in Britain. There were three English glass cones by 1792, when it made both bottles and crown glass, and a steam engine was installed in 1801. The works was controlled until 1792 by James Dunlop, tobacco merchant and landowner, and from 1838 by James Christie of the Calder Ironworks. The Verville Glassworks in Glasgow, established in 1776 by the statistician Patrick Colquhoun, made flint crystal table glass until 1835. Its single English glass cone was a landmark. The works at Alloa, with its 79 feet (24 m) high cone, produced tablewares and enamelled items, and probably dates from the 1770s.

Almost a thousand people were employed in 1841 in Scottish potteries, most of them on the coalfields, where many potteries dated from the 1770s. There were clusters around Glasgow and Edinburgh, and at Alloa and Greenock. The Delftfield Pottery at Glasgow, which made tin-glaze earthenware, was established in 1748 by a company that included the tobacco merchant Lawrence Dinwiddie and his brother Robert, who was governor of Virginia in the 1750s. James Watt was a partner in the 1760s and gave advice even after he moved to Birmingham. William Young was apprenticed at Delftfield, became senior partner, and introduced the manufacture of porcelain, but the works closed in 1824. The pottery at Cumnock was built in 1792, probably to make pots for the stamping and potting process at a forge that was never completed. From about 1830 it produced mottoware, dishes inscribed with sayings such as 'Oatmeal grains mak Scotsmens brains'.

A coal-using industry that had no significant parallel elsewhere in Britain was the refining of oil from cannel coal and, after 1858, from oil-bearing coal-measure shales. The industry was founded by the chemist James Young, who patented his process in 1850, and set up a refinery at Bathgate in 1851. By 1865 three million tons a year of oil-bearing shale were being mined in West Lothian, where immense 'bings', made up of the pinkish-red waste from the process, soon dominated the landscape. In 1865 Young set up Young's Paraffin Light & Mineral Oil Co., with a plant at Addiewell near Bathgate. He retired to Wemyss Bay in 1870, but the industry did not reach its peak output until 1913. Today, despite extensive removal of the gigantic bings in the 1960s and 1970s, enough examples remain to give a clear impression of the scale of this unique industry – and perhaps the finest of all, the so-called Five Sisters at Addiewell, has been designated a nature reserve because of its rare and diverse flora.

In Scotland the large-scale manufacture of bricks and tiles began in the mid-nineteenth century. Carron and other early coke-fuelled ironworks used refractory bricks from Stourbridge, but the foundations of the Scottish industry were works producing draining tiles, the first of which began production at Cessnock, Ayrshire, in 1826. More opened after the invention of cylindrical clay drainage pipes in 1843. The Garnkirk Fireclay Company, established in 1832, was the largest in Scotland in 1850. Larger works, with banks of kilns producing drainage pipes, sanitary ware and refractories, were mostly built after 1870.

In the Highlands coal mining at Brora in Sutherland, begun in the sixteenth century, was revived in the late eighteenth century as part of the Leveson-Gower family's intended regeneration of the region. Coal was used to boil salt, but the removal of salt duties in 1823 caused the closure of the colliery in 1828, although it was re-opened in 1872. Coal was also being mined at Machrihanish in Argyll in 1700. A short canal was built in 1794 to serve the mine, which worked until 1856. The sinking of a new pit in 1877 led to the construction of the six-mile, 2 ft 3 in. (0.7 m) gauge Campbeltown & Machrihanish Railway. Distilleries consumed much of the output of both mines.

The output of Scottish coal mines increased from about 2.7 million tons in the mid-1820s to 7.4 million in 1854, due largely to the expansion of iron making after the introduction of hot blast in 1828. Many of those who invested in blast furnaces around Coatbridge accumulated their capital by raising coal and selling it in Glasgow. When Monkland ironmasters turned to Ayrshire in the 1840s they sank mines for coal as well as for iron ore. Mines in Fife grew substantially after 1872 when they produced 1.55 million tons, or 10 per cent of Scottish output. The Fife Coal Company found new markets by taking coal by rail to Methil and other North Sea ports. Production in Scotland almost doubled between 1754 and 1870, but increased almost three-fold in the next three decades to exceed 33 million tons by 1900, when the industry employed more than 100,000 men. It is appropriate that Scotland's mining museum at Newtongrange represents the large-scale industry of the decades after 1870. Monuments of its earlier history include pumping engine houses at Prestongrange, Devon Colliery near Alloa, and Blacksyke near Kilmarnock.

◁ The Five Sisters, around a mile north-west of West Calder, West Lothian. Around twenty such 'bings' remain in the landscape south-west of Edinburgh, as monuments to the oil-shale industry that prospered here into the twentieth century. The Five Sisters are now a scheduled historic monument.

The coalfields of Yorkshire

The coalfield that extends from Yorkshire into Nottinghamshire and Derbyshire was exploited on only a modest scale in 1700, and much of it was not significantly developed until after 1870. In 1854 the 333 collieries in the West Riding produced 7.75 million tons of coal and employed 21,030 miners. Many Yorkshire mines provided fuel for local needs, including those of textile-mill owners and finishers of woollen cloth, but those between Leeds, Wakefield and Sheffield supplied distant markets and supported coal-hungry manufactures. The first steam engine on the coalfield was installed by John Hirst in 1735 at Greasbrough, near Rotherham, where coal was being carried on 'Newcastle roads' (that is, railways) by 1763. Developing technology enabled deep coal workings to follow the eastward dip of the seams, and in the 1850s and 1860s pits were sunk near Rotherham and Barnsley where prospectors aimed to reach the Barnsley (or Top Hard) Seam, which could be up to 7 feet 6 inches (2.3 m) thick, and whose coal was suitable for firing boilers. The High Hazel Seam above it was favoured as domestic coal, and the Thorncliffe seam below it was used in gasworks and coke ovens. The Barnsley Seam was worked at Kilnhurst from 1858, at Kiveton Park from 1866, and at Manvers Main and Denaby Main, then the most easterly colliery in Yorkshire, from 1868.

The explosions at the Barnsley Oaks Colliery in 1866 were the worst coal-mining disaster in England. The mine was notoriously dangerous: a methane explosion had already killed 73 men there in 1847. The first of three explosions in 1866 occurred on 12 December, after which rescue parties brought out some men from the vicinity of the shaft bottom as well as the bodies of those who had been killed. After the rescuers re-entered the mine the following day there were two further explosions, one of which is depicted in this contemporary image. In all some 361 men lost their lives.

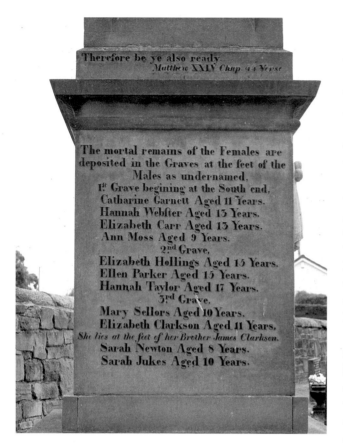

The mortal remains of the Females are
deposited in the Graves at the feet of the
Males as undernamed,
1st Grave begining at the South end,
Catharine Garnett Aged 11 Years.
Hannah Webster Aged 13 Years.
Elizabeth Carr Aged 13 Years.
Ann Moss Aged 9 Years.
2nd Grave,
Elizabeth Hollings Aged 15 Years.
Ellen Parker Aged 15 Years.
Hannah Taylor Aged 17 Years.
3rd Grave,
Mary Sellors Aged 10 Years.
Elizabeth Clarkson Aged 11 Years.
She lies at the feet of her Brother James Clarkson.
Sarah Newton Aged 8 Years.
Sarah Jukes Aged 10 Years.

Therefore be ye also ready.
Matthew XXIV Chap. 44 Verse

The face of the memorial to the Huskar accident in the churchyard at Silkstone, Yorkshire, which lists the women and girls killed in the tragedy.

Women worked underground in Yorkshire until the practice was forbidden by the Mines Act of 1842. Witnesses at the inquiry that preceded the Act testified that girls worked as trappers and hurriers (the Yorkshire term for those who drew corves loaded with coal) not only in isolated workings but in the most productive mines around Barnsley. An inrush of water at the Huskar Pit, Silkstone, on 4 July 1838 drowned eleven girls aged between 8 and 17, as well as fifteen boys between 7 and 16. The south Yorkshire pits were also notoriously gassy. An obelisk outside All Saints, Darfield, commemorates 189 men and boys who were killed by an explosion at the Lundhill Colliery in 1857, while the figure of an angel alongside the Darfield–Barnsley road is a memorial to the 361 men killed at the Oaks Pit in 1866.

Improvements in inland navigation enabled the carriage of Yorkshire coal to distant markets. An Act of 1699 authorised the Aire & Calder Navigation Company to extend navigation on the Aire from its tidal limit at Knottingley to Leeds (completed in 1700) and on the Calder from Knottingley to Wakefield (reached in 1704). By 1830 numerous branch canals and tramroads connected collieries and quarries with the river Aire over the 11¼ miles between Leeds and Castleford, and with the river Calder on its 12½-mile course from Wakefield to the confluence. From 1758 John Smeaton directed the construction of the Calder & Hebble Navigation, allowing navigation upstream to Halifax, while in 1774 the trustees of Sir John Ramsden obtained authority to build a waterway from the Calder at Cooper's Bridge to Huddersfield. Other canals eventually extended navigation through the Pennines to Lancashire.

The Selby Canal, completed in 1781, ran from the river Aire at West Haddlesey to Selby, the lowest bridging point on the river Ouse, and became an outlet for woollen cloth from the West Riding. It was superseded from 1826 by a canal, designed by George Leather, from Knottingley to Goole. This encouraged the Aire and Calder Navigation Co. to build a new town at Goole, which prospered as a coal port. In 1863 William Bartholomew introduced the compartment boats called 'Tom Puddings', and their associated hydraulically operated hoists, which carried coal to Goole until 1985.

The river Don reached its confluence with the Ouse near Goole by way of the Dutch River, whose eighteenth-century course was shaped by floods of circa 1688. In 1700 the Don could only be navigated to Doncaster for nine months of the year, but Acts of Parliament of 1726–27 empowered Doncaster Corporation to improve the river upstream from its tidal limit at Barnby Dun, while the Hallamshire Cutlers' Company took responsibility for continuing the navigation towards Sheffield. Vessels could reach Rotherham by 1740 and Tinsley by 1751, although it was not until 1819 that a canal into the heart of Sheffield was completed. New cuts were subsequently made on the Don, including one that linked the river to Greasbrough, which was financed by the 2nd

Inland navigation to the Lincolnshire town of Horncastle became possible with the canalisation of the river Bain, completed in 1802. Warehouses for general cargo stand at the head of navigation, but Horncastle also became a market for coal from Yorkshire.

Humber keels on the Stainforth & Keadby Canal, close to the lock by which it enters the river Trent at Keadby.

Marquis of Rockingham and built by William Jessop. Inland navigation in south Yorkshire was substantially improved by three waterways sanctioned in 1793. The Barnsley Canal, opened in 1799, extended from the river Calder downstream of Wakefield to a five-arch masonry aqueduct over the river Dearne at Hoyle Mill, north of Barnsley. A further section, opened in 1802, led to a basin at Barugh, terminus of a tramroad from coal mines at Silkstone. The Dearne & Dove Canal, opened in 1804, connected the Barnsley Canal near the Dearne Aqueduct with the river Don at Swinton, and had branches to Worsborough and Elsecar. The Stainforth & Keadby Canal, opened in 1802, linked the Don near Thorne with the river Trent, providing access to waterways in Lincolnshire.

The expansion of the waterways network southeastwards across Lincolnshire and down the Trent Valley was crucial to the developing market for Yorkshire coal, giving it a very competitive position. Improvement of the Trent began when a cut was dug around Newark in 1773. An Act of 1783 placed the river under the authority of the Company of Proprietors of the Trent Navigation, whose engineer was William Jessop, and within two years a 68-mile towpath from Shardlow to Gainsborough was completed. The 46-mile Chesterfield Canal, authorised in 1771 and opened in 1776, joined the Trent at West Stockwith. The Foss Dyke, the oldest man-made waterway in England, extends 11 miles from the Trent at Torksey to the river Witham at Lincoln, and was improved in the 1760s by John Grundy junior and John Smeaton, who also, under an Act of 1762, carried out works on the Witham between Lincoln and Boston. The improvement of the river Welland from 1772 enabled vessels to reach Spalding, Market Deeping and Stamford. Works on the river Ancholme from Ferriby Sluice to Bishopbridge Wharf near Market Rasen were completed in 1778, and from 1800 a canal linked the Ancholme with Caistor. The navigation from Tetney Haven on the Humber to Louth enabled vessels to reach Louth by 1770. Sleaford was linked to the waterways network in 1794 by the canalisation of the river Slea, and Horncastle by works on the river Bain, completed in 1802. Navigation and land reclamation in

Lincolnshire were closely linked, and large boats could access many villages along drainage channels.

These waterways created a market for water-borne West Riding coal that extended from Ripon, across the plain of York and through Lincolnshire, to the western edges of Nottinghamshire and the borders of Northamptonshire. Around every bridge and ferry grew up coal merchants' yards, lime kilns, brick and tile works and malthouses. In market towns Yorkshire coal fired gas retorts, provided steam for the pumps of breweries, and the prime movers of engineering shops, oil mills and whiting works. It fired the boilers of pumping engines that drained and made fertile the wetlands, and the engines of those penny capitalists who invested in threshing machines and, from the 1860s, in steam-ploughing sets. The waterways were the arteries by which old trades and technologies were stimulated and new ones diffused.

There were communities of vessel owners, boat people and boat builders at Goole, Knottingley and Castleford, and at Thorne, the red-brick town between the river Don and the Stainforth & Keadby Canal. There were 22 vessel owners at Knottingley in the 1820s, and there in the 1860s about 300 people were involved in building, repairing and working boats. Coal boats were crewed both by men from the colliery districts and by boatmen from Lincolnshire who delivered grain or potatoes to Yorkshire and returned with coal.

In 1861 the census enumerators listed 260 boats on the Barnsley Canal and the river Don, at Mexborough,

Knottingley, Castleford, Thorne and Stainforth, including 36 from Sheffield and Rotherham and 25 from Hull. Some came from the west, from Wakefield and Mirfield, and some from Beverley in the East Riding. More than 50 were from Lincolnshire, from Gainsborough, Butterwick and Stockwith on the Trent, Walkeringham on the Chesterfield Canal, Louth, Horncastle and Boston, Bishopbridge on the Ancholme, and Saxilby on the Foss Dyke, as well as from the city of Lincoln.

Crowle and Keadby, at the junction of the Stainforth & Keadby Canal and the river Trent, were staging points for keels passing between Yorkshire and Lincolnshire. The census lists 26 vessels in the two villages, five being from Thorne and eight from Lincolnshire, including boats from Martin on the Horncastle Navigation and Brigg on the Ancholme. There were 25 vessels on the Trent between the Humber and Gainsborough and on the Foss Dyke, four of them from Yorkshire, while boats from Knottingley and Goole were on the Ancholme, the Louth Navigation and at Spalding.

Coal was also carried on the rivers Ouse, Derwent, and Hull, on the Beverley Beck, made navigable in 1726, and on the Pocklington Canal, authorised in 1815. In 1861 the thirteen vessels near Beverley included one from Knottingley and two from Worsborough. There were 17 boats in and around Selby, and 18 at York of which 14 were engaged in the coal trade, three of them taking coal upstream to Ripon. The development of Goole enabled sea-borne Yorkshire coal to

◀ The Beverley Beck was one of many waterways that enabled coal from the mines around Barnsley to customers in Lincolnshire and the East Riding of Yorkshire. It extends less than a mile from Grovehill Lock on the river Humber into the town of Beverley, and was made accessible to Humber keels by the construction of a lock as part of a drainage project in 1802. Traffic on the Beck increased substantially during the nineteenth century even after the opening of main-line railways.

PHOTOGRAPH: CARNEGIE, 2005

compete with that from Tyneside and Wearside, and in 1861 there were vessels from Goole at King's Lynn, Wisbech, Woodbridge, Mistley and Maldon.

Collieries in Yorkshire also prospered from the growth of manufactures. The smiths and cutlers of Hallamshire used coal that was taken to Sheffield in 'open boats'. The Milton and Elsecar Ironworks, the Park Gate forge, and the blast furnaces at Holmes all consumed large quantities. Many of the grates, ranges and fenders that characterised Victorian houses were made in Rotherham, where the ironfounder William Owen had 800 employees in 1861. Pattern makers, moulders, cupola tenters, fender buffers, kitchen-range fitters and 'Berlin blackers of iron grates' lived in the area. Sickles and scythes were manufactured around Beighton in the Rother Valley by firms varying in size from a three-man business to that of Thomas Staniforth, who had 146 workers. Other forges produced components for railway vehicles. The locomotive works of the South Yorkshire Railway at Mexborough opened in 1855, and built two locomotives in 1861–62, but from 1864 was used for repairs and overhauls. At Brinsworth brass founders, chasers and lacquerers including migrants from Birmingham made chandeliers as well as taps and pipes. Coke from Elsecar was commended in 1849 by ironfounders from St Ives (Huntingdonshire) and Northampton, and the Great Northern Railway's inspector of coal, working from Elsecar in 1861, probably bought coke to fire locomotives.

The 70 foot (21.5 m) high English glass cone at Catcliffe, built in 1740 by William Fenney, is evidence of the importance of glass making in Yorkshire. About two dozen people were employed in the manufacture of bottles there in 1861, some of them from South Shields. The New York glassworks at Brinsworth employed 43 people; there were more than 50 glass-makers at Kimberworth; and nearly 200 in two bottle factories at Mexborough and Swinton, while a glass-maker from Kingswinford near Stourbridge employed 52 hands at Barnsley.

Swinton was described in 1839 as 'the chief seat of china and earthenware manufacture in the North of England'. In 1841 there were 1,039 potters in the West Riding, 4.2 per cent of the United Kingdom total. The

△ The Waterloo Kiln, the only surviving structure of the Rockingham Pottery.

Don Pottery at Swinton was established in 1801 and managed by William and John Green of the Leeds Pottery, who for a period from 1810 made porcelain. It was sold in the 1830s to Samuel Barker. In 1861 more than 300 pottery workers lived in Mexborough and Swinton. The Kilnhurst Pottery, which dated from 1746, employed 90 hands and produced earthenware into the twentieth century. Other works included the Newhill Pottery near Wath-on-Dearne, the Rawmarsh Pottery established about 1790 by William Hawley, and the Holmes Pottery which from 1850 employed more than 60 people making glazed earthenware.

The celebrated Rockingham Pottery originated in 1747 as a producer of tiles and common pots, situated on Swinton Common. By 1787 the partners included members of the Green family from Leeds, and it produced chocolate-coloured tea and coffee sets. In 1806 ownership passed to John and William Brameld, who began to make porcelain. After a crisis in 1825 was averted by support from the 4th Earl Fitzwilliam, the name Rockingham and the red griffin mark from the Wentworth crest were adopted. The Bramelds were embarrassed by an order for a 200-piece dessert service for King William IV, for which they received

£5,000, much less than the cost of production. The works closed in 1842, and by 1860 some of its buildings were being used for grinding flint. In 1916 they were said to be 'a ruinous and sad spectacle', although a bottle oven of 1815 remains.

Transport systems in the Yorkshire coalfield in the eighteenth century focused on Ferrybridge and Knottingley, where the Great North Road crossed the Aire & Calder Navigation. River-based trades in timber and grain stimulated the growth of sawmills, corn mills, maltings and breweries. The quarrying, burning and marketing of limestone, and the manufacture of whiting, occupied 80 people in Knottingley and 40 in nearby Brotherton in 1861. Mining in the adjoining communities of Featherstone and Castleford employed more than 500 men, and grew rapidly after the sinking of Featherstone Main Colliery in 1868. Featherstone became notorious as the place where the military killed two miners on 7 September 1893, and in 1957 it was portrayed as 'Ashton', an archetypal mining community, in the book *Coal is Our Life*.

Pottery manufacture around Knottingley began on a large scale in the 1790s. The Knottingley Pottery was established in 1792 by William Tomlinson, and in 1796 David Dunderdale issued a pattern book for his Castleford Pottery, where he made classically inspired stoneware. Eight earthenware manufacturers in Castleford in 1861 employed 300 people making black, blue and white, and lustre wares, and local flint millers provided them with materials. There were many links with potteries in north Staffordshire. Ralph Wedgwood from Burslem was a partner at Knottingley in the 1790s, and migrants from Fenton, Hanley, Longton and Tunstall lived in the area in 1861. The manufacture of glass bottles, using locally produced lime and sand, began about 1810, and by the 1870s Castleford produced about 16 million bottles a year, many of which were exported. More than 500 people worked in 1861 for ten glassmakers whose products included carboys for chemicals and bottles for medicine and aerated waters.

The townships of Holbeck and Hunslet, the most urban part of the Yorkshire coalfield, are bounded by the bend of the river Aire downstream from Leeds Bridge. In 1700 folds lined with houses were clustered at the bridge foot along the bifurcating routes to Wakefield, Dewsbury and Halifax. The completion of the Aire & Calder Navigation stimulated the construction of wharfs, and in 1776, after the Leeds & Liverpool Canal was opened as far as Gargrave, a

A view of Leeds from the south published *circa* 1860. The numerous kilns provide evidence of the presence of potteries, glassworks and other coal-using industries in Holbeck and Hunslet.

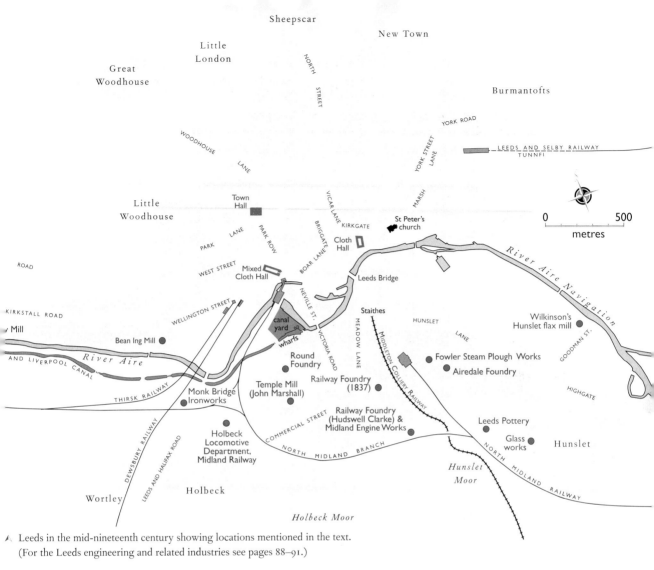

⌃ Leeds in the mid-nineteenth century showing locations mentioned in the text.
(For the Leeds engineering and related industries see pages 88–91.)

terminal warehouse was built alongside its first lock. A two-mile railway from Middleton Colliery ended near Leeds Bridge. It belonged to Charles Brandling, who owned pits near Newcastle-upon-Tyne and employed a viewer, Richard Humble, from Tyneside. Authorised in 1758, the double-track line with a gauge of 4 feet (1.23 m) opened on 20 September of that year, when 'the Bells were set a-ringing, the Cannons of our fort fired, and a general joy appear'd in every face'. A directory of 1817 observed that Leeds 'is principally supplied with coal from the pits at Middleton'. The colliery accounts suggest that domestic consumption rose from 28,000 tons in 1771 to 53,000 in 1801, and industrial consumption from 5,000 tons to 8,000 tons. Between 1811 and 1814 the annual sale of coal at the

terminal staithes was 88,000 tons. About 80 people worked underground and on the surface at Middleton Colliery in 1773, but it expanded to employ 230 by 1793 and 380 by 1820.

Holbeck and Hunslet developed a characteristic coalfield economy. In the 1860s most colliers worked at small mines, such as those of Joseph Fowler, who employed 22 people including his own ten-year-old son, and Charles Grosvenor, who employed 26 people in his colliery and brickyard. Steam-driven spinning and weaving mills, cloth-finishing works, foundries and forges all consumed coal on a substantial scale. The Leeds Pottery near the Middleton Railway was founded in 1770 by John and Joshua Green, in partnership with Richard Humble from Middleton Colliery.

The publication in 1783 of a pattern book in English, French and German indicated the company's ambitions, and it traded profitably with Russia. The pottery specialised in white-bodied, lead-glazed earthenware following classical precedents, and prospered for 60 years, but its workforce diminished from 400 to 300 in the 1850s, and it closed in 1878. The Hunslet Hall Pottery was opened shortly before 1792 and produced creamwares. A gazetteer of 1837 listed nine earthenware manufacturers in Leeds, all but one of them in Hunslet. In 1861 the industry employed at least 500 people, including mould turners, saggar makers, slip makers, cave men, turners of potters' wheels and lathes, handlers, carriers-off, dippers, sorters and packers, and makers of stone bottles.

Glass making also consumed coal in Hunslet. The principal glasshouses, near Hunslet village, were worked from about 1800 by John Bowers whose family by the 1850s owned a flint glass and bottle works, two crown window glass factories, and a chemical works producing alum, copperas, nitric, hydrochloric and sulphuric acids, as well as coal mines. They employed many of the crucible makers, glass-founders, glass-gatherers, blowers of crown glass, bottle blowers, glass cutters and crate makers who lived in Hunslet, but several other concerns operated in the area in the 1860s including Wood & Doyle, managed by three brothers from Brierley Hill whose 30 employees made flint glass. There were two paper works, a soapworks, several brickyards, tanneries and malthouses, as well as the Holbeck locomotive sheds of the Midland Railway and the city gasworks. Steam engines powered textile mills, iron forges and engineering shops, and were also employed to grind grain, press oil seeds, crush clay for brick making, pulp rags for paper making, saw timber and operate printing presses.

Most of Hunslet's workers lived in scattered blocks of back-to-back terraces filling plots that had once been fields alongside the radial routes, a rather different pattern from the regimented terraces that characterised Leeds north of the river Aire. This was an urban coalfield comparable in many respects with the areas around Walker or Wearmouth in the North East, but wholly different from those mining areas where headstocks were surrounded by fields, and where colliers kept company with ploughmen and cowherds.

The East Midlands seams

Coal mining was well established in the East Midlands by 1700. Indeed, the first known railway built to carry coal in Britain was working at Wollaton Park near Nottingham in 1604, and collieries in that area were still productive in the mid-nineteenth century. In 1692 John Houghton knew of pits up to 120 feet (37 m) deep at Denby, Heanor and Smalley, and learned that in summer, when the roads were dry, coal from Heanor was carried south to Northamptonshire. In the middle of the eighteenth century Angerstein noted pits up to 180 feet (55.4 m) deep along the road from Chesterfield to Sheffield. A steam pumping engine was supplied in 1735 by the Coalbrookdale Company to mines at Smalley. Mining was stimulated by the construction of three canals radiating from Langley Mill. The Erewash Canal, opened in 1779, extended 11¾ miles to the river Trent, near its junction with the Loughborough Navigation at Sawley. The Cromford Canal, opened in 1794, ran 14½ miles to Cromford, passing under the watershed between the Erewash and Derwent valleys in the 3,000-yard Butterley Tunnel. The Nottingham Canal, opened in 1796, passed from Langley Mill along the eastern side of the Erewash Valley before turning east toward Nottingham. These canals opened up markets to the south and, for example, in 1835 coal from Shipley was being sent by narrow boat to Newport Pagnell and Buckingham.

Before 1850 mining extended along the north–south axis formed by the rivers Erewash and Rother, which from 1862 was followed by the Erewash Valley and North Midland railways. The Erewash rises near Kirkby-in-Ashfield and flows south from Pinxton past Ironville, Codnor, Eastwood, Ilkeston, and Sandiacre to join the Trent at Long Eaton, and for many miles forms the border between Nottinghamshire and Derbyshire. The Rother rises near Pilsley and flows north past Chesterfield, Staveley and Eckington to its confluence with the Don at Rotherham. The dip of the

The railway junction at Clay Cross where the North Midland Railway from Derby, to the right, opened in 1839, was joined by the Midland Railway's extension of its Erewash Valley line, opened from Pye Bridge in 1862 (see page 142). Many of the coal mines and ironworks in the area were developed by partnerships of which George Stephenson was a member, and the great engineer spent his last years at nearby Tapton Hall.

Prince's Street, Eastwood, part of the mid-nineteenth-century group of terraced housing for coal miners which D. H. Lawrence called 'The Backs'. Lawrence's birthplace is a short distance away in Victoria Street.

coal seams is from west to east, and most productive mines in the early nineteenth century were west of the axis on the Derbyshire side. As deeper shafts became feasible, more collieries were sunk in Nottinghamshire. Thus, although Mansfield came to be regarded in the twentieth century as a coalfield town, a textile company that was disposing of a steam engine in 1793 complained of 'the Excessive Scarcity of Coal in our Neighbourhood', and the railway to Pinxton, opened in 1819, was intended to deliver coal to the town's malthouses.

The longwall system of mining was used by the mid-eighteenth century and in 1812 about 50 pits were wound by steam engines. At the Cinderhill (or Babbington) Colliery in the Leen Valley at Basford, sunk by Thomas North from 1841, coal was raised by wooden tandem headstocks from a 654-foot (201 m) shaft that was fitted with guide rods and lined with iron tubbing. Coal was moved underground on railways, and the pit was ventilated by an underground furnace. George Stephenson leased the Tapton estate north of Chesterfield in 1838, the year after he had established a company to exploit minerals discovered at Clay Cross during the construction of his North Midland Railway. Robert Stephenson severed the family connection with the business, but it prospered as the Clay Cross Company, and by 1854 had opened four collieries. In 1861 Clay Cross was a mining community with a population in excess of 3,000. The company, owned from 1871 by Sir William Jackson, sank more pits in the 1860s and 1870s. Richard Barrow of the Staveley Company opened Speedwell Colliery in 1841, Hopewell and Hollingwood in 1843, Springwell in 1853 and Seymour in 1858, and by 1865 these together were producing 743,000 tons *per annum*. The population of Staveley increased from 2,926 in 1835 to 6,831 in 1861. Such growth also encouraged the founding of new settlements. In the four rows that comprised Seymour Cottages were 130 houses, all occupied in 1861 by coal miners. The majority of the 833 inhabitants were of local origin, but there were migrants from Dawley and Benthall in Shropshire; Gornal, Greets Green and Netherton in the Black Country; Hetton and South Shields in Co. Durham; and Leigh and Wigan in Lancashire. Miners in the 102 houses that made up Speedwell Terraces included incomers from Cambridgeshire, Suffolk and Devon, as well as men bred as colliers at West Bromwich, Wallsend and Bedworth.

Mining in Nottinghamshire and Derbyshire expanded from the 1840s because coalmasters found new markets, particularly in London, that they could readily supply by rail. The first consignments were despatched south from Clay Cross in 1846 via the North Midland and Midland Counties lines to Rugby and then by canal, but by 1850 coal was being sent directly to London by rail, and from 1868 the Midland Railway had its own independent route to the capital. The Clay Cross Company, which carried more coal to London than any other Derbyshire concern, despatched 385,632 tons in 1870. In the following decades railway companies fought strenuously for the privilege and profit of taking the region's coal to London.

In the 1860s mines along the western edge of the coalfield were mostly small. The road from Chesterfield towards Chatsworth was lined with small pits, brownware potteries, textile factories and workshops, terraces of workers' cottages and allotment gardens, and about 70 miners at Ashover were employed raising fuel for a lead smelter and lime kilns. In the hills east of the river Derwent miners were numerous at Pentrich, Heage,

Denby and Horsley Woodhouse, while about 100 lived in the vicinity of Belper.

The growth of mining in the Erewash Valley was described by D. H. Lawrence, son of a butty at Eastwood. Lawrence recalled 'an extremely beautiful countryside, just between the red sandstone and the oak trees of Nottingham, and the cold limestone, the ash trees, the stone fences of Derbyshire. To me, as a child and a young man, it was still the old England of the forest and agricultural past.' The parish commons were enclosed by an Act of 1792, and Lawrence reflected that before his birth Eastwood was 'a small place of cottages and fragmentary rows of little four-roomed miners' dwellings, the home of the old colliers ... who worked in ... mines with an opening in the hillside into which the miners walked, or windlass mines, where the men were wound up one at a time, in a bucket, by a donkey'. Such mines were working when his father was a boy, and he saw their remains in his own childhood.

The interests of two families were amalgamated in 1787 to form Barber, Walker & Co., the company that Lawrence called Carston Waite, which controlled seven collieries in Eastwood by 1807, and continued until nationalisation in 1947. Eastwood Hall was the home of the family established by Joseph Walker, of the Rotherham iron-founding family. The Barbers lived at Lamb Close Hall, on which Lawrence modelled Shortlands in *Women in Love*. The company offices occupied the building that is now the Durban House Heritage Centre. Mining was transformed from the 1850s. The Eastwood mines produced less than half a million tons of coal in 1848, but 2 million in 1871 and 16 million in 1900. Nevertheless, the collieries remained within a rural landscape. Lawrence described how

down the valleys of the brooks from Selby and Nuttall, new mines were sunk, until soon there were six pits working. From Nuttall, high up on the sandstone among the woods, the railway ran, past the ruined priory of the Carthusians and past Robin Hood's Well down to Spinney Park, then on to Minton, a large mine among corn-fields, from Minton across the farm-lands of the valleyside to Bunker's Hill, branching

St Pancras Station, seen here under construction, was opened in 1868 and symbolised the Midland Railway's advance from the provinces into the capital. The train shed was designed by William Henry Barlow, the Midland's consulting engineer, and the latticed ribs of the roof were provided by the Butterley Company from Derbyshire. The roof was erected with the aid of a giant moveable timber scaffold and measured 100 ft high and 240 ft wide. The platforms were constructed of iron plates on a girder grid supported by 688 iron columns on brick piers. The air of ostentation was increased by Sir George Gilbert Scott's hotel erected on the Euston Road frontage of the station. Nevertheless, for all this display, the principal motive of the Midland Railway's extension to London was to carry coal to the metropolis, and until the 1960s huge quantities of coal travelled from the marshalling yard at Toton on the border of Nottinghamshire with Derbyshire, through Leicester, Kettering, Bedford and St Albans, to yards in north London.

off there, and running north to Beggarlee and Selby, that looks over at Crich and the hills of Derbyshire; six mines like black studs on the countryside, linked by a loop of fine chain, the railway.

Fewer than a thousand people were living in Eastwood in 1801, but nearly 2,000 in 1861, about 300 of whom worked in pits, and about 90 in framework knitting. Many miners lived in The Breach, built by Barber Walker, ranks of brick cottages looking eastwards towards Greasley. Lawrence called them 'The Bottoms', and described 'the little front gardens with auriculas and saxifrage in the shadow of the bottom block, sweet-williams and pinks in the sunny top block … between the long lines of ash-pits went the alley where the children played and the women gossiped and the men smoked.'

James Knighton, born in Eastwood about 1780, experienced great changes in coal mining and his community. From the age of eight, before learning to write, he drove gin horses that were drawing coal from a pit. At eleven he began to draw waggons underground, with a belt and chain, along wooden tracks subsequently replaced by iron rails, receiving a shilling for each 12-hour shift. He commenced 'man's work' at 14, holing underneath the seam of coal prior to its being hacked down. When he was about 40 his body was scorched by a methane fire, and ten years later an injury caused by a roof fall prevented him from working for three years. He was still working underground at 65 when he broke his collarbone.

Greasley, whose church tower is visible from Lawrence's birthplace, was the largest parish in Nottinghamshire. Its population rose from 2,968 in 1801 to 6,210 in 1861, when 1,175 people were employed

▲ The pit at Brinsley, once the workplace of D. H. Lawrence's father, was 780 ft (238 m) deep, and began production in 1872, when its wooden tandem headstock came into use. After the closure of the colliery the headstock was removed for preservation at the Lounds Hall Museum (closed in 1989), but it has since been re-erected in an area of parkland where there is little other evidence that there was once a coal mine.

▼ 'Old Crown China Works' by William Mosley (1890). William Duesbury had built a national reputation for his 'Crown Derby' wares in the late eighteenth century. In 1848 some of the workforce moved to this site in King Street and revived the company as 'The Old Crown Derby China factory'.

PHOTOGRAPH BY CARNEGIE, WITH PERMISSION OF DERBY MUSEUMS AND ART GALLERY

▼ Horses hauling coal waggons alongside the Derby Canal at Little Eaton. This photograph dates from *circa* 1908.

© NATIONAL RAILWAY MUSEUM/SCIENCE & SOCIETY PICTURE LIBRARY

▲ Belper was primarily a textile town from the late eighteenth century, dominated by the cotton-spinning mills erected by the Strutt family, but it lay on the edge of the Derbyshire coalfield, and several coal-based industries flourished there, including pottery manufacture and the making of nails. The Strutts erected several nailmakers' shops in their housing developments, of which this is an example, which gave employment to the husbands and fathers of women and children who were employed in large numbers in the mills. These were a tiny proportion of the 162 nailers' shops which William Bamford counted in the town in 1821.

in coal mining and more than 200 in framework knitting. Puddlers and shinglers from the ironworks at Codnor Park lived in New Brinsley, and 20 men were mining iron ore on Newthorpe Common. Most of Greasley's immigrants, brickmakers from Derby and Leicester, miners from the Black Country, and several Irish families, lived in the 40 houses in Holden Square. Today the re-erected headstocks of 1875 from Brinsley High Park Colliery, where Lawrence's father worked, stand among unthreatening grassy mounds.

In many communities framework knitters and lace-makers lived alongside coal miners. The population of Heanor exceeded 4,000 by 1861, with 650 miners, 350 people engaged in framework knitting, and more than 100 in lace making. Smalley was already a mining village in the 1690s, but only a dozen colliers lived there in 1861, alongside 120 framework knitters. In Codnor, with a population of 4,100, there were more than 600 coal miners and over 100 ironstone miners; the ironworks of the Butterley Co. employed about 70; and more than 80 people were involved in frame-work knitting. In Kirkby-in-Ashfield framework knitting provided employment for more than 550 of the population of nearly 3,000, with only just over 200 working in the pits. In Sutton-in-Ashfield, a renowned mining community in the twentieth century, there were scarcely two dozen colliers in 1861, but more than 2,500 people worked in framework knitting.

Mining expanded into Nottinghamshire in the 1860s. There were 21 collieries in the county in 1860 and 26 by 1869, while 16 more opened in the 1870s. Output rose from 732,666 tons in 1862 to 1.57 million in 1867. By 1871, 16,405 miners employed in Derbyshire pits were producing 5.1 million tons *per annum*. The Staveley, Sheepbridge, Butterley and Stanton iron companies became powerful forces in coal mining, while furnaces, forges and foundries provided a consistent demand for coal. More than 600 men were making nails in Belper in 1861; there were makers of spades, shovels, scythes, sickles, garden forks and nails at Eckington and Staveley, and foundries at Belper and Chesterfield, while three companies at Langley Mill made castings, axles and springs for railway waggons.

Chesterfield was an archetypal coalfield town, although an ancient borough with a spacious market place and a venerable parish church. It had well-appointed shops and inns, and was a base for Scots travelling drapers. Traditional industries include flour-mills, malthouses, a fellmonger's yard and a tannery. The town's population increased from 4,267 in 1801 to 6,212 in 1841. Collieries and potteries flourished in 1700, and the establishment of the Griffin Foundry in 1777 by John and Ebenezer Smith began a long history of boiler making and engineering. Manufacturing was stimulated by the opening of the Chesterfield Canal in 1777 and from 1840 by a skein of competing railways. In the mid-nineteenth century coal miners lived in every quarter of the town. There were blast furnaces to the north and south. Framework knitting was signif-icant in the eighteenth century, but fewer than 20 knitters worked in the parish in 1861, although other textile enterprises flourished including the steam-powered Holymoor Mill where 190 employees made cotton thread; a lace factory with 214 employees; an elastic web factory; and the 'Bump Mill' established in the 1790s at Brampton Moor, which produced candle-wick. In 1839 John Robinson set up a factory making pillboxes, and by the 1860s it also manufactured cotton lint for medical purposes. In 1755 Angerstein observed three potteries making the salt-glaze brown earth-enware, usually called Nottingham Ware, and in the 1860s about 400 potters in the Chesterfield area made brown, yellow and black salt-glaze teapots, treacle jugs and jelly moulds.

Joseph Bourne, son of a stoneware potter from Belper, began to make salt-glazed wares at Denby from 1809 after a seam of clay was discovered in 1806 during the construction of the turnpike road from Derby to Alfreton. By 1861 he employed nearly 100 people at Denby and Belper and was succeeded by his son Joseph Harvey Bourne, whose widow continued the business until 1898, introducing the manufacture of kitchenwares and art pottery. The Crown Derby porcelain works was established in the 1740s, when the Huguenot Andrew Planche worked there. In 1756 he formed a partnership with William Duesbury, a north Staffordshire potter, and John Heath, a banker. Duesbury acquired the Chelsea Pottery in 1770 and closed it in 1784, taking craftsmen and equipment to Derby. The Derby works prospered under the management of his son, William Duesbury II, and a decline after his death was followed by a revival under Robert Bloor from 1811. John Coke who had been impressed by porcelain made in Saxony, established a porcelain factory at Pinxton near the newly opened Cromford Canal, in 1796, powered at first by a steam engine, but later by a waterwheel. Coke was joined briefly by the celebrated William Billingsley, born in Derby and apprenticed at the Derby works, but he left in 1799. The Pinxton pottery produced light, translucent porcelain, and at its peak employed 50 people, but it closed in 1812–13 and its buildings became dwellings for colliers. Billingley's career was notoriously peripatetic, and between 1799 and 1802 he established a pottery at Mansfield, before moving to Lincolnshire, Worcester, South Wales and ultimately to Shropshire.

South Derbyshire and north Leicestershire

The coalfield that straddles the boundary between Leicestershire and Derbyshire already had a long history in 1861, at which date more than 1,600 miners were recorded as working there. In 1700 the mines of the Beaumont family at Coleorton, two miles east of Ashby-de-la-Zouch, were a celebrated source of coal which was distributed by packhorse through the Midlands. Longwall operation was introduced before 1700, probably by miners from Shropshire. A steam engine near Measham was working by 1720 and more were erected in the 1720s. The Coalbrookdale Company provided parts in 1730 for a pumping engine at Coleorton and in 1732 for another at Measham. About 50 miners worked at Coleorton in the 1860s, when some of the coal they produced was used by a pot manufacturer who employed 27 people.

Joseph Wilkes, lord of the manor of Measham from 1783, vigorously propounded the gospel of 'improvement'. The son of a farming family, he gained a reputation as scientific agriculturalist and founder of the Smithfield Society, and as partner of the first Sir Robert Peel in his cotton-manufacturing enterprises at Fazeley and Tamworth. Wilkes was an active trustee of turnpike roads, a proprietor of the Trent and Soar navigations, and established at Measham a bank, a covered market, a coaching inn, two multi-storey cotton mills and a tannery. He invested in coal mines and was a pioneer in the application of steam winding at collieries. He devised 'Wilkes's Gobs', bricks of approximately twice the normal size ($11\frac{1}{2} \times 5\frac{1}{2} \times 4\frac{1}{2}$ ins) which were intended to reduce the duty payable on bricks under legislation of 1785. He supported the

The principal coal-using industries on the coalfield that extends from south Derbyshire into north Leicestershire were ceramics works. The one significant ironworks in the area, the furnace at Moira, operated for only two campaigns, in 1806–07 and 1810–11. The structure was subsequently adapted as housing and is now preserved.

The coalfield around Measham and the settlements that gained the name of Coalville prospered in the early nineteenth century, their coal conveyed to distant markets by the Ashby Canal and the Leicester & Swannington Railway, which was extended into the Midland Railway's route from Leicester to Burton-on-Trent. Profitable traffics in coal, ceramics and beer led the Midland and the LNWR to construct a line from the latter's main line at Nuneaton to Moira, from which trains could run to Ashby-de-la-Zouch and Burton, with a branch from Shackerstone Junction to Coalville. The line was opened in 1873, when this photograph was taken, but it was never profitable and lost its passenger services in 1931.

Ashby-de-la-Zouch Canal, but was nervous that local mines produced insufficient coal to sustain it, and his own companies became entangled in litigation after his death.

The Ashby-de-la-Zouch Canal was authorised in 1792 and was opened in 1802 from Marston Junction on the Coventry Canal to Moira, but the intended northwards extension to the Trent was never built. Much of its prosperity was due to the sinking in 1804 of Moira Colliery, named after the 2nd Earl Moira. Its coal found markets in southern England, the extent of which is revealed by the origins of the 33 narrow boats moored there on census night in 1861, 22 being from places on the Oxford Canal, the river Thames and the Wilts & Berks Canal. On the same night boatmen from Measham and Moira were moored at Abbot's Langley, Hemel Hempstead and Boxmoor on the Grand Junction Canal. At about the time the colliery opened, a blast furnace was constructed with an arched charging ramp spanning the canal. It worked for only two campaigns in 1806–07 and 1810–11, and the spaces under the charging bridge and the engine houses were adapted as dwellings. The canal company paid no dividend until 1827–28.

Large-scale mining east of Measham began in 1822 with the sinking of a pit at Long Lane, the settlement that by 1833 was called Coalville. From 1832 it

was served by the Leicester & Swannington Railway, which was designed by Robert Stephenson to carry coal and stone eastwards to Leicester and included two inclined planes. The line originally accommodated passengers only in mixed trains. After being taken over by the Midland Railway in 1845–46 it became part of the company's route from Burton-on-Trent to Leicester. The inclined plane at Bagworth was abandoned in 1848, but loaded waggons were hauled uphill from 1833 on the Swannington incline by a Horseley Company engine which worked until 1947, and which is now displayed at York. Mining entrepreneurs included John Ellis, chairman of the Midland Railway from 1849 until 1858, after whom the village of Ellistown was named.

Iron smelting at Moira failed, but there were other industrial customers for coal. A lime yard with about 40 kilns on the Calke Abbey estate at Ticknall was linked with the Ashby Canal by a railway that passed over an arched stone bridge of 1802 and through a 138-yard cut-and-cover tunnel. Brick making became more significant than in most coalfields. It was reckoned in the 1880s that about 70 per cent of the national output of sewer pipes came from Swadlincote, and refractory bricks and chimney pots were made on a large scale. By 1860 more than 60 miners and quarrymen extracted clay for ceramics works, while brickworks employed

Moira Colliery took its name from the landowner, Francis Rawdon-Hastings, 2nd Earl Moira and from 1816 1st Marquis o Hastings. It was sunk, alongside the Ashby Canal, from 1804, and within a few years became one of the most profitable in the coalfield. While the sinking was in progress a mineral spring was discovered, and soon afterwards the Moira Baths building was constructed, with an adjacent hotel, but people seeking a health cure or recreation found the surroundings of a working colliery uncongenial, and from the 1820s spa water was instead conveyed by canal and tramway to the Ivanhoe Baths, 3½ miles east at Ashby-de-la-Zouch, which opened in 1822. Beyond the colliery are two kilns used in the manufacture of ceramics for which the coalfield was famous.

An example of 'Measham Ware', pottery made from a straw coloured clay and decorated with flowers, produced in the south Derbyshire/north Leicestershire coalfield. This example is held in by the Ironbridge Gorge Museum. There are settlements called Old Park in several English coalfields; the one named on the teapot lies just over a mile north of Ashby-de-la-Zouch.

more than 170. In 1871 Edward Ensor employed 98 men and boys in the manufacture of firebricks, sewer pipes and chimney pots. The brick and tile company at Whitwick Colliery was founded in 1827, and was managed from 1859 by George Smith, who agitated for the improvement of the working conditions of canal boat people and brickmakers, published in 1871 *The Cry of the Children from the Brickyards of England*, and secured legislation restricting employment in the industry of children under ten.

Tickney ware, named after Ticknall, was usually black-glazed. It was widely distributed in the early eighteenth century and there were 20 potters in the village in 1861, a small proportion of about 650 people then employed in potteries in the coalfield. 'Measham ware', made from straw-coloured clay covered with a dark treacly glaze, and decorated with coloured flowers, was popular with canal boat people. Black, brown and yellow wares were also produced, together with the blue-banded pottery called 'Cornish' ware, made at Church Gresley. The area became famous for kitchen utensils, yellow-glazed mixing bowls and pie dishes. Useful, health-ensuring and sometimes beautiful ceramic products emerged from the confusion of waste tips, chimneys, beehive-shaped kilns and stunted bottle ovens that could still be observed from trains passing Swadlincote as late as the 1960s.

Warwickshire

The Warwickshire coalfield extended 20 miles north and north-west from Coventry (Eliot's *Middlemarch*) through Bedworth, Atherstone and Nuneaton to Polesworth and Tamworth. North of Bedworth is the watershed, from which streams drain north towards the river Anker and the Trent, while those to the south flow to the Avon and the Severn. The subtle intermixture of agriculture, mining and textile manufacturing in the coalfield was portrayed by George Eliot:

the land would begin to be blackened with coal-pits, the rattle of handlooms to be heard in hamlets and villages. Here were powerful men walking queerly with knees bent outward from squatting in the mine, going home to throw themselves down in their blackened flannel and sleep through the daylight, then rise and spend much of their high wages at the ale-house with their fellows of the Benefit club; here the pale eager faces of handloom weavers, men and women, haggard from sitting up late at night to finish the week's work, hardly begun till the Wednesday. Everywhere the cottages and the small children were dirty, for the languid mothers gave their strength to the loom; pious Dissenting women, perhaps, who took life patiently, and thought that salvation depended chiefly on predestination, and not at all on cleanliness. The gables of Dissenting chapels now made a visible sign of religion and of a meeting-place to counterbalance the ale-house, even in the hamlets. … The breath of the manufacturing town, which made a cloudy day and a red gloom by night on the horizon, diffused itself over all the surrounding country, filling the air with eager unrest. Here was a population not convinced that old England was as good as possible.

Coal mines in Warwickshire were some of the first to be drained by steam engines. In 1700 Sir Richard Newdigate, oppressed by debts and ambitious to build a new country house, invested in coal mines at Griff, six miles north of Coventry, that were drained by waterwheels, a windmill and horse gins. After his death the mines were leased by Richard Parrott and George Sparrow, who installed a steam engine in 1714 and another in 1729–30.

The coalfield's lifelines were the road from Coventry through Bedworth to Leicester, turnpiked in 1754, and the Coventry Canal, opened from Bedworth to Coventry in 1769 and from Atherstone in 1771. With the Oxford Canal, it was part of a network that linked the Midlands with London and the South. Its junction with the Oxford Canal was established at Longford (Hawkesbury Junction) in 1777, the year before the Oxford was opened to Banbury. The line north to Fradley Junction on the Trent & Mersey was completed in 1790, the same year that the Oxford Canal was extended from Banbury to the Thames. The Coventry Canal was also joined by the private Newdigate and Griff canals, built respectively in 1773 and 1787 by Sir Roger Newdigate of Arbury Hall to enable boats to reach his collieries. Other mines were linked to the waterway by tramroads. The canals enabled Warwickshire mine owners to develop markets in Oxfordshire, Berkshire and Northamptonshire.

In 1861 there were boats moored in the coalfield from Berkshire, Oxfordshire, Northamptonshire and towns alongside the Grand Junction Canal in Hertfordshire. New pits continued to be opened through the nineteenth century, among them the Charity Colliery sunk in 1831 by the Bedworth Coal & Iron Company, which hoped to exploit the iron ore in the coal measures, and built an unsuccessful blast furnace where its tramway approached the Coventry Canal. Nevertheless, there were 139 ironstone miners in Bedworth in 1861 extracting ore for smelting in the Black Country, where it was delivered by boats like those from Oldbury and Netherton moored at Exhall. Coventry was fringed by coal-consuming brickyards and lime kilns. The narrow boat *Providence* of Uxbridge – at Chilvers Coton on census night in 1861 – appears to have been collecting bricks for the London area. The principal ceramics works were near Tamworth, where by 1851 about 350 people made blue bricks, chimney pots, quarries (i.e. floor tiles), and drainage pipes. Children as young as eight years old loaded and unloaded kilns. A company was established at Glascote in 1847 by Charles Canning and John Gibbs to manufacture glazed sewer pipes and, as Gibbs & Canning, began in 1867 to make architectural terracotta, providing materials for the Royal Albert Hall, Manchester Town Hall and the Victoria & Albert Museum.

In the scattered settlements extending from Hawkesbury Junction through Exhall, Bedworth and Nuneaton to Tamworth, coal miners lived alongside silk workers, domestic weavers of tapes and ribbons, foundrymen and boilermakers, and at Atherstone with makers of hats. Bedworth, with a population of 5,656 in 1861, came to be regarded as the centre of the Warwickshire coalfield, but in the 1860s the 500 miners in the town comprised less than 10 per cent of the population, compared with about a third who made textiles. By contrast the 184 coal miners among the 872 inhabitants of Baddesley Ensor comprised 21 per cent of a population that included scarcely any textile workers. The northerly extremity of the coalfield, the ancient borough of Tamworth, flourishing as a market town but in decline as a textile-manufacturing centre, was the home of 180 miners. A colliery at Exhall was managed by a Tynesider who had worked at Seaton Delaval, Wigan and in North Wales. Most coalmasters, however, were natives of the Black Country, among them Samuel Spruce from Wolverhampton, Thomas Caldecott from Oldbury, William Nowell from Wednesbury, and William Perrens from Kingswinford, all of whom employed more than a hundred miners.

The Black Country

The Black Country coalfield extends in an arc from 10 to 16 miles in length, north and west of Birmingham. Most of it lay in Staffordshire, but Stourbridge and Dudley were in Worcestershire, while Halesowen was a detached portion of Shropshire until 1844. The Black Country coalfield is divided by the north–south ridge that includes Castle Hill at Dudley and Sedgley Beacon. The river Stour to the west and the river Tame to the east provided water power, which was scarce in the central part of the region. Coal from the 10 yard (9 m) 'thick' seam was used by nailmakers, locksmiths, lorimers and scythe makers, but in 1700 it could be employed neither for smelting iron ore nor for refining pig iron into wrought iron (see below, Chapter 7). The forges and the three blast furnaces of the region used charcoal and were situated on streams to the east and west. Coal was not carried in large quantities to customers at a distance, although the potential of Black Country mines was recognised as early as the 1660s by those who planned to make the river Stour navigable

THE DUDLEY PORT IRON WORKS, THE PROPERTY OF MESSRS. PLANT AND FISHER.

Ironworks were some of the principal customers for the coal raised from the mines of the Black Country. The Dudley Port Ironworks of Plant & Fisher was one of the smaller forges in the region, producing wrought iron from 20 puddling furnaces and three rolling mills. The image shows the importance of the canal network to industry in the area, with boats with cabins which were probably taking iron to distant customers, day-boats without cabins which probably bought in raw materials, and an early canal steamboat.

to the river Severn. Coal production expanded from the mid-eighteenth century, and Raybould estimated that the output of coal in the region in 1800 was about 840,000 tons, increasing to 3.1 million tons, or 13.2 per cent of national output, by the late 1820s and to about 5 million by 1850.

The use of mineral fuel in blast furnaces and forges, and the application of steam engines to drive bellows, slitting mills, rolling mills and hammers, allowed iron making to grow in the Black Country, which

abounded in the key raw materials. In the late 1750s John Wilkinson built a coke-fuelled blast furnace at Bradley which became the nucleus of a large and influential ironworks. Others followed his example. The growth of iron making increased demand for coal, although not all seams were suitable for furnaces and forges, and relatively cheap fuel could be supplied to other industries and to distant customers.

The region's remarkable canal system originated in 1769 when the Birmingham Canal linked collieries at

Wednesbury with central Birmingham, and the navigation was extended until by 1860 it comprised 159 route miles, with no fewer than 550 private basins, far more than in any other emerging conurbation. Its main line across Smethwick summit was improved in several stages, until in the 1820s Thomas Telford excavated a deep cutting accommodating a 40 foot (12.3 m) wide waterway. Subsequent developments included the opening in 1844 of the Tame Valley Canal, so that long-distance boats could avoid the congested locks at Farmer's Bridge, and the completion in 1858 of the Netherton Tunnel – with twin towpaths and gas lighting – providing an alternative route to the older Dudley Tunnel through the central ridge. The canals served as the circulatory system of the coalfield. Almost all mines, ironworks and other industrial installations established between 1790 and 1850 were linked to the canals, and from the 1850s 26 basins were built where coal delivered by narrow boats from canal-connected pits was loaded onto railway waggons for despatch to distant destinations. Many of the region's boatmen and boatwomen carried bulk materials in day-boats.

Wolverhampton, Dudley, Stourbridge and Walsall were all ancient towns. Even in the seventeenth century they had markets and concentrations of retailers and professional men, and by 1700 were home to ironmongers who distributed raw materials

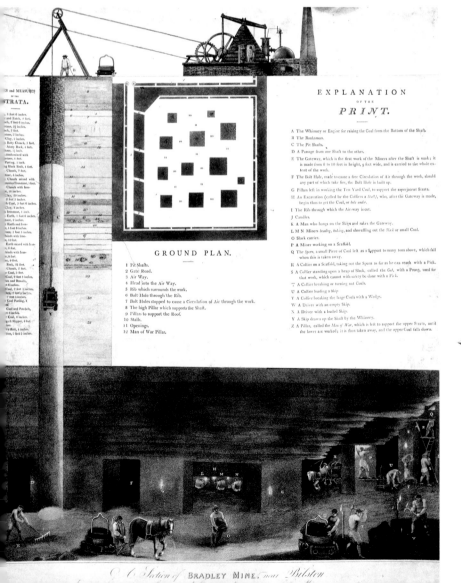

A section of a mine at Bradley near Bilston, including images of the surface installation and the coalface, engraved by F. Eglinton after an original by D. Morris, and published in 1808. It provides evidence that steam winding had become almost universal by that time in coal mines of significant size, and shows something of the unique methods of mining used to extract the ten-year seam of coal in the Black Country.

for the manufacture of hardware and collected finished products. At that time much of the Black Country was still open heathland, its fringes settled by metalworkers who lived in squatter-like holdings in communities such as that conserved at Mushroom Green. The enclosure of common lands established land-holding rights, making possible the construction of large industrial complexes, but the pattern of settlement remained notably haphazard. Angus Bethune Reach observed in 1849 that:

> The coal population … live, sometimes in poor detached cottages, sometimes in detached rows or clusters of houses, sprinkled here and there amidst the rubbish waste, or along the roads – sometimes in overgrown villages, of each portion or *quartier* of which a smelting or forging work forms the nucleus.

The cleanliness, the furnishings and the demeanour of the population, particularly of women, were unfavourably contrasted by commentators with those of Northumberland and Durham. Most local entrepreneurs left the provision of housing to market forces, and cottages were built, or old ones rebuilt, almost randomly on common land. In individual fields a few landowners laid out small grids of closely packed streets that were lined with two-storey brick terraces, but that process, too, was piecemeal and uncoordinated. Many people walked several miles between their homes and their workplaces.

Some coal and iron concerns in the Black Country were large, and comparable with the Lilleshall or Butterley companies, but one of the characteristics of the region, a source of both strength and weakness, was the prevalence of small firms. Gilbert Gilpin observed, during the crisis in the iron industry that followed the Napoleonic Wars, that because landed property in south Staffordshire was much divided, proprietors turned their resources to immediate account, banding together with clerks and tradesmen who could raise a few hundred pounds to provide capital for building furnaces or forges. Because their resources were limited, and they depended entirely on their investment, they continued production by lowering prices when orders were scarce.

➤ Cobb's Engine House, two miles south of the centre of Dudley, housed a Newcomen-type engine built as late as 1831, which pumped water up the 525 ft (162 m) shaft of the Windmill End Colliery. The engine worked until 1928 and two years later was moved to the Henry Ford Museum at Dearborn, Michigan. It is one of the outstanding monuments of the Black Country coal industry.

➤ Industries in Birmingham and the Black Country were served by the Birmingham Canal Navigation which was continually improved and extended from the time it opened until the late 1850s. In 1860 it comprised some 159 route miles. Maintenance of much of the system was managed from these Gothic-style workshops at Icknield Port.

Black Country colliers consistently complained, particularly during the Chartist-inspired troubles of 1842, about sub-contracting in the mines, the 'butty' system (see above, page 210). The worst features may have been mitigated in the years that followed, but sub-contracting was entrenched in the social structure, and was also used in other industries. In 1861 a bundler of hoop iron who lived near the Bromford Ironworks employed two men, and must certainly have been a sub-contractor, as were the 'Butty Stone Getters' at quarries at Lower Gornal, a pattern maker with four employees, and a ball furnacemen with two – his work involved heating wrought-iron scrap balls prior to re-rolling, and could have had no independent existence outside a large forge.

Nineteenth-century travellers found Oldbury one of the least appealing places in England. The parish lies on the ten-yard seam at the centre of the Black Country and had about 16,000 inhabitants in the 1860s. The original line of the Birmingham Canal passes through it, and is carried on the Steward Aqueduct over Telford's new line of the 1820s. The new canal was quite soon paralleled by the Stour Valley line of the London & North Western Railway, and the Great Western Railway reached Old Hill from Stourbridge in 1866. The vitality of heavy industry was indicated by the building, as late as 1858, of a canal basin that came to be called the 'Chemical Cut'.

Many men from Oldbury – rollers, catchers and bundlers of iron, puddlers, underhand puddlers, shinglers and hammermen – worked at the Bromford Ironworks, originally water-powered, where by 1870 John Dawes & Sons had 69 puddling furnaces. Iron foundries included the Griffin Foundry of Hunt Brothers, established in 1839, which produced architectural ironwork and vessels for chemical manufacturers. At the Brades Steel Works of William Hunt & Sons, dating from the mid-eighteenth century, melters, cutters, polishers and hardeners of steel made spades, shovels, hoes and scythes. Oldbury's other, and extraordinarily varied, metal products in the 1860s included coffin furniture, gun locks, nuts, bolts, screws, rivets, railway spikes, swords and bayonets.

South of the Stour Valley Railway was a carriage and waggon company established in the late 1850s by R. W. Johnson, a contractor who also owned a waggon repair works at Bromsgrove. Johnson found Oldbury attractive because iron could be obtained from 30 rolling mills within a two-mile radius. In the 1860s the carriage-building shop was the longest in Britain, when it was constructing sleeping carriages with teak bodywork, mounted on bogies, for the East Indian Railway. It was surrounded by sawmills and shops for planing, grooving and boring wood.

Oldbury's atmosphere was badly polluted by several chemical works. On its western border was the glassworks established in 1822 by Robert Lucas Chance, which ten years later adopted the technology for making sheet glass that had been developed in France by Georges Bontemps. In 1851 the Chance works provided the immense quantity of glass that was needed to clad the Crystal Palace. Oldbury residents employed there included blowers, gatherers, flatteners, grinders, cutters and polishers of sheet, crown and ornamental glass. In 1835 the company built a plant at Oldbury to make sodium carbonate for glass making, and this expanded to produce sulphuric acid. In the 1860s the plant employed salt-cake furnacemen, black-ash workers, white-ash driers, brown-ash workers, copperas makers, ammoniac workers, vitriol makers, coopers and packers of washing soda. The chemist Arthur Albright became a partner in 1842 with John and Edmund Sturge of Selly Oak, manufacturers of potassium chlorate, and after 1844 of white phosphorus supplied to makers of matches. In 1850 production was transferred to the canalside at Oldbury, but in 1854 Albright's partnership with the Sturges was terminated and he took a new partner, John Edward Wilson. The firm, called Albright & Wilson from 1856, produced white and red phosphorus and subsequently manufactured other phosphorus-based products. Bone-burners were prominent among the employees in the 1860s.

But Oldbury's economy was yet more diverse. A cement works was opened on the 'Chemical Cut', while on the western edges of the parish were deep pits from which clay was extracted for the making of bricks, roofing tiles and drainage pipes. In 1861 the principal manufacturer was Joseph Hamblet, employer of 80 men, whose wife kept the *Old Swan* in Church Street. Miners of coal and iron ore lived all over

James Foster, who managed John Bradley & Co., was the most influential ironmaster in the West Midlands in the early and mid-nineteenth century, with furnace complexes and forges in both Shropshire and the Black Country, as well as many mines where coal and iron ore were extracted. The core of his business was the New Foundry at Stourbridge, established alongside the Stourbridge Canal from 1819.

Chain making on a domestic scale was one of the characteristic industries of the western part of the Black Country coalfield. This three-hearth chainmakers' shop stands in the Mushroom Green conservation area near Brierley Hill. The pulley above the door allowed completed chain to be passed outside the shop, leaving more working space within.

Oldbury in the 1860s, as did makers of breeze or 'gleeds', the small cokes used in smiths' hearths.

The *Boat* public house at Oldbury was a focal point for canal boatmen from Oxford, who collected coal from and delivered grain to the Black Country. About 50 boatmen were living ashore in Oldbury in 1861. Boat builders included men born at Banbury, Braunston, Lichfield and Worcester. Thomas Darby, who kept a public house and occupied 40 acres, employed six men in a road haulage business, four of them carters who lived in.

South-west of Oldbury lay Rowley Regis, a parish of nearly 4,000 acres encompassing Blackheath, Cradley Heath, Old Hill and Tividale, with a population in 1861 of almost 20,000. The hard dolerite called 'Rowley Rag', quarried around Turner's Hill, was shaped into paving slabs and transported to towns all over the canal network. A concentration of chain and anchor makers extended from Cradley northwards through Halesowen and Rowley Regis to Netherton, where Lloyds' Staffordshire Proving House for anchor chains stood on Primrose Hill.

A lithographic print by Louis Haghe after an original by R. Bridgens depicting the Galton Bridge that had been designed by Thomas Telford to carry a road across the deep cutting by which he had taken the Birmingham Canal through the Smethwick summit. The castings, spanning 150 ft, were supplied by the Horseley Company from nearby Tipton, and the bridge opened for traffic in 1829. On the canal are three horse-drawn barges, one of them Pickford No. 3, and another steered by a woman.

© SCIENCE MUSEUM/SCIENCE & SOCIETY PICTURE LIBRARY

Men whom the enumerators called 'Thick Coal Miners' worked the ten-yard seam. There were blast-furnacemen and forgemen in Rowley, as in most Black Country parishes, and many were engaged in making tubes, used as gaspipes and later for bicycle frames. A tinplate works at Tividale, owned by William Williams from Neath, employed 157 people in rolling, cleaning, rubbing, shearing and sorting. There were scythe smiths, scythe platers and scythe grinders, makers of spades, shovels and pincers. Breech makers, breech-pin makers, barrel grinders and ramrod makers were involved in making guns, while most British makers of Jews' harps worked in Blackheath.

Nail making occupied many Black Country people. Most of the inhabitants of Over End, Virgins End and Mares Green, ancient nail-making hamlets in West Bromwich, still followed the trade in 1841, but there were fewer nailers in the parish 20 years later when cut wrought-iron nails and nails cast from malleable iron were being produced in factories. In Upper and Lower Gornal and parts of Sedgley some nailers still laboured in their own homes in 1861, and the infrastructure of a domestic system remained in place. Men worked as factors, reckoners, weighers, bagging weavers and nailers' tool menders, and there were warehouses in Sedgley and Lower Gornal. Several nail factors lived on Dudley Road, Upper Gornal, among them Eliza Tinsley, a 48-year-old widow, who supposedly put out work to 3,000 domestic workers.

The borough of Dudley encompassed an ancient market town and many hamlets. Its population in 1861

approached 45,000, but was beginning to decline. It had mines, blast furnaces and forges, but Dudley's distinctive products were vices, anvils, augers, safes, brass pipes and taps, iron bedsteads, fenders and fire irons. Unusually, large numbers of itinerant sellers stayed in Dudley and traded their wares in the hamlets. Lodgers at one public house included travellers in baskets and mats from Abingdon, and a London-born fish hawker. There were Irish hawkers of crockery, drapery and salt, while about 40 Scottish itinerant drapers lived in Victoria Terrace.

Stourbridge was also an ancient town, within the parish of Old Swinford. Glass making was established to the north at Wordsley before 1700, and by 1800 the banks of its newly constructed canals were lined with English glass cones. At Stourbridge table glass was manufactured on a large scale, but some companies also made sheet glass and bottles. In 1835 there were ten glass manufacturers in the area, together with seven makers of the refractory clay pots used in glass making, some of whom also made retorts for gasworks and chemical plants. The New Foundry in Bradley Road, Stourbridge, built in 1820 by John Urpeth Rastrick for his partner, the ironmaster James Foster, is an imposing 197 × 49-foot (60 × 15 m) building with wrought-iron rafters and massive cast-iron tie beams, in which cast bosses accommodated the tops of pillar cranes. Lye Waste, which originated as a settlement of squatters whose rights to remain were recognised in an Enclosure Act of the 1780s, was by the 1860s a centre for making galvanised buckets and baths.

West Bromwich in 1801 was a parish of just under 6,000 acres, with a population of 5,687. Its nucleus around the Old Church overlooked the valley of the river Tame, and most of its population lived in hamlets with the suffix 'Green' or 'End', scattered across heathlands to the west. On 13 June 1776 Arthur Young observed 'one continued village of nail makers', while a resident in 1836 recalled the old cottages, 'little better than a temporary hut, wattled with sticks and plastered in some cases with mud, covered with branches of trees, straw, turf and the like materials, most of these had but one apartment, some few with two'. There were old-established iron forges on the edges of the parish, but nail making was the predominant trade. In the 1770s three ironmongers distributed more than 1,000 tons of rods per year to be made into nails.

The blowing-in of coke-fuelled blast furnaces, the building of canals, and the expansion of coal mining stimulated growth throughout the Black Country, but two particular factors influenced the development of West Bromwich. First, the road through the parish from Birmingham to Wednesbury was turnpiked in 1727 across remnants of common fields and heathland 'where rabbits burrowed in great numbers'. Second, an area alongside the road of some 387 acres was the subject of an Enclosure Act implemented in 1804. On either side of this road, between the edge of the Earl of Dartmouth's Sandwell Park and the bifurcation of the roads to Wednesbury and Dudley at Carters Green, the commissioners laid out 40 foot (12 m) wide side roads creating plots for residential or industrial use. The main road was further improved from 1815 under the direction of Thomas Telford as part of the Holyhead Road.

West Bromwich prospered from new kinds of manufacturing, producing components and consumer goods. In 1782 John Izon moved his foundry from Birmingham to the canalside on the southern edge of the parish, and in 1791 Archibald Kenrick, a Birmingham buckle maker, established a foundry by the canal at Spon Lane. His products included coffee mills – a West Bromwich speciality – and by 1830 he employed 400 people. The making of springs and spring balances began in the early nineteenth century. John Salter, founder of a dynasty prominent in the

town's history, was employing 47 people in 1851 making spring balances, roasting jacks and pocket steel yards. Heavier springs for coaches were being manufactured by 18 firms in 1851, five of whom also made hinges for railway vehicles. James Russell of the Crown Tube Works in Wednesbury took out a patent in 1823 for making boiler tubes, and within the next 20 years tube making took root in West Bromwich. In 1844 John Spencer patented a method of making corrugated iron sheets by hot and cold rolling, and erected the Phoenix Ironworks on the Balls Hill branch canal. Many people were employed in two exceptionally large concerns,

⅄ The locomotive *Agenoria*, built in 1829 by Foster, Rastrick & Co. at the New Foundry, Stourbridge, for the Shutt End Colliery (or Pensnett) Railway at nearby Kingswinford, where it worked until 1864 when it became part of the collection of the Science Museum, London. It is now in the National Railway Museum, York. Its sister locomotive, *Stourbridge Lion*, built in 1828, was exported to the United States.

the glassworks of Chance Brothers in neighbouring Smethwick, and the gasworks at Swan Village, begun in 1825 and completed in 1829, which supplied gas to Birmingham, Bilston and Darlaston.

After the enclosure the main road, now named High Street, was soon lined with shops and prestigious dwellings, and by 1841 more than 120 properties stood on what had previously been open heathland. In 1834 the street had 'the air and bustle of a market town'. Retailers included nine grocers and ten drapers, together with chemists, bakers, butchers, shoemakers supplied by a currier, tailors, watchmakers, a wine merchant and a printer. The professions were represented by three doctors, two solicitors and a surveyor, while the Dudley & West Bromwich Bank occupied a prominent position. Shopkeepers included men from Mildenhall, Wisbech, Manchester, Cheltenham, Charwelton (Northamptonshire) and Llanymynech. Christ Church, a chapel-of-ease to the distant parish church, was built on the High Street in 1828, and by the mid-1830s there were Baptist, Independent, Wesleyan, Primitive Methodist and Roman Catholic places of worship in the vicinity. The principal social centre was the *Dartmouth Hotel*, opened on 14 January 1834. Fourteen substantial mansions were listed in West Bromwich in 1837, most of them occupied by ironmasters or manufacturers, and the parish was described in 1849 as 'a west end suburb for the retired and thriven iron and coal masters, carriers and factors

of the mining district which surrounds it'. A sizeable town had emerged in a largely new location in the space of only forty years.

However, because of its increasingly industrial character West Bromwich, like so many other manufacturing towns, soon ceased to be attractive to the wealthy. The 4th Earl of Dartmouth left Sandwell Park in 1853 to live at Patshull Hall, allowing the south-west corner of the park to be divided into plots for middle-class housing. Archibald Kenrick lived in Roebuck Lane, but his sons, though continuing the family hardware business, settled at Edgbaston, Birmingham's most select suburb. The Izon family sold the estate around 'The Lodge' in 1867, enabling the land to be used for a town hall, public baths and a hospital. Other families who had lived on High Street were tempted by rising land values to sell up and move elsewhere, while the comfort of those living in villas in the western parts of the parish was threatened by vast excavations for clay. The town gained its borough charter in 1882, became a county borough in 1888, and saw a flowering of civic culture under the leadership of the ironfounder Alderman Reuben Farley, investor in many businesses, five times mayor, Poor Law guardian, and supporter of the building society, the mechanics' institute, the YMCA, choral, temperance and horticultural societies and the football club. Farley believed that, 'It was a man's duty in his native town … to do all he could to improve the

'The Black Country' near Bilston, 1869. Engraving by G. Greatbach after H. Warren RA, showing a scene of heavy industry at night, with fire from gas outlets. Bilston, which is now part of Wolverhampton in the West Midlands, was an area dominated by coal mining and iron manufacturing. Published by W. Mackenzie, Glasgow.

condition of the people … to make the lives of the people brighter and happier.'

Many who made money in West Bromwich were less inclined to live there. Nevertheless the transformation of the parish was dramatic. The population multiplied almost ninefold in 70 years, growing to 47,918 in 1871 and to 59,538 in 1901, at a time when many Black Country communities were declining. A writer in 1895 called West Bromwich 'the Chicago of the Midlands', remarking that 'few English towns have risen so rapidly into the front rank of municipal life'; its rise, however, was typical neither of Black Country towns, nor of coalfield towns generally. The transition from obscurity to fully fledged independent borough, with a complete range of amenities and demonstrable civic pride, was shared by few coalfield communities anywhere in Britain.

The estates of the Ward family, earls of Dudley, provide the principal example of seigniorial enterprise in the Black Country. Five Enclosure Acts passed between 1776 and 1799 enabled the earls to develop mining and iron making on their estates around Stourbridge, Dudley and Kingswinford. The family promoted the Dudley and Stourbridge canals and by 1800 had leased several canal-side plots for the building of blast furnaces. Their Round Oak Works, opened in 1855, became highly profitable, especially because all the materials for iron making could be obtained from the earl's mines and quarries nearby. The Black Country's most significant early railway, the Pensnett Railway, ran across the estate linking Ashwood Basin on the Staffordshire & Worcestershire Canal with industrial concerns around Brierley Hill. Opened in 1829, with edge rails laid to 4 ft 8½ in. gauge, it included several self-acting inclined planes. Horses were the motive power on level sections, but the locomotive *Agenoria*, built at the New Foundry, Stourbridge, and now displayed at York, was employed on one two-mile stretch.

Elsewhere on the Black Country coalfield, Wolverhampton was a wealthy town whose economy was dominated by the manufacture of hardware; Walsall specialised in metalwork for saddlers; and Willenhall was a lock-making parish where the Children's Employment Commission in 1841 found 'two vast masses of stagnant filth and putrescence sufficient to breed a plague throughout the whole of England'. It is difficult to envisage the impact on those who lived in the area of the perpetual smoke or the disordered landscape. The parliamentary commissioner Thomas Tancred observed in 1843, as he travelled from Birmingham to Wolverhampton, that

The houses, for the most part, are not arranged
in continuous streets, but are interspersed with
canals, crossing each other at different levels;
and the small remaining patches of the surface
soil occupied with irregular fields of grass or
corn, intermingled with heaps of the refuse of
mines or of slag from the blast furnaces. …
The whole country might be compared to a
vast rabbit warren.

In 1829 J. W. M. Turner portrayed the fire, smoke and chaos around Dudley Castle, and the young James Nasmyth reflected gloomily the following year, as he surveyed the view from the castle, how

The venerable trees struggle for existence under
the destroying influence of sulphuric acid;
while the grass is withered and the vegetation
everywhere blighted. I sat … and looked down
upon the extensive district, with its roaring and
blazing furnaces, the smoke of which blackened
the country as far as the eye could reach; and
as I watched the decaying trees I thought
of the price we had to pay for our vaunted
supremacy in the manufacture of iron.

Coal and pottery in the north Staffordshire coalfield

The mines in the Vale of Trent produced only a small proportion of the coal extracted in Britain. Output figures for north Staffordshire were commonly conflated with those for the Black Country, but statistics for 1826–28 suggest that 456,500 tons, or 1.94 per cent of national output, came from the area. In

The polite outward face of a characteristic north Staffordshire potbank, with a waggon arch, a Venetian window above it, together with a pediment, containing a plaque, and a cupola with a bell that could summon workers to their shifts. This was probably the Hill Works, built by John and Richard Riley in 1814. Behind the formal fronts were yards with untidy mixtures of kilns, ovens and workshops.

1856 some 1.3 million tons were mined, a figure that increased by 1864 to more than 3 million, or 3.2 per cent of national output. Coal was used in salt-works at Weston-on-Trent, Shirleywich and Ingestre to the south, and at Church Lawton and Wheelock to the north, and until the mid-eighteenth century Staffordshire mines supplied coal for boiling salt in the Cheshire 'wiches'. Several ironworks also flourished in the nineteenth century. Nevertheless, it was the pottery industry that dominated this coalfield throughout the period from 1700 to 1870.

In 1750 Pococke observed that on Madeley Hill on the watershed between the Weaver and the Trent west of Newcastle-under-Lyme he came across 'that clay for which this country is so famous and is us'd in making the common earthenware, bricks, tyles and pipes for conveying water', commenting that 'they bake 'em in kilns built in shape of a cone, which make a very pretty appearance there being great numbers of them in all the country beyond Newcastle'. He noted that some potters used white ball clay from Poole, and flints from Lincolnshire, that they produced fine white and red pottery as well as utilitarian products, and that itinerant hawkers purchased wastelings or seconds. Whatley observed in 1750 that Burslem was 'noted for the manufacture of pots to hold butter'. The exuberantly decorated slipware chargers made by Thomas Toft of Burslem are evidence that before 1700 potters sought to sell their ware to the fashionable classes. Demand for cups and pots for drinking tea and coffee increased after 1700. One of the justifications for building the Trent & Mersey Canal was that potters in Burslem and surrounding places made 'various kinds of stone and Earthenwares which are carried out at great expense to all parts of the kingdom and exported to our islands and colonies in America and to almost every part of Europe'. By the middle of the eighteenth century, therefore, 'The Potteries' was an industrial area of fast-growing importance, and with a highly distinctive and recognisable identity.

As in any other developing industrial area communications were a key element in economic change. Those through the Vale of Trent were improved by, among other changes, the turnpiking of the road from Derby through Uttoxeter and Stoke to Newcastle-under-Lyme in 1759, and the opening of the Trent & Mersey Canal in 1777. Tramroads were soon carrying coal to the canal. In 1792 Lord Torrington was impressed by the horses and asses he saw in the streets of Stoke, by the intersecting canals, and by men whitened with powdered china clay. By 1870 new settlements had grown up away from the old village centres at, for example, Etruria, and Longport and Middleport along the Trent & Mersey Canal.

The populations of Burslem, Fenton, Hanley, Longton, Stoke and Tunstall grew rapidly, and marginal land, open heaths and commons, roadside verges and village greens came to be covered with

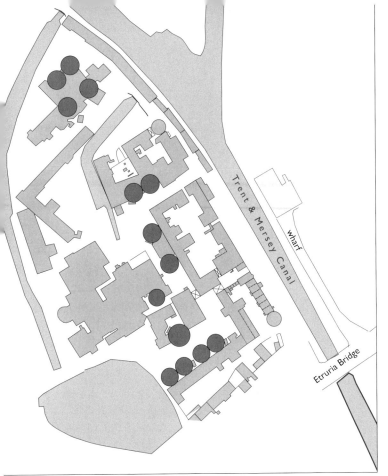

A plan adapted from the Ordnance Survey map of 1877 showing Josiah Wedgwood's Etruria Works as they appeared after more than a century of growth and adaption, with at least 14 bottle ovens and numerous workshops behind the formal façade that faces the Trent & Mersey Canal. The road crossing Etruria Bridge – the turnpike from Leek to Newcastle-under-Lyme – was a significant factor in the location of the works.

The façade of the Etruria factory, built for Josiah Wedgwood to the design of Joseph Pickford and opened on 13 June 1769. The waterway in the foreground is the Trent & Mersey Canal, of which Wedgwood was a prominent promoter. Its surface was originally level with the ground floor of the factory. The polite frontage, as in other north Staffordshire potbanks, hid an untidy array of kilns and workshops around the yard behind (as shown on the map, left). The cupola with its bell resembles those that were used to embellish some contemporary cotton mills. Nearby, on the opposite bank of the canal stood Shelton Bar, one of north Staffordshire's principal ironworks.

cottages, while farmyards were filled with kilns and workshops. A map of Burslem of about 1740 shows 28 pot banks and numerous heaps of discarded 'wasters' (that is, unusable wares). Fifteen years later Angerstein observed 30 potteries in Burslem producing white, black, red and tortoiseshell wares, and remarked that makers of lead-glaze pottery used coal-measure clays while producers of whitewares employed ball clay from the Isle of Purbeck combined with ground flints. Some master potters brought together their employees and separated the different stages of the manufacturing process. Ivy House, Burslem, built by Thomas and John Wedgwood in 1750, was the first pottery 'factory', and was used between 1759 and 1762 by Josiah Wedgwood before he moved to the Bell Works (which was named after the bell that summoned its employees). In 1769 Wedgwood built the Etruria Works on the banks of the Trent & Mersey Canal where it was crossed by the turnpike road from Leek to Newcastle-under-Lyme. The factory was capped by a cupola containing a bell, just like an Arkwright-style cotton mill, and he assigned workers to clearly defined specialist tasks. He did not mechanise the manufacturing of pottery, but placed the process in

purpose-built works which were separate from his home (which was a mansion, overlooking the site, designed by Joseph Pickford). The specialisation of labour and the geographical separation of place of production from place of residence were among the key ingredients of new industrial structures, and at Stoke these were demonstrated at an early date. Steam power was introduced to the pottery industry in 1772 when John Turner of Lane End used a Newcomen engine to pump water back over a waterwheel which powered throwing engines and lathes. His example was followed in 1782 by the Spode factory, and in 1784 Josiah Wedgwood installed a Boulton & Watt engine at Etruria to drive clay and flint mills and colour-grinding pans.

Manufacturers developed new ranges of products, such as Wedgwood's black basalt and Jasper wares. Ironstone china, a form of stoneware, was first made in 1800 by William Turner of the Lane End Pottery and subsequently by Josiah Spode, Charles James Mason of Lane Delf, and George and Job Ridgway of Shelton. The manufacture of porcelain was introduced at the New Hall Pottery, Shelton, in 1782, after the company purchased the patent rights

A lithograph by T. Brooks showing the buildings of Enoch Wood & Sons, makers of earthenware pottery, at Burslem, north Staffordshire. After working for Josiah Wedgwood, Wood set up his own business in 1783, when he was 24, in partnership with his cousin Ralph Wood. The numerous chimneys and bottle ovens are evidence of the enormous quantities of coal consumed by the potbanks of north Staffordshire.

granted to William Cookworthy. The production of bone china was introduced at Etruria by Josiah Wedgwood II. The new wares were publicised by orders from royalty, particularly by the Green Frog Service which Catherine the Great commissioned from Josiah Wedgwood, and which is now displayed in the Hermitage in St Petersburg.

By 1800 the characteristic Staffordshire potworks had a polite outward face, an ordered range of two- or three-storey buildings along a street, with three bays standing proud of the rest, topped by a pediment, and pierced by a waggon arch, usually with a Venetian window above it. Behind the formal frontage was a yard surrounded by bottle ovens which, because their working life was no more than 30 years, were constantly being rebuilt, and also by potters' and saggar makers' workshops, warehouses, packing rooms, crate makers' shops, and usually a steam-engine house. William Adams's Greengates Pottery in Tunstall, built in the 1780s, was one of the first to follow this pattern. The surviving entrance block of Enoch Wood's Fountain Works at Burslem is pedimented and has a Venetian window, but other parts, now demolished, were extravagantly Gothick. The Portland Works at Sutherland Road, Longton (1861) follows the same pattern, as does the nearby building which houses the Gladstone Pottery Museum. Interspersed with potworks, and equally productive of smoke, were preparation works, where clay was milled by steam power, and bones and flints were calcined in kilns, as at the mill built by Jesse Shirley in 1857, now the Etruria Industrial Museum.

Even by the standards of Victorian industrial conurbations the Potteries was notoriously unhealthy, in part because of exceptionally heavy smoke pollution, and living conditions were made worse by the condition of many potworks. The Children's Employment Commission of 1841, which examined 127 potteries, found that 25 were large, recent, well built and well ventilated; 64, employing between 50 and 100 people each, had working rooms which were low, damp, dirty and ill-ventilated; and conditions in the remaining 38 were even worse. Only after the Factory Acts Extension Act of 1864 did legislation significantly impact on working conditions. The German J. C. Kohl wrote of the approach to Burslem and Hanley in 1842:

The surrounding hills are all crowned with lofty columns and the huge pyramids of the chimneys, and with the great rounded furnaces, of which dozens are often seen close together, looking like colossal bomb mortars. The high roofs of the drying houses, the magnificent warehouses and the massy walls that enclose the whole great establishment or 'workhouse bank' with piles of clay, flints, bones, cinders and other matters, serve rather to strengthen the illusion. … Between the great workhouse banks lie scattered the small houses of the shopkeepers, the workmen, the painters, the engravers, the colourmen and others, while here and there the intervals are filled up by churches and chapels, or by the stately houses of those who have grown rich by pottery.

The impact of the industries of the Potteries was strongly felt in the rural hinterland. In 1776 the Trent & Mersey Canal Co. received authority to build the 17-mile Caldon Canal from Etruria to Froghall, which opened in 1779. It also constructed a 14-mile tramroad from Cauldon Low to Froghall, descending 649 feet (247 m) in the course of its journey. The line was altered several times and by 1802 was a double-track plateway with five self-acting inclines. It was acquired in 1847 by the North Staffordshire Railway, and by the 1860s was a line of 3 foot 6 inch (1.08 m) gauge with three inclined planes. The canal and plateway served the quarries around Cauldon Low, the source of prodigious quantities of limestone. Some limestone was burned in canal-side kilns at Consall Forge and Froghall. In the Churnet, Trent and Moddershall valleys watermills ground flints, bones, and colours for decorating pottery, while paper mills made tissue paper for transfer decoration. In the woodlands around Cheddleton and Dilhorne and on Cheadle Common craftsmen made the 'Staffordshire crates' in which ceramic wares were despatched to customers. Collieries extending in a circuit around Cheadle were worked from the 1770s, and subsequently supplied nearby copper smelters. The coalfield revived after the sinking of Parkhall Colliery in 1873, and more than 300 miners were at work there in 1881.

A complete industrial landscape: the Lancashire coalfield

Coal mining in Lancashire grew more rapidly after 1750 than in any other part of Britain. An output of about 350,000 tons in 1750, representing 6.7 per cent of national output, increased to 900,000 tons or 10.2 per cent by 1775, and to 1.4 million tons by 1800. By the late 1820s the county was extracting about 4 million tons a year, more than 13 per cent of the British total. By 1854 output (including that of mines in Cheshire) approached 10 million tons, 13 million in 1861, nearly 15 million in 1871, and over 20 million (15.7 per cent) by 1875. The number of miners in Lancashire and Cheshire exceeded 20,000 in 1841, increased to 46,300 by 1861 and to 54,500 by 1871. There were 534 pits in the county in 1880.

Over much of Lancashire and north Cheshire collieries extracted fuel that satisfied local domestic needs and fired the boilers of nearby textile mills. The radical politician and writer Samuel Bamford

A coal-mining landscape at Hindley, Lancashire, which has much in common with those in other coalfields. Both of the principal collieries here – Hindley and Strangeways Hall – appear to be served by mineral railways as well as by sidings from the routes of the main-line companies. The miners and their families were accommodated in terraces, including a group of three small squares. Subsidence had obviously created many large and small pools on the surface.

PHOTOGRAPH BY CARNEGIE, REPRODUCED BY COURTESY OF THE COUNTY ARCHIVIST, LANCASHIRE ARCHIVES

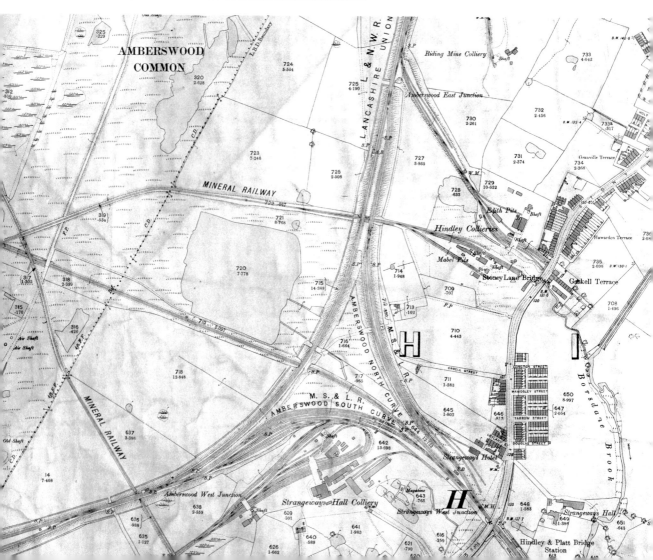

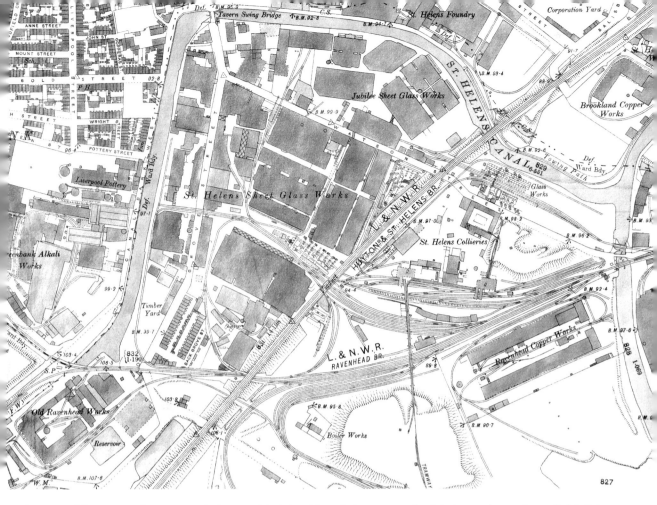

This is one of the most significant spots in the history of the industrial revolution. At Ravenhead, in the area that was later called St Helens, around the head of the Sankey Brook Navigation, John Mackay established the British Plate Glass Works from 1773 and the Ravenhead Copper Works from 1780. This late nineteenth-century map shows the continuing significance of the glass and copper industries in the area, a century after Mackay's time, as well as the importance of the mines that provided fuel for those industries, and for the alkali works that provided an essential raw material for glass making, the potteries and the St Helens Foundry, whose products included the Rory O'More Bridge of 1863 in Dublin. The map also shows how the London & North Western Railway had built sidings, many of them with tight curves, to gain access to works in the area.

recalled Christmas celebrations at Middleton north of Manchester about 1810, when the weaver might offer the collier spiced currant loaf and ale, with the greeting, 'Thou deserves whatever thou canst get. I live and work here in cheerful day and sunlight; thou spendest thy life in constant danger, and in little dark cells underground. Come, don't need inviting. Thou art heartily welcome, and canst never be too greatly paid for thy labours.' In the early 1860s miners lived all over Middleton, many of them working in pits owned by James Haigh, who lived in no particular

luxury at Radcliffe Cottage on the road to Rochdale. Similarly there were coal miners in Accrington, Bacup, Horwich, Nelson and Rawtenstall, areas dominated by cotton manufacturing. Most coal workings were on a modest scale, and a typical owner was Adam Mason of Horwich, who employed 24 men and 8 boys in 1861. In some parts of Manchester – at Newton Heath for example – colliers lived alongside cotton spinners, ironfounders and people following many other trades. However, the coal industry of the south-western part of the county was of a different character and sustained furnace-based industries that were essential – if unlovely – parts of the British economy. In 1700 there were coal mines among the peat mosses that in 1868 were to become the borough of St Helens. The Sankey Brook Navigation, authorised in 1757, opened two years later, and extended to Fiddler's Ferry in 1762, was the first stimulus to growth. It was promoted by salt traders and, with the river Weaver which was made navigable in 1732, enabled coal from St Helens to be taken to salt refiners in Cheshire. Huge quantities of Lancashire coal made the short waterborne journey across the Mersey estuary and up the Weaver to Northwich. The balancing flow was of white salt: the quantity shipped down the Weaver increased from 20,000 tons in 1760 to 40,000 in 1780 and exceeded 100,000 tons by 1800. In the 1830s every colliery proprietor in the St Helens area also owned saltworks in Cheshire.

John Mackay, a Scot involved in the salt trade from the 1760s, developed interests in mining in St Helens and brought two coal-hungry industries to Ravenhead at the terminus of the canal. The Ravenhead Copper Works of 1780 ensured that the area was in the mainstream of a fast-developing industry. Much more significant in the long term, though, was glass making. There were glasshouses in the St Helens area before 1700, using coal and local sand, but the British Plate Glass Co., incorporated in 1773, brought to Britain the process of casting glass for mirrors and windows which had been first used at St Gobain. The great Ravenhead casting hall, a cathedral-like building 339 × 50 feet (104 × 46 m), cost £60,000 and was the largest industrial structure in Britain at the time. From the late 1780s the grinding machinery was worked by a Boulton & Watt engine, the drive for which was apparently designed by James Watt himself. The first glass was cast in 1776, but the works did not prosper until the enterprise was transformed from 1792 by a new manager, Robert Sherbourne, who used up waste glass or cullet, employed covered melting pots which saved heat, and introduced emery to the grinding processes. On Sherbourne's appointment, George Mackay, brother of John, left the company to join a crown glass company at nearby Eccleston. The manufacture of flint glass began in 1822 when John William

Bell established a works in a disused foundry, and in 1826 the St Helens Crown Glass Co. began production in a glass cone modelled on those at Dumbarton, with William Pilkington as a partner. From 1841 Pilkington adopted the method of making cylinder glass brought to Britain by Robert Lucas Chance, for which he recruited Belgian workers. New grinding machines from Nasmyth's foundry at Patricroft were developed by Henry Deacon, but he left in 1851 to work at Widnes. From 1849 the company was called Pilkington Brothers. The Union Plate Glassworks and the Manchester & Liverpool Plate Glass Company at Sutton Oak both began production in the 1830s. The window glass companies profited from growing demand after the repeal of the Window Tax in 1851: weekly output at Pilkingtons rose from 80 tons a week in 1851 to 150 tons only three years later. Glass making on Tyneside declined and by the 1860s 75 per cent of British window glass was made by three companies, Pilkingtons, Chance of Smethwick, and Hartley of Sunderland. Glass making employed 3,764 people in St Helens in 1881.

The British Plate Glass Company initially used alkali pearl ash from the United States, although one investor, Thomas Dundas, encouraged the use of Lord Dundonald's alkali process. From the 1820s, though, plants using the Leblanc process grew up in St Helens, where Irish migrants tolerated the foul working conditions involved. James Muspratt set up an alkali works in his native Dublin on receiving an inheritance in 1818, moved to Liverpool in 1822, and in 1828, in partnership with Josias Gamble, an Irishman who studied at Glasgow University, built an alkali works at Gerard's Bridge on the Sankey Canal.

A similar works at Sutton was built in 1839 by Andrew Kurtz, who had fled from his native Würtemburg to Paris and then United States before settling in Britain. The business passed to his son Andrew George Kurtz, a patron of the arts in Liverpool. Joseph Crosfield, a Quaker who set up a soapworks at Warrington in 1814, was making candles on a large scale by 1830. In 1836, with his brother James and others, he bought a disused alkali works at St Helens, leasing the land on which the Gamble & Muspratt works had stood. St Helens was at the centre of the agitation that led in 1863 to the Alkali Works Regulation Act, but after 1870 the principal developments in alkali manufacturing took place at Widnes.

There were potteries in St Helens throughout the eighteenth and nineteenth centuries, most of them making mugs and stoneware bottles, but in 1846 Henry Doulton, son of the Lambeth potter John Doulton, began producing glazed pipes and other sanitary appliances, which were in increasing demand as sanitation in cities was improved. About 1850 Doulton acquired the Greenbank Pottery, St Helens, and the firm employed most of the 600 people engaged in ceramics manufactures in the borough in 1881.

Collieries in St Helens supplied more distant markets from the 1830s. The St Helens & Runcorn Gap Railway, opened in 1833, ran to a dock at Widnes on the river Mersey. It provided competition for the Sankey Navigation, but the two amalgamated in 1845 and enjoyed a monopoly until the joint company was absorbed by the London & North Western Railway in 1864. In 1830 almost all the coal leaving St Helens went to the Cheshire wiches, but in 1846, of 693,000 tons carried by railway or canal, 183,000 tons were shipped to Cheshire salt refineries, and 440,000 tons went down the river for coastwise transit, export or to fire the boilers of steamships. By 1881 coal mining in St Helens employed 3,000 people.

Liverpool profoundly influenced manufactures on the south Lancashire coalfield. Its ocean-going ships carried Lancashire products to Africa and the Americas, and brought to the Mersey tobacco, sugar and palm oil as well as raw cotton and, from the 1830s, copper ore, all of which were raw materials that required some form of processing. Coasting ships arrived with clay, flints and ore, and took away coal, copper products, wire, salt, glass, pottery and soap. Liverpool was a magnet for the coal trade. Its first turnpike, of 1725, covering the eight-mile road to the market town of Prescot on the edge of the coalfield, was specifically intended to benefit the coal traffic, and it was said in 1760 that 'colliers' carts and horses … fill the roads all the way to Liverpool'. Lamps at toll-gates even enabled coal waggons to pass through in the hours of darkness. Coalmasters also gained access to the port by inland navigations. Thomas Patten I, a

Images published in 1886 illustrating the manufacture of soap at the works of Joseph Crosfield & Co. at Warrington. The importance of water transport in the economy of the Lancashire coalfield is illustrated in the central picture.

Warrington merchant dealing in tobacco, sugar, tea and slaves, made the tidal upper Mersey estuary navigable from Runcorn to Bank Quay, and between 1721 and the late 1730s the construction of the Mersey & Irwell Navigation enabled boats to reach Manchester. The river Douglas, from Wigan to the sea, was made navigable in 1742, but it was sold in 1771 to the Leeds & Liverpool Canal, which used it to gain access to Wigan, and completed its line from Liverpool to the junction with the Douglas at Newburgh in 1774. The Duke of Bridgewater's Canal reached the Mersey at Runcorn in 1776. Liverpool was the best-connected port in England in the 1790s, uniquely able to benefit

⚲ A late nineteenth-century map illustrating the extraordinary concentration of alkali and other chemical works at Widnes on the north bank of the river Mersey, which flows across the south-east corner of this map. The other principal waterway is the extension of the Sankey Canal to the riverside at Spike Island, opened in 1833. The St Helens & Runcorn Gap Railway, a 'hybrid' line, also opened in that year, and within several decades the area was crossed by a maze of lines and sidings.

PHOTOGRAPH BY CARNEGIE, REPRODUCED BY COURTESY OF THE COUNTY ARCHIVIST, LANCASHIRE ARCHIVES

from its overseas and coasting trade as well as its proximity to coal reserves. By the late 1790s about 350,000 tons of coal a year were delivered to Liverpool, more than half the output of the south Lancashire pits, and nearly six times as much as the Bridgewater Canal took to Manchester.

In the late eighteenth century Liverpool was not just a busy port town; for a time it was the primary manufacturing centre of the Lancashire coalfield. Coal-using industries flourished there. In 1755 Angerstein noted four saltpans, ten potteries making earthenware for America, and four glasshouses, as well as five sugar refineries and ten tobacco works. The boiling of rock salt began in 1696 and continued until the late eighteenth century. By 1790 there were eight

sugar refineries, three glassworks, four iron foundries, a sulphuric acid plant and four cotton mills, while the 39 furnaces of the Liverpool Copper Works consumed annually up to 12,000 tons of coal. In 1700 several local potteries produced delftware, and the manufacture of soft-paste porcelain was introduced in 1756 by Richard Chaffers. The Herculaneum Pottery at Toxteth was founded in 1796 by Samuel Worthington and operated until 1841, making creamware and porcelain, much of which was exported. Manufacturing industry flourished in Liverpool in the 1790s, using coal delivered by water from its hinterland to fire furnaces, kilns and boilers and to provide heat for refiners and brewers. Nevertheless even before 1800 the city's economy was changing. The copper works closed in

1794 and the salt pans in 1798, while pottery manufacture declined. More coal was exported, and more was consumed in furnace-based industries nearer the collieries. Nineteenth-century Liverpool was essentially an entrepôt, and it was not until much later in the twentieth century that new manufacturing industries were to be attracted to the area.

Coal-based manufactures also prospered in Warrington, a thoroughfare town where the key north–south route in north-west England crossed the Mersey at the head of tidal water. Angerstein saw Thomas Patten's copper works, ten workshops making pins using brass wire from Bristol, as well as sugar refineries. Travellers noted the manufacture of sailcloth, huckaback and other forms of coarse linen.

Long before the eighteenth century Wigan had been a manufacturing centre, notable from the sixteenth century for its bell founding, metal working and pewter making as well as for its very early coal mines at Haigh and elsewhere. By the turn of the eighteenth century Wigan was celebrated for its cannel coal, and for the 1,000-yard long Great Haigh Sough that was constructed in the 1660s by Sir Roger Bradshaigh to drain local mines. Angerstein visited iron forges and nailers' shops in the vicinity. The Haigh Ironworks was established in 1789 and in 1870 Wigan was the principal iron-working centre in Lancashire, while the gigantic Trencherfield and Swan Meadow mills are evidence that cotton spinning also flourished in the town. Wigan's growth was chiefly due to its role as the commercial centre of that section of the coalfield, where according to one calculation 1,020 shafts were sunk to extract coal from 25 workable seams. The Wigan School of Mining was founded in 1857. The town's population increased from 10,989 in 1801 to 37,658 in 1861 and 48,192 in 1881. By 1870 most of its mines were controlled by the Wigan Coal & Iron Co., one of the largest companies in Britain, which was formed from 1 July 1865 by an amalgamation of the collieries of the Earl of Crawford and the Pearson & Knowles Coal & Iron Co.

Widnes, which in the mid-eighteenth century was a sparsely populated riverside hamlet in the parish of Prescot, was transformed from the 1840s into one of the principal centres of chemical manufacture in Britain. It stands across the river Mersey from Runcorn, on the peninsula called Spike Island. In 1814 Thomas Telford planned a suspension bridge between the two shores, but they remained unconnected until the completion of the railway bridge in 1868. The population of Widnes in 1841 was just 2,209, but grew by the 1890s to almost 60,000. In 1888 it was described, notoriously, as 'the dirtiest, ugliest and most depressing town in England', and its atmospheric pollution – principally from hydrochloric acid gases – was exceptionally severe, and its lifeless watercourses frequently ran with diluted acid. The surrounding landscape was a blasted waste, enlivened by vast white mounds of the alkaline residues, known locally as 'galligoo'.

The Sankey Canal and the St Helens & Runcorn Gap Railway both opened to Spike Island in 1833. In 1847 John Hutchinson, who had studied in Paris with A. G. Kurtz, established a Leblanc plant at Widnes Dock where he employed 100 people by 1851 and 600 by 1865. He also built the West Bank Dock and let plots on Widnes Marsh and Moor to other manufacturers. Hutchinson's first manager, Henry Deacon, left in 1853 to form a partnership with William Pilkington, making alkali on a nearby site. Between 1854 and 1876 Deacon obtained 29 patents relating to alkali manufacture, and from 1855 his partner was Holbrook Gaskell, with whom he had worked at Nasmyth's foundry at Patricroft and who experimented with an ammonia sodium process to make alkali. William Gossage, a druggist from Lincolnshire, was a partner from 1830 at the British Alkali Works at Stoke Prior in Worcestershire. In 1836 he developed the 'Gossage Tower', by which hydrochloric acid gas produced in the Leblanc process could be condensed instead of being released into the air. After a nomadic career he moved to Widnes in 1850 to set up a copper smelter, but began to make alkali, and in 1852 was granted the first of several patents for making soap. In 1857 with James Hargreaves he developed a white mottled soap which became nationally branded as Gossage's Soap, and by 1870 his products accounted for half the soap exports from the United Kingdom. John McClellan, the Liverpool-born son of a Scots draper, established a factory at Widnes in the same year as

Hutchinson, producing borax and later making soda ash, saltcake and bleaching powder. His daughter married Henry Brunner, who worked for Hutchinson, as did her brother-in-law John Brunner and Ludwig Mond, who in 1873 formed Brunner Mond & Co., which transformed the British chemical industry by adopting the vastly more efficient ammonia soda or Solvay process.

The coalfields of North Wales

The North Wales coalfield extends over 160 square miles from the Dee estuary through Buckley, Wrexham, Ruabon and Chirk to Ifton and Trefonen in Shropshire. Its output figures are often conflated with those of South Wales or Lancashire. Mines in North Wales developed early, and were employing four Newcomen engines by 1733, but through the eighteenth century it consistently produced less than 2 per cent of national output. Coal was taken by road to Chester, although the Ellesmere Canal, which was authorised in 1793, was intended to cross the coalfield from Shrewsbury to the Dee. As completed, it provided only a round-about route to Chester, but fulfilled local demands for domestic fuel and agricultural lime. The railway from Chester to Shrewsbury, which began as the North Wales Mineral Railway, opened in 1848, and from 1854 was part of the Great Western Railway. The Ruabon Coal Company, formed by Sir Daniel Gooch in 1856, provided traffic for the GWR by supplying coal to distant customers. Ironworks in North Wales consumed large quantities of coal, as did lead smelters on Deeside. Otherwise the principal coal-using manufactures were the potteries around Buckley, which produced lead-glaze wares sold all over Wales. Some were already in production in 1700, several opened in the 1730s and 1740s, and by 1818 the industry employed 230 people.

The Forest of Dean

The Forest of Dean, the dissected plateau between the Severn and the Wye, with a 35-square-mile coal basin at its centre and pockets of rich haematite iron ore, is an ancient royal demesne where free miners enjoy rights to extract minerals unparalleled elsewhere in Britain. East and West Dean, the 23,000 acres that once comprised the royal demesne, had a population of 7,014 in 1831, rising to 17,801 in 1861, and 20,861 in 1871. The growing population was accommodated in encroachments on Crown land, of which 134 were recorded in 1752, 585 in 1787, and 1,462 – occupying more than 2,000 acres – in 1834. From 1838 the Crown conceded ownership of encroachments made before 1787 to the occupiers, and many cottagers subsequently purchased their holdings. The settlement pattern remained one of straggling hamlets, although Cinderford, which was laid out around an ironworks from the 1830s, had urban characteristics, while Coleford was an historic town surrounded by terraces accommodating miners and ironworkers.

On the edge of the Forest the Wye Valley was viewed in the 1780s and 1790s by wealthy travellers who hired covered boats, well stocked with provisions, which took them from Ross through Monmouth to Chepstow. Stebbing Shaw in 1788 learned that the woodland on the steep slopes was cropped every twelve years for charcoal, and observed lime kilns on the slopes below Goodrich, coal workings at Lydbrook and ironworks around Tintern Abbey.

In 1776 Arthur Young declared that 'Few countries are more truly rich than this vast waste; for it contains in the first place a fertile soil, fine timber, lime, iron and coals to burn and smelt them', but innovations were applied tardily. Mining operations were numerous but on a very small scale – there were over 100 coalpits in the 1780s but collectively they employed only between 400 and 500 men and produced 94,000 tons of coal per year, less than 200 tons each on average. The first steam pumping engine in the Forest was not installed until 1754, and tramroads were only built from the 1790s, the first by the ironmaster James Teague, who realised that 'foreigners' could bring to the Forest both capital

Hills and scattered woodland near Two Bridges in the Forest of Dean. Much of the coal extracted in the Forest of Dean came from small mines, often adits, in clearings areas such as this.

An adit, or drift mine, at Connop, typical of hundreds in the Forest of Dean, that had recently been abandoned in the 1970s.

and expertise. A West Indies merchant from Bristol, Edward Protheroe, became the leading coalmaster in Dean. By 1831 his Parkend Company managed 32 pits and employed more than 500 men. The coalfield retained many aspects of its unique history. By the 1860s most coal and iron ore was produced at mines with steam pumping engines, but adits were still being worked by free miners, and some minerals were transported by carriers and muleteers who also worked small farms. Mining was linked with such forest trades as hoop making, bark shaving and the burning of charcoal. The output of coal in Dean increased during the nineteenth century, from 145,000 tons in 1841 to 590,000 tons in 1860 and 838,000 tons in 1871, when it accounted for about 0.7 per cent of national output. Iron ore output also increased, rising from 18,872 tons in 1841 to a peak of 192,074 tons in 1860, when much of it went for smelting to South Wales.

Early railways, rather than internal colliery lines, stimulated the coalfield economy. The port of Bullo Pill on the west bank of the Severn was brought into existence by the Forest of Dean Railway, a 4 ft (1.23 m) gauge plateway through the Forest which opened in 1809 and was extended to Cinderford by 1833. There were quays and a tidal basin at Bullo Pill, which prospered by exporting coal and stone. The company was taken over in 1850 by the South Wales Railway, when the plateway was converted to broad gauge and linked to the SWR main line. The Severn & Wye Tramroad, authorised in 1809–10, ran from Lydbrook near the Wye through Norchard and Parkend to a harbour at Lydney which opened on 17 March 1813. Trade with Bristol, Barnstaple, Bridgwater and other Bristol Channel ports continued through the nineteenth century. The plateway became a broad-gauge railway in 1868 but was converted to standard gauge in 1872.

Coal mining and industry around Bristol

The coalfield around Bristol produced about 90,000 tons of coal in 1700, and 170,000 in 1775, after which output doubled within 25 years, reached 480,000 tons in 1815 and 600,000 tons, or 2.74 per cent of the national output, in the late 1820s. By 1860 the figure had reached 942,000 tons. The coalfield provided energy for the great port of Bristol, for England's archetypal spa resort, Bath, and for the smelting and fabrication of non-ferrous metals. The mines lay within a triangle of about 240 square miles with its angles at Cromhall in the north, Frome in the south-east and Nailsea in the south-west. In the eighteenth century the best-known mines were on common land at Kingswood, between Bristol and Bitton, where the remains of the shallow pits visible in 1873 have now been covered by suburban development. John Wesley regarded the Kingswood colliers as a disorderly community, 'neither fearing God nor regarding man'. Mines north of Bristol gained access to the city by two early railways, the Avon & Gloucestershire completed in 1828, and the contemporary Bristol & Gloucestershire. Mining was revived in the nineteenth century by Handel Cossham, a self-taught geologist who worked pits 2,000 feet (616 m) deep at Parkfield and Speedwell. Kingswood miners in the 1860s lived alongside people following all the occupations of a diversified manufacturing city – cotton spinners, quarrymen, papermakers, nailers and hatters.

Coal was discovered in 1763 at Radstock, Somerset, and by the mid-1790s there were 26 pits there, employing 1,500 men and boys and producing more than 75,000 tons *per annum*. Production was stimulated by the 18-mile Somersetshire Coal Canal, opened in 1805 from the Kennet & Avon Canal to basins at Timsbury and Paulton. Tramroads linked the canal to collieries in and around Radstock. The canal was profitable, and by 1820 was carrying 100,000 tons of coal *per annum*. Colliery owners developed distant markets, and boats from Abingdon, Reading and Newbury were loading coal at Timsbury in April 1861. At Paulton, where a waste tip called 'the Batch' remains a brooding presence in the landscape, 294 (15 per cent) of the 1,958 inhabitants in 1861 were

miners; there were 618 among the 3,836 inhabitants of Midsomer Norton, and 487 among the 3,260 who lived in Radstock. There were steam engines at most pits, and coal was used to fire brick- and lime kilns and coke ovens.

Travellers in 1728 and 1750 recorded that there were 15 glasshouses in Bristol, and a Swede in 1760 counted 12 English glass cones from a viewpoint on Totterdown Hill. There were 12 glasshouses in 1794, but only 4, including those at Nailsea, survived in 1833. By the 1880s all had merged into a single bottle-making company. Window glass and drinking-glasses were made in Bristol, but bottles were produced in exceptionally large quantities. In the early eighteenth century bottles were sent annually, during the cider and perry season, to towns in Worcestershire. One Severn barge in 1705 conveyed consignments of up to 24,000 bottles. Glass making at Nailsea was established in 1788 by John Robert Lucas. He built a second English glass cone in 1790, and by 1836 the factory was employing 120 people. In 1861 there were 113 coal miners in Nailsea and 94 glassmakers, including men from Portobello near Edinburgh, Dumbarton, St Helens and South Shields, and two from France. Most made window glass, although Nailsea became particularly well known for jugs, dishes and rolling pins in flecked green glass. A daughter of J. R. Lucas married William Chance, a partner at Nailsea. Their son Robert Lucas Chance brought John Hartley from Dumbarton to Nailsea. Hartley followed him to the works he founded at Smethwick, in 1827, and Hartley's sons from 1836 made window glass at Sunderland.

Bristol delftware was celebrated in the eighteenth century, but Bristol was also notable for a short time for the manufacture of porcelain. For eight years between 1770 and 1778 William Cookworthy, the first potter in England to make true porcelain (see above, pages 216–17), operated the Castle Green Porcelain Works, but it closed after he sold the patent rights to the Newhall company in Staffordshire. Nevertheless the pottery industry continued to thrive in Bristol, where by 1861 more than 150 people were involved in the manufacture of stoneware, whiteware and redware.

Coal and industry in the Valleys: the South Wales coalfields

A 15-ton lump of coal reposes beneath a shelter in the public park that was once the ornamental grounds of Bedwellty House, Tredegar, built in 1818 for the ironmaster Samuel Homfray. It was cut for the Great Exhibition, but proved too heavy to be transported to the Crystal Palace in London. This monument symbolises the dominant industry of the Valleys, the dramatic, deeply cut, steep-sided clefts through which a grand sequence of rivers – the Llwyd, Ebbw, Sirhywi, Rhymni, Taf, Cynon, Nedd, Ogwr, Llynfi, Tawe and Llwchwr – descend from the Brecon Beacons to the Bristol Channel. For most twentieth-century Englishmen this was a region rarely if ever visited, but about which popular images abounded. It was perceived to be characterised by chapel-going, clubs that allowed drinking on Sundays, rugby union football and male voice choirs. There were traditions of communal solidarity, whose hopes were enshrined in the National Health Service, and in state-of-the-art collieries such as Maerdy, part of an industry which was believed – at least by some – to belong to the people. It was portrayed by Humphrey Jennings in *Spare Time* in 1939 and *Diary for Timothy* in 1945. To a young English historian in 1962 train journeys from Newport through Bargoed and Dowlais Top to Talyllyn Junction, from Pontypool Road over the Crumlin Viaduct and through Quaker's Yard, Aberdare and Hirwaun to Neath, and from Neath Riverside through Pantyffordd and Onllwyn to Brecon, were a revelation. Here were terraces snaking up smoke-filled valleys, punctuated by chapels, cinemas, schools, and institutes that fostered self-improvement as well as billiards, with allotments stretching up the slopes towards sheep-grazed mountains. On the valley floors rugby grounds were interspersed with collieries, from which tank locomotives eased lines of loaded coal waggons warily downhill towards the coast and which returned noisily with the empties.

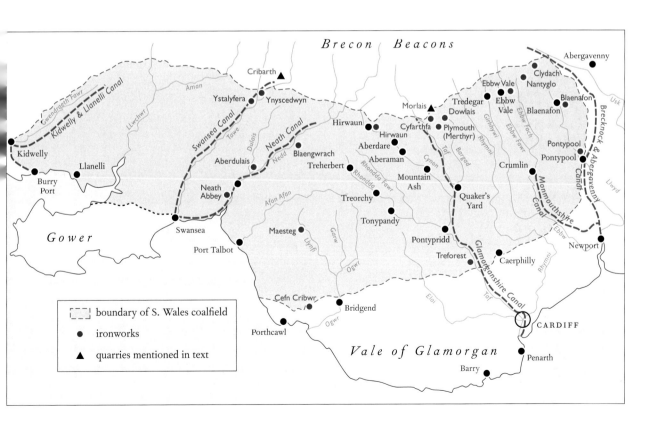

The modest scale of the coal industry in South Wales before the closing decades of the eighteenth century is illustrated by this image of a mine near Neath, wound by a horse gin and set in an almost entirely rural landscape.

An engraving by Thomas Cartwright after an original by Edward Pugh showing the stone viaduct carrying the tramway from collieries in the valleys of the Afon Ebbw and Afon Sirhowy and the ironworks at Tredegar and Sirhowy to the port of Newport. A train hauled by three horses has just come off the viaduct. Alongside the bridge was the works of the Union Copper Company.

Such is the strength of these images of the Welsh Valleys that it is easy to assume that South Wales was always one of Britain's principal sources of coal, but in 1700 the valleys were rural and outstandingly beautiful. At that time the region's collieries produced only about 80,000 tons of coal, no more than 2.6 per cent of national output. Some was shipped to Ireland and to harbours around the coast from Cardigan to Exeter, while culm and anthracite for malting were taken up the river Severn to the English Midlands. The output of coal rose by 1750 to about 140,000 tons, due largely to new demands for fuel generated by the fuel-hungry pumping engines in Cornish mines and the smelting of copper around Swansea, but the Valleys still produced less than 3 per cent of national output. The building of coke-fuelled blast furnaces from the 1750s, and of coal fired forges from the 1780s, stimulated an increase to 650,000 tons in 1775, 1.7 million tons in 1800, 2.75 million in 1815 and 4.4 million, or 14.5 per cent of national output, in 1830.

The canals in South Wales and their associated tramroads were actually built primarily to sustain iron making, by conveying raw materials and taking pig and bar iron to the docks. They were promoted by ironmasters including Richard Crawshay and Samuel Homfray. The Glamorganshire Canal was opened over the 25½ miles from Merthyr to Cardiff in 1794, the 11-mile Monmouthshire Canal from Pontnewydd to Newport in 1799, the 13-mile Neath Canal about 1795, the associated Tennant Canal in 1825, the 16-mile Swansea Canal in 1798, and the 33¼-mile Brecknock & Abergavenny Canal from Pontymoile on the Monmouthshire Canal to Brecon, in 1812. Railways on the Shropshire pattern were built near Neath in the 1690s, and a century later a profusion of iron tramroads carried materials to ironworks from sources inaccessible to water transport. The Sirhowy tramroad, a 4 ft 2 in. (1.28 m) gauge plateway, opened in 1805 and with the Nine Mile Point tramroad, opened the following year, provided a 25-mile route from Newport to Sirhowy which included a 32-arch sandstone viaduct over the flood plain of the Afon Ebbw at Risca. Tramways similarly extended the influence of the Brecknock & Abergavenny and Swansea canals.

In 1801 William Coxe commented on the customary annual whitewashing of Monmouthshire houses, which added to the neatness and cheerfulness of the landscape, thereby identifying one of the uses of limestone from quarries around the edges of the coalfield. Limestone was also used in blast furnaces, and lime was applied on farmland, both on the good agricultural land of the Vale of Glamorgan and the Usk Valley, and on moorland in process of 'improvement'. The huge quarries at Morlais north of Merthyr are evidence of the hunger of the Plymouth, Penydarren and Dowlais Ironworks for fluxing stone. Lime kilns are prominent along the Brecknock & Abergavenny Canal, at Goytre, Govilon and Talybont, and it has been estimated that as many as 54 once stood alongside the Swansea Canal. At Cribarth Mountain, above the Tawe Valley, 30 quarries gained access to the Swansea Canal by a tramroad system that included 18 inclined planes, and on Carnau Gwynion, near the headwaters of the Afon Nedd, a walled enclosure encompasses the remains of 161 lime kilns.

⚹ Stone blocks without iron rails: the remains of the Morlais Tramroad built in the early nineteenth century to deliver limestone to the blast furnaces at Merthyr Tydfil.

There were several potteries at Swansea, the first being the Cambrian Pottery founded in 1764 which made wares similar to those produced by Josiah Wedgwood. William Dillwyn, a Pennsylvania Quaker, leased the works when touring Wales as an anti-slavery campaigner, and his son Lewis Weston Dillwyn owned it from 1810. Swansea porcelain was made there between 1814 and 1817. Dillwyn's son, Lewis Llewellyn Dillwyn, managed the pottery from 1836 and took over the adjacent Glamorgan Pottery in 1838, but closed the operation in 1870. He was MP for Swansea from 1855, a partner in the Landore Spelter Works and the Landore-Siemens Steel Company, and a director of the Great Western Railway. The closure of the Glamorgan works led to the establishment in 1839 of the South Wales Pottery at Llanelli, which worked until 1875. The celebrated pottery at Nantgarw on the Afon Taf was established in 1813, when its partners included the eccentric and ever-itinerant William Billingsley. He worked at Swansea from 1814 but returned in 1817 and for three years produced wares of superlative quality, before moving to Shropshire. The works was revived from 1833 and made earthenware, stoneware bottles and tobacco pipes until 1920.

This tinted lithograph published in the 1850s by Newman & Co. of London shows bustling activity in the port of Swansea. The foundation of the prosperity of the city sometimes known as Copperopolis was the two-way trade with Cornwall, taking coal to ports such as Hayle and Portreath, and returning with cargoes of copper ore. Swansea had the densest concentration of copper-processing works in the British Isles, which continued in production using imported ores after supplies from Cornwall had diminished. Coal mined in the Swansea area was also used in ironworks and potteries, and substantial quantities were exported.

© SCIENCE MUSEUM / SCIENCE & SOCIETY PICTURE LIBRARY

The burning of limestone in kilns to produce lime for agriculture was important on the northern edge of the South Wales valleys as it was wherever coalfields adjoined agricultural regions. This group of restored limekilns stands alongside the Brecknock & Abergavenny Canal at Goytre, near Blaenavon.

In 1850 more than 100 South Wales collieries were using water balances for winding. At the top of a shaft an empty 'tram', or waggon for use underground, was shunted onto a platform beneath which was a tank filled with water, while at the foot of the shaft was an identical platform on which stood a waggon, loaded with coal, beneath which was an empty tank. When the brake was released the empty waggon would descend while the full waggon and tank were raised to the surface. At the bottom of the shaft the water was released from the tank into a drainage adit or a sump from which it was pumped to the surface. The most spectacular illustration of the principle, although not at a colliery, was installed by James Ashwell at Blaenavon Ironworks about 1841.

In the nineteenth century coal mining became the major force for economic growth in South Wales. The amount of coal shipped rose from 608,237 tons in 1819 to 1.29 million tons in 1839, while output rose by more than 90 per cent between 1830 and 1854, reaching 8.5 million tons, produced by more than 30,000 miners. Much of the growth was due to the use of the superb Welsh 'steam coal' for ships' boilers, favoured by the Admiralty because it burned with a minimum of smoke. Output rose to 11 million tons in 1864, and 16.5 million tons ten years later, and by 1913 had reached 56.8 million tons, almost 20 per cent of UK output. It was estimated in 1847 that of an annual production of 6 million tons about 30 per cent was shipped, 47 per cent was used in iron making, 11 per cent in processing copper and tin, and 12 per cent in chemical works, principally coke ovens.

A new generation of entrepreneurs developed the coal resources of the Valleys. The richest, although not strictly an entrepreneur, was the 2nd Marquis of Bute, who owned the land upon which Cardiff developed as the metropolis of the coalfield and also much coal-rich land in the Rhondda valleys. Then there was David Davies, a sawyer from Llandinam in mid-Wales, who became a railway contractor and from 1864 opened coal mines in the Rhondda. He eventually employed about 5,000 miners, and established the Ocean Coal Company in 1887, from which he was known as 'Davies yr Ocean'. David Davis, a grocer from Hirwaun, sank the Blaengwawr Colliery from 1841, the Abercwmboi pit from 1851, and Ferndale from 1862. Explosions at the latter killed 178 miners in 1867 and 53 in 1869. William Thomas Lewis, son of an engineer at Merthyr, worked for the Bute estate, but from the 1870s acquired his own pits in the Rhondda Valley and founded Lewis Merthyr Consolidated Collieries Ltd. Thomas Powell inherited a timber business at Newport, but in 1840 sank the first deep shaft in the Aberdare Valley and had 16 collieries when he died in 1863. The business was continued by the Powell Duffryn Steam Coal Co., whose moving spirit was Sir George Elliot from Co. Durham, who had managed Wearmouth Pit in the late 1830s. He assembled a consortium which bought Thomas Powell's collieries, and in 1867 purchased the mineral-rich Aberaman estate from Crawshay Bailey. The company became one of the most influential in South Wales, exporting across the world.

Richard Cory, of Bideford, Devon, owner of a coasting vessel, opened a ship-chandler's business in Cardiff in 1838 and began ship broking several years later. With his sons John and Richard II he set up Richard Cory & Sons, owners of ships, coal merchants and exporters, colliery agents and ship brokers. From the late 1860s they owned collieries in the Rhondda, Ogmore, Neath and Aberdare valleys, and became the principal coal shipping business in South Wales as well as the owners of a huge fleet of railway waggons. The firm of John Cory & Co. was formed by another ship-owner, John Cory of Padstow, who moved to Cardiff in 1872 and owned 21 steamers when he died.

Iron-making companies turned to coal as a source of profit. In 1837 Matthew Wayne of the Gadlys Ironworks formed, with his sons, the Merthyr-Aberdare Steam Coal Company. He was regarded as the first man to send coal from Aberdare to Cardiff, and his obituary recorded that 'to him more than to anybody else Aberdare owes unquestionably its present prosperity, as he it was who first found out and brought to the notice of the public the valuable properties of its steam coal'. Crawshay Bailey bought land in the Rhondda and at Mountain Ash at agricultural prices, and in 1847 also invested in the Aberaman estate, although the full value of its mineral resources was only to be exploited by Powell Duffryn after 1867. By the 1870s the Cyfarthfa, Ebbw Vale, Blaenavon, Rhymney and Tredegar companies were as well known for their coal as for their iron.

Cwm Rhondda symbolised the steam-coal boom in South Wales. The streams that flow down the Rhondda Fawr and Rhondda Fach join at Porth and flow into the Taff at Pontypridd. The valleys were sparsely populated until mining for outside markets began in 1819. In 1851, at a time when only 951 people were living in the valley, agents of the Bute estate demonstrated that deep seams of coal could be worked, and over the next three decades more than 30 collieries were sunk, which by 1884 were producing annually 5.5 million tons of coal. The population of Rhondda grew to almost 17,000 by 1871, and reached 113,000 in 1901, by which date it was the second largest urban community in Wales. But it was not a true town, rather a long sequence of linear terraces and hillside mining villages

which spread mile after mile along the valley linking nucleated semi-urban places with evocative names – Treherbert, Treorchy, Tonypandy, and Tylorstown.

While canals and tramroads facilitated the growth of iron working in the Valleys, coal mining relied upon standard-gauge railways to carry the produce of collieries to the coast for shipping. Tramroads in South Wales did not use chaldron waggons, and coal-shipping docks were characterised by hoists and tipplers rather than staithes. The Taff Vale Railway, extending 24 miles from Cardiff to Merthyr, was promoted by Sir John Josiah Guest, Crawshay Bailey, Thomas Powell and Anthony Hill. Although its engineer was Isambard Kingdom Brunel, it was built to standard gauge. The line opened, with an extension into the Rhondda Valley, in 1840–41, and the track was doubled in 1857. It was the prototype of other lines that ran down the Valleys to the coast – the railway network of South Wales was distinctive for the small, independent and often highly profitable companies operating in the coalfield, while in certain valleys by the 1880s several competed for the lucrative traffic, sometimes building long, expensive (and very wet) tunnels under the intervening ridges to gain access to neighbouring sections of the coalfield. Even in the 1870s there were many shorter branch lines serving side valleys.

Coal shipping ports were essential to the South Wales economy. Pre-eminent among them was Cardiff, the metropolis of the coal trade, whose population grew from about 2,000 in 1801 to 10,000 by 1841, 33,000 by 1861, and, after boundary extensions, to 57,000 in 1871 and 83,000 in 1881. Shipping of coal began at the Bute West Dock (1839), which was followed by the East Dock in 1855–59 and the Roath Basin in 1874. Some coal-owners, anxious to avoid the powers exercised by the Bute estate in Cardiff, promoted other ports, in co-operation with the railway companies which sought independent access to the sea. The docks at Penarth, served by the Taff Vale Railway, were opened in 1865, and construction of docks at Barry, supported by the Ocean Coal Co. and the Barry Railway Company, began in 1884. The Town Dock at Newport was opened amid boisterous festivities in 1842 and extended in 1858. In 1865 Sir Charles Morgan formed the Alexandra (Newport and South Wales) Docks & Railway Company, which opened the North Dock in 1875, worked railways and took over the Town Docks in 1884. Newport's population grew from less than 7,000 in 1801 to almost 50,000 by 1881. The docks at Porthcawl were built in the 1820s by the owners of the 4 ft 7 in. (1.4 m) gauge Duffryn Llynvi & Porthcawl Railway, and the settlement around the floating dock of 1839 came to be called Port Talbot. The dock at Briton Ferry, where the Afon Nedd enters Swansea Bay, was opened in 1861, and subsequently taken over by the Great Western Railway.

Swansea, with a population of almost 20,000, was the largest of the South Wales ports in 1800. It prospered from copper smelting, and had pretensions as a resort. The North Dock was created by diverting the Afon Tawe in 1852, the larger South Dock opened in 1859, and the Prince of Wales Dock was built in 1879–80. The city's population grew to 68,000 in 1861, 90,000 in 1871 and 111,000 in 1881. At Llanelli, where anthracite was shipped throughout the eighteenth century, Pemberton's Dock was built between 1794 and 1804 and further docks in 1834 and 1859. Pembrey New Harbour, later known as Burry Port, was linked to the anthracite mines of the Gwendraeth Valley by the Kidwelly & Llanelly Canal, authorised in 1812, and taken over from 1861 by the Burry Port & Gwendraeth Valley Railway. Some wrought-iron tub boats from the canal remain in the breakwater.

Conclusions

The principal British coalfields had much in common. The larger collieries, with the exception of those in the North East, used the longwall method of working by 1800. All adapted the principal innovations in technology: pumping by Newcomen and later by other steam engines; the steam winding engine; the safety lamp; wrought-iron chains, and wire ropes for haulage; underground railways; and by the 1860s ventilation fans. In every coalfield by 1800 there were early railways, usually conveying coal to navigable water. Women did not work underground in most coalfields, and the practice became illegal in any case in 1842. The same Act prohibited the employment of boys under ten. Most miners worked in the coalfields where they grew up, but managers, particularly from the North East, tended to be migratory, and some movements of families from rural areas to the mining districts can be identified.

Every coalfield provided domestic fuel for local customers and for small-scale manufactures, but some experienced rapid increases in production when transport facilities significantly improved or when coal-using industries sprang up. Between 1700 and 1830 around 4–5 per cent of coal mined in England, Scotland and Wales was exported to Ireland and foreign countries, but with the coming of the steamship that amount rose significantly. By 1830 nearly 20 per cent of coal raised was being used in iron making, but none of the other significant coal-using industries – copper smelting, salt refining, glass, pottery, alkali and town-gas manufacture – used more than 2 per cent of the national output.

Aneurin Bevan famously described Britain as a tiny island 'almost made of coal and surrounded by fish'. Between 1700 and 1870 the British learned how to use that coal.

➤➤ The engraving and map of 1855 show the ironworks at Falkirk alongside the Forth & Clyde Canal which was established in the second decade of the nineteenth century by men from Carron. In 1848 it passed into the ownership of the Kennard family. It produced numerous cast-iron utensils for household use, and industrial plant such as sugar pans, as well as armaments and the castings for the Crumlin Viaduct (see pages 120–2). The cupola furnaces where iron was melted would have been situated in the Furnace House adjacent to the steam engines that powered their fans. Molten iron would have been poured into moulds prepared in the adjacent moulding shops. Castings would have been finished in the workshops between the main block and the canal, and assembled – with any necessary wrought-iron components from the smiths' shops and wooden components from the sawmill – in the fitting shop. The canal would doubtless have been used for the despatch of finished products, but the presence of a stable block shows the continuing importance of horses, probably mainly for transport within the works.

MAP BY COURTESY OF THE NATIONAL MUSEUM OF SCOTLAND; ENGRAVING © SCIENCE MUSEUM/SCIENCE & SOCIETY PICTURE LIBRARY

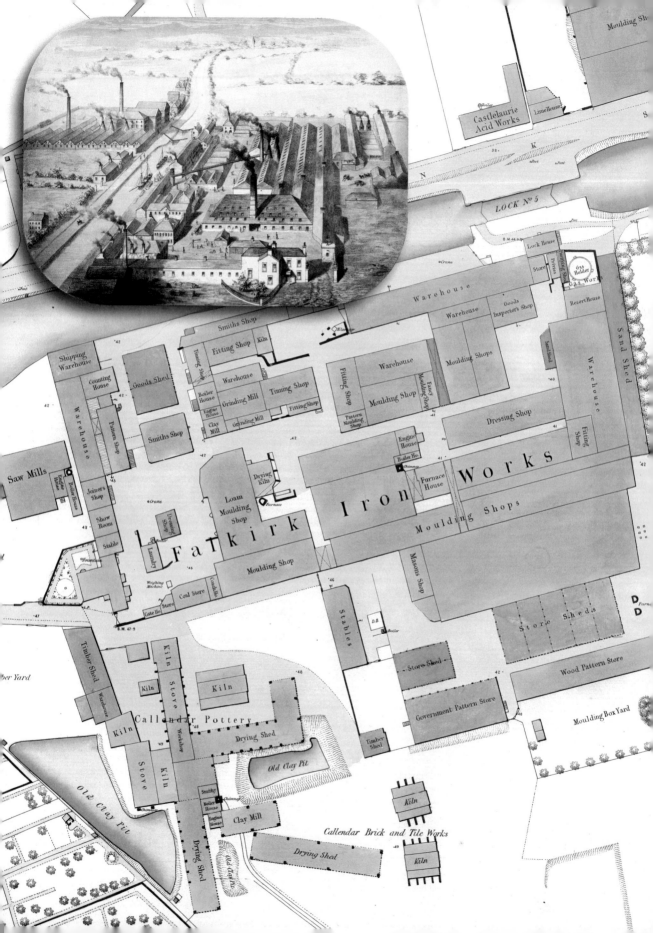

7

'Iron in the blood':
the making of iron and steel

'Of iron are the tools which make the country rich in peace – the plough share and the spade; with iron she multiplies ten thousand-fold, by her machinery, the strength of her hands. We cook our food in iron vessels over iron ranges. Of iron are the weapons that have made us powerful in war – the sword, the shell, the cannon. With iron we span gulfs of the great sea; of iron we are building ships like towns to ride upon the deep. ... The present strength of Britain, we may very reasonably say, is due to the fact that this fortunate country has more iron in its blood than any other.'

HOUSEHOLD WORDS, QUOTED IN GEORGE MEASOM, *THE OFFICIAL ILLUSTRATED GUIDE TO THE GREAT WESTERN RAILWAY*, C.1862

O F ALL THE MATERIALS of the industrial age, iron was the most celebrated and the most evident. Iron was essential in the development of every industry, providing most of the parts from which steam engines, machine tools and textile machines were manufactured, as well as the frames for factory buildings, spectacular roofs for railway stations, and the hull plates for great new steamships such as the SS *Great Britain*. In civil engineering some enthusiasts in the age of the Iron Bridge and the Pontcysyllte Aqueduct considered its possibilities to be boundless. More prosaically, iron grates, pots and kettles could be found on and around the domestic hearths of all but the poorest families. And, more broadly, colonial expansion was made possible by iron weapons and tools. Iron was at the forefront of industrialisation, and there were few entrepreneurs in any branch of industry who were more single-minded than the ironmakers Abraham Darby II, John Wilkinson, Richard Crawshay and the brothers Baird. Enormous iron and steel plants came to dominate the Black Country, parts of Yorkshire and Clydeside, and areas like the South Wales valleys and the upland moors of County Durham that had been but sparsely populated at the beginning of the eighteenth century.

By the 1860s Britain had become the dominant force in European iron making, but this was after a long period of innovation and investment in which the output of British blast furnaces increased around 130-fold in the hundred years after 1788. In 1700 Britain did export iron products, but much of the pig iron and wrought iron from which these were made had been imported. The most prominent of

291

early eighteenth-century manufacturers, Sir Ambrose Crowley, who died in 1713, imported much of his iron from Sweden and Russia, as did the cutlers and edge-tool makers of Sheffield and Hallamshire. Crowley had interests in blast furnaces and forges, but he was essentially a consumer rather than a producer of iron, which is indicative of Britain's role in the European iron trade in 1700. This chapter examines the astonishing expansion of Britain's iron and steel industries in the 170 years that followed.

Developments in the technology of iron making

The methods used in Britain in 1700 to make iron were not employed in every part of Europe. In the western Mediterranean, from Bergamo across Lombardy, Tuscany and Provence to Catalonia, ironmasters used 'Bergamasque' blast furnaces, whose flat fronts were retained by wrought-iron bars stretched between masonry towers. These furnaces employed the scarcely credible technology of the water *trompe* – in which a blast of air was generated by water cascading down a trumpet-shaped pipe – to blow blast furnaces and forge hearths. In France molten iron from the blast furnace was cast not into pigs but as a *saumon*, a flat fish-shaped plate. In Sweden, which produced about half of Europe's iron, the industry was controlled by the State and the Jernkontoret, the ironmasters' association. Swedish iron in 1700 – and still in the 1860s – was used in Sheffield to make steel by the cementation process. Angerstein, who toured Britain in 1753–54 on behalf of the Jernkontoret, shows that there was no single market for iron, but rather a multiplicity of niche markets. At warehouses in London he saw trading in Spanish and Russian as well as Swedish iron, and steel imported through the Netherlands from Remscheid, and noticed that American pig iron was melted in the capital's foundries. In the West Country he saw Swedish iron at Bridport, Exeter and Plymouth, but found that iron from Bilbao was favoured for horse-shoes and gun barrels. Foundries in Bristol, meanwhile, used scrap from Holland, while at Whitehaven he found that about 200 tons *per annum* were being imported from Siberia through St Petersburg, and used chiefly for tyres, while 30 tons a year arrived from Sweden, to be used for wheel nails and horseshoes.

Not all wrought iron was made using the same method. The ancient bloomery method, by which wrought iron was made direct from the ore, was no longer of economic consequence in Britain by 1700, although it continued elsewhere, in 'Catalan forges' in the Basque provinces and the French département of Ariège (but not in Catalonia itself) and *stückofen* in Styria, while bloomeries produced iron at Clintonville in the Adirondacks until as late as 1890. In Britain at the start of the eighteenth century virtually all the iron used was first smelted from the ore in blast furnaces to produce cast or 'pig' iron and then further refined into wrought iron by heating and hammering

⊲ A cementation furnace which is conserved in the centre of Sheffield.

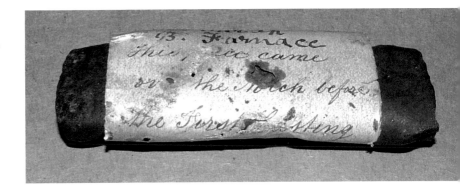

A portion of pig iron, 80 mm height × 30 mm, taken from the first run at the newly opened 'Sarah' blast furnace at the Plymouth Works, Merthyr, in 1850.

BY COURTESY OF CYFARTHFA CASTLE MUSEUM

in finery-and-chafery forges. The technology was introduced to Sussex before 1500 by migrants from the Pays de Bray, between Dieppe and Beauvais, and it subsequently spread to other parts of England. The early eighteenth-century blast furnace was a masonry structure, with a shaft supported by four arches, such as those that remain at Rockley near Barnsley and Charlcott in south Shropshire. A furnace operated continuously, being fed with iron ore, fuel and the limestone that was used as a flux. Air was blown in by water-powered bellows, and molten iron and slag were usually tapped twice daily. The blast furnace produced cast iron, a form of the metal with a carbon content of between 1.8 and 4.5 per cent. In Britain this was cast as the liquid metal flowed into a 'runner', a depression in a bed of sand from which branched channels called 'sows', extending from which were smaller channels: this system was thought to resemble piglets feeding from a sow. The first recorded use of the term 'pig iron' was in 1665.

The principal demand in 1700 was for wrought iron, the commercially pure form of the metal, strong in tension but weak in compression, which could be used for horseshoes, tools, nails and locks. Wrought iron was refined from pig iron in an establishment generally called a forge, which in 1700 usually consisted of two hearths. At the finery hearth the iron was melted with charcoal using an air blast provided by water power, and was decarburised by a secondary air blast, which required considerable skills from the finer. The resultant iron was than pounded under a water-powered hammer, which expelled impurities, a process known as 'shingling', then reheated in a chafery hearth before being hammered into a relatively pure lump of metal called a 'bloom'. Much of the iron produced in 1700 was taken to slitting mills, where blooms were hammered into bars and then rolled into strips between cylindrical iron rolls powered by waterwheels. The strips were then passed through pairs of counter-rotating shafts on which were collars which acted as rotary shears, cutting them into rods that could then be used by nailers. Slitting mills were introduced in England from the Liège region in the sixteenth century.

Traditional charcoal-fired furnaces

The charcoal-based iron industry was not declining in 1700. Its voracious appetite for charcoal was met by the management of woodlands and – contrary to the myth which was frequently rehearsed at the time, and has found its way into many histories published in more recent times – it did not deprive the Royal Navy of timber for its shipbuilding programmes. In 1717 there were about 75 blast furnaces in Britain, with an annual production of about 25,000 tons, a mean of 300 tons *per annum*. Up to 130 forges refined pig iron into wrought iron, the form in which 90 per cent of the metal was used. About 30 furnaces and rather more forges formed a network centred on the river Severn. Fourteen furnaces in the Weald were in blast, while there were nine or ten in Derbyshire and Yorkshire. The number of charcoal-fired furnaces reached a peak of about 82 in 1725–29, with an estimated total output of 29,000 tons. The number of furnaces fell to just

△ The Cyfarthfa Ironworks, Merthyr, painted by the local artist Penry Williams, *circa* 1825. In the distance is the row of seven blast furnaces that formed the core of the works, while in the foreground is one of the small iron bridges built in the 1790s by Watkin George.

over 70 by 1750, though with only a slight decline in output. By 1760, 63 furnaces were producing about 24,000 tons. Fewer than 60 furnaces were working during the 1760s, no more than 40 by 1780, and only two dozen remained in blast in 1790, with an output of at most 10,000 tons.

The mid-eighteenth-century decline was most evident in the Weald of Kent, Sussex and Surrey, which had been the most productive iron-making region in Britain during the previous century. Here ore from local sources was smelted with charcoal from the extensive local woodlands, but supplies of ore were diminishing and wood was in demand for other purposes. The list compiled by John Fuller in 1717 details 14 furnaces in Kent and Sussex, of which

10 were in blast. Some furnaces were blown out, but new ones were built and old ones revived until the Seven Years War of 1755–63. The relative prosperity of the furnaces rested on specialisation in the casting of ordnance, and masked a decline in the refining of Wealden pig into wrought iron. The number of finery- and-chafery forges fell from 21 in 1667 to 13 in 1717. At several furnaces there were boring mills for finishing cannon, including Pippingford where archaeologists uncovered the beam-slots for a track with the four cast-iron wheels of the boring carriage, and Stream, where a boring bar was found which is now displayed in Lewes Museum. Cannon were dragged, with very great difficulty, towards London: in 1743 one iron-master wrote, 'have gotten 20 9-pounders to Lewes …

The complex of buildings at Newland, about a mile north-east of Ulverston, which includes, on the left, the substantial remains of a blast furnace, built from 1746 on an established water mill site, which worked until the 1890s. A forge was added in 1783 and a rolling mill in 1799.

The Duddon blast furnace in the parish of Broughton-in-Furness, established in 1736, which continued working until 1867. Charcoal was used as its fuel and the bellows were water-powered. The furnace itself is to the right of the picture, while to the left are the extensive barns for the storage of charcoal made in the local woodlands.

these 20 have torn the roads so that nothing can follow them and the country curse us heartily.'

The ordnance trade shrivelled away after 1763, for ironmasters in the Midlands and Scotland had seized the opportunities provided by the demands of the government for guns during the Seven Years War. A Wealden furnace which once made cannon was said by 1777 to be 'in decay and it is feared the manufactory at Carron [near Falkirk] will prevent its return'. Only two furnaces in the Weald worked after 1790, and the last, at Ashburnham, was blown out in 1813. Wealden forges were no longer significant by 1750, but the last continued until 1820. Flour mills, paper mills and silk-throwing mills were built on the sites of ironworks, while 'hammer ponds', as reservoirs were called (whether or not they powered hammers), were incorporated into parks or drained and used to grow hops. The beds of such ponds provide the best field evidence of the sites of Wealden ironworks, but the church of SS Peter and Paul, Wadhurst, contains 30 memorials that were cast in iron between 1617 and 1790.

The vitality of the charcoal-iron industry was evident in Cumbria, where six charcoal blast furnaces were built in the 36 years after 1711. A blast furnace was constructed about 1711 on the Cunsey Brook near Windermere by ironworkers from Cheshire, which stimulated local men to build the furnace at Backbarrow the following year. The Backbarrow Company opened a furnace at Leighton, north of

Carnforth. The blast furnace at Nibthwaite bears the date 1736, and Duddon Furnace was completed in the same year. The Newland Furnace near Ulverston was built in 1747 by Richard Ford and partners, who also constructed the pier that eighty years later became the nucleus of Barrow-in-Furness.

Haematite ores from Cumbria were transported to furnaces where fuel and power for smelting were abundant, from Parton near Whitehaven to Bersham near Wrexham from 1747, and from Whitehaven via Chepstow and the river Severn to Horsehay in Shropshire in 1759–62. Several furnaces designed to smelt haematite were constructed in the Scottish Highlands. Two of the 1720s in Inverness-shire were short-lived, but the Lorn Furnace at Bonawe, 14 miles east of Oban, established by the Newland Company in 1753, worked until 1873, while the Cralechan Furnace on Loch Fyne produced iron between 1755 and 1813. The Dyfi Furnace on the Afon Einion near Machynlleth, built in 1755, used Cumbrian haematite ore with locally burned charcoal and remained in production for more than 40 years. Archaeological evidence suggests that Dyfi and Cralechan were built by the same masons.

There are remains of at least eight charcoal-fired blast furnaces in Ireland, most of them built in the seventeenth century by Englishmen, including the economist Sir William Petty and Charles Coote, Earl of Mountrath. They used charcoal from woodlands which were felled and cleared rather than managed. Those at Muckross, Co. Kerry; Dromod, Co. Cavan; Mountrath, Co. Laois; and Enniscorthy, Co. Wexford, worked into the second half of the eighteenth century.

Harrison Ainslie & Co., the company that worked the Newland Furnace near Ulverston, persisted in making charcoal-blast pig iron, acquiring the Backbarrow furnace in 1818, and Duddon in 1828, as well as working Bonawe in Scotland, and establishing a short-lived furnace at Warsash, Hampshire, in 1868. Duddon ceased working in 1857, Bonawe in 1873 and Newland in 1891, but iron was smelted with charcoal at Backbarrow until 1921. Some forges used charcoal to produce wrought iron with the specific qualities sought by makers of guns, chain, wire and tinplate. Those at Hampton Loade and Eardington in Shropshire worked respectively until 1866 and 1889 as part of John Bradley & Co., one of the largest Midlands iron-working companies. Charcoal iron plates were made in the 1870s at the Wilden, Cookley and Broadwaters forges. Charcoal wrought iron was also produced in finery hearths in large, principally puddling forges, in Shropshire and South Wales.

Coke and coal replace charcoal

At the start of the eighteenth century a typical blast furnace might produce 10 or 15 tons of pig iron a week during an annual 'campaign' of 30–40 weeks through the winter months, when water power for the bellows could be assured. The most productive furnace listed by John Fuller in 1717 had an annual output of 600 tons. If urgent orders were received when water was short, as happened at several Wealden furnaces in 1743, waterwheels were adapted as treadmills. Campaigns were also extended by pumping water that had passed over the waterwheels back into the pools from which it had flowed, a practice initiated at Coalbrookdale in the 1740s with horse pumps, then with a steam engine. In the middle of the eighteenth century a series of technological improvements assisted the process: from the 1750s new furnaces had bellows powered by waterwheels from which water was recycled, and from the mid-1770s steam engines were used to power bellows directly, freeing blast furnaces from the seasonality and intermittence that dependence on water power implied. From about 1760, too, ironmasters used cast-iron cylinders rather than leather-and-wooden bellows. Fuel supply was the other constraint on the operation of blast furnaces. At Coalbrookdale between 1709 and 1714 Abraham Darby I showed that it was possible to use coke to produce iron which could be used to make castings, although this iron was unsuitable for refining into wrought iron. Not until the 1750s did his son, Abraham II, produce pig iron that could be sold to forgemasters. He also increased capacity, so that by 1756 his furnace at Horsehay profitably produced up to 22 tons per week, which, since it was not blown out in the summer months, represented an annual output of more than 1,100 tons. Incremental changes further increased output. In 1771 each furnace at Horsehay produced up to 29 tons of iron a week, and by 1805 one furnace was making 43 tons a week, representing an annual output of more than 2,000 tons as productivity steadily increased.

Coke blast furnace output in Great Britain

Date	Number of furnaces in blast	Total output	Mean annual output per furnace
1788	53	48,200 tons	909 tons
1791	85	80,704	949
1806	162	250,406	1,545
1823	237	417,566	1,762
1830	333	615,917	1,850
1843	378	1,348,158	3,567
1852	497	2,701,000	5,435
1872	715	6,743,000	9,429

In 1828 James Beaumont Neilson demonstrated at the Clyde Ironworks that the efficiency of a blast furnace could be improved by heating the air blast before it was blown through the *tuyeres* (wrought-iron or copper tubes) into the furnace. The standard means of heating air *en route* to the furnace became the regenerative stove named after Edward Alfred Cowper, who patented it in 1857 and applied it at the Clarence Ironworks in 1860. In 1849 George Parry, chemist at the Ebbw Vale Ironworks, devised the bell and hopper system of charging, by which the top of a furnace could be closed, which saved energy and allowed gases to be drawn off to heat boilers or hot blast stoves. Iron ore, coke and limestone were deposited on the bell, which was briefly lowered to allow them to fall into the furnace. Blast furnace productivity also increased as a result of developments in mechanical engineering, as lifts and inclined planes worked by steam and hydraulic power were applied to raise materials to charging platforms.

Coal largely replaced charcoal in the refining of wrought iron during the eighteenth century. At some forges in the 1750s chaferies were fired with coal or coke, but this presented few problems since they only reheated iron. Some ironmasters adopted 'buzzing', the reworking of scrap wrought iron, which gave forgemen experience of reverberatory furnaces. A buzzing furnace was one of the first structures installed at Thomas Botfield's new forge at Old Park in east Shropshire in 1789–90. The first process for refining wrought iron with coal to be widely adopted was 'stamping and potting', which involved heating broken pieces of pig iron in refractory pots. The West Bromwich ironmasters John Wright and Richard Jesson were granted a patent for it in 1773, but a similar process had also been patented by Charles and John Wood in 1761 and 1763. John Wilkinson mediated between them and other ironmasters who were making wrought iron with coal.

Henry Cort and the puddling process

Henry Cort was a facilitator who effectively brought together several processes, and he might be regarded as the Richard Arkwright or the Josiah Wedgwood of wrought-iron manufacture. He worked at an insignificant forge at Funtley (then *Fontley*) in Hampshire, but was aware of reverberatory furnaces and knew that Thomas and George Cranage had used one to make wrought iron at Coalbrookdale in the 1760s, apparently with unsatisfactory results. He took out patents in 1783 and 1784 for 'puddling' iron and related processes which he demonstrated to ironmasters. Puddling was adopted with enthusiasm in South Wales, but taken up more slowly in Shropshire, partly because companies had invested in stamping and potting, and partly because of the conservatism of forgemen. Nevertheless, by 1800, although some stamping and potting continued, Cort's process was the accepted method of refining wrought iron.

A puddling furnace consists of two compartments, one for a coal fire separated from one for metal by a wall or 'firebridge', at the end of which a flue drew across heat which melted the iron. The puddler stirred the molten iron with a bar through an aperture with a counter-balanced door, until the iron was decarburised and became putty-like in consistency. It was then gathered together, removed and 'shingled' under a hammer, before being rolled into 'puddled bar' or 'muck bar', which was subsequently rerolled. At many forges pig iron intended for puddling was first melted in a coke-fired refinery hearth which removed its silicon and some of its carbon. Puddling initially required about 40 cwt of pig iron to produce half that weight of wrought iron, but during the 1820s the Black Country ironmaster Joseph Gibbons developed 'wet puddling', in which furnaces were lined with slag containing iron oxide. The oxygen in this combined with the carbon in the pig iron to form carbon monoxide, with a violent reaction from which the process gained the alternative name of 'pig boiling'. Wet puddling enabled a ton (20 cwt) of wrought iron to be produced from 21 cwt of pig. The efficiency of forges was further improved by waste heat boilers, introduced in 1827 by John Urpeth Rastrick, which used heat generated by puddling furnaces to generate steam for rolling mill engines and hammers.

Cort also patented the use of grooved rolls in rolling mills, which enabled wrought iron to be rolled into round and square rods, or 'angle iron'. In his time a rolling mill had a pair of rolls, and when the iron had passed through it had to be returned to the other side

A painting of 1792 by Julius Caesar Ibbetson showing the working of iron at Merthyr Tydfil. A mass of wrought iron, probably from a puddling furnace, is being shingled under a hammer to remove slag.

Part of the melting shop at the Abbeydale Industrial Hamlet, Sheffield, showing a furnace in which crucibles filled with blister steel were placed so that the steel would melt. The resultant crucible steel was subsequently 'teemed' into ingot moulds.

The eighteenth-century steelworks, with its cementation furnace, at Derwentcote, County Durham.

in a 'dead pass'. By 1815 the three-high mill, in which iron was also rolled on the return pass (which involved less loss of heat), had been developed in Staffordshire. Other incremental improvements to mill technology included the 'guide mill', introduced before 1820, in which the final pass rolled the iron into a different shape of the same cross-sectional area as the penultimate pass, thus avoiding 'fins' on its side. In the 1780s forges, like furnaces in the previous decade, were freed from their dependence on water power by the application of rotative steam engines to work hammers and mills. From the 1840s the Nasmyth steam hammer supplanted helve or tilt hammers for shingling.

Puddling was the principal means of manufacturing wrought iron for 80 years, and was used into the third quarter of the twentieth century. In Britain it remained unmechanised, and dependent on the pragmatic skills of puddlers, which were acquired by practice and guarded as a trade secret. One of the rules of a club formed by ironworkers at Tredegar in 1831 was that each member promised not to teach his trade to others without permission. By the early 1870s there were more than 8,000 puddling furnaces in the United Kingdom, some in very large establishments: 151, for example, at Consett and 161 at Dowlais. A heat of iron normally lasted two hours, and it was customary for puddlers, their underhands, shinglers and the rollers of puddled bar to work six heats, making a twelve-hour shift. Received wisdom held that puddlers could not follow their trade beyond their forties, although census evidence suggests that some were still making iron into their sixties.

New steel-making technologies

The word 'steel' applies to several alloys of iron and carbon (other forms of steel in which iron was alloyed with metals such as manganese, chromium and vanadium became important later). In 1700 it meant what is now called carbon steel, used in cutlery and edge tools. This was made in a cementation furnace, a conical structure up to 60 feet (18.5 m) high. Bars of wrought iron were packed with alternating layers of charcoal in sandstone 'chests', which were sealed with debris from the bottoms of grinders' troughs. The chests were heated for several days, after which the bars, by now with blistered surfaces (hence 'blister steel'), were removed and rolled, or broken into pieces, piled, reheated and welded together under a hammer to produce 'shear' steel. Two cementation furnaces remain in Sheffield, but the best-preserved example is Derwentcote Furnace in Co. Durham which worked from c.1720 until c.1890. Blister steel was ideal for making the edges of tools and weapons, but was unsuitable for springs. From 1740 Benjamin Huntsman, a Lincolnshire clockmaker who settled in Sheffield, devised a process in which blister steel was re-melted in crucibles at a temperature of 1,600°C, which required a powerful draught provided by a tall chimney. After several heatings the molten steel was poured into an ingot mould. Crucible steel was superior to blister steel for making turning tools, razors, wires and springs, but it could only be made from blister steel, and therefore most steelworks built after 1750 had both cementation and crucible furnaces, differentiated by round and rectangular chimneys respectively.

The first of many alloy steels that supplanted crucible steel for engineering tools was devised in 1868 by R. F. Mushet.

In 1856 Henry Bessemer, who had made innovations in textiles, glass making and sugar refining, read to the British Association a paper entitled 'On the manufacture of malleable iron and steel without fuel', which proved to be the beginning of far-reaching changes. The puddling process had limitations. The size of bar that could be produced was limited by the amount of iron that a puddler could work in one heat, and numbers of puddlers could not easily be increased in times of high demand. While doing research on gun barrels, Bessemer blew air through molten iron in his bronze-powder works in London, and found that after a violent exothermic reaction the resultant metal, subsequently called 'mild steel', had most of the qualities of wrought iron, and that it could potentially be produced on a large scale. He patented the process, which stimulated others to experiment further, and generated animated correspondence in the provincial and technical press. Several ironmasters installed Bessemer 'converters', the pear-shaped crucibles carried on trunions in which iron was melted for the process. It nevertheless became evident that the process was flawed. Bessemer's experiments had been carried out with phosphorus-free pig iron, and he had lined his converter with non-siliceous refractory bricks, but it proved impossible to make steel of quality with phosphoric ores in acid-lined furnaces. Further, the rapid absorption of oxygen by the iron prevented it from settling in the ingot mould. Robert Mushet solved the latter problem by adding *spiegeleisen*, a compound of iron, manganese and carbon which absorbed oxygen, and which could be imported from Germany. However, haematite ores were free of phosphorus, and most of the works that successfully used the Bessemer process were in Cumberland or Furness,

⊲ The manufacture of mild steel by the Bessemer process involved melting pig iron or scrap in a pear-shaped 'converter' and blowing air through it. This Bessemer converter, once used at Workington, now guards the entrance to the Kelham Island Industrial Museum in Sheffield.

where such ores were abundant. Steel rails proved to last longer than those of wrought iron, and the London & North Western Railway installed a Bessemer plant at Crewe in 1865.

Other means were devised of making mild steel. Sir William Siemens, the German scientist who lived in England from the 1840s, developed a regenerative furnace, in which hot gases from a furnace heated a honeycomb-like maze of refractories, which subsequently heated air that was in turn blown into a furnace. By having two such mazes he could heat one while the other gave up its heat, and the flows could be reversed at intervals to keep up a continuous current of hot air. The regenerative furnace had been designed for glass making, but in 1863 the Frenchman Émile-Pierre Martin applied it to the making of steel. Siemens set up an experimental works to demonstrate the process in Birmingham in 1866, took out a patent for the 'open hearth' furnace in 1867, and in 1869 opened a works employing the process at Landore near Swansea.

In 1879 Sidney Gilchrist Thomas demonstrated the 'basic Bessemer' process, which he had developed at Blaenavon, in which, by lining a converter with a basic instead of an acid lining (in practice with dolomite), it was possible to make mild steel with phosphoric ores, while the resultant 'basic slag' could be used as a fertiliser. Basic linings were also used in open-hearth furnaces. Most of the principal ironmakers installed steel-making plant, and those who had recently invested in puddling forges found it difficult to gain a return on their capital. In 1877 the Board of Trade approved mild steel as a material for bridges, and it was used with spectacular effect in the Forth railway bridge, which was completed in 1890.

How iron was used

Perhaps the most familiar and enduring uses of iron were structural castings. Cast-iron bridges, aqueducts, and columns in factories and railway stations, help to define our image of the period. Smaller practical and decorative objects were also made from cast iron. The process of casting was, by 1700, well known and relatively straightforward. Liquid iron from a blast furnace would be ladled into moulds to form useful pots and kettles or decorative fire backs. As early as the 1540s iron cannon were being cast in Sussex, while the iron tomb of a Bringewood ironmaster at Burrington (Herefordshire) dates from 1619. Until the early eighteenth century iron pots were cast in 'loam', a mixture of sand, clay, straw and horse manure, but in 1707 Abraham Darby I, then working at Bristol, began to cast in sand. The new process enabled a five-gallon bellied pot to be made with only two-thirds of the iron formerly used. In the seventeenth century most iron castings were made at blast furnaces, but by 1710 there were foundries (workshops where castings

A moulder in an iron foundry, ladling molten iron from what appears to be a cupola furnace on the left, into a mould box. A shovel used for filling mould boxes with sand, and tongs with which hot castings could be lifted, are also visible, as is a firegrate which was doubtless one of the products of this particular foundry. The engraving comes from the *Book of English Trades* of *circa* 1810.

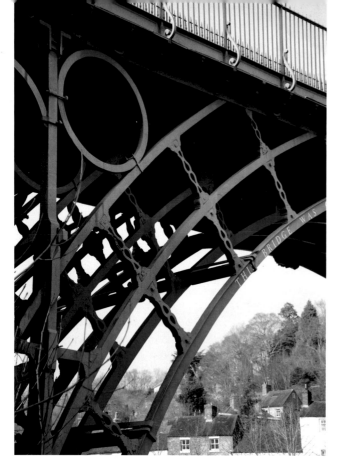

⤺ The Iron Bridge across the river Severn near Coalbrookdale in Shropshire was assembled from castings of various sizes fitted together by techniques such as shouldered dovetail joints that were commonly used by carpenters.

were made by melting pig iron or scrap brought from elsewhere) in Bristol, Dublin, London and Newcastle-upon-Tyne. From the 1720s cast iron was used for steam engine cylinders. It was also employed for architectural purposes, such as the railings around St Paul's Cathedral, which were fixed in 1714; from the 1770s in bridges; and from the 1790s for the frames of buildings. Before 1700 most castings were made with molten iron direct from the blast furnace, but Abraham Darby I used a reverberatory furnace known as an 'air furnace' in which pig iron or scrap was melted, which enabled larger castings to be made with fewer impurities. Air furnaces were still used in the 1860s, particularly for melting large items of scrap, but they were largely superseded by 'cupolas', which were shaft furnaces blown by several tuyeres, of the kind patented in 1794 by John Wilkinson. The cupola made possible the establishment of foundries throughout Britain.

Some of the iron rolled in British mills in the nineteenth century was used to manufacture tinplate, useful for many purposes because of its resistance to rust. Iron sheets coated with tin were first made in Bavaria in the fourteenth century, and imported tinplate was used in Britain in the sixteenth century. Its production was advocated by Andrew Yarranton, and by 1697 John Hanbury was rolling 'black plates', suitable for tinning, at his forge near Pontypool. The work of the Frenchman René Réamur, who demonstrated that plates could be cleaned with acid prior to being dipped in tin, was known in England by 1728, and by 1750 tinplate was being made at several works in South Wales. Tinplate workers traded in most towns. Richard Kempster, who died in Bridgnorth in 1756, made candlesticks, graters, coffee pots, dripping pans and lanterns, and his probate inventory lists 181 plates each worth 3*d*., and also 920 rivets. The principal manufacturers in London around 1800, Jones & Taylor of Tottenham Court Road, employed as many as 150 men. In the nineteenth century demand from the United States increased, particularly for kettles, washbowls and roofing sheets for frontier shacks and, after the discovery of oil in Pennsylvania in 1859, for cans for petroleum products. The output of tinplate in the United Kingdom, which was around 4,000 tons *per annum* in 1805, increased to 37,000 tons in 1850; 77,000 tons in 1860; and exceeded 150,000 tons by 1871. British tinplate production was the greatest in Europe, and until the 1890s the scale of American production was of little consequence – which resulted in a good export market. Of 84,000 tons produced in 1865, 75 per cent was exported, 49,000 tons (58 per cent) to the United States. Most tinplate works had only one or two rolling mills and technological innovation in other aspects was slow: the steam engine installed at Landore in 1851 was supposedly the first to drive a tinplate mill, and even in 1886 some 46 of the country's 346 tinplate mills were water-powered. Most tinplate works were in South Wales, but individual plants flourished in other iron-working areas.

A process for coating sheets of wrought iron with zinc was patented in France in 1829 by Stanislaus Sorel, and soon afterwards Henry Crawford in England was granted a patent for a process, universally called galvanising, in which iron was first pickled in acid, then washed, then dipped in zinc ammonium chloride, and subsequently in molten zinc. The process was adopted in the Black Country, where the characteristic galvanising shed had a high pitched roof with louvres along its whole length. Zinc was melted by coke fires. Galvanising was used to coat builders' ironware, ships' fittings, domestic hollowware, and the corrugated sheets that provided temporary accommodation on the frontiers of empire.

Iron making in Shropshire and the West Midlands

Woodland management and coppicing could provide a renewable source of charcoal, but in densely populated countries such as Britain these supplies could not readily be increased. From the seventeenth century, therefore, attempts were made to utilise coal, which was available in what appeared to be limitless quantities, for metallurgical processes. The best publicised trials were carried out by Dud Dudley who obtained patents before the Civil War, and in 1665 published *De Metallum Martis*, a report on experiments as well as an appeal for sponsorship. One of Dudley's experiments – a furnace at Dudley which was blown by a horse-mill and continued work until 1676 – was financed in part by Sir Clement Clerke of Launde Abbey, Leicestershire. Sir Clement, in association with his son Talbot, became involved with patents and associated litigation relating to the use of reverberatory furnaces for smelting lead and copper. In 1693 he had interests in 'The Company for Making Iron with Pit coal', which built a short-lived blast furnace at Cleator, Cumberland, the following year. (For iron making and industry in Cleator and elsewhere in west Cumberland, see pages 340–3.) The company contracted with Shadrach Fox, who worked the blast furnace at Coalbrookdale from 1696, for the supply of shot, for which the iron was probably smelted with coal: we know, for example, that in 1701, when Fox's brother Thomas managed the furnace at Wombridge in present-day Oakengates, coal was stocked there.

Mineral fuel was applied to the smelting of metallic ores in the late seventeenth century and its use in iron making was therefore a relatively small step into the unknown. The research of Peter King has shown the link from Sir Clement Clerke, through the Company for Making Iron with Pit coal, to Coalbrookdale and other ironworks in Shropshire. The blast furnace at Coalbrookdale was severely damaged by an explosion, probably in 1706, after which Shadrach Fox left England for Russia. It was leased and rebuilt by Abraham Darby of Bristol, whose activities before 1708 reveal how contemporary iron making was part of a wider spectrum of metallurgical activity. A Quaker, born near Dudley, Darby was apprenticed to a maker of malt mills in Birmingham, and in 1698

The ruins of the Madeley Wood furnaces, the only Shropshire ironworks of the 1750s of which there are significant remains, on the banks of the river Severn near the Iron Bridge.

moved to Bristol. About 1702 he formed a partnership with other Quakers to operate a brassworks at Baptist Mills on the north-east outskirts of the city. Darby's first recorded link with Shropshire was in 1706 when he witnessed the purchase of a Quaker meetinghouse at Broseley in the Severn Gorge. He was involved in the establishment of a brassworks in Coalbrookdale, to which shipments of calamine, the zinc oxide used in brass making, appear to have begun in that year. He also set up a copper smelter in Coalbrookdale, and in 1710 leased copper mines at Harmer Hill near Shrewsbury. Darby worked an iron foundry in Cheese Lane, Bristol, from 1703, and in 1707 took out his patent for casting bellied pots. He melted iron at Cheese Lane in an 'air furnace', a reverberatory furnace of the type with which he was familiar from brass and copper works, for which he purchased pig iron from blast furnaces at Blakeney, Redbrook and Guns Mill in the Forest of Dean. He was aware of the work of Dud Dudley, for a manuscript copy of *De Metallum Martis* was kept in the family archive.

From October 1708 Darby rebuilt the blast furnace at Coalbrookdale, probably aware that Shadrach Fox had previously fired it with mineral fuel, and put the furnace in blast in January 1709. For this he purchased coal locally and 'charked' it into coke, perhaps following the example of Shadrach Fox, but for five years there were difficulties and experiments. He tried buying pig iron from the Forest of Dean, mixing coke with charcoal and peat, and using coke made at Bristol and coal from Neath. At last, by 1714 the venture was successful, and shipments of castings increased. In 1715 Darby built a second blast furnace, enabling him to increase his output. He had patented his process for casting bellied pots, but did not seek legal protection for his method of smelting with coke, probably because it was known that he was building on the experience of others – it was no secret, indeed, for in 1710 the lessees of mines in Dawley, a mile from Coalbrookdale, had agreed to supply coal for coking to the blast furnace at Kemberton.

Darby's motivations and the breadth of his interests in working metals are revealed by his involvement with Tern Forge, which was built in 1710 in what is now Attingham Park, between Shrewsbury and

Coalbrookdale. It included a finery-and-chafery forge, mills for rolling brass plates and hoop iron, a slitting mill and a steel furnace. Darby's brother-in-law, Thomas Harvey, called it 'the first Joint Work of this kind in England', the term 'joint work' indicating that both iron and brass were being processed. Darby had probably intended that pig iron from Coalbrookdale would be refined into wrought iron at Tern, and that brass from Coalbrookdale would be rolled there. These objectives were not realised. Coke blast pig iron could not readily be refined into wrought iron, while the death of Jeffrey Pinnell, a partner both at Tern and Coalbrookdale, and an authority on brass rolling, led to a contraction of non-ferrous activities. In 1714 the bargeowner who carried most of Darby's traffic took 'twelve stones for brass workes' and a ton of tools down the river Severn to Bristol. This apparently marked the end of brass making in Coalbrookdale, although the copper smelter probably worked until Darby's death in 1717. For more than three decades the two blast furnaces at Coalbrookdale were outside the mainstream of the iron industry, while Tern became a conventional finery-and-chafery forge until its landlords, who resided nearby and were fatigued with the sound of its forge hammer, declined to continue its lease. The buildings were demolished in 1756.

The iron industry of the West Midlands underwent many changes in the 1750s. In 1754 the second Abraham Darby leased land for mining in Great Dawley and, with his partner Thomas Goldney III, blew in a coke-fired blast furnace at Horsehay, two miles north of Coalbrookdale, from which he supplied pig iron to forges in the Stour Valley. This breakthrough into the market for pig iron for forging was probably due to some sort of innovation in furnace technology developed at Coalbrookdale in the early 1750s, perhaps an advance in blowing techniques or a more studied selection of ores. Darby and Goldney blew in another furnace at Horsehay in 1757, and constructed two more at Ketley, a few miles to the north, the first of which worked from 27 January 1758. Partnerships, including local mine owners, built blast furnaces at nearby Madeley Wood and Lightmoor, and a new company was established to manage iron making on the Willey estate of the Forester family.

The new ironworks depended on steam power and railways. The furnace bellows were powered by waterwheels, but these used water that was recycled using steam-powered pumps (for the adoption of this technology see above, pages 53–4). Railways had been carrying coal to Severnside wharfs for 150 years, but the first worked by an iron company was constructed by the Coalbrookdale partners in 1749. Railways delivered raw materials to all the furnaces built in the 1750s, and the connected lines of the Coalbrookdale partners extended eight miles from Donnington Wood to the Severn.

The construction of nine profitable coke blast furnaces in Shropshire within five years had profound effects on the iron trade nationally and locally. In 1764 the 2nd Earl Gower formed a company to exploit the mines on his Lilleshall estate, in which his partners were John Gilbert, agent to the Duke of Bridgewater (builder of the eponymous canal) at Worsley, and Thomas Gilbert, his agent at Lilleshall, solicitor to the Bridgewater estates, and MP for his pocket borough of Newcastle-under-Lyme. A lesser landowner, anxious to share in the boom, wrote in 1757 that 'everybody is building furnaces'. Abraham Darby II, in a letter to Thomas Goldney III in July 1760, calculated that the annual output of iron before the Horsehay furnace was blown in was 9,000 tons, and that it had doubled in five years. His figures do not accord with historians' statistics, but that he made such a calculation demonstrates his awareness of the magnitude of the changes he had initiated.

Technological and managerial changes continued. In 1776 John Wilkinson demonstrated that a steam engine could blow a blast furnace directly, using a water balance, freeing iron smelting from its dependence on water power. In the 1780s Boulton & Watt rotative engines were applied to drive rolling mills, slitting mills and forge hammers, and Wright and Jesson and then Henry Cort devised ways of using coal in forging wrought iron. The new companies of the 1750s combined iron working with mineral extraction. In the 1780s they developed integrated ironworks, where minerals were taken in at one end and machines, architectural and engineering castings, and wrought-iron bars and plates were sold to customers at the other. A writer in 1802 described the ironworks of Carron, Coalbrookdale and South Wales as 'unequalled perhaps in Europe for the union which they present of the whole series of the operations in iron manufacture from the first quarrying or collecting of the ore the ultimate manufacture of it into all that diversity of implements which it furnishes for the use of the arts and of human life in general'. Writing from the United States in 1795 Joseph Priestley remarked that, in contrast to those in England, American ironworks were all 'upon the old plan. … No one here has got into the way of connecting all the processes in one concern. The ore is carried to the furnace, the pigs some miles to the chafery, the bars some miles to the mills and so on.'

In 1800 Thomas Telford observed that the number of blast furnaces in the Shropshire coalfield 'exceeds any within the same space in the Kingdom'. There were 14 coke blast furnaces in Shropshire in 1775, which might have been capable of producing in excess of 12,000 tons *per annum* (about 40 per cent of national output), while in 1788 the 21 coke and 3 charcoal furnaces in the county were making nearly 25,000 tons of iron, or about 38 per cent of national output. By that time, however, iron making elsewhere was expanding, and although in 1796 the 23 works in Shropshire made nearly 33,000 tons of iron, this represented rather less than 30 per cent of the national output, and in 1805–06 nearly 55,000 tons represented just 22 per cent of an expanded national output. For two decades after the opening of the Iron Bridge in 1781, Coalbrookdale attracted visitors who marvelled at a series of industrial sights, including flame-topped furnaces among the cliffs of the Severn Gorge, several iron bridges, canal and railway inclined planes, foundries and cannon-boring mills, and tunnels giving access to geological curiosities and factories making exquisite porcelain. Underpinning these spectacles were nine iron-working companies which from 1755 had applied new technologies and devised new forms of management.

After 1815 the prosperity of the region waxed and waned with the economic cycles. Ironmasters adopted innovations tardily, but the trend of production was upwards until 1869, when a peak output of nearly 200,000 tons amounted to less than 2 per cent of the

John Wilkinson, the most eminent of late eighteenth-century ironmasters. A portrait by Lemuel Francis Abbot.

John Wilkinson's memorial at Lindale in Furness, near to his home and much-improved estate at Castle Head.

iron made in Great Britain. The Botfield family's Old Park Company was nationally influential between 1800 and the late 1850s, when it fragmented. The Lilleshall Company, formed in 1802 as successor to Earl Gower's partnership of 1764, produced pig and wrought iron that commanded premium prices, and from the 1850s made steam engines and pumps for international markets. The Coalbrookdale Company produced pig and wrought iron until the 1880s, but achieved fame through its foundry which contributed notably to the Great Exhibition.

The pattern set in Shropshire was followed in the Black Country, Lancashire, South Wales and Scotland. The agent of transfer to Staffordshire was John Wilkinson. In the words of Telford Wilkinson was 'king of the ironmasters'. Like Isambard K. Brunel, Wilkinson has suffered less from his detractors than from his admirers, some of whom have fallen into the trap of exercising their own fantasies or perpetuating myths about the man and his achievements. Wilkinson could be difficult to deal with – a 'hard hearted,

malevolent old scoundrel ...' according to Lord Dundonald – but his was a commanding presence in four iron-working regions. He was an 'improver' of landscapes, the patron of many innovations, in London a powerful advocate of the iron trade in his dealings with politicians and the military, and a respected figure in continental Europe. His father, the Durham-born pot founder Isaac Wilkinson, had worked at Little Clifton and Backbarrow before purchasing the Bersham furnace near Wrexham in 1753. After schooling at Kendal, and a spell in Liverpool, John Wilkinson became a partner in 1757 in the New Willey Ironworks in Shropshire, and by 1774 controlled it. A decade later French aristocrats were impressed by his immense wealth. He installed a cannon-boring mill at Willey, and by May 1775 had supplied a steam engine cylinder to a customer in the Netherlands. In 1779–80 he built new furnaces at Snedshill in present-day Oakengates, which were blown by steam engines without any use of water power. Snedshill pig went to forges in the Stour Valley, and the foundry cast floor-plates for copper works at Macclesfield, St Helens and the Greenfield Valley in Flintshire. Wilkinson significantly influenced the building of the Iron Bridge, invested in the Shropshire, Shrewsbury and Ellesmere canals, and launched the first of a fleet of iron boats on the river Severn in 1787. He was involved in the iron trade at Wilson House near his estate at Castle Head, Grange-over-Sands. From 1766 he controlled the Bersham Ironworks, where he manufactured cylinders for steam engines, one of which remains at Le Creusot, where it was taken by his brother, William Wilkinson, who also had shares in Bersham. When William returned to

Britain he considered that Bersham's prosperity was threatened by projected furnaces on the adjacent Brymbo estate, which his brother had purchased in 1792. The ensuing litigation was settled by arbitrators who awarded William over £8,000 but allowed John to buy out his share in Bersham.

John Wilkinson built a coke-fired blast furnace at Bradley near Bilston, Staffordshire, in the late 1750s, but it was of little consequence until new construction began about 1772. By 1803 the Bradley works consisted of several blast furnaces, a puddling forge and steam-driven mills rolling bars and sheets. The young Joseph Priestley wrote to Wilkinson in 1790 that he thought

A large-scale Ordnance Survey map of the 1880s showing the site of John Wilkinson's ironworks at Bradley in the years of its decline. The pair of blast furnaces at Barbor's Field appear still to have been working but the three Bovereux furnaces had probably been blown out for the last time. The six 'ironworks' were probably all, in Black Country usage, forges where wrought iron was refined from pig iron or scrap by puddling. The Bradley site appears to have been broken up after Wilkinson's death in 1808. In 1872 two blast furnaces were still working, but were under different ownership from two forges and a tinplate works. This concentration of ironworks grew up in the late eighteenth and early nineteenth centuries along part of the original line of the Birmingham Canal Navigation which had been by-passed by a new stretch of canal built by Thomas Telford in the 1820s, although it remained in use for local traffic. The more easterly of the two railways is the Birmingham, Wolverhampton & Dudley line of the Great Western Railway, opened in 1854 and originally broad-gauge, while the more westerly is the Oxford, Worcester and Wolverhampton line, one of the key routes in the 'Battle of the Gauges' (see pages 186–8), which by the 1880s was owned by the Great Western.

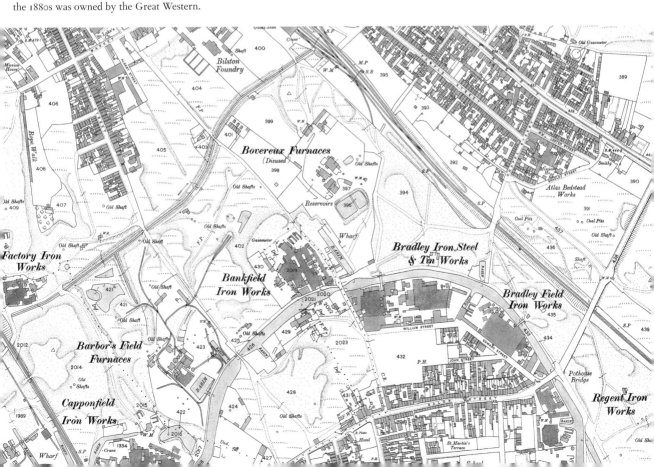

THE CONEYGRE IRON WORKS, THE PROPERTY OF THE EARL OF DUDLEY.

⌐ The three Coneygre blast furnaces near Tipton belonged to the earls of Dudley and were reputed to produce some of the best pig iron in
the Black Country. The ramps carrying raw materials to be loaded into the tops of the furnaces are readily visible, as are the façades of the
three casting houses into which molten iron from the furnaces was tapped into pig beds. As in other Black Country images the canal boats
with cabins used for long-distance transport can be distinguished from the day-boats that were used for local journeys.
BY COURTESY OF THE IRONBRIDGE GORGE MUSEUM TRUST

it the first ironworks in the world, 'where so many
improvements are daily making'. The litigation that
characterised Wilkinson's career continued after his
death: he had fathered three children in his seventies,
and his nephew contested his estate with them. Only
the Brymbo works continued but, his innovations
apart, Wilkinson's main legacy was the iron industry
of the Black Country.

Iron working in western Britain in 1750 revolved
around Bewdley on the river Severn, where pig iron
was traded from furnaces in the Forest of Dean, South
Wales, Shropshire, north Staffordshire, Cheshire,
Cumberland and Furness, and from Sweden, Russia,
Spain and America. Some pig iron was sent upstream
for refining in Shropshire and mid-Wales, but much of
it went to forges along the river Stour. These produced
iron used by smiths on the Black Country to make
nails, locks and chains, and by manufacturers of more

valuable items in Birmingham. The many thousands
of people involved in the hardware trades of the West
Midlands added substantially to the value of the iron
made in the region's furnaces and forges. The hardware they produced was exported to many parts of
the world, and the spades, shovels and buckets that
they made helped to transform agriculture and civil
engineering in Britain and in the nation's distant colonies. Thomas Foley, whose toga-clad effigy adorns the
rococo parish church at Great Witley, owned several
forges in the Stour Valley, as did Richard Knight, who
worked at Coalbrookdale in his youth. From the 1730s
Knight used Lower Mitton forge to make tinplate
and the Broadwater Works in the 1750s made steel in
cementation furnaces with wrought iron from Sweden
and Russia.

The accounts of the Knights' forges provide many
insights into the iron trade. In the 1730s ore for the

A diagrammatic representation of calcining kilns, supposedly near Coalbrookdale. In kilns of this kind iron ore was heated, which drove off moisture, sulphur and carbon dioxide and also separated some waste materials. Ore is shown being delivered from a mine along a horse tramway to the kilns, and calcined ore is being loaded on to a plateway waggon in the foreground.

furnace at Bringewood was carried 10 miles from Titterstone Clee, and 20 miles from Shirlett near Much Wenlock. Pig iron for Bringewood Forge, some of it from the blast furnace at Halesowen, was carried overland from Bewdley. Black plate was carried in the opposite direction from Bringewood to Lower Mitton. The trading network spanned two continents: the pig iron used at Mitton in 1735–36 came not only from the Forest of Dean, Scotland, and Charlcott and Willey in Shropshire, but also from Principio and Baltimore in America, while in the 1740s the Knights used iron from Russia, from Maryland and Tubal in America, and from north and South Wales, Shropshire and Backbarrow. Coke blast pig iron from Coalbrookdale was used for the first time at Wolverley Forge in 1754–55, and thereafter the Coalbrookdale partners sent pig iron from Horsehay to Wolverley, Cookley and Whittington, and later to Mitton and Bromford. In 1758 the Knights' forges received iron from Ketley, and in the 1760s from John Wilkinson. By the 1790s, however, many charcoal blast furnaces that had supplied the Stour Valley had been blown out. In 1802–08 iron came from eight works in Shropshire, from Brierley and Dudley Wood in the Black Country, and from Varteg and Blaenavon in South Wales. The forges themselves also saw changes: coal was used by 1750 in chaferies;

from the 1770s some adopted stamping and potting; some began puddling in the 1790s, although a few persisted with a form of finery using charcoal; and some switched to steam power. The longevity of certain sites was remarkable: Whittington, Cookley, Broadwaters, Wilden and Hyde, already old in 1700, were still operating in 1872, and some continued into the twentieth century.

The example set by John Wilkinson at Bradley near Bilston was followed by many Black-Countrymen from the 1790s. The brothers Parker built furnaces at Tipton Green in 1783, and William and Richard Crofts leased land at Kingswinford for the Old Level furnaces in the following year. In 1788 six coke blast furnaces in the region produced 4,500 tons of iron, and in 1791 fifteen made 7,800 tons. By 1806 there were 25 works with 42 furnaces, making nearly 50,000 tons of iron annually, almost 20 per cent of national output. In 1839, 108 furnaces made 338,730 tons of iron, and by 1852 159 furnaces produced 725,000 tons, about 27 per cent of national output. A peak was reached in 1856 with an output of 777,000 tons. Output fluctuated in the 1860s but then declined. The boom year of 1871 was the last in which output exceeded 700,000 tons and it was never more than 500,000 tons after 1873. A high proportion of Black Country iron was refined into wrought iron, and pig iron was imported from Shropshire for the same purpose. By 1870 there were 2,160 puddling furnaces in the district. In the 1850s canal boats delivered limestone from the Vale of Llangollen, haematite from Cumbria that had been transshipped on the Mersey, ores from north Staffordshire, and ironstone from Northamptonshire. A commentator remarked in 1869 that, 'the quantity of ironstone being sent into south Staffordshire from other districts is something wonderful', but such a spectacle distracted attention from the fast-diminishing mineral resources of the region. When contemplating the shipping of iron ore into the Black Country the prescient Harry Scrivenor had asked as early as 1854, 'Is not this, as regards south Staffordshire, the beginning of an end?'

Black-Countrymen influenced the growth of iron making throughout Britain. The Homfray family prospered in South Wales, while Charles Attwood and the brothers Dawes established works in Co. Durham and Yorkshire, but of equal importance were the legions of furnace keepers, puddlers and shinglers from Tipton, Oldbury, West Bromwich and Dudley who took their skills to Elsecar, Park Gate, Carnforth and elsewhere.

North Staffordshire

Iron making in north Staffordshire was significant throughout the period 1700–1870. In 1717, for instance, we know that there were blast furnaces at Madeley, Church Lawton (Grange) and Meir Heath, and ten forges were refining wrought iron. The Meir Heath furnace, with the forges at Consall, Oakamoor and Chartley, formed the Foley partnership's Staffordshire works. In the 1670s Plot described the manufacture of frying pans near Newcastle-under-Lyme, and Angerstein observed that wrought iron for the process came from two forges in Cheshire. However, Meir Heath furnace was blown out in 1762; Grange and Madeley had both closed by 1780, and the number of forges in the region was similarly reduced.

Smelting of iron with coke began in the 1780s when Sir Nigel Gresley leased a site in Apedale to Abraham Parker of Tipton and his brother, where by 1789 they were working a blast furnace whose stack remains. In 1792 the Silverdale Iron Co. built furnaces two miles south, on the estate of the Sneyd family. The works were managed together in the mid-nineteenth century, and worked until 1902. In 1796 the output of the north Staffordshire furnaces remained less than 2,000 tons, but by 1839 ten furnaces were making 18,200 tons of pig iron, 1.45 per cent of the national output. By 1854 the total increased to 104,000 tons (3.4 per cent of the national total), reaching 218,000 tons in 1864, and a peak of 303,000 tons, or 5.1 per cent of British output, in 1870, at which date there were 40 blast furnaces, and 480 puddling furnaces in ten forges. Output never again exceeded 300,000 tons, but remained near that level through the 1890s.

North Staffordshire was rich in iron ore. In 1861 about 650 ironstone miners worked in the parishes of Cheadle, Cheddleton, Ipstones and Kingsley in the Churnet Valley. The crews of 16 canal boats loading iron ore at Ipstones were from the Black Country, but ore for north Staffordshire works was probably delivered by day-boats. Ore was also extracted from the coal measures, and about 70 ironstone miners worked in Tunstall in 1861 and 30 in Norton-on-the-Moors.

John Gilbert became aware of the minerals discovered during the construction of the Harecastle Tunnel on the Trent & Mersey Canal, and in 1786 purchased an estate where, in about 1800, his son built a 20-bedroom mansion named Clough Hall. The estate was purchased in 1812 by Thomas Kinnersley, a banker from Newcastle-under-Lyme who provided capital for leading potters, and his agent, Robert Heath I. They built coke-fired blast furnaces on the site. Robert Heath II left Clough Hall in 1854 to set up furnaces at Biddulph Valley, and by 1870 was the dominant figure in the north Staffordshire iron trade, the owner of four furnaces at Norton-in-the-Moors and four at Biddulph Valley, and of forges where there were 143 puddling furnaces. In 1877 he bought and demolished the furnaces at Clough Hall and made coke on the site for his other ironworks.

The Shelton Bar Company originated in 1841 when the 1st Earl Granville blew in three blast furnaces at Etruria, in the heart of the Potteries; after 1852 the second earl constructed a model forge. In 1872 the complex included 8 blast furnaces, 94 puddling furnaces and 7 rolling mills. It produced plate, used by shipbuilders and railway companies, mixing haematite from Barrow with local ironstone and pig iron from the Lilleshall Company with that from its own furnaces.

The north Staffordshire ironworks exchanged ore and semi-finished iron with Black Country works, and the two regions were linked by migration. Of 250 ironworkers in Tunstall in 1861 more than 70 originated from Tipton, Oldbury, West Bromwich and neighbouring parishes, while Black-Countrymen comprised 68 of the 195 resident ironworkers at Biddulph Valley.

Volcanoes in the Valleys: iron making in South Wales

On 9 July 1844 Carl Gustav Carus, friend of Goethe, painter, professor of anatomy, and physician to King Friedrich Augustus II of Saxony, visited Merthyr Tydfil. He thought it an extraordinary place:

we saw everywhere smelting houses and forges, little railways and canals for the conveyance

of the iron from one place to another. In one valley we saw below a canal and a railway for locomotive engines. … And what mountains of dross were piled up! Certainly the quantity of iron produced in these mountains must be enormous! … Above the flaming chimneys of the blast furnaces the heated air trembled,

⚐ The sense of drama provided by the large ironworks in South Wales in the mid-nineteenth century is readily apparent in this view of Dowlais, painted by George Childs in 1840, at a time when there were 18 furnaces within the works, which in total employed about 2,500 men.

and made the outlines of the mountains of dross behind them appear wavy. I could not help imagining these mountains of dross to be volcanoes, and the blast furnaces little burning craters.

His royal master, Augustus II himself, demanded to view the ironworks at night:

> We therefore went out again after ten o'clock, and were first conducted to a height above the town, whence we had a view of five or six of these works where fires are constantly kept up by night as well as by day. One might imagine oneself in the land of the Cyclops. … Whilst viewing in the dark night behind these glowing works, the high volcanic-looking cones of those mountains of dross which I have noticed, wonderfully illuminated by the red flames, one's fancy might easily represent at one time a blazing fortress, at another a burning castle, at another the fiery city of Pluto as represented by Dante.

At this date the 40 or so ironworks of South Wales – mostly clustered along the heads of the Valleys from Blaenavon to Hirwaun and in the Vale of Neath – included about 150 blast furnaces which produced annually about half a million tons of pig iron, around 36 per cent of the national output. It was then the principal iron-working area in Britain, and profits were such that Sir Josiah John Guest of Dowlais was regarded as worthy to entertain a monarch, whose tour also included stays at Woburn Abbey and Chatsworth.

Yet South Wales had not been a significant iron-working area in 1700. About 30 charcoal blast furnaces worked in Wales between the sixteenth century and 1750, most of them short-lived, and in 1717 the seven in South Wales were making a total of only 2,000 tons. Charcoal-fuelled and water-powered forges were dispersed widely across the principality; there were 13 in South Wales in 1717 and 11 in 1749–50. This was not a region where men had generations of experience of iron making, and it lacked the infrastructure of blacksmiths, ropemakers, builders and transport contractors that could be taken for granted in Coalbrookdale, the Black Country or County Durham. The Welsh ironworks of most consequence in 1700 was at Pontypool, in the valley of the Afon Llwyd, and had been established in the 1570s by Richard Hanbury. John Hanbury II enlarged the forge and built a rolling mill, supposedly designed by his agent Thomas Cooke of Wolverley, and is credited with introducing tinplate manufacture into Britain, as well as improving methods of drawing iron wire. In 1717 Hanbury's blast furnace produced 400 tons a year and his forge 350 tons, while in the 1750s its annual output of about 700 tons made it one of the most productive in Britain. In the 1740s pig from the furnace was sent to the Mitton and Cookley forges, and from about 1732 tinplate from the

◁ The ruins of the ironworks at Hirwaun, showing a section through a characteristic eighteenth-century blast furnace located at the foot of a retaining wall, from which it was fed with materials, delivered to the site by early railways.

This view of 'Cyfarthfa House and Works', painted around 1791 by William Pamplin, Richard Crawshay's gardener, illustrates the significance of the Glamorganshire Canal which carried the output of the Cyfarthfa Ironworks to Cardiff and the coast.
BY COURTESY OF CYFARTHFA MUSEUM

forge was used by Hanbury's agent, Edward Allgood, to make japanned wares which were manufactured at Pontypool until about 1822. Angerstein remarked that 'everything [is] kept very secret and strangers forbidden'. The ironworks was in due course adapted to use mineral fuel. There were four blast furnaces by 1839 when the forge still specialised in refining iron for tinplate and wire. The Hanburys owned the works until 1851, and it was sold to the Ebbw Vale Co. in 1864.

The success of Abraham Darby II in the 1750s, in smelting with coke pig iron that could be refined into wrought iron, stimulated investments in the Valleys by English capitalists. Some were men who had prospered in the Midland iron trade; others had made fortunes in the City of London. Ironworks lay along the heads of the Valleys, where, by happy coincidence, iron ore and bituminous coal outcropped, and where the coal measures met the carboniferous limestone. John Maybury, a member of a dynasty of hammermen who worked at forges all over Britain and in the American colonies, leased land in 1757 at Hirwaun alongside the Afon Cynon, and built a water-powered blast furnace, perhaps the first in South Wales to be fired with coke. Almost immediately a charcoal-fired furnace at Brecon in which the Mayburys had

interests was blown out. By 1813 the works at Hirwaun included two blast furnaces blown by a Boulton & Watt engine, a forge with ten puddling furnaces and a rolling mill powered by a Trevithick engine. The Crawshay family purchased the works in 1819 and added two more blast furnaces, but they relinquished their interest in 1859 after which the furnaces worked only spasmodically.

The first of four ironworks on the edge of Merthyr was built at Dowlais in 1759, and produced iron from 1760. Its partners included merchants from Bristol, the ironmaster Isaac Wilkinson, and Edward Blakeway, partner in the Willey Ironworks. In 1767 John Guest of Broseley was appointed manager of what was still a modest concern. He was succeeded by his son Thomas Guest who introduced steam power and made Dowlais into a very large ironworks.

The Cyfarthfa works on the western side of Merthyr was initially financed from the City of London, with profits made by trading across the Atlantic and in the Baltic. It was built on a 4,000-acre holding leased in 1765 by the immensely rich Anthony Bacon, a native of Whitehaven who worked with an uncle in Maryland, and presided from London over the shipping of African slaves to America and the importation of tobacco and molasses. His first partner was William

△ The rolling mills at one of the great ironworks at Merthyr (either Dowlais or Cyfarthfa) as they would have appeared to Dr Carus during his nocturnal visit with the King of Saxony in 1844. The stands of one of the rolling mills are clearly shown on the right, near to what appears to be the steam engine that drove the mill. The pen and wash drawing is by Thomas Hornor and was completed about 1817.

Brownrigg, a doctor practising at Whitehaven, who had studied at Leiden, experimented with mineral waters in Germany, and who entertained Benjamin Franklin in 1771. Brownrigg's brother-in-law, Charles Wood, supervised the construction of a blast furnace and a stamping and potting forge. Wood, the son of the ironmaster William Wood, had worked in Jamaica and at the Low Mill forge near Egremont. He wrote a day-by-day commentary on his experiences, which tells us that he made a contract with three masons on 18 August 1766 to build a blast furnace and was preoccupied with obtaining supplies of Cardiff lime and of alder poles for scaffolding. Hauling timber in a region without metalled roads was difficult, but he obtained a pair of oxen, controlling them with a beech yoke made by his sawyers. When a waggon became stuck on Merthyr Common in May 1766 the horse was brought home and the oxen were despatched to retrieve the vehicle. Bricks were delivered to the site on sleds. Wood found it difficult to discipline his workers, noting

on 30 August 1766 that seven of his masons were drunk at an alehouse. He was aware that he was an outsider in Welsh society, observing that William Edwards, the bridge builder, 'knows most of the masons in this and the neighbouring County, and can procure where we cannot'. Wood also faced problems with the weather, observing on 26 May 1766 that it was 'a close morning, with small rain, like dew', a phenomenon familiar to all who have done fieldwork in the Valleys. Rain often made brick making impossible. After the buildings were finished Wood stayed as managing agent at Cyfarthfa until his death in 1774.

Cyfarthfa prospered by supplying cannon to the East India Company and from 1773 to the Board of Ordnance, which led Anthony Bacon into a partnership with Richard Crawshay, a Yorkshire-born trader in Baltic iron, who bought out Brownrigg's share in the Ordnance contract in 1777. When Bacon died in 1786 there was confusion over the inheritance, and by 1791 Crawshay controlled the company. He moved to

Cyfarthfa in 1792 and over the next 18 years shaped it in his image. He was the first ironmaster enthusiastically to adopt the puddling process, for which he obtained a licence from Henry Cort in 1787. By 1794 the works included two blast furnaces, eight puddling furnaces, three fineries, three balling furnaces and a rolling mill. From 1791 he employed the engineer Watkin George, who created at Cyfarthfa a showground of spectacular innovations and was celebrated in song.

A pioneering iron bridge across the river Taff was completed in 1793 for the Cyfarthfa Ironworks. Known as Pont-y-Cafnau – the 'Bridge of Troughs' – the bridge was designed as a combined aqueduct and rail bridge. The deck, supported by a pair of large cast-iron king-post A-frames, carried the waggonway that was used to deliver limestone from a nearby quarry to the blast furnaces. Below this a trough carried water to power machinery. At the centre of the A-frames a support carried a second aqueduct to convey water to the waterwheel powering the blowing cylinders of the furnaces. The bridge is 24 feet 5 inches (7.5 m) long, precisely the span of the cast-iron trusses that roofed the forge at Cyfarthfa. George designed four other iron bridges in the vicinity. J. M. W. Turner painted one in 1797, and another, dismantled in the 1970s, has since been re-erected and placed outside the birthplace of the musician Joseph Parry in Chapel Row, one of the few workers' terraces that remains from the early years of Cyfarthfa.

By 1806 an output of 10,460 tons of pig iron made Cyfarthfa the most productive ironworks in Britain. Richard Crawshay, 'Moloch the Iron King', accepted no man as an equal (in 1807 even the talented Watkin George left to join the Hanburys at Pontypool) and told a visitor to Cyfarthfa in 1797 that he 'bent his whole mind upon being a perfect iron-master'. There were three blast furnaces by 1796, a fourth was added the following year, and in 1801 a subsidiary group was built at Ynysfach, a mile to the south. Crawshay moved within a circle of ironmasters, whose portraits he commissioned. A gathering at his dinner table in the summer of 1790 included John and William Wilkinson, William Reynolds, Joseph Priestley the younger and the 9th Earl of Dundonald. He entertained visitors from Russia, always appears of have had his own way in disputes over mineral rights and water supply, enthusiastically supported the Glamorganshire Canal, and left a fortune of £1.5 million.

Richard Crawshay was conscious that he belonged to a generation who had established an iron industry that dominated Europe. He wrote in 1790:

we work all with Fossil Coal – my Blast Furnaces are 60 feet high, each Furnace produces about 1400 Tons *per annum* – we make use of Air [i.e. puddling] Furnaces instead of Finerys, when the Metal is brought to nature, instead of Hammers, we put it between a pair of Rolls & crush it like a paste.

William Crawshay I inherited his father's estate, but left the management of the ironworks to *his* son, William Crawshay II, the 'iron king', who commissioned the crenellated Cyfarthfa Castle in 1824–25. The management subsequently passed to the fourth generation, Robert Thompson Crawshay, a fervent opponent of trades unions, who transferred the main focus of the company from iron making to coal mining. Annual output by 1864, when five of the eleven furnaces had been adapted for hot blast, exceeded 50,000 tons of pig, while the forges and mills, which drew power from five waterwheels as well as several steam engines, produced 1,200 tons of puddled bars per week. In 1872 the forge comprised 72 puddling furnaces and seven mills. R. T. Crawshay closed the furnaces and forge in 1875 and left Cyfarthfa Castle in 1889, but the works was fitfully revived until 1919. The bases of four furnaces and the engine house remain at Ynysfach, while there are remnants of six furnaces at Cyfarthfa. The passage behind them, through which blast pipes once carried air from the bellows to the tuyeres, is still capable of inspiring awe.

The Plymouth Ironworks in Merthyr was begun by John Guest and Isaac Wilkinson in 1763 on land leased from the Earl of Plymouth, and was sold to Anthony Bacon in 1766 and leased after his death to Richard Hill. His son Anthony Hill was regarded as the most scientific of ironmasters, and Plymouth iron commanded a premium price. After his death the works continued in other ownership until 1875. The ironworks at Penydarren was built from 1784 on land leased from Anthony Bacon by Jeremiah and Samuel, the sons of Francis Homfray of Wollaston and members of another family with a long history in the Midlands iron trade. Iron was made at Penydarren until 1875.

Dowlais became one of the largest ironworks in Britain. Thomas Guest succeeded his father in 1785 when the works comprised just two blast furnaces. He built more furnaces, began a forge in 1801, and invested in Boulton & Watt engines. By 1808 there were four blast furnaces and a forge with four refineries, 20 puddling furnaces and 10 balling furnaces. His son Josiah John Guest had a thorough understanding both of iron-working technology and of the commercial aspects of the iron trade. By 1840 there were 18 blast furnaces at Dowlais, and the company employed 1,000 coal miners, 1,000 raising iron ore and 2,500 ironworkers. The Big Mill that opened in 1830, measuring 240 × 210 feet (74 × 65 m), exported rails to the United States from 1832, and rolled 20,000 tons in 1835. Another forge, the Goat Mill, begun in 1857, included two rolling mills that could produce 1,700 and 700 tons of rails per week. Specimens of its products were displayed at the International Exhibition of 1862. Josiah John Guest was elected the first MP for Merthyr in 1832, and gained his baronetcy in 1838. Even in the 1830s local mines were unable to supply sufficient ore to the furnaces, which by the 1860s were being charged with ore from Cumberland, Furness, the Forest of Dean, Northamptonshire and Spain. Bessemer converters were installed from 1865, and Siemens open hearth furnaces from 1871, but 161 puddling furnaces made Dowlais the largest forge in Britain. After 1888 the company concentrated investment at Cardiff, but iron making continued at Dowlais until 1930. The only buildings remaining from the time when Dowlais was the principal ironworks in Wales are a Palladian stable block of 1820, and the library of the 1850s, designed by Sir Charles Barry as a memorial to Sir Josiah John Guest.

Rich archaeological evidence of how ironworks were established in the Valleys remains at Blaenavon, which in 1806 was second in output only to Cyfarthfa.

There, three furnaces were built between 1789 and 1792 by partners from the West Midlands, Thomas Hill, Thomas Hopkins and Benjamin Pratt, on land leased from the 2nd Earl of Abergavenny. A fourth was added by 1805 and a fifth by 1823. The combined output increased from 16,882 tons in 1823 to 26,872 tons in 1858. Above the furnaces was the 200-yard long Upper Yard where raw materials were unloaded from tramroad waggons and packhorses, and men and women worked 12-hour shifts shovelling coal into coke ovens, breaking limestone and ironstone, feeding calcining kilns, and charging materials to the blast furnaces. Farther north is evidence of the methods by which iron ore was obtained in the 1790s. Off the road to Abergavenny are scours on areas of commonland that was let by the ironmasters in 'patches' to individuals, who created small pounds from which water was released suddenly, carrying away top soil to reveal nodules of ore (a technique not dissimilar to that of the lead-mining 'hushes', see pages 353, 373). Scours depicted on a map of 1812 can still be identified on the ground today. The practice probably ceased when the Keeper's Pond was built as a forge reservoir in 1817–18. From 1859 the company built an ironworks on the valley floor alongside the railway, and the furnaces on the original site were used for the last time soon after 1900.

The Blaenavon Company's tramroad system totalled 35 route miles by 1837. A line built in 1793 to Pontnewynydd linked the works with the Monmouthshire Canal, opened in 1796. Before 1798 a ravine near the furnace was crossed by an eight- or ten-arched viaduct, which was drawn by Sir Richard Colt Hoare and subsequently covered by industrial waste. An alternative outlet to the waterway system was provided by a tramroad built in 1817–18 by Thomas Hill II, which ran to a wharf on the Brecknock & Abergavenny Canal at Llanfoist. Spectacular earthworks mark its course around the bleak slopes of the Blorenge, and a tunnel driven through the mountain in about 1815 enabled waggons of limestone to reach the furnaces from quarries two miles north.

The first forge in the Blaenavon area was built about 1804 at Cwmavon, two miles south of the furnaces near Forge Row, a terrace of 1804–06. It closed between

An engraving of the blast furnaces at Blaenavon from a watercolour by Sir Richard Colt Hoare, which was published in 1801 when the works was only a few years old. Above the three furnaces are the charging houses where materials were being prepared for tipping into the furnaces. The casting houses stand in front of the furnaces, and between them is the blowing engine house with two round chimneys. There is an adit mine for coal on the right, while to the right ground is being removed prior to the building of two more furnaces. The elevated structure may have contained a trough taking water to the boilers of the blowing engine, and, as the appearance of a woman with a basket on her head suggests, it may also have been used for conveying coal or for taking sand for the pig beds.

1817 and 1822 when the company constructed a works in a wild landscape at Garnddyrys, alongside a tramroad two miles north-east of the furnaces. There, only forbidding crags of slag, earthworks, and two dry reservoirs remain of the forge. The puddling furnaces and a rolling mill were worked by men from 34 houses which all disappeared after production ceased in 1863.

Close to the blast furnaces are Stack Square and Engine Row, solid houses of the early 1790s in a style familiar in the English Midlands. They were probably built to attract skilled men, but they are not representative of the first generation of housing at Blaenavon. A shortage of accommodation is suggested by Colt Hoare's picture of the tramroad viaduct which shows dwellings within the arches, and a roof over the viaduct doubtless intended to keep the dwellings dry. Higher up the hillside, Bunkers Row, which is now demolished, was originally a terrace of 20 single-storey back-to-back dwellings of mean dimensions, probably designed for unskilled workers. Detached larders stood outside each house. In about 1860 the

terrace was rebuilt as ten through-houses with higher outside walls. The first of about 225 houses of a standard design, with a kitchen and small bedroom on the ground floor and a sleeping room above, were built in the 1820s; some remain. Archdeacon Coxe observed in 1801 that Blaenavon had 'the appearance of a small town, surrounded with heaps of ore, coal and limestone, and enlivened with all the bustle and activity of an opulent and increasing establishment'.

Construction of furnaces in the Clydach Gorge, three miles north of Blaenavon on land leased from the 5th Duke of Beaufort, began in 1793. There were two furnaces by 1813, and four by 1844, which were blown by a waterwheel and a Boulton & Watt steam engine. The works may never have been profitable, but it did produce iron for more than 60 years. The remains of the four furnaces and the archway of the charging house are highly picturesque. Alongside the Afon Clydach is a row of 'dual' houses, a two-storey terrace built into the hillside above a basement row of one-room dwellings opening in the opposite (downhill) direction, the latter providing some of the dampest family accommodation in the region.

The works at Nant-y-glo was established in 1791 when the Blaenavon partners, having leased land in excess of their requirements, sub-let part of it to Harford, Partridge & Co. whose manager, Richard Summers Harford, erected furnaces which were put into blast in 1795. In 1811 the site was sold to Joseph Bailey and Matthew Wayne, both of whom were enabled to invest by legacies in the will of Richard Crawshay who died in 1810. Bailey, one of Crawshay's nephews, supposedly tramped from Wakefield to take up employment at Cyfarthfa, and inherited a minority share of the partnership which he sold to William Crawshay I. Wayne was Richard Crawshay's highly regarded furnace manager at Cyfarthfa, and used his master's bequest of £100 as capital in the Nant-y-glo partnership. In 1820 Wayne sold his shares to Crawshay Bailey, Joseph's younger brother.

The brothers made Nant-y-glo one of the principal works in South Wales. Their outlet was a tramroad to Govilon Wharf on the Brecknock & Abergavenny Canal, where the company's iron warehouse of 1821 remains. In 1833 they purchased the Beaufort furnaces, two miles north-west, and six years later worked eight blast furnaces at Nant-y-glo and six at Beaufort, profiting from the buoyant demand for wrought-iron rails. Crawshay Bailey sold both works for £4 million in 1871, but the successor company closed Beaufort in 1873 and Nant-y-glo in 1874. The Baileys were regarded as the least humane of the South Wales ironmasters – Joseph Bailey so feared his workers' wrath during the unrest of 1816 that he built two round towers above Nant-y-glo, where his family and trusted employees would have sheltered had there been an uprising. Their superiority was visibly asserted in Bayliss Row, a terrace built in the 1820s on the hillside with all the windows facing uphill so that Crawshay Bailey's house and pleasure grounds in the valley below were not overlooked. In 1837 he bought a mineral-rich but unexploited estate at Aberaman in the Cynon Valley, where he erected blast furnaces in 1845 and a forge by 1847. The estate was sold in 1867 to the Powell Duffryn Coal Company which abandoned the ironworks.

Matthew Wayne also became a partner in an ironworks at Gadlys in the Aberdare Valley, where the first furnace worked from 1828. Three more were operating in 1850, when a tinplate works was built alongside. His son Thomas built a blowing engine

▼ The terrace of 'dual' houses alongside the blast furnaces at Clydach. The downhill façade shows three storeys, but the top two consisted of conventional houses that faced uphill. The doors at ground level gave access to single-room dwellings that were excessively damp and, when the furnaces were operating, constantly swathed in smoke and sulphurous fumes.

▲ The ruins of the complex at Clydach, three miles north of Blaenavon, where four blast furnaces were constructed between 1813 and 1844.

The blast furnaces at Ebbw Vale which were at the centre of the extensive network of ironworks in South Wales built up in the mid-nineteenth century by Abraham Darby IV, of the family most famous for their links with Coalbrookdale. This photograph of 1893–95 shows characteristic blast furnaces of the mid-nineteenth century, with masonry bases and the upper parts of refractory bricks held together by wrought-iron plates.

Abraham Darby IV also acquired the six blast furnaces at Abersychan. This quadrangle of buildings appears to have comprised the mechanical engineering workshops of the complex, and against the wall to the left is what appears to be a small air furnace used for melting iron for castings.

house and two furnaces in 1855–56 which remain, but his family's interests turned to mining coal and the ironworks closed in 1866.

The famous ironworks at Ebbw Vale was built in 1790 and by the late 1830s had grown to include four furnaces and a puddling forge. Jeremiah Homfray, brother of Samuel Homfray of Penydarren, was sole original owner, but Harford, Partridge & Co. took shares in the company in 1792 and Homfray departed in 1796. In 1818 James Harford acquired the three blast furnaces at Sirhowy, two miles west, and constructed a tunnel through which pig iron could be taken to Ebbw Vale. The Harfords encountered trading difficulties in 1842, and in 1844 sold Ebbw Vale to Abraham Darby IV of Coalbrookdale. He steadily expanded his Welsh iron empire during the next twenty years: in 1849 he took over the Victoria Ironworks (1839) farther down Ebbw Vale; in 1852 he bought the six blast furnaces of the British Iron Co. at Abersychan, in the valley of the Afon Llwyd; in 1857 he acquired the nearby Pentwyn Ironworks (1825); and from 1864 he took over the venerable ironworks at Pontypool, which until 1839 had been worked by the Hanburys. In 1863 Darby's company leased 75,000 acres, had 19 blast furnaces, 192 puddling furnaces and 1,200 workers'

dwellings, and was producing 100,000 tons of iron rails a year. Bessemer converters were installed at Ebbw Vale before he retired in 1873. The conglomerate he created was substantially larger than the Coalbrookdale Company and in 1872, with 19 blast furnaces and 237 puddling furnaces, was comparable in size to the whole Shropshire iron industry. Thereafter the company rationalised its activities. Pentwyn closed in 1869, Sirhowy in 1879, and Abersychan in 1881. Pontypool, with its historic specialisms in tinplate and iron for wire drawing, continued rather longer, and Ebbw Vale survived many crises until its final closure in 2002.

The Tredegar Ironworks, less than two miles from Ebbw Vale, was established in 1797–1800 by Samuel Homfray on land leased from his father-in-law, Sir Charles Gould Morgan. A blast furnace was working in 1803 when puddling furnaces were also under construction. Homfray built a mansion in Bedwellty Park in 1818, and by 1822 worked five furnaces at Tredegar. His sons Samuel and Watkin managed the works after his death, but the family connection ceased in 1868 when the 9 blast furnaces and 80 puddling furnaces passed to a partnership that included Joseph Whitworth and Henry Pochin. A steel plant was built

Francis Crawshay, second son of William Crawshay II, took charge of the Hirwaun Ironworks which the family acquired in 1819, and of a new tinplate works established in the 1820s at Treforest. He had an interest in Druidism, and learned the Welsh language to communicate with his workpeople. After Hirwaun closed in 1859, and Treforest in 1867, he spent his remaining years at Sevenoaks, Kent.

in the 1880s, but the energies of the Tredegar Iron & Coal Co. were devoted increasingly to coal mining; iron making at Tredegar ceased in 1891.

There were also ironworks in the valley of the Afon Ogwr. The works at Cefn Cribwr near Bridgend, one of the best-preserved blast-furnace complexes in the region, was built in the 1770s by John Bedford. It was rebuilt in the 1820s, although smelting appears to have ceased as early as 1836. The ironworks at Tondu, built after 1820, prospered from 1854 under the management of James Brogden, a member of a Furness family who shipped ore to South Wales. He supervised the construction of the harbour at Porthcawl in 1864–67. The ironworks at Maesteg was built from 1828, and by 1848 included 3 blast furnaces, 72 coke ovens and a foundry casting railway chairs. The works was acquired in 1862 by the Llynvi Vale Iron Co., owners

of the nearby Cambrian Ironworks which dated from the late 1830s, and in 1872 both passed under the control of the Brogden family's Llynvi, Tondu & Ogmore Coal & Iron Co., which ceased operation in 1878.

The principal technological change in the South Wales iron industry in the mid-nineteenth century was the charging of uncoked anthracite and later bituminous coal direct to the blast furnace, which was made possible by hot blast. The process was developed from 1836–37 by George Crane at the Ynyscedwyn Ironworks in the Swansea Valley, built on the site of a charcoal iron furnace that he acquired in 1823. Some 36 anthracite-fired blast furnaces were built in southwest Wales, but the technology was difficult to manage and rarely yielded profits. The Venallt Ironworks at Blaengwran in the Vale of Neath consisted of two blast furnaces built between 1839 and 1842 to smelt iron ore with anthracite, but it closed by 1854 when the site, where the engine house remains, was adapted to produce patent fuel. The Banwen Ironworks, three miles north, where two furnaces and an engine house still stand, was built in 1845–48, but may only have produced 80 tons of pig. The principal impact of Crane's process was experienced in Pennsylvania. David Thomas, manager at Ynyscedwyn, migrated to the Lehigh Valley in 1839 and used anthracite to smelt iron with spectacular success.

Tinplate manufacture was concentrated in the western valleys, where the works at Ynyspenllwch was operating in 1747. The industry grew prodigiously in the nineteenth century, and there were 90 works in South Wales before the imposition of tariffs on imports to the United States in the 1890s. Most used iron produced in South Wales. Some of the most impressive remains are those of the iron-framed open smithy at Treforest, near Pontypridd, part of a works developed by William Crawshay and his son Francis Crawshay. The largest concern was reputedly the Ystalyfera Iron and Tinplate Works, which operated between 1838 and 1885 and had 12 mills and 11 anthracite-fired blast furnaces. At the picturesque waterfalls at Aberdulais the visible remains are those of the Aberdulais Tinplate Co., founded in 1830, parts of which continued until 1939. Hot and cold rolling-mills

A copper token struck around 1792 showing the tapping of the blast furnace at the Carmarthen Ironworks, which were established by Robert Morgan in 1748. The furnace was water-powered and was situated on a small stream flowing into the Afon Towy. Iron ore, coal and limestone could be delivered either by road or by ship. A forge was built alongside the furnace soon after 1748 and a tinplate mill was added before 1777. The works continued to produced tinplate until 1900.

and pickling and annealing areas have been conserved at the Kidwelly Tinplate Works, which began in 1737 and continued until the 1940s.

Relatively few iron companies in South Wales produced steam engines. The beam winding engine of 1861 from Newbridge Colliery, now displayed on the Treforest campus of the University of Glamorgan, came from Varteg, and 11 locomotives were built at Tredegar between 1832 and 1853. The Neath Abbey Ironworks was founded in 1792 by partners who included George Croker Fox, a Falmouth Quaker, and two of his brothers, and Peter Price, a Quaker trained at Coalbrookdale who had worked at Carron and in America. He managed Neath Abbey from 1801 and was succeeded in 1817 by his son, Joseph Tregelles Price. Neath Abbey supplied many engines to Welsh ironworks – Penydarren and Blaenavon (1819), Cyfarthfa (1833), Nant-y-glo (1836), Dowlais, Rhymney and Maesteg (1838), Clydach (1840), Cwmavon and Gadlys (1845), Sirhowy (1849), Aberdare (1852), and Plymouth (1865). Locomotives were built there for Ebbw Vale (1832), Dowlais (1832–38) and Plymouth (1864). The works closed in 1885, but two blast furnaces of 1793 still stand. Neath Abbey's apprentices included Benjamin Baker, designer of the Forth Bridge, and David Thomas, pioneer of anthracite-fired blast furnaces.

Most ironworks in South Wales prospered by selling wrought iron and capitalising on opportunities during the Napoleonic Wars when supplies from Sweden and Russia were interrupted, and from the 1830s with the demand for rails for main lines. Welsh foundry iron had a good reputation, and in 1849 Blaenavon pig was used at foundries at Northfleet, Limehouse and Ipswich, and Beaufort iron at Southampton and Bridgwater, while Clydach pig was preferred at Plymouth.

In 1830 the 113 blast furnaces in South Wales produced 277,643 tons of pig iron, more than 40 per cent of the national output. Output grew rapidly, but the relative position was not sustained – in 1854, 169 furnaces at 48 sites made 750,000 tons, but this now represented just 24 per cent of the national figure. The peak of 985,000 tons in 1859 represented 27 per cent of national output, but that level was not exceeded until 1.46 million tons was reached in 1871. Although this was a time of prosperity for the iron industry, that represented only 16 per cent of national output. Production then fell to 818,000 tons in 1873, and that level was not exceeded until 1880. The decline was in part due to a shortage of ore, and in part to the intro-duction of Bessemer steel making, for which much Welsh pig was unsuitable. The use of pig iron made from phosphoric ores was made possible by the 'basic Bessemer' process, developed at Blaenavon by Sidney Gilchrist Thomas and Percy Carlyle Gilchrist, but it was more beneficial to ironmakers in the United States than to those in Wales. Many of the historic ironworks in the Valleys were closed after 1871, and production was sustained by works on the coast, which smelted imported ores.

North Wales

In North Wales charcoal-fired blast furnaces were working in 1700 at Ruabon and at Plas Madoc near Wrexham, from which pig iron was being sent to Cookley in the 1740s. The furnace at Bersham was built by Charles Lloyd in 1719, and from 3 December 1721 was fired with coke. In the 1730s it passed to the control of Richard Ford and Thomas Goldney III of Coalbrookdale, and in 1753 was purchased by Isaac Wilkinson who by 1762 was casting steam engine cylinders. John Wilkinson was a partner from 1755, and after his father settled in South Wales in 1763 energetically developed the works, casting cannon and steam engine cylinders as well as pots and pans, and providing training for the offspring of his friends, including the young James Watt who 'studied at the college of Bersham'. Aikin, writing in 1795, described the works as 'among the first of the kind in the kingdom'. Wilkinson bought the adjacent Brymbo Hall estate in 1792 and began to build furnaces, which led to the dispute with his brother, after which he controlled both works. Bersham was offered for sale in 1813 but never worked again and the site was leased to a papermaker in 1818.

The Brymbo works were taken over in 1842 by a company that included the engineer Henry Robertson and the brothers William Henry and Charles Edward Darby of Coalbrookdale. Steel was made there until 1990, and one of Wilkinson's furnaces remains. In 1872 there were six blast furnaces on the North Wales coalfield between Plas Kynaston, overlooking the Pontcysyllte Aqueduct, to Mostyn on the Dee estuary. Iron making contributed significantly to the prosperity of North Wales, although the region produced only about one per cent of national output.

The ancient iron-making industry of Dean

In 1700 the Forest of Dean was a productive iron-working area. John Fuller in 1717 listed eight blast furnaces producing annually 2,850 tons of iron, more than the output of the ironworks in the Weald or in Shropshire, and about 10 per cent of national output. In 1677 Andrew Yarranton described Forest pig as 'of the most gentle, pliable, soft nature, easily and quickly to be wrought into manufacture'. The non-phosphoric ores from the Forest produced 'tough' (the word has a specific meaning in the trade) pig iron which could be refined into wrought iron which combined strength and ductility, comparable with that from Sweden. The Ironworks in Partnership, established by Philip Foley in 1692, controlled most works in the Forest. Yarranton observed that pig iron from Dean was taken up the river Severn to forges in the Stour Valley, Shropshire and mid-Wales. Fuller listed 15 forges in the vicinity of the Forest, some of which used iron from charcoal-fired blast furnaces in South Wales. The forge at Lydbrook made Osmund iron for the Foleys' wire-drawing works at Tintern. The Dean furnaces also produced acceptable foundry iron. Between 1705 and 1711 'pot iron' was made at Blakeney, while firebacks were cast at Guns Mill and railings at Bishopswood. Angerstein observed that haematite from the Lake District and slag from Roman and medieval bloomeries were charged to blast furnaces in Dean.

The Forest's contribution to national output diminished as production expanded elsewhere, but iron making remained significant in the 1860s. In 1788 four charcoal-fired blast furnaces produced 1,600 tons of iron, about four per cent of the national output. Charcoal was abundant in the Forest, but charcoal blast furnaces gradually ceased working. Guns Mill was adapted for paper manufacture in 1743; the furnace at Flaxley closed about 1802, and Redbrook in 1816. Bishopswood was abandoned by 1814, Lydney by 1810, and the furnace on the Angiddy Brook above Tintern from 1828.

Coke smelting was introduced in the 1790s. At the initiative of Thomas Teague a blast furnace was built at Cinderford from 1795, and began production in 1797 or 1798, but ceased working in 1806. Furnaces at Parkend built in 1799 closed about 1807. The Whitecliff Furnace, built by James Teague with partners from Shropshire, made iron from 1801–02. A second furnace was added in 1808, but the works was abandoned by 1812. Moses Teague overcame difficulties in using coke made from Dean coal and re-opened the Parkend furnace in 1824. Cinderford was re-opened in 1829, taken over by William Crawshay II in 1838, and worked until 1894, while the Ebbw Vale Co. built furnaces in the 1830s and 1840s at Ruspidge and Oakwood. Four blast furnaces in the Forest in 1840 produced 15,500 tons of iron, and Griffiths in 1872 listed ten. Some ancient water-powered forges specialising in iron for wire drawing and tinplate manufacture were still working in 1870.

Some highly significant developments in iron-working technology took place in the Forest of Dean as a result of the activities of the metallurgist David Mushet – who discovered Black Band ironstone in his native Scotland – and his son Robert Forester Mushet. The former began to work at the Whitecliff furnace in 1810, but soon afterwards established the Forest or Darkhill Ironworks, a largely experimental establishment where he had a cupola furnace and facilities for making crucible steel. Robert Mushet took over the works after his father's death in 1847. It was he who demonstrated that the Bessemer steel-making process could be improved by the addition of *spiegeleisen*. At Darkhill, Mushet produced the experimental ingot from which the first steel rails were rolled at Ebbw Vale before being laid by the Midland Railway at Derby. His enterprise was enlarged in 1862 as the

One of the two blast furnaces at Morley Park.

The remains of Whitecliff Furnace in the Forest of Dean.

The Cannon Mill foundry in Chesterfield, which bears the date 1816, although it was probably built by the Smith family before the end of the eighteenth century. The machinery in the mill was powered by a waterwheel.

Titanic Steel Co., but although he developed self-hardening (tungsten) steel in 1868, his works closed in 1874. Mushet became involved in a long struggle with Sir Henry Bessemer for recognition of his contribution to steel making: when living in Cheltenham in 1881, he justifiably informed the census enumerator that his occupation was 'Co-inventor of steel rails with Sir Henry Bessemer'. Darkhill was the least typical of the Forest of Dean ironworks, but in the context of the history of technology it was easily the most important.

Iron making in the East Midlands

Ironstone occurs in the coal measures through the Erewash and Rother valleys on the eastern border of Derbyshire, where four charcoal-fuelled blast furnaces were working in 1700. Another was built at Melbourne in the 1720s, but all were blown out by 1800. The landowner Francis Hurt built a charcoal blast furnace at Alderwasley in 1764, and later attempted to use coke as its fuel but abandoned his experiments in 1780. The adjacent forge continued, and a few workers produced sheet iron there in the 1860s. In 1767 Hurt purchased Morley Park near Heage and built a furnace that he fired with coke and blew by steam power. His son leased it in 1811 to John and Charles Mold, who rebuilt it and constructed another alongside it in 1825. The furnaces produced pig iron until 1875, and their gritstone stacks remain. Two coke-fired furnaces were built at Stonegravels, Chesterfield, in 1780 and two at Wingerworth in 1782. The region produced just over 10,000 tons of pig iron in 1806 and more than 34,000 tons from 14 furnaces in 1839. By 1870 there were 49 furnaces at 14 works. Derbyshire pig iron was well suited to foundry work and, apart from two small forges in Derby, the only puddling establishments in the county were those of the Whittington, Sheepbridge and Butterley companies where there were 87 puddling furnaces in total.

In 1755 John Smith, whose father had been Master Cutler in 1722, founded the Griffin Works at Brampton, Chesterfield. By the end of the century his sons had opened mines for coal and ironstone, and established the Adelphi Ironworks at Duckmanton. In 1806 the Smiths made 1,700 tons at Griffin and 900 tons at Adelphi. They cast cylinders for Boulton & Watt and for Francis Thompson of Ashover. The Griffin Works closed in 1833, and the Adelphi furnaces in 1845, but the Cannon Mill of 1816 remains.

At the southern end of the coalfield the first ironworks at Stanton-by-Dale opened in 1791 but quickly went bankrupt. It was revived in 1846 when Benjamin Smith and his son Josiah, from Duckmanton, leased coal, ironstone and clay mines and built three blast furnaces. They in turn went bankrupt in 1849, but the works was continued by their creditors as the Stanton Iron Company and prospered under the management of a banker, George Crompton. The company worked collieries and became a major influence in the coal industry.

The expansion of iron making in the Erewash Valley began with the establishment of the Butterley Company. The Cromford Canal, opened in 1793, runs north from Langley Mill in the Erewash Valley through Butterley Tunnel into the valley of the Amber. While it was under construction Benjamin Outram and Francis Beresford, the company's solicitor, purchased the 200-acre Butterley Hall estate near Ripley, which was rich in coal and iron ore, together with limestone rocks at Crich, 3½ miles north-west. They constructed a blast furnace in 1791 and the following year with William Jessop and John Wright, a Nottingham banker, concluded a partnership agreement. They built a foundry alongside the blast furnace and established a lime and limestone business based on the quarries at Crich, which were linked to the canal at Bullbridge. They leased additional land at Codnor Park in the Erewash Valley in 1796, and in 1810 built a blast furnace there, the nucleus of a second ironworks. By 1805 the company was producing 1,766 tons of iron *per annum*, and employed about 800 people. Six cottages built at Codnor Park in 1797 became the nucleus of a new community, Ironville, which was enlarged into a model village in the 1830s.

The blast furnaces at Butterley were reconstructed in 1838 beneath an imposing stone retaining wall which survives. By 1848 the annual production of pig

The office block of the Sheepbridge Iron Company which dates from 1857.

iron from six furnaces at Butterley and Codnor Park was more than 20,000 tons. The company produced castings for Vauxhall Bridge in London in 1813–16 and for a bridge at Lucknow in India in 1816. William Brunton worked for the company between 1808 and 1821. The son of a Dalkeith clockmaker, he became a colliery viewer, then worked in the fitting shops at New Lanark before entering the employment of Boulton & Watt at the Soho Foundry. After leaving Butterley he managed the Eagle Foundry in Birmingham. By 1870 the Butterley Co. had 8,000 employees working at its blast furnaces, the 42 puddling furnaces at Codnor Park, and a foundry at Langley Mill, but its 15 collieries were becoming its principal preoccupation. By the early 1860s output of coal exceeded 700,000 tons *per annum*, much of which was taken southwards by rail. The company prospered under the management of Francis Wright, who became senior partner in 1830 and had interests in the Midland Railway. The company's outstanding monument is the 6,894 tons of ironwork it supplied for the magnificent train shed at St Pancras.

Two eminent figures were associated with the Riddings Ironworks near Alfreton, built by Thomas Saxelby & Co. from 1800. From 1805 it was managed by David Mushet, succeeded by James Oakes who owned the works from 1818 and ran it in a paternalistic manner. In 1847 Oakes built a plant to refine the oil that seeped from local mine workings and here, from 1848, he employed James 'Paraffin' Young, founder of the Scottish shale oil industry. In 1830 the company had three blast furnaces and 500 employees. Walter

Mather, who had worked charcoal-fuelled furnaces and forges in Derbyshire, built coke blast furnaces at Staveley from 1783, which benefited from the proximity of the Chesterfield Canal. The works passed in 1815 to George Hodgkinson Barrow and in 1840 to his brother Richard Barrow. The business employed more than 3,000 men in 1861, and became a joint stock company in 1864, when its seven furnaces produced 13,000 tons of pig iron and its five collieries extracted 800,000 tons of coal. The company was managed by Charles Markham, son of a Northampton solicitor who worked for the Midland Railway at Derby and married the daughter of Sir Joseph Paxton. The company's prosperity depended increasingly on its coal mines and its foundries, which produced nearly a thousand upright columns for the building that housed the 1862 International Exhibition in London. The Sheepbridge Ironworks, whose offices bear the date 1857, consisted in 1872 of five blast furnaces and a forge with 27 puddling furnaces. It was founded by David Chadwick, and the chemist, Henry Davis Pochin, best known for his process for clarifying rosin, which enabled the manufacture of white soap, and for a filler made from china clay used in paper making. He subsequently quarried china clay in Cornwall, and with his brother Samuel Davenport Pochin established the Croft Stone & Brick Co. in Leicestershire. He had interests in iron making at Tredegar, represented Stafford in Parliament from 1868, and established Bodnant Gardens on the estate that he purchased in North Wales in 1874.

Sheffield: cutlery, iron and steel

Sheffield, nine miles north of Sheepbridge, stands a little apart from the mainstream of British iron making. While the products of British furnaces and forges dominated international markets in 1870, Sheffield's cutlers and steelmasters continued to import many of their raw materials. Warehouses stacked with Swedish Danemora or Oregrund wrought-iron bars for making crucible steel could still be photographed in 1900 at Firth's Iron Wharf and Jessop's Swedish Iron Store. Sheffield's principal manufactures in 1700 had been cutlery and edge-tools, and its iron- and steel-making industries took precedence only from

The Globe Works in Sheffield was built in 1825 for Ibbotson & Raebank, edge tool manufacturers. This was an integrated works with its grinding machinery powered by steam engines, and the building incorporated the owner's dwelling, whose porch can be seen on the right. Charles Cammell was among the many steel masters who gained experience at the works. After passing through the hands of many owners, and suffering an arson attack in the 1970s, the works is now restored as the Globe Business Centre.

The Pond Works in Sheffield, one of many that produced crucible steel for cutlery and edge tools. The conical tops of cementation furnaces used for the manufacture of blister steel can readily be recognised. The tall chimney probably provided draught for the furnaces used for refining blister steel into crucible steel.

the mid-Victorian period. The two industries need to be perceived separately, although some business concerns were involved in both activities. At Sheffield, as at Remscheid and Solingen in the Bergisches Land, hammer forges produced cutlery, tools and weapons from the Middle Ages onwards. The metal-working region embraced Hallamshire, the ancient district which included the parishes of Sheffield and Ecclesfield and the chapelry of Bradfield, and extended across the Derbyshire border to Eckington and Whittington. From 1624 an Act of Parliament placed control of the making of cutlery with the Company of Cutlers in Hallamshire.

Sheffield's population increased from 14,500 in 1736 to 46,000 in 1801. Carriers went regularly to London; the principal roads radiating from the city

Shepherd's Wheel, one of many water-powered grinding shops on the streams above Sheffield.
PHOTOGRAPH: CARNEGIE

'Interior of a tilt,' an oil painting by Godfrey Sykes which shows hearths used for heating wrought iron or steel and a water-powered tilt hammer of the kind much used in Sheffield and elsewhere for shaping the iron.
© SCIENCE MUSEUM/SCIENCE & SOCIETY PICTURE LIBRARY

The Sheaf Works in Sheffield, opened by William Greaves in 1823, which, along with the Globe Works (see page 326) was one of the first purpose-designed cutlery factories, and which, like the Globe Works, presented an elegantly formal façade to the outside world.
PHOTOGRAPH: CARNEGIE

The Cyclops Works in Sheffield, built by Charles Cammell in the early 1840s, the first of many such works alongside the railway to Rotherham. As the conical tops of cementation furnaces indicate, this was a works that produced carbon steel for the manufacture of cutlery and edge tools, but from 1861 Cammell began to roll mild steel rails at the works.
BY COURTESY OF THE IRONBRIDGE GORGE MUSEUM TRUST

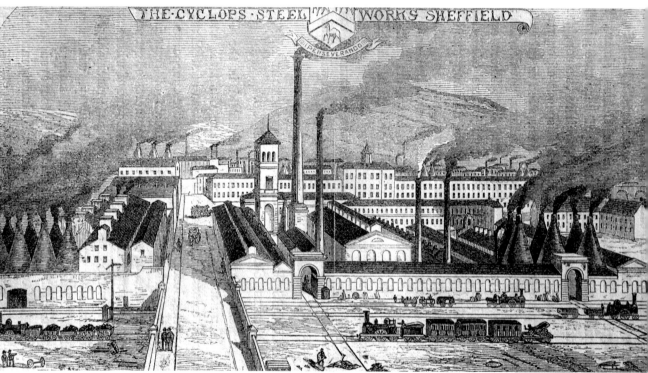

were turnpiked from 1756, and the supply of coal for smiths' fires was improved as navigation on the river Don was extended. Sheffield's most precious natural resource was its abundant water power, and by 1800 more than 100 waterwheels were employed grinding cutlery and edge tools. However, steam power was used for grinding from 1786, and by the 1850s more than 100 steam engines were working. There was much sub-contracting in the cutlery trade, and some 'public wheels' supplied tenants with room and power in return for rent. The first cutlery 'factory' is recognised to have been the Sheaf Works, opened by William Greaves in 1823. In 1850 it was one of five cutlery firms that employed more than a hundred people. Sheffield's population grew to 185,000 in 1861 and exceeded a quarter of a million by the mid-1870s. Manufacturing followed traditional patterns and distinctive local specialisations: table knives and scissors were made in the city; scythes at Norton; sickles at Eckington; files, table forks, gimlets and braces-and-bits at Ecclesfield; and spring knives at Worrall.

A prospect of Sheffield drawn in 1737 shows only two conical cementation furnaces, but their numbers multiplied after Benjamin Huntsman's discovery of 1740 enabled crucible steel to be made from the blister steel they produced. The scale of steel making increased from 1838. New works in the Don Valley multiplied existing technology, with rows of conical cementation furnaces alongside tall buildings containing crucible furnaces, with rectangular stacks up to 40 feet high. In 1835 Sheffield produced about 10,000 tons of crucible steel, a total that increased tenfold in the next 40 years. Sir John Brown, having profitably manufactured spring railway buffers, built the Atlas Works in Savile Street from 1857, and in steel making began to use his own puddled iron rather than Swedish bars. Charles Cammell built the Cyclops Works, the first along the railway to Rotherham, before 1845, while Thomas Firth and his son Mark developed the Norfolk Works, which included Sheffield's largest rolling mill. Thomas Jessop established the Brightside works in 1835 and exported cutlery steel to the United States. The largest plant of this kind was the River Don works of Naylor, Vickers and Co. which, under the management from the 1850s of Thomas and Albert Vickers, could make 15,000 tons of crucible steel *per annum*.

Mild steel was unsuitable for cutlery and edge tools, but Henry Bessemer opened a steelworks in Sheffield in 1858, and John Brown in 1860 and Charles Cammell in 1861 began to roll mild steel rails at their existing works. Brown opened a new mill in 1863 where he rolled armour plate, which he was selling to the Royal Navy by 1871. His company purchased the Clydebank Ship-building & Engineering Co. in 1899, and was best known in the twentieth century for shipbuilding. The steel-making company established by Charles Cammell followed a similar course, amalgamating in 1903 with William Laird, the Birkenhead shipbuilder). Naylor, Vickers & Co. manufactured steel shafting for ships from 1868 and screw propellers from 1872, and from the 1880s produced artillery. In 1871 Samuel Griffiths listed 91 Bessemer converters in Great Britain, of which 22 were in the Sheffield area. This marked the peak of Sheffield's importance in

The Sheffield area. The tributaries of the Don provided a good source of water power for grinding wheels.

the production of mild steel. In that year, it has been estimated, the major steelmakers of Sheffield were exporting to the USA around three times the amount of steel as the entire domestic US output. Subsequently the city's steelmakers concentrated on carbon steels and then on alloy steels, used in trades which were already well established in 1700.

Beyond Sheffield: iron making elsewhere in west Yorkshire

Iron making in the West Riding of Yorkshire was important throughout the eighteenth and nineteenth centuries, although it was not the region's principal industry, and the output of West Riding works never exceeded 10 per cent of the national total. Four charcoal-fuelled blast furnaces were listed in 1717, when up to ten forges were working. The Spencer family of Cannon Hall, Barnsley, were as influential in Yorkshire as the Foleys were in the West Midlands. Through marriage, John Spencer I and his son John II acquired estates in Cawthorne that were rich in coal and iron ore, as well as shares in several ironworks. By the 1740s the family had interests in nine groups of ironworks in Yorkshire and north Derbyshire, including Rockley Furnace in Worsborough which worked until the 1740s and still stands, Kirkstall Forge, and Wortley Top Forge, which produced railway axles until 1929, and is conserved. The Spencers controlled the whole process from raw material to finished product: they produced nails – chiefly for sale in London – made from rods slit in their slitting mills from wrought iron

which had been refined in their forges from pig iron smelted in their blast furnaces using ore produced in their mines. In the 1740s William Spencer employed 120 nailers. From 1717 the forge at Colne Bridge was leased by William Westby Cotton who developed a rival concern, including a blast furnace at Bretton and the forge at Kilnhurst. There was competition for charcoal in the region, and no prospect of increasing its supply. The result was that William Spencer withdrew from the iron trade in 1748, and most of Yorkshire's charcoal-fuelled furnaces had been blown out by 1780.

The celebrated ironworks at Rotherham was established by the three sons of Joseph Walker, nailmaker and farmer of Grenoside, in the parish of Ecclesfield north of Sheffield. Samuel and Aaron Walker built an air furnace in 1741 behind the family home, where they melted scrap iron to cast pots. In partnership with the third brother, Jonathan, and John Booth, a nail chapman, they set up a foundry at Masbrough in 1746–48, and in 1757 leased the Holmes estate, where there was already an ironworks. They rebuilt the blast furnace, added two more, and by 1782 had a Boulton & Watt engine to recirculate the water that provided power for the bellows. They began to manufacture cannon in 1772. By 1782, when the enterprise passed to the next generation, it included three blast furnaces at Holmes, as well as a foundry which cast parts for the iron bridge demonstrated by Tom Paine in London in 1790–91, and for the bridges at Sunderland, Staines, Yarm, and Southwark. Lord Torrington, witnessing the boring of a howitzer in 1792, observed that 'Mr Walker is, with his ironworks in this neighbourhood, what Sir Richard Arkwright is with his cotton works in Derbyshire'. Samuel Walker was also a partner in a leadworks at Newcastle-upon-Tyne, while his son Joseph was a co-founder of Barber, Walker & Co., the Nottinghamshire coal-mining company. The family was involved in banking from 1791–92, and in the early 1820s transferred its iron-making interests to Gospel Oak, Tipton.

An ironworks at Park Gate, north of Rotherham, which opened in 1823, subsequently became the

The small Low Mill blast furnace at Silkstone, near Barnsley, was built to smelt local iron ore with coke about 1820, but it appears to have operated only for about two years, and for that reason provides good evidence of furnace construction and technology of the early nineteenth century.
BY COURTESY OF DAVID HEY

property of Samuel Beel, whose sons incorporated the Park Gate Iron Co. in 1864. Initially it was a puddling forge, using pig iron from the Holmes blast furnaces, but a mill for rolling rails was built in 1845, and in the 1850s many of the plates for I. K. Brunel's *Great Eastern* were produced there. By 1872 Park Gate included 5 blast furnaces, 90 puddling furnaces and 6 rolling mills, and the company continued to work the Holmes furnaces. The workforce at Park Gate in 1861 included puddlers from Tipton, Oldbury and West Bromwich, and furnacemen from Merthyr and Brynmawr.

From 1782 the 4th Earl Fitzwilliam encouraged industrial development at Elsecar, between Rotherham and Barnsley. There were rich mines of ironstone at nearby Tankersley Park, served by a branch of the Dearne & Dove Canal, opened in 1804. In 1795–1800 John and William Darwin from Sheffield built two blast furnaces at Elsecar. Walkers of Rotherham built a furnace about a mile to the west which was the nucleus of the Milton Ironworks, taking its name from the Fitzwilliams' Northamptonshire estate. In 1824 the works passed to William and Robert Graham, whose foundry made the cast-iron beam supplied in 1836 for the engine at Elsecar New Colliery and the Leawood Pump on the Cromford Canal in 1849. Darwin & Co. went bankrupt in 1827, and the Elsecar works was then directly controlled by the Fitzwilliam estate until 1849, when it was leased to the Black Country ironmasters William and George Dawes, who had works at Oldbury and West Bromwich. They also took over the Milton Ironworks and worked both until the furnaces were blown out in 1883. A once open-sided rolling-mill building with a 70-foot (21.5 m) span wrought-iron roof remains at Elsecar, as do many ironworkers' houses, including Old Row and Station Row built before 1801, and the 28 dwellings in Reform Row completed in 1837 which were commended by a parliamentary commission. In 1870 the combined works included 6 blast furnaces, 61 puddling furnaces and 10 rolling mills. More than 100 of the 400 ironworkers in Elsecar in 1861 had been born in the Black Country, including puddlers, shinglers and sheet-iron rollers from Tipton, Oldbury, West Bromwich and Bradley.

A charcoal-fired blast furnace was worked by the Spencers at Chapeltown, south-west of Elsecar,

Workshops that once formed part of the Elsecar Ironworks.

Cottages in Reform Row, Elsecar, which date from 1837.

but was blown out in the 1770s. Two coke-fuelled furnaces were built there in 1793, on the land of the 4th Earl Fitzwilliam, by George Newton and Thomas Chambers, from 1789 partners in the Phoenix Foundry in Sheffield. Coal and iron ore initially came from shallow workings in the surrounding woodland. The furnaces were the nucleus of the Thorncliffe Ironworks, whose products included castings for Tower Bridge and for the Eddystone Lighthouse. By

↗ The huge complex of the Bowling Ironworks near Bradford, around 1870, when it produced crucible steel as well as the wrought-iron boiler plates for which it was famous.

the 1890s Newton Chambers employed 8,000 people in its mines, ironworks and coal distillation plants.

The forge complex at Stocksbridge, in the narrow valley of the river Don ten miles north-west of Sheffield, was established in a former cotton mill in 1842 by Samuel Fox, a Derbyshire man who had been apprenticed to a wire drawer at Hathersage. In 1851 Fox designed the Paragon umbrella frame made of U-sections of steel wire, and in 1855 began to make frames for crinoline dresses from wire rolled in a similar manner. He produced his own crucible steel from 1854, and in 1862 the works included two cementation furnaces, a crucible melting shop, rolling mills and four-storey buildings, probably for wire drawing. In 1862 Fox built a Bessemer steel plant that by 1870 was making rails, springs and rods for railway companies. The Stocksbridge works remained in production in 2012.

Farther north in the West Riding, the particular qualities of the local iron ore enabled two ironworks near Bradford to produce plate which makers of steam engines throughout Britain were proud to use in their boilers. The blast furnace built at Bowling in 1788 was the nucleus of a complex which by 1872 included 6 blast furnaces, 21 puddling furnaces, a steel plant with 100 crucible pot furnaces, and mills for rolling plates, bars and tyre iron. It employed about 1,000 workers and 2,000 miners. The nearby Low Moor works, founded by the mineralogist Joseph Dawson, was built around 1791, the date displayed on a surviving octagonal office building. In 1872 it included 8 blast furnaces, 40 puddling furnaces and 7 rolling mills, producing what Samuel Griffiths regarded as 'the most valued iron in the kingdom'. The workforce in 1861 consisted overwhelmingly of men born in the immediate locality, who lived among coal miners and spinners, weavers and finishers of worsted cloth, manufacturers of cards for wool combing, and engineers making textile machinery. The principal owner, Charles Hardy, oversaw the works from Odsall House. In the 1820s the Low Moor company took over the Shelf Ironworks, established in 1794 by Aydon and Elwell, one of whose early employees was John Banks, the popular lecturer on science and designer of the elliptical cast-iron beam for steam engines. The foundry supplied about 20 swivelling bridges to canal and dock companies between 1804 and 1824, as well as iron bridges at Sowerby Bridge and Horsforth. Bowling closed in 1898, but Low Moor made iron until 1928

The Kirkstall Forge on the river Aire upstream from Leeds was active in the 1580s, produced nailers' rods around 1700, and made spades and shovels in the 1780s, before turning to forging axles for carts in 1798. From the 1830s it specialised in axles and wheels for railway vehicles, in hydraulic machinery and steam hammers, one of which, dating from the 1860s, is preserved in railway workshops at Melbourne, Victoria. The forge continued in production until 2002. Ironworks were also established in the mid-nineteenth century at Monk Bridge in Leeds, Farnley, Ardsley, Beeston Manor and Hepworth. In 1872 the West Riding's 45 blast furnaces provided only 4.6 per cent of national output, but their significance lay in the unique qualities of some of their products. Boiler plate from Low Moor and Bowling and umbrella ribs from Stocksbridge had no equals.

Iron making in lowland Lancashire

Ironworks in south Lancashire were few but important. The Lancashire industry is recorded inconsistently in statistical returns, which makes quantitative assessment difficult. A charcoal-fuelled blast furnace was built at Holme Chapel between Todmorden and Burnley about 1700 by Robert Wilmott but closed about 1750. Carr Mill furnace at Ashton-in-Makerfield worked with charcoal between about 1720 and 1751 and was briefly revived as a coke-fuelled works in 1759, when its partners included George Perry of Coalbrookdale. Much of the wrought-iron made in Lancashire, whether refined from pig or re-worked from scrap, was used for making tools, nails or wire.

Park Bridge Ironworks on the river Medlock near Ashton-under-Lyne was established in the 1780s by Samuel Lees, and was subsequently managed by his widow. Wrought iron was rolled into forms for which there was a ready sale in Lancashire, including rivets and rollers for textile machines. Park Bridge village, with terraced cottages of the 1850s and 1860s, a Mechanics' Institute of 1863 and the church of St James of 1866, is largely intact, and the ruins of the

➤ An engraving by Watkins after an original by Harwood, showing the works of Rothwell, Hick & Rothwell at Bolton, Lancashire, around 1832. The firm was established in 1830 and, inspired by the Rainhill Trails, began to manufacture steam locomotives. Benjamin Hick left to set up his own works in Bolton in 1832, but the foundry continued to build steam locomotives until 1864. In all they built around 200 locomotives, many going for export. In 1866 the company won '… the contract for the construction and erection of eight beam engines for £54,570, and are proceeding with the work at their foundry at Bolton' for the Abbey Mills pumping station in London.

ironworks, which closed in the 1940s, are interpreted at a visitor centre.

The ironworks on the Haigh Hall estate was established in 1789, incorporating the forge at Brock Mill where Angerstein observed the melting of scrap to provide wrought iron for making hoes, shovels and sugar-cane knives for the West Indies. By the mid-1790s two blast furnaces provided pig for a foundry that produced shot and shell for the Forces, sugar mills, and castings for steam engines, one of which, with classical detailing and bearing the date 1818, was recorded in 2009 at a sugar plantation in Haiti. Smelting ceased at the Haigh works from 1856, after which it was managed by Henry Birley who employed 490 men and boys in 1861 producing bar iron and mining tools. In 1858, on the east bank of the Leeds & Liverpool Canal, the 24th Earl of Crawford built the Kirkless Ironworks, which in 1865 was incorporated in the Wigan Coal & Iron Co., an amalgamation of the earl's collieries with other companies. By 1870 the ironworks included ten blast furnaces, rolling mills, and engineering workshops which manufactured locomotives between 1865 and 1912. Notwithstanding the size of Wigan Coal & Iron, the Lancashire iron industry remained of modest size in the 1870s. Iron ore was smelted at the six blast furnaces of the Ditton Brook Iron Co. built in 1862, but the works was adapted as a grease factory by 1900. Nineteen forges in lowland Lancashire in 1872 had only 338 puddling furnaces between them. Most were parts of large engineering concerns such as the textile machinery manufacturers, Platt Bros of Oldham, and the Gorton plant of the Manchester, Sheffield & Lincolnshire Railway. (See pages 340 ff. for the iron industry of Furness.)

The Irish and Scottish iron-making industries

Iron smelting had a modest presence in nineteenth-century Ireland. A coke-fired furnace was built in 1788 at Arigna, Co. Roscommon, on the site of a charcoal-fired works. It was blown by a Boulton & Watt engine, but worked spasmodically, and closed in 1838. Two coke-fired furnaces were built in 1852 at Creevelea, Co. Leitrim, on the site of another charcoal furnace. They worked for less than five years but were briefly revived in 1861–62 using peat as fuel. One of the two still stands.

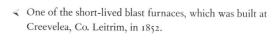
◁ One of the short-lived blast furnaces, which was built at Creevelea, Co. Leitrim, in 1852.

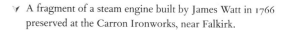
▽ A fragment of a steam engine built by James Watt in 1766 preserved at the Carron Ironworks, near Falkirk.

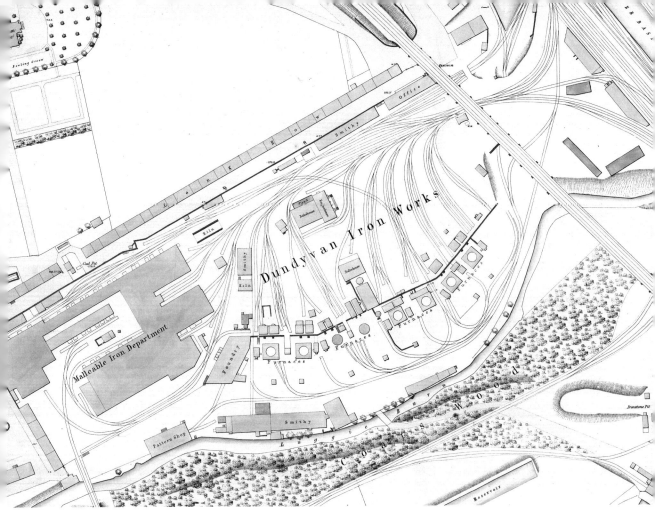

A map of the Dundyvan Ironworks, Coatbridge, in 1858, showing eight blast furnaces with adjacent structures square in plan, which were probably hot blast stoves – it was the development of hot blast techniques that made it possible to smelt the Scottish Black Band ores. The Cowper Stove, usually circular in plan, which was the usual means of providing hot blast in the late nineteenth century, was only invented in 1857. The 'Malleable Iron Department' to the west of the complex would have contained puddling furnaces for refining wrought iron and rolling mills for shaping it into rails or plates.

In Scotland iron working grew substantially after 1820. Scottish bloomeries had been productive in the Middle Ages, but in 1700 it is probable that less iron was being smelted in Scotland than in Ireland. Charcoal-fired blast furnaces smelting haematite from the Lake District were built in the 1720s and 1730s in Argyll and Inverness-shire. The first coke-fired blast furnace in Scotland, at Carron Ironworks on the Firth of Forth near Falkirk, was blown in on 1 January 1760. Its partners included John Roebuck and Samuel Garbett, John Glassford, a Glasgow tobacco merchant who owned 25 ships, and William Cadell, a merchant trading in iron with Russia and Sweden. John Smeaton designed new waterwheels and blowing cylinders in 1767, and if the company had not encountered financial difficulties James Watt might have developed the steam engine at Carron. T. S. Aston remarked, perhaps mischievously, that the lighting of the furnace 'may serve to mark, for those who like to be precise in such matters, the beginning of the industrial revolution in Scotland'. Furnaces were built in Lanarkshire and in Ayrshire in the next 50 years, but they scarcely amounted to a revolution. Carron prospered on armaments, but in 1773 the Admiralty refused to take more of its guns.

Production was re-organised by Charles Gascoigne, Garbett's son-in-law and managing partner from 1769, who improved the short-barrelled 'carronade', originally invented by Robert Melville, which was produced until the early 1850s. Under threat of bankruptcy, Gascoigne migrated in 1786 to Russia where he established ironworks and was given a title.

Svedenstierna proves a revealing account of iron making in Scotland in 1803. At Carron there were five blast furnaces, cupolas and air furnaces, boring mills for cannon and steam engine cylinders and a small forge, all surrounded by a wall, and the Swede observed that, 'one cannot in any circumstances get to see these works'. William Cadell's descendants worked the Cramond Ironworks on the edge of Edinburgh, where water-powered forges and rolling mills produced spades and shovels from scrap imported from Holland

and steel from Russian and Swedish iron. *En route* to Glasgow he visited the Wilsontown Ironworks, founded in 1779 by John and William Wilson, which closed in 1782 but re-opened in 1784 after advice from men from Coalbrookdale. It closed again in 1812, but was worked between 1821 and 1842 by William Dixon. Svedenstierna visited the Clyde Ironworks at Tollcross, established in 1786 by John Mackenzie, who had been dismissed as manager of Wilsontown in 1782, and saw three blast furnaces, a foundry for cannon, and a forge opened after a workman gained experience at Coalbrookdale. The Clyde works was taken over in 1810 by James Dunlop, and smelted iron ore until 1978. On his way south Svedenstierna saw three blast furnaces on Lord Dundonald's estate at Muirkirk, but not, apparently, the nearby Glenbuck Ironworks which had been established in the 1790s by John Rumney and which closed in 1813. Nor did he visit the three furnaces of 1802 at Shotts, nor the nearby Omoa furnace, built in the 1790s and named after the fortress of San Fernando de Omoa in Honduras, captured in 1779 by the landowner Colonel William Dalrymple. Svedenstierna hoped to meet the already famous David Mushet but found that he had left the Clyde Ironworks for the Calder Works, Coatbridge, which had been established in the 1790s. It was purchased in 1801 by William Dixon, a Northumbrian coal viewer, with whom Mushet formed a partnership before he left for Derbyshire and the Forest of Dean.

Three years after Svedenstierna's visit the output of Scottish blast furnaces totalled 22,840 tons, or 9.4 per cent of the national output, but by 1823 it had increased only to 24,500 tons, or 5.4 per cent. Svedenstierna observed that the charge at Carron included nodules collected on the shores of the Firth of Forth, and that Scottish furnaces generally lacked supplies of ore. Mushet in 1801 identified

Summerlee Iron Works

◁ The blast furnaces at the Summerlee Works at Coatbridge, like those at Dundyvan, were ranged in a line, and raw materials were delivered to them at a high level by standard-gauge railways. The use of hot blast techniques was pioneered at Summerlee. After the works closed in 1926 the remains were covered over, but have been partly excavated in recent years.
BY COURTESY OF THE NATIONAL LIBRARY OF SCOTLAND

the Black Band ironstone, found in proximity to commonly worked seams of coal, but it could not then be smelted. However, Scottish iron making was transformed from the 1820s by developments at the Clyde Ironworks. In 1824 James Beaumont Neilson experimented by heating the blast before it entered the furnace, achieving economies in fuel consumption and enabling the smelting of Black Band ores. Hot blast was installed at the Clyde works, whose partners Colin Dunlop and John Wilson took shares in Neilson's patent of 1828, which lasted, although challenged, until 1843. Blast furnaces then proliferated in the parishes of Old and New Monkland around the towns of Coatbridge and Airdrie, an area served by the Monkland Canal, which had opened in 1791. Much of the capital invested in ironworks came from men of humble origins who had leased land for mining, and profitably sold coal that was transported to Glasgow by canal. One ironmaster in 1864 declared:

> There are few districts in Scotland in which
> the results of individual energy are so fully
> exemplified as in Coatbridge. It may be
> indeed said to have been the cradle of the iron
> manufacture of the kingdom; and, in bringing
> up and recording the events of the past, and
> the names of the enterprising few who, by
> their science and skill, explored and searched
> the earth, and expended their capital to benefit
> their fellow-men, we shall find their names not
> amongst the great or the titled, and we will
> not require to search amongst parchments of a
> century back to trace their genealogy. It is from
> the ranks of the ploughmen, the blacksmiths,
> the mechanics the weavers and the miners of
> the district that they have sprung.

Alexander Baird, a farmer in Monkland, leased mining rights on several estates from 1816, and in 1826 began working mines at Gartsherrie, which from 1829 were served by a branch canal. His sons William and James Baird built a blast furnace which began work on 4 May 1830. By 1842 there were 16 furnaces at Gartsherrie, producing more than 100,000 tons of iron per year. The Bairds became influential. William Baird

was MP for Falkirk Burghs from 1841, chairman of the Caledonian Railway, governor of the Forth & Clyde Canal, and had an estate in Fife. William Dixon applied hot blast at the Calder Ironworks, built blast furnaces at Calderbank and Chapelhall, and became involved in litigation with Neilson. The Dundyvan Ironworks was founded in 1833 by Colin Dunlop and John Wilson of the Clyde Ironworks, and controlled by the latter after Dunlop's death. The Summerlee Ironworks, where the foundations of four furnaces and five hot blast stoves are displayed in a heritage park, was founded in 1835, and controlled by Neilson's family from the 1850s. The Carnbroe works began making iron in 1838, and the Langloan furnaces were built from 1841. There were 49 blast furnaces at Coatbridge in 1861, most of them with puddling forges alongside the furnaces. By 1864 there were other substantial iron-using works in Coatbridge: six puddling forges producing bar iron, rails and boiler plate; the North British Ironworks which specialised in wrought-iron axles; two manufacturers of iron tubes; two substantial foundries; and the only tinplate works in Scotland. The area was transformed within two decades as ironworkers were accommodated in ranks of single-storey cottages: the population of Old Monkland rose from 9,580 in 1831 to 27,332 in 1851, when the census recorded that 36 per cent of the population of Coatbridge were of Irish birth. The minister wrote in 1840:

> The population of this parish is at present
> advancing at an amazing rate, and this
> propensity is entirely owing to the local coal
> and iron trade, stimulated by the discovery of
> the black band of ironstone and the method
> of fusing iron by hot blast. New villages are
> springing up almost every month, and it is
> impossible to keep pace with the march of
> prosperity and the increase of the population.

If any place in Britain experienced an 'industrial revolution' it was Coatbridge in the 1830s and 1840s. The landscape was as terrifying as Merthyr and Coalbrookdale had been in earlier times. It was disturbing, even to one of the Gartsherrie family. Robert Baird wrote in 1845:

‘There is no worse place out of hell than this neighbourhood.’ Justin Parkes’ painting of the Gartsherrie Ironworks at night gives credence to the sentiment expressed by Robert Baird, one of the family who prospered most from the profitability of iron making around Coatbridge.

There is no worse place out of hell than this neighbourhood. At night the groups of blast furnaces on all sides might be imagined to be blazing volcanoes at most of which smelting is continued on Sundays and weekdays, day and night, without intermission. From the town comes a continual row of heavy machinery: this and the pounding of many steam hammers seemed to make even the very ground vibrate under one's feet. Fire, smoke and soot with the roar and rattle of machinery are its leading characteristics; the flames of its furnaces cast on the midnight sky a glow as if of some vast conflagration. Dense clouds of black smoke roll over it incessantly and impart to all its buildings a peculiarly dingy aspect. A coat of black dust overlies everything.

By the mid-1840s all the land around Coatbridge that could be exploited for coal and iron ore was controlled by the iron companies, and those who wished to expand looked to Ayrshire. The most bizarre development was the establishment in 1845 by the Bairds of an ironworks on the estate of the 13th earl of Eglinton, the host in August 1839 of the Eglinton Tournament, a shambolic revival of medieval jousting. Within sight of Eglinton Castle the Bairds built three (and by 1858 eight) blast furnaces and a puddling forge. In 1856 their Eglinton Company took over the Muirkirk furnaces which dated from 1787 and the Lugar furnaces of 1845. They also gained control of the Blair and Portland ironworks in Ayrshire. The partners in the Carnbroe Ironworks invested at Glengarnock, Ayrshire, in 1843, where they built 14 blast furnaces by 1872, and in 1854 they acquired a site at Ardeer to build another four. While other Coatbridge ironmasters invested in Ayrshire, John Wilson of Dundyvan leased land near Carron in 1845 to build the Kinneil Ironworks. Andrew Miller observed in 1864:

> The fruits of industry from this district have spread from Calder to Govan, from Gartsherrie to Eglinton and Blair, from Dunyvan to Kinniel, Lugar and Muirkirk, from Carnbroe to Glengarnock and Ardeer.

Henry Houldsworth, the Glasgow cotton spinner, established machine shops alongside his spinning mill at Anderstone, and in 1836 leased mining rights in Shotts. He built the Coltness Ironworks at Newmains in 1837, which by 1864 consisted of twelve blast furnaces, and from 1848 invested in the Dalmellington Ironworks in Ayrshire, where an Italianate blowing engine house still stands.

In 1852, as capital invested in Ayrshire furnaces began to yield profits, 775,000 tons of pig iron were being smelted in Scotland, some 28.7 per cent of the national output. The proportion diminished subsequently, and in 1868 Dundyvan was the first of the Coatbridge works to close. In 1864 1.16 million tons represented 24.3 per cent of the national figure, and the 1.2 million in 1870 just 20.2 per cent. In 1872 iron was smelted in Scotland at 29 works, in which there were 155 blast furnaces, of which 130 were in blast. There were 565 puddling furnaces in Scotland, some adjacent to furnaces but others in specialist forges. Production fell to 806,000 tons in 1874, only 13.5 per cent of national output. Some ironworks began to make steel, but more were closed before 1900.

The growth of Scottish iron making in the 1830s disturbed some comfortable patterns in the British iron trade. In 1849 Scottish foundry iron was being used by founders at Mansfield, Stowmarket, Dartford,

Perhaps the most significant consequence of the growth of iron making in Scotland was the stimulus it gave to the building of iron ships in yards along the river Clyde. This view of *circa* 1860 shows the Govan yard of Robert Napier, 'the father of Clyde shipbuilding'.

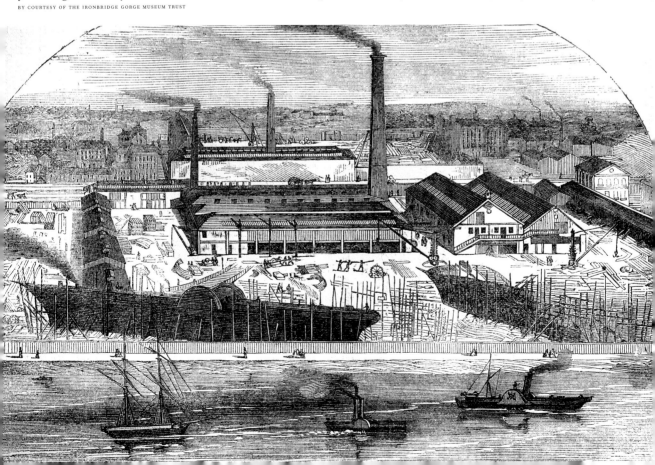

Reading, Poole and Plymouth, that from Calder, Shotts and Gartsherrie being particularly commended. In the long term, however, the importance of Scottish iron making lay not in English market towns but in the shipyards and engineering workshops of Clydeside. The iron passenger ship *Vulcan*, built for the Forth & Clyde Canal Co. in 1818, began a tradition of building iron ships in western Scotland, stimulated from the 1830s by increasing supplies of suitable iron. In the seven years 1846–52 some 233 steam vessels with iron hulls were built on the Clyde, a mean of 33.3 per year; but in the seven years 1862–68, less than two decades later, the total had increased to 1,494, or 213.4 ships per year. Other forms of heavy engineering

also prospered. In 1836 William Neilson, brother of the inventor of hot blast, established one of the many locomotive building works in Glasgow. Between 1800 and 1960 some 26,000 steam locomotives were constructed in the city. Robert Napier began making marine steam engines in 1823, and was subsequently called the 'father of Clyde shipbuilding'. William Arrol established a works at Dalmarnock in 1872, where he initially specialised in boiler making and then in structural steel, bridges and cranes. While Scottish companies dominated iron making for a relatively short time, their customers – primarily the engineers and shipbuilders on Clydeside – prospered for more than a century.

Iron in west Cumberland and Furness

The first ironworks established in Cumberland in the nineteenth century was at Cleator Moor, four miles from the west coast. Much of the parish was enclosed

between 1815 and 1825, but parts of the moor remained open common. The population increased from about 400 in 1801 to 818 in 1821, with the establishment of a

The iron and steel works of the Barrow Haematite Company at Barrow-in-Furness. Pig iron made from the phosphorus-free haematite ores of Furness was particularly suitable for steel making by the Bessemer process, introduced in 1856. The company blew in its first blast furnace at Barrow in 1859, and by 1872 had 16 blast furnaces, 18 Bessemer converters and 7 rolling mills. When the works was at its peak the furnaces produced up to a quarter of a million tons of pig iron annually.

A map showing the Barrow Haematite Works in 1893, with the blast furnaces, circular in plan, ranged in a line on the western side, interspersed with Cowper hot blast stoves, also circular in plan but of smaller diameter. The lengthy sheds of the steelworks containing Bessemer converters are to the east. It is evident from the map that raw materials were delivered to the iron and steelworks by standard-gauge railways.

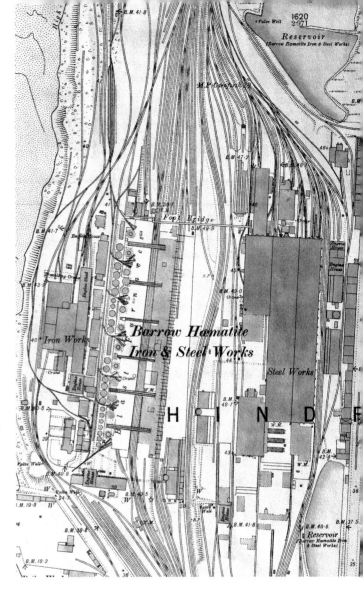

flax mill by Henry Birley, but Cleator was described in 1828 as 'a retired and rather pleasant village'. However, about 60 miners were extracting haematite in 1841, and in the following year the Haematite Ironworks Co. began to build blast furnaces on Cleator Moor. Within twenty years it employed 500 ironstone miners, when the population of the parish reached 3,995. In the late 1850s three blast furnaces employed about 80 men and produced about 500 tons of pig iron per week, and six furnaces were in blast by 1872. The iron company constructed terraced housing for its workers, but many cottages were built on the open moorland in deplorable circumstances: in 1857 six people died from sulphur dioxide poisoning caused by rain penetrating the broken slag upon which their homes had been constructed. The flax mill was revived by the Unitarian Thomas Ainsworth and employed 250 people by 1861, many of them wives and daughters of miners and furnacemen. The managers of the ironworks and mines came from Northumberland, Scotland and Cornwall, but more than 500 Irish-born people lived in the Cleator Moor district in 1851, and in 1861 four lodging-houses provided accommodation for young and single Irish flax workers and ironstone miners – in that year almost 60 per cent of the population was Irish-born. Another lodging-house accommodated migrants from the Isle of Man. The ironworks at Cleator Moor continued to operate until 1926, after which the district became one of the most socially deprived in Britain.

The phosphorus-free haematite ore of Furness (then part of Lancashire) and west Cumberland was particularly suited to the Bessemer process of steel making. The Oldside furnaces at Workington were blown in soon after Bessemer's revelation of his discovery in 1856, and the furnaces at Harrington worked from 1857. Five furnace complexes were established at Workington between 1862 and 1875, two at Maryport in 1868 and 1875, the works at Millom in 1867, the Lonsdale plant at Whitehaven in 1872, and the furnaces at Parton in 1872 and Distington in 1878. The first Bessemer plant in the region was installed at the West Cumberland works in 1872. By 1881 there were 49 furnaces in west Cumberland producing more than 100,000 tons of pig iron annually, but the boom was short-lived, because the Gilchrist-Thomas steel-making process worked with phosphoric pig iron, and Cumberland producers faced competition from imported Spanish ores.

The most spectacular growth was at Barrow-in-Furness, whose favourable situation enabled it to develop into a fully fledged town, comparable with Middlesbrough. Barrow, a hamlet in Dalton parish in the Furness hundred of Lancashire, had a population of about 250 in 1841, when industrial activity centred on a quay to which carters delivered iron ore for shipment to South Wales and the Black Country. The Furness Railway, opened in 1846, took over the work of the carters. The railway was extended to join the Ulverston & Lancaster Railway, opened in 1857, which, with long viaducts over the Kent and Leven estuaries, linked Furness to the national network. The growth of Barrow was supported by two of its dominant landowners, the dukes of Devonshire and Buccleuch – the Devonshire Dock opened in 1867, and the Buccleuch Dock in 1873. Nevertheless, development was principally due to a generation of entrepreneurs. Among these was James Fisher, who established a shipping line in 1847 to carry ore and slate. His company had 70 ships by 1868, developed links with the Baltic, the Mediterranean and North America, and generated revenue that was invested in shipbuilding. Another was Henry William Schneider, who managed an ore mine at Whiteriggs from 1839, and in 1841 began to send ore to Barrow. With his partner, the Scot Robert Hannay, he discovered new deposits in 1850. James Ramsden was apprenticed with Bury, Curtis & Kennedy, the Liverpool engineers, before becoming locomotive superintendent of the Furness Railway in 1846. He was general manager of the company from 1857 and managing director from 1866. The railway and the enterprise of Schneider, Hannay and Fisher stimulated iron-ore mining. Exports of ore from Barrow rose from 75,000 tons *per annum* in the early 1840s to 182,000 tons by 1849, and to more than half a million tons by 1860, when more than 1,000 iron-ore miners worked in the vicinity. When addressing the Iron & Steel Institute at Barrow in 1903, the Scottish-born steel magnate Andrew Carnegie recalled that the qualities of haematite ore from Furness were appreciated in Pittsburgh.

The Furness Railway supported the construction across the Pennines of the South Durham & Lancashire Union Railway, which opened in 1862, and delivered coking coal from Co. Durham. The principal beneficiary of the new railway was the Barrow Haematite Iron Co., established by Schneider and Hannay with the support of Ramsden, which blew in its first blast furnace in 1859. The company used hot blast to produce pig iron that was suitable for Bessemer steel making, and by 1861 had four blast furnaces working, and employed more than 170 men at the furnaces, and 500 ore miners. By 1872, with 16 furnaces, 18 Bessemer converters and 7 rolling mills, it was the largest British producer of Bessemer steel. The company sold steel rails to American railroad companies, despatching the first consignment of 450 tons to New York in one of Fisher's vessels. In 1871 Ramsden and others established the Barrow Ship-building Co., which used plate from the steelworks. The yard's first ship, Ramsden's yacht *Aries*, was launched in 1873, and 90 vessels were completed over the next eight years.

The stone terrace which Ramsden built at Salthouse in 1849 to accommodate railway employees was the nucleus of the town. The railway company purchased 7,000 acres for development in 1854, and two years later drew up plans for urban development, with the principal streets 60 feet (18.5 m) wide, much more generous than in most British cities. Sites were set aside for a market, public buildings and places of worship. Barrow became a borough in 1867, with Ramsden as its first mayor. The corporation met in the Furness Railway Co. offices, and the Gothic town hall, designed by the Belfast architect William Henry Lynn, was not completed until 1887. Ramsden supported the Barrow Building Society, which laid out streets where the idiosyncrasies of small speculators' developments can readily be recognised. Jute mills were established from 1869 providing employment for the town's women, and mills were also built to grind grain from the American prairies. Migrants from many parts of Britain sought their fortunes in Furness. Miners at Dalton, four miles inland from Barrow, included engineers and fitters from Camborne, Redruth and Gwennap, while blastfurnacemen had come from Tipton, Bilston and Sedgley in the Black Country, and from Ketley and Dawley in Shropshire. Scots migrants were accommodated in tenement blocks similar to those in Glasgow and Dundee. Barrow's population grew from 3,135 in

1861 to 18,911 in 1871 and 47,249 in 1881. In 1872 a visitor, reflecting on 18 years of change, commended the 'imposing shops, hotels; thousands of well-built houses; wide streets, running as they ought at right … elegant churches and chapels of all denominations abounding.' Growth subsequently faltered, but to the *New York Times* in 1881 Barrow appeared, 'a city of marvellous growth to be likened only to the Western cities of America'.

The furnaces at Carnforth, where the Furness Railway joins the main west-coast line from Lancaster to Carlisle, were effectively part of the Furness iron industry. Four blast furnaces were built in the 1860s by the Carnforth Haematite Iron Co. on land belonging to the Earl of Dudley, and used ore brought by rail from the west. Bessemer steel making began in 1872. Workers lived in a village originally built after 1861 called Dudley (now Millhead) where most of the inhabitants in 1881 were immigrants from the Black Country. The last furnace here worked until 1929.

Ironstone along the Jurassic Ridge

In 1850 iron making was a coalfield activity, and the coalfields remained the principal centres of production thereafter, but the discovery in the 1850s of ores in the oolitic limestone resulted in a proliferation of blast furnaces across the rural shires. Samples of Northamptonshire ore were displayed at the Great Exhibition in 1851; the extraction of ironstone at Blisworth and Wellingborough began soon afterwards; and by 1854 ore was being taken to Black Country furnaces. Thomas Butlin blew in a furnace in 1853 at Wellingborough, where his brother and partner employed 120 men in 1861. Northamptonshire's second furnace, close to the Grand Junction Canal and the railway at Heyford, was built by George Pell who had interests in lime burning, brick making and selling coal, and employed 160 men in the 1860s. Others who invested in the industry included William Butlin, owner of an engineering works in Northampton; William Ball, the Ulster-born proprietor of a foundry at Rothwell; C. H. Plevins, who had interests in ironworks in Derbyshire and Nottinghamshire; and Samuel Griffiths, chronicler of the iron industry, who for a time worked the Heyford furnace. He observed in 1873 that 'Northamptonshire, during the last fifteen years, has become a very important district for iron ore'. The county's output was then 779,314 tons, nearly 5 per cent of the national total. Much of it was despatched to the Black Country or to the Erewash Valley, providing cargoes for canal boats which had been deprived of more lucrative traffics by railway competition. But iron was also produced locally – furnaces were blown in at Finedon in 1866, Irthlingborough and Stowe in 1866, Islip in 1871 and Hunsbury Hill in 1873. By the 1880s Northamptonshire produced over 200,000 tons of pig iron a year, about 3 per cent of national output.

➤ The track of the tramway at Seend, Wiltshire, used to carry ironstone to the short-lived local blast furnaces, and then to a wharf on the Kennet & Avon Canal for onward shipment to South Wales.

In the early 1850s ironstone was uncovered during railway construction around Westbury, Wiltshire, and colliers from Radstock began to extract it in 1857. The Westbury Iron Co. built blast furnaces which in 1861 were directed by a manager from Co. Durham and employed more than a hundred men, including migrants from Bilston, Tipton, Backbarrow and Merthyr. Three blast furnaces were constructed from 1857 at Seend alongside the Kennet and Avon Canal. They used coke from South Wales and Somerset and employed about 50 men in 1861. The plant was demolished after difficulties were encountered in operating the furnaces, and ore from the quarries was subsequently despatched to South Wales.

Iron ore was discovered in the Leicestershire Wolds and in Lincolnshire in the 1850s. Charles Winn of Nostell Priory, Wakefield, owned an estate in Frodingham, including the townships of Scunthorpe and Appleby. His son, Rowland, had samples of ironstone analysed in 1859, and persuaded William and George Dawes of Elsecar Ironworks to begin mining, which they did in July 1860. Ore was initially taken to Yorkshire, but the brothers leased land from Winn and built three furnaces, the first of which was blown in during May 1864. Rowland Winn built six streets that were the nucleus of the town of Scunthorpe. A Leeds brickmaker, Joseph Cliff, worked a blast furnace from 1865, and the following year the North Lincolnshire Iron Co. built another at Frodingham Warren. In 1871 seven furnaces in the Scunthorpe area produced more than 30,000 tons of iron. By 1880 21 furnaces were making in excess of 200,000 tons, and steel making in Scunthorpe remains significant in the twenty-first century.

Iron in the North East: Tyneside, Weardale and Cleveland

The country's greatest ironmaster at the beginning of the eighteenth century was Sir Ambrose Crowley, and his business activities provide an interesting case study for the early phases of iron making in Britain. The son of a Quaker blacksmith from Stourbridge, Crowley was apprenticed to an ironmonger in the City of London. He made hardware in London, but in 1683 moved his manufacturing activities to Sunderland, although he continued to live in the capital, while the hub of his business was a depot at Greenwich. From 1690 he established new works in Co. Durham, extending along the river Derwent about two miles from its confluence with the Tyne to Winlaton. By 1707 this site included two forges, two slitting mills, two cementation furnaces, and smithies forging hoes, anchors, harpoons, frying pans, saws and patten rings. It was said that he employed a thousand men, many of them outworkers making nails. Crowley obtained iron on the London market, from British, Swedish and Russian sources, and transported it as ballast in collier ships returning to the North East. He gained contracts for supplying anchors, nails, tools, hinges

◁ One of the first coke-using ironworks in the North East was at Lemington, on the north bank of the river Tyne a short distance upstream from Newcastle, where the Tyne Iron Co. constructed a pair of blast furnaces about 1800. The two men appear to be tapping a blast furnace, but the most intriguing feature of the image is the small steam locomotive that was probably employed to move away waggons loaded with pig iron.

and locks to the Royal Navy – the scale of which may be gauged by the fact that he was owed £50,000 by the Navy Board at the time of his death in 1713 – but his son John Crowley developed a peace-time trade with Charleston, South Carolina, exporting the axes, spades, ox-chains, cane-cutting knives and hoes that were used in growing tobacco, sugar and rice on slave worked plantations. In 1755 Angerstein learned that the works supplied 300 tons of edge tools annually to the East India Company, and that orders for production were received from Greenwich every ten weeks. He observed a foundry casting flat irons and pans from scrap cannon imported from Holland, and a finery-and-chafery forge refining annually about 250 tons of wrought iron from English and American pig, although that was insignificant in comparison with the 1,950 tons of Russian and Swedish iron used in the smithies. The Crowley enterprise, from 1788 known as Crowley, Millington & Co., continued in the 1860s, by which time some much larger iron-making concerns were developing in the North East.

Iron making in the North East initially depended on ores from the coal measures, but supplies were less abundant here than in other coalfields. The Tyne Iron Co. built two blast furnaces at Lemington, near Newcastle, about 1800; three were constructed at Birtley, ten miles south, in 1827–28; and there was a single furnace at Wylam, near the Tyne west of the city, in 1844. The Derwent Iron Co. built furnaces in the mid-1830s which passed into other ownership, but the company constructed the first of seven blast furnaces at Consett in 1839–40, intending to use local ores. In 1844 the Weardale Iron Co. completed a furnace at Stanhope, and in 1845–46 built the first of five furnaces at Tow Law, nine miles south of Consett, which were intended to use both coal-measure ores and those from veins in nearby limestone hills. In the late 1830s ironmasters turned to ores from the Yorkshire coast. A trial cargo of 55 tons was received at Birtley on 18 May 1836, and from 1837 a partner in the Tyne Iron Co. at Lemington began to use nodules that had been collected on beaches near Whitby. Samples of ore from Grosmont, inland from Whitby, and from Kettleness on the coast, were tried at Wylam in 1838–39, when the Consett works also began to use ore

from the area. In 1842–43 Losh, Wilson & Bell built a furnace at Walker which was intended to smelt ores from north Yorkshire, and ore from this source was used by 1857 in the company's five furnaces. Farther south, furnaces were blown in at Hartlepool in 1839 and at Thornaby in 1840.

The development of large-scale iron making in Cleveland was initiated by John Vaughan, the Worcester-born son of a Welsh ironworker, who worked as a puddler at Dowlais, then in Carlisle, before his appointment in 1832 as manager of the Walker Ironworks. In 1841 he set up the Vulcan Ironworks in Middlesbrough with Henry Bolckow, a Mecklenburger then trading in Newcastle, refining Scottish pig iron in puddling furnaces. On 14 February 1846 they began to smelt iron ore at Witton Park, near newly opened pits around the inland terminus of the Stockton & Darlington Railway at Escomb. Witton Park prospered using local coking coal and ores from Cleveland. By 1857 the complex consisted of 93 coke ovens, 4 blast furnaces and a forge that could roll 700 tons of rails and 140 tons of plates per week. There were five blast furnaces and more than a hundred puddling furnaces in 1872, but the works closed in 1884. The inhabitants of Escomb were predominantly locally born coalminers, but Witton Park in 1861 was a community almost entirely made up of more than 400 ironworkers and their families, coke burners, blastfurnacemen, puddlers, shinglers, rollers of slabs, and labourers employed in shearing, straightening, dressing and boring holes in rails. More than 150 (37 per cent) were Irish-born, many of them finding their first homes in Co. Durham at lodging-houses kept by Irish landlords. About a quarter were Welsh, including many from Merthyr, Dowlais and Nant-y-glo whose religious needs were met by ministers from Anglesey and Cardiganshire. Black-Countrymen included puddlers and shinglers from Bilston, West Bromwich and Wednesbury.

In 1850, after years of scientific prospecting, John Vaughan and John Marley, a mining engineer, discovered a rich source of iron ore on Eston Moor. The following January Bolckow and Vaughan established a mine, and in 1852 set up blast furnaces at Eston and Middlesbrough. In 1864 Bolckow, Vaughan became a limited company with a capital of £5.5 million. Other companies followed their example. The thick seams of ore could be exploited relatively easily by drifts. Mines were opened in an arc extending through Middlesbrough, Saltburn, Loftus, Whitby, Grosmont, Battersby and Guisborough and from the coast to Rosedale, where a range of calcining kilns forms a striking monument. The Tyneside ironmasters Losh, Wilson & Bell from Walker developed the Lofthouse Mines at Skinningrove from 1859, while Bell Brothers of Wylam began mining at Normanby in 1853 and worked the Cliff Mines from 1860. The furnaces at Jarrow were built in 1857 by Charles Palmer, and those

he took over at Wallsend in 1856 relied on Cleveland ores.

More Cleveland ore was smelted in and around Middlesbrough, where coking coal from Co. Durham was easily accessible. More than 40 blast furnaces were built between 1850 and 1861. Griffiths in 1872 calculated that there were 104 in Cleveland and more than 140 in the North East broadly defined. Bells built the Port Clarence furnaces north of the Tees in 1862, and Sir Isaac Lowthian Bell became an acknowledged leader of Cleveland industry. William Hopkins and Thomas Snowdon opened the Teesside Ironworks in 1853, and William Cochrane, a Coseley-born coal

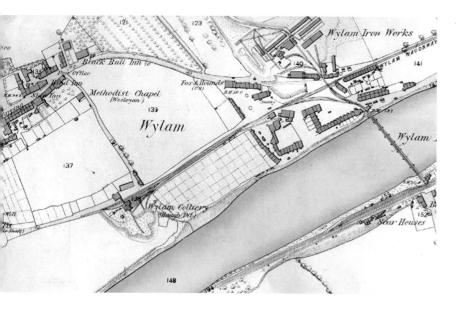

A map published around 1860 of Wylam on the river Tyne, showing Wylam Colliery, where the fathers of both Timothy Hackworth and George Stephenson were employed, and where William Hedley built the locomotive *Puffing Billy* in 1813 (see page 61). The single blast furnace at the Wylam Ironworks was built at some time before 1844, but was blown out for the last time in 1864. Part of the Wylam Waggonway can also be seen here. This early waggonway was built in the mid-eighteenth century to deliver coal from Wylam and a number of other local collieries to the staithes at Lemington five miles farther down the north bank of the Tyne.

The imposing remains of the iron ore calcining kilns at Rosedale.

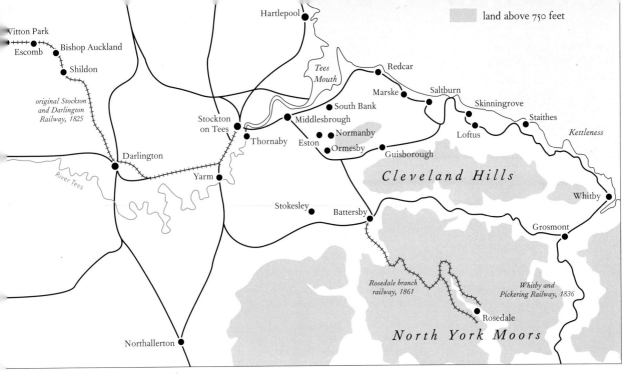

Labels on map: Vitton Park, Escomb, Bishop Auckland, Shildon, original Stockton and Darlington Railway, 1825, Hartlepool, Tees Mouth, Redcar, Saltburn, Marske, Skinningrove, Staithes, South Bank, Middlesbrough, Stockton on Tees, Normanby, Loftus, Kettleness, Thornaby, Eston, Ormesby, Darlington, Yarm, Guisborough, Cleveland Hills, River Tees, Whitby, Stokesley, Battersby, Grosmont, Rosedale branch railway, 1861, Whitby and Pickering Railway, 1836, Northallerton, Rosedale, North York Moors

⋏ The iron-mining and -working area of Cleveland.

master from Elswick, built a furnace at Ormesby in 1854. Bernhard Samuelson, a Hamburg-born Jew, who had directed a foundry at Tours and owned agricultural engineering works in Banbury, built the first part of his South Bank works in 1854. He was introduced to John Vaughan at the Cleveland Agricultural Show in 1852 by C. B. Dockray, the civil engineer who built the first railway to Banbury. Middlesbrough's population grew from 7,431 in 1851, to 19,416 in 1861, and 55,934 in 1881.

Pig iron made with Cleveland ores had too high a phosphorus content for use in Bessemer steel making, and large sums were invested in puddling forges. Samuel Griffiths remarked of Cleveland that 'the manufacture of malleable iron has become a great staple', and listed more than 2,000 puddling furnaces in the North East. Samuelson produced 3,000 tons of iron per week at South Bank in 1870 when he began building the Britannia Ironworks, a forge with a capacity of 1,400 tons of puddled iron per week which shared the name of his foundry at Banbury. He sold it in 1879 to Arthur Dorman and Albert Long after he had tried to make steel by the Siemens-Martins process at South Stockton. In 1873 firms in the North East

produced 340,000 tons of wrought-iron rails, but with competition from steel rails the output in 1897 was only 6,749 tons, and by 1896 only 300 puddling furnaces remained. Bolckow, Vaughan built a Bessemer plant in 1876, but the future success of the Teesside ironworks depended on the Gilchrist-Thomas open-hearth process demonstrated by its inventors at Eston in 1879. A succession of amalgamations followed from which Dorman Long emerged as the dominant company in the region.

Ironworks were also established in the hills of South Durham as railways – the first being the Stanhope & Tyne of 1834 – created links with the coast. Charles Attwood, whose family was involved in the iron trade at Halesowen, moved in 1809 to Gateshead where he worked in glass making. Through contacts with lead-mining entrepreneurs he realised that the iron carbonate ores found in Weardale were of high quality and situated close to the Durham coalfield. He became managing partner of the Weardale Iron Co., established in 1842 with capital from Barings' Bank, which in 1845 began construction of five blast furnaces at Tow Law, an area of open moorland in the parishes of Wolsingham and Brancepeth. The company headquarters, now

Consett Iron Works. (1065)

⋏ The first blast furnaces at Consett in the hills of County Durham were built by the Derwent Iron Co. in 1839–40. The works grew rapidly in the late nineteenth century, bringing in iron ore first from Cleveland and then from overseas. This postcard is evidence of its enormous size by the early years of the twentieth century. The works closed in the 1980s.
BY COURTESY OF GEORGE NAIRN

Attwood Place overlooks the playing field where the ironworks once stood. More than 600 miners and iron-workers, about 10 per cent of them Irish-born, lived at Tow Law in 1861, in two-storey rubble stone cottages built in twos and threes along the main street. The company also developed collieries, the first of them the Black Prince mine, and linked its enterprises by a private railway. In 1860 Attwood acquired mining rights in Wolsingham, where there was a traditional manufacture of spades, edge tools and butchers' steels employing about 30 men in 1861. Subsequently he established blast furnaces and a forge at Tudhoe, nine miles south-east of Tow Law. The company's iron was suited to the Bessemer process, and Attwood himself took out a patent for casting steel in 1862 for which he built a plant at Wolsingham, and sought advice from Sir William Siemens. A Siemens furnace was built at Tow Law by Attwood's manager, William Shaw, and worked from Christmas Day 1867. Nearly 400 miners in 1861 were extracting iron ore from mines in the parish of Stanhope.

The Derwent Iron Company's blast furnaces at Consett, built in 1839–40, were scarcely viable when they used local ores. Nodules from Whitby had to be transshipped several times, as did Cleveland ores

delivered from 1851. In 1857 the Northumberland & Durham District Bank, to which the company was indebted, hit a crisis which led to restructuring in 1864. The new directors closed the satellite blast furnaces at Crookhall, a mile from the main works, and at Bradley near Leadgate, and rebuilt the seven furnaces at Consett, equipping them with Cowper stoves, and installing eight beam blowing engines, four of them from the Lilleshall Company. The landmark 250 foot (77 m) high chimney, which exhausted furnace waste gases, was inaugurated on 28 May 1868. In 1872 more than 150 puddling furnaces in the company's colossal forge were producing wrought iron that was rolled into plates for shipbuilding and rails for use in the United States and the Colonies but, as one director recalled, 'About 1876 came the extinction of the iron rail trade and the substitution of steel rails'. Thereafter the company concentrated on shipbuilding plates, and erected Siemens Martin steel furnaces in 1882. In 1872 the Consett company formed a consortium with the Dowlais Co., Krupp of Essen and the Ybarra Co. in Spain to work haematite mines near Bilbao. Once steel making began the Consett furnaces ceased using Cleveland ore, and by 1893 they were charged only with Spanish ore. A town, whose development was controlled from 1864 by a Local Board of Health, grew up around the ironworks. One of its longest terraces was called Staffordshire Row, which suggests that its first workers were from the Black Country, but there was subsequently an inward migration of Irishmen, and in the 1840s and 1850s Consett was riven by sectarian conflicts. In spite of its reliance on imported ore delivered on steeply graded railways Consett continued to produce iron and steel into the second half of the twentieth century.

The Weardale Coal & Iron Co.'s works at Tudhoe, using coking coal from nearby pits, was established on open moorland in 1853 with the intention of producing bars and plates from pig smelted from Weardale ores. Tudhoe's population rose from 400 in 1851 to 1,359 in 1861 and to more than 5,000 by 1871. The works included 56 puddling furnaces in 1872 providing wrought iron for five rolling mills. By 1861 there was a labour force of more than 400, some from the Black Country, some from Shropshire, and several from South Wales and the Forest of Dean. More than half were Irish-born, probably the highest percentage at any ironworks in the North East. The works made steel by 1890, but closed in 1901. The nearby Ferryhill Ironworks, designed to use ore from Rosedale in Cleveland, was established by James Morrison in 1859, and by 1872 comprised eight blast furnaces. The company collapsed in 1879, and the works closed in 1890 after less than 30 years. The iron industry in Cleveland and the North East was at a pinnacle of prosperity in 1870, but that prosperity was soon tempered.

Conclusions

In the 170 years reviewed in this book iron making in Britain changed utterly. In 1700 furnaces and forges had been fired with charcoal; in 1870 coal was the fuel used in almost every British ironworks. In 1700 bellows and mills had been universally worked by water power, and most ironworks were located alongside streams in the depths of the countryside; by 1870 the landscapes around Coatbridge, Merthyr and Middlesbrough were dominated by furnaces and forges, billowing smoke and raging flames. In 1870 steam engines powered almost all the industry's machinery, although some waterwheels still turned at works that continued to operate on ancient sites. In 1700 Britain's furnaces and forges had not been able to meet the demands of the nation's iron-working craftsmen, whose needs had to be met by imports; but in 1870 the British iron industry dominated world markets, and only the specialist requirements of steelmakers were fulfilled by imported iron. Some iron-making companies, following the precedent set by Abraham Darby II in Shropshire in the 1750s, had grown into very large integrated concerns; some of them, such as the Crawshays of Cyfarthfa, major producers of coal; others, such as the Butterley Co., builders of bridges, steam engines and other heavy engineering products. Over the period iron displaced wood as the material used in the construction of machinery and transmission systems, and such characteristic symbols of the industrial revolution as the steam locomotive, the spinning mule and the Lancashire loom were essentially iron artefacts. Other iron objects – hardware from the Black Country, cutlery and edge tools from the Sheffield region and, above all, rails from numerous rolling mills – formed a large proportion of Britain's exports, and ironworks provided the materials for the growing shipbuilding industries of north-east England and Clydeside. The technologies that had been developed in Britain – coke smelting, puddling, grooved rolls and methods of making mild steel – were adopted wherever iron was made on a large scale. The Lancashire Forge, a modification of the finery-and-chafery process observed by a Swedish metallurgist near Ulverston in Furness, was widely used in the ancient ironworks of Dalarna and other provinces of Sweden, while the use of anthracite in blast furnaces, which had been pioneered in South Wales, was one of the cornerstones of the iron industry of Pennsylvania. Iron was at the heart of the industrial revolution, and it is fitting that the outstanding monuments of mid-nineteenth-century Britain – the Britannia Bridge, Saltaire Mill and St Pancras Station – should have been structures which were made of iron.

Many mines of non-ferrous ores were situated in remote and mountainous areas and at great distances from the main centres of population. Perhaps none is more remote than the copper workings at Allihies, at the western tip of the Beara Peninsula, 80 miles from Cork. The mines were directed by Cornishmen who built the characteristic Cornish engine house, high on the side of the mountain above the bay, as well as the Methodist chapel that stands amid the tailings from ore dressing near the sea shore and which now accommodates a visitor centre.

8

Precious veins: non-ferrous metals

'Rattling, the adamantine chains & hooks heave up the ore,
In mountainous masses plung'd in furnaces, & they shut & seal'd
The furnaces a time & time.'

WILLIAM BLAKE, *VALA* OR *THE FOUR ZOAS*

BRITAIN was one of Europe's principal sources of tin, copper and lead throughout this period, but the fortunes of those working the three metals followed very different paths. Cornwall was the most important European source of tin in 1700 and remained so, although the development of tin mining was constrained in the late eighteenth century by surging demands for Cornish copper. British mines produced a smaller but substantial proportion of Europe's lead and were buoyant in 1870. However, while the production of tin and lead increased steadily, the rise of the copper industry was meteoric. Copper working in 1700 was on an insignificant scale and depended on the expertise of migrants. By the mid-eighteenth century, however, the industry was exploiting new sources of ore, establishing smelting and fabricating works on the coalfields, and making products such as copper sheathing for wooden ships, and bolts and brass axle bearings, which influenced the development of wider technologies.

The ores of these three non-ferrous metals were mined and smelted in broadly similar ways, and the technologies developed in the principal areas of production – at first in the Bristol region and then in west Cornwall and the North East – spread to other areas through sales of machines and the migration of skilled personnel. 'Captains' from Cornwall and members of the Literary and Philosophical Society of Newcastle-upon-Tyne were influential wherever metallic ores were mined.

By accident of location, the mining of metals flourished in some of the most remote parts of the British Isles. The activity populated desolate mountain areas which are now resorts only of ramblers, sheep or those who watch or shoot birds. It created the tortured landscapes around Carn Brea and Parys Mountain. Metal working stimulated the growth of the second city of Wales, had an influential presence in Bristol, Newcastle-upon-Tyne, Chester, Derby and Shrewsbury, exploited the power of tumbling cascades in the Greenfield Valley and more placid waters in the Home Counties, and created landmarks – in the form of the two shot towers flanking Waterloo Bridge – that were visible from the Palace of Westminster.

The two shot towers which framed the southern approach to Waterloo Bridge in London. The one to the west (i.e. on the left) survived to be part of the Festival of Britain exhibition in 1951, and was demolished eleven years later. Somerset House is on the far side of the river Thames. Here the illustrator features a number of ceremonial barges on the river, taking part in the Lord Mayor's Procession from the Guildhall in the City up river to Westminster.

The restored waterwheel at the Killhope lead ore crushing mill near to the head of Weardale in County Durham. The wheel is 33 feet 6 inches in diameter and was installed around 1860. It originally drove four sets of rollers. This waterwheel, the largest of several in use here at one time, now forms an exhibit at the North of England Lead-mining Museum.

A primitive form of buddle used to wash lead ore in Northumberland in the early nineteenth century.

Miners pursued veins of non-ferrous ores by 'stoping', sinking shafts or driving adits into hillsides and then cutting out ore from the veins they encountered in a series of steps (or 'stopes') either above or below a haulage tunnel. Nevertheless, 'streaming' – the extraction of metallic deposits from river-borne silts – was a significant source of tin ore in Cornwall, while the ores of Parys Mountain were mostly worked instead from open pits. In the northern Pennines 'hushing' was widely used, whereby small streams and gulleys were dammed to form ponds; the temporary dams were then broken, and the resultant torrent of water tore away the overburden, hopefully to expose ore-bearing veins beneath. In parts of Swaledale and elsewhere the landscape has been changed quite markedly and visibly by this process (see page 373). In some areas, such as the northern Pennines, methods of working changed relatively little through the eighteenth and nineteenth centuries, although advances in geological understanding and developments in dressing and smelting technologies contributed to growth. Elsewhere increases in production were driven by the application of steam power.

However they were raised, ores had to be separated from stones. Thus, between Truro and Chacewater in 1750 Richard Pococke observed women and children breaking ore and separating tin and copper. Separated ores were crushed to produce concentrates for smelting, a process in which the degree of sophistication depended upon the value of the metal. One method of crushing was by 'stamps', often with cast-iron heads, that were held upright in wooden frames and raised by the action of a cam on a horizontal shaft, usually driven by a waterwheel, and which was then allowed to fall on the material to be crushed. In 1698 Celia Fiennes saw tin ore being pounded by stamps until it was as fine as the finest sand, and by 1738 the London Lead Company was using stamps on its dressing floors on Alston Moor. An alternative was the horse-powered edge runner mill, of which an example remains in Derbyshire at the Odin Mine, Castleton. From 1805 copper ore was treated in the Cornish Roll, a mechanised crusher designed by John Taylor and first manufactured by the Mount Foundry at Tavistock.

Lead and tin ores could be separated from waste by 'jigging' – shaking the crushed mineral in water – which might be done in a 'hotching tub' of the kind displayed at Killhope in upper Weardale, a tank filled with water in which material in a sieve was jerked up and down vigorously. The ores, with their much greater specific gravity, sank to the bottom of the layer of crushed and powdered material. Lead and tin ores might be separated further from waste by 'buddles', containers through which water flowed, carrying away the lighter materials and leaving the ore. Trunk buddles, series of connected boxes, were widely used by the early nineteenth century, and from the 1820s circular buddles were developed, in which a mineral-bearing slime was fed on to the middle of a circular sloping platform and deposited in a surrounding trough. The Brunton Buddle, named after William Brunton, was a continuous cloth-belt separator for dressing fine slime ores. The high value of tin ore justified the use of shaking tables – inclined surfaces usually vibrated by water power – on which heavier ore particles would shake downwards. Dressing plants extended along streams wherever ores were mined.

The tin industry

The mineral resources of southern Britain were known to the merchants of antiquity. We know that the Phoenicians sailed to Cornwall for tin, while Julius Caesar made enquiries of the islands before his invasion in 54 BC: 'Tin is found in the inland regions, iron on the seacoast; but the latter is not plentiful … [The Britons] use imported bronze.' By the time of our study, between 1700 and 1870, Cornish mines remained the principal source of tin in Europe. In the mid-nineteenth century about a third of the world's supply came from south-west England, an increasing proportion of it from mines along the Tamar Valley extending across the border into Devonshire. Tin ore was also obtained by 'streaming', recycling the silts deposited in watercourses. A streaming works in the 1790s could be three-quarters of a mile long and 300

One of the principal uses of tin was in the manufacture of tinplate, used for numerous household utensils in the eighteenth century, but from the early nineteenth century for cans in which food could be preserved. This tin of roast veal was manufactured in 1823 by the London firm of (Bryan) Donkin, Hall & Gamble for the expedition of 1824–25 in search of the North-West Passage that was led by Rear Admiral Sir William Edward Parry. The 7 lb can was opened in 1939 by its then owners, The British Food Manufacturing Industries Research Association.

© SCIENCE MUSEUM/SCIENCE & SOCIETY PICTURE LIBRARY

yards wide. Tin was used in pewter, in printers' type, in mirrors, and in glazes for ceramics; by 1700 it was also being used to coat plates of wrought iron rolled at the Pontypool mill of John Hanbury. The demand for tinplate increased, and in 1870 Britain was the world's principal producer.

Pewter is an amalgam in which three or four parts of tin are usually mixed with one of lead. It was cast in moulds, and the resulting pieces were turned and hammered. Worn wares could be recycled readily.

Pewter plates, dishes and candlesticks were omnipresent in English households in the early eighteenth century. Their manufacture was regulated by the Pewterers' Company of London, who recognised about 1,250 manufacturers, trading in most substantial towns, while groups unacknowledged by the company flourished in Wigan and Walsall. The inventory of a Ludlow pewterer of the 1690s reveals the threat from makers of ceramics, for among his kettles, dishes, chamber pots and candlesticks were potters' wares from the Clee Hills, Burslem and the Netherlands. The substitution of pottery for pewter was one of the principal changes in English households between 1700 and 1850, although manufacturers reputedly prospered by supplying pewter tankards to public houses.

Documentary evidence exists for the production of refined metallic 'white tin' because it was used in coinage, and while the figures may not reveal the

Exposures of metallic ores in the cliffs near the village of Botallack, about seven miles north-west of Penzance, were known from early times, but the Botallack Mine, which extended under the sea at 1,500 ft below the surface, was established in the early nineteenth century. A 30-inch steam pumping engine by Harvey of Hale was installed in 1823 but may have replaced an earlier engine. There were several other mines in this area, including the celebrated Levant Mine where an engine of 1840 by Harvey of Hale is preserved *in situ*. From an engraving of 1872.

© SCIENCE MUSEUM/SCIENCE & SOCIETY PICTURE LIBRARY

complete output of the industry, they do indicate trends of production. Output of metallic tin in the first decade of the eighteenth century varied between 1,114 and 2,176 tons, but did not reach 2,000 tons again until 1748. It then remained steady through the 1750s, exceeded 3,000 tons in 1766 and remained at that level for several decades, before reaching 4,120 tons in 1817 and over 5,000 in 1824. That method of recording ceased in 1837, but the *Mineral Statistics* published from 1854 show a rise from about 6,000 tons in that year to more than 10,000 in the early 1860s, and output remained at that level in 1870. In 1841 some 5,706 Cornishmen and 130 Cornish women were mining tin, less than half the 11,639 men and 2,098 women in the county who were employed extracting copper. Elsewhere, 150 worked tin deposits on the eastern side of the river Tamar in Devon.

Traditionally, tin was smelted in blowing houses, thatched stone buildings sheltering cylindrical stone furnaces, with water-powered bellows. Tin concentrate and charcoal were placed in the furnace in layers, and more were added as the metal melted and was collected in stone troughs, from which it was ladled into heated iron pots. Damp charcoal was added, causing slag to rise to the surface where it could be skimmed off. The metal was then ladled into moulds and afterwards into pots into which green applewood was inserted, creating turbulence which separated more slag. Droplets of tin lodged in the roof were recovered by periodically burning the thatch. Although tin was also smelted in reverberatory furnaces from about 1700, some blowing houses were still working in 1870. Refined tin was cast in granite moulds into blocks weighing about 300 lbs. These were taken to the stannary towns – Truro, Liskeard, Helston, Lostwithiel and Penzance – where they were weighed, numbered, assayed and stamped. Richard Warner saw blocks piled in the streets of Penzance in 1808. The ancient industry was carefully regulated by the Stannary Courts, in part because of the value of the product but also because a wealth of traditional practice and custom had grown up during the medieval period.

The tin and copper mines of Cornwall

West Cornwall was the source of most of Britain's tin, but its mines also produced copper ore, about 6,000 tons annually by 1720. Richard Warner observed in 1799 that although tin remained lucrative it was of secondary consideration because of the growth of copper mining. He described the legendary opening of the Wheal Virgin copper mine at Gwennap in 1757, when the ore mined in the first fortnight sold for £5,700. Some mines produced both minerals, and most significant developments in Cornish mining were associated to some extent with both industries. Even in 1700 the landscape here was distinctive. Celia Fiennes travelled to Land's End past Redruth 'mostly over heath and downs which was very bleak and full of mines'. In 1775 the Pennsylvania Quaker Jabez Maude Fisher stayed with William Cookworthy and described the scenery around Redruth: 'the land [is] most barren in the midst of a country of downs and moors, the bowels of which have been ransacked, turned inside out and every particle of worth, if it had any, carried off.' He went 734 feet (226 m) underground at Dolcoath, where he observed 'the place was too terrible to be viewed without fright and astonishment'. Richard Warner found the mining area around Carn Brea 'a country whose very entrails have been torn out by the industry of man … here everything is upon a grand scale.' 'Mining,' he wrote, 'penetrates into the earth and covers the neighbouring soil with unproductive rubbish. It proceeds to poison the brooks around with its mineral impregnations, spreads far and wide the sulphurous smoke of its smelting houses, blasting vegetation with their deleterious vapours, and obscuring the atmosphere with infernal fumes of arsenic and sulphur.' In the 1850s Walter White observed from Carn Brea 'a hungry landscape, everywhere deformed by small mountains of many-coloured refuse; traversed in all directions by narrow paths and winding roads, by streams of foul water, by screaming locomotives with hurrying trains; while wheels and whims, and miles of pumping rods, whirling and vibrating, and the forest of tall beams. … Giant arms of steam engines swing up and down,

Minerals were worked from the Carclaze Mine, about two miles north of St Austell, for more than 400 years. This engraving of the early nineteenth century shows the importance of water power at the mine, in the foreground for dressing ore, and possibly also for pumping water from the workings.

The landscape of mining area around Redruth and Camborne was one of the most dramatic in Britain. This engraving of around 1860 shows a mine with a characteristic Cornish engine house, probably accommodating a pumping engine, and a winding engine house nearby, while in the foreground water is being used to dress ore. In the distance is Carn Brea, the granite tor topped by the 90 feet high monument to Francis Basset, Baron de Dunstanville, who died in 1835 after championing the interests of Cornish miners to government for many years.

and the stamping mills appear to try which can thunder loudest.'

Many technological developments in Cornwall were stimulated by the high cost of fuel in a county with relatively limited timber and located far away from coalfields. Celia Fiennes observed that turfs were used in smelting ores in 1698, and near St Austell in 1754 Angerstein saw blowing houses fuelled with charcoal.

Coal-fuelled copper smelters were established at Hayle from 1757–58, worked by about 150 men in the 1790s, but most Cornish copper ore was shipped unsmelted to Neath and Swansea. A two-way trade developed across the Bristol Channel, exchanging Welsh coal for Cornish copper and copper ore. Six steam pumping engines were installed at Cornish mines before 1733, and a further 80 before 1780. Angerstein observed

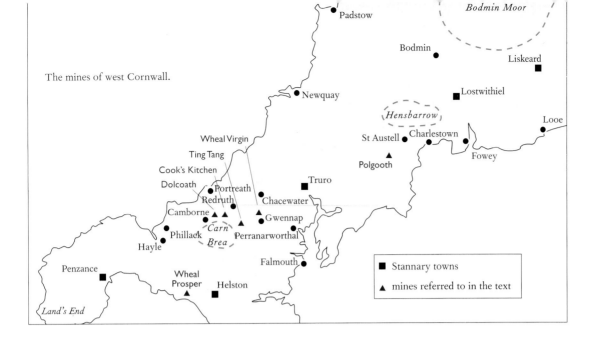

The mines of west Cornwall.

Stannary towns ■

mines referred to in the text ▲

numerous steam engines and had conversations about others in 1754. Boulton & Watt energetically sought to sell engines in Cornwall between 1780 and 1800. The first worked at Chacewater from 1777, the second at Ting Tang, Gwennap, from 1778, and about 90 were operating in 1800. The relative efficiency of the engine enabled mining to take place at greater depths. A visitor in 1788 to the 684 foot (210 m) deep Polgooth Mine was told that it could not be pumped without its Boulton & Watt engine. High fuel costs stimulated Cornish engineers to improve the efficiency of the steam engine, but application of the innovations of Arthur Woolf, Edward Bull and Jonathan Hornblower was retarded by the determination of Boulton & Watt to protect their patents. The beam pumping engine in its most efficient form, the Cornish engine, was perfected in 1811–12 by Richard Trevithick, and Cornish engineering companies prospered, providing the mundane day-to-day requirements of local mines, as well as the occasional very large engine. (See above, pp. 79–80.)

The Dolcoath Mine near Camborne was one of the largest and most productive in Cornwall. Copper was being worked there as early as 1720, and by 1778 workings extended 600 feet below the surface. Dolcoath was one of the Cornish copper mines which closed as a result of competition from Parys Mountain between 1787 and 1799. By the 1830s copper ores in the workings were running out, but shafts were driven deeper to find lodes of tin ore which were profitably exploited from the 1850s, and by 1882 the workings were 1,260 feet deep. The mine eventually closed in 1920.

The largest Cornish mines were imposing concerns. In 1796 Charles Hatchett noted that about 700 were employed underground and on the surface at Polgooth, and 340 at Cook's Kitchen. At Dolcoath in 1808 a 200 hp Boulton & Watt engine and two others pumped water from the workings; there were five winding engines; and 1,600 workers produced each month between 60 and 70 tons of copper and £30 worth of tin. The monthly cost of coal was £700, of timber and cordage £300 each, of candles £200, of gunpowder £150, and iron £150. By the 1860s the shaft was 3,000 feet deep, the mine employed 1,200 men and had ten steam engines, seven waterwheels and a 'man engine'.

Cornish miners developed a profound understanding of mining technology. One of their achievements was the 38-mile Great County Adit, begun in 1748, which drained mines near Redruth. Cornishmen improved steam engines, applied wire rope haulage from 1840 and made many innovations in the dressing of ores. From 1842 they began to improve access to workings by installing 'man engines', systems of rods in access shafts reciprocated by water- or steam power on which there were steps, from which miners stepped off at each change of direction on to staging affixed to the shaft walls or on to a step on a parallel rod at the end of its stroke. They also took their skills to every continent.

Bristol and brass

Brass, the result of alloying copper with zinc, was widely used in 1700 for the manufacture of household utensils. During the eighteenth century it was increasingly employed by mechanical engineers for

bearings, and there were small brass foundries in most engineering works. By the 1870s it could be found in many forms in most households, as taps, as fittings on furniture, and above all in the characteristic Victorian bedstead. London and Birmingham became the principal centres for making brass artefacts, but the city where the manufacture of the metal itself was pioneered was Bristol.

Some Cornish copper was used to make brass in Bristol, where it was combined with calamine (zinc ore) from the Mendips. In 1760 Ferrner found the Mendip mines unimpressive, with many small shafts spread across land whose ownership was minutely subdivided, and today the visible traces of the industry are limited – a stone chimney at Shipham is a rare monument of calamine mining. Lead was also worked in the Mendips, principally at Charterhouse, where after a period of decline it was revived in the mid-nineteenth century. New dressing technologies were introduced, flues were built, and lead-rich slags from earlier periods were re-smelted. These industries were modest in scale: in 1861 between 60 and 70 miners were living in Shipham, Rowberrow and Blagdon, together with half a dozen smelters.

Brassmakers in Bristol initially utilised the skills of immigrants who had come from the region around La Vieille Montagne (Altenberg) near Aachen. Brass rods and 'battery' goods (beaten copper shaped into pots and pans) were traded by Bristol merchants

The Saltford Brass Mill near Bristol, which was built in the early eighteenth century and continued operating until the 1920s.

Much of the brass produced from copper and zinc from smelters in the British Isles was formed into useful articles by manufacturers in Birmingham. Most such manufacturers operated from small workshops but some, including Winfield & Son, established in 1829, had large factories with formal frontages to the outside world. This engraving depicts the factory in 1860 when the Winfields employed about 700 workpeople: according to the article it was 'a model manufactory and for completeness, extent, and good order it would perhaps be difficult, if not impossible to find any large industrial establishment to surpass it'.

MESSRS. WINFIELD AND SON'S MANUFACTORY, BIRMINGHAM.

in Africa, and brass was used for making pins at Gloucester, for wool-combing cards, and for many purposes in Birmingham. Between 1700 and 1702 the Bristol Brass Wire Company set up a works at Baptist Mills. Its partners included: Nehemiah Champion, a merchant; Abraham Darby I, who subsequently set up an iron foundry in Cheese Lane, before moving to Coalbrookdale in 1708; and John and Thomas Coster, who from 1692 smelted copper at Redbrook in the Forest of Dean. In 1706 the Brass Wire Company set up two water-powered works at Keynsham on the river Avon and the river Chew. The company was eventually controlled by the descendants of Nehemiah Champion, and was the largest of several concerns in Bristol, producing annually in the 1720s about 300 tons of brass at six works – the mill that remains at Saltford was built in 1721. The company took over

the Redbrook works from the Costers in 1734; in 1738 William Champion patented a means of producing metallic zinc, a difficult task given the volatility of the metal; and in 1746 he built the works at Warmley, to which industrial spies tried in vain to gain entrance. By the early 1760s the company was vertically integrated, with 22 copper-smelting furnaces, 15 brass furnaces, 5 water-powered battery mills, a wire mill and rolling mills, and at Warmley there was a steam engine which recirculated water. Nevertheless, after heavy borrowings it became bankrupt in 1769. Most of the works continued to operate, but the Bristol brass industry was never again so prosperous. By the 1780s most brass was made by alloying zinc and copper metals in crucibles in reverberatory furnaces, and the use of calamine diminished. The mills at Saltford and Keynsham operated until the 1920s.

A copper revolution

Copper smelters and battery works (in which hammers formed copper and brass into sheets) were established in the 1730s, 1740s and 1750s in Lancashire and Cheshire, in the Greenfield Valley in Flintshire, and in the Home Counties, but the copper industry was shaped particularly by the development of smelting around Swansea and Neath, by the exploitation of newly discovered ore deposits on Anglesey, and by the substantial increase in demand generated by the use of copper sheathing on the hulls of ships from the third quarter of the eighteenth century onwards. Before the 1850s there are no reliable output figures for refined copper or copper ore, but we do know that the amount sold publicly in Cornwall increased almost fourfold between 1726–35 and 1766–75, and continued to increase, reaching a peak in 1845–48. By the 1770s about 90 mines in Cornwall were producing copper ore, 20 of them of significant size. Metallic copper output in the United Kingdom rose from an estimated 1,000 tons *per annum* to 7,000 tons during the eighteenth century, while in the late 1850s output from British ores averaged slightly less than 20,000 tons a year. The import of copper ore began in the 1830s, exceeded 40,000 tons by 1840, and was more than 100,000 tons in most years in the 1860s. The output of British ore reached a peak of 361,300 tons in 1856, remained above 200,000 tons until 1865, fell below 100,000 tons after 1870, and by 1885 was negligible. In Cornwall the extraction of copper ore ceased to be significant, although the county remained Europe's principal source of tin.

The first copper smelter in the Swansea Valley, White Rock at Landore, began operation in 1717. The growing coal trade with Cornwall increased return shipments of copper and copper ore. From the 1770s ores from Anglesey were also smelted in the area. Swansea, a medieval borough of modest size built around a castle, had become a port of regional significance, but in the course of the eighteenth century copper smelting transformed it into one of Britain's principal industrial cities. It developed along the banks of the Afon Tawe, which was navigable upstream to Landore. The river was used through the nineteenth century, and a meander was bypassed by the 840-yard New Cut in 1840–45. Navigation was extended in the 1790s by the construction of the Swansea Canal, which ran 15 miles to Ystradgynlais. With associated waterways it provided outlets for coal mines in the upper reaches of the Tawe Valley, and improved access to copper works on the lower stretches. The Neath Canal, extending 13 miles down from Glynneath to Giant's Grave near Briton Ferry, also dates from the 1790s, while the Tennant Canal, opened in 1824, linked the Neath Canal with the docks at Swansea. Wooden railways were constructed in the mid-1750s, supplying coal to several copper smelters. A line built in 1762 included a tunnel, and Sir John Morris ordered iron rails from Coalbrookdale in 1776. Between 1756 and 1783 about 13 route miles of surface railway were built in the Swansea area, generally of the Shropshire type west of the Tawe, and of the broader gauge Newcastle-style (see above pp. 221, 229–30) to the east.

Increased production of copper had consequences for many branches of manufacturing. It enabled, for example, the construction of large vessels for brewing and distilling such as this pot still installed in the early nineteenth century in the distillery established in a building designed as a woollen mill at Midleton, Co. Cork.

The Hafod Copperworks was established alongside the river Tawe in Swansea by the Cornishman John Vivian in 1810, and in the mid-nineteenth century was supposedly the largest copper works in the world. The two engine houses from which the rolling mills were driven date from 1860–62 and 1910. Many copper slag blocks were used in the construction of the extensive boundary walls. The works closed in 1980.

BY COURTESY OF RCAHMW

The typical copper works in Swansea or Neath had banks of kilns, in which ore was calcined, and a high-roofed hall, with honeycombed brick ventilators in the gable ends, filled with the reverberatory furnaces which were typically used for smelting copper from about 1700. The Hafod Copperworks, built at Landore in 1808–09 by the Cornishman John Vivian, had a smelting hall measuring 380 × 46 feet (117 × 14.2 m), with 24 furnaces. Works with rolling mills required power, usually provided by steam engines.

Most copper companies provided accommodation for some of their employees, but many workers lived in squatter-type cottages amid coal shafts on unenclosed commons. The 1841 census recorded 210 such cottages on the hillside common at Graig Trewyddfa near Morriston, whose occupants included 97 copper workers and 140 coal miners. At the other extreme

Morriston itself, established from 1768 by Sir John Morris, had a double grid plan of wide streets devised by the bridge builder William Edwards. 'Morriston Castle', four crenellated towers, each four storeys in height, linked by three-storey blocks enclosing a central courtyard, provided accommodation for 40 families, and was completed by 1773. The remaining cottages at Morriston date from the nineteenth century, as do those at Trevivian, or Vivian's Town, built in the late 1830s by John Henry Vivian. There the first phase comprised 48 catslide houses of local sandstone, rendered, with blocks of copper slag as quoins.

The copper smelters along the banks of the rivers Tawe and Neath created noxious pollution. Ayton observed in 1813 that above the copper works 'is not a blade of grass, a green bush, nor any form of vegetation, volumes of smoke, thick and pestilential, are seen

An aerial view of the workings for copper ore on Parys Mountain, Anglesey. In the lower part of the picture are some of the ponds used for the extraction of copper sludge by galvanic action from the cupriferous water drained from underground workings.

BY COURTESY OF RCAHMW

'The junction of the Mona and Parys Mountain Copper Mines', painted by Edward Pugh in 1790. Extraction of ore from the eastern part of the mountain by Charles Roe's Mona Company began in 1768. Ten years later the Parys Mountain Company was established to work the western part. The division between the areas worked by the two companies can still be observed, although from 1785 the Anglesey solicitor Thomas Williams, sometimes called the 'Copper King', who was prominent in the Parys Mountain Co., came to control all the workings in the area. The painting shows something of the flimsy wooden scaffolds by which miners gained access to lodes of copper in the rock faces.

BY COURTESY OF THE NATIONAL MUSEUM OF WALES

∧ The landscape of Parys Mountain in the early twenty-first century is unequalled for its colourful aridity.

crawling up the sides of the hills which are as bare as a turnpike road'. He saw filthy women with ragged clothes breaking up coal for the smelters. When visiting Vivian's Hafod works in 1819 Michael Faraday observed that the billowing clouds of smoke ascending the valley were filled with sulphur and arsenic. Even in the 1950s the lower Swansea Valley was notorious as perhaps the most polluted and environmentally despoiled place in the British Isles.

There was growing demand for copper plates for brewery vats and other industrial containers, for ingots that could be beaten into pots and pans for export, and for copper for brass making, but the innovation that most stimulated the industry was the use of copper to sheathe the bottoms of ships. The Royal Navy sailed increasingly in tropical waters, where wooden hulls were damaged by the teredo worm (*tereda navalis*) which releases bacteria that digest cellulose. In 1761 the Navy experimented with copper sheathing on the hull of the frigate *Alarm*, on duty in the Caribbean. The experiment worked, but it was soon found that iron bolts reacted galvanically with the copper plates, as a result of which several other vessels were lost. The Navy realised that copper bolts, made from bar copper, were needed. William Forbes, copper contractor to the Royal Navy, adapted Henry Cort's process for rolling iron to the rolling of copper bars, after which Thomas Williams, working with two Birmingham brassmakers, devised a way of strengthening the rolled bars by drawing them through steel draw plates. Both processes were in use by 1784, when the Admiralty ordered that all the Royal Navy's new ships should be sheathed in copper sheets to be held in place by copper bolts. For example, in 1780 HMS *Victory* was brought in to be sheathed in 3,923 sheets of copper each measuring 4 feet × 14 inches (1.23 × 0.36 m).

At Macclesfield a copper works was built from 1758 on common land leased from the corporation by Charles Roe. There, using local coal, he smelted ore from Coniston, Ecton (Staffordshire) and Alderley Edge. In 1764 Roe leased part of Parys Mountain on Anglesey and on 2 March 1768 his agents discovered the 'Golden Venture', an abundance of low-grade copper ore that could be extracted easily. His Mona Company worked the eastern part of the hill, but in 1778 a new concern, the Parys Mountain Company, established to exploit the ores to the west, began operations. It was controlled by the Anglesey solicitor, Thomas Williams of Llandinam, who also gained control of the eastern part of the mountain when Roe's lease expired in 1785. The mine required an investment of £62,000 in three years, but by 1789 was recording a profit of £19,000 *per annum*. In 1779 the Parys Company leased land for a smelter at Ravenhead on the Sankey Canal and Williams purchased the Upper Bank works at Swansea, which dated from the 1750s. In 1780 he completed mills in the Greenfield Valley near Holywell, initially for rolling copper from Ravenhead and Upper Bank into plates and wire, and later rolling sheathing and bolts for ships. In 1786 some remission of duties on the coastal shipping of coal encouraged the delivery of coal to Amlwch, on the north coast of Anglesey. It was used on Parys Mountain for calcining ores, and later in smelters at Amlwch. The Mona Company also operated a smelter at St Helens and mills in the Greenfield Valley.

Thomas Williams came to dominate the copper trade. The outflow of copper ore from Anglesey depressed the price of Cornish ore and in 1785, with John Wilkinson and others, he established a company to buy and process that ore. Between 1787 and 1792 Cornish mine owners could only market their ore through Williams's company, giving him an effective monopoly, only ended as a result of the agitation of Boulton & Watt and Birmingham brass manufacturers. Williams remained a dominant figure, bringing together the expertise that enabled the production of copper bolts for the Royal Navy. He controlled smelters at St Helens, purchased others in South Wales, and owned a sulphuric acid plant in Liverpool.

He had mills and battery works in the Greenfield Valley, and purchased the copper mills at Wraysbury near Windsor, and the Temple Mills near Marlow.

Parys Mountain transformed the economy of copper working and became one of the most dramatic of all industrial landscapes. While Ironbridge, Blaenavon and New Lanark have been mellowed by time, Parys Mountain continues to shock the observer. The scoured summit is devoid of vegetation except for some gorse, heather and brambles at the margins. There are no slugs under the stones, and birds search in vain for prey. Rocks are pink, purple, autumnal brown and grey. Some are splintering, others blown with bubbles of air like slag or certain brands of chocolate. Water is ochreous and the strata exposed on the cliff faces appear to have been grotesquely twisted in some primeval upheaval. The mountain was worked by quarrying and by adits and shafts, of which 145 are shown on a map of 1786. A narrow embankment divides the two sections of the hill. From the rims of the pits men swung on ropes to set explosive charges. The displaced rock was raised in kibbles and broken by gangs of women and children before being put into bags and taken to Amlwch. Rectangular kilns for calcining the ore, between 10 and 20 yards wide and as long as 50 yards, with walls 4 feet high, were built from about 1778 by the Mona Company. They were filled with ore which was covered with stones and sealed with clay to smoulder for six months. The fumes were drawn through condensers where sulphur was deposited. Later kilns at the mine and at Amlwch were conical and about 27 feet (8.3 m) high. Copper was also produced by dipping scrap iron in pits filled with cupriferous drainage water from the mines. The copper sulphate in the water caused the iron to dissolve by galvanic action, leaving a copper-rich sludge which could be smelted. Some 1,500 people were working on Parys Mountain in the 1790s. Visitors were impressed by the vivid tints of the rock and the constant rumble of explosions, but above all by the barren landscape. Richard Ayton found 'all vegetation is blighted and tarnished by the poisonous fumes from the copper works … and on the ridges of the Parys Mountain the land is utterly bare and reduced to a frightful desert.' Sir Richard Colt Hoare in 1801 described the mountain as 'one of the most sublime and interesting scenes I ever beheld'.

The peak of production had passed by 1800, and in 1810 Colt Hoare found that the bustle and the rumbling of explosions which he had observed only nine years earlier had diminished. Richard Ayton wrote of Amlwch in 1813 that, 'This wretched town stands in the midst of a hideous scene of desolation; the country round looks as if it had been blasted by a horrid pestilence and raises in the mind no images but of misery and famine.' From 1811 the mine was directed by John Henry Vivian, who employed 600 people in 1815. The depression intensified, and a visitor commented in 1839 that the mines, worked then by about 300 people, were a wreck of what they had once been. The census in 1841 recorded only 256 copper miners on Anglesey. Copper ore from Caernarfonshire was smelted at Amlwch, and Parys Mountain enjoyed a further phase of modest prosperity from 1857 under the direction of Charles Dyer. About 250 miners were mining copper on the mountain in 1881, while about 20 young women dressed ore, and more than 20 men worked at the smelter.

Farther north Thomas Patten I set up a copper smelter at Bank Quay, Warrington, about 1717, and his family subsequently became partners in the Cheadle Company. A separate 'Warrington Company', formed in 1755, smelted copper and made bangles at Warrington which were used by traders for the purchase of slaves and manufactured pots and other receptacles from copper and brass sheet in a battery works in the Greenfield Valley. In 1772 the company leased land for a smelter on the banks of the Sankey Canal, and seven years later the Parys Mountain Company leased a nearby site at Ravenhead from John Mackay. The Warrington Co. works had closed before 1785, when Thomas Williams purchased the site and smelted ore mined by the Mona Mine Company. The two works, with the British Plate Glass Co., consumed most of the output of the mines of the St Helens coalfield. In 1784 Ravenhead was taking in about 12,000 tons *per annum* of ore and producing about 1,000 tons *per annum* of copper, and in 1795 the two works reputedly smelted a total of 20,000 tons of ore annually. The Ravenshead works then included a brass plant, and one of its products was small copper bars, of which 30 tons a week were exported to China. A 'pirate' steam engine was supplied to the works by John Wilkinson. The St Helens smelters were closed in 1815 after the decline of production on Parys Mountain, but smelting was revived from the 1830s using ores imported into Liverpool from Cuba and Chile. A smelter was built near Ravenhead by the company known from 1832 as the Bolivar Mining Association, and another by the British & Foreign Copper Company at Sutton Oak. Both developed symbiotic relationships with local producers of sulphuric acid, who used copper pyrites. Further works were erected in the mid-nineteenth century, evidence of their existence being provided by the slag block walls of the church of St Peter, Parr, designed by J. Medland Taylor in 1865.

Copper working began in the Greenfield Valley of North Wales in the 1740s when Thomas Patten's Warrington Company set up mills known as the Battery Works. At the lower end of the valley Thomas Williams completed a rolling mill in 1780, erected a hammer mill to make bolts for fixing sheathing on ships in 1783, and in 1785 took over the works of the Warrington Company. A second rolling mill with three cast-iron waterwheels and, appropriately, a copper roof, was built in 1787, and the following year the company built the Meadow Mills to produce copper rollers for printing textiles. One writer commented that Williams, 'that useful and active character, with unparalleled speed, covered the lower part of the stream … with buildings stupendous in extent, expense and ingenuity of contrivance'. Richard Warner wrote in 1798 of the stream that cascaded down the valley that, 'this torrent works one large corn mill, four cotton manufactories … a copper and brass work, one under the firm of the Mona Mine Company, the other under that of the Parys Mine Company, hammer mills, where copper, brewing and other vessels are manufactured, a mill for drawing off copper wire, a calcinary of calamine and a building for making brass'. The British & Foreign Copper Co. retained a plant in the valley in the 1830s and 1840s.

Thomas Patten I became a partner from the 1730s in the Cheadle Brass & Copper Company, established to supply brassworkers in Birmingham. Copper and

The water power of the Greenfield Valley was first applied to the working of copper in the 1740s when Thomas Patten of the Warrington Company set up the 'Battery Works' (i.e. a series of rolling mills) shown in this aerial photograph. Thomas Williams of the Parys Mountain Company built a rolling mill in the valley in 1780, added a hammer mill for fabricating copper bolts in 1783, and in 1785 took over the Battery Works. These works became one of the principal sources of the copper sheets applied to the hulls of British ships and of the bolts employed to fix them.

brass making prospered at Cheadle where Patten's company and its later competitors used coal from local mines. Ore was obtained from the mine at Ecton, in the Staffordshire Peak District, believed in 1777 to be one of the richest sources of copper in Europe, which was managed by the Duke of Devonshire's estate from 1760 until its closure in 1817. The estate worked a smelter between 1770 and 1818 near Whiston, 12 miles south-east of Ecton, where blocks of slag remain, built in to cottage and garden walls. By 1775 brass was being made at Brookhouses near Cheadle, Staffordshire, for which calamine was obtained from the Peak District. In 1734 Thomas Patten II built a mill for drawing brass and copper wire at Alton, which was working in 1775 but was subsequently adapted for paper making. Its leat was occupied from 1811 by the Uttoxeter Canal. From 1794 until about 1840, at a brassworks outside Stone, set up by George, 2nd Baron Vernon, copper and brass wire were made from ingots cast at Cheadle.

It was powered by a waterwheel and a 36 hp steam engine. In about 1790 the Cheadle Company adapted a tinplate works at Oakamoor on the river Churnet to smelt and roll copper. From 1850 the company scaled down its smelter at Brookhouses and sold the Oakamoor works to Thomas Bolton & Sons of Birmingham, who made tubes for locomotive boilers and wires for telegraphy. The company employed 170 people in 1881, and when space for expansion in the narrow valley was exhausted, built a works at nearby Froghall.

Charles Roe's reaction to the discovery of copper ores on Anglesey was to build smelters at Congleton and Bosley near Macclesfield, and in 1767 at Toxteth, Liverpool. After his death in 1781 his company was managed by his son William Roe. Lord Torrington in 1790 thought that the copper works had stimulated the growth of Macclesfield, but found that 'mixing, melting and flat'ning the copper' was 'a most unwholesome employ, for which the workmen, I think are meanly pay'd'. The company failed to renew its lease on Parys Mountain and ceased to mine at Coniston in 1795, but sought other sources of ore, in Caernarfonshire and Ireland, for which it opened a smelter at Neath. The Toxteth smelter closed in 1793, those at Macclesfield in 1801, and in 1811 the company's interests at Neath were sold to the Cheadle Company.

In 1841 there were 432 copper miners in Caernarfonshire, rather more than the 256 on Anglesey. Workings at Llanberis, and at Drwys-y-Coed in the Nantlle Valley, began in 1768, and continued into the nineteenth century, as did operations on the Great Orme where the copper ore had been worked in the Bronze Age. The ores were smelted at Amlwch, and later at Swansea. At Drwys-y-Coed there remain tiny shelters around anvils on which women and girls – 'coparledis' – broke up the ore with hammers, while the present-day model yacht pond on the west shore at Llandudno, overlooked by the statue of Lewis Carroll's White Rabbit, was once part of the washing floor of the Great Orme mines.

Copper mining was widespread in Ireland where in 1854 there were 277 non-ferrous metal mines. The 1841 census listed 3,996 Irish people involved in mining, including 721 in Co. Wicklow, 439 in Co. Tipperary, 416 in Co. Kilkenny, 385 in Co. Waterford, and 321 in Co. Cork, most of whom would have been working non-ferrous ores. In 1778 copper mines around Avoca in the Wicklow Mountains were operated by the Cronebane Co., whose partners were linked with the Macclesfield Co. In 1811 the mines were leased by Williams Brothers of Perranarworthal, Cornwall, who worked them until 1884, chiefly for pyrites. The mines employed at their peak about 2,000 men, and were linked by tramway to the port of Arklow. On the coast of Co. Waterford near Bunmahon the Knockmahon Copper Mines Company excavated 12 miles of water-courses in the 1830s to provide power and drainage for its workings, which at that time employed up to 1,200 men. A Cornish engine house remains on the cliff top at Tankardstown. Copper ores were also worked in Co. Tipperary, particularly at Lackamore when an extensive water-power system was created in the 1850s. The mining region around Mount Gabriel near

The remains of one of the copper mines at Ballydehob (Beal an da Chab) on the south coast of County Cork.

Ballydehob (Beal an da Chab), Co. Cork, extended 12 miles from Skibbereen to Schull. At Ballydehob itself are remains of a mine and its dressing floors and the ruins of workers' cottages. The landscape of copper working at Allihies at the extremity of the Beara Peninsula is one of the most evocative in the British Isles (see the photograph on page 350). The mine began about 1812 and once employed 1,200 people. Its prosperity was destroyed by the Great Famine, when many miners died, but operations continued until the 1880s. Several engine houses remain, one at great height on the side of a mountain, while the beach is surfaced with tailings from an ore-dressing plant. A museum housed in a Methodist chapel built by Cornishmen in 1845 was opened by the Irish president in 2007. After the Famine many Irish miners migrated to contribute to the development of mines in Michigan and Montana, and to more modest operations at Coniston, Lancashire.

There were also brass and copper enterprises in the Home Counties. Jacob Momma from Stolberg established a brass works in 1649 at Esher, worked in the early eighteenth century by William Dockwra, partner in the Costers' smelters at Redbrook. Defoe described three water-powered mills near Marlow where brass was made and beaten with hammers into pots and pans. One, the Temple Mill, was purchased in 1788 by Thomas Williams, who employed Samuel Wyatt to design the nearby Temple House, protected by a 164 yard (150 m) fence of slate pillars from North Wales. Temple Mills produced copper bolts and sheets in the 1840s, but had been adapted to make paper by 1852. In 1790 Williams bought the mills at Wraysbury, near the confluence of the Thames and the Colne below Windsor, where brass and copper were worked until 1820, when paper mills were built there. In 1803 Robert Spedding erected a new works on a site at Harefield, which had been used for working copper since 1781, and imported copper from Neath to make sheet, bolts and bars. The mill was working in 1861, but soon it too was converted to paper making. Coppermill Lane near the river Lea in Walthamstow takes its name from a water-powered works built from 1808 by the British Copper Co., to which copper ingots were delivered from Landore by ship and rolled into sheets. The mill worked until 1857, when its site was taken over by the East London Waterworks Company.

In the Lake District significant copper mining was started in the 1580s by German miners, under the auspices of the Mines Royal Company. Ore was extracted at Coniston by them in the late sixteenth century and again by Charles Roe between 1758 and 1795. It was revived in the 1820s in the amphitheatre formed by the frequently cloud-topped mountains flanking the Old Man of Coniston, where terraces of waste materials, bubbling streams that once washed ore or drove waterwheels, rugged stone cottages and blocks of slag remain as witness to past endeavours. The new enterprise was begun in 1824 under the direction of John Taylor, a native of Norwich who had worked in Derbyshire, Cornwall and Wales, and supervised operations at Grassington for the Duke of Devonshire. He directed the driving of the Deep, or Horse, Level at Coniston, and his manager, John Barratt, drained old workings and developed new ones on Tilberthwaite Fells two miles to the north. Sixteen waterwheels drained the mines in 1870 when workings

extended 1,600 feet (493 m) below the surface. The revival of mining stimulated the building of the branch railway from Foxfield to Coniston in 1859, but the output of ore never equalled the peak of 3,569 tons achieved in 1856, and by 1864 was less than 2,000 tons. Two agents at Coniston were Cornishmen, from St Mewin and Gwennap. John Barrett was born at Redruth, and his two sons at Grassington. Many Irishmen migrated to Coniston after the Famine – the 1861 census recorded 252 miners and 46 ore dressers in the area, 86 (29 per cent) of them Irish-born.

From the mid-nineteenth century the copper industry was shaped by imported ores. Demand for brass continued, particularly from Birmingham, while the growth of railways increased demand for copper tubes for locomotive boilers and for brass bearings, and the development of electric telegraphs required copper wire and brass instruments.

Precise figures for the output of copper ore in the United Kingdom are available only from 1854, and show an all-time peak, of 361,300 tons, in 1856. Output was just over 230,000 tons *per annum* in 1859–61, falling to 198,300 in 1865 and 106,700 in 1870, and never reached 100,000 tons again, dropping below 50,000 tons in 1883. While copper mining peaked in the mid-nineteenth century, however, the output of metallic copper from smelters rose, from 22,000 tons in 1850 to 80,000 tons in 1880. The copper industry came to be dependent on imported raw materials. Imports of copper ore were negligible before 1830 and did not exceed 100,000 tons before 1862. After some fluctuations, the total in 1889 exceeded 250,000 tons, while the import of crudely smelted 'blister' copper increased from less than 4,000 tons in the 1850s to more than 40,000 tons in the late 1880s. Initially Spain was the principal source of imported ore and copper. The changing nature of the industry is illustrated by the rise of the Tharsis Sulphur & Copper Company, founded in Glasgow in 1866 by John Tennant. The fortune of the Tennant family had been made by manufacturing bleach powder during which process they used sulphur to produce their own sulphuric acid. Sulphur compounds, often found in association with deposits of copper ore, were used in making the acid, which led Tennant to buy the Tharsis copper mines in Spain. He established the company's first copper smelter at St Rollox, Glasgow, in 1866. Within six years he had seven copper-smelting works in Britain, including plants at Jarrow on Tyneside, at Widnes and in the Black Country. Demand for copper was increasing rapidly in the late nineteenth century with the growth of telecommunications and later of the electrical supply industry. The British copper industry continued to prosper, but it could no longer depend on native raw materials.

The lead industry

If the history of the copper industry between 1700 and 1870 was tumultuous, the working of lead was characterised by continuity. Lead had been worked for centuries in most of the areas where it was mined when the industry reached its peak in the 1860s. On display in Derby Museum there is a 65 kg ingot or 'pig' of lead dating from the Roman period that was found at Yeaveley, south of Ashbourne, and which was probably mined near Wirksworth; another ingot, of similar weight, stamped with the names of Vespasian and Titus, can be dated to AD 76 was found at Hints Common, Staffordshire, and is now in the British Museum. More than 10,000 tons of metallic lead were exported in most years between 1700 and 1750, and the trend was subsequently upwards, reaching almost 20,000 tons *per annum* in 1768–69 and 1789–90. The level fluctuated after 1800, and did not again exceed 20,000 tons until 1842. It did so in only five years before 1862, but exports surged thereafter. The total reached 48,400 tons in 1869 and remained above 40,000 in most years until 1900, although these buoyant figures depended upon increasing imports of ore. A French observer in 1830 calculated that about 43 per cent of Europe's output of lead was made in Britain. National output figures are only available from 1845, when 78,300 tons of ore were raised in mines in the United Kingdom, and 52,700 tons of metallic lead were produced by the smelters. Ore production rose to 102,000 tons in 1851, and was less than 90,000 tons in only one year in the next twenty. Small quantities of other metallic ores – zinc, manganese and copper, and some iron ore – were also extracted in the principal lead-mining areas. The value of the silver found in some lead ores made its separation viable, while the extraction of fluorspar and barytes sustained some mines after lead working ceased.

One important factor in the development of the lead industry was the establishment of The London Lead Company. This company originated in 1692, when a group of entrepreneurs (most of them Quakers)

➤ This diagram from the 1842 Report of the Children's Employment Commission on Lead Mines in Durham, Northumberland and Cumberland, shows a 'cupola', a coal-fired reverberatory furnace for smelting lead ore, in which heat from the fire in one chamber, on the left, was drawn over the ore in the adjacent chamber and out through the flue on the right, which, in some cases, led into a lengthy chimney climbing a hillside. The puddling furnace, used to produce wrought iron from pig iron, and the air furnace, used for melting iron for castings, worked on the same principles. The word cupola was also applied to the fan-driven furnace used from the 1790s for melting iron, which worked on different principles.

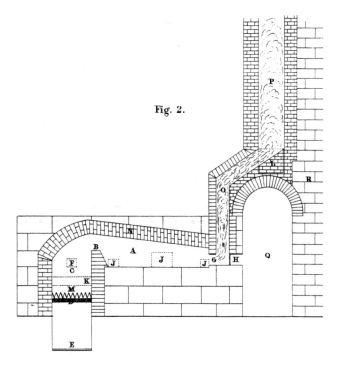

Fig. 2.

This late medieval carving of a lead miner on the wall of the church of St Mary, Wirksworth, is evidence of the long history of lead mining in Derbyshire.
PHOTOGRAPH: CARNEGIE

for its workpeople, and during crises in 1800 and 1815–17 sustained their food supplies. The company remained prosperous in 1870, but subsequently ran down its activities and was wound up in 1905.

The most common lead ore is galena, or lead sulphide (PbS), which has a high specific gravity, is easy to identify, is relatively easy to dress, and in addition to lead ore might also contain silver, zinc, cadmium, antimony, arsenic or bismuth. The process of 'dressing' involved the crushing of the material brought from the mine and the separation of the valuable ores from the useless rock with which they were mixed. Dressing was usually carried out by a flotation process. Most ore was smelted near the mines from which it was extracted, but the processing of metallic lead was a largely urban industry. Galena was smelted either in an ore hearth, a furnace in which it was mixed with dried wood (white coal) or a mixture of peat and charcoal and blown with water-powered bellows, or in a cupola, a coal-fired reverberatory furnace (introduced for this and other purposes in the late seventeenth century) which was charged with calcined galena. The lead-rich slags from a cupola were usually re-melted in another furnace called a slag hearth. Both types of smelter continued in use in the nineteenth century. The best preserved ore hearth is at Froggatt Wood, eight miles south-west of Sheffield.

took leases of several mines. In 1704 they acquired the charter of the defunct 'Company for Smelting Down Lead with Pitcoal', and in 1705 took over a partnership which had a smelter at Ryton-on-Tyne and mines on Alston Moor. The company acquired interests in Derbyshire, Teesdale, Cumberland, the Isle of Man and Flintshire. It was an unusual institution by 1800, resembling more the Hudson's Bay Company than other manufacturing companies such as Boulton & Watt or Richard Arkwright & Co. It built roads and provided housing and social facilities

The lead industries of Derbyshire and the northern Pennines

In 1700 the extraction of lead ore in Derbyshire was already a long-established industry. The barmote court which still meets in Wirksworth to settle mining disputes, and similar courts which convened at Bradwell, Eyam, Monyash and Tideswell, originated in the thirteenth century. The 'rakes', resembling crudely dug railway cuttings where miners followed veins across the countryside – such as those at Dirtlow and Tideslow – cannot readily be dated, but certainly existed at the time of eighteenth-century enclosures.

And there were complaints in the seventeenth century that demands for fuel for smelting caused the devastation of local woodland.

The lead industry in Derbyshire evolved gradually between 1700 and 1860. Many mines were drained by 'soughs', sloping tunnels which took water from mines to rivers or streams, in the construction of which the county's miners were particularly skilled. About 30 of consequence were built before 1700, including the Cromford Sough begun in the 1670s.

The five-mile Meersbrook Sough, draining mines around Wirksworth into the river Derwent, was begun in 1772 (the date inscribed on the portal through which it enters the river) but completed only in 1846. About 200 soughs were identified in the late nineteenth century, and that from the Magpie Mine to the river Wye at Ashford was begun as late as 1873. The first steam pumping engine in Derbyshire appears to have been built in 1717 at Winster, where a visitor on 28 September 1730 observed three engines pumping. The first cupola smelter in Derbyshire was built at Ashover in 1735, but ore hearths remained in use until the 1780s. The London Lead Company had mines at Winster and in Darley Dale, but by the 1780s had relinquished most of its interests in Derbyshire. In 1809 John Farey counted 292 lead mines in Derbyshire, and 18 cupola smelters. Thirteen steam engines were being used for pumping in 1777, and several engines built by Francis Thompson of Ashover were installed in the 1790s. Cornish engines, such as those at the High Rake Mine in Little Hucklow, Magpie Mine in Sheldon, and the Mandale Mine in Lathkill Dale, were built to drain new or revived workings from the 1840s.

The Derbyshire lead field extended from the confluence of the Amber and the Derwent near Crich, west through Wirksworth to the river Dove and the Staffordshire border, and north-west past Bonsall, Winster, Sheldon, Eyam and Tideswell to Castleton. There were 1,333 lead miners in the county in 1861, but the number had fallen to 871 by 1881, although some substantial mines were revived. Among the principal mining communities were Wirksworth and Middleton-by-Wirksworth, where there were more than 400 miners in 1861. Farther north, Bonsall Moor is pock-marked with hundreds of shallow lead mine shafts with their accompanying spoil tips. About 100 lead miners in Bonsall parish lived alongside about 150 framework knitters, 50 cotton factory workers and 20 papermakers. Another 100 miners and labourers at smelthouses lived in Arkwright's Cromford and neighbouring Matlock, where the Banbury-born brothers Frederick, Joseph and Thomas Stevens were pioneers in processing barytes, used in the manufacture of paper, rubber and linoleum. There were many miners in the northern part of the county, in such parishes as Youlgreave, Stoney Middleton, Eyam, Great Hucklow and Bradwell, near Castleton and around Derbyshire's most easterly lead mines at Ashover. The Barmaster of the High Peak, head of the Barmote Court, lived in Little Longstone. His neighbours included two 'writing clerks to the Barmaster', which suggests that the court remained busy. The nature of the workforce is evidence of the measured growth of the industry. The majority of Derbyshire lead workers were locally born, as were the agents who directed them, although a few migratory Cornish agents and engineers found employment in the county. Stoney Middleton was the only community where there were significant numbers of migrants, most of them Irish.

Galena occurs in vertical veins in the upper

Magpie Mine, 3½ miles west of Bakewell, is the outstanding monument of lead mining in Derbyshire. Lead ore was worked here for more than two centuries, and the latest surviving structures date from the 1950s. A Newcomen pumping engine was installed before 1824, and in 1827 a record output of 800 tons of galena was recorded. The mine was re-organised from 1839 by the eminent mining engineer John Taylor. Surviving buildings include the prominent engine house of 1869–70, and the chimney of 1840 alongside it.
PHOTOGRAPH: CARNEGIE, 2005

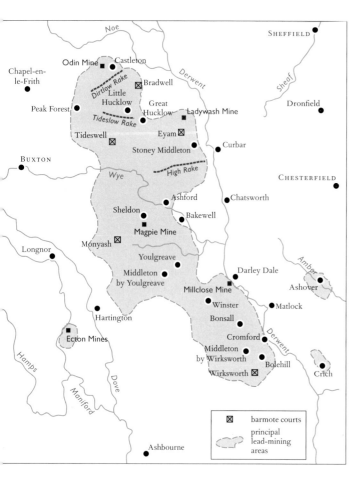

surprised that steam engines had yet to be used in the mines. Fuel for smelters came from peat bogs or the tiny mines that produced moorland coal. Power on most dressing floors was provided by waterwheels. Lengthy flues taking fumes from smelters to chimneys high on the sides of the mountains are a distinctive feature of the Pennines, although they were used elsewhere. Pennine ores are relatively rich in silver, and from the 1790s increasing attention was paid to the separation of the precious metal from the lead, for which a new process was devised in 1833 by Hugh Lee Pattinson. It was adopted at most smelters in the region, and the London Lead Company paid him £1,050 for the right to use the technology.

The lead-mining communities of the north Pennines were distinctive, with evidence of dual occupations. In many places mining was associated with the quarrying of stone or slates (which here meant sandstones or grits which split into thin slabs). Moorlands and open commons were often divided into smallholdings of between 5 and 20 acres whose farmers also mined lead ore, or provided carts for carrying it. Many mines were in exceptionally remote locations – the

reaches of the valleys of the rivers which rise in the Pennines and flow into the Yorkshire Ouse – Nidderdale, Wharfedale, Wensleydale, Swaledale and Arkengarthdale. Deposits extend northwards from the Yorkshire Dales through Teesdale and Weardale to the valley of the North Tyne, and westwards to Alston Moor over the border with Cumberland. In 1841 about 5,000 people were mining lead in the North Riding, Co. Durham, Northumberland and Cumberland. Because of the topography, with deep valleys giving ready access to exposed metalliferous veins, most mines were adits, and the modern landscapes of these regions lack the imposing engine houses that may be seen elsewhere, in Derbyshire and mid-Wales. The mining companies operated sawmills to shape timber for shoring shafts and adits. John Marshall, passing through Wensleydale and Swaledale in 1800, was

Swathbeck Mines near the head of the Tees were at 2,500 feet (770 m) above sea level – and parliamentary reports of the 1840s describe 'bunkhouses' at remote mines in which miners slept on weeknights, returning to their homes at weekends. (There is little evidence of them in the 1861 census, perhaps because the count was undertaken on a Sunday night.) While nineteenth-century lead-mining ventures in Wales and Shropshire were notoriously speculative, the mines of the northern Pennines were consistently productive, and the two principal companies, the London Lead Company and the Blackett-Beaumont group were managed with prudence; investments were made in new technology, and the upland lead-mining communities enjoyed, subject to swings in the trade cycle, a century of relatively prosperous stability. By the mid-nineteenth century those communities consisted largely of families who had grown up in the dales.

About 250 men were working in lead mines and smelters in Nidderdale in 1861, most of them in and around Pateley Bridge, including those employed at the Prosperous and Cockhill smelters on Greenhow Hill on the watershed between Nidderdale and Wharfedale. A few miners extracted ore from a scatter of small workings that extended to the head of the dale. The smelthouse at Grassington in Wharfedale, one of the first in Yorkshire where there were cupola smelters, was completed in 1792 and was enclosed within an imposing wall, like a colonial fortress. A flue built in the 1850s rises 150 feet (46 m) to a 60-foot (18.5 m) chimney on the side of the dale. Grassington is part of the parish of Linton where about 250 people were involved in mining or smelting lead in 1861, including the assay master, a Cornishman from Chacewater. More than 80 miners worked at Kettlewell and in workings farther north in the dale. In Wensleydale, the valley of the river Ure, the most easterly lead mines were near the confluence with the river Cover. Mines in Coverdale and farther north in Cotterdale provided coal for smelting lead, principally at the Keld Heads smelt mill, from which a flue extended nearly two miles up the moor. More than 200 lead miners were working in Wensleydale in 1861, the majority of them in the village of Redmire.

The landscape of Swaledale above Richmond is rich

The lead-mining districts of the Yorkshire Dales.

in evidence of lead working. On the upper stretches of Gunnerside Gill near Keld deep gullies running down the hillsides are evidence of 'hushing'. This was a process in which workers would break a temporary dam they had constructed on a stream in order to 'hush' or wash away the spoil to expose the usually vertical lead veins. In the same area Friarfold Rake and Forefield Rake show the process of excavating vertical veins of ore to shallow depths, following the lines of veins across country and thereby creating distinctive

The lead smelthouse at Grassington, completed in 1792. The flue, built in the 1850s, ascends 150 ft up the hillside to a 6 feet high chimney.

The smelt mill at Old Gang in the upper part of Swaledale, about 14 miles west of Richmond (Yorkshire), one of the most remote industrial sites in England, where the smelting of galena began about 1797 and continued for more than a century.

The Grinton smelt mill on the Cogden Gill, showing its peat store and the 1,100 ft long flue that ascends to a chimney on the hillside. The smelt mill worked from the 1780s until 1870.

trenches. In 1861 more than 800 men were employed mining, dressing and smelting lead ore in the townships westwards from Richmond to the head of the dale. Lead working also occupied the majority of those who lived in the 14,256-acre parish of Arkengarthdale, on either side of the Arkle Beck which descends from hills over 2,000 feet high to join the river Swale at Grinton. About 70 men in the area were employed at scattered coal workings such as Tan Hill Colliery, working the 'moor coal' which was used with peat in smelting mills. Some of the wives and daughters of lead miners worked at ore-dressing plants, but more than a hundred earned extra income by knitting stockings in their homes, a very long-standing domestic craft in the Yorkshire Dales. While one farmer in Arkengarthdale tended 4,000 acres, most of the holdings were small, and farmers either worked in the mines or provided services for the mining companies. In the Whaw area about a dozen farmers with holdings of between two and twelve acres worked in the mines, while two were employed at a smelter, and others worked as carters taking pig lead to navigable water and later to railway sidings. Hushing transformed the landscape of the valley – the hillside west of Langthwaite is scarred by the Stodart and Hungry Hushes, great ravines up to 250 feet (77 m) deep and totalling almost two miles from end to end.

Through Swaledale and Arkengarthdale there are waste tips, and tracks on the hillsides, and many-times-inundated remnants of dressing floors along the streams. In their heyday the mining communities were thriving and substantial places: Muker, Gunnerside and Keld had doctors, public houses, shops, cloggers and shoemakers, tailors, schools and places of worship, as well as the offices, dry stores, and the sawmills of the mining companies. The ruins of the smelters are impressive. Lead was smelted at Marrick over many centuries, but the remnants of the smelter actually date from a rebuilding of the 1860s. The Grinton smelt mill on the Cogden Gill worked from the 1780s until 1870. Its peat store remains, with a 1,100 foot (339 m) long flue ascending to a chimney on the hillside. The Surrender smelt mill, at a height of nearly 1,300 feet on the Barney Beck which joins the river Swale at Healaugh, was established in the late eighteenth

century, rebuilt in 1840, and worked until about 1880. The surviving features include the waterwheel pit, the piers of its peat store and a lengthy flue with two chimneys. The most evocative remains are those of the Old Gang smelt mill, which once included four ore furnaces smelting 2,000 tons of lead *per annum*. A long sequence of pillars remains from the massive peat store, 390 × 21 feet (119 × 6.5 m), which could hold sufficient fuel to fire the smelter for three years (see page 43). At a lower level are the remains of the smelter building and of the hearths within it, while there are several adits on the sides of the valley. No occupied buildings are within sight, and the most obvious living creatures are usually grouse and sheep. The Old Gang Lead-mining Co. operated until 1906.

Beyond the high hills and moorland at the head of Arkengarthdale the streams drain northwards towards the river Greta, which near Barnard Castle joins the river Tees flowing south-eastwards from Cross Fell, which at almost 3,000 feet is the highest part of the Pennines. upper Teesdale had mining communities. Barnard Castle, with a population of about 5,000 in 1861, was a market town whose principal manufactures were textiles, but among its people was a profusion of hawkers who perambulated the dales selling earthenware, pots and pans, small wares, draperies, shoes and spectacles. At Copley, five miles north, was a smelter – with a chimney bearing the date 1832 – which consumed ores from the estates of the dukes of Cleveland, whose seat was Raby Castle. More than 200 people were engaged in mining and smelting lead in the townships between Barnard Castle and Middleton-in-Teesdale. Among them were men employed at the Blackton smelt mill at Eggleston, built by the London Lead Co. in 1775, and rebuilt in the 1820s. This, the company's only smelt mill in Teesdale, was a complex of many buildings, ergonomically designed so that materials moved down the slope and did not require lifting, with a flue rising to a chimney on the hillside. The company employed the Pattinson process to separate silver from metallic lead.

The London Lead Company began mining in Teesdale in 1753, establishing its local headquarters in Middleton-in-Teesdale in 1815, and in 1833–34 built Masterman Place, a range of 25, two-storey stone-built

workers' houses designed by Ignatius Bonomi and arranged in small groups. In 1861 Middleton House was the home of Robert Walton Bainbridge, who had the grand title of 'Superintendent of the Lead Company Works in the North'. Middleton parish extended over 40,250 acres as far as Alston and the Cumberland border. Its population of 1,537 in 1801 grew to 3,091 in 1831, 3,769 in 1861 and reached a peak of 3,823 in 1871, falling substantially after 1881. In 1861 more than 600 miners lived in Middleton and in Holwick on the opposite bank of the Tees, together with more than 200 washers, dressers and smelters. More than 80 miners occupied small farms, while other farmers carried ores and concentrates between mines, washing floors and the smelter.

The road up Teesdale climbs to 1,962 feet (604 m) beneath Stack's Rigg before descending the valley of the South Tyne through the lead-mining community of Garrigill. Another route, coming up Weardale from the east, rises to 2,090 feet (644 m) above Killhope before passing through Nenthead and down the valley of the river Nent, which joins the South Tyne at Alston. The market town of Alston was the centre of a Cumberland parish of 36,967 acres, little of which was cultivated, but Alston Moor was a notably rich source of metallic ores, and its history was intricately linked with that of Weardale. The most powerful force in lead mining at Alston and Nenthead was the London Lead Company. In 1700 the Alston estate was owned by the 3rd Earl of Derwentwater, but he was beheaded after supporting the Old Pretender in 1715, and it passed first to the Crown and then in 1735 to the Commissioners of Greenwich Hospital, who the following year leased most of the mining rights to Colonel George Liddell. In 1737 he built the first smelt mill at Nenthead. The London Lead Company took over Liddell's leases in 1745, and thereafter the company's agents decided every fourth month which veins were to be worked, which partnerships should work them, and the rates to be paid for the ore produced. In 1768 there were 119 lead mines in Alston parish, of which 103 were leased out by Greenwich Hospital.

Nenthead, a virtually new community, was the centre of the London Lead Company's operations. With its strong Quaker ethos, the company built housing for its workers from 1825 together with allotment-style gardens, a market hall, an inn, a clock tower and a shop that took ready money, rather than a 'truck' shop that accepted only company tokens. A school was opened in 1819 and a reading room in 1833, and by 1847 the company enforced compulsory attendance for the children of its workpeople. Innovations in dressing and smelting were made by Thomas Dodd, the company's mines agent between 1785 and 1816. It built three roller-crushers at Nent Head in 1813 and by 1817 was using iron railways underground and on its washing floors. Under the direction of Joseph Dickinson Stagg, manager of the smelt mills from 1842, a condenser was installed to draw furnace gases through water chambers, depositing particles of lead. A building housing the Pattinson process for recovering silver was constructed in 1839, and projects of the 1850s included a dry store for tools, candles, fuses and gunpowder, engineering workshops and a timber yard, while jaw crushing machines were introduced from 1867. The London Lead Company worked at Nenthead until 1882. It was calculated that 1,100 people were employed in mining in Alston in 1800. The Nent Force Level, an 8-foot (2.5 m) square adit of which parts were accessible in boats, extends about 2½ miles from Alston to Nenthead and was begun in 1776

at 890 feet (274 m) above sea level under the direction of John Smeaton. In 1815 work ceased but was recommenced 270 feet (83 m) higher and it was completed as far as the Rampgill Vein at Nenthead in 1839.

In the 1850s the mines on Alston Moor were producing between 5,000 and 10,000 tons *per annum* of lead ore, together with some zinc blende and calamine, and copper and iron ores. There were 55 mines on the moor in 1851, but almost half the output of 5,151 tons of lead ore came from the two largest, and the production levels recorded at 23 of them was less than 20 tons. The population of the parish of Alston was more or less stable at about 6,500 between 1831 and 1861, but declined substantially after 1871. In 1861 1,230 of the men of the parish were mining, dressing

⟨ The lead-mining districts of the northern Pennines.

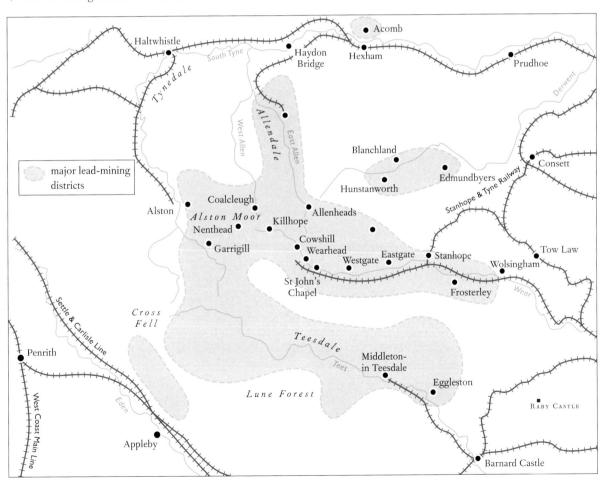

and washing ores and 40 worked at smelters. A small woollen mill in the town of Alston provided work for about 30 women.

The other significant lead-mining partnership in the north Pennines area, usually called the Blackett-Beaumont Company, originated in 1696 with the granting of a lease of mines in Weardale to Sir William Blackett who was succeeded by the Beaumont family. In 1801 the London Lead Company leased mines at Stanhope and elsewhere in upper Weardale, but exchanged the latter for some Blackett-Beaumont workings in 1847 in order to concentrate their activities around Stanhope – the largest parish in Co. Durham, extending over 60,875 acres. In 1861 lead working in Stanhope, Wolsingham, Huntstanworth and Edmondbyers employed more than 1,800 people, while from the 1840s iron ore was mined in Wolsingham by Charles Attwood's Weardale Iron Co. The traffic generated by coal mining, limestone quarrying and lead mining prompted early railway construction: from 1834 the area was served by the Stanhope & Tyne Railway which descended into Weardale by inclines at Crawley and Weatherhill, and extended 38 miles to South Shields, and by the Weardale Railway from Bishop Auckland which reached Frosterley in 1847, Stanhope in 1862 and Wearhead in 1895.

The lead-mining communities were scattered along the valley, from Wolsingham through Frosterley, Stanhope, Eastgate and Westgate, St John's Chapel, Ireshopeburn, Wearhead, Cowshill, Killhope, and over the watershed to Nenthead. One of the principal smelters was the Lintzgarth Mill, built by the Blacketts in 1737, on the bank of the Rookhope Burn which joins the Wear at Eastgate. A six-arch viaduct over the burn carried the flues which rise 1½ miles to a chimney 1,528 feet (470 m) above sea level on Redburn Common. The very well-preserved dressing floors at Killhope, now the North of England Lead-mining Museum, served mines opened by the Blackett-Beaumont Company in 1853. The 33 ft 6 in. (10.3 m) diameter iron waterwheel that dominates the site was built by W. G. Armstrong of Newcastle for an Allendale mine in 1859 and moved to Killhope, where it drove crushing rollers, in 1877. Ramshaw in Huntstanworth parish was the centre of operations of the Derwent Lead Mines, which were revived in 1805. In contrast to the iron-working settlements east of Stanhope, the lead-mining communities of Weardale were exceptionally stable, the vast majority of people having been born in the hamlets where they lived or in neighbouring settlements. New roads to Alston built in the 1820s reduced the area's isolation, but this was always a bleak and harsh environment.

The river East Allen rises on Burtree Fell, north of Cowshill on the road from Stanhope to Alston. The sources of the river West Allen are near Coalcleugh about a mile north of Nenthead. The two join about three miles north-west of Allendale town and flow north to the Tyne. This was another major lead-mining district. The mines at Allenheads produced 55,785 tons of ore between 1729 and 1795, and 200,032 tons between 1800 and 1896 (the figures for 1796–99 are missing). Thomas Sopwith, a writer on mining, became mine surveyor for the London Lead

◁ Remains of the ore-washing plant, on the river West Allen at the Coalcleugh Mine, about two miles north-east of the conserved site at Killhope.

⚲ This watercolour, entitled 'Grating', shows broken ore being washed in a buddle.

© SCIENCE MUSEUM / SCIENCE & SOCIETY PICTURE LIBRARY

Company in 1845 and subsequently its chief agent at Allenheads. Allendale was a large parish with eight 'grieveships' extending to 37,267 acres. Its population in 1861 totalled 3,454, of whom 355 were lead miners, 88 washers and dressers, and 107 smelters. Lengthy adits are explored by cavers; water gushes through the ruins of the washing floors at Coalcleugh; and the Blackett-Beaumont Company's smelt mill at Allendale is notable for an Armstrong hydraulic engine. The most impressive surviving monuments of lead working are the immense flues at the north end of the valley, extending 2½ miles to two chimneys 1,505 feet (464 m) above sea level on open moorland. As in Weardale the population was stable, but in May 1849 some 58 miners and their families, blacklisted during an industrial dispute, left Liverpool aboard the *Guy Mannering en route* for mines in Wisconsin and Illinois.

The Blackett-Beaumont Company also owned mines in Haydon Bridge parish, seven miles north of Allendale, where there were collieries and an engineering works. The lead workings were centred on a smelter at Langley built in 1768 by the Commissioners of Greenwich Hospital, and expanded thereafter. In 1858 the smelt mill was worked by Shield & Dinning,

who refined silver from the metallic lead, produced raw materials for lead paint, and manufactured bone manure. In 1861 there were 123 lead miners in the parish and 46 workers at the smelter. About 50 men worked in 1861 at lead mines and a smelter north of the Tyne at Acomb near Hexham, and more than 30 at a smelter owned by Sir Edward Blackett at Fallowfield.

As we have seen, lead deposits are often found in association with other metals. For example, zinc ores from Alston were smelted at a spelter (i.e. zinc) works at Tindal, six miles east of Brampton on the banks of the Coalfell Beck amid the collieries owned by the earls of Carlisle and worked by James Thompson, who in 1837–40 employed *Rocket* (of Liverpool & Manchester fame, see pages 86, 146, 182) on the railway that served them. The smelter was established in 1845 by James Henry Attwood and supplied with coal by a self-acting inclined railway. The mines on Alston Moor in 1856 produced 257 tons of zinc blende and 120 tons of calamine. The works employed about 50 men in the 1860s. Ores were calcined in 28 reverberatory furnaces until they became zinc oxide, which was mixed with small coal and fired at high temperatures to produce gaseous zinc which was distilled into liquid zinc in refractory containers. The smelter was worked after Attwood's death by the Nenthead & Tynedale Lead & Zinc Co. and closed in 1895. Fumes destroyed the vegetation around the site and until the 1950s the ground was littered with retort sherds.

West of Middleton-in-Teesdale lead ore was mined around Brough, and more than 130 miners were employed on the slopes of Hilton Fell and Murton Fell east of Appleby. Farther west in Cumberland more than a hundred people in 1861 mined, dressed and smelted lead ores around Keswick. In Patterdale mining on the banks of the Red Tarn Brook below Helvellyn on the western side of Ullswater began in the eighteenth century. Sinking of the Greenside Mine commenced in 1818, and 95 miners were recorded there in the 1861 census. The agent was William Phillips from Gwennap. Greenside Mine worked until 1962, when it was the last 'traditional' lead mine in the whole of the British Isles.

Lead production in Scotland, Man and Ireland

The only significant source of non-ferrous ores in Scotland was around Wanlockhead and Leadhills in the Lowther Hills near the headwaters of the river Clyde. The extraction of lead, and at times of zinc and silver and even gold, began in the seventeenth century, and the produce of the mine was subsequently smelted at a mill whose remains have been conserved, together with a waterwheel, a steam engine and a unique water-powered beam engine. A library was established in Leadhills in 1741 and the Miners' Reading Society Library in Wanlockhead in 1756. Production on a diminishing scale continued into the twentieth century. The Museum of Lead Mining at Wanlockhead preserves evidence both of mining technology and of the social and cultural life of this isolated industrial community.

The Isle of Man was a significant source of metallic ores in 1870, producing some 2,500 tons *per annum* of lead and silver ore, 500 tons of copper ore and 9,000 tons (some 20 per cent of British output) of zinc ores. There were only 355 miners on the island in 1841 but the scale of working increased in the following decade. The outcrop at Laxey was discovered about 1780, and levels were subsequently driven into the hillside. A new company was formed in the 1820s when waterwheels were installed to drain the workings. The most monumental and celebrated was the *Lady Isabella*

waterwheel (the 'Laxey Wheel'), erected in 1854 by Robert Casement (see page 51). The pitch-back wheel is 72 feet 6 inches (22 m) in diameter, with 168 buckets, and the pump rods which it worked were carried on a viaduct of 34 stone arches. From it the washing floors of the Laxey mine extended a mile as far as Agneash village. The mine employed about 500 men between the 1850s and the early 1880s. Most were Manx-born, although several Cornishmen were present and a few Irishmen worked on the dressing floors. Lead ore was also worked at Foxdale near Peel in the eighteenth century. The Foxdale Mine Company was formed in 1823 on the initiative of lead processors from Chester and controlled the largest of several workings which by 1880 employed about 250 men underground and 180 on the surface, producing annually 3,500 tons of ore.

There were also workings for lead in Ireland, particularly around Silvermines in Co. Tipperary, where a Cornish engine house and dressing floors remain, and at Ballycorus, Co. Dublin, where the Lead-mining Company of Ireland established a smelter and processing works in 1805 which was supplied from Glendalough and other mines in the Wicklow Mountains, and worked until the 1920s. A mile-long flue climbs the hillside to an 80-foot (24.6 m) granite chimney.

Lead mining in Shropshire and Wales

The lead-mining region of south Shropshire presents contrasts with the northern Pennines. Its rise in the eighteenth century was rapid, producing a land-scape characterised by imposing engine houses, and

 The engine house at the Old Grit Mine in Shropshire which probably accommodated a Boulton & Watt pumping engine installed in 1783.

 The labour force and waterwheel of the Nant-bwlch-yr-heirn Mine in the Conwy Valley, North Wales, photographed around 1875.

it was the subject of reckless speculation in the mid-nineteenth century. Large-scale mining began in the 1730s at the Bog Mine, in wild country west of the Stiperstones, from which ore was taken for smelting near Coalbrookdale. A Boulton & Watt pumping engine was erected in 1777. In the 1780s John Lawrence established the White Grit Co., which successfully worked several mines, but the family was beset with lawsuits after 1815. The richest mine in the region, and one of the most productive in Britain, was at Snailbeach. Extraction began in 1761, and the Snailbeach Mining Co., formed in 1782, worked the mine for a century. Snailbeach was prosperous in 1870, with an annual output of more than 3,000 tons of lead ore, but other ventures were less successful. Activity at the Bog Mine was renewed in 1839 with

the installation of a 370 hp steam pumping engine, the *Queen Victoria*, supplied by the Coalbrookdale Co. Crowds swarmed over the hills on inauguration day, cannon were fired, and visitors feasted on ale, bread and cheese while being serenaded by harpists and fiddlers. The mine closed in 1844 and was re-opened in 1856 by a fraudulent company that went into liquidation three years later.

The output of Shropshire lead mines reached a peak of 7,932 tons of ore in 1875, fuelling the speculative investment that provided capital for several imposing engine houses – which saw little use – built under the direction of the Cornish engineer Arthur Waters. Several smelters with ore hearths were built at the foot of the hills around Pontesford, fortuitously close to mines in the Shrewsbury coalfield, but

The remains of the extensive dressing floors of the Cwmystwyth lead mine, a large network of adit and shaft workings about 15 miles inland from Aberystwyth. The mine was worked in the Middle Ages, enjoyed a prosperous period in the 1780s and another from 1848 under the direction of John Taylor. Further investments were made in the late 1890s, and the ruins of the offices, houses and the dressing floors which treated ores from a crushing mill powered by water turbines and a Pelton waterwheel lie above the remnants of earlier dressing systems. It would have been excessively expensive to transport coal for a steam engine to such a remote spot, and the site demonstrates the continuing importance of water power in remote parts of Britain even in the late nineteenth century.

in 1862–63 the Snailbeach Co. built a reverberatory smelter on the hillside half a mile from the mine, from which a flue led to a chimney on the hillside which also served the boilers of a Cornish pumping engine erected in 1856. The output of the Shropshire mines declined in the 1880s, but workings for fluorspar and barytes continued into the twentieth century.

In Wales most lead working in the eighteenth century was in the north-east, where the Prince Patrick mine was sunk in 1728 on Halkyn Mountain. The London Lead Company set up a smelter at Gadlis in 1702 which it worked until the 1780s. John Wilkinson took over the productive mine at Minera near to his Bersham Ironworks in 1788, and in 1789 built a short-lived smelter at Brymbo. In the 1840s Taylor re-organised operations at Minera, amalgamating eleven mining companies, and improving drainage by the construction of the Deep Day Level, completed in 1847. Several leadworks were established in the Greenfield Valley from the 1750s, including the River Bank works, built by Birmingham interests in 1785, which calcined calamine for brass making and smelted lead ore. Halkyn Mountain remained an important source of ore. John Taylor, acting as agent for Lord Grosvenor, installed an ore-crushing mill in 1823, and

from 1829 he improved pumping arrangements and enlarged the Holywell drainage level to accommodate a horse tramway. Several smelters, for calamine as well as for lead ore, worked along the shore of the Dee estuary in the mid-nineteenth century. At Flint 300 men were working at three smelters in 1833. In 1841 63 per cent of the 2,289 people engaged in lead mining in Wales lived in Flintshire.

A rich vein of lead ore was discovered in 1692 at Llangynog in Montgomeryshire, near the head of the Tanat Valley. At first the ore was smelted nearby, but in the 1720s a furnace was built at Pool Quay, the head of navigation on the river Severn. This used ore from other mines and worked until 1762. The opening of the Ellesmere and Montgomeryshire canals and the prospect of main-line railways stimulated interest in Montgomeryshire lead mines. There were only 83 lead miners in the county in 1841, but 1,100 in 1851 and nearly 1,500 by 1871. Numbers increased after the discovery in 1865 of a rich vein of ore at Van near Llanidloes, a mine which was exceptionally prosperous and employed more than 600 men in the late 1870s. Farther west in Cardiganshire and Carmarthenshire there were 619 lead miners in 1841. The mine at Cwmystwyth, perhaps the richest source of lead in Wales, worked from the 1740s, enjoyed renewed prosperity under the direction of John Taylor from 1848, and continued into the twentieth century. Lead ore was also found in the Gwydir ore field on the west side of the Conwy Valley and on the Lleyn Peninsula where an engine house of 1779 at Penrhyn Du accommodated a Boulton & Watt pumping engine. Mines from both areas sent ore to the smelter at Gadlis.

Lead processing in towns and cities

Lead ore was usually smelted near the mines in the uplands where it was dug, but metallic lead was processed in large towns. Lead could be rolled into sheets for roofing or extruded into pipes. Lead shot was made in shot towers, the invention of William Watts of Bristol who patented the concept in 1782. A shot tower was usually about 180 feet (55 m) tall. Pig lead would be melted in small furnaces at different heights according to the size of shot required, and arsenic was added to make it fall as droplets rather than a continuous stream. It was poured through perforated copper screens and fell as spheres into vats of water. At most processing works there were ovens for producing the red lead (lead oxide) which was used in glass making and varnishes, and chambers for making white lead (basic lead carbonate) for pottery glazes and paints.

Lead was processed in Newcastle-upon-Tyne from the early eighteenth century, and in 1778 a partnership was formed between Samuel Walker I (of the Rotherham iron-working family) and Richard Fishwick and Archer Ward, both from Hull. They leased land at Elswick where they began producing white lead in 1788, installed a steam-powered rolling mill, and in 1797 added a 174-foot (53.5 m) shot tower which remained until 1969. The Elswick complex, the largest of several on Tyneside, had a 930-foot (286 m) frontage to the river Tyne by the 1880s, when it included white-lead chambers, rolling mills, red-lead ovens and hydraulic pipe presses, with power provided by a 35 hp steam engine. Customers included coach-makers in Newcastle and glassmakers on Tyneside and Wearside.

In 1788 William Watts, with Philip George, a Bristol brewer and distiller, and a banker, formed Watts, George & Co. and built a shot tower in Commercial Road (now Upper Ground), Lambeth, on the south bank of the river Thames. Watts went bankrupt after speculating in property, but George continued the works at Redcliff Hill, Bristol, where Watts's original tower was still in use in 1870. In 1794 he sold the Lambeth works to Walkers, Maltby & Co., a London branch of the Walker company from Newcastle. It was formed in 1785, with Thomas Maltby, whose family had long been involved in the London lead trade, as a partner. The company rolled sheet lead on a mill installed by Joseph Bramah and powered by a 36 hp steam engine, and later made pipes with five hydraulic presses. Thomas Maltby withdrew from the company in 1824 and in 1826 opened a rival works with a shot tower on Belvedere Road, west of Waterloo Bridge. The new works was taken over by Walkers in 1839. The shot tower, a famous London landmark, in use until 1949, was a feature of the Festival of Britain in 1951, and remained standing until 1962. Walkers also had a plant at Islington which produced white lead. It was sold to Thomas Maltby in 1824, and after 1837 it supplied London markets with chemicals from Elswick.

In 1799–1800 the Walker partnership built a works with a 168-foot (51.7 m) shot tower and a white-lead plant at Chester, well placed to process lead from smelters on the Dee estuary. It stood beside the Chester Canal, along which by 1805 coal could be delivered from mines around Ruabon. The workforce numbered more than 150 in 1840. Walkers took over the Dee Bank smelter in the 1830s and rebuilt it in 1840–41 with a red-lead plant and a rolling mill. The partners also opened a white-lead works at Derby in the early 1790s, which they operated until 1839 when it was sold to the company established by William Cox in 1806. Cox erected a 149-foot (45.9 m) shot tower in 1809 and his works was still operating in 1870.

Lead processing in Shrewsbury had its origins in London. A London plumber, Thomas Burr, moved to Shropshire between 1811 and 1813. He used lead from local smelters to extrude pipes, and built a tower to make shot, while retaining an interest in the trade in the capital. In 1829 he purchased the flax-weaving mill that had been built by Charles Bage. It was developed by his sons between 1836 and 1852 into a complex which included a lead-rolling mill, a melting furnace and casting bed, a hydraulic pipe-making machine, two steam engines, and plant for producing white lead and red lead. More than 60 people were employed in 1861, and the works continued until 1894. By the 1850s the Burrs were also working the Commercial Road plant in Lambeth. They used the shot tower until 1870, and the works passed to others before it was demolished in 1935.

Conclusions: mining and processing

Metalliferous mining declined dramatically after the 1870s as overseas mines, many of them developed by Cornish engineers, began to export their produce to Britain, sharply reducing the prices that British miners could obtain for their ores. The economic fortunes of many upland communities deteriorated because of falling production, and this was exacerbated by external competition on other fronts too. Overseas

An engraving of *circa* 1860 of the leadworks in Derby of Cox, Brothers & Co., centred round a 149 ft shot tower. In 1846 Bagshaw's Directory lists the company as 'lead merchants mfrs. of white lead, lead pipe & shot, Morledge & Mill hill', while at the London Exhibition of 1862 the company exhibited 'Red, white, and orange lead, shot, lead pipes, plates of Derbyshire silver, etc.'.

THE PATENT SHOT WORKS, THE PREMISES OF MESSRS. COX BROTHERS AND CO.

producers also provided competition for agricultural products of the upland regions – Canterbury Lamb from New Zealand was sold in increasing numbers of shops in the 1880s. Most of the textile factories that had been established between 1790 and 1810 in the remote uplands were never prosperous, and the majority had closed by the 1830s, while long-established textile manufactures, such as that of woollen stockings in the area around Kirkby Stephen, were threatened by factory production elsewhere. The populations of many upland communities were lower in 1970 than they had been a century previously. But the decline of non-ferrous mining hit these areas particularly hard. Annual production figures, available from 1845, show that output of lead ore exceeded 100,000 tons in 1851 and 1856, and in each year between then and 1872, was, with one exception, over 90,000 tons. Thereafter decline was swift: output never passed 60,000 tons after 1882, or 50,000 tons after 1888, and in 1904 was only 24,600 tons. The output of copper ore had sharply declined before 1870, and while the production of tin ore reached a peak of 16,272 tons in 1871, it fell thereafter, and in 1896 was less than 10,000 tons. While mining declined, companies processing and fabricating non-ferrous metals continued to prosper and expand.

The metals industries present many contrasts between stability and feverish change, but all were affected by technological innovations in the eighteenth and nineteenth centuries. They provided self-sufficiency within Britain in a range of essential materials, and, by exporting, contributed substantially to the balance of payments. Taken together they were a powerful part of the economy.

The concentration of cotton-spinning mills at Ancoats in Manchester, alongside Union Street and the Rochdale Canal was the subject of one of the most powerful images of the industrial revolution, the work of George Pyne, published in 1829, and the mills remain one of the most impressive sights in industrial Britain. In the centre here is the eight-storey Sedgwick Mill built between 1818 and 1820.

9

'The spinners' ardent toil':
the textile industries

'It was the Spinners' ardent toil
That raised our happy nation
And plac'd this little sea-girt isle
In a superior station.'

BLACKBURN MAIL, 28 NOVEMBER 1804

AMONG the sectors that contributed to Britain's industrialisation, textiles stands above all others. The cotton industry, particularly of Lancashire, was the world's pre-eminent textile-manufacturing trade for a century and a half from the 1770s; woollen goods from Yorkshire and elsewhere had a much more venerable history and continued in importance throughout our period; linen, flax and silk, too, added to the bewildering variety of Britain's manufacturing output of yarns, cloths and clothing. The textile industry was a 'leading sector' in Britain's industrial revolution, which shaped developments in the wider economy and, indeed, in society at large.

The textiles sector was so important because of four salient factors. First, there was the sheer size of the industry. By 1861 some 452,000 people were employed in the cotton sector alone, as well as 173,000 in making fabrics from wool, 94,000 in the linen industry and 52,000 in silk manufacture – in all, over three-quarters of a million people from a national workforce of between 10 and 11 million. Second, as we shall see, textile production was very widespread, with fabrics of many types being produced in almost every part of the United Kingdom. Third, the manufacture of textiles was famously stimulated by technological innovations. It was one of the first and most important industries to experience significant mechanisation: in spinning, weaving, and the printing of fabrics. Finally, the textiles sector conspicuously brought into existence a new whole way of working, a factory system qualitatively different from what had gone before and which acted as a prototype for other industries. During the eighteenth century, indeed, textile entrepreneurs created large buildings accommodating series of processes, where workers could be closely managed in the performance of specialised tasks. Manufacturers began to use advanced water-power systems and steam engines to drive their machines. They imported raw materials from distant parts of the world, and supplied export markets where their ultimate customers included poor people as well as élites.

It is easy to interpret the history of textile manufacturing as a steady upward graph which continued to rise after the 1860s. Yet there were sage voices, such as that of Francis Moore in 1782, which cautioned against too great a reliance on cotton, arguing that, 'cotton can be no staple, because England does not produce a single ounce': foreign manufacturers closer to the cotton-growing regions were sure to be at an advantage in due course. A generation later, in 1815, Robert Owen found great cause for concern in the country's reliance on the industry:

> this single branch of British manufactures
> has become of vital national importance.
> It is interwoven with all that relates to the
> employment of our population, of our capital,
> and of our shipping; and all that concerns our
> national credit, our solvency, and our domestic
> peace, contentment and security … [but]
> the boldest and most far-seeing minds in the
> community cannot contemplate any serious
> vicissitude befalling it, without the utmost
> alarm and terror.

Yet this was also an industry where old technology and customary practices were intertwined with the new, where the archaic was sometimes as significant as the innovative, and domestic or small-scale production just as important as the huge new factory. Like the product of a Jacquard loom, the industry's history encompasses many paradoxical strands. There is, however, no denying the sector's central role in the industrial revolution in many parts of the British Isles.

The export of wool and later of woollen cloth had been one of the principal and enduring strengths of the British economy during the Middle Ages, and through the sixteenth and seventeenth centuries. Textile manufacturing was widespread in 1700, and was the subject of frequent comment by early eighteenth-century travellers. Celia Fiennes, for example, noted the woollen cloth trade in Devizes, the making of baize in Colchester, of damasks and crapes in Norwich, of cloth for plaids in Kendal, and of serges in Exeter. She was impressed by the wealth gained in Leeds from manufacturing woollen cloth, and in Manchester from trading in linens and cotton. Daniel Defoe, who also travelled extensively around the country, observed that textile manufactures in Norwich provided employment in the city's hinterland and recorded silk working by Huguenots in Canterbury, flannel production in Salisbury, and 'the serge manufacture of Devonshire', centred on Exeter, where fabrics were brought to be finished and exported to Holland, Spain and Italy. In crossing Blackstone Edge from Rochdale to Halifax, Defoe saw smallholdings, whose occupiers combined farming with making woollen cloth, in a countryside 'infinitely full of people; those people all full of business'. Whatley observed the manufacture of flannels in Abergavenny, fustian in Carlisle, serges in Kettering, narrow cloth in Kington and woollen yarn in Liskeard. These accounts emphasise not only the very widespread distribution of textile production, but also the existence of numerous local specialisms, cloths which were identified with – and often named after – particular towns and districts.

Textiles were effectively marketed through the shops of mercers who, in every town, sold goods from outside the locality, hardware, paper, and chemicals (such as whiting, pitch and ochre) from elsewhere in Britain, sugar, spices, tobacco and spirits from overseas, and fabrics and haberdashery which were both home-produced and imported. Probate inventories give a vivid picture of their wares, as the following examples indicate. In 1716 Thomas Allen of Midhurst, Sussex, had black broad cloth from Wiltshire or Gloucestershire and fustian that could have come from Lancashire, as well as white Persian sarsnet (a soft, silky material used for linings and dresses), striped Scotch cloth (a type of linen), printed calicos, striped muslin, cotton waistcoating and handkerchiefs, and worsted stockings, nightcaps and children's mittens. In 1700 Benjamin Wright of Wellington, Shropshire, stocked black and spotted serge, blue linsey, white crepe, coloured fustian, and white Osnabriggs (a coarse linen named after the German city). In 1673 Gruffyth Wynne of Caernarfon had stock worth more than £250, including flowered satin ribbons, black paragon (a mixture fabric that was often printed) and red paragon bodices, yellow sarsnet, Warrington cloth (a coarse linen), glazed calico, and broad cloth worth seven shillings a yard. Alexander Ethersey, who died in Buckingham in 1706, had fabrics and haberdashery worth about £1,000, including silks and mohair, cloth from Tamworth, Kidderminster and Yorkshire, linen from Hamburg, and black broad cloth also valued, like Wynne's, at seven shillings a yard.

The textile industries in Britain had long been important, but during the eighteenth century the quality, range and competitiveness of their products were transformed by a series of technological innovations which had wide-ranging implications right across society. These innovations brought changes in every sector of the textile industry, but most of them were applied first in the production of cotton, and of necessity they must form the starting point of our survey of textile manufacturing.

Innovations in cotton machinery

Sellar and Yeatman declared that, 'The Industrial Revolution would never have occurred but for the wave of great mechanical Inventors, e.g. Arkwright, who invented the Spinning Jenny, or unmarried textile working girl; subsequently however this kind of work was done by mules, the discovery of a man called Crompton.' Innovations in textile manufacturing long ago became an historical cliché, but familiarity does not imply insignificance, and inventions do merit examination. The most familiar of these innovations, whatever their subsequent applications, concerned cotton and took place in Lancashire, particularly around Bolton and Blackburn. By 1700 Lancashire weavers were producing mixture fabrics combining cotton and linen yarns, and by 1750 were making fabrics entirely of cotton. There was a ferment of innovation in the Lancashire towns in the mid-eighteenth century, even if some inventors fled elsewhere to avoid the attentions of machine-breakers, those who felt their traditional livelihoods were threatened by mechanisation.

↗ The patent drawings for the machine for spinning cotton that was devised by Lewis Paul and John Wyatt, who built a factory to produce cotton in Northampton which was unsuccessful. The principle of using rollers to draw out fibres was used by Richard Arkwright in his water-frame.
CARNEGIE COLLECTION

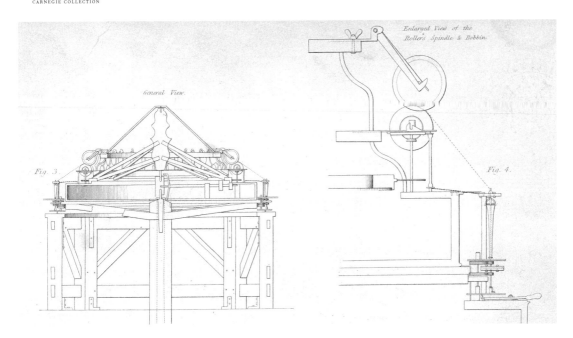

John Kay, born near Bury, Lancashire, was apprenticed as a maker of reeds, the comb-like devices that keep warp threads separate on a loom. Kay developed a reed made from polished wire rather than the reeds from which they derive their name or from cane, and in 1730 made a machine for cording and twisting worsted yarn. Then in 1733 Kay obtained a patent for a 'flying shuttle' which allowed weft to be passed through warp threads more quickly and over a greater width of cloth, effectively doubling the speed of weaving on the handlooms of the day. His device was widely copied even before his patent expired in 1747.

Parliament refused to help him recoup the money that was his due, and he spent the latter decades of his life in France. The operation of looms was further improved by the drop box (a container which houses shuttles for wefts of various colours), the invention of his son Robert Kay. The proliferation of looms with flying shuttles in the mid-eighteenth century increased the demand for yarn, and this in turn gave a powerful economic stimulus to the innovation and development of new machinery that could spin yarn more quickly and economically.

James Hargreaves, weaver and carpenter, lived in

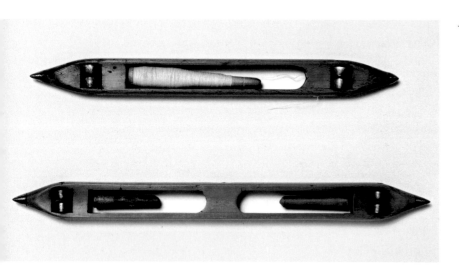

◁ Two shuttles designed for use on the flying shuttle loom and patented by John Kay in 1733. They have iron-tipped ends, rollers underneath to reduce friction, and one has two pins to weave a two-ply thread. This type of shuttle speeded up weaving (since the shuttle no longer had to be passed laboriously by hand across the loom) and made possible the production of broader cloth, since the width had previously been limited by the span of the weaver's arms.
© SCIENCE MUSEUM/SCIENCE & SOCIETY PICTURE LIBRARY

THE SPINNING JENNY.

◁ The spinning jenny, the invention of James Hargreaves, a hand- or sometimes horse-powered multiple spinning machine that was a significant improvement upon the spinning wheel. The spinner would turn the large driving wheel with his right hand, causing the spindles to rotate, while managing the draw bar, with which he controlled the drafting of the threads, with his left hand. (See also the illustration on page 20.)
CARNEGIE COLLECTION

Engraved by T.E.Nicholson.

Blackburn, and in 1764 produced the first 'jenny', a spinning machine with a carriage that was moved outwards by the spinner, drawing and twisting the roving, and then moved back to wind the spun yarn onto rotating spindles. The name probably derives from dialect pronunciation of the word 'engine', which at the time was used for any mechanical device. The first of Hargreaves' jennies had eight spindles, but there were twice as many on the version which he went on to patent in 1770, and machines with up to 120 were built subsequently. After encountering opposition to new machinery in Lancashire, Hargreaves moved to Nottingham, where he prospered modestly until his death but gained no reward for his innovation. The spinning jenny could only produce coarse yarns used in wefts, but it did enable substantial increases in productivity. It could be worked by hand or by horse-power, and jenny shops accommodating ranges of machines proliferated. In 1778 a Chorley man observed the local enthusiasm for spinning machinery, whether worked by waterwheels, by hand or by horse power. The jenny remained significant in textile manufacturing in some areas for another century.

In 1769 a 'new Piece of Machinery never before found out ... for the making of Weft or Yarn from Cotton, Flax and Wool' was patented by Richard Arkwright, a peruke maker born in Preston who worked in the Bolton area from about 1750; from 1762 he had a business which involved travelling in Nottinghamshire and Derbyshire. Arkwright's influential water-frame drew upon the invention of John Wyatt, a Birmingham carpenter who later worked for Matthew Boulton, and his partner, Lewis Paul, son of a Huguenot physician, who between 1742 and 1761 operated an unprofitable water-powered cotton mill in Northampton. However, by drawing the roving through four sets of paired rollers and winding it by means of a flyer onto a rotating spindle, Arkwright succeeded in both drawing and twisting the yarn. Arkwright employed a Warrington clockmaker John Kay (not to be confused with John Kay, inventor of the flying shuttle) to make the machine. Kay had worked with Thomas Highs from whom, it is alleged, the idea of paired rollers rotating at different speeds may have been taken, but Richard Hills has demonstrated that the machines which Arkwright supposedly copied had flaws and that as a viable machine the water-frame can rightly be adjudged to have been Arkwright's invention. James Watt sagely remarked that 'whoever invented the spinning machine, Arkwright had the most difficult part which was making it useful'. Arkwright and Kay were working in Preston in January 1768, but later in the year Arkwright moved to Nottingham where he found investors to provide him with capital, and in 1769 set up a horse-powered spinning factory in the Hockley area.

Of greater significance even than his invention of the water-frame, Arkwright developed and perfected a comprehensive system for the production of yarn from raw cotton which could be applied in water-powered or later in steam-powered factories. He was obviously aware of the buildings which were already used for throwing silk at Derby and Congleton, and from 1 August 1771 leased land for a mill at Cromford in Derbyshire powered by the Bonsall Brook and the Cromford Sough. A letter of 2 March 1772 concerning window fittings suggests that the building was then nearing completion. The ferment of ideas about textile machines in Lancashire encompassed new methods of carding, and Arkwright was concerned to mechanise this process too. He was granted a patent in 1775 for a series of preparation processes – opening and cleaning cotton, carding, and the creation of slivers and rovers. He made it possible to process raw cotton almost entirely by machine, and within the bounds of one factory, into yarn that could then be despatched for use by weavers. His achievement, summarised in Rees' *Cyclopaedia*, was to introduce into cotton manufacture 'a system of industry, order and cleanliness, till then unknown in any manufactory where great numbers were employed together, but which he so effectually accomplished that his example may be regarded as the original of almost all similar improvement'. The validity of the 1775 patent was contested in 1781, and finally reversed in 1785 enabling others to utilise Arkwright's developments. The pattern that Arkwright had first established at Cromford was followed by other entrepreneurs, who built cotton-spinning factories in many parts of Britain and farther afield.

Samuel Crompton, born to a family of spinners, lived at Hall i'th'Wood, a sixteenth-century house near Bolton, Lancashire. He attempted to improve the jenny, and in 1779 completed a spinning 'mule' which combined the moving carriage of the jenny with the rollers of the water-frame. He lacked the money to take out a patent and received meagre reward for the expertise which he shared with cotton manufacturers. Parliament granted him £5,000 in 1812, but his subsequent ventures failed. A fully mechanised self-acting version of the mule was perfected by Richard Roberts between 1825 and 1830, and went on to become the principal means of spinning yarn. As it proliferated

in the 1830s it initiated large-scale changes in cotton spinning, because it enabled one mule-tenter with two or three boys to operate as many as 1,600 spindles.

A powered loom was invented by the clergyman-poet Edmund Cartwright in 1784. He had studied at University College, Oxford, and became interested in textile machinery after a conversation at Matlock Bath in 1784 which followed a visit to Arkwright's mills at nearby Cromford. He patented his loom in 1785 and set up a weaving factory in Doncaster, but his business became bankrupt in 1793. He subsequently carried out experiments in agricultural improvement at Woburn for the 5th Duke of Bedford, and in 1809 was

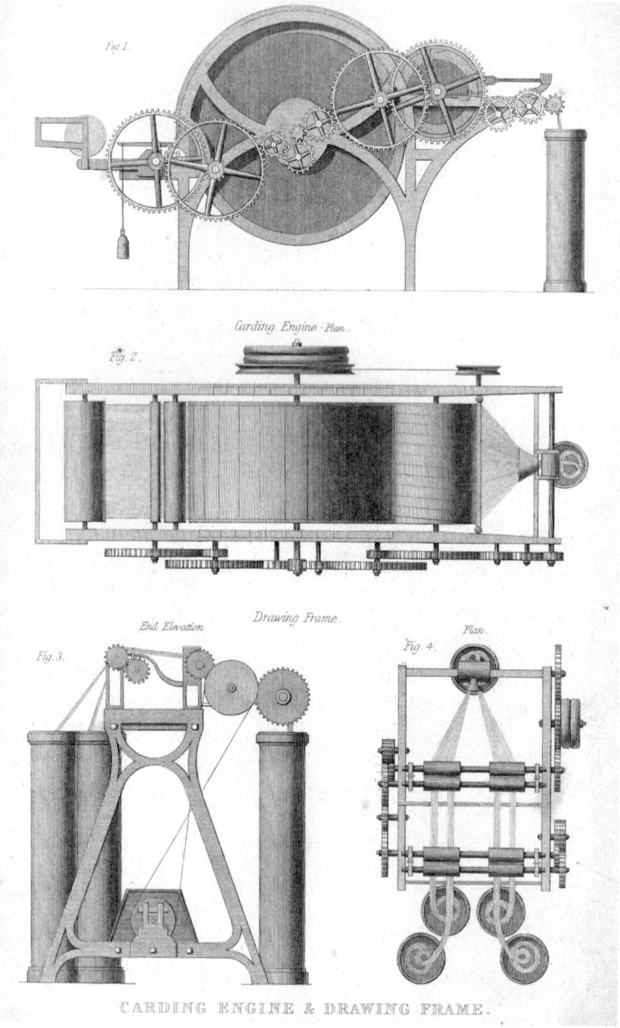

Fig.1.

Carding Engine - Plan.

Fig.2.

End Elevation. *Drawing Frame.* *Plan.*

Fig.3. *Fig.4.*

CARDING ENGINE & DRAWING FRAME.

⤺ Arkwright was responsible not just for the water-frame but for a series of machines that made it possible to accommodate in factories the whole series of processes for transforming raw cotton into yarn for the weaver, and to work most of them by water- or steam power. Among his most significant innovations was the carding machine, seen here in an illustration from Edward Baines, *The History of the Cotton Manufacture in Great Britain* (1835).

⤼ Samuel Crompton. The spinning 'mule' that he invented was adopted very widely but, without patent protection, Crompton did not prosper from it personally.

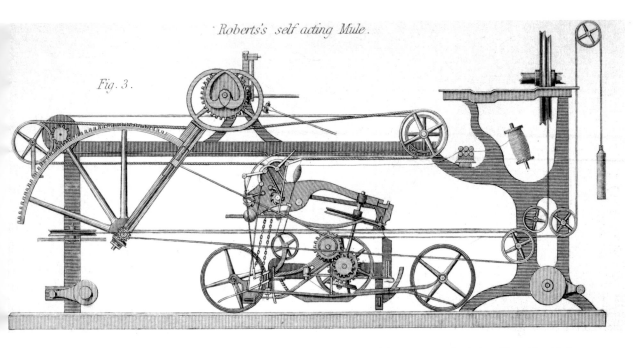

Roberts's self acting Mule.

Fig. 3.

A drawing by J. W. Lowry published in the 1830s showing the self-acting version of the spinning mule, designed by Richard Roberts, an iron machine which was mass-produced in great quantities in Lancashire engineering works from the 1820s. Ranks of such mules filled the spinning floors of many textile mills in Lancashire and elsewhere.

Like the self-acting mule, the powerloom by the 1820s could be produced in very large numbers. This picture of a factory in Stockport, north-east Cheshire, in 1830 shows line after line of such looms, all powered by leather belts attached to overhead shafts which would have been worked by a distant steam engine. The supervisors are male, the weavers young women.

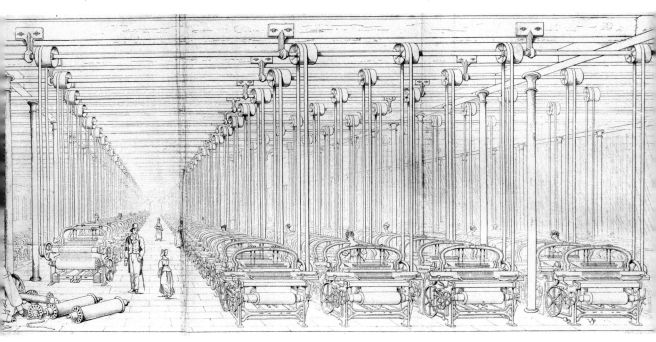

▲ The best known of the portraits of Richard Arkwright, by Joseph Wright of Derby. His prosperity shines out of the picture, while by his left hand is a model of his water-frame.

in which it could be adapted to new purposes. By 1828 a Macclesfield newspaper acknowledged that 'M. Jacquard's looms [are] now generally used throughout the three kingdoms for every figured article woven in looms'. Nevertheless the application of mechanical power to weaving progressed slowly. It took many years to devise powerlooms that could weave blankets, carpets and multi-coloured fabrics, and in some places handloom weaving continued into the second half of the nineteenth century.

Methods of finishing fabrics also changed from the late eighteenth century. Cloth was traditionally treated with sour milk (lactic acid) and whitened by sunlight on bleach greens, but from 1785 the Savoyard chemist Claude Louis Berthollet demonstrated that bleaching could be achieved with chlorine compounds. Through the 1790s Charles Tennant, a weaver from Ayrshire, took out patents for the manufacture of bleaching powder, then regarded as a hypochlorite of lime. His method involved passing chlorine gas over hydrated lime which was spread over the floors of lead-lined chambers. In 1799 he opened a factory to manufacture bleaching powder at St Rollox, on the north-eastern side of Glasgow, which became one of the largest industrial plants in Scotland. Bleachworks consumed large quantities of clean water and were characteristically located on valley floors upstream from discharges of polluting effluent, and many carried on finishing processes other than bleaching. In the Pennine valleys of Lancashire and Yorkshire the bleaching trade was often a key element of the local textile economy, and bleachworks could be very extensive, with a major impact upon the topography. At Wallsuches near Bolton, for example, a bleachworks was established in 1777 by the Ridgway Brothers. By the mid-1840s the extensive complex included a large 'lodge' (or reservoir), created by damming the shallow valley upstream from the works, together with two smaller reservoirs and three long rectangular ponds, with a network of canal-type feeders, leats and sluices, and small coalpits to provide fuel. Almost the entire infrastructure survives intact, as do most of the late eighteenth- and early nineteenth-century buildings, among them Wallsuches House, a fine property built at the end of the eighteenth century for John Ridgway on

given a grant of £10,000 by the House of Commons, after which he retired to Kent. Stockport was at the centre of improvements to the powerloom in the early nineteenth century, by William Horrocks, William Radcliffe and others. In 1822 the Manchester engineer Richard Roberts patented a loom made in iron which was subsequently mass-produced.

About 1800 the Frenchman J. M. Jacquard perfected a loom that could weave fabrics with complex patterns, controlling groups of warp and weft yarns by using perforated pattern cards through which needles passed to lift and lower the warp ends according to the pattern of holes punched in them. The loom was used in British textile-manufacturing communities from the 1820s, and loom carpenters quickly devised ways

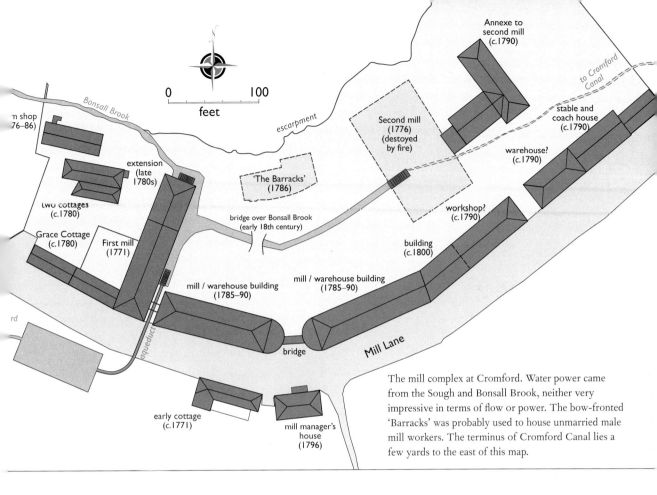

The mill complex at Cromford. Water power came from the Sough and Bonsall Brook, neither very impressive in terms of flow or power. The bow-fronted 'Barracks' was probably used to house unmarried male mill workers. The terminus of Cromford Canal lies a few yards to the east of this map.

the south side of the works, with landscaped grounds extending down to the brook.

The techniques for printing calico fabrics were introduced to the British Isles from India, although they also had origins in Egypt and South America. In the eighteenth century patterns carved on wooden blocks were impressed on fabrics by hand, but from the 1780s a method was developed by which designs were etched on copper plates which were fixed on to cylinders, and pieces of cloth, stitched together and inscribed with the names of their owners for identification, would be drawn by water- or steam power through an elaborate system of pattern, inking and drying rollers. There were about 170 calico printworks

in England and Scotland by the 1860s, and they added substantially to the attractiveness of – and thus to the revenue gained from – cotton fabrics. The spread of printing had widespread and unexpected repercussions. When Needwood Forest in Staffordshire was enclosed from 1801 many of its 148,170 holly trees were felled to be used for rollers in calico printworks in Manchester. The fulling of woollen cloth had been water-powered since the late Middle Ages, but the process of calendering – providing the final pressed finish for textiles by passing fabrics through the hot or cold rolls of a machine called a calender – came to be powered by water and subsequently by steam in the late eighteenth century.

Cotton mills: a revolution in factory working

Richard Arkwright's Cromford Mill was an immediate success and for more than 20 years was steadily extended. The first mill building, of local gritstone,

measured 93 × 26 feet (28.5 × 8 m), was 11 bays long and of five storeys, and was powered by an overshot wheel to which water was delivered by an aqueduct. A second mill was added in 1776–77, of 16 bays and six storeys with an attic above, whose water was conveyed by a massive culvert. Warehouses were built in the late 1780s, and by 1790 the potential for further expansion was limited by the constraints of the site.

'The profits arising from the machinery of Sir Richard Arkwright were so considerable, that it frequently happened, in different parts of the country, that the machinery was employed for the whole four-and-twenty hours,' according to Sir Robert Peel in 1816. John Byng (later Viscount Torrington) wrote evocatively of the changing of the shifts at Cromford:

I saw the workers issue forth at 7 o'Clock, a wonderful crowd of young people … a new set

then goes in for the night, for the mills never leave off working. … These cotton mills, seven stories high, and fill'd with inhabitants, remind me of a first rate man of war; and when they are lighted up, on a dark night, look most luminously beautiful.

Arkwright and his family invested in other mills in Derbyshire, and from the 1780s in Scotland, while from 1776 his partner Jedediah Strutt built mills farther south in the Derwent Valley. The revocation of Arkwright's patents in 1785 stimulated a rush of mill building that extended through Lancashire and the Midlands, and reached even some of the most remote parts of the British Isles. By 1788 there were about 200

꜀ The hamlet of Mottram in the Pennine foothills about eight miles east of Manchester grew from a cluster of houses on top of a hill around a church in 1750 to a long street of 127 houses in 1795 when this map showing several cotton mills was published in John Aikin's *Description of the Country from 30 to 40 miles round Manchester.*

꜀ One of those mills (towards the bottom of the map) was constructed about 1790 upstream from Broad Bottom Bridge by Kelsall and Marsland. Aikin wrote, 'This pile of building has much injured the picturesque beauty of the view, concealing a fine wood in which the river loses itself', but others saw mills as sources of prosperity, and as structures that were romantic in their own right.

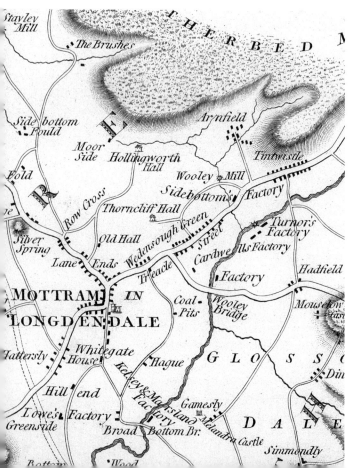

Arkwright-style mills in Great Britain; his technology was taken to the United States in 1789 by Samuel Slater, and to Germany in 1784 by Johann Gottfried Brugelmann.

The proliferation of multi-storey, mechanically powered spinning mills is only one aspect of the expansion of textile manufactures in the late eighteenth century. It is, however, one of the most important. The Arkwright-style mill required power, initially provided by waterwheels, and the locations of the first generation of spinning factories were determined by which ancient water mills happened to be available for sale or leasing. The shortage of suitable sites led cotton masters to consider the use of steam power. From the 1740s ironmasters had been using steam engines to pump water from below waterwheels back to the upper reservoir for re-use by the wheel, and when Arkwright built the Haarlem Mill at Wirksworth in 1780, he adopted a Newcomen engine to operate in this manner. About 1782 Arkwright with partners built Shudehill Mill in Miller Street, Manchester, with a five-storey main building measuring 200 × 30 feet (60.9 × 9.1 m), to which power was supplied from a 30 foot diameter waterwheel, whose water was recirculated by pumps worked by a steam engine. By 1791 the engineer Joshua Wrigley had installed engines for similar systems at 13 mills in Manchester.

However, the advent of the Watt rotative engine in 1782 made it possible for the first time to contemplate using steam power to drive the textile machinery directly – in 1785 George Robinson and his son James installed a Boulton & Watt engine at their mill at Papplewick, Nottinghamshire, which is acknowledged as the first rotative engine to drive machinery in a cotton factory. Robey and Kanefsky calculated that 468 steam engines were installed at textile mills between 1780 and 1800, although until the 1820s steam power was still of less consequence than water power as a means of working textile machinery. By avoiding the need to locate mills on reliable watercourses, the rotative engine made possible the proliferation of textile factories in towns. As Sir Robert Peel the elder remarked in 1816, 'owing to the present use of steam power in factories … large buildings are now erected, not only as formerly on the banks of streams, but in

Water-powered textile mills in the Derwent Valley.

the midst of populous towns.' Peter Gaskell believed it was in the first five years of the nineteenth century that steam became the usual source of power for new textile factories, which thereafter were increasingly built in towns. Urban mills, especially in the coalfields of Lancashire, gradually supplanted the water-powered factories which had grown up on scattered rural sites in many parts of Britain.

Another of Arkwright's innovations was that his mills often worked into, and sometimes through, the hours of darkness and therefore required artificial lighting, initially by candles or oil lamps. Some mill owners favoured the oil lamp invented by the Swiss

Aimé Argand in which the wick was mounted between a pair of metal tubes and surrounded by a cylindrical glass chimney. The lamp was promoted in Britain in the 1780s with the help of Matthew Boulton and James Watt. After William Murdock's demonstrations of the illuminating properties of coal gas in the 1790s, Boulton & Watt installed gas lighting systems at many large textile mills, although a survey of Gloucestershire mills in 1833 showed that 4 were lit entirely with candles, 6 with lamps, 18 with candles and lamps, one with lamps and gas, and only one entirely with gas. Most early textile factories were heated by domestic-style open fires, or by systems which drew warm air from ground-floor stoves through flues with outlets just below ceiling levels on working floors. The circulation of warm air was aided by the draughts created by small fireplaces. The owner of Stanley Mill near Stroud described in 1833 the numerous fires about the factory which made it smell like a cook-shop when workpeople fried bacon for their lunches. The Salford Twist Mill, built by George Augustus Lee in 1800, was heated by steam passing through the hollow cast-iron columns that formed the building's structure, and in the next two decades Boulton & Watt provided more than 20 similar systems in mills which had boilers for supplying steam engines.

An Arkwright-style mill could accommodate several hundred workpeople, and required a sanitation system. At first privies were located on working floors, but in Masson Mill they were grouped around a staircase in a projecting part of the front of the building. In many subsequent mills, including Murrays' Mill in

⌄ Masson Mill, built by Richard Arkwright from 1783 about a mile from his Cromford Mills, expressed his growing wealth and self-confidence. It was powered by the river Derwent rather than by the combination of the Bonsall Brook and a sough from a lead mine that worked his first mills. Its frontage was ornamented with eight Venetian windows, three Diocletian windows and a cupola, and in the decades that followed several other textile entrepreneurs built mills that had some of the features of country houses.

⌃ Oxford Mills, Ashton-under-Lyne, built for spinning cotton in 1845 and 1851 by Thomas and Hugh Mason, showing in the corner of the courtyard a staircase turret of the kind that provided access to mill floors without occupying space that could be used for machines, and which usually included lavatories as well as stairs.

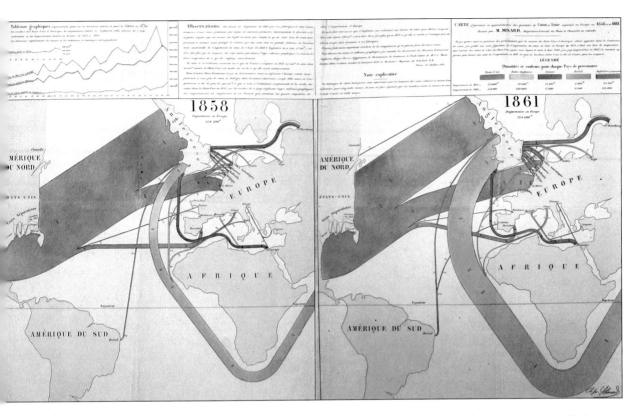

Charles Minard's maps of 1858 and 1861 are graphical representations of the quantities of cotton imported into Europe (principally the United Kingdom) at those dates. We know from other sources that raw cotton consumption (that is, imports retained in the UK and not re-exported) had increased by a factor of 200 from the 1740s to the 1840s.

Manchester, and Calver Mill in Derbyshire, they were located within staircase turrets, which left the main floors clear for machines. Materials could usually be carried on staircases, but by the 1830s elevators called *teagles* were employed in some Lancashire mills. Most textile factories expressed social discipline by means of a bell in a turret or a clock within a pediment, emphasising that owners required punctuality and regular attendance. A high external wall was an insurance against theft and the intrusions of machine-breakers, but also defined an area where authority rested with the mill owner. The significance of this kind of demarcation was revealed in a description of one of several fustian mills in Warrington in 1863, of which it was said, 'on the principle of the factory [this] works is the only one with all the premises shut off within gates'.

As we have seen, spinning machinery brought work-forces together in factories from the later eighteenth century, while weaving remained a largely domestic industry. It was the powerloom that eventually made possible the concentration of weaving in factories. One of the earliest purpose-built weaving mills was a single-storey building measuring 90 feet (27.4 m) long and 30 feet (9 m) wide, and with a vaulted brick roof, built in Shrewsbury for weaving linen by Charles Bage in 1815–16. Most early weaving mills were probably multi-storey buildings imitating current practice in spinning. In Glasgow a weaving factory in Graham Square, built about 1835, was a six-storey, 9 × 3 bay structure, with wooden floors supported by cast-iron columns. A weaving mill requires good lighting and heavy floor loadings (because of the huge weight of ranks of looms). While the first could be obtained in a multi-storey building, it could also be achieved in a north-lit, single-storey shed, which avoided the problem of floor loadings and gave greater structural stability. The characteristic saw-tooth profile of these weaving sheds' roofs is one of the defining images of the industrial revolution. The origins of such north-lit sheds – in which natural light is maximised without admitting direct sunshine – are not fully understood, but Waterside Mill, Langfield, Yorkshire, was specifically built in 1829 to house powerlooms. Specialist buildings for cotton weaving, often called sheds, were being built in Lancashire in the 1820s and covered many acres of the north-east of the county by the 1850s.

Factories were hungry for labour, sometimes in places without a ready supply. In remote locations spinning masters provided accommodation for hastily recruited workforces, predominantly women and children. Some mill owners, including the Strutts at Belper, provided premises where adult men could follow different, non-textile occupations. In Shrewsbury John Marshall found it difficult to recruit skilled workers and advertised in 1800 for an engineman, 'preferably accustomed to a Boulton & Watt engine'. In 1809 he sought 20 flaxdressers, offering piecework terms, and specifying that applicants should belong to the 'Hecklers' Club', indicating that ambitious entrepreneurs had sometimes to contend with established custom, in this case with the traditional practices of itinerant flaxdressers. Most entrepreneurs hoped that settled communities would develop around their mills, with children succeeding parents in work.

Between 1780 and 1830 some owners recruited orphan children in the care of their parishes, both locally and from distant cities. Thus, John Marshall recruited 82 from London for Ditherington Mill at Shrewsbury, and also took on parish apprentices from nearby villages. Apprentice houses were built at most mills where significant numbers were employed. The best known is at Quarry Bank Mill, Styal, eleven miles south of Manchester, where Samuel Greg recruited 150 children from London. In the 1830s Andrew Ure observed that the girl apprentices at Styal were recruited locally and from Chelsea but chiefly from Liverpool. Two apprentice houses remain at Ditherington, on the edge of Shrewsbury, one constructed soon after 1800 outside the perimeter of the site, the other built from 1812 within the boundary. Its size suggests that John Marshall expected to continue to recruit parish apprentices, but he appears not to have done so. The practice had diminished by 1820, although the owners of Cressbrook Mill between Buxton and Bakewell did take on children from Liverpool, Chester, Southampton and Bristol in the 1820s, and recruited some from Leicester as late as the 1850s. At the silk mill at Tring, Buckinghamshire, where the apprentice house remains, the 1861 census records 45 female apprentices aged between 12 and 17 (all but one of whom had been born in central London) living under the supervision of a 'master and matron of apprentices'.

Many of the mills that took apprentices were located at a distance from towns and main roads. The linen factory at Wildboarclough near Macclesfield hired 73 during its brief existence in the late 1790s. John Whitaker's Greenholme cotton mill at Burley-in-Wharfedale took 100 apprentices from London alone, some of whom continued there willingly as adult workers. John Birch employed 256 apprentices from London to make cotton at Backbarrow near Ulverston. In Derbyshire substantial numbers were taken on at Edale, Tideswell and elsewhere. While John Marshall employed apprentices at Shrewsbury, he had none at his Leeds mills; nor were London apprentices employed elsewhere in Leeds. However, the employer who took on the most London apprentices was William Toplis, who engaged no fewer than 762 for his cotton mill at Cuckney, north of Mansfield. The case of Robert Blincoe, from St Pancras in London, who was apprenticed from 1803 and worked until 1817 at Litton Mill in Derbyshire, made the practice notorious after a journalist publicised his story in a pamphlet, but it is fair to say that some apprentices were well treated and those at rural mills probably fared better than they would have done as orphans in urban parish workhouses or on city streets. In 1841 the Derbyshire mill owner John Smedley expressed a preference for millhands who, by completing apprenticeships at other mills, had shown themselves honest, industrious and respectable in their conduct.

Divergent patterns of growth and production in the cotton industry

Erasmus Darwin wrote of Richard Arkwright that 'by giving perpetual employment to many thousand families he has increased the population, and been productive of greater commercial advantages to this country, and contributed more to the general benefit of mankind, in so short a period of time, than any other single effort of human ingenuity'. It is indeed easy to perceive the growth of textile manufacturing in such revolutionary terms. The construction of multi-storey steam-powered mills, whose owners imposed rigorous discipline on their workpeople, created the 'factory system' which was described and defined by social commentators in the 1840s.

By the early years of the nineteenth century there were several cotton manufacturers operating on a large scale. The various mills owned by Arkwright employed perhaps 1,800, while the Strutts had around 1,500 and Robert Owen at New Lanark perhaps 1,700. But many operations were very much smaller than this. In 1792 John Byng noted that in Accrington, 'every vale swarms with cotton mills; some not bigger than cottages'. Evidence given to Parliament in 1816 showed that only seven mills had more than 600 workers, and that most had between 100 and 300 each. Two years later, a list compiled by the mill owners contained the names of 337 mills with a mean number of 170 employees. H. D. Fong calculated that in 1838 the average number of workers per factory in Lancashire varied between 78.1 in Oldham and 237.7 in Black-burn; in Manchester the average at that date was 216.3.

Textile manufacturing also developed by evolutionary means. In many cases, including at Cromford and Belper, 'factories' developed over time, as buildings accumulated around an original nucleus. Elsewhere, different models might develop and endure. For example, some entrepreneurs would not build a central manufacturing facility at all, preferring instead to distribute raw materials to domestic workers for spinning or weaving, and to receive the goods back after processing. Such places could be strikingly different from the urban warehouses of Lancashire or the mansion houses of clothiers in Gloucestershire. In some cases a concentration of a few spinning jennies or handlooms in a workshop might trigger growth that would eventually result in a factory. Alternatively, an ancient site might form the nucleus for later development. From the Middle Ages onwards, for example, fulling mills had employed water power to finish woollen cloth, and from the 1770s their water-wheels were also employed to work scribbling (or carding) machinery for wool; in due course spinning and weaving might take place on the premises. Thus, a form of factory would emerge by piecemeal development. In linen manufacturing, too, comparable concentrations of activity might occur around bleach greens. Nor was all development through the adoption of new machinery or technologies. Elements of the factory system, including the assembling of a sizeable workforce and the imposition of workplace discipline, might be introduced by bringing together hand-operated machines in a fairly primitive building that lacked any power system. Thus, in 1818, a Macclesfield ribbon manufacturer argued that the concentration of looms in a factory could increase quality and lower costs even if they were not powered. It seems that the proliferation of technologically unsophisticated means of production was just as significant as the building of modern multi-storey mills.

For a time the demand for the textiles produced by these new means was insatiable. Many memoirs attest to the frantic expansion of cotton production around Manchester about 1780, and the evidence they provide is now corroborated by archaeological data. The industrial archaeologist Mike Nevell has identi-fied two modes of production. In the first, domestic textile manufacturing was combined with farming and organised on a family basis. The architectural and archaeological expression of such growth was the addition of workshops or loomshops to farmsteads and cottages. In many Pennine and Lancashire townships such family-based farmstead and weaving operations became widespread and common. The second mode of work was merchant capital production, a dispersed form of production under centralised control in which clothiers put out work to spinners, weavers and finishers working in their homes. In this case, growth can be seen through the building of three-storey buildings that usually comprised both living and working accommodation. Hundreds of these were built in the Manchester region. William Radcliffe of Mellor near Stockport recalled in 1828 the atmosphere of the fifteen years after 1788 when 'the old loomshops being insufficient, every lumber room, even old barns, cart houses and outbuildings of every description were repaired, windows broke through the old blank walls, and all fitted up for loomshops. This source of making room being at length exhausted, new weavers' cottages with loomshops rose up in every direction, all immediately filled.' Fortunately for architectural historians, the durability of millstone grit, the usual building material in the region, has ensured the survival of archaeological evidence of this time of growth.

The changes of this period can be illustrated by the example of Saddleworth. The parish lies eleven miles north-east of Manchester, around the headwaters of the river Tame; in 1700 Saddleworth had a population of about 2,000. It was in the West Riding of Yorkshire, but lies west of the Pennine ridge and had many links with Lancashire. Memorably, Ammon Wrigley said that Yorkshire got its brass (i.e. money) and Lancashire got its sewage. As early as the 1720s up to 75 per cent of the male population were engaged in textiles, and this proportion increased as population grew. Farmsteads with the characteristic multi-light windows that admitted daylight for the spinner or handloom weaver were built from the early seventeenth

century. From the 1770s there was a surge in the construction of three-storey workshops, and by 1800 blocks were being built specifically to accommodate families and their looms, in some cases with workshops extending over two or three dwellings, exemplifying the 'merchant capitalist' mode of production. Some farmstead buildings were heightened or had wider windows or taking-in doors inserted, to make possible the operation of more spinning jennies or handlooms, while lean-to dyehouses and cropping sheds were added, and tenters were erected in fields. Saddleworth illustrates that one aspect of the industrial revolution in textiles was a frantic expansion of domestic production. The parish also provides evidence of the evolution of powered factories. From the 1770s it was possible to use machines in scribbling (or carding) wool, and several fulling mills were adapted for carding. Carders and their families made their homes among the machinery, just as other families had looms or spinning jennies in their living quarters. Ammon Wrigley, the Saddleworth poet, recalled that

it was customary for the carder and his family to live in the mill, generally in one corner of the scribbling room, the living and sleeping apartment being divided from the machines by pieces of pack sheeting or canvas, sewn together and strung across the room from wall to wall. All the warmth in winter came from small fireplaces at each gable end; even now

◁ High Kinders, Saddleworth, an example of the evolutionary growth of a manufacturing complex. The three- and four-storey buildings date from the mid-seventeenth century to the mid-nineteenth. The taking-in door in the angle between the two main blocks is approached by a cantilevered stone staircase. The single-store block in the foreground was used for dyeing. High Kinders was once occupied by seven families all engaged in manufacturing textiles.

A block of cottages at New Delph, Saddleworth, constructed along a new turnpike road *circa* 1800. It originally consisted of four dwellings, each of two rooms and built two-on-two. The upper dwellings were approached from the high level at the rear, and two loomshops ran across the second and third floors. The dwellings were originally rented to four handloom weavers.

Part of Brownhill Mill, Saddleworth, showing the 'little cottage chimney' dating from the time when it was the home of a carder, his wife and six children. The building was later used as a tannery.

some of our ruined old mills have little cottage chimneys on their roofs.

He reflected:

> No more the carder makes his home
> Within the Carding Room
> No more the weaver's porridge can
> Is hung against the loom.

At Shore Mill, in the hamlet of Delph, built in 1782, and at Brownhill Mill there is archaeological evidence of Wrigley's 'little cottage chimneys', and the census returns show that carders did indeed make their homes within carding rooms. In 1841 a carder lived in Brownhill Mill with his wife, six children aged between 13 and 22, all engaged in working wool, and three younger children. In Saddleworth the 'domestic system' involved not just manufacturing in dwellings, but also the use of purpose-built manufactories as habitations.

Many new water-power systems were excavated in the late eighteenth century to operate textile mills. All but 5 of the 36 fulling mills in the Greater Manchester area were built after 1760, most of them after 1780. Evidence has been found of 387 water- and steam-powered textile plants that worked in Greater Manchester in the eighteenth century. Of those, 219 were cotton-spinning mills, fewer than a quarter of which were of the Arkwright type, and in addition there were large numbers of shops with spinning jennies or mules which were worked by animal or human power.

The Greater Manchester area demonstrated the wide range of experiences which was typical of other areas too. The growth of the industry is reflected in the quantity of raw cotton consumed annually in Britain, which between 1800 and 1804 varied between 52 and 61 million pounds but between 1820 and 1824 did not fall below 120 million pounds. Booming output figures hid a variety of production methods and organisational structures. There were many different ways to make an industrial revolution.

Weaving cotton cloth on handlooms

The powerloom was adopted gradually, and at a significantly later date than powered spinning. Therefore, most of the surging production of yarn that emerged from spinning factories of various kinds between 1780 and 1820 had to be woven on hand-powered looms, by handloom weavers whose numbers, in Britain, reached a peak of about 240,000 in 1820. More than 130,000 signed a petition in 1807 calling for a minimum wage, and no fewer than 15,000 were present at a demonstration in Manchester the following year. For several generations handloom weavers enjoyed high prices, a relatively good standard of living, and were able to benefit from generally high and increasing demand for the product of their looms. After 1820, however, the number of powered looms increased very rapidly: Edward Baines estimated that there were 2,400 power-looms in British factories by 1813, 14,150 by 1820 and 115,552 by 1835. More recently Goeff Timmins and Douglas Farnie showed that although handloom weavers, like other textile workers, suffered during times of recession, there were still opportunities in the trade in the late 1830s. From that time onwards,

▶ Cotton handloom weaving flourished in central Lancashire, where substantial stone-built cottages, such as these in Church Street, Ribchester, four miles from Blackburn, dating from 1798, retain characteristic features such as cellar or ground-floor loomshops.

▲ Size Cottages, Albert Street, Lower Wheelton near Blackburn. The archaeology of these buildings is evidence both of the prosperity and of the decline of handloom weaving in central Lancashire. To the right is a house with a cellar loomshop, characteristically approached by a flight of steps leading to the front door. It is neatly constructed of dressed stone, and the protruding stones on the left indicate that it had once been intended to add more dwellings to the terrace in the same style. It appears that when the terrace was eventually extended handloom weaving was no longer prosperous, and the house on the left not only lacked a loomshop but was built with much inferior stonework.

though, an ever greater proportion of the demand for cheaper cotton fabrics was met by factories using powerlooms. The profitability of handloom weaving plummeted, and the number of handloom weavers in Lancashire fell from between 150,000 and 190,000 in 1821, to about 30,000 in 1861, but even in the 1850s they remained a substantial presence, and still formed majorities in some communities. The decline in handloom weaving was neither uniform nor predictable: sometimes the owners of integrated works had some yarn woven on powerlooms, but put out the rest to domestic handloom weavers. In places, handloom weavers adapted their skills, turning to the manufacture of finer grades of cotton (which could not be woven on early powerlooms) while others began to weave silk (which was not yet mechanised). Census returns suggest that from the 1840s the children of handloom weavers chose not to follow fathers in the trade, but to take up other occupations. Handloom weaving therefore became an ageing workforce, whose numbers in Lancashire had declined to 10,000 by 1871.

There is plentiful visual evidence in central Lancashire for the expansion of handloom weaving between 1780 and 1820. Many hundreds of cottages were built with rooms intended for weaving, but in the lowlands they do not resemble the stone buildings with multi-light mullioned windows familiar in the higher Pennines. Loomshops might be in cellars, where the damp atmosphere, which made it easier to work cotton, compensated for the lack of natural light, or on the ground floors of cottages, alongside living rooms. In 1977 Timmins identified many handloom weavers' cottages in central Lancashire, grouped in small colonies and established in the early nineteenth century. Those at Guide and Mellor, south-east and north-west of Blackburn, had ground-floor loomshops, each lit by two windows on the opposite side of the entrance from the living room, which had just one window. The weavers' houses at Waterloo, south of Bolton, have ground-floor loomshops lit by long, three-light windows. The Club Houses at Horwich, west of Bolton, consist of terraces totalling about 150 dwellings, with cellar loomshops, some of which have front doors approached by flights of up to seven steps, which enabled the insertion of windows to illuminate

John Horrocks built a spinning mill that came to be called the Yellow Factory in Preston in 1791, which proved to be the nucleus of a huge cotton-making complex, including four other large multi-storey mills and numerous smaller workshops, collectively known as the Yard Works. This view is from Charles Hardwick's *History of Preston*, published in 1857.

From the 1790s John Horrocks' spinning mills produced cotton yarn that was woven by handloom weavers, many of them living in terraced houses with cellar loomshops, such as these examples in Mount Pleasant. As cotton fabrics came to be woven on power looms in factories many cellar loomshops were converted into single-room family dwellings.

Handloom weaving persisted in rural parts of central Lancashire well into the third quarter of the nineteenth century. Top o' th' Lane at Brindle is a lengthy terrace, constructed in several phases, which in 1861 comprised about 30 dwellings, some with ground-floor and some with cellar loomshops; many were occupied by handloom weavers.

△ Handloom weavers' cottages of various dates off Revidge Road, Blackburn.
PHOTOGRAPH: CARNEGIE

➤ Houses in Nelson Street, Horwich, near Bolton, incorporating cellars lit by windows alongside the steps up to the front doors where handloom weavers could work. Nelson Street forms part of the 'Club Houses' built by a terminating building society around 1800.

the cellars. These houses were constructed by a terminating building society, and one group bears the date 1801. Few handloom weavers remained in Horwich in 1861, when the principal entrepreneur in the district was Christopher Howarth who employed 405 people at his bleachworks and 204 in his coal mines. There are similar cottages with cellar loomshops at Lower and Higher Wheelton, south-west of Blackburn. In the lengthy terrace called Top o'th'Lane at Brindle, five miles south-east of Preston, some cottages have cellar loomshops, with front doors approached by up to six steps, while others have ground-floor shops. Both kinds are illuminated by three-light windows. There were about 30 dwellings in the terrace in 1861, with a population of 156 of whom 136 were born in Brindle, and most of the remainder in contiguous parishes. Of a working population of 78, no fewer than 73 were weavers, of whom 48 were described as handloom weavers of cotton. This was a textile working community as settled as any company village, and it was still engaged in domestic manufacturing in 1861.

Nigel Morgan showed that handloom weaving was also an urban phenomenon, and that in excess of 1,000 and perhaps as many as 3,000 houses with cellar loomshops were built in Preston, and similar numbers in other Lancashire towns. An ancient town at the lowest

bridging point on the river Ribble, Preston was a place of resort for the gentry of Lancashire in the eighteenth century, but became a textile-manufacturing centre after John Horrocks and his brother Samuel built the three-storey Yellow Factory, just to the east of the old town centre, for spinning cotton in 1791. There were 16 mills in the town in 1825, 46 in 1847 and 71 in 1862, and the town's population increased from 11,887 in 1801 to 68,537 in 1851. The textile labour force in 1847 amounted to 13,851, about half of them women and girls. The mean workforce at mills in the town was about 300, a relatively high figure, and two companies, Horrocks Miller & Co. with 2,000 employees and Swainson & Birley with 1,400, were exceptionally large. When the first spinning mills were opened they produced yarn that was put out to handloom weavers working in their homes, and the inclusion in a directory of 1818 of a list of more than 200 weavers indicates their status as independent tradesmen. While handloom weavers suffered in times of depression, it was remarked in 1836 that, 'The demand for handloom weavers generally was scarcely ever so brisk as at the present moment. The fact is manufacturers are hawking their work, which is chiefly of the common description, to be woven from house to house, and offering higher wages.'

One of the most imposing cotton factories in Lancashire was the Fishwick Mill of Swainson & Birley (sometimes referred to as the 'Big Factory') at Preston, built around 1823. Sitting on a bluff overlooking the river Ribble to the south of the town, this large mill was drawn by Thomas Allom to illustrate Baines' 1835 history of the cotton industry. (See also the illustration of mule spinning at this mill, page 30.)

Morgan demonstrated that some weavers lived in over-crowded conditions in dwellings crammed into the burgage plots in the core of the medieval town, but in two areas, around Friargate and near Samuel Horrocks' Lark Hill House, there were numerous cottages with loomshops, some in cellars with front doors approached by flights of steps, and some approached by internal staircases. Almost all the houses with cellars were built before 1825 during the period when the first generation of spinning mills came into operation, and many of the weavers listed in the 1818 directory lived near the Horrocks mills. Many handloom weavers remained in the area in 1851, but by then there were powerlooms in Preston. By 1882 the 73 mills in the town employed about 28,000 hands, but while some new mills were built thereafter the industry ceased to grow significantly. In Preston, as in Manchester and other Lancashire towns, the demise of handloom weaving led to a deterioration in living conditions as cellar loomshops were let instead as family dwellings. One sale notice, for houses in Snow Hill, Preston, in 1843, explained that, 'The Cellars attached to the houses … having distinct and exclusive entrances from the front of the street, are capable of being let and enjoyed with or without the houses to which they belong'.

Cotton manufacturing across Lancashire

By the 1860s the Lancashire cotton industry was changing. Around Blackburn, Burnley, Accrington and Colne in the north, spinning declined while weaving expanded. In the south weaving continued to expand, but was overshadowed by a spectacular growth in spinning. Growing specialisation was expressed architecturally in multi-storey spinning mills, mostly designed by architects from Oldham. Many were constructed of the characteristic shiny Accrington engineering brick, and had load-bearing steel frames, floors of polished hardwood supported on concrete beams or brick arches, large areas of

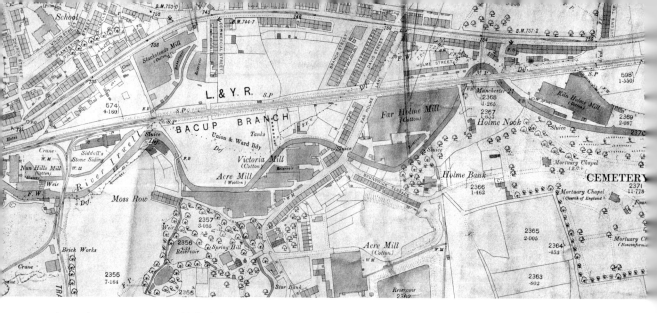

This Ordnance Survey map published in 1893 showing Stacksteads, between Rawtenstall and Bacup, portrays a landscape not untypical of many parts of industrial Lancashire. There are eight cotton mills along this short stretch of the river Irwell. The housing that accommodated the millworkers included considerable numbers of back-to-back dwellings, including lengthy terraces on the south side of the main road to the east of the map, as well as some through-houses of simple rectangular plan, and some tunnel-back houses of more recent date.

glass within curtain walls, towers (which were often elaborately ornamented) carrying water tanks for sprinkler systems, and detached steam-engine houses from which machinery was powered by rope drive systems. Such mills were built in many places in Lancashire, but the principal concentrations were around Oldham and Bolton.

The weaving towns in the north were characterised instead by single-storey, north-lit sheds, although in older communities they were interspersed with multi-storey mills which had originally been built to house spinning machinery. Both kinds of factory were built to formulae: spinning mills to house a certain number of spindles with the appropriate number of associated machines; and weaving sheds to accommodate ranks of looms. The preserved Queen Street Mill at Harle Syke in Burnley was one of four in a development of 1894, and housed more than a thousand looms driven by line shafting and belts from a steam engine, which had been made at nearby Nelson. The valleys of the rivers and streams draining the moorlands were lined with calico printworks and bleachworks, as well as paper mills which used waste from cotton working, and older water-powered spinning mills. On smaller upland streams water-powered bobbin mills were common.

The prosperity of the Lancashire cotton industry depended on numerous other trades, among them the manufacture of wooden bobbins. There were many bobbin mills in the Lake District, but two flourished at Hurst Green in the Ribble Valley near Clitheroe. This photograph of one of them was taken by the pioneer photographer Roger Fenton, probably on a trip to his family, who owned it, in 1858.

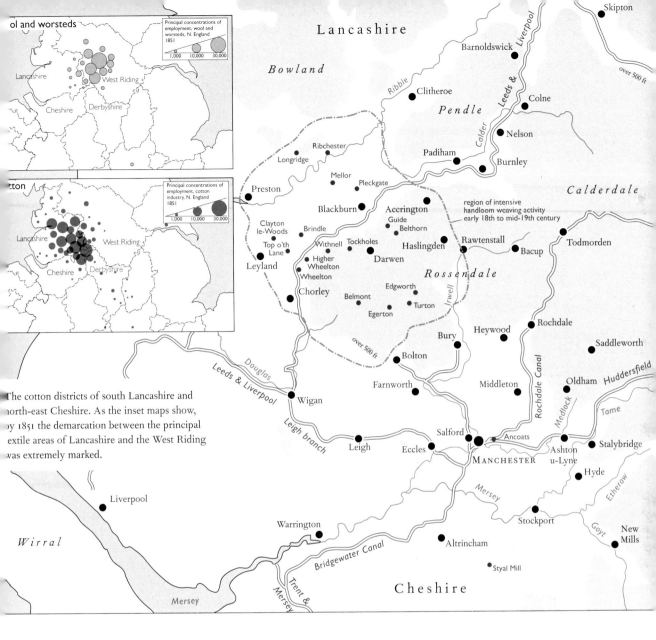

The cotton districts of south Lancashire and north-east Cheshire. As the inset maps show, by 1851 the demarcation between the principal textile areas of Lancashire and the West Riding was extremely marked.

The traditional view is that Yorkshire was a woollen-manufacturing region, Lancashire a cotton one. Yet this rule was never hard and fast. As we shall see, cotton mills were not unknown in Yorkshire, while in many Lancashire communities mills working silk, woollens or flax were interspersed with cotton factories, their owners doubtless appreciating the services provided by the infrastructure that was in place mainly to serve cotton manufacturers. There were, indeed, 99 woollen mills in Lancashire in 1835 and 125 in 1867. Many of them were around Rochdale, producing flannel, but they were found all over the county. Cotton manufacturers benefited from the presence of mills (known as 'condenser' mills) which processed discarded fibres from carding and other preparation processes to produce yarns for towelling and the cheaper forms of bed linen.

Many cotton manufacturers were able to obtain coal from local mines, although some mills were alongside canals which brought fuel from more distant collieries – and from the 1840s some works had their own railway sidings. Coal was used in the lowlands to fire brick-kilns whose products were used in mills and housing. In the uplands stone quarries provided building materials as well as flags for mill floors and paving streets. Farther afield, the slate quarries of Wales and the Lake District produced the roofing materials for tens of thousands of terraced houses.

In Lancashire the number of cotton mills increased from 856 in 1841 to 1,451 in 1856, of which 591 were involved with spinning, 344 in weaving, and the remaining 516 were integrated. The sections that follow illustrate the broad variety of textile communities in the county.

Middleton

The township of Middleton, seven miles from Manchester, specialised in the manufacture of silk, and handloom weaving persisted there into the second half of the nineteenth century. The community is documented in the autobiographical writings of Samuel Bamford and the observations of Angus Bethune Reach. Born in 1788, Bamford grew up in the home of his uncle, a silk weaver, a modestly comfortable dwelling consisting of a living room attached to which were a workshop accommodating four looms, a kitchen and buttery, with sleeping chambers above. The living room was furnished with rush-bottom chairs, a clock in a mahogany case, a corner cupboard and an oaken chest of drawers, together with a barometer and pictures of biblical subjects. Bamford's uncle regularly walked to Manchester to deliver the handkerchiefs he had woven and to collect yarn for future work. He walked deliberately 'with a stick in his hand, his green woollen apron twisted round his waist, his clean shirt showing at the open breast of his waistcoat, his brown silk handkerchief wrapped round his neck, a quid of tobacco in his mouth and a broad and rather slouched hat on his head'. He was followed by his nephew, with a rough jacket, knee breeches, strong stockings and shoes, and open-collared shirt, and, with the prospect of seeing the big city, 'pleasure and glee in my heart

and countenance'. Uncle and nephew waited while other weavers received attention from the 'putter-out' at the warehouse, and usually took lunch in the *Hope & Anchor*, before returning with other Middleton weavers, in a group large enough to deter footpads.

Bamford recalled that in the opening years of the nineteenth century work ceased at Middleton around Christmas and the New Year. Finished work was despatched to the warehouse and the house scrupulously cleaned before ale was tapped and currant loaves sliced. Boys played football and the young enjoyed carol singing, ghostly stories and sliding on ice. Holidays were observed on Shrove Tuesday and on Mid-Lent Sunday, and most of Easter Week was taken up with the election and subsequent misrule of the 'Lord Mayor of Middleton'. The first of May was a time for settling remembered grievances, and Whitsun was marked by the drinking of specially brewed ales, but the principal annual festival was the 'wake' commencing with rush bearing on the third Saturday in August, which was followed by a week of festivities, most of which involved drinking so that by the Thursday only the dregs of the wakes-keepers were staggering about. After the wakes, as days shortened, loom-houses were lit with candles.

Forty years later Reach found that most Middleton men were still silk handloom weavers, some of whom

<< While Middleton near Manchester was famous for its handloom weavers who worked silk, in the mid-nineteenth century some large cotton-spinning mills were built there, some of which, the Dane Mills, appear on this share certificate of 1873 issued for the Middleton & Tonge Cotton Mill Co. The certificate is hand-signed by the company's directors and secretary.
© SCIENCE MUSEUM/SCIENCE & SOCIETY PICTURE LIBRARY

also cultivated smallholdings. He observed houses well furnished, with solidly built chairs and chests of drawers, scrubbed deal tables and kitchen ranges, although loom-houses usually had earthen floors and some accommodated chickens as well as textile machinery. Weavers were bemoaning the fall in prices for their cloth over twenty years, but one of them commended the domestic system, which enabled him to control his children and introduce them gradually to the loom, and another in his seventies concluded that the standard of living in Middleton was higher in 1849 than it had been in his youth. Reach was impressed by the eagerness of weavers to read, by their pride in their skills and by their appetite for politics, reflected in the naming of children after Henry 'Orator' Hunt and Feargus O'Connor.

Oldham

Oldham, a hilltop township seven miles from Manchester, away from the principal early transport routes across the Pennines, was well supplied with coal from local mines. The parish included the hamlets of Royton, Shaw, Chadderton and Lees, and adjoined Saddleworth, as we have seen a vibrant centre of enterprise in the eighteenth century. Oldham had a strong plebeian identity, and most of its cotton masters rose from the ranks of millhands. Textile manufacturing grew from the late eighteenth century as it did in the region generally. There were 7 steam-powered mills in the district in 1800, 19 in 1818 and 96 in 1856. Oldham responded effectively to the Cotton Famine of 1861–65: when supplies of raw cotton from America were halted, and under the guidance of John Platt, its mills adopted Egyptian cotton and even constructed new buildings. By 1871 there were more spindles in Oldham than in any country outside the United States. Further booms in mill construction in 1873–75 and in 1904–08 enabled Oldham to uphold its position, much of its capital being raised by limited liability companies. In the years before the First World War the 'Oldham Limiteds' came to hold a dominant position in the international cotton trade. Oldham's mill architects, Abraham Henthorn Stott, his son Sir Philip Sydney Stott, his brother Joseph Stott, Edward Potts and Frederick William Dixon designed mills in Lancashire and overseas. One of the first built by the Stott family was Houldsworth's Mill at Reddish, consisting of two five-storey blocks used for spinning, separated by a central warehouse and office block, all in the Italianate style.

➤ Cotton mills depicted on an Ordnance Survey map of the Westwood area of Oldham, on the road to Rochdale, published in 1893. Most of the houses follow simple rectangular plans suggesting that the area was developed in the 1850s or earlier. The reservoirs, necessary to provide water for the boilers of steam engines, are a prominent feature of the landscape. Oldham was one of the most remarkable of the cotton towns, undergoing a dramatic expansion of spinning capacity from the 1860s onwards. The Sun Mill in Chadderton (1860–62) had 60,000 spindles and set an example for others to follow. In the period 1870–77 the new joint-stock 'Oldham Limiteds' contributed greatly to an increase of 2.2 million spindles in the town.

PHOTOGRAPH BY CARNEGIE, REPRODUCED BY COURTESY OF THE COUNTY ARCHIVIST, LANCASHIRE ARCHIVES

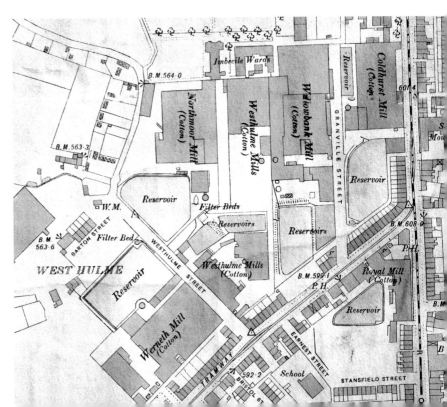

Oldham was also the world's principal centre for the manufacture of textile machinery. The firm founded in 1822 which was built up from 1846 by John Platt and became Platt Bros & Co. from 1854, perfected designs for carding machines, roving frames and self-acting mules, and by the 1890s employed 15,000 people at two works in the town. The second largest firm developed from a workshop making rollers for spinning machines opened in the 1790s by Samuel Lees and subsequently managed by his son Asa Lees who gave it his name. Both companies were substantial in 1870 and grew significantly afterwards. From the 1860s three builders of steam engines also flourished in the town.

Bolton

By the end of the seventeenth century the market town of Bolton, nine miles north-west of Manchester at the confluence of several tributaries of the river Croal, was already an established centre of textile manufacturing. Bolton lay at the centre of a parish of more than 33,000 acres, and the population of the whole area grew under the stimulus of an expanding cotton manufacture. It was a hub of innovation in the mid-eighteenth century, of developments in spinning machines, and of experiments with fabrics, such as the cotton velvets made by Jeremiah Clark in the mid-1750s, the quiltings manufactured by Joseph Shaw from 1763, and the muslins made from 1780 by Thomas Ainsworth.

The population of the town, a little over 5,000 in 1773, had doubled by 1789, reached 17,416 by 1801, and increased by almost three and a half times to 60,393 by 1851. The population of the parish rose from 19,826 in 1801 to 73,905 by 1841, an even greater rate of increase.

In 1818 nineteen mills employed 3,262 people. The streams running into the Irwell provided water power and process water for calico printworks and bleach yards. Coal came from workings on Smithills Moor north-west of the town. By 1851 about 80 cotton mills were working in the area, employing over 10,000 people, almost 60 per cent of them women. Some mills were very large, including one five-storey building

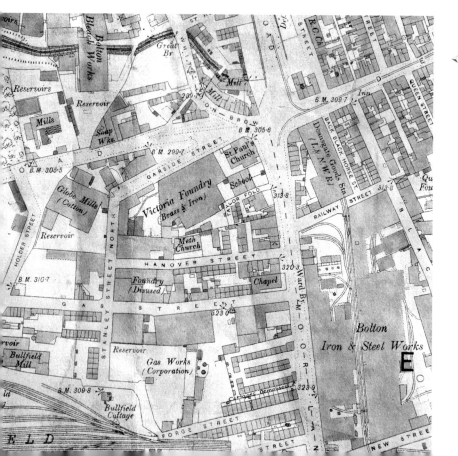

An Ordnance Survey map of the central part of Bolton published in 1893, showing the complexity of the economy of one of the larger towns in the Lancashire textile region. While there are several cotton mills, almost certainly spinning mills, there is also a substantial bleachworks, and a factory making soap, which was used in large quantities in finishing textiles as well as for personal hygiene. There is a large iron and steel works, three foundries, one of them disused, and a gasworks alongside the railway. As in Oldham there are numerous reservoirs. The housing is varied, including some back-to-back terraces (for example, to the west of Moor Lane and on Gas Street) and some quite spacious dwellings which by 1893 were in locations in which they would have suffered severely from pollution, and were probably tenemented.

PHOTOGRAPH BY CARNEGIE, REPRODUCED BY COURTESY OF THE COUNTY ARCHIVIST, LANCASHIRE ARCHIVES

286 feet long and 60 feet broad (88 × 18.5 m). Fifty-three of the mills were steam-powered, employing on average 48 hp. The principal products were cotton twills, shirtings, quiltings and muslins. They were finished at eight bleaching grounds, six calico print-works, and more than twenty dyehouses. There were also two silk manufacturers and a flax-spinning mill in the parish, together with several paper manufacturers using waste cotton. Textile manufacturers were supported by makers of combs, rollers, reeds, shuttles, spindles and skips, together with sizers, and dealers in yarn and cotton waste.

In addition, more than 3,000 men were employed in foundries and machine shops, most of which made textile machinery. The most eminent of them, Dobson & Barlow, was established in 1790 and occupied an imposing factory in Kay Street which was built in 1846. The Soho Ironworks of Benjamin Hick & Son, opened in 1833, was celebrated for its mill engines. From the 1860s Bolton was increasingly dominated by towering multi-storey mills.

The influence of cotton manufacturing on rural Lancashire by 1844 is illustrated by the course of the Bradshaw Brook which rises on Turton Moor and flows east of Bolton to join the river Croal at Darcy Lever. In 1844 it passed two operating collieries and some shafts already abandoned, and numerous sandstone quarries. In the course of just four miles, from Bradshaw Bridge to the Croal, the brook was lined with three corn mills, two large cotton mills, three bleachworks, a calico printworks and the enormous Bradshaw Hall Print & Bleach works.

Bacup

In Rossendale, 18 miles north of Manchester, Bacup lies near the Yorkshire boundary in a fold between the hills from which spring the tributaries of the river Irwell. Most of Bacup's mills and many of its houses were built of stone quarried from the hills, and the drift mines of the Hogshead Colliery and other nearby pits produced fuel for local consumption. Textiles were made in the area in the eighteenth century, and a group of three-storey weavers' cottages stands near Irwell Mill. Carding mills for wool were built from the 1780s. A yeoman, John Lord, whose family were subsequently involved both in mining and cotton, was working a spinning mill by 1789, and three more were operating by 1794. Machine-breakers in Rossendale destroyed more than a thousand looms during the county-wide wave of violent industrial unrest in 1826, but seven integrated cotton mills, with self-acting mules and powerlooms, were built in the 1830s.

Bacup's population in 1861 totalled nearly 15,000. Some handloom weavers continued to work in the area, and the changes in spinning were reflected by, for example, a household in which a son of 37, a self-acting minder, lived with his 70-year-old father, a hand-mule cotton spinner. The census of 1861 recorded 12 cotton spinners and manufacturers, between them employing 2,547 people; the largest business had 856 employees, the smallest 11. Between 1824 and 1865 some 35 cotton mills of up to four storeys were built, mostly of stone. The Irwell Springs calico printworks was developed from 1813 on the site of a fulling mill, while a dyeworks specialised in Turkey Red fabrics. The woollen industry employed about a hundred people, principally around Tunstead Mill. Textile manufacturers could draw on the skills of a machine maker who employed 12 men, an engine smith with 10, and an ironfounder with 7. By 1861 Bacup was a settled community, with few migrants from farther afield than adjacent parishes. Eight of the twelve cotton manufacturers were born in the township of Newchurch-in-Rossendale, which included Bacup. Manufacturing in Rossendale suffered severely during the Cotton Famine, and later in the nineteenth century some mills in the area were adapted to produce footwear. (See also the map on page 408.)

Power-weaving communities

The townships of Old and New Accrington lay five miles east of Blackburn, and in 1800 amounted to no more than a village in which there was nevertheless a considerable manufacture of woollens. Cotton spinning and particularly calico printing led to a rapid rise in population, and by 1861 almost 17,000 people lived in the two townships, which had become a sizeable town and was incorporated as a borough in 1878. The majority were weavers of cotton, although there were some spinners, as well as calico printers, bleachers and dyers. The census reveals that the workforces employed by 24 cotton manufacturers ranged from 39 to 679 and totalled 4,333. The Broad Oak Printworks, established in the early 1790s in the valley of the Warmden Brook, had 12 printing machines, and employed 850 workers in 1846, while the Baxenden Printworks, adapted in 1799 from a wool-carding mill, operated seven machines. Calico print workers included chemists, engineers, pattern drawers, engravers, block cutters, sewing machine workers, cotton piece numberers, hooking room workers, back tenters to printing machines and calender men. Several dyeworks in the town used ground madder. The Globe Works, founded in 1853, made spinning machinery, and its workforce increased from 500 in 1866 to 3,800 in 1902.

Nelson, on the southern side of the river Calder between Burnley and Colne, was a weaving community that grew up in the townships of Great and Little Marsden, where there were coal mines and stone quarries. The turnpike from Burnley to Skipton, much of it on an entirely new alignment, opened through the valley in 1755, the Leeds & Liverpool Canal followed in 1796, and a small hamlet grew up at a road junction on the turnpike. The Lomeshay Mill was built for wool spinning as early as 1780, and became the headquarters of William Ecroyd & Sons,

who by 1861 employed 500 people and made cotton as well as worsteds. The Barrowford corn mill on the opposite side of the river was adapted for cotton spinning by Abraham Hargreaves. His diary reveals that John Wesley preached nearby on 18 April 1784; the first spinning frames were set up on 8 May; and by September he was seeking customers at Blackburn. Most growth in Nelson came after the opening in 1849 of the East Lancashire Railway. There was already a station at Marsden near Huddersfield, and to differentiate them the ELR called the Lancashire one after the *Lord Nelson* pub at the nearby road junction. Thus the emergent community acquired its name. Soon afterwards Walverden Mill, which included both a three-storey spinning block and a stone-built weaving shed, was opened. The Pendle Street Room & Power Co. Ltd built several factories, including the Reedyford Mill and Pendle Street Shed of 1855, which enabled entrepreneurs with limited capital to establish businesses. In 1861 the community was overwhelmingly concerned with weaving cotton on powerlooms. The largest cotton company was that of Joseph Tunstill who employed 600 people, but five cotton firms in the townships each employed fewer than 50 people. There were no bleach or calico printworks in the vicinity, although mordants were manufactured at a chemical works at Hollin Bank and even in a relatively remote community such as Nelson there was a mechanical engineering company employing 40 people. Most of Nelson's growth came after 1870.

Manchester as 'Cottonopolis'

Manchester can be interpreted at several levels; in the 1860s it was a great city with a population of 380,000, the centre of a developing conurbation of over 1.5 million people. The Free Trade Hall (1854) and its town hall, built between 1867 and 1877, expressed its municipal pride; there were well-stocked shops, and innumerable small-scale manufacturers of consumer goods. In 1700 Manchester, with a population of about 5,000, was a significant centre of textile marketing, as it had been since the mid-sixteenth century. Early development was clustered along the banks of the rivers Irwell, Medlock and Irk and the Shooters Brook, which in the middle decades of the eighteenth

century provided power for spinning machines and process water for printing, dyeing and bleaching. The first spinning factory to utilise steam power in the city was Richard Arkwright's Shudehill Mill of 1780, where a steam engine – whose boiler flues were served by what was possibly the city's first high factory chimney – recirculated water which had passed over the waterwheel. Many more mills were constructed in the decades that followed, most of them filled with spinning mules.

The mills in Ancoats, depicted in George Pyne's engraving of 1829, are particularly significant. For half a century they were among the largest textile

The cotton mills alongside Union Street and the Rochdale Canal at Ancoats, Manchester, depicted on a watercolour of the early nineteenth century. From left to right are the Long Mill, the Old Mill and the eight-storey Sedgewick Mill (see also page 386). These mills belonged to McConnel & Kennedy, the largest cotton-spinning firm in Manchester. The canal opened in 1804. The vessel in the foreground is distinctly different from the narrow boats of the Midlands waterways depicted elsewhere.

REPRODUCED FROM MCCONNEL & CO. LTD, *A CENTURY OF FINE SPINNING, 1790–1913*

The Union Street mills, Ancoats, belonging to the large firms of McConnel & Kennedy and Murrays. From left to right, McConnel & Kennedy's Long Mill (built in two stages in 1805 and 1806, A), their 'Old Mill' of 1797 (B) and Sedgwick Mill (1818, C) and Sedgwick New Mill (D, 1868). The integrated 'Murray Street Mill' complex consists of Murrays' Old Mill (E, 1798) and Decker Mill (F, 1802) along the canal frontage, their New Mill on Jersey Street (G), the Murray Street block (H, around 1804–06), and the doubling mill of 1842 (I). Note the canal basin within the Murrays' mill complex, which was entered via a tunnel under the road. (See also the map on page 494.)

PHOTOGRAPH BY CARNEGIE, REPRODUCED BY COURTESY OF
THE COUNTY ARCHIVIST, LANCASHIRE ARCHIVES

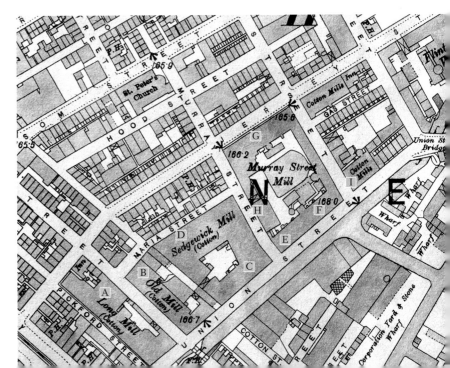

McConnel & Kennedy's cotton mill, from a drawing dated 1800. James McConnel was born in Scotland in 1762 and came to Lancashire when he was 19, initially as a machine maker. When a customer failed to pay for a pair of McConnel's mules, he decided to set them to work himself. In 1791 he entered a partnership to make machines and to work cotton on their own account. McConnel & Kennedy occupied several mills before building this, the Old Mill in Ancoats, in 1797, powered by a Boulton & Watt steam engine. (See also map on page 415.)

REPRODUCED FROM MCCONNEL & CO. LTD, *A CENTURY OF FINE SPINNING, 1790–1913*

One of the imposing mills in the vicinity of Little Ireland, the Chorlton Twist Mill in Oxford Road, depicted on an engraving published in 1829. The mill was built by Samuel Marsland who headed a syndicate that laid out a network of streets in Chorlton on Medlock providing suitable sites for textile mills. Unlike many of Manchester's spinning mills Chorlton Mill was not connected directly to the canal system. It did, however, draw water from the Medlock for its steam engines, and this early fireproof mill also boasted two basement levels, the upper of which had tunnels to connect with the company's other mills nearby.

AUTHOR COLLECTION

Brunswick Mill, Ancoats. This was one of the largest of Manchester's mid-nineteenth-century mills. The main production facility occupied the taller U-shaped buildings; the three-storey frontage linking the two wings was used for warehousing. The only significant architectural embellishment was to the archway that led into the mill's courtyard. At 92 metres the 28-bay building was extremely long for the time. This view is from Bradford Road; on the far side of the mill 35 loading bays led directly out on to the Ashton-under-Lyne Canal.

REPRODUCED FROM H. BANNERMAN & SONS, *THE STORY OF THE SPINDLE*, 1895

The Exchange in Manchester, the international hub of the cotton trade in the mid-nineteenth century. The building seen here was the second on this site, having replaced an earlier structure of 1792 in 1809. It was enlarged and rebuilt in the 1860s, by which time it was said to be the largest trading room in the world, able to accommodate up to 3,000 merchants.

The foundry, best known as Peel, Williams & Peel, was established in Miller Street, off Shude Hill in Manchester about 1797–1800 but soon moved to the Phoenix Foundry on nearby Swan Street. The firm acquired a second site, the Soho Foundry at Ancoats, about 1810. The company gave up the Phoenix Foundry in the 1820s or early 1830s. It grew to be a very large engineering concern employing several hundred workers. Peel, Williams & Peel provided the plant for the gasworks in Manchester as well as numerous steam engines for textile mills and other industrial concerns. The firm remained in business until soon after 1887.

Little Ireland, from the first edition Ordnance Survey map. This area along the banks of the Medlock was notorious and therefore well documented. Like many other parts of northern industrial towns it shows the close proximity of housing and industry. The area's nickname came from the large Irish population that had come to Manchester in the early nineteenth century: by 1851 Manchester had over 50,000 residents of Irish birth. To the west of this map we see Chorlton Mills and to the south-east the Oxford Road Twist Factory.

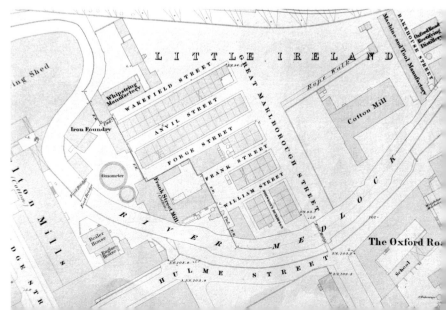

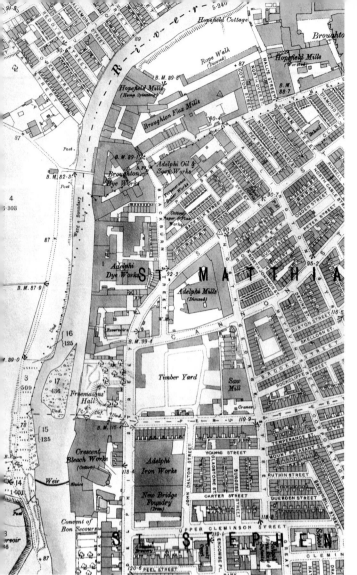

'Smoke consuming at Ancoats, Manchester', a poster published about 1820 illustrating the extent of smoke pollution in Manchester (as in other northern cities).
© SCIENCE MUSEUM/SCIENCE & SOCIETY PICTURE LIBRARY

Industry along the banks of the Irwell in Salford. Along this stretch of the river we see mills for weaving worsted and flax and for spinning hemp, two large dyeworks and a soap factory, a sawmill, a bleachworks, the Adelphi Iron Works and the New Bridge Foundry. Little wonder that many northern rivers became heavily polluted. (See also map on page 494.)

factories in Britain. They were seen by many visitors to Manchester and assumed, wrongly, to be representative of textile mills generally. In the 1780s James McConnel and John Kennedy had migrated from Scotland to Manchester, and in 1790 they established a company which built its first mill at Ancoats. It was located in the grid of streets that had been laid out beside the line of the soon-to-be-completed Rochdale Canal. The mill was a steam-powered factory designed to accommodate spinning mules; like the first major extension of the complex, the Old Mill of around 1810, it has been demolished. In contrast, the eight-storey Sedgwick Mill of 1818–20, one of the most impressive buildings in Manchester, survives. This,

the oldest remaining building on the site, stands alongside the five-storey New Sedgwick Mill of 1868 and twentieth-century buildings that replaced the original mills. The brothers Adam and George Murray also migrated from Scotland in the 1780s, spun cotton in room-and-power mills, then from 1798 established a complex south-east of the McConnel & Kennedy works. The Old Mill of 1798 and the Decker Mill of 1802, both of seven storeys, the six-storey New Mill of 1804, and warehouses of 1806 formed a quadrangle around a branch of the Rochdale Canal, whose main line, linked to the basin by a tunnel, opened during the period of construction. Murrays' mills were powered by two Boulton & Watt steam engines and, like their

Chorlton New Mill was built by the Birley family from the 1790s, and overlooked the notorious working-class district known as Little Ireland. The mill was taken over in the 1860s by Charles Mackintosh & Co., who used it for the production of waterproof fabrics.

neighbours, specialised in producing fine yarns for handloom weavers in Scotland. In the early 1820s the Beehive Mill, consisting originally of two six-storey blocks providing room and power for aspirant entrepreneurs, was built on the south bank of a branch canal which served a coal wharf in Bengal Street. A fourth imposing mill in the area was the seven-storey Brownsfield Mill by the main line of the Rochdale Canal, west of Great Ancoats Street.

On the opposite side of the city centre the Chorlton New Mill stands within a similar grid of streets. It was built by the Birley family from the 1790s, but its most imposing building, an eight-storey block on Cambridge Street, dates from 1814, and was powered by a Boulton & Watt engine. A 12-bay fireproof block on Hulme Street was added in 1818 and a powerloom weaving shed in 1829. The mill overlooked the notorious housing in Little Ireland, and was taken over in the 1860s by Charles Macintosh & Co. for the production of waterproof fabrics. There were similar mills on the other side of the river Irwell in Salford, such as the factory built at Pendleton in 1783 by William Douglas and George Augustus Lee's iron-framed Salford Twist Mill of 1799–1802.

The Murrays employed 1,215 people in 1816, McConnel & Kennedy 1,020, and Philips & Lee of Salford 937. These were the largest mills in the conurbation and the ones that most impressed visitors. However, 24 of the 86 mills in Manchester and Salford had fewer than 200 employees. It was calculated in 1818 that the mills in Manchester, Salford and Eccles provided employment for 19,913 people and until about the middle of the century Manchester was the dominant cotton-manufacturing centre in Lancashire, although cotton spinners formed a small part of its textile workforce which included people involved in printing, dyeing and bleaching cotton, silk manufacturing, and the making of fustians, waterproof fabrics and smallwares (tapes and braids). The infrastructure for textile manufacturing included spindle forgers, roving fly makers, bobbin turners, shuttle tip makers, reed rib makers, and Manchester's engineering industry. Cotton manufacturing in Manchester reached its peak in 1853, by which date there were more than 100 mills. Most subsequent investments in buildings were in the surrounding region, and by 1883 there was a sense that textile manufacturing – as distinct from trading – could no longer provide the city's engine of growth.

The four-mile course of the Medlock through Manchester in 1831 illustrates many aspects of the textile industry. The river extends just ten miles from its sources in the hills east of Oldham to its confluence with the river Irwell. It enters Manchester from the east and is crossed by the Ashton Canal before turning south near Chappells Cotton Mill and a sulphuric acid works. At the next bend the Holt Town Cotton Mills, with some back-to-back housing, lay on its north bank. It passed between two dyeworks, before flowing beneath Ancoats Bridge on the road to Ashton near

Barton's Cotton Mill. The river veers north beyond the bridge, with Taylor & Chatwell's cotton mills and a dyeworks to the north, and a large printworks to the south. Four more dyeworks, the Hanover Cotton Mill, the Mayfield Printworks, a tannery, a paper mill and the Ardwick Printworks lined its meandering banks before it was crossed by Ardwick Bridge on London Road. Its subsequent circuitous course passed the Ardwick Bridge chemical works, which occupied both banks, three more cotton mills, the town manure yard, a ropewalk, and the New Garratt Print Works, before it was crossed by Brook Street. Along the stretch to Oxford Road were a dyeworks and a timber yard on the north bank and two cotton mills to the south. Beyond Oxford Road the Medlock passed through one of the principal concentrations of cotton mills in Manchester – the Oxford Road Mill, Fairweather's Mill, Latham's Mill, Runcorn's Mill, Marsland's Mill and Birley's Mill – and the notorious Little Ireland. Beyond Cambridge Street were five cotton mills, two dyeworks, two chemical works, a size works, a brewery, an ironworks and a gasworks before the river's junction with the Bridgewater Canal. After passing beneath the Castlefield railway terminus in a tunnel the Medlock entered the river Irwell. This was the river that de Tocqueville called the 'Styx of the new Hades'.

By 1840 Manchester was the undisputed commercial capital of the cotton industry, not merely the 'sovereign mistress' of 280 cotton-producing communities within a radius of 12 miles but also the international centre of the trade. The first cotton exchange was opened in 1729, but through the eighteenth century the centre for textile trading remained at Blackwell Hall in London, while most cotton brokers worked from Liverpool. Nevertheless, in 1800 there were many warehouses of the kind visited by Samuel Bamford's uncle, and increasing numbers of manufacturers from outside Lancashire found it expedient to keep premises in Manchester. The number of warehouses increased from 120 in 1772, to 726 in 1820 and 955 in 1829. In 1815 57 warehouses on Cannon Street provided accommodation for 106 separate firms. The focus of the market for cotton cloth moved from London to Manchester after 1818, and the transfer of cotton broking from Liverpool was marked by the formation of the Cotton Brokers' Association in Manchester in 1841. Merchants from Germany, the Netherlands, Switzerland, France and Italy had settled in Manchester by 1835, and were followed by men from Russia and southern Europe. John Scholes has shown that the overall number of foreign merchants in Manchester grew from 20 in 1800 to 390 in 1870, by which date their numbers included 143 Germans and 167 Greeks. By 1853 there were 1,683 warehouses in the city, and in 1861 some census enumerators used the specific category *Manchester* warehouseman. The vast warehouses in the Venetian style in Portland Street date from the 1850s, but the first of the even larger palaces of textile commerce that line Whitworth Street were not built until the 1890s. They did no more than reflect a long-established commercial hegemony.

Lancashire in 1870

The Lancashire cotton industry continued to grow after 1870. It remained a powerful force in the British economy right through to the 1960s, and much recent scholarship about the industry has been devoted to its more recent history. Some of its characteristic buildings, such as Oldham-style spinning mills and weaving sheds extending over many acres, were built after 1870. Geographically, the later nineteenth century also saw shifting patterns within the county. In 1870 the growth of such communities as Shaw and Nelson was still gathering momentum, while in other parts of Lancashire the industry had ceased to expand and was even beginning to contract. The decline in manufacturing in Manchester was quoted as one reason for the city's investment in the Ship Canal in the 1890s. Growth in Preston came to an end by the 1880s, while some mills in Rossendale were adapted to produce slippers and shoes. But the impact of cotton, and its many associated and dependent industries and trades, was profound and permanent. New towns had been created and medieval market centres transformed beyond all recognition. The population of the county increased more than fourfold between 1801 and 1871, from 673,000 to 2,819,000, and rose

Henry Bannerman & Sons also owned the North End and River Meadow mills at Stalybridge. The five-storey North End Mill was built with stone in 1851, together with a single-storey weaving shed. River Meadow Mill on the opposite side of the river Tame was a four-storey structure. There were 80,000 mule spindles in the two mills in the late nineteenth century producing medium-fine counts of twist and weft using Egyptian and American cotton. North End Mill has been demolished but River Meadow Mill survives and has been adapted to new uses.

An engraving of India Mill in Darwen, near Blackburn, which was built by Eccles Shorrock. The chimney, 288 feet (88 metres) high, was inspired by Italian architecture, and was built between 1864 and 1868 at a cost of £12,000. Many mill owners built such chimneys, competing with each other to construct the tallest. A blockade of the cotton-producing southern states because of the American Civil War stopped cotton imports to Britain and led to unemployment and famine in the northern textile towns. Shorrock went bankrupt and died of ill health. The mill finally closed in 1991.

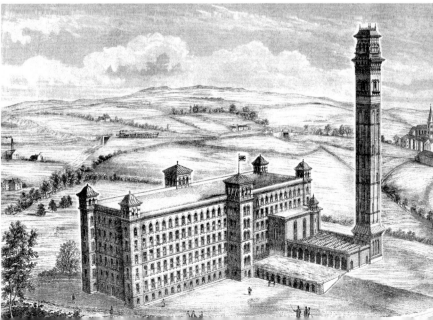

further to 4,373,000 by 1901. The jurist and historian James (Viscount) Bryce, who explored Lancashire as a schools commissioner, reflected in 1868:

The county has, so to speak, taken a sudden leap out of one age into another. ... The

speed with which this region has increased in wealth and population finds no parallel except in America or Australia, and the phenomena which have accompanied its growth are exactly those which are observed at this moment in our newest colonies.

Cotton across the Midlands

The Arkwright spinning mill appeared to offer boundless opportunities for acquiring wealth, and the market for cotton yarns among the hosiers of the east Midlands was particularly enticing. James Hargreaves settled in Nottingham, and his spinning jenny was then described as a machine for making yarn for hosiery. The jenny was in fact incapable of producing the fine yarns demanded by a fashion-orientated market in Nottingham, but for a generation it was used to produce coarser yarns in upland Derbyshire. Richard Arkwright was also drawn to Nottingham, securing the support of the leaders of the hosiery trade – Samuel Need in Nottingham and Jedediah Strutt in Derby. The success of the water-frame led Arkwright himself to build mills at Cressbrook, Bakewell and Wirksworth in Derbyshire, while the Strutt family invested at Belper, Milford and Derby, and other entrepreneurs in Nottinghamshire. By 1800 there were about 40 Arkwright-style cotton mills in the two counties, and about 30 elsewhere in the Midlands. Some were of major significance, such as those at Papplewick, and others were built as far south as Warwick and Lutterworth.

The Peel family provided a link between Lancashire and the Midlands. Robert 'Parsley' Peel was a dealer in linen/cotton mixture fabrics used for printing. He adapted a barn at Intack, east of Blackburn, to accommodate 20 spinning jennies for James Hargreaves, whom he protected from machine-breakers before his departure for Nottingham. After 1774, when statutory constraints on printing were eased, Peel set up a printing works at Church, near Blackburn, and in 1770 opened a manufacturing warehouse for carding and spinning yarn for calico handloom weavers. In 1780, after the warehouse was destroyed by machine-breakers, he established a cotton mill with water-frames at

Burton-on-Trent but continued to invest in Lancashire and about 1787 built an integrated spinning, weaving and printing works at Bolton with Thomas Ainsworth. Peel built three mills at Burton-on-Trent on sites made available by the Trent Navigation authorities.

His son, the first Sir Robert Peel, established his own business in Lancashire from the 1770s, introducing 'that order, arrangement and subdivision which form the marked characteristics of the factory system'. He acknowledged his debt to Arkwright, remarking that 'We all looked up to him and imitated his mode of building'. In 1790 he invested £15,500 in the purchase of property in Tamworth, which enabled him to become the borough's MP. He also built several water-powered spinning mills there, and in 1791, with Joseph Wilkes of Measham, purchased land at Fazeley a mile south of the town where, as part of a comprehensive programme of improvement, he built water-powered factories for spinning, weaving, printing and bleaching, and constructed terraced housing for his workpeople. The mills were managed by Edmund, the younger brother of the second Sir Robert Peel, the prime minister, but passed out of the family's hands in 1841. Part of the enterprise was taken over by the Tolson family from Wakefield, who built a five-storey mill in 1883, and manufactured tapes at Fazeley until the last years of the twentieth century. By 1800 the Peels were working 23 mills in Blackburn, Bolton, Bury, Burton-on-Trent and in the Tamworth area. However, after the Napoleonic Wars the spinning industry declined in the Midlands. In 1833 there were three mills in the Nottingham area, with others farther north around Mansfield, but most of those farther south had closed. Nevertheless, the textile industry continued to prosper in the relatively isolated communities created by Arkwright, his partners and successors in the valleys of the river Derwent and its tributaries.

The textile industry in Derbyshire extended upstream from the county town, where the river Derwent powered the mills, to the source of the river in the High Peak. There, textiles were only one element in the local economy, alongside lead mining and quarrying. In Derby itself the Lombes' silk mill remained in operation in 1870, together with more recent silk and tape mills. The Derwent had powered various mills at Darley Abbey two miles north of the city since the Middle Ages. Robert Bage, the son of a paper-maker, was born in the hamlet, and William Duesbury ground flint there to make porcelain. The Quaker Thomas Evans worked corn, flint and paper mills at Darley Abbey in the 1770s. In 1782 he constructed a new weir and subsequently built the first cotton mill on the site, the 17-bay Long Mill, which was followed by the Middle Mill of 1796–1800, the fireproof East Mill of 1818–19 and the West Mill constructed shortly after-wards by Walter Evans. The buildings of the cotton-manufacturing community established from 1792 have survived almost intact, a mixture of two- and three-storey terraces, some of great elegance, intermixed with cluster houses, blocks of four relatively spacious dwellings, with large gardens, which were reputedly occupied by senior staff. The church of St Matthew was built in 1818 and the Regency-style school in 1832, by which time the village had a population of 1,170. By the 1850s Evans & Co. specialised in cotton for sewing, mending and knitting.

Five miles further upstream the mills at Milford were worked by the Strutt family. Jedediah Strutt, son of a South Normanton farmer, patented the Derby rib machine for making hosiery in 1759. He was the leading hosier in Derby and provided capital for Richard Arkwright. The family's cotton-spinning business was developed by his three sons William (concerned chiefly with technological development); Joseph, who lived in Derby and was responsible for commercial matters; and George Benson, who managed the mills at Belper and Milford. Jedediah Strutt built the first of the Milford mills on the site of an iron forge he had purchased in 1781. He constructed the Hopping Mill weir in 1799–1801, and for housing

The silk mill in Derby built in 1721 by John and Thomas Lombe. This was one of the most significant developments in silk manufacturing in England, but it also provided a pattern for factory production that was followed by manufacturers of cotton in Derbyshire later in the eighteenth century.

used land made available by an enclosure award in 1791. The community at Hopping Hill included two stone three-storey terraces of 28 and 29 houses, built in 1792–97, and a back-to-back terrace built into the hillside in 1818–20. Only a dyehouse of 1832 and some small buildings remain of the mill complex, which was demolished about 1960.

Two miles north of Milford is Belper, where the Strutts developed a cotton-spinning complex from 1776. To the first mill was added the North Mill, built in 1784–86 and destroyed by fire in 1803. William Strutt used iron columns in a mill at Derby in 1792–93, in a warehouse at Milford, and in the 200 foot (62 m) long, six-storey West Mill of 1793–96 at Belper. His corre-spondent Charles Bage built the Ditherington flax mill in Shrewsbury in 1796–97 with a frame wholly of iron, and in 1804 Strutt rebuilt the North Mill at Belper in similar fashion. The first mill was replaced in 1810–11 by the five-storey South Mill, while the Round Mill, which appeared to derive from Jeremy Bentham's concept of the panopticon, was commenced in 1803 but only came into production in 1816. The Strutts invested large sums in water power, constructing the picturesque horseshoe weir in 1797. Their workers' colonies were commended by Andrew Ure who wrote that 'this manufacturing village has quite the picturesque air of an Italian scene, with its river, overhanging woods and the distant range of hills'. The Strutts' enterprise was one of the largest anywhere in the cotton industry, employing 1,813 people in 1818. The housing included the Long Row of 1792–97, originally 77 houses in three sandstone terraces, two of which were broken by the construction of the North Midland Railway in 1840, and five blocks of 'cluster houses' on the pattern of those at Darley Abbey, built from 1805 and each comprising four dwellings with extensive gardens. Cotton mills principally employed women and children, and the Strutts built several nail shops which provided employment for the males of those families living in their cottages, as well as a Unitarian chapel in 1788.

The Arkwright-style mill at Lea Bridge, six miles north of Belper, was built in 1783–84 by Peter Nightingale and Benjamin Pearson (who had worked for Arkwright) and was powered by the Lea Brook which also worked a lead smelter and rolling mill owned by Nightingale. The mill was taken over in 1818 by the Smedley family and subsequently produced yarns for woollen garments.

Arkwright's first mills impressed all who saw them, particularly when they were illuminated at night, or when the juvenile labour force emerged from their gates, and his community at Cromford was a cause of much – generally favourable – comment. By 1790 the expansion of Cromford Mill had come up against the constraints of the site, but Arkwright built a second complex, Masson Mill, on the river Derwent to the north. The first houses built by Arkwright in Cromford, perhaps dating from 1777, appear to be the 27 terraced dwellings on either side of North Street which have multi-light windows on their upper floors, illuminating shops which could have accommodated looms or frames for male workers whose partners and children were employed at the spinning mills. However, most of the houses are of other types: there are 36 two-storey and 83 three-storey cottages. Arkwright himself lived from 1776 in Rock House, a stone-fronted dwelling built for him by Peter Nightingale that overlooks the mills, but about 1790 he commissioned the mansion called Willersley Castle, from which the mills cannot be seen. It remained incomplete at the time of his death in 1792.

The hub of commercial activity in Cromford was the *Greyhound*, a three-storey pedimented inn completed in 1776 overlooking a market place lined

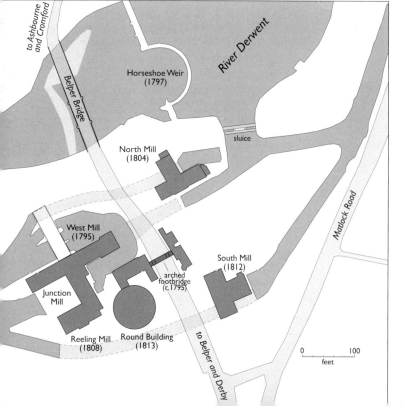

Strutt's mills at Belper, showing the complex system of watercourses that was developed to power the mills. Rees' *Cyclopaedia* described the mills at Belper as being 'on a scale and most complete we have ever seen, in their dams and their water works', and even today the weirs and sluices (⋎) form an impressive sight.

with buildings designed as shops, including two ranges of single-storey shambles of which one survives. Arkwright established a weekly market in 1790. The church of St Mary, within the grounds of Willersley Castle, was completed in 1797, and includes a vault containing Arkwright's remains. The village school was built by Richard Arkwright II in 1832. The Cromford Canal, which extends 14½ miles to the hub of the East Midlands canal system at Langley Mill, was opened in 1794, and Cromford's comparative isolation was finally ended by the building of a new turnpike road from Belper, authorised in 1817. Richard Arkwright II retained the Cromford and Masson mills but sold his father's shares in other ventures in order to invest in land and government stocks. The management of the mills passed to other members of the family, who did not invest. Many machines dating from the time of Richard Arkwright I remained in use in the 1850s, by which time they were exceedingly antiquated, and by 1870 the Arkwrights occupied only part of Cromford Mill. In the 1880s Masson Mill was successfully adapted to manufacture sewing cotton, while cotton working at Cromford Mill ceased in 1891. About 200 cotton workers lived in Cromford in 1861, by which date only ten heads of households in North Street were employed in the mills. More than 300 lived in other parts of the parish of Matlock, many of whom were employed in bleaching and the manufacture of tapes and candlewick at mills in Lumsdale.

A little more than a mile south of Cromford is the market town of Wirksworth where in 1780 Arkwright built the Haarlem Mill, at which water was recirculated by a steam engine. In 1861 Wirksworth was a town of about 3,700 people in a parish that included several populous lead-mining hamlets. Haarlem Mill was adapted in the 1820s to produce tape, the town's principal manufacture by 1861, occupying several other mills and providing employment for more than 250 workers. Wirksworth's mills were notorious for the production of red tape for the civil service. In 1861 a small cotton-spinning mill two miles north-west of Matlock, built in 1785, was being used to spin flax, and employed about 90 people. In 1778 Arkwright built a cotton mill on the edge of Bakewell on the river Wye, where he employed 300 people in 1789. Lord

The Cromford Canal, opened in 1794, linked Arkwright's cotton-manufacturing enterprises with the Midlands waterway network. The warehouse was built soon after the canal opened for Nathaniel Wheatcroft who became the principal canal carrier. The lean-to shed which protected goods from the elements, was added in 1814.

The two long gritstone terraces that comprise North Street, Cromford, contain 27 dwellings, and were the first erected by Richard Arkwright *circa* 1776. The long-light windows on the upper storeys illuminate attics that were used by men for weaving or framework knitting while their wives and children worked at Arkwright's mills.

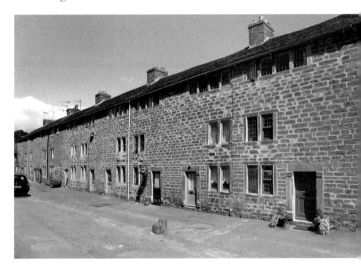

Torrington admired the mill pool, but was refused entrance in 1790 for fear that his presence would 'disturb the girls'. The labour force numbered only about 120 in 1861 when the town was better known as a resort. Fire destroyed the mill in 1868.

Cressbrook Mill, four miles north-west of Bakewell, originated as a spinning mill powered by the Cress Brook near its confluence with the river Wye. It was

A cotton-spinning mill was built at Bamford on the river Derwent from 1782, and rebuilt after a fire in 1791. Some 240 people were employed there in 1861. The importance of water power at Bamford is evident from the photograph, while on the side of the mill are good examples of the turrets used to accommodate staircases and lavatories, freeing the mill's floors for laying out machinery.

The Boar's Head Mills at Darley Abbey, on the Derwent just north of Derby were developed for cotton spinning from the 1780s by the Evans family. The mill buildings are exceptionally well preserved, and the adjoining company village comprises terraces and cluster houses, and includes a particularly elegant school building of 1832.

The elegant building at Cressbrook Mill, Derbyshire, erected by Francis Phillips in 1814-16. Since the photograph was taken it has been adapted as apartments.

built by Arkwright in 1783, destroyed by fire in 1785, and subsequently rebuilt by Richard Arkwright II. An elegant building powered by the river Wye, with cast-iron internal columns and a frontage of 12 bays with a four-bay pediment section topped by a cupola, was added in 1814–16 by Francis Phillips. Between 1810 and 1830 the managers employed 300 parish apprentices from London, and a house to accommodate them was built in 1817. In 1861 the mill was the property of Manchester-born Henry McConnell and employed about 300 people. It worked until 1963 and has since been adapted as housing. A mile upstream on the river Wye is Litton Mill, a two-storey stone cotton factory built in 1782 by Ellis Needham and Thomas Frith, and rebuilt in 1874 after a fire. It was notorious as the location of the alleged sufferings of the apprentice Robert Blincoe who worked there between 1803 and 1814. He alleged, some years later, that apprentices were expected to crawl beneath machines that were still working, that they were poorly housed and fed, and that their overseers treated them brutally. Henry Newton, the owner in 1861, employed 297 hands working cotton and worsted. Litton Mill continued working into the second half of the twentieth century. The six-storey stone Calver Mill on the river Derwent four miles north of Bakewell dates from 1803–04 and replaced a cotton mill of 1785. A new wheelhouse was added in 1834 with a pair of 22 foot (6.7 m) diameter waterwheels each generating 80 hp. The mill is notable for its latrine turrets and for its surviving 36-pane cast-iron framed windows. About 140 people worked there in 1861. It was used for textiles until 1923, and is now adapted as apartments.

Six miles upstream on the Derwent is the mill at Bamford, a mixture of three- and four-storey stone buildings on a site used for cotton spinning from 1782. It was rebuilt after a fire in 1791 by Samuel Moore, a Manchester mill owner, and his son William Moore and employed 240 people in 1861. Near the head of the Derwent's tributary, the river Noe, is Edale Mill, a four-storey gritstone building that was used for carding, spinning and doubling cotton from the late 1790s. It was used for cotton manufacturing until 1934 and, like others in the Peak District, is now adapted as holiday apartments.

The mills of the Derwent Valley transformed people's view of manufacturing in the late eighteenth century, impressing with their size and also with the way they transformed the landscape, perhaps most noticeably at night when they were lit up. These factories were welcomed by those who favoured deferential social attitudes, but others recognised the harmful effects on children of compelling them to tend machines for many hours of each day. The long-term impact of Arkwright's enterprises was equally significant. Many mills in the Midlands had short lives, but most of those around the Derwent Valley manufactured textiles for more than a century, some for two centuries.

Arkwright's influence extended across the river Dove into Staffordshire. A mill at Tutbury was adapted to spin wool in 1782, but the following year the partners erected a five-storey building nearly 200 feet (62 m) long for spinning cotton; a fireproof extension was added in 1829. The mill worked until 1888, was used from 1891 until 1968 to manufacture plaster, and was demolished in 1972. The confusingly named Tutbury Mill at Rocester was built by Arkwright from October 1781. It was enlarged in the nineteenth century when steam engines were installed, although waterwheels powered some machines until 1878. Textile production continued here until 1985. John Cooper adapted corn and leather dressing mills at Mayfield west of Ashbourne to spin cotton in 1793. By the 1820s there were mills on either side of the river Dove, one in Derbyshire and one in Staffordshire. The Hanging Bridge Mill was rebuilt in 1866 and was still used for

textiles in 2008. John Cooper also built a cotton mill in 1784 at Woodseaves, on the Bradbourne Brook two miles north of Ashbourne. By the 1880s it employed about 50 people doubling cotton and worked until 1908 when it was demolished.

The transition from domestic to factory production is graphically illustrated at Tean Hall Mills near Cheadle, the most significant of several tape factories close to the Derbyshire/Staffordshire border. In 1747 John and Nathaniel Phillips learned how to construct looms for weaving tapes, known variously as 'Dutch', 'ribbon' or 'engine' looms. They distributed yarn to weavers working in their own homes from a timber-framed house of 1613 and a small Baroque mansion. A seven-bay, three-storey building with a pediment topped by a cupola, in the manner of an Arkwright spinning mill, was added about 1816. In the 1820s it became possible to drive Dutch looms with steam power. Immediately the Phillips family concentrated production in a vast five-storey mill in the classical style, extending over 23 bays and powered by a Boulton & Watt steam engine. It was designed by the Manchester engineer George Augustus Lee, who calculated that it would accommodate 450 looms, and that since one weaver would be able to take charge of two looms, labour costs would be halved. The pattern of work at Upper Tean suddenly changed from domestic labour – with yarn distributed from the various warehouses – to disciplined attendance on machines in what was then one of the largest factories in Britain. Tapes were made at Upper Tean until the end of the twentieth century, and the 1823 mill is now adapted as housing.

The spread of cotton

Cotton manufacturing could also be found beyond the heartlands. In 1754 Angerstein judged that Carlisle's trade was 'feeble and of little importance', although the weaving of fustian, a fabric in which cotton and linen were mixed, was already established in the city. Carlisle's population in 1801 numbered only about 9,000 but it grew rapidly with the establishment of cotton mills along the river Caldew, which flows northwards beneath the city's western walls to join the river Eden. 'To this sweet stream,' observed one writer

in 1803, 'Carlisle owes half its wealth.' The building of water-powered spinning mills was matched by the creation of colonies of handloom weavers. At some point the surviving stone-built cottages in St John Street appear to have incorporated loomshops. Carlisle benefited from cheap coal from the earl of Carlisle's mines near Brampton, ten miles to the east. By 1861 Carlisle had a population of nearly 30,000, of whom more than 4,000 were engaged in cotton and woollen manufacture.

The growth of cotton manufacturing dates from 20 November 1790 when the three sons of the check manufacturer Richard Ferguson leased six acres at Warwick Bridge, on the river Eden five miles east of the city, and built the three-storey water-powered Langthwaite spinning mill. They leased it in 1809 to their brother-in-law Peter Dixon and his sons, who constructed a four-storey extension and a new reservoir, and in 1832 added a steam engine. In 1836 the Dixons constructed the seven-storey Shaddon Mill, with an iron frame designed by Sir William Fairbairn, which dominates the western side of Carlisle. The mill measures 224 feet × 58 feet (69 × 18 m), while its chimney, the dominating landmark in the city, is 350 feet (97 m) high. From 1837 the Dixons' home was Holme Eden, a red sandstone calendar house (365 windows, 52 chimneys, 12 passageways and 7 entrances) designed in the Tudor style by John Dobson and overlooking the Langthwaite Mills.

Carlisle's textile manufacturers specialised in checks and ginghams and similar cotton fabrics, some of which were reputedly exported to clothe slaves in the southern United States. Other manufacturers produced calico prints and cotton twine, girth cloths and linen, and some also wove woollen cloth. In 1847 there were four large spinning mills in Carlisle in addition to that at Warwick Bridge, together with two at Dalston, six miles south-west, and another, with a calico printworks, at Cummersdale two miles south. There were also eight weaving factories and several bleaching and finishing works. Some were very large concerns. In 1861 William Parker employed nearly 500 people making checks and ginghams, while Edward McGibbon's integrated cotton manufactory had a workforce of 700. John Hargreaves, one of the principal woollen cloth manufacturers, had 97 employees. By 1861 most weaving factories used steam looms, but handloom weavers were still numerous. Merchants dealing in yarn and finished cloth traded in Carlisle, and there were manufacturers of shuttles, heddles, bobbins, reeds and harnesses. In Carlisle proper there were more than 4,000 textile workers in 1861, with about 300 more in Stanwix and other parishes to the north, and more than 600 at Dalton and Cummersdale.

The textile industry in Carlisle grew deep roots in its region. The weaving of cotton checks and ginghams at Brampton began in the 1780s. Mills were built and in 1861 cotton manufacturing employed more than 300 people in the town. Cotton manufacturing was also established at Penrith in the early nineteenth century, but subsequently declined, although one firm employed more than 40 people in 1861. On the Cumberland coast the influence of check and gingham manufacturers from Carlisle was intermingled with older traditions of working hemp and flax. By the late 1820s there were seven check and gingham manufacturers in Wigton, as well as a calico printworks and a woollen mill. In 1861 about 400 of its 4,000 inhabitants were employed in the manufacture of cotton. Like the roots of a tree, the textile manufacturing extended farther – more than 90 cotton handloom weavers worked in their own homes in the villages between Wigton and the coast, though the textile industry was less prosperous around Maryport. Marshall listed several flax manufacturers in the area and observed a cotton mill, but in 1814 it was standing derelict, and by the 1860s the only textile workers in the town were canvas-weavers supplying local sailmakers. A cotton mill at Cockermouth gave employment in 1861 to about 130 people. In south Cumbria there were mills employing between 50 and 100 people at Ulverston, Finsthwaite and Backbarrow, and near Penny Bridge.

Cotton manufacturing became one of the principal occupations in the Greenfield Valley in Flintshire, one of Britain's most abundant sources of water power. John Smalley, one of Arkwright's partners, built the Yellow Mill in 1777 using stone from the ruined Basingwerk Abbey, and his sons opened the Upper Mill in 1783, the Lower Mill in 1785, and the Crescent Mill in 1790. With the contemporary growth of copper works the valley became one of the most significant concentrations of industry in the late eighteenth century.

While Yorkshire was famed most for its woollens, cotton was also a significant part of the Yorkshire textile industry from the 1780s, when the potential profits from Arkwright's processes seemed boundless. Some mills were adapted in the early nineteenth century to produce woollens, but between 1835 and

Two of the cotton mills in the Greenfield Valley, Holywell, North Wales, from an aquatint by J. White. In the foreground is the Upper Mill of 1783, with a clock in the pediment and a cupola with a bell on the roof, symbols of the work disciplined imposed in textile factories. In the background is the Crescent Mill of 1790.

1903 between 13 and 20 per cent of the county's mills were actually used by cotton manufacturers. Some Yorkshire cotton manufacturers produced warps for worsted fabrics. Mills built at Hull in 1837 and 1847, and the one significant cotton mill in Bristol, opened in 1838, are discussed in Chapter 11 (pages 510, 513).

Men with capital also built mills in some very remote places. In about 1794 unknown entrepreneurs built a carding and spinning mill powered by a 14 foot (4.26 m) diameter waterwheel on the site of Prescot Forge in the Clee Hills of Shropshire. Attempts were made to sell it between 1804 and 1827, but its sole memorial was the name 'Factory' given to nearby houses. A mill was built about 1800 alongside the river Eden at Kirkby Stephen by venturers who probably hoped to supply yarn to the many stocking knitters in the vicinity. It failed, and after use by a silk-throwing concern and another cotton-spinning company, the

building was adapted in the 1830s as the union workhouse. The stone-built Yore Mill at Aysgarth in Wensleydale was built in 1783 by seven partners, including John Pratt, whose father made a fortune in London operating hackney carriages. The mill began to spin in 1786, was offered for sale in 1814, was ruinous in 1820 and was destroyed by fire in 1852. A three-storey mill with a 22-foot (6.8 m) waterwheel at Gayle near Hawes in upper Wensleydale was built in the early 1780s by Oswald and Thomas Routh. It had a short life as a cotton mill, but was later used for spinning flax and then for worsted yarns. A four-storey mill at Malham, in Wharfedale, was built in 1785, ceased spinning by 1820 and was derelict by 1841. Mills in Galloway, at Ballasala on the Isle of Man, and in remote parts of Ireland and the Scottish Highlands all testify to the seemingly limitless prospects that appeared to be offered by cotton spinning from the 1780s.

The Scottish cotton industry

The Scottish lowlands were, after Lancashire, the most important centre of cotton production in Britain. Much of the financial and technological expertise that was the foundation of the industry came from linen manufacturing, which was widespread in the eighteenth century and was encouraged from 1727 by the Board of Trustees for Fisheries and Manufactures. Output of linen rose three-fold in volume and four-fold in value between 1736 and 1770, and Glasgow became Britain's principal centre of linen trading, supplying markets in England and the American colonies. Cotton

was being spun in Glasgow in the late 1770s, and the South Woodside Mill on the river Kelvin was working by 1784. Nevertheless, Richard Arkwright's celebrated visit to Glasgow and the Falls of Clyde in October 1784 is customarily seen as the beginning of Scottish cotton manufacturing. David Dale established the community at New Lanark the following year, and mills were soon constructed at Catrine, Deanston and Stanley. The process of change and the links with earlier forms of manufacturing are epitomised in the conserved cottage at Kilbarchan near Paisley, which

↗ The handloom weaver's cottage at Kilbarchan, four miles west of Paisley, conserved by the National Trust for Scotland. It was built in 1723 by the linen weavers Andrew John and Jenat Bryden, whose names are inscribed over the front door. It was later used by weavers of cotton fabrics.

was built for a linen handloom weaver but later used by a weaver of cotton.

Cotton manufacturing expanded quickly. According to one reckoning there were 19 cotton mills in Scotland in 1788, but a survey of 1793 recorded 39 powered by water in the west of the country alone. Six years later there were nine steam-powered mills in Glasgow and another nine in Paisley. Imports of cotton into the Clyde ports increased in value from £150,000 *per annum* in 1770–74 to £7.5 million in 1801, but import figures do not accurately reflect the rate of growth of the industry since much of the cotton yarn worked in Scotland came from the Manchester firms of A. & G. Murray and McConnel & Kennedy and was used in the weaving of shawls and other fine fabrics. While powerlooms were installed in many mills, the number of Scottish handloom weavers continued to increase until about 1840, as migrants into the Lowland towns were drawn into the trade.

The first steam-powered cotton mill in Glasgow began working in 1792. Henry Houldsworth went to Glasgow from Nottingham in 1799 to manage a water-powered cotton mill, which he subsequently purchased, and in 1804 he constructed a large spinning mill, similar to the Salford Twist Mill, which was probably the first fireproof building in Scotland. James Cleland's statistics in 1831 suggested that a third of the occupied population of Glasgow was involved in cotton textiles. One of the first effective Scottish trades unions was organised by Glasgow spinners from about 1805. The union succeeded, during a succession of sometimes violent disputes in the 1820s, in maintaining a standard of living that was comfortable relative to that of handloom weavers or flax workers in eastern Scotland. Some new factories were built – multi-storey Oldham-style spinning mills designed by the Stotts and also north-lit weaving sheds – but by 1870 Glasgow was no longer comparable with Manchester as a cotton-manufacturing centre.

Paisley is similar in many respects to the Lancashire towns of Bolton and Oldham. In 1700 it was a centre for linen manufacturing, with a population of about 4,500 – which increased to 7,000 in 1755, 31,000 in 1801 and 57,000 in 1831. By then it was the fourth largest burgh in Scotland, and perhaps half the population were dependent on weaving. The extent of the industry is indicated by the spread of early mills around the town: the Roadlie Mill at Neilston built from 1790, the six-storey Old End Mill at Johnstone of 1787, at Milliken Park the six-storey Cartside Mill of 1792 with its Venetian windows, and the Calderpark Mill of *c*.1790 at Lochwinnoch. Paisley's specialisms came to be shawls inspired by Indian designs, first of silk then of fine cotton woven on Jacquard looms, and thread, which was made principally by Clark & Co. at the Anchor Mills, founded in 1812, and J. & P. Coats at the Ferguslie Mills, founded in 1826. The manufacture of cotton thread in Paisley began in the 1820s and went on to become the town's principal industry in the decades after 1870.

Rural-manufacturing communities were a distinctive feature of the Scottish cotton industry. New Lanark was important as a large complex but also as an influence on the social development of industrial communities, a theme that is considered below in Chapter 14. Arkwright was a partner with George Dempster in Stanley Mills established in 1785, six miles north of Perth, but he withdrew from the venture after a nucleus of workers had been trained. The complex

James Black & Co. were Scotland's principal calico printing firm. Their original works was at Alexandria, Glasgow, but from 1835 they acquired and greatly enlarged another printworks at Dalmonach, Dunbartonshire, on the banks of the Monkland Canal. This engraving of *circa* 1860 also provides a good impression of the cabinless day-boats which were employed on the canals of central Scotland.

includes the Bell Mill, a five-storey brick building with a bell cupola, completed by 1790, the East Mill built in 1802–09, and the fireproof Mid Mill of 1823–28. The lade (leat) powered seven waterwheels until 1921, and the mill worked until 1989. At its gates is an elegant company village of solidly constructed two-storey stone terraces. The Adelphi Mill at Deanston on the river Teith, seven miles north-west of Stirling, was established in 1785 by the brothers Archibald and John Buchanan. The latter had been an agent for Arkwright, selling his twist in Scotland, while the former had served an apprenticeship at Cromford. The mill was designed according to Arkwright's principles, although spinning jennies were used alongside water-frames, and subsequently mules were introduced. Trainee workers from Deanston or Stanley may have comprised the party of about 40 North Britons from Perth (or Perthshire) who arrived at Cromford to the sound of bagpipes in May 1785. The Deanston mill was sold by the Buchanans in 1793 and taken over in 1808 by James Finlay & Co. Its principal surviving buildings date from 1827, when the capacity of the water-power system was increased, and until 1949 the lade powered four 36 foot (11 m) diameter

waterwheels. In the mid-nineteenth century the mills employed about a thousand people. Cotton manufacturing ceased in 1965, and the buildings now form part of a distillery.

The Ballindalloch Mill at Balfron on the Water of Endrick, 16 miles north of Glasgow, was established by the local landlord in association with the Buchanan brothers in 1789–90, and was managed by Archibald Buchanan after he sold Deanston in 1793. Spinning mules produced yarn for weavers working more than 300 looms in the parish in 1841, although a calico printworks established nearby in the 1790s proved unprofitable because of the high cost of transporting coal. The mill complex on the river Ayr at Catrine was established from 1785 by David Dale in partnership with Claud Alexander of Ballochmyle, who had made a fortune as paymaster-general in India. It was managed for a time by Archibald Buchanan. Cotton was manufactured until 1968, but the twist mill, notable for its Venetian windows, was destroyed by fire in 1963.

The mill powered by the river Clyde at Blantyre was built from 1785 by a company whose partners included David Dale. It developed into an integrated complex, spinning, weaving and dyeing cotton, and employed 750 workpeople in 1816. The explorer and missionary David Livingstone was born in Shuttle Row, and the mill's counting house is now the nucleus of the David Livingstone Centre. Three of the rural mills – Ballindalloch in 1793, Catrine in 1801 and Deanston in 1808 – came under the control of James Finlay & Co. and were managed by the founder's son Kirkman Finlay. The owners of the mills had strong incentives to create settled communities, for they found it difficult to persuade migrants from the Highlands to adapt to the demands of the factory system: at Catrine it was suggested that setting a Highlander at a loom was like putting a deer to the plough.

A cotton-spinning mill at Rothesay on the Isle of Bute was opened in 1779, reputedly the first in

Scotland. The industry flourished under Robert Thom: from 1800, when steam power on the island proved not to be viable, he rebuilt the water-power system. By the 1850s there were five mills at Rothesay, one of five storeys, which gave employment to 1,215 people, but the industry declined as the town developed as a resort. There were only about 160 cotton workers there in 1881, and the last mill closed soon afterwards. Cotton mills at Gatehouse of Fleet in Galloway were established from 1785 by the Yorkshire cattle dealer John Birtwhistle and managed by his son Alexander. By 1850 they had been adapted for other purposes. A 12-bay, three-storey building now accommodates The Mill on the Fleet arts centre.

Attempts to establish cotton working in the Highlands are considered in Chapter 14 (see page 593).

The cotton industry in Ireland

Cotton spinning also spread rapidly in Ireland in the 1780s, with spinning works at Dublin, Belfast, Slane, Blarney and Glasheen. Irishmen were already experienced in constructing large multi-storey buildings for milling grain. When cotton mills were successfully established, bleachworks followed, and employment was provided for handloom weavers. The industry prospered for a generation, particularly around Belfast, where entrepreneurs established water-powered spinning mills, and handloom weavers made the transition

from linen to cotton. The process was reversed after the peace of 1815 and particularly after the financial crisis of 1825. Cotton manufacturing continued at a few centres in the south (as described in Chapter 14), but in the Belfast area spinning mills were either adapted to produce linen yarn or went out of business. Weaving, based on yarns imported from England, declined less rapidly. By 1841 only about 6,000 people in Ireland were engaged in manufacturing cotton, about 2 per cent of the total in the United Kingdom.

◁ The cotton industry flourished in Ireland, particularly in Ulster, for a generation from the 1780s, but fell into decline after 1815, which in the northern counties was accompanied by an expansion of factory-based linen production. This ruined cotton mill near Ballynure, Co. Antrim, provides evidence of a remarkably short-lived industry.

The silk industry

Silk, the fine soft thread secreted by silkworm caterpillars (*Bombyx mori*) when forming cocoons, was imported from China or the Middle East, usually in skeins of several thousand yards. It was wound onto bobbins, then 'thrown' or twisted into yarn ready for weaving. Silk fabrics were normally dyed, and often printed. In 1700 the principal centre of silk manufactures was in Spitalfields in London, where it was established by Huguenot refugees after the revocation of the Edict of Nantes in 1685. Their imposing early eighteenth-century houses still stand in Elder Street and Fournier Street, and many silk workers remained in Spitalfields in the nineteenth century.

Silk manufacturers were the first textile producers to use water power for purposes other than fulling. In 1702 Thomas Cotchett, a Derby solicitor, asked the engineer George Sorocold to build a three-storey mill, 62 feet long, that would be equipped with Dutch machines. The venture was unsuccessful, but one of Cotchett's employees, John Lombe, went to Piedmont, observed innovative methods of doubling silk, and returned with detailed drawings. Despite more than a hint of industrial espionage, Lombe was granted a patent in 1719, and at Derby in 1721, with his brother Thomas, he built a five-storey mill which can be regarded as a significant progenitor of Arkwright's system: a multi-storey textile mill with a single power source. Lombe's mill at Derby was 101 feet (33.5 m) long and 39 feet (12 m) wide, in which a large workforce worked silk-throwing machines, whose foundations were set on the ground floor and extended through the first two storeys, while smaller doubling machines were ranked on the three floors above. The mill operated for almost two hundred years until a fire in 1910, after which it was rebuilt on the original foundation arches but with three storeys instead of five. It now houses the Derby Industrial Museum. The Derby silk mill quickly achieved celebrity, and was imitated in Stockport, where the Logwood Mill was built in 1732 by a former employee of the Lombes. Raw silk, particularly 'tram', the coarser quality used for weft, was also thrown by hand. It was reckoned in 1765 that 7 mills in England used the machines developed by the Lombes, but there were about 60 where tram was thrown.

⌐ Elder Street, Spitalfields, on the eastern side of the City of London was laid out in the 1720s. A deed of 1724 refers to 'the street intended to be called Elder Street'. Almost every house consisted of a basement, three storeys and a roof garret, often used for weaving silk. While the frontages are impressive, most of the houses were only one room deep.

⌐ Fournier Street, Spitalfields, was also laid out in the 1720s, and was initially settled by Huguenot refugees who brought silk manufacturing to this part of London. Many of the houses have panelled rooms and elaborately carved staircases and fireplaces, but the well-lit attics were used for working silk. At the western end of the street is Nicholas Hawksmoor's magnificent Christ Church, Spitalfields, which was built between 1714 and 1720.

Silk making developed through several advances in technology. Steam power was applied to throwing and ultimately to weaving, and powered spinning (as distinct from throwing) of silk was introduced at Galgate, Lancashire, in 1792. Jacquard looms enlarged the range of products that could be woven in the 1820s. The ceiling height in the Victoria Mills, Macclesfield, built in 1823, is 12 feet 6 inches (3.8 m) compared with an average of 8 feet 2 inches (2.5 m) in other mills in the town, suggesting that it was designed to accommodate the controls of Jacquard looms (which were mounted above the loom itself). A Macclesfield engineer announced in 1828 that he had been manufacturing Jacquard for six years, and assured potential purchasers that he had an agency agreement with Jacquard of Lyons. Silk makers enjoyed protection from foreign competition until the signing of W. E. Gladstone's commercial treaty with France in 1860. The numbers employed in silk factories increased from 31,000 in 1835 to a peak of 56,000 in

1856, but had declined to 52,000 by 1861 and to 41,000 by 1867, and with some fluctuations continued to fall, although the output of broad-piece goods increased through the 1860s and 1870s.

The principal centre of silk working in Britain was the upland region extending 20 miles from Macclesfield through Congleton and Leek towards Cheadle, passing from Cheshire into Staffordshire and including the valleys of the Bollin and the Dane, both tributaries of the Mersey, and the river Churnet, which flows into the Dove and ultimately the Trent. Water power for textile manufacturing was abundant in the region, and modest supplies of coal were used from the late eighteenth century in steam-driven factories. Across this whole area in the early eighteenth century silk was woven into ribbons, or used, sometimes in embroidered patterns, to cover padded buttons made with wooden or horn moulds. Other buttons were covered with linen, horsehair and ox-hair. Tagged leather laces called 'Congleton points' were the

⅄ The 18-bay, 5-storey Union Mill in Statham Street, Macclesfield, one of seven silk mills constructed in the town between 1811 and 1831 that were adorned with pediments. This was a period of investment and prosperity, described by one silk manufacturer as 'the highest point of perfection'. Union Mill has been demolished, and only one of the pedimented mills now remains.

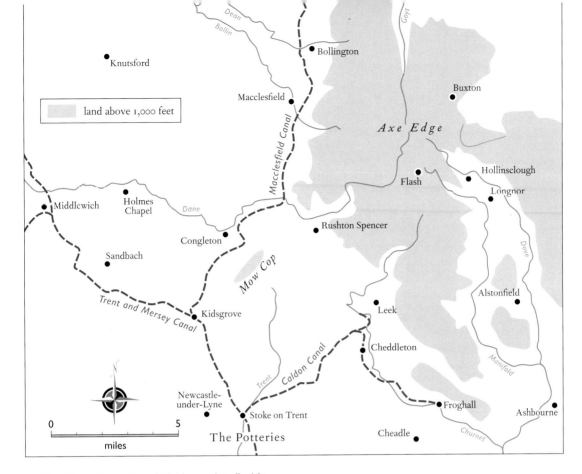

⋏ The silk-working region of Cheshire and Staffordshire.

traditional 'manufacture' of Congleton. With pottery from nearby Stoke-on-Trent, ribbons, buttons and laces were carried to distant parts of England by hawkers who lived in the upland parish of Alstonefield between Leek and Buxton.

The most spectacular silk mill of the eighteenth century was constructed at Congleton in 1753 by a partnership headed by Nathaniel Pattison, a London silk merchant who had links with the Lombes. The five-storey, 29-bay building was 240 feet long, 24 feet wide and 48 feet high (74 × 7.4 m × 14.8 m), and housed eleven circular throwing machines on the lower floors, each about 12 feet (3.6 m) in diameter and about 19 feet 8 inches (6.0 m) high. Its first waterwheel was installed by James Brindley. The first silk factory in Macclesfield was the four-storey, water-powered 'Button Mill' built in 1744 at Park Green by Charles Roe, who based the design on 'a perfect model of the silk mill at Derby'. It accommodated six

circular throwing machines. The son of a clergyman from Castleton, Derbyshire, Roe was an inspirational citizen and entrepreneur. He settled in Macclesfield before 1742, married the daughter of a silk merchant, and began copper smelting in the town. He paid for the building of Christ Church in 1775, and his memorial there relates that he 'carried on the Button and Twist Manufacture in this town with the most active Industry, Ingenuity and Integrity, and ... established here ... the silk and copper manufactories by which many thousands of families have since been supported'. A second silk mill was built in 1769 on Sunderland Street, and by one calculation 119 textile mills were erected in Macclesfield and Congleton between 1784 and 1826. Some were substantial buildings with powered machinery, but many were 'shades', small workshops accommodating hand-worked or horse-powered machines. An advertisement in 1812 offered for sale 'a building used as a silk mill with ...

↖ Cottages in Pitt Street, Macclesfield, which appears to have been
built when handloom weaving of silk in the town was ceasing to be
a domestic occupation. Only one building in the street has weavers'
attics.

in Silk Street, Congleton … together with a horse
wheel with cast-iron gearing … together with two
useful ponies which have been accustomed to work
the said mill'. Nevertheless, by 1780 the pattern for
water- and later steam-powered silk-throwing mills
was established. The weaving of broad silk fabrics
was introduced in Macclesfield during the 1790s, and
steam power was adopted by 1810. Cotton mills were
built in the region following the annulment of Richard
Arkwright's patents in 1785, but after 1815 several of
these were adapted to work silk.

The typical mill built between 1780 and 1830 was
of three or four storeys, rectangular or L-shaped in
plan, with wooden internal frame and roof structure,
and heated either by stoves or open fires through vents
to each floor, or by piped steam. Most were plain in
appearance, but between 1811 and 1831 seven pedimented factories were built in Macclesfield, of which

only the Chester Road Mill survives. These elegant
buildings reflected the prosperity of a period which
the silk manufacturer John Brocklehurst II called the
'highest point of perfection'. Yet most silk fabrics were
woven by hand. A survey of 1836 reported that only 414
powerlooms were used to weave silk in Cheshire, and
even in 1849 it was said that they were used only in the
production of coarse fabrics. In 1824 it was reckoned
that there were 550 master weavers, working in their
own homes, in Macclesfield, but many of the 4,000
looms working in the town in 1840 were provided by
employers and congregated in unpowered workshops.

The predominance of handloom weaving was
reflected by the building of 'garret houses', considerable numbers of which can still be seen in Macclesfield,
Congleton and Leek. There were about 600 in
Macclesfield, the majority constructed during the first
quarter of the nineteenth century when, according to
a contemporary, 'weavers carried everything with a
high hand; if a new house was built, the upper storey
was generally prepared with large windows fit for
a weaver's workshop.' The characteristic house was
of three storeys, of red brick, with a roof of stone
flags (although after the canal opened in 1831 Welsh
slate was used instead). Doorways and the entrances
to passages have arched heads. The large-windowed
garret workshops were usually accessed by wooden
steps entered through trapdoors. In 1849 Reach
inspected a house where there were five treddle-looms
and a Jacquard loom in the workshop, which produced
silk handkerchiefs. Most garret houses were built spec-
ulatively in groups of three or four, but there were
some longer terraces. In later developments isolated
three-storey garret houses stand proud in terraces of
two-storey cottages. Until the 1970s the relationship
between factory and domestic production was vividly
reflected in the streets of Macclesfield, where elegant
pedimented mills were still surrounded by ranks of
garret houses.

The population of Macclesfield increased from
around 6,000 in 1754 to 8,743 in 1801, then expanded
by 40 per cent in the first decade of the nineteenth
century, 44 per cent in the second and 30 per cent in the
1820s, to reach 23,129 in 1831. This was followed by a
decade of stagnation in the 1830s, and decline in the

1850s. The population of Congleton grew from 3,861 in 1801 to 6,400 in 1821 and reached a peak of 12,344 in 1861, after which it too declined. The population change of these towns therefore closely reflected the fortunes of the silk industry. The first mills in Leek were built soon after 1800, and by 1835 seven factories with 119 powerlooms employed 744 people. A near-contemporary directory listed 17 'silk manufacturers', many of whom operated from small workshops. The population of the parish grew from 6,810 in 1801 to 10,780 in 1831 and 13,294 in 1851.

Like landed estates, silk mills in Macclesfield, Congleton and Leek were managed by 'stewards', an occupation distinct from that of overlooker. Some tasks, particularly printing and dyeing, were sub-contracted. Reach recorded that an 'undertaker' in Macclesfield rented houses in which he installed looms that were worked by tenant weavers, who fulfilled his orders, but that they in turn employed journeymen and took on apprentices. However, some undertakers worked at the loom themselves. In 1841 more than 8,000 people, 47 per cent of them women and girls, worked in silk making in Macclesfield, comprising 65 per cent of the employed population. The census of 1861 recorded four employers of more than 200 silk workers in Macclesfield, four in Congleton and four in Leek, but the median number employed by companies in Macclesfield was just 19, in Congleton 45 and in Leek 32.

Most manufacturing took place in the three towns, but there was some elsewhere. The largest rural concerns were dyehouses, at Rushton Spencer and Cheddleton, employing respectively 30 and 75 people in 1861. More than a hundred silk button makers worked in the upland townships of Flash, Heathylee and Hollinsclough. There was some manufacturing in nearby towns. About 170 silk workers lived alongside miners, copper workers and tape weavers in Cheadle in 1861, but there the industry disappeared before 1881; a manufacturer at Sandbach employed more than 300 people; and 60 people worked silks at Middlewich. Silk working was a minor part of the textile industry elsewhere in north-west England, particularly at Middleton near Manchester and at Galgate, south of Lancaster, where the mill

established in 1792 employed about 200 people in 1861. Silk making was supported by an infrastructure of pattern designers, machine makers, reed makers, harness knitters, makers of bobbins, reeds and spools and card cutters. It also had much wider connections – thus, most spinners of silken yarns in Cheshire and Staffordshire had links with Coventry.

Macclesfield had an Evangelical tradition that was encouraged by Charles Roe and given impetus by the Revd David Simpson, son of a Yorkshire farmer who was involved with other Evangelicals, including Rowland Hill at St John's College, Cambridge. He was ordained in 1771, appointed curate at St Michael, Macclesfield, in 1772, and in 1779 Charles Roe presented him with the living of Christ Church. Simpson, a friend of John Wesley, was interested in Sunday schools and in 1796 his follower, John Whitaker, founded a school which taught adults as well as children. It proved popular, and in 1814 an imposing ten-bay, four-storey building was opened. It now houses Macclesfield's heritage centre. In its first year it had 2,451 pupils and about 200 volunteer teachers but, although theoretically non-denominational, its success exacerbated tensions between Anglicans, who felt excluded from the enterprise, and dissenters.

Some were dismayed that writing was taught alongside reading, but its benefits were extolled by Adam Rushton who, having begun work at a twisting mill at the age of eight, was later delighted to learn about popular science, Homer and America. He reflected about learning to write: 'no engineer, architect, inventor, discoverer or commander could have felt more exquisite pleasure.' The Sunday school was also an instrument of social control, priding itself according to one committee member that it instilled 'loyalty, honesty and submission to employers'. David Simpson denounced Jacobins, Tom Paine and the theatre, and the declared objective of the school in 1825–26 was 'not to make the children of the labouring classes discontented with their situations, to encourage a spirit of insubordination and to raise them above their fellows in the same rank of life with themselves … it teaches humility, patience and resignation and is calculated to fit its subjects to act a useful part in their allotted station in life.' Nevertheless, the school, and those in other manufacturing towns that met in undistinguished buildings, contributed substantially to the creation of a working-class culture rooted in learning and respectability. The Chartist *Northern Star* commented in 1838 that 'If the poor in this country are generally well informed, able to converse freely and rationally on many literary subjects, we owe it to the Sunday schools in which they have learned to read'.

Manufactured silk took many forms – broad fabrics for garments, braids, laces, ribbons, bindings and trimmings, ferret (a stout tape used for garters), gimp (a form of twist), ties, cravats, scarves, sashes and shawls. Individual places often specialised in particular products, as the experience of Coventry demonstrates. The city's principal manufactures between 1700 and the 1860s were silk ribbons, gauzes, trimmings and some broad fabrics. The Rochefoucaulds observed in 1786 that most of the inhabitants, including many women, made ribbons in their own homes, and that young children carried out ancillary tasks. Silk working employed more than 10,000 of the city's 36,000 people in 1851 but only about 8,000 of a population of 41,000 in 1861, by which time the trade was declining because the 1860 treaty with France removed duties on imports

⋎ Cottages with attics high enough to accommodate the control mechanisms of Jacquard looms – nos 1–7 Hurst Road, Longford, Coventry, built in the second quarter of the nineteenth century.

to Britain. In 1835 there were six silk throwsters in Coventry, 77 ribbon-manufacturing businesses and 13 silk dyers, as well as makers of shrouds and trimmings, and builders of looms. Joseph Hart, whose family controlled the city's largest ribbon business, employed 400 men and 580 women and girls in 1861. Most weavers worked in their own homes, some in the picturesque half-timbered and gabled houses that were destroyed by the Luftwaffe on the night of 14–15 November 1940, and some in suburbs such as Radford and Foleshill, growing beyond the unenclosed open fields. Most looms were worked manually, and the 1861 census records the occupations of many teenage boys as 'turns a loom'. In 1851 more than 80 per cent of Coventry silk workers were locally born, although there had been inward migration from Spitalfields, Bethnal Green, Macclesfield and Reading. The outlook of ribbon workers was conservative. A newspaper observed in 1853 that, 'Little enterprise is manifested by the master manufacturer, and still less by the operative weaver. … They seem to jog on in the old style in which their grandfathers pursued their trade, and to trust to foreign skill to provide them with new ideas, or to an indulgent government to continue protection.' Nevertheless, the Jacquard loom was welcomed in Coventry, and in the suburbs of Stoke and Longford there are still cottages with high-ceilinged upper storeys which could accommodate the looms' control mechanisms. In 1857 John and Joseph Cash built an innovative 'cottage factory' alongside the Coventry Canal, in which weavers living in their own homes could employ power from a steam engine to operate machinery in upper-storey workshops, but only 48 of the planned 100 dwellings were completed, and in 1862 the workshops were converted into a single factory extending above the living quarters.

Silk working extended ten miles northwards from Coventry through Bedworth to Nuneaton. More than 1,800 silk workers lived at Bedworth in 1861. Many were domestic workers, some of whose characteristic homes remain in Rye Piece, but Thomas Rowbotham employed more than 250 in a throwing mill at Colleycroft. About 3,000 of Nuneaton's population of about 10,500 were silk workers, as were 660 of the 1,859 inhabitants of Bulkington, two miles east of Bedworth.

Blockley, Gloucestershire, at the northern end of the Cotswolds, was a village with abundant water power and was a centre of silk throwing for nearly two centuries, supplying yarn to weavers in Coventry. Up to a dozen mill buildings can still be recognised in the village, although most have been adapted as dwellings. Westmancotts Mill, seen here, was one of the last to close, in the 1880s.

Three brooks provided water power for silk working at Blockley, on the northern edge of the Cotswolds, where the first silk mill began production in 1718. Blockley yarn was supplied to weavers in Coventry. By 1820 more than 300 people were working in six mills, and the population rose from 1,569 in 1801 to 2,596 in 1861, but declined thereafter as mills closed. More than 400 villagers were employed in silk manufacture in 1851, of whom about 350 were female, 30 of them aged ten or less. Many were wives of agricultural workers, but some were single female lodgers from nearby parishes. The number employed fell to fewer than 200 in 1871, and from the 1870s the mills were adapted to other purposes – an iron foundry, a piano factory, and a workshop where about 50 women used sewing machines to make linen collars.

A chain of silk mills extended through the Cotswolds. The Burton (or Avon) Mill at Malmesbury was built in the 1790s by an entrepreneur who hoped to make broad cloth without the restrictions imposed by trade associations in Trowbridge and Bradford-on-Avon. It was taken over in the 1850s by a Derby company, which used it for silk manufacturing; in the 1880s the firm employed more than a hundred people. There was a small silk-throwing works at Tetbury in 1861, a winding mill employing 100 at Brimscombe, a factory at Winchcombe with 58 work-people, and a mill at Chipping Campden, later used by C. R. Ashbee's Guild of Handicrafts, which had a workforce of just six.

The silk industry in London declined. Manufacturers began to move production to Hertfordshire, Essex and Suffolk in the 1780s (when French visitors noted that silk working in Sudbury was funded by London merchants). Wage rates fell from the 1790s, and by the 1820s silk working in the capital was a sweated trade, albeit a substantial one. Several manufacturers lived in Spital Square in 1861, among them George Foot who employed 200 people, Henry Soper who employed 88, and his son, also Henry, who employed 300. The products of London silk workers included velvets, fringes, artificial flower petals, tassels, trimmings, umbrella covers and garters.

George Courtauld, a member of a Huguenot family, set up a silk business in Spitalfields, but became a Unitarian, opposed the government during the American War, and spent the years from 1785 to 1794 farming in Kentucky. After returning to England he converted a corn mill at Pebmarsh, Essex, into a silk mill in 1798, and in 1809 moved to Braintree where he similarly adapted another mill to specialise in crepe for mourning clothes. He returned to America in 1818, leaving the business to his son Samuel and his partner and cousin Peter Taylor. From 1819 Samuel Courtauld adapted the last baize factory in Bocking to work silk, and in 1825–28 built steam-powered mills at Bocking and Halstead, the latter adapted from the town corn mill. His manager was Stephen Beuzeville, whose Huguenot family had worked silk at Spitalfields for more than a century. By 1850 the company employed more than 2,000 people in three mills, including that at Halstead, where Samuel Courtauld made his home at Gosfield Hall. By 1861 more than 1,250 of Halstead's population of nearly 7,000 were engaged in throwing

silk and weaving crepe. Braintree and Bocking were said in 1855 to 'form one continuous town extending for a mile on the road from Chelmsford to Halstead'. In 1861, of their joint population of 7,989, some 1,281 were directly engaged in silk working, including throwsters, crepe weavers, silk velvet weavers, figured silk weavers and tambour weavers.

At Haverhill about 600 people were employed in 1861 in various branches of textiles, including cotton weaving and the manufacture of the light brown linen fabric known as drabbet, but 450 worked in silk factories, 230 of them in that owned by John Lester. Coggeshall and its surrounding villages were also involved in silk working, about 200 people making tambour lace for which patterns were embroidered on fabrics stretched on drum-shaped frames, about the same number weaving silk velvet, and 660 employed in the throwing mill of John P. Hall. At Sudbury and the neighbouring Essex parish of Ballingdon textile manufacturing employed 1,140 of a combined population of 5,786. The majority wove silk velvet and satin and fabrics for umbrellas, although some worked worsteds and cotton. In 1855 it was reckoned that there were about 700 looms in the Sudbury area, and substantial houses of the mid-nineteenth century with well-illuminated attics for weaving remain in Girling Street and New Street. More than a hundred were

employed in a steam-powered silk mill at Hadleigh in 1861 and more than 40, including an 'instructor in silk weaving', in a factory at Lavenham.

The industry also flourished in Hertfordshire. For example, more than a hundred were employed in 1861 at a steam-powered mill in Rickmansworth; there were 280 workers at Thomas Shute's Wigginhall Mill at Watford; 230 at the Abbey Mill in St Albans founded by John Woollam in 1802; and about 200 in a steam-powered factory at Aylesbury in Buckinghamshire. In 1825 a silk mill began operation at Tring, and by 1840 this was worked by David Evans & Co. of Cheapside, who employed 500 people. They, with the aid of a 25 hp steam engine called *Venus*, built by Peel, Williams & Peel, produced yarn from skeins imported from Italy, China and Bengal; the weaving took place in London, Manchester and Coventry. Even in Berkshire, where over many decades silk manufacturing was said to have been disappearing, 14 people were working in 1861 at a mill in Newbury. The elegant water-powered silk mill at Whitchurch in Hampshire, which is conserved, was built about 1800 and used for silk manufacture from about 1830. In 1838 just over a hundred people were employed there, 39 of them children under thirteen. There was an almost contemporary silk mill at Whitchurch, in Shropshire, a 143 foot (44 m) long building of two storeys, alongside the Ellesmere Canal, powered by a 10 hp steam engine by Galloway of Manchester. It was adapted as a warehouse before 1851. Mills producing silk were established – and closed – between 1750 and 1850, at Sherborne, Sutton-in-Ashfield, Chesterfield, Sheffield and Ludlow among other places.

Flax, hemp, linen and jute

Flax and hemp were utilised in many fabrics in 1700 – in the best linens, the cambrics, lawns and hollands used for apparel, bedding and table napkins; in the coarse huckaback and hurden fabrics used for mundane household tasks; and for sailcloth, canvas, sackings and tarpaulins. In the first stages of manufacture flax stems were 'retted', by soaking them in water to decompose the gum that binds them together; they were then subjected to 'braking' by rollers, before 'scutching', in which wooded blades scraped away gummy residue. These processes were mechanised by 1700, and a water-powered scutch mill is displayed at the Ulster Folk Museum. The scutched stems were divided by heckling (or combing) into the 'line', the long fibres employed in finer fabrics, and the short fibres, known as 'tow', 'nogs' or 'hurds', used in coarser forms of cloth. Beetling, the equivalent of the fulling process used in the finishing of woollens, could also be powered by water, as in the mill preserved at Wellbrook near Cookstown, Co. Tyrone. Both types of mill became the focus of manufacturing systems in which most spinners and weavers worked in their own homes. The consumption of linen was growing in 1700 and, since much of the demand was met by imports, the visionary Andrew Yarranton suggested that flax warehouses, schools to teach spinning, dwellings for weavers, and bleaching yards should be among the features of the new towns that he envisaged at waterway junctions.

Much of the yarn produced commercially in the early eighteenth century was for mixture fabrics such as fustian, druggets and linsey-woollsey. Pococke observed at Manchester in 1750 'a great manufacture … of linen and cotton which for spinning and reeling employs most of the country round'. Much of the hempen and flaxen yarn used in Lancashire in the mid-eighteenth century was imported from the Continent, while yarn from the Netherlands and the Baltic stimulated manufactures along the Humber. In

➢ In the Irish linen industry beetling was a finishing process equivalent to fulling in the manufacture of woollen cloth. The process could readily be mechanised, as in this mill which was powered by the Rathmore Burn on Snipe Island, near Dundary in Co. Antrim, which has been adapted as a dwelling house. Beetling mills, like the scutching mills used in the preparation of flax for spinning, sometimes became the nuclei of substantial linen factories.

The 'Muckle House' at Spittalfield, Tayside, built in 1767 as the hub of a system of domestic textile manufactures which included and extended beyond the cottages ranged around it.

A view of a bleaching mill in Ireland published in 1791, one of *Twelve Engraved Plates Depicting the Various Stages in the Production of Linen in Ireland* by William Hincks which first appeared in 1782. At this time cloth was usually bleached by treating it with sour milk before exposing it to sunlight on a bleaching green. Claude Louis Berthollet demonstrated in 1785 that chlorine compounds could be used for bleaching, but it was only after Charles Tennant took out a patent for bleaching powder in 1799 that practices began to change substantially.

1794 Arthur Young observed flax spinning and linen weaving at Barton-on-Humber and the manufacture of sacking at Gainsborough. In Scotland linen production was centred on bleacheries and on water-powered mills such as the remote Lintmill of Boyne, eight miles east of Banff. The emergence of more ambitious systems of production is illustrated by the 'Muckle House' at Spittalfield near Caputh (between Dunkeld and Blairgowrie) on Tayside, a five-bay, two-storey building built in 1767 that was a focus for spinners and weavers working in their own homes, including the single-storey cottages ranged around the adjacent green.

In 1780 Arthur Young observed that linen manufactures were the great staple of Ireland. After 1696 Irish merchants could export linen to England free of duties, and production was encouraged by the Board of Trustees of the Linen Manufacturers of Ireland, established in 1711, who built the White Linen Hall in Dublin in 1728. Large quantities of linen from Ireland were handled at Chester, where a linen hall was built by city merchants in 1778. At Blarney, near Cork, Young saw a textile-manufacturing community of about 90 cottages established from 1765 by Major James St John Jefferyes, which produced cotton and woollen as well as linen fabrics. The manufacture of the latter centred round a scutch mill and a bleachery. Young described the processing on small farms in Co. Armagh of flax imported from Riga, Königsberg (Kaliningrad) and St Petersburg. On the estate of the 1st Marquis of Lansdowne at Ballymote, Co. Sligo, he observed a 'manufactory' developed from 1774 around a beetling mill which processed the fabrics produced from 90 looms, which went to the spectacular bleachery established by the marquis's brother, Thomas Fitzmaurice, at Lleweni near Denbigh.

The growth of the linen industry in Ireland was constrained in the late eighteenth century. Young thought that its spread into the countryside, where wages were low, inhibited the take-up of mechanisation, while John Marshall believed that growth was limited after the Union of 1800 by the Corn Laws, which led Irish farmers to grow grain rather than flax. In the Belfast area capital was diverted from linen manufacturing for a generation by the growth of cotton spinning.

In County Durham linen manufacturing flourished in Darlington throughout the eighteenth century. Angerstein visited a scutch mill there, and observed that raw materials were imported from Holland, enabling weavers to make fabrics for sheets, tablecloths and women's petticoats, as well as coarse cloths and waistcoating. John Kendrew, a Darlington optician, and

The Linen Hall in Dublin, opened in 1728, which was the focus of the activities of the Linen Manufacturers of Ireland, a body established in 1711. The engraving, one of *Twelve engraved plates depicting the various stages in the production of linen in Ireland* by William Hincks was published in 1791. It shows linen merchants and manufacturers standing by boxes and bales of linen awaiting exportation. Hincks referred to the linen trade as 'the beneficial staple of our country'.

Thomas Porthouse, a watchmaker, achieved modest success in mechanising the spinning of flax when in 1787 they patented a machine developed from Richard Arkwright's water-frame. They began to spin yarn in a water mill that Kendrew also used to grind glass. By the mid-1790s three of the twelve mills on the 13-mile stretch of the river Skerne passing through Darlington were used for spinning yarn, and the manufacture of linen was said to exceed that of any town in England. Linen was also produced in Knaresborough and adjacent parts of Nidderdale, and during the 1790s mechanised spinning mills were set up elsewhere in Yorkshire, at Beverley, Conisbrough, Ripon and Bingley. Mills were also built in the Lake District, and the first mechanised flax-spinning mill in eastern Scotland began working at Inverbervie in 1787, to be followed by water-powered mills at Douglastown in 1789 and Kinghorn in 1792, and the first mills in Dundee which were working by 1793.

The linen industry was transformed by John Marshall in the same way that cotton manufacturing was revolutionised by Richard Arkwright. Marshall was the son of a Leeds merchant who traded in linen, then an insignificant part of the local economy. From 1782, when he superintended the construction of a new warehouse, he acquired a taste for building. His father's death in 1787 provided an inheritance sufficient for him to live in frugal idleness, but he preferred to enter into 'more hazardous schemes'. He was transparent about his ambitions, reflecting at the age of 31 that he set up a company 'not with the desire of getting money but with the ambition of distinguishing myself', while acknowledging that he was drawn to mechanised flax spinning by the fortunes that had been made from cotton spinning. He reflected that he had sought 'an employment where there was a field for exertion and improvement, where difficulties were to be encountered and riches to be obtained by overcoming them'.

Marshall established a partnership with Samuel Fenton, his late father's partner, and Ralph Dearlove, a linen manufacturer from Knaresborough, and set up a water-powered spinning mill at Adel, four miles north of Leeds. They used machinery based on that of Kendrew and Porthouse, whose suit alleging the infringement of their patent was settled out of court in 1794. Difficulties with the machines were solved by the employment of Matthew Murray, the millwright whose skills were one of the foundations of mechanical engineering in Leeds. He took out a patent for

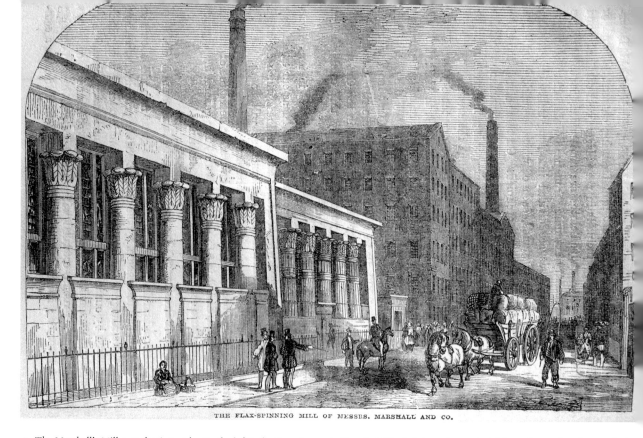

THE FLAX-SPINNING MILL OF MESSRS. MARSHALL AND CO.

The Marshall's Mill complex in Leeds. On the left is the Egyptian-style Temple Mill of 1838–43, beyond which, to the north and towards the city centre, are iron-framed multi-storey blocks erected in the 1820s, and beyond them the earlier buildings in the complex, the first of which date from the 1790s. From George Measom, *The Official Illustrated Guide to the Great Northern Railway* (1861).

flax-spinning machinery in 1790, and the following year Marshall and his partners built a mill on Water Lane on the southern side of Leeds. During the financial crisis of 1793, touched off by the outbreak of war with France, Marshall had to buy out his partners, to borrow money to meet obligations, and to sell stocks of flax accumulated in warehouses at Hull, but worked long hours while 'Matthew Murray exerted his talents and made some great improvements'. By 1792 he had links with the brothers Thomas and Benjamin Benyon, woollen cloth merchants from Shrewsbury and fellow Unitarians, and in December 1793 entered into a partnership with them. They gave up their former business and Thomas Benyon moved to Leeds, where a second mill was completed in 1795 but suffered a fire in February 1796. Production resumed in July 1796, but a decision had been taken to construct a mill at Ditherington, Shrewsbury. It was designed by Charles Bage with an iron frame that

was heralded as fireproof (see page 118). A Boulton & Watt steam engine was installed in the Shrewsbury mill during July 1797, and production was in progress by the following November. The partnership lasted until June 1802 when Marshall, frustrated by what he perceived as the ineffective management of Benjamin Benyon, bought out Bage and the brothers, who proceeded to establish a parallel business with iron-framed mills at Holbeck, Leeds, and Castlefields, Shrewsbury.

Marshall's was the outstanding business in the British flax industry. It expanded along the thoroughfare in Leeds which gained the name Marshall Street, with a succession of buildings culminating in the Temple Mill of 1838–43, a single-storey, top-lit shed with façades in the Egyptian style to the design of Ignatius Bonomi. While it is best known for its ornamental features, Temple Mill is also important because it demonstrated that heavy machines could best be accommodated in single-storey buildings, a principle that was slowly recognised in jute manufacturing and other branches of textiles. Wooden-framed spinning machines were replaced by iron frames that carried about three times as many spindles. During the 1830s the wet-spinning process, by which flax roving was passed through steam to neutralise pectose gum that adhered to it, enabled the separation of fibres for finer spinning. A version of the process had been used secretly in Leeds from about 1816, and Marshalls adopted it from 1827. Temple Mill was designed specifically to accommodate wet spinning, which came to be used by most other flax spinners. Much of the linen yarn spun in Leeds was woven into fabrics in Barnsley, 24 miles to the south, but from the 1790s some machine-spun flax had been made into thread used in making footwear, clothing, saddlery and carpets. The Shrewsbury mill produced thread from its earliest years, but from the 1830s Marshalls also manufactured substantial quantities in Leeds.

By the 1820s Leeds could be regarded as 'the principal town in England for flax-spinning', although the industry was over-shadowed by the city's woollen manufactures. In 1836, 64 of 152 British flax mills were in the West Riding of Yorkshire, 34 of them in Leeds. The Leeds factories were also larger, employing an average of 200 people, while the average in the West Riding was 66, and in south-west England 31. The foundation of the Leeds industry was the range of small, unspectacular firms that provided, for a time, a nursery for new talent. The Scot William Brown observed such mills in 1821: 'they are old, irregular-looking houses seemingly much disfigured with alterations and additions … some of the smaller ones are even made out of … old dwelling houses.' He exempted from this description the premises of John Marshall and the Benyons, and some other flax spinners in the city worked in similarly imposing buildings. Moses Atkinson and John Hives, who had worked with Marshall, set up a partnership in 1823, rebuilt a mill of the 1790s previously used for cottons and woollens, and expanded the complex with a six-storey, 20-bay block in 1833. John Wilkinson spent a decade spinning flax in cramped rented premises before constructing the monumental seven-storey Hunslet Mill.

The Hunslet mills alongside the Aire Navigation in Leeds, built in 1838–40 for the flax manufacturer John Wilkinson, who for ten years previously had worked in inconvenient rented premises. By 1847 Wilkinson employed 1,500 female workers in the largest single-build mill in Leeds. Flax was spun in the seven-storey iron-framed block on the right. Some of the ancillary buildings are of later date. As the Leeds flax industry declined in the 1870s the mill was adapted for the manufacture of woollens. From George Measom, *The Official Illustrated Guide to the Great Northern Railway* (1861).
AUTHOR COLLECTION

The weaving industry at Barnsley was reputedly established in 1744, when William Wilson began to put out yarn to domestic workers. The trade increased from the early nineteenth century in response to the availability of supplies of linen yarn from spinners at Leeds, but some manufacturers also used cotton and silk yarns. Thirty-four linen manufacturers were listed in the town in the 1830s. Products included patterned linens, which were designed by several artists resident locally, damasks, towelling, sheeting and coarse huckabacks. The powerloom was introduced in 1837, although handloom weaving of some fabrics continued long afterwards. By 1850 there was a concentration of mills, most of them initially water-powered, in Peel Street. Taylor's Row, of which only photographic evidence remains, was a lengthy terrace with cellar loomshops, built in the early nineteenth century for handloom weavers of linen, many of whom still lived there in 1861. It took its name from the Taylor family of Dodsworth Hall, who controlled what was probably the largest business in the district, employing 1,200 people by 1861; by 1880 they had 400 powerlooms in a mill in Peel Street. Linen manufacturing rested on an infrastructure of dye- and bleachworks, of bobbin, shuttle and reed makers, and engineers who made powerlooms. The linen industry grew elsewhere in Yorkshire. From the 1790s water-powered mills were built near Pateley Bridge, Ripon and Knaresborough, and in 1835 Francis Stabler constructed a steam-powered, iron-framed integrated linen factory at Lawrence Street, York.

However, by the 1840s linen manufacturing was principally a Scottish industry. In 1831 nearly 16,000 people in England and Wales were engaged in flax and linen production, more than half of them in Yorkshire, but the industry at that date employed almost 46,000 in Scotland. It extended from Wigtown and Berwick to Banff and Elgin, but the principal centres were Aberdeen and Dundee. The Dundee industry suffered setbacks in the early nineteenth century, but a prediction in 1821 – that the passion for improvement among Scottish flax spinners would within a decade enable them to overtake their English competitors – proved to be remarkably prescient. Between 1822 and 1834 six mills in Dundee were enlarged and fourteen new ones went into production. Within three years from 1834 three very large iron-framed mills were constructed in the city. The total amount of power utilised in flax spinning increased from about 150 hp in 1821 to 1,436 hp in 1836. The rate of growth slackened subsequently, and Dundee's largest producer went bankrupt in 1842, but as flax spinning declined jute manufacture expanded to take its place, while in Aberdeen the linen industry was displaced by woollen manufacturing.

Jute from Bengal was first spun mechanically in 1832 at the Chapelshade Works, Dundee. Jute carpets were being woven in the city by about 1840, and the first purpose-designed jute mills probably date from around 1851, after which several mills in the city advertised that they worked both jute and tow. The most striking feature of the large mills built in Dundee was the construction of mansard cast-iron framed attics, in the Gothic style, which provided well-lit accommodation where imperfections in yarn could readily be spotted as it was being wound on powered machines. One of the first was the four-storey, 23-bay Upper Dens Mill of 1851–52, and similar mills were constructed through the 1860s and into the 1870s. As manufacturers turned to jute they found it necessary to construct single-storey buildings to house the heavy machinery needed for preparing materials for spinning, and from 1865 began to take advantage of the relative cheapness of land by building single-storey sheds for spinning, something almost unknown in other branches of the British textile industry, where multi-storey spinning mills were the norm.

Most jute was woven in the 1850s in handloom factories, of which there were 25 in Dundee in 1858. One example in Dons Road was a three-storey building in which warps were dressed with starch or size and dried on the top floor where there were wide louvred openings, similar to those in the drying loft of a tannery. Some handloom factories continued to be built into the 1870s, but powerloom weaving was gradually adopted for jute, building on the experience gained by linen weavers. The characteristic Dundee weaving shed had a double-pitched roof to catch as much sunlight as possible, quite unlike the typical north-lit cotton-weaving sheds of Lancashire. The Camperdown Works, established in 1850, was steadily expanded in the next 20 years and eventually employed more than 5,000 people. Its High Mill, built between 1857 and 1868, is 40 bays long and of three main storeys, with a basement below and a cathedral-like traceried cast-iron Gothic attic above. With its 282 foot (82 m) high polychrome brick campanile chimney, called Cox's Stack, it remains one of the outstanding features of the Dundee cityscape.

Every textile factory built in Dundee between 1793 and 1907 was powered by steam. These comprised a linen mill of 1793 by a Newcomen engine working machines by a crank mechanism; four subsequent

Jute being woven in a the weaving shed of Dens Works, Dundee. This factory was owned by Baxter Bros & Co. Ltd, the largest linen and jute manufacturers in Dundee in the half-century after 1840, at times employing as many as 4,000 workers.

works powered by Boulton & Watt engines, of which one, a sun-and-planet engine of 1799, still survives; at least one by Fenton, Murray & Wood; and from 1810 principally by engineers based in the city. Most of the world's jute-weaving machinery in the late nineteenth century was made in Dundee, and the city had a symbiotic relationship with jute growing and manufacturing in India, where from the 1870s mills were built along the banks of the river Hooghly near Calcutta with Scottish capital and using construction techniques as well as machines from Dundee.

Jute was a relatively small segment of the British textile industry in relation to cotton, woollens or to the linen trade from which it grew. It was nevertheless of importance as the foundation of the linoleum trade, centred on Kirkcaldy in nearby Fife, which for three generations provided the standard floor covering for working- and middle-class dwellings throughout Britain. Linoleum was patented in 1863 by Frederick Walton of Staines and manufactured in Kirkcaldy. In 1828 Michael Nairn opened a four-storey handloom factory there, weaving linen, but in 1847 he turned to making floor cloths and began to make linoleum on jute-based canvas from 1877. In England the economy of Lancaster was transformed from the 1850s, and more particularly from the 1870s, by the establishment of factories producing oilcloths and floor-coverings on a large scale.

When he passed through Cumberland in 1800 John Marshall found thriving manufactures of linen thread, checks and osnabrugs (coarse linen fabrics named after the German city of Osnabrück). In 1754 hemp and flax put out by merchants in Carlisle were being spun 15 miles to the south-west at Wigton, where there were seven manufacturers in 1800. Marshall noted six flax mills in Whitehaven, and in 1809 Joseph Bell and John Bragg built an iron-framed flax-spinning mill there, similar to those at Leeds and Shrewsbury. The building was used for its original purpose for only a few years, but two other flax mills in Whitehaven were still working in the early 1860s, making both thread and fabrics. John Marshall saw the 1,500-spindle flax-spinning mill of Hornby, Bill & Birley at Egremont, where flax manufacture in 1861 gave employment to nearly 200 of the town's 3,481 people. The flax mill worked by Thomas Ainsworth at Cleator employed the wives and daughters of Irish ironworkers on Cleator Moor – about 250 worked there in 1861. Textile manufacturing had deep roots in Cockermouth, on the river Derwent, which had a population of just over 7,000 in 1861. Water power was abundant and worked corn mills and spade mills as well as textile factories, which employed about 700 people, of whom about 450 worked with flax. At Heversham south of Kendal 96 people were employed in 1861 at a flax and hemp mill.

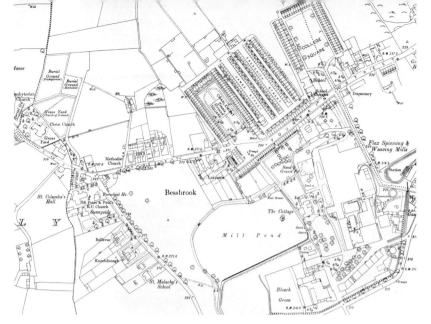

A section of the 1906 Ordnance Survey map, showing the flax-spinning and -weaving mills at Bessbrook as well as the estate housing. (See also below, pages 595–6.)

Barracks Mill, Catherine Street, Whitehaven, an iron-framed flax-spinning factory built in 1809 by the Quaker entrepreneurs Joseph Bell and John Bragg. A substantial proportion of the first generation of iron-framed textile factories were designed for spinning flax. The building is so named because it was once a militia barracks. It has passed through many other uses and is now adapted as apartments.

The first water-powered flax-spinning mill in Ireland was built by the Nicholson family at Bessbrook, Co. Armagh, in 1813. During the Napoleonic Wars the commercial focus of the linen trade moved from Dublin to Belfast, but the industry grew substantially only from the mid-1820s, with the building of factories to accommodate wet spinning. In 1841 the manufacture of flax and linen in Ireland employed 135,303 people, more than two-thirds of the total number of linen workers – 197,057 – in the United Kingdom. There were 28 mills in the Belfast region by 1851, many of them steam-powered, but spinning factories also flourished in Navan and Drogheda. Production

was stimulated by the resurgence of traditional Irish linen manufactures that required fine yarns, pattern damasks, cambrics for women's dresses, baby clothes and handkerchiefs, made by such companies as William Sprott & Co., established in 1850 in Dromore, and fabrics that could be used by the shirt- and collar-making companies in Londonderry. The introduction of powerlooms increased demand further.

Several firms exemplify this period of expansion. John Grubb Richardson, a merchant who bought 'brown' linen cloth and bleached it before putting it on the market, built spinning and weaving mills at Bessbrook near Newry from 1846. The Annesborough

Mills and Greenvale Bleachworks, three miles from Dundrum, County Down, developed around an 80-acre bleach green that had been opened in 1800 by James Murland. He subsequently became involved with spinning and weaving, built mills in the 1820s, and in 1836 constructed a huge stone mill, 240 × 50 feet (74 × 15 m) with three working floors and an attic storey. By 1870 the site extended over 229 acres. Steam engines were employed in the summer months, but in winter water power was almost sufficient to turn the machinery. Murland and his successor provided over 100 solidly constructed cottages for their workpeople, although the community lacked the paternalistic overtones of Bessbrook. Linen manufacture was revived in the 1860s in the Cork area with the construction from 1866 of the Millfield factory that was modelled on practice in Belfast. Powerloom weaving of linen began on a large scale in the Belfast area in the early 1860s, while bleaching and finishing also came to be organised in sizeable units. The industry was one of the factors that stimulated the growth of the city, from 53,000 people in 1831 to 208,000 in 1881. In the late nineteenth century Irish manufacturers served extensive overseas markets and while the industry had declined in Leeds, Belfast had become one of the world's principal seats of linen manufacturing.

The growth of flax spinning resulted in a decline in yarn imports, from 17,000 tons *per annum* in 1771 to only a thousand tons in 1830, while imports of unworked flax increased from 12,000 tons in 1787 to 50,000 tons by 1830. Exports of linen cloth also increased. Before 1790 the annual total had never exceeded 12,000 yards (10,972 m) but through the 1820s the level did not fall below 24,000 yards (21,945 m) and reached 100,000 yards (91,440 m) in 1849. Exports never fell below that during the remainder of the century, but the peak of 200,000 yards (182,880 m) was reached in 1864, and subsequent growth was constrained by competition

from abroad, particularly from Belgium. While the linen industry prospered in Ireland in the 1860s, it withered in Yorkshire, especially after John Marshall's death in 1845. Several mills in the North Riding ceased to work flax from the 1830s; after the deaths of the brothers Benyon their huge Shrewsbury mill was demolished in 1836–37; those who took over their Leeds works were declared bankrupt in 1861; and John Wilkinson's Hunslet Mill was adapted for woollen manufacturing from the early 1870s.

John Marshall's wealth enabled him to put capital into his mills throughout his life and to make other investments, in property and, in his last years, in railway shares. About 1811 he bought the Hallsteads estate on Ullswater, where he built a house and developed interests in landscape gardening and agriculture. He purchased Headingley House, Leeds, in 1818, and leased a London residence in Berkeley Square in 1825. His properties in the Lake District were valued at £66,500 in 1825, and by 1840 he had settled each of his five sons on estates around Ullswater where they enjoyed hunting and climbing. In the 1850s, however, the business entered a period of terminal decline. It was interrupted by occasional modestly profitable years, allowing investments such as the installation of new steam engines at Shrewsbury in 1875, but the business was wound up in 1886 with the closure of the Leeds and Shrewsbury mills by the Rugby-educated grandsons of the founder, John Marshall III and Stephen Marshall. In a pessimistic business climate they apparently decided to give up the cares of business for an exhilarating life around Ullswater. But differently motivated, differently educated managers might have developed new products and exploited new markets as did their contemporaries in Ireland and Flanders, and in the English cotton and woollen industries.

Wool and woollens

Cloth was made from woollen yarn in most parts of the British Isles in 1700 and that was still the case in 1870. The term 'woollen' can be applied to any fabric woven from woollen yarn, but it is usually employed – as here – to refer to fabrics made from short-staple (i.e. short-fibred) wool, prepared by carding, as distinct from worsted, which is made from long-staple wool prepared by combing so that the fibres lie parallel to each other. Worsted yarn can be used for knitting hosiery as well as weaving cloth. It is named after the village in Norfolk where the fabric originated, and was manufactured in the eighteenth century, but the most significant area of production came to be the West Riding of Yorkshire. When a piece of woollen cloth came from the weaver it was cleaned or scoured with fullers' earth (fine-grained clay, usually hydrated aluminium silicate, from the Weald or Bedfordshire) which removed oil, size and dirt. A second treatment during which the fabric was pummelled by heavy hammers had the effect of thickening the fabric. Fulling was mechanised from the late Middle Ages. Afterwards cloth was dried, usually by being stretched on tenter frames, goalpost-like structures which can be seen on eighteenth-century maps around the edges of towns such as Exeter, and 'burlers' picked out remaining pieces of foreign matter or knots tied during weaving. The nap on the cloth was raised by teasels arranged in frames called handles, and was then cut with large pairs of hand-worked shears. With worsted the process differed since the object was to show the weave clearly and distinctly. After shearing cloth was inspected and pressed.

Many innovations which had originated in the cotton industry were adopted by makers of woollen cloth, and by 1870 most manufacturing of woollen fabrics was factory-based, although some manufacturers used the new machines to meet purely local needs. For instance, the carding mill at Church Stretton employed only six or seven workers in the 1860s, and produced blankets and suitings for farmers (often in exchange for wool). Other rural mills worked on a similar basis. The growth of the industry depended on increasing supplies from sheep breeders such as Robert Bakewell whose Leicester sheep produced long wool suitable for worsteds. In southern England the improvement of the Southdown breed produced short-fibred wool for woollens. Merino wool was imported from Spain from the 1770s onwards and in the nineteenth century manufacturers brought in wool from familiar breeds raised in the colonies, and from exotic beasts in every continent. Annual wool imports rose about five times from 7.7 million pounds in 1800–04 to 35.3 million in 1830–34, almost 70 per cent of which came from Germany – much of it merino wool. By 1865–69 the total imported annually reached 236,000 million pounds, of which 57 per cent came from Australia.

Despite the geographical ubiquity of the industry,

The landscape of domestic woollen manufactures in upland Yorkshire: Pecket Well near Hebden Bridge.

The piece halls of the West Riding symbolised the dynamic growth of woollen and worsted manufacturing in the late eighteenth century. Individual clothiers would rent the small individual shops within the halls for display of pieces of cloth to wholesale merchants. The magnificent piece hall at Halifax, designed by Thomas Bradley, opened in 1779 and was initially prosperous, but by the 1820s only about two-thirds of its 314 rooms were occupied; from 1868 it was used as a market by the Corporation. It is the only one of the major piece halls that still stands and is now a major attraction, used for retailing and as a venue for events.
PHOTOGRAPH: CARNEGIE

in 1870 the trade in woollens and worsteds was dominated by the manufacturers of the West Riding of Yorkshire. For example, in 1851, there were almost 71,000 worsted workers in Yorkshire but the number exceeded 1,000 in only three other counties – Lancashire, Leicestershire (where worsted yarns were used in hosiery) and Norfolk. The Yorkshire woollen-manufacturing area extended from Saddleworth to Wakefield and from Penistone into the Dales. Its marketing centres were Leeds, Wakefield and Huddersfield, and in the era of factory production Leeds dominated its finishing trades. Particular places had specialisms – narrow cloths in Huddersfield, white cloths and blankets around Dewsbury, and coloured cloths around Leeds – while in the nineteenth century the trade in recovered wool (shoddy and mungo) was concentrated around Batley and Dewsbury. Worsted manufacture mostly took place north of a line between Huddersfield and Pudsey, particularly in and around Bradford and Halifax. There are imperfections in the figures recorded by the Yorkshire quarter sessions of woollen cloth treated at fulling mills, but they show that the quantity of narrow cloth processed between 1740 and 1819 more than doubled, while that of broad cloth increased over seven-fold.

In the 1720s Daniel Defoe described the landscape of woollen manufactures in Yorkshire when he made his way over an ill-signed route in characteristically foul weather across Blackstone Edge from Rochdale to Halifax, making note of such things of interest as dwellings scattered across small holdings, the 'people all full of business', the cheapness of coal, and the use of water for dyeing, scouring and fulling. Clothiers carried their finished fabrics to urban markets, established in Halifax, Leeds and Wakefield before 1700, usually in the manner shown in George Walker's picture of 'Cloth-makers' in *The Costume of Yorkshire* of 1814 – one piece (around 30 yards long) on the back of a packhorse. Defoe described how trading took place in Leeds over trestle tables, with merchants seeking fabrics whose colours and patterns matched the demands of their clients. The process was formalised after 1750 with the building of cloth or piece halls where individual clothiers hired small shops for the display of their products. The Mixed Cloth Hall at Leeds opened in 1758, the city's White Cloth Hall in 1775, and halls at Huddersfield in 1766, Penistone in 1768, Bradford in 1773 and Wakefield in 1778. The surviving Piece Hall in Halifax was designed around a 91 × 110 yard (83 × 101 m) courtyard by the architect Thomas Bradley and opened on New Year's Day 1779. It included 315 rooms, those on the upper levels accessible along galleries behind colonnades of Tuscan round columns. Its history reflects changes in the industry. For about 35 years it fulfilled the functions for which it was intended, but by the 1820s fabrics were marketed in different ways and fewer than 200 of its rooms were occupied by 1830. While it remained a

TEXTILES 451

Ranks of looms in one of the weaving mills near Halifax, operated by Edward Akroyd, probably the mill at Copley. From George Measom, *The Official Illustrated Guide to the Great Northern Railway* (1861). On the left of this image are lines of Jacquard looms. Late nineteenth- and early twentieth-century photographs show that overhead loom heads with a large number of hooks might need to be positioned at a greater height than shown in this image.

Warehouses lining the approach to the main station at Dewsbury that were once used for the reception of materials from many countries that were used in the manufacture of shoddy.

spectacular venue for celebrations and performances, it lost its original purpose and in 1868 it became the property of Halifax Corporation who used it as a market.

From the 1770s Yorkshire fulling mills were enlarged to accommodate scribbling (i.e. carding) machines. One of the features of the West Riding industry was the prevalence of 'company mills', small enterprises in which clothiers combined to prepare and finish wool, which they spun and wove on other premises. Each partner paid for work at regular prices and shared in the mill's annual profits. By 1789 there were, by one reckoning, 36 mechanised scribbling mills in the West Riding, and their number increased six-fold in the next decade. Benjamin Gott's Bean Ing Mill in Leeds of 1792 was a steam-powered plant that included spinning rooms, two-storey ranges of loomshops, and even a mill for grinding dyewoods. It set a pattern of integration that was subsequently followed, albeit gradually, in many Yorkshire mills. The iron-framed four-storey, 23-bay Armley Mill of 1805–07, rebuilt by Gott after a fire in an earlier building, was originally used only for scribbling and fulling.

At several mills built from the 1790s handloom weavers were accommodated in multi-storey blocks. At first the powerloom was adopted slowly, but after

1850 the number increased rapidly and there were more than 30,000 by 1874. About 160 mills were built between 1819 and 1835, by which date there were 406 in Yorkshire. The size of buildings increased, and some mills incorporated mechanised mule spinning, but the scale of operation remained modest, and a parliamentary report of 1833 found that most woollen mills employed fewer than 50 workers, and very few had more than 75. In the worsted trade there were 22 mills by 1800, 54 by 1815, and 204 by 1835, when the mean number of workers was 82, rather higher than in the woollen branch. In all, 610 woollen and worsted mills have been identified as working in the West Riding in 1835, in total employing more than 40,000 people. Woollen manufacturing utilised 8,890 hp, of which 30 per cent was generated by 241 waterwheels and the remainder by 308 steam engines. Worsted manufacturers had access to 4,060 hp, of which just over 20 per cent came from 102 waterwheels and the remainder from 159 steam engines.

During the period from 1835 to 1865 the woollen branch expanded rapidly – there were 899 woollen mills in Yorkshire by 1867, employing 62,300 people – but many handloom weavers remained active in the 1860s, and a quarter of the looms in the fancy woollen trade in Huddersfield in 1866 were worked by hand. Woollen yarn was usually spun on mules, while powerlooms produced increasingly complex forms of woollen cloth, blankets, carpets and intricately patterned shirtings. The number of worsted mills increased from 204 in 1835 to 516 in 1871, and of employees from 17,816 to 109,557. Worsted yarn was usually spun on modified water-frames called throstles. The number of powerlooms increased from 30,856 in 1850 to 48,905 in 1871, while handlooms had largely disappeared from the worsted trade by 1860. During the 1840s, too, its focus shifted from Leeds to Bradford, where the number of merchants increased from 25 in 1837 to 157 in 1861, matching the remarkable rise in population from 13,000 in 1801 to 104,000 in 1851 and 146,000 in 1871.

The most significant technological development was the mechanisation of wool combing, the work of Samuel Lister and Sir Isaac Holden during the 1850s. From the 1860s the nature of the industry changed with the widespread use of fine merino wools. The extent of that change was expressed in Lister's Manningham Mills, where the most monumental buildings date from the 1870s. Bradford developed a comprehensive infrastructure supporting the worsted trade. The

'Worstedopolis' powered by steam. The many chimneys of Bradford are portrayed here in an engraving of 1869 by Henry Warren. To the right is one of the city's many multi-storeyed mills, while in the foreground is a quarry for stone or brick clay for the construction of yet more houses and factories.

Wool Exchange, designed like most of the city's buildings of the period by Lockwood & Mawson, was built between 1864 and 1867. Oates Ingham & Sons, finishers and dyers, occupied a site of seven acres in the early 1860s, where their 400 staff produced cotton warps and worsted yarns, and Joseph Mitchell made mohair and other specialist yarns at his Valley Mill, and patented a machine for spinning mottled yarn. The engineer George Hodgson, whose works dated from 1849, supplied the powerlooms for Saltaire, and developed an export trade with continental Europe. Worsted exports were usually handled by merchants, and the area called Little Germany is filled with warehouses in the Italianate style, mostly built for German merchants between 1860 and 1874.

In 1813 Benjamin Law of Batley developed a process by which finely shredded rags were mixed with virgin wool to make yarn called 'shoddy', which was used in heavy woollens such as blankets. The poorest grade was known from about 1857 as 'mungo'. The area around Batley, Dewsbury and Ossett was known by the 1860s as 'the great shoddy metropolis'. Shoddy manufacture stimulated recycling throughout Britain, and rail-served warehouses at Batley and Dewsbury received bales of rags from all over the country and from continental Europe. Most of the latter, regardless of their country of origin, were despatched from Antwerp. Batley, 6½ miles south-west of Leeds, had a population in 1861 of 14,170. Some 367 people, most of them women, were engaged in trading, sorting and grinding rags, and were employed by 45 dealers. Batley's 35 woollen spinners and manufacturers employed 3,036 people. Sixteen firms had fewer than 20 workers, but three had more than 300, including Joseph Olroyd who employed 655. There were 16 blanket manufacturers with a total workforce of 173. Batley also had the engineering infrastructure characteristic of most Yorkshire textile communities, with two ironfounders, employing 27 and 36 men, three machine makers, a bobbin manufacturer, and makers of teeth for rag machines, as well as two local colliery proprietors, one with 237 employees and the other with 110.

Morley, three miles north-east of Batley, illustrates

Manningham Mill, Bradford, displays the self-confidence of the West Riding textile industry at the end of our period. It replaced an earlier building destroyed by fire in 1871 and was designed by local architects Andrews & Pepper, for Samuel Cunliffe Lister, who was initially a worsted manufacturer. He contributed substantially to the development of wool-combing technology and devised machines for making silk waste into velvets and poplins which were used in Manningham Mill. The mill produced velvet for coronations and parachute silk during the Second World War. Production ceased in 1992 and the buildings, as the poster in this 2005 photograph shows, are being adapted as apartments.

the variations between textile communities in the West Riding. Morley had a population of 6,840 in 1861 but grew sufficiently to be granted borough status in 1885, followed in 1895 by the opening of one of England's most splendid town halls. The town's most significant factory is the Crank Mill, a steam-powered mill three storeys high and extending over seven bays, built for the 2nd Earl of Dartmouth in the early 1790s and providing scribbling and fulling facilities accessible to any local clothier. Only the cylinder of the engine was enclosed, and the crank and flywheel were exposed on the gable wall. There were coal miners throughout the parish with a concentration at Low Common. The shoddy industry had an insignificant presence in 1861, but 33 woollen spinners and manufacturers employed 998 people. The infrastructure comprised makers of shuttles and bobbins and a mechanical engineer employing 69 men.

Sowerby and Sowerby Bridge were twin settlements in the ancient parish of Halifax, one on a hilltop above the river Calder, the other around an ancient crossing of the river near its confluence with the Ryburn, and the junction of the Calder & Hebble Navigation with the Rochdale Canal. Sowerby had long associations with textiles: stone-built cottages with multi-light mullioned windows remain in its streets, and Wood Lane Hall of 1649 is an imposing clothier's house. Sowerby Bridge grew from a scatter of houses in 1830 into a community of more than 7,500 people by 1871. The rivers powered old-established fulling mills, and the navigation brought coal. Sowerby Bridge Mills, built in the 1790s, included a four-storey, 13-bay loomshop with broad windows providing light for a multitude of handlooms. The textile economy was varied. In 1861 there were several woollen (or wooling, in the local vernacular) mills, and several producing worsted, cotton factories producing cotton warps for worsted manufacturers as well as calicos and cashmeres, and several silk mills. The principal employers were William Ranson, woollen manufacturer, whose workforce exceeded 700, and William Morris, worsted spinner, who employed 254. Handloom weavers produced fabrics in which cotton and woollen, or cotton and silk, yarns were mixed, and worsted and cotton mixtures were woven on powerlooms. Other products included carpets and shoddy, both woven on powerlooms, blankets, fustian and waterproof oil cloths. There were pressers, burlers, tenterers and dyers of woollens and block printers of cottons. The associated infrastructure included makers of shuttles, cards, reeds and heddles, a logwood grinder, manufacturers of acids, a maker of belts for driving machines, and several engineering concerns, including Wood Bros, who made steam engines and Henry Broadbent, supplier of lathes. The Bank Foundry of Timothy Bates & Co., established in 1786, was managed in the 1850s and 1860s by Joseph Pollitt, a kinsman of the founder, who in 1865 took as his partner Eustace Wigzell. The son of an East India Company captain, Wigzell was apprenticed with John Penn & Sons in Greenwich and worked for the Russian government in Ekaterinburg. He was prevented from returning to Russia by the Crimean War, worked again for John Penn, and as a partner at Sowerby Bridge made the firm of Pollitt & Wigzell famous for its mill engines.

Mirfield, on the Calder nine miles downstream from Sowerby Bridge, had a population of 5,041 in 1821 which increased to 12,869 in 1871. In 1861 five colliery proprietors employed just over 200 men, and along the river was a community in which about 100 men made their livings working and building boats. Five woollen manufacturers between them employed more than 500 people; a cotton factory producing yarns and warps employed 81; and the manufacture of carpets, blankets and hearthrugs occupied about 400. Mirfield's worsted manufacturers worked with alpaca and mohair. There were four small engineering concerns in the town, and some considerable milling and malting establishments using grain delivered by barge.

The area extending five miles south from Bradford through the Spen Valley to Cleckheaton, encompassing the Bowling and Low Moor Ironworks and the mines that supplied them, was also important for textiles. Cleckheaton itself had a population of 4,299 in 1841 when it was celebrated for the manufacture of cards for wool carding and for manufacturing cloth for army uniforms. By 1861 the population of the townships in the Spen Valley exceeded 37,000. This was the heartland of the worsted industry, and 23 worsted manufacturers in 1861 employed 3,461 people, a mean of more than 150. The fabrics produced by designers, spinners, weavers, croppers, pressers and dyers of stuffs or worsteds, and woven on power-looms, included alpaca. Worsted manufacturers also used cotton warps provided by several local firms.

There were three specialist wool-combing companies, one employing more than 100 people; 19 makers of cards employing altogether 122; and four makers of card setting machines who had 75 employees. Cards were made for cotton and flax manufacturing as well as for worsteds, and several card makers in the hamlet of Scholes also farmed holdings of up to nine acres. Card makers depended on wire manufacturers, among them James Cockroft of Scholes who employed 24 and James Bateman of Parkhouse who had 49 workers. Three woollen firms employed fewer than 130 people between them. Flannel was made in the area by eleven small-scale producers who employed just 40 people. Other products included carpets, blankets, army cloth and India-rubber fabrics. The infrastructure included boilers of size, starch manufacturers, makers of healds, reeds and slays, oil merchants, and a dozen engineering

companies which between them employed 573 people. The Spen Valley has never been fashionable, but it was as focused on manufactures as any part of Britain.

The worsted industry included an area that *is* fashionable – the Worth Valley, extending four miles south from its confluence with the Wharfe at Keighley to Haworth, where the 1861 census records the aged Patrick Brontë spending his last months in the parsonage after his children had predeceased him. As a curate in Shropshire in 1810–12 Brontë had experienced the impact of industry upon society, with the growth of iron making, and later he saw it in Yorkshire. The population of Haworth and the neighbouring community of Oxenhope totalled 5,276 in 1861. Elizabeth Gaskell observed in 1857 that the landscape from Keighley to Haworth, of villas, rows of workmen's houses, great worsted factories with an occasional old-fashioned farmhouse, all abundant with grey stone, could hardly be called 'country' for any part of the way. Giles & Goodall identified 26 mills in the area, the earliest of which were water-powered factories of the 1790s, built to spin worsted

Lumbfoot Mill from the north-west. The first mill on the site just west of Haworth, in the West Riding, was built in 1797, but it was demolished and replaced by a new mill between 1854 and 1858. Despite being flooded in 1864, it was still much the same in 1914 when this photograph was taken. This view shows the spinning mill on the left and the single-storey weaving shed on the right. The engine room and its chimney can be seen beyond the spinning mill.

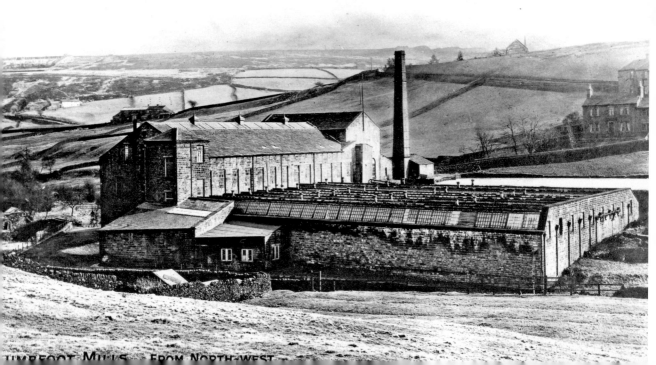

LUMBFOOT MILLS FROM NORTH-WEST

The Ebor Mill at Haworth, established *circa* 1819, when its centrepiece was a three-storey, seven-bay spinning mill. It was expanded by new owners in the 1850s, and again in 1887 when the six-storey, 18-bay building which now dominates the site was constructed. It remained throughout its working life an integrated worsted mill, which took in wool to be combed, spun, woven and finished on the site.

PHOTOGRAPH: CARNEGIE, 2005

yarn. The three-storey water-powered Ebor Mill was built for worsted spinning by Hiram Craven about 1819, when the yarn it produced was put out to hand-loom weavers. About 1850 it passed into the hands of Merrall Bros who owned several worsted factories in the area. Haworth had a range of retailers, including makers of clogs and bakers of oat bread; 20 or so men hewed flagstones in quarries; and about a dozen miners extracted coal at Oxenhope; but the main business of the Worth Valley was the manufacture of worsteds, combing wool (much of it still by hand in 1861), spinning worsted yarn, producing cotton warp, and weaving 'stuff', almost entirely on powerlooms.

The self-confidence of the Yorkshire textile industry was expressed in its civic buildings, not only in Leeds, Bradford, Halifax and Huddersfield but in smaller towns such as Morley and Todmorden, and across the region in dissenting chapels, mechanics' institutes and mills built in styles that were beyond the utilitarian, such as the four-storey, fireproof New Ing Mill at Batley of 1863, whose corner tower has a crenellated parapet. The sheer might of the industry is perhaps best appreciated at Saltaire, whose social

significance is discussed in Chapter 14. Eight years after the ceremonial opening of the mill in 1853 Titus Salt's community consisted of 447 houses occupied by 2,510 people. Only 165 – 6.6 per cent – originated outside Yorkshire, and many of those were from Colne just over the Lancashire border. There were several families from Dolphinholme, Lancashire, where mechanised worsted spinning originated, and 26 individuals from Norfolk. While there were many Irish migrants in central Bradford there were only ten at Saltaire. Many of the long-distance migrants followed occupations outside the mill, particularly schoolteachers and railwaymen. Wool combing was mechanised, mules were used for spinning, and fabrics were woven on powerlooms. Cotton was used for warps, and some silk and mohair were worked, but extensive use was made of alpaca, whose processing occupied nearly 100 of the workforce. Saltaire remains as an expression of the philanthropy of its founder, but the recruitment of such a large and so skilled a workforce almost entirely from the West Riding is one of the best indications of the contemporary prosperity of worsted manufacturing.

Woollens elsewhere in England

The woollen industry (including worsteds) was the most widespread of the textile trades. The Yorkshire industry accounted in 1867 for more than half the

woollen mills in the British Isles, but the pockets of manufacturing elsewhere were far from insignificant. In 1841, for example, as many as 6,000 people were engaged in the woollen industry in Gloucestershire and Wiltshire, more than half that number in Somerset, and around 2,000 in Devon. Woollen textiles were made in many other communities in England – carpets in Kidderminster and Wilton, woollen 'stuffs' in three mills in Darlington, and in a three-storey mill at Acklington Park, Northumberland, which employed 47 people in 1861.

Most factories in Gloucestershire, Wiltshire and Somerset were integrated plants which incorporated specialist buildings such as the handle house (for drying frames filled with teasels) which remains at Trowbridge, piered drying-houses of the kind sketched by Karl Friedrich Schinkel at Wotton-under-Edge (of which an example still stands at Stanley near Stroud) and the wool stoves that can be seen at Melksham and Frome. The making of woollen cloth in the Stroudwater Valley and around Wotton-under-Edge was well established in 1700, and in the 1720s Defoe observed clothiers' premises extending for nearly 20 miles alongside the river Frome. From the 1790s fulling mills became the nuclei of factories, as carding and spinning machines were installed. Of 33 Gloucestershire companies in 1833, 13 had erected new buildings since 1800, and 4 had rebuilt older structures. By 1860 most cloth was being woven on powerlooms, but some handloom weavers remained at work. The mill of 1813 at King's Stanley is exceptional among the Gloucestershire mills. Its ornate iron frame appears to have been designed to accommodate more shafting than was ever installed, to power processes that were not mechanised for many decades. In the

➢ The wool stove at Melksham, one of the few survivors of many similar structures that were used in the West of England woollen cloth industry. Wool and woollen fabrics were bleached in the eighteenth century by wetting them and heating them in stoves with shallow pans of sulphur. The stoves could also be used for drying finished fabrics.

➢ Handles are wooden frames in which teasels are fixed for raising the nap on woollen cloth. Water was poured over them during the process, and they were placed to dry in buildings through which air could flow through louvers of chequered brickwork. This building at Trowbridge is the only complete example of a handle house in England, although some fragments do remain at other woollen mill sites.

Phoenix Mill, Staverton, near Trowbridge, the flagship mill of the Wiltshire woollen cloth industry, rebuilt in 1825 after a fire with a phoenix above its pediment. It was adapted as a condensed milk factory in 1897–98 by the Anglo-Swiss Condensed Milk Co., and was reduced to two storeys by Nestlé International which owned the site from 1905. The picture showing war surplus lorries carrying churns of milk dates from *circa* 1919.

1830s its labour force of about 900 was the largest in Gloucestershire, and its five waterwheels, supplemented from 1822 by a 40 hp Boulton & Watt steam engine, produced more power than was available at any other mill in the area. The elegance of the building may have been intended to impress visitors approaching the owners' mansion house, but the spectacle was destroyed within a decade by the erection of the steam engine. The only comparable complex locally is New Mills, Kingswood near Wotton-under-Edge, which was built at about the same time and also had five waterwheels. The motives for building such mills are difficult to determine. They may have been a response to the threat of Luddism in 1812–13 or an assertion of the place of clothiers in county society. Whatever the case, Stanley Mill illustrates the complexities and paradoxes of industrial development.

The Wiltshire woollen industry had much in common with that of Gloucestershire, but from the late eighteenth century most of its manufacturers specialised in lighter fabrics, although those in Bradford-on-Avon persisted with broadcloths. As in Gloucestershire, machine carding and spinning began before 1800, but handloom weaving persisted into the mid-nineteenth century. Manufacturing grew in Trowbridge, where the availability of coal delivered by canal stimulated the installation of steam engines. In 1861, 655 of the 5,442 inhabitants of Westbury were involved in manufacturing woollen cloth – mule spinners, handloom and powerloom weavers,

shearmen, handlesetters, fullers and dyers. In both Gloucestershire and Wiltshire investment in factory building, steam power and new textile technology continued into the mid-nineteenth century, but while individual firms might prosper the woollen industry as a whole ceased to grow.

Eighteenth-century Taunton and Exeter were centres for the finishing and marketing of woollen cloths, particularly the serges that were made across Somerset and Devon. The pattern of the industry changed from 1790s, and by 1870 most production took place in large but isolated mills. Some 39 were recorded in Devon in 1838, although their total labour force numbered only 1,810, an average of 46, and some must have been very small. The number of mills declined to 21 in 1850 and 18 in 1871, while the labour force fell to 825. Investment continued – the four-storey spinning block at Tonedale Mills dates from the 1860s, the mill at Culmstock was rebuilt in 1877–78, and the beam engine at Coldharbour Mill, Uffculme, was installed in 1867 – but the industry as a whole stopped expanding.

In Oxfordshire woollen fabrics were made in and around Banbury, Witney and Chipping Norton. Manufacturers in Banbury by the 1790s specialised in plush, a range of fabrics (largely mixtures of cotton or worsted warps with silk, worsted or mohair wefts) whose common feature was a long pile, which for many varieties was cut. The trade declined from the 1840s, when about 100 weavers with a larger number of dependants migrated to Coventry. There were four woollen manufacturers in Chipping Norton in the 1790s, taking in cloth from weavers working in their own homes, but by 1851 the descendants of one of them, Thomas Bliss, had built an integrated factory. After a fire it was replaced in 1872 by a spectacular mill with a central chimney stack in the Tuscan order, designed by the Bolton architect George Woodhouse. By 1881 this employed 581 people, many of them migrants from other textile-producing regions. The Witney Blanket Weavers' Company received a royal charter in 1711 and a decade later erected a hall where blankets made in the town from yarn spun in the surrounding region were weighed and measured. The trade was reckoned to be declining in 1807 but revived with the introduction of carding and spinning machinery, and evolved into a factory-based industry, in which from the 1850s several companies employed steam engines, self-acting mules and powerlooms. Like tweed production at Chipping Norton, the manufacturing of blankets at Witney flourished into the second half of the twentieth century.

Norwich was the hub of a system of worsted manufacturing in the eighteenth century, and although this was then eclipsed by competition from the West Riding it remained significant. Production was concentrated in Norwich itself, where yarns were produced from cotton and silk as well as from wool, although worsted yarn was brought in from Yorkshire. There were eleven worsted mills in Norfolk in 1851, employing about 1,400 workers. Remaining buildings include a three-storey factory that accommodated handloom weavers, the six-storey room-and-power factory called the New Mill built by the Norwich Yarn Company in 1839, and the Albion Mill of 1836–37 which produced worsted yarn. About 1860 the firm of Willett, Nephew & Co. introduced a new fabric which superseded bombazines for mourning garments. Colchester in the eighteenth century was a centre for the production of bays (baise). The last manufacturer went out of business in the 1830s, although worsted spinning continued a little longer elsewhere in Essex.

Woollen manufacturing was widespread across the Lake District. At Keswick several manufacturers provided work for about 70 people, rather fewer than the 90 people who made pencils in the town, while about 50 makers of woollens were among the 700 textile workers in Cockermouth. Kendal had a well-established textile trade by 1700, and its guild companies still flourished in 1800. The town was bountifully supplied with water power by the river Kent and its tributaries, and was a place of thoroughfare, where routes to Sedbergh, Kirkby Stephen and Ambleside left the road from Lancaster to Carlisle. Celia Fiennes remarked in 1698 that Kendal Cotton (a green woollen cloth) was used for blankets in England and for plaids in Scotland. Travellers in 1750 observed that Kendal cloth was traded throughout England and that fabrics woven in the town were supplied to plantation owners in the West Indies to clothe slaves. By the 1790s there were 17 manufacturers of woollen and mixture fabrics in Kendal, one cotton mill, one maker of worsteds and one of checks, and four stocking manufacturers. Ancillary traders included dyers, shearmen, bobbin, shuttle, reed, card and comb makers, logwood grinders, soap boilers and millwrights.

In the 1820s Kendal's products included baizes, serges, waistcoating, carpeting and cotton wicks, as well as hosiery. The population grew from 8,984 in 1821 to 10,395 in 1851, and in 1861 nearly 1,250 people in Kendal and its vicinity were employed in woollen manufactures. Their products included tweeds, worsteds, trousering, Guernsey frocks, rugs for railway carriages, Brussels and Venetian carpets and hand-knitted hosiery, and the larger mills employed steam- as well as water power. The woollen manufacturer Charles Braithwaite employed about 500 people; the carpet maker John Whitwell had 226 workers; and the woollen manufacturer John Wilson 267; but manufacturing in Kendal derived its strength from a multitude of concerns with between 10 and 20 workers.

More than 60 bobbin mills in the Lake District formed a significant part of the textile industry in the mid-nineteenth century. In 1861 about 100 bobbin makers lived in Staveley, north-west of Kendal; Robert Hutchinson Fell employed 70 at Troutbeck Bridge; and Charles Horrax had 24 at Stock Ghyll Mill, Ambleside. At Gilpin Mill, five miles west of Kendal, George Rushford combined bobbin manufacture with farming and Methodist local preaching, and accommodated in his household eight apprentice bobbin makers and a sawyer. Bobbin manufacture also flourished in the valleys of the rivers Leven and Crake, the southern outlets of Windermere and Coniston Water. At the preserved Stott Park Bobbin Mill, built in 1835, the miller and his family shared their accommodation in 1861 with five live-in bobbin turners, and eleven bobbin-turner apprentices aged between 11 and 20.

The woollen industry in Wales

The manufacture of coarse woollen webs occupied a substantial proportion of the working population of Wales in 1700, and the sales of webs from Merioneth were said about 1750 to realise sums approaching £40,000 *per annum*. The trade conformed to established customs overseen by the Drapers' Company of Shrewsbury which had effectively controlled it since the 1620s. Each Thursday, Welshmen in blue coats and striped linsey waistcoats sold cloth to drapers in The Square in Shrewsbury, until the end of the market was marked by the ascent of members of the company into the upper room of the market hall. The cloth was finished by shearmen in Shrewsbury, taken by road to Blackwell Hall, and traded internationally, to the poorer regions of Europe and to slave plantations in the Americas. The formal market ceased about 1795 and the Drapers relinquished the lease of the hall in 1803, but Shrewsbury traders continued their involvement. In 1833 one draper met an order from the East India Company for 20,000 yards of Welsh flannel, and a warehouse in the town, offered for sale in 1865, was said to have been used for many years for the storage of woollen cloth.

The Yellow Mill of 1777 in the Greenfield Valley, Flintshire, demonstrated to Welsh manufacturers the advantages of powered machinery. The first water-powered woollen mill was reputedly built near the iron forge at Dolobran on the Afon Vyrnwy north-west of Welshpool in about 1789, and ten years later about 40 carding engines were said to be working in Montgomeryshire. In 1797 a market was established at Welshpool, and manufacturers began to concentrate on the production of flannels. The most striking development of the years that followed was the growth of Newtown, where there were fewer than 1,000 people in 1801 but 2,038 in 1821 and 3,785 in 1851, with about another thousand in the suburb of Pen-y-gloddfa north of the river Severn. The wholesale market for flannel was moved to Newtown in 1832, and another market opened at Llanidloes in 1836. By 1838 six factories in Newtown employed 192 people, including outworkers, but in all 672 people were involved in the trade, producing for 75 manufacturers and employing 700 looms. Townspeople prided themselves on living in what they termed the 'Leeds of Wales'. Textile manufacturing also expanded in Llanidloes, whose population grew from 3,145 in 1821 to 4,604 in 1851. Flannel making in Montgomeryshire probably reached its peak in the 1850s after the introduction of power-looms, but thereafter population growth ended, and the Van lead mine became the focus of local economic activity.

The flannel-manufacturing region is notable for the Chartist-inspired riots on 30 April 1839. Chartists had caused concern to the authorities in Montgomeryshire for eight months. Some, apparently anticipating a

▾ A flannel-mill alongside the river Severn at Llanidloes near to the spot where the Chartists assembled in 1839.

rising in Merthyr, had collected guns, staves, pikes and daggers that had been fashioned from flannel-weavers' spindles. Three London policemen along with an officer from Newtown were sent to Llanidloes, where the blowing of horns summoned Chartists to assemble. Magistrates panicked and ordered the arrest of leaders, who were held in the *Trewythen Arms* until it was stormed by their followers. For several nights disciplined Chartists kept order in the town before the arrival of troops. Deep inter-communal sentiments were aroused. There was resentment at the presence of Metropolitan policemen but, as 'quiet men', they were left unharmed while a hated officer from Newtown was beaten up. Some of the special constables were farmers from the parish of Llangurig, with whom the men of Llanidloes had ancient feuds. Some 33 of the Chartists were rounded up and tried in July, most receiving short prison sentences. The 2nd Earl of Powis observed during the incident the virtues of governmental restraint and the advisability of removing responsibility from magistrates. As deputy lieutenant of Shropshire he handled the Chartist strike of 1842 in the Coalbrookdale coalfield with tact and

skill, avoided disorder, and earned the commendation of the Home Secretary in the letter from which is taken the epigraph to Chapter 1.

Woollen manufacturing also flourished in the Teifi Valley in Carmarthenshire around Dre-fach Felindre, where the nine-bay, two-storey Cambrian Mill now houses the National Wool Museum. Woollen cloth was made in the region throughout the eighteenth century, but from the 1820s carding machines were installed at fulling mills; small factories, the largest employing no more than 100 people, became the focus of manufacturing. The industry prospered with the growth of coal mining in the South Wales valleys, which created a market for shirts of stout fabrics, suitable for miners, as well as for shawls, blankets and hosiery. The industry reached its peak between 1880 and 1910.

In Ireland woollen manufacturing was generally overshadowed by the linen industry, although woollens were produced in many areas, and from the 1790s carding and spinning machines were employed in some places. In 1874 there were 70 woollen mills in Ireland, although together they employed only 1,500 people.

The Scottish woollen industry

In Scotland there were several pockets of woollen manufacturing, and the industry received government support between 1780 and 1830 as a means of providing employment for the poor. In the 1830s there were about 100 woollen mills, most of them water-powered, employing about 3,500 people, and by 1851 some 182 with 9,500 workers. The number of power-looms increased from 247 in 1850 to 9,708 in 1871. There were almost 200 mills in 1870 and by 1874 they employed 27,700 people. Aberdeen was a flax-spinning city in the early nineteenth century, but its principal factories, including Broadford Mill which incorporated an iron-framed spinning mill of 1808, began to make woollens. Grandholm Mills, originally a flax-spinning complex of 1793–94, was adapted for woollen production and enlarged through the nineteenth century by J. & J. Crombie, a large concern that specialised in overcoating. A firm at Elgin made fabrics from rare fibres. The industry also flourished in the

Ochils north of the Firth of Forth where about a third of Scotland's wool was being spun in 1850. Strude Mill at Alva, an astonishing six-storey pedimented building of 1827, appears to have been designed to accommodate handloom weavers. There were other mills at Tillicoultry and Alloa.

However, the largest concentration of woollen manufactures in Scotland was in the towns along the river Tweed and its tributaries the Gala Water, Ettrick Water and the river Teviot, including Innerleithen, Galashiels, Hawick, Selkirk and Melrose. The earliest woollen mill in the region is probably the Caerlee Mill at Innerleithen, a four-storey structure built by one-time blacksmith and ironmaster in Shropshire, Alexander Brodie, in 1788–90, apparently to house spinning jennies. In Galashiels five fulling mills were adapted to spin woollen yarn between 1791 and 1805. Stocking frames were introduced at Hawick in 1771, and the manufacture of hosiery became a significant element in the region's woollen industry. Investment in textiles was stimulated by building of the North British Railway's 'Waverley' route, which opened from Edinburgh to Hawick in 1849, and was finally completed to Carlisle in 1862. The prosperity of the region was based on specialisation in quality products, particularly tweed fabrics, for which the wool from Cheviot sheep was particularly suited, and knitwear.

Lace and hosiery

At the beginning of the eighteenth century socks and stockings were knitted for the national market in several areas: around Kendal and the north-west extremity of the Yorkshire Dales, at Tewkesbury and Godalming, and in parts of Dorset, Northamptonshire and the North Riding. Thomas Pennant memorably described how in Bala women gathered to gossip and knit stockings, in summertime carrying on their craft seated on the prehistoric burial mound of Tomen-y-Bala. By 1851 the hosiery industry employed 65,500 people, most of them working in their own homes in Derbyshire, Leicestershire and Nottinghamshire, where the trade flourished from the early eighteenth century as hosiers moved north from London to avoid restrictions imposed by the Framework Knitters' Company. By 1782 some 20,000 frames were being used in Great Britain, about 90 per cent of which were in the East Midlands, and by 1812 the total had increased to almost 30,000. William Felkin, the historian of the trade, calculated in 1844 that more than 42,000 frames were in use in the British Isles, around 90 per cent of them in Derbyshire, Leicestershire and Nottinghamshire.

The large-scale manufacture of hosiery depended on the stocking frame, which had been invented in 1589 by the Revd William Lee of Calverton, Nottinghamshire, and in the following three centuries the subject of numerous incremental improvements. Cotton stockings were first produced on a stocking frame by a Nottingham knitter in 1730, using yarn imported from India. In 1758–59 the Sutton-in-Ashfield hosier Samuel Unwin gained a prize from the Society of Arts for his improvements to the stocking frame, while Jedediah Strutt of Belper was awarded a patent for the Derby rib machine, on which fashionable ribbed stockings could be knitted. In 1764 frames were adapted to make eyelet holes, in 1767 to produce velvet, and in 1769 to manufacture brocade.

By 1800 some stocking frames were complex machines built by framesmiths, who practised in all the principal hosiery-manufacturing towns and villages and were supplied by local makers of needles and of

'The Art of Stocking Frame Work Knitting', an engraving from the *Universal Magazine*, published in 1750, showing two women, one spinning yarn, the other winding bobbins, and a man knitting stockings on a knitting frame. The nature of the building and the place of publication suggest that this is an image of one of the framework-knitting households in London which were numerous in the mid-eighteenth century.

the lead weights called sinkers. Each frame was built to suit a particular yarn – worsted, cotton or silk, and in due course merino, angola, alpaca or lambs' wool – and machines were adapted to knit gloves, shirts, vests, shawls, cravats, drawers, children's hoods and night caps. Most garments produced on frames had to be stitched up, so some of the women employed in hosiery manufacture worked as seamers, as did many young children. The character of the industry changed during the Napoleonic Wars. The traditional pattern of work, in which the knitter went to the hosier's warehouse to collect yarn on a Monday, and returned on a Saturday afternoon with what he had produced, was abandoned early in the nineteenth century. Thereafter, distribution and collection came to be controlled by 'bag hosiers'. Middlemen and people unconnected with the trade invested in stocking frames, which were rented to knitters, a practice that created many grievances. The trade suffered during the economic crises of the 1830s and 1840s – a commentator in 1835 remarked that 'the stockinger and the manufacturer generally seem to have been left in the backwash

of industrial progress', and in 1845 a government commissioner blamed the depression in the trade on an irregular supply of work, an over-supply of knitters, the employment of women and young children at low wages, and the practice of frame renting. There were fears that the quality of much English hosiery was insufficient to command international markets.

Making hosiery remained a largely domestic occupation into the 1860s. It has been calculated that in 1851 there were framework knitters in 220 parishes in the East Midlands. The principal centres were Leicester, with more than 4,000 frames, and Nottingham with nearly 3,500 and almost 1,400 in nearby Arnold; there were also 1,750 in Hinckley, 906 in Loughborough, 700 in Derby, 594 in Ilkeston, 421 in Belper and 821 in Mansfield. In many villages a few knitters lived alongside agricultural workers and sometimes coal miners, but the quintessential framework-knitting communities were large villages where knitters were the dominant occupational group. Felkin's survey revealed 1,209 frames in Shepshed, 550 in Wigston, 501 in Kirkby-in-Ashfield and 1,968 in Sutton-in-Ashfield.

➢ A rear view of No. 238 Alfreton Road, Nottingham, reveals that its upper storey once served as a knitter's or lacemaker's workshop.

➢ A single-storey workshop which forms part of No. 6 Britannia Street, Shepshed.

Many former hosiers' workshops can be identified in Shepshed, where in 1861 more than 1,200 of the 3,600 people were engaged in knitting. They were supported by a dozen framesmiths and makers of needles and sinkers. The pattern in neighbouring villages such as Long Whaddon, Hathern and Belton was similar. At Calverton, home of the Revd William Lee, there were 430 knitters, some 31 per cent of the population of 1,372. In Windles Square, which had two rows of hosiers' cottages with wide ground-floor windows, dating from 1834, all but one of the heads of the 27 households recorded in the 1861 census were framework knitters, the only exception being the Scottish keeper of a beerhouse. Some two-storey knitting workshops remain in the village, as does a knitter's cottage bearing the date 1857, evidence of the longevity of domestic hosiery manufacture. At Ruddington, where the museum provides the best evidence of the workshop phase of the industry, there were 343 frames in 1844, and in 1861 some 29 per cent of the parish's 2,283 inhabitants were engaged in knitting. Ruddington was an open village where many cottagers combined farming with other occupations. Although Sutton-in-Ashfield, Nottinghamshire, was best known in the twentieth century as a mining community, in 1861 fewer than two dozen colliers lived in the parish – but almost 2,400 people (about 32 per cent) were engaged in knitting, together with 40 framesmiths and makers of parts.

Hosiery factories were being built at Wigston, four miles south of Leicester, in the early 1890s at the same time that a traditional two-storey knitting shop was erected at the rear of a hosier's house of seventeenth-century origins. The workshop and the house now comprise a museum of framework knitting. Abundant evidence suggests that Wigston was a poverty-stricken community in the mid-nineteenth century, with a surplus of labour both in agriculture and framework knitting. In 1861 almost 900, or 35 per cent, of its 2,521 inhabitants, were engaged in knitting garments that included cotton, worsted and lambs' wool shirts, gloves and children's socks. Many seven- and eight-year-olds were working, and one girl of four was recorded as a sewer of socks. The village economy was transformed after 1870 with the

One of the workshops that houses the framework knitting museum at Ruddington.

construction of railway workshops, a foundry and footwear and hosiery factories.

Jacquard mechanisms were applied to frames from 1841, and in 1825 William Kelly opened the Bow Bridge Mills in Leicester which produced elastic braid. The larger frames could no longer be accommodated in knitters' houses, and in some communities workshops were established with room for a dozen or more frames. It was a small step from such workshops to factories, where frames could be powered by steam engines. The first of these was opened at Loughborough in 1839 by Arthur Paget. In 1851 Hind & Mundella, employers of only 44 knitters in 1844, built a factory in Nottingham that had galleries resembling those in the Crystal Palace – in 1857 they employed 300 people and were putting out work to about 3,000 domestic knitters. The firm was known from 1864 as the Nottingham Manufacturing Company, and subsequently opened a factory in Chemnitz – 'the Saxon Manchester' – as well as expanding in Loughborough. Another influential company, I. & R. Morley, had an imposing warehouse in Wood Street, Nottingham, and operated factories in Leicester, Loughborough and Sutton-in-Ashfield. From 1860 its owner was the

THE PATENT STARCH WORKS OF MESSRS. THOMAS HALL, SONS, AND CO.

Liberal politician Samuel Morley. The first factory in Hinckley, with 40 circular frames, was opened by Thomas Payne in 1855. One of the most significant in Leicester was the St Margaret works, built from 1865 by Edwin Corah, where a 50 hp steam engine powered knitting machines and 77 sewing machines used for seaming, while 28 hand frames were retained for special orders.

The move towards factory production was accelerated by the patent granted in 1864 to William Cotton, for a device that enabled stockings or other products to be automatically narrowed or widened as they were knitted on powered machines. Cotton licensed manufacturers to use his patent machines, and in the 1870s set up a factory in Loughborough to produce them. The machine transformed the industry and was adopted in other countries – there were more than 10,000 in Saxony by 1900. The introduction in the 1860s of the sewing machine, which could be used to finish knitted garments, also made it logical to concentrate production in factories. By 1871 there were 120 steam-powered hosiery factories in England, and in the next two decades the industry became almost entirely factory-based. In 1890 aged stockingers in Leicester were reduced to selling firewood. The demise of domestic knitting was accelerated by the Education Acts of 1870 and 1876 which, by imposing compulsory attendance at school, deprived knitters of the services of young children, and by anti-truck legislation of 1874 which made frame-rent illegal. Many hosiers from the 1870s established small

factories equipped with Cotton machines and sewing machines. These were largely operated by women, who comprised nearly 75 per cent of the industry's labour force by 1911.

Framework knitting spread westwards into Derbyshire during the eighteenth century. The industry had only a modest presence in the county town, and no Derbyshire village was as dominated by knitting as Sutton-in-Ashfield, Wigston or Shepshed. At Crich about 10 per cent of the 2,800 inhabitants were framework knitters in 1861, many working in alpaca or merino. Abraham Dawes accommodated seven male framework knitters, aged between 25 and 37 and making merino shirts, in his home on Town Street. In the industrial parish of Bonsall, near Matlock, the 1,290 inhabitants included more than 150 framework knitters, as well as more than 100 lead miners and smelters, about 50 cotton mill workers and 22 papermakers. Bonsall's framework knitters produced stockings, shirts, dresses, drawers and pantaloons in cotton, angola, merino and silk.

Several Derbyshire hosiers developed large businesses. In 1803 George Brettle became a partner in a company which controlled 1,000 frames in 1812, 4,000 in 1829 and 6,000 in 1844. In 1834–35 he built a three-storey distribution warehouse that survives in Chapel Street in Belper, and his firm became well known for its knitted garments. In 1818 the Smedley family took over the cotton mill at Lea Bridge, which they used for spinning woollen yarn. John Smedley adapted it to make merino and angola yarns, from which knitters

Springfield Mill at Sandiacre, on the banks of the Erewash Canal, seven miles west of Nottingham, illustrates the prodigious growth of the lace industry in Nottinghamshire in the late nineteenth century. The four-storey mill, some 400 feet long, bears the date 1888 and was built for T. Hooley Ltd. It provided tenemented accommodation for individual lacemakers, and power was distributed to working areas throughout the building from a central steam engine. Staircase turrets at the back of the building provided access to the working floors.

made quality garments. More than 120 people were working in 1861 at what was then called the Angola Factory.

The manufacture of machine-made lace evolved from the hosiery industry, and became equally significant in the East Midlands. Crude net was produced on knitting frames from the 1760s, and in 1778 a Nottingham framesmith took out a patent for a machine that could make point net. The most significant innovation was the bobbin net machine, patented in 1808 and then in many respects improved by John Heathcoat. He built a factory at Loughborough, where his machines were destroyed by Luddites on 28 June 1816, after which he moved his business to Devon. The industry continued to grow in the East Midlands, particularly after Heathcoat's patent expired. There were about 1,000 bobbin net machines in Nottingham in 1823 but five times as many in 1833, and the number of lacemakers in Derbyshire, Leicestershire and Nottinghamshire almost doubled from 11,334 in 1831 to 22,026 in 1851. The first steam-powered lace factory appears to have been a four-storey, 168 foot (52 m) long building in Derby, built by Boden & Morley in 1825.

Lace making grew largely as a domestic industry in the first half of the nineteenth century. Campion has shown that the houses with purpose-built workshops along Mansfield Road in Nottingham were insufficient to accommodate the number of lacemakers in the area, and that many must have worked in normal houses or in workshops outside their homes. Lace

making also prospered in Loughborough and Derby, and in the coalfield west of the river Erewash, around Ilkeston and Heanor, where in 1861 nine manufacturers employed a total of over 50 people in silk lace making, although these were outnumbered by about 300 framework knitters. The largest lace works in 1861 had 170 machines, but from 1870 colossal lace factories, some of them designed to be tenemented, were constructed west of Nottingham, at Long Eaton and Draycott.

John Heathcoat transformed the economy and the appearance of Tiverton, previously a market town and a place of quiet resort for half-pay officers and clergy without cure of souls. He established his business in a cotton mill dating from 1790, where his machinery was powered by a waterwheel, 25 feet (7.7 m) wide and 25 feet in diameter. By the 1850s the factory employed about 1,500 people – throwsters, reelers, twisters and winders of silk, flossers, bankers, separators, skeiners and measurers of lace, together with clerks, errand girls and more than a dozen smiths and fitters. By repute many of Heathcoat's employees from Loughborough migrated to Tiverton, but there is little evidence in census returns to suggest a mass migration – although in 1861 there was still a core of engineers and overseers with origins in Loughborough, Shepshed and Leicester, most of whom had married local women. By the time of his death Heathcoat appears to have created a workforce that was stable and largely self-perpetuating, and Heathcoat Fabrics remains in business. The appearance of the mill changed after a fire in 1936, but the brick terraces in Heathcoat Square, Loughborough

Street and Melbourne Street are evidence of the impact of manufacturing upon a previously placid town.

Tiverton contrasts with Honiton, the traditional centre of lace making in Devon. By the 1860s the trade was suffering from competition from machine-worked lace, but remained substantial. It appears to have been an entirely female industry: not only were the lace-makers (rather more than 160 of them in 1861) women, but also the seven lace manufacturers, a lace dealer and a lace designer. Lace making employed about 750 people in the 1860s in the parishes between Honiton and the river Exe.

It also grew in the South Midlands, as a scattered, hand-worked, proto-industrial manufacture, the antithesis of the Nottingham industry. In 1841 the 11,374 laceworkers in the East Midlands counties represented 37.6 per cent of the national labour force in the industry, while there were 10,380 in Bedfordshire, Buckinghamshire, Northamptonshire and Oxfordshire. Twenty years later the 22,020 lacemakers in the East Midlands represented a smaller proportion (34.6 per cent), while the number in the South Midlands had grown to 28,415 (44.6 per cent of the workforce in Great Britain). The industry was spread across the four counties, in such towns as Wellingborough (with more than 130 lacemakers in 1861), Thame (58) and Bicester (77), and also flourished in open villages such as Desborough and Blisworth, in the forest hamlets of Whittlewood, and places in the Chilterns including Chinnor, where there were about 250 lacemakers. The labour force was almost entirely female and was based on village lace-schools, such as that kept by two sisters at Kingston Blount, Oxfordshire, at which girls were introduced to the craft at an early age. The industry peaked in the 1850s. The number of lacemakers in Northamptonshire fell from 10,364 in 1851 to 8,221 in 1861, and to fewer than a thousand by 1891. The number in Bedfordshire increased in the 1850s but decreased from 6,728 in 1861 to 4,792 in 1881. Today there are few relics of the industry apart from the collections of lace in the museums at Northampton, Olney and Bedford.

Conclusions: leading the industrial revolution

In the mid-Victorian era much of the discussion about the spectacular growth of industry concerned textile factories, in particular cotton mills. Great new industrial buildings accommodating large numbers of workers had sprung up in most regions of the country, and the Arkwright-style factory was emblematic of the economic, social and workplace changes of Britain's industrial revolution. Closer examination of the industry reveals a complex interplay between technological change and social and economic developments. Large-scale investments in factories, often with new settlements, grabbed the attention of contemporaries; yet there were also many more modest investments in workshops or small numbers of machines within existing but expanding communities; and in many regions and sectors domestic production endured alongside mechanised manufacturing – albeit in gradual decline – for a surprisingly long time.

Some outstanding buildings – Masson Mill at Cromford, Stanley Mill in Gloucestershire, Saltaire Mill, the Gidlow Works of 1863–65 at Wigan which was designed by George Woodhouse for John Rylands – are more than functional. Their grand scale and architectural pretention can reveal something of the motives of the builders and of the whole rationale of industrialisation. Textile factories can also represent other aspects of industrialisation. New Lanark, for example, epitomises enlightened philanthropy, while at Temple Mill, Leeds, we see a combination of the owner's satisfaction after a long career and a determination to continue innovating, while Litton Mill raises questions about the consequences of enforced child labour.

Textile mills of this era can be seen as agents of economic progress or as means of enforcing slave-like labour. Some factories were indeed scenes of repression. Some cotton masters earned, and deserved, a reputation for callous pursuit of profit, while in literature the factory system was often blamed for the subordination of workers to the inexorable rhythms of a spinning mule or power loom. Despite this, many textile employers provided employment that workers

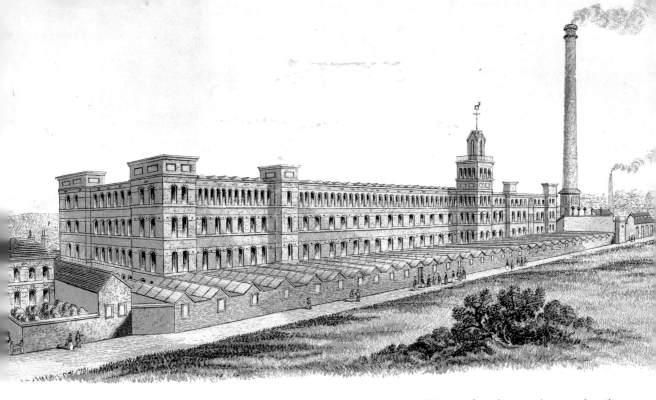

The cotton mills at Wigan were some of the largest in Lancashire, although the town stands a little apart from the county's principal textile districts. Gidlow Mill, designed by the Bolton architect George Woodhouse, was built in the mid-1860s for John Rylands, better known as the founder of the library that is now part of the University of Manchester. It was a colossal integrated mill, and this engraving shows distinctly the traditional multi-storey spinning mill, the extensive north-lit sheds accommodating weavers, and the chimney for the boilers that provided steam for the mill's engine.

FROM A CONTEMPORARY PRINT

found acceptable, with wages that were high in relation to those paid in comparable occupations, while a few created communities which — at least for employees with a deferential outlook — offered living conditions that were exceptionally enlightened for the time.

The effects of the textile industry on consumption were also significant. Exports of textiles were important, but the products of mills also had a profound impact in the British Isles. As early as 1805 David Macpherson wrote in his *Annals of Commerce* that the growth of cotton spinning after 1785 began a new era, not just in the economy but also in the dress of both sexes. He commended the qualities of printed calicos, muslins, cotton and silk stuffs for waistcoats, and cotton stockings. Dr Matthew Webb, a surgeon who since 1806 had lived among the miners and ironworkers of Ketley Bank, Shropshire, told a parliamentary commission in 1842 that living conditions had improved during his working lifetime, partly because of the reduction in scrofula, typhus and scarletina brought about by greater cleanliness which was the consequence of 'the cheapness of cotton, linen and woollen apparel'.

Textile factories and all they represent — mechanisation, the congregation of large numbers of people in places of work, the imposition of strictly enforced hours of labour and rigid workplace discipline — are central to our understanding of the nature of Britain's industrial revolution. Some workers undoubtedly felt trapped or oppressed by the new factory system, particularly in the early, 'heroic' phases of industrialisation, but in a general social and economic sense there were certainly some favourable consequences. For good or ill, the textile mills of the late eighteenth century changed for ever the world of work and many aspects of society at large.

10

Rags to riches:
a revolution in paper

'... thou hast caused printing to be used, and, contrary to the king, his crown and dignity, thou hast built a paper mill.'

JACK CADE, HENRY VI PART 2, IV, VII, 35.

THE facts, the figures, and the history, of the industrial revolution were recorded on paper. From the copious quantities preserved in archives and libraries, historians and conservators are familiar with many different types. Some papers were inexpensive and crude, others costly: the varied papers on which probate inventories were drafted; the blue paper of account books bound with paste board; the formal letters inscribed with quills on laid watermarked paper or faintly legible on flimsy tissues from one of James Watt's copying machines; the octavo leaves on which the thoughts of John Banks and Thomas Tredgold were printed; and, perhaps most importantly, the sheets upon which newspaper editors laid out advertisements and local news, or intelligence of railway openings. Textile products were wrapped by manufacturers and by retailers, in brown capp paper. Pasteboard boxes protected jewellery, watches, cutlery and medicinal pills. Children learned to read and to measure from primers and chapbooks, and the Bibles that shaped many lives were printed on thin sheets made at Wolvercote, Bathford or in the Gade Valley. Queen Victoria wrote letters, and J. M. W. Turner made sketches on paper from the Turkey Mill near Maidstone. Political demonstrations, circus performances, charity sermons and lectures were publicised on posters, printed on paper that might be vivid orange or purple.

The paper-making industry was thus an important component in the manufacturing history of the British Isles, one that hitherto has rarely been given the attention it deserves.

In 1700 there were about 100 paper mills in England, most of which made brown, blue or grey papers for wrapping. Huguenot migrants began to make white writing paper before 1700, and the Company of White Papermakers, established in 1686, had eight mills by 1698. It was wound up soon afterwards, but its mills probably continued in operation. Paper making in England expanded until by 1720 received opinion held that about two-thirds of demand was being met by domestic suppliers. Defoe wrote in 1712 that 'paper manufacture in Britain is a small but improving thing'. The Society of the White & Printing Paper Manufactory of Scotland was established in 1694 by Nicholas Dupin, a Frenchman who had attempted to set up linen-making enterprises in England and Ireland. Two mills which were opened near Edinburgh continued working after the company was wound up in 1703.

Paper making depended upon water power, and since there was strong competition with other trades for suitable riparian sites, some mills were situated in remote locations, although paper was made at most places where water power was plentiful, such as in the Greenfield Valley, at Blarney, along the Waters of Leith and at Ludlow and Derby. Paper mills had symbiotic relationships with cities, which were the sources of the rags they used as raw materials as well as being the principal markets for their products. Within 40 or so miles of London there were concentrations of paper mills in both 1700 and 1870. Defoe observed that mills in the Loddon Valley produced printing paper for newspapers, journals and pamphlets, but not very much fine paper for bound books or writing. Some papermakers, on the other hand, found distant markets. In 1730 the mill at Claverley, Shropshire, produced several grades of paper, one of which was used for printing, and supplied customers in Stafford, Worcester, Birmingham and Dublin. In Scotland most mills were close to Edinburgh where the establishment of the *Edinburgh Gazette* in 1698, the *Edinburgh Courant* in 1718, and the *Scottish Magazine* in 1739, created a demand for paper that could be used for printing; the proprietors of newspapers eventually owned several paper mills. Similarly most of the 50 or so paper mills established in Ireland by 1780 were near Dublin or Cork. The Irish House of Commons was proud that its journals were printed on white Irish paper.

At the beginning of the eighteenth century mercers sold a variety of paper products. Most stocked pasteboard, but kept it with haberdashery wares since it was used for making headdresses and in pressing cloth. Writing paper was logically kept with ink. Most mercers sold alphabets, hornbooks, construing books, chapbooks and primers for children, as well as Bibles, psalters and prayer books for adult customers. All kept the capp paper that was used for wrapping.

Traditional paper mills were water-powered and required pure water for processing. The usual raw material was rags, which might be discarded clothing

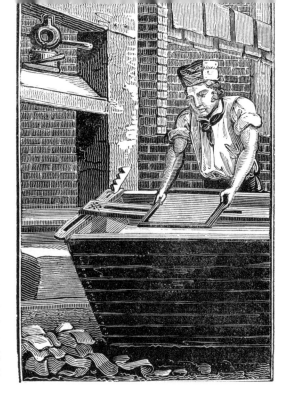

'The Paper Maker' from the 1824 edition of *The Book of English Trades*. A vatman is dipping a mould into a vat of pulp (or 'stuff'). On lifting it out he will give it a shake to set the fibres and remove excess water, remove the 'deckle' (wooden frame) and turn the mould to deposit the wet sheet of paper on a piece of felt. A pile of felts is visible near the screw press to the left of the picture, and sheets that have been pressed are hanging up to dry above the vatman's head.

or waste from textile manufacturers or tailors, or old ropes (known as 'cordage'). In 1861 a 35-year-old woman at Farleigh, Kent, was employed as an oakum-picker in a local paper mill. When Richard Fosbrook of Alveley, Shropshire, died in 1730, his estate included best rags worth £5, second-quality rags worth four guineas, and cordage to the value of £12. Bartholomew Smith, an Englishman who set up a paper mill near Aberdeen, announced in 1751 that he would provide the region with fine and coarse paper, brown paper and pasteboard, and that he would visit Aberdeen market weekly to buy flaxen and hempen rags by the stone weight. Since his undertaking was 'beneficent to the country', he expected people to save materials for his works.

Rags were sorted and cut up, usually by women,

and were pulped by stamps, ranges of up to five cam-operated wooden hammers set above troughs. There were usually several troughs in line so that rags could be moved from one to another as they were soaked. The hammers in the first would be shod with spikes to fray the cloth, while those in the last had plain wooden heads so that fine fibres would not be lost. The technology was developed in Italy in the sixteenth century, and was used to make fine-grade papers until the twentieth century. The materials were beaten in water to produce pulp or 'stuff' which was mixed in vats, into which a 'vatman' dipped a mould made up of a grid of fine wires and a wooden frame or 'deckle'. On lifting out the mould he gave it a practised shake to set the fibres and drain away most of the water. The deckle was removed and the mould turned with an adept rocking motion to deposit the wet sheet of paper on a piece of felt. Felts and paper were stacked by the 'coucher'; when a 'post' of 144 sheets of paper and interleaved felts was built up it was pressed in a wooden screw press. The paper was hung to dry in a loft. Some types of paper were smoothed with metal plates or sized, if intended for writing.

Most new paper-making concerns were sited on established mill sites. The manufacture of woollen cloth was declining in south-east England, and millwrights could readily adapt shafts that had worked fulling stocks to power stamps for pounding rags. Most mills in 1700 had only one vat, but some were much larger. As early as 1679 Timothy West's business was of considerable size: he worked both the corn and the paper mills at Horton, Buckinghamshire, had 23 pairs of moulds worth £12, felts worth £4, material for paper making worth £140, and a stock of complete paper worth £945 10s. In 1713 William Goodshire at Thorney Mill, Buckinghamshire and Drayton Mill, Middlesex, had equipment and raw materials worth £150, and finished white and brown paper valued at more than £300.

Demand for paper increased as printers proliferated in market towns. Most were small businesses producing bill headings, menus, invitations, tickets, posters, pamphlets and the occasional book. Some, in county towns, ventured into the production of four-page weekly newspapers printed on single sheets. A Norwich printer was pleased in 1701 that he could obtain printing paper from Taverham Mill, four miles west of the city. The economic significance of provincial printers was modest. They employed only one or two workpeople, and their machines were hand-operated, but they did enable townspeople to communicate with one another and with the wider world.

The mechanisation of paper making

The principal technological change in paper making in the mid-eighteenth century was the introduction from the 1730s of the 'Hollander beater', a machine developed in the Netherlands in the late seventeenth century which consisted of a trough fed with water and rags or other fibres, in which rotated a solid wooden roller fitted with iron knives or teeth which beat the fibres into a pulp. Hollander beaters gradually replaced stamps in most mills, although they tended to produce shorter fibres, and thus weaker paper, and the metal blades could contaminate the pulp, the result of which might be foxing on the pages of books many years later. Wove paper was made in moulds where the parallel lines of wire were replaced by a mesh. John Baskerville, the Birmingham typographer, produced an edition of Virgil on wove paper in 1757 which was acclaimed through Europe. It was possibly made at the Turkey Mill in Kent by John Whatman, whose son James produced the $52\frac{3}{4}$-inch × $31\frac{3}{4}$-inch Antiquarian sheet for the Society of Antiquaries of London, intended for engravings.

From about 1740 there was a significant increase in the quantity of quality paper being made in England. In the 1780s the mill at Taverham in Norfolk specialised in writing and printing paper, including Elephant and Atlas sizes. There was a proliferation of mills with four or five vats, including the West Mills at Newbury, the Throstle Nest Mill near Manchester, and Wolvercote Mill near Oxford. Measuring output from the levels of duty charged shows that production of paper increased from less than 3,000 tons *per annum* in England and Wales between 1700 and 1720 to more than 5,000 in the late 1750s, over 6,000 for the first time in 1765; it doubled in the next three decades, exceeding 12,000 tons in 1796.

Angerstein saw Hollanders working at Wookey in Somerset, in the Forest of Dean at the mill which displaced the Guns Mill blast furnace, in the Greenfield Valley, and at Chopwell, Co. Durham. He commended the white paper made with the pure water of the river Axe at Wookey, but observed that iron in the water dictated that paper mills on the river Derwent in Co. Durham could make only wrapping paper. He also noted that a mill at Egremont in Cumberland found its markets in Ireland. In 1785 the brothers La Rochefoucauld visited Birmingham and on the recommendation of Joseph Priestley visited the workshop of Henry Clay, who in 1772 had patented a process for making paperboard by pasting together several sheets of brown paper. Clay's paperboard could be worked like wood with saws and files. It was heat-resistant and could be made waterproof by painting, varnishing or japanning. It was used for buttons, tea trays, caddies,

ladies' work-boxes and snuffboxes, and the thicker grades were employed in the panels and roofs of coaches. Clay had been apprenticed to John Allport, a Birmingham drawing master, and established his own workshop in New Hall Street in 1772. He moved to London in 1802, but his business in Birmingham was continued by Jennens & Betteridge, whose factory in 1844 was described as one of the finest and most interesting in the town.

From the 1790s there were substantial changes in technology. Twelve steam engines were set to work at paper mills between 1780 and 1800. The first was probably installed for Richard Howard and Thomas Houghton at Wilmington, near Hull, in 1786, and the first in Scotland at Lasswade near Edinburgh in 1803. The same year a steam-worked mill was built at Aberdeen, and in 1805 William Balston set up the Springfield Mill near Maidstone, powered by a Boulton & Watt engine whose beam survives. From the beginning the mill had ten vats; it employed 100 people in 1835 and about 250 in 1861. All but the smallest mills

⋌ A plan made in 1808 by the London engineers Bryan Donkin & Co. for the continuous paper machine patented the previous year by the brothers Henry and Sealy Fourdrinier.

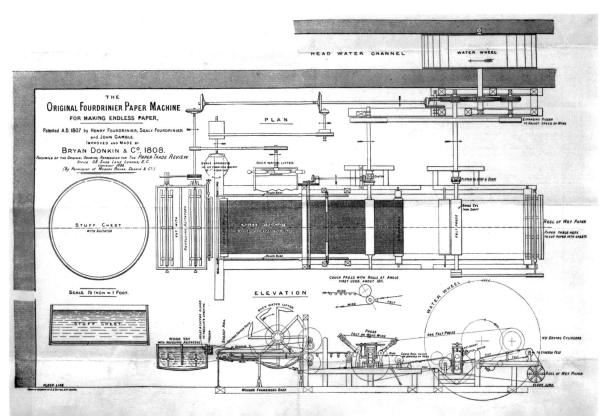

employed steam engines by 1860, if only to supplement water power. Chlorine was used for bleaching paper at Lasswade in 1791, and there was controversy about methods of bleaching and the infringement of patents during the rest of the decade. In 1800 Charles Tennant patented bleaching powder, as important for papermakers as it was for textile manufacturers.

A hand-operated machine for making paper in lengths up to about 12 feet was invented in France in 1798 by Nicholas-Louis Robert. By 1801 rights in the machine were owned by the London stationers Henry and Sealy Fourdrinier, who in 1802 commissioned John Hall, a Dartford ironfounder, to construct a machine from Robert's drawings. Hall's brother-in-law, the engineer Bryan Donkin, took the initiative in manufacturing the machine, and the Fourdriniers financed the workshop that he established in Bermondsey. In a Fourdrinier machine liquid pulp was poured onto a continuous web of wire mesh, forming, as the water drained away, a sheet which was passed onto a continuous felt blanket, before being pressed between several pairs of rollers, and wound damp into a roll, after which it was cut and dried in a loft. The Fourdriniers made paper at Frogmore Mill in Hertfordshire from 1803, and commenced production at Two Waters Mill in 1805. They calculated in 1806 that one of their machines reduced the cost of a hundredweight of paper from 16s. to 3s. 9d. They invested in research and obtained patents in 1803 and 1807, but were declared bankrupt in 1810. Some 41 licences for machines were granted, at £350 *per annum* each, between 1807 and the expiry of the patents in 1822. There were 89 machines working by 1835 and 267 by 1850, but many of those who bought machines, including Tsar Alexander of Russia, failed to meet their obligations. In 1837 a Parliamentary Select Committee recommended that the Fourdriniers' contribution to paper making merited reward, and in 1840 they received £7,000, which was supplemented by a subscription from the paper trade. Nevertheless, the brothers died in obscurity.

Fourdrinier machines were exported to France and Germany and from 1827 to the United States. The first in Ireland was delivered in 1807 to J. B. Sullivan's Dripsey Mill near Cork. The first in Scotland worked at Peterculter, near Aberdeen, from 1811, and there were machines at 23 of Scotland's 52 mills by the 1820s. The first in Wales was installed at William Hill's mill in the Greenfield Valley in 1821. Donkin made numerous improvements to the Fourdrinier machine. In 1822 he began to use steam-heated cylinders which dried paper continuously, an idea that had been patented by Thomas Bonsor Crompton in 1820. Crompton made paper at Farnworth Bridge, Lancashire, in a mill worked by his ancestor Richard Crompton who was making paper on the site in 1700. Thomas Crompton installed three Fourdrinier machines and built machines for other papermakers after the patents expired. With Enoch Taylor he patented a rotary cutter for paper in 1828. Much of the paper from Farnworth Bridge was used in newspapers, including the London *Morning Post*.

An alternative technology appeared within a few years. John Dickinson, offspring of the Superintendent of Ordnance Transports at Woolwich and the daughter of a Huguenot silk weaver from Spitalfields, was apprenticed as a stationer and began to trade in paper. In 1809, with the publisher George Longman, he purchased Apsley Mill on the river Gade which had been adapted for paper making by George Stafford, one of his suppliers. The same year he patented a cylinder-mould paper-making machine, in which fibre from a suspension containing pulp was deposited on a wire-covered cylinder partially submerged in a vat. The machine was successful, and Dickinson acquired more premises – a former corn mill at Nash in 1810–11, a textile mill at Batchworth about 1818, Home Park Mill in 1826, and Croxley Mill, Watford, in 1830. The cylinder-mould machine was competitive with the Fourdrinier machine, but the large machines of the late nineteenth century were based on principles established by the Fourdriniers.

Other innovations followed the development of paper-making machines. In 1807 John Dickinson patented a form of cartridge paper which was employed by British artillerymen in the Napoleonic Wars, and was subsequently used for the tube sections of shotgun cartridges, for drawing, and in the endpapers of books. Dickinson also produced the tough but thin paper used in the Pocket Reference Bible published by Samuel Bagster in 1812–13. In 1827 Louis Aubrey of the Two Waters Mill obtained a patent for weaving an endless web of wire with which paper could be produced on a machine with watermarks like those on hand-made paper. Dickinson also took out patents for paper for copperplate printing and for veneered paper. Most letters in 1800 were folded and sealed with wax before being despatched in the post, but in 1830 the Treasury held a competition for an envelope, the winner being the painter William Mulready whose design used Dickinson's silk thread paper. Mulready also designed the officially approved envelope issued in 1840 when Rowland Hill launched the Penny Post. John Dicksonson & Co. produced envelopes with ready-gummed flaps from about 1850. Blotting paper was first made about 1795 by William Russell Slade at Hagbourne Mill, Berkshire, but his invention was scarcely exploited until Thomas Burch Ford, who had married into the family, took over the mill in 1855 and displayed its products at the Paris Exhibition of that year. From Lady Day 1859, Ford leased Snakeley Mills near Loudwater where he made blotting paper on Fourdrinier machines.

Mechanised paper mills transformed the economy of the valley of the river Gade in Hertfordshire as much as the cotton mills of Richard Arkwright and the Strutts transformed that of the Derbyshire Derwent. The Gade flows south from the Chiltern Hills through Gaddesdon, Two Waters, Hemel Hempstead and King's Langley to Watford where it is joined by the river Colne which passes Redbourn and St Albans on its descent from the chalk uplands. The Colne proceeds south through Rickmansworth, Harefield and Uxbridge to join the Thames at Staines. From Hemel Hempstead to Uxbridge the Gade and Colne are followed by the Grand Junction Canal. Paper mills flourished along the canal and the rivers between Rickmansworth and Hemel Hempstead. There were more than 250 papermakers in 1861 at Rickmansworth, Croxley Green, Chorley Wood and Sarratt, more than 70 in Watford, and over 200 at King's Langley and Abbot's Langley, among them two of the partners in John Dickinson & Co., which employed 468 hands. More than 400 papermakers, including punchers, stampers, folders, gummers and black borderers of envelopes, lived in Hemel Hempstead.

Estimates of the number of mills in Britain vary, but all figures show the same trend. There were 507 in England and Wales in 1831, but only 362 in 1847, and 274 in 1870. The number in Scotland increased slightly, to 52 in 1860, while that in Ireland halved from 52 to 26 in the same period. In 1881 there were 324 paper mills in the British Isles. Output grew, from 17,059 tons in 1805 to 74,500 tons in 1855, an increase of 437 per cent, due principally to mechanisation. The amount of paper made by hand fell, from 16,502 tons in 1805 to 14,278 tons in 1810 and 4,164 tons in 1855. Such was the rate of adoption of mechanised techniques, that while hand-made paper accounted for 75 per cent of the total output in 1810, it had declined to 45 per cent in 1825, and only 6 per cent in 1855. Nearly 8,000 people were engaged in making paper in the United Kingdom in 1841: 5,690 in England and Wales, 1,470 in Scotland and 713 in Ireland.

Patterns of paper making

Between 1800 and 1830 paper manufacturing showed contradictory tendencies. The installation of paper-making machines, the application of steam power and the ability of inland waterways to transport coal, rags and finished products created mills that were unprecedentedly large. At the same time the number of paper mills grew from about 430 in England and Wales in 1800 to a peak of about 560 in 1820. Many were small, single-vat, hand-operated mills set up on water-power sites vacated by other industries, and, against the long-term trend, the output of hand-made paper increased marginally between 1820 and 1825. Most small mills made wrapping papers, which were in increasing demand as shops proliferated between 1800 and 1820. A petition in 1802 observed that wrapping paper was 'made in remote places by men of small capital'. Mill sites no longer used by other trades that were adapted to paper making in this period included the slitting mill at Tibberton, which was used as a paper mill from 1804. Head Weir Mill at Exeter was converted from fulling in 1787 and became a substantial paper mill, while Burneside Mill near Kendal, a woollen mill, was adapted to make paper in 1833. From the 1830s the process was reversed and paper mills were adapted to other purposes, most reverting to corn milling. The mill at Ballymagart, Kilkeel, County Down ceased working about 1829, was adapted as a scutch mill, then from 1846 as a corn mill. A paper mill was built on the site of the charcoal-fired blast furnace at Bouldon in Shropshire about 1790. Only two papermakers were living in the hamlet by 1841, and the waterwheel was driving a corn mill before 1850. About 20 mills were working in Shropshire in 1820, most of them producing wrapping paper, but writing paper was made at Hopton Wafers, glazed boards at Longnor, paper for book printing at Ludford, blue sugar paper at Ludford and Tibberton, and filter and blotting paper at Neen Savage. No more than three mills remained in 1880 and only one survived in 1900.

The same tendencies can be observed in Oxfordshire. Hazelford Mill at Broughton was converted from fulling to making paper in the eighteenth century but was closed in the 1850s. The nearby mill at North Newington produced paper from the 1680s, and

employed 20 people in 1861 making the stiff, blue foolscap paper used in government offices. Thomas Ward Boss recalled the passage through Banbury in the 1830s of cumbersome waggons, loaded with bales of rags, making their way to the mill, which was adapted to make superphosphate fertilisers in the 1860s. Deddington Mill made paper from 1684, but employed only two or three people in the 1850s and by 1870 was again a corn mill. The mill of the 1680s at Hampton Gay was worked by steam from 1873; nine people were working there in 1881 but it closed soon afterwards. Those at Shiplake and Rotherfield Peppard installed steam engines by 1871, but had closed by 1900. Meanwhile mills around Oxford prospered. Thomas Routledge pioneered the production of paper from esparto grass at Eynsham, while the mill at Wolvercote made white paper for books as early as the 1680s. It was steam-operated from 1811, soon after the opening of the Oxford Canal, and by 1881 was employing nearly a hundred people. Sandford Mill, adapted to make paper in 1826 and purchased by Oxford University Press in 1880, operated on a similar scale.

One of the principal concentrations of paper mills in southern England was in the Wye Valley in Buckinghamshire. Several mills were adapted after 1800 from other kinds of manufacture – from corn mills, from cotton spinning at Taplow, gunpowder blending at Eggan's Grove, iron working at Colne Bridge, and rolling copper at Wraysbury. Three local mills with paper-making machines were attacked during the Captain Swing riots of 1830. More than 200 people were employed making paper and millboard around Marlow in 1851, 119 of them at James Spicer's Glory Mills, Wooburn. In 1861 the total exceeded 260. Buckinghamshire mills produced papers for writing, and sheets that could be bound together in ledgers and printed books. By 1860 most mills had machines; many supplemented water with steam power; and several manufactured millboard.

Nearly a thousand papermakers worked in Kent in 1841. The proximity of London and the availability of cordage from Chatham Dockyard enabled the industry to flourish, particularly along the river Medway and its tributaries. The first English paper mill had supposedly been built at Dartford in 1588,

The buildings of Ludford (Temeside) Mill, on the edge of Ludlow, a site where paper was made for most of the period between 1700 and 1870. The mill was adapted in the 1880s for the roller milling of grain.

and in 1861 more than 100 men and 200 women were engaged in paper making there. In 1861 Maidstone was a garrison town, the centre of county administration, and had the usual industries of a market town – milling, malting, brewing, leather processing and engineering – but paper making was the predominant industry, employing about 700 people in the neighbourhood. The mill at Taverham on the river Wensum near Norwich was operating by 1701. It had four vats in 1807 when a Fourdrinier machine was installed. The equipment was renewed in the 1840s, and in 1847 the mill was taken over by a company whose principal partner was John Thadeus Delane, editor of *The Times* from 1841 until 1877. The mill employed about 60 people in 1861, working day and night shifts producing white and brown paper. The mill provided paper for *The Times*, for the *Oxford English Dictionary* in 1884, and for the Revised Version of the King James Bible the following year. Taverham, the last paper mill in Norfolk, closed in 1899.

Paper making in Devon prospered in the valley of the river Culm and particularly at Bradninch, eight miles north of Exeter, a former market town of about 2,000 people where two mills employed about 300 people in 1861. It was a settled community where almost all the papermakers were locally born, although men from Bradninch found employment in distant parts of England. In Somerset more than 100 papermakers worked in 1861 at mills in the vicinity of Wells and Wookey Hole.

Paper making flourished in the vicinity of textile manufacturing, because cotton waste could be used as a raw material, and cotton producers were customers for wrapping papers. Thus, in 1861 more than 50 people worked at John Cockburn's paper mill at Allen Wood near Carlisle, which used waste from the nearby Warwick Bridge cotton mills, while John Long's mill at Ulverston, also near cotton mills, employed 28. There were several mills near Cromford, and in 1861 about 50 papermakers lived there or in nearby Matlock and Bonsall. Peckwash Mill near Duffield was built about 1800 by Thomas Tempest. A terrace of 14 houses for employees was constructed in the 1850s, and paper making in the area employed more than 50 people in 1861. The Alder Mill near Tamworth, owned

The paper mill at Horton Kirby on the river Darenth upstream from Dartford was established in the 1820s by Henry Hall, brother of John Hall the Dartford engineer who built Fourdrinier machines, on a site previously occupied by corn mills and an iron forge. The mill produced paper for many journals including the *Tatler* and the *Illustrated London News*. It was taken over in 1872 and subsequently much enlarged by the firm of Spalding & Cudlipp, originally wholesale stationers in London. The 230-feet chimney was built in 1881, and by 1890 the mill employed about 400 people. The advertisement also shows that Spalding & Cudlipp made paper by hand at Rush Mills, Hardingstone, near Northampton, and that they had agents in France, India and Australia.

© SCIENCE MUSEUM/SCIENCE & SOCIETY PICTURE LIBRARY

by Charles Fisher, employed about two dozen people and used waste from local textile mills.

New paper mills in Lancashire were attracted by the proximity of bleachworks as well as the demand for paper from textile manufacturers and the availability of cotton waste. In 1841 the industry in Lancashire employed 677 people, of whom 168 were women. By 1851 there were 22 mills in the county, including two of the largest in Britain, at Bridge Hall and Farnworth. The size of the Withnell Fold mill, established in the early 1840s on the banks of the Leeds & Liverpool Canal, is indicated by the 29 cottages ranged in five rows that once housed its workforce. Eleven papermaking machines were working at the Bridge Hall Mills, Bury, in the 1880s. A 'paper mill cotton dresser' was among the employees at the steam-powered paper mill at Haigh near Wigan in 1861.

There was also a substantial paper industry, employing more than 500 people in 1841, in the West Riding of Yorkshire, where mills around Barnsley used waste from linen manufactories. The Old Mill at Barnsley, powered both by water and steam, employed 17 people in 1861. Onesacre Mill at Wharncliffe Side had 33 employees, and there were two steam-powered paper mills in Hunslet, one employing 32 people making glazed paper, paper bags and paper boxes. One of the largest mills in Yorkshire, at Richmond, which employed more than 100 people in 1861, was established by Henry Cooke who as a young man had worked the Egglestone Abbey Mill in Co. Durham.

By the 1790s Scottish paper mills were producing more than 1,000 tons *per annum*, including writing paper, tissue paper, pasteboard, the calendar paper used for pressing cloth, and cartridge paper for hosiery manufacturers. The principal concentration was around Edinburgh, particularly in the valley of the North Esk where there were five paper mills in 1767. The mill at Lasswade originated about 1750 and was celebrated for its white writing paper. In 1802 Svedenstierna found it neat and well fitted. Rags were cut by children and old people on tables which were ranged around the walls of a room and fitted with vertical knives. A steam engine drove machinery for washing rags and the rollers that crushed them, and chlorine was used for bleaching. Of the other mills on the North Esk, Polton had five vats by 1767, Melville four in 1793 and six in 1814, and by 1832 nine mills on the river employed ten Fourdrinier machines. While the numbers of mills in England, Wales and Ireland diminished after 1820, the total in Scotland increased slightly, and 57 were still working in 1870. Output in Scotland first exceeded 2,000 tons in 1818, rose to more than 3,000 tons by 1825, and continued to increase rapidly, reaching 20,000 tons in 1860.

Many women were employed in paper making, principally as cutters or sorters of rags or as sorters and packers of paper. In small mills the inflow of rags could be inconsistent, and such work could be combined with seasonal labour in the fields. The subordinate role of women, and the assumption that they required supervision, is indicated by job titles such as 'overlooker of paper women' and 'overlooker of rag women' at Bradninch and Wookey. Male papermakers, and the engineers and millwrights who installed and maintained machines and power systems, could easily migrate to places where their talents were best rewarded.

Itinerant workers in the mid-nineteenth century fall into two categories. Some left small mills on the point of closure, while others exploited the skills they had acquired at large mills. Those at Kettlebrook Mill, Warwickshire, included several from Kemberton, Shropshire, where the paper mill had closed in the 1840s. A papermaker from Cleobury Mortimer, where several mills ceased before 1850, worked at Wookey Hole. There were papermakers from North Newington and Deddington at Loose near Maidstone. Successful mills, Bradninch, Wookey Hole, Taverham, Winchcombe, and those in the Medway, Gade and Loddon valleys, were nurseries of talents, from which papermakers and managers found employment across the country. In 1861 papermakers in Maidstone included men from High Wycombe, Wooburn, Marlow, Cromford, Bradninch, Winchcombe, Rickmansworth, Taverham, Bathford, Wookey Hole and Tamworth. The manager of the Eynsham Mill was a Scot, and the paper manufacturer at Hampton Gay a native of Whalley, Lancashire.

The manufacture of paper, whether by hand or machine, depended on the availability of fine wires for moulds or machines, and wiremakers often set up business in the vicinity of paper mills. Six wiremakers are recorded in the 1861 census as living around Winchcombe, near the large paper mill at Postlip, and there were wire drawers and makers of paper moulds in Barnsley and Maidstone. Suppliers of raw materials were also part of the infrastructure of the paper industry. In 1861 a dealer in flax waste and rags was lodging at East Malling, a 'straw agent for paper-making' at Wells, and a buyer of rags near Taverham.

Paper products were essential in the workings of some manufacturing industries. Thus, tissue paper was used for pressing fabrics, for transferring designs onto pottery, and for copying letters on machines of the type patented by James Watt in 1780, while glazed paper was employed in pressing woollen cloth. The millboard used for book covers was being made in

England by 1720. Pasteboard cartons were manufactured from 1817, and folding cartons from the 1860s. The introduction of Jacquard looms in the textile industry from the 1820s necessitated the production of hole-punched cards. Patterns for complex fabrics, such as those used for bedspreads and figured window curtains, required up to 8,000 cards, and whole floors of mills in Macclesfield had to be given over to their storage. In Nottingham cards for Jacquard-controlled lace-making machines were prepared by people such as the 'Jack Hard Puncher' who lived in Radford. Other workers in Nottingham prepared pasteboard for lace bonnets.

Developments in paper making after 1850

Papermakers were given a compelling incentive to increase production by the repeal of the stamp duty on newspapers in 1855, and the removal of excise duties on paper, defined by Sir Edwin Chadwick as the 'taxes on knowledge'. Newspapers proliferated as the removal of the duties made it possible for them to be sold for no more than a penny. In 1851 561 newspapers were being published in England, of which 17 were dailies, totals which by 1867 had increased, respectively, to 1,294 and 84.

Esparto grass, grown in Spain and North Africa, was supposedly first used in Britain for paper making in 1850. Within a decade it was being employed at several mills; paper made from it was exhibited in the International Exhibition of 1862, and its use expanded in the years that followed. Eynsham Mill near Oxford had fewer than a dozen employees in the 1840s, but was enlarged under the management of Thomas Routledge, who took out patents for the use of esparto grass in 1856 and 1860. He employed 63 people in 1861. Machinery was worked by steam and water power, and workers included sorters of esparto fibres. Routledge was born in Kilburn, and spent his early adult life in Camberwell. In 1860, with John Evans, manager of the John Dickinson mills, he bought the Ford Mill at South Hylton near Sunderland which was opened in 1838. In 1841 there were about 30 papermakers in South Hylton, about half of them Irish. Rags remained the principal raw material, but in 1851 a 24-year-old Irish spinster was employed as a 'grass sorter', indicating that esparto grass might already have been in use. After 1860 Ford Mill became one of the principal esparto-using mills in Britain, and esparto imports into nearby Newcastle increased from 1,224 tons in 1860 to 9,534 tons in 1862. By 1871 it employed more than 60 people, several of them grass cleaners. In the 1860s Routledge himself moved from Eynsham to Claxheugh Grove at South Hylton, while in 1861 the managing clerk came from Oxford, and other employees included people from Hampton Gay, Wolvercote and Eynsham, Marlow, Flintshire, Scotland and Ireland. About 140 papermakers lived in South Hylton in 1881. The mill supplied 'half stuff', thick sheets of pulped esparto that were made into paper at other mills, including John Dickinson's works in Hertfordshire. The use of esparto expanded elsewhere, and by 1870 mills in Scotland were using 44,000 tons *per annum* compared with only 18,000 tons of rags and less than 200 tons of other materials. By 1861 straw was being used for paper making at Samuel Hook's Snodland mill, where an innovative approach to manufacture is also indicated by the presence of a chemical department and alkali makers.

The use of china clay as a filler, from 1807, was another significant technological development. By 1858 seven pits around Hensbarrow in Cornwall were producing clay specifically for papermakers. In 1855 Henry Davis Pochin of the Sheepbridge Ironworks developed a process whereby china clay was dissolved in sulphuric acid to produce alum cake, for use in paper making. He subsequently invested in china-clay workings near St Austell, and his company was one of the major producers until its merger with English China Clays.

Many workers in paper flourished in cities. In the City Road area of London in 1861 there were makers of paper bags, envelopes, fancy boxes, pocket books, pill boxes, account books and linings for jewel cases, as well as embossers of paper, enamellers of card, book-edge gilders and map colourers. In central Manchester

⚹ William Cherry's printworks in Dublin which produced a wide range of commercial stationery, including paper bags, envelopes and account books. From George Measom, *The Official Illustrated Guide to the Great Southern & Western and Midland Great Western Railways of Ireland* (London: Measom, 1866).

there were makers of similar goods as well as workers in warehouses that supplied paper to textile manufacturers. About 1854 William Cherry saw an opportunity in Dublin, acquiring the Seville Works, which had previously been used for building railway waggons. By 1866 he employed 300 people in printing and the manufacture of paper bags, bound account books and envelopes. In 1839 John Bradbury Robinson set up a factory in Chesterfield to make pill boxes, and his company, which employed 183 people in 1861, displayed its cardboard products in the International Exhibition of 1862. In Nottingham in 1861 there were manufacturers of fancy linen and hosiery boxes, one of whom employed 28 people. By 1865 millboard made at Llangenni, Breconshire, was used not just for bookbinders' board but also as soles for slippers.

The paper industry remained widely dispersed in 1870. Many small mills still worked in remote locations, but the introduction of esparto grass hastened a tendency to concentrate production in large mills close to the coast. This trend accelerated in the 1880s with the introduction of wood pulp as a raw material. The number of mills declined while output increased: in 1850 about 400 mills in Great Britain produced 100,000 tons of paper, but in 1900 fewer than 300 mills were making over six times as much.

❧

Paper making was central to the economic growth of the eighteenth and nineteenth centuries. Its output increased prodigiously due to the introduction of machines that could only be constructed with the skills of ironfounders, forgemen, fitters and wire drawers. The transformation of the industry depended on innovations from Europe – the Hollander beater in the mid-eighteenth century, and the paper-making machine which, while its development was due to the Fourdriniers and Bryan Donkin, was the invention of the Frenchmen Nicholas-Louis Robert. Growth also owed much to new products developed by John Dickinson and others. The pattern of paper manufacturing established in England between 1800 and 1820 was subsequently copied in other countries. Paper was vital in many industries, but above all it made possible the diffusion of information, reflected in Samuel Johnson's description of the English in 1781 as 'a nation of readers'.

PART III

Towns, cities, and communities

A panorama of Liverpool in the 1870s. Britain's second port (after London) shared many of the characteristics and problems of the country's other rapidly expanding urban centres, including over-crowding, insanitary housing, inadequate water supplies or public health amenities. But Liverpool also boasted some fine new buildings, including a Georgian town hall, the Customs House, St George's Hall and industrial buildings such as Albert Dock. Today Liverpool has more listed buildings than any city outside London.

11

Great cities, old and new

'The great difficulty in the management of the poor is in great cities. It is there that vice has spread her temptations, and pleasure her seductions and folly her allurements. ... It is to these great marts of human corruptions that the base and profligate resort from the simplicity of country life.'

SIR ARCHIBALD ALISON [1845?]

'Young towns, towns which are rarely or never mentioned in our early history ... have, within the memory of persons still living, grown to a greatness which this generation contemplates with wonder and pride, not unaccompanied by awe and anxiety.'

T.B. MACAULAY, *THE HISTORY OF ENGLAND*, 1848.

THE WORLD, it seemed, had never seen such sights before. The largest industrial towns of the British Isles (some of which became cities in the formal sense only after 1870) were new to human experience. This was not mainly because of their size or their population — there had been populous, extensive and insanitary urban spaces in all periods since antiquity — but because of their spectacular and unprecedented rates of growth, their high population densities, the increased segregation of social classes, and, most important, the nature of the social and economic activities of their inhabitants. Britain's towns and cities were all different: in this chapter we look at some of the classic 'Victorian cities', those which made their livings by manufacturing or trade.

Urban historians of the past half-century, notably Asa Briggs and H. J. Dyos, and more recently Tristram Hunt, have published extensively on the broad phenomenon of what has often been termed the 'Victorian city'. It is not the purpose of this chapter to recount their findings, but rather to describe the characteristics of particular places, and to highlight the diversity of experience. To help make sense of the complexity, one can describe Britain's towns and cities in terms of a broad urban hierarchy, ranging from, at the bottom, small provincial settlements, up through a host of medium-sized industrial or partly industrial towns, right up to the large regional cities such as Glasgow, Manchester or Birmingham and, finally, to London, which in all periods was unique, both in its size, its economic nature and its pace of activity. Within each stratum of this hierarchy each town was individual in character, different in economic and social circumstances. The result was, and is, a rich and varied tapestry of experience across the country.

Similarly, no two cities had identical roles in industry or manufacturing. No other city could claim the '1,000 trades' of Birmingham; Manchester specialised in textiles, while Sheffield produced cutlery and steel, and such specialisms shaped each town's relationships with nearby medium-sized towns (such as, respectively, Bolton or Rotherham) which were involved in the same sectors. This chapter also explores the distinctive characteristics of places that may often be misleadingly coupled together in historical discussion: Glasgow and Edinburgh, Liverpool and Manchester, Dublin and Cork. Yet the great cities of nineteenth-century Britain did have much in common: all had to find solutions to questions about drainage, the provision of clean drinking water and the control of noxious trades; and all had extensive ranges of shops and small-scale manufacturers of consumer goods.

Macaulay's epigraph to this chapter shows that, like modern historians, contemporaries were fascinated by rapidly expanding towns. Circumstances in the late 1830s and early 1840s – economic depression, outbreaks of cholera, revelations about child labour in factories and mines, political agitation by the Chartists, and a growing realisation by professionals and by some politicians of the extent of urban squalor – led to debate among the educated classes about the 'condition of England'. The phrase was coined by the Scottish historian Thomas Carlyle in *Chartism* (1839) and expanded upon in his 1843 polemic *Past and Present*. He drew attention to issues such as inequality, social dislocation and spiritual malaise, caused, he thought, by unbridled manufacturing wealth:

> The condition of England … is justly regarded
> as one of the most ominous, and withal one of
> the strangest, ever seen in this world. England
> is full of wealth, of multifarious produce,
> supply for human want in every kind; yet
> England is dying of inanition. With unabated
> bounty the land of England blooms and grows;
> waving with yellow harvests; thick-studded
> with workshops, industrial implements, with
> fifteen millions of workers, understood to be
> the strongest, the cunningest and the willingest
> our Earth ever had …

Yet this wealth was spread very unequally, in fact immorally. Rich and poor had never been driven so far apart in social experience or in economic means. The growth of materialism, laissez-faire policies, and rampant capitalism, had all undermined the sense of social cohesion that Carlyle instinctively felt had existed in former times.

The images which illustrated these debates were urban. For in towns and cities a dense congregation of people made the problems all too visible: here one could hardly avoid witnessing the harsh inequalities, or the lack of spiritual well-being, bemoaned by Carlyle. No one could doubt that many people in cities lived in over-crowded squalor, and apologists for the factory system had to plead that it was socially beneficent in isolated communities away from smoke, stench and temptation. Yet these harsh realities of life were never the only themes of Britain's urban history, and they should not blind us to the positive developments which can be enumerated: the cultural achievements of Victorian cities in architecture, the establishment of libraries, museums and galleries, the patronage of music and exhibitions, and the diffusion of knowledge through learned societies, were all formidable.

The growth of cities was not a uniquely British phenomenon. Léon Faucher, when declaring the 1840s to be the age of great cities, coupled London, Manchester and Liverpool with Paris, Amsterdam, Vienna, Naples, Madrid, New York, St Petersburg and Moscow. Nevertheless, the spectacular urbanisation of Britain during the eighteenth and first half of the nineteenth centuries was a phenomenon on an unprecedented scale, and its social, economic and geographical impact was more profound than in any other country. In 1700 most British towns and cities remained within their medieval limits, with increasing populations accommodated by building in the courts and yards in historic centres or medieval suburbs. During the eighteenth century, though, most towns began to burst their ancient bounds – a few, such as Edinburgh or Bath, with formally planned developments of architectural distinction. Friedrich Engels thought one of the unique features of London was that it was a 'city in which one can roam for hours without leaving the built-up area and without seeing the slightest sign of the approach of open country'. London was unique, and most other cities of the mid-nineteenth century would have seemed small by comparison. In the industrial heartlands of Lancashire, the West Riding and the West Midlands were many substantial manufacturing and commercial towns which did not attract the attention bestowed on Birmingham or Leeds; among them Rochdale, Wigan, Huddersfield, Halifax, West Bromwich and Walsall. From such towns as these, and even from Glasgow and Manchester, open hillsides were visible (when smoke or fog allowed), and open countryside was accessible from most city centres within no more than an hour's walking.

Cities were centres of trade and commerce. One of the most significant trades was the purchase of energy, and one unifying feature was that the means of conveying coal to cities were improved radically from the eighteenth century onwards. Meanwhile, certain kinds of commerce could stimulate or encourage manufacturing. Tobacco processing and sugar making, for example, developed in cities that traded with the Americas, particularly Glasgow and Liverpool. In others textile-finishing processes were concentrated within the towns, particularly in warehouses, where fabrics were measured and pressed before being exposed for sale. In the eighteenth century most consumer goods, clothing, furniture and footwear, were made by the individual craftsmen who could be found in every town. In larger places there were complex systems of sub-contracting, by which a shoemaker or tailor might act sometimes as a master, and at others undertake work for a more prestigious craftsman. Relatively large businesses supplying such goods were developing by the 1860s, some of them factory-based. In cities there were also concentrations of sophisticated customers – in Manchester in 1861, for example, we know that the range of paper products included fancy boxes, paper tubes, hat boxes and paper bags, and there were makers of fenders, plaster figures, cigars, butchers' skewers and paraffin who would not have found sufficient custom in smaller towns.

In every town some trades, such as milling, malting and tanning, required specialist buildings but employed relatively few workers, and during the eighteenth century breweries were established in almost every town. In the early eighteenth century a few foundries in London, Dublin and Bristol made castings, but by 1800 foundries had grown into engineering concerns capable of producing steam engines and machines for manufacturing, and by 1850 they could be found in most towns. Some forms of manufacturing, such as metal working in Birmingham, Wolverhampton and Sheffield, glove making in Worcester, and hosiery in Nottingham and Leicester, were focused on cities where wholesalers distributed raw materials and collected the products of surrounding regions in warehouses. In the West Riding these functions were performed in impressive piece halls. Exchanges where the raw materials for textile manufacturing were traded were also a feature of the larger cities – in Manchester and Liverpool, for example – as were places where products were authenticated: silver at the Assay Office of 1773; and guns at the Proof House of 1813 in Birmingham.

Great cities were naturally places of thoroughfare, the foci of transport routes, and places where travellers were accommodated. Some were 'towns of passage', places where migrants lingered *en route* to new lives. The Irishmen mining copper at Coniston or making iron at Tow Law doubtless used other places as staging points on their journeys. Such movements often followed family connections, as did those of migrants from the Caribbean and the Punjab in Brixton and Southall in the 1950s. Moving from a rural area to a city before possibly finding employment within its hinterland, was a commonplace of eighteenth- and nineteenth-century working-class experience. The most obvious employment opportunities for under-skilled migrants from rural areas were in jobs involving fetching and carrying – for example, the numerous porters at markets, wharfs and warehouses. In older cities entry into such occupations might be protected by established customs; in most there were systems of casual labour in which racial, religious or family connections as much as strength, intelligence and dexterity determined each morning whether a man might work.

Trade, commerce, industry, and the buying and selling of goods: these were the foundations of the great urban explosion of the industrial revolution.

Urban thinking

Cities generated ideas as well as trade. We have already seen some examples of this: the role of Newcastle-upon-Tyne, for example, in the diffusion of mining and other expertise; the influences that emanated from the universities of Edinburgh and Glasgow; and the generation of developments in mechanical engineering in London, Birmingham, Manchester and Leeds.

One important example is Birmingham's Lunar Society, which began to assemble about 1765 after its leading figures had been brought together by the need to discuss canal business, although the name was adopted later. This informal body, which never had more than 15 members, met most months at the full moon, assembling at Matthew Boulton's Soho House around a well-laden table at two o'clock, and staying until about eight, spending the post-prandial hours examining geological and botanical specimens, scientific instruments, plans and models. Its members included Matthew Boulton, Erasmus Darwin, Thomas Day (an active campaigner against slavery), Richard Lovell Edgeworth, John Fothergill (a merchant apprenticed in Königsberg and Boulton's partner between 1762 and 1782), Samuel Galton junior (armaments manufacturer and Quaker), James Keir the chemist, William Murdock, Joseph Priestley, William Small (a Scots-born doctor who taught mathematics to Thomas Jefferson at Williamsburg, Virginia), Jonathan Stokes, botanist, James Watt, Josiah Wedgwood, John Whitehurst the Derby horologist, and William Withering, physician and botanist. An outer circle who attended occasionally and were in regular contact with some of the members included Sir Joseph Banks, John Baskerville the typographer, Dr Joseph Black, Benjamin Franklin, Robert Augustus Johnson (chemist and clergyman), William Reynolds, John Roebuck, John Smeaton, John Waltire, John Wilkinson, and the painter Joseph Wright of Derby.

Many scientific and technological innovations were discussed around the society's table. This was the most influential provincial grouping of the eighteenth century, but unlike the Society of Arts, the Royal Society, and some philosophical societies, its activities diminished from the 1780s, and its books were dispersed by lottery in 1813.

The Derby Philosophical Society was its offshoot, founded by Erasmus Darwin when he settled in Derby in 1783. Its members included Robert Bage, William and Jedediah Strutt, Josiah Wedgwood, and John Whitehurst. The society acquired books, scientific instruments and fossils, which passed to the city museum in 1858. The Manchester Literary & Philosophical Society, meanwhile, was founded in 1791. Its early history was shaped by the chemist John Dalton, who became a member in 1794, was appointed secretary in 1800 and served as president from 1817 until his death in 1844. Dalton introduced to the society the young Robert Owen. Later members included William Fairbairn and Joseph Whitworth. The Leeds Literary & Philosophical Society was founded in 1819. John Marshall was its president from 1820 to 1826 and Benjamin Gott from 1831 to 1833, and members included Edward Baines, proprietor of the *Leeds Mercury* and MP for the city, and his son Sir Edward Baines, historian of the textile industries. The influence of philosophical societies was extended by such itinerant lecturers as John Waltire and John Banks, but the role of such bodies in fostering thinking that led to social and economic change is difficult to measure. Many manufacturers, even in cities where they flourished, were not members, and the genesis of ideas was often unrelated to formally constituted organisations. A Nottingham lace manufacturer commended to a parliamentary commission in 1841 'the ideas we have from being congregated together'.

Living quarters

In most towns and cities population increased at a prodigious rate during the industrial revolution period, the consequence of a rising birth rate and of inward migration. Construction could not always keep pace with the population increase, and, as many contemporaries pointed out, population densities could be astonishingly high by both earlier and later standards. Alongside the resident population there would arrive in cities a host of visitors, rural traders, itinerant workers and shoppers, which all combined to produce an intensity of street life which it is difficult for a twenty-first-century European to comprehend, although something of it might yet be seen in the cities of India or China. The sellers of food on the streets of Manchester in 1861 give some indications of this — there were hawkers of oatcakes, vegetables, fruit and fish, makers of potted beef, boilers of 'toffy' and makers of sweetmeats.

Some families preferred cellars to other dwellings because of their proximity to the streets. Charitable projects in provincial cities, as in London, had relatively little impact on the lives of those who lived on the streets, and long after 1870 city life was portrayed by the founder of the Salvation Army as a sea in which three million people were threatened by waves of starvation, unemployment, drunkenness, pawnshops, beggary, prostitution, suicide and anarchy.

Each city in the British Isles had a characteristic style of working-class dwelling, and in many places more commodious dwellings in the same style accommodated members of the middle class. Many of the poor lived in tenemented dwellings that once had been occupied by wealthy families, and in most cities there were areas, like the Potteries in west London, where people lived in shack-like cottages amid brick clay pits and heaps of urban refuse. Most working-class houses were constructed in small groups by speculative builders, who either sold the property to landlords or kept it themselves as an investment — the kind of person described by Thomas Cubitt in 1840 as 'a little shopkeeper class of person who has saved a little money in business'. Demand for inexpensive rented accommodation was high, and in periods of prosperity developers built cheaply and quickly, creating in essence the 'slums' of future decades. Many did not own the freeholds of the land on which they built, and therefore had no incentive to construct high-quality dwellings. Engels was quite clear on this point in as far as it affected parts of Manchester:

The outer walls, those of the cellar, which bear the weight of the ground floor and roof, are one whole brick thick at most, the bricks lying with their long sides touching; but I have seen many a cottage of the same height, some in process of building, whose outer walls were but one-half brick [i.e. *circa* 4½ inches] thick. … The object of this is to spare material, but there is also another reason for it; namely, the fact that the contractors never own the land but lease it, according to the English custom, for twenty, thirty, forty, fifty, or ninety-nine years, at the expiration of which time it falls, with everything upon it, back into the possession of the original holder, who pays nothing in return for improvements upon it. The improvements [i.e. the houses] are therefore so calculated by the lessee as to be worth as little as possible at the expiration of the stipulated term. And as such cottages are often built but twenty or thirty years before the expiration of the term, it may easily be imagined that the contractors make no unnecessary expenditures upon them.

A high proportion of residents in Edinburgh, Glasgow, Aberdeen and Dundee lived in multi-storey tenement blocks, a form of building dictated by Scottish land law. There were subtle differences in forms of building between the four cities, but in all of them some tenement blocks were well designed by eminent architects, while others were over-crowded and unhealthy. The tenements built in Barrow-in-Furness have already been noted (see page 342). Newcastle's typical dwelling was the two-storey flat that, in certain configurations, presented the unnerving spectacle of four adjacent doors in a front elevation. In 1900 over half the dwellings on Tyneside were of that type. Working-class dwellings on Wearside were wholly different. In Sunderland there were many hundreds of one-storey, two-room deep cottages built in long terraces. These were still being built in the 1880s when a group of streets at Roker were named after members of Gladstone's cabinet of 1880–85. Intermingled with single-storey terraces were rows of catslide houses, built at much the same time. Dublin and Cork were also characterised by single-storey terraces.

Back-to-back housing was most prevalent in

the West Riding of Yorkshire (especially in Leeds and Bradford), some towns in Lancashire, and the industrial Midlands – where they were numerous in Birmingham, but curiously almost unknown in nearby Wolverhampton, Walsall and Dudley, highlighting the wide variations often apparent between neighbouring places. Maurice Beresford argued convincingly that in Leeds the back-to-back was determined historically, by the building of parallel blind-back terraces on the burgage plots of the medieval town, and the long narrow fields enclosed in the seventeenth century that shaped cul-de-sac developments from the 1780s. Yet Nottingham and Birmingham, where back-to-backs were equally prevalent, had different topographical histories, and some back-to-back terraces, such as those of c.1760 at New Dale, Shropshire, were built despite there being no constraints of space. The back-to-back had an evil reputation by the 1840s, when its construction ceased in Manchester, and the Local Government Act of 1858 enabled councils to prohibit building of new back-to-backs. The lack of through-ventilation was a particular reason for its condemnation by those who espoused the miasmatic theory of the spread of epidemic disease. Nevertheless, in Leeds it was so much the established house type that it continued to be built into the twentieth century, and in other West Riding towns building continued after 1870. In Sheffield most houses were of the 'through' type, but the city's principal idiosyncrasy was the open spaces at the backs of terraces, which were used communally and included ashpits and blocks of privies. In Liverpool the typical dwelling was within an enclosed court. In towns and cities where the numbers of hand-loom weavers multiplied from the 1780s many houses were built with cellar loomshops which, when the trade was displaced by factories with powerlooms, became family dwellings, known in Dundee as 'sunk flats'.

Agitation for the improvement of urban living conditions, the 'health of towns question', was stimulated by high death rates, and particularly by the epidemics of cholera that swept across Britain between 1831–32 and 1866–67, although in some places from the mid-eighteenth century Improvement Acts did ameliorate living conditions where there was political will. The Public Health Act of 1848 enabled the establishment of local boards of health which were able to survey housing problems and take measures towards their resolution by the enforcement of bye-laws concerning matters such as the size of new dwellings, the availability of drainage facilities, ceiling heights and the widths of streets and back alleys. Boards of health could take responsibility for whole towns, disregarding ancient borough or parish boundaries. Some local authorities found that water supplies were available from private companies; others established municipal systems, and all, in due course (in some places not until the 1850s or 1860s), constructed sewage-disposal systems.

Working people's houses from the late eighteenth century onwards can be recognised on early Ordnance Survey maps; if not back-to-back in form, they were usually square or rectangular in plan, and might be of two or three storeys. From about 1850 the 'tunnel back' house, a four-room dwelling with a rear extension comprising a scullery on the ground floor and a third bedroom above, was built in substantial numbers in every sizeable town. When they were built in long terraces their back yards or gardens were accessible through the 'tunnels' which gave the house-type its name. They were built in many sizes and with an infinite variety of degrees of external ornamentation. In larger towns and cities they were built, according to bye-laws, in serried ranks with front and back lanes of uniform width. Architects have observed that the tunnel-back form is an inefficient means of enclosing space, and it was ridiculed by the Garden City Movement. Meakin in 1905 commended houses at Port Sunlight in which 'the unsightly "back addition" is entirely dispensed with'.

The establishment of a local board of health did not guarantee that housing in a town would be healthy and commodious. There was resistance to the imposition of standards, which were seen as inhibiting enterprise and economic growth, and as infringements of landowners' rights to do as they wished with their property. Overcrowding and squalor in particular vicinities could be blamed on the individuals who lived there, but individuals were powerless to provide a water supply or drainage facilities. Nigel Morgan described struggles in Preston during which individual landowners attempted to prevent the appointment of a medical officer of health and the imposition of bye-laws. He showed that bye-laws of 1876 and an Improvement Act of 1880 resulted in significant improvements in the quality of housing built subsequently, although living conditions in the town as a whole remained unhealthy, and in the 1880s infant mortality remained higher than in any other major town in Britain. In most cities public-health legislation ultimately ensured that new building was of acceptable quality. Older housing might benefit from sewerage systems or new water supplies, but alternatively could remain extremely unhealthy – landlords could refuse to connect their cottages to sewers, and oblige their tenants to continue drawing water from wells, springs or rivers. Some poor-quality housing might be demolished as a consequence of schemes to build railways, roads, markets or other public buildings. In London the construction of the railway termini, for instance, swept away extensive areas of working-class dwellings, as had the Regent Street development. No compensation, alternative housing or right of appeal were granted to those tenants who were displaced, and even by 1870 local authorities could do scarcely anything to rehouse the very poor. In most towns all that was possible before the 1890s was some thinning-out of congested housing or the conversion of back-to-backs into through dwellings.

The walls of all but the most expensive houses in cities were constructed with materials that were obtained locally – bricks made from local clay, or stone in places such as Burnley, East Lancashire, Bradford and Stamford, where there were quarries nearby. Roofs were almost always made with imported softwoods, and most were covered with slate or stone flags, although in some areas ceramic tiles were preferred. The railway system made possible more ostentatious ornamentation of frontages, with Bath stone, marbles from Derbyshire, terracotta from Hathern, Stamford or Tamworth, or the ornamental sandstone lintels and sills shaped at the Robin Hood Colliery south of Leeds. The railways also made almost ubiquitous Welsh or Cumbrian slate as a relatively inexpensive roofing material.

Large parts of some cities and towns were from the 1850s laid out by Freehold Land Societies, originally conceived by a James Taylor, a Birmingham Liberal, as a means of creating Liberal votes in county parliamentary constituencies by developing estates of small freehold properties on the fringes of towns. Taylor propagated his ideas energetically. A society would invite subscriptions from the public, limiting the number of shares that any individual could hold. A plot of land was acquired which, when services were laid out, was divided into plots for distribution to members, usually by ballot. On some estates there was a 'front row', facing a main road, where plots were larger and where subscribers were obliged to build houses of higher value than on other streets. The appearance of Freehold Land Society estates is distinctive. They usually follow a grid pattern and typically consist of short terraces of up to six houses, mixed with smaller groups and even individual houses of different dates. Sometimes the owner of several adjacent plots would leave one as garden ground; in 2010 it may remain in cultivation or be the site of a twentieth-century bungalow. Freehold Land Society estates can readily be recognised in Banbury, Kidderminster, Oxford, Lancaster, Preston, Northampton and Shrewsbury, and there are many in Birmingham. Their existence may be revealed by such names as 'Freehold Street', 'Freetown' or 'Union Street'. Some societies aided small-scale speculators rather than owner-occupiers, and some, as in Aston Park, Birmingham, facilitated the creation of middle-class enclaves in which there were resident domestic servants in most households.

In several cities aristocratic or gentry landowners controlled certain areas and allowed building under covenants which ensured that dwellings of high values were constructed, as on the Calthorpe estate on the western side of Birmingham, or in The Park in Nottingham, or the estates of the earls of Derby in Liverpool.

Foul living conditions were not exclusive to large manufacturing cities. Most towns suffered the ravages of cholera in 1832 and for the next few decades. Overcrowded accommodation, polluted water supplies and a lack of drainage could be found in market towns which were unaffected by industry, and in the less favoured areas of stylish resorts and the stateliest of historic towns. Oxford and Cambridge, for example, had much in common apart from their universities. Each had a population of about 28,000 in 1851. Oxford was the focus of road transport services to London from most of Wales (since the lowest bridging point on the river Severn was at Gloucester) and from large parts of the West Midlands, while Cambridge fulfilled a similar role for much of East Anglia. Both were significant inland ports. In Oxford the poor, of the parish of St Thomas, west of the city and the university, many of them transient poor, experienced living conditions analogous to the worst that could be found in manufacturing towns, as did those who lived in the Newmarket Road area of Cambridge. A cheap terrace of a dozen two-room cottages erected on an ill-drained meadow on the edge of a town such as Dorchester, Totnes or Ludlow, with only two privies, a water supply polluted by a graveyard and a tannery, and an average of perhaps as many as eight inhabitants to a house, might disturb a few local doctors or ministers, but it was scarcely a novelty since the poor in such towns had suffered similar conditions for centuries past. Many acres of such housing on the edges of Manchester and Leeds came to trouble the conscience of the nation.

Capital cities

The two ancient capital cities provide contexts in which to consider urban growth. After the Act of Union of 1707 Scots MPs travelled to Westminster, but the centre of the Scottish ecclesiastical and legal system remained in Edinburgh; it was still a garrison city, and as the gathering point for Scotland's nobility and gentry it was served by ambitious retailers. Its university, in the age of the Scottish Enlightenment, influenced economic and social developments throughout the British Isles. In the Old Town are tall tenement-like buildings, some of seventeenth-century date. Planning of the New Town, north of Nor' Loch, began in 1765. The original proposals by James Craig were subsequently modified, and many of the most distinguished buildings were built several decades later.

Manufacturing in Edinburgh, as in London, was dominated by breweries, whose output in 1832 was five times those in Glasgow; in 1896 it was 11 times larger, and comprised about 80 per cent of the beer brewed in Scotland. Distilling was also carried on in Edinburgh; the baronial-style Caledonian Distillery of 1855 was the largest in the country. Most working-class people lived in tenement blocks of up to six storeys, which tended to be larger and deeper than those in Glasgow, and could be baronial or classical in style. Between 1861 and 1876 the Edinburgh Co-operative Building Co. built 11 terraces of two-storey flats at Stockbridge, adorned with insignia of the building trades.

Until 1920 the port of Leith on the Firth of Forth was administratively separate from Edinburgh. It was

◁ For centuries Edinburgh has been the seat of the Scottish legal system and Church. Its castle, which dominates this view, was the home of one of Britain's principal garrisons. The medieval heart of the city was separated from the eighteenth-century new town by the Nor' Loch, which was drained in the early nineteenth century. Three railway companies built stations in the area in the 1840s which were replaced from 1868 by the North British Railway's Waverley Station. Two years later the Caledonian Railway constructed its own Prince's Street Station.

an ancient burgh, its core a tangle of warehouses, tenements and merchants' mansions crowded within sixteenth-century fortifications near the mouth of the Water of Leith. The port's Baltic and whaling trades prospered in the eighteenth century and stimulated the growth of boat building and its attendant trades. The first wet docks were constructed in the second decade of the nineteenth century and provided space for warehouses, timber yards and glassworks. Coal was exported, particularly to Russia and Scandinavia, and returning colliers brought cargoes of sawn timber. Dock construction continued in the mid-nineteenth century. The Quayside Mills of 1825 were the first of many corn mills around the harbour, and from the 1880s new mills began to produce flour from Canadian grain.

Dublin was a colonial capital, in the eighteenth century the social centre for a land-owning class,

A late nineteenth-century plan of the port of Leith showing the tangled streets of the town's medieval core and the space for trading activities created by the construction of wet docks. The construction of the Edinburgh Dock was about to begin at the time the map was published. As the map shows, Leith docks were approached by railways from two directions. Leith was home to many industries, including the milling of grain, pottery and glass making, whaling and the distilling and bonding of whisky.

CARNEGIE COLLECTION

The Guinness brewery at St James's Gate, Dublin, founded in 1759, after just over a century of growth in the early 1860s, when it extended over 59 acres. From George Measom, *The Official Illustrated Guide to the Great Southern & Western and Midland Great Western Railways of Ireland* (London: Measom, 1866).

BY COURTESY OF THE IRONBRIDGE GORGE MUSEUM TRUST

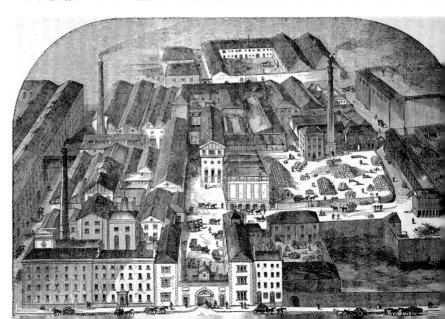

many of whom held estates on both sides of the Irish Sea – and after the merging of the English and Irish parliaments in 1800, an increasingly uneasy community. The elegance of Dublin's central areas was due to the Commissioners for the Making of Wide and Convenient Streets, who between 1757 and 1840 laid out new thoroughfares and set standards for developers. The architect James Gandon was responsible for the Customs House of 1781–91, the Four Courts of 1786–96, the King's Inns of 1795–1816, and the extension to the Houses of Parliament on College Green (now the Bank of Ireland) which was the work of Sir Edward Lovett Pearce. The river Liffey was crossed by the Mellows (Queen's) Bridge of 1764–68, designed

by Charles Vallancy, and by Gandon's O'Connell (Carlisle) Bridge of 1791. The crossings of the early nineteenth century were iron spans, the Wellington footbridge of 1816 cast at Coalbrookdale, the Sean Heuston (King's) Bridge of 1827–28, designed by George Papworth and cast at the city's Royal Phoenix Ironworks, and the Rory O'More (Victoria & Albert) Bridge, a single iron arch with Romanesque detailing, supplied in 1858 by Robert Daglish's foundry at St Helen's. Dublin was Ireland's principal port for trade with the rest of the British Isles, and its harbour was improved following plans made by William Bligh. The South Wall was completed in 1790 and the North Wall in 1820–25. The docks designed by James Gandon

There were important distilleries as well as breweries in the Irish capital. This engraving published in 1845 shows the whiskey distillery of William Jameson & Co. in Marrowbone Lane. To the rear of the site are the extensive multi-storey bonds, found at most distilleries, in which whiskey (or whisky, in Scotland) was matured in casks.

Characteristic single-storey working-class dwellings in the Portobello area of Dublin, close to the banks of the Grand Canal.

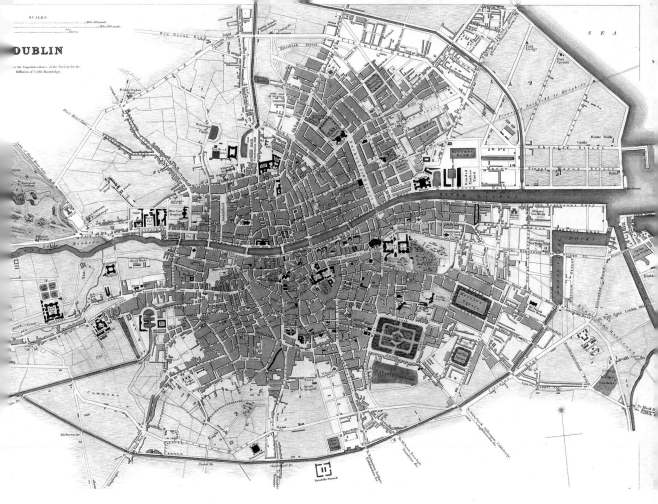

A map of Dublin published in 1836 by Baldwin & Cradock. This was before the construction of railways, but the docks at Ringsend on the south bank of the river Liffey and at the North Wall on the north bank can readily recognised, as can the Grand Canal which extended from the former around the south side of the city, and Royal Canal which traced an arc to the north.

CARNEGIE COLLECTION

and William Jessop and built in 1792–96 at Ringsend, where the Grand Canal joined the river Liffey, were the most extensive in contemporary Europe, and other docks were built on the north bank of the river near its junction with the Royal Canal.

Dublin's population grew from about 9,000 to about 200,000 between 1700 and 1800 and had reached 254,810 by 1851, 263,751 in 1861 and 267,727 in 1871. Most of its working class were employed in the provision of services, and larger manufacturing concerns were few. The most celebrated was founded in 1759 by Arthur Guinness, who leased a small brewery on the western side of the city. From 1799 the company brewed stout, which by the 1830s could be bought in almost every town in Great Britain

(in 1861, for instance, the Dublin Porter Warehouse in Bristol employed 11 men). By that time the brewery extended over 59 acres, and only four British breweries consumed more malt. Textile manufacturing in Dublin was dominated by one of the city's leading retailers, Pim Brothers of Great George Street. The company's enterprises included a weaving factory that made fashionable fabrics incorporating silk yarns, a dyeworks, and the Greenmount spinning mill which employed more than 600 people. Another retailing concern, the ironmongers Joshua Edmundson & Co., operated the Stafford engineering works whose products included gas equipment for country estates.

The observation of Friedrich Engels that 'the poorer districts of Dublin are among the ugliest and

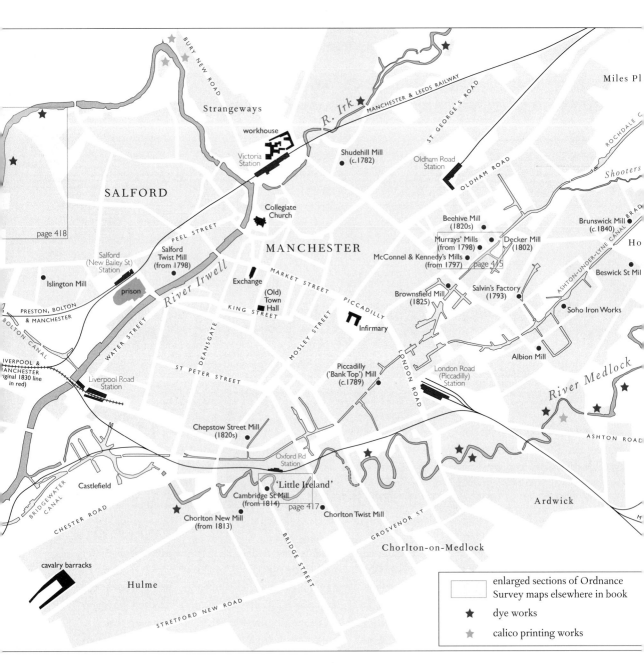

Map labels (clockwise/by region):

BURY NEW ROAD

Strangeways

Miles Pl

R. Irk

MANCHESTER & LEEDS RAILWAY

ST GEORGE'S ROAD

ROCHDALE C

workhouse

Shudehill Mill
(c.1782)

Oldham Road
Station

OLDHAM ROAD

Shooters

Victoria
Station

SALFORD

Collegiate
Church

Beehive Mill
(1820s)

Brunswick Mill
(c.1840)

Bra

page 418

MANCHESTER

Murrays' Mills
(from 1798)

Decker Mill
(1802)

Ho

PEEL STREET

McConnel & Kennedy's Mills
(from 1797)   page 415

ASHTON-UNDER-LYNE CANAL

Beswick St Mil

Salford
(New Bailey St)
Station

Salford
Twist Mill
(from 1798)

Exchange

MARKET STREET

Brownsfield Mill
(1825)

Salvin's Factory
(1793)

Soho Iron Works

Islington Mill

prison

(Old)
Town
Hall

PICCADILLY

River Irwell

KING STREET

PRESTON, BOLTON
& MANCHESTER

Infirmary

Albion Mill

MOSLEY STREET

River Medlock

BOLTON CANAL

LIVERPOOL &
MANCHESTER
(original 1830 line
in red)

WATER STREET

DEANSGATE

ST PETER STREET

Piccadilly
('Bank Top') Mill
(c.1789)

LONDON ROAD

London Road
(Piccadilly)
Station

Liverpool Road
Station

Chepstow Street Mill
(1820s)

ASHTON ROAD

Oxford Rd
Station

BRIDGEWATER
CANAL

Castlefield

'Little Ireland'

page 417

Ardwick

Cambridge St Mill
(from 1814)

Chorlton Twist Mill

CHESTER ROAD

Chorlton New Mill
(from 1813)

GROSVENOR ST

M

BRIDGE STREET

Chorlton-on-Medlock

cavalry barracks

Hulme

enlarged sections of Ordnance
Survey maps elsewhere in book

★ dye works

★ calico printing works

STRETFORD NEW ROAD

Manchester around 1850, showing the locations of significant cotton mills, dyeworks and printworks, as well as the town's topography and principal transport infrastructure. According to an early census by Thomas Percival in 1773 the town's population was 23,000. By 1851 it stood at 401,000 (including Salford across the Irwell). Léon Faucher in 1844 described Manchester as 'the most extraordinary settlement, the most interesting, and in some respects the most monstrous that social progress had yet produced'. To him and others Manchester epitomise the phenomenon of dense urban development built in association with large new factories. On this map only the most important, significan or noteworthy of the cotton factories are shown. As well as manufacturing, Manchester also developed a dominant role in the trading of cotton; some of the largest and the most notable surviving buildings around the city centre are the warehouses where textile goods were displayed and sold as well as stored. The significance of the canal network is obvious, with many mills either fronting a canal or having sho branches built right into the factories. The original terminus of the Liverpool & Manchester Railway, at Liverpool Road, is also shown.

most revolting in the world' may not have been based on first-hand observation but it was not unduly exaggerated. Many of Dublin's poor lived in tenements in substantial houses which had been abandoned by the wealthy. The more prosperous, together with the city's armies of clerks, occupied tunnel-back houses similar to those in English cities. There were also large areas of single-storey houses. Some, like the birthplace of Sean O'Casey at No. 9 Innisfallen Parade, appear to have consisted of little more than one principal room. O'Casey conveys the tensions of late nineteenth-century Dublin, when soldiers paraded 'like figures taken out of a toy-box' on royal birthdays, but were confined to barracks to avoid provoking disorder on other occasions. Manufacturing in Dublin probably had a lesser presence than in any British city of comparable size, yet the city's death rate was the highest, an indication that urban squalor was not simply the consequence of the growth of manufacturing industries.

Towns of the North and the Midlands

Manchester, with Salford on the opposite bank of the river Irwell, was perceived around 1840 as the symbol of the economic energy which had been unleashed in previous decades, and of the social ills that were epitomised in the 'Condition of England' question. In 1843 Carlyle wrote of 'ever toiling Manchester, its smoke and soot all burnt'. Faucher in 1844 considered Manchester 'the most extraordinary settlement, the most interesting and in some respects the most monstrous that social progress had yet produced', and the same year J. G. Kohl asserted that, 'never since the world began was there a town like it, in its outward appearance, its wonderful activity, its mercantile and manufacturing prosperity and its remarkable moral and political phenomena'. When Sidonia in Disraeli's *Coningsby* declared that the age of ruins was past, his companion asked if he had seen Manchester.

Manchester grew during the eighteenth century from a market town where textiles were traded into a manufacturing city, initially of three-storey loom-shops and from 1780 of steam-powered textile mills, including by 1810 some buildings of extraordinary size. (Manchester's role in the textile industry is discussed in Chapter 9.) Its population grew from 94,876 in 1801 to 237,832 in 1831 to 339,000 in 1861. Its role as a commercial rather than a manufacturing centre was observed by Hugh Miller in 1846, who wrote, 'We see whole streets of warehouses, – dead, dingy, gigantic buildings, barred out from the light, and, save where here and here a huge wagon stands, lading or unlading, under the mid-air crane'.

Working-class housing of the late eighteenth and early nineteenth centuries has long ceased to be occupied, although some buildings survived to be surveyed before they were demolished, cocooned in commercial properties, and there have been some archaeological excavations of housing sites. A house in John Street, one of 138 built in the 1820s in a development called Irk Town, was condemned in 1903 but survived in industrial use until 1982. The four-room two-storey houses with cellar dwellings beneath were clearly unhealthy from the time they were built, and Irk Town was the subject of disparaging remarks by Engels and A. B. Reach. Excavations in George Leigh Street, Ancoats, revealed the existence of rows of back-to-back houses, single-room in plan, with the spaces in between filled in with a further back-to-back row. The older dwellings were remodelled into through-houses in the 1880s and the infilling demolished.

One of the most notorious concentrations of squalor in Manchester was in Little Ireland, a group of back-to-back terraces comprising Wakefield Street, Anvil Street, Forge Street, Frank Street and William Street within a bend on the Manchester side of the river Medlock. Interspersed with the crumbling houses were a whip-string factory, an iron foundry, and a small cotton mill (see map on page 417). On the Chorlton-on-Medlock side of the river were several large textile mills built on a grid of streets that had been laid out in the 1790s. The most imposing were erected for H. H. Birley (who led the Yeomanry during the 'Peterloo Massacre' of 1819). In the 1820s the Birley family went into partnership with Charles Mackintosh in a mill which was visited by the King of Saxony in 1844.

Friedrich Engels, the son of a cotton manufacturer from the Wuppertal, arrived in Manchester at the age of 22 in 1842. His radical views were reinforced by what he saw of the factory system and the evils which he considered it to have engendered. While parts of his account of the condition of the working class were based on secondary sources, he knew Manchester well after living in the town for some years, and gaining local knowledge from Mary Burns, an Irish-born mill girl who took him to places where he might have feared to tread unaccompanied. He was appalled by the cottages of Little Ireland; his well-known published account can largely be corroborated from other sources, and it retains its power to shock:

The most horrible spot (if I should describe all the separate spots in detail I should never come to the end) lies on the Manchester side, immediately south-west of Oxford Road, and is known as Little Ireland. In a rather deep hole, in a curve of the Medlock and surrounded on all four sides by tall factories and high embankments, covered with buildings, stand two groups of about two hundred cottages, built chiefly back to back, in which live about four thousand human beings [i.e. an average of 20 per house], most of them Irish. The cottages are old, dirty, and of the smallest sort, the streets uneven, fallen into ruts and in part without drains or pavement; masses of refuse, offal and sickening filth lie among standing pools in all directions; the atmosphere is poisoned by the effluvia from these, and laden and darkened by the smoke of a dozen tall factory chimneys. A horde of ragged women and children swarm about here, as filthy as the swine that thrive upon the garbage heaps and in the puddles. In short, the whole rookery furnishes such a hateful and repulsive spectacle as can hardly be equalled in the worst court on the Irk. The race that lives in these ruinous cottages, behind broken windows, mended with oilskin, sprung doors, and rotten door-posts, or in dark, wet cellars, in measureless filth and stench, in this atmosphere penned in as if with

a purpose, this race must really have reached the lowest stage of humanity …

Similar accounts were written by Kohl and by de Tocqueville, who called the area a 'watery land which nature and art have contributed to keep damp'.

The unhealthiness of the environment was exposed by Dr James Kay, who was born in Rochdale, studied in Edinburgh and worked in Dublin before practising in Manchester during the first cholera epidemic of 1832. Known as James Kay-Shuttleworth after his marriage in 1842, he was influential as a civil servant in the development of popular education, and in 1861–65 was vice-chairman of the relief committee during the Lancashire 'cotton famine'. His work drew attention to streets that were unpaved and houses that were undrained and unventilated and surrounded by pigsties. He pointed out that Mancunians with the abilities and contacts to improve conditions mostly lived away from squalid areas. Segregation within the working class was perceived by Reach in 1849, who observed that in prosperous times the Manchester operative need never want – he was accustomed to eat 'flesh meat' regularly, often sealed with potatoes in a pasty. He noticed that workers leaving Birley's factory were well dressed and well shod, suggesting that they lived in unostentatious comfort. It is doubtful whether those he saw were making their way to Little Ireland, for much of Manchester's squalor arose from its role as a 'town of passage', a magnet for migrants which provided an abundance of unskilled casual work. Reach visited most of the city's working-class areas and acutely observed the differences between them. Working men uniformly lived in two-storey dwellings, some of which in the older areas had cellars beneath, but they were not to be found in more recently built quarters. Better furnishings, he observed, went with better housing, 'a very fair proportion of what was deal in Ancoats was mahogany in Hulme', where he saw wallpapered rooms with corner cupboards, glass and china ornaments, small steel engravings, sometimes a barometer, and almost always a clock. Reach concluded that of Manchester's squalor was due to its rapid growth after the erection of mills, when speculators ran up housing which was insanitary from the time it was first occupied.

When the large-scale Ordnance Survey map was published in 1849 there were many concentrations of back-to-back houses in Manchester and Salford. In the grids of streets north and south of the Ancoats mills, built from the 1790s, back-to-back terraces were intermingled with through-houses with steps at their fronts, indicating that they probably included cellar loomshops. Cellar dwellings, as in Preston, were the consequence of the boom in handloom weaving of the 1780s and 1790s.

The construction of new back-to-backs in Manchester was prohibited in 1842 and few were built thereafter. In Hulme, commended by Reach, many streets already laid out were not built-up in 1849. Few of the completed houses were back-to-backs, and only a small number had cellar loomshops. The majority were parallel terraces with narrow back alleys between them, very like the 'bye-law houses' built in many cities after the establishment of boards of health. Manchester's outer suburbs were spacious and drew favourable comments. Aikin commended the merchant houses in Ardwick Green, which he thought resembled the West End of London. Mogg was impressed in 1840 by rows, terraces, places and parades which embraced 'every style of architecture, interspersed with villas in the Italian style, and Swiss and Gothic cottages of considerable beauty'. Victoria Park off Oxford Road, an enclosed estate in the manner of London's squares, was established by Act of Parliament in 1837. In the 1840s it attracted many prominent Mancunians, particularly members of the Anti-Corn Law League, and remained a private estate until the 1890s.

Manchester became a corporate borough in 1838, and with the authority that was provided by subsequent sanitary legislation the city's built environment did begin to change. The tenth anniversary of the repeal of the Corn Laws was marked in 1856 with the inauguration of the Free Trade Hall, designed by Edward Walters. In 1853 Manchester received city status and four years later it hosted a vast and memorable art exhibition on the site of the present Old Trafford football ground. The Hallé Orchestra played at the Free

Trade Hall from 1858, and a decade later construction began of Alfred Waterhouse's magnificent town hall, whose interiors symbolise the splendours and the contradictions of Victorian urban life. Nowhere were those contradictions more evident than in Manchester. Aspects of the city horrified visitors, and the extent of the degrading conditions in which many people lived was quantified by Kay. Nevertheless, just as the factories in Ancoats were not typical cotton mills, so the living conditions in Little Ireland were not characteristic of those of Manchester's working class, many of whom lived in tolerable comfort, even if under an almost permanent pall of smoke.

Leeds did not attract attention in the 1840s in the way that Manchester did. The town's roles in the textile industry and mechanical engineering, and its place in a coalfield, are discussed above (pages 88–91, 248–50). It was a compact town until the 1770s, but underwent two periods of exceptional growth, in 1772–93 and 1821–31, the increasing population being first accommodated by the erection of houses infilling yards and folds, but in the mid-1780s the first streets of two-storey back-to-back houses were built. The back-to-back terrace became the characteristic Leeds working-class dwelling, at first to the east of the ancient centre then, after attempts to create elegant middle-class neighbourhoods at the west end were frustrated by industrial pollution, in that direction too. Most of the great textile mills of Leeds were built in isolation, and quickly surrounded by back-to-backs. Many working-class people found these houses congenial – one man told Reach they were better than through-houses because 'one heats the other like two in a bed'. But the squalor in the east end of Leeds was equalled in scarcely any other city, albeit derived from the lack of drainage rather than the house type.

Kohl found Leeds 'a dirty, smoky, disagreeable town … perhaps the ugliest and least attractive town in England'. Reach, who was familiar with bad housing conditions, wrote that he had plodded through 'streets in which the undisturbed mud lay in wreaths from wall to wall', where pigs treated any open space as a sty, and where privies were ruinous and horribly foul.

John Freeth in 1769 described Birmingham as 'the great Mechanic Warehouse of the World'. The city prospered by working metals, which for the most part had been smelted elsewhere, using the skills of its artisans and power obtained from the river Rea and the Hockley Brook. The opening of the canal from Wednesbury in 1769 provided a source of cheap coal, and Birmingham became the (often congested) hub of the Midlands canal system, while later the junctions between the different railway companies at Curzon Street and Lawley Street in 1837–42 were at the centre of the developing national network. The Soho Manufactory and the engine business of Boulton

and Watt, together with the Lunar Society, brought contacts with innovative thinking throughout the British Isles. Parts of eighteenth-century Birmingham, particularly the streets north of Colmore Row leading to the church of St Paul, Hockley, had a distinct air of elegance, while the fine town hall of 1834, designed by Joseph Hansom and Edward Welch, shows that the city had acquired a sense of civic pride. Birmingham's population rose from 70,670 in 1801 to 143,986 in 1832 and 344,000 in 1871.

Kohl and other travellers of the 1840s contrasted

Birmingham, with the surrounding parishes later incorporated within the city, had a population in 1861 of about 350,000. This map, published in 1864, shows that several areas which were thoroughly urbanised by 1900, such as Bordesley Green, Adderley and Harborne, remained largely rural. There was a clear distinction between the dense networks of streets in the manufacturing quarters to the north, east and south, and the spacious and ordered suburban development on the Calthorpe Estate in Edgbaston to the west. It also portrays the ambitious development of villas in Aston New Town, south of the park that surrounds Aston Hall, whose pretensions were frustrated by the proliferation of odoriferous or noxious manufacturing processes. As in other large cities, there were substantial institutions on the suburban fringes, such as the workhouse and lunatic asylum at Winson Green. The map shows the Rotton Park reservoir of the Birmingham Canal Navigation (marked 'Canal Reservoir') from which water flowed into the original level of the canal across Telford's new line of the 1820s over the Engine Arm Aqueduct (see page 114), and portrays the Duddeston Viaduct (see page 187) as if it were carrying traffic.

Birmingham with Manchester, observing a city of workshops rather than factories – a view that was basically sound and echoed by such historians as Asa Briggs and Maxime Berg. Manufacturers produced buckles and buttons, guns, snuff boxes, medals, corkscrews, gimlets and bradawls, axes and hoes, pencil cases, chandeliers, gold and silver chains, tubes, wire, brass fittings for cabinets and coffins, whistles and numerous other 'toys'. Although Matthew Boulton demonstrated, by building the Soho Manufactory in 1761, that metal items could effectively be produced in a large factory, most Birmingham goods continued to be made in workshops. The Soho Manufactory was closed in 1848 and demolished in 1863. Joseph Gillott began to use machinery to manufacture pens in the 1830s, and in 1839–40 built the substantial Victoria Works, where 500 people were employed in 1870. George Elkington's electro-plating concern in Newhall Street employed about 500 in 1850, and about 1,000 in 1880, chiefly makers of jewellery and cutlery. But otherwise, and rather similar to the cutlery sector in Sheffield, small concerns remained characteristic of the city and there were some 700 workshops in the Jewellery Quarter alone in 1880.

Until the 1860s the predominant house type in working-class areas of Birmingham was the back-to-back, most commonly built around a court, with access via a 'tunnel' through-houses fronting a street. There were between 9 and 22 houses in the various courts in the area around the conserved back-to-back houses in Inge Street, which was built up between 1802 and the 1830s. Increasing numbers of tunnel-back houses were built as Birmingham expanded from the 1850s, but there were still 43,000 back-to-back houses in the city in 1914. Pollution was a major problem here as elsewhere. Kohl's comment as he left Birmingham in 1842 might apply to any city where there were coal-based manufactures: 'I was delighted to have a clear view of the sky again. In Birmingham you can form no speculation on the weather. The rain is not felt till it has worked its way through the smoke and the sun shows himself only as a yellow patch. Sunrise and sunset, stars and moonlight are things unknown.'

In the mid-eighteenth century Nottingham was celebrated for its sociability, for the assemblies, concerts and race meetings attended by wealthy people who lived in elegant houses lining its principal streets. It was a river port, handling substantial traffic on the Trent, and was well supplied with fuel from collieries in its immediate vicinity. From 1796 the Nottingham Canal provided a direct link with the coalfields on the Nottinghamshire/Derbyshire border, and associated waterways made connections with other parts of the Midlands. Nottingham prospered with the hosiery trade, and the market for yarn attracted both Hargreaves and Arkwright to the city. Cotton factories flourished in the late eighteenth century and some were still working in 1870, chiefly providing yarn for hosiery and lace workers. Lace making expanded from the 1820s and by 1870 was increasingly a factory-based industry.

The nature of the city changed with the growth of manufacturing. The population increased from about 7,000 in 1700 to about 12,000 in 1750, but the development of Nottingham, like that of Cambridge, Coventry and Leicester, was shaped by the geography of its ancient common fields, which were not enclosed until an Act of Parliament of 1845. The parishes beyond the common land consequently experienced rapid growth in the early nineteenth century. The population of Lenton, whose common fields were enclosed in 1796, grew from 893 in 1801 to 5,589 in 1851, while that of Radford, enclosed in 1768 and 1798, from 2,269 to 12,637 in the same period. The population of Nottingham itself almost doubled in forty years, from 28,861 in 1801 to 52,164 in 1841, but the constraints imposed by the girdle of unenclosed common fields meant exceptional densities of building in the city itself: in 1841 some 11,612 houses were crammed into just 530 acres. In 1831–32 more than 7,000 of those dwellings were back-to-backs, most of them in courts entered by tunnels no more than three feet wide. The city centre was no longer a place of sociability, and a parliamentary commission in 1845 found over-crowding worse than in any other industrial town. The Enclosure Act of 1845, which released 1,069 acres of common land, began a process of improvement, making land available for housing, and regulating the standard of new housing, effectively ending the construction of back-to-backs.

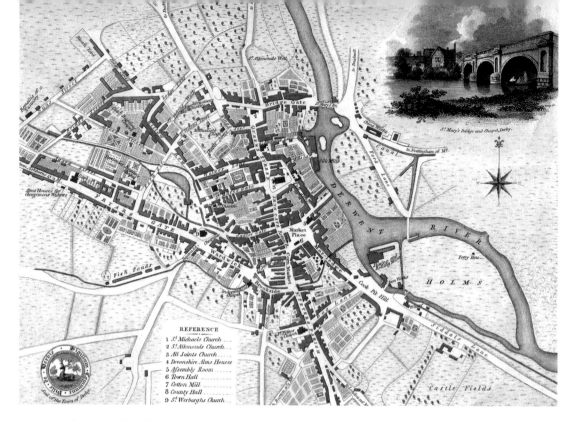

⋏ A map of Derby published by Cole & Roper in 1806. The town's population was only about 12,000, but it was already an important industrial centre. Derby was well supplied with water power, and the silk mill on the river Derwent established in 1721 set the pattern for multi-storey factories in every sector of the textile industry. Cotton spinning and tape weaving were important in the early nineteenth century, as well as pottery manufacturing and lead processing. From the 1840s Derby also became the hub of the Midland Railway.

The availability of building land made possible the demolition of older commercial property, which in turn enabled the construction from the 1850s of the imposing warehouses that comprise the city's 'Lace Market'. The commissioners also set aside 130 acres for recreational and open space, north of the centre.

An elegant suburb, The Park, grew up in Lenton parish, once the deer park of Nottingham Castle. Some plots were offered for sale from 1807, but major developments began in the 1820s at the instigation of the 4th Duke of Newcastle, and were continued under the 5th Duke who succeeded in 1851 and appointed the celebrated Nottingham architect Thomas Chambers Hine as surveyor in 1854. The basic layout was established by the 1860s, but many plots were not occupied for several decades. It remains one of the best preserved of all High Victorian suburbs.

Derby was still a small town in 1801, with a population of fewer than 11,000 (compared with about 7,000 three decades earlier), but by 1871 more than 50,000 people were living in the borough with more than 11,000 in contiguous areas beyond its boundaries. It was a thoroughfare town, the meeting point of several roads including the main route from London to Manchester and Glasgow. The improvement of the river Derwent in 1721 provided a navigable link with the river Trent. Derby was notable for the variety of its industries. Its silk mill was built in 1721; Jedediah Strutt began to manufacture hosiery there in 1759; and by the 1860s its townscape was dotted with multi-storey mills producing ribbons, lace, and silk, woollen and elastic fabrics. Unlike Nottingham, whose town authorities showed little desire to allow a railway to be built into the town, Derby chose to become an important railway town, the hub of the Midland Railway, which erected its locomotive and

There were coach-building workshops in almost every town of consequence in the mid-nineteenth century. The works of Herbert and Arthur Holmes at Derby was a relatively large enterprise. As in most such works, carriages were assembled in first-floor workshops from components which had been fabricated on the ground floor. The engraving shows clearly the ramps by which completed vehicles were eased down into the courtyard.

BY COURTESY OF THE IRONBRIDGE GORGE MUSEUM TRUST

The cast-iron arch of 1878 which carried the Great Northern Railway over Friargate in Derby bears the city's coat of arms. It was a product of the local foundry of Andrew Handyside, which happened to be a substantial enterprise of national significance, but smaller bridges in many parts of the country were cast by market-town foundries of modest size. This was perhaps the last cast-iron bridge that was of any consequence, and it was erected almost exactly a century after the Severn had been spanned by the Iron Bridge near Coalbrookdale.

PHOTOGRAPH: CARNEGIE

carriage works in the city, together with some housing for its workers. James Eastwood & Sons made loco-motives and carriages at the Litchurch Works, which employed several hundred people in 1861, when it was fulfilling export orders from France, Russia, the United States and Australia. The Britannia Foundry, taken over in 1848 by the Scot Andrew Handyside, is well known for its ornamental and structural iron-work, including the bridge of 1878 which carried the Great Northern Railway over Friargate, but it also produced steam engines and machinery for breweries, collieries, waterworks, and the government arma-ments works at Woolwich and Enfield. The Union Foundry was established in 1785 and in the 1860s the grandsons of the founder claimed that the planing

machine had been invented there. The Morledge and Mill Hill works operated in the 1860s by William Thomas Cox comprised one of the largest lead-processing concerns in Britain.

Derby is actually one example of a widespread and important urban type – the middle rank of manufac-turing town – which has recently been given renewed attention by historians such as Jon Stobart and Stephen Caunce. With populations ranging roughly between 50,000 and 120,000 in 1871, these were acknowledged centres of manufacturing and commerce. As indus-trialisation progressed such towns could be found in surprising numbers in parts of the North and the Midlands. In particular, Caunce identifies 'an intense but discontinuous urban belt [which] stretches across

Britain's narrow waist, from Liverpool to Hull … a central zone only 70 miles long by 30 wide … which forms one of the Europe's greatest population concentrations'. Often separated by only a few miles, these individual industrial towns might well harbour fierce economic and social rivalries, but they also thrived on common trading links and shared networks of contacts and expertise, their ruling and manufacturing elites coming together in trade organisations, or meeting for business and social exchange in larger regional centres such as Manchester or Leeds. In these towns could be found some of the greatest economic dynamism and some of the densest clusters of industry.

Some of these medium towns, such as Norwich, Preston and Nottingham, although experiencing industrial growth, had long been regarded as regional capitals. Some, including Blackburn, Bolton, Halifax, Huddersfield, Oldham, Stockport and Wolverhampton, were ancient market towns of modest size where manufacturing had stimulated rapid growth. A substantial proportion of Britain's manufacturing capacity was concentrated in such places. Three notable examples, Bath, Blackpool and Brighton, were resorts, while two, Plymouth and Portsmouth, housed Royal Navy dockyards. The inhabitants of Sunderland gained their livings by mining and shipping coal, but also by using coal to make pottery and glass. Swansea was a coal-shipping port, but also the principal centre of copper working in Britain. Some towns were wholly new creations of the industrial revolution period, including the ports of Birkenhead and Middlesbrough, West Bromwich, the only large town of the West Midlands coalfield that was not an ancient market town, and the six 'towns' which from 1925 made up the city of Stoke-on-Trent. Many towns in Lancashire, Yorkshire and the West Midlands, which had grown rapidly during the industrial revolution, achieved municipal status in the decades after 1870, but steadily lost their powers to govern themselves during the second half of the twentieth century.

Facing the Atlantic

Liverpool was often coupled with Manchester in accounts of industrial England, but the two cities were (and still are) very different. Liverpool prospered and began to grow in the eighteenth century from the Atlantic trade, processing tobacco and sugar, handling imported cotton, and deriving wealth from the slave trade that took place 3,000 miles away. Improvements to the inland-waterways system gave it direct communication with the principal industrial communities in the North and the Midlands. Its civic pride was expressed in the town hall built to the design of the elder John Wood in 1749–54. Liverpool was one of the first ports to have a wet dock for trading purposes, in 1715, and the area of its docks system, as described above, quadrupled between 1824 and 1860, when it became the pre-eminent west-coast port in Britain. The rise of coal-based manufactures from the 1750s and their decline from the 1790s is discussed in Chapter 6. In the nineteenth century Liverpool was a city where goods were handled rather than made, although processing industries such as sugar refining had a considerable presence, and several engineering companies profited during the first decades of main-line railways. Liverpool was pre-eminently a town of passage, through which Irish people travelled *en route* to other parts of England, and where many – Irish, Scots, Welsh, English and east Europeans – awaited passages overseas. Liverpool also became the long-term home of very large numbers of Welsh and Irish migrants, reflected in many Welsh language newspapers and chapels and a multitude of Roman Catholic churches and schools.

Liverpool's characteristic working-class dwellings were three-storey back-to-back houses arranged around enclosed courts. They were often structurally integrated with houses fronting main streets, through which tunnels provided access. Most had cellars which were let as separate dwellings. The layout is largely explained by the high cost of land, the supply of which was controlled by three great landed estates. Occupied cellars, of which there were 1,728 in the city in 1790, were a fashion. Taylor showed that to dig a cellar probably cost more than enclosing the same space in a building above ground, and in the 1840s rents for

A panorama of Liverpool from an imaginary viewpoint above Birkenhead published in 1847 by the London company established by Rudolf Ackermann. The Albert Docks complex stands almost at the centre of the waterfront, with the Canning Dock behind it. The panorama also shows the Brunswick, Queen's, Salthouse, Waterloo and Clarence docks, and prominent buildings include St George's Hall, the Town Hall and the New Custom House. The course of the Leeds & Liverpool Canal can be seen to the top left of the image.

cellars were as high as those for first-floor rooms. Faucher remarked that street life was a dominant factor in the lives of Liverpool's young people – one father told him he preferred living in a cellar because it was close to the street for his children.

Geography allowed Glasgow, too, to prosper from maritime trade and transatlantic connections. Defoe described Glasgow as the emporium of the west of Scotland, 'a large, stately, and well-built city … one of the cleanliest, most beautiful, and best-built cities in Great Britain'. Perhaps more than any other city in the British Isles, Glasgow exemplifies the paradoxes of the period between 1700 and 1870. It was a city where living conditions were squalid, where systems of casual labour created perpetual uncertainty for working people, and where sectarian antagonisms were endemic. It was equally a city of outstanding architecture: the Trades Hall of 1794 by Robert Adam, Hutchesons' Hospital of 1802–05, the Royal Exchange of 1829 by David Hamilton, and the Caledonia Road

Free Church of 1856–57 and the church in St Vincent Street of 1859, both by Alexander 'Greek' Thomson, are buildings of exceptional quality. The same architects were responsible for numerous warehouses, tenements and villas. Glasgow was one of the first cities to bring in clean water from the mountains, with the pipeline from Loch Katrine opened in 1859.

In the eighteenth century Glasgow's prosperity was drawn from the Atlantic trade, particularly from the processing of tobacco and sugar from the Caribbean which were exchanged for Scottish glass, pottery, textiles and candles. Scottish (that is, Glasgow) merchants exercised a stranglehold over much of Caribbean trade and grew exceptionally rich as a result. There were also substantial trades with European ports. The proceeds of trading enabled the creation of a new town west of the ancient city, where large, fashionable stone mansions and terraces were constructed over extensive areas off the Great Western Road. The Clyde Navigation Trust, established in

1809, made it possible for ocean-going ships to reach Glasgow, but until the Kingston Dock was opened in 1867 they could only berth at riverside quays. The Monkland Canal, opened in 1791, supplied Glasgow with coal, and provided access via its junction with the Forth & Clyde Canal to other parts of the Lowlands.

Cotton spinning developed on a large scale from the 1780s and remained a substantial and still-expanding industry in 1870, although by then Glasgow was relatively less important in the cotton trade than previously. Engineering prospered, particularly the building of iron ships, marine engines, sugar-processing machinery, bridges, copper vats and railway locomotives, of which more were built in Glasgow than in any other British city. Macquorn Rankine, Professor

of Civil Engineering and Mechanics at Glasgow from 1855, fostered creative co-operation between the university and engineers.

The St Rollox Chemical Works, established in 1799 by Charles Tennant, became one of Glasgow's largest industrial concerns (see page 394). Tennant's partner until 1814 was Charles Mackintosh, who patented his process for making waterproof fabrics in 1823. By 1840 the works, then managed by John Tennant, employed 500 men, included more than 100 retorts and furnaces, and consumed 600 tons of coal a week. It could be located by the 435 foot (134 m) high Tennant's Stalk or Tennant's Lum, a chimney designed by Macquorn Rankine to carry away noxious fumes. Dodd described the works in 1847:

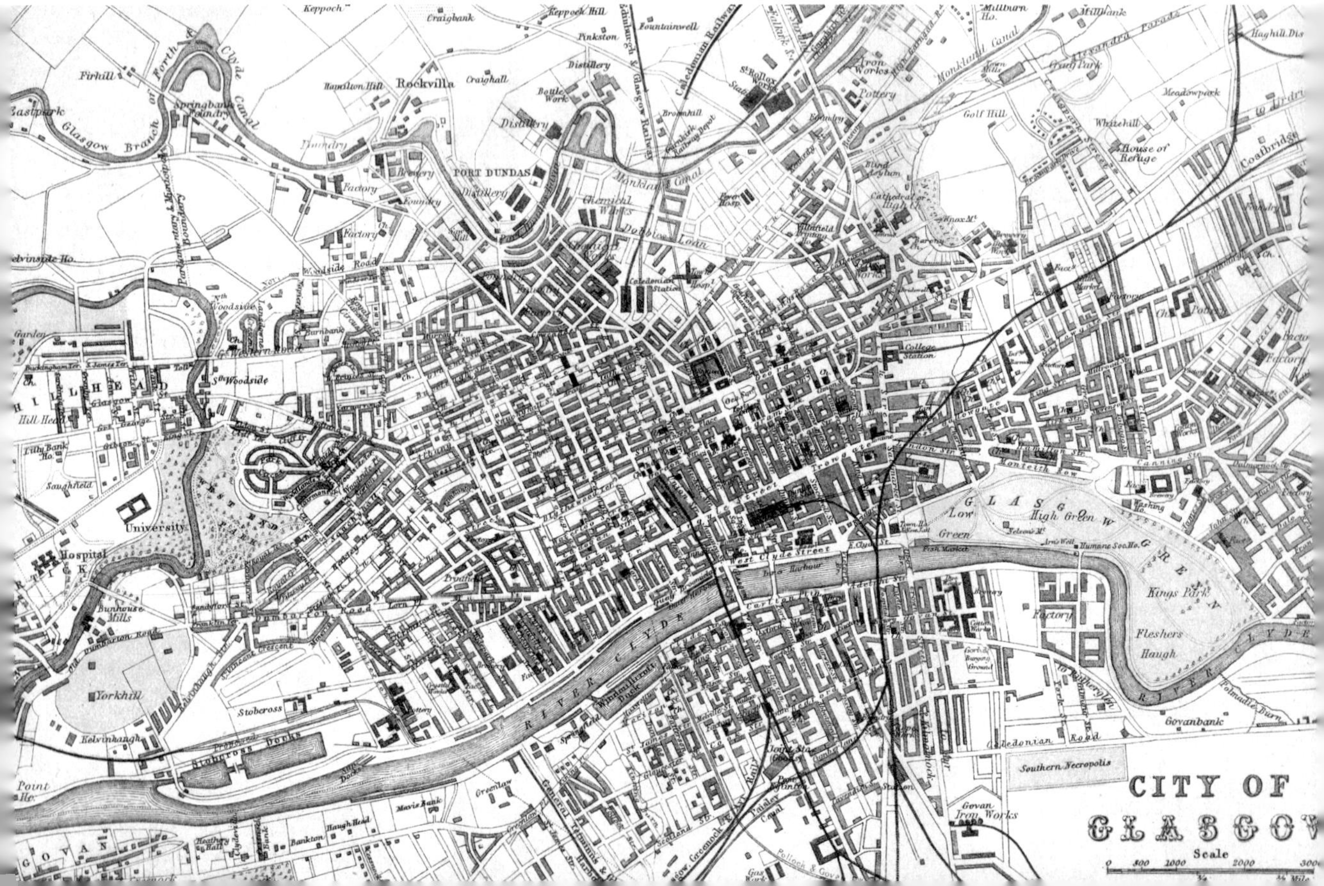

This map, published in 1878, portrays a city whose population had grown from 77,000 in 1801 to 522,000 in 1871. The grids of tenement-lined streets that characterised many parts of Glasgow are clearly evident, as are streets which were laid out but not yet built up. The map marks several of the largest factories, including (top, centre) the chemical works at St Rollox alongside the Monkland Canal, the city's principal source of coal, and near to its junction with the Forth & Clyde Canal. By the 1870s railways reached Glasgow from most directions, and the city became one of Britain's principal producers of steam locomotives. Glasgow had prospered as a port trading particularly with the Americas, but ships had to be loaded and unloaded at riverside quays until the construction of the Kingston Dock only eleven years before the map was published.

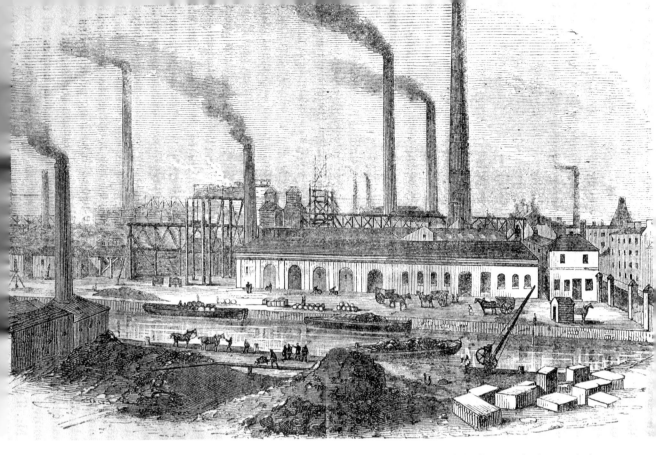

The St Rollox Chemical Works, established in 1799–1800 by Charles Tennant for the manufacture of bleaching powder, became the largest industrial enterprise in Glasgow. The 435 ft chimney, known as Tennant's Stalk or Tennant's Lum, was one of the city's landmarks. The factory stood on the north bank of the Monkland Canal, which delivered most of the 600 tons of coal consumed by its furnaces each week.

They are, necessarily, black and dirty, and as infernal in appearance as we can well imagine any earthly place to be. The heaps of sulphur, lime, coal and refuse; the intense heat of the scores of furnaces in which the processes are going on; the smoke and thick vapours which dim the air of most of the buildings; the swarthy and heated appearance of the men; the acrid fumes of sulphur and the various acids which worry the eyes, and tickle the nose and choke the throat; the danger which every bit of broad-cloth incurs of being bleached … form a series of notabilia not soon to be forgotten.

John Tennant opened a chemical plant on Tyneside, and in 1866 established the Tharsis Sulphur & Copper Works whose first plant was at St Rollox. The chemical concern employed 2,000 people at St Rollox in 1879.

The tenement was the principal form of middle-class as well as working-class accommodation in Glasgow. Its form derives from long traditions of building residential blocks of four or more storeys, and from the Scottish system of land holding which involved commitments to paying feu duty rather than the outright sale of property. Most tenements were built of stone, some of it from the builders' own quarries, although brick was used for staircase towers on the back elevations. The architectural style of many tenement blocks was derived from the Renaissance palaces of Rome and northern Italy, and Robert Adam and Alexander Thomson were among the architects who designed them. Though some were architecturally distinguished, they were as much subject to overcrowding as other forms of working-class housing, one consequence of which was the 'ticketing' of houses which became obligatory in 1866. All houses of three apartments or fewer were measured and their capacity fixed and inscribed on a metal plate on the door. By the 1880s there were 23,228 ticketed apartments in the city.

Cork was another of the principal Atlantic ports in the eighteenth century; reputedly it had the world's largest market for butter and it enjoyed thriving trades in grain, beef hides and the provisioning of ships. Craftspeople made silverware, glass and lace which competed with the products of Europe's most fashionable cities. Cork's natural harbour enabled it to become Ireland's chief link with continental Europe

and the wider world. Trade was controlled from the elegant Custom House of 1814–18 and handled at numerous stone warehouses on the riverside quays. Cork's population grew from about 25,000 in 1700 to about 80,000 a century later. A variety of industries flourished there. In 1800 leather processing was carried on at 40 tanneries; the river Lee with its tributaries, the Glasheen and Curragheen, provided power for numerous flour mills; and the trade in malt was larger than that in Dublin. The porter brewery established by William Beamish and William Crawford in 1791–92 was the largest in Ireland until overtaken by the Guinness brewery in 1833, and there were several other substantial breweries, as well as some distilleries. There were capable mechanical engineering firms in the city, particularly Richard Perrott & Sons, established in 1810, who operated the Hive Iron Works in Great George's Street, a boiler works at Wandesford Quay, and a water-powered forge at Curraheen. By 1860 the firm was making steam engines, rollers for gunpowder works, waterwheels, turbines, equipment for paper mills, breweries and distilleries, and flour-dressing machines that were exported to Australia. The King Street Ironworks, opened in 1816, made structural ironwork, including that of 1830 which remains at the Midleton Distillery outside the city. The Vulcan Foundry, established in the 1820s, specialised in the manufacture of suspension waterwheels and associated transmission systems. Cork shipbuilders were pioneers in the construction of iron vessels. The linen industry in Munster was smaller than in Ulster but none the less significant, and Cork was its trading centre. There were also four substantial glassworks in the early nineteenth century, whose workers included men from Stourbridge and Tyneside. Cork was a less prosperous city in the nineteenth century than in the eighteenth. It suffered severely during the economic downturn which followed the Napoleonic Wars and again during the Famine. Much employment was on a casual basis, and immigration from the country-side exercised a downward pressure on wages. As in Dublin the construction of single-storey terraced dwellings continued into the late nineteenth century. A quadrangle of such cottages stands on the North Mall alongside the Lee, while Madden's Buildings in

▼ The Hive Iron Works of Richard Perrott & Sons, depicted in four views of *circa* 1866. The first two images show the formal façades which the works presented to the outside world, but the third image depicts a machine shop with a substantial lathe, a drilling machine and other machine tools, while the fourth provides evidence of the large-scale milling machinery for which the company was famous. From George Measom's *The Official Illustrated Guide to the Great Southern & Western and Midland Great Western Railways of Ireland* (London: Measom, 1866).

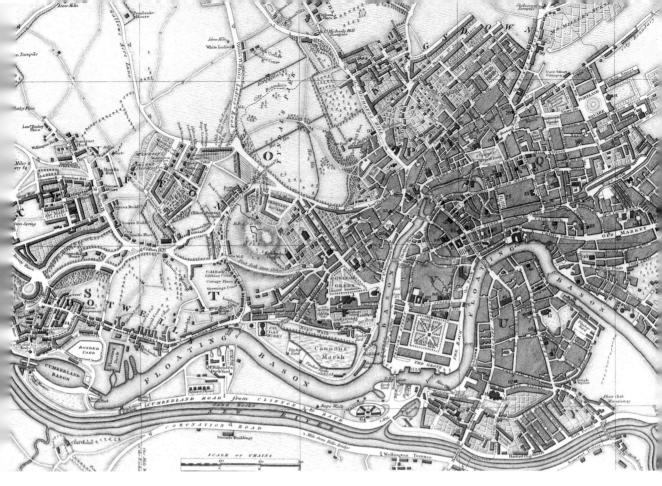

Watercourse Road comprise 76 one-storey cottages in four parallel rows, constructed in 1886.

In the eighteenth century Bristol derived much of its living from the triangular Atlantic trade, as its vessels shipped English textiles and hardware to Africa, conveyed slaves thence to the Americas, and returned to Bristol with sugar, tobacco and hardwoods which were processed around its harbour and in its hinterland. For a period Bristol was England's second port, and through coastal shipping and inland navigation determined patterns of trade in large parts of western Britain. It is a commonplace observation that in the nineteenth century Liverpool handled a growing proportion of the Atlantic trade, and of other trans-oceanic commerce. This was in part because

facilities for handling ships at Bristol, while adequate in the age of sail, proved difficult to improve. William Jessop drew up a plan, implemented in 1802–09, by which the river Avon was dammed at Rownham and its course re-directed from Totterdown through a New Cut, providing permanent high water at the traditional quays along the Avon and the Frome in the 'Floating Harbour'. Brunel gave advice on the prevention of silting, but the delays in the launching of his revolutionary SS *Great Britain* showed how difficult it was to accommodate sea-going ships of increasing size at wharfs that were located eight miles from the open estuary up a winding river. The *Great Britain* was formally 'launched' by the Prince Consort on 19 July 1843, but only in December the following

year could she leave the dock in which she had been built (and where she now once again reposes, see page 152). Trade expanded in spite of the difficulties, the net tonnage of foreign goods imported increasing from 129,254 in 1850 to 206,723 in 1860, although in 1877 the opening of the first dock at Avonmouth marked the beginning of a move from the city to the sea. (Increasing ship size and an inconvenient river would result in similar moves in port facilities elsewhere, such as from Lancaster to Glasson Dock at the mouth of the Lune; down the Thames from London to Tilbury; and farther towards the mouth of the Mersey at Bootle and Seaforth.)

Bristol's industry was characterised by its variety. In 1860 Measom listed the city's manufactures as glass, sugar, iron, brass, floorcloths, vinegar, tobacco, ships, cocoa, carriages, manures, agricultural implements, and earthenware. Coal was plentiful locally, and miners lived among other working people, particularly in the northern part of the city. On census night in 1861 the Sailors' Home in Queen's Square sheltered mariners from the Austrian Empire, Denmark, France, Germany, Spain, Sweden and the United States. Shipbuilding prospered, together with the making of anchors, blocks, chains, masts, ropes and sails.

Numerous ship-owners, West Indies, Indian, Russian and Australian merchants, colonial brokers and dealers in tea, coffee, India rubber, brandy and wine, mahogany, cedar and dyewoods, lived in the fashionable parts of the city. These areas, including the spa resort of Clifton, had a population comparable to that of Bath, with many retired merchants, East India Company officials, ship-owners and military officers, as well as stockbrokers, lawyers and people deriving their income from land in Australia or Barbados, Canadian bonds, iron, tin and copper mines, and shares in shipping and railway companies. More than 30 Anglican clergy 'without cure of souls' were resident in Clifton in 1861, as well as 15 incumbents from parishes as distant as Huddersfield and Brighouse. As in Bath a significant part of the population provided recreation for the wealthy: actors, baths attendants, 'professors' of foreign languages, bath-chair proprietors, dancing masters, billiard markers, and comedians. The wealthy were also served by goldbeaters, silversmiths, engravers on marble, 'embroiderers on satin and other costly materials', ostrich-feather manufacturers, jewellers from Prussia, a cigar dealer from Hamburg, and figure makers from Tuscany.

Coach making was a substantial industry in Bristol, with many small companies and several large ones, including the Bristol Wagon Works Company, one of whose founders in 1851 was John Fowler, whose role in Leeds was discussed earlier (page 91). Coachmakers drew on the specialist skills of spring manufacturers, weavers of coach lace and fringe, and carriage-lamp

The Great Western Factory in Bristol was one of the largest cotton mills in Britain, although it was an isolated venture, located at a considerable distance from the centre of the cotton trade in Manchester. It was built in 1838 at a time when Bristolians looked forward with optimism to increasing trade with the Americas, and it employed 1,570 people in 1861. In spite of its isolation, it remained in production until 1926.

makers. The timber trade was carried on in many yards and at many sawmills, some of which specialised in hardwoods, veneers, dyewoods or deals. A merchant dealing in timber hoops employed 140 men in 1861.

The old-established trade in grain flourished. There were several large flour mills, supported by manufacturers of millstones and starch manufacturers. The leather trade was immense, with numerous skin yards, tanneries, and curriers, and specialist craftsmen who made straps, gaiters, whips and horse collars, as well as boots and shoes. Richard Drake's tannery employed 70 men in 1861. At several drapers' shops on College Green and Wine Street dressmakers and milliners as well as sales assistants were among substantial numbers of live-in employees, as many as 66 in one establishment.

More than a dozen tobacco companies were active in the city in the 1790s and almost as many in the 1860s, but the most prosperous was that formed by Henry Overton Wills I, son of a Salisbury watchmaker, who became a partner in a Bristol business in 1786 and took it over as Wills & Co. from 1789. After his death it was managed by his sons William Day Wills and H. O. Wills II, who introduced steam power from 1861, and in 1871 began to manufacture cigarettes as well as pipe tobacco and snuff. Beaters-up, cutters, finishers, sorters, spinners, strippers and turners of tobacco lived in many parts of the city.

Conrad Finzel from Frankfurt-am-Main set up an innovative sugar refinery in Bristol in 1836 in which he used a centrifuge to dry crystallised sugar as it came from vacuum pans, thus obviating the need to make sugar loaves. His plant occupied more than two acres and incorporated its own bone-charcoal works by the time of his death in 1859. From the 1870s it faced competition from refineries in London, Liverpool and Glasgow, and it closed in 1881. In 1853 Finzel built Clevedon Hall (originally called Frankfurt Hall), but much of the profit from the business was spent on an orphanage on Ashley Hill. Another sugar manufacturer, William Stock, employed 84 men in 1861. One sugar works manager came from Aachen, but most refinery employees were locally born.

The well-known typographer Joseph Fry began making chocolate in 1759. Two years later he took over an existing company, and established a factory in Union Street in 1777. It was managed from 1795 by his son Joseph Storrs Fry I, who patented a process, powered by a Boulton & Watt engine, for grinding cocoa beans, and used hydraulic presses designed by Joseph Bramah to squeeze chocolate extract from cocoa. By 1830 Fry was producing solid eating chocolate, and under the management of the founder's grandsons it marketed moulded chocolate bars from 1847, chocolate cream bars from 1866 and Easter eggs from 1873. In 1861 the firm employed 141 people, about half of them women.

Brass making and lead working in Bristol are discussed above (see pages 358–9). Several brass mills of the early eighteenth century were still working in the 1860s, and the city's leadworks continued to produce pipes, sheet, shot and white lead, as well as refining silver during the smelting process. Ironworks included galvanising concerns, wire rollers and rivet makers. Charles Lambert's pin-making company employed 300 people in 1861, and there were specialist manufacturers of cut nails, heel tips and horse nails.

Textile manufacturing in Bristol was overshadowed by the Great Western Cotton Factory on Barton Hill, one of the largest in Britain. Its five-storey spinning mill extended for 30 bays, while weaving took place in a vast single-storey shed. It was built as late as 1838 during a period of optimism about trade with the United States following the launch of the steamship *Great Western*. The partners included Archibald Vickers from Manchester, Charles Sage from Hawarden (who had worked in the West Indies), and William Naish, a member of a well-known Bristol manufacturing family who in the 1820s had been producing hosiery and sewing-thread. In 1861 the mill's workforce comprised 1,570 people. It remained in production until 1926 and was demolished in 1968. Smaller enterprises were engaged in manufacturing woollen cloth, spinning hemp and flax, weaving canvas, sacking and cocoanut fibres, working horse-hair and weaving, printing and painting floor cloths.

Mechanical engineering flourished in Bristol. In the eighteenth century some of the first iron foundries that were not parts of blast-furnace complexes were active in the city, and Bristol's contacts with ironworks in Shropshire ensured that its entrepreneurs were acquainted with the potential of the steam engine. Thomas Goldney III installed a Coalbrookdale engine to pump water for the fountains outside his mansion at Clifton in 1764–66. Between 1830 and 1960 mechanical engineers in Bristol built 4,200 steam locomotives, more than were produced in Derby or in London. The foundation of the industry was an array of small and medium-sized firms, foundries and smithies, each employing up to 40 people. Henry Stothert from Bath set up a manufactory of locomotives and other iron machinery in the city in 1836–37 and took Edward

Slaughter into partnership in 1839. Their enterprise was known from 1844 as the Avonside Ironworks. Slaughter studied in Paris, was apprenticed at the Canal Ironworks in Limehouse, and worked with I. K. Brunel on the Great Western Railway. Avonside built main-line locomotives as well as the industrial shunters for which it was well known in the twentieth century. Its products included the Fairlie locomotive *James Spooner* built for the Festiniog Railway in 1872. In 1861 the Slaughter enterprise employed 778 men. Henry Stothert became a partner in a shipbuilding concern which from 1851 occupied the Hotwells Dockyard and continued to build ships until 1933. The Atlas Engine Works was set up by Fox Walker & Co. in 1864. It specialised in the construction of small tank locomotives, of which about 400 were built in 20 years. It was taken over from 1880 by Thomas Peckett and continued building steam locomotives until 1958. Other companies in Bristol made agricultural machinery and scale beam weighbridges. Engineering concerns in 1861 drew skilled labour from many parts of Britain: boilermakers from Neath, Liverpool, Sunderland, Leeds and Manchester; and engine fitters from the Forest of Dean, Newcastle-upon-Tyne, Hayle, Preston and Scotland.

Chemicals produced in Bristol in 1861 included sulphuric acid, alkali, alum, lamp black and phosphorus, as well as various chemical-based consumer goods. Soap making using imported olive oil was well established in the eighteenth century. Thomas Thomas, a migrant from Wales, opened a soap company in 1824 which was known from 1845 as Christopher Thomas & Bros. The company built a red-brick factory in the Florentine style in the 1880s, and from 1898 was celebrated for its 'Puritan' soap. Phosphorus was used to make matches in a factory large enough to employ specialist matchbox makers. The products of alkali works included washed crystals, and a factory employing nine men made washing blue. Blacklead was manufactured for cleaning grates. Bristol manufacturers produced superphosphate fertilisers and pressed linseed oil at mills whose by-product was cattle cake. There were several firms of tar distillers in the city, the most notable that of William Butler who in 1843 became a partner in a company which he controlled from 1863.

Factory production of consumer goods was expanding in Bristol in the 1860s. There were factories where foremen supervised sewing machinists, where products included ready-made garments, waterproof clothing, corsets and baby linen. Many regarded themselves, not as tailors or dressmakers, but as makers or cutters of shirts, waistcoats, vests, trousers or cloth caps. One staymaker employed 400 hands. Boots, shoes and slippers were manufactured on an increasingly large scale. A shoe manufacturer in Dorset Street employed 120 people; another, whose family had fled from the French Revolution, employed 125 in York Road; and James Durham claimed to employ 1,000 hands, although clearly not in a single factory. Food manufacturers included makers of ships' and fancy biscuits, a vinegar works large enough to employ a steam engine, and a warehouse known as a cheese 'factory'. Furniture was also being manufactured on a large scale. Numerous cabinet-making concerns employed between 20 and 50 people each, and specialist concerns made looking glasses, pianos, window blinds, mattresses and iron bedsteads. Nevertheless, the growing availability of consumer goods scarcely affected many of the city's working class, who continued to seek the necessities of life from old clothes shops, general dealers in wearing apparel, and street hawkers of fruit, vegetables, fish, cheese and pastries.

An east-coast metropolis: Hull

The ports of the east coast had rather different characteristics. Britain's busiest and largest maritime trading centre, London, was a port of global significance which traded with all parts of the known world, but it shared some characteristics with places farther north. Most east-coast ports enjoyed some trade with southern Europe and the Americas, but such places as Yarmouth, King's Lynn, Sunderland, Newcastle-upon-Tyne, Leith, Dundee and Aberdeen tended to look principally east, to the Netherlands, Germany, the Baltic and Scandinavia, and north towards the Arctic. Their development was shaped by the innovations of the industrial revolution period, such as wet docks, improvements to inland navigation, mainline railways, and the establishment of mechanical engineering works. All formed part of far-reaching supply chains that provided British industry with many of its raw materials, such as iron, pitch and hemp, and supplied house builders throughout Britain with abundant softwoods from the Baltic and Scandinavia. As we have seen, the Tyne, with Newcastle at its heart, was by far the most important coal-shipping port in the country, but all the east-coast ports were involved in this trade to a greater or lesser extent. Another increasingly important trade in Hull, Yarmouth, Aberdeen and Leith, together with Lowestoft and Grimsby, in the late nineteenth century was that of industrial fishing. In most east-coast ports, too, there were textile factories, many of which, at least initially, processed raw materials imported from traditional trading partners in northern Europe.

Kingston-upon-Hull provides an illuminating example of a busy east-coast port. With a population of 122,000, it was large – it counted among the dozen largest cities in the British Isles in 1871 – and a study of its varied trade patterns and industries sheds light on aspects of industry hitherto not considered, as well as its important role in inter-continental migration which was of such global significance in this period.

Hull grew from a place of modest size in 1700 to be regarded a century later as the third port in England. Its principal trades were with Germany, the Netherlands, the Baltic and Scandinavia. Some of its trades, such as the import of Swedish iron for Sheffield steelmakers and of timber, flax and hemp from the Baltic, and the export of lead, Pennine millstones and woollens made in the West Riding, were long lived. There were consuls in the port in 1861 from Denmark, France, Norway and Sweden, interpreters of Italian and Greek, a settled minister of the German Lutheran Church and an agent for the Grand Russian Railway Co. There was also some trade with Spain and Portugal. Sugar was being refined at Hull in the 1670s, and by 1790 there were two substantial sugar-houses, while tobacco manufacture, introduced in the 1720s, was being carried on at four mills by the 1780s. Sugar was still being refined in the city in 1861. The river Trent, the Aire & Calder Navigation and numerous canals provided Hull with direct routes, plied by keels, sloops and lighters, to the mining and manufacturing areas of Yorkshire and the Midlands. A Manchester source described Hull in 1795 as 'the key through which our manufactures can alone find a passage for the markets of Germany, Switzerland and the borders of Italy', while Svedenstierna remarked that it 'has in the last few years risen to an almost unbelievable degree of prosperity through the extended trade and manufacture of Great Britain'. Continuity rather than revolutionary change characterised the city's economy. Many manufactures in the 1860s were dependent upon the traditional trades of the port, but some were focused on consumer products.

Hull lies 25 miles from the North Sea on the north bank of the Humber estuary, at its confluence with the river Hull. The Dock Company of Kingston-upon-Hull was established in 1774. Construction of the first dock, later known as the Old Dock, began in 1775 and it received its first ship on 22 September 1778. Capacity was enlarged by the opening of the Humber Dock in 1809, the Junction Dock in 1829, and the Railway and Victoria Docks by 1851. Docks opened the prospects of trading to more merchants, since only those with premises on the waterfront previously had access to wharfage facilities. The amount of cargo handled rose from 109,491 tons in 1775 to 1,058,107 tons in 1863, and subsequently increased at a faster rate than either London or Liverpool.

Much of Hull's prosperity in the late eighteenth century was due to whaling ships, working principally off the coasts of Greenland. Whaling was encouraged by government subsidy from 1733. Between 1752 and 1772 Hull ships brought in 171,907 tons of whale oil, an average of 88 tons per ship per trip. The trade reached its peak in 1818–19, and in 1820 60 vessels each earned more than £5,000 per trip, although the dangers of the industry were highlighted when ten ships were lost in the following year, and another six were wrecked in 1830. The size of the fleet fell from 25 in 1834, to 15 in 1835 and just 3 in 1837, and it disappeared afterwards. Hull had gained substantial revenues, although at daunting cost in lives, from a trade which not only provided the capital for other enterprises in Hull, but was essential to many manufacturing processes throughout Britain. Whale oil was used in lamps, as a lubricant, in dressing flax and as a source of tallow, while whale bone was employed in corsets and within industry, for example as brushes for cleaning boiler flues.

As in Liverpool and Glasgow, one of the most notable trades in the port was in people – the passage of emigrants from Germany, the Baltic and eastern Europe to distant continents and particularly to the United States. The number of migrants was increased from 1843 by the services of the Wilson shipping line of Hull, and from 1840 by the opening of railways which carried migrants to London, Glasgow and Southampton, but above all to Liverpool, where they took ships for their intended destinations. The North Eastern Railway constructed a special emigrant waiting room at Paragon Station in 1871 and by one calculation 2.2 million migrants passed through Hull between 1836 and 1914.

Hull's expanding working-class population was accommodated from the late eighteenth century in back-to-back houses in courts, but a board of health was constituted in 1851, and from 1854 its bye-laws insisted that each new house must have open space at the back. The construction of back-to-backs ceased, but until the 1890s builders and speculators continued the traditional pattern of building houses in courts at right angles to the road.

The most important manufacture in Hull, the crushing of seeds to produce linseed oil and cattle cake, was established by the early eighteenth century. More linseed and cotton seed was imported at Hull than at all other British ports combined. In 1754 Angerstein noted 13 oil mills, some horse-driven and some using wind power, and windmills were reckoned to be the chief source of power for seed crushing in 1823. From 1795 the Bramah hydraulic press was used to extract the last drops of oil from residues. Joseph Pease, whose oil mill was his chief concern from 1740, was the outstanding entrepreneur in the trade. He established Hull's first bank in 1754, and his grandson Joseph Robinson Pease I and great-grandson Joseph Robinson Pease II were prominent in mercantile

Martin Samuelson, son of a Jewish family who migrated to England from Hamburg, set up an engineering works in Hull in 1849, at the same time that his brother Bernhard (from 1882 Sir Bernhard) began to manufacture agricultural implements at Banbury before becoming one of the leading figures in the iron trade of Cleveland. Martin Samuelson's first products, hydraulic presses for the manufacture of oilcake, were designed for a traditional Hull industry, but from 1854 he began to build iron ships, and, as this image shows, made vessels of considerable size for the Atlantic trade.

affairs in Hull – several warehouses in the port bear the initials 'JP'.

Oil crushing, and the manufacture of white and red lead and colouring materials from the Pennines, brought down the river Trent, stimulated the growth of paint manufacturing. The availability of oil also made possible the growth of soap making on a large scale, while the manufacture of putty, using whiting from the chalk hills of the East Riding, was another use of linseed oil.

Flax and hemp were also imported into Hull in large quantities and were used in linen manufacturing elsewhere in Yorkshire, and in Hull itself by makers of canvas and sacking. Cotton manufactures were initially linked with flax working. The Hull Flax & Cotton Mill Company was formed in 1837 and made cotton fabrics on a large scale. The Kingston Cotton Mill Co. was established ten years later and constructed a 501 foot (154 m) long, 80 foot (25 m) wide, five-storey mill. Like the Great Western Cotton

Co. in Bristol, these were large but isolated concerns. Neither proved prosperous. The Hull company finally closed in 1866 and the Kingston company in 1894, both, according to one judgment, as a consequence of failures in management rather than because spinning cotton in Hull posed particular difficulties.

Shipbuilding was an essential part of the Hull economy. Some 23 ships were built there for the Royal Navy between 1739 and 1774. Most were of modest size but they included the very large HMS *Temple* of 1,421 tons, which was completed in 1759. Arthur Young observed six or seven shipyards in 1796, as well as makers of masts, blocks and sails. Martin Samuelson, brother of Bernhard Samuelson, MP and Cleveland ironmaster, set up an engineering company in Hull in 1849, initially making hydraulic presses for manufacturing oilcake. He diversified into building iron ships in 1854 and within seven years had constructed 49 steam and sailing vessels, including steamships of up to 3,000 tons for the Atlantic trade. In 1864 he sold out to a new company which closed the yard in 1866. The other large shipbuilding concern was that of C. & W. Earle, founded in 1852–53, which had built 100 steamships by 1866. Sub-contractors included many shipsmiths, anchorsmiths, rivet makers, blockmakers, riggers and makers of steam gauges. Boilermakers were drawn from many parts of Britain including London, Derby, Liverpool, Argyll, Lanarkshire and Co. Down.

Thomas Reckitt of Wainfleet was a member of a Quaker family who travelled in America, and strongly supported the abolition of slavery. Isaac Reckitt, one of his many sons, worked in the grain trade in Boston and Nottingham, and in 1840 took over a starch business in Hull, where he employed 51 people in 1851. He diversified into importing, and later manufacturing, 'washing blue' or ultramarine, which was synthesised in 1827 by the French chemist Jean-Baptiste Guimet, who baked a mixture of china clay, sodium carbonate and sulphur at extreme temperatures, producing a substance used in the nineteenth century principally in laundries and paper making. Washing blue was

also made in Bristol and in a former cotton mill of 1785 at Backbarrow. The business employed up to 300 people in 1861, and after the death of Isaac Reckitt in the following year it was continued by his three sons. Reckitts were pre-eminently manufacturers of consumer goods, sold to householders for everyday use. In the early 1860s they were making biscuits by machinery, using imported grains; black lead; and starch and wash blue which was sold to housewives in small linen parcels called 'dolly bags'.

The increasing availability of fish affected working-class living standards from the 1860s. Hull's fishing fleet in 1845 consisted of only 21 sailing smacks of up to 30 tons, but within ten years had grown to 110 smacks of up to 34 tons. Many fishermen migrated to the Humber from the south coast – in 1861 there were more than 50 from Thanet and Dover and as many as 100 from Devon, about half of them from Brixham, as well as men from Grimsby, Yarmouth, the Thames estuary, Hastings and Cornwall. Most came with their families, and were supported by netmakers and dealers from their native ports. By 1875 there were three times

One of the great changes in the building industry in the course of the nineteenth century was the adoption of Portland Cement in place of lime mortars. Portland Cement is made from clay and either limestone or chalk. The materials are mixed and fired in a kiln where the lime, alumina and silica combine to form a clinker which is cooled, mixed with gypsum to stabilise the cementiteous compounds, and then pulverised in ball mills. The works of George and Thomas Earle, originally established on the banks of the river Hull at Wilmington in 1821 became one of the largest cement works in England, and used supplies of blue clay from Barton-on-Humber and of chalk from the Yorkshire Wolds, both delivered by rail.

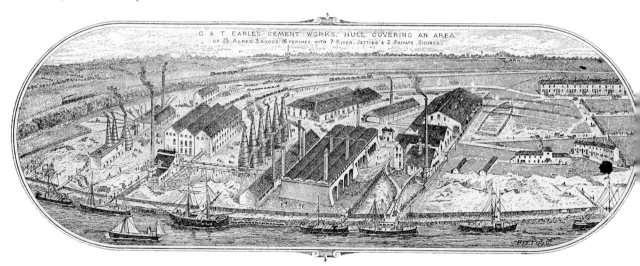

G. & T. EARLES CEMENT WORKS, HULL COVERING AN AREA OF 13 ACRES, 3 ROODS, 16 PERCHES, WITH 7 RIVER JETTIES & 2 PRIVATE SIDINGS.

as many smacks as in 1855, and the average vessel was almost twice as large. Trawlers were introduced from 1858, but their numbers did not rise quickly until the 1880s. From 1858 ice was used to keep fish fresh, while many of the herring landed were preserved by curing. Fish merchants used overnight trains to distribute their wares across England and Wales. Hull became an archetypal industrial fishing port from the late 1850s, a distinct type of town, with facilities for handling fresh fish, for preserving it by curing and smoking, for the profitable use of inedible parts, and for the servicing of fishing fleets.

Conclusions

The great cities of the British Isles in the 1860s had much in common, and many of their shared characteristics had been shaped by the industrial developments of the previous 170 years. All, for example, had improved access to energy and better forms of transport and communication. In all of them there had developed mechanical engineering industries. Within each city, however, there could be found sharp contrasts between areas of architectural elegance and districts of foul, over-crowded and unhealthy living conditions; and all had large groups both of their permanent and their itinerant populations who experienced low wages and insecure employment. By the 1860s, partly because of the increasing impact of national legislation, all were beginning to ensure that new developments were not intrinsically unhealthy. Some cities had large-scale manufacturing industries, while others handled the commerce generated by such industries. All had consumers with sophisticated tastes whose demands were met by networks of small manufacturing workshops and imposing retail shops.

These complex communities functioned in ways that were comparable in many respects with the cities of antiquity, or of the Renaissance, and they were, as a class, different from contemporary towns devoted almost entirely to manufacturing – they were major industrial centres, but were also much more than that.

The poles of urban experience in the mid-nineteenth century were the slums of Little Ireland or the east end of Leeds, and Cuthbert Brodrick's town hall of 1858 in Leeds or that designed by Alfred Waterhouse and built in 1869–77 in Manchester. Urban squalor was not a new phenomenon in eighteenth- and nineteenth-century Britain; nor was it entirely the consequence of the rise of mining and manufacturing. Of the cities considered above, the worst overall living conditions were probably in Dublin, which was the least industrialised. Industrialisation and urbanisation are not the same phenomenon.

But the rise of industry did increase the sheer scale of squalor. The submerged tenth in a city of 200,000 people were more visible and obvious, and generated more hazards to health, than a tenth of the population of a town of 9,000. The most obvious economic development of the eighteenth century was the widespread use of coal, which created urban living conditions which West Europeans now find it difficult to comprehend. Yet industry also generated expertise which enabled the alleviation of squalor and disease – once there was sufficient political will – through the paving of streets, the building of sewers and pumping stations, and the construction of pipelines from sources of pure water in the uplands. Industry also created communal wealth which was sometimes expended wisely in buildings and on activities that fostered science and culture, in a manner that seems as alien in the twenty-first century as the squalor of the slums. *The Times* on 30 October 1896 discussed the elements of local corporate unity which 'In its most pronounced form it is found in some great towns in Yorkshire, Lancashire and the neighbouring counties … its presence begets a public spirit fruitful in all manner of good civic deeds, a wholesome rivalry between communities, and a healthy local pride without which England would be much poorer than it is.' This broad vision of the civic virtue of the 'Victorian city' is one that endures in the public consciousness to this day.

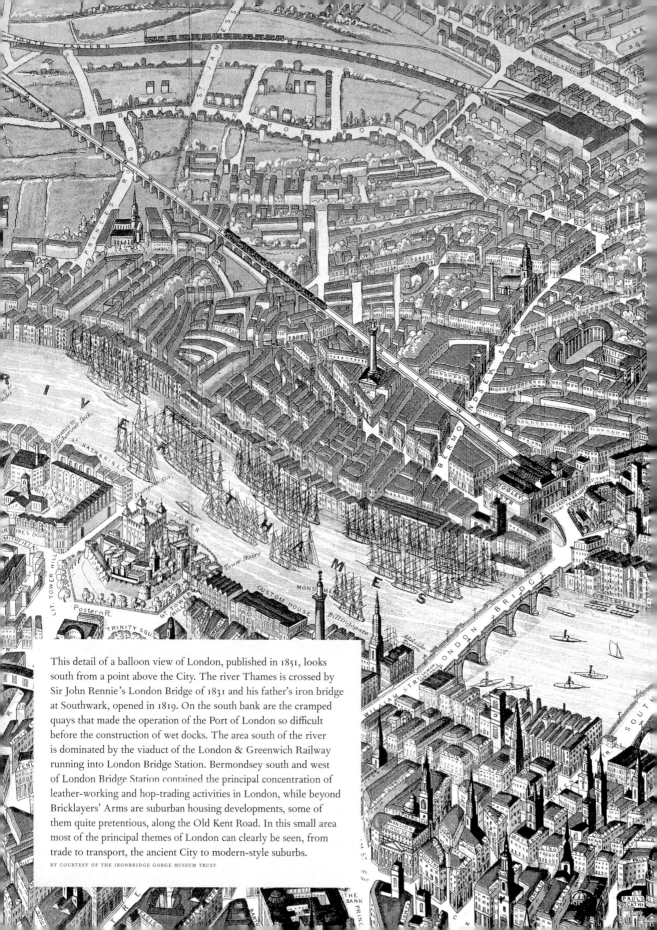

This detail of a balloon view of London, published in 1851, looks south from a point above the City. The river Thames is crossed by Sir John Rennie's London Bridge of 1831 and his father's iron bridge at Southwark, opened in 1819. On the south bank are the cramped quays that made the operation of the Port of London so difficult before the construction of wet docks. The area south of the river is dominated by the viaduct of the London & Greenwich Railway running into London Bridge Station. Bermondsey south and west of London Bridge Station contained the principal concentration of leather-working and hop-trading activities in London, while beyond Bricklayers' Arms are suburban housing developments, some of them quite pretentious, along the Old Kent Road. In this small area most of the principal themes of London can clearly be seen, from trade to transport, the ancient City to modern-style suburbs.

12

Capital industries: manufacturing in London

'I know nothing more imposing than the view one obtains of the river when sailing from the sea up to London Bridge.'

FRIEDRICH ENGELS, *THE CONDITION OF THE WORKING CLASS IN ENGLAND* (1845)

L ONDON'S ROLE in Britain's industrial revolution was as important in its way as that of Birmingham, Lancashire or South Wales, although this centrality has not always been appreciated. The influential French historian Fernand Braudel, for example, believed that capital cities were present during the industrial revolution only as spectators, while J. L. Hammond considered that the industrial revolution was 'a storm that passed over London and broke elsewhere'. The capital did indeed lack cotton mills, collieries and blast furnaces, but the prosperity of miners, manufacturers, clothiers and merchants all over Britain depended upon London for the marketing and consumption of their products: by far the largest market in the British Isles, London had an enduring economic importance. T. C. Barker remarked that, 'In the interpretation of the Industrial Revolution too much attention is paid to making things, especially to making things in factories, not enough to buying and selling or to providing services of all kinds, which are also wealth generators'. The purpose of this chapter is to illuminate some of the roles of the capital within the national economy, and to show their relationships with developments elsewhere. The boundaries between retailing and manufacturing and between manufacturing and warehousing, between manufacturing and London's trading, military and resort functions, were indistinct. Many craftsmen working in their own homes or small workshops processed materials and made components for others in complex webs of sub-contracting.

In part London was important because of its size and economic power. During the whole of the period from 1700 to 1870 London was the largest city in Europe. The historical demographer Professor Sir Tony Wrigley estimated that its population rose from 570,000 in 1700 to 675,000 by the middle of the eighteenth century, and to 900,000 by 1801. It had exceeded a million by 1811, approached two million in 1841, reached 2.8 million in 1861 and 3.2 million in 1871, and exceeded 4.5 million by the end of the century.

The city grew rapidly from the mid-sixteenth century until the 1660s, but growth between 1700 and 1750 was fitful, with six mortality crises between 1714 and 1740–41, and until the late eighteenth century deaths still exceeded births. Large parts of the booming metropolis were exceedingly unhealthy and insanitary, and migration into the city was the primary reason for the city's rapid growth in the second half of the eighteenth century. Some improvements in public health resulted from legislation, and possibly from the development of greater immunity to diseases then current, but some areas remained exceptionally unhealthy in 1870, and the city's entire population suffered from smoke pollution and the threat of infections that were water-borne or spread from pockets where living conditions were squalid. The immigrants who sustained London's growth were many and very varied. The influence of Huguenots has already been remarked upon many times. Germans dominated sugar manufacturing in the nineteenth century, while other individuals from abroad brought understanding of particular technologies. The capital was ever more accessible to people from the provinces, so transport improvements encouraged migration. Stagecoaches, packhorses, waggons and drovers regularly made their way to London in 1700, albeit not as rapidly as in the 1820s. Nobility and gentry and their servants went to the capital for the social season. On completing their apprenticeships young craftsmen sought experience 'on the tramp', particularly from tradesmen in London. Young women from all over Britain lived and worked at dress-making and millinery establishments in the West End, while some from mining areas worked each summer in London's market gardens.

Wages in eighteenth-century London were relatively high, which attracted many migrants seeking a better life. High wages also led to the re-location of some manufactures, such as silk throwing, framework knitting, watch making and porcelain production, to the Midlands where labour was cheaper, but all left behind some presence in the capital. Watches and watch-parts were made at Prescot and Coventry, but numerous watchmakers worked in London, where some diversified into making scientific instruments. Many silkworkers still worked in Spitalfields in the 1860s. Porcelain manufacture was important only between the 1740s and the 1770s, but several hundred potters still plied their trade in the capital in the 1860s.

Crucially, most of the entrepreneurs from provincial England, Scotland, Wales and Ireland that have been discussed in earlier chapters were assiduous in maintaining connections with London. Thus, from 1788 Sir Richard Arkwright kept a house at no. 8 Adam Street. John Wilkinson had a gun wharf and leadworks in Rotherhithe, while his fellow Shropshire ironmasters Abraham and Samuel Darby operated a foundry in the 1770s near to the *George* in Southwark. Companies with premises in Upper Thames Street in the 1860s included the Swansea copper smelters Vivian & Sons and Pascoe Grenfell & Sons, the Hartley Bottle Co. and Ayre's Quay Bottle Co. from Sunderland and the Carron and Weardale iron companies.

London was described and portrayed by many writers, most notably by Henry Mayhew, John Hollingshead, George Dodd, Charles Booth, George Augustus Sala and Charles Dickens. Writers tended to concentrate on the wealth generated from the court, the city or government or, in dramatic contrast, the poverty of the capital's 'submerged tenth'. What drew less attention was London's industry. Between the extremes of wealth and poverty were hundreds of thousands of people who made their livings in the city – some of them comfortable livings – in manufacturing and associated activities.

The changing topography of London

Friedrich Engels was amazed by London's size. The City of London and Westminster, separate entities since the Middle Ages, had spread until they were joined as a single conurbation during the eighteenth century, while, south of the river, Southwark and Bermondsey expanded in economic importance as in population. London's topography was shaped by new bridges: Westminster (1750), Blackfriars (1769), Vauxhall (1816), Waterloo (1817) and Southwark (1818); the Rennies' new London Bridge replaced the

Vinegar was a very important preservative in the eighteenth and nineteenth centuries. The five great vinegar manufactories in London, four of which were on the Surrey side of the river Thames, rivalled in size the capital's breweries. The works on Bankside, on the medieval estate of the bishops of Winchester, was supposedly used for vinegar manufacture from the seventeenth century. It was acquired by Robert, Arthur and William Pott in 1790. In the mid-nineteenth century it fronted Southwark Bridge Road between the church of St Saviour and the Barclay Perkins brewery. Like other works in London malt was made into fermented wort or 'gyle', which was made into vinegar (or subjected to acetification) in a vinegar field, an extensive area in which hundreds of casks, each holding more than 100 gallons, were ranged on wooden bars resting on brick piers. The casks were filled by hoses and, after a spell of several weeks or even months, were emptied by siphons into troughs along which the vinegar flowed into tanks in one of the buildings on the edge of the 'field'. From the tanks steam-operated pumps removed it into vats, after which it was filtered or brightened. In the early twentieth century the Pott concern was amalgamated with the Beaufoy company whose works was at south Lambeth.

multi-arched medieval London Bridge in the early 1830s. All required new approach roads. Blackfriars Road was built at the same time as the bridge, extending about a mile south to St George's Circus from which radiated a web of other roads. The opening of Vauxhall Bridge in 1816 led within two years to the construction of the Camberwell New Road. Southwark Bridge Road was cut through existing streets and buildings to give access to the new bridge in 1819. Other roads were driven through slums, with the triple purpose of eradicating poor-quality housing (by driving its occupants elsewhere), improving transport facilities, and creating plots for development. New Oxford Street passed through the 'rookeries' of St Giles in the 1840s, and among subsequent schemes was Holborn Viaduct, built by William Heywood in 1863–69. The civil engineer James Elmes advocated such a policy in 1827, urging the formation of 'healthy streets and elegant buildings instead of pestilential alleys and squalid hovels; by substituting rich and varied architecture and park-like scenery for paltry cabins and monotonous cow-lairs; by making solid roads and public ways scarcely inferior to those of ancient Rome.'

London's first railways terminated on the fringes of the built-up area. Locomotive sheds and freight depots at places such as Stratford and Bricklayers' Arms, and entwinements of tracks at Willesden and Battersea, occupied large areas, creating noise and smoke. Robert Stephenson's Round House of 1847 at Chalk Farm is one of the few remnants of London's engine sheds. Railways caused further upheaval when lines were extended to termini nearer the centre, projects that impelled several companies towards bankruptcy. The South Eastern Railway drove a line of 1 mile 68 chains above the streets of Southwark to its Charing Cross Station, opened in 1864. Its bitter rival, the London, Chatham & Dover Railway, raised funds recklessly for its line through south London and across the Thames at Blackfriars, which also opened in 1864. The company was embarrassed by the financial crash of 1866, and its affairs were in Chancery for five years afterwards. Both schemes destroyed many houses and commercial premises, as did the extension of the North London Railway from Kingsland to Broad Street, completed in 1865, and the Great Eastern Railway's line from Bishopsgate to Liverpool Street, opened in 1874.

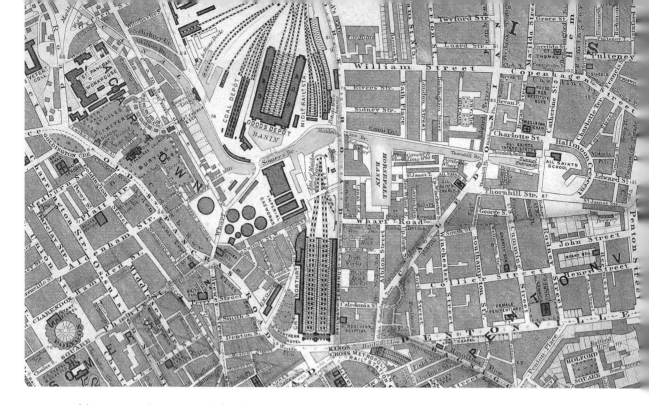

A map of the area around King's Cross before the construction of the Midland Railway's St Pancras Station (see page 253), immediately west of Old Pancras Road. The Great Northern Railway's passenger station was opened on 14 October 1852, replacing a temporary station a little to the north (see page 133). The map portrays the extensive King's Cross freight depot, including the staithes from which coal was emptied through the bottom doors of the hopper waggons used in the first decades of coal carrying on the GNR. The map shows clearly the function of the freight depot as an interchange between the railway and the Regent's Canal. The eastern part of the depot was occupied by the Midland Railway whose trains from 1857 gained access to London by using the Great Northern's tracks from Hitchin. From 1868, with the opening of St Pancras and its associated freight warehouses and yards, the Midland had no need for these facilities. Alongside the GNR freight depot is the Imperial Gasworks (see page 523), one of the largest in London. On the south side of Pentonville Road is the station of the underground Metropolitan Railway. The area is full of small-scale industrial enterprises, shaping iron and making a variety of products including black lead and tiles.

Manufacturing was *relatively* less significant in London than in provincial cities because the service sector and the financial, legal, medical and government activities of the capital occupied so much space and employed so many people. London was also a garrison city, on a large scale by British standards. Barracks and the military and naval hospitals at Chelsea and Greenwich were prominent, and many army and navy officers lived in the capital. There were government industrial establishments in east London, the Royal Mint, the Arsenal and Dockyard at Woolwich and the Victualling Yard at Deptford. London's hospitals, prisons, residential schools, workhouses, and public and private lunatic asylums were also numerous and large. The Middlesex County Lunatic Asylum at

Hanwell had 1,779 inmates in 1861, and in January of that year the Marylebone workhouse accommodated 2,039 indoor paupers. The Marshalsea prison for debtors was relocated on Borough High Street in 1811, and new prisons included Millbank Penitentiary of 1816 and Pentonville of 1842. The varied presence of the State was evident on the north side of Trafalgar Square where, behind William Wilkins' National Gallery of 1838, stood St George's infantry barracks and the St Martin's workhouse. The six-acre site in the Strand where George Edmund Street's Royal Courts of Justice were built between 1868 and 1882 cost £1.45 million, and 450 houses had to be demolished before construction commenced. Similar displacement had taken place in Nash's Regent Street development.

Trade and the city

London was the pre-eminent centre for financial dealings and international trade. The Stock Exchange, overseas trading companies, insurance offices and other financial institutions occupied most of the City and in 1870 employed many clerks who lived in increasingly distant suburbs. The Sun Fire Office, formed in 1708, and the Exchange Assurance Co. were the two largest insurance companies in England during the eighteenth century, and had few competitors before the establishment of the Phoenix Company in 1782, while the society of Lloyds, the informal body that assembled from about 1688 in Edward Lloyd's coffee house and from 1744 at the Royal Exchange, was the principal source of cover for shipping. The expansion of the docks on the Thames after 1800 is described in Chapter 4.

Overseas trade in 1700 was shaped by chartered companies, the largest of which was the East India Company. Established in 1600, the company ruled much of India until its powers were taken away by the Government of India Act of 1858; it was finally dissolved in 1874. The company also traded with China, and was managed from East India House in Leadenhall Street, which was rebuilt in 1799–1800 by Richard Jupp. The company's pensioners lived, for the most part comfortably, in many parts of England in the 1860s. Another important institution, the Company of Merchant Adventurers of London, was chartered in 1407 and traded chiefly to Hamburg and the Netherlands. It lost its privileges in 1689, but members, often called the Hamburg Company, continued trading to that city. The Eastland Company was established in 1579 and traded with the Baltic countries, chiefly through the ports of Elbing (Elblag), Danzig (Gdansk) and Königsberg (Kaliningrad), exchanging English cloth for timber, tar, flax and grain. The company's monopoly ended in 1673 and it had effectively ceased trading by the 1750s. The Royal African Company was established in the seventeenth century and was principally a slave-trading concern, for a time managed by the future king James II. It lost its monopoly in 1698, and in 1731 gave up slaving for trading in ivory and gold dust in present-day

Ghana. It was dissolved in 1752 but was succeeded by the African Company of Merchants which operated until its abolition in 1821. The Levant Company, established in 1581, traded principally with Aleppo in present-day Syria, but also with Constantinople (Istanbul), Alexandria and Smyrna (Izmir), and the Venetian empire. It chiefly exported textiles and metals and brought to London silk, cotton, dried fruit, spices, wool, soft leather and barilla, the alkaline grasses from the Mediterranean coast used in soap making. The company lost its monopoly in 1754 and was dissolved in 1825.

One company with a very mixed reputation was the notorious South Sea Company which was formed in 1711 and enjoyed trading rights in the Spanish empire in America; between 1713 and 1750 it operated the *asiento*, the right to supply African slaves to the Spanish colonies. Within 25 years the company purchased some 34,000 slaves of whom 4,000 died on the Atlantic crossing. The company's chief function, however, was the funding of government debt, as a Tory competitor to the Whig Bank of England, and in 1720 it was the centre of the speculation that caused the South Sea Bubble crisis. The company survived, trading until 1763 and being involved in the management of government debt until the 1850s.

The Hudson's Bay Company received its charter in 1670 and for two centuries opened up the territories that now comprise Canada, trading chiefly in fur. In 1771 one of its employees, Samuel Hearne, former naval officer and expert in navigation, was the first European to reach the Arctic overland. While exploration continued in the nineteenth century monopolistic trading was steadily undermined, and in 1870 the company's privileges were relinquished, although it continued to trade. Another venerable City institution, which had originated in 1356, was Blackwell Hall in Basinghall Street, the hub of the woollen cloth trade. Its buildings were destroyed by fire and rebuilt from 1672, with an eight-bay, three-storey frontage, behind which were two courtyards lined with warehouses. Factors at Blackwell Hall supplied raw wool to manufacturers and furnished working

The Honourable East India Company, the most eminent of London's trading companies, ruled much of the sub-continent from India House on Leadenhall Street, completed in 1729, until its functions were taken over by the government in 1858. This aquatint shows a well-attended sale in 1809. India House was demolished in 1861.
© MUSEUM OF LONDON

The great sociologist Charles Booth, whose *Life and Labour of the People in London was published* in 1886–1903 compiled a series of maps showing the degree of poverty across the city, indicated on a colour scale of seven or eight (according to date) gradations, ranging from black, 'the lowest class, vicious or semi-criminal', through light blue, poor, with 18s.–21s. per week for a modest family, to yellow, 'upper-middle and upper class, wealthy'. While the maps relate to the period of his researches they also throw light on earlier decades. This map extends from Hoxton and Bow in the north, southwards to the Tower and to Limehouse.
© CHARLES BOOTH/MUSEUM OF LONDON

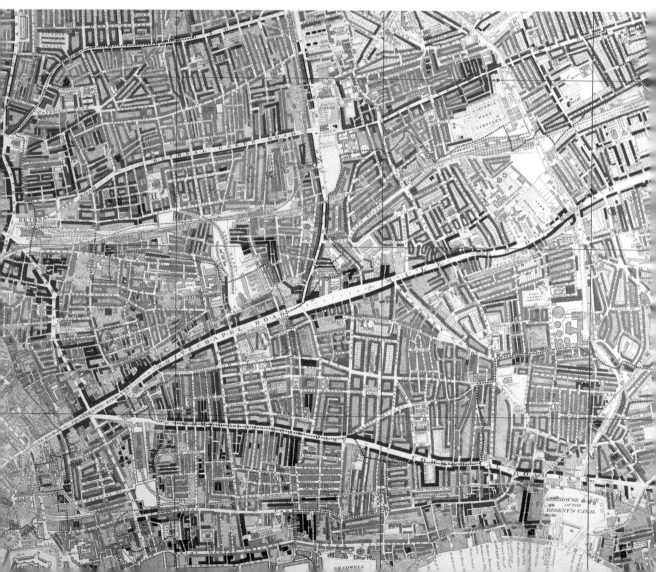

capital for manufacturing woollen cloth for which they subsequently found markets. Many waggons from the provinces made their way laboriously to Blackwell Hall with bales of cloth. Blackwell Hall ceased to operate in 1820, to be succeeded by the Wool Exchange and a cluster of wholesale warehouses around Cannon Street. All these many trading institutions had gone by the 1860s, but, apart from slaving, the businesses they represented continued. Throughout the period from 1700 to 1870 they delivered materials for a host of London trades, and provided custom for many provincial manufacturers.

London as showcase

Of all Europe's capitals, London was the best provided with energy. The seaborne carriage of coal from Tyneside and Wearside, discussed in Chapter 6, was established by 1700 and remained prosperous in 1870, by which date coal was also reaching London by rail from the Midlands. London also took full advantage of the steam engine. A Newcomen engine was erected at the York Buildings waterworks at Chelsea in 1726, and although bankruptcy necessitated its removal in 1732, a pair of engines was constructed nearby by a rival company in 1741–42. They were publicised by an engraving published by John Boydell in 1752. Robey and Kanefsky found that 139 steam engines were installed in London during the eighteenth century, a total exceeded by only six English counties.

The Chelsea engines are evidence of London's role as a showcase for new technology; another example of this were the Albion Mills near Blackfriars Bridge, which had been built from 1786 by the architect Samuel Wyatt, with steam power supplied by Boulton & Watt and mill-work by John Rennie. Twenty pairs of mill-stones were capable of grinding 20 bushels of wheat each hour, and the mills became something of a tourist attraction, one of the industrial wonders of the age. The destruction of the mills by fire in 1791 was welcomed by some tradesmen, who saw it as the symbol of a system of manufacturing alien to the customs of the capital. The prototype iron bridge designed by Tom Paine, described in Chapter 4 (see pages 112–13, 282, 523), was displayed at the *Yorkshire Stingo* public house near Paddington between May 1790 and October 1791, and Richard Trevithick's *Catch-me-who-can* locomotive famously ran on a circuit in Bloomsbury in 1808. As it was being built on the banks of the Thames at Millwall in the 1850s, Brunel's *Great Eastern* was a spectacle on the skyline of east London.

Innovators were drawn to the capital. From 1852 the Patent Office was centred on Southampton Buildings near Holborn. Other influential institutions were the Royal Society, and the Society for the Encouragement of Arts, Manufactures and Commerce (the Society of Arts), founded in 1754 by William Shipley, which offered premiums for designs and projects, encouraging research into dyestuffs, woodland management and cartography. From 1769 until the 1840s the Society arranged annual displays of new industrial devices. Many provincial manufacturers became fellows of the Society. Subsequently London became the centre of the activities of the professional engineering bodies – the Institution of Civil Engineers from 1818 and the Institution of Mechanical Engineers from 1877.

London was also a showcase for public utilities, including the water supply and drainage systems discussed in Chapter 4. Gas lighting was introduced by Frederick Winsor, a Brunswicker who had observed the use of gas in France. In 1807 he demonstrated its potential by illuminating one side of Pall Mall. In 1812 he formed the Gas Light & Coke Co., but afterwards moved to Paris, and the company's successful development from 1814 was due principally to Samuel Clegg, a Mancunian who was apprenticed at the Soho Manufactory. Clegg installed gas lighting in textile mills at Sowerby Bridge, and invented the lime purifier that was used in gasworks. By the 1860s there were gasworks all over London. The Gas Light & Coke Co. works in Westminster extended from Horseferry Road to Great Peter Street. Other installations included the Phoenix works near Blackfriars and in Bermondsey, the Imperial works between the throats of King's Cross and St Pancras stations, the City of London works by the Victoria Embankment, and the West Ham works on the bank of the Channelsea River. Smaller works

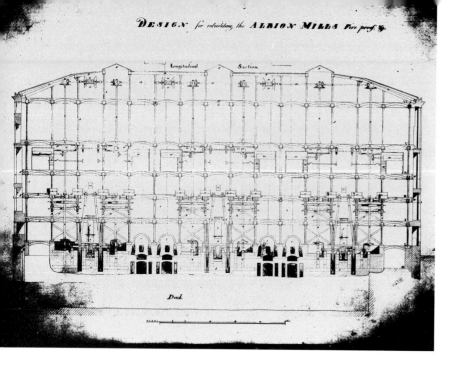

DESIGN *for rebuilding the* ALBION MILLS *fire proof.*

Longitudinal Section.

Dock.

served the Victoria and Surrey Commercial Docks, and there were three in Shoreditch near the Regent's Canal. The Gas Light & Coke Co. works on the East Ham marshes began production in 1870, came to occupy 550 acres, and was named Beckton after Simon Adams Beck, the company's governor. Most gasworks on the south bank came under the control of Sir George Livesey's South Metropolitan Gas Company, which built the 150-acre East Greenwich works from 1884. The establishment of large works in east London stimulated the growth of chemical works which produced disinfectants, insecticides and dyestuffs from by-products.

London's roles in mechanical engineering, lead processing, textiles and the paper industry are discussed in Chapters 3, 8, 9 and 10, and other manufacturing industries are discussed below. Concentrations of activity in certain areas – watch making in Clerkenwell, sugar refining in Whitechapel, coach making in Long Acre – elided gently into neighbouring districts.

Many Londoners walked to their places of work, some for considerable distances, from Newington Causeway to the Royal Mint, or from Soho to a clerks' office in the docks. The pioneering urban historian H. J. Dyos described the 'halfpenny hatches' in Camberwell, the footpaths between main roads which enabled commuting clerks to shorten their walk to

the City and the West End. Polluting industries using imported raw materials grew up in Whitechapel near the docks, and by 1870 were expanding across the river Lea into Essex. An extraordinary concentration of manufacturing flourished on the south bank between Deptford and Lambeth. Dodd observed that Southwark was 'as distinguishable at a distance for its numerous tall chimneys and the clouds of smoke emitted by them as London is for its thickly congregated church-spires'. In 1870 the streets at the south end of London Bridge were the centre of leather processing and the hop trade – there were no fewer than 15 hop warehouses within 500 yards of London Bridge Station in 1873. The area also included an iron foundry, a wire manufactory, two steam flourmills, two breweries, two distilleries, an India rubber works, a ropery, a black lead and emery works, and factories making glue, pins and hats. Farther west, around Newington Causeway, lived many clerks who worked in the City, the Woolwich Arsenal or in the docks, as well as assemblers of French millstones, and the makers of steel pens and mathematical instruments, iron bedsteads, glass, pewter toys, floor cloths and window blinds.

The example of Sir Ambrose Crowley cited above (pages 344–5) offers a good example of the complex interrelationships that were possible. This prominent

Worcestershire-born ironmaster was apprenticed in London and in later life went on to serve as high sheriff of the City. He continued to live in London and had his business headquarters there. He also used the London market to obtain his raw materials of iron, but at the age of just 25 had set up his manufacturing operations in the North. London was the business centre, vital for networking and trade – both domestic and foreign – but the dirty work of furnace and forge was far away in Co. Durham.

Retailing and manufacturing in London

London's shops were famous throughout Europe. 'The stranger in London,' wrote a German visitor in 1786, 'will be struck with astonishment when he sees the riches and the variety of innumerable kinds of merchandise displayed before his eyes in thousands of well-fitted-up shops, for I believe there is no city in the world which in this respect can be compared to London. ... Manufactories are dispersed all over the Kingdom, but almost the fourth part is in London, watchmakers, jewellers, gold and silver workers, printers, bookbinders, silk weavers, sugar refiners.'

Much industrial activity in London related to the supply of consumer goods, whose manufacture was intertwined with retailing. London suppliers, indeed, served wealthy customers all over Britain. Their role is illustrated by the ironmaster Abraham Darby III, who purchased hats, shoes and stockings on visits to London in the 1780s. When he died in 1789 his possessions included a six-fold screen with maps which was 'handsome and London-made', a weather glass made by Adams (either George Adams senior or his son George junior) of Fleet Street, instrument makers to His Majesty, who might also have made Darby's Leyden jars. He also had an eight-day clock in a mahogany case by Lamb & Webb of London, and a pair of 12-inch diameter globes made by James Ferguson, who in 1755 had taken over the business of the celebrated globe maker John Senex of Fleet Street.

John Mechi, whose Bolognese father fled Paris during the French Revolution, was born in 1801 and in his teens became a clerk in a city merchant house involved in the Newfoundland trade. He opened a cutlery shop in Leadenhall Street in the City in 1827, moving to no. 4 in 1830. He sold scientific instruments and made a fortune from his 'patent magic razor strop'. He took over another business in 1855 which enabled him to trade at the prestigous address of 112 Regent Street; in 1859 his manager Charles Bazin became his partner. The company specialised in boxes (still highly valued), made in various materials and accommodating toiletries, decanters and writing materials. In contrast with the practices of other London retailers, discounts were not offered, and the execution of 'country orders ... upon remittance or reference' could be significant to the business. Mechi began to farm at Tiptree Hall, Essex, and wrote on agricultural improvement.

SAME PRICES CHARGED AT BOTH ESTABLISHMENTS & ANY ARTICLE EXCHANGED IF NOT APPROVED.

ALL PRICES MARKED IN PLAIN FIGURES & NO DISCOUNT.

MECHI & BAZIN'S

ESTABLISHMENTS,

4, LEADENHALL STREET, &
112, REGENT STREET, LONDON

Appropriate and useful PRESENTS, from 5s. to £200 each, are exhibited at these Establishments, consisting of DRESSING CASES, WORK BOXES, WRITING DESKS, DESPATCH CASES, the new TRAVELLING BAG, fitted with materials for the TOILET, the WRITING and WORK TABLE; PAPIER MACHE WARES, INKSTANDS, FRENCH BRONZES, PORCELAIN VASES, FANS, SCENT BOTTLES and CASES, BAGATELLE TABLES, CHESS BOARDS and CHESSMEN, RETICULES, very usefully fitted, NEEDLES, CARD CASES, and an immense assortment of other useful and elegant bijoux, embracing a collection of upwards of £30,000 value.

EVERY ATTENTION & CIVILITY WILL BE SHEWN TO INSPECTING VISITORS WHETHER PURCHASORS OR NOT.

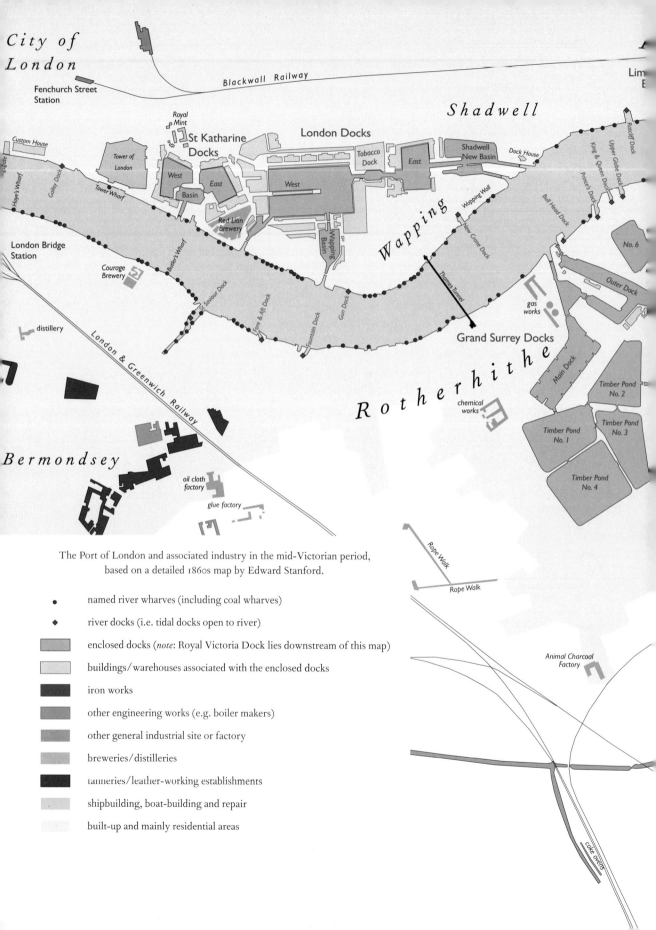

City of London

Fenchurch Street Station

Blackwall Railway

Lim E

Custom House

Tower of London

Royal Mint

St Katharine Docks

London Docks

Shadwell

Dock House

Ratcliff Dock

Hope's Wharf

Galley Dock

Tower Wharf

West Basin

East Basin

West

Tobacco Dock

East

Shadwell New Basin

King & Queen Dock

Upper Globe Dock

Prince's Dock

No. 6

Red Lion Brewery

Wapping Wall

Bull Head Dock

London Bridge Station

Courage Brewery

Butler's Wharf

Wapping Basin

Wapping

New Crane Dock

Outer Dock

distillery

Saviour Dock

Lyne & Aft Dock

Fountain Dock

Gun Dock

Thames Tunnel

Grand Surrey Docks

gas works

Main Dock

Timber Pond No. 2

London & Greenwich Railway

Bermondsey

Rotherhithe

chemical works

Timber Pond No. 1

Timber Pond No. 3

oil cloth factory

glue factory

Timber Pond No. 4

The Port of London and associated industry in the mid-Victorian period, based on a detailed 1860s map by Edward Stanford.

Rope Walk

Rope Walk

- named river wharves (including coal wharves)

◆ river docks (i.e. tidal docks open to river)

enclosed docks (*note*: Royal Victoria Dock lies downstream of this map)

buildings/warehouses associated with the enclosed docks

iron works

other engineering works (e.g. boiler makers)

Animal Charcoal Factory

other general industrial site or factory

breweries/distilleries

tanneries/leather-working establishments

shipbuilding, boat-building and repair

built-up and mainly residential areas

coke ovens

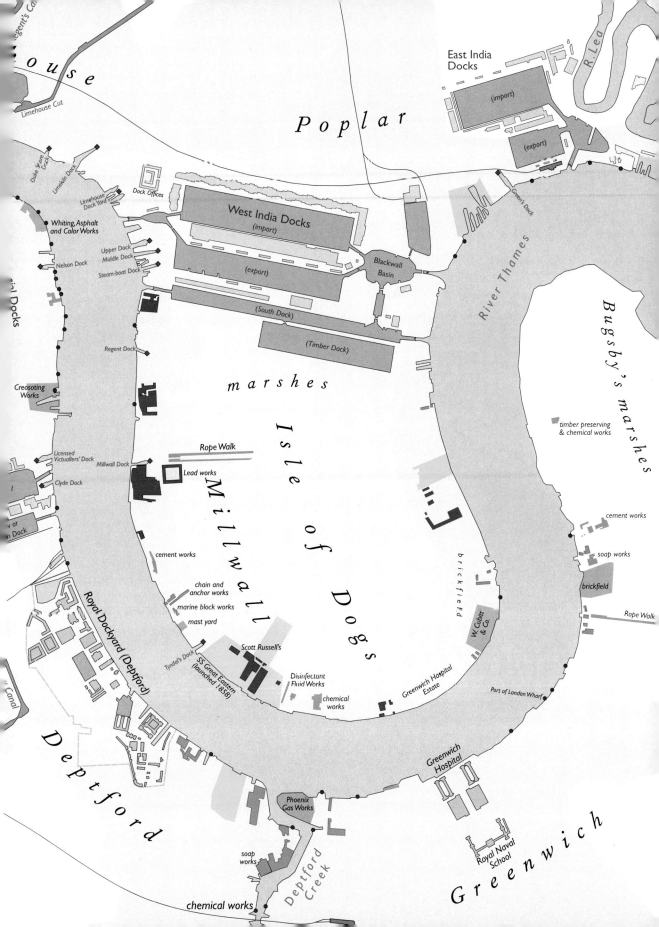

Limehouse Cut

Regent's Can...

...ouse

Duke Shore Dock

Limekiln Dock

Dock Offices

Whiting, Asphalt
and Color Works

Upper Dock
Middle Dock

Nelson Dock

Steam-boat Dock

...ial Docks

Creosoting
Works

Licensed
Victuallers' Dock

Millwall Dock

Clyde Dock

...y or
...n Dock

Regent Dock

Poplar

East India
Docks

(import)

R. Lea

(export)

Green's Dock

West India Docks
(import)

(export)

Blackwall
Basin

(South Dock)

River Thames

(Timber Dock)

marshes

Bugsby's marshes

timber preserving
& chemical works

Isle

Rope Walk

Lead works

cement works

of

cement works

Millwall

soap works

chain and
anchor works

brickfield

Dogs

marine block works

mast yard

Royal Dockyard (Deptford)

Tyndal's Dock

Scott Russell's

SS Great Eastern
(launched 1858)

Disinfectant
Fluid Works

chemical
works

brickfield

W. Cubitt
& Co.

Rope Walk

Greenwich Hospital
Estate

Port of London Wharf

...Canal

Deptford

Greenwich
Hospital

Phoenix
Gas Works

Royal Naval
School

soap
works

Deptford Creek

Greenwich

chemical works

Many Victorian Londoners wore second-hand clothes obtained from establishments such as this shop in Seven Dials near Covent Garden, one of the poorest parts of central London. The photograph dates from 1877.

© NATIONAL MEDIA MUSEUM / SCIENCE & SOCIETY PICTURE LIBRARY

Many clients of London shops were less wealthy than Abraham Darby, but rich enough to be regular customers, visiting shops to order goods similar to those on display or to buy ready-made items of, for example, clothing or furniture, that might need modification. This demand was met by an army of workers, many operating in their own homes, others in small workshops, and some on retailers' premises. In the tailoring trade a distinction was made between 'honourable' tradesmen, who had garments made on their own premises at standard rates, and 'dishonourable' men who gave out work to 'sweaters' to be done at lower prices. Mayhew calculated in 1849 that only about 3,000 of 21,000 tailors in London were 'honourable'. One sweater to whom he spoke had two men living and working with him, but the average sweater

employed about six individuals, and could make a satisfactory living from their labours without working himself. Sweated workers were paid below the regular rates and were charged for their food and their accommodation, which was usually in garrets. In London there was also a trade in ready-made goods, known in the garments sector as the 'slop business'. Mayhew visited a first-floor workshop, approached along a court crowded with herring stalls, where he found seven men and two girl tailors sitting cross-legged on the floor sewing coats for 'ready-made houses or slop sellers'. They explained that a single tradesman could not get work from a wholesale warehouse because he would not be able to offer the security that a sweater could provide. During the nineteenth century garment manufacture in London became specialised, and in every working-class area there were makers of shirts, waistcoats and trousers, many of whom worked under sweated conditions.

Boundaries between retailing and manufacturing were indistinct, and in the 1860s scarcely any of the clothes, furniture and footwear made in London came from factories with powered machines. George Dodd observed in 1840 that, 'We have no "coat-factories" nor "boot factories", no assemblages of men in large many-storied buildings, manufacturing coats and boots with those appliances of machinery and division of labour which distinguish a factory. Both are handicraft employments, which can be carried on at the home of the workman.'

Much of the evidence collected by Mayhew and his collaborators, and by Charles Booth, attests to the poverty of tradesmen and tradeswomen who had no alternative but to work for sweaters or middlemen engaged in slop business. It was believed by many, moreover, that conditions worsened between 1815 and 1840. Schwarz suggested that sweating had its origins in the mid-eighteenth century or earlier, and in reality it is doubtful whether London tradespeople ever enjoyed a golden age. Not least, the nature of small-scale manufacturing in a capital city made it susceptible to threats. Middlemen could put out work to provincial manufacturers, as when footwear wholesalers ordered shoes from Northamptonshire. New technology also threatened jobs, as happened

One of the great State enterprises in the London area, the gunpowder works at Waltham Abbey. This range of buildings of about 1850 consisted of six gunpowder blending shops, each with stout walls and a flimsy roof that would be blown off in any explosion without damaging the adjacent shops. The machinery in each shop was powered by a steam engine in the tall building in the centre of the range. The blending shops were used in the mid-twentieth century for experimental work on rocket propellants.

with the introduction of steam-driven circular saws in the timber trade. Such threats might successfully be resisted over limited periods, on the grounds that they were contrary to established custom, but in the longer term the impact could be severe. London always offered refuge to the poor, from the British Isles and continental Europe, and it was easy for rates to be undercut by entrepreneurs exploiting the vulnerability of newcomers, who had no resources but their labour. The impact of migrant workers is illustrated by two adjacent households in Richmond Buildings, Soho, recorded in 1861: one was occupied by eight tailors from various parts of Germany, the other by an upholsterer from Dresden, two goldsmiths from St Petersburg and Belgium, and tailors, from Mecklenburg, Baden, Hanover, Bohemia, the Hague and Oslo.

London's roles as garrison city and as a port of embarkation for military personnel *en route* for overseas postings created many manufacturing jobs in addition to those at Woolwich, Deptford, Enfield Lock and Waltham Abbey. There were several army contractors in London, whose precise activities are difficult to fathom, but army tailors, tailoresses, clothiers and makers of trimmings (particularly epaulettes) were numerous in the parish of St Martin-in-the-Fields, and military embroiderers and makers of military caps all over the city. A military plumassier, a craftsman who worked with feathers, lived in Soho, and there was a maker of military gold and silk sashes in Gloucester Street. Military tailors also supplied police forces,

prisons and organisations such as the East India Company. According to Mayhew makers of uniforms were forced to live in poverty. He explained that colonels of regiments were granted annual clothing allowances for their men – £6 10s. 3d. for a cavalry drummer and £2 6s. for an infantry private – but that the sums paid out amounted to much less. A colonel could thereby make a profit of £600 *per annum* on his men's uniforms. Makers of military 'accoutrements' (all a soldier's equipment other than his arms and his uniform – buttons, spurs and belts, for example) worked all over London.

Some of the largest 'manufacturing' establishments in the garment sector were London's fashionable retail stores. In 1841 about 20,000 women were employed in dress making and millinery. Many dressmakers and milliners were living in at large stores, as were sales assistants, cashiers and porters. There were also discrete but sizeable dress-making and millinery concerns catering for the wealthy, with few external signs that they were shops. Mayhew described one with a richly curtained and carpeted showroom, attended by a footman and French assistants. Above was a first-floor workroom with three long deal tables, at which sat young ladies working on garments. Their sleeping quarters were on the second floor. Even at fashionable establishments, though, some work was put out to women working in squalid conditions in garrets, and beyond the prestigious stores in the West End extended a hierarchy of second- and third-class establishments. There were also warehouses where garments, especially bonnets, were mass-produced for export to the colonies.

Mayhew's estimate that three-quarters of London's dressmakers and milliners had grown up in the country is confirmed by census returns. For example, at 59–62 Oxford Street, the drapery store of Grant & Gask, the 1861 census recorded 34 male and 5 female assistants, 6 milliners, 5 porters and 8 domestic servants, all supervised by a housekeeper. Of the 45 milliners and assistants, only 7 had been born in the London area; 19 came from elsewhere in England, 11 from Scotland, one each from Ireland, Wales, the Isle of Man, Switzerland and Canada, and 3 from Paris. At the Peter Robinson linen drapery store (103–108 Oxford Street) there were 32 male assistants, 24 female assistants, milliners and mantle makers, 6 clerks and cashiers, 10 porters and watchmen and 5 domestic servants. Of the 62 assistants and craftswomen, 7 were from London, 48 from 18 different English counties, 3 from Wales, 2 from Scotland, and one each from France and Jersey. The staff included John Lewis, a 24-year-old assistant from Bridgwater, who worked for Peter Robinson until he opened his own shop in 1864. Elizabeth Ramage, a 67-year-old widowed dressmaker lived at 26–27 Portman Street, where she employed her two daughters and 32 other young women, of whom 11 were from Scotland, 5 from London, one from Ireland and one from Jamaica. William Bacon, a draper of 44–46 Old Compton Street, employed 70 people, including 39 males and 7 females who lived in. Some similarly large shops flourished in the suburbs, at such places as Newington Causeway where one drapery establishment in 1861 was managed overnight by a senior assistant in charge of 66 male and 9 female live-in staff.

Several innovative developments in retailing combined shopping with entertainment. 'At the head of its class' in 1842 was said to be the 'bazaar' at 4–6 Soho Square, opened on 1 February 1816 by John Trotter, who had prospered as an army contractor during the Napoleonic Wars. He converted his four-storey, seven-bay warehouse into a 'bazaar', with open mahogany counters ranged on either side of aisles on two floors of the building. They were rented on a daily basis by about 200 young women, who sold millinery, gloves, lace and jewellery, often made in their own homes. In 1861 the matron – a 55-year-old spinster from Leith – insisted that the women adopt a plain and modest style of dress. During the social season Trotter's bazaar, which traded until 1889, attracted custom from carriage-owning families. The Pantheon, between Oxford Street and Great Marlborough Street, was an eighteenth-century theatre which was adapted as a bazaar in 1834. It included a picture gallery and stalls selling the products of London's workshops – millinery, children's toys, dresses, sheet music, pocket books, ceramic ornaments and artificial flowers. As in the Soho Bazaar, each counter was attended by a young woman. The Pantheon, which closed in 1867, included an aviary, tanks filled with goldfish, and a conservatory with pot plants. The Lowther Arcade was described as 'a tube of shops running from St Martin's Churchyard into the Strand', comparable with the tube in which Robert Stephenson carried the Chester & Holyhead Railway over the Menai Straits. It was celebrated for toys, especially Noah's Arks, 'those Edens of wooden zoology'; jewellery, including brooches with portraits of Marie Antoinette, Jenny Lind, Oliver Cromwell and Louis Kossuth; and as the 'Bagdad of housekeeping odds and ends, including Windsor soap, French coffee pots, scent bottles and fans'. The Pantechnicon off Belgrave Square and the Baker Street Bazaar were points of sale for second-hand carriages. The former also sold furniture, wine and toys, while the latter incorporated Madame Tussaud's exhibition of waxworks.

A particularly dynamic development was the store opened in 1863 at 31 Westbourne Grove by the Yorkshireman William Whiteley, who perceived that profits might be gained by providing for the occupants of fashionable Bayswater. His shop expanded into neighbouring properties and by 1867 comprised 17 departments. Many of its 622 employees in 1872 were accommodated in dormitories operated under a regime of severe discipline. Many others supplied the store from their homes or from workshops. In 1881 Whiteley declared his occupation as 'Universal Provider'.

Precious materials, precision goods and music

London craftsmen also produced many products using imported gold, silver, precious stones, ivory and tropical hardwoods. Such manufactures depended on complex systems of sub-contracting. Gold and silver, for example, were beaten and refined in workshops, to be used by jewellers and makers of clocks and watches. Brass-founders, finishers and chasers worked all over London, many making mundane fittings for plumbers and gas fitters, but some providing precision parts for mechanical engineers and instrument makers. Turners of ivory, ebony and mahogany, meanwhile, supplied cabinetmakers, and provided parts used by instrument makers and makers of jewellery boxes. London's glass workers were among the most skilled in Europe, providing mirrors for cabinetmakers and others, and lenses and ground glass for makers of telescopes. Gun making was a work of assembly that traditionally drew on the skills of independent makers of barrels, locks, stocks and cases. Some of the most significant craftsmen in London produced anatomical, astronomical, drawing, mathematical, surgical and navigational instruments. The development of the chronometer by London watchmakers, including John Harrison and Thomas Earnshaw, made possible the voyages to the distant countries which produced the imports on which such manufactures were based.

The music 'industry' in London between 1700 and the 1860s was in part a manufacturing activity, concerned with wood, metals and paper, but it also provided livings for performers, copyists and teachers. The manufacture of pianos underwent a process that can reasonably be called an 'industrial revolution'. Many craftsmen and musicians contributed to its development, but the transformation of piano making into an industry can be observed through the evolution of the Broadwood company, which originated when Burkat Shudi migrated from Switzerland to London in 1718, and was apprenticed to a maker of harpsichords. He opened a workshop in 1728 and in 1765 supplied the instrument played in London by the nine-year-old Mozart. John Broadwood migrated to London from the Lothian Hills in 1761, eight years later married Shudi's daughter, became his partner in 1771, and inherited a share of the business when Shudi died in 1773. From about 1777 Broadwood made pianos in harpsichord cases and commissioned research from the Royal

➤ John Broadwood was not the only large-scale manufacturer of pianos in London. D'Almaine & Co. were publishers and retailers of sheet music with a shop at 20 Soho Square. They also had an extensive business in manufacturing musical instruments, including flutes and clarinets, and produced pianos in this factory in Chilton Street off the Bethnal Green Road. It is a remarkably well-lit building, indicating the precision work necessary in making keys and fixing strings.
© THOMAS HOSMER SHEPHERD/MUSEUM OF LONDON

Society into their workings. In 1784 he produced more pianos than harpsichords and ceased making the latter from 1793. He left a fortune which was inherited by his son, James Shudi Broadwood, and grandson, Henry Fowler Broadwood, who joined the board in 1836. The company leased land in Westminster in 1823, and by 1840 their factory extended 100 yards from gates in Horseferry Road, through several quadrangles, to an entrance in Holywell Street. Workshop-made parts were assembled into instruments, which were taken to showrooms in Great Pulteney Street, where they were finished and tuned. In 1840 the company employed about 400 people at Horseferry Road, 150 at the showrooms and others making small parts in their own homes or workshops; the firm was among London's twelve largest employers of labour. Many of Broadwoods' materials were imported through the Port of London. Mahogany came from Honduras and Spain; ivory, used as a veneer on limewood to make white keys; ebony, used solid in black keys; and felt made from Hungarian wool. The factory also used native beech and sycamore, vellum and leather readily available in London, and wire of 14 thicknesses. Wood was turned on lathes renowned for their sophisticated design. Broadwood & Co. prided themselves on their settled, skilled workforce. There was a fire at Horseferry Road in 1856, but the factory was rebuilt,

and the company remained in Westminster until 1902. Horseferry Road was a factory of outstanding size and reputation, but pianos were also manufactured in other parts of London, as were other instruments: guitars and violins in Westminster; flutes off St Martin's Lane; clarinets and concertinas in Islington. Many organ builders were based in London, too, including Thomas Robson of St Martin's Lane who had 15 employees in 1861. In 1851 the almost 3,000 makers of instruments in London represented more than 80 per cent of the national total. Those living in Soho in 1861 included four Germans in Bateman's Buildings, three from Lyons in Frith Street, a French violin maker, and makers of brass instruments from Germany and Ireland.

The service sector of the music industry could be found in Soho and on the northern side of Oxford Street, where in one group of streets in 1861 96 people gained their livings from music, manufacturing and selling instruments, composing, copying, engraving, publishing and selling scores, performing, and teaching. 'Professors' of music in the area originated in Belgium, the Netherlands, Breslau, Dublin and the Isle of Man. German musicians who toured the provinces regarded London as a base, and the 1861 census reveals that a nonet from Nassau spent census night at a public house in Wardour Street.

Brewing

As we have seen, cotton mills dominated the landscape in Ancoats, as did blast furnaces in Merthyr Tydfil, but London's breweries were the capital's most prominent industrial buildings. From the 1720s until the 1860s their characteristic product was a heavy, dark porter. Brewing benefited from the application of science: the use of thermometers from the 1760s, and of hydrometers from the 1770s; the rolling of copper sheets, which made possible the construction of larger vats; and steam power which was used for pumping and for driving machines.

Whitbread's brewery in Chiswell Street, near the border of the City in Islington, was one of London's most important breweries. The Porter Tun Room there measures 160 × 60 feet (49.3 × 18.5 m), has a

spectacular king-post roof completed in 1784, and is now part of a conference centre. Samuel Whitbread had established his brewery on the site from 1750 around an existing house. By 1760 he was producing 64,000 barrels *per annum*, and the brewery was the second largest in London. A Boulton & Watt steam engine was being installed by John Rennie when the French aristocrats, the brothers La Rochefoucauld, visited the brewery in 1785. It pumped water and beer, and drove rollers crushing malt, an Archimedes screw lifting crushed malt into hoppers, agitators in vats, and hoisting gear. It worked until 1887 and since 1888 has been exhibited in Sydney where it is now displayed at the Power House Museum. The brewery's annual production expanded to 202,000 barrels in 1796, and

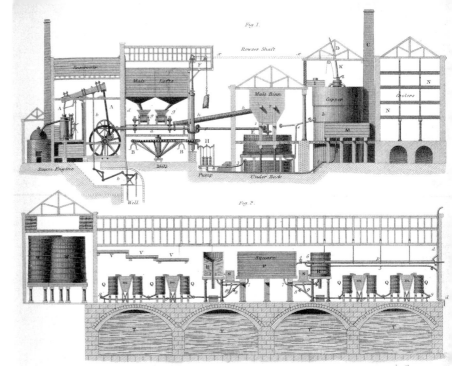

From the 1750s until long after the end of the period covered in this book, Whitbread's brewery in Chiswell Street was one of the largest in London. This engraving, based on drawings made by John Farey jnr in 1810, shows elevations of the inside and outside and a cross-section of the Porter Brewery, idealised in places so that all the equipment can be seen at once. The steam engine (A) drives the great wheel (B, with harnesses), which in turn drives the malt grinders (G), lifting tackle (F), Archimedean screw (H) and rouser chains in the copper (via the overhead shaft X). The second elevation, taken at right angles to the first, shows some of the fermenting tuns and the huge, stone-lined basement cisterns. Brewing was big business in the capital.

it remained among the capital's largest in 1870. When he died in 1796 Whitbread left more than £1 million. He was succeeded by his son Samuel Whitbread II, the Whig politician and opponent of slavery, who invested in the Southill estate in the family's native Bedfordshire, where the mansion was redesigned by Henry Holland. The popularity of porter waned from the 1860s, but bottling plant, installed at Chiswell Street from 1868, enabled Whitbread's lighter beers to become national brands.

In the mid-nineteenth century the Black Eagle brewery of Truman, Hanbury, Buxton in Brick Lane, Spitalfields, occupied six acres. It was more than three decades old in 1700, and from 1722 was managed by Benjamin Truman whose name became a brand. Sampson Hanbury was a partner from 1780. His nephew, Thomas Fowell Buxton, MP, prison reformer and opponent of slavery, was involved in management from 1808, introduced steam power, and developed national markets. In the 1860s the brewery consumed more malt than any other in London, drew its water from wells 850 feet (262 m) deep, and was proud of its 80 draymen, supposedly taller and heavier by two stone than guardsmen. Many of the brewery buildings in Brick Lane still stand and have been adapted for retailing and recreational purposes.

The Thames riverbank boasted several highly visible industrial buildings. Among them was the Anchor Brewery, which dominated Southwark's riverside. Ralph Thrale worked there for twenty years and became owner in 1729, repaying the money he borrowed within eleven years. His son Henry Thrale was married to Hester (née Salusbury), friend of Samuel Johnson, who, when acting as executor of Thrale's will in 1781, remarked, 'We are not here to sell a parcel of boilers and vats but the potentiality of growing rich beyond the dreams of avarice'. The business was purchased by John Perkins, its manager, and David Barclay of the banking family, and as Barclay Perkins was one of London's largest breweries until its closure in 1955. Its output in 1840, 361,321 barrels *per annum*, was larger than that of Truman Hanbury at 263,295 or Whitbread at 218,828. In 1850 the site extended over ten acres and employed 430 men and 160 dray horses. Its principal brewhouse measured 225 × 60 feet (69.3 × 19.5 m), and was open to a great height, with no intervening floors or partitions. Two towering buildings were linked across a street by a suspension bridge. Steam engines of 45 and 30 hp provided power for pumps and machines. Barclay Perkins did not own the land between the brewery and the river, and in the 1840s gangs of porters had to be employed carrying malt from barges in 1.5 cwt sacks up several flights of stairs to a warehouse.

The Horseshoe Brewery towered above the junction of Tottenham Court Road and Oxford Street and was celebrated for its 'black beer'. It originated in 1764 and was purchased in 1809 by Sir Henry Meux. In 1785 several porter vats, 22 feet (6.8 m) high and each bound by 29 iron hoops and holding 20,000 barrels of porter, were installed at the top of the building. On 17 October 1814 an iron hoop snapped; the contents exploded outwards, causing the collapse of other vats, and approximately 2.75 million pints of beer cascaded into St Giles, demolishing two houses. Nine people died, one of them from alcohol poisoning having drunk copiously from the torrents gushing down the streets. In 1865 the Horseshoe Brewery used about half the malt consumed at the Anchor and Black Horse breweries, but was nevertheless a large concern. It was demolished in 1922.

Many other breweries in London would have been regarded as exceptionally large manufacturing concerns had they been located in the provinces, among them the Lion Brewery established on the South Bank in 1837 (whose Coadstone lion adorns the approach to Westminster Bridge); the Stag Brewery in Pimlico, in which James Watney became a partner in 1837; and the Mortlake Brewery, purchased by Watneys in 1889. Brewing enterprises in London, like those in Edinburgh and Dublin, grew because they were at the nodal points of transport systems, and could easily obtain grain and fuel. They had customers close at hand, easily supplied by horse-drawn drays, and could readily gain access to distant markets in Britain, and overseas with such products as Russian Stout.

The brewery in Upper Thames Street, which from 1866 stood next to Cannon Street Station, occupied a site which supposedly had been used continuously for brewing from 1431. From 1759 the brewery was directed by Felix Calvert, and after his death in 1802 by his son Nicholas; from 1860 the firm was known as the City of London Brewery Co. In 1785 the brewery was the second largest in London after Whitbread's, but for most of the nineteenth century it was sixth or seventh in the hierarchy. The company acquired a brewery in Fulham in 1919 and three years later ceased brewing in the City. The buildings in Upper Thames Street were used for storage until 1941 when they were destroyed by bombs. This image shows the brewery *circa* 1820.
© ROBERT B. SCHNEBBELIE/MUSEUM OF LONDON

↳ This view of the Falcon Glassworks, Holland Street, Blackfriars, shows the interior of the English glass cone that was added to the complex about 1820. The central flue is supported on columns and surrounded by small glass furnaces from which glass blowers are taking liquid glass.

© MUSEUM OF LONDON

Leather and glass

London was the principal centre of leather processing in Britain. The capital city had greater access to raw materials than any other town. Smithfield produced hides and skins as a by-product of the capital's appetite for meat, while hides were also imported: we know that a tannery visited by Dodd used skins that had come from as far away as Switzerland, Germany, North Africa, the East Indies, the Cape of Good Hope and Asia Minor. The industry was also helped by the fact that London had many consumers of leather: coachmakers, harness-makers and bookbinders; millwrights who installed leather belting; families whose members could afford more than one pair of shoes or boots; people rich enough to buy writing cases, cigar cases or billiard tables; cavalry officers requiring chamois breeches; lawyers needing parchment for deeds and covenants; and people whose daily tasks required the protection of aprons or heavy gloves. The political economist James McCulloch, indeed, rated leather as the most important material in the economy, after cotton, wool and iron.

The significance of imports is symbolised by the Skin Floor, or the Tobacco Dock, in the London Docks, which once contained 210,000 square feet (19,500 sq m) of working space. It was built in 1811–14 to the design of Daniel Alexander, with a roof supported by a grid of tree-like iron columns, standing above a cavernous brick-vaulted undercroft. The upper part was designed to handle tobacco, and the cellars for wines and spirits, but for most of its working life the building was known as the Skin Floor and was used for the storage of hides from Australia.

In 1841 more than 900 people, almost all adult males, worked in London's tanneries; about 90 per cent of them in or near the Leather Market in Bermondsey, which opened in 1833. Other workers in the area included curriers, sellers of hides and skins, dealers in bark, leather-dyers and enamellers, and

Bermondsey was the principal area of leather working in eighteenth- and nineteenth-century London. This image taken by the 23-year-old amateur photographer Geoffrey Bevington depicts work in progress at his family's business and was displayed on their stand at the International Exhibition of 1862. The firm of Bevington & Sons was established in 1795 and had premises at Neckinger Mills, Bermondsey, and St Thomas's Street, Southwark. The photograph shows sheep skins intended for use as rugs being cleansed and pared.

© GEOFFREY BEVINGTON/MUSEUM OF LONDON

The Skin Floor (or Tobacco Dock) in the London Docks is one of the most astonishing buildings in the Port of London. It was built in 1811–14 to the design of Daniel Alexander, initially as a bonded store for imported bales of tobacco, but for most of its working life it served as a warehouse for hides imported from Australia. Its roof was supported by lines of bifurcating iron columns of the kind seen here, while its brick-vaulted undercroft has the atmosphere of a cathedral crypt. After the closure of the London Docks the Skin Floor was adapted for retailing in 1984–89.

makers of parchment, as well as those concerned with other by-products from meat markets – such as wool staplers and warehousemen, hair and flock manufacturers, dealers in horns and hooves, and manufacturers of glue and neats' foot oil. The low-lying marshy areas to the south of the Thames were ideal for leather processing. In 1850 Mayhew described the leather-working streets of Bermondsey, the peculiar smells of raw hides and of the dark, chocolate-coloured liquors in tan pits, and the clicking of steam engines turning bark mills. Characteristic buildings were grouped around pits, 'long and sometimes high and always black and wooden structures, without glass windows, but with boards that can be closed or opened to admit air at pleasure'. Yards were filled with new and spent bark, heaps of leather off-cuts for gluemakers, and horns for comb makers and cutlers. Curriers prepared skins and tanned hides for shoemakers, saddlers and

coachmakers and, according to Mayhew, could be recognised by their blue flannel trousers, jackets and aprons and their superior boots.

Glass was made in London from the seventeenth century, and 19 of 66 glass manufacturers listed in the *Universal British Directory* in the 1790s were in the capital. The 1,000-strong glass-working labour force in London in 1841 was of similar size to those in Lancashire and the North East. Many were involved in cutting or shaping glass, but glass making took place on a considerable scale. Until 1780 the principal works were at Vauxhall. The glassworks by Falcon Wharf on the south bank near Blackfriars Bridge dated from the seventeenth century. It was taken over in 1803 by the firm of Pellatt & Green, managed in the mid-nineteenth century by Apsley Pellatt, who wrote books on glass making and developed encrustation as a means of decoration. When Dodd visited the Falcon

Industry developed around the suburban fringes as well as in the centre of London. Walkers, Maltby & Co. (see page 383) opened a lead-processing plant adjacent to a popular public house, the *Rosemary Branch*, at Islington in 1783, building two windmills in 1786 and 1792 to grind white lead, used in making paint. By 1835 the windmills had been replaced by a 20 hp steam engine. At that time the plant had about 50 employees, two-thirds of them women, whose health was supposedly less affected by toxic fumes than that of men.

WATERCOLOUR, 1795, BY JULIUS CAESAR IBBETSON
© JULIUS IBBETSON/MUSEUM OF LONDON

works in 1840, Pellatt was using sand from Lynn in Norfolk and Alum Bay, and Australian sand that had arrived as ballast, together with American alkali, probably pearl ash. The three cylindrical kilns within the quadrangle of buildings were fired with coke, burned from Northumberland small coal in coke ovens on the premises. Stourbridge clay was used to make melting pots; when worn out these were ground up in a horse-powered mill and the materials re-used. The works produced drinking-glasses, cruets, decanters, claret jugs and lampshades, many of them engraved, which were displayed in a showroom in St Paul's churchyard. Pellatt also supplied phials and four-sided perfume bottles. Other London glassmakers produced bottles for beer and vinegar. The capital's principal sources of plate glass were the Albion Cast Plate Glass

Manufactory across Blackfriars Road, established about 1789 by Alexander Black, and the Thames Plate Glass Works, opened in Glasshouse Place, Poplar, in 1835 and closed in 1874, when, reputedly, its employees emigrated to make glass in New Albany, Indiana.

Dodd remarked that Pellatt supplied glass to astronomers and opticians. The makers of scientific and surgical instruments used lenses and ground glass; mirrors with bevelled edges were employed in cabinet making; and the jewellery trade produced jewelled silver hand mirrors and ornamental lamps. In 1794 two London glassworkers specialised in coach-glass. Nevertheless, London was not self-sufficient in glass products, and most of the leading provincial manufacturers had depots in the capital.

Engines, carriages and ships

London's role in the diffusion of engineering expertise is discussed in Chapter 3. The capital was one of the country's principal sources of machines, and in the 1820s engineering employed about 10,000 men in London. In 1753 Angerstein noted: 'Travelling home to the Royal Exchange by boat, a distance of two English miles, I saw, on the south bank of the Thames, iron foundries, a factory making white lead, glass-works ...' Maudslay & Field supposedly had 800 workers in 1851,

while some shipbuilders employed several hundred, but most establishments were foundries or machine shops employing fewer than twenty. Four railway companies constructed locomotive and carriage works in the capital. The Eastern Counties (from 1862 the Great Eastern) Railway opened its works on a 31-acre site at Stratford in 1847 and produced its first locomotives in 1851. Its workforce in 1861 included men who had come from Tipton, Glasgow, Cornwall,

Leeds and Newcastle. The London & Southampton (later the London & South Western) Railway workshops near the passenger terminus at Nine Elms were opened in 1838, constructed locomotives from 1843, and moved to a new site in 1861–65. Carriage building was transferred to Eastleigh in 1891, to be followed by locomotive construction in 1908–10. The London, Chatham & Dover Railway built a works at Longhedge Farm, Battersea, in 1863 and constructed locomotives there from 1869 until 1904, after which it became part of the Stewart's Lane engine shed. The North London Railway's locomotive and carriage shops at Bow dated from 1853, and locomotives were built

there from 1863. The principal private builder was George England, a native of Newcastle-upon-Tyne who set up the Hatcham Ironworks in Pomeroy Street, New Cross, in the 1840s and, with many craftsmen from the North East, sold locomotives to railway companies in Britain and abroad. The works supplied locomotives to the Festiniog Railway in 1863–64, and in 1869 constructed for the company the celebrated double-ended locomotive *Little Wonder*, designed by Robert Fairlie. In all, some 2,700 steam locomotives are known to have been built in London, the majority before 1900. Other substantial foundries included the Manor Ironworks of Holbrook & Co. in Manor Street,

Robert Fairlie was a talented engineer, who proposed the construction of articulated locomotives in a paper of 1864. In 1862 he eloped with the 19-year-old daughter of George England, of the Hatcham Ironworks in south London. In court he claimed to have received his father-in-law's assent to the marriage, but it was revealed that England's own wife had been born out of wedlock, and that he therefore had no right to withhold consent to Fairlie's marriage. Despite this, business relationships between Fairlie and England appear to have prospered. The Hatcham Ironworks constructed the Festiniog Railway's first Double Fairlie locomotive (page 588), *Little Wonder*, in 1869, and as a result of its success the railway was permitted to build further locomotives of this type without paying patent royalties.

NATIONAL LIBRARY OF WALES

Hooper & Co. originated as Adams & Hooper in 1805 and were among the best known and most successful of London coach-building companies. The landau became popular around the time of Queen Victoria's coronation in 1838. This example was designed by George N. Hooper, and the drawing dates from 1855. Hooper & Co. moved from building horse-drawn carriages to providing bodies for motor cars, which they continued to do until 1959.

© SCIENCE MUSEUM/SCIENCE & SOCIETY PICTURE LIBRARY

Chelsea, whose skilled labour force included men from Cornwall, Leeds, Dudley and Ripley, and the works at Greenwich and Deptford of John Penn, who supplied engines for 735 ships during his working lifetime.

In many ways coach building was the archetypal London industry. For coachbuilders there was a strong local market, including export agents and visiting aristocrats and gentry who spent time in the capital. The industry could also draw on a wide range of specialist supplies, readily available in London as nowhere else. London was the focus of Britain's transport system, both by road and sea, as well as later by rail, and the capital's coach manufacturers were able to prosper from a large and expanding market.

Carriages were commonly used in London by 1700, and Chapter 5 details the expansion of stage, posting and mail coach services during the eighteenth century. Statistics demonstrating the growth of short-distance road transport after the coming of railways are provided by the carriage duty: in 1834 duty was paid in the United Kingdom for almost 100,000 two- and four-wheeled carriages, increasing to 205,000 by 1854, to 272,000 by 1864 and to 410,000 by 1874. Many of these vehicles were built in London. In 1851 there were as many as 4,948 coachbuilders, more than 30 per cent of the national total. London coachmakers supplied vehicles for use in the provinces, including stagecoaches, opulently furnished vehicles for aristocrats and, in the nineteenth century, cabs and hackney carriages. Quality carriages were exported by the East India Company and to America, and some coachmakers fulfilled orders from aristocratic and royal families in continental Europe. Members of the trade also made fire-engines, omnibuses, invalid chairs and babies' perambulators, and in 1861 one bath-chair maker employed a dozen men.

Many advances in coach making were made during the eighteenth century. Crucible steel made possible the manufacture of superior springs, and in 1804 Obadiah Elliott of Lambeth introduced the steel elliptical leaf spring, which he improved with the aid of a grant from the Society of Arts. Erasmus Darwin and Richard Lovell Edgeworth were among many enthusiasts who proposed improvements in coach construction. Charles Hatchett, son of John Hatchett,

a Long Acre coachmaker, was a polymath who mixed on equal terms with the leading figures in the industrial revolution. In 1794 a coachmaker attributed to John Hatchett improvements in design used by almost every member of the trade. Samuel Hobson, who from about 1824 took over Hatchett's workshop, made further improvements, reducing the heights of wheels, lengthening coach bodies and hanging them lower, and substituting a double step to the door for a three-step ladder.

Coach building involved many skills and overlapped several other trades. The carriage or chassis was constructed from wrought iron by coach smiths and vice-men, incorporating springs and wheels that had been made by specialist wheelers. A coach body usually had an ash frame with panels of mahogany, and a roof which by the late eighteenth century might be of paperboard. The lining or trim was usually of woollen cloth stuffed with horsehair, but of silk or fine leather in vehicles designed for the wealthy. Fittings were prepared by coach- and harness-platers, and in 1861 we learn of one specialist 'coach finisher' who employed six people in Devonshire Street, Marylebone. Coaches were elaborately painted, and those for public service or for the wealthy had heraldic inscriptions executed by specialists.

Coach making benefited from the presence in the capital of leading coaching entrepreneurs, including William Chaplin, who in the 1830s had five yards from which he leased vehicles, and 1,300 horses, to stagecoach operators. Mailcoaches, introduced from 1786 by John Palmer, were smaller vehicles, and advances in technology enabled the reduction of their weight by 1820 to no more than 16 cwt. About 700 were operating when coaching reached its zenith about 1830. All were made by Besant & Vidler of Millbank, who also hired them to contractors and serviced the vehicles during layover periods. In the eighteenth century most carriages plying for hire were second-hand private vehicles, but builders began to produce specialist hackney carriages. Joseph Aloysius Hansom, architect of Birmingham Town Hall and founder of *The Builder*, designed a 'patent safety cabriolet' in 1835 and formed a company to manufacturer the vehicle that was to immortalise his name, although the company actually produced a design by John Chapman. By 1870 the principal builder of Hansom cabs was the company established in 1864 in Wolverhampton by Henry Forder, who had showrooms in St Martin's Lane, London.

Coachbuilders worked in most parts of London, but throughout our period the trade was concentrated in Long Acre, north of Covent Garden. Many well-known companies were there at the time of the 1861 census, including Henry Turrill at 22–23 Long Acre, who employed 27 men and made three coaches for the Marquesses of Bute (now displayed at Arlington Court near Barnstaple). His neighbours included Charles Saunders at no. 14, with 13 employees, Robert Silk at nos 8–9 with between 50 and 60, John Allen at no. 72 with 10, and Henry Hall at nos 97–98 with 26. More than 100 men directly involved in coach making lived in Long Acre and adjacent streets, including coach draughtsmen, spring makers, body makers, coach lace weavers, lining makers, coach trimmers, coach carvers and makers of carriage lamps. Coach making also involved suppliers who had customers in other trades, such as harness and varnish makers, oil and colour men, brassfounders and engravers of brass, upholsterers, wheelwrights, heraldic painters and India rubber workers, who supplied brake blocks.

Just as London was Britain's premier port, so, until the 1860s, it was the nation's principal centre for shipbuilding. There were just over 20,000 shipbuilders (excluding caulkers and other allied occupations) in Great Britain in 1841, of whom 11 per cent were in London, most of them in Poplar. By repute shipwrights were intelligent, received high wages, and effectively maintained protective practices. Most built

John Penn was a mechanical engineer who became the principal supplier of marine engines to the Royal Navy. He succeeded to the management of the engineering company John Penn & Sons when his father died in 1843, and began to specialise in marine engines. He displayed his management skills at the beginning of the Crimean War in 1854 when he supervised the production of 90 engines of 60 hp for gunboats to be deployed in the Baltic, parts for which were made in machines shops all over the country. During his career he produced engines for 735 ships, including HMS *Warrior*, and was twice president of the Institution of Mechanical Engineers. At its peak John Penn & Sons employed 1,800 people at Greenwich and Deptford. Like Henry Maudslay in a previous generation he was responsible for training large numbers of mechanical engineers (see also page 455).

HMS *Warrior*, launched on 29 December 1860 and commissioned on 1 August 1861, was the Royal Navy's first iron-hulled, armour-plated battleship, and at 9,210 tons was the largest warship of her time. She was built at the Thames Ironworks, Blackwall, an indication of the supremacy of London shipbuilders in the mid-nineteenth century. New developments quickly made her obsolete, and she had been downgraded within a decade and used for coastguard duties and then as a naval educational establishment and as an oil store. A campaign for her restoration began in 1967 and twenty years later she was returned to Portsmouth.

wooden vessels and regarded with hostility those who built iron steamships. London shipbuilders were best known in the eighteenth century for building for the East India trade, although the Thames was lined with small yards, where barges and lighters were made for use on the river and in coasting.

A shipyard at Millwall was opened in 1839 by David Napier, cousin of Robert Napier, the pioneer of iron shipbuilding on the Clyde (see page 340). Before moving to London, David Napier built the boiler for *Comet* in 1812, and constructed steamships in Scotland. Jacob and Joseph d'Aguilar Samuda established the firm of Samuda Brothers by the mouth of Bow Creek in 1843, but moved in 1852 to a more spacious site at Cubitt Town on the Isle of Dogs. Alfred Yarrow began building steam launches at Folly Wall on the Isle of Dogs in 1865. One of the largest companies in London was the Thames Ironworks, established in 1837 by Thomas Ditchburn, a shipwright, and Charles Mare, a naval architect, which from 1838 operated at Bow Creek. Within a few years their yards extended over 14 acres, and in 1847 they established a site at Canning Town, where they had rolling mills, and capacity to build vessels of up to 4,000 tons. They employed 3,000 people when they built the steamship *Himalaya* for the P & O Line in 1853 and HMS *Warrior* (the navy's first iron-hulled, armour-plated warship) in 1860. The greatest achievement of London shipbuilders was the construction of Brunel's *Great Eastern*, begun by John

Scott Russell, naval architect, secretary of the Society of Arts, commissioner of the Great Exhibition, and an accomplished scholar in fluid dynamics. He acquired the site of Napier's shipyard, laid down the keel in May 1854, and went bankrupt in 1856. The vessel was launched at the fourth attempt in January 1858 after hydraulic rams had been acquired from the company recently established in Birmingham by the Cornish engineer Richard Tangye. The ramp upon which *Great Eastern* was built was uncovered in the 1980s and can still be seen in Napier Avenue, Millwall.

While *Great Eastern* was not eclipsed in size until the end of the century the average size of iron steam-ships grew steadily, and launching was increasingly problematic in a narrow river busy with shipping. Iron plates could be delivered to London by sea, but ship-builders on Tyneside, Wearside and Clydeside were closer to forges and rolling mills. London's role as a shipbuilding centre was further undermined by the financial crisis of 1866, when it was calculated that 30,000 men were unemployed in Poplar. This decline was exacerbated by the Admiralty's decision to close the royal dockyard at Woolwich in 1869. Some ship-building continued – the 714-ton sailing clipper *Ambassador*, of composite iron and wood construction was built at Rotherhithe in 1869 (its hull survives in Chile), and the Thames Ironworks built ships until 1912 – but other yards either closed or moved elsewhere. The great days of shipbuilding on the Thames were over.

⋏ A detail of 'Building the Great Leviathan', an oil painting by William Parrott showing I. K. Brunel's great steamship the SS *Great Eastern* nearing completion on the riverbank at Millwall on the Isle of Dogs, not long before its much delayed launching on 31 January 1858. The decision to construct the largest steamship of its time in a London yard reflects the pre-eminence of the capital's shipyards in the mid-nineteenth century. It is also worth noting how the Brunel's ship towers over the other vessels in the Thames.

NATIONAL MARITIME MUSEUM

Sugar importing and processing

Processing sugar was another quintessential London activity. Imports of raw sugar increased from about 500,000 cwt in 1700 to about 3 million in 1800, and the proportion re-exported diminished as consumption in Britain increased. Sugar refineries were established in several locations on the west coast, but the industry had a substantial presence in London. The most significant technological development, the use of vacuum pans heated by steam, was the work of the aristocrat chemist Edward Charles Howard, brother of the 12th Duke of Norfolk – he was invited by Charles Ellis, 1st Baron Seaford, to investigate the refining of sugar, and he patented his process in 1812.

Most of the capital's sugar-processing works were in Whitechapel. In 1873 there were eight refineries in the area, lofty buildings with many small windows, within which George Dodd observed 'an extraordinary quantity of pipes and tubes of various sizes traversing the premises in every direction'. Brown sugar was imported in hogsheads and delivered by waggons from the West India Docks. Refineries used large quantities of water, usually raised from wells by steam pumps,

as raw sugar was dissolved in cisterns and treated with lime water before being filtered through cotton bags and decoloured, using 'animal charcoal' made by heating bones in retorts at several nearby works. After boiling in Howard's patent copper vacuum pans the solution was poured into conical moulds laid out on the upper storeys to allow syrup to drain out (it was reboiled to produce an inferior grade of sugar). Most sugar in the mid-nineteenth century was sent to shopkeepers as conical sugar loaves: the bases of the loaves were scraped and left to harden for several days before they were wrapped in paper and dried in ovens, then rewrapped in blue paper ready for sale. Many of the refineries in Whitechapel closed in the 1870s, after which sugar making was concentrated at the enormous new Tate & Lyle plant in Silvertown in Newham.

No London industry was more the preserve of migrants than sugar processing. While the laborious task of filling moulds was traditionally done by Irishmen, the majority of sugar-refiners or boilers in Whitechapel were Germans, more than 400 of whom were recorded in the 1861 census in the parish of St

George-in-the-East. About half were recorded simply as German but more than 150 were from Hanover, 30 from Prussia, 10 from Hamburg, with others from Frankfurt-am-Main, Bremen, Kassel and Schleswig. Many were single men in their twenties who lived at German lodging-houses, or at the refineries. German seamen and groups of German musicians also stayed in Whitechapel, and there were several German shops and beerhouses, one of them the headquarters of a German friendly society. There were German churches (both Lutheran and Catholic), German bread bakers, shoemakers, tailors, cigar makers and carpenters, a sausage manufacturer from Heidelberg, and even some German prostitutes.

Bricks and stones

While subject to the fluctuations of the trade cycle, the building trade between 1700 and 1870 generally prospered as London expanded. At the beginning of the eighteenth century much of the land surrounding the built-up area consisted of clay which, using the ready supply of coal from the North East, could be used to produce bricks. Shallow clay workings extended over areas that were subsequently used for housing. By 1850, though, bricks were also being brought into London from elsewhere. In the Medway Valley local clays, with the addition of coal ashes and street sweepings from London, were shaped and fired with sea-borne coal to produce bricks that were taken away by barge. Another source was in Middlesex, deliveries being made along the Paddington branch of the Grand Junction Canal. The wharfs at Little Venice and Bull's Bridge, where the branch joined the line to Brentford, were concerned chiefly with building materials. Vessels took bricks into London and returned with ashes or dust. There were 41 boats at the Paddington basin on 7 April 1861, of which the cargoes of 34 are known: of these, 15 were carrying bricks, and 5 were loaded with ashes, breeze or dust for brick making. Of 23 boats around Bull's Bridge, 20 were carrying ashes or bricks. Lime and gravel were also taken by canal into the Paddington basin. Inconsistencies in census enumeration make it difficult to measure the size of the industry, but it was clearly extensive. More than 220 makers of bricks and tiles lived in Hillingdon in 1861, many of them in a hamlet called Starve All. In Hayes, with a population of 2,636, there were more than 250 brickmakers, most of them at Yeading. In Norwood, which included Southall, there were over 100, but brickfield labourers were under-recorded. The movement of bricks by rail from Bedfordshire and the Soke of Peterborough only began after 1881.

London drew in materials from many other parts of the British Isles, unloaded from coasting vessels or lighters at wharfs along the Thames and cut, shaped and sometimes polished in adjacent yards before being passed to builders. Slate was brought from North Wales, the Lake District, and Delabole in Cornwall; stone from the isles of Portland and Purbeck; and paving stones from Yorkshire and Poole. There were several stoneyards along the Regent's Canal. Marble arrived from several sources, and the Westminster Marble Works, where much of it was polished, was almost as extensive as the adjacent piano factory. Building materials also arrived by rail – thus, in 1861 John Hencote, a young man from Bath, was making his living as a Bath Stone agent, employing seven men near Paddington Station.

London's housing

From the Great Fire in 1666 onwards, building in London was subject to regulations. These were renewed in the London Building Act of 1844, which established the Metropolitan Buildings Office, whose powers passed in 1855 to the Metropolitan Board of Works. Building regulations were intended to restrict the spread of fires, and gave houses in London distinctive characteristics. Most eighteenth-century dwellings, from the fashionable squares in Bloomsbury to the mean terraces in Bethnal Green, had flat fronts, with the lower slopes of roofs concealed by plain pediment walls. Terraced houses in the nineteenth century had party walls, sufficiently thick to withstand fire for two hours, which extended through and stood proud of tiled or slated roofs.

Many houses in London built for relatively wealthy people were cascaded to other uses within a generation or so, and in all but the most fashionable areas many sizeable dwellings were tenemented. In the outer suburbs mansions standing in several acres might be occupied by only two generations of a family before being either demolished to make way for estates of more modest dwellings or passing to institutional use. In the West End working people (whose labour was essential to the functioning of the city and the fashionable residences) tended to live in courts off the principal streets. Their equivalent in new suburbs such as Bayswater were the mews cottages interspersed among fashionable terraces. In purely working-class areas the characteristic dwellings were the 'flat-fronted' two-up two-down terraced cottages, a type of housing that extended over hundreds of acres of Bethnal Green and adjacent areas. While on plans these may appear reasonably spacious, they were frequently subject to multi-occupation, and some were badly built. In his documentary film *Housing Problems* of 1935, Sir Arthur Elton depicted labourers pushing down the walls of cottages of this kind with minimal exertion.

The most distinctive features of housing in central London in the nineteenth century were multi-storey apartment blocks built by charitable bodies, although such dwellings accommodated only a small proportion of London's working class, and scarcely any of the destitute for whom they were supposedly intended. These dwellings originated with the formation of two charitable societies. The Metropolitan Association for Improving the Dwellings of the Industrial Classes was established in 1841 and built blocks in the Old St Pancras Road and Spicer Street, Spitalfields. The Society for Improving the Condition of the Labouring Classes was founded in 1844 and completed its first building in Lower Road, Pentonville, in 1846. The society's architect, Henry Roberts, made a profound impression on housing in London. His career displays two parallel concerns of the members of philanthropic societies intent on improving working-class housing. They wished to provide accommodation

for respectable working men that would avoid their having to stay at common lodging-houses where, it was perceived, they would be exposed to disease, crime and vice. They also tried to accommodate families in dwellings not subject to multi-occupation, which could be let profitably at rents that could be afforded by those on average wages. By 1851 Roberts was known as the architect who 'built a great many of the new Lodging Houses in London'. He became involved with providing accommodation for single men when he designed the now-demolished Destitute Sailors' Asylum in Well Street, Whitechapel, opened in 1835. He regarded it as 'the prototype of the improved lodging houses'. He designed a model lodging-house in George Street, Bloomsbury, which was opened by Prince Albert in May 1848. The following year he built for the SICLC a five-storey block of tenements, surrounding a courtyard and approached by balconies, in Streatham Street near the British Museum, which set a pattern for other charitable schemes. For the Great Exhibition he designed a pair of model three-bedroom cottages in modular form that could be extended vertically or horizontally to form tenement blocks or terraces. Since 1851 the cottages have stood near the Oval, and other examples were built at Windsor, Abbots Langley, Tunbridge Wells and elsewhere. In 1852–53 Roberts designed St George's Buildings, Bourdon Street, Mayfair, for the builder John Newson, and provided him with plans for five further blocks. From 1853 Roberts lived abroad, but the multi-storey tenement block became a feature of the London landscape. The Metropolitan Association continued building, and one of its blocks, Gatcliff Buildings in Chelsea, finished in 1867 bears the name of the association's secretary. Columbia Square, four 5-storey blocks, completed between 1859 and 1862 on the site of Nova Scotia Gardens, a dustyard purchased in 1857 by the banking heiress Angela Burdett-Coutts, was designed by Henry Darbishire who became architect to the Peabody Trust. Alongside the square Darbishire built the extravagantly Gothic Colombia Market, completed in 1869. The most active provider by 1870 was the Peabody Trust, established in 1862 by George Peabody, an American banker who settled in London in 1827 and financed the US display

The energy unleashed into house building around London in periods when money was available for investment is portrayed in the etching published in 1829 by George Cruikshank, 'London going out of town, or the March of Bricks and Mortar'. In the foreground is a triumphant army of robotic bricklayers and hod-carriers advancing towards the brick kilns in the centre of the image. Clay for brick making was dug from pits that were soon afterwards filled with domestic rubbish. To the left are ranges of completed or semi-completed houses, while to the right the representatives of the countryside – cows, sheep and trees and haystacks with legs – are taking flight.

at the Great Exhibition. The Peabody Trust's first block was completed on the corner of Folgate Street, in Whitechapel, in 1864, and by 1875, when almost 4,000 people lived in Peabody dwellings, there were also blocks in Islington, Shadwell, Horseferry Road and Lawrence Street, Chelsea. There was continuity between Roberts' work, that of the Peabody Trust, and the apartment blocks built by Rowland Plumbe and others after the establishment of the London County Council in 1889.

Some argued that philanthropy was counter-productive, and that the provision of dwellings should be based on sound commercial principles. In 1872 Octavia Hill alleged that people transplanted to healthy and commodious homes would pollute and destroy them. While inaction would certainly have allowed housing conditions to deteriorate, it was a valid criticism of philanthropic projects that they did nothing to aid the poorest workers and still less the capital's street people. Hollingshead observed that occupants at Streatham Street were 'sharp-sighted

tenants from outside districts who are a little more advanced in cleanliness and civilization, and are quick to see where ten shillings worth of comfort is selling at less than half price', their relative prosperity indicated by their ability to pay rent promptly. The construction of apartment blocks could cause as much disruption to the housing of the poor as the building of railways or new roads: according to Hollingshead, they never improved the neighbourhoods in which they were built since 'the costermongers, the street hawkers, the industrious poor are still rotting up their filthy, ill-drained, ill-ventilated courts, while well-paid mechanics, clerks and porters, willing to sacrifice a certain portion of their self-respect, are the constant tenants of all these model dwellings'. In 1857 the existing inhabitants of Nova Scotia Gardens had to be cleared from their homes to make way for the new scheme, and when the first two wings of Columbia Square were completed Hollingshead observed that 'the industrious poor of Bethnal Green are very sparingly represented in them'.

Hollingshead's observations are borne out by the census. In 1861 there were 54 dwellings in the Streatham Street block, of which 3 were untenanted. The other 51 were occupied by 215 people, a mean occupancy rate of 4.22 people per flat, better than most working-class dwellings in London. Only two flats accommodated as many as eight people, and four had only one occupant. Only about half the heads of households were London-born, and most were skilled tradesmen (including seven coach and harness makers, six carpenters and joiners, four compositors, three clerks, two tailors, a coppersmith, a piano key maker and a vellum book-binder). The SICLC's Lodging House in George Street may have removed some respectable young men from the dirt and temptations of common lodging-houses, but it did nothing for those who found the common lodging-house a substitute for the workhouse. There were 98 inmates at George Street on 7 April 1861, all male, and 57 of them were under 40. Thirty-five were born in the London area, 13 in Ireland, 5 in Scotland, 2 in France and one each from St Thomas in the West Indies, India, and Philadelphia. Almost all followed skilled trades or well-paid occupations, including several coachmakers, an ornamental glass cutter, a brass musical instrument maker and two collectors of rents.

Spreading suburbs

In the early nineteenth century London was a uniquely large city: none of the great northern towns had more than one-tenth of London's population. London's suburbs were a new creation, a product of the second half of the eighteenth century. Their nature was determined to a large extent by the random influence of landownership, and they were (and are) a varied patchwork – from the squares of Bloomsbury, built by the Russell family, dukes of Bedford in the eighteenth century, and the formality of Belgravia and Pimlico, laid out in the nineteenth century by Thomas Cubitt, to enclaves of the very poor, engaged in recycling or brick making. As early as 1836 *Chambers' Edinburgh Journal* remarked on the unsettled, uneven nature of suburbs, where there was always 'something new, raw and sprawling' with 'a quality of spic and span which does not somehow excite veneration', a characteristic feature being 'houses whose sides betray that they were intended to have others stuck upon them'. Even such an elegant development as the Paragon at Blackheath, begun in 1793 and finished in 1813, was affected by cessations of building caused by the Napoleonic Wars.

Although multi-occupancy was common in London, there was a general acceptance that the family dwelling was the norm. Most houses were built in greyish brick with roofs of Welsh slate. By the 1840s bay windows were providing variety from the usual flat-fronted dwellings, even in working-class districts, while decorative features abounded on middle-class houses – columns with elaborate capitals, decorative balconies, stained and frosted glass, and carved barge boards. Suburban streets show a pattern of restless change in the detailing of ornamentation. Many houses were constructed by small-scale builders as speculations, or on behalf of speculators. The spread of housing could be perceived in military terms: 'The main army,' wrote one commentator in 1861, 'is preceded by an advance of villas ... seizing a few picked positions. Then come the more solid ranks of the semi-detached ... along the high roads and in the neighbourhood of railway stations.' A suburb might accommodate the carriage class until horsebuses, trams or railways arrived, at which point residents in large villas might move to more secluded spots.

Dormitory areas gradually extended. The first omnibus services were introduced by George Shillibeer in 1829, from the *Yorkshire Stingo* on the Marylebone Road to the City, and in 1836 it was observed that a merchant working near the Bank of England might live with his family at Paddington, Clapham, Brixton or Wandsworth, up to six miles away, and travel daily by omnibus. On May Day 1844 the significance of the omnibus trade was expressed by a procession of more than 40 vehicles owned by John Wilson, the principal proprietor, who arrayed his drivers in new suits, decked the harnesses with rosettes and nosegays, and with three bands circulated through

Islington before driving to Henley for a day's recreation, leaving 12 buses to maintain services in London. The London General Omnibus Company was formed in 1856, but there was fierce competition for traffic – within a few years buses from Camberwell were crossing the Thames every five minutes. By the 1860s the cost of a daily journey by omnibus was supposedly within the reach of better-paid clerks, and public transport, increasing numbers of buses, then trams and suburban trains, came to cater for a middle-class and even a working-class clientele, rather than the wealthy individuals who had patronised the services run by Shillibeer and Wilson. In 1850 the *Railway Times* disparaged the omnibus suburbs and asked,

'Who would prefer living at Paddington, Islington, Kingsland or Walworth if, he could for the same cost, reside at Kingstead, Banstead Downs, Stanmore Common, Bushey Heath, Northfleet, Slough, Epsom, Hainault Forest, Barnet or Reigate?' The impact of railways on suburban travel was nevertheless limited; it was not until the 1880s that railway companies deliberately sought working-class commuting customers, although street trams had begun to make a significant impact on suburbs in the late 1860s.

The Artizans', Labourers' and General Dwellings Company was established in 1867 by the self-made drainage contractor William Austin. Its president until 1875 was the 7th Earl of Shaftesbury, and it established a

Working-class dwellings in fashionable London. St George's Buildings, a tenement block in Bourdon Street, Mayfair, designed by Henry Roberts and built in 1852–53 for John Newson, a native of Woodbridge, Suffolk, who made a fortune in London, at first from road-sweeping contracts and then as a building contractor who constructed many houses on the Grosvenor estate in the West End.

The cottages designed on a modular system by Henry Roberts that were displayed outside the Crystal Palace at the Great Exhibition in 1851, and re-erected at Kennington in 1853.

The block of model homes for families in Streatham Street near the British Museum, designed by Henry Roberts for the Society for Improving the Condition of the Labouring Classes and constructed in 1849. It was not quite the first such block in London, but is the oldest that survives.

second pattern of philanthropic building, the suburban cottage estate. The formation of the society was in part a reaction to the building of railways through densely inhabited areas in the 1860s. The company's first estate was built from 1872 on a 42½-acre pig farm near Clapham Junction Station. The tree-lined streets and red-brick terraces, ornamented with polychrome patterns and Gothic detailing, were designed by Robert Austin, the company architect until 1877. The estate's 1,135 houses are approached between cottages with corner turrets, which gives it something of the exclusive character of more pretentious suburbs. It was named after Shaftesbury, to whom it represented 'a new era in the progress of working men ... a town on all the modern principles of sanitary arrangements with recreation grounds, clubs, schools, libraries, baths and no public houses.' Shaftesbury Park provided housing of good quality for working families, but only for those who earned enough to pay relatively high rents. The company built further estates at Queen's Park, Kilburn, from 1875; Noel Park, Woodgreen, from 1881; and Leigham Court, Streatham, from 1889.

In a pioneering study of Victorian suburbs, published in the mid-1960s, H. J. Dyos drew attention to the numbers of commuting clerks in Camberwell. The 1861 census reveals that in streets near Peckham Park Road there were clerks serving an astonishing variety of bodies, including the War Office, the Inland Revenue, the Bank of England, assorted lawyers, East India traders, the Madras Railway, hop merchants, leather merchants, ironmongers, goldsmiths, and a telegraph company. A similar group settled beyond the river Lea in Essex. In 1861 the householders in the streets north of Forest Gate Station, on the Great Eastern main line opened in 1840, included clerks employed by ship brokers, shipping agents, bakers, silk warehouse owners, East Indies traders, tobacco companies, stationers, booksellers, railway companies and a religious society. By contrast, residents in Bayswater and the smarter areas of Paddington were *employers* of clerks, and the occupational structure resembled that of Bath, except that householders were more likely to be working than retired. They included army and navy officers, senior civil servants, members

of the Stock Exchange, clergy without cure of souls, merchants trading with Portugal, South America, the West Indies, India, the Baltic and Australia, and dealing in wine, brandy, flax and marble, one proprietor of the gasworks in Delhi, and an exiled Russian journalist.

London's roughest suburbs recycled its waste, the size of London giving its recycling industries a visibility which they lacked in smaller cities. In *Hard Times* Charles Dickens refers three times to the House of Commons as 'the national dust-yard', where Thomas Gradgrind sifted at the parliamentary cinder-heap without turning up many precious articles. He obviously knew that these references would resonate with his readers. In 1849–50 Mayhew explained that the collection of ash from London's tens of thousands of coal fires was a parish responsibility, and calculated that dust collecting employed about 1,800 people. Contractors paid for the privilege of collecting in the eighteenth century, but by the 1840s would only do it *for* payment. Dust was taken to yards in filth-encrusted carts and dumped on volcano-like conical heaps to await sifting, usually by women and children. The soft white ashes, called 'soil', were used as a fertiliser on marshy soils – in the 1840s mainly around Barking. The coarse cinders, or 'breeze', used for brick making, were carried by boat to the brickfields of Middlesex and Kent. Old bricks found among the dust were used as hardcore for roads in housing developments, while scrap metal was stamped into fastenings and corner reinforcements for trunks. All over London marine-store dealers collected scrap for iron foundries, bottles used as cullet by glassmakers, rags for papermakers, bones for burners of animal charcoal and old shoes used by shoemakers as filling and in the manufacture of Prussian Blue dye. Dust-yards were located on the fringes of the built-up area, many near the canals. Some, overtaken by tides of building, remained as enclaves within middle-class neighbourhoods. In *Our Mutual Friend* Dickens described 'a tract of industrial suburban Sahara, where tiles and bricks were burnt, bones were boiled, rubbish was shot, dogs fought, and dust was heaped by contractors'. One such enclave was 'The Potteries' (Pottery Lane) off Holland Park Avenue, described by Hollingshead – an area of about nine acres where groups of cottages named after their builders lined tracks that were rivers of mud. Many building workers and casual labourers lived there, and many women did laundry work, but the predominant occupations were brick making, which employed more than 30 people in 1861, dust sifting, dealing in old bottles, old bricks and recycled fat, and pig feeding (or pig training) which employed about 30 men and involved collecting kitchen waste from clubs and hotels and rendering it in coppers, separating fat for sale to tallow chandlers and feeding the residue to the pigs. The area's public houses, the *Earl of Zetland* and the *Victory*, were centres for bird fanciers and sports involving pugnacious dogs. Hollingshead encountered a 'village Hampden' who, resenting the attitude of philanthropists towards such communities, declaimed that 'a working man goes to his coffee shop, reads his newspapers, and is not such a fool as he's often made out'. The Sultan Street area of Camberwell was a similar enclave where cottages had been built on plots originally leased for gardening. The land was used by keepers of pigs and cows, and some houses accommodated Irishmen working in a glue factory. In a similar area near Maudslay's engineering works high rents were extorted from iron moulders and pattern makers for houses surrounded by dust heaps, and adjacent to a yard let out annually as winter quarters for the 'yellow smoking boxes upon wheels' that were the homes of travelling showmen.

The collection of second-hand clothing occupied many people in London. In the eighteenth century the celebrated centre of the trade was in Monmouth Street, between Shaftesbury Avenue and St Martin's Lane, but by the 1840s its focus had shifted to the area around Petticoat Lane adjacent to the Cutler Street warehouses of the East India Company, who regularly complained about the nuisances created thereby. Wholesalers in the area supplied retailers of second-hand clothes all over London and also compressed clothes into bales which were exported to Ireland, Holland and Belgium.

The rougher fringes of London also provided depots for horse transport. As early as 1731 it was estimated that there were more than 15,000 draught horses in addition to saddle horses in London when the nobility and gentry were resident during the social season. The demise of stagecoaching and waggoning resulted in the demolition of most of the inns associated with those trades, but not to any diminution of the numbers of horses in London. Many proprietors of cab, Hackney carriages and omnibuses had homes and stables among market gardens and brickfields in the suburbs.

Conclusions: London as an industrial centre

Engels referred to London as 'the commercial capital of the world [which] created the gigantic docks in which are assembled the thousands of ships which always cover the river Thames'. But London was more than a centre of commerce. Industry in London can be perceived in a long chronological context, as a series of trades, frequently interdependent, in which many jobs were hereditary. Some produced goods of high value; in others workers were subject to the threat of undercutting. In the particular context of the years between 1700 and 1870, technological innovations from elsewhere were taken up quickly in London – the steam engine, the rolling mill, the English glass cone, the shot tower, the vacuum process for refining sugar, the steam sawmill, the use of copper sheets in brewing vats, steel springs for carriages, and building iron ships. For the most part, companies using such innovations were neither the biggest nor the most celebrated of their kind, but the concentrations of varied manufactures in Southwark, Whitechapel, Battersea and, by 1870, West Ham, had few equals.

London had many roles in the eighteenth and nineteenth centuries: the seat of government, the law courts and the monarchy, the hub of the social and recreational world of the rich and famous, a garrison city, an entrepôt for international trade, and one of Europe's most glittering concentrations of retailers. All these functions dovetailed with the many and varied manufactures described above. While some Londoners made their livings by other means, the majority were as much 'a manufacturing people' as the citizens of any other town in Great Britain.

13

Towns of a different kind: resorts

'Towns in which wealth created elsewhere is expended for purposes of health and recreation.'

T. B. MACAULAY

ETWEEN 1700 and 1870 the provision of services and facilities for recreation, tourism and health treatments became an industry in its own right. One of the most important themes of this period was a gradual increase in opportunities for leisure and for travel, farther and farther down the social scale. Eighteenth-century resorts might be patronised by gentlefolk emulating royal or aristocratic visitors, but by the end of the nineteenth century increasing numbers of people of more modest social standing and means were making day, weekend or holiday trips, often by rail, to inland and seaside resorts in many parts of the country. Pensioners from the armed forces, the civil service or the East India Company, the retired or the independently wealthy were still keen to take up residence in the genial surroundings of Bath, Cheltenham, or Harrogate, but less privileged people – and less genteel pastimes – could now be found in popular and readily accessible resorts such as Blackpool or Brighton. The resorts of the British Isles, like its people, came in many different forms. This chapter considers these varied communities and the ways in which their development was intertwined with the industrial society that was growing throughout the country.

Resorts were among the fastest growing towns of the eighteenth and nineteenth centuries, providing livelihoods for many people. Their growth was shaped by entrepreneurs and was made possible by technological innovations, including the pumping engine, the steamship, main-line railways and the ability of civil engineers to construct embankments, bridges and piers. By the 1860s leisure resorts were catering for a broad clientele, including families whose wealth came from mines and manufacturing, working people whose horizons had been widened by newspapers, books and popular entertainers and, most important, people with fortunes derived from investments, the armed forces, or from working overseas. Resorts had provided access to health-giving mineral waters long before 1700. Ancient Romans had reclined at *Aquae Sulis* on the site of Bath, and the curative properties of spa waters were described in Elizabethan tracts. The traveller Celia Fiennes was an informed critic of the spas that were fashionable in 1700. At Epsom she observed lodging-houses around the wells and was impressed with the facilities for riding and driving with coaches. Harrogate, where she drank with difficulty a quart of water on two consecutive mornings, was pervaded by a smell of sulphur. She found the hot baths at Buxton intimidating, but enjoyed the scenery of the Peak.

At Tunbridge Wells in Kent she noticed ample lodgings, coffee houses, and the distinctive wooden items known as Tonbridge ware. She was repulsed by the steamy air around the hot springs of Bath, but did appreciate good lodgings, the quality of the flesh and fish, the decorum of the bathing facilities, the music and dancing, and pleasant green walks. She participated in a masque on 23 April 1702 which replicated the coronation of Queen Anne. By this date Bath was already more famed for its pleasures than for its cures, and the town came to rely more upon the genteel taking up residence in the town than upon visitors.

Bath's example was imitated by Cheltenham and Leamington, and later by Harrogate, Malvern and Buxton. Wherever there was mineral water, and at some places where there was not, entrepreneurs sought profit by providing for visitors or genteel residents. Some towns prospered by accommodating those anxious to view mountains, caves, gorges and waterfalls. The medicinal benefits canvassed in the mid-eighteenth century, which could be gained initially from drinking and subsequently from bathing in sea-water, were endorsed by George III at Weymouth from 1784 and in 1791 at Sidmouth, and by the Prince Regent at Brighton. Scarborough, with mineral waters as well as beaches, prospered. Brighton, a small fishing town in 1700, had become a fashionable resort with almost 7,500 people a century later: in 1851 it was a major urban area with 67,673 inhabitants. After 1800 the faster-growing resort towns were those on the coast – Augustus Granville, the authority on mineral cures and the settings in which they were taken, admitted in 1840 that 'no one can deny that mineral waters for the last 30 years have been growing out of fashion' – but inland resorts continued to grow, albeit slowly, and the curative properties of their waters was still a significant attraction even in the 1860s.

A model for the development of resorts suggests that growth came in four stages, at each of which it could be halted. First, the resources – curative waters, beaches for bathing, or spectacular scenery – were 'discovered' and visited by a few. Second, local investment provided access and accommodation. Next followed speculative external investment – in the case of Bath, in the form of capital from London. The final stage, the development of mass tourism, occurred when the built environment took precedence over natural attractions. A model based on social factors would put first the attraction of health-giving waters, then a growth of numbers on whom discipline was imposed by masters of ceremonies, followed by the proliferation of long-term accommodation for people with assured incomes from investments, and finally the diversification of the economy, with the growth of a working-class employed in services, the development of retailing, and the beginnings of manufacturing.

Bath: the archetype

The hot spring waters at Bath became popular before 1700 after visits by Mary of Modena (wife of James II) and the future Queen Anne. The Harrison Assembly Rooms, completed in 1708, were the first in a long series of investments in new facilities. Building prospered when interest rates were low, particularly in 1726–32, 1753–58, 1762–71 and 1785–92. *A Practical Dissertation on Bath Waters*, which appeared in four editions between 1707 and 1764, was written by Dr William Oliver, also inventor of the Bath Bun and the Bath Oliver biscuit. He settled in Bath in 1728, and in 1738–42 was one of the founders of the Bath General Hospital. His three partners were equally influential. The Cornishman Ralph Allen settled in Bath by 1712, having made one fortune as the contractor who improved provincial postal services, and making another as owner of the mines and quarries at Combe Down which provided the honey-coloured stone from which eighteenth-century Bath was constructed. Richard 'Beau' Nash, the celebrated dandy and entrepreneur, became Bath's master of ceremonies in 1705, re-organised transport within the city, improved the quality of entertainments and, by establishing rules of conduct, widened access to social occasions. By forbidding duelling and the carrying of swords he made the resort safer for refined gentlewomen and also for gambling, by which he gained and lost his own fortune. The Bath-born architect John Wood the elder

From 1731 Ralph Allen conveyed stone for the construction of prestigious buildings in Bath from his quarries on Combe Down to the banks of the river Avon along a wooden railway, which descended in all about 500 feet. The relatively narrow gauge, and the low-sided waggons with wheels of cast iron, followed contemporary practice in the Shropshire coalfield. Horses pulled the empty waggons uphill, while the loaded waggons descended by gravity, controlled by apparently effective brakes. For many years the railway was one of Bath's principal attractions, but it was scrapped amid popular protests after Allen's death in 1764. As seen here, the railway passed the Palladian Prior Park House which was built for Ralph Allen from 1734 to the design of John Wood the elder. The house is now occupied by a Roman Catholic college, while the extensive landscape garden, originally laid out by the poet Alexander Pope, is managed by the National Trust. This engraving, published by John Bowles & Son in London in 1752, is one of the earliest representations of a railway in polite art.

PHOTOGRAPH CARNEGIE, BY COURTESY OF BATH LIBRARY

Sir William Pulteney (né Johnstone) was one of the richest men in the kingdom and an influential figure in national politics. He was the third son of Sir James Johnstone, who held estates in the Scottish Borders. He trained as a lawyer, and served as MP for Cromartyshire from 1768 to 1774 and for Shrewsbury between 1775 and his death in 1805. In 1760 he married the heiress to the estates of the earls of Bath and changed his name to Pulteney when she succeeded to her inheritance in 1767. Three of his spheres of activity are of particular significance here: he was over many years a patron of Thomas Telford; he energetically developed his wife's inherited property in Bath, and he was governor of the British Fishing Society, founded in 1786 (see below, page 593), which built three fishing harbours in the Scottish Highlands and from 1803 laid out the southern part of the town of Wick, which was named Pulteneytown, and where a distillery still produces a fine whisky under the name 'Old Pulteney'.

BY COURTESY OF THE IRONBRIDGE GORGE MUSEUM TRUST

designed the north side of Queen Square in 1728–34, the King's Circus in 1754–69 and Ralph Allen's home at Prior Park in 1741. His son John Wood the younger built the Royal Crescent in 1767–75. In the last quarter of the century Sir William Pulteney developed his wife's Bathwick estate and commissioned the construction in 1769–74 of the bridge designed by Robert Adam that took his name.

The hot springs remained a unique feature of Bath, but in 1747 a French commentator observed that 'the company at these waters are always in good humour … the principal virtue of the bath is derived from the society of those who use them.' Bath was celebrated as a marriage market, though also as a setting for adultery, for beneath its genteel surface was a turbulent underworld. This partly centred on prostitution: in 1771 Smollet referred to the 'nymphs' of Avon Street, a development of the 1730s that failed to retain respectable residents and later included a notorious concentration of common lodging-houses. Nevertheless, by 1800 Bath was increasingly a place of genteel residence for the wealthy, and some even complained that the numerous clergy contributed to the deflation of gaiety. In 1801, with a population of 33,000, Bath was among the dozen largest towns in England. It grew rapidly in the next 20 years but

The Royal Crescent in Bath was designed by John Wood the younger and built between 1765 and 1775. This development of only 30 dwellings became one of the most influential factors in the prosperity of Bath, setting a standard for architecture of the highest quality in housing which equalled or even surpassed that achieved in the city's public buildings.

PHOTOGRAPH CARNEGIE, BY COURTESY OF BATH LIBRARY

more slowly thereafter, reaching 53,000 in 1841, and declined slightly in the next two decades. The Great Western Railway, which from 1841 connected Bath with London and Bristol, failed to bring the increased number of visitors that had been anticipated.

There was no other town like Bath, but the 1861 census reveals patterns characteristic of all resorts. There were nine hotels with live-in staff, of whom there were 15 at the *York House* and 10 each at the *Greyhound* and the *Castle*, as well as 220 inns, some of which accommodated guests. So numerous were respectable lodging-houses that a directory of 1864 declined to list them. They even included establishments in the Royal Crescent and Queen Square. Domestic servants comprised the most numerous occupational group – the census lists 65 male and 286 female resident servants in the 82 fully occupied houses in the Circus, the Royal Crescent and Queen Square. The presence of so many maidservants accounts for the extraordinarily high ratio of females to males in the city: about 150 : 100 in the late nineteenth century. Freelance servants included the 44 waiters listed in the 1864 directory, women who 'went out washing' (a distinct group from 'washerwomen', who took washing in), daily governesses, cleaners of lace and shawls, and jobbing gardeners. An 'intelligence office for servants' was one of a dozen servant registries, while a training school for female servants in Brunswick Place had 18 pupils. Residents and visitors were served by numerous doctors and several hospitals. Bathing establishments employed about 50 people, including drivers of pumping engines and attendants who helped people in and out of the water. A 'Missionary to the Chairmen and Flymen' preached to those who provided short-distance transport. The manoeuvrable tricycle carriages called 'bath-chairs' were being made by James Heath from about 1750. These made sedan chairs obsolete, and in 1860 some 160 were available for hire. In the same year 50 proprietors operated light horse-drawn carriages or 'flies'.

Education comprised a substantial part of the Bath economy. There were many boarding schools, but the city's specialism was the teaching of 'accomplishments' by 'professors' of languages, drawing, fencing, music and dancing; in Bath there were also many sellers of sheet music, and pianoforte tuners. Entertainment provided livings for about 100 professional musicians in Bath in 1861, including a Hanoverian band, instrumentalists from Nassau and the Palatinate, vocalists from Liverpool, Scotland, Ireland, Genoa, Rome, Vienna and Boulogne. The impresario William Manders visited Bath in April 1861 with his Grand National Star Menagerie, whose staff included Marimo Maccomo, an Angolan who came to England via the United States in 1857, and who was customarily billed as 'the African Lion Tamer, Tiger Tamer and Snake Charmer'. Recreational establishments ranged from the Athenaeum and the Literary Institution to billiard rooms. Painters of portraits, landscapes, watercolours and miniatures lived in the city, along with sculptors, Italian figure makers, a jet-ornament manufacturer and a dealer in Swiss carvings; by 1864 there were also 24 photographers.

The principal shops in Bath were very large. One drapery establishment employed 92 people, and 19 staff lived in at another. Clothing was made by independent tailors and dressmakers, and the plethora of army officers provided work for a specialist military tailor. Bakers specialised in Bath Olivers and Bath Buns, and luxury businesses that would not have been viable in most towns included bullion dealers, Morocco case makers, furriers and pearl stringers. The principal boot and shoemakers employed up to 30 people. Cabinet-making businesses were larger than in most towns (one workshop employing 41 and another 29), while eleven men worked for a chair and sofa manufacturer. Furniture was renovated by 'jobbing upholsterers', while 'brightsmiths' installed and renovated elegant fireplaces in Regency houses.

Bath's economy was shaped by the demands of its genteel long-term and medium-term residents. Analysis of those residents reveals few traces of the 'industrial revolution' that transformed other parts of Britain. Many were annuitants, fundholders and property holders, and some owned land in Ireland or Australia. Some were railway shareholders, and a few had interests in docks or gas undertakings, but most investments in industry were at one remove, channelled through financial institutions. There were few manufacturers from the Midlands or the North – the retired cotton manufacturer from Stalybridge and the Scottish papermaker were unusual figures in Bath. But there were officials from the Inland Revenue, the Office of Woods, and the Board of Health, men who had made their livings as bankers, stockbrokers or West India Merchants, and eight admirals, six generals and numerous colonels and commanders, either serving, or on half-pay, or retired. There were former East India Company surgeons, engineers, artillery and cavalry officers, judges and inspectors of hospitals. Women

⚹ A bath-chair is a light carriage mounted on three or four wheels, usually accommodating just one passenger who steered by means of a tiller operating on the front wheel or wheels. Most were pushed by hand, although some were drawn by donkeys or ponies. They first appeared in Bath in the 1750s and soon began to supersede sedan chairs. The first manufacturer was supposedly James Heath, and for many years his company was one of the principal manufacturers. Bath-chairs were employed in large numbers in most resorts and 160 were available for hire in Bath in 1860.
PHOTOGRAPH CARNEGIE, BY COURTESY OF BATH LIBRARY

householders included 31 of 83 heads of households in the Circus, the Royal Crescent and Queen Square. Many were spinsters, daughters of wealthy families, but some were widows, and others were married to men posted overseas. Ministers of almost all varieties of religion then practised in England lived in Bath – Jewish synagogue readers, Roman Catholic priests, ministers of Congregationalist, Baptist, Unitarian, Wesleyan, Primitive Methodist, United Methodist and Moravian chapels, and a bishop of the Catholic Apostolic Church. Eight city missionaries, two scripture readers and a 'Bible woman' ministered to people below the threshold of respectability. If there were more dissenting ministers than in most cities, the proportion of Anglican clergy was even greater. Apart from those serving local churches, there were about 50 clergy by chance or by choice 'without cure of souls', together with about 30 who held benefices elsewhere, including the Dean of Salisbury, who resided with his family and five servants in Brook Street, and the incumbents of St Bartholomew, Wilmslow; St George, Stamford; All Saints, Wing; St Lawrence, Eyam; and Christ Church, West Bromwich. Bath's genteel residents were overwhelmingly people who had prospered from land, from financial dealings and overseas trade, and from lucrative service in the armed forces or in India.

Bathing, piers and promenading: Britain's coastal resorts

While Bath is internationally celebrated, Britain's best-known resorts are located around its coasts. They have varied origins, as fishing hamlets, harbours of refuge, military bases and packet ports. One of the first to develop was Scarborough, on the bracing North Sea coast of Yorkshire, which was both spa and coastal resort. Its mineral springs were the nucleus from which it grew. In 1698 the corporation built a sea-wall and a cistern for the spa waters, and by 1736 visitors were taking promenades and riding in carriages as well as bathing in the sea. The town had a population of 6,409 in 1801, doubling by 1851 and increasing further to 18,357 in the next decade. Granville in 1841 detailed the advantages which Scarborough enjoyed: it was situated amid lofty cliffs in the shadow of a castle; its mineral springs were adjacent to a 'convenient and luxurious sea-bathing shore'; sea-bathing arrangements were commendable; and the spa baths were well fitted up. The promenade had been improved by the engineer James Walker, using techniques that foreshadowed the Thames Embankment; a pier was constructed in 1826; and access to the spa from the

➤ Visitors began to take the waters at Scarborough after the discovery of a spa at the foot of the cliffs to the south of the town in the 1620s. The town grew as a resort and had the advantage by the late eighteenth century of being able to offer both spa waters and the newly fashionable consumption of, or bathing in, sea-water. By the time this engraving was published in 1791 Scarborough had all the amenities of a fashionable resort – theatre, library, reading rooms and assembly rooms – and in the following decade the town gained an iron bridge which saved visitors from having to climb down and up its rugged hills and a museum whose collection was tended by the great geologist William Smith (see above, pages 144–5).
SCARBOROUGH MUSEUMS AND GALLERY

town was provided by the iron Cliff Bridge, 414 feet (128 m) long and 75 feet above a chasm, built by public subscription in 1827. The arrivals of fashionable visitors were duly gazetted, and a two-day race meeting was held on the sands every August. Boats took visitors for cruises, and Castle Howard, Rievaulx Abbey and Flamborough Head could all be reached by carriage. In 1861 there were 17 hotels in Scarborough and about 240 lodging-houses, and 80 jet makers provided souvenirs or gifts. Foreign vessels in the harbour provided a lively spectacle during the herring season. Libraries were available and Scarborough's history could be studied in the book published by Thomas Hinderwell in 1798 and reprinted in 1837. William Bean's display of fossils and shells was said to be unparalleled. The museum, housed in a rotunda in the classical style, was arranged by the geologist William Smith. It was opened in 1829 by the Philosophical Society, whose objective was 'to give energy, concentration and effort to native talents to examine the great laboratory of the earth'. Unsurprisingly, genteel residents included the families of cloth manufacturers from places such as Dewsbury, Keighley and Wakefield.

The atmosphere of the late eighteenth-century coastal resort was recreated in 1880 by Thomas Hardy in *The Trumpet Major*. Crowds at Budmouth (Weymouth) waited for the appearance of the king and queen. Girls tripped along the esplanade, watching the sea, the cliffs and the soldiers. Fashionable visitors paraded in ruffles and finery, while the beach swarmed with bathing-machine attendants wearing wristbands inscribed 'God save the King'. Weymouth prospered from the patronage of George III, whose statue is still a feature of its promenade.

Brighton, in 1785 a fishing village with a fleet of fewer than 50 smacks, similarly benefited from the presence of George III's son the Prince of Wales, subsequently the Prince Regent and from 1820 King George IV. He visited Brighton in 1783, and in 1787 stayed at a farmhouse which conveniently accommodated his liaisons with Maria Fitzherbert. The prince's presence made Brighton fashionable. Lord Torrington in 1788 enjoyed exploring bookshops, had a good meal accompanied by bottles of claret and port, and was impressed by the assembly room where actors were

due to perform Shakespeare's *Henry IV*. He nevertheless found the town a place of bad company, frequented by 'a harpy set of painted harlots'. The prince's farmhouse was enlarged in the classical style from 1787 by Henry Holland, before being transformed between 1815 and 1822 by the construction of the Pavilion, designed with an exterior in an Indian style and an interior by John Nash that mixed Indian with Chinese themes. After the death of George IV the Pavilion remained a royal residence, but Queen Victoria did not find it congenial and it was sold by the Crown in 1850 to the municipality, and became assembly rooms. It set a pattern for ostentation in seaside architecture which was copied in many coastal communities, but it was by no means a popular building. William Cobbett compared it with the Kremlin.

Cobbett also observed that Brighton's proximity to London, which could be reached by noon on a coach leaving not particularly early in the morning, made it popular as a place of residence for commuting stock jobbers, as well as a place of resort for pleasure-seekers. Brighton was also celebrated as a garrison town, with a battery on the front that was manned by the Royal Artillery until 1858. The barracks at Preston on the road to Lewes originated as temporary accommodation when Napoleon threatened invasion, but became a permanent cavalry base after the peace of 1815. 'Brighton Camp' (or 'The Girl I left behind me') was one of the most popular of popular songs. Around the barracks was a concentration of 'low, shabby, nasty houses, irregularly built', which accommodated, among others, dealers in second-hand clothes who traded in the civilian garments of new recruits when they were kitted out with uniforms. Brighton was also a packet port with as many as nine sailing vessels plying to Dieppe, which were joined by a steamboat in 1822. The following year the 380-yard long Chain Pier was built to the design of Captain Samuel Brown, originally as an embarkation and disembarkation point for the packets. The pier became as famous as the Pavilion. It was painted by J. M. W. Turner and by John Constable. It served as a promenade from which visitors could view Brighton as if from the sea, and a camera obscura and other facilities were provided for their entertainment. The railway to London, opened

The first section of what is now called the West Coastway route from Brighton to Portsmouth and Southampton was opened as far as Shoreham in May 1840, a year before the completion of the main line from London to Brighton. It was extended to Worthing in 1845, to Chichester in 1846, and to Portsmouth in 1847. This engraving shows the great crowds who usually assembled to see the openings of early railways. The depth and ruggedness of the cuttings is perhaps exaggerated.

The Chain Pier at Brighton is an outstanding instance within the recreation 'industry' of the medium becoming the message. It opened in 1823 to the design of suspension bridge pioneer Captain Samuel Brown (see page 117) as a utilitarian means of access to packet boats, enabling them to moor in relatively deep water. This engraving of 1824 shows how quickly it became an attraction in its own right, a promenade from which (paying) visitors could view Brighton as if from the sea. In due course a camera obscura and other entertainments were provided. The Chain Pier fell out of fashion, and its demolition was already in prospect when it was destroyed by a storm in 1896. The entrance kiosks shown in this image remain intact to this day.

There were few railway stations closer to the sea than Ramsgate Harbour. The South Eastern Railway opened its line to Ramsgate from Canterbury in 1846, but its rival the London, Chatham & Dover reached the Thanet resort in 1863, building a four-platform terminus alongside the harbour that was reached down a 1 in 75 gradient and through a 1,630-yard tunnel. Unsurprisingly the line was difficult to operate, and the station was closed by the Southern Railway in 1926 as part of a rationalisation of rail facilities in Thanet. It subsequently became an amusement park and zoo by the name of 'Merrie England'.

in 1841 and from 1846 part of the London, Brighton & South Coast Railway, made day trips from the capital easily possible; by the 1860s trains were covering the 50¾ miles in 75 minutes. Developers built houses that accommodated both visitors and long-term residents. To the east the suburb of Kemp Town was developed from 1823 on the initiation of Thomas Reed Kemp, MP for Lewes. He was forced by his creditors to flee to Paris in 1837, but the estate was built and expanded by the great contractor Thomas Cubitt who lived there from 1846 until his death in 1855. The leisure industry prospered in Brighton; the population increased from 7,000 in 1801 to 24,000 in 1821 and 90,000 in 1871, a rate of growth matched in few manufacturing towns. Brighton lacked a spa and developed later than Scarborough, but in many respects it was the archetype of the seaside resort, just as Bath was the archetype of the spa, and the citizens of many other coastal communities aspired to emulate its success.

The old fishing communities of Ramsgate and Margate developed as resorts from the late eighteenth century when hoys – ships which delivered goods from London – began to carry passengers. A voyage usually lasted eight hours, but Charles Dibdin observed that since 'high, low, rich, poor, sick and sound are all huddled together without discrimination, it cannot be very agreeable [or] very delicate for fine ladies'. In 1749 the Admiralty designated Ramsgate a harbour of refuge, where passing vessels could shelter during tempestuous weather, and John Smeaton built its first pier. Paddle-steamer services began in 1815, and it was possible in the 1880s to take boats to Tilbury, Dover, Calais and Boulogne. Ramsgate has a Regency ambience with streets named after Wellington and Nelson and one called the Plains of Waterloo. Wellington Crescent on the cliff top is built in grey-yellow brick in the neo-classical style, with four-storey houses in the centre and three-storey houses at each end. Liverpool Lawn is a curving terrace of 19 three-storey houses, with the royal arms in relief on a central pediment. But by the mid-nineteenth century genteel residents preferred villas to terraces. Vale Square is overlooked by Christ Church, designed by George Gilbert Scott and consecrated in 1847. On the eastern side is a brick terrace of 9 three-storey houses, with

bow windows on each floor, but to the north and south are villas of the 1840s and 1850s. Ramsgate's population in 1821 totalled just over 6,000, but 30 years later it was nearly 15,000, and it exceeded 22,000 by 1881. The South Eastern Railway, which reached Ramsgate from Ashford in 1846, and the London, Chatham & Dover Railway, whose line to Ramsgate Harbour opened in 1863, greatly increased the attractiveness of the town, both for visitors and residents. Ramsgate catered first for those who wished to drink sea-water for the benefit of their health, then for those wishing to bathe, and subsequently for people wealthy enough to settle to enjoy the benefits of the facilities, which by 1861 included bathing machines, warm baths, coffee houses, billiard tables, dancing and music 'academies', shops called bazaars, bath-chairs, a show featuring Mr Punch, and a concentration of prostitutes in Vincent Place. Genteel residents included annuitants, fundholders, retired officers, and numerous clergy including absentee incumbents from Padgate and Rochdale in far-away industrial Lancashire.

In the mid-eighteenth century Margate was described as 'a fishing town resorted to lately by company to drink sea water'. The Royal Sea Bathing Infirmary was founded in 1791 as bathing supplanted sea-water drinking. Margate flourished partly because of its beaches, its sunrises and sunsets, and the prospects of passing ships, and partly because of investment in the harbour wall, built in 1815 under the direction of John Rennie. The town's facilities included a theatre, assembly rooms and a museum. In 1835 James Newlove lowered his son into a hole encountered while digging a duck pond and discovered passages of inexplicable origin, lined with millions of shells, forming a grotto which became a popular attraction. J. M. W. Turner found inspiration in the quality of the light at Margate, and enjoyed observing the vigorous activity before the daily morning departure of the steam packet for London. Margate's population, about 7,000 in the 1820s, exceeded 10,000 by 1861 and almost doubled in the next twenty years. A borough from 1857, with two railways opened in 1846 and 1863, Margate was a place of residence for the wealthy retired, in which people gained livings as keepers of lodging-houses, pastry cooks, attendants at the baths, carriage proprietors,

Dover was a resort of some consequence in the mid-nineteenth century, as well as a garrison town and a packet port. This view of 1837 shows the prominence of the Castle, the sheltered artificial harbour from which vessels regularly crossed the Channel, and, in the distance, some of the terraces and hotels that accommodated visitors and wealthy long-term residents.

bath-chairmen and artists, although it also remained a working port providing posts for coast guards, pilots, boat builders, fishermen and oyster dealers.

Birchington, a smaller Thanet resort, had a population of 537 in 1801 which grew to 1,373 in 1881. Perhaps its greatest contribution to the distinctive character of coastal resorts is that by that time it included the first seaside bungalow estate. In rural Bengal the word 'bungalow' meant a peasant hut, but the meaning changed, to a single-storey house in India intended for Europeans, and then to a holiday home, originally for families who could afford servants, whose occupants sought to avoid noisy attractions. The first seaside bungalows were built at Westgate, the quieter end of Margate, in 1869–70. The first bungalow estate, on the cliff tops at Birchington, was laid out in the early 1870s by the architect Sir John Taylor on behalf of the land-owner John Seddon, author of *The Ancient Domestic Architecture of Kent*. The plans for prefabricated buildings were taken from *Designs & Examples of Cottages, Villas and Country Houses*, written in 1857 by John Weale, London's leading architectural publisher. The streets are named after figures in literature, science and industry, and the bungalows provided opportunities for inhaling bracing sea air, gazing at passing boats and appreciating restless waves. The promoters believed that 'people at the seaside are for the most part intent on doing nothing, and the object is to do this in as great a variety of ways as possible'. Residents on the estate included Sir Erasmus Wilson, the dermatologist, and Dante Gabriel Rossetti.

Dover grew as a resort from 1827 when Marine Parade was built as a speculation. Granville in 1840

regarded its recently constructed houses as 'fit for patrician inmates'. In 1861 the town included numerous 'lodging-houses', as boarding places for holidaymakers were known in Kent – in later years they were called 'apartments' to distinguish them from *common* lodging-houses. The needs of holidaymakers and wealthy residents were met by Bath-chairmen and fly proprietors, bazaar keepers, shell dealers and librarians, by proprietors of bathing machines, billiard markers, donkey men and 'professors' of music, singing and languages. Dover was also a military base, accommodating more than 2,500 army personnel in 1861, and the presence of active soldiers and sailors attracted those who had retired, including General Sir Francis Cockburn who spent 12 years in Canada fostering settlement in what became Ontario, and George, 3rd Earl Cadogan who entered the Royal Navy at the age of 13, dashingly commanded HMS *Havannah* in the Adriatic in 1812–15, and became Admiral of the Blue in 1857. Dover was also the principal packet port for France. The bustling activity of its harbour added to the town's attractions, and accommodating long-distance travellers before and after cross-Channel journeys provided additional income for its hotels and boarding houses.

Most of the first generation of English seaside resorts were in southern England, and depended on road transport or ships for their initial success. From the 1830s main-line railways and the demands of those who lived in the manufacturing areas of the North, the Midlands and Clydeside transformed communities along many other stretches of the British coast into places catering for the leisure needs of substantial sections of the population.

The first chalybeate spring in Cheltenham was discovered in 1716, and such was the demand for its water from local people that the farmer who owned the site began to charge for access. Its setting was enhanced from 1743 by the planting of an avenue of elm trees, seen in this engraving. The spring was called the Royal Well after King George III took the waters in 1788, one of the events which stimulated the growth of Cheltenham as an inland resort.

The 3 ft 6 in. gauge Gloucester & Cheltenham Railway, authorised in 1809, ran from the terminus of the Gloucester & Berkeley Canal to Cheltenham and to quarries on Leckhampton Hill, which supplied stone for many of Cheltenham's most prestigious buildings. The railway included several inclines on Leckhampton Hill, including the one portrayed in this engraving of *circa* 1830 past the Devil's Chimney, a well-known local landmark and destination for walks.

Taking the waters: inland spas and resorts

Inland spas also prospered. King George III drew attention to Cheltenham when he took the waters there in 1788. The population of the town scarcely exceeded 3,000 in 1805, but in 1809 Henry Thompson, a London financier, opened the Montpellier Spa. Other spas were soon established, a promenade was laid out, and a social programme offered. Large areas were then developed by Thompson's son Pearson, before he emigrated to Australia in 1849. By 1851 Cheltenham was a major town, with 35,051 people.

From a few cottages in 1801, the Warwickshire hamlet of Leamington Priors became a town with a population of 18,529 in 1861. In 1700 mineral waters were taken in a modest establishment in what became Bath Street, but in 1784 the shoemaker and poet Benjamin Satchwell discovered a second spring, and baths opened two years later. More springs were found, and their waters were commended by doctors. In 1808 the first houses were built on the property of Edward Willes, on the north bank of the river Leam, and the completion of the Pump Room in 1813–14 stimulated building. The town followed a regular pattern, with streets laid out at right angles to the Parade, a broad boulevard rising up the slope from the pump rooms to Beauchamp Square. Streets to the east were planned in 1827 by John Nash and James Morgan, while Lansdowne Crescent, 25 five-storey Regency-style houses, was built in 1835 by William Thomas, a Suffolk-born architect. Leamington began as a town of terraces in the classical style, but soon became one of villas which by the 1850s were usually of brick dressed with stone, with Gothic arches and high soaring gables. It was also notorious as a town of false starts and bankruptcies – even now, incomplete terraces remain as evidence of the risks involved in building a resort. A successful resort also required accommodation for short-term guests. The 100-bedroom *Williams's* (later the *Regent*) *Hotel* opened in 1819; by 1861 more than 100 lodging-houses also catered for respectable visitors. Samuel Sidney observed in 1851 that Leamington was also well located for tourist visits to Stratford-upon-Avon, Warwick and Kenilworth. Following patronage by Princess (later Queen) Victoria, the town's name was graced from 1838 with the prefix 'Royal' and with the suffix 'Spa'.

The Stray is an area of 200 acres which, under the enclosure award for the Forest of Knaresborough of 1778, remained accessible for visitors taking the waters at Harrogate's various spas. According to the Act, 'all persons whomsoever shall and may have free access at all times to the … springs, and be at liberty to use and drink the waters …' One of the earliest known mineral springs at Harrogate, the Tewit Well, remains under a dome on the Stray. These open spaces were a popular area for promenading by visitors to the spa.

PHOTOGRAPH CARNEGIE, BY COURTESY OF THE YORKSHIRE ARCHAEOLOGICAL SOCIETY

HARROGATE, THE STRAY FROM RIPON ROAD. 9.525. H.V.

Leamington's prosperity owed much to the physician Henry Jephson. Born near Mansfield, he studied at St George's Hospital, practised in Leamington in 1818, and completed his qualification at the University of Glasgow in 1827. Thereafter he attracted to Leamington 'an army of invalids and would-be invalids', by prescribing moderate eating and abstinence from stimulants, together with regular consumption of the waters. By 1850 his annual income was estimated to be over £20,000. The gardens which took his name were laid out in 1834. Like most successful resorts, Leamington also attracted private schools, including Leamington College, designed in the Tudor style by David Squirehill in 1847. Measom considered that Leamington's shops rivalled for size and convenience those of the metropolis, and attributed the town's growth to 'the means of entertainment and recreation so plentifully provided by the resident population'. In 1861 residents in Leamington included significant numbers of people who had prospered in manufacturing, including an earthenware manufacturer from Hanley, a cotton-spinner from Darwen, a needlemaker who employed 350 men at Redditch, a chandelier maker from Birmingham and an ironmaster from Wednesbury.

In 1770 the spa at Harrogate was, according to Smollet, 'treading upon the heels of Bath in the articles of gaiety and dissipation', but its growth before 1860 was constrained. Granville considered that it remained a village while Cheltenham and Leamington had become towns, and even in 1861 its off-season population was just 5,558. The Duchy of Lancaster, who owned and controlled much of the land upon which the spa and town were located, consciously developed its estate from 1840, and the Pump Room and the *Crown*, *White Hart* and *Clarendon* hotels date from that time. The resort was spaced around the 200 acres of land called the Stray, left open after enclosure in 1778. Visitors in 1861 were accommodated at 14 hotels and 140 lodging-houses, and the usual resort recreational facilities were available, as well as an observatory. Harrogate's genteel residents included shipbuilders and iron merchants from Co. Durham, cotton manufacturers and calico printers from Lancashire, edge-tool manufacturers from Sheffield, and manufacturers of woollens and worsteds from the West Riding. Harrogate may not quite have been a town in 1861, but by 1901, when its population exceeded 26,000, its urban status could not be doubted.

Hydropathy

There are hotels called 'hydros' throughout the British Isles. These reflect a mid-nineteenth-century fashion for hydropathy (now 'hydrotherapy'). The application of water to the body by sponges or wet sheets with the object of soothing pains was popularised from the 1820s by Vincenz Priessnitz of Grafenburg (Jesenik in the Czech Republic). The practice was publicised by Captain R. T. Claridge, who published

a book on Priessnitz's work, undertook lecture tours in Scotland and Ireland, and wrote that 'the year 1842 may be considered as a new era in the mode of curing disease in this country'. This was scarcely true in a medical sense, but his work considerably influenced the development of resorts. Claridge had been preceded at Grafenburg by Dr James Wilson, who in 1837 met James Manby Gully, a fellow-student of medicine with Charles Darwin at Edinburgh. Wilson and Gully set up a hydropathic establishment in 1842 at Malvern, then a spa of modest pretensions but which grew substantially. The company established in London in 1792 by Jacob Schweppes began to bottle Malvern water in 1850, and brought it to national prominence by selling it at the Great Exhibition.

The first hydropathic centres in Scotland and Ireland were opened in 1843; the *Glenburn* at Rothesay by Dr William Patterson, and the Turkish baths at Blarney, constructed for Dr Richard Barter. The latter was associated with similar ventures elsewhere in Ireland: one opened at Bray in 1859, in ostentatious buildings designed by William Dargan, and a short-lived establishment at Ennis, Co. Clare, was built in 1869–70. In Scotland nine further hydropathic establishments were established before 1870, four of them built by limited liability companies.

The most celebrated hydropathic spa in England was at Matlock, located on the river Derwent just a mile north of Cromford Mill. Fashionable people had been taking the waters there as early as the 1690s. A visitor in 1755 found its atmosphere less lively than the 'gay flutter and extravagance' of Bath and Tunbridge Wells, but he enjoyed an evening cruise on the river Derwent, serenaded by French horns. There were only 13 lodging-houses at Matlock Bath in 1831, but it subsequently flourished as a day resort after the railway from Derby opened in 1849. The older village of Matlock, with a population of 4,252 in 1861, also developed into a health resort. John Smedley revived his father's hosiery firm in the 1820s, and settled near the family's factory at Lea Bridge, three miles to the south. He took an interest in hydropathy from 1847 and in 1851 advised Ralph Davis who was setting up a hydropathic establishment at Matlock. Smedley bought the business in 1853 and he and his successors extended it into a great range of gritstone buildings, now the offices of Derbyshire County Council. In 1861, when more than 40 staff attended to about 80 visitors, an observer noted that 'the grounds are ... laid out in terraced walks and landscape gardening, highly ornamental ... the invalid may take walking exercise and enjoy himself at pleasure in these extensive grounds.' By 1868 seven other hydros were operating in Matlock. Tourist gifts and souvenirs were provided by a dozen marble and spar manufacturers. Henry Watson perfected a water-powered lathe for turning marble and spar in 1751, established a workshop at Ashford, and corresponded on geological matters with

John Whitehurst of the Lunar Society. His son White Watson laid out a botanical garden at Bakewell, sold minerals and fossils at a 'museum' at Matlock Bath, and supplied specimens to other Lunar Society members including Erasmus Darwin, William Strutt and Josiah Wedgwood. Natural wonders were essential to the visitor experience: guides led visitors through caves and up a zigzag path to the Heights of Abraham.

A variety of resorts

British resorts are not susceptible to sweeping generalisation. They vary enormously in their origins, their character, and the ways in which they developed. Some were leisure resorts first and foremost, while others had wider economic roles. Some were principally for the wealthy and for long-term residents, while others catered for day- or weekend-trippers. Some were well served by railways, while others sought to protect their exclusivity.

But resorts did share certain characteristics. For all of them growth was made possible by transport facilities. The seven-mile section of the road from Bath towards London was turnpiked as early as 1707, and after 12 further Acts of Parliament the whole 125½-mile route was thus managed by 1743. Brighton also depended initially on road transport. The first turnpike to the town was authorised in 1770, and the routes from the capital (varying between 51 and 58 miles) were further improved after the Prince Regent built the Pavilion. By 1821 eighteen coaches were plying daily between Brighton and London, completing the journey in about six hours. New roads instigated predictable social changes. Lord Torrington remarked in 1787 that improved roads in the Vale of Glamorgan made Swansea a bathing place, and introduced 'strolling players and all other mischiefs'.

Steamships were responsible for the emergence of resorts in Thanet, Essex, and on Clydeside. In *Sketches by Boz* (1836) Charles Dickens gave several glimpses of steamboat travel down the Thames from London. 'One of the most amusing places we know is the steam-wharf of the London Bridge, or St Katharine's Dock Company, on a Saturday morning in summer, when the Gravesend and Margate steamers are usually crowded to excess …' And when Mr Tuggs, a rotund London grocer of modest means, inherits £20,000 his family decides that they really must get away from the city. But where to go?

'Gravesend?' mildly suggested Mr Joseph Tuggs. The idea was unanimously scouted. Gravesend was low. 'Margate?' insinuated Mrs Tuggs. Worse and worse – nobody there, but tradespeople … 'Ramsgate?' ejaculated Mr Cymon, thoughtfully. To be sure; how stupid they must have been, not to have thought of that before! Ramsgate was just the place of all others. Two months after this conversation, the City of London Ramsgate steamer was running gaily down the river. Her flag was flying, her band was playing, her passengers were conversing; everything about her seemed gay and lively. – No wonder – the Tuggses were on board.

Other resorts grew after the opening of railways. Excursion trains fostered the growth of resorts that catered for day-trippers, such as Matlock Bath, Southend-on-Sea and Clacton-on-Sea. Excursion traffic came at the dawn of the railway age: as early as September 1831 a special train took Sunday School children from Manchester to Liverpool, and the train hired by Thomas Cook on 5 July 1841 to take temperance enthusiasts from Leicester to a demonstration at Loughborough was the foundation of a travel company. George Neele, a manager on the South Staffordshire Railway from 1849, thought that the Great Exhibition popularised cheap excursions, and reflected, 'We exploited Lichfield extensively using its cathedral as the attraction for excursion trains'. The numbers could be astonishingly large. On Trinity Monday 1853 staff at Shrewsbury station collected 32,000 tickets from excursionists arriving for the town's ancient 'show'; in 1882 a total of 420,000 visitors arrived by train to enjoy the week's festivities of Preston Guild. Some coastal resorts were deliberately planned with the railway in mind. These included Saltburn, which was serviced

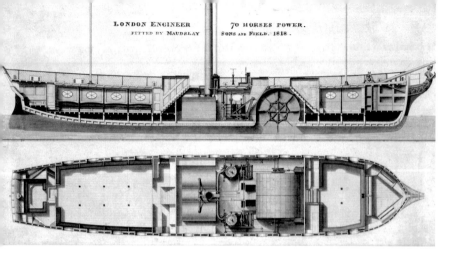

LONDON ENGINEER 70 HORSES POWER. FITTED BY MAUDSLAY SONS AND FIELD. 1818.

Excursion trains helped stimulate the development of resorts. They were running on the Liverpool & Manchester Railway soon after its opening in 1830, though in popular mythology the first was organised by Thomas Cook, founder of the travel company, carrying passengers from Leicester to a temperance meeting in Loughborough in 1841. Temperance was also popular in the mining districts of Cornwall: this 1855 engraving shows a train heading west on the West Cornwall Railway near Redruth past the Dunstanville Monument on Carn Brea (see page 356). Between Truro and Penzance this line was then of standard gauge but was converted to broad gauge in 1866–67 after the opening of the Cornwall Railway across the Royal Albert Bridge in 1859 linked it with lines in England. Excursions of this kind gave rise to the popular song (to the tune of 'Clementine'):

> *Happy Camborne, Happy Camborne*
> *Where the railway is so near,*
> *And the engines show how water*
> *Can accomplish more than beer.*

West Cornwall Teetotal Gala Excursion Train passing the Redruth Viaduct.

from the late 1850s by the Stockton & Darlington Railway Co.'s line. Twelve miles from Middlesbrough, Saltburn gained a pier, pleasure grounds, assembly rooms and the spacious railway hotel, the *Zetland*. Other towns, including Fleetwood, Barry and Silloth, were reached by railway for the purposes of developing port facilities, and the idea of catering to holidaymakers was secondary. In 1841 Weston-super-Mare became the first resort to which a branch line was specifically constructed; others – to Scarborough, Blackpool, Southport, Eastbourne and Torquay – followed in the same decade. Unfortunately passenger statistics do not survive in sufficient number or detail to allow objective analysis of the impact of the railways on the fortunes of such resorts. In the case of Blackpool, the classic

northern holiday resort, the sheer weight of anecdotal evidence makes it clear that their impact was huge, particularly towards the end of the century; in other places it appears to be less clear-cut.

Evangelical clergy vehemently opposed Sunday excursions. The Congregationalist Dr Joseph Parker, then minister at Banbury, caused outcry when he wrote in a tract in 1855 that Sunday excursionists included 'the dirtiest, silliest, laziest and poorest of the working population'. Some excursions were characterised by anarchic vigour. When in 1848 a train from Oldham Mumps to Blackpool was advertised at 1s. for ladies and 1s. 6d. for gentlemen the station was besieged by a crowd of two thousand, many of them men in drag. At Sowerby Bridge in 1858 the station staff filled four

In the summer of 1847 Queen Victoria and Prince Albert travelled to Scotland in the royal yacht, *Victoria and Albert*. Their northward voyage included a call in the Isles of Scilly (see below, page 585), but on their return they left the yacht at Fleetwood and boarded a train for London. The port of Fleetwood at the mouth of the river Wyre in Lancashire was planned by the landowner, Sir Peter Hesketh Fleetwood, who employed Decimus Burton to lay out spacious streets and to build elegant terraces and the *North Euston Hotel*, visible on the left of this picture. The new town stood alongside a railway from Preston opened in 1840. It was intended to be a packet station at which travellers to and from Scotland could transfer between train and boat. Victoria's journey, arriving in the port on 20 September and departing by train the following morning, epitomised Sir Peter's intentions, but the completion of the Lancaster and Carlisle Railway over Shap Fell – a vital link in the west-coast line from London to Scotland – undermined the venture. Fleetwood revived after 1870 under the aegis of the Lancashire and Yorkshire Railway as an industrial fishing port and as a packet station for Belfast and the Isle of Man.

parcel trucks with intoxicated bodies after the annual excursion of the local Temperance Society returned from Liverpool. By contrast, members of mechanics' institutes often studied geology or history in advance of excursions to particular destinations. The tickets available for excursion trains often allowed passengers to return home on normal services after a stay of several days, helping to introduce the lower orders to the idea of residential holidays.

In terms of their plan and visual character, resorts were shaped by pre-existing patterns of land holding. Some owners encouraged planned developments, as at Southport and Eastbourne. Where there was no controlling landlord, such as at Blackpool, building could be haphazard. There were building workers in every resort, their way of life portrayed in Robert Tressell's *The Ragged Trousered Philanthropists*, which was set in Mugsborough (Hastings) around 1906. Civil engineers built piers, embanked promenades, bridged chasms, and provided access from cliffs to beaches. The first lift to a beach was installed at Saltburn in 1860. The word 'esplanade', originally an open space between a castle and the town it protected, came to mean instead a levelled area designed for promenading. The healing reputations of waters and the celebrity of doctors remained powerful attractions in the 1850s and 1860s, and convalescent homes became the nuclei of some resorts. Access to the sea required investment in bathing machines, described at Margate in 1805 as:

> four-wheeled carriages, covered with canvas, and having at one end of them an umbrella of the same material which is let down to the surface of the water, so that the bather descending from the machine by a few steps is concealed from the public view, whereby the most refined female is enabled to enjoy the advantages of the sea with the strictest delicacy.

There were hot and cold bathing facilities at coastal and inland resorts. In Brighton in the 1860s there were tepid baths at 77 East Street for men and at no. 78 for women. Landowners, local boards of health or public subscribers invested in gardens, networks of cliff walks, or areas of greensward surrounding bandstands provided by foundries such as Macfarlane's of Glasgow. A resort also required investment in lodginghouses and from the 1850s in imposing hotels, as well as in assembly rooms, theatres and concert halls. There was much interest in food associated with the coast, with oysters, jellied eels, shrimps, crabs, lobsters, whelks and mussels. Preparing shellfish for sale was a significant local trade at, for example, Lytham and Southport. Kippers and bloaters could be taken home from day trips. Resorts required short-distant transport, in bath-chairs, hackney carriages or the 'cars' that ferried people across Leamington. Walks or rides were attractive, if they terminated at a particular point, such as the 'little cake houses where you have fruit syllabubs and summer liquors' which delighted Celia Fiennes at Bath, or Uncle Tom's Cabin north of Blackpool.

Relationships between fishermen, visitors and their hosts were ambiguous. Smacks drawn up on beaches and nets hung up to dry created picturesque atmospheres, while images of sailing fleets offshore could be evocative, and fishermen took visitors for trips in boats. Nevertheless, fish gutting was hidden from view in genteel resorts. At many places there was a continuing relationship with the military. The presence of the army at Dover or the Royal Navy at Portsmouth was overwhelming, but batteries along the south coast, including some martello towers built during the Napoleonic Wars, were still manned in the 1860s by Royal Artillerymen. Several cannon were removed when the battery at Brighton was dismantled in 1858, but at Eastbourne 144 soldiers were manning the Circular Redoubt (now the town museum) in 1861. At Seaford two gunners and two bombardiers with their families were based around a martello tower (also now a museum), and at Lyme Regis the East Cliff Battery with its two 24-pounders remained in the care of a Royal Artillery sergeant. Parades and military pageants added to a resort's attractions, and the presence of serving units made resorts attractive as places of residence for retired officers.

Granville commended the attractive powers of waterfalls and towering cliffs and crags, and of historic abbeys, castles and mansions. Processions of passing ships interested visitors, as did wrecks such as that of the *Atlantique* of Nantes, beached at Brighton in June 1860. Displays of antiquities, minerals and fossils varied in quality between stalls selling shells or fossils and William Smith's museum at Scarborough. Exotic live animals were exhibited at resorts by itinerant menageries. The showman 'Lord' George Sanger opened the Hall-by-the-Sea with a menagerie at Margate, and a similar establishment, the Amphitheatre at Ramsgate. Shops were larger at resorts than in other towns of similar size, and fancy bazaars and similar establishments flourished in less refined places, many selling ceramic or wooden items imported from Germany. The manufacture of jet ornaments employed more than 300 people in Whitby and its vicinity in 1861. Resorts provided markets for painters of landscapes and portraits, and for photographers, some of whom established portable darkrooms on promenades.

Piers were essential features of aspiring coastal resorts by the 1860s. Brighton's Chain Pier of 1823 was the first to be more than a landing stage, providing shelters, shops and entertainments. Many piers drew inspiration from Brighton's Royal Pavilion, with architecture that combined function with spectacular fantasy. Eugenius Birch designed many, including those at Eastbourne (1866–70), Clevedon (1860), the North Pier at Blackpool (1863) and the West Pier at Brighton (1866). Piers enabled promenaders to view resorts as if from the sea, and created new venues for entertainments and retailing.

By the 1860s resorts were identified with particular social classes. At inland spas such as Matlock and Malvern there were distinctions between quarters where genteel residents and long-term visitors took the waters and those which provided amusements for day-trippers arriving by rail. Granville observed in 1841 that 'the upper & wealthier classes [are] driven away from every point on the coast by facilities offered to the "everybody" and the "anybody", of congregating in shoals at the same watering place, creating bustle, noise, confusion and vulgarity'. The quest for exclusivity is exemplified by the development from the 1860s of Cliftonville and Westgate on either side

The coastal battery at Lyme Regis which was still manned by the Royal Artillery in 1861.

The tomb of the circus proprietor 'Lord' John Sanger at Margate, Kent. His brother 'Lord' George Sanger, depicted in a toga on his adjacent memorial, opened some of the most prominent centres of entertainment in the Thanet resorts from the early 1870s, the Hall by the Sea at Margate, which included a menagerie, and the Amphitheatre at Ramsgate.

of what had become the plebeian resort of Margate. It was a matter of pride that excursion trains never called at Westgate Station, and it was observed in 1879 that 'A great number of the houses belong to residents who either live there all the year round or make it their autumn quarters. ... Westgate is somewhat rigidly exclusive in its tastes and strongly aristocratic in its feelings and ambition – a sort of Mayfair by the sea.' A Thanet writer in 1881, extolling the virtues of the bungalow estate at Birchington, defined the ambience that exclusive resorts were intended to avoid: 'the perfect repose of the place is unruffled by the noisy seaside attractions. There are no German bands ... no distressing niggers [i.e. nigger minstrels] on the shore, and no donkey-drivers in the roads.' Nor were there cheap excursionists. Birchington-on-Sea had no jetty, no assembly rooms, nor a 'Tivoli' nor a 'Ranelagh', not even a tea-garden. It was 'an uncontaminated play-ground for large families and a secluded sanatorium for invalids'.

Hotels and lodging-houses were prominent features of resorts. The word 'hotel' was first applied to '*The Hotel*' (now the *Royal Clarence Hotel*) opened in Exeter in 1768, but the use of the term spread slowly. There were hotels in coastal resorts before 1800, but new ventures of the 1850s and 1860s were on a larger scale. The *Pavilion* was built by the South Eastern Railway after it reached Folkestone in 1843 and remained the resort's premier hotel until the 1890s. In 1881 its guests included Sir Edward Watkin, the railway director, then overseeing the construction of the abortive Channel Tunnel. The *Burlington Hotel* at Eastbourne was built in 1851, and ten years later its 25 guests included the brewer, China merchant and MP Robert Culling Hanbury, and Sir Rowland Hill, founder of the Penny Post. Most hotels built by railway companies were places of transit, but some, such as the *Seabrook* (later the *Imperial*) at Hythe, built before 1860 by the South Eastern Railway, catered for long-term visitors and stimulated the development of resorts. The North

Eastern Railway built the *Zetland Hotel* at Saltburn to the design of William Peachey in 1863, and in 1864 Thomas Savin of the Cambrian Railways commissioned the Gothic Revival architect John Pollard Seddon to adapt Castle House at Aberystwyth as a palatial hotel, opened in 1865 and closed, after Savin's bankruptcy, a year later. It was sold to the University of Wales in 1872.

The *Grand Hotel* replaced the artillery battery on the seafront at Brighton and opened in 1864. Designed in the Italian Renaissance style by John Whichcord, it was lavishly ornamented with Minton tiles and 230 marble chimney-pieces. It had smoking rooms, billiard rooms, segregated coffee rooms for ladies and gentlemen, and five hydraulic lifts, the first in the English provinces. The *Ilfracombe Hotel*, a vast building in polychrome brick in the French Gothic style, was designed by the London architect M. C. W. Horne, and completed in 1867. The same year saw the opening of the *Grand Hotel* at Scarborough, designed by Cuthbert Brodrick on the calendar principle, and constructed with six million yellow bricks around towers representing the four seasons, with 52 chimneys and 365 rooms, including those on the attic floors for guests' servants, and extending 160 feet from the roof to the foundations on the seaward side.

The *Granville Hotel* at Ramsgate is equally monumental. Augustus Welby Pugin, the prophet of the Gothic Revival, moved to Ramsgate in 1843, built a house in the Gothic style, and constructed the Roman Catholic church of St Augustine with a monastery adjoining. His son Edward Welby Pugin built the *Granville* from 1869. The hotel is constructed in grey-yellow brick with a seven-storey tower and crenellated chimneys through which passed steam from Turkish baths. Sea-water was piped direct to guests' bathrooms. The hotel was partly the cause of Pugin's bankruptcy in 1873; it was then bought by Edmund Davies, who laid out the nearby Victoria Gardens, and built new roads to give direct access to the shore.

The seaside and inland spas were central to the attractions of early resorts. Later transport facilities and changing perceptions of mountain scenery stimulated the growth of resorts in, for example, the Lake District, and north and mid-Wales. Between 1752 and 1782 fourteen Acts were passed placing roads north of the Wye under the control of turnpike trusts. Some trusts built new roads that enhanced access to the coast, and stagecoach services, initially running only in the summer months, began from Shrewsbury to Barmouth and Aberystwyth in the 1790s. The completion in 1827 of a new road through Llanbrynmair reduced the journey time between Shrewsbury and Aberystwyth from 15 to 13 hours. The Welsh coast was frequented by Welsh and Shropshire gentry. A spinster from Admaston near Shrewsbury regularly spent the season at Aberystwyth where in 1802 and 1806 she found pleasant companions, content with bathing and strolling, and not enthusiastic about participating in gambling, balls and plays, but in 1803 there was little company, and continuous rain for six weeks prevented bathing. In 1813 Ayton reflected in Aberystwyth that the fashion of sea bathing 'lays out streets of stone and builds houses of brick in places which seemed … to be doomed to an eternity of unpaved lanes and mud walls'. At Barmouth there were bathing machines by 1787 and the *Corsygedd Arms* in 1805 accommodated '30 persons most of fortune and fashion'. A new town was proposed in 1825 at Aberdovey, 'one of the most delightful situations for bathing in the kingdom'. At Towyn, the *Corbet Arms* was seen as chiefly attractive to 'economical farmers'. The Chester & Holyhead Railway, opened in 1850, served Rhyl, of which one observer commented in 1848, 'I do not believe there is another place so good in the country … a traveller like me is a sojourner here and has visited the South of France, Spain, Mexico &c and says he prefers the atmosphere to any of them.'

At Llandudno the land in the shadow of the Great Orme was enclosed by an Act of Parliament of 1849, which awarded 832 of the 955 acres to the first Baron Mostyn whose descendants developed the town after the establishment of an Improvement Commission in 1854. A branch linked Llandudno to the Chester & Holyhead line in 1858, and in the same year a pier opened, facilitating the arrival of steamers from Liverpool. A visitor in 1853 saw a 24-bedroom hotel and a crescent of fourteen houses under construction in a 'beautifully situated and thriving locality … evidently destined soon to vie with the most famed

Improvements to a resort's facilities can sometimes destroy the very features that first made them attractive. John Ruskin famously protested on these grounds against the construction of the Manchester, Buxton, Matlock and Midland Junction Railway through the beauties of Monsal Dale. Here we see the construction of the 533-yard Headstone Viaduct in Monsal Dale, with the wooden centrings for the five 50-foot span arches awaiting the laying of the stone voussoirs. The line was opened to Buxton in 1863 and became in due course the Midland Railway's route from Manchester to London. It closed in 1968: perhaps Ruskin would have approved of the disused Monsal Dale section being used by walkers and cyclists?

watering places'. But some projected resorts failed to prosper. Above the sands at Borth, on the estuary of the Afon Dyfi, Thomas Savin built terraces in the 1860s flanking the approach to the railway station. Borth did not grow into a resort, but Savin's development epitomised contemporary perceptions of the growth of seaside towns:

> [Alice] was up to her chin in salt water. Her first idea was that she had somehow fallen into the sea, 'and in that case I can go back by railway', she said to herself. Alice had been to the seaside once in her life, and had come to the general conclusion that wherever you go on the English coast you find a number of bathing machines in the sea, some children digging in the sand with wooden spades, then a row of lodging houses, and behind them a railway station.

There could also be opposition to opening up areas of natural beauty. Most famously in 1844 the poet William Wordsworth led a fierce but ultimately failed campaign of resistance against the construction of a railway line from Kendal into the heart of the Lake District at Windermere. 'The projectors have induced many to favour their schemes,' he claimed in his first letter to the *Morning Post*, 'by declaring that one of their main objects is to place the beauties of the Lake District within easier reach of those who cannot afford to pay for ordinary conveyances.' He argued that only minds properly educated in matters of culture and contemplation could properly appreciate the beauties of the area, and that this would likely be beyond the capacity of ordinary holidaymakers brought by the train.

The mechanisms by which resorts were planned or developed could vary enormously. Some, such as Blackpool, were 'open' communities in the sense that development was uncontrolled by any civic authority or single land-holding interest. Others, such as Harrogate, Fleetwood, Buxton or Eastbourne, were 'closed' communities, more carefully planned and controlled by a guiding hand. In 1861 Blackpool was a community of about 3,600 people. It had been commended by William Hutton in 1788, and in 1812 a commentator extolled its beach, 'a bolder and more unbroken expanse of sea rolling in upon this particular point than is to be seen anywhere else upon this sand-bound coast'. Visitors arrived in carts, while some walked 50 miles from Manchester. Granville in 1841 found that many of the 3,000 summer visitors came from Preston, less than 20 miles away, and that the hotels were closed in the winter. Blackpool was not

Blackpool was already a successful resort in 1870s, but it grew at a phenomenal rate in the following decades and such was its magnetic attraction in 1893, the year before the opening of the Tower, that it was advertised by the Midland Railway which could only send trains there over long stretches of line owned by other companies. Blackpool benefited from the practice in many northern industrial parishes of retaining 'wakes', annual holidays, often on patronal festivals, during which many factories were closed for a week for maintenance of the machinery. Railway companies put on special trains to convey families to coastal resorts, and particularly to Blackpool.

Some nineteenth-century seaside piers were built on wooden uprights, but that at Southport, opened on 2 August 1860 and designed by James Brunlees, was an iron structure whose columns are evident in this engraving. The pier is almost a mile long, second only in length to that at Southend. A pier was a particularly appropriate feature at Southport, where the sea was always distant at low tide. Some bathing machines are visible on the right.

a genteel resort, although in the third quarter of the eighteenth century it had clear pretensions to such a status. Granville took dinner at *Nixon's Hotel* with 'a motley of honest-looking people', including an ironfounder from the West Riding and a none-too-prosperous Oporto merchant from Liverpool. He was nevertheless impressed with the investment that had been made in sea-walls and houses facing the sea. There were ten hotels in April 1861, although only the *Clifton Arms* with 24 guests and the *Victoria Arms*

which accommodated two cotton manufacturers with their families appeared to be trading out of season. There were more than 170 lodging-houses, many kept by families whose male heads followed other occupations – joiners, gardeners and tailors. Two men kept donkeys for hire, and a public baths employed two or three attendants, but the seasonal nature of employment was indicated by a man whose occupation was given as 'Keeps a Post Horse in Summer – Labourer in Winter'. The railway came in 1846, and the fragmented pattern of landownership provided opportunities for enterprise, but created a haphazard pattern of buildings – there was no overall plan or effective control of development – and delayed the provision of amenities. Blackpool's first permanent theatre opened in 1859, the North Pier in 1863 and the South Pier in 1866. By the mid-1860s it was accommodating 25,000 visitors at the summer peak. It became a vibrant playground for Lancashire's working class, but its principal growth came after 1870.

The resort of Southport could not have been more different from Blackpool, its Lancashire neighbour. In 1835 Sir George Head was travelling to Liverpool on the Leeds & Liverpool Canal packet boat. At Scarisbrick Bridge he observed omnibuses and luggage carts waiting to convey passengers to Southport, 'a watering place near the Ribble'. Unlike Blackpool's chaotic development, progress in Southport was controlled by the Hesketh and Bold families. Regulated street widths ensured the growth of an attractive and spacious resort, rich in gardens. An innkeeper reputedly erected a driftwood beach hut in 1792, a hotel was built in 1798, and in 1805 the construction of Wellington Terrace marked the beginning of Lord Street, the town's principal axis. Southport's population reached 10,097 in 1861, and it continued to prosper, particularly after the construction of a hydropathic centre.

Other resorts similarly benefited from aristocratic patronage. The population of Folkestone almost doubled in the two decades after the railway arrived in 1843, reaching nearly 10,000 in 1861 and almost 20,000 in 1881. The 3rd Earl of Radnor was responsible for the regularity of the streets, lined with large and comfortable villas, hotels and boarding houses. Residents in 1881 included the 6th Earl of Glasgow and the 11th Earl Dundonald, and many wives with absentee husbands contracting in India, building railways in South America or prospecting for minerals in Russia. The development of Eastbourne was shaped by the dukes of Devonshire, particularly by William Cavendish, 7th Duke, who succeeded to the title in 1858. A guide book was published in 1787 and by the 1790s there were circulating libraries and billiard rooms, but the population in 1801 was less than 2,000. The sea-wall was built, creating a promenade, from 1848, the railway opened the following year, and in 1861 Eastbourne's population approached 6,000.

The dukes of Devonshire were also responsible for the inland resort of Buxton. It was well known as a spa in the eighteenth century, but its population in 1841 was only 1,569. Growth was stimulated by the building of the *Royal Hotel* in 1849–52. The baths were rebuilt in 1852–53, the Quadrant laid out in 1853–64, and a park was designed by Sir Joseph Paxton.

Other towns sought to emulate the prosperity of resorts, or indeed anticipated their characteristics. Some county towns, such as Nottingham, Durham, Preston and Bury St Edmunds, were celebrated for the gaiety of their society in the eighteenth century, as were Ludlow and Stamford, to which gentry flocked by choice, not because attendance was required at quarter sessions. Their seasons revolved around race meetings which provided opportunities for socialising at public breakfasts, card parties and cockfights. Assembly rooms, whether of unquestioned elegance, such as that built at the *Lion Hotel*, Shrewsbury, by the lawyer John Ashby in the 1770s, or of the dismal kind described by Elizabeth Gaskell in *Cranford* (thought to be based on Knutsford, Cheshire) enabled county families to meet in the winter to dance and play cards. The 'mouldy odour of aristocracy' at Cranford spread to other towns in the 1830s, as improved communications drew land-owning families to London. Alan Everitt observed that by 1700 a class of 'pseudo-gentry' had emerged, people with independent incomes that were not derived from country estates, the annuitants and fundholders found in resorts and in smaller numbers elsewhere. The *Banbury Guardian* in 1852 encouraged the building of houses suitable for persons of private fortune since 'it would be a wise step to encourage the residence amongst us of those who come to spend not to get money'. Ludlow was known in 1805 as a clean town with handsome shops where 'many of the inhabitants live on their fortunes'. Nevertheless, a pamphleteer in 1810 urged townspeople to invest to create a resort. Ludlow was set in beautiful country and was well supplied with provisions. Water from local springs could be heated to provide hot baths and made medicinal by the addition of sulphur compounds. Crescents and terraces could be built on nearby common

land, and a house might be adapted as assembly rooms. Ludlow would become a place of retirement for warriors fighting Napoleon, and the entrepreneur who brought this about would surely gain a peerage. By 1861 Ludlow accommodated some retired officers, unbeneficed clergy and superannuated clerks of the Exchequer, and had an assembly room of 1840, but it was not primarily a resort. In *Catherine Furze*, set in a Midlands town in the 1840s, Mark Rutherford describes a recently built development called 'The Terrace', which contained a dozen houses in the classical style. Its first residents included a doctor, a brewer and a wholesale grocer, and it was the desired residence of the aspiring wife of an ironmonger. The contemporary Rutland Terrace in Stamford, built in high-quality stone, succeeded in attracting genteel residents rather than tradesmen. The heads of 13 of its 20 households in 1851 were women living on investments, while the seven male householders comprised a solicitor, banker, retired grocer, former naval officer, proprietor of houses and two clergymen.

Several rail-served 'day resorts' such as the Blisworth Pleasure Gardens near Northampton, developed close to towns. The best known was Pavilion Gardens on the Isle of Dogs, alongside the North Woolwich railway terminus opened in 1847. By 1869 the gardens included a ballroom, an open-air dancing platform, a maze, butts for archery and rifle shooting and an open-air theatre. Visitors arrived by steamer as well as by train and for several decades were entertained by musical acts, balloon ascents and

firework displays. On the opposite bank of the Thames Rosherville Gardens, developed from 1837 in a disused chalk pit at Gravesend, had similar attractions, and was 'justly celebrated', according to one writer in 1858, 'as the most beautiful public gardens in the kingdom'.

Another particular type of new community was the Clyde steamboat resort. Resorts on Clydeside were closely connected to mining and manufacturing, and their growth was the consequence of the steamship and the railway. At Largs, for example, a fishing community with a sheltered harbour on the Ayrshire coast, the construction of a pier in 1834 enabled steamboats to bring visitors down the Clyde from Glasgow. Handloom weaving of plaids occupied some families, but by 1861 this was essentially a resort, with six hotels, boarding houses, hirers of boats and genteel residents who included an underwriter at Lloyds, a sugar broker, and several shipbuilders.

Dunoon on the Cowal peninsula had a pier by 1820, enjoyed direct steamship services to and from Glasgow by the 1840s, and by the 1880s had quicker services by steamer to Gourock and thence by rail. Its development was initiated by James Ewing, Lord Provost of Glasgow, a founder of Glasgow Bank in 1805, West Indies merchant, sugar trader and plantation owner. He built Castle House (now the museum) from 1822 and other wealthy merchants and manufacturers constructed villas. They included carpet manufacturers, cotton spinners, calico printers, shawl manufacturers, colliery managers, ironfounders and shipbuilders. There were 18 hotels in Dunoon by 1880, and numerous lodging-houses, as well as the artists, teachers of accomplishments, boat hirers and billiard markers that could be found in most resorts.

Rothesay, on the island of Bute, grew up under the shadow of Mount Stuart House, home of the 2nd and 3rd Marquesses of Bute, landlords of Cardiff. Rothesay's population approached 8,000 in 1870, when its prosperity was said to depend almost entirely upon its character as a watering place and as a place of retirement for merchants and manufacturers from Glasgow, Falkirk, Hawick and Paisley. There was much investment in the 1870s; the headquarters of the Archaeological and Physical Society opened in 1873; the Royal Aquarium, which included rocks illustrating Bute's geology, was completed in 1875–76; and a public hall in 1879. The principal boat hirer operated 17 vessels, and visitors could also view the scenery of Bute from cabs, carriages and omnibuses. Much of Rothesay's growth was due to Alexander Bannatyne Stewart, collector of paintings and orchids, whose Rothesay-born father made a fortune from a Glasgow grocery business established in 1826. The Clyde estuary was an early centre for the building and the use of steamboats, but the area also prospered from the popularity of yachting. Stewart was flag officer of the Royal Northern Yacht Club whose headquarters were at Rothesay; crew members lived in all three resorts, and a yacht building yard flourished at Largs.

In Ireland the principal coastal resort was Bray, 12 miles south of Dublin. Genteel Dubliners were settling there by 1800, and from 1854 it was served by the Dublin & Kingstown Railway. Guests at the hotels and boarding houses along its promenade could bathe in the shadow of the 650 foot (200 m) high Bray Head and enjoy excursions to the scenic delights and historic monuments of the Wicklow Hills.

On the far north coast the harbour at Portrush, Co. Antrim, was constructed from 1827 by Sir John Rennie, and a railway from Coleraine opened in 1855, but the electric tramway to the Giant's Causeway was not built until the 1880s. The most successful Irish resort was Killarney, beside the lakes and mountains of south-western Ireland in Co. Kerry. The first steps towards providing accommodation for visitors in the wild countryside were taken by the 4th Viscount Kenmare, who lived there for twelve years directing road making and the building of boats for hire, and leasing plots for the construction of inns. Kerry was ravaged by the Great Famine, but the restoration of Killarney's fortunes began in 1861 when Queen Victoria visited with an entourage of more than 100. By 1900 the town's population exceeded 6,000.

Killarney was the most successful mountain and lake resort in the British Isles. The English Lake District lacked a single urban centre but had many small resorts. Dibdin observed in 1801 the importance to the thoroughfare trade of Kendal of *Laker*s, 'those persons who go out of curiosity to visit the lakes'. In 1861 Keswick was described as 'the fashionable resort of a great number of strangers in the summer months'. There were lodging-houses for respectable guests, of whom there were few in April, although visiting entertainers included a German band and a Glaswegian fiddler. Several men made their livings as guides and boatmen, taking out anglers and those who wished to view the scenery from Derwentwater.

No resort in the Scottish Highlands proper matched the success of those around the Clyde estuary or of Killarney, although the establishment from 1848 by Queen Victoria and Prince Albert of a home in Deeside at Balmoral provided the kind of royal patronage for the region that in previous generations had brought celebrity and economic success to Bath, Weymouth and Brighton. The distance of the Highlands from the principal centres of population, the lingering traumas of the Clearances (see below, Chapter 14) and the determination of aristocratic landlords to preserve the mountains and moors for field sports made the growth of popular tourism almost impossible in this period.

Manufacturing in resort towns

The growth of resort facilities supplanted manufacturing in some towns. In others prosperity encouraged the establishment of manufactures which gave winter employment. In the case of Matlock Bath mere

An unlikely product of the resort of Bath, a curved jib steam crane, of the type designed by William Fairbairn, constructed by Stothert & Pitt and erected in Bristol docks in 1875. It now forms part of the city's industrial museum. Stothert & Pitt's works were on Lower Bristol Road, Bath. Nearby were the 1859 premises of Isaac Pitman's publishing and printing establishment. Pitman was noted as the inventor of shorthand, and his company came to be significant employer in the city better known for its Roman and Georgian spas.

coincidence led to an inland spa developing in close proximity to several great spinning mills including Arkwright's Masson Mills. Small harbours declined as the fishing industry was concentrated in Grimsby, Fleetwood, Hull and Aberdeen, although Yarmouth flourished both as resort and as industrial fishing port. Rothesay was a fishing port and a textile-manufacturing centre as well as a resort. The making of 'Honiton' lace gave employment in 1861 to many people in the small resorts of south Devon. Leamington was celebrated for the kitcheners made by William and Sidney Flavel. In Bath the engineering company Stothert & Pitt grew from a foundry set up on the premises of the ironmonger George Stothert, and from 1827 managed by his son Henry Stothert who in 1844 took into partnership Robert Pitt. The company moved to premises on the Lower Bristol Road in 1857, and employed about 100 men in 1861, by which time it had a reputation as a supplier of cranes. Engineering also prospered at Brighton, where the London, Brighton & South Coast Railway established its locomotive works in 1852, and even at Blackpool the mechanical engineer John Parrott employed more than 20 men in 1861.

Many coastal resorts were beginning to grow rapidly in 1870, and the principal inland spas were still flourishing, although railways failed to bring prosperity to such aspirant watering places as Tenbury Wells, Willoughby and Llanwrtyd Wells. Bournemouth, perceived by Thomas Hardy as 'Sandbourne',

a fashionable watering place with two stations, piers, groves of pines, promenades and covered gardens, 'a new world in an old one … a city of detached mansions; a Mediterranean lounging-place on the English Channel', grew from a scattered community of fewer than 700 people in 1841 into a town of 38,000 by 1891. James Brogden, the Furness ore shipper who built Porthcawl harbour and the railway serving it in 1865–67, adapted his family residence as a hotel and built an esplanade. His ambitions were curbed by bankruptcy, but Porthcawl prospered nevertheless. On the Lincolnshire coast, Skegness and Mablethorpe lacked railways in 1861, when the former was a community of fewer than 300 with one boarding house. It grew after the railway arrived in 1873 in accordance with a plan prepared in 1877 for the 9th Earl of Scarborough, while Mablethorpe developed around a convalescent home.

By 1870 the leisure industry was firmly established, and much growth was still to come. Increasing numbers of people were able to travel to a wide range of destinations, including day-trippers to Brighton; Wakes weeks' holiday-makers to Blackpool; and retired gentlefolk to Bath. The affluence and the transport networks brought by industrialisation in the period up to 1870 had played important roles in the development of these very British resorts.

14

Creating communities: calculations and aspirations

'... we fixed upon a place near Newry. ... It had ... the admirable condition, in my sight, of enabling us to control our people and to do them good in every sense.'

John Grubb Richardson

HOWEVER MUCH they shared the same technologies, industrial communities in the British Isles differed in their housing, their culture, their inheritance from the past, and sometimes even their language. The Warwickshire coalfield described by George Eliot was quite different from that of Nottinghamshire portrayed by D. H. Lawrence, and neither resembled the mining villages of County Durham or the valleys of South Wales. The object of this chapter is to examine the forces which created distinctive industrial communities, whether they were the legacies of past events, the ambitions of entrepreneurs, or the objectives of 'Improvers'. Particular attention is paid to communities created on what were perceived as the margins of the national economy, and on those which were planned, with practical or idealistic motives, to set patterns that might be imitated by others. Such places were exceptional, but they illuminate what was happening elsewhere.

'Open' and 'close' communities

The distinction between 'open' and 'close' (or 'closed') villages, often remarked in the mid-nineteenth century and 'rediscovered' by historians in the 1960s, illuminates the nature of industrial as well as agricultural communities. Settlement in close villages was controlled by landlords. Farm labour was provided by 'indoor servants', workers who lived in farmhouses, or by labourers from elsewhere travelling daily; cottages were inhabited only by gamekeepers, whippers-in and stockmen who might be required overnight. Many landlords pursued deliberate policies of depopulation, demolishing cottages when they became vacant, thus

reducing poor rates (which remained chargeable to the individual parish until 1865). Such policies also ensured that the poor and their wretched dwellings were invisible from the windows, terraces and carriage drives of stately homes. In open villages, by contrast, the pattern of land holding was dispersed; with no central control, owners of small properties could cram closes with cottages to rent; populations increased; and poor rates were high. The distinction between open and close parishes was made by James Caird, the chronicler of English agriculture, who described how labourers were driven from close parishes under the control of one or two large proprietors and forced to compete for limited numbers of cottages elsewhere. Thomas Hardy, in *Tess of the d'Urbervilles*, made a triple distinction between villages cared for by their lords, villages of freeholders or copyholders cared for by themselves, and villages uncared for, either by themselves or by their lords. Unregulated 'open' parishes were often perceived to be the resorts of criminals and unmarried mothers. Castle Acre in Norfolk was known as 'the coop of all the scrapings in the country, for if a man or a woman do anything wrong they come here, and they think that by getting among them here they are safe'. In 1784 the Rochefoucaulds observed that its houses were 'dirty and badly built and not even fit to be in France'. An 'open' village usually had a beer shop, and, in contrast to close parishes where the primacy of the Established Church was often unchallenged, most had dissenting chapels.

Some open 'villages' were communities of squatters who had built cottages on common land, such as village greens, heaths, marshes and hillsides. The erection of cottages on commons is documented from the sixteenth century, and it was believed that if a house could be erected in one night with smoke coming from the chimney before sunrise the cottager had a right to stay. In 1805, for example, a collier occupied a cottage on the edge of the recently enclosed Lyth Hill Common near Shrewsbury. It stood within an enclosure of about an acre upon which he and his wife grew potatoes, wheat, peas, beans and cabbages, and kept a pig, while the collier worked seasonally for local farmers. One of the cottages on Myddle Wood Common in Shropshire dates from 1581, and in the eighteenth century the surrounding community included tailors and weavers as well as farm labourers, while women made their livings as midwives and by baking cakes for sale.

The common in Clee St Margaret on the slopes of Brown Clee remains unenclosed to this day. Those settled in holdings of one or two acres on its edges in the 1850s included carpenters, stone masons, quarrymen, lime burners, coal miners, coal hauliers, sawyers and the keeper of a cider house. The parish of Alstonefield in north Staffordshire extended over 23,249 acres and rises to 1,535 feet (473 m). In its four upland townships 10,000 acres were unenclosed in 1700. Many cottages

were built around the hamlet of Flash by hawkers who travelled to sell ribbons from Leek, buttons from Macclesfield and smallwares from Manchester in distant parts of England. Parliament was told in 1786 that they had converted 'a barren and wild spot to a rich and fertile circuit'. Hawkers' circuits were similar in many respects to the Evangelical 'connexions' of the mid-eighteenth century, when the Staffordshire uplands were a fertile nursery for Methodism, and in the nineteenth century when Mow Cop became the St Peter's Square of Primitive Methodism. The Rochefoucaulds were surprised in 1784 to observe uncultivated commons near London, but learned that the poor had immemorial rights to cut bracken and brushwood here. However, 70 parishes a year were being cleared, ensuring that 'in a few years all will be in proper cultivation'. Between 1793 and 1820 alone about a million acres of common lands, together with twice as much land in open fields, were enclosed, effectively curtailing the expansion of many communities involved in manufacturing and mining.

Some significant mining and manufacturing areas were made up of open communities. A Birmingham newspaper in 1754 observed of the Black Country that, 'The chief quantities of coal, iron and other foods of this country are carried by men who rent small farms into which these parts are very much divided. They raise little or no corn except for their own subsistence expecting to pay their rents and subsist themselves principally by carriage and generally keep five or six horses … for that purpose.' Patterns of open, squatter-like settlement similarly characterised parts of the Potteries, the textile manufacturing areas in the Pennines, and parishes such as Bonsall where several industries flourished.

Nineteenth-century literature abounds in descriptions of open communities. Mark Rutherford in *Catherine Furze* describes 'a rough lath-and-timber thatched house at Abchurch, a place to which labourers were driven because houses were very scarce on the farms in that part, and landlords would not build'. A Nonconformist chapel stood at a nearby crossroads. In *Alton Lock* Charles Kingsley described 'a knot of thatched hovels all sinking and leaning every way but the right, the windows patched with paper, the doorways stopped with filth, which surrounded a beershop', while in George Eliot's *Silas Marner* the weaver 'worked at his vocation in a stone cottage that stood among the nutty hedgerows near the village of Raveloe and not far from the edge of a deserted stone pit'.

The less respectable suburbs of market towns such as Thetford, Louth and Coggeshall were reservoirs of labour for rural parishes, serving the same functions as 'open' villages. Hardy described Mixen Lane, the rough suburb of Casterbridge (Dorchester):

> the Adullam of all the surrounding villages … the hiding place of those who were in distress and in debt and trouble of every kind. Farm-labourers and other peasants who combined a little poaching with their farming, and a little brawling and bibbing with their poaching, found themselves sooner or later in Mixen Lane. Rural mechanics too idle to mechanise, rural servants too rebellious to serve, drifted or were forced into Mixen Lane. The lane and its surrounding thicket of thatched cottages stretched out like a spit into the moist and misty lowland. Much that was sad, much that was low, some things that were baneful, could

be seen in Mixen Lane. Vice ran freely in and out certain of the doors of the neighbourhood; recklessness dwelt under the roof with the crooked chimney; shame in some bow windows; theft (in times of privation) in the thatched and mud-walled houses by the sallows. … Yet amid so much that was bad needy respectability had also found a home.

Such 'open' suburbs could be found on the edges of most towns. In Rock Lane, a braided straggle of cottages on a hillside from which it is possible to look westwards to the elegant streets of Ludlow, were brickmakers, knife grinders, tinkers, tailors and shoemakers. The 'rough suburb' of Headington Quarry on the eastern side of Oxford was analysed by the late Raphael Samuel. It originated as single-storey quarrymen's shacks on waste land among the stone quarries. In the nineteenth century people made their livings from brick making, poaching, rabbit catching, well digging, horse dealing, laundry work for colleges, selling dripping collected from college kitchens, and working with carts.

In 1834 Francis Witts described Cranham, eight miles from Gloucester, where two potteries provided employment for about ten people, making garden pots,

A characteristic West Midlands squatter cottage built on common land at Hayton's Bent in the parish of Stanton Lacy near Ludlow. Many such cottages had massive chimney stacks to which were attached rooms of relatively flimsy construction. This cottage was built at an unknown date before 1772. The surrounding area was enclosed in the early nineteenth century

Scattered squatter-like settlement at Rock Lane, a 'rough suburb' of the elegant town of Ludlow.

milk pans and earthenware pipes. 'A stranger,' he said, 'would suppose the place to be a peaceful rural abode of good will and honest simplicity, but Cranham has no resident gentleman or clergyman, and the habits of the people are thievish and gross.' Another example is Juniper Hill, near Brackley, portrayed by Flora Thompson as 'Lark Rise', which 'consisted of about 30 cottages and an inn, not built in rows but dotted anywhere within a more or less circular group'. The cottages had been thrown up when heathland in the parish of Cottesford had been enclosed in the 1820s, and served as a reservoir of labour for nearby farmers.

The status of nineteenth-century open and close communities was rooted in the past. Between 1589 and 1607 the Fiennes family of Broughton Castle, Oxfordshire, brought into their own hands almost all the land in the township of Broughton, while granting long leases and creating freeholdings in the adjacent hamlet of North Newington. Broughton retains the neat appearance of a close village. In 1861 there were scarcely any craftsmen or dissenters among its 213 inhabitants. Its two large farms employed 37 workers, but only 21 labourers lived in the township. North Newington, meanwhile, had a population of 428 in 1861, and was a characteristic open village. There freeholders were numerous and dissent was strong. Only ten women worked as domestic servants while there were 22 in Broughton. Six farms, four of less than 40 acres, employed 52 labourers, but 83 farmworkers lived in the parish. Six men and 14 women worked at the paper mill, and craftsmen included carpenters, shoemakers, hurdle makers, blacksmiths and a wheelwright, while a baker kept a beerhouse and the innkeeper doubled as a butcher.

Seigniorial enterprise

Some 'close' industrial communities were the creations of philanthropic aristocrats, concerned to provide employment for the poor. A visitor in 1773 was impressed by the village of Lowther near Penrith, on the estate of the 1st Earl of Lonsdale, where a round stone building was used for carpet weaving. A bleachery built in the 1780s by Thomas Fitzmaurice at Lleweni near Denbigh included an arcaded crescent, 400 feet in extent, with a loggia in the centre and a pavilion at each end, designed by Thomas Sandby. For about 30 years it processed fabrics from the family's Irish estates. A worsted spinning mill at Louth, built by a landowner in the 1780s, was intended to provide employment and reduce poor rates. Inveraray, built from 1745 for the 3rd Duke of Argyll, was a more ambitious project with similar objectives.

Landowners who established 'close' communities hoped to create settled deferential populations, where children would succeed their parents as farm workers and household servants and who would not be disturbed by alcohol, sexual licence, dissenting religion or radical politics. Owners of manufactories had similar objectives. By the mid-nineteenth century the London Lead Company had established communities in Weardale and Teesdale where almost all lead miners and smelters were locally born. Similarly, some of the first master cotton spinners were commended for the peaceable communities whose growth they had fostered. Peter Gaskell in 1836 praised 'magnificent factories surrounded by ranges of cottages, often exhibiting signs of comfort and cleanliness highly honourable to the proprietor and the occupants' which could be observed in Derbyshire, Cheshire, Lancashire and the Glasgow region, and affirmed that the objective of providing housing for factory workers was the creation of a peaceable, self-perpetuating labour force: 'Around many mills a fixed population has arisen, which is as much a part and parcel of the property of the master as his machinery. The rapid improvement in the last has put an end to the necessity for new labourers, and thus little colonies are formed under the absolute government of the employer.'

Andrew Ure considered that the best consequences of factory labour could be observed at rural mills which afforded regular employment over the years to the same families. He commended the example of the community around the Strutts' mills at Belper which, he observed, for half a century had 'furnished steady employment and comfortable sustenance to a population of many thousand individuals'.

A commentator on the Irish cotton-manufacturing community at Prosperous, County Kildare, in 1783 observed that 'sober and diligent workmen naturally fall into constant employment under masters who know their value', and were consequently seldom willing to join new employers, while it was necessary for entrepreneurs quickly to discharge men who appeared to be drunkards, idlers or the leaders of cabals. At New Lanark in the 1790s David Dale retained his workforce during difficulties caused by a fire and financial losses in London, paying wages when there was no work, and asserting that he was 'keeping together the people and particularly the children'.

The works at Bromborough Pool in Cheshire provides an informative example. The founder, William Wilson, belonged to the family of Scottish ironmasters who established Wilsontown, north-east of Lanark on the road to Edinburgh. When the ironworks there closed in 1812 he went to London to trade with Russia. Then, in 1830, he became a partner in a candle-making company named after a fictitious Edward Price, with a factory at Vauxhall. Developments in chemistry enabled the manufacturing costs of candles to be reduced and their lighting efficiency increased, while the abolition of the Candle Tax in 1831 increased opportunities for manufacturers. Whereas tallow-chandlers in market towns and mining communities made candles by dipping, the Price company developed technology for large-scale production in moulds. The research of the French chemist Michel Eugène Chevreuil showed that the solid and liquid components of fats could be separated by mixing with a strong alkali. This process, 'saponification', was already being used by soap manufacturers, but George, son of William Wilson, developed it by distilling fats using high-pressure steam and vacuum pans. The company first prospered by distilling coconut oil from Ceylon, but by 1840 used waste products including skin and bone fat, and it later employed palm oil from West Africa. From 1854 the principal raw material was paraffin wax made from petroleum from Burma and, after 1859, from Pennsylvania. Wilson was adept at marketing, and sold thousands of candles to be displayed in front-room windows on the occasion of Queen Victoria's coronation in June 1838. The firm

became a joint stock company, Price's Patent Candle Co., in 1847. In 1853 Wilson's sons, George, the chemist, and James, who like his father was an enthusiastic Evangelical, established a factory and company village at Bromborough Pool on the Wirral peninsula, conveniently situated for the supply of palm oil that had been imported into Liverpool. By 1861 more than 90 houses had been erected, the majority with living room, kitchen and scullery on the ground floor, and three bedrooms above. Each had a garden, and they were generously spaced around a cricket field and a bowling green. The Wilsons persuaded many of their workpeople to move from London to Merseyside. More than 170 men worked at the factory, 50 of whom were natives of London, mostly skilled workers from Battersea and Lambeth. Twenty-one candlemakers aged between 15 and 19 were accommodated in part of a mansion called Court House, under the tutelage of Edmund Hampson, curate of Bromborough and chaplain to the company. Bromborough Pool showed that it was possible for a strongly motivated entrepreneur to establish a stable workforce, even in a tumultuous area such as south London, and even to transfer it effectively to a new location.

The industrial communities that conformed most closely to the model of the 'close' villages were New

Some of the original houses at Bromborough Pool Village, in Manor Place.

Substantial stone-built cottages in Union Street which form part of the Ashworths' cotton-spinning community at Egerton near Bolton.

Eagley and Egerton, three miles north of Bolton. The water-powered New Eagley Mill was built in 1793 by the Quaker John Ashworth, and the mills prospered under the management of his sons Henry and Edmund. New Eagley mill was raised to six storeys soon after 1818, with a waterwheel from William Fairbairn, and Egerton Mill, commenced by others, was acquired in 1829. The brothers believed in unconstrained private enterprise, and Henry vigorously supported the Anti-Corn Law League. During the controversies of the 1840s the mills became a showpiece displaying the best features of the factory system. Aristocratic opponents of the League sought to find faults, while Free Trade propagandists lavished praise on the working and living conditions there. William Cooke Taylor, a propagandist for the Anti-Corn Law League, was particularly complimentary about the two settlements in 1842 in a book on which an account by the French politician Léon Faucher may be based. Geoffrey Timmins has shown that some housing was purchased by, rather than built by, the Ashworths, and that the houses were not of uniform quality. Nevertheless, some cottages had up to four bedrooms, pantries, water-boilers and ovens, with lavatories in walled back yards, and piped water from 1835. Most are built in local stone in small groups facing on to stone-flagged streets, and some have low-pitched Regency-style roofs. Communal buildings included schools, a library, a newsroom, several chapels and a cookshop providing bread and pies, but public houses were excluded. The Ashworths promoted thrift, sobriety, regular attendance at public worship, and cleanliness, which they ensured by

Almost nothing remains of one of the most celebrated industrial communities of the early nineteenth century, the textile community at Mellor, on the northern edge of Derbyshire, built by Samuel Oldnow, which was lavishly praised by contemporary commentators. Near the site today are the so-called 'Roman Lakes', which were the reservoirs for the mill's water power. Oldnow's Mill itself was destroyed by fire in 1892, but traces of its massive masonry have been found, as shown in this photograph, during recent excavations.

PHOTOGRAPH: CARNEGIE

inspections. Workers were well paid and generously provided with holidays by the standards of the time. In 1849 Reach commented that 'Here is no grime nor squalor. The people are hard-working labourers, but they live decently and fare wholesomely. There is no ragged wretchedness to be seen, no ruinous and squalid hovels.' Edmund Ashworth observed in 1839 that 'The man who has a well-furnished house is a more trustworthy servant than one who lives in a cellar or single room with almost no furniture, but the workman who lives in his own house is better than either', and the brothers encouraged home ownership.

Other textile communities that attracted attention included Quarry Bank, near Wilmslow, developed by Samuel Greg, which had a variety of housing all in open surroundings but of different dates, and those around the mills of Samuel Oldnow at Mellor (then on the western extremity of Derbyshire) and David Whitehead at Hollymount near Rawtenstall. The most-commended colonies were in isolated locations where owners had no choice but to provide housing, and where the lack of alternative employment eased the imposition of work discipline. The use of water power, even if supplemented by steam, meant that smoke caused less pollution than in towns. In most cases the proprietors lived on the spot. Many of the sources relating to such communities were written to promote Free Trade and the interests of manufacturers. A writer describing Portlaw near Waterford remarked in 1852 that 'one glance at the exterior of the village and the great establishment would have been enough to put to flight the miserable nonsense that some people nurse in their brains as to the unhappy condition of those who are employed in mills and factories'. For workers who could accept such patterns of discipline they were doubtless satisfying places in which to live.

The founders of two communities established in west Yorkshire in the 1850s had contrasting beliefs. Edward Akroyd, a Halifax worsted manufacturer, inherited £1.75 million from his father in 1847. He built Copley, a 'model' community of two terraces of back-to-back cottages near the river Calder, and by 1861 employed 4,500 workpeople in several mills. From 1859 he constructed a community named Akroydon on the hill north of Halifax, adjacent to Hayley Hill Mill and to his home at Bankfield Hall. The houses were the work of a local architect, but George Gilbert Scott designed the magnificent church of All Saints. Akroydon is laid out around a square imitating what Akroyd and Scott believed to be the plan of an old Pennine village. The stone cottages have Gothic detailing, and Akroyd was said to be 'desirous of keeping up the old English notion of a village – the squire and the parson as head, and then the tenant farmers and lastly the working population'. He believed that good living conditions produced sobriety and peaceable temperaments, and that the rural village of mythology was a better place to live than the industrial town. The Gothic style was adopted because 'the taste of our forefathers pleases the fancy, strengthens the house and home attachment and entwines the present with memories of the past'.

While Akroyd was an Anglican, Sir Titus Salt, whose model mill community near Shipley is rightly famous, was a Congregationalist, and he preferred the Italianate to the Gothic style in architecture. Salt did not yearn for an idyllic past but looked to a future made better by the fruits of manufacturing. Born in Morley in 1803, he settled from 1822 in Bradford, one of the fastest growing towns in Britain, where he manufactured alpaca and other new fabrics. He had planned to retire on his 50th birthday, but in 1850 resolved to create a new community, which he named Saltaire, north of Bradford alongside the river Aire and the Leeds & Liverpool Canal. His huge mill, designed, as was the village, by the Bradford architects Lockwood & Mawson, was opened in 1853, when he proclaimed that, 'I hope to draw around me a population that will enjoy the beauties of this neighbourhood – a population of well-paid, contented, happy operatives … nothing shall be spared to render the dwellings of the operatives a pattern to the country.' The mill expressed the virtues of provincial and dissenting England. At 545 feet (168 m) it was longer than the nave of St Paul's, and its 250-foot (77 m) chimney was higher than the Monument to the Great Fire in London. By the 1870s Saltaire comprised 800 cottages with a Congregational Church of 1859, a school, alms-houses and a hospital of 1868, and an institute and a

⌄ Saltaire Mill exemplifies the self-confidence of many manufacturers in the mid-nineteenth century. Titus Salt (he was created baronet in 1869) had already made a considerable fortune in the Bradford worsted trade when, in 1850, he resolved to build alongside the river Aire, 'a first-rate manufacturing and commercial establishment', with dwellings alongside where he hoped to attract a 'population of well-paid, contented happy operatives … that will enjoy the beauties of this neighbourhood'. The six-storey mill, 545 feet (166 m) long, was designed, as was the nearby housing, by the Bradford architects, Lockwood & Mawson, and William Fairbairn was responsible for the power-transmission system inside the factory. When this engraving was published in 1869 most of the 800 houses that comprised the mill community had been built, but Salt did not designate the area east of the river Aire as a public park until 1871. The mill closed in 1986 and the following year was bought by the entrepreneur Jonathan Silver, who redeveloped it to accommodate offices, shops, flats and the gallery devoted to the works of Bradford-born artist David Hockney.

© SCIENCE MUSEUM/SCIENCE & SOCIETY PICTURE LIBRARY

park completed in 1871. Salt's community accepted in an optimistic spirit the rise of manufacturing. At the opening ceremony the mayor of Bradford observed, with characteristic high-Victorian enthusiasm, that 'they had built palaces of industry equal to the palaces of the Caesars; instead of hand labour they had, to the utmost, availed themselves of the almost miraculous resources of mechanical science.'

Improvement

Salt and Akroyd were concerned to shape the conduct of their employees. Others conceived their mission as the shaping of landscapes, the creation of aesthetically satisfying vistas or useful enterprises in areas which seemed offensively unproductive. Some found that, ultimately, they also had to change people. Sir George Crew, when contemplating enclosure in Alstonefield in 1839, remarked that 'no land which is capable of being cultivated can be allowed to be idle for the gratification of the eye'. Matthew Boulton, reflecting on his career in Birmingham, remarked, 'I founded my manufactory upon one of the most barren commons in

England, where there existed but a few miserable huts filled with idle, beggarly people, who by the help of the common land and a little thieving made shift to live without working. The scene is now entirely changed. I have employed a thousand men, women and children in my aforesaid manufactory, for nearly thirty years past.' Jabez Maude Fisher observed that Boulton's factory was 'like a stately palace of some duke ... the whole scene is a Theatre of Business. ... Men women and children full of employment according to their strength and docility. ... All seem like one vast machine.'

Entrepreneurs and landlords considered that 'improvement' brought benefits to the poor. John Bishton, ironmaster and agent to the 1st Marquis of Stafford, observed in 1794 that unimproved commons bore chiefly gorse, bushes and fern, that their miserable huts and ill-cultivated plots afforded 'trifles' to men and their families, and that the daughters of cottages too readily became poverty-stricken unmarried mothers instead of useful servants. W. G. Hoskins and L. D. Stamp pointed out that the unconsidered trifles of common dwellers, digging pebbles from under the clay or turf from bogs, keeping beehives, collecting goose feathers, juniper berries and rushes, and cutting stone, enabled them to make adequate if undeferential livings.

The rationale of Improvement was expressed by Sir John Sinclair who wrote in 1826 of 'the spectacle ... of a people naturally possessed but of few territorial resources, and living in a bleak and unpropitious climate, employing their activity, their constancy and

Improvement in the lowlands – the manor of Fazeley in the valley of the river Tame in Staffordshire which was transformed in the 1790s by the first Sir Robert Peel and Joseph Wilkes. Streams were re-directed to drain agricultural land which had not previously been especially productive, to provide water power for four new textile factories, and to create lakes providing vistas from Drayton Manor (later to be the home of Peel's son, the prime minister). They also built terraced housing for the textile workers, much of which still remains. Textiles were manufactured at Fazeley until the late twentieth century, and the five-storey steam-powered Fazeley Mill was constructed in 1886.

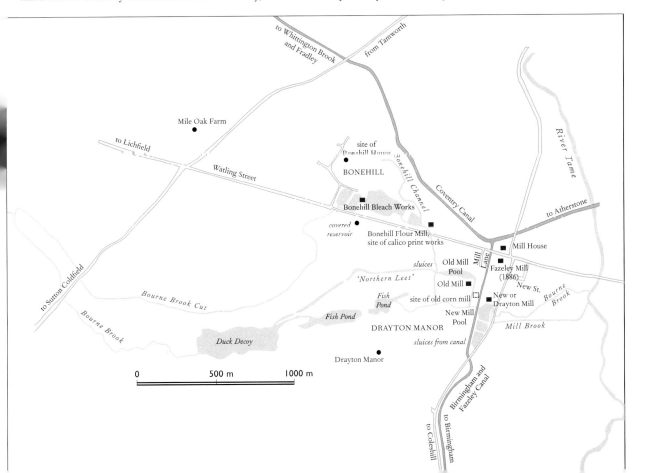

their genius in triumphing over a sterile soil – directing their attention to the riches of the mind … and making agricultural, manufacture and commerce, instruction morality and liberty flourish together.' This sentiment was shared by entrepreneurs. Richard Crawshay was concerned with 'Improvement' in the Valleys in respects other than just the construction of ironworks. He was a founder of the Glamorganshire Agricultural Society, corresponded with Sir John Sinclair about agricultural innovations, and invested in a woollen manufactory at Bridgend, opened in 1792, which failed to prosper. John Wilkinson, Crawshay's frequent correspondent, applied from 1778 the principles of Improvement to his estate at Castle Head in Furness. He constructed a dyke across the estuary of the river Winster which enabled 500 acres of land to be drained and made productive. He created a spectacular walled garden adjoining his mansion, on a rocky eminence which he covered with rich soil. He planned to install a steam engine that would pump fresh water for irrigating crops and salt water in which he, his family and guests could take baths. Visitors to the estate included Joseph Priestley, Erasmus Darwin, Matthew Boulton and Josiah Wedgwood.

Improvement could also be applied in the lowlands. From 1791 the first Sir Robert Peel, in collaboration with Joseph Wilkes of Measham, purchased land at Fazeley on the banks of the river Tame near the junction that had been made in 1789 between the Birmingham and Coventry canals. By excavating pools and channels they created many acres of productive farmland, provided an ornamental setting of lakes and woodland for Peel's mansion, Drayton Manor, and replaced an ancient corn mill with four water-powered factories in which cotton was spun, woven, bleached and printed. They built a village of spacious dwellings for those who worked in the mills. Wilkes followed a similarly wide-ranging programme of Improvement at Measham itself, establishing collieries, cotton mills, a bank, brickworks, roads and canals.

Harbours featured prominently in the Improvement agenda. Arthur Young regarded Mistley in Essex as 'one of the most interesting places to be seen in England'. The estate, overlooking the Stour estuary, was owned by Richard Rigby, whose fortune was derived from plantations in Antigua and Jamaica. Rigby was a notoriously corrupt politician, of whom it was remarked that he left to his descendants 'nearly half a million of public money', compiled in his capacity as Paymaster General to the Forces between 1764 and 1784. Among other things, the mansion was the setting for orgies, whose participants supposedly included prominent politicians. Rigby was an innovative farmer, built hothouses to grow grapes, peaches and pineapples, and planned a sea-bathing spa at Mistley which did not materialise, although he did create a successful port where manufactures prospered. An inn, brick houses, and a church designed by Robert Adam, stood near quays and a wet dock, where trade in corn, coal and lime flourished. Moorings were provided for whaling ships, a boatyard built 32-gun frigates, and Mistley became one of the principal malting centres in the eastern counties.

In Cornwall, at the other end of the country, Charlestown near St Austell was established in 1791 when the landowner Charles Rashleigh commissioned John Smeaton to construct a harbour, including a wet dock. Some copper ore was shipped, but Charlestown became principally a place of despatch for china clay, which was delivered by carts, taken to Liverpool by sea, and thence by canal to the Potteries. Around the dock grew up a shipyard, a rope walk and fish cellars, while there was a substantial import trade in coal, leading one visitor to remark that one side of the harbour was coated in white dust and the other in black.

Improvement at the margins

Improvement was most significant in marginal areas. For example, Augustus Smith applied the gospel of Improvement in the Isles of Scilly. The son of a banker with an estate in Hertfordshire, Smith leased the islands as lord proprietor in 1834. He laid out farms of viable size, opened schools, built a quay in the harbour at St Mary's and tried to eradicate smuggling by offering well-paid employment in shipbuilding and the victualling of passing ships. He also carried out clearances, forcing poor inhabitants to move to the mainland. He established his home at Tresco Abbey, creating terraced gardens shielded by a belt of *Cupressus macrocarpa* and adorned with exotic plants. Smith's achievements were applauded in 1847 when the royal yacht paused in the islands *en route* for Scotland. Improvement was more fully realised in 1859 when a sailing packet was replaced by a paddle steamer and the opening of the Royal Albert Bridge enabled trains to cross from Cornwall to England. Steamships and railways stimulated the development during the 1860s of the trade in narcissi, by which the islands prospered in the late nineteenth century.

Roundstone (Cloch na Ron), 48 miles north-west of Galway City, was an attempt to apply the doctrine of Improvement in the boglands of Connemara. It was laid out by Alexander Nimmo, a native of Fife who studied at Edinburgh, knew Thomas Telford and wrote with him the article on 'Bridges' in Brewster's *Cyclopedia*. On Telford's recommendation he went to Ireland in 1811, was employed in Connemara from 1813, and from 1820 was engineer for the Commissioners for Irish Fisheries. He built more than 30 piers on the Galway coast and nearly 250 miles of roads. Roundstone was developed from the 1820s, a Franciscan monastery was established there in 1835, and 75 houses were occupied by 1840, some of them by Scottish fishermen. Nimmo also mapped bogs in Co. Kerry in 1811–13 as a prelude to the re-organisation of settlement planned by the Bogs Commissioners.

Another area that could be regarded as marginal was the Ogwen Valley in Gwynedd, where from 1790 Richard Pennant, first Baron Penrhyn, employed capital accumulated from sugar plantations in Jamaica to transform the landscape between Tryfan and the sea near Bangor, initially through enclosures. In 1782 he bought out those who had leased slate workings on his land and retained them as waged employees. Disciplined extraction of slate replaced haphazard methods of working on open commons. A harbour, Port Penrhyn, was constructed in 1790 and accommodated vessels of up to 300 tons. A road was driven in 1791 up the western side of the pass of Nant Ffrancon, and extended in 1800 to Capel Curig, where Pennant

built an inn which attracted visitors seeking the fashionably sublime mountain scenery. His road was replaced in 1804 by a turnpike on the opposite side of the valley which was itself reconstructed after 1815 as part of the Holyhead Road. Innovative agricultural techniques were applied on newly enclosed land and several literary travellers visited a model dairy which had milk pans of Queensware. Before 1798 Penrhyn established a 'factory' where slates were fashioned into gravestones, chimneypieces and writing slates. A water-powered mill ground flints from southern England into powder, used at the Herculaneum Pottery in Liverpool. From 1801 a railway with three inclined planes linked the principal quarry with Port Penrhyn. Pennant's obituarist wrote in 1808 that 'by the creation of an active and extensive traffic, the materials of which were drawn from his own estates, employment and food have been given to thousands'. By 1850 the Penrhyn enterprises employed about 2,000 men.

Lord Penrhyn created an industry that flourished elsewhere in Gwynedd, and was copied in other remote parts of the British Isles as well as in distant Pennsylvania. Slate was sold overseas and roofed the housing of industrial workers throughout Britain. It became a commodity that was handled, along with coal, salt and lime, by canal-side merchants throughout England. Slate was extracted from some 400 locations in North Wales, but most came from large-scale workings established between 1780 and 1800, at Penrhyn, the Nantlle Valley, the Dinorwic quarry at Llanberis, and around Blaenau Ffestiniog, with smaller but substantial operations farther south near Talyllyn, Corris and Dinas Mawddwy. By 1870 there were up to 15,000 slateworkers in North Wales, although the numbers employed varied with the trade cycle.

Slate-working communities varied in character. At some quarries barracks (*barics*) were built, most of which provided accommodation that would have been cramped for small families and was severely over-crowded in the boom years of the 1860s and 1870s. The Anglesey barracks at Dinorwic, built in 1869–73 and condemned as unfit for occupation in 1937, now forms part of the National Slate Museum. In other places quarrymen occupied squatter cottages on open commons. Quarrying communities, with such

The Penrhyn Quarry near Bangor which was a centrepiece of the programme of 'Improvement' in the Ogwen Valley initiated from 1790 by Richard Pennant, first Baron Penrhyn. This image of *circa* 1842 shows clearly the method of working the quarry as a series of uniform galleries about 60 feet high, which was used in other very large slate workings in North Wales, as well as the railway system that was essential to the operation of such a large concern.

The remnants of slate-working settlement on Mynydd Cilgwyn in the Nantlle Valley Gwynedd.

names as Nazareth, Caesarea and Carmel, retained a deeply Welsh identity, and popular verse preserved an assumption that quarry owners and managers were Englishmen dependent on the skills of their Welsh employees:

> Mewn gweithfeydd sydd yma'n Nghymru
> Gwelir Saeson yn busnesu;
> Rhaid cael Cymry i dorri'r garreg,
> Nid yw'r graig yn deall Saesneg.

> In workplaces here in Wales
> See Englishmen interfering
> But you must get Welshmen to break
>   the rock,
> For the rock does not understand English.

The stepped gallery system of quarrying was introduced at Penrhyn between 1800 and 1825. From 1800 inclined planes were used there to move slate, and water-balance inclines were working in North Wales from the 1830s. Waste tips became features of the

The Cob, the great embankment south-east of Porthmadog, was part of the improvement of the Treath Mawr, the sands around the mouth of the Afon Glaslyn from the sea, carried out by William Alexander Madocks. The embankment was completed in 1811, providing a route by road to the packet port he planned at Porth Dinllaen. Subsequently a tramway, the precursor of the Festiniog Railway, was built across the Cob to carry slate from quarries at Blaenau Festiniog to Madocks' harbour at Porthmadog.

landscape, mountainous in scale at Penrhyn, Dinorwic and Blaenau Ffestiniog, and unmistakable evidence of slate working at smaller quarries. Buildings in which blocks of slate were sawn were constructed from about 1800, originally housing machines whereby iron bars were moved to and fro by cranks lubricated by a paste of water and sand, which was the cutting agent, and from the 1850s accommodating powered saw tables. Roofing slates were finished by hand in cabins (*gwaliau*). Railways carried slate blocks within quarries and took finished products to the coast.

The principal slate-working centres were industrial sites of impressive magnitude. At Gilfach Ddu, now the National Slate Museum, the workshops of the Dinorwic quarry were built in 1870 at the interchange between the 23-inch (0.6 m) gauge railway system used in the quarries and the 4-foot (1.21 m) line that led to the coast at Y Felinneli (Port Dinorwic). The workshops line a quadrangle, which has the appearance of a forbidding colonial fortress, and drew power from a huge waterwheel. The demands of extractive industry stimulated the growth of engineering enterprises. Small workshops were operating near Penrhyn and at Pen-y-Groes before 1820, and foundries flourished at Porthmadog, but the principal works was the De Winton Union Ironworks in Caernarfon which grew after Thomas Jeffreys Parry de Winton became a partner in 1853. Its products included waterwheels, saw tables, marine engines, air compressors, and, from the 1870s, vertical-boilered locomotives – and it built the waterwheel at Gilfach Ddu.

Ships from western Wales carried slate all round the British coast and to distant countries. As in other marginal areas, merchant shipping became a livelihood. Small locally built wooden sailing ships from Pwllheli, Porthmadog, Barmouth, Aberdyfi, Aberystwyth and Aberaeron, crewed by men from Caernarfonshire, Merioneth and Cardiganshire, sailed to northern Europe, the Caribbean and the Gulf of Mexico. Crews of sailing vessels from Caithness, the Western Isles, the Shetlands, the Isle of Man and the Channel Islands earned their livings in a similar manner.

The slate-working technology which was developed in North Wales was applied on Valentia Island, the most westerly inhabited island in Europe. There a slate quarry was opened in 1816 on the estate of Maurice FitzGerald, 18th Knight of Kerry and a Whig politician. The manager from 1827 was a Welshman, John Jones, probably from the Nantlle Valley. From 1840 a new settlement, Knightstown (An Chois) was built on the island to the design of Alexander Nimmo. Its nucleus was the *Valentia Hotel*, opened in 1830 but subsequently renamed the *Royal Hotel*. The quarry employed about 500 men in the 1840s and was producing 2,000 tons of slate *per annum* in the 1860s. Slate was also extracted at the Ormonde Quarry in Co. Kilkenny and the Victoria Quarry in Co. Tipperary, where there are tombstones inscribed in Welsh. The principal source of slate in England was the Lake District, and architects used green slates from Coniston or Honister for decorative effect in many substantial Victorian villas. Many of the slates that roofed Glasgow and Edinburgh originated in quarries worked from 1693 at Ballachulish on the south side of Loch Leven. Slate blocks were taken by railway to the side of the loch where they were split, and the completed slates carried south by ship.

The port of Aberaeron, south of Aberystwyth, was founded by the Revd Alban Jones Gwynne and also drew inspiration from principles of Improvement. Alban Thomas, a Hampshire clergyman, moved to Cardiganshire in 1797 after the death of his first wife. He married an heiress cousin in 1805, inherited the Monachty estate from another cousin, and took the name Gwynne. In 1807 he obtained an Act of Parliament permitting the construction of a harbour, of which the first pier was completed in 1809. His son, Colonel Alban Gwynne, laid out a square around a town hall, and commissioned the Shrewsbury architect Edward Haycock to build the church of Holy Trinity. He also built a woollen mill and a forge renowned for its shovels, and let plots to retailers, among them John Roberts, draper, of Manchester House. A shipyard in the harbour constructed 65 vessels between 1830 and 1870, and sea captains made their homes in Regency houses overlooking Cardigan Bay.

One of the most ambitious 'Improvement' projects was concerned with the 15,000 acres of Fforest Fawr, the Great Forest, in Brecknockshire, enclosed from 1817 and bought in 1819 by John Christie, a London indigo merchant. Christie surrounded his property with a 44-mile stone wall, and in 1821–22 built the 36-mile Brecon Forest Tramroad linking collieries, limestone quarries and a model sheep farm; there were several depots, with lime kilns, stables, warehouses and terraced cottages. He was bankrupt in 1827, but the tramroad was continued by others.

In 1798 William Alexander Madocks, a Denbighshire landowner, began to purchase parts of Traeth Mawr, the great sands around the mouth of the Afon Glaslyn east of Criccieth. He obtained parliamentary sanction in 1803 for a road across the sands towards Porth Dinllaen on the Lleyn peninsula, which he envisaged as a packet port for Ireland accessible without crossing the as yet unbridged Menai Straits. On the north shore of the estuary he laid out Tremadog, potentially a thoroughfare town, whose main streets were pointedly named 'London' and 'Dublin'. It included a market place, a town hall that could accommodate theatrical performances, a Gothic church, a dissenting chapel, a water-powered woollen manufactory and an inn. The Cob, an embankment completed in 1811, closed off the sand from the sea. The first quays of a new harbour, later called Porthmadog, were constructed in 1824. The 13-mile gravity-worked Festiniog Railway from the slate quarries at Ffestiniog crossed the Cob from 1836, and was operated after 1863 by steam locomotives. The influence of developments on the margins of the British economy was exemplified by the double-bogie, double-ended but single firebox locomotive, patented in 1864 by Robert Fairlie, used with much publicity on the Festiniog Railway from 1869, and subsequently supplied to railways in Sweden, Russia, Burma, New Zealand, Mexico and the United States.

The integrated objectives that characterised the doctrine of Improvement were revealed by Madocks in reviewing Traeth Mawr: 'I employ my mind incessantly in thinking how to compass those important objects necessary to complete the system of improvements in Snowdonia, any one of which wanting the rest lose half their value.'

The Fens

At first sight the mountains of Snowdonia and Brecknockshire appear to have little in common with the million acres of flat peatland in Cambridgeshire, Huntingdonshire, Lincolnshire and Norfolk, yet William Madocks became MP for Boston in 1802 and employed the Fenland engineer James Creassy on the initial stages of the Cob, and Telford and Rennie were among engineers involved with Fenland drainage projects. The modern Fens were the creation of inland navigation, of coal and the steam engine, and are as much a landscape of Improvement as Traeth Mawr. In the Middle Ages the area was wooded marshland. The first significant drainage work was the construction in the 1490s of Morton's Leam, a new course of the river Nene between Stanground near Peterborough and Guyhirn, directed by Cardinal John Morton. Large areas were drained by Vermuyden in the seventeenth century, and Enclosure Acts in the century after 1750 made provision for drainage schemes. Enclosure involved the construction of unbending roads alongside drainage channels and the building of new farmsteads designed to accommodate sheep and cultivate arable crops. Some holdings were very large – 1,347 acres at Holbeach, 1,200 at Littleport, 920 at Swaffham Bulbeck, five of more than a thousand acres at Lakenheath. In some parishes commissioners laid out cottage holdings which chiefly housed self-employed craftsmen. Enclosure also created a class of landless labourers, most of whom lived in the larger villages and market towns. High food prices and the downward pressure on wages after the peace of 1815 led to riots in Littleport and Ely,

savagely repressed by militia and a troop of the First Dragoons under the direction of parson magistrates. Five captured rioters were hanged at Ely on 28 June 1815, and nine were deported to Australia.

The principal drainage channels were open to inland navigation and delivered coal for brick and lime kilns and for the proprietors of steam threshing engines, most of whom were cottagers. The 1861 census reveals the 70-ton *Transit* of Lincoln, *en route* with 'general goods' from Lincoln to Sibsey, at Kirkstead Wharf on the Witham; the *George & Susannah* of Spalding, a 21-ton barge, at Holbeach Creek; a 6-ton coaster the *James & Ann* of Boston at Gedney; and a 14-ton lighter from Boston at Deeping St James. Some owners and crewmen were called 'coal boaters', indicating the significance of the principal inward cargo. It was difficult for manufacturing industry to flourish in a sparsely populated region, but there were engineering works in the market towns of Spalding, Chatteris and Holbeach, while more than 100 worked at Martin Aitken's steam-powered flax factory at Pinchbeck. Forty were women, who otherwise could find employment only as 'maids of all work' in farmhouses, or, seasonally, on the land. Steam-engine houses and drivers' cottages interrupt the flatness of the landscape. Some drivers were locally born, but many, like head teachers of National Schools, station masters and Methodist ministers, were incomers; from Edinburgh at Pode Hole, from Warsop (Notts) at Manea, and men from Butterley and Ripley who tended Butterley Co. engines, at Mepal and Stretham.

Improvement in the Highlands

In 1700 Lowland Scots and Englishmen knew little of the Highlands, a tribal and martial society where landholders held allegiances to the chiefs of their clans whom they followed into battle, sometimes to further the interests of the British Crown, but in 1715 and 1745 in support of pretenders to that crown. Highlanders were perceived as potentially over-mighty subjects, a threat to an unmilitaristic country. The last inter-clan battle, between Campbells and Sinclairs, was fought

near Wick in 1680, and on 13 February 1692 Campbells notoriously massacred 38 MacDonalds at Glencoe. Gaelic was universally spoken in the Highlands, and most families lived in 'black houses' with turf roofs, heated by open peat fires and shared with cattle and poultry. Trade with the outside world was limited to the exchange of black cattle for meal (a trade always constrained by rustling), and the collection of kelp which served as alkali for makers of soap and glass in

England and the Lowlands. Most clothing, candles, and footwear were crudely made from local materials. The rising of 1745 was disastrous for all who took up arms against the king, and for many who did not. The defeat of the Jacobites at Culloden in 1746 was followed by prohibitions on carrying firearms, wearing traditional dress and playing pipes, and the judicial powers of clan chiefs were removed. Samuel Johnson remarked that 'there was perhaps never any change of national manners so quick, so great and so general as that which has operated in the Highlands by the last conquest and the subsequent laws'. There were signs that Highland society was changing. General George Wade found labour for building roads by offering wages sufficiently high to tempt men away from their holdings and their allegiances to chiefs, and capitalist-style sheep farms were established from the 1750s. A survey of 1771 showed that families were already emigrating to the colonies.

Landowners enthusiastic about scientific farming formed the Highland Agricultural Society in 1784, and in some areas patterns of farming developed similar to those employed by the best practitioners in the Lowlands. Sir John Sinclair perceived that

Improvement depended upon changes in land holding, believing that the only economic use for the interior was for large-scale sheep farming, and that people should be encouraged to settle on the coast around new harbours which could shelter fishing boats and, through coastal shipping, stimulate new manufactures. Sinclair wrote of 'the necessity for reducing the population in order to introduce valuable improvements and the advantages of committing the cultivation of the soil to the hands of a few'. He was among those who from 1790 introduced to the Highlands the Cheviot sheep, bred by James Robson. The removal of tenants to create large-scale sheep farms accommodating Cheviots caused a rising near Dingwall in 1792. Its leaders were presumed to be Jacobins but they enjoyed local support, and those tried and found guilty were inexplicably released from prison.

Clearances took place in two principal phases, between 1782 and 1820 and between 1840 and 1854. The notorious events in Sutherland between 1807 and 1821 epitomise relationships between the margin and the mainstream of the British economy. Most of the county belonged to Elizabeth, the surviving child of William Gordon, 17th Earl of Sutherland, who, with his wife, died at Bath the year after their daughter's birth. In 1785 the heiress married George Granville Leveson-Gower, 2nd Marquis of Stafford and, in his final months 1st Duke of Sutherland, who witnessed the French Revolution as ambassador to Paris between 1790 and 1792. In 1803 he inherited the family's holdings in Shropshire, including much of the Coalbrookdale coalfield, and the Trentham estate in Staffordshire encompassing part of the Potteries. In the same year he also inherited a lifetime interest in the enterprises of his uncle, the 3rd Duke of Bridgewater. The Marquis received more than £2 million from the Bridgewater enterprises alone in the 30 years after 1803, and held government stock to the value of £1.1 million when he died. From 1812 his affairs were managed by his 'commissioner', James Loch, a member of a family of diminished gentry from Drylaw, near Edinburgh, friend at the University of Edinburgh of Sydney Smith and Henry Brougham, and disciple of Adam Smith. Loch learned estate management at the Blair Adam estate of his uncle, the lawyer and politician William

⌄ The harbour at Lybster, south-west of Wick, was among many constructed on the Scottish coast with the intention of encouraging large-scale fishing. Lybster prospered under the patronage of the British Fisheries Society from 1810, and in 1829 the landowner Captain Temple F. Sinclair financed the construction of a new stone-built harbour, which by 1845 was the home port for 283 vessels. Storms inflicted damage on several occasions, necessitating new works, and by 1900 fishing in that part of Scotland was declining.

Adam, grandson of the architect William Adam. Loch wrote in 1814 that his master's territories were 'a Kingdom and ought to be considered in this light by those he employs', and exercised his formidable talents on behalf of the Leveson-Gowers for the rest of his life. The marquis and his son rebuilt the family homes, employing Sir Jeffrey Wyatville at Lilleshall, and Sir Charles Barry at Trentham Hall and Dunrobin, Co. Sutherland, and in 1827 he bought from the government the unfinished mansion opposite Buckingham Palace intended for the indebted Frederick, Duke of York. The Leveson-Gowers completed the house, named it Stafford House (now Lancaster House) and under the 2nd Duke of Sutherland and his wife it was one of the social hubs of political London.

Loch found that clearance of tenants from the Sutherland properties had begun in 1807. Patrick Sellar, another Edinburgh law graduate and factor to the estate from 1809, leased land on his own account for a sheep farm at Strathnaver and gave tenants notice to quit in January 1814. In June they were expelled with barbarity, the details of which are obscured by the emotions that the clearance subsequently generated. Some accounts suggest that men with dogs swept the valley, burning houses while old people, unable to escape, were still inside. Sellar was tried and acquitted for the atrocities in 1816, but remained guilty in public opinion. More cottages were burned during clearances in Sutherland from 1819 and, by the most modest estimate, the countess's factors expelled between 5,000 and 10,000 people between 1807 and 1821 to make room for sheep. Interest in the Clearances has focused on Sutherland, where the establishment of sheep farms and the resettlement of tenants on the coast, sustained by the marquis's fortune derived from industrial England, were at times carried out in an inhumane and barbaric manner.

The motivations of Improvers in the Highlands were not purely selfish. Loch defined his objectives as 'to render this mountainous district contributory as far as it was possible to the general wealth and industry of the country, and in the manner most suitable to its situation and peculiar circumstances. To convert the former population of these districts to industrious and regular habits and to enable them to bring to market

Dunrobin, the palatial mansion, rebuilt by Sir Charles Barry, from which the Leveson-Gower family managed their estates in County Sutherland.

a very considerable surplus quantity of provisions for the supply of the large towns in the southern parts of the land, or for the purposes of exportation.' The physical problems in the Highlands were no more difficult than those which civil engineers overcame elsewhere, but the objectives of the Improvers could be achieved only by changing attitudes, and relationships were charged by the received wisdom among Lowland Scots that Highlanders were less than civilised. In 1824 John MacCulloch described the charred black ruins of cottages as 'the former hamlets of the idle and useless population', while Loch wrote of obstacles to Improvement 'arising out of the prejudices and feelings of the people themselves'. Some Highlanders evidently preferred life on their tiny plots to more comfortable living elsewhere, contradicting Adam Smith's view that it was 'the uniform, constant and uninterrupted effort of every man to better his own condition'. Loch was also responsible for the Leveson-Gower manor of Ketley in Shropshire where building was unsupervised in the eighteenth century. He found that accommodation was little better than the huts in Co. Sutherland. The worst houses were demolished,

The great iron bridge over the Dornoch Firth built by Thomas Telford in 1812 is a good indication of the impact that infrastructure projects using the latest technology could have on the economy of marginal regions. According to Samuel Lewis in 1846, Bonar had increased 'in extent and importance, especially since the erection of the great iron bridge in 1812, and vessels now trade to it [the nearby harbour at Criech], of from thirty to sixty tons' burthen, importing meal, coal, and lime, and exporting fir-props, wool, oak-bark, corn, and salmon'.

One of the warehouses that line the harbour at Helmsdale.

The ruins of the Arkwright-style textile mill at Spinningdale showing its setting on an inlet of the Dornoch Firth.

and others improved with chimney pots, dormer windows and drip moulds following an estate-house style. Poachers and those deemed idle or promiscuous were deprived of their tenancies, and in 1833 Loch's henchmen rounded up and killed 500 bulldogs owned by cottagers, part of a programme designed 'to breed up a steady, industrious and moral set of persons, resistant to the vice of radicalism'. Loch was pleased that re-settled Highlanders at Helmsdale lived in well-built cottages which were no longer shared with animals and that they were paying attention to cleanliness, but when colliers from Staffordshire sent to Brora in 1815 complained that they had to lie at night in straw and could not buy bread, he had to remind his subordinate that 'colliers are accustomed to many comforts unknown to the Highlanders … without which you cannot expect them to remain'.

Despite all the ambitious plans and massive expenditure of time and money, the Clearances in Sutherland were unprofitable. The estate yielded no net income between 1812 and 1822, and economic conditions deteriorated as numbers of herring diminished, while the price of kelp fell from £20 per ton in 1808 to £3 per ton in the 1830s following the introduction of the Leblanc process for alkali manufacture. The scale of investment by the Sutherland estate diminished after the death of the 1st Duke in 1833. Further clearances were enforced between 1840 and 1854, particularly in Ross-shire, but that period was dominated by the effects of the Potato Famine, which had less impact in Sutherland than in other counties, possibly as a result of the Clearances. The tide of emigration swelled from 1850.

Settlements around the coast bear witness to the ambitions of the Improvers. The government funded the harbours and roads, which were built for the Commission for Highland Roads and Bridges under Telford's supervision, and the construction of the Caledonian Canal. The Sutherland estate also built many roads without parliamentary assistance, as well as fostering coal mining at Brora, and from 1814 developing the fishing port of Helmsdale, where houses, an inn, a fish-curing works and a boatyard were constructed around a harbour designed by John Rennie. The iron bridge over the Dornoch Firth at Bonar, built by Telford in 1812, brought prosperity to the adjacent harbour at Criech, which by 1846 was importing coal, lime and meat, and despatching cargoes of pit props, wool, oak bark, corn and salmon. The British Fisheries Society, founded in 1786, established communities at Ullapool in Wester Ross, Tobermory on Mull and Lochbay on Skye. Pulteneytown, south of Wick, took its name from the society's governor, Sir William Pulteney, whose career illustrates further links between 'the margins' and the mainstream. Born William Johnston into a gentry family from Dumfriesshire, he studied law at Edinburgh where he knew Adam Smith, David Hume and Robert Adam. In 1760 he married Frances Pulteney, niece of the 1st Earl of Bath, and took her surname when she inherited the family fortune. Pulteney was MP for Shrewsbury from 1774, and employed Thomas Telford to adapt Shrewsbury Castle as an elegant home. He developed land in Bath, in the Caribbean, and in New York State. Pulteneytown was laid out from 1803 according to a plan by Telford and by 1846, when it had warehouses, fish-curing yards, an iron foundry and a floating dock, it had a settled population of 3,132.

Sir John Sinclair hoped that textiles would give Highlanders 'the opportunity of tasting the sweets and advantages of labour'. The cotton-manufacturing community called Spinningdale was established in the 1790s on the 18,000-acre Skibo estate on the Dornoch Firth, purchased in 1786 by George Dempster, who once spoke of 'converting Sutherlandshire into Lancashire'. A partnership that included David Dale and George Macintosh, the Glasgow dyer, built 20 cottages and a mill which employed about 100 people, but it proved difficult to impose work discipline, and the building was destroyed by fire in 1806, leaving ruins which include two features characteristic of Arkwright-period spinning mills – a latrine turret and a Venetian window. Textile manufactures proved more prosperous in the burgh of Cromarty. In 1765–67 George Ross, a lawyer who had become rich in London as an army contractor, bought the estate centred on Cromarty at the tip of the Black Isle peninsula between the Moray and Cromarty firths. He built the once-elegant Cromarty House, and constructed a two-storey, 25-bay hempen cloth

▲ George Ross's development at Cromarty: the former hempen cloth factory, now converted to housing.

▼ The harbour at Cromarty.

factory, a three-storey 5-bay brewery, and a forge that made nails and spades from imported Russian iron. He promoted herring fishing from Cromarty harbour and built a quadrangular hogyard, a source of pork which was salted and exported. Heathland on the Black Isle was planted with trees or enclosed to make barley fields, cultivated by ploughmen from Buckinghamshire whose wives established a lace school. By 1846 the herring fishing was in decline, but the textile mill employed 150 people, and pork worth £20,000 *per annum* was being exported from Cromarty harbour.

Communities in Ireland

Many attempts were made to create manufacturing communities in Ireland. Lt Col Robert Brooke, born in Co. Kildare, served in India from 1764, and from 1780 used capital accumulated there to invest in a cotton-manufacturing settlement adjoining the unbending turnpike road that crosses the Bog of Allen from Clane to Allenwood. The enterprise, optimistically called Prosperous, used carding machines, spinning jennies and looms brought from Manchester, and initially the fabrics found a ready sale in Dublin. Subsequently Brooke found it difficult to buy machines, some of his weavers proved to be drunkards, and his products encountered competition from imports from Lancashire. Nevertheless, in 1783 an Irish observer considered Prosperous 'a little Manchester which has sprung up in three years space', and was delighted 'to see one of those great manufactures, the pride, the boast and endless sources of riches to England, at once established and firmly rooted amongst us'. The enterprise was faltering in 1788 when Brooke accepted the post of governor of St Helena. The men of Prosperous were United Irishmen and the village was the scene

◁ The terrace of cotton workers' houses built at Prosperous in 1780.

The enormous flax-spinning mill at Bessbrook near Newry, built from 1846–47 by John Grubb Richardson. It was the flagship mill of the Ulster linen industry, and around it Richardson hoped to create a pliant and moral workforce that would be protected by the isolation of the site from the temptations and vices of urban life. (See also the map on page 448.)

of a battle with the British army on 24 May 1798; by 1837 Prosperous seemed 'little more than a pile of ruins' – though the sturdily constructed cottages of 1780 still stand.

The community planned by Edward Stratford, 2nd Earl of Aldborough at Stratford-on-Slaney in Co. Wicklow, was more ambitious. Stratford, whose family home was in Co. Kildare, had an enthusiasm for architecture, and from 1775 developed a community with spinning mills, a calico printworks and bleach greens, and supposedly some 400 houses, the whole planned on the model of Bath. He also invested in Stratford Place, off Oxford Street, London, and in the 1790s in Aldborough House, Dublin. His enterprise in Co. Wicklow failed, although another company was spinning cotton and printing calico at Stratford in the 1830s.

The model cotton-manufacturing community established from 1825 by David Malcolmson at Portlaw, on the river Clodagh 12 miles from Waterford, was

more successful. Malcolmson, a Quaker born at Lurgan, had prospered in corn milling at Clonmel. He acquired the mill site at nearby Portlaw in 1825 and began production the following year with 260 workers in a single-storey factory, part of which was top-lit, with machinery powered by several water-wheels. The factory was enlarged and employed about 800 people in 1835 and 1,362 in 1850. Malcolmson and his sons established a model community which from the 1840s consisted of four principal streets radiating from a square. Some of the houses, which still stand, had roofs of tarred calico made at the factory. The enterprise was fully integrated, taking in raw cotton, delivered by barge from Waterford, and producing fabrics that were dyed and printed on the premises. In the 1850s the company supplied export markets and was competitive with Lancashire firms, but the American Civil War initiated a period of difficulties, and the company collapsed in 1877.

Bessbrook, the linen-manufacturing community

near Newry established from 1846–47 by John Grubb Richardson, was planned as a means of avoiding the labour problems that Brooke encountered at Prosperous. Richardson, who was related to the Malcolmsons, came from a Quaker family long-established in the linen trade, and decided to extend his bleaching and wholesaling business by building spinning and weaving mills. He was shy of taking responsibility for a factory population in Belfast and determined to build at Bessbrook, a site with ample water power in a district where flax was cultivated and where he could control his workpeople. He built high-quality accommodation for some 4,000 people, using the local blue granite (also used in Manchester Town Hall). The settlement included allotments, a dispensary, library, billiard room, assorted shops, sports fields, and places of worship for several denominations. There were no pawnshops and no public houses, and Richardson hoped that such a community would not require policing.

The prospects for innovative communities – and indeed the whole nature of society and the economy in large parts of Ireland – were changed for ever by the Great Famine of the late 1840s. Rising population, growing underemployment, and a dependence on the potato as almost the sole means of sustenance had created the potential for widespread starvation in the desperately poor counties along the western and south-western seaboard. There had been serious food shortages in Mayo in 1831 and Donegal in 1836,

but in the late autumn of 1845 the potato blight, *phyrophthora infestans*, became evident in main crop potatoes. It infected the whole crop of 1846, and the direct effects were felt into the early 1850s. There was extreme starvation in the west, and the whole country was affected as starving men, women and children flocked eastwards in search of food. Nevertheless, the accustomed exports of grain and dairy produce to England from the prosperous farmlands of the Irish midlands continued. The belated efforts of government to alleviate the situation by importing maize and by programmes of public works proved largely futile; in 1849 an emaciated population was scourged by cholera which began in Belfast; and thousands of peasants in the west were evicted by the agents of England landowners. About a million people died as a result of the famine and related diseases and another million had emigrated by 1851: Ireland's population fell by about 21 per cent in just six years. Large-scale emigration continued in the decades that followed: the population had exceeded 8 million in 1841, but was only 4.4 million in 1911. The impact of the famine was greatest in Munster and Connaught, where population fell, respectively, by 22.5 and 28.8 per cent during the 1840s. Irishmen had been migrating to work in industry long before 1845, but the presence of so many Irishmen and women in the industrial regions of Scotland and England by the 1860s, remarked upon many times in the chapters above, was the direct consequence of the Great Famine.

Moravian communities

Communities that can loosely be labelled 'utopian' reflect alternative patterns of economic and social organisation. Settlements with a religious or ideological basis can either attempt to proselytise, or they can fit quietly into existing society and endeavour to stimulate emulation by example. Ideology does not always coincide with economic feasibility; strongly motivated individuals tend to be disputatious, and some utopian communities were short-lived. Nevertheless, even those with brief lifespans deserve attention, for their implied critiques of existing society can be enlightening.

Long-lived communities deserved particular respect, and the four Moravian settlements in Great Britain have existed for more than two centuries. The Church of the Moravian Brethren, founded by Jan Hus in 1457, was almost obliterated during the Thirty Years War. It was refounded in 1722 by Ludwig von Zinzendorf, who established its headquarters on the estate in Saxony that he named Herrnhut (the Lord's watch). From 1732 ministers were despatched on foreign missions, and they arrived in Britain during the early stages of the Evangelical revival. Histories of many dissenting congregations reveal that they originated in the 1730s when a few individuals met, usually on secular premises, to discuss religious matters. Some sought pastoral guidance from ministers who were establishing 'connexions' of like-minded groups between whom they circulated, of whom George Whitefield and John Wesley were the best known. In Georgia in 1735 Wesley was impressed by the serenity of the Moravians, and after his 'conversion' in 1738 he visited Herrnhut. The Moravian settlements grew up within this pattern of itinerancy.

Benjamin Ingham, born at Ossett, near Wakefield, knew Wesley at Oxford and travelled with him to Georgia and Hernnhut before they quarrelled in 1740. He developed a connexion in Yorkshire and in 1742 placed the societies within it under the care of the Moravian Brethren. The following year he bought for them a 22-acre estate at Pudsey which was named Fulneck, after the town of Fulnek in Moravia. Zinzendorf visited Britain in 1743 where he met John Cennick, who preached for Wesley. Cennick subsequently visited Saxony and ministered in Dublin. He was ordained deacon in the Moravian Church in 1749 and settled near Ballymena, where by 1755 he had built up a committed congregation of 46 and a larger following. After his death the Moravians leased land at nearby Gracehill for a settlement, which was constructed from the mid-1760s. The community at Ockbrook, five miles east of Derby, had similar origins. A group of serious Christians were meeting in the village in 1739 and one of their number heard a Moravian minister preaching at the market cross in Nottingham. The group requested pastoral guidance, and the Moravians sent a minister from Yorkshire in 1740; a congregation was formally constituted in 1750, and building of the settlement began the following year. In 1755 the Moravians formally recognised a congregation at Dukinfield, east of Manchester,

and in 1785 the Revd Benjamin Latrobe established a settlement around a church which he designed at nearby Fairfield. Four Moravian communities were thus established within 40 years in areas that were experiencing industrial growth. Moravian congregations also flourished in Bath, Leominster and Bedford, among other places.

The Moravian settlements are similar in appearance and ethos. Each is centred on a chapel, around which are houses for single Brethren and Sisters, schools with boarding facilities, and, at Fulneck, a house for widows. A visitor described Gracehill in 1794, when about 50 families totalling 300 people lived there. The church stood in the centre with houses for the sisters and brothers on either side; there was an inn and a warehouse where goods were sold at set prices. Self-sufficiency was an acknowledged objective of the Moravian settlements. Small areas of land were cultivated, and each had basic food shops, shoemakers and tailors, together with doctors and watchmen. The women who lived in the Sisters' houses were celebrated embroiderers. Many residents worked in the predominant local industries – cotton manufacture at Fairfield, woollens at Fulneck, linens at Gracehill and framework knitting, particularly of gloves, at Ockbrook. In 1861 there were 113 boarders at the school at Fulneck, 63 at Fairfield and 47 at Ockbrook. The settlements showed that it was possible in a quietist manner to establish communities with particular ethical and educational standards amid a changing industrial society, part of a wider community extending across the British Isles and beyond. The three English settlements in 1861 included people born in all the other three and at Gracehill. There were teachers at Ockbrook, Fulneck and Fairfield who were born at Herrnhut, and one from Baden at Ockbrook, while 14 of the boarders at Fulneck were born in the Caribbean.

Robert Owen: New Lanark and after

The mill community at New Lanark near the Falls of Clyde originated in 1784, when David Dale took Richard Arkwright to view the site. The first mill began production the following year. By the mid-1790s the water-powered complex comprised four

mills containing 6,000 spindles, and several tenement blocks accommodating workers. In 1800, when about 2,000 people were living at New Lanark, it was already regarded as an exceptional place, not least because David Dale was concerned about the education of the

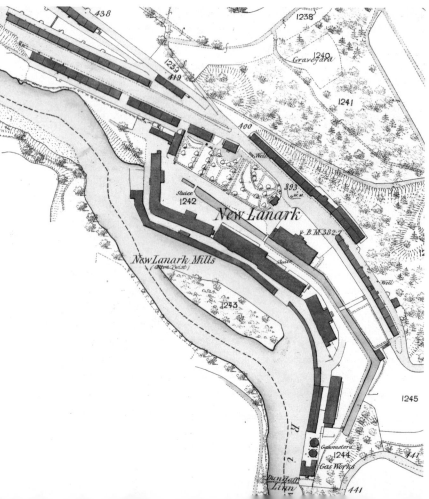

An engraving which helps to show why visitors to New Lanark in the early nineteenth century found it such an impressive community. The mills were established in 1785 by David Dale and managed by Robert Owen between 1800 and 1824. The town of Lanark is visible on the hilltop. The mills have many of the characteristics of Arkwright-style cotton factories in other parts of Britain, but the workers were housed in tenement blocks similar to those in Glasgow. By the early 1970s New Lanark had fallen into a state of dismal dereliction, but a trust has overseen the conservation of its buildings and their adaptation to a range of new uses – housing, a hotel, heritage and commercial – a task that was substantially complete by 2005. New Lanark is now a UNESCO World Heritage Site.

This late nineteenth-century OS map clearly shows the water-power system (see also page 50). The main lade emerges from a tunnel (bottom right) and runs past the mills before running beneath Mill No. 1 to rejoin the Clyde downstream.

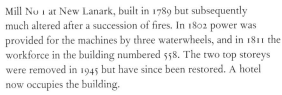

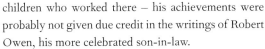

Mill No 1 at New Lanark, built in 1789 but subsequently much altered after a succession of fires. In 1802 power was provided for the machines by three waterwheels, and in 1811 the workforce in the building numbered 558. The two top storeys were removed in 1945 but have since been restored. A hotel now occupies the building.

One of the tenement blocks at New Lanark, the Wee Row, built in the mid-1790s. It has been used as a hostel by the Scottish Youth Hostels Association since 1994.

Robert Owen's school at New Lanark, built in 1817, where his enlightened ideas about education were put into practice. The building is now a museum.

PHOTOGRAPHS: CARNEGIE

children who worked there – his achievements were probably not given due credit in the writings of Robert Owen, his more celebrated son-in-law.

Robert Owen was born in 1771 at Newtown, Montgomeryshire, before factory-based flannel manufacturing was established there. He worked in his teens for a linen draper in Stamford, then in London and Manchester, where he became involved in cotton manufacturing and managed the Bank Top mill, owned by Peter Drinkwater. In 1796 he became managing partner of the Chorlton Twist Company. He gained acquaintance with Unitarian followers of Joseph Priestley, and joined the Manchester Literary & Philosophical Society. On business visits to Scotland he met Ann, daughter of David Dale, and married her in 1799, after acquiring shares in the company. Owen managed New Lanark, with impressive effect, from 1800 until 1824. He slowly dispensed with the labour of parish apprentices, appointed new supervisors, and brought discipline (which he called 'government') to the labour force, many of whom were refugees from the Highland Clearances. He took measures to prevent theft, limit drunkenness and promote cleanliness.

Owen may have exaggerated some of the management problems he had faced. Most of the workforce in 1800 he characterised as 'a collection of the most ignorant and destitute from all parts of Scotland … generally indolent, and much addicted to theft, drunkenness and falsehood.' He described how he had constructed new housing, and planned to accommodate in a new institution a school, communal eating facilities, drilling for boys, and regular lectures. The establishment of an infant school was motivated not just by idealism but also because it freed women to work in the mills. In 1816 he completed the Institution for the Formation of Character, the building which symbolised his social thinking.

From 1812 this perspective was more influential than his entrepreneurial success, for his relationships with partners showed that he could be reckless in financial matters. In that year Owen published *A Statement regarding the New Lanark Establishment*, an appeal for investment – his stewardship of funds originating with Archibald Campbell of Jura was subject to scrutiny. The pamphlet was successful and by attracting new investors he was able to buy the business from the former partnership. Other publications followed; the *First Essay on the Formation of the Human Character* in 1813, and three subsequent essays, *An Address to the Inhabitants of New Lanark* in 1816, and *Reports to the County of Lanark* in 1820. In them he expressed enlightened views on education, derived from the Swiss Johann Pestalozzi and Philip von Vellenberg and the Alsatian Johann Oberlin whom he visited in 1818. He argued that instruction for children should be rendered a pleasure, and that children should never be led to believe without reasoning. He looked back to a perceived idyllic past, concluding that the manufacturing system had so far extended its influence that 'ere long, the comparatively happy simplicity of the agricultural peasant will be wholly lost amongst us'. He proposed the establishment of communities of about a thousand people, occupying accommodation within parallelograms with kitchens and dining rooms for communal eating, schools and lecture rooms, infirmaries, lodgings for guests, and communal dormitories for children. Each community was to be set within an estate of up to 1,500 acres, to be worked by spade cultivation.

His ideas were influential. Owenite groups were formed in manufacturing towns and villages all over Britain, setting up People's Halls of Science and Philosophical Halls, and contemplating communities of the kind for which Owen provided a blueprint. In 1824 Owen gave up the management of New Lanark and sailed to the United States, where in January 1825 he purchased a settlement in Indiana established by followers of the Würtemburg-born millenarian George Rapp. It was named New Harmony, and attracted many adherents, but quickly foundered, and Owen returned to Britain in June 1827.

Several Owenite communities were established in the British Isles. Abram Combe, an Edinburgh tanner, visited New Lanark and as a result in 1825 founded a community at Orbiston, a 200-acre estate nine miles east of Glasgow. His partner was A. J. Hamilton, an army officer who had seen spade cultivation at the pauper colonies established from 1816 at Willemsoord in the Netherlands. The principal commercial enterprise at Orbiston was a foundry, but there were also printers, farmers and several craftsmen. A four-storey

stone building housed 1,000 people with communal dining facilities and leisure rooms. The community collapsed under pressure from creditors after Combe's death, and no traces remain of the buildings. A community at Ralahine, Co. Clare, was set up by the landowner John Scott Vandeleur who had met Owen in Dublin. Under the management of the Englishman, E. T. Craig, 618 acres were worked by 52 tenants and during two years when harvests were good the community prospered. It faltered after gambling debts caused Vandeleur's bankruptcy in 1833, and Craig's plans to utilise the water resources of the estate to power manufacturing concerns were never realised.

Owen's proposals also influenced William Hodson, a retired mariner and Methodist who farmed at Upwell in the Cambridgeshire Fens. In 1837 he opened a school in Wisbech, where E. T. Craig served as headmaster, and in 1839 purchased a 200-acre estate alongside the Old Bedford River at Manea Fen, where he established a community on Owenite principles, with dormitories for children, communal dining rooms, uniforms of Lincoln Green, and possessions held in common. Up to 40 people could take tea at the top of a 60-foot observatory tower looking across the Fens to Ely Cathedral. The community worked a windmill and a brickfield, and published a journal, *The Working Bee*, whose attitudes to social class caused offence to local clergy. Craig moved there from Wisbech, but Hodson spent much of his time lecturing elsewhere and after a breakdown of discipline the community broke up in December 1840. The colony was taken over by local people, and by 1861 the only trace of Hodson's venture was the continuation of brick making, which employed four men.

At a congress in London in 1835 Owen formed the Association of All Classes of All Nations, a legally constituted body, which published the *New Moral World*, had 50 branches by December 1838, and in 1839 leased land for the colony of Queenwood at Tytherley on the chalk uplands in Hampshire. The foundations of the principal building, Harmony Hall, were laid on 30 August 1841. The colony was established as a joint stock company requiring capital, which Owen found difficult to raise because of his perceived hostility to established religion. The luxury of Harmony Hall, a three-storey structure of 80 rooms with stained-glass windows, a ballroom with a richly embellished ceiling, a long vine wall and a central heating system that did not work, aroused resentment among the colonists. The land at Queenwood was incapable of sustaining substantial numbers of people and, as at Manea, there were disagreements between the colonists, some of whom were committed communitarians from Manchester, Bradford and Sheffield. By 1844 the community was collapsing and in 1847 Harmony Hall was adapted as a college. The community failed because whereas at New Lanark Owen had provided benefits for his workpeople out of profits, at Queenwood they were taken from capital before revenues had been generated. Many working-class radicals believed that the collapse of Queenwood was a failure of capitalism, and while proposals for a return to the land continued to resonate, from the mid-1840s more energy went into co-operative trading than into communities. Nevertheless the enthusiasm with which Owen's proposals were greeted reflected a wish to cultivate the land, and to combine cultivation with manufactures or crafts, and some found Owen's communitarianism attractive.

The Chartists

Between 1838 and 1842 the Chartist movement brought together dissidents of all kinds, including political reformers disappointed by the results of the 1832 Reform Act, protesters against the Poor Law Amendment Act of 1834, miners, factory employees, and domestic workers with varied particular grievances, temperance advocates, Owenites and political opportunists. Asa Briggs aptly described it as a 'snowball movement'. The unwelcoming reception given to the petition presented to Parliament in 1842 as well as the improving economic situation caused the movement to lose impetus and fragment. However, the Chartist Land Company was launched in 1845 by Feargus O'Connor, editor of the *Northern Star*, perhaps as a means of maintaining his status within a declining movement. Subscriptions, raised through Chartist branches, allowed the purchase of estates upon which four-acre smallholdings were distributed by ballot. On each plot stood a cottage (to O'Connor's design) and at the centre of each community was a school. The first estate, at Heronsgate near Rickmansworth, was acquired in March 1846. The estate was 'inspected' in August by a procession from Hyde Park Corner, while bands played the 'Chartist Land March'. The first settlers arrived on May Day 1847. Subsequently estates were built at Charterville near Minster Lovell in Oxfordshire, at Snigs End and Lowbands near Tewkesbury, and at Dodford near Bromsgrove, where a cottage is conserved. The financial basis of the Land Company was unsound, and it collapsed in 1851, but its success in attracting subscriptions shows that the life of a rural smallholder appealed to at least some of the working class. The estates passed into other ownership after 1851, and the school buildings were sold. At Charterville, on a windswept hill, and Snigs End and Lowbands, on heavy clay, it was intrinsically difficult to make a living on four acres. There were about 40 cottages at Snigs End and almost twice as many at Lowbands, but by 1861 most were occupied by locally born agricultural labourers. Only a handful of cottagers from more distant parts remained, including people from Nottingham, Hyde (Cheshire), Axminster, and Ashburton (Devon). About two dozen cottagers appear to have made all or part of their livings from their original holdings. There were six shoemakers, two carpenters, a cabinetmaker and a tailor, while about a dozen women made leather gloves in their homes. In 1861 Heronsgate had 30 cottages, but the school had become a pub, the *Land of Liberty*. Nine cottagers appear to have lived by cultivating their original plots, and another was working 36 acres and employing a labourer. Six heads of households were farm workers and five were building craftsmen. Among the cottagers were individuals from Kidderminster, Burton-on-Trent, Wigan, Trowbridge and Neath. Heronsgate became a residential suburb, while Dodford achieved a measure of prosperity supplying fruit and vegetables to Birmingham in the 1880s and 1890s.

The Chartist colonies provide the best archaeological record of attempts to create smallholdings,

⌄ One of the cottages designed by Feargus O'Connor at the Chartist colony at Snig's End near Tewkesbury, Gloucestershire.

⌄ The former school at Snig's End, now a public house called the *Prince of Wales*. Similar buildings survive at Lowbands and Charterville.

characterised by the phrase 'Three acres and a cow' used by Jesse Collings in the general election of 1885, but there were other such schemes. One example was 'Enoch's Colony', a group of eight cottages at Sibford, Oxfordshire, founded in 1849–50 by John Enoch, a Quaker clock repairer who had been impressed by Charterville. A plot of 1½ acres was attached to each cottage, but by 1873 all the tenants were working other land and following other occupations – a country carrier, a thatcher, a sawyer, a highways foreman and a shoemaker. One had prospered and moved to a farm of 20 acres. And while various projects deliberately sought to create communities of smallholders, many thousands of families still made their livings in 1870 on holdings of a few acres on commons or former commons, which they cultivated while also making shoes, mining coal, carting lead ore, shaping slates or firing pots.

Industrial communities

This chapter has concentrated on those industrial communities that were celebrated, those motivated by concepts of Improvement, chiefly on the margins, and those established with utopian motives. Entrepreneurs who developed 'model' settlements sought to create stable, socially controlled communities in the tradition of rural 'close' parishes. Improvement schemes on the margins show that intelligent men could perceive that prosperity might arise from mining and manufactures and from the application of the skills of engineers, and that they hoped, not just to make profits for themselves, but to re-shape, as they saw it beneficially, the lives of those who worked for them. Utopian settlements can be interpreted as critiques of industrial society, showing that it might be possible for communities to subsist comfortably but with different occupational and economic structures. Their limited success shows that such communities required shared objectives and favourable locations. The attraction of such schemes suggests that divisions between urban and rural, and between manufacturing and agriculture, may have been less sharp than historians sometimes suggest. Navvies working on the Peak Forest Canal in 1794 and the Birmingham & Liverpool Junction Canal in 1827 were attracted away by the prospect of harvesting, and during the Chartist-inspired coal strike in Shropshire in 1842 it was revealed that miners who were 'good harvest men' were always willingly spared in August. Working-class memoirs contained numerous references to people who went home annually to participate in village feasts and fairs, but a desire to reconnect with the rhythms of the agricultural years was not the same as a yearning to return to the condescension and oppression of life ruled by landowners.

15

Epilogue:
a revolution in context

'In this queer jumble of the old England and the new I came into consciousness.'

D. H. LAWRENCE (BORN 1885).

T HE ECONOMIC FORCES which transformed many of the communities discussed above were far from spent in 1870. Railway construction continued; the output of iron was still increasing; most sectors of the textile industry continued to expand; and coal mines were opened on Cannock Chase, in the Leen Valley of Nottinghamshire, in Fife and Kent, and in other areas not previously exploited. Nevertheless, in the landscape there was plentiful evidence of industrial ventures which had failed or whose course was run – the mine on Parys Mountain, working on a much reduced scale in 1870; the abandoned Arkwright-style mills in remote valleys where cotton had never been spun profitably; canals where encroaching reeds and rushes were rarely disturbed by passing boats. Some activities which in 1700 were prosperous and flourishing had now ceased altogether – the spinning of worsted yarn in rural Norfolk, for example, or the smelting of iron in the Weald, where communities that once resounded to the clang of water-powered hammers were now peaceful backwaters.

Changing manufactures

The years around 1870 were a time of significant change in industry and society. Most people still bought clothing, footwear, furniture and food that had been made locally, even if fabrics came from Lancashire or Yorkshire, thread from Paisley and wood from overseas. However, the sewing machine, introduced in Britain in 1857, was beginning to transform clothing and footwear manufacture. Hosiery had long been marketed nationally, but its manufacture was increasingly factory-based, and the range of products extended to include shirts and vests. The development of large-scale production of garments was hesitant.

Thus, Long's Building in Devizes, sometimes called Wiltshire's first textile factory, had no power system and appears to have been built in the 1780s as a warehouse for garments produced domestically, although it served that purpose for only a short time. John Hyde of Abingdon employed 1,400 people making garments in 1851, most of them women working in their homes in surrounding villages. But Hyam Hyam of Colchester, a pawnbroker in 1823 and a clothes dealer by 1826, set up a company with his sons which by 1870 was manufacturing clothing on an industrial scale, at the Abbey Gate Works. Another Colchester firm, founded by Thomas Hammond in 1854, supplied international markets with suits and trousers, and in 1864 wholesale tailoring companies in Colchester were reckoned to be employing 2,000 women and 200 men. Londonderry was already a significant centre of shirt manufacturing when the five-storey factory of Tillie & Henderson was built near Craigavon Bridge in 1856. By 1861 there were specialist makers of shirts, waistcoats or trousers in most large towns. Subsequently the mass-production of clothing brought great changes, particularly in the East End of London and in Leeds, creating more employment for women, providing opportunities for immigrant entrepreneurs, and indirectly improving the health and comfort of large sections of the population – though not necessarily those who actually worked in a trade notorious for sweated labour.

The making of boots and shoes was also on the verge of transformation in 1870. Footwear made in Northampton was 'sent beyond the seas' in 1750, but Northampton remained a comparatively small town with a population of only 7,020 in 1801, although it grew to 26,657 in the next 50 years. By that time footwear was the 'manufacture' of most towns in Northamptonshire, although it was organised on a domestic basis. Growth was stimulated by military contracts and by outsourcing from traders in London. Production increased from the late 1850s with the introduction of sewing machines and other machinery. The construction in 1857 of a three-storey Italianate warehouse and an imposing factory in Campbell Square, Northampton, indicated a growth in the scale of production. The numbers employed in boot and shoe manufacture in Northamptonshire increased from 13,254 in 1851, 6.2 per cent of the total population, to 41,644, 12.4 per cent of the population, in 1901. Until the 1890s manufacturing was divided between factories and domestic workshops, and in the 1880s housing developments, such as the grid of streets off Rockingham Road in Kettering, might include workshops at the ends of gardens – there were more than 2,000 in Kettering alone. By 1891 Northamptonshire, with only 1.1 per cent of the population of England and Wales, had 14.5 per cent of the country's shoemakers. Factory-based manufacturing of footwear became established in pockets elsewhere in Britain,

in Rossendale, around Stafford, in Norwich and in Kendal, and manufacturers developed marketing systems based on chains of shops and rail distribution. Craftsman shoemakers remained ubiquitous in 1870 but decreasingly so in 1900.

If there was a revolution in the British dairy industry it took place in the years 1870–73, when innovatory enterprises were established at Longford, Semley, Chippenham and Aylesbury, setting patterns of operation that continued for more than a century. The first identifiable cheese factory in England was opened at Longford near Derby in 1870, using American methods and managed by an American of Dutch descent. The first wholesale depot intended to supply milk to London was built alongside the railway at Semley, Wiltshire, in 1871. Factories producing canned condensed milk, using the process developed in the United States by Gail Borden, were opened at Chippenham and Aylesbury by the [American] Anglo-Swiss Condensed Milk Co.

Around the end of our period, fishing became concentrated in large ports – Aberdeen, Fleetwood, Grimsby, Hull, Lowestoft and Yarmouth. From these places fresh fish was quickly distributed by rail, but they were also where fish was preserved by smoking, salting and canning, and where factories processed waste parts of the catch into fertilisers and stock feed. The smell of herring was traditionally associated with common lodging-houses, which were resorts of the very poor, and from the 1860s fish-and-chip shops began to multiply. Fish became a significant part of the working-class diet. Another staple was carbohydrates, and similarly milling, which had gradually adopted steam power from the 1780s, was transformed after an exhibition in 1881 demonstrated the potential of roller milling, invented by a Swiss, developed in Hungary, and first adopted on a large scale in the United States. Some inland mills adopted the new technology, which is displayed at Caudwell's Mill at Rowsley, Derbyshire. Many small rural mills closed, but large new mills were constructed beside the docks at London, Birkenhead, Avonmouth, Manchester, Newcastle, Leith, Dublin and Cork. The pattern of manufacturing biscuits was set by the Royal Navy. As early as the 1820s biscuits were mass-produced at the Royal Victoria Victualling

Yard at Deptford and Sir John Rennie's monumental mill and bakery building at the Royal William Yard at Plymouth. Civilian manufacturers used similar technology, but the success of companies such as Huntley & Palmer of Reading, Carrs of Carlisle, W. & R. Jacob in Dublin and George H. Frean and James Peek in Bermondsey also depended on imaginative marketing, innovative packaging, advertising and intelligent use of the railway system. Dietary standards also improved as a result of the import of bacon, eggs and dairy produce from Australia, New Zealand, Canada and the United States, as well as from Germany, the Netherlands and Scandinavia, where much of the produce came from co-operative ventures of small farmers, which were also successful in dairying districts in Ireland, but not in England.

Furniture manufactures serving national markets gradually supplanted cabinetmakers supplying local people from small workshops. Chair making in the Chilterns became a large-scale manufacture centred on High Wycombe where there were 21 chairmakers by the 1830s. Machinery was introduced from the 1860s, and the trade benefited from well-publicised orders for seating for great events in London. One chairmaker in 1861 employed 160 and another 130 people, but the median size of a factory labour force was around 30. Specialist manufacturers provided chair backs, cane and varnish, and local engineers made chair-making machinery. There were more than 30 manufacturers in the town in the 1870s, and their output could reach 4,700 chairs per day.

Books were also mass-produced as printers moved away from London. Hazel, Watson & Viney relocated to Aylesbury in 1867, and employed more than 200 people a decade later. They recruited compositors from many parts of Britain, but also employed young local women in folding, binding and packing books. William Clowes began printing off the Strand in 1803, used steam presses from 1823, and created one of the largest printing concerns in London which printed half a million copies of the catalogue for the Great Exhibition. His successors began to print at Beccles in 1873, where they invested substantially in American technology.

Charles Wilson pointed out that one feature of industrialisation was the emergence of entrepreneurs who 'fulfilled in one person the functions of capitalist, financier, works manager, merchant and salesman'. Entrepreneurs continued to emerge, taking advantage of the new technologies of the late nineteenth century, and exploiting newly perceived markets. The changes which led to the supply of new clothing and footwear and an increasing range of foodstuffs to working-class people were as much in retailing as in manufacturing, and were brought about both by the inspiration of entrepreneurial shopkeepers and by the motivation of those who managed co-operative societies. The supply of boots, shoes, clothing, food and furniture to families all over Britain depended on chains of shops and on distribution by rail. J. D. Chambers remarked that industrialisation brought losses but many gains, since 'whatever the merits of the pre-industrial world may have been they were enjoyed by a deplorably small proportion of those born into it'. Developments in the manufacture of consumer goods and a revolution in retailing spread those gains more widely.

The wider world

By 1870 Britain was no longer the only workshop of the world. The application of technology from the United States was a common feature of developments in the manufacture of consumer goods in the second half of the nineteenth century. The writer Elihu Burrit, born in the clock-making town of Bristol, Connecticut, was in the far north of Scotland in the early 1860s when,

almost within sight of the Orkneys, I heard the clatter of the reaping machine. ... It has travelled fast and far since 1851 when it first made its appearance in Europe in the Crystal Palace as one of the wild impracticable 'notions' of American genius. In Wick I visited a newspaper establishment and saw in operation one of the old 'Columbians' or the American printing press, surmounted by the Eagle of the Republic. The sewing machine is in all the towns and villages on the islands.

Not only were the new manufactures largely based on the sewing machine, and on specialist American technology used in dairying, printing and furniture manufacture, but the markets for established British manufactures were changing. Visitors to railway museums in continental Europe will observe locomotives made in Britain in the 1840s and 1850s, but those of later decades, if not produced in the countries in which they ran, were mostly made in Germany, while manufacturers in Glasgow, Manchester and Leeds looked instead to markets in India and the colonies. New heavy industrial regions such as Pennsylvania, the Ruhrgebiet and the Donetsk Basin were emerging in 1870, making use of British experience, but in some cases, as in Siegerland and Styria, building on centuries-old traditions of manufacturing that were alien to British custom. Industrial areas of a different kind, where manufacturing generated less smoke, subsequently grew up in Bavaria, Würtemburg and California.

The effects of industrial growth could be seen throughout the British Isles, but proto-industrial patterns of production persisted. In Oxfordshire in the 1860s, for example, there were long-established manufacturing activities: quarrying in the countryside, milling grain, tanning and malting in the market towns. During the eighteenth century a canal was built through the county and Oxfordshire was criss-crossed by turnpike roads and, from the 1840s, by railways. In the towns there were breweries with pumps worked by steam engines and tuns fabricated from sheets of copper. Mechanical engineering works melted pig iron and forged wrought iron brought by rail or canal, shaping it on machine tools made in London or Manchester. Most of the county's ancient paper mills were on the verge of closure but three near Oxford employed large numbers of people and used technologies only recently devised. The making of textiles was transformed into a factory-based industry in Witney and Chipping Norton, but migrated away from Banbury. In spite of such changes, manufactures that were proto-industrial in character still employed

several thousand people – lace around Bicester and Thame, leather gloves around Woodstock, Witney and Charlbury, the sewing of garments for John Hyde's clothing enterprise in Abingdon, and the turning of parts for chair manufacturers in the Chilterns. To the east in Bedfordshire and Hertfordshire the extensive straw-plaiting industry remained a largely domestic occupation in the 1860s. In the West Midlands the last cottages built specifically for domestic chain making, in Paint Cup Row, Dudley, were constructed in 1906. In Oxfordshire in 1870, as in most counties, agricultural labourers remained the largest occupational group, and many young sons of labourers trekked to find employment of whatever kind in nearby towns, in the big cities, or in the colonies or the United States.

Kendal is a town whose industrial prosperity was shaped as much by its history, by a tradition of entrepreneurship, as by its natural resources. Its varied manufactures, discussed above (see page 460), proved resilient. The remark that 'notwithstanding many inconveniences which this town has ever laboured under, the manufactures have all along continued to flourish, and have of late years been greatly increased by the spirit and industry of the inhabitants' was as true in the 1860s, when factory-based shoe making was expanding, as when it was made in the 1790s. By contrast some iron-working and coal-mining settlements prospered only as long as the industries that sparked their growth were viable. Other places, Runcorn, St Helens and West Bromwich, grew from very little by continuously adopting new technologies. Many of the developments that contributed most to gross national product happened at places far below the horizon of metropolitan recognition, at Sirhowy, Hetton-le-Hole, Gwennap and Glengarnock.

Collins showed that the industrial revolution stimulated growth in upland regions until about 1870, but not thereafter. After then most upland regions declined, although some areas, including parts of the West Riding and Cumbria and the South Wales valleys, were drawn more or less permanently into the mainstream of the economy. Elsewhere there had been extensive depopulation, the consequence of the Highland Clearances and the Great Famine, and after 1870 of the collapse in prices for metallic ores. Just as the

THE EFFINGHAM WORKS, THE PROPERTY OF MESSRS. YATES, HAYWOOD, AND DRABBLE.

The Effingham Works of Yates, Haywood and Drabble at Masborough, Rotherham, depicted here in an engraving of the early 1860s, was one of the most imposing industrial complexes of its time. The firm originated in 1823 when some of the Yorkshire activities of the Walker family (see above, page 330) were taken over by James Yates, who in the ensuing years had several partners, and worked from several sites in the Rotherham area. In 1846 he formed a partnership with George Haywood and John Drabble, and the company subsequently built the Effingham Works for the manufacture of stove grates on the site of a demolished flax mill. The works consisted of three ranges of buildings parallel to Thames Street in the foreground. Beyond the third range was a glassworks, with an English glass cone, to the right, and a blacking works and a small iron foundry to the left. The company passed through a series of takeovers in the twentieth century, and finally ceased trading in 1970, but the buildings fronting Thames Street still stand. From G. Measom, *The Official Illustrated Guide to the Great Northern Railway* (1861).

consequences of industrialisation could be observed on the margins, so could the consequences of the Clearances and the Famine be observed in industrial communities, among Highlanders and Irishmen in Glasgow, the Irish at Cleator Moor and Coniston, and in market towns where Irishmen and women continued to keep lodging-houses long after their principal customers ceased to be gangs of farm labourers from Clare or Kerry escaping the Famine. The pressures on agricultural communities caused by enclosure were exemplified in the families from the Newmarket area settled in Pelton. Evidence of the communities of the skilled created by industrialisation is shown by the migratory habits of north Staffordshire potters, of puddlers from South Wales, Shropshire and the Black Country, of glassmakers from Dumbarton, South Shields and St Helens, the presence of viewers from Northumberland wherever coal was mined, and of Cornish 'captains' wherever metallic ores were extracted.

Many in the 1860s took an optimistic view of the society, perceived to be focused on manufacturing, that had been created since 1700. Several iconic structures – the Crystal Palace, Robert Stephenson's tubular bridges, Saltaire, the SS *Great Eastern* – symbolised this view. So did expressions of civic pride, such as the Free Trade Hall in Manchester completed in 1856 and Leeds town hall opened in 1858, or of satisfaction with what was being achieved in public health, expressed in the waterworks in Perth or the Abbey Mills pumping station. Measom reflected at the Effingham Works at Rotherham, 'a solid three-storey edifice of about the length of the *Great Eastern*', that such colossal manufactories 'tell of increased comfort for the people of the country; they make us sure that their products are becoming less and less costly', offering 'unequivocal testimony to the growing wealth of the nation', and pondering where customers were to be found for the beautiful and long-lasting grates produced there. In one sense Yarranton's suggestion of the 1680s that 'England should be the Empory and Store House of the World' had become true.

Changes after 1870 were as much social as economic. Eric Hobsbawm described the emergence of a working class rather different from that which had expressed its identity during the Napoleonic Wars and in the era of Chartism. It was associated with huge manufacturing establishments, such as the Great Western works at Swindon or the Elswick engineering complex, and it was increasingly concentrated in large cities – there were 36 British cities with more than 100,000 people in 1911 compared with just 10 in 1851. Industries such as coal mining and railways were increasingly perceived on a national scale. Working men became followers of professional sport, and wearers of cloth caps, which were being manufactured on a large scale by 1861 in most cities, in Bristol as well as Leeds. Annual holidays, particularly at Blackpool, became part of the culture of those in regular employment.

Some of the staples of the economy in 1870, with their associated social disciplines and assumptions, continued for another century. Choking fog still engulfed a coking plant near Aberdare in 1980; spinning mules made in Huddersfield and Dobcross looms still clattered in Stanley Mill (Gloucestershire) in 1986; and steel was still rolled in a hand-operated mill at Priorslee until about 1980. The demolition of what was (incorrectly) thought to be Birmingham's last back-to-back house was celebrated in the early 1960s, and shortly afterwards attempts to preserve the last court dwellings in Liverpool proved unavailing. In some respects the Britain of 1870 seems more alien than that of 1700. Communities across the country were focused with what now seems astonishing single-mindedness

on particular forms of manufacturing, on framework knitting in Sutton-in-Ashfield, on smelting iron in Coatbridge, on making locomotives at Swindon, or mining coal at Pelton. The country was indeed populated by a 'manufacturing people'.

Industrial growth between 1700 and 1870 left many scars on the landscape. The urban squalor that visitors observed in Little Ireland was equalled in many cities across Europe that were not primarily industrial, and hesitant steps were already being taken in 1870 to improve living conditions. The 'Wigan Alps', and other areas routinely polluted over many decades by smoke or the dumping of waste, remained features of the landscape well into the twentieth century, and some deserted industrial sites, notably Parys Mountain, still retain an element of almost Gothic drama. In 1934 Priestley was appalled to find the people of Shotton, Co. Durham, living under perpetual clouds of smoke from a smouldering pit heap, and thought that conditions in 'Rusty Lane' (Spon Lane), West Bromwich, made the whole pomp of government a miserable farce. Peter Hennessey, an historian of the twentieth century, observed that British cities in 1945 'still bore the scars and configurations of the world's first industrial revolution which turned us into a nation of urban dwellers'. Some environmentalists have interpreted the British industrial revolution as the beginning of the destruction of the planet, and it is possible that at some time in the twenty-first century it will be expedient to apologise for it, just as apologies have been made for the Slave Trade and the Irish Famine, although by whom and to whom the apology might be made is a matter for speculation. The 'victims' might be seen as members of unhappy communities in once prosperous British coalfields or mill towns, as well as coastal dwellers in the tropics threatened by rising sea levels.

Berg and Hudson concluded in 1992 that 'The Industrial Revolution was an economic and social process which added up to much more than the sum of its measurable parts'. In some respects it is difficult to disagree with this statement, and it is supported by the many technological and social cross-currents described above. The changes in the British economy and British society between 1700 and 1870 had no obvious precedents, and certainly set patterns which

The perpetual shroud of smoke that surrounded a coke plant south of Aberdare, photographed in April 1980.

were imitated elsewhere. The events chronicled in this book were influential throughout the world: railways enabled the colonisation of whole continents; Ghent and Łódź became the 'Manchesters', respectively, of Belgium and Poland. Yet it can be misleading to indulge in rhetorical superlatives about 'world firsts'. Mining and manufacturing took place in many countries long before 1700, and the experience of industrialisation in the United States, Germany and India since 1870 has been significantly different from that in Britain, even if the technologies applied have been similar. Manchester, New Hampshire, was a cotton-working city, yet it has little else in common with Manchester, Lancashire; the differences between the paternalist landscape of Le Creusot and the open settlements of the Black Country are more apparent than the similarity of the technologies employed, and the sense of patient iron working over many centuries

at Engelsberg and other *bruks* in Dalarna, makes many of the enterprises of the British 'Industrial Revolution' seem as transitory and short-lived as copper mining on Parys Mountain.

This study has avoided using the term 'industrial revolution' in such a way as to imply that it was an uncontrollable process like a volcanic eruption or a typhoon, or an animate being with its own identity and will. Rather, it is a convenient term by which to refer to the sum of many people's actions. The object of the book has not been to offer a 'big idea', to complete in fewer than ten words the sentence 'The industrial revolution occurred because …', but rather to set out what changes occurred in mining and manufacturing in the British Isles between 1700 and 1870 and their impact on particular communities and on society at large. It is for readers to decide whether, in the end, they wish to call this an 'industrial revolution'.

The end

Glossary

adit: a type of mine in which a horizontal or nearly horizontal tunnel is driven into a hillside to gain access to minerals.

air furnace: a reverberatory furnace used for melting pig iron or cast-iron scrap before casting it into moulds, used in England by the early eighteenth century, and generally superseded by the cupola furnace.

alkali: in an industrial context, sodium carbonate, or soda ash, Na_2CO_3, used in the manufacture of soap and glass.

alloy steels: steels to which elements other than carbon have been added to impart properties required for particular purposes; examples are manganese steel and nickel steel.

animal charcoal: the calcined bones of animals that had been slaughtered for meat, used for filtering in industrial processes, particularly in sugar refining.

anthracite: a non-bituminous, clean-burning coal found in Britain principally in the western valleys of South Wales; used in malting and domestic heating and to a limited extent (in Britain) in iron smelting.

assembly rooms: public rooms in resorts, used for card playing, dancing and social gatherings generally. They might be funded by public subscriptions or, as private ventures, as appendages to inns or hotels.

atmospheric railway: a railway provided with a cast-iron tube laid between the rails, along the top of which was a slit sealed with a leather flap: the vehicles had pistons suspended into the tube. After air had been exhausted from the tube by pumps, the vehicles were propelled along the rails by atmospheric pressure; the technology was not widely adopted.

back-to-back house: a dwelling within a terrace consisting of a double row of houses sharing a common back wall; because of the lack of through-ventilation, which was seen as essential for health, these houses were widely condemned.

ball clay: clay of high plasticity and firmness which is one of the raw materials of porcelain. Deposits, which result from the decomposition of granite, are found in Dorset and Devon.

barilla: a source of alkali. Ashes containing 12–24 per cent sodium carbonate, obtained by burning coastal grasses, chiefly from the Mediterranean coasts of France and Spain. Used in making soap until the mid-nineteenth century.

bark mill: a mill used for shredding bark for use when tanning leather.

battery works: an establishment in which water-powered hammers shape sheets of metal, particularly brass and copper, either for use in wire making or into hollow ware such as kettles or pans.

bazaar: the traditional place for retailing in the cities of the Ottoman Empire, but in nineteenth-century Britain an establishment offering cheap goods, either within a covered or open market on in a conventional shop, often with exotic decor enticing custom.

beetling mill: a mill in which flax is crushed by rollers in the preparatory stages of linen production.

bell pit: a type of mine in which a shaft was sunk, usually up to 30 feet (10 m) deep, and the mineral worked out, usually in a circular fashion, to form a bell-shaped void. Such mines usually had short lives and they often left damp, saucer-shaped depressions in the landscape when they were abandoned.

Bessemer process: a method of making mild steel from molten pig iron by blowing air through it, developed by Sir Henry Bessemer from 1856.

billets: wooden logs that were traded as firewood; or rolled or forged semi-finished pieces of iron or steel in section up to 5 × 5 inches. Pieces of larger section are called blooms.

black plate: a wrought-iron (or, later, mild-steel) rolled plate ready for tinplate making, but before being 'pickled' (i.e. cleaned with acid).

blast furnace: a shaft furnace, usually for smelting iron ore, which operated continuously. Ore was charged in layers with fuel (usually charcoal or coke, but sometimes anthracite) and a flux (almost always limestone). Air from bellows operated by water- or steam power, was blown in through pipes called tuyères. In the period reviewed in this book molten 'pig' iron was usually tapped from blast furnaces twice a day.

bleaching, bleaching powder: the whitening of cotton and linen yarn and cloth by the action of sunlight and air; or by the use of chemicals, particularly bleaching powder, patented in 1800 by Charles Tennant, which is produced by the action of chlorine on hydrated lime and was originally regarded as 'hypochlorite of lime' ($Ca(ClO)_2$).

blister steel: hardenable steel suitable for knives and cutting tools, made by carburising wrought-iron bars for several days in a cementation furnace; the name derived from the blisters which formed on the surface of the steel within the furnace.

bloomery furnace: a charcoal-fired furnace used for the direct reduction of iron ore to produce wrought iron, or, in some cases, steel. Of no significance in the British Isles after 1700.

bobbin: a spool or pin around which yarn is wound for use in weaving or knitting.

Boulton & Watt engine: a steam engine – built under the supervision of the partnership, formed in 1774, of Matthew Boulton and James Watt – which incorporated the features that were protected under Watt's patent of 1769, particularly the separate condenser, which represented a significant advance over the 'atmospheric' engine. The patents were extended in 1775 to expire in 1800. Until the partners opened the Soho Foundry in 1796 they customarily supplied customers only with drawings, valves and the services of skilled erectors, the larger parts of engines being supplied by various foundries.

breastshot wheel: a waterwheel on which the water flow was directed at or just above or below the mid-point of the wheel. John Smeaton showed in 1759 that the overshot wheel was of superior efficiency to the undershot, but that the breastshot wheel in many circumstances was a workable compromise.

broad-gauge railway: a railway of wider gauge than the British standard of 4 ft 8½ in (1.435 m), used in particular to refer to the 7 ft 0¼ in (2.14 m) gauge employed by I.K. Brunel on the Great Western Railway, but no longer used by that company after 1892.

buddle: a series of containers through which water flowed, carrying away lighter waste from crushed metallic ores. Trunk buddles, in use by 1800, consisted of three interconnected boxes. Circular buddles were used from the 1820s.

butty: a sub-contractor, particular in a coal mine.

buzzing: a name used from the second half of the eighteenth century for a process by which scrap wrought iron was re-worked in a reverberatory furnace.

calamine: a zinc ore, zinc carbonate ($ZnCO_3$), usually found in association with lead ores, principally in the Mendip Hills. It was used in brass making, for which smelting into metallic zinc was unnecessary.

calender: a machine equipped with rollers that provides the final pressed finish for textiles or paper.

calico: a plain, usually white cotton fabric that could be used for printing, originally by wooden blocks but from the 1780s by powered machines with copper cylinders.

carding: The process of preparing wool, raw cotton or hackled hemp or flax for spinning by removing impurities and straightening the fibres. Hand carding was done with a pair of boards covered with leather through which were struck fine wire hooks or points to catch the fibres as one board was pulled gently across the other. A carding machine was one of the key elements in the factory system of producing cotton yarn developed by Richard Arkwright in the 1760s.

Cast iron: iron with a carbon content between 1.8 and 4.5 per cent, used in a foundry to make castings. Pig iron, the product of a blast furnace, is a form of cast iron.

cementation furnace: a furnace in which bars of wrought iron, packed into refractory clay vessels and heated by charcoal fires, were carburised to make blister steel which was suitable for the manufacture of edge tools.

centring: the temporary frameworks, usually wooden, on which wedge-shaped stone voussoirs were erected in order to form arches.

chaldron: a measure used in the shipping of coal from north-east England. From 1686 a Newcastle chaldron approximated to 53 cwt (2,700 kg), while a London chaldron was approximately 25.5 cwt (1,300 kg). From about 1750 the term often referred to a chaldron waggon, one of the high-sided, bottom-discharging vehicles used on early railways in the North East. Until the late eighteenth century chaldron waggons were usually worked singly, each one pulled by a horse, but they were subsequently marshalled in trains.

china clay: a highly refractory clay, also called kaolin, an essential raw material in the manufacture of porcelain, and from the mid-nineteenth century used in paper manufacture. The principal deposits in Europe are in Cornwall.

close(d) community: a village where one landlord was able to control settlement, in particular to prevent the settlement of families who might become paupers.

club houses: a term that usually means dwellings constructed through the agency of a building society.

cluster house: one of a group of four houses in quadruplex form within a single block, of approximately square plan, and set in a spacious garden. The best-known examples were provided for skilled workers in Derbyshire textile mills.

coadstone: a high-quality terracotta imitating stone used for statues and architectural detailing made in Lambeth, London, by the firm established by Eleanor Coade.

coal drop: a development of the staithe, on which a coal waggon was lowered by a counterbalanced platform to a ship where the coal was discharged, thereby avoiding breakage of the coal. Invented by William Chapman in 1800 and first applied at Wallsend in 1812.

compound engine: a steam engine that uses the same steam successively to drive pistons in high-pressure and low-pressure cylinders.

condenser (i): the part of a steam engine in which steam exhausted from the cylinder was converted back to water by being cooled. In the Newcomen engine condensation took place within the cylinder. One of the principal innovations made by James Watt was the separate condenser, usually installed at a lower level than the cylinder, which increased the thermal efficiency of the engine.

condenser (ii): a device employed from the mid-nineteenth century to extract metal from the smoke from lead smelters by drawing it through water, avoiding the expense of long flues.

condenser (iii): at a condenser cotton mill waste from carding and other stages of manufacture is, after further cleaning, spun into yarn suitable for the cheaper forms of bed linen and towelling.

copperas: a name applied to sulphates of several metals, but principally to ferrous sulphate ($FeSO_4$) or green vitriol, used in dyeing and tanning.

Cornish engine: a condensing beam engine, of the type introduced by Richard Trevithick in 1811–12. The Cornish engine was efficient, and examples continued to be built into the twentieth century.

crown glass: glass made by cutting a blown cylinder, spinning it into a disc, annealing it, then cutting it into panes. Crown glass in windows can be recognised by the arcs of circles visible on its surface.

crucible: a refractory open-mouthed vessel, approximately 2–3 feet in size, used for heating materials in various industrial processes, but particularly in the manufacture of glass and steel.

crucible steel: carbon steel made by a process introduced at Sheffield by Benjamin Huntsman in 1740, by which blister steel was broken into small pieces and melted in a refractory clay crucible in a coke-fired furnace. Once the process was complete steel in the crucible could be poured into a small ingot mould.

cullet: waste glass that was re-used to make new glass.

cupola (i): a shaft furnace, operating intermittently, fired with coke and blown by three or four tuyères, used for re-melting pig iron or scrap in a foundry. It was patented in 1794 by John Wilkinson, although the invention is generally attributed to his brother, William Wilkinson.

cupola (ii): a reverberatory furnace for smelting lead, normally coal-fired in the British Isles where it was first used in the seventeenth century.

cupola (iii): an architectural term for a dome-shaped structure mounted on columns, often used on factories to protect a bell.

currier: one who carries out the process by which leather produced by a tanner is rendered supple and suitable for use by shoemakers or saddlers. The process entails soaking, scraping and the treatment of the leather with tallow or oil.

delftware: a hard, translucent white-bodied form of earthenware.

'depot': a recess of the kind used alongside the Holyhead road in North Wales in which broken stone was stored before being applied to the surface of the road.

Diocletian window: a semi-circular window divided into three lights by two vertical mullions, also known as a thermal window, a feature of Palladian architecture in eighteenth-century Britain.

rabbet: a light brown linen fabric, manufactured particularly in East Anglia.

Dutch loom: a form of loom used for making ribbons and tapes used at Tean Hall, Staffordshire, from 1747 and powered by steam engines from the 1820s.

English glass cone: a conical structure of a kind introduced in the early eighteenth century, enclosing a glass kiln or kilns, which acts as a funnel to increase draught.

faggots (i): bundles of twigs bound together and traded for the use of bakers in bread ovens.

faggots (ii): bundles of small wrought-iron bars heated and welded under a hammer to make a shaft or other forging.

finery-and-chafery forge: a forge, usually charcoal-fuelled and water-powered, in which pig iron was decarburised with the aid of an air blast in a finery hearth, then shingled under a hammer into a 'half-bloom', then reheated in a chafery hearth before being hammered into a form suitable for slitting or some other method of reworking. The process was gradually superseded by puddling.

flash lock: a form of lock on a river which increased the depth upstream and had a gated opening. When the gate was opened a flash of water would surge downstream raising levels over shallows and enabling boats travelling upstream to be drawn through the gates, sometimes with the use of winches.

flat (i): a term commonly used for an apartment, deriving from the Scottish word for a floor or storey within a house.

flat (ii): a sailing vessel used in inland navigation, normally prefixed by the name of a river such as 'Mersey flat' or 'Humber flat' or by the name of the commodity usually carried, as in a 'deal flat', used for transporting softwoods. The masts could often be lowered to help negotiate obstacles. Cf. *lighter*.

flint glass: a form of glass in which flint from chalk deposits was used as a source of silica, that evolved into the lead crystal glass used in the eighteenth century for table wares. Now principally applied to optical glass.

floating dock, floating harbour: an artificially enclosed area of water in which ships can be moored at anchor at all states of the tide while being loaded or unloaded. Sometimes also known as 'wet' docks, in contradistinction to dry docks used in ship repairing.

flue: specifically a chimney but widely used to refer to any conduit for conveying smoke and gases heated in industrial processes. It refers particularly to the vaulted passages constructed from the late eighteenth century in upland regions to convey exhaust gases from lead smelters that terminated in chimneys positioned on hilltops. Powerful draughts could be generated in such flues, some of which were up to five miles long.

forge (i): a works where the finery-and-chafery, the stamping-and-potting or the puddling process was used to refine pig iron or scrap into wrought iron.

forge (ii): a works where wrought iron or steel were shaped by hammers or presses, the smallest examples of which were blacksmiths' smithies.

foundry: a works where metal is melted and poured into moulds to make castings. When unqualified the term is normally taken to refer to an iron foundry.

Fourdrinier machine: the first effective machine for manufacturing paper, invented by the brothers Fourdrinier and patented in 1801 and 1807.

Freehold Land Society: a form of building society first established in Birmingham from 1848 by James Taylor. Money was raised from subscribers to purchase land which was divided into plots that were often distributed to members by ballot. Many such societies became vehicles for small-scale speculators rather than a means to owner occupation.

fulling: a vigorous working of woollen cloth in a solution of water with a fulling agent (urine, fuller's earth, or soap) to produce controlled shrinkage and to compact and felt the fibres. Water-powered fulling mills, with large wooden hammer beams called fulling stocks were used in the British Isles from the late Middle Ages.

fustian: a term which applied to various types of fabric from the fourteenth century, but which by 1800 meant a coarse cloth made from cotton or flax and used for outer garments, essentially one with a cut pile like corduroy. 'Fustian Jackets' became a synonym for the English working class by *circa* 1840.

flying shuttle: The invention of John Kay in 1733, the 'fly' or 'flying' shuttle was a system of devices by which the thread of the weft was passed through the threads of the warp without having to be handled by the weaver. On either side of the loom were boxes in which the shuttle could be caught after it had been sent through the warp, leaving behind it a trail of weft. Sliding above each box was a 'hammer' that was pulled to send the shuttle back through the warp.

galena: lead sulphide (PbS), the ore which is the principal source of lead.

haematite: a high-grade iron ore (Fe$_2$)$_3$, found particularly in Cumbria, characteristically red in colour with nodules shaped like kidneys.

handloom: a non-mechanised loom of any kind. Typically a single handloom might be located in a domestic work environment, within a cottage, but large numbers of handlooms might also be brought together in loomshops. The plight of handloom weavers, thrown out of work, or whose earnings were depressed, by the introduction of powerlooms in the second quarter of the nineteenth century, was widely perceived as a social problem.

headstock: the frame at the top of the shaft of a mine on which the winding apparatus is mounted.

helve hammer: a heavy cast-iron hammer, powered by a shaft from a waterwheel or a steam engine, used for shingling iron or making heavy forgings.

Hollander beater: a beating machine consisting of a rectangular trough in which revolved a large roller fitted with knives, used to macerate and beat rags into pulp for the traditional manufacture of paper. Introduced in the Netherlands in the mid-seventeenth century and in England by 1740.

horse gin: a device powered by one or more horses or donkeys walking round a circular track and harnessed so as to turn a large toothed wheel which turned smaller wheels operating machinery. Widely used throughout the period from 1700 to 1870.

hot blast: the process by which air from the blowing engine of a blast furnace is heated in stoves before entering the furnace, developed by the Scot James Beaumont Neilson and introduced in 1828.

hoy: a small sailing vessel used in coasting trades for both freight and passengers, particularly from London to ports in the Medway estuary, the Isle of Thanet and other parts of the Kent coast.

huckaback: a coarse linen fabric with a rough surface, used particularly for towels.

hurds: the shortest fibres of flax or hemp, otherwise noggs or tow, used to make coarse fabrics, particularly the sheets and other linen used by poor people in the seventeenth and eighteenth centuries.

hurrier: A term, used particularly in the Yorkshire coalfield, for children who hauled coal in corves (baskets) from the face where it was cut to the main roadways where it was loaded into railway waggons that carried it to the shaft bottom.

hushing: a method of exposing veins of ore in which surface soil is removed by a torrent of water, usually accumulated behind a dam at the head of a gulley.

hybrid railway: a name applied to railways of the early nineteenth century that had some but not all of the five attributes of main-line railways, i.e. specialised track, a measure of public control, public access, mechanical traction and the carriage of passengers.

hydraulic accumulator: a means of providing constant pressure in a hydraulic power system and of storing the energy within the system, developed by Sir William Armstrong from 1851. A ram or piston in a cylinder compresses the fluid in the hydraulic system. On top of the ram a yoke carries ballasted bins to create an artificial head of water. Control chains on the bins actuate pumps to maintain the head.

hydraulic cement: cement which will set under water, usually made from argillaceous limestone (a clayey limestone with hydrated aluminium silicate) or chalk marl. Used in England by the 1750s.

Improvement: the concept, popular in the late eighteenth and early nineteenth centuries, of developing land to maximise its use for industry and agricultural, as well as to enhance its aesthetic appeal.

inclined plane: a slope, usually with rails, across which a vehicle can be moved between two relatively flat stretches of railway, or by which a boat can be transferred from one kind of waterway to another. Inclined planes were usually powered by steam engines, but where the predominant traffic was downhill they could be self-acting.

ingot: metal cast in a mould ready for re-working. An iron or steel ingot would be rolled or forged. An ingot of a non-ferrous metal might be re-melted.

Jacquard loom: a loom with a control mechanism which involves the use of perforated pattern cards, invented by J. M. Jacquard *circa* 1800, and introduced in the British Isles in the following decades.

jet: a hard, compact, black form of lignite, found particularly in North Yorkshire, which takes a brilliant polish and is used in the manufacture of toys and tourist souvenirs.

keel (i): the longitudinal member of the frame of a ship on which the rest of the frame is constructed.

keel (ii): an open, oar-propelled boat used to carry coal from wharfs on the upper reaches of the rivers Tyne and Wear to sea-going ships, particularly at Shields or Sunderland, with a capacity of about 21 tons.

keel (iii): the name applied to craft on the river Humber and its associated waterways, usually measuring about 58 ft × 14 ft.

laminated ribs: ribs of a bridge or similar structure made from successive layers of wood or metal.

Lancashire boiler: a form of cylindrical boiler developed by Sir William Fairbairn and others in the 1840s, with two flues that could be fired alternately in two furnaces to prevent the formation of smoke, but also providing an increased heating surface.

lathe: a machine for 'turning', by gradually feeding a single-point cutting tool against work rotating about a horizontal axis, producing principally cylindrical, but also flat and conical or threaded surfaces.

lattice beam: a beam fabricated from wooden, wrought-iron or steel strips, crossed and fastened together, with open spaces left between.

leat: an artificial channel conveying water to a mill, usually cut around a natural fall on a river or stream. In Scotland usually called a lade.

Leyden jar: electrical apparatus used by scientists and many amateur polymaths with scientific interests. A glass jar coated with tin foil inside and out, with an electrode rod passing through its mouth was given an electric charge generated by a friction machine, by which the inner and outer surfaces stored equal but opposite charges. The jar was developed in the 1740s in Germany, and in the university city in the Netherlands (now Leiden) from which it takes its name.

lighter (i): an unpowered vessel of shallow draught into which goods were unloaded from sea-going ships, that might also be used generally for the movement of goods within a port. Widely used at the Port of London, both on the river and in the docks.

lighter (ii): a type of dumb barge usually measuring 42 ft × 10 ft used on navigations in the Fens in England, and, measuring 62 ft × 14 ft, on the inland navigations in the north of Ireland.

line: the longest fibres of flax or hemp separated from the coarse fibres (hurds, tow, noggs) by the process of hackling.

longwall: a system of mining coal or iron ore developed in Shropshire from the seventeenth century and used in most British coalfields except in north-east England. A system of tunnels was created which enabled the whole of a seam to be removed, the resulting void (or 'gob' or 'goof') being held up with pit props and filled with waste.

mail coach: a small and fast horse-drawn coach for carrying mail introduced in 1784 by John Palmer, Surveyor and Comptroller General of the Post Office, which carried small numbers of passengers from 1791.

malleable iron (i): a term often used loosely and misleadingly to apply to wrought iron.

malleable iron (ii): cast iron that has been annealed by heating it with powdered iron ore for several days, making it possible to cast the iron into nails, hinges etc. Used in England from the 1790s.

man engine: a system used from the early nineteenth century to enable miners to go to and from their work, principally in metalliferous mines. Systems of wooden rods were reciprocated by water power and later by steam engines, and miners were able to ascend or descend shafts by stepping on and off steps which were formed at intervals on the rods.

mansard roof: a roof with a double slope, the lower longer and steeper than the upper, taking its name from the seventeenth-century French architect François Mansart.

methane: a highly flammable gas (CH_4), and a source of constant danger in many coal mines where it is known as 'fire damp'.

mild steel: steel containing between 0.10 and 0.20 per cent carbon, first manufactured by Sir Henry Bessemer in 1856, and subsequently by the open hearth process developed by Sir William Siemens. From the 1880s the work of S. G. Thomas enabled iron made from phosphoric ore to be used in steel making. Mild steel is used widely in vehicles, machines and for constructional purposes.

mungo: the poorest grade of shoddy, usually made from hard rags or felted materials. New mungo was made from unused waste, such as tailors' clippings, old mungo from used garments. The term was first used in 1857.

narrow boat: the standard vessel of the waterways of midland England, whose dimensions were fixed at a meeting of canal proprietors at Lichfield on 15 December 1769. A narrow boat measures 70 ft × 7 ft, and usually has a cabin 10 ft long at the stern. The capacity was up to 35 tons, although loads were generally in the region of 20 tons. From the 1820s if not earlier there was living accommodation on board. The vessels used on the broad waterways in northern England (and on some in the south) were about 14 ft in beam.

narrow-gauge railway: strictly speaking a railway with a gauge of less than the standard gauge of 4 ft 8½ in (1.435 m), but many gauges were used for short periods in the 1830s and 1840s, and the term generally means a line with a gauge of less than 3 ft 6 ins (1.1 m) used to penetrate mountain regions or for cheapness.

Newcomen engine: a steam engine of the type developed by Thomas Newcomen, the earliest known application of which dates from 1712. The piston propelled a balanced beam to which a pump was attached, by admitting steam at atmospheric pressure into a cylinder. The steam was then condensed by a water jet, allowing the piston to be forced into the cylinder by atmospheric pressure – hence the name 'atmospheric' engine by which it is often known. The principle of the engine was protected by patent until 1733, and construction of Newcomen engines continued into the nineteenth century.

night soil men: scavengers who collected the contents of earth closets in towns. Usually the contents were emptied into a pile outside a house, to be collected by cart at night and subsequently used as fertiliser on farms or market gardens.

noggs: a synonym for hurds.

north-lit shed: a single-storey building, often of considerable width as well as length, usually with windowless walls and with columns carrying a steel-framed roof of saw-tooth pattern, aligned so that the fenestration within it faces north to avoid glare from direct sunlight within the workplace. This building type was used in Lancashire by the 1820s and became the characteristic powerloom weaving shed of the northern part of the county. In the late nineteenth century the north-lit shed was used for many kinds of manufacturing throughout the British Isles.

oakum: loose fibres obtained from untwisting old rope, used in caulking ships. Picking oakum was a task often imposed on prisoners or the inmates of workhouses.

open community: a village or scattered community where there was no controlling landlord, and where incomers could readily settle.

open hearth furnace: a method of making mild steel introduced by Sir William Siemens in the 1860s, an alternative to the Bessemer process. Iron was melted in a hearth fired from the opposite ends by coal gas. The waste combustion gases passed from the hearth through a range of refractive regenerators en route to the flue. When the direction of firing was reversed, the combustion air would be preheated by passing it through the regenerators before mixing with the fuel. A second set of regenerators would be heated as the waste gases passed out of the hearth, and would be used in turn to heat combustion air when the direction of firing was again reversed.

ore hearth: a furnace for smelting lead in which the ore and the fuel (usually dried wood or a mixture of peat and charcoal) were mixed. An ore hearth was blown with bellows that were usually water-powered.

overshot wheel: a waterwheel rotating in an anti-clockwise direction. Water was carried above the wheel and delivered to buckets just below the top. Overshot wheels were more efficient than undershot, and could be powered by relatively small streams.

packet boat: a vessel plying at regular intervals between two or more ports, for the conveyance of mails, particularly diplomatic despatches, as well as parcels and passengers. The term was applied to vessels sailing between Holyhead and Ireland in the seventeenth century, and for a time from 1816 referred to ships sailing regularly between Britain and North America. Passenger boats on canals both in Great Britain and Ireland were also called packets.

paper board: a material made by a process patented by Henry Clay in 1772 in which sheets of brown paper were pasted together. Paper board could be sawed or filed, and made waterproof by painting, varnishing or japanning. It was made into boxes, buttons and trays and the thicker grades were used for the roofs of coaches.

parish apprentice: a pauper child in the period before the Poor Law Amendment Act of 1834 who was placed by parish authorities with the owner of a textile mill or other industrial establishment. The term 'apprenticeship' did not imply that the child would be taught a skilled trade.

patching: a synonym for hushing, used particularly in South Wales.

Pattinson process: a process devised by Hugh Lee Pattinson in 1833 for the recovery of silver from metallic lead that was widely used in the northern Pennines.

piece hall: a large wholesale market for the sale of 'pieces' of finished cloth, usually divided into booths. Piece halls were built in most of the principal towns in the West Riding of Yorkshire in the eighteenth century. The most significant surviving example is at Halifax.

pig iron: cast iron in the form in which it came in the period before 1870 from a blast furnace, ready for re-melting in a forge or a foundry. The name derives from the shape of the moulds into which it was traditionally cast when tapped from the furnace, which were said to resemble piglets feeding from a sow. In other countries iron from a blast furnace was moulded in different ways, in France into a fish-shaped slab called a *saumon* (salmon).

pillar-and-stall: a method of mining coal or other bedded mineral in which tunnels are driven into the solid mineral leaving pillars to support the roof. Coal was extracted from specific stalls for which miners were paid by piece work.

'pirate engine': a steam engine that was deemed to infringe James Watt's patents that were valid until 1800.

plateway: railway track incorporating the angled iron rails used by John Curr from the 1780s. Rails might be of cast iron or wrought iron. Sleepers might be stone blocks, of wood or of either form of iron.

plush: a fabric with a long, stiff pile, which might incorporate silk, mohair, woollen or worsted yarns. It was used for liveries and for upholstery.

porcelain: a collective name for pottery made with more or less translucent bodies, produced in China in or before the ninth century AD. Knowledge of how to make porcelain spread across Europe from Dresden in Saxony in the mid-eighteenth century. True porcelains are made of materials which when fired produce white-bodied wares. Hard porcelains have clay bodies; feldspar within the clay body acts as a flux. Soft porcelains are earthenwares that have been made translucent by the addition of flux in the form of soda, potash, marble or bone ash.

post chaise, *post horse*: a vehicle or beast available for private hire at an inn; a licence would be issued under which the innkeeper was obliged to provide carriages for hire and to have available replacement horses for carriages hired elsewhere. In England the cost of travelling by post coach in the 1780s was approximately three times the stagecoach fare. A post coach might be driven by the hirer or by a postilion.

post mill: a windmill in which the entire body of the mill can be rotated to face the wind on a vertical post supported by a trestle or sill, which in surviving examples is often supported on masonry or brick piers and is sometimes covered by a round brick housing.

pound lock: the principal means employed on European waterways since the Renaissance of transferring boats between different levels of a waterway. A chamber, whose walls are usually set on piles and tied together with cross beams, is enclosed at either end by gates. Water is let in or out through sluices so raising or lowering boats in the lock.

probate inventories: lists of people's possessions made after their deaths, which can often be valuable sources for the history of material culture before *circa* 1760.

puddling: a means of forging wrought iron from pig iron in a reverberatory furnace, with coal as its fuel, patented by Henry Cort in 1784, which within twenty years became the principal means of making wrought iron in the British Isles. Of equal importance in the process was Cort's development of a rolling mill with grooved rolls.

putting: the movement of coal from the face where it was cut to haulage ways in mines, either on railways or in baskets attached to children by girdles and chains.

rake: a vertical vein of metallic ore, usually lead, occurring between walls of rock, and excavated from deep trenches several miles long, often over many centuries.

reciprocating steam engine: a steam engine that was capable only of a reciprocating motion, such as that required for working a pump. Cf. *rotative steam engine*.

red lead: lead oxide (Pb_3O_4), which was used in glass manufacture and varnishes, and was usually made in urban leadworks by a process involving the use of two sets of ovens.

regenerative furnace: a furnace in which the air from bellows is heated by passing it through a maze of refractory bricks, itself heated by waste gases from the furnace. Usually there were two refractory mazes, one of which would be heated with gases from the furnace while air was blown through the other. The open hearth furnace used in steel making is an example.

reverberatory furnace: a furnace in which the flame is directed from a chamber containing the fire across a wall made of refractory materials into a second chamber containing the material being heated, at the far end of which is a flue. The air furnace, the puddling furnace and the cupola used for melting non-ferrous metals are examples.

rolling mill: a device consisting of two or more sets of rolls accommodated in housings and rotated by water, steam or later by electric power, in which hot or cold metal, principally iron or steel, is elongated and formed into particular sections according to the form of the rolls. Rolling can produce rounds, squares, angles, plates, sheets and H- or I-sections (for the American market).

room-and-power mill: a factory, usually intended for the manufacture of textiles, in which entrepreneurs were able to lease space to accommodate their own machinery and workers and pay for power that was provided by a central, commonly used prime mover.

rotative steam engine: a steam engine capable of turning machinery, driven by the crank, patented by James Pickard in 1780, or the sun-and-planet motion devised by James Watt the following year.

roving: The phase of textile production that precedes spinning. A rove or roving is a fine web of a textile fibre, usually cotton or wool, which has been carded and is awaiting spinning. Rovings of wool are often joined to increase their strength in a machine called a slubbing billy or, later, a condenser.

schooner: a type of sea-going sailing vessel widely used in the eighteenth and nineteenth centuries, which had at least two masts, each of two parts. It was powered by gaff and boom sails, both receiving the wind on either side according to the direction of the wind relative to the direction in which the ship was sailing.

scribbling: a synonym for carding.

scutch mill: an establishment in which flax was struck with a flat wooden blade to scrape away gummy residue and hard pieces of the stalk.

shoddy: a woollen fabric made from yarn produced by tearing woollen rags to shreds with the addition of some new wool. The process was established in Batley, Yorkshire, in 1813.

shot tower: a tower, typically about 180 feet high, used for making lead shot of uniform size. Pig lead was melted in small furnaces at different heights according to the size of shot required, with some arsenic added to prevent the lead falling as a continuous stream. Molten lead was poured from various heights through perforated copper screens, falling as spheres into a vat of water below. The process was patented by William Watts of Bristol in 1782.

shuttle: A component of a weaving loom used for passing the thread of the weft from one edge of the cloth to the other between the threads of the warp. (*q.v.* flying shuttle)

slag: the waste product of smelting or forging metal, most commonly a vitreous material with a high silica content.

slipware: pottery decorated with slip, a suspension of fine particles in water, which was commonly produced in Britain from the mid-seventeenth century.

slitting mill: a two-stage process for the production of narrow rods for nailers and other smiths from blooms of wrought iron, used in the Liège area by 1500 and patented in England in 1588. The bloom was hammered into the shape of a bar and then passed between two plain cylindrical iron rolls, powered by a waterwheel. The strip was then passed through counter-rotating shafts on which were collars which acted as rotary shears.

sough: a sloping tunnel that drained water from a mine to a natural watercourse on the surface.

spandrel: the roughly triangular space between an arch and the straight-sided figure enclosing it; most commonly the abutment and deck of a bridge.

spelter: an alternative name for zinc.

spinning jenny: the first practical multiple-spindle spinning machine, patented by James Hargreaves in 1770. While the operator moved the carriage out, the roving was drawn and twisted; when the carriage was moved back, the yarn was wound on to the rotating spindles. Early machines contained around 16 spindles. Jennies could be used for either wool or cotton. Many workshops were established in the late eighteenth century to accommodate these hand-powered machines. Cf. *water-frame*.

spinning mule: a powered spinning machine that combined the drafting rollers of Richard Arkwright's water-frame with the moving carriage of James Hargreaves's spinning jenny. It was invented by Samuel Crompton in the 1770s, but large-scale production began in the late 1820s with the development of the self-acting mule by Richard Roberts. A single mule, moving backwards and forwards every 15 seconds or so, could contain over 1,000 spindles and could be worked by a single minder and two assistants. Continued in use in Britain into the twentieth century.

sprit-sail barge: a barge whose sail is extended by a sprit, a small boom or pole which crosses the fore and aft sail diagonally from the mast to the upper hindmost corner of the sail, which it extends and elevates.

squatter settlement: dwellings built on common land, which might be open heath, a roadside verge or a village green. Common land belonged to the lord of the manor, although he could not alienate it. A squatter settlement could be controlled by the annual imposition of fines in a manorial court since rents could not be charged. Squatter plots were usually irregular in shape and many were bounded by low earthen banks.

stagecoach: a coach that ran at specific times between specific places, with changes of horses after each stage of about twelve miles. The term was first used in the late seventeenth century. Stagecoaches were substantial vehicles, which from about 1750 carried passengers outside.

staircase turret: a turret on the side of a factory (usually a textile mill) which accommodated a staircase, and usually lavatories as well, permitting the whole of a floor to be occupied by machinery.

stamping-and-potting: a coal-fired method of making wrought iron from pig iron patented by John Wright and Richard Jesson in 1773, in which broken pieces of pig iron were heated in clay pots. Much used until displaced by the puddling process from about 1800.

stamps: water- or steam-powered machines for crushing metallic ores, particularly those of tin, copper and gold, used from the early eighteenth century. Heavy wooden 'stampers', often with cast-iron heads, and held upright in wooden frames, were raised by the action of a cam on a horizontal shaft.

standard gauge railway: in Great Britain, a railway of the 4 ft 8½ in. gauge derived originally from practice in the coalfield of north-east England, used on the Liverpool & Manchester Railway, and subsequently on other main lines, and enshrined in law by the Railway Regulation (Gauges) Act of 1846. In Ireland a standard gauge of 5 ft 3 ins (1.6 m) was adopted.

steam hammer: a hammer, invented by James Nasmyth in 1839, which operated vertically, powered by a steam cylinder in the apex of an A-frame, with the anvil located between the two upright members of the frame.

streaming: the extraction of minerals from deposits of silt in rivers and streams, using buddles or similar devices, used in Cornwall, particularly for the extraction of tin ores.

suspension bridge: a bridge in which the deck is hung from cables slung between two anchorages over towers or piers at either end. This form of construction was known in ancient China, was introduced on a small scale in Europe in the eighteenth century, and substantially developed in the years after 1800. Thomas Telford's Menai Bridge, completed in 1826, demonstrated the potential of suspension bridges for spanning great distances, beyond the capabilities of other form of construction.

sweated trades: the manufacture of goods, especially clothing, in cities, particularly in London, by workers employed at very low wages, below the accepted rates, which might be further reduced by charges made for accommodation and food.

tambour: the French word for drum, and for a type of lace, generally of silk, for which patterns were embroidered on fabrics stretched on drum-shaped frames.

tenement: a legal term of land ownership (literally, the holding of a tenant) that came to apply to a separately occupied room or set of rooms within a subdivided house, or in Scotland to the multi-storey blocks of dwellings characteristic of Dundee, Edinburgh and Glasgow, and to individual apartments within such blocks.

terracotta: large blocks of pressed clay, typically buff or red in colour, widely made in Great Britain in the mid- and late nineteenth century, and used on such prestigious buildings as the Wedgwood Institute in Burslem, Manchester Town Hall, and the Natural History Museum, but also, on a modest scale, in many suburban dwellings.

thoroughfare town: a town where many inhabitants made their livings by catering for passing travellers.

throstle: a modified form of the water-frame (*q.v.*).

tilt hammer: the earliest form of powered hammer which comprised a hammer head at one end of a haft and a fulcrum in the centre. It was operated by cams on a shaft connected to a waterwheel or a steam engine. Widely used in the iron trade to deliver light blows in rapid succession.

tinplate: wrought-iron or steel sheet, thinly coated with tin, first produced in the British Isles in the early eighteenth century. Sheets, suitably prepared, were immersed in baths of molten tin, and then dried. The tinplate industry was particularly important in the western valleys of South Wales.

tow: a synonym for hurds.

tower mill: a form of windmill in which a stone or brick tower supports a revolving cap in which the sails are set, introduced to Europe about the fourteenth century.

tram: the coarser fibres of raw silk, normally used as weft, and commonly thrown by hand.

tramway: from the late eighteenth century a small or temporary railway, typically serving an industrial establishment or connecting to another transport system such as a canal, but from the 1860s applied to systems of public transport in which passenger-carrying vehicles ran on rails powered by horses, steam or cables, and later by electric traction.

trow: a name given to the larger types of vessel operating on the river Severn and its tributaries, applied particularly to vessels that could sail on the estuary waters downstream from Gloucester.

tub boat: a small vessel, often box-shaped, usually employed on a canal using inclined planes, frequently worked in 'trains', and measuring 18–21 feet long and about 5 feet wide.

tubular bridge: a bridge consisting of a colossal hollow beam with a road or railway running through it. The most notable examples in the British Isles were the Britannia and Conwy bridges on the Chester & Holyhead Railway.

tunnel-back house: a two-up, two-down dwelling extended by a rear extension in which were a scullery on the ground floor and a third bedroom above, commonplace in most towns from the 1850s.

turnpike road: the word turnpike originally meant a gate, and the term was applied to the barriers erected across roads by trusts empowered by Act of Parliament to collect rolls from travellers and apply the income to the improvement of the roads. The first turnpike act in England was passed in 1663, but the system only began to spread in the 1690s. The powers of turnpike trusts gradually passed to highway boards in the second half of the nineteenth century, and then to county councils, and none remained by 1900.

tuyère: a nozzle through which air is forced into a furnace, supplied with air by a tuyère pipe.

two-storey flat: an apartment with its own front door on either the ground or first floor of a terrace, the characteristic working-class and lower-middle-class dwelling in Newcastle-upon-Tyne, which was also built in some nearby mining communities. The type had evolved by 1850 and continued to be built in the twentieth century.

undershot wheel: a waterwheel rotated in a clockwise direction with buckets located in a stream flowing beneath it. In theoretical terms undershot wheels were less efficient than overshot but on sizeable rivers they could be a satisfactory source of power.

Venetian window: a window with three openings, the central one arched and wider than the others, a feature of Palladian architecture in eighteenth-century England. Also called a Serliana.

viewer (colliery): a term used principally in north-east England, and especially in the eighteenth century, for a mining engineer, one who could oversee and manage the sinking and operation of a colliery.

waggonway: the usual term for a wooden (or later an iron) industrial or mineral railway in north-east England.

warp: the threads which are extended length-wise in a loom.

water balance: a device for raising minerals from a mine shaft or lifting vehicles or boats between two levels of a railway or canal. A tank, counterbalanced with the load, is filled with water so that its greater weight causes it to descend, raising the load. When the water was discharged the process could be repeated.

water-frame: a powered machine for spinning cotton, incorporating a series of rollers that turned at different speeds, which gradually drew the cotton fibres before being spun onto bobbins. Originally developed by Thomas Highs and John Kay, the water-frame was patented in 1769 by Richard Arkwright, who put it into successful commercial practice at his spinning mill at Cromford, Derbyshire.

weft: the threads that cross from side to side in a piece of cloth on a loom, at right angles to the warp threads with which they are interlaced.

wet dock: a synonym for a floating dock, as distinct from a dry dock which was a chamber from which water could be drained after a ship had been floated in to allow repair work to take place.

wet spinning: a process used in the preparation of fine linen yarns in which flaxen roving passes through a trough of heated water. Patented in France in 1815, and used in the Leeds flax industry from the 1820s.

white lead: basic lead carbonate ($2PbCO_3$, $Pb(OH)_2$), made by rolling up thin plates of lead and suspending them above pots of vinegar, a process that originated in Venice in the seventeenth century; the most important constituent of paint between 1700 and 1870 and into the twentieth century.

worsted: well-twisted yarn made from long-staple (or long-fibred) wood, combed so that the fibres lie parallel to each other. The term was used in the Middle Ages and derives from Worstead, ten miles north of Norwich. From *circa* 1800 the chief centre of worsted manufacture was around Bradford, Yorkshire.

wrought iron: a commercially pure form of iron, containing virtually no carbon, and fibrous in texture due to threads of slag. Until the development of mild steel from the 1850s the usual material for nails, locks and chains, for structural sections used in tension, and for machine parts.

Further reading

Abbreviations

BusH	*Business History*	OUP	Oxford University Press
CBA	Council for British Archaeology	*PMA*	*Post-Medieval Archaeology*
CUP	Cambridge University Press	RCAHMS	Royal Commission on the Ancient & Historical Monuments of Scotland
D&C	David & Charles (Newton Abbot)		
EcHR	*Economic History Review*	RCAHMW	Royal Commission on the Ancient & Historical Monuments of Wales
EH	English Heritage		
HM	*Historical Metallurgy*	RCHME	Royal Commission on the Historical Monuments of England
HMSO	Her Majesty's Stationery Office		
IAR	*Industrial Archaeology Review*	*TNS*	*Transactions of the Newcomen Society*
LecUP	Leicester University Press	*T&C*	*Technology & Culture*
LivUP	Liverpool University Press	*TexH*	*Textile History*
MUP	Manchester University Press	*TLH*	*The Local Historian*
ODNB	*Oxford Dictionary of National Biography*	*TTS*	*Transactions of the Thoroton Society*
		VCH	*Victoria County History*

1. Introduction: a manufacturing people

The literature on the Industrial Revolution is vast, and successive academic controversies, over standards of living, the nature of output growth and capital formation, have generated many more articles than can be listed here. This bibliography includes the printed sources of which conscious use has been made, but omits some articles whose essential arguments are included in books by the same authors.

The earliest significant text is A. Toynbee, *Lectures on the Industrial Revolution of the Eighteenth Century in England* (London: Rivington, 1884). It is important to acknowledge the long-term influence of four introductory works, T. S. Ashton, *The Industrial Revolution, 1760–1830* (OUP, 1948) and its sequel, J. D. Chambers, *The Workshop of the World* (OUP, 1961), E. J. Hobsbawm, *Industry and Empire* (Harmondsworth: Penguin, 1969) and P. Mathias, *The First Industrial Nation* (London: Methuen, 1969). M. Berg, *The Age of Manufactures: industry, innovation and work in Britain* (2nd edn, London: Routledge, 1994); M. Berg and P. Hudson, 'Rehabilitating the Industrial Revolution', *EcHR*, vol. 45 (1992); N. F. R. Crafts, *British Economic Growth During the Industrial Revolution* (OUP, 1985); J. Horn *et al.* (eds), *Re-conceptualizing the*

Industrial Revolution (Boston: MIT Press, 2006–07); P. Hudson, *The Industrial Revolution* (London: Arnold, 1992); P. Joyce, *Works, Society and Politics* (London: Harvester, 1980); P. K. O'Brien and R. Quinalt (eds), *The Industrial Revolution and British Society* (CUP, 1993); E. A. Wrigley, *Continuity, Chance and Change: the character of the Industrial Revolution in England* (CUP, 1988) and E. A. Wrigley, 'The Divergence of England: the growth of the English Economy in the 17th and 18th centuries', *Transactions of the Royal Historical Society* (2000), are among the works that have helped to re-shape thinking on the subject in recent decades. S. King and G. Timmins, *Making Sense of the Industrial Revolution* (MUP, 2001) is an enlightening summary of key issues, and includes an extensive bibliography.

Many aspects of British history not discussed in detail here are covered in masterly fashion elsewhere: the foundations of the financial system in P. G. M. Dickson, *The Financial Revolution in England, 1688–1756* (London: Macmillan, 1967); the rise of British identity in L. Colley, *Britons: forging the nation, 1707–1836* (London: Vintage, 1996); the international context in E. Jones, *The European Miracle:*

environments, economics and geopolitics in the history of Europe and *Asia* (CUP, 1981); rural history in O. Rackham, *The History of the Countryside* (London: Dent, 1986); slavery in H. Thomas, *The Slave Trade: the history of the Atlantic slave trade, 1440–1870* (new edn, London: Phoenix, 2006) and J. Walvin, *Black Ivory: a history of British slavery* (London: Fontana, 1993); management in S. Pollard, *The Genesis of Modern Management* (London: Arnold, 1965); the Empire in D. Cannadine, *Ornamentalism: how the British saw their Empire* (London: Penguin 2001); the international context in R. C. Allen, *The British Industrial Revolution in Global Perspective* (Cambridge University Press, 2009); espionage in J. R. Harris. *Industrial Espionage and Technology Transfer: Britain and France in the eighteenth century* (Aldershot: Ashgate, 1998); and class in E. P. Thompson, *The Making of the English Working Class* (London: Gollancz, 1963). There is an extensive literature on demography, stemming from E. A. Wrigley and R. S. Schofield, *The Population History of England, 1541–1871* (London: Edward Arnold, 1981), which also includes E. A. Wrigley, R. S. Davies, J. E. Oeppen and R. S. Schofield, *English Population History from Family Reconstitution* (CUP, 1997). Some issues in historical demography are summarised in R. A. Houston, *The Population History of Britain and Ireland, 1500–1750* (Basingstoke: Macmillan, 1992). Recent works on the roles of women in industry include K. Honeyman, *Women, Gender and Industrialisation in England, 1700–1870* (New York: St Martin's Press, 2000) and D. Valenze, *The First Industrial Women* (Oxford University Press, 1995).

There are many works on industrial monuments. Outstanding among them is N. Cossons, *The BP Book of Industrial Archaeology* (3rd edn, D&C, 1993). J. Butt and I. Donnachie, *Industrial Archaeology in the British Isles* (London: Elek, 1979) stands out for its coverage of both Great Britain and Ireland and K. Falconer, *Guide to England's Industrial Heritage* (London: Batsford, 1980) provides authoritative accounts of monuments east of Offa's Dyke and south of Hadrian's Wall. Industrial landscapes in England and Wales are discussed in B. Trinder, *The Making of the Industrial Landscape* (3rd edn, London: Phoenix, 1997), while M. Stratton and B. Trinder, *Industrial England*

(London: Batsford/English Heritage, 1997) analyses types of industrial buildings.

An English historian must acknowledge his shortcomings when examining the histories of Ireland, Scotland and Wales. L. M. Cullen, *An Economic History of Ireland since 1660* (2nd edn, London: Batsford, 1987) and C. Rynne, *Industrial Ireland, 1750–1930: an archaeology* (Wilton, Co. Cork: Collins Press, 2006) have proved helpful texts on Ireland, as have G. D. Hay and G. P. Stell, *Monuments of Industry: an illustrated historical record* (RCAHMS, 1986); J. R. Hume, *The Industrial Archaeology of Scotland, I, The Central Lowlands* (London: Batsford, 1976); J. R. Hume, *The Industrial Archaeology of Scotland, II, The Highlands and Islands* (London: Batsford, 1977); T. C. Smout, *A History of the Scottish People, 1560–1830* (London: Fontana, 1987); T. C. Smout, *A History of the Scottish People, 1830–1950* (London: Fontana, 1987) on Scotland. Monuments in Wales are described in G. M. Rees, *The Industrial Archaeology of Wales* (D&C, 1975) and economic history in A. H. Dodd, *The Industrial Revolution in North Wales* (3rd edn, Cardiff: University of Wales Press, 1971) and A. H. John, *The Industrial Development of South Wales, 1750–1850* (2nd edn, Cardiff: Merton Priory Press, 1995).

Works of reference include the complete Ordnance Survey 1:50,000 coverage of Great Britain and many older maps; the *Oxford Dictionary of National Biography*; the *Oxford English Dictionary*; B. R. Mitchell (with P. Deane), *Abstract of British Historical Statistics* (CUP, 1962); J. Langton and R. L. Morris, *Atlas of Industrializing Britain, 1780–1914* (London: Routledge, 1987) and B. Trinder (ed.), *The Blackwell Encyclopedia of Industrial Archeology* (Oxford: Blackwell, 1992).

The quotation that begins the Preface is from W. H. Auden, 'Letter to Lord Byron', *Collected Longer Poems* (London: Faber, 1968), that from Sir James Graham at the start of Chapter 1 from National Library of Wales, *Calendar of Letters and Documents Relating to the Chartist Riots in Montgomeryshire in the Possession of the Rt Hon Earl of Powis* (Aberystwyth: National Library of Wales, 1935) and that which ends it from E. Gibbon, *Gibbon's Autobiography* (ed. M. M. Reese, London: Routledge & Kegan Paul, 1970).

2. Fuelling growth: the unleashing of energy

Broad questions about energy are considered in R. L. Hills, *Power in the Industrial Revolution* (MUP, 1970); R. L. Hills, *Development of Power in the Textile Industry from 1700 to 1930* (Ashbourne: Landmark, 2008); A. E. Musson, 'Industrial motive power in the United Kingdom 1800–70', *EcHR*, 2nd ser., vol. 29 (1976); A. E. Musson and E. Robinson, *Science & Technology in the Industrial Revolution* (MUP, 1969); R. Samuel, 'The Workshop of the World: Steam Power and Hand Technology in mid-Victorian Britain', *History Workshop Journal*, vol. 3 (1977) and G. N. von Tunzelmann, *Steam Power and British Industrialization to 1860* (Oxford: Clarendon Press, 1978). The authoritative work on water power is T. S. Reynolds, *Stronger than a Hundred Men: a history of the vertical waterwheel* (Baltimore MD: Johns Hopkins University Press, 1983). Studies of particular aspects of animal-, water- and wind-power include W. Fairbairn, *A Treatise on Mills and Millwork* (London: Longman, Green, Longman & Roberts, 1861–63); W. Fairbairn, 'On Waterwheels with Ventilated Buckets', *Minutes of the Proceedings of the Institution of Civil Engineers*, vol. 8 (1849);

J. K. Major, *Animal-Powered Engines* (London: Batsford, 1978); J. Shaw, *Water Power in Scotland, 1550–1870* (Edinburgh: John Donald, 1984); J. Smeaton, *An Experimental Enquiry Concerning the Natural Power of Water and Wind to Turn Mills and Other Machines depending on Circular Motion* (London: I. & J. Taylor, 1794, 2nd edn 1796; 3rd edn 1813); L. Syson, *British Water Mills* (London: Batsford, 1965); T. Telford, '*Telford on Mills*, MS with drawings by William Jones, Library of the Institution of Civil Engineers'; R. Wailes, *The English Windmill* (London: Routledge & Kegan Paul, 1954); M. Watts, 'John Padmore's Cranes at Bath and Bristol', *Bristol Industrial Archaeology Society Journal*, 8 (1975); P. N. Wilson, 'The Waterwheels of John Smeaton', *TNS*, vol. 30 (1955–57).

Sources for the development and application of steam power include J. S. Allen, 'The Introduction of the Newcomen Engine from 1710 to 1733', *TNS*, vol. 42 (1969–70), vol. 43 (1970–71), vol. 45 (1972–73); D. B. Barton, *The Cornish Beam Engine* (Truro: Bradford Barton, 1969); M. Boldrin and D. K. Levine, *Against Intellectual*

Monopoly (CUP, 2008); J. Farey, *Treatise on the Steam Engine* (London: Longman, 1827; repr. D&C, 1971); J. R. Harris, 'The Employment of Steam Power in the Eighteenth Century', *History*, vol. 52 (1967); R. L. Hills, *Power from Steam: a history of the stationary steam engine* (CUP, 1988); R. L. Hills, *James Watt I, His Time in Scotland, 1736–74* (Ashbourne: Landmark, 2002); R. L. Hills, *James Watt II, The Years of Toil, 1775–85* (Ashbourne: Landmark, c.2005); R. L. Hills, *James Watt III, Triumph through Adversity, 1785–1819* (Ashbourne: Landmark, c.2006); J. Kanefsky and J. Robey, 'Steam Engines in 18th century Britain: a Quantitative Assessment', *T&C*, 21 (1980); L. T. C. Rolt and J. S. Allen, *The Steam Engine of Thomas Newcomen* (rev. edn. Ashbourne: Landmark, 1997); J. Tann (ed.), *The Selected Papers of Boulton & Watt*, vol. 1 (London, Diploma, 1981); J. Tann, 'Arkwright's Employment of Steam Power: a note of some new evidence', *BusH*, vol. 21 (1979); H. S. Torrens, 'New Light on the Hornblower and Winwood Compound Steam Engine', *Journal of the Trevithick Society*, vol. 9 (1982); H. S. Torrens, 'Some Newly Discovered Letters from Jonathan Hornblower (1753–1815)', *TNS*, vol. 54 (1982–83).

Sources on the coal industry appear in the bibliography for Chapter 6, but to them should be added R. Thorne, 'The Great Northern Railway and the London Coal Trade', in M. Hunter and R. Thorne (eds), *Change at King's Cross* (London: Historical Publications, 1990) and, for the significance of peat, P. R. Bjorling and F. T. Gissing, *Peat: its use and manufacture* (London: Griffin, 1907).

Sources on particular places include S. D. Chapman, 'Sutton Old Mill', *Journal of Industrial Archaeology*, vol. 2 (1965); F. D. Price, 'A North Oxfordshire Parish and its Poor: Wigginton, 1730–1830', *Cake & Cockhorse*, vol. 2 (1962); F. D. Price (ed.), *The Wigginton Constables' Book, 1691–1836* (Banbury Historical Society, 1971); M. Reed (ed.), *Buckinghamshire Probate Inventories, 1661–1714* (Aylesbury: Buckinghamshire Record Society, 1988); F. W. Steer, *Farm and cottage inventories of Mid-Essex 1635 to 1749* (2nd edn, Chichester: Phillimore, 1969); Sir J. Sinclair, *Analysis of the Statistical Account of Scotland* (Edinburgh: Constable, 1825); A. Young, *General View of the Agricultural of the County of Essex* (2 vols, London: Sherwood, Neely & Jones, 1813).

There is enlightening material on many sources of energy in R. G. W. Anderson and J. Jones (eds), *The Correspondence of Joseph Black* (Ashgate, 2012).

3. Making machines

The best general studies of mechanical engineering are A. F. Burstall, *A History of Mechanical Engineering* (London: Faber, 1963); R. A. Buchanan, 'The Diaspora of British Engineering', *T&C*, vol. 27 (1986); A. E. Musson, 'The Origins of Engineering in Lancashire', *Journal of Economic History*, vol. 20 (1960); E. Musson and E. Robinson, *Science and Technology in the Industrial Revolution* (MUP, 1969); L. T. C. Rolt, *Tools for the Job* (rev. edn, London: Historical Metallurgy Society, 1986); W. Steeds, *A History of Machine Tools* (OUP, 1969).

Useful studies of individual engineers and firms include T. S. Aston, *An 18th-century Industrialist: Peter Stubs of Warrington, 1756–1806* (MUP, 1939/1961); J. Coad, *The Portsmouth Block Mills: Bentham, Brunel and the start of the Royal Navy's Industrial Revolution* (EH, 2005); E. S. Dane, *Peter Stubs and the Lancashire Hand Tool Industry* (Altrincham: Sherratt, 1973); J. Tann (ed.), *The Selected Papers of Boulton & Watt*, vol. 1 (London: Diploma Press, 1981); S. B. Donkin, 'Bryan Donkin, FRS, MICE, 1768–1855', *TNS*, vol. 27 (1949–50); Sir D. Gooch, *The Diaries of Sir Daniel Gooch* (1892; repr. Stroud: Nonsuch, 2006); E. Vale, *The Harveys of Hayle* (Truro: Bradford Barton, 1966); J. F. Petree, 'Maudslay, Sons & Field as General Engineers', *TNS*, vol. 15 (1934–35); S. Smiles (ed.), *James Nasmyth: Engineer – an autobiography* (London: John Murray, 1883); J. A. Cantrell, *James Nasmyth and the Bridgewater Foundry: a study of entrepreneurship in the early engineering industry* (Manchester: Chetham Society, 1984); R. L. Hills, *Life and Inventions of Richard Roberts, 1789–1864* (Ashbourne: Landmark, 2002); A. E. Musson, 'Joseph Whitworth and the growth of mass production engineering', *BusH*, vol. 17 (1975); T. R. Harris, *Arthur Woolf: a Cornish engineer, 1766–1837* (Truro: Bradford Barton, 1966).

Material on Wolverton is taken from F. B. Head, *Stokers and Pokers* (London: John Murray, 1849) and B. West, *Town of Trains: the story of Wolverton Works* (Buckingham: Barracuda, 1983) and other railway towns are discussed in P. Billson, *Derby and the Midland Railway* (Derby: Breedon, 1996); J. Cattell and K. Falconer, *Swindon: the legacy of a railway town* (London: HMSO, 1995); W. H. Challoner, *The Social and Economic Development of Crewe, 1780–1923* (MUP, 1950); D. K. Drummond, *Crewe: railway town, company and people, 1840–1914* (Aldershot: Scolar, 1995); A. S. Peck, *The Great Western Railway at Swindon Works* (Poole: Oxford Publishing Co., 1983); J. Simmons, *The Railway in Town and Country, 1830–1914* (D&C, 1986) and B. J. Turton, 'The Railway Towns of Southern England', *Transport History*, vol. 2 (1969).

4. Comprehending structures: the evolution of civil engineering

The history of the engineering professions is described in R. A. Buchanan, *The Engineers: a history of the engineering profession in Britain, 1750–1914* (London: Kingsley, 1989) and P. Corfield, *Power and the Professions* (London: Routledge, 1995). Civil engineering is covered specifically in M. Chrimes (ed.), *The Civil Engineering of Canals and Railways before 1850* (Aldershot: Ashgate, 1997); R. C. Cox, *Civil Engineering Heritage: Ireland* (London: Thomas Telford, 1998); G. Watson, *The Smeatonians: the Society of Civil Engineers* (London: Thomas Telford, 1989) and G. Watson, *The Civils: the story of the Institution of Civil Engineers* (London: Thomas Telford, 1988).

There are many studies of individual engineers. For William Adam see J. Gifford, *William Adam, 1689–1748: the life and times of Scotland's universal architect* (Edinburgh: Mainstream, 1989); for Brunel see S. Brindle, *Brunel: the man who built the world* (London: Weidenfeld & Nicholson, 2005); R. A. Buchanan, *Brunel: the life and times of Isambard Kingdom Brunel* (London: Hambledon, 2002); A. Pugsley (ed.),

The Works of Isambard Kingdom Brunel: an engineering appreciation (London: Institutions of Civil Engineers, 1976); L. T. C. Rolt, *Isambard Kingdom Brunel: a biography* (London: Longmans Green, 1957) and A. Swift, *The Ringing Grooves of Change: Brunel and the coming of the railway to Bath* (Bath: Akeman Press, 2006). Fairbairn's career and thinking can be studied in his own works: *An Account of the Construction of the Britannia and Conway Tubular Bridges* (London: John Weale, 1849); *On the Application of Cast and Wrought Iron to Building Purposes* (London: John Weale, 1854); *Iron: its history, properties and processes of manufacture* (London: A. & C. Black, 1861) and *The Life of Sir William Fairbairn, partly written by himself and completed by William Pole* (London: Longman, 1877). The best account of Hartley is in N. Ritchie-Noakes, *Jesse Hartley: Dock Engineer to the Port of Liverpool, 1824–60* (Liverpool: National Museums & Galleries on Merseyside, 1980), and C. Hadfield and A. W. Skempton, *William Jessop: Engineer* (D&C, 1979) is the only modern study of Jessop. Macadam can be studied in R. Devereux, *John Loudon Macadam: chapters in the history of highways* (OUP, 1936) and J. L. Macadam, *Remarks on the Present System of Road Making* (4th edn, London: Longman, 1816). For Rennie see C. T. G. Boucher, *John Rennie, 1761–1821* (MUP, 1963). C. Hadfield, *Thomas Telford's Temptation* (Cleobury Mortimer: Baldwin, 1993) is a valuable corrective to the 'spin' in T. Telford, *The Life of Thomas Telford, Civil Engineer*, ed. J. Rickman, London: J. & L. G. Hansard, 1838), and is also important for the study of Jessop. See also A. Penfold (ed.), *Thomas Telford: Engineer* (London: Thomas Telford, 1980). K. Downes, *Sir John Vanbrugh: a biography* (London: Sidgwick & Jackson, 1987) and V. Hart, *Sir John Vanbrugh: storyteller in stone* (London & New Haven: Yale University Press, 2008) are authoritative sources on their subject. For Whitworth see G. W. Oxley, 'Robert Whitworth (1737–99): Canal Engineer of Calderdale', *Transactions of the Halifax Antiquarian Society*, vol. 8 (2000).

The standard works on turnpike roads are concerned with administration rather than engineering, but H. Parnell, *A Treatise on Roads* (London: Longman, 1838) contains a wealth of information about how roads were improved. One of the principal projects is detailed in J. Quartermaine, B. Trinder and R. Turner, *Thomas Telford's Holyhead Road* (York: CBA, 2003), while D. McClure, *Tolls and Tacksmen* (Ayr: Ayrshire Archaeological & Natural History Society, 1994) provides a Scottish perspective.

Understanding the history of bridges begins with T. Ruddock, *Arch Bridges and their Builders, 1735–1835* (CUP, 1979), which should be supplemented with N. Cossons and B. Trinder, *The Iron Bridge: symbol of the Industrial Revolution* (2nd edn, Chichester: Phillimore, 2002); J. R. Hume, 'Cast Iron and Bridge-building in Scotland', *IAR*, vol. 2 (1978) and G. Prade, *Ponts et viaducts remarquables d'Europe* [*Remarkable European bridges and viaducts*] (Poitiers: Daniele Brissaud, 1990). Important original sources are W. H. Barlow, 'On the Existence (Practically) of the Line of Equal Horizontal Thrust in Arches and the Mode of Determining it by Geometrical Constructions', *Minutes of the Proceedings of the Institution of Civil Engineers*, vol. 5 (1846); E. Clark, *The Britannia and Conway Tubular Bridges* (London: Day, 1850); C. Labelye, *A Short Account of the Methods made use of in Laying the Foundation of the Piers of Westminster Bridge* (London: W. Straham, 1739); C. Labelye, *A Description of Westminster Bridge* (Dublin: G. & A. Ewing, 1751). Understanding of the development of cast-iron

frames for buildings has substantially changed in recent decades. The best starting points are R. S. Fitzgerald, 'The Development of the Cast Iron Frame in Textile Mills to 1850', *IAR*, vol. 10 (1988) and the collected studies in R. J. M. Sutherland (ed.), *Structural Iron, 1750–1850* (Aldershot: Ashgate, 1997). Important original sources include E. Hodgkinson, 'Theoretical and experimental researches to ascertain the strength and best forms of iron beams', *Memoirs of the Literary and Philosophical Society of Manchester*, 2nd ser., vol. 5 (1831); C. Hutton, *Tracts on Mathematical and Philosophical Subjects* (3 vols, London: Rivington, 1812); G. Snell, 'On the Stability of Arches, with Practical Methods for Determining, According to the Pressures to which they will be Subjected, the best Form of Section, or Variable Depth of Voussoir, for any Given Intrados or Extrados', *Minutes of the Proceedings of the Institution of Civil Engineers*, vol. 5 (1846) and T. Tredgold, *A Practical Essay on the Strength of Cast Iron* (2nd edn, London: J. Taylor, 1824).

C. Hadfield, *The Canal Age* (D&C, 1968) and N. Crowe, *English Heritage Book of Canals* (London: English Heritage & Batsford, 1994) are starting points for the history of canals. Detailed studies of canal engineering include J. Andrew, 'Canal Pumping Engines', *IAR*, vol. 15 (1993); P. S. M. Cross-Rudkin, 'Constructing the Staffordshire & Worcestershire Canal, 1766–72', *TNS*, vol. 75 (2006); D. Tew, *Canal Inclines and Lifts* (Gloucester: Alan Sutton, 1984). R. Hunt, *Oration delivered at Pontcysyllte Aqueduct on its first opening, November 16th 1805, to which is affixed a Letter addressed to the Rt Hon The Earl of Bridgewater* (Shrewsbury: Eddowes, 1806) is a key original source. The development of port installations is detailed in I. S. Greeves, *London Docks, 1800–1980: a civil engineering history* (London: Thomas Telford, 1980); A. Jarvis, *Liverpool Central Docks, 1799–1905: an illustrated history* (Stroud: Sutton, 1991); J. Pudney, *London's Docks* (London: Thames & Hudson, 1975) and N. Ritchie-Noakes, *Liverpool's Historic Waterfront* (London: HMSO, 1984). The Fens are discussed in H. C. Darby, *The Draining of the Fens* (CUP, 1966); R. L. Hills, *Machines, Mills and Uncountable Costly Necessities: a short history of the drainage of the Fens* (Norwich: Goose, 1967) and C. Taylor, *The Cambridgeshire Landscape* (London: Hodder & Stoughton, 1973). Works on utilities in cities include G. Amey, *The Collapse of the Dale Dyke Dam, 1864* (London: Cassell, 1974); J. F. La Trobe Bateman, *History & Description of the Manchester Waterworks* (Manchester: T. J. Day, 1884); G. M. Binnie, *Early Victorian Water Engineers* (London: Thomas Telford, 1981); S. Halliday, *The Great Stink of London: Sir Joseph Bazalgette and the cleansing of the Victorian metropolis* (Stroud: Sutton, 1999).

For contracting, see: T. Coleman, *The Railway Navvies* (London: Hutchinson, 1965); I. Harris, 'Shropshire Navvies: the builders of the Severn Valley Railway', in B. Trinder (ed.), *Victorian Shrewsbury* (Shrewsbury: Shropshire Libraries, 1984); W. Mackenzie, *The Diary of William Mackenzie, the first international railway contractor* (ed. D. Brooke, London: Thomas Telford, 2000); C. Walker, *Thomas Brassey: railway builder* (London: Muller, 1969) and M. Morris, 'Towards an archaeology of navvy huts and settlements of the Industrial Revolution', *Antiquity*, vol. 68 (1994).

S. Winchester, *The Map that Changed the World* (London: Viking, 2001) reveals the relationship between civil engineering and geology.

5. Changing horizons: transport in an industrial society

H. J. Dyos and D. H. Aldcroft, *British Transport: an economic survey from the seventeenth century to the twentieth* (LecUP, 1871) provides an overall view of transport developments.

The standard works on turnpike roads are W. Albert, *The Turnpike Road System in England, 1663–1840* (CUP, 1972) and E. Pawson, *Transport and Economy: the turnpike roads of eighteenth-century Britain* (London: Academic Press, 1977), but S. and B. Webb, *The Story of the King's Highway* (London: Longman, 1913) has a wider timespan, and remains valuable for legal and administrative aspects of the road system. D. Gerhold, *Carriers and Coachmasters: trade and travel before the turnpikes* (Chichester: Phillimore, 2005) and D. Hey, *Packmen, Carriers and Packhorse Roads: trade and communications in North Derbyshire and South Yorkshire* (LecUP, 1980) are outstanding studies of roads around 1700. Accounts of coaching inns include A. Everitt, 'The English Urban Inn, 1560–1760', in A. Everitt (ed.), *Perspectives in English Urban History* (London: Macmillan, 1953); D. Lloyd, P. Howell and M. Richards, *The Feathers* (Ludlow Historical Research Group, 1986) and W. A. Champion, 'John Ashby and the History and Environs of the Lion Inn, Shrewsbury', *Shropshire History & Archaeology*, vol. 75 (2000). The standard account of coaching in Ireland is M. Bianconi and S. J. Watson, *Bianconi: king of the Irish roads* (Dublin: Allen Figgis, 1962). Books which looked back nostalgically to the golden age of coaching such as C. G. Harper, *The Manchester and Glasgow Road* (London: Palmer, 1907); C. G. Harper, *The Holyhead Road* (2nd edn, London: Chapman & Hall, 1902) and W. C. A. Blew, *Brighton and its Coaches* (London: Nimmo, 1894) contain much valuable information. A. Everitt, 'Country Carriers in the Nineteenth Century', *Journal of Transport History*, new ser., vol. 3 (1976) describes a humble but none-the-less important form of public road transport. The last days of coaching are discussed in C. Evason, 'Downhill Journey: stage-coaching in Shrewsbury, 1833–1861', in B. Trinder (ed.), *Victorian Shrewsbury* (Shrewsbury: Shropshire Libraries, 1984). F. M. L. Thompson, *Victorian England: the horse-drawn society* (London: Bedford College, 1970) revolutionised thinking about horse-drawn transport in the railway age. Sources for inventories of inns include M. Reed (ed.), *Buckinghamshire Probate Inventories, 1661–1714* (Buckinghamshire Record Society, 1988), and the Banbury waggon is described in T. W. Boss, *Reminiscences of Old Banbury* (1903; repr. *Cake & Cockhorse*, vol. 16 (2004)).

Original sources on waterways include H. R. de Salis, *Bradshaw's Canals and Navigable Rivers of England and Wales* (London, Blacklock, 1904; repr. D&C, 1969); J. Priestley, *Historical Account of the Navigable Rivers, Canals and Railways of Britain* (London: Longman, 1831; repr. D&C, 1969). Studies of river navigations include D. Hussey, *Coastal and River Trade in Pre-Industrial England: Bristol and its region, 1680–1730* (University of Exeter Press, 2000); M. Prior, *Fisher Row: fishermen, bargemen and canal boatmen in Oxford, 1500–1900* (Oxford: Clarendon Press, 1982); R. Stone, *The River Trent* (Chichester: Phillimore, 2005); D. Summers, *The Great Ouse: the history of a river navigation* (D&C, 1973); B. Trinder, *Barges and Bargemen: a social history of the Upper Severn Navigation, 1660–1900* (Chichester: Phillimore, 2005); B. Trinder and N. Cox (eds), *Miners & Mariners of the Severn Gorge: the probate inventories of Benthall, Broseley, Little Wenlock & Madeley* (Chichester: Phillimore, 2000); T. S. Willan,

The Navigation of the Great Ouse (Bedford: Bedfordshire Historical Society, 1942) and T. S. Willan, *River Navigation in England, 1600–1750* (2nd edn, MUP, 1964). Coastal shipping is covered in T. S. Willan, *The English Coasting Trade, 1660–1750* (2nd edn, MUP, 1967) and ports in G. Jackson, *The History and Archaeology of Ports* (Tadworth: World's Work, 1983). The history of canals is considered generally in C. Hadfield, *The Canal Age* (D&C, 1968) and on a regional basis in the 'Canals of the British Isles' (D&C) series which Hadfield edited. Two studies of individual canals have been particularly useful in this study: H. J. Compton, *The Oxford Canal* (D&C, 1976) and A. H. Faulkner, *The Grand Junction Canal* (Rickmansworth; Walker, 1993). J. D. Porteous, *Canal Ports: the urban achievement of the canal age* (London: Academic Press, 1977) is the standard work on the subject, and C. Giles, *Stourport-on-Severn: pioneer town of the canal age* (EH, 2008) is a more recent account of one port. Social aspects of the canals are covered in W. Freer, *Women and Children of the Cut* (Mold: Railway & Canal Historical Society, 1995); H. Hanson, *The Canal Boatmen, 1760–1914* (MUP, 1975) and G. Smith, *Our Canal Population: a cry from the boats with a remedy* (London: Haughton, 1878). Canal (and railway) politics are analysed in F. C. Mather, *After the Canal Duke: a study of the industrial estates administered by the trustees of the Third Duke of Bridgewater, 1825–1872* (Oxford: Clarendon Press, 1970) and in E. Richards, *The Leviathan of Wealth: the Sutherland fortune in the Industrial Revolution* (London: Routledge & Kegan Paul, 1973). C. G. Lewis, 'Hugh Henshall, 1734–1816', *TNS*, vol. 76 (2006) details the career of a key figure in canal carrying, an aspect of which is illuminated in M. Nevell and J. Walker, *Portland Basin and the Archaeology of the Canal Warehouse* (Tameside: Tameside Metropolitan Borough Council, 2001).

The foundation of scholarship on early railways is M. J. T. Lewis, *Early Wooden Railways* (London: Routledge & Kegan Paul, 1970), to which should be added the proceedings of four annual conferences, A. Guy and J. Rees (eds), *Early Railways: papers from the First International Early Railways Conference* (London: Newcomen Society, 2001); M. J. T. Lewis, *Early Railways 2: papers from the Second International Early Railways Conference* (London: Newcomen Society, 2003); M. R. Bailey (ed.), *Early Railways 3: papers from the Third International Early Railways Conference* (Sudbury: Six Martlets, 2006); G. Boyes (ed.), *Early Railways 4: papers from the Fourth International Early Railways Conference* (Sudbury: Six Martlets, 2010). S. Hughes, *The Archaeology of an Early Railway System: The Brecon Forest Tramroads* (RCAHMW, 1990) is a meticulous study of one of the most ambitious lines of its kind. See also I. Ayris *et al.*, 'The Archaeological Excavation of Wooden Railway Remains at Lambton "D" Pit, Sunderland', *IAR*, vol. 20 (1998) and C. J. A. Robertson, *The Origins of the Scottish Railway System, 1722–1844* (Edinburgh: John Donald, 1983).

The starting points for studying standard-gauge railways are J. Simmons, *The Railway in England and Wales, 1830–1914: the system and its working* (LecUP, 1978); J. Simmons, *The Railway in Town and Country, 1830–1914* (D&C, 1986); J. Simmons, *The Express Train and other Railway Studies* (Nairn: David St John Thomas, 1994); J. Simmons, *The Victorian Railway* (London: Thames & Hudson, 1995). M. Robbins, *The Railway Age* (Harmondsworth: Penguin,

1965) is a collection of perceptive essays. Railway termini are considered in G. Biddle and J. Spence, *The British Railway Station* (D&C, 1977); M. Binney, M. Hamm and A. Foehl, *Great Railway Stations of Europe* (London: Thames & Hudson, 1984) and A. A. Jackson, *London's Termini* (D&C, 1969), while the best studies of individual stations are S. Brindle, *Paddington Station: its history and architecture* (EH, 2004) and J. Simmons, *St Pancras Station* (rev. edn with chapter by R. Thorne, London: Historical Publications, 2003). Other types of railway building are considered in M. Binney and D. Pearce (eds), *Railway Architecture* (London: Orbis, 1979) and M. Hunter and R. Thorne (eds), *Change at King's Cross: from 1800 to the present* (London: Historical Publications, 1990). The social and topographical consequences of railway construction are discussed in J. R. Kellett, *The Impact of Railways on Victorian Cities* (London: Routledge & Kegan Paul, 1969); R. H. G. Thomas, *London's First Railway: the London & Greenwich* (London: Batsford, 1972) and A. Swift, *The Ringing Grooves of Change: Brunel and the coming of the railway to Bath* (Bath: Akeman Press, 2006). Works on railway towns are listed under Chapter 3.

Original sources quoted in this chapter include 'On the Canal' in *Household Words* (11 Sept. 1858), 'The Memoirs of Peter Mottershead, Mason City, Iowa', *Locomotive Engineers' Journal* (May 1908), and British Parliamentary Papers· *Report of the Commissioners on Railway Gauges, Oxford, Worcester & Wolverhampton and Oxford & Rugby Railway Bills*, 1845, XI.

6. Coal mining and coalfield industries

The standard works on the coal industry are the official histories, J. Hatcher, *The History of the British Coal Industry, I, Towards the Age of Coal* (Oxford: Clarendon Press, 1993); M. W. Flinn, *The History of the British Coal Industry, II, 1700–1830: The Industrial Revolution* (Oxford: Clarendon Press, 1984); R. Church, *The History of the British Coal Industry, III, 1830–1913: Victorian Pre-eminence* (Oxford: Clarendon Press, 1986), which should be supplemented by an important article, S. Pollard, 'A New Estimate of British Coal Production, 1750–1850', *EcHR*, vol. 33 (1980), and by J. Benson, *British Coal Miners in the Nineteenth Century: a social history* (Dublin: Gill & Macmillan, 1980). A. R. Griffin, *Coalmining* (London: Longman, 1971) provides an introduction to mining technology, and two works by R. L. Galloway, *A History of Coal Mining in Great Britain* (London: Macmillan, 1882; repr. D&C, 1969) and *Annals of Coal Mining and the Coal Trade* (Colliery Guardian, 1898; repr. D&C, 1971) remain valuable.

Original sources on mining in north-east England include J. C., *The Compleat Collier: or the whole art of Sinking, Getting and Working Coal-Mines &c as is now used in the Northern Parts, especially about Sunderland and Newcastle* (London: G. Conyers, 1708; repr. Newcastle: Frank Graham, 1979); T. Robertson (ed.), *A Pitman's Notebook: the diary of Edward Smith, Houghton colliery viewer, 1749–1751* (Newcastle: Frank Graham, 1970); C. von Oeynhausen and H. von Dechen, *Railways in England, 1826 and 1827* (ed. C. E. Lee and K. R. Gilbert, Cambridge: Heffer/Newcomen Society, 1971) and N. Wood, *A Practical Treatise on Railroads* (London: Knight & Lacey 1825). A. Guy and F. Atkinson, *West Durham: the archaeology of industry* (Chichester: Phillimore, 2008) is an informative study of part of the region. Important articles include A. Raistrick, 'The Steam Engine on Tyneside 1715–78', *TNS*, vol. 17 (1936–37) and A. W. Skempton and A. Andrews, 'Cast-Iron Edge-rails at Walker Colliery, 1798', *TNS*, vol. 48 (1974–75).

The standard work on the Shropshire coalfield is B. Trinder, *The Industrial Revolution in Shropshire* (3rd edn, Chichester: Phillimore, 2000), which can be supplemented by the original sources in B. Trinder (ed.), *The Most Extraordinary District in the World: an anthology of visitors' impressions of Ironbridge, Coalbrookdale and the Shropshire coalfield* (3rd edn, Chichester: Phillimore, 2005); B. Trinder and J. Cox (eds), *Yeomen and Colliers in Telford: the probate inventories of Dawley, Lilleshall, Wellington & Wrockwardine* (Chichester: Phillimore, 1980); B. Trinder and N. Cox, *Miners and Mariners of the Severn Gorge: the probate inventories of Benthall, Broseley, Little Wenlock & Madeley* (Chichester: Phillimore, 2000) and by J. Alfrey and K. Clark, *The Landscape of Industry: patterns of change in the Ironbridge Gorge* (London: Routledge, 1993). For the river Severn see B. Trinder, *Barges and Bargemen: the social history of the Upper Severn Navigation* (Chichester: Phillimore, 2005), and for early railways M. J. T. Lewis, *Early Wooden Railways* (London: Routledge & Kegan Paul, 1970) and B. Trinder, 'Recent Research on Early Shropshire Railways', M. J. T. Lewis (ed.), *Early Railways 2: papers from the Second International Early Railways Conference* (London: Newcomen Society 2003). On the smaller Shropshire coalfields see B. Trinder, *The Industrial Archaeology of Shropshire* (Chichester: Phillimore, 1996).

Coal mining in the north of Ireland is covered in A. Steward, *Coalisland, Co. Tyrone in the Industrial Revolution, 1800–1901* (Dublin: Four Courts Press, 2002), and the Cumberland industry in J. V. Beckett, *Coal and Tobacco: the Lowthers and the economic development of West Cumberland, 1660–1760* (CUP, 1981). Scottish coalfields are described in A. B. Campbell, *The Lanarkshire Miners: a social history of their trade unions* (Edinburgh: John Donald, 1979); G. Douglas and M. Oglethorpe, *Brick, Tile and Fireclay Industries in Scotland* (RCAHMW, 1993); J. Lindsey, *The Canals of Scotland* (D&C, 1968); E. Lord, 'Slavery in Scotland? Scottish collieries, 1606–1799', *TLH*, vol. 37 (2007); M. Oglethorpe: *Scottish Collieries: an inventory of Scotland's coal industry in the nationalised era* (RCAHMS, 2008); J. Turnbull, *The Scottish Glass Industry, 1610–1750* (Edinburgh: Society of Antiquaries of Scotland, 2001) and C. Whatley, *The Scottish Salt Industry, 1570–1850: an economic and social history* (Aberdeen University Press, 1987).

C. Hadfield, *The Canals of Yorkshire and North-east England* (2 vols, D&C, 1972/1973) describes the waterways of the Yorkshire coalfield, while N. Dennis, F. M. Henriques and C. Slaughter, *Coal is Our Life* (London: Eyre & Spottiswoode, 1957) provides a view of the area as relevant to the nineteenth century as to the twentieth.

Quotations from D. H. Lawrence are from *Sons and Lovers* (World Classics edn, 1995) and A. A. M. Inglis (ed.), *D. H. Lawrence, A Selection from Phoenix* (Harmondsworth: Penguin, 1971). Other sources for the East Midlands coalfield include S. D. Chapman, 'Muted Paternalism: the Barber Walker Co. & its Collieries in West Nottinghamshire, 1700–1900', *TTS*, vol. 107 (2003); J. Farey, *A General View of the Agricultural and Minerals of Derbyshire* (3

vols, London: Board of Agriculture, 1811–17); H. Green, 'The
Nottinghamshire & Derbyshire Coalfield before 1850', *Journal of the
Derbyshire Archaeological & Natural History Society*, vol. 56 (1935);
A. R. Griffin, 'Thomas North: Mining Entrepreneur Extraordinary',
TTS, vol. 76 (1972); D. Hey, *Derbyshire: a history* (Lancaster:
Carnegie, 2008); C. Owen, *The Leicestershire and South Derbyshire
Coalfield, 1200–1900* (Ashbourne: Moorland/Leicestershire Museums,
1984) and J. E. Williams, *The Derbyshire Miners: a study in industrial
and social history* (London: Allen & Unwin, 1962). The quotations
from George Eliot come from *Felix Holt: the radical* (Blackwood edn,
n.d.), and material on the Coventry Canal from C. Hadfield, *The
Canals of the East Midlands* (D&C, 1966), and on Gibbs and Canning
from M. Stratton, *The Terracotta Revival: building innovation and the
image of the industrial city in Britain and North America* (London:
Gollancz, 1993).

The standard works on the Black Country are T. J. Raybould,
*The Economic Emergence of the Black Country: a study of the Dudley
Estate* (D&C, 1973); M. B. Rowlands, *Masters and Men in the West
Midland Metalware Trades Before the Industrial Revolution* (MUP, 1975);
R. H. Trainor, *Black Country Elites: the exercise of authority in an indus-
trialized area, 1830–1900* (OUP, 1993) and *VCH Staffordshire*, vol. 17,
West Bromwich, Smethwick and Walsall (OUP, 1976).

Material on north Staffordshire is drawn from D. Baker, *Potworks:
the industrial architecture of the Staffordshire Potteries* (RCHME, 1991);
R. Christiansen and R. W. Miller, *The North Staffordshire Railway*
(D&C, 1971); C. Hawke-Smith, 'The Potteries Landscape, 1500–1820
AD', *Staffordshire Archaeological Studies*, new ser., no. 4 (1987);
D. M. Palliser, *The Staffordshire Landscape* (London: Hodder &
Stoughton, 1976); A. D. M. Phillips (ed.), *The Potteries: continuity and
change in a Staffordshire conurbation* (Stroud: Sutton, 1993); R. Sherlock,
The Industrial Archaeology of Staffordshire (D&C, 1976); D. M. Smith
'Industrial Architecture in the Potteries', *North Staffordshire Journal of
Field Studies*, vol. 5 (1964); L. Weatherill, *The Pottery Trade and North
Staffordshire, 1660–1760* (MUP, 1971).

An abundance of scholarship chronicles the Lancashire coalfield,
including B. L. Anderson and P. J. M. Stoney, *Commerce, Industry and
Transport: studies in economic change on Merseyside* (LivUP, 1983);

T. C. Barker, *The Glassmakers: Pilkington: the rise of an international
company, 1826–1976* (London: Weidenfeld & Nicholson, 1977);
T. C. Barker and J. R. Harris, *A Merseyside Town in the Industrial
Revolution: St Helens, 1750–1900* (LivUP, 1954); A. J. Fenwick,
Chemical Classics: some founders of the chemical industry (2 vols, London
and Manchester: Sherratt & Hughes, 1906); D. W. F. Hardie, *A History
of the Chemical Industry in Widnes* (London: Imperial Chemical
Industries, 1955); P. Hyland, *The Herculaneum Pottery: Liverpool's
forgotten glory* (LivUP, 2005); J. Langton, *Geographical Change
and the Industrial Revolution: coalmining in south-west Lancashire,
1590–1799* (CUP, 1979); J. Langton, 'Liverpool and its Hinterland
in the late eighteenth century', in B. L. Anderson and P. J. M. Stoney
(eds), *Commerce, Industry and Transport: studies in economic change
on Merseyside* (LivUP, 1983); J. Langton, 'The Industrial Revolution
and the Regional Geography of England', *Transactions of the British
Institute of Geographers*, vol. 9 (1983).

Works on the Forest of Dean include C. Hart, *The Industrial
History of Dean with an Introduction to its Industrial Archaeology*
(D&C, 1971); S. Mills *et al.*, *A Guide to the Industrial Archaeology of
Gloucestershire* (Telford: Association for Industrial Archaeology, 1992);
R. Millward and A. Robinson, *Landscapes of Britain: the Welsh Marches*
(London: Hodder & Stoughton, 1971); H. G. Nicholls, *The Forest of
Dean: an historical and descriptive account* (London: Murray, 1858) and
VCH Gloucestershire, vol. 5 (Oxford University Press, 1966). Bristol
and the Somerset coalfield are covered in A. Buchanan and N. Cossons,
The Industrial Archaeology of the Bristol Region (D&C, 1969);
K. Clew, *The Somersetshire Coal Canal and Railways* (D&C, 1970) and
C. G. Down and A. J. Warrington, *The History of the Somerset Coalfield*
(Radstock: Radstock Museum, 2005).

Works of particular relevance to coal mining in South Wales
include S. Hughes *et al.*, *Collieries of Wales: Engineering & Architecture*
(RCAHMW, n.d.); A. H. John, *The Industrial Development of South
Wales, 1750–1850* (2nd edn, Cardiff: Merton Priory Press, 1995);
J. B. Lowe, *Welsh Industrial Workers' Housing, 1775–1875* (Cardiff:
National Museum of Wales, 1977) and W. G. Thomas, *Welsh Coal
Mines* (Cardiff: National Museum of Wales, 1977).

7. 'Iron in the blood': the making of iron and steel

The best summary of the iron industry remains J. R. Harris, *The British
Iron Industry, 1700–1850* (Basingstoke: Macmillan Education, 1988), and
the most fluent explanation of its technology is W. K. V. Gale, *Iron and
Steel* (London: Longmans, 1969) with which should be coupled the
same author's *The Iron and Steel Industry: a dictionary of terms* (D&C,
1971). Three earlier economic histories also contain important material:
T. S. Ashton, *Iron and Steel in the Industrial Revolution* (MUP, 1951);
A. Birch, *The Economic History of the British Iron and Steel Industry,
1784–1879* (London: Cass, 1967) and C. K. Hyde, *Technological
Change and the British Iron Industry, 1700–1870* (Princeton: Princeton
University Press, 1977). The development of puddling is considered in R. Hayman, 'The Cranage Brothers and Eighteenth-century
Forge Technology', *HM*, vol. 38 (2004); R. Hayman, 'Charcoal Iron-
making in Nineteenth-century Shropshire', *EcHR*, vol. 61 (2008)
and R. A. Mott, *Henry Cort – the great finer, creator of puddled iron*

(London: The Metals Society, 1983). W. E. Minchinton, *The British
Tinplate Industry: a history* (Oxford: Clarendon Press, 1957) is the
standard work on the subject. P. Riden, *A Gazetteer of Charcoal-fired
Blast Furnaces in Great Britain in Use Since 1660* (Cardiff: Riden, 1987)
and P. Riden, 'Eighteenth-century Blast Furnaces: a New Checklist',
Journal of the Historical Metallurgy Society, vol. 12 (1978) are essential
works of reference.

The Wealden industry is described comprehensively in H. Cleere
and D. Crossley, *The Iron Industry of the Weald* (LecUP, 1985), but
was also the subject of a remarkable pioneering study by E. Straker,
Wealden Iron (London: Bell, 1931). J. Dinn, 'Dyfi Furnace Excavations,
1987–92', *PMA*, vol. 22 (1988) is an important archaeological
study. The principal sources for the career of Abraham Darby I
are B. Trinder, *The Industrial Revolution in Shropshire* (3rd edn,
Chichester: Phillimore, 2000); N. Cox, 'Imagination and Innovation

of an Industrial Pioneer: the first Abraham Darby', *IAR*, vol. 12 (1990); P. W. King, 'Sir Clement Clarke and the Adoption of Coal in Metallurgy', *TNS*, vol. 73 (2001) and entries in *ODNB*. For John Wilkinson see the article by John Harris in *ODNB* and N. C. Solden, *John Wilkinson, 1728–1808: English ironmaster and inventor* (Lewiston, NY: Edwin Mellen Press, 1998). The standard work on the Stour Valley forges and associated undertakings is L. Ince, *The Knight Family and the British Iron Industry* (Birmingham: Ferric Publications, 1991), and the Black Country is also covered in M. B. Rowlands, *Masters and Men in the West Midland Metalware Trades Before the Industrial Revolution* (MUP, 1975) and T. J. Raybould, *The Economic Emergence of the Black Country: a study of the Dudley Estate* (D&C, 1973). For ironworks in south Shropshire see B. Trinder, *The Industrial Archaeology of Shropshire* (Chichester: Phillimore, 1996).

The chief sources for iron making in South Wales are J. P. Addis, *The Crawshay Dynasty* (Cardiff: University of Wales Press, 1957); M. Atkinson and C. Baber, *The Growth and Decline of the South Wales Iron Industry, 1760–1880* (Cardiff: University of Wales Board of Celtic Studies, 1987); M. Elsas (ed.), *Iron in the Making: Dowlais Iron Company Letters, 1782–1860* (Cardiff: Glamorgan County Council, 1960); C. Evans (ed.), *The Letterbook of Richard Crawshay, 1788–1797* (Cardiff: South Wales Record Society, 1990); C. Evans, 'The Labyrinth of Flames': work and social conflict in early industrial Merthyr Tydfil* (Cardiff: University of Wales Press, 1993); J. Gross (ed.), *The Diary of Charles Wood of Cyfarthfa Ironworks, Merthyr Tydfil, 1766–1767* (Cardiff: Merton Priory Press, 2001); L. Ince, *The South Wales Iron Industry, 1750–1885* (Birmingham: Ferric Publications, 1993); L. Ince, *Neath Abbey and the Industrial Revolution* (Stroud: Tempus, 2001); A. H. John, *The Industrial Development of South Wales, 1750–1850* (2nd edn, Cardiff: Merton Priory Press, 1995); J. B. Lowe, *Welsh Industrial Workers' Housing, 1775–1875* (Cardiff: National Museum of Wales, 1977); P. Wakelin, *Blaenavon Ironworks and World Heritage Landscape* (Cardiff: Cadw, 2006); P. Wakelin, 'Scouring the Land: Early Iron Ore Extraction at Blaenavon', *Monmouthshire Antiquary*, vol. 12 (1996). For the Dean ironworks see C. Hart, *The Industrial History of Dean with an Introduction to its Industrial Archaeology* (D&C, 1971); B. L. C. Johnson, 'The Foley Partnerships: the iron industry at the end of the charcoal era', *EcHR*, 2nd ser., vol. 4 (1952); S. Mills *et al.*, *A Guide to the Industrial Archaeology of Gloucestershire* (Telford: Association for Industrial Archaeology, 1992); H. G. Nicholls, *Iron-making in the Olden Times* (London: Bartlett, 1866); F. M. Osborn, *The Story of the Mushets* (London: Nelson, 1952) and *VCH Gloucestershire*, vol. 5 (OUP, 1966).

Iron making in Sheffield is covered in D. Bayliss (ed.), *A Guide to the Industrial Archaeology of South Yorkshire* (Telford: Association for Industrial Archaeology, 1995); K. C. Barraclough, *Sheffield Steel* (Sheffield: Sheffield City Museums, 1989); K. C. Barraclough, *Benjamin Huntsman, 1704–76* (Sheffield City Libraries, 1976); K. C. Barraclough, *Steel-making before Bessemer* (2 vols, London: Metals Society, 1981/1984); J. L. Fearns, 'The Walker Company of Rotherham', *Industrial Archaeology* vol. 12 (1977); D. Hey, *The Rural Metalworkers of the Sheffield Region* (LecUP, 1972); D. Hey, *The Fiery Blades of Hallamshire: Sheffield and its neighbourhood, 1660–1740* (LecUP, 1991) and S. Pollard, *A History of Labour in Sheffield* (LivUP, 1959). One of the principal iron-making enterprises in Leeds is discussed in G. Davies, M. Stenton, R. Fitzgerald and R. Kinchin-Smith, *Monk Bridge Ironworks* (York Archaeological Trust, 2011). Sources for Furness included A. G. Banks, *H. W. Schneider of Barrow and Bowness* (Kendal: Titus Wilson, 1984); M. Boden, *Furness Iron* (EH, 2000) and J. D. Marshall, *An Economic History of Furness, 1711–1900, and the Town of Barrow, 1757–1897, with an Epilogue* (1958; repr. 1981, Beckermet: M. Moon). For the Lancashire industry see A. Birch, *The Haigh Ironworks, 1789–1856: a nobleman's enterprise during the Industrial Revolution* (Manchester: John Rylands Library, 1953); J. Langton, *Geographical Change and the Industrial Revolution: coalmining in south-west Lancashire, 1590–1799* (CUP, 1979) and M. Nevell and J. Walker, *The Park Bridge Ironworks and the Archaeology of Wrought Iron in North-West England, 1600–1700* (University of Manchester Archaeology Unit, 1999), and for the Scottish industry A. Miller, *The Rise and Progress of Coatbridge and Surrounding Neighbourhood* (Glasgow: Dundyvan Ironworks, 1864); D. L. Smith, *The Dalmellington Iron Company* (D&C, 1967). John Marley, 'Cleveland Ironstone … Its Discovery, Application and Results in Connection with the Ironworks in the North of England', *Transactions of the Institution of Mechanical Engineers*, vol. 5 (1856–57) is the classic account of the industry's origins.

8. Precious veins: non-ferrous metals

The ubiquitous John Taylor is well described in R. Burt, *John Taylor: mining entrepreneur and engineer, 1779–1863* (Ashbourne: Moorland, 1977). Cornish mining is covered in D. B. Barton, *A History of Copper Mining in Cornwall and Devon* (Truro: Barton, 1961) and D. B. Barton, *A History of Tin Mining and Smelting in Cornwall* (Truro: Barton, 1967).

The standard works on the copper industry are T. C. Barker and J. R. Harris, *A Merseyside Town in the Industrial Revolution: St Helens, 1750–1900* (LivUP, 1954); S. G. Checkland, *The Mines of Tharsis: Roman, French and British enterprise in Spain* (London: Allen & Unwin, 1967); K. Davies and C. J. Williams, *The Greenfield Valley* (Hawarden: Clwyd Record Office, 1977); D. Gwyn, *Gwynedd: Inheriting a Revolution: the archaeology of industrialisation in North-West Wales* (Chichester: Phillimore, 2006); J. R. Harris, *The Copper King: a biography of Thomas Williams of Llandinan* (LivUP, 1964); S. Hughes, *Copperopolis: landscapes of the early industrial period in Swansea* (Aberystwyth: RCAHMW, 2000); G. Malmgreen, *Silk Town: industry and culture in Macclesfield, 1750–1835* (Hull: Hull University Press, 1985); D. M. Palliser, *The Staffordshire Landscape* (London: Hodder & Stoughton, 1976); T. Pennant, *The History of the Parishes of Whiteford and Holywell* (London: White, 1796); and R. R. Toomey, *Vivian and Sons, 1809–1924* (Birmingham: Garland, 1985).

Lead mines in northern England are described in R. T. Clough, *The Lead Smelting Mills of the Yorkshire Dales and Northern Pennines* (2nd edn, Keighley: privately published, 1980); R. Fieldhouse and B. Jennings, *A History of Richmond and Swaledale* (Chichester: Phillimore, 1978); A. Guy and F. Atkinson, *West Durham: the archaeology of industry* (Chichester: Phillimore, 2008); B. Jennings (ed.), *A

History of Nidderdale (3rd edn, Pateley Bridge: Nidderdale History Group, 1992); A. Raistrick, *Two Centuries of Industrial Welfare* (2nd edn, Ashbourne, Moorland, 1977); A. Raistrick, *The West Riding of Yorkshire Landscape* (London: Hodder & Stoughton, 1970); A. Raistrick, *The Lead Industry of Wensleydale and Swaledale* (2 vols, Ashbourne: Moorland, 1975); A. Raistrick and B. Jennings, *Lead Mining in the Pennines* (London: Longman, 1973), those in the Isle of Man in L. E. Garrad, *et al.*, *The Industrial Archaeology of the Isle of Man* (D&C, 1972), and those in Wales and Shropshire in F. Brook and M. Allbutt, *The Shropshire Lead Mines* (Ashbourne: Moorland, 1973), R. Burt, P. White and R. Burnley, *The Mines of Shropshire and Montgomeryshire with Cheshire and Staffordshire: metalliferous and associated minerals, 1845–1913* (University of Exeter Press, 1990); P.-L. Coste and A. A. Perdonnet, 'Traitement metallurgique des minerais de plomb en Angleterre' [Smelting of Lead Ores in Reverberatory Furnaces as performed in Great Britain], *Annales des Mines*, vol. 7

(1830; repr. Eindhoven, De Archaeologische Pers, Eindhoven, 1987); A. H. Dodd, *The Industrial Revolution in North Wales* (3rd edn, Cardiff: University of Wales Press, 1971); W. J. Lewis, *Lead Mining in Wales* (Cardiff: University of Wales Press, 1967); R. Millward and A. Robinson, *Landscapes of North Wales* (London: Hodder & Stoughton, 1978); D. M. Rees. *The Industrial Archaeology of Wales* (D&C, 1975) and B. Trinder, *The Industrial Archaeology of Shropshire* (Chichester: Phillimore, 1996).

For the brass industry see A. Buchanan and N. Cossons, *The Industrial Archaeology of the Bristol Region* (D&C, 1969); J. Day, *Bristol Brass* (D&C, 1973); J. Day, 'The Continental Origins of Bristol Brass', *IAR*, vol. 7 (1984). The standard work on pewter manufacture is J. Hatcher and T. C. Barker, *A History of British Pewter* (London. Longman, 1974), and lead processing is comprehensively described in D. J. Rowe, *Lead Manufacturing in Great Britain* (London: Croom Helm, 1983).

9. 'The spinners' ardent toil': the textile industries

The quoted inventories are published in B. Trinder and J. Cox (eds), *Yeomen and Colliers in Telford: the probate inventories of Dawley, Lilleshall, Wellington and Wrockwardine* (Chichester: Phillimore, 1980), and M. Reed (ed.), *Buckinghamshire Probate Inventories, 1661–1714* (Aylesbury: Buckinghamshire Record Society, 1988). Dr Nancy Cox supplied copies of those of Allen and Wynne.

The literature on textile manufacturing and textile mills is vast. The classic works are E. Baines, *History of the Cotton Manufacture in Great Britain* (London: Fisher & Jackson, 1835; repr. London: Cass, 1966); E. Baines, *An Account of the Woollen Manufacture of England* (London: W. Mackenzie, 1875; repr. D&C, 1970); T. Ellison, *The Cotton Trade of Great Britain* (1886; repr. London: Cass, 1968); W. Radcliffe, *Origins of the New System of Manufactures commonly called Power Loom Weaving* (Stockport: Thomas King 1828); William Felkin, *A History of the Machine-Wrought Hosiery and Lace Manufactures* (London: Longman Green, 1867; repr. D&C, 1967); G. Turnbull, *A History of Calico Printing in Great Britain* (Altrincham: Sherratt, 1951); A. P. Wadsworth and J. de L. Mann, *The Cotton Trade and Industrial Lancashire, 1600–1780* (MUP, 1931).

General surveys of the industry include S. D. Chapman, *The Cotton Industry in the Industrial Revolution* (London: Economic History Society, 1972); S. D. Chapman, 'Fixed Capital Formation in the British Cotton Industry, 1770–1815', *EcHR*, 2nd ser., vol. 23 (1970); M. M. Edwards, *The British Cotton Trade, 1780–1815* (MUP, 1967). J. Addy, *The Textile Revolution* (London: Longman, 1976) is a useful collection of documents.

J. Tann, *The Development of the Factory* (London: Cornmarket, 1970) provides an introduction to early textile mills, while two studies by the former Royal Commission, C. Giles and I. Goodall, *Yorkshire Textile Mills: the buildings of the Yorkshire textile industry, 1770–1930* (HMSO, 1992); M. Williams, *Cotton Mills in Greater Manchester* (Preston: Carnegie, 1992) have an significance beyond the regions they describe. An important theme in factory development is discussed in C. Giles, 'Housing the Loom, 1790–1850: a study of industrial building in a transitional period', *IAR*, vol. 16 (1993), and early mills are analysed in S. D. Chapman, 'The Textile Factory before Arkwright:

a typology of factory development', *Business History Review*, vol. 48 (1974). K. Honeyman. *Child Workers in England: parish apprentices and the making of the early industrial labour force* (Farnham: Ashgate, 2007) reflects practices in several sectors and regions.

Richard Arkwright's life is described in S. D. Chapman, 'The Arkwright Mills – Colquhoun's Census of 1788 and Archaeological Evidence', *IAR*, vol. 6 (1981–82); R. S. Fitton, *The Arkwrights: spinners of fortune* (MUP, 1989); R. S. Fitton and A. P. Wadsworth, *The Strutts and the Arkwrights* (MUP, 1958); R. L. Hills, *Richard Arkwright and Cotton Spinning* (London: Priory, 1973); J. Tann, 'Arkwright's Employment of Steam Power: a note of some new evidence', *BusH*, vol. 21 (1979) and G. Unwin, *et al.*, *Samuel Oldknow and the Arkwrights* (Manchester: MUP, 1924). C. Aspin, *The Water Spinners* (Helmshore Local History Society, 2003) is a comprehensive survey of Arkwright-style mills, while Derwent Valley Mills Partnership, *Nomination of the Derwent Valley Mills for Inscription on the World Heritage List* (Matlock: Derwent Valley Mills Partnership, 2000) provides an authoritative account of Arkwright's influence in Derbyshire.

Studies of Lancashire and Cheshire include O. Ashmore, *The Industrial Archaeology of Lancashire* (D&C, 1969); O. Ashmore, *The Industrial Archaeology of North-West England and Where to Find It* (MUP, 1982); C. Aspin and S. D. Chapman, *James Hargreaves and the Spinning Jenny* (Helmshore, 1964); S. Bamford, *Early Days* (London: Simpkin, Marshall & Co., 1849); D. Beattie, *A History of Blackburn* (Lancaster: Carnegie, 2007); D. Bythell, *The Hand Loom Weavers* (CUP, 1969); R. L. Greenall, *The Making of Victorian Salford* (Lancaster: Carnegie, 2000); D. Gurr and J. Hunt, *The Cotton Mills of Oldham* (Oldham Cultural & Information Services, 1983); I. Haynes, *Cotton in Ashton* (Tameside Libraries & Arts Committee, 1987); I. Haynes, *Stalybridge Cotton Mills* (Manchester: Neil Richardson, 1990); I. Haynes, *Mossley Textile Mills* (Manchester: Neil Richardson, 1996); R. McNeil and M. Nevell, *A Guide to the Industrial Archaeology of Greater Manchester* (Telford: Association for Industrial Archaeology, 2000); N. Morgan, *Vanished Dwellings: early industrial housing in a Lancashire cotton town: Preston* (Preston: Mullion, 1990); A. E. Musson, 'The Origins of Engineering in Lancashire', *Journal* of Economic History, vol. 20 (1960); M. Nevell, 'The Archaeology of Industrialisation and the Textile Industry: the example of Manchester and the south-western Pennine uplands during the 18th century (Part I)', IAR, vol. 30 (2008); M. Nevell (ed.), From Farmer to Factory Owner: models, methodology and industrialisation (Manchester: CBA North West, 2003); M. Nevell and D. George (eds), A Guide to the Industrial Archaeology of Lancashire (Telford: Association for Industrial Archaeology, 2007); M. Nevell and J. Walker, Tameside in Transition: the archaeology of the Industrial Revolution in two North-west lordships, 1642–1870 (Tameside Metropolitan Borough Council, 1999); M. B. Rose (ed.), The Lancashire Cotton Industry: a history since 1700 (Preston: Lancashire County Books, 1996); W. J. Smith, Saddleworth Buildings (Saddleworth Historical Society, 1987); J. G. Timmins, Handloom Weavers' Cottages in Central Lancashire (Lancaster: University of Lancaster, 1977); J. G. Timmins, The Last Shift: the decline of handloom weaving in nineteenth-century Lancashire (MUP, 1993); J. F. Wilson (ed.), King Cotton: a tribute to Douglas A. Farnie (Lancaster: Crucible, 2009).

The Midlands cotton industry is considered in S. D. Chapman, The Early Factory Masters (D&C, 1967); S. D. Chapman, 'The Peels in the Early English Cotton Industry', BusH, vol. 11 (1969); N. Greatrex, 'The Robinson Enterprises at Papplewick, Nottinghamshire, Parts I & II', IAR, vol. 9 (1986–87); A. Menuge, 'The Cotton Mills of the Derbyshire Derwent and its tributaries', IAR, vol. 16 (1993); M. Stratton and B. Trinder, 'The Foundations of a Textile Community: Sir Robert Peel at Fazeley', TexH, vol. 26 (1995).

The best introduction to the flax industry is provided by W. G. Rimmer, Marshall's of Leeds, Flax-spinners, 1788–1886 (CUP, 1960), to which should be added B. Trinder, 'Ditherington Flax Mill – a Re-evaluation', TexH, vol. 23 (1992); B. Trinder, The Industrial Archaeology of Shropshire (Chichester: Phillimore, 1996) and H. J. Mackenzie, The Story of Barnsley Linen (Barnsley: Hickson, Lloyd & King, 1949). Irish textile manufacturing is discussed in G. H. Bassett, County Down Guide and Directory (1886; repr. Belfast: Friar's Bush Press, 1988); G. Camblin, The Town in Ulster (Belfast: William Mullen, 1951); F. Hammond, Antrim Coast and Glens: industrial heritage (Belfast: HMSO, 1991); W. A. McCutcheon, The Industrial Archaeology of Northern Ireland (Belfast: HMSO, 1980); S. Rothery, A Field Guide to the Buildings of Ireland (Dublin: Lilliput, 1997) and C. Rynne, Industrial Ireland, 1750–1930: an archaeology (Wilton, Co. Cork: Collins Press, 2006).

The most recent account of the silk industry in Macclesfield and Congleton is A. Calladine and J. Fricker, East Cheshire Textile Mills (London: RCHME, 1993) to which should be added M. Fletcher, 'Old Mill Congleton Cheshire – Brindley's Grand Design', IAR, vol. 20 (2008), while the history of Leek and of Alstonefield is detailed in M. W. Greenslade (ed.), VCH Staffordshire, vol. 7, Leek and the Moorlands (OUP, 1996). The social history of Macclesfield is considered in Gail Malmgreen, Silk Town: industry and culture in Macclesfield, 1750–1835 (Hull: Hull University Press, 1985), while Sunday schools are examined in a national context in T. W. Lacquer,

Religion and Respectability: Sunday schools and working-class culture, 1780–1850 (New Haven: Yale University Press, 1976). A. Rushton, My Life, as Farmer's Boy, Factory Lad, Teacher and Preacher, 1821–1909 (Manchester: S. Clarke, 1909) describes life in Macclesfield towards the end of its period of rapid growth. J. Prest, The Industrial Revolution in Coventry (OUP, 1960) places the ribbon industry in its urban context, while B. Trinder, 'Sent to Coventry: the great migration of Banbury plush weavers', Cake & Cockhorse, vol. 17 (2008) identifies a significant migration of textile workers. Mill sites in eastern England are discussed in J. Booker, Essex and the Industrial Revolution (Chelmsford: Essex County Council, 1974); D. Alderton and J. Booker, The Batsford Guide to the Industrial Archaeology of East Anglia (London: Batsford, 1980) and D. C. Coleman, Courtaulds: an economic and social history (2 vols, OUP, 1969).

Accounts of the woollen industry include M. L. Baumber, From Revival to Regency: a history of Keighley and Haworth, 1740–1820 (Keighley: Crabtree, 1983); K. Falconer, 'Mills of the Stroud Valleys', IAR, vol. 16 (1993); G. Firth, Bradford and the Industrial Revolution (Halifax: Ryburn, 1990); D. Gregory, Regional Transformation and Industrial Revolution: a geography of the Yorkshire woollen industry (London: Macmillan, 1982); P. Hudson, The Genesis of Industrial Capital: a study of the West Riding wool textile industry, c.1750–1850 (CUP, 1986); D. T. Jenkins and K. G. Pointing, The British Wool Textile Industry, 1770–1914 (London: Heinemann, 1982); J. de L. Mann, The Cloth Industry in the West of England from 1640 to 1880 (Oxford: Clarendon Press, 1971); K. Ponting, The Woollen Industry of South-west England (Bath: Adams & Dart, 1971); M. Stratton and B. Trinder, 'Stanley Mill, Gloucestershire', PMA, vol. 22 (1988); J. Tann, Gloucestershire Woollen Mills (D&C, 1967). A. H. Dodd, The Industrial Revolution in North Wales (3rd edn, Cardiff: University of Wales Press, 1971) discusses the industry in Montgomeryshire.

Modern works which discuss the hosiery and lace industries include D. Hey, Derbyshire: a history (Lancaster: Carnegie, 2008); W. G. Hoskins, The Making of the English Landscape: Leicestershire (London: Hodder & Stoughton, 1957); D. M. Smith, The Industrial Archaeology of the East Midlands (D&C, 1965) and VCH Leicestershire, vol. 4, The City of Leicester (OUP, 1958).

Studies of the Scottish textile industries include W. Brown, Early Days in a Dundee Mill, 1819–1823 (ed. J. Hume, Dundee: Abertay Historical Society, 1980); A. J. Cooke, 'Richard Arkwright and the Scottish Cotton Industry', TexH, vol. 10 (1979); A. J. Cooke, 'Cotton and the Scottish Highland Clearances: the development of Spinningdale, 1791–1806', TexH, vol. 26 (1995), A. J. Cooke (ed.), Stanley: its history and development (Dundee: University of Dundee Department of Extra-Mural Education, 1977); J. Hume, The Industrial Archaeology of Scotland, I, The Lowlands and Borders (London: Batsford, 1976); J. Hume, The Industrial Archaeology of Scotland, II, The Highlands and Islands (London: Batsford, 1977); G. M. Mitchell, 'The English and Scottish Cotton Industries', Scottish Historical Review, vol. 22 (1925) and M. Watson, Jute and Flax Mills in Dundee (Dundee: Hutton Press, 1990).

10. Rags to riches: a revolution in paper

The standard works on the industry are D. C. Coleman, *The British Paper Industry, 1495–1860 – a study in industrial growth* (Oxford: Clarendon Press, 1958); A. H. Shorter, *Paper-making in the British Isles: a historical and geographical study* (D&C, 1971) and A. D. Spicer, *The Paper Trade: a descriptive and historical survey from the commencement of the nineteenth century* (London: Methuen, 1907). Informative surveys include S. Freese, *The Watermills of Buckinghamshire* (ed. M. Farley, E. Legg and J. Venn, Aylesbury: Buckinghamshire Archaeological Society, 2007); J. M. Preston, *Industrial Medway: an historical survey* (Rochester: Preston, 1977); J. Shaw, *Water Power in Scotland,* 1550–1870 (Edinburgh: John Donald, 1984); J. J. Sheahan, *History & Topography of Buckinghamshire* (London: Longman, 1862) and A. G. Thompson, *The Paper Industry in Scotland* (Edinburgh: Scottish Academic Press, 1974). Individual companies are discussed in J. Evans, *Time and Chance: the story of Arthur Evans and his forebears* (London: Longmans Green, 1943); J. Evans, *The Endless Web, John Dickinson & Co. Ltd, 1804–1954* (London: Cape, 1955) and C. Porteous, *Pill Boxes and Bandages: a documentary biography of the first two generations of Robinsons of Chesterfield, 1839–1916* (Chesterfield: Robinson, n.d. c.1961).

11. Great cities, old and new

Two volumes of the *Cambridge Urban History*, P. Clark (ed.), *The Cambridge Urban History of Britain, II, 1540–1840* (CUP, 2000) and M. Daunton (ed.), *The Cambridge Urban History of Britain, III, 1840–1950* (CUP, 2000) are the best guide to the topics discussed in this chapter, and can be supplemented with P. Borsay, *The Eighteenth-century Town: a reader in English urban history, 1688–1820* (London: Longman, 1990); A. Briggs, *Victorian Cities* (Pelican edn, Harmondsworth: Penguin, 1968); D. Cannadine, *Lords and Landlords: the aristocracy and the towns, 1774–1967* (LecUP, 1980); C. W. Chalklin, *The Provincial Towns of Georgian England: a study of the building process, 1740–1820* (London: Arnold, 1974); P. J. Corfield, *The Impact of English Towns, 1700–1800* (OUP, 1982); R. Dennis, *English Industrial Cities of the Nineteenth Century* (CUP, 1984); H. J. Dyos (ed.), *The Study of Urban History* (London: Arnold, 1968); H. J. Dyos and M. Wolff (eds), *The Victorian City: images and realities* (2 vols, London: Routledge & Kegan Paul, 1973); R. J. Morris and R. Rodger, *The Victorian City: a reader in English urban history, 1820–1914* (London: Longman, 1993) and R. Porter, *Enlightenment Britain and the Creation of the Modern World* (London: Penguin, 2001); T. Hunt, *Building Jerusalem: the rise and fall of the Victorian city* (London: Weidenfeld & Nicolson, 2004).

General works on housing and public health include S. D. Chapman, *The History of Working-class Housing: a symposium* (D&C, 1971); C. Creighton, *A History of Epidemics in Britain* (2nd edn, 2 vols, London: Cass, 1965); E. Gauldie, *Cruel Habitations: a history of working-class housing, 1780–1918* (London: Allen & Unwin, 1974); N. Morgan, *Deadly Dwellings: housing and health in a Lancashire cotton town: Preston, 1840–1914* (Preston: Mullion, 1993); S. Muthesius, *The English Terraced House* (London: Yale University Press, 1982); D. Rubinstein, *Victorian Homes* (D&C, 1974); J. G. Williamson, *Coping with City Growth During the English Industrial Revolution* (CUP, 1990) and A. S. Wohl, *Endangered Lives: public health in Victorian Britain* (London: Dent, 1983). For urban colonies see J. D. Marshall, 'Colonisation as a Factor in the Planting of Towns in North-West England', in H. J. Dyos (ed.), *The Study of Urban History* (London: Arnold, 1968); G. Timmins, 'Textile Colonies and Settlement Growth in Lancashire, c.1780–c.1850', in J. F. Wilson (ed.), *King Cotton* (Lancaster: Crucible, 2009). T. Hunt, *Building Jerusalem: the rise and fall of the Victorian city* (London: Phoenix, 2005) splendidly details the consequences of civic pride, and can be supplemented with C. Cunningham, *Victorian and Edwardian Town Halls* (London, Routledge & Kegan Paul, 1981).

T. M. Devine, *The Tobacco Lords: a study of the tobacco merchants of Glasgow and their trading activities, c.1740–1790* (Edinburgh: 1975); A. Gomme and D. Walker (eds), *The Architecture of Glasgow* (2nd edn, London: Lund, 1987); J. R. Hume, *The Industrial Archaeology of Glasgow* (Glasgow: Blackie, 1974); J. R. Hume, 'The St Rollox Chemical Works', *Industrial Archaeology*, vol. 3 (1966); G. Stamp, *Alexander 'Greek' Thomson* (London: Laurence King, 1999) and F. Worsdall, *The Glasgow Tenement: a way of life* (Glasgow: Richard Drew, 1989) are among the many studies of Glasgow. Material on Manchester is provided by S. Clark, 'Chorlton Mills and their Neighbours', *IAR*, vol. 2 (1978); S. Clark and A. D. George, 'A Note on "Little Ireland", Manchester', *Industrial Archaeology*, vol. 14 (1979); J. Kay, *The Moral & Physical Condition of the Working Classes employed in the Cotton Manufacture in Manchester* (London: J. Ridgway, 1832); A. Kidd, *Manchester* (3rd edn, Lancaster: Carnegie, 2006); I. Miller and C. Wild, *A. & G. Murray and the Cotton Mills of Ancoats* (Lancaster: Oxford Archaeology North, 2007); J. Roberts, *Working-class Housing in Nineteenth-century Manchester: the example of John Street, Irk Town, 1826–1936* (Manchester: Neil Richardson, 1984); R. A. Smith, *A Centenary of Science in Manchester* (London: Taylor & Francis, 1883); M. Spiers, *Victoria Park, Manchester: a nineteenth-century suburb in its social and administrative context* (MUP, 1976) and S. Taylor and J. Holder, *Manchester's Northern Quarter: the greatest meer village* (London: English Heritage, 2008). For Leeds see M. Beresford, *East End, West End: the face of Leeds during urbanisation, 1684–1842* (Leeds: Thoresby Society, 1988); E. K. Clark, *The History of 100 Years of the Leeds Philosophical & Literary Society* (Leeds: Jowett & Sowry, 1924) and D. Fraser (ed.), *A History of Modern Leeds* (MUP, 1980), and for Nottingham J. V. Beckett (ed.), *A Centenary History of Nottingham* (2nd edn, Chichester: Phillimore, 2006); J. D. Chambers, *The Vale of Trent, 1670–1800: a regional study of economic change* (CUP, 1958) and R. Church, *Economic and Social Changes in a Midlands Town: Victorian Nottingham, 1815–1900* (London: Cass, 1966), for Derby, P. Elliott, *The Derby Philosophers: science and culture in British urban society, 1700–1850* (MUP, 2009) and E. Robinson, 'The Derby Philosophical Society', *Annals of Science*, vol. 9 (1953), and for Birmingham, J. Cattell and B. Hawkins, *The Birmingham Jewellery Quarter: an introduction and guide* (EH, 2000); C. Chinn, *Birmingham: the great working city* (Birmingham: Birmingham City Council, 1994); M. Dick (ed.), *Matthew Boulton: a revolutionary player* (Studley: Brewin, 2009); P. M. Jones, *Industrial Enlightenment: science, technology and culture in British urban society, 1700–1850* (Manchester University Press, 2008); J. Money, *Experience and Identity: Birmingham and the West Midlands, 1760–1800* (MUP, 1977); R. E. Schofield, *The Lunar Society of Birmingham: a social history of provincial science and industry in eighteenth-century England* (Oxford: Clarendon Press, 1963); J. Uglow, *The Lunar Men: the friends who made the future* (London: Faber, 2002) and C. Upton, *Living Back-to-Back* (Chichester: Phillimore, 2005).

For housing in Liverpool the best guide is I. C. Taylor, 'The Court and Cellar Dwelling: the eighteenth-century origin of the Liverpool slum', *Transactions of the Historical Society of Lancashire and Cheshire*, vol. 122 (1970–71) while works on the docks are listed above under Chapter 4. For Cork see A. Bielenberg, *Cork's Industrial Revolution, 1780–1880* (Cork: Cork University Press, 1991) and C. Rynne, *The Industrial Archaeology of Cork City and its Environs* (Dublin: Stationery Office, 1999), for Bristol, C. Harvey and J. Press, *Studies in the Business History of Bristol* (Bristol Academic Press, 1988); D. Hussey, *Coastal and River Trade in Pre-industrial England: Bristol and its region, 1680–1730* (Univeristy of Exeter Press, 2000); C. A. Macinnes, *Bristol: a gateway of Empire* (London: Arrowsmith, 1939; repr. D&C, 1968); W. E. Minchinton (ed.), *The Trade of Bristol in the Eighteenth Century* (Bristol Record Society, 1957); P. K. Stembridge (ed.), *The Goldney Family: a Bristol merchant dynasty* (Bristol Record Society, 1998) and H. Torrens, *The Evolution of a Family Firm: Stothert & Pitt of Bath* (Bath: Stothert & Pitt, 1978), and for Hull, G. Jackson, *Hull in the Eighteenth Century: a study in economic and social history* (OUP, 1972); B. Reckitt, *The History of Reckitt & Sons Ltd* (1958) and *VCH County of York East Riding*, vol. 1, *The City of Kingston-upon-Hull* (OUP, 1969).

For discussion of medium-sized industrial towns see: S. Caunce, 'Northern English industrial towns: rivals or partners?', *Urban History*, vol. 30 (2003); S. Caunce, *Complexity, Community Structure and Competitive Advantage within the Yorkshire Woollen Industry, c.1700–1850* (Leeds University Business School, 1997); J. Stobart, *The First Industrial Region: north-west England, c.1700–60* (Manchester University Press, 2004).

12. Capital industries: manufacturing in London

The classic nineteenth-century surveys of London by Mayhew and Booth are detailed below. Enlightening studies of London's history include P. Ackroyd, *London: a biography* (London: Chatto & Windus, 2000); G. Stedman Jones, *Outcast London: a study in the relationships between classes in Victorian society* (OUP, 1971); D. Olsen, *The Growth of Victorian London* (London: Batsford, 1976); R. Porter, *London: a social history* (London: Penguin, 2000); J. White, *London in the Nineteenth Century: 'a human awful wonder of God'* (London: Vintage, 2008). Three incisive articles are T. C. Barker, 'Business as usual? London and the Industrial Revolution', *History Today*, vol. 39 (1989); J. Langton, 'The Industrial Revolution and the Regional Geography of England', *Transactions of the British Institute of Geographers*, vol. 9 (1983) and E. A. Wrigley, 'A Model of London's Importance, 1650–1750', in P. Abrams and E. A. Wrigley (eds) *Towns in Societies* (CUP, 1978).

Manufactures are analysed in D. Barnett, *London: hub of the Industrial Revolution: a revisionary history, 1775–1825* (London: Tauris, 1998) and L. D. Schwarz, *London in the Age of Industrialisation: entrepreneurs, labour force and living conditions, 1700–1850* (CUP, 1992), and particular industries in T. R. Gourvish and R. G. Wilson, *The British Brewing Industry, 1830–1980* (CUP, 1994); A. McConnell, *Jesse Ramsden (1735–1800): London's leading scientific instrument maker* (Aldershot: Ashgate, 2007). P. Mathias, *The Brewing Industry in England, 1700–1830* (CUP, 1959); A. D. Morrison-Low, *Making Scientific Instruments in the Industrial Revolution* (Aldershot: Ashgate, 2007); D. J. Rowe, *Lead Manufacturing in Great Britain* (London: Croom Helm, 1983); E. Stirling, *The History of the Gas Light & Coke Company, 1812–1949* (London: Benn, 1949); G. A. Thrupp, *History of the Art of Coach-Building* (London: Kerby & Endean, 1876) and D. C. Watts, *A History of Glass-making in London* (London: Watts Publishing, 2008). E. Williamson and N. Pevsner, *The Buildings of England: London Docklands: an architectural guide* (Harmondsworth: Penguin, 1998) is an excellent guide to buildings in the docks. For transport see T. C. Barker and M. Robbins, *A History of London Transport*, vol. 1, *The Nineteenth Century* (London: George Allen & Unwin, 1963).

For housing see J. S. Curl, *The Life and Works of Henry Roberts, 1803–1876: architect* (Chichester: Phillimore, 1983); J. N. Tarn, *Working-class Housing in 19th-century Britain* (London: Lund Humphries, 1969); S. Wohl, *The Eternal Slum: housing and social policy in Victorian London* (London: Arnold, 1977), and for suburbs H. J. Dyos, *Victorian Suburb: a study of the growth of Camberwell* (LecUP, 1973); A. Saint, *et al.*, *London Suburbs* (EH, 1999); G. Tindall, *The Fields Beneath: the history of one London village* (London: Phoenix, 1998). Demographic aspects are considered in J. Landers, *Death and the Metropolis: studies in the demographic history of London, 1670–1830* (CUP, 1993). Brick making for London is described in J. M. Preston, *Industrial Medway: an historical survey* (Rochester: privately published, 1977) and M. Robbins, *Middlesex* (Chichester: Phillimore, 2003). The account of Wilson's omnibus procession comes from *Pictorial Times* (1844). Two panoramic views from the Elton Collection at Ironbridge, *A Balloon View of London, as seen from Hampstead*, published by Banks & Co., Holborn, 1 May 1851 and *A Panorama of London and the River Thames* have proved valuable sources on industrial history.

13. Towns of a different kind: resorts

The epigraph comes from T. B. Macaulay, *The History of England* (Everyman edn, London: Dent, 1906). The starting point for studying resorts is A. B. Granville, *Spas of England and Principal Sea-Bathing Places, I, The North; II, Midlands and South* (London: Henry Colburn, 1841; repr. Bath: Adams & Dart, 1971).

General studies of the subject include P. Borsay, 'Health and

Leisure Resorts, 1700–1840', in A. Brodie and G. Winter, *England's Seaside Resorts* (EH, 2007); P. Clark (ed.), *The Cambridge Urban History of Britain*, vol. 2, *1540–1840* (CUP, 2000); A. Everitt, 'The English Urban Inn, 1560–1760', in A. Everitt (ed.), *Perspectives in English Urban History* (London: Macmillan, 1953); R. W. Malcolmson, *Popular Recreations in English Society, 1700–1850* (CUP, 1973) and J. A. R. Pimlott, *The Englishman's Holiday* (London: Faber & Faber, 1947).

The most recent of many studies of Bath is G. Davis and P. Bonsall, *A History of Bath: image and reality* (Lancaster: Carnegie, 2006). Inland resorts are described in T. Brighton, *The Discovery of the Peak District* (Chichester: Phillimore, 2004) and L. F. Cave, *Royal Leamington Spa: a history* (Chichester: Phillimore, 1988), while Anon (W. P. R.), *A Short Address to the Inhabitants of Ludlow* (Ludlow: The Author, 1810) is an enlightening account of how resorts might develop. General studies of coastal resorts include A. Brodie and G. Winter, *England's Seaside Resorts* (EH, 2008); B. Goodall, 'Coastal Resorts: development and re-development', *Built Environment*, vol. 18 (1992); F. Gray, *Designing the Seaside* (London: Reaktion, 2006); K. Lindley, *Seaside Architecture* (London: Hugh Evelyn, 1973); G. Shaw and A. Williams (eds), *The Rise and Fall of British Coastal Resorts* (London:

Pinter, 1997); J. K. Walton, *The English Seaside Resort: a social history, 1750–1914* (LecUP, 1983); J. Walvin *Beside the Sea* (London: Allen Lane, 1977). Studies of particular resorts include D. Cannadine, *Lords and Landlords: the aristocracy and the towns, 1774–1967* (LecUP, 1980); T. Hinderwell, *The History and Antiquities of Scarborough* (York: Blanchard, 1798, 3rd edn with a memoir of the author, Scarborough: Bye and London: Whittaker, 1837); A. D. King, *The Bungalow: the production of a global culture* (London: Routledge & Kegan Paul, 1984); A. Mayhew, *Birchington and its Bungalows* (Canterbury: 1881) and J. K. Walton, *Blackpool* (Lancaster: EUP/Carnegie, 1998).

Original sources used here include L. Carroll, *Alice in Wonderland* (1865); R. T. Claridge, *Hydropathy or the Cold Water Cure as practised by Vincenz Priessnitz* (London: James Madden, 1842); R. Russell, *A Dissertation on the use of Sea-Water in the Diseases of the Glands* (London: W. Owen, 1755) and E. Shanes, *Turner's Rivers, Harbours and Coasts* (London: Chatto & Windus, 1981). There is material on the role of railways in promoting holidays in R. Christiansen and R. M. Miller, *The Cambrian Railways* (D&C, 1967); George P. Neel, *Railway Reminiscences* (London: McCorquedale, 1904; repr. Wakefield: EP Publishing, 1974) and T. Normington, *The Lancashire & Yorkshire Railway* (Manchester: Heywood, 1898).

14. Creating communities: calculations and aspirations

Open and closed communities are discussed in J. Caird, *English Agriculture in 1850–51* (London: Longman, Brown, Green & Longmans, 1852; see also 2nd edn with introduction by G. E. Mingay, Farnborough: Greg, 1968); R. Gough, *The History of Myddle* (ed. D. Hey, Harmondsworth: Penguin, 1981); D. Hey, *An English Rural Community: Myddle under the Tudors and Stuarts* (LecUP, 1974); K. Jones, M. Hunt, J. Malam and B. Trinder, 'Holywell Lane: a squatter community in the Shropshire coalfield', *IAR*, vol. 6 (1982); B. A. Holderness, '"Open" and "Close" Parishes in England in the Eighteenth and Nineteenth Centuries', *Agricultural History Review*, vol. 20 (1972); D. Mills, 'English Villages in the Eighteenth And Nineteenth Centuries: a sociological approach', *Amateur Historian*, vol. 6 (1965); R. Samuel, *Village Life and Labour* (London: Routledge & Kegan Paul, 1975); E. P. Thompson, *Whigs and Hunters: the origin of the Black Act* (Harmondsworth: Penguin, 1977); E. P. Thompson, *Customs in Common* (London: Penguin, 2993); B. Trinder, 'The Open Village in Industrial Britain', in M. Nisser, ed, *The Industrial Heritage: Transactions of the Third International Conference on the Conservation of Industrial Monuments*, vol. 3 (Stockholm: Nordiska museet, 1978) and C. Ward, *Cotters and Squatters: housing's hidden history* (Nottingham: Five Leaves, 2002). The account of Broughton is drawn from *VCH Oxfordshire*, vol. 9 (OUP, 1969), and that of Alstonefield from *VCH Staffordshire*, vol. 10 (OUP, 1996).

Sources for the seigniorial enterprises discussed here include R. Balgarnie, *Sir Titus Salt Bt: his life and its lessons* (London: Hodder & Stoughton, 1877); R. Boyson, *The Ashworth Cotton Enterprise: the rise and fall of a family firm, 1818–80* (OUP, 1970); G. Darley, *Villages of Vision* (London: Architectural Press, 1975); A. Raistrick, *Two Centuries of Industrial Welfare* (2nd edn, Ashbourne: Moorland, 1977); J. Reynolds, *The Great Paternalist: Titus Salt and the growth of nineteenth-century Bradford* (London: Maurice Temple Smith, 1983);

M. B. Rose, *The Gregs of Styal, 1750–1914: the emergence and development of a family business* (MUP, 1977); G. Timmins, 'Housing Quality in Rural Textile Colonies, c.1800–c.1850: The Ashworth settlements revisited', *IAR*, vol. 22 (2000), while those of a later generation are chronicled in B. Meakin, *Model Factories and Villages: ideal conditions of labour and housing* (London: T. Fisher Unwin, 1905).

Aspects and applications of the gospel of Improvement are analysed in P. Jenkins, *The Making of a Ruling Class: the Glamorganshire gentry, 1640–1790* (CUP, 1983); W. G. Hoskins and L. G. Stamp, *The Common Lands of England and Wales* (London: Collins, 1964); N. C. Solden, *John Wilkinson, 1728–1808: English ironmaster and inventor* (Lewiston NY: Edwin Mellen Press 1998); M. Stratton and B. Trinder, 'The Foundations of a Textile Community: Sir Robert Peel at Fazeley', *TexH*, vol. 26 (1995). The concept of the margins is discussed in E. J. T. Collins, *The Economy of Upland Britain, 1750–1950* (Reading: Centre for Agricultural Study, 1978); D. Gwyn, 'The Narrow-Gauge Nations: industrial archaeology beyond the leading sectors', *IAR*, vol. 19 (2007).

For Improvement in the Scillies see S. Llewellyn, *Emperor Smith: the man who built Scilly* (Wimborne Minster: Dovecote Press, 2005), and for Irish projects G. Camblin, *The Town in Ulster* (Belfast: William Mullen, 1951); J. Kelly, 'Prosperous and Irish Industrialisation in the late Eighteenth Century', *Journal of the County Kildare Archaeological Society*, vol. 16 (1985–86); R. W. Lightbrown, *An Architect Earl: Edward Augustus Stratford (1736–1801), 2nd Earl of Aldborough* (Kilkenny: OLL Editions and Irish Georgian Society, 2008); K. Villiers-Tuthill, *Alexander Nimmo and the Western District: emerging infrastructure in pre-famine Ireland* (Galway: Connemara Girl Publications, 2006); N. P. Wilkins, *Alexander Nimmo: master engineer, 1783–1832* (Dublin: Irish Academic Press, 2009).

Aspects of change in Wales are considered in E. Beazley, *Madocks* and the Wonder of Wales (London: Faber, 1947); D. Gwyn, 'The Industrial Town in Gwynedd: a Comparative Study', Landscape History, vol. 24 (2002); D. Gwyn, Gwynedd: Inheriting a Revolution: the archaeology of industrialisation in north-west Wales (Chichester: Phillimore, 2006); E. Hughes and A. Eames, Porthmadog Ships (Llanrwst: Gwasg Carreg Gwalch, 2009); S. Hughes, The Archaeology of an Early Railway System: the Brecon Forest Tramroads (RCAHMW, 1990); M. Jones, 'Y chwarelwyr: the slate quarrymen of North Wales', in R. Samuel (ed.), Miners, Quarrymen and Saltworkers (London: Routledge & Kegan Paul, 1977); J. Lindsay, The History of the North Wales Slate Industry (D&C, 1974).

Changes in the Fens are discussed in H. C. Darby, The Draining of the Fens (1940); R. L. Hills, Machines, Mills and Uncountable Costly Necessities: a short history of the drainage of the Fens (Norwich: Goose, 1967); J. Ravensdale, Liable to Floods (CUP, 1974); A. Peacock, Bread or Blood (London: Gollancz, 1965); J. Ravensdale and R. Muir, East Anglian Landscapes: past and present (London: Michael Joseph, 1984).

The starting points for consideration of the Highlands are J. Prebble, The Highland Clearances (London: Secker & Warburg, 1963) and E. Richards, The Highland Clearances (Edinburgh: Birrlin, 2000), which can be supplemented by standard works on Thomas Telford, and by A. J. Cooke, 'Cotton and the Scottish Highland Clearances: the development of Spinningdale, 1791–1806', TexH, vol. 26 (1995); J. Dunlop, The British Fisheries Society, 1786–1893 (Edinburgh: John Donald, 1978); J. Evans, The Gentleman Usher: the life and times of George Dempster, 1732–1818 (Barnsley: Pen & Sword, 2005); R. Mitchison, Agricultural Sir John: the life of Sir John Sinclair of Ulbster (London: Geoffrey Bles, 1962) and Sir John Sinclair, Analysis of the Statistical Account of Scotland (Edinburgh: Tait, 1831). E. Richards, The Leviathan of Wealth: the Sutherland fortune in the Industrial Revolution (London: Routledge & Kegan Paul, 1973) and E. Richards, 'The Social and Electoral Influence of the Trentham Interest, 1800–62', Midland History, vol. 3 (1975–76) bring together the Leveson-Gower's activities in Co. Sutherland with their interests in the industrial Midlands, while a protagonist in those affairs wrote J. Loch, An Account of the Improvements on the Estates of the Marquis of Stafford in the Counties of Stafford and Salop and on the Estate of Sutherland (London: Longman, 1820).

For the Famine in Ireland see C Woodham Smith, The Great Hunger: Ireland 1845–49 (London, Penguin edn, 1991) and C Kincaly, The Great Irish Famine: impact, ideology and rebellion (Basingstoke: Palgrave, 2002).

Utopian communities in general are discussed in W. H. G. Armytage, Heavens Below: utopian experiments in England, 1560–1960 (London: Routledge & Kegan Paul, 1961), and the Owenite movement in I. Donnachie, Robert Owen of New Lanark and New Harmony (East Linton: Tuckwell, 2000); R. G. Garnett, Co.-operation and the Owenite socialist communities in Britain, 1825–45 (MUP, 1972); R. Owen, A Statement Regarding the New Lanark Establishment (Edinburgh: Moir, 1812; repr. Glasgow, Molendinar, 1973); R. Owen, A New View of Society and Other Writings (ed. J. Butt, London: Everyman, Dent, 1972) and E. Royle, Robert Owen and the Commencement of the Millennium: a study of the Harmony community (MUP, 1998). For the Moravian communities see J. E. Hutton, A History of the Moravian Church (London: Moravian Publication Office, 1909) and R. White, A History of Gracehill (Gracehill: privately published, n.d., c.1993). The Chartist Land Company is discussed in O. Ashton, R. Fyson and S. Roberts (eds), The Chartist Legacy (Woodbridge: Merlin, 1999); A. Briggs (ed.), Chartist Studies (London: Macmillan, 1959); A. M. Hadfield, The Chartist Land Company (D&C, 1970); E. Royle, Chartism (3rd edn, London: Longman, 1996); D. Thompson, The Chartists (Hounslow: Temple Smith, 1984); P. Searby, 'Great Dodford: The Later History of the Chartist Land Scheme', Agricultural History Review, vol. 16 (1968) and K. Tiller, 'Charterville and the Chartist Land Company', Oxoniensia, vol. 50 (1985).

Epilogue: a revolution in context

General works on the Industrial Revolution are listed in the bibliographical notes for Chapter 1, and to them should be added N. Crafts, 'British Industrialisation in and International Context', Journal of Interdisciplinary History, vol. 19 (1989); E. J. Hobsbawm, 'The Making of the Working Class, 1870–1914', in E. J. Hobsbawm, Uncommon People: resistance, rebellion and jazz (London: Abacus, 2007) and C. Wilson, 'The Entrepreneur in the Industrial Revolution in Britain', History, vol. 42 (1957).

There is an extensive literature on the growth of consumer goods industries which includes J. Booker, Essex and the Industrial Revolution (Chelmsford: Essex County Council, 1974); J. Burnett, Plenty and Want: a social history of diet in England from 1815 to the present day (Harmondsworth: Pelican, 1968); W. B. Clowes, Family Business, 1803–1953 (Beccles: Clowes, 1953); G. Jones, The Millers: a story of technological endeavour and industrial success 1870–2001 (Lancaster: Carnegie, 2001); P. Mathias, Retailing Revolution (London: Longmans, 1967); L. J. Mayes, The History of Chair-making in High Wycombe (London: Routledge & Kegan Paul, 1969); B. Trinder, 'The Archaeology of the British Food Industry, 1660–1960: a preliminary survey', IAR, vol. 15 (1993); VCH Northamptonshire, vol. 8 (OUP, 2008) (for the boot and shoe industry) and J. K. Walton, Fish and Chips and the British Working Class (LecUP, 1992). The quotation by Hennessy is from P. Hennessy, Never Again: Britain, 1945–1951 (1992; Penguin, 2006), 164.

Original sources

Considerable use in this study is made of accounts of Britain by eighteenth- and nineteenth-century travellers, and by one or two from the twentieth century. Details of works quoted are as follows:

Aikin, A., *Journal of a Tour through North Wales* (London: J. Johnson, 1797).

Aikin, J., *A Description of the Country from Thirty to Forty Miles round Manchester* (London: John Stockdale 1795; repr. D&C, 1968).

Andrews, W. *see* Chancellor

Angerstein, R. R., *R. R. Angerstein's Illustrated Travel Diary 1753–1755: Industry in England and Wales from a Swedish Perspective* (trans T. and P. Berg, London: Science Museum, 2000).

Ayton, R., *A voyage around Great Britain undertaken in the summer of 1813* (2 vols, London: Longman, Hurst, Rees, Orme & Brown, 1814–23);

Baines, E., *History, Directory & Gazetteer of the county palatine of Lancaster* (2 vols, Liverpool: W. Wales, 1824–25; repr. D&C, 1968);

Banks, J. *see* Broadbridge

Bingley, W., *North Wales delineated from two excursions through all the interesting parts of that country during the summers of 1798 and 1801* (London: Longman & Rees, 1804).

Blaikie, A., *A Scottish Farmer's Ride through England 100 years ago* (Selkirk: Lewis, 1906).

Blanc, Mon (Jean Bernard) L'Abbe le, *Letters on the English and French Nations* (London: J. Brindley 1747).

Booth, C. (ed.), *Life and Labour of the People in London* (London: Macmillan, 1892–97).

Borrow, G., *Wild Wales* (Everyman edn, London: Dent, 1958).

Boswell, J., *Journal of a Tour to the Hebrides with Samuel Johnson* (1785, Everyman edn, London: Dent, 1958).

Bray, W., *A Sketch of a Tour into Derbyshire and Yorkshire* (London: B. White, 1778).

Broadbridge, S. R., 'Joseph Banks and West Midland Industry', *Staffordshire Industrial Archaeology Society Journal*, vol. 2 (1971).

Buckmaster, J., *The Village Politician: the life-story of John Buckley* als *Buckmaster* (London: Fisher Unwin, 1897; repr. Horsham: Caliban, 1982).

Burritt, E., *A Walk from London to John O'Groats* (London: Sampson, Low, Son & Marston, 1864).

Burritt, E., *Walks in the Black Country and its Green Border-Land* (London: Sampson Low, 1868).

Byng, J., 5th Viscount Torrington, *The Torrington Diaries* (ed. C. B. Andrews, London: Eyre & Spottiswoode, 1934).

Campbell, J., *A Political Survey of Britain* (London: the Author, 1774).

Carlyle, T., *Chartism* (London: J. Fraser, 1840).

Carus, C. G., *The King of Saxony's Journey through England and Scotland in the year 1844* (London: Chapman & Hall, 1846).

Chadwick, E., *The Sanitary Condition of the Labouring Population of Great Britain*, ed. M. W. Flinn (Edinburgh University Press, 1965).

Chancellor, V. (ed.), *Master & Artisan in Victorian England: The Diary of William Andrews and the Autobiography of Joseph Gutteridge* (London: Evelyn, Adams & Mackay, 1969).

Cobbett, W., *Rural Rides* (Everyman edn, 2 vols, London: Dent, 1957).

Colquhoun, P., *A Treatise on the Wealth, Power & Resources of the British Empire* (London: Mawman, 1814–5).

Coste, P.-L. and Perdonnet, A. A., 'Traitement metallurgique des minerais de plomb en Angleterre'. *Annales des Mines*, vol. 7 (1830); repr.: *Smelting of Lead Ores in Reverberatory Furnaces as performed in Great Britain, 1830* (Eindhoven: De Archaeologische Pers, n.d.).

Coxe, W., *An Historical Tour in Monmouthshire* (London, T. Cadel junr & W. Davies, 1801).

Darwin, E., *The Botanic Garden* (London: J. Johnson, 1791).

Defoe, D., *A Tour through England and Wales* (Everyman edn, 2 vols, London: Dent, 1959).

Dibdin, C., *Observations on a Tour through almost the whole of England and a considerable part of Scotland in a series of letters* (London: Goulding, 1801–02) [Charles Dibdin the Elder, 1745–1814].

Dodd, G., *Days at the Factories: or the Manufacturing Industry of Great Britain described* (London: Knight, 1843; repr. Wakefield: EP, 1975).

Dodd, G., *et al.* (eds), *The land we live in: a pictorial & literary sketch-book of the British Empire* (4 vols, London: C. Knite, 1847–50).

Dupin, C., *Voyages dans la Grande-Bretagne depuis 1816* [Journeys in Great Britain since 1816] (Parish: Bachelier, 1825–26).

Dupin, C., *The Commercial Power of Great Britain* (London: C. Knight, 1825).

Elmes, J., *Metropolitan Improvements* (London: Jones, 1827).

Engels, F., *The Condition of the Working Class in England* (ed. W. O. Henderson and W. H. Chaloner, Oxford: Blackwell, 1958).

Faraday *see* Tomos

Farington, J., *The Farington Diary* (ed. James Greig, London: Hutchinson, 1922–28).

Faucher, L., *Etudes sur l'Angleterre* [Studies on England] (2 vols, Paris: Guillaumin, 1845)

Fenton, R., *Tours in Wales 1804–13* (ed. J. Fisher, London: Bedford Press, 1917).

Ferber, J. J., *An essay on the Oryctography of Derbyshire, a province of England* (1765, published in German 1776), in Pinkerton, *General Collection* (see below).

Ferrner *see* Woolrich

Field *see* Hall

Fiennes, C., *The Journeys of Celia Fiennes* (ed. C. Morris, London: Cresset Press, 1947).

Fisher, J. M., *An American Quaker in the British Isles: the travel journals of Jabez Maude Fisher, 1775–1779* (ed. K. Morgan, Oxford: Oxford University Press/British Academy, 1992).

Gaskell, P., *Artisans and Machinery* (London: Parker, 1836; repr. London: Cass, 1968).

Gilpin, J., *Journals and Notebooks, 1790–1801* (MS in State Archives, Harrisburg, Penn).

Godwin, G., *Town Swamps and Social Bridges* (1859, Victorian Library edn, LecUP, 1972).

Gonzales, Don M., *The Tour of Don Manuel Gonzales of Lisbon* (1730) in Pinkerton, *General Collection* (see below);

Goodrich, S., *Letters from Simon Goodrich to General Sir Samuel Bentham* (Science Museum, London, Goodrich Collection).

Granville, A. B., *Spas of England and Principal Sea-Bathing Places, I, The North; II, Midlands and South* (London: Henry Colburn, 1841; repr. Bath: Adams & Dart, 1971).

Griffiths, G., *Going to Markets and Grammar Schools* (London: Freehan, 1870).

Griffiths, G., *Reminiscences and Records during Ten Years Residence in the Midland Counties from 1870 to 1880* (Bewdley: Griffiths, 1880).

Gutteridge, J. *see* Chancellor

Hall, J. W., 'Joshua Field's Diary of a Tour in 1821 through the Midlands', *TNS*, vol. 6 (1925–26).

Hanaford, P., *The Life of George Peabody* (Boston, MA: B. Russell, 1870).

Harrall, T., *Picturesque Views of the Severn* (2 vols, London: Whittaker, 1824).

Hassell, J., *Tour of the Grand Junction* (London: J. Hassell, 1819).

Hatchett, C., *The Hatchett Diary* (ed. A. Raistrick, Truro: Bradford Barton, 1967).

Haussez, Baron C. le M. de L., *Great Britain in 1833* (Philadelphia: Mielke, 1833).

Head, Sir Francis Bond, *Stokers and Pokers* (London: John Murray, 1849).

Head, Sir George, *A Home Tour through the Manufacturing Districts of England in the summer of 1835* (London: J. Murray, 1836; repr. London: Cass, 1968).

Henderson, W. O., *Industrial Britain under the Regency: The Diaries of Escher, Bodmer, May and de Gallois 1814–18* (London: Cass, 1968).

Hoare, Sir R. C., *The Journeys of Sir Richard Colt Hoare through Wales and England 1793–1810* (ed. M. W. Thompson, Gloucester: Alan Sutton, 1983).

Hollingshead, J., *Ragged London in 1861* (London: Dent, Everyman: 1986).

Holt, J., *A General View of the Agriculture of Lancashire* (London: Nicol, 1795).

Hudson, D., *Munby: Man of Two Worlds: the life and diaries of Arthur J. Munby, 1828–1910* (London: Abacus, 1974).

Hutchinson, W., *Excursion to the Lakes with a Tour through part of the northern counties, 1773–74* (London: J. Wilkie, 1776).

Hyde, C. K., 'The Iron Industry of the West Midlands in 1754: Observations from the Travel Account of Charles Wood', *West Midlands Studies*, vol. 6 (1973).

Jefferies, R., *Hodge and his masters* (1880, Fitzroy edn, 2 vols, London: MacGibbon & Kee, 1966).

Jefferies, R., *The Hills and the Vale* (1909, pbk edn, OUP, 1980).

Kalm, P., *Pehr Kalm's Account of his visit to England on his way to America in 1748* (trans. J. Lucas, London: Macmillan, 1892).

Keating, P., ed, *Into Unknown England 1866–1913: Selections from the Social Explorers* (London: Fontana, 1976).

Kielmansett, Count F. von, *Diary of a Journey to England in the years 1761–62* (London: Longmans, 1902).

Kohl, J. G., *Ireland, Scotland and England* (London: Bruce, 1842).

Lewis, S., *A Topographical Dictionary of England* (London: Lewis, 1845).

Lewis, W., and Chisholm, A., *Specimens and Observations in a journey thro' some parts of England July 21 to August 6, 1768* (Keele University, Wedgwood Archives 39–28405)

Loveday *see* Markham

Macaulay, T. B., *The History of England from the accession of James II* (London: Dent, 1906).

Markham, S., *John Loveday of Caversham 1711–1789: the life and tours of an eighteenth-century onlooker* (Wilton: Michael Russell, 1984).

Marshall, J., *John Marshall's tour book to Scotland 1800* (University of Leeds, Brotherton Library, Marshall MS 200/62).

Marshall, J., *John Marshall's tour books to Cumberland 1800–07* (University of Leeds, Brotherton Library, Marshall MS 200/63).

Marx, K., and Engels, F., *On Britain* (Moscow: Foreign Languages Publishing House, 1962).

Mavor, W., *A Tour in Wales and through Several Counties of England performed in the summer of 1805* (London: R. Phillips, 1806).

Mavor, W., *The British Tourist's Companion* (3rd edn, 2 vols, London, Phillips, 1809).

May, J. G., 1814 *see* Henderson

Mayhew, H., *London Labour and the London Poor* (London: Griffin, Bohn, 1861–2; repr. Dover, New York & Constable, London, 1868).

Mayhew *see also* Thompson, E. P., and Yeo, E. (eds)

Measom, G., *The Official Illustrated Guide to the Great Eastern Railway* (London: Measom, 1865)

Measom, G., *The Official Illustrated Guide to the Great Northern Railway* (London: Measom, 1861)

Measom, G., *The Official Illustrated Guide to the Great Western Railway* (London: Measom, 1865).

Measom, G., *The Official Illustrated Guide to the Great Southern & Western and Midland Great Western Railways of Ireland* (London: Measom, 1866).

Measom, G., *The Official Illustrated Guide to the London & North Western Railway* (London: Measom, n.d.).

Mill, J. S., 'Walking Tour of Berkshire, Buckinghamshire, Oxfordshire & Surrey, 3–15 July 1828', *The Collected Works of John Stuart Mill* (ed. J. M. Robson, Toronto: University of Toronto Press, 1988).

Miller, H., *First Impressions of England and its People* (London: John Johnston, 1847);

Mogg, E., *Mogg's Handbook for Railway Travellers or Real Iron-Road Book* (2nd edn, London: Mogg, 1840).

Moritz, C. P., *Journeys of a German in England: a walking-tour of England in 1782* (ed. R. Nettel, London: Eland, 1983).

Morton, H. F., *Strange Commissions for Henry Ford* (York: Herald, 1946).

Munby *see* Hudson

Nasmyth *see* Smiles

Newte, T. (Anon), *A Tour of England and Scotland in 1785 by an English Gentleman* (2 vols, London: Robinson, 1788).

Oeynhausen, C. von, and Dechen, H. von, *Railways in England 1826 & 1827* (ed. C. E. Lee and K. R. Gilbert, Cambridge: Heffer, 1972).

Orwell, G., *The Road to Wigan Pier* (1937, Harmondsworth: Penguin, 1962).

Peacock, G., *Memoir of Dr Thomas Young* (London: John Murray, 1855).

Pennant, T., *Tours in Wales from 1778* (Caernarfon: Humphreys, 1883).

Pennant, T., *The Journey from Chester to London* (London: B. White, 1782).

Phillips, J., *A General History of Inland Navigation* (London: Taylor, 1792).

Philp, R. K., *A History of Progress in Great Britain* (London: Houlston & Wright, 1859).

Pinkerton, J., *A General Collection of the best and most interesting voyages and travels in all parts of the World* (London: Longman, Hurst, Rees & Orme, 1808–14).

Pococke, R., *The Travels through England of the Revd Richard Pococke* (ed. J. J. Cartwright, London: Camden Society, 1888/1889).

Postlethwayt, M., *A Universal Dictionary of Trade & Commerce translated from the French of Jacques Savary* (London: Knapton, 1751).

Priestley, J. B., *English Journey* (London: Heinemann, 1934).

Raumer, F. von, *England in 1835* (London: J. Murray, 1836; repr. Shannon: Irish Universities Press, 1971).

Razzell, P. E., and Wainwright, R. W., *The Victorian Working Class: Selections from Letters to the Morning Chronicle* (London: Cass, 1973).

Reach, A. B., *The Yorkshire Textile Districts in 1849* (ed. C. Aspin, Helmshore Local History Society: 1974).

Reach, A. B., *Manchester and the Textile Districts in 1849* (ed. C. Aspin, Helmshore Local History Society, 1972);

Reach *see also* Razzell and Wainwright

Robertson, D., *A Tour through the Isle of Man* (London: E. Hodson, 1791).

Sanger, G., *Seventy Years a Showman* (1910, Fitzroy edn, London: MacGibbon & Kee, 1966).

Scarfe, N., *A Frenchman's Year in Suffolk, French impressions of Suffolk life in 1784* (Woodbridge: Boydell/Suffolk Records Society, 2003).

Scarfe, N. (ed.), *Innocent Espionage: the La Rochefoucald Brothers' Tour of England in 1985* (Woodbridge: Boydell, 1995).

Schinkel, K. F., *Reise nach England, Schottland und Paris im Jahr 1826* [*Journey to England, Scotland & Paris in the year 1826*] (ed. G. Riemann, Munchen (Munich): C. H. Beck, 1986).

Shaw, S., *A Tour to the West of England by the Rev. S. Shaw* (London: Robson, Clark & J. Walker, 1789).

Sherrard, R. H., *The White Slaves of England* (London: Bowden, 1897).

Sidney, S., *Rides on Railways* (London: Orr, 1851; ed. B. Trinder, Chichester: Phillimore, 1973).

Simond, L., *Journal of a Tour and Residence in Great Britain during the years 1810 and 1811 by a French Traveller* (Edinburgh: Constable, 1815).

Simpson, S., *The Agreeable Historian or the Compleat English Traveller* (London: Walker, 1746).

Skrine, H., *Two successive Tours throughout the whole of Wales with several of the adjacent English counties* (London: Elmsley & Bremner, 1798).

Smiles, S., *James Nasmyth: Engineer – An Autobiography* (London: John Murray, 1883).

Somerville, A., *The Autobiography of a Working Man* (1848, Fitzroy edn, London: MacGibbon & Kee, 1967).

Southey, R., *Journal of a Tour in Scotland in 1819 in the company of Thomas Telford and John Rickman* (ed. C. H. Herford, London: John Murray, 1929).

Southey, R., *Letters from England by Robert Southey* (ed. J. Simmons, London: Cresset, 1951).

Spence, E. I., *Summer Excursions through parts of Oxfordshire, Gloucestershire, &c.* (London: Longmans, Hurst, Rees & Orme, 1809).

Spiker, S. H., *Travels through England, Wales & Scotland in the year 1816* (London: Lackington, Hughs, Harding, Mavor & Jones, 1820).

Stowe, H. B., *Sunny Memories of Foreign Lands* (London: T. Nelson, 1854).

Strauss, G. L. M., *et al.*, *England's Workshops* (London: Groombridge, 1864).

Svedenstierna, E. von, *Svedenstierna's Tour in Great Britain, 1802–03* (ed. M. W. Flinn, D&C, 1973).

Taine, H., *Taine's Notes on England* (ed. E. Hyams, London: Thames & Hudson, 1957).

Taylor, W. Cooke, *Notes on a tour in the manufacturing districts of Lancashire* (London: Duncan & Malcolm, 1842).

Thompson, E. P., and Yeo, E. (eds), *The Unknown Mayhew: Selections from the Morning Chronicle, 1849–50* (Harmondsworth: Penguin, 1973).

Tocqueville, A. de, *Journeys to England & Ireland* (ed. J. P. Mayer, London: Faber, 1958).

Tomos, D., *Michael Faraday in Wales* (Denbigh: Gwasg Gee, n.d. c.1973).

Universal British Directory (London: Champanne & Whitrow, 1791).

Ure, A., *The Philosophy of Manufactures* (1835, 1861 edn, London: Bohn 1861).

Vallancey, C., *A Treatise on Inland Navigation* (Dublin: G. & A. Ewing, 1763).

Vancouver, C., *A General View of the Agriculture of Devon* (London: Board of Agriculture, 1808).

Vaughan, R., *The Age of Great Cities: or Moral Society viewed in its relation to Intelligence, Morals and Religion* (London: Jackson & Walford, 1843).

Warner, R., *A Walk through some of the Western Counties of England* (London: Robinson, 1800).

Warner, R., *A Tour through the Northern Counties of England and the borders of Scotland* (2 vols, London: Robinson, 1802).

Warner, R., *A Tour through Cornwall in the autumn of 1808* (London: Wilkie & Robinson, 1809).

Warner, R., *A Second Walk through Wales in August and September 1798* (4th edn, London: Robinson, 1813).

Wendeborn, F. A., *A View of England towards the close of the 18th century* (published in Germany, 1786, London: G. G. J. & J. Robinson, 1791).

Whatley, S., *England's Gazetteer* (3 vols, London: J. & D. Knapton, 1751).

White, W., *A Londoner's Walk to the Land's End and a trip to the Scilly Isles* (London: Chapman & Hall, 1855).

Witts, F. E., *The Diary of a Cotswold Parson* (ed. D. Verey, Gloucester: Alan Sutton, 1986).

Wood, C., *The Diary of Charles Wood of Cyfarthfa Ironworks, Merthyr Tydfil, 1766–67* (ed. J. Gross, Cardiff: Merton Priory Press, 2001).

Wood, C.: see also Hyde.

Woolrich, A. P. (ed.), *Ferrner's Journal, 1759/60: An Industrial Spy in Bristol* (Eindhoven: de Archaeologische Pers, n.d.).

Wordsworth, W., *Guide to the Lakes* (1835, ed. E. de Selincourt, OUP, 1970).

Yarranton, A., *England's Improvement by Sea and Land*, vol. I (London: Everingham, 1677), vol. II (London: Parkhurst, 1681).

Young, A., *Tours in England and Wales* (London: LSE Reprints, 1932).

Young, A., *A Tour in Ireland made in the years 1776, 1777, 1778 and brought down to the end of 1779* (London: Cadell, 1780).

Young, A., *A General View of the Agriculture of Essex* (London: Richard Phillips, 1807).

Young A., *A General View of the Agriculture of Oxfordshire* (London: Sherwood, Neely & Jones, 1813; repr. D&C, 1969).

Websites:

Among the most useful websites used in this study are:

www.british-history.ac.uk

www.copac.ac.uk

www.ExploreEnglandsPast.org.uk

www.historicaldirectories.org

www.storyoflondon.com

www.victoriacountyhistory.ac.uk

Museums and conservation projects:

The following are contact details of museums and conservation projects mentioned in the text:

Abbeydale Industrial Hamlet, Abbeydale Road South, Sheffield S7 2QW, www.simt.co.uk

Arlington Court and the National Trust Carriage Museum, Arlington, Barnstaple, Devon EX31 4LP.

Beamish Museum, Beamish, Co. Durham, DH9 ORG, museum@beamish.org.uk

Big Pit National Coal Museum, Blaenafon, Torfain NP4 9XP, www.museumwales.ac.uk/en/bigpit

Black Country Living Museum, Tipton Road, Dudley, West Midlands, DY1 4SQ, www.bclm.co.uk

Blaenavon World Heritage Site, Church Road, Blaenavon, Torfaen NP4 9XP, www.world-heritage-blaenavon.org.uk

Caudwell's Mill, Rowsley, Matlock, Derbys DE4 2EB, www.caudwellsmill.co.uk

National Coal Mining Museum, Caphouse Colliery, New Road, Overton, Wakefield WF4 4RH, www.ncm.org.uk

Cheddleton Flint Mill, Cheddleton, Staffordshire, ST13 7HL.

Crofton Pumping Station, Crofton, Marlborough, Wilts, SN8 3DW. www.croftonbeamengines.org

Cromford: The Arkwright Society, Cromford Mill, Mill Lane, Cromford, Matlock, Derbys DE4 3RQ, www.arkwrightsociety.co.uk

Crossness Engines Trust, Old Works, Crossness STW, Belvedere Road, Abbey Wood, London SE2 9AQ, www.crossness.org.uk

Dogdyke Pumping Station, Bridge Farm, Tattershall LN4 4JG, www.dogdyke.com

Elsecar Heritage Centre, Wath Road, Elsecar, South Yorkshire S74 8HJ, www.elsecar-heritage-centre.co.uk

Etruria Industrial Museum, Lower Bedford Street, Etruria, Stoke-on-Trent ST4 7AF, www.stoke.gov.uk

Gladstone Pottery Museum, Uttoxeter Road, Longton, Stoke-on-Trent ST3 1PQ, www.stoke.gov.uk

Helmshore Mills Textile Museum, Holcombe Road, Helmshore, Rossendale BB4 4NP, www.lancashire.gov.uk/museums

Ironbridge Gorge Museum, Coach Road, Coalbrookdale, Telford TF8 7DQ, www.ironbridge.org.uk

Kew Bridge Steam Museum, Green Dragon Lane, Brentford, Middlesex TW8 OEN, www.kbsm.org

Long Shop Museum, Main Street, Leiston, Suffolk IP16 4ES, www.longshop.care4free.net

Museum of Science & Industry, Liverpool Road, Castlefields, Manchester M3 4FP. www.mosi.org.uk

National Railway Museum, Leeman Road, York YO26 4XJ, www.nrm.org.uk

National Slate Museum, Llanberis, Gwynedd LL55 4TY, www.museumwales.ac.uk

North of England Lead Mining Museum, Killhope, nr Cowsgill, Upper Weardale, Co. Durham DL13 1AR, www.killhope.org.uk

Queen Street Mill Textile Museum, Queen Street, Harle Syke, Burnley BB10 2HX, www.lancashire.gov.uk/museums

Rosedene (Chartist cottage), Victoria Road, Dodford, Bromsgrove, Worcs B61 9BJ, www.nationaltrust.org.uk

Ruddington Framework Knitters' Museum, Chapel Street, Ruddington, Nottingham, www.rfkm.org

Ryhope Engines Museum, Waterworks Road, Ryhope, Sunderland SR2 OND, www.ryhopeengines.org.uk

St Fagans National History Museum, Cardiff CF5 6XB, www.museumwales.ac.uk/en/bigpit

Science Museum, Exhibition Road, South Kensington, London SW7 2DD, www.sciencemuseum.org.uk

Scottish Mining Museum, Lady Victoria Colliery, Newtongrange, Midlothian EH22 4QN, www.scottishminingmuseum.com

Stott Park Bobbin Mill, Finsthwaite, Newby Bridge, Cumbria LA18 8AX, www.english-heritage.org.uk

Stretham Old Engine, Stretham, Ely, Cambridgeshire CB7, www.strethamoldengine.org.uk

Thinktank, Millennium Place, Curzon Street, Birmingham, B4 7XG, www.thinktank.ac

Ulster Folk & Transport Museum, Cultra, Hollywood, BT18 OEU, www.nmni.com/uftm

Weald & Downland Open Air Museum, Town Lane, Singleton, Chichester PO18 OEU, www.wealddown.co.uk

Wigston Framework Knitters' Museum, 42/44 Bushloe End, Wigston, Leicester LE18 2BA, www.wigstonframeworkknitters.co.uk

Wollaton Hall, Wollaton Park, Nottingham NG8 2AE, www.nottinghamcity.gov.uk

Index

The dates of birth and death of individuals are shown where they are known

Peers of the realm are indexed by family names with cross references to titles.

The names of towns and villages in the British Isles are followed by their ancient (i.e. pre–1974) counties;

places abroad by the countries in which they are situated in 2012.

For definitions of technical terms see glossary

A

B

C

D

E

F

G

H

I

J

K

L

M

N

O

P

Q

S

T

U

V

Wood, David (1761–1820),
  engineer 88–9
Wood, Charles (1702–74),
  ironmaster 38, 101, 297, 314
Wood, Enoch (1759–1840), potter
  272–3
Wood, John (d. 1779), ironmaster
  297
Wood, John, the elder (1704–54),
  architect 502, 551–2
Wood, John, the younger (1728–
  82), architect 552–3
Wood, Nicholas (1795–1865),
  colliery viewer 90, 219, 227
Wood, Ralph (1748–95), potter
  272
Wood, Sancton (1815–86),
  architect 194
Wood, William, millwright 91
Wood, William (1671–1730),
  ironmaster 314
Woodbridge, Suffolk 100, 156,
  247, 547
Woodcroft, Bennet (1803–79),
  founder of Patent Museum
  151
wood fuel 41, 44

Woodhead Tunnel 142, 143
Woodhouse, George (1829–83),
  architect 460, 468–9
Woodnorth, Peter, potter 236
wood pulp 480
Woodseaves, Derbys 427
Woodstock, Oxon 606
Wookey, Som 473, 477–8
Woolf, Arthur (1766–1837),
  engineer 69, 79–80, 357
Woollam, John, silk manufacturer
  440
woollen cloth 89, 378, 387–8,
  449–63, 472, 511
Worcester 46, 96, 117, 169, 265,
  346, 471, 485
Wordsley, Staffs 266
Wordsworth, William (1770–
  1850), poet 569
Workington, Cumb 238, 300, 341
Wormleighton, Warks 165
Worrall, Yorks 329
Worsborough, Yorks 246, 330
Worsley, Lancs 123, 159, 162,
  169, 305
Worsted, Norf 450
worsteds 449–57, 463, 603

Worth, river 456–5
Worthing, Sussex 557
Wortley, Col A. Stuart 182
Wortley Top, Yorks xii, 330
Wostenholm, George (1800–76),
  cutler 21
Wotton-under-Edge, Gloucs
  458–9
Wraysbury, Berks 364, 476
Wrexham, Denbs 95, 180, 306,
  306, 322
Wright, Benjamin (d. 1700),
  mercer 388
Wright, Francis (1806–73),
  ironmaster 325
Wright, John, ironmaster 297, 305
Wright, Joseph (1734–97), painter
  11, 394, 486
Wright, Joseph (d. 1859), carriage
  builder 72
Wrigley, Ammon (1861–1946),
  poet 402–3
Wrigley, Sir Edward Anthony
  (b. 1931), historian 24–5,
  517–18
Wrigley, Joshua (d. 1810),
  engineer 397

Wrockwardine Wood, Salop
  231–2
Wrocław (Breslau), Poland 532
Wuppertal, Germany 496
Würtemburg 33, 600, 606
Wyatt, Sir Matthew Digby (1820–
  77), architect 194
Wyatt, John (1700–66), cotton
  spinner 389, 391
Wyatt, Samuel (1737–1807),
  architect 368, 523–4
Wyatt, William (d. 1835), architect
  70, 78
Wyattville, Sir Jeffrey (1766–
  1840), architect 591
Wye, river (Bucks) 476
Wye, river (Gloucs/Mon) 33,
  120, 181, 286
Wye river (Derbys) 371, 425–6
Wylam, Northumb 60, 86, 111,
  345–6
Wynne, Gruffyth (d. 1673),
  draper 388
Wyre, river 21, 565

Y

Yarm, Yorks 113, 119, 330
Yarmouth see Great
  Yarmouth
Yarranton, Andrew (1616–84),
  visionary 15, 118, 121, 302,
  322, 441, 608
Yarrow, Alfred (1842–1932),
  shipbuilder 541

Yates, James (1798–1881),
  ironfounder 607
Ybarra, Spain 348
Yeading, Middsx 543
Y Felinneli (Port Dinorwic) 156,
  587
Ynyscedwyn, Glam 320
Ynysfach, Glam 315

Ynyspenllwch, Glam 320
York xii, 87, 192, 257, 446
  National Railway Museum
  189, 192, 257, 267, 269
Yorkshire Coalfield 243–50
Youlgreave, Derbys 371
Young, Arthur (1741–1820),
  agriculturalist 37, 44, 49, 97,

203, 267, 280, 442, 513,
  584
Young, James (1811–83), chemist
  242, 325
Ynyscedwyn Ironworks 320
Ystalfera, Glam, 320
Ystradgynlais, Glam 181

Z

zinc 304, 358–9, 369, 377, 379–80, 382
Zinzendorf, Ludwig von (1700–60), religious leader 596–7